Map pages south

6

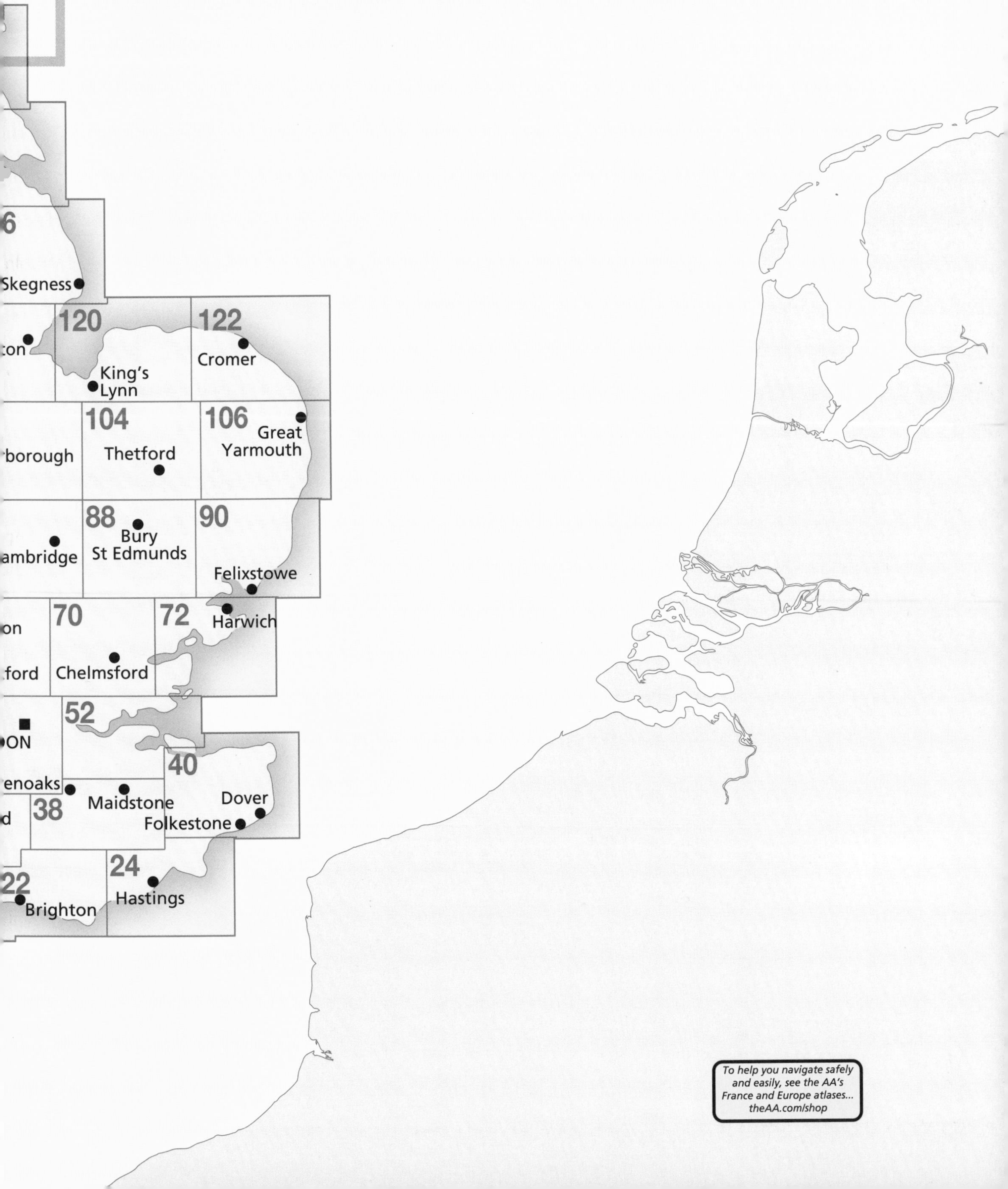

Skegness●

●ton

120

King's
●Lynn

122

Cromer●

104

●borough   Thetford
●

106

Great
Yarmouth●

88

●ambridge   Bury
St Edmunds
●

90

Felixstowe
●

70

●on

●ford   Chelmsford
●

72

Harwich●

52

■
●ON

●enoaks

40

38

Maidstone
●

Dover●

Folkestone●

●d

22

24

Hastings●

●Brighton

Atlas contents

Scale 1:148,000 or 2.34 miles to 1 inch

Map pages south	inside front cover
Route planner	II–VII
Atlas symbols	VIII–1
Road maps 1:148,000 scale	2–283
Channel Islands 1:100,000 scale	9
Isle of Man 1:200,000 scale	154
Orkney Islands 1:450,000 scale	275
Shetland Islands 1:450,000 scale	281
Western Isles 1:480,000 scale	282–283
Restricted junctions	284–285
Index to place names	286–368
County, administrative area map	286–287
Map pages north	inside back cover

15th edition June 2014

© AA Media Limited 2014
Original edition printed 2000.

Cartography:
All cartography in this atlas edited, designed and produced by the Mapping Services Department of AA Publishing (A05184).

This atlas contains Ordnance Survey data © Crown copyright and database right 2014 and Royal Mail data © Royal Mail copyright and database right 2014.

Publisher's notes:
Published by AA Publishing (a trading name of AA Media Limited, whose registered office is Fanum House, Basing View, Basingstoke, Hampshire RG21 4EA, UK. Registered number 06112600).

All rights reserved. No part of this publication may be reproduced, stored in a retrieval system, or transmitted in any form or by any means – electronic, mechanical, photocopying, recording or otherwise – unless the permission of the publisher has been given beforehand.

ISBN: 978 0 7495 7607 3.

A CIP catalogue record for this book is available from The British Library.

Disclaimer:
The contents of this atlas are believed to be correct at the time of the latest revision, it will not contain any subsequent amended, new or temporary information including diversions and traffic control or enforcement systems. The publishers cannot be held responsible or liable for any loss or damage occasioned to any person acting or refraining from action as a result of any use or reliance on material in this atlas, nor for any errors, omissions or changes in such material. This does not affect your statutory rights.

The publishers would welcome information to correct any errors or omissions and to keep this atlas up to date. Please write to the Atlas Editor, AA Publishing, The Automobile Association, Fanum House, Basing View, Basingstoke, Hampshire RG21 4EA, UK. E-mail: roadatlasfeedback@theaa.com

Acknowledgements:
AA Publishing would like to thank the following for their assistance in producing this atlas:
RoadPilot Information on fixed speed camera locations provided by and © 2014 RoadPilot® Driving Technology. Crematoria data provided by Cremation Society of Great Britain. Cadw, English Heritage, Forestry Commission, Historic Scotland, Johnsons, National Trust and National Trust for Scotland, RSPB, The Wildlife Trust, Scottish Natural Heritage, Natural England, The Countryside Council for Wales.

Printer:
Printed in Dubai by Oriental Press

REPUBLIC
OF
IRELAND

DUBLIN
Dún Laoghaire
(Apr–Sept)

To help you navigate safely
and easily, see the AA's
Ireland atlases...
theAA.com/shop

Rosslare
Harbour

Holyhead
Anglesey
Bangor
Caernarfon
Bethesda
Pwllheli
Abersoch
Porthmadog
SNOWDONIA
A5025
A55
A5
A487
A4086
A470
A497
A496

Llandudno
Colwyn Bay
Conwy
Abergele A55
Betws-y-coed
Denbigh
A525

Rhyl
Holywell
Queensferry
Mold
Ruthin
A494
A55

LIVERPOOL
Birkenhead
Widnes
Ellesmere Port
Northwich
Chester
Crewe
Nantwich

Formby
Crosby
St Helens
Warrington
Runcorn
John Lennon
Knutsford
M58
M62
M60
M56
M57
A580
A550
A41
A51
A534
A49
A53

Ormskirk
Skelmersdale
Wigan
Bolton
Bury

Market
Drayton
Newport
A518
A5
A529
A41

Barmouth
Dolgellau
A470
A493
A487

Bala
Llangollen
Oswestry
Wrexham
A5
A483
A495
A525
A5
A49

Shrewsbury
Welshpool
A458
A483
A5

Newcastle-
under-Lyme
A53

Machynlleth
A489
Newtown
A470
A489

Church
Stretton
Bridgnorth
A49

WOLVERHAMPTON
Telford
M54
A442
A518
A454

Cardigan Bay

Aberystwyth
WALES
Llangurig
A485
A44
A470
A483

Rhayader
Knighton
A488
A4113
Ludlow
A49

Leominster
A49
A4112

Stourbridge
Hales
Kidderminster
Bromsg

Aberaeron
Tregaron
A487
A485
A482

Llandrindod
Wells
A483
A44
Kington
A481

Builth
Wells
A470
A438
Hay-on-Wye
A438
A4103

Worcester
A44
Great
Malvern
A449

Cardigan
Newcastle
Emlyn
A484
A486
Lampeter
A485

Llandovery
A40
Brecon
A470
A479

Hereford
Ledbury
A49
M50
Tewk
A40

Fishguard
St Davids
PEMBROKESHIRE
COAST
Haverfordwest
Milford Haven
Pembroke Dock
Pembroke
A487
A40
A478
A4076
A477
A40
A477

Carmarthen
St Clears
Tenby
A48
A40
A483

Llandeilo
BRECON BEACONS
A4067
A470
A465

Abergavenny
A40
Monmouth
Ross-on-Wye
A49
A466
A40

Gloucester
M50
Strou
M5

Llanelli
Swansea
Port Talbot
M4
Neath
Pontypridd
A465
A4061
A470
A48
Bridgend

Merthyr
Tydfil
Cwmbran
Chepstow
Newport
CARDIFF
Clevedon
A470
A449
A48
M48
M49
M4
M32
A420

Cardiff
Weston-
super-Mare
Avonmouth
BRISTOL
Bath
Bristol
A368
A37
A361
A420

Bristol Channel

Lundy

Ilfracombe
Lynton
Minehead
Cheddar
Wells
Shepton
Mallet
Frome
A371
A37
A371

Barnstaple
EXMOOR
A39
A361
A396
Bridgwater
Glastonbury
A39
A303
A372

Bideford
Great
Torrington
South
Molton
A361
A358
M5
Taunton
Wincanton
A303

Newton
Abbot
Tiverton
A358
A30
Yeovil
Ilminster
Crewkerne
Sherborne
A37
A303
A351

Bude
Holsworthy
Hatherleigh
A3072
A388
A386
A377
Crediton
Chard
Axminster
A30
Blandford
Forum
A354

Launceston
Okehampton
A30
DARTMOOR
A382
Exeter
M5
Honiton
Bridport
A35
A30
A3052

Wadebridge
Bodmin
Tavistock
A386
A38
A380
Exmouth
Dawlish
Teignmouth
Lyme
Regis
Dorchester
A35
A354

Newquay
Liskeard
Buckfastleigh
Plymouth
Newton Abbot
Torquay
Paignton
Weymouth
Fortuneswell
A392
A30
A390
A38
A391

St Austell
Lostwithiel
Saltash
Torpoint
PLYMOUTH
Totnes
Dartmouth
Kingsbridge
A3058
A391
A379

Redruth
Truro
Camborne
A30
A390
A39
A3083

Penzance
Land's
End
Helston
Falmouth
A394
A39
A30

Lizard

Santander
(Mar–Oct)
Roscoff
St Malo (Nov–Mar)

Guernsey
Jersey
St-Malo

ENGLISH

Legend

— Motorway
— Toll motorway
— Primary route
dual carriageway
— Primary route
single carriageway
— Other A roads
— Vehicle ferry
— Fast vehicle ferry
or catamaran
National Park

Route planner

Rotterdam (Europoort) Zeebrugge

Esbjerg
Hoek van Holland

Dieppe

Cherbourg
Guernsey
Jersey
St-Malo
Caen (Ouistreham)
Le Havre
Bilbao
Santander

Cherbourg (May–Sept)
Le Havre

Cherbourg (Mar–Oct)
Santander
Gijón

Dieppe

Dunkerque

Calais

CALAIS / COQUELLES TERMINAL

CHANNEL TUNNEL TERMINAL

Strait of Dover

CHANNEL

ENGLAND

FRANCE

The Wash

THE BROADS

SOUTH DOWNS

PEAK DISTRICT

NEW FOREST

Isle of Wight

Place names (selection):
Huddersfield, Thorne, Scunthorpe, Humberside, Grimsby, Barnsley, Doncaster, Robin Hood Doncaster Sheffield, Bawtry, Brigg, Cleethorpes, Louth, Mablethorpe, Rotherham, Glossop, Stockport, SHEFFIELD, Worksop, Retford, Gainsborough, Market Rasen, Buxton, Bakewell, Chesterfield, Lincoln, Horncastle, Skegness, Matlock, Alfreton, Mansfield, Leek, Ashbourne, Ilkeston, Newark-on-Trent, Sleaford, Boston, DERBY, Long Eaton, Loughborough, Grantham, Spalding, Bourne, King's Lynn, Sheringham, Cromer, Hunstanton, North Walsham, Fakenham, Aylsham, Burton upon Trent, Uttoxeter, East Midlands, Melton Mowbray, Stamford, Wisbech, Swaffham, Dereham, Norwich, Caister-on-Sea, Lichfield, Oakham, March, Downham Market, Great Yarmouth, Tamworth, LEICESTER, Wigston, Peterborough, Chatteris, Ely, Thetford, Attleborough, Lowestoft, Walsall, Hinckley, Market Harborough, Bungay, Beccles, BIRMINGHAM, Nuneaton, Corby, Kettering, Huntingdon, Bury St Edmunds, Diss, Southwold, COVENTRY, Rugby, Northampton, St Neots, Newmarket, Stowmarket, Aldeburgh, Royal Leamington Spa, Cambridge, Woodbridge, Warwick, Daventry, Bedford, Haverhill, Sudbury, Ipswich, Stratford-upon-Avon, Towcester, Brackley, Milton Keynes, Royston, Halstead, Felixstowe, Evesham, Banbury, Leighton Buzzard, Baldock, Stevenage, Braintree, Harwich, Chipping Norton, Bicester, Dunstable, Luton, Bishop's Stortford, Colchester, Stow-on-the-Wold, Witney, Aylesbury, Hertford, Harlow, Clacton-on-Sea, Cheltenham, Burford, Thame, Hatfield, Chelmsford, Witham, Maldon, Cirencester, Oxford, High Wycombe, St Albans, Brentwood, Burnham-on-Crouch, Faringdon, Abingdon-on-Thames, Watford, Basildon, Southend-on-Sea, Swindon, Wantage, Beaconsfield, LONDON, Canvey Island, Sheerness, Margate, Marlborough, Maidenhead, Slough, City, Tilbury, Gravesend, Ramsgate, Devizes, Newbury, Reading, Windsor, Bracknell, Heathrow, Richmond, Dartford, Rochester, Chatham, Kent International, Sandwich, Staines-upon-Thames, Swanley, Croydon, Sevenoaks, Maidstone, Canterbury, Deal, Woking, Leatherhead, Redhill, Tonbridge, Ashford, Dover, Basingstoke, Farnham, Guildford, Dorking, Reigate, East Grinstead, Royal Tunbridge Wells, Folkestone, Andover, Alton, Gatwick, Crawley, Crowborough, Hythe, New Romney, Amesbury, Winchester, Petersfield, Billingshurst, Horsham, Heathfield, Tenterden, Salisbury, Romsey, Eastleigh, Midhurst, Uckfield, Rye, Wilton, Southampton, Arundel, Shoreham-by-Sea, Lewes, Hastings, SOUTHAMPTON, Chichester, Worthing, Brighton, Bexhill, Eastbourne, Ringwood, Lymington, Gosport, Portsmouth, Bognor Regis, Newhaven, Bournemouth, Christchurch, Cowes, Ryde, Swanage, Freshwater, Newport, Sandown, Shanklin

0 10 20 30 miles
0 10 20 30 40 kilometres

To help you navigate safely and easily, see the AA's France and Europe atlases…
theAA.com/shop

NORTHERN IRELAND

REPUBLIC OF IRELAND

IRISH SEA

Firth of Clyde

Firth of Forth

Solway Firth

LOCH LOMOND AND THE TROSSACHS

LAKE DISTRICT

SNOWDONIA

Major places:

EDINBURGH, GLASGOW, Paisley, Greenock, Stirling, Dunfermline, Motherwell, East Kilbride, Kilmarnock, Carlisle, LIVERPOOL, BELFAST, DUBLIN, Dún Laoghaire, Larne

Inveraray, Callander, Crieff, Auchterarder, Dunblane, Alloa, Kinross, St Andrews, Cupar, Glenrothes, Kirkcaldy, Rosyth, Falkirk, Airdrie, Livingston, Dalkeith, Dunbar, Helensburgh, Dumbarton, Dunoon, Largs, Ardrossan, Irvine, Kilwinning, Troon, Prestwick, Ayr, Maybole, Girvan, Cairnryan, Newton Stewart, Stranraer, Cumnock, Strathaven, Lanark, Biggar, Peebles, Galashiels, Selkirk, Hawick, Jedburgh, Kelso, Thornhill, New Galloway, Dumfries, Castle Douglas, Annan, Moffat, Langholm, Lockerbie, Longtown, Brampton, Penrith, Alston, Maryport, Cockermouth, Workington, Keswick, Egremont, Ravenglass, Millom, Windermere, Ambleside, Kendal, Sedbergh, Kirkby Lonsdale, Barrow-in-Furness, Morecambe, Heysham, Lancaster, Fleetwood, Blackpool, Clitheroe, Preston, Southport, Ormskirk, Skelmersdale, Formby, Crosby, Bolton, Wigan, St Helens, Warrington, Widnes, Runcorn, Birkenhead, Ellesmere Port, Northwich, Chester, Crewe, Nantwich, Newcastle under Lyme, Market Drayton, Whitchurch, Oswestry, Shrewsbury, Welshpool, Newport, Telford

Colonsay, Jura, Islay, Port Askaig, Port Ellen, Kennacraig, Tarbert, Lochgilphead, Arran, Campbeltown

Isle of Man, Ramsey, Peel, Douglas, Castletown, Isle of Man (Ronaldsway)

Holyhead, Anglesey, Bangor, Caernarfon, Bethesda, Llandudno, Conwy, Colwyn Bay, Abergele, Rhyl, Holywell, Mold, Denbigh, Ruthin, Queensferry, Betws-y-coed, Pwllheli, Abersoch, Porthmadog, Bala, Llangollen, Wrexham, Barmouth, Dolgellau

(May–Sept) (Mar–Oct) (Apr–Sept) (Nov–Mar) (Mar–Oct)

To help you navigate safely and easily, see the AA's Ireland atlases...
theAA.com/shop

Motorway
Toll motorway
Primary route
dual carriageway
Primary route
single carriageway
Other A roads
Vehicle ferry
Fast vehicle ferry
or catamaran
National Park

0   10   20   30 miles
0   10   20   30   40 kilometres

Eyemouth
Berwick-upon-Tweed
Wooler
Alnwick
Amble
Morpeth
Ashington
Newcastle
North Shields Tynemouth
South Shields
NEWCASTLE UPON TYNE
Gateshead
SUNDERLAND
Consett
Chester-le-Street
Durham
Hartlepool
Bishop Auckland
Stockton-on-Tees Middlesbrough
Barnard Castle
Darlington
Richmond Scotch Corner
Durham Tees Valley
Guisborough Whitby
NORTH YORK MOORS
Leyburn Northallerton
Thirsk
Helmsley Pickering
Scarborough
Ripon
Easingwold Malton Filey
Harrogate
Otley Wetherby York Bridlington
Keighley Driffield
BRADFORD LEEDS Selby Market Weighton
Halifax Beverley
Wakefield Goole KINGSTON UPON HULL
Huddersfield Pontefract Killingholme
Barnsley Thorne Scunthorpe Immingham
Oldham Doncaster Humberside Grimsby
MANCHESTER Rotherham Brigg Cleethorpes
Glossop Robin Hood Doncaster Sheffield
Stockport SHEFFIELD Bawtry Market Rasen Louth Mablethorpe
PEAK DISTRICT Worksop Gainsborough
Buxton Retford Lincoln Skegness
Bakewell Chesterfield Horncastle
Leek Matlock Mansfield
Ashbourne Alfreton Newark-on-Trent Boston
STOKE-ON-TRENT Ilkeston Sleaford The Wash Sheringham Cromer
Stafford DERBY Grantham Hunstanton North Walsham
Uttoxeter NOTTINGHAM Spalding King's Lynn Aylsham
Stone Long Eaton Bourne Fakenham
Burton upon Trent East Midlands Loughborough Dereham Norwich Caister-on-Sea
Rugeley Melton Mowbray Wisbech Swaffham THE BROADS
Lichfield Oakham Stamford Norwich Great Yarmouth
LEICESTER

Amsterdam (IJmuiden)
Rotterdam (Europoort) Zeebrugge

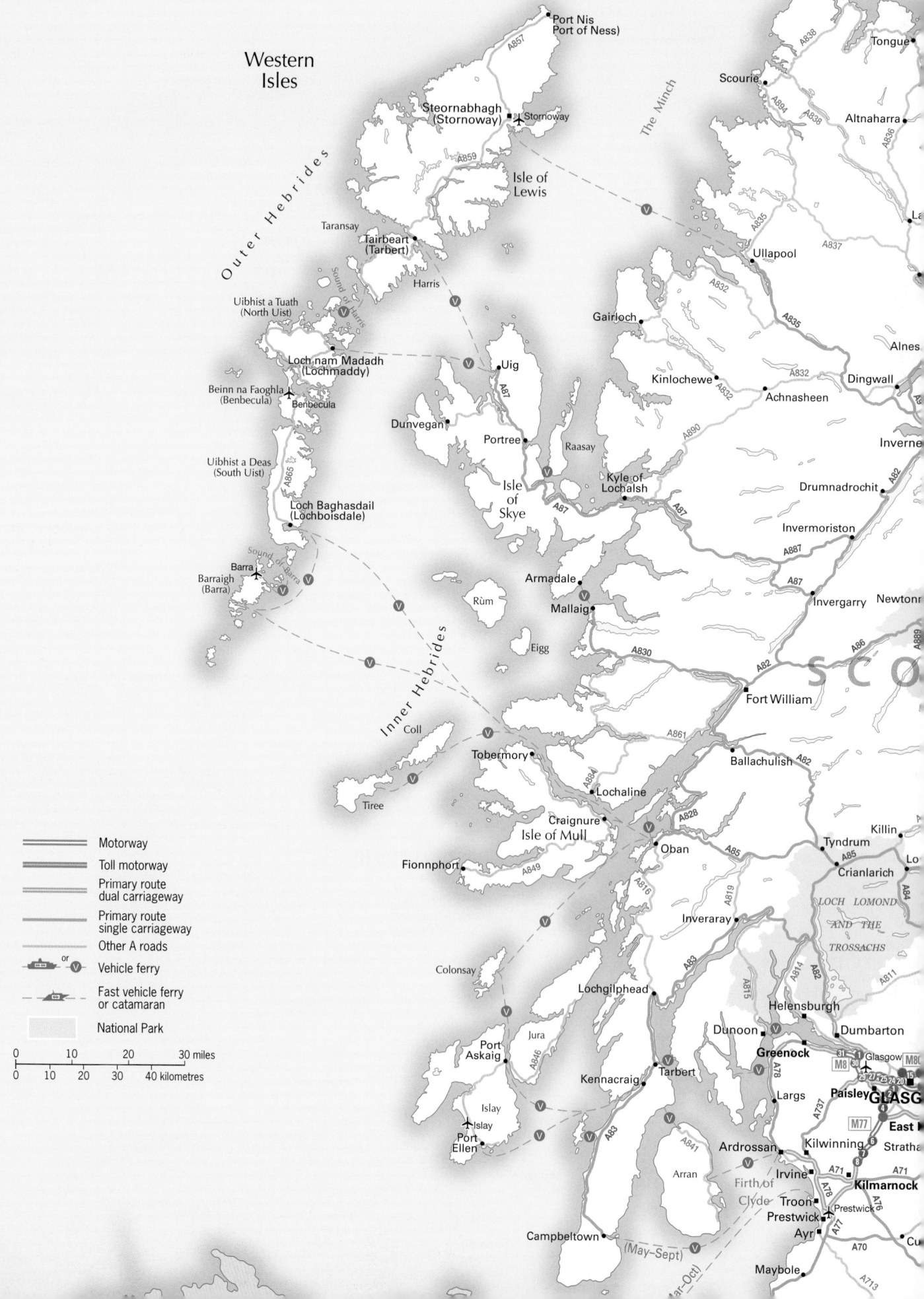

Western
Isles

Outer Hebrides

Port Nis
Port of Ness)

The Minch

Scourie

Tongue

Altnaharra

A838

A836

A894

Steornabhagh
(Stornoway)

Stornoway

Isle of
Lewis

A857

A837

Ullapool

A835

A859

Taransay

Tairbeart
(Tarbert)

Gairloch

A832

Harris

Kinlochewe

A632

Achnasheen

A832

Dingwall

Uibhist a Tuath
(North Uist)

Sound of Harris

Uig

Dunvegan

A850

A87

Portree

Raasay

A890

Drumnadrochit

A82

Inverne

Loch nam Madadh
(Lochmaddy)

Beinn na Faoghla
(Benbecula)

Benbecula

Isle
of
Skye

Kyle of
Lochalsh

A87

Invermoriston

A887

Uibhist a Deas
(South Uist)

A865

Armadale

A87

Invergarry

Newtonr

A82

Loch Baghasdail
(Lochboisdale)

Mallaig

Rùm

Sound of Barra

Eigg

A830

A86

A889

Barra

Barraigh
(Barra)

Inner Hebrides

Fort William

S C O

Coll

Tobermory

A861

Ballachulish

A82

Tiree

Lochaline

A884

Killin

Craignure
Isle of Mull

A828

Oban

A85

Tyndrum

A85

Lo

A84

Fionnphort

A849

Crianlarich

LOCH LOMOND
AND THE
TROSSACHS

A816

Inveraray

A819

A82

A815

A83

A914

A82

A811

Colonsay

Lochgilphead

Helensburgh

Dunoon

Dumbarton

Port
Askaig

Jura

A846

Tarbert

Greenock

Glasgow

M8

M80

A78

Kennacraig

Islay

Largs

Paisley

GLASG

Islay

A83

A737

M77

East

Port
Ellen

Ardrossan

Kilwinning

Stratha

A841

Irvine

A71

Kilmarnock

Arran

Troon

Prestwick

A77

Firth of
Clyde

Campbeltown

(May–Sept)

Ayr

A70

Cu

Maybole

A713

FERRY INFORMATION

Hebrides and west coast Scotland
calmac.co.uk   0800 066 5000
skyeferry.co.uk
western-ferries.co.uk   01369 704 452

Orkney and Shetland
northlinkferries.co.uk   0845 6000 449
pentlandferries.co.uk   0800 688 8998
orkneyferries.co.uk   01856 872 044
shetland.gov.uk/ferries   01595 743 970

Isle of Man
steam-packet.com   08722 992 992

Ireland
irishferries.com   08717 300 400
poferries.com   08716 642 121
stenaline.co.uk   08447 70 70 70

North Sea (Scandinavia and Benelux)
dfdsseaways.co.uk   08715 229 955
poferries.com   08716 642 121
stenaline.co.uk   08447 70 70 70

Isle of Wight
wightlink.co.uk   0871 376 1000
redfunnel.co.uk   0844 844 9988

Channel Islands
condorferries.co.uk   0845 609 1024

Channel hopping (France and Belgium)
brittany-ferries.co.uk   0871 244 0744
condorferries.co.uk   0845 609 1024
eurotunnel.com   08443 35 35 35
ldlines.co.uk   0844 576 8836
dfdsseaways.co.uk   08715 229 955
poferries.com   08716 642 121
myferrylink.com   0844 2482 100

Northern Spain
brittany-ferries.co.uk   0871 244 0744
ldlines.co.uk   0844 576 8836

EMERGENCY DIVERSION ROUTES

In an emergency it may be necessary to close a section of motorway or other main road to traffic, so a temporary sign may advise drivers to follow a diversion route. To help drivers navigate the route, black symbols on yellow patches may be permanently displayed on existing direction signs, including motorway signs. Symbols may also be used on separate signs with yellow backgrounds.

For further information see www.highways.gov.uk, trafficscotland.org and traffic-wales.com

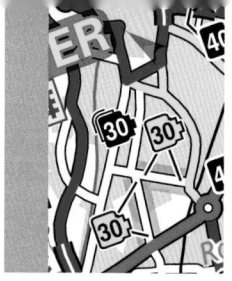

Atlas symbols

Motoring information

M4 Motorway with number	**30** Safety camera site (fixed location) with speed limit in mph
T4 **Toll** Toll Toll motorway with toll station	**40** Section of road with two or more fixed safety cameras, with speed limit in mph
11 Motorway junction with and without number	**50** **50** Average speed (SPECS™) camera system with speed limit in mph
3 Restricted motorway junctions	**V** Fixed safety camera site with variable speed limit
S Fleet Motorway service area	▼ 5 ▼ Distance in miles between symbols
Motorway and junction under construction	or **V** Vehicle ferry
A3 Primary route single/dual carriageway	Fast vehicle ferry or catamaran
11 Primary route junction with and without number	Railway line, in tunnel
3 Restricted primary route junctions	─○─✕─ Railway station and level crossing
S Primary route service area	├┼┼┼┼┼┼┤ Tourist railway
BATH Primary route destination	✈ Ⓗ Airport, heliport
A1123 Other A road single/dual carriageway	Ⓕ International freight terminal
B2070 B road single/dual carriageway	**H** 24-hour Accident & Emergency hospital
Minor road more than 4 metres wide, less than 4 metres wide	**C** Crematorium
Roundabout	**P+R** Park and Ride (at least 6 days per week)
Interchange/junction	City, town, village or other built-up area
Narrow primary/other A/B road with passing places (Scotland)	628 ▲ Spot height in metres
Road under construction/ approved	637 Lecht Summit Mountain pass
├═════┤ Road tunnel	Sandy beach
Toll Road toll	National boundary
──→ Steep gradient (arrows point downhill)	County, administrative boundary

Touring information
To avoid disappointment, check opening times before visiting.

Scenic route	Farm or animal centre	Rugby Union national stadium
Tourist Information Centre	Zoological or wildlife collection	International athletics stadium
Tourist Information Centre (seasonal)	Bird collection	Horse racing
Visitor or heritage centre	Aquarium	Show jumping/equestrian circuit
Picnic site	RSPB site	Motor-racing circuit
Caravan site (AA inspected)	National Nature Reserve (England, Scotland, Wales)	Air show venue
Camping site (AA inspected)	Local nature reserve	Ski slope (natural)
Caravan & camping site (AA inspected)	Wildlife Trust reserve	Ski slope (artificial)
Abbey, cathedral or priory	Forest drive	National Trust property
Ruined abbey, cathedral or priory	National trail	National Trust for Scotland property
Castle	Viewpoint	English Heritage site
Historic house or building	Hill-fort	Historic Scotland site
Museum or art gallery	Roman antiquity	Cadw (Welsh heritage) site
Industrial interest	Prehistoric monument	Other place of interest
Aqueduct or viaduct	Battle site with year 1066	Boxed symbols indicate attractions within urban areas
Garden	Steam railway centre	World Heritage Site (UNESCO)
Arboretum	Cave	National Park
Vineyard	Windmill	National Scenic Area (Scotland)
Country park	Monument	Forest Park
Agricultural showground	Golf course (AA listed)	Heritage coast
Theme park	County cricket ground	Major shopping centre

G · H · J · K · L · M

1 · 2 · 3 · 4 · 5 · 6 · 7 · 8

St Breock
Egloshayle
Tredethy
Croanford
Hellandbridge
Waterloo
Temple
Candbell Lake
Park
BROWN DOWN
Cheesewring
Minions
Starts Open-Air Theatre Do

Treneague
Sladesbridge
Pencarrow
Colquite
Helland
Millpool
Caradon Mining District
Common Moor
Darite
w's Nest

Burlawn
Washaway
Lane End
Warleggan
Mount
Cardinham
St Neot
Golitha Falls
King Doniert's Stone
Tremar
St Cleer
Mer
Trethevy Quoit

Hay
Polbrock
Brocton
Dunmere
Cooksland
Pantersbridge
Lampen
Carnglaze Caverns
St Cleer
Trembraze
B3254

Ruthernbridge
Boscarne
Tregawne
Nanstallon
St Lawrence
Fletchersbridge
Tredinnick
Ley
Tredinnick
Doublebois
Dobwalls
Li ard
Trembraze

Withiel
Tremore
Retire
Bodmin
Bodmin & Wenford Railway
A38
13
Moorswater
Trevelmond
Lamellion
A38

Lamorick
Tregullon
Lanivet
West Taphouse
Middle Taphouse
East Taphouse
St Pinnock
Moorswater
Paul Corin's Magnificent sic Machines

Victoria
Higher Town
Bokiddick
Cutmadoc
Lanhydrock
Sweetshouse
Braddock
1643
Boconnoc
Herodsfoot
St Keyne
Trewi

Criggan
Lockengate
Bodwen
Helman Tor
Penhale
Restormel Castle
Couch's Mill
Porfell Wildlife Park
Duloe
Widegates

Carbis
Bugle
Tredinnick
Lostwithiel
Milltown
Bocaddon
Lerryn
Muchlarnick
Tredinnick
Sandplace
Morval
Tredi
La

Whitemoor
Carnsmerry
Rosevean
Treverbyn
Lanlivery
Castle
Lanreath
St Veep
Pelynt
St Martin
Monkey S

Stenalees
Carthew
Wheal Martyn
Penwithick
Trethurgy
Luxulyan
Luxulyan Valley
Tywardreath Highway
Penpillick
Treesmill
Golant
Penpoll
Trenewan
Trelawne
A387

hole
oalla
Ruddlemoor
Carclaze
Tregrehan Mills
St Blazey
Eden Project
Tywardreath
Torfrey
Lanteglos Highway
Trenewan
Model Village
Portlooe
Porthallow

St Austell
Trewoon
Boscoppa
Holmbush
St Blazey Gate
Par
Biscovey
Polmear
A3082
B3269
Bodinnick
Crumplehorn
Polperro
Looe or St George's Island

Mewan
Polgooth
Tregorrick
Porthpean
Carlyon Bay
Charlestown
Polkerris
Menabilly
Fowey
St Catherine's Castle
Polruan
Lansallos
Polperro
Talland Bay
Looe B

Sticker
London Apprentice
St Austell Bay
GRIBBIN HEAD
Lantic Bay
Pencarrow Head
Lantivet Bay
South West Coast Path
Gribbin Head - Polperro Heritage Coast

Levalsa Meor
Rescorla
Trenarren
Black Head

Ewe
Towan
Pentewan
Lost Gardens of Heligan
Mevagissey Bay

Kestle
Tregiskey
Penare Point

Mevagissey
Portmellon
Chapel Point

arrick
Gorran High Lanes

cassa
Gorran Churchtown

Treveor
Gorran Haven

winger
Maenease Point

Penare

Bay
DODMAN POINT

A30
A38
A390
A391
A389
A387
B3254
B3268
B3269
B3273
B3274
B3359
B3252
B3253

0 1 2 3 4 5 miles
0 1 2 3 4 5 6 7 8 kilometres

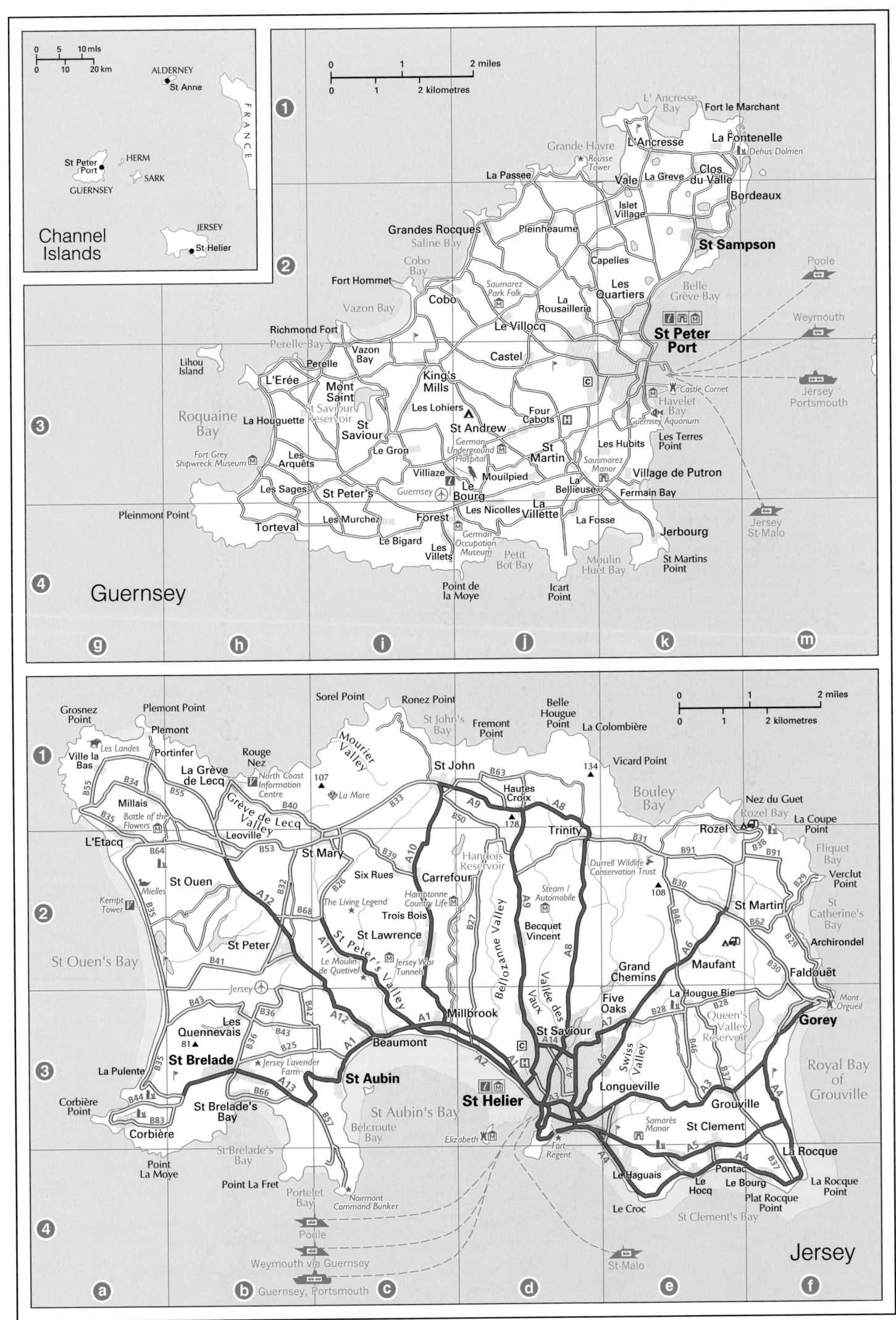

0 5 10 mls
0 10 20 km

ALDERNEY
St Anne

FRANCE

St Peter
Port   HERM
            SARK

GUERNSEY

Channel
Islands

JERSEY
St Helier

Guernsey

0   1   2 miles
0   1   2 kilometres

L' Ancresse
Bay
Fort le Marchant
L'Ancresse
La Fontenelle
Dehus Dolmen
Grande Havre
Rousse
Tower
Clos
du Valle
La Passee
Vale   La Greve
Islet
Village   Bordeaux
St Sampson
Grandes Rocques
Pleinheaume
Saline Bay
Poole
Cobo
Bay
Capelles
Les
Quartiers
Belle
Grève Bay
Weymouth
Fort Hommet
Saumarez
Park Folk
La
Rousaillerie
St Peter
Port
Cobo
Le Villocq
Vazon Bay
Richmond Fort
Castel
Perelle Bay
Vazon
Bay
Jersey
Portsmouth
Perelle
King's
Mills
C
Castle Cornet
Lihou
Island
L'Erée
Mont
Saint
St Saviour
Reservoir
Les Lohiers
Four
Cabots
H
Havelet
Bay
Guernsey Aquarium
Roquaine
Bay
La Houguette
St
Saviour
St Andrew
German
Underground
Hospital
St
Martin
Les Hubits
Les Terres
Point
Fort Grey
Shipwreck Museum
Les
Arquêts
Le Gron
Villiaze
Mouilpied
Sausmarez
Manor
Village de Putron
Jersey
St-Malo
Les Sages
St Peter's
Guernsey
Le
Bourg
La
Bellieuse
Fermain Bay
Pleinmont Point
Les Murchez
Forest
Les Nicolles
La
Villette
La Fosse
Jerbourg
Torteval
Le Bigard
German
Occupation
Museum
St Martins
Point
Les
Villets
Petit
Bot Bay
Moulin
Huet Bay
Point de
la Moye
Icart
Point

g   h   i   j   k   m

Jersey

0   1   2 miles
0   1   2 kilometres

Grosnez
Point
Plemont Point
Sorel Point
Ronez Point
Belle
Hougue
Point
La Colombière
Plemont
Ville la
Bas
Les Landes
Portinfer
Rouge
Nez
Mourier
Valley
St John's
Bay
Fremont
Point
Bouley
Bay
Nez du Guet
La Grève
de Lecq
North Coast
Information
Centre
107
La Mare
St John
B63
Hautes
Croix
A8
Vicard Point
134
Rozel Bay
La Coupe
Point
Millais
Battle of the
Flowers
B55
Grève de Lecq
Valley
B40
B33
B50
A9
128
Trinity
B31
Rozel
B38
B91
Fliquet
Bay
Verclut
Point
L'Etacq
B64
Leoville
B53
St Mary
B39
A10
Handois
Reservoir
Durrell Wildlife
Conservation Trust
108
B91
B30
St Martin
B29
St
Catherine's
Bay
St Ouen
Mielles
B32
A12
B68
B26
Six Rues
Carrefour
Hamptonne
Country Life
Steam /
Automobile
A9
B46
Maufant
B62
Archirondel
Kempt
Tower
B35
The Living Legend
Trois Bois
Becquet
Vincent
A6
B30
Faldouët
St Peter
A12
B41
St Lawrence
St Peter's Valley
Jersey War
Tunnels
Bellozanne Valley
Vallée des
Vaux
Grand
Chemins
La Hougue Bie
B28
B28
Mont
Orgueil
St Ouen's Bay
Jersey
Le Moulin
de Quetivel
Grouville
Gorey
B43
B36
Les
Quennevais
81
B43
B25
Millbrook
Five
Oaks
A7
Queen's
Valley
Reservoir
B46
B37
Royal Bay
of
Grouville
St Brelade
B42
A11
A1
St Saviour
A14
Swiss
Valley
A4
La Pulente
Jersey Lavender
Farm
A13
Beaumont
St Aubin
C
A1
H
A3
Longueville
B27
Grouville
B35
B44
Corbière
Point
St Brelade's
Bay
B66
St Helier
A3
A6
St Clement
B37
La Rocque
Corbière
B83
B57
St Aubin's Bay
Elizabeth
Fort
Regent
A4
Samarès
Manor
A5
A4
La Rocque
Point
Point
La Moye
St Brelade's
Bay
Belcroute
Bay
A2
Le Haguais
Le Bourg
Pontac
Plat Rocque
Point
Point La Fret
Portelet
Bay
Noirmont
Command Bunker
Le Croc
Le
Hocq
Le Bourg
St Clement's Bay
Poole
St-Malo
Weymouth via Guernsey
Guernsey, Portsmouth

a   b   c   d   e   f

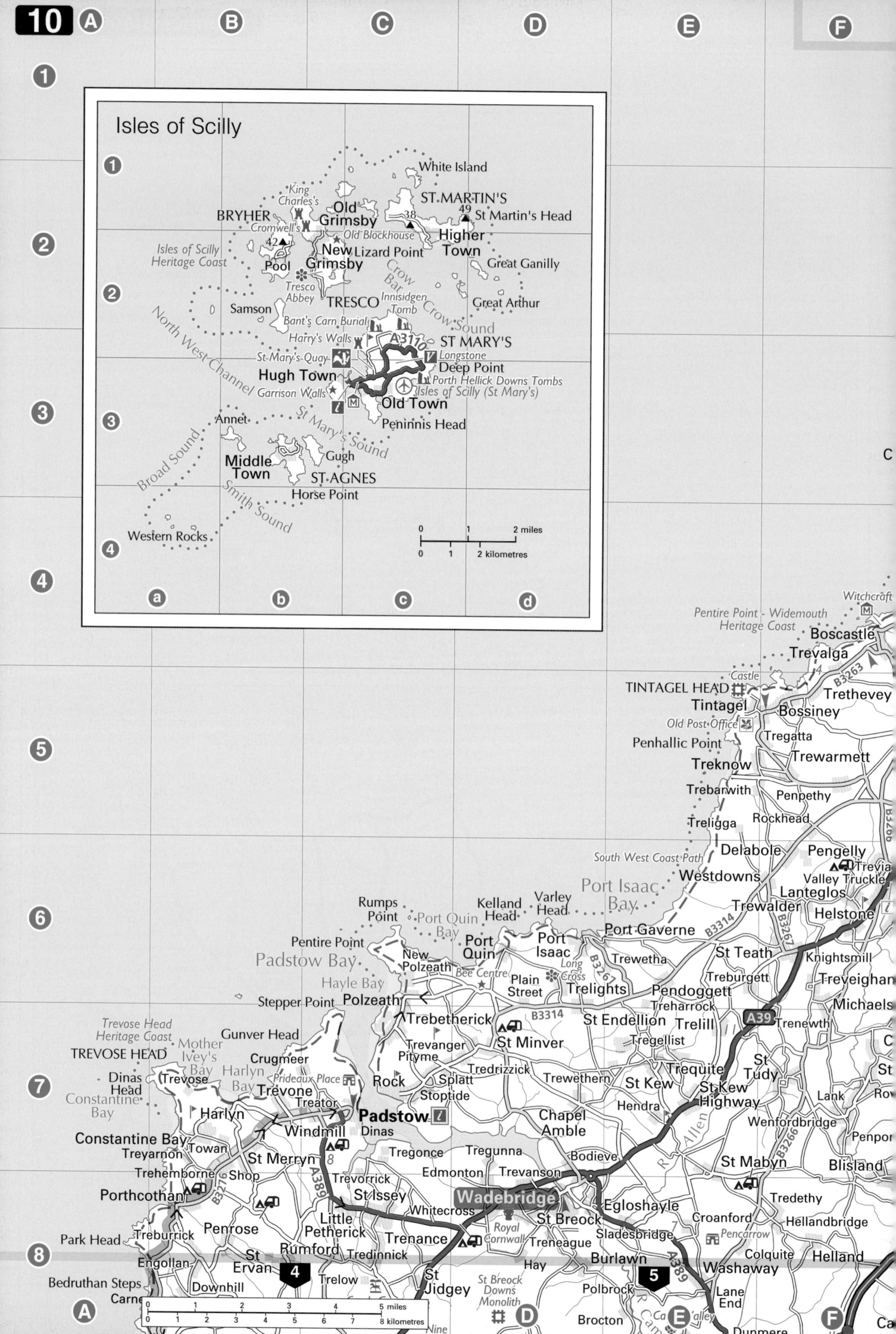

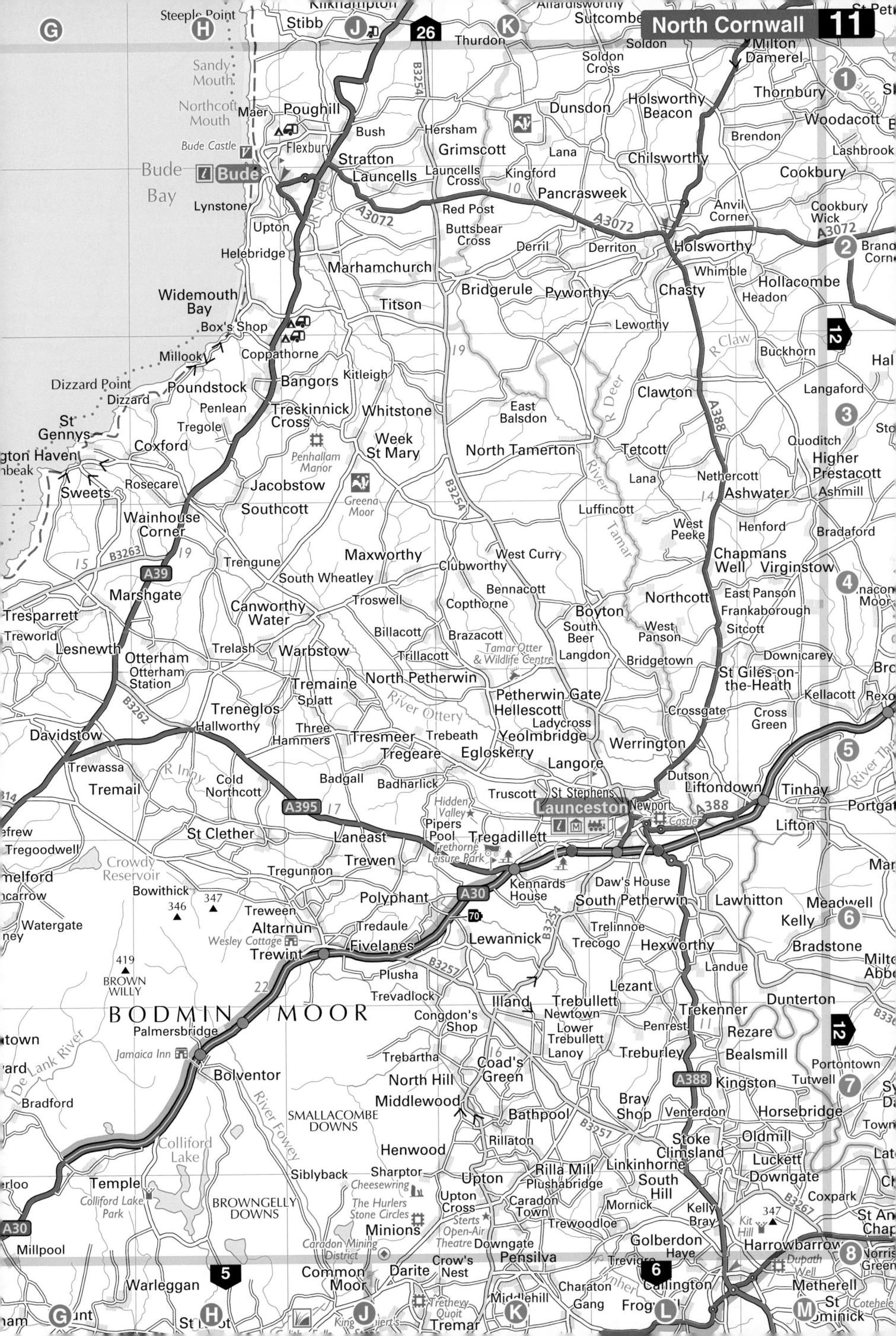

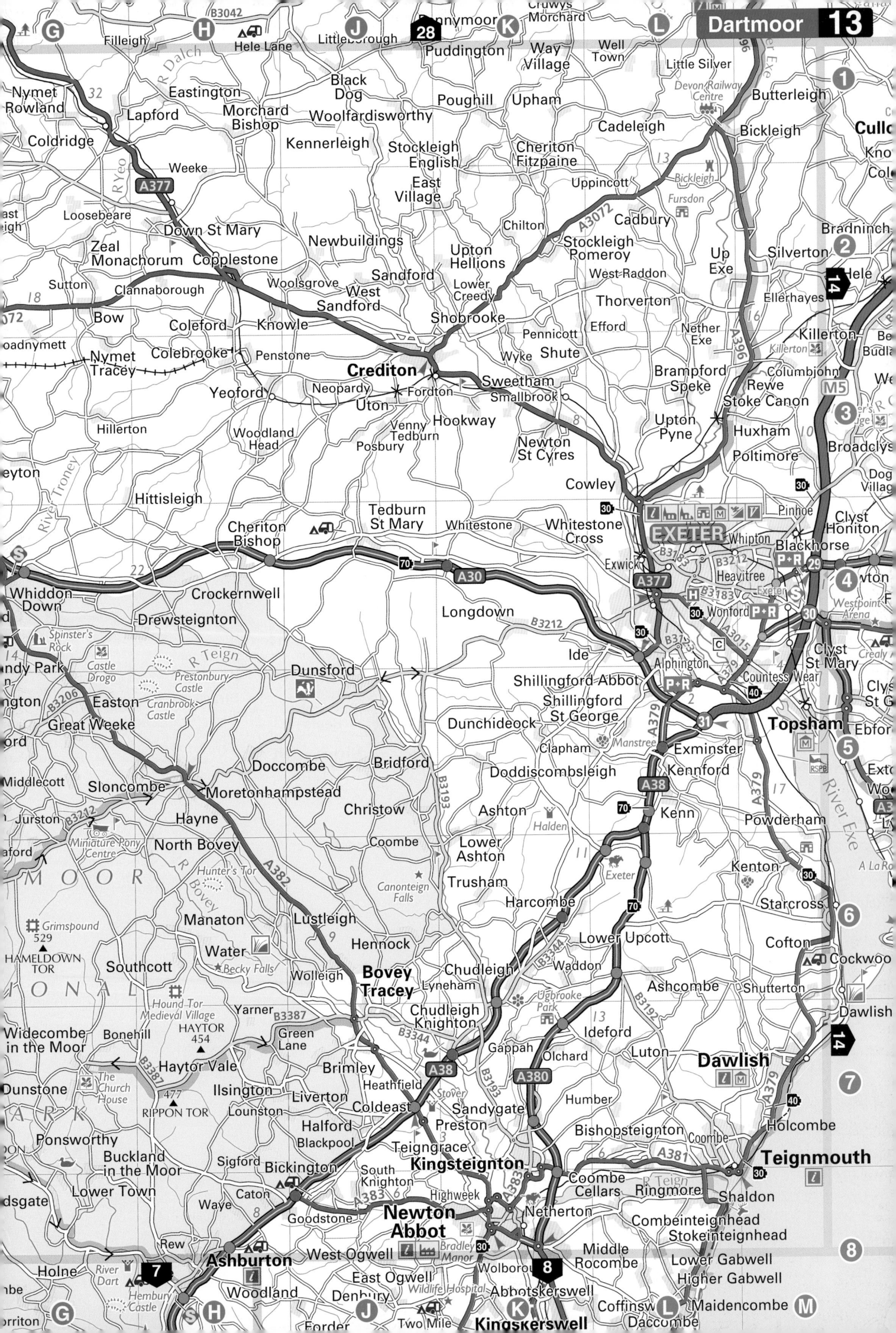

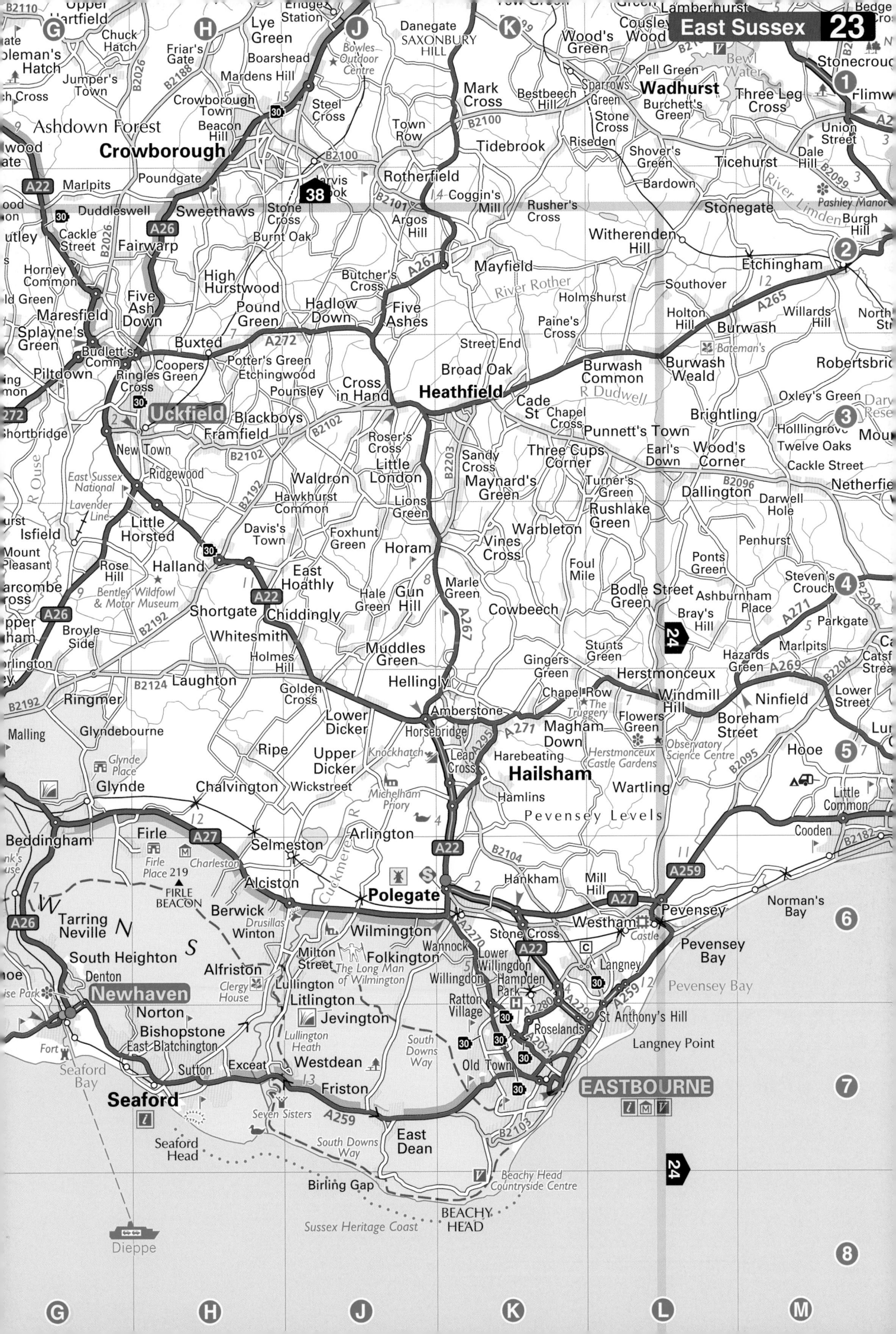

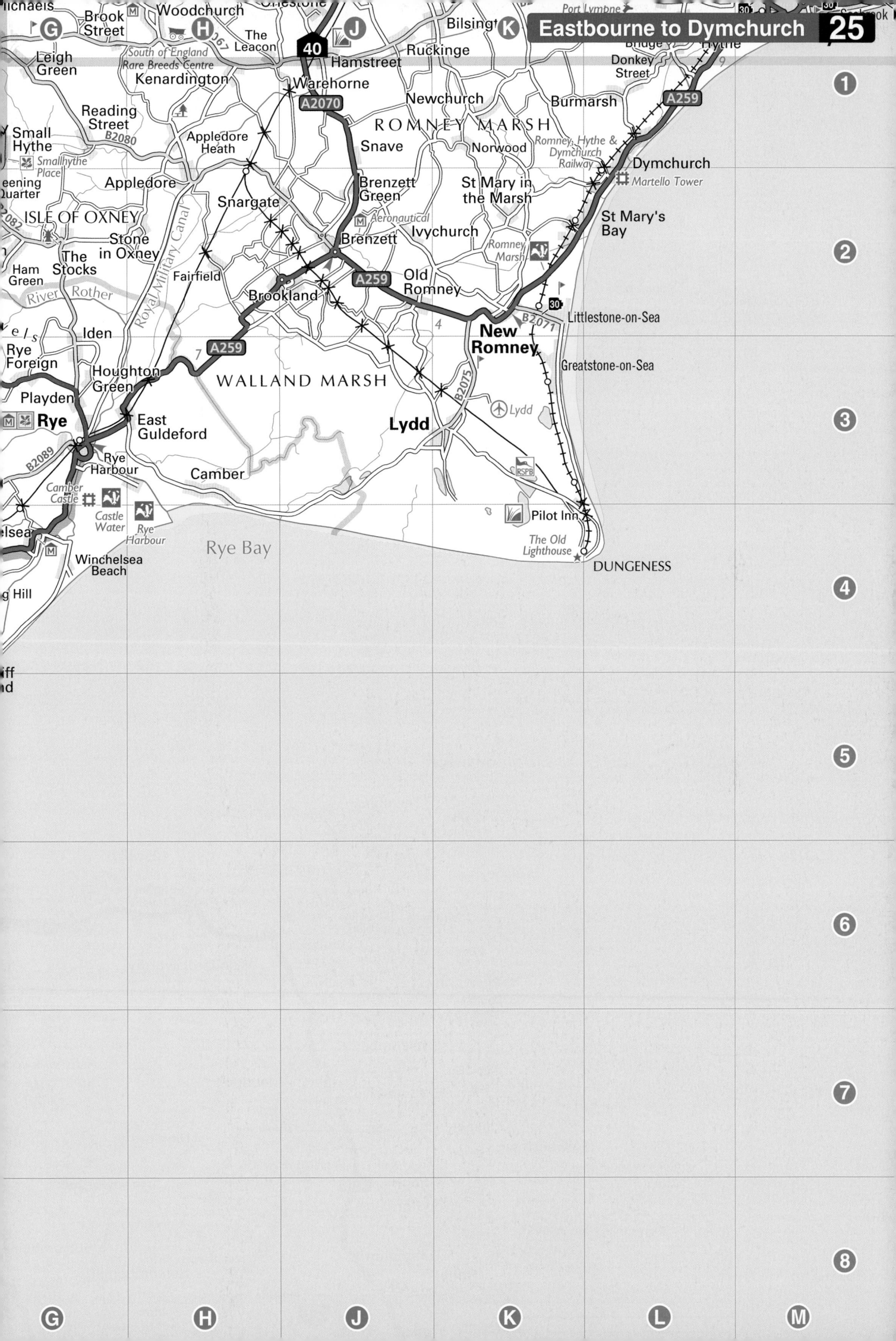

A B C D E F

1

North West
Point

*Lundy
Heritage Coast*   LUNDY

2   ▲ 142

Marisco
Surf Point

Shutter Point

3

4

B A R N S T A P L E

O R

5   HARTLAND POINT   *Shipload
Bay*   B I D E F O R D   B A Y

Titchberry   Brownsham

Damehole
Point   *Hartland Abbey
& Gardens*   Clovelly   *Hartl
Heritage*

Stoke   Velly   Buck's
Mills

Hartland Quay   Hartland   B3248   Higher
Clovelly   H

*Spekes Mill
Mouth*   *Docton Mill
Gardens*   Buck's
Cross   A39

6   Milford   Philham   *Milky Way*   Par

Elmscott   Edistone   Woolfardisworthy   Cranford   Parkha
Ash

Hardisworthy   Tosberry

South
Hole   Welcombe   Meddon   Ashmanswort

Mead   Darracott   East
Putford

7   Gooseham
Mill   Woolley   *Gnome
Reserve* ★   Wes
Putfo

Gooseham   Eastcott   16   East
Youlstone   Dinworthy   Colscott

Morwenstow   West Youlstone   Bradworthy

Higher Sharpnose Point   Shop   A39   Kimworthy   Sutcombe

*South West
Coast Path*   Woodford   *Tamar
Lakes*   Alfardisworthy   Sutcombe

Lower Sharpnose Point   Kilhampton   Sutcombemill

8   Steeple Point   Stibb   Thurdon   Soldon   *River*

A   0   1   2   3   4   5 miles
0 1 2 3 4 5 6 7 8 kilometres   D   11   E   Soldon
Cross   F

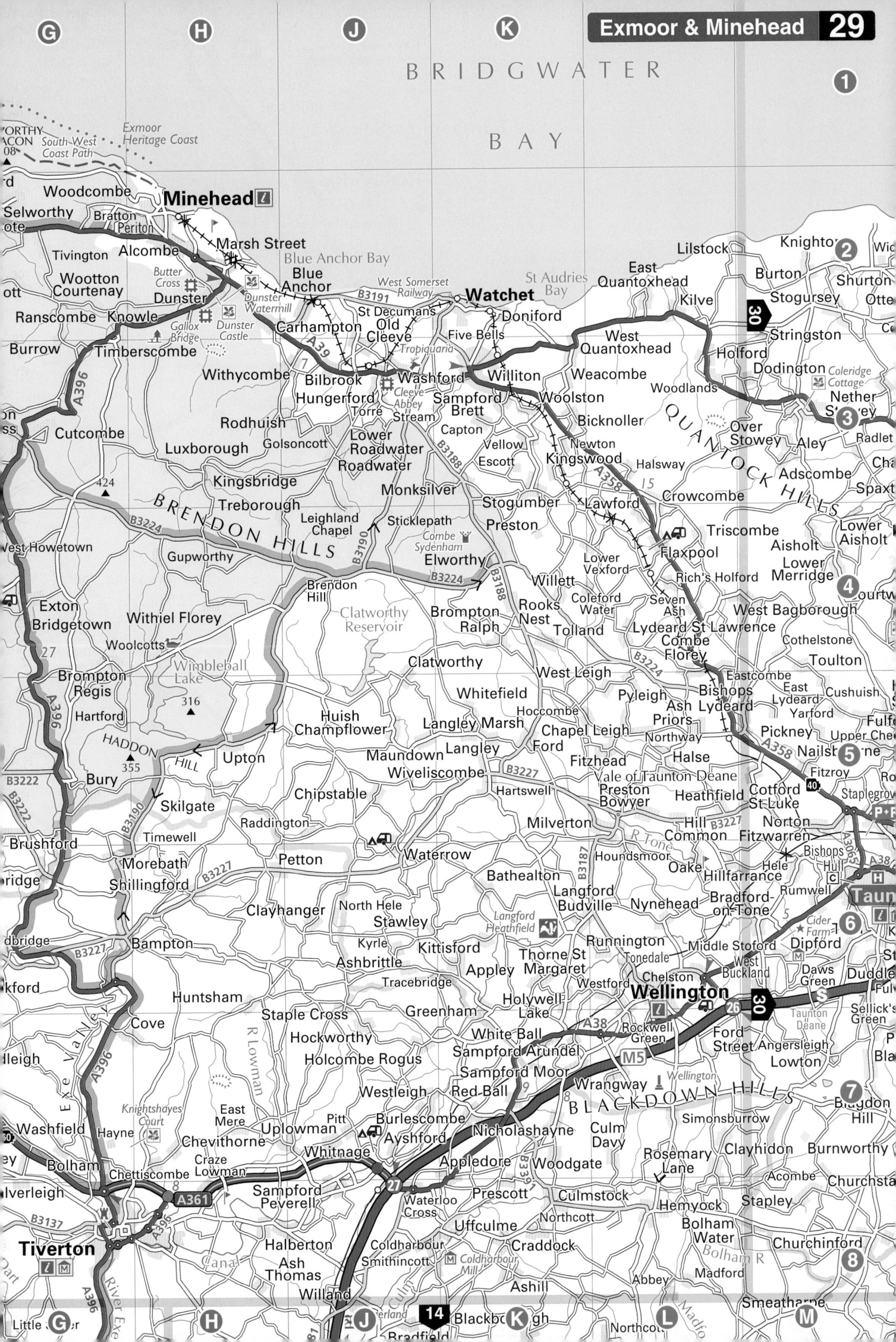

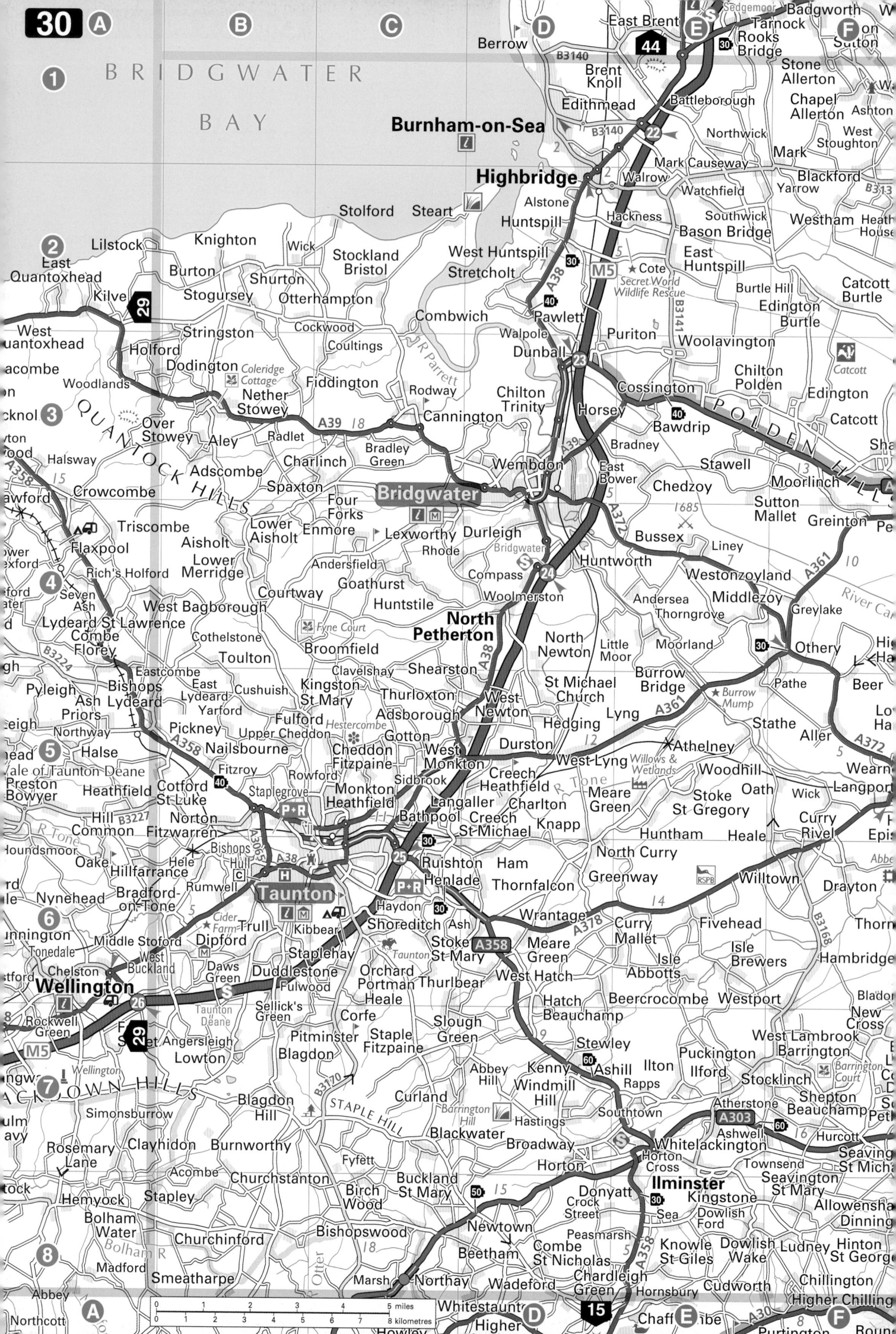

45 **J** **K**

Chewton Mendip · Bathway · Easton · Clapton · Chilcompton
B3135 · B3114 · B3139 · Stratton-on-the-Fosse · Kimersdon · A362

G Draycott **H** · Priddy · East Water · Emborough · Gurney Slade · Downside · Holcombe · Highbury · Newbury · Upper Vobster · Mells **1**

Clewer · Cocklake · Green Ore · Binegar **30** · Nettlebridge · Ham · Vobster · Coleford · Whatley · Little

Rodney Stoke · Old Ditch · Ebbor Gorge · Westbury-sub-Mendip · Wookey Hole · **A37** · Ashwick · Oakhill · Stoke St Michael · East End · Downhead · Little Elm · Chantry · Castle

Wedmore · Latcham · Easton · Lower Milton · Walcombe · West Horrington · Leigh upon Mendip

Bagley · Theale · Panborough · Henton · Burcott Mill · Wookey · Dulcote · Dinder · Downside · Darshill · Shepton Mallet · Dean · Leighton · Cloford **2** · Catch · A361

Bleadney · Yarley · Worth · Coxley Wick · **Wells** · Croscombe · West Compton · Charlton · Cranmore · East Cranmore · Trudoxh... · East Somerset Railway

Westhay Moor · Lower Godney · Upper Godney · Polsham · Coxley · Worminster · North Town · West Compton · Pilton · East Compton **40** · Prestleigh · Chesterblade · Higher Alham · West Town **32** · Wanstrow · A359

Meare · Stileway · Meare Fish House · Godney · North Wootton · Westholme · Royal Bath and West Showground · Stoney Stratton · Westcombe · Batcombe · Upton Noble **3** · SEAT HILL

Northload Bridge · **Glastonbury** · Brindham · Glastonbury Tor · Street on the Fosse · Pylle · Evercreech · Milton Clevedon · South Brewham · North Brewham

Northover · Edgarley · Havyatt · West Pennard · East Pennard · Hembridge · Wraxall · Ditcheat · Lamyatt · West End · Bruton · King Alfred's Tower

Walton · Asney · **Street** · Butleigh Wootton · West Bradley · Woodland Street · Coxbridge · Tilham Street · Parbrook · Huxham Green · Stone · **A37** Alhampton · Hornblotton Green · Clanville · Wyke Champflower · Ansford · Cole · Redlynch · Stoney Stoke

Compton Dundon · Baltonsborough · Gosling Street · Catsham · Southwood · Four Foot · Hornblotton · Alford · Lovington · Castle Cary · Pitcombe · Shepton Montague · Charlton Musgrove

Dundon · BRADLEY HILL · Barton St David · Silver Street · West Lydford · East Lydford · Wheathill · Galhampton · Bratton Seymour · Wincanton · Bayford

Stembridge Tower Mill · Littleton · Kingweston · Keinton Mandeville-on-Fosse · Lydford · Foddington · Yarlington · **A371**

Pitney · **Somerton** · Charlton Mackrell · Charlton Adam · Babcary · North Barrow · South Barrow · Brookhampton · Woolston · **A303** · Lattiford · **Wi...** **5**

Upton · South Hill · Catsgore · Midney · Lytes Cary Manor · Kingsdon · Haynes International Motor · Little Weston · North Cadbury · Blackford · Holton · Compton Pauncefoot · Maperton · North Cheriton

Long Sutton · Knole · **A372** · Downhead · **50** · West Camel · Sparkford · Queen Camel · Wales · South Cadbury · South Cheriton · Horsington · Abbas Comb **6**

Little Load · Long Load · Northover · Ilchester · Podimore · Bridgehampton · Chilton Cantelo · Sutton Montis · Marston Magna · Charlton Horethorne · Stowell · Templecombe · Yenston

Milton · Stapleton · Coat · Ash · **A303** · Tintinhull Garden · RNAS Yeovilton · Fleet Air Arm · Yeovilton · Limington · Ashington · West Mudford · Adber · Rimpton · Corton Denham · Sandford Orcas · Milborne Wick · Henstridge Ash **32**

Martock · Hurst Priory · Stoke sub Hamdon · Chilthorne Domer · Yeovil Marsh · Draycott · Mudford Sock · Mudford · Up Mudford **30** · Trent · Poyntington · Milborne Port · Henstridge · A30 · A357

Norton sub Hamdon · Montacute · Montacute House · Odcombe · Tintinhull · Thorne Coffin · **40** · Preston Plucknett · Over Compton · **Yeovil** · Nether Compton · Stallen · Oborne · Purse Caundle · **7**

Little Norton · Chiselborough · Brympton · West Coker · Barwick · Bradford Abbas · North Wootton · **Sherborne** · Sherborne Castle and Gardens · Old Castle · Goathill · Haydon · Stalbridge Weston · Stourton Caundle

Wigborough · East Chinnock · Burton · Thornford · Folke · Bishop's Caundle · Lydlin...

Middle Chinnock · Hardington · Hardington Moor · East Coker · Sutton Bingham · Stoford · Lillington · Longburton · Caundle Marsh · Holwell **8**

Crewkerne G · Haselbury Plucknett · Pendomer · Ryme Intrinseca · Beer Hackett · Knighton · Boys Hill · Crouch Hill · Pleck · Packers... · King's... **M**

North Perrott · **15** · **H** · Closwo... · **J** · Hamlet · **K** · Holnest · **16** · **L** · East Pulham · Hazel...

A B C D E F

32

Stratton-on-the-Fosse
Carlton
Kilmersdon
Hardington
Laverton
Lullington
Cton
Brokerswood
Bratton
Bratton Camp
 Ilbrook

1

Downside
Holcombe
Newbury
Highbury
Upper Vobster
A362
45
Buckland Dinham
Oldford
Beckington
Berkley
Rudge
Standerwick
Penleigh
46
Westbury
White Horse
878
TENANTRY D

ttlebridge
Ham
Coleford
Vobster
Mells
Great Elm
B3090
Clink
Dilton Marsh
A3098
A36
Chalford
Westbury Leigh
Dilton
A350
WARMINSTER DOWN

Leigh upon Mendip
Whatley
Little Green
Frome
Chapmanslade
Lye's Green
Corsley
7
S
212
Warminster
WARMINSTER DOWN

Stoke St Michael
East End
Downhead
Chantry
Little Elm
Lower Whatley
Nunney
Little Keyford
Elliots Green
Lane End
Corsley Heath
Cold Harbour
A36
208
BATTLESBURY HILL
Boreham
198
SCRATCHBURY HILL

2

Mallet
Dean
Leighton
Nunney Catch
Cloford
Tytherington
East Woodlands
West Woodlands
Longleat
A362
8
Crockerton
Bishopstrow
Norton Bavant
Heytesb

Doulting
Cranmore
A361
Trudoxhill
Lower Marston
West Woodlands
West Woodlands Showground
Longleat Forest CenterParcs
Shear Cross
Sutton Veny
Knook

Chesterblade
East Cranmore
31
West Town
Wanstrow
Witham Friary
Horningsham
Newbury
Longbridge Deverill
Tytherington
Corton
Boy Sher

3

Stoney Stratton
Westcombe
Batcombe
Upton Noble
A359
Gare Hill
Pottle Street
Hill Deverill
Brixton Deverill
176
TYTHERINGTON HILL

Milton Clevedon
North Brewham
SEAT HILL
Maiden Bradley
BRIMSDOWN HILL
A350
Monkton Deverill
Pertwood

amyatt
West End
South Brewham
Kilmington
Kilmington Common
LONG KNOLL
Kingston Deverill
Chicklade

Wyke Champflower
Bruton
King Alfred's Tower
Kilmington Street
Norton Ferris
KEYSLEY DOWN
60
Berwick St Leonard

4

Ansford
Dovecote
Cole
Redlynch
Hardway
Stourhead
Stourton House
Stourton
West Knoyle
Upton
Hindon
Fonthill Gifford

Pitcombe
Stoney Stoke
Gasper
Zeals
Mere
Burton
The Green
East Knoyle
Tuckingmill
Tisb

Castle Cary
Barrow
Coombe Street
Wolverton
Barrow Street
Holloway
Newtown
East Ha

Bratton Seymour
Shepton Montague
Penselwood
Charlton Musgrove
Bleak Street
Queen Oak
Silton
Huntingford
Milton on Stour
Sedgehill
A350
West Hat

5

Yarlington
Woolston
Bayford
B3081
Wincanton
Bourton
West Bourton
Silton
A371
Stoke Trister
Hale
Cucklington
Wyke
North End
Semley

A303
Holton
Lattiford
Gillingham
Ham Common
Motcombe
Old Wardour Castle
Ar

Blackford
Compton Pauncefoot
bury
Maperton
North Cheriton
Buckhorn Weston
Langham
Sandley
Bugley
Knap Corner
Enmore Green
Ivy Cross
Shaftesbury
Ludwell
Donhead St Andrew
West End

6

Charlton Horethorne
South Cheriton
Horsington
Abbas Combe
Kington Magna
West Stour
A30
Donhead St Mary
Charlton

Stowell
Higher Nyland
East Stour
Stour Row
Guy's Marsh
Cann
West Melbury
Melbury Abbas
Fontmell and Melbury Downs

Milborne Wick
ord Orcas
Templecombe
Yenston
Lower Nyland
10
Fifehead Magdalen
Stour Provost
Todber
Margaret Marsh
Hartgrove
Compton Abbas
Ashmore
Fontmell Down

yntington
Milborne Port
Henstridge Ash
Henstridge Marsh
Moorside
East Orchard
Woodbridge

7

athill
Old Castle
31
Stalbridge
Purse Caundle
Walton Elm
West Orchard
Bedchester
Fontmell Magna
Sutton Waldron
New To

Sherborne Castle and Gardens
Haydon
Stalbridge Weston
Stourton Caundle
Hinton St Mary
Manston
Iwerne Minster
Stubhampton

Oborne
A30
6
Allweston
Bishop's Caundle
Lydlinch
Bagber
A357
Sturminster Newton
Hammoon
Gold Hill
Fontmell Parva
A350
Iwerne Courtney or Shroton
CRANBORNE C
Tarrant Gunvil

8

orth tton
Folke
A3030
Caundle Marsh
Holwell
Fifehead Neville
Pleck
Rivers Corner
Fiddleford
Child Okeford
Hambledon Hill
Little Hanford
Tarrant Hinton

Longburton
Boys Hill
Crouch Hill
King's Stag
Sturminster Common
Okeford Fitzpaine
Shillingstone
Hanford
Ash
T nt
L neston

Holnest
Sandhills

0 1 2 3 4 5 miles
0 1 2 3 4 5 6 7 8 kilometres

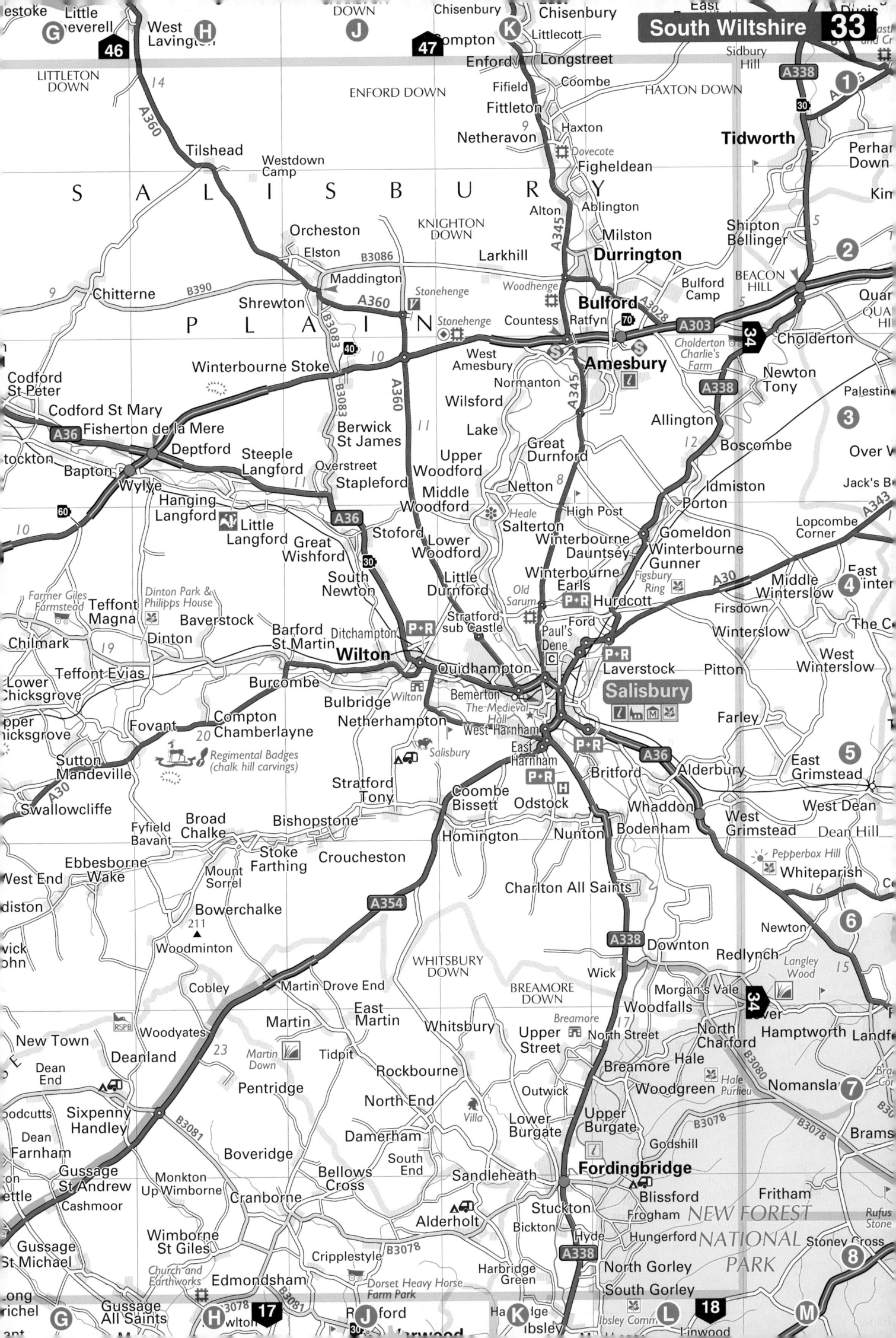

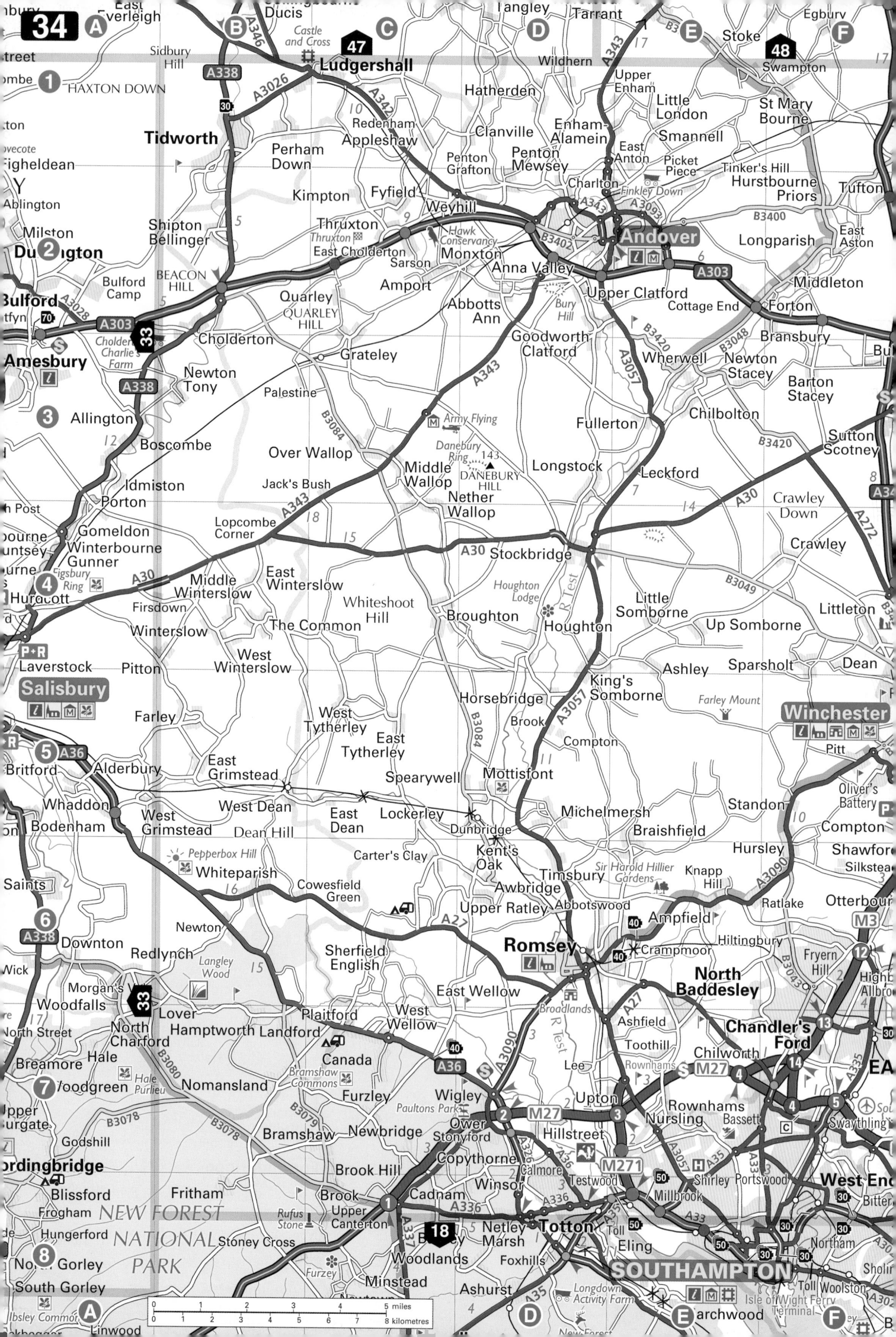

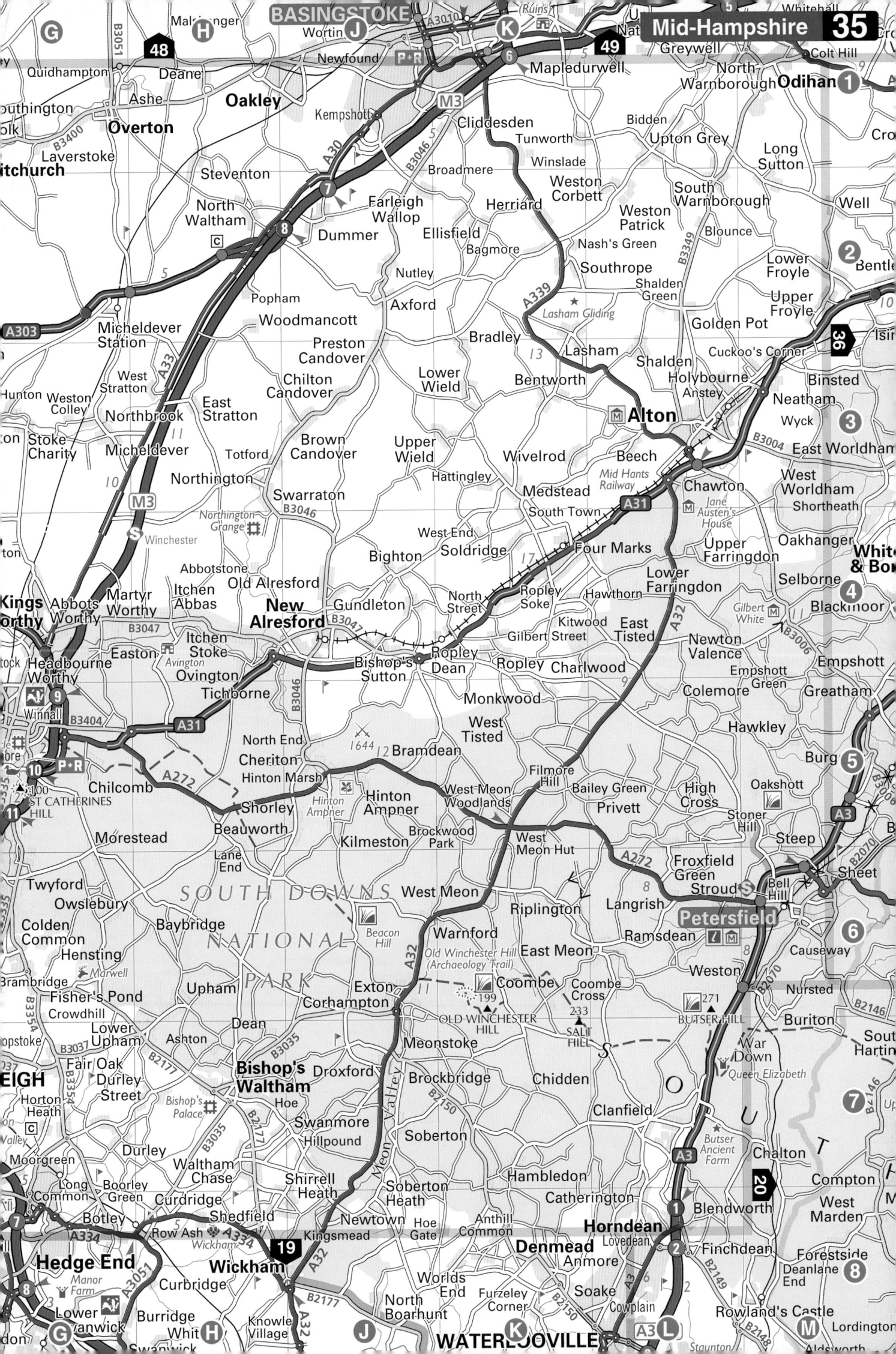

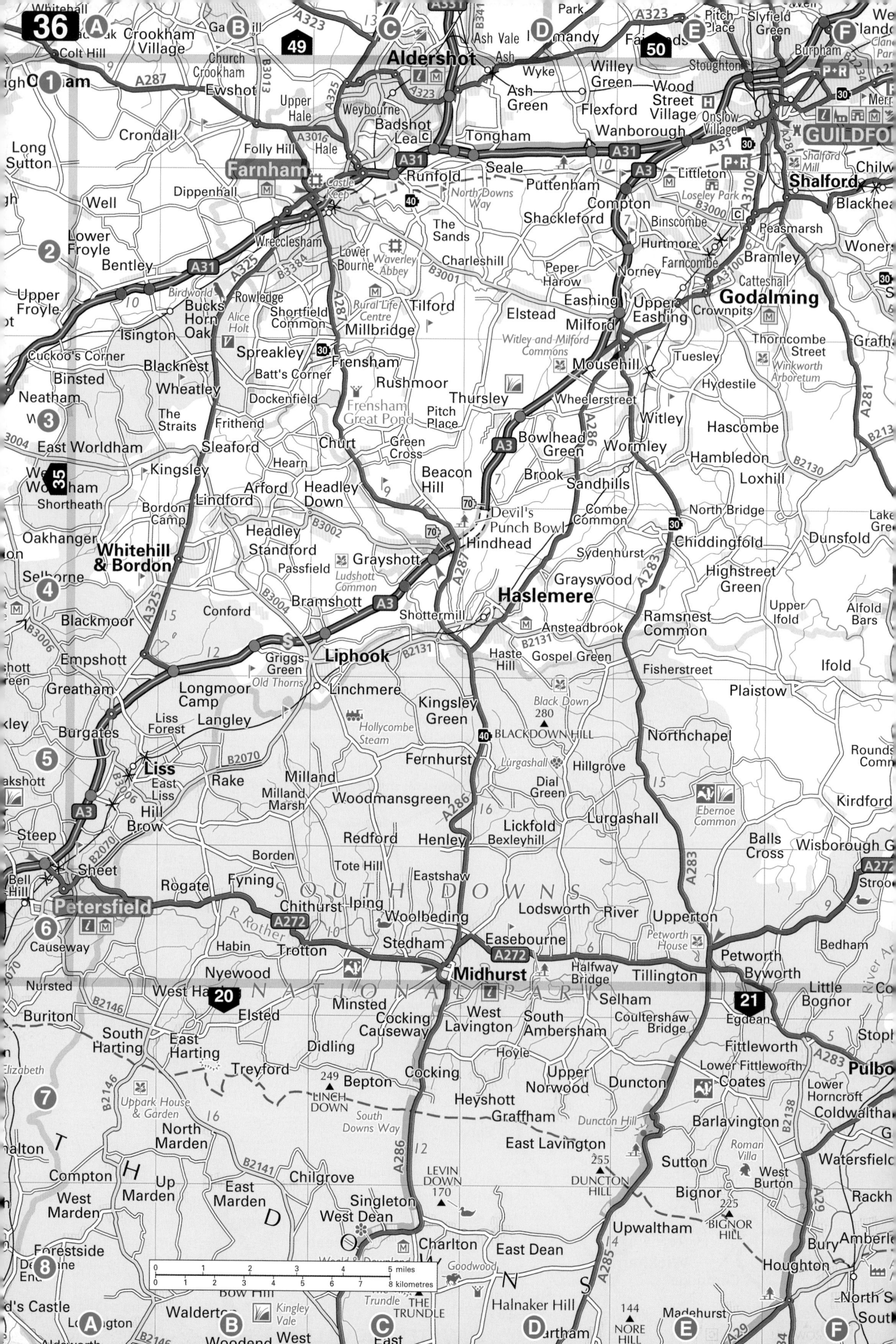

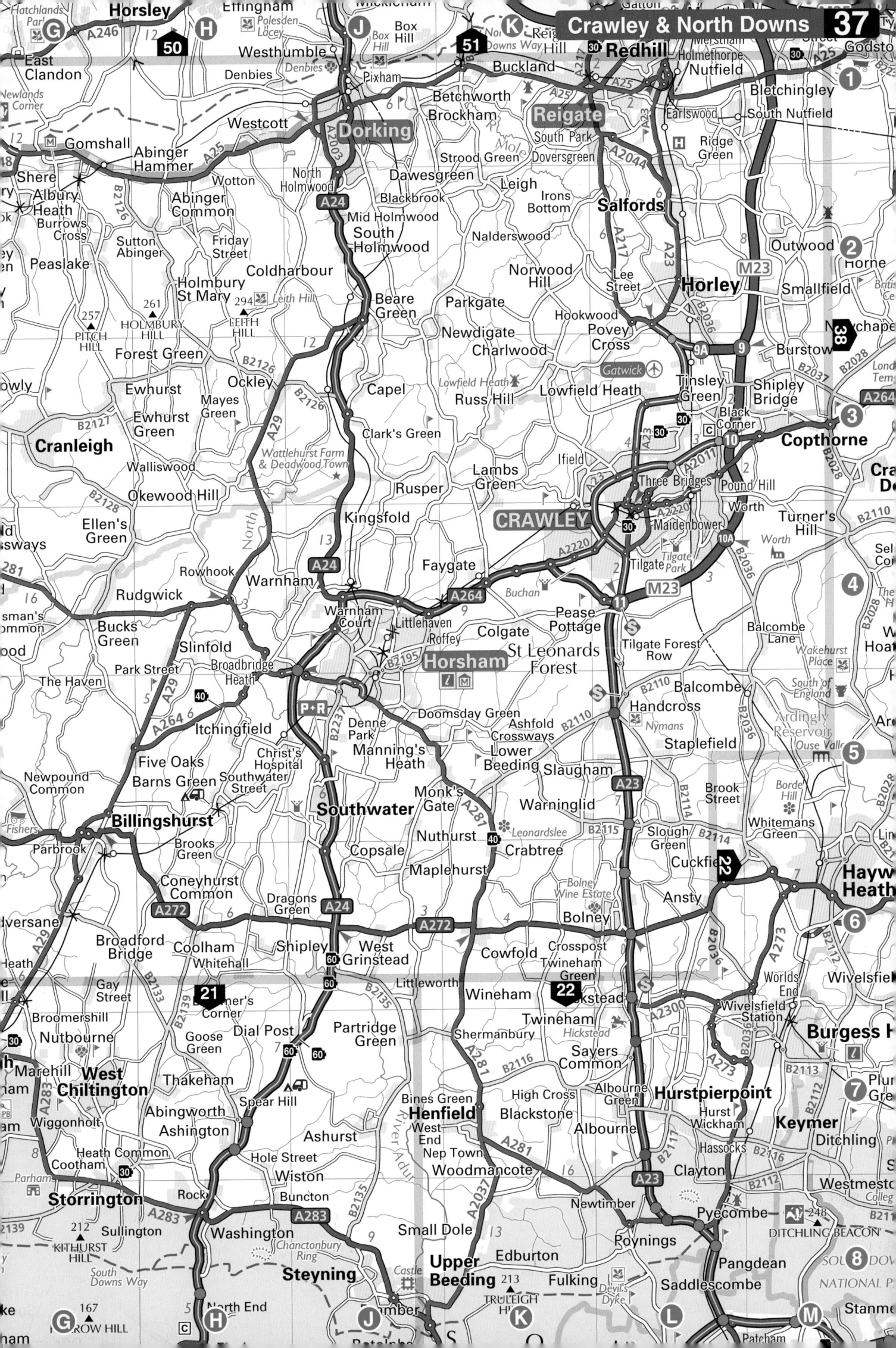

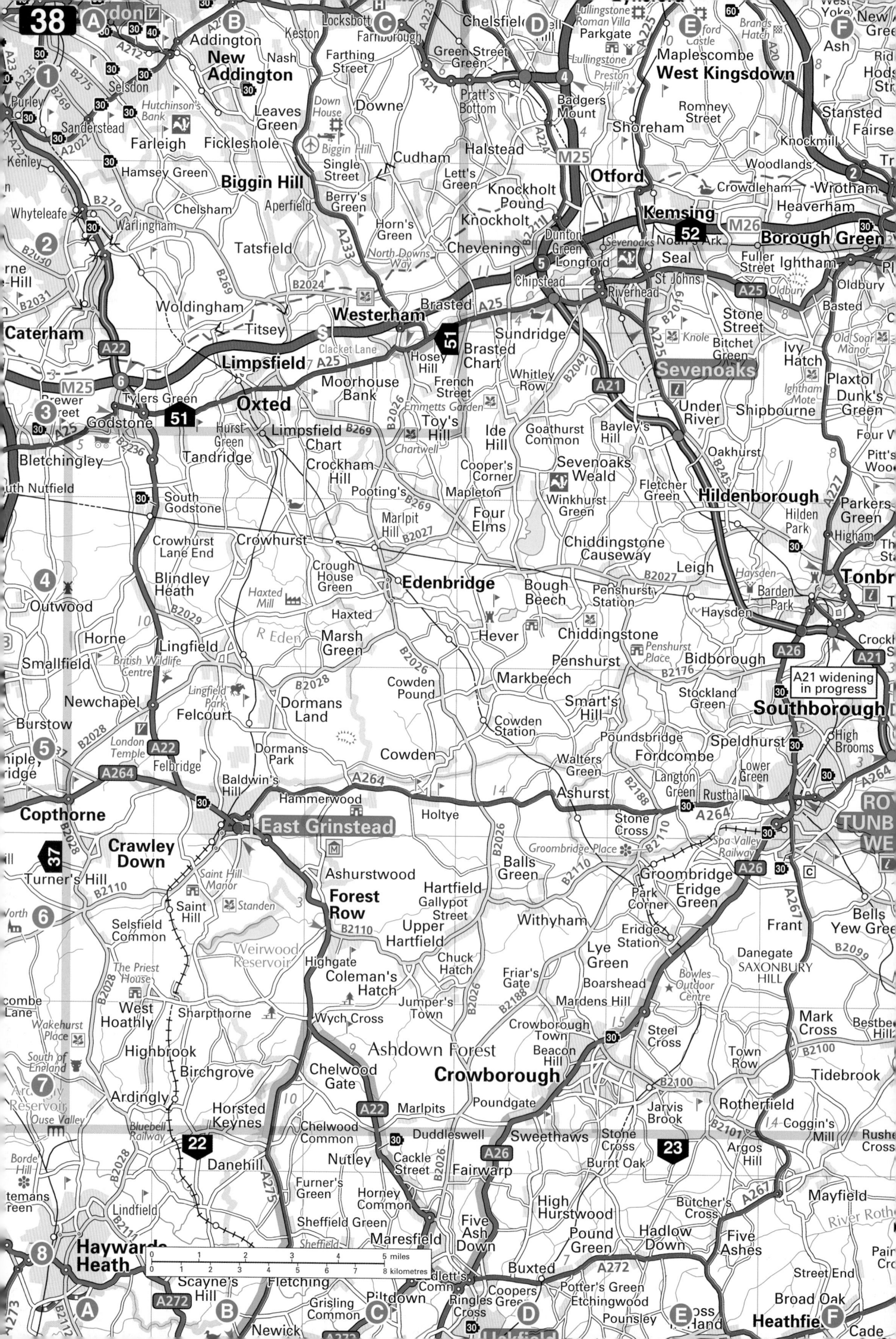

Sitting...

Snodland · **Aylesford** · **Ditton** · **West Malling** · **MAIDSTONE** · **Bearsted**

Priestwood Green · Upper Halling · North Halling · Halling · Wouldham · Walderslade · Capstone · Hempstead · Meresborough · Hartlip · Chestnut St · Chalkwell · Borden · Tunstall · Bapchild · Rodmersham · Rawling Street · Dungate

Harvel · Culverstone Green · Paddlesworth · Holborough · Lords Wood · Lidsing · Bredhurst · Guildstead · Kemsley Street · Danaway · Oad St · Hearts Delight · Highsted · Rodmersham Green

Vigo · Birling · Ryarsh · Trosley · Burham · Blue Bell Hill · Kit's Coty · Westfield Sole · Dunn Street · Stockbury · South Green · Stiff Street · Silver Street · Bexon · Bredgar · Milstead

Addington · Leybourne · Larkfield · New Hythe · Eccles · Tyland Barn · Boarley · Boxley · Kent Event Centre · White Horse Wood · Thurnham · Bicknor · Swanton Street · Frinsted · Doddington · Wichling

Little Comp · Offham · St Leonard's Street · East Malling · Allington · British Legion Village · Ware Street · Grove Green · Detling · Hucking · Broad Street · Wormshill · Ringlestone · West Street · Payden Street

Kings Hill · Herne Pound · East Malling Heath · Barming Heath · Tovil · Willington · Shepway · Otham · Sutton Street · Hollingbourne · Eyhorne Street · Leeds · Broomfield · Harrietsham · Woodside Green · Lenham

Soar · Mereworth · Wateringbury · Kent Street · Teston · East Barming · Dean Street · Loose · Boughton Green · Langley · Cock St · Chart Corner · Otham Hole · Five Wents · Kingswood · Chartway Street · Leadingcross Green · Sandway · Lenham Heath

West Peckham · Nettlestead · Nettlestead Green · Goose Green · Yalding · Coxheath · Linton · Boughton Monchelsea · Chart Sutton · Chart Hill · Sutton Valence · Chartway Street · Liverton Street · Platts Heath · Grafty Green

East Peckham · Hale Street · Hunton · Benover · Chainhurst · Stile Bridge · Boughton Malherbe · Egerton · Egerton Forstal

Barnes Street · Snoll Hatch · Hop Farm Family Park · Beltring · Mockbeggar · Underling Green · Little Pattenden · Cross-at-Hand · Milebush · Rabbit's Cross · Farthing Green · Plumtree Green · Jubilee Corner · Potter's Forstal · Pembles Cross · Boughton Malherbe · Mundy Bois

Five Oak Green · Rhoden Grn · Fowlhall · Collier Street · Queen Street · Great Pattenden · Little Cheveney · Wanshurst Green · Sweetlands Corner · Hawkenbury · Southernden · Swift's Green · The Quarter

Paddock Wood · Whetsted · Claygate · Pearson's Green · Marden · Marden Thorn · Staplehurst · Headcorn · Wheeler's Street · Biddenden Green · Chambers Green · Maltman's Hill · Pluckley Station

Matfield · Mile Oak · Marden Beech · Iden Croft Herbs · Frittenden · Sinkhurst Green · Lashenden · Smarden Bell · Smarden · Romden Castle · Wissenden

Brenchley · Horsmonden · Corks Pond · Castle Hill · The Corner · Winchet Hill · Grovenhurst · Curtisden Green · Knox Bridge · Hareplain · Standen · Curteis Corner · Stede Quarter · Further Quarter · Middle Quarter · Haffenden Quarter

Hazel Street · Broad Ford · Colliers Green · Three Chimneys · Cranbrook Common · Wilsley Pound · Sissinghurst Castle · Biddenden · Woolpack · High Halden

Goudhurst · Spelmonden · Finchcocks · Iden Green · Glassenbury · Wilsley Green · Union Mill · Sissinghurst · Goose Green · Arcadia · London Beach · Hoathly · Lamberhurst · Scotney Castle · Riseden · Kilndown · Golford · Golford Green · East End · St Michaels · Redbrook Street

Hook Green · Lamberhurst Down · Cousley Wood · Bewlbridge · Bedgebury Cross · Cranbrook · Goddard's Green · Biddenden · Parkgate · Bewl Water

Stonecrouch · Bedgebury National Pinetum · Hartley · Benenden · Beacon Hill · Tenterden · Leigh Green

Wadhurst · Three Leg Cross · Flimwell · High Street · Gill's Green · Iden Green · Benenden · Strood · The C.W. Booth Collection of Historic Vehicles · Small Hythe · Chapel Down Winery · Small Place

Burchett's Green · Union Street · Hawkhurst · Highgate · Gun Green · Dingleden · Rolvenden · Peening Quarter

Shover's Green · Ticehurst · Dale Hill · The Moor · Four Throws · Standen Street · Rolvenden Layne · Pashley Manor

Bardown · Stonegate · Burgh Hill · Hurst Green · Merriments · Sandhurst · Kent & East Sussex Railway · Newenden · Wittersham · Ham Green · The Stocks

Witherenden Hill · Etchingham · Bodiam · Bodiam Castle · Linkhill · Sandhurst Cross · Great Dixter House & Gardens · Northiam · Rother Levels

Southover · Holton Hill · Burwash · Willards Hill · Northbridge Street · Salehurst · Ewhurst Green · Four Oaks · Beckley · Clayhill · Peasmarsh · Rye Foreign

Burwash Weald · Robertsbridge · Staple Cross · Cripp's Corner · Collier Green · Horns Cross · Millcorner · Bodiam

Bateman's · Dudwell · Darwell · Oxley's Green · Isle of Oxney · River Rother

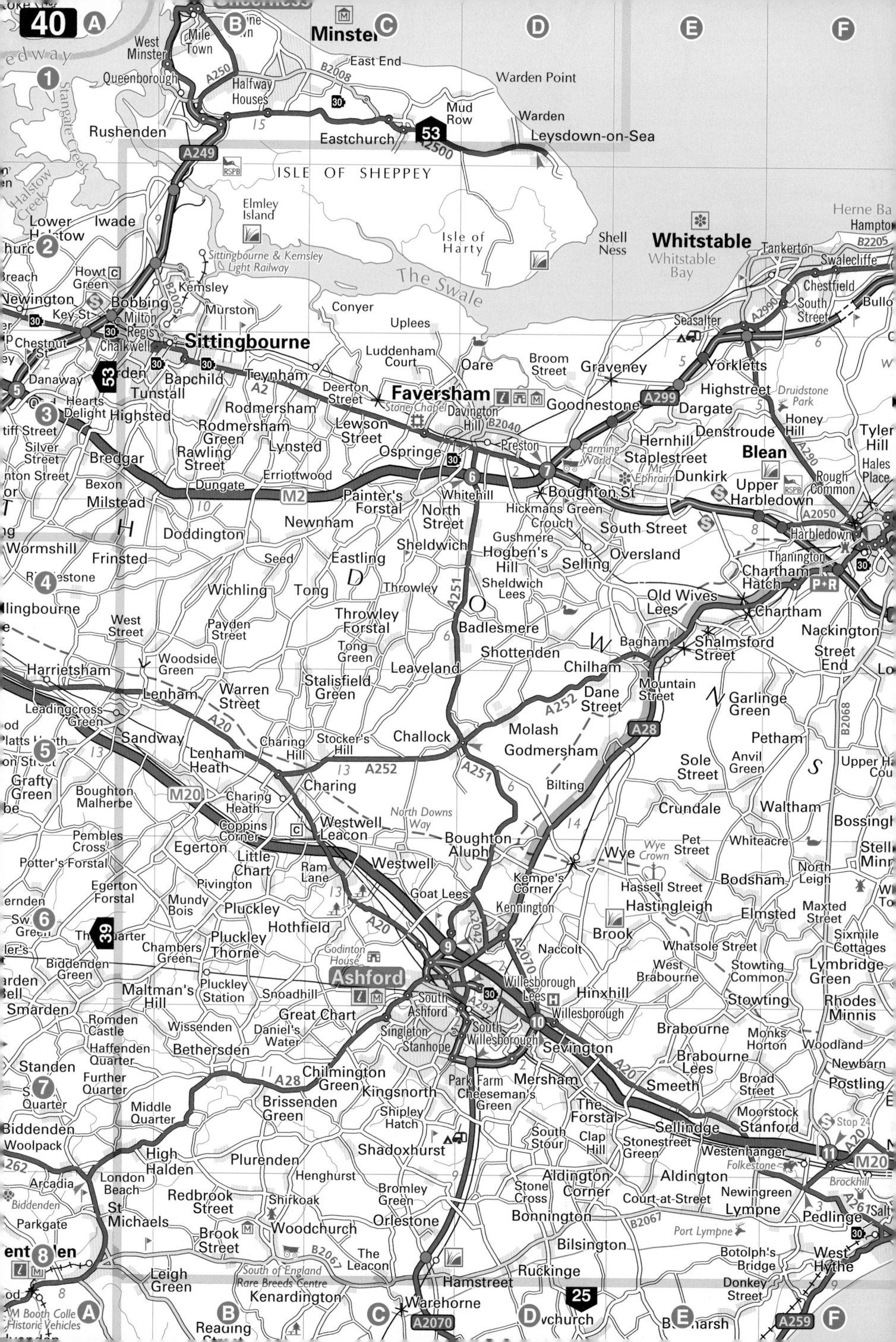

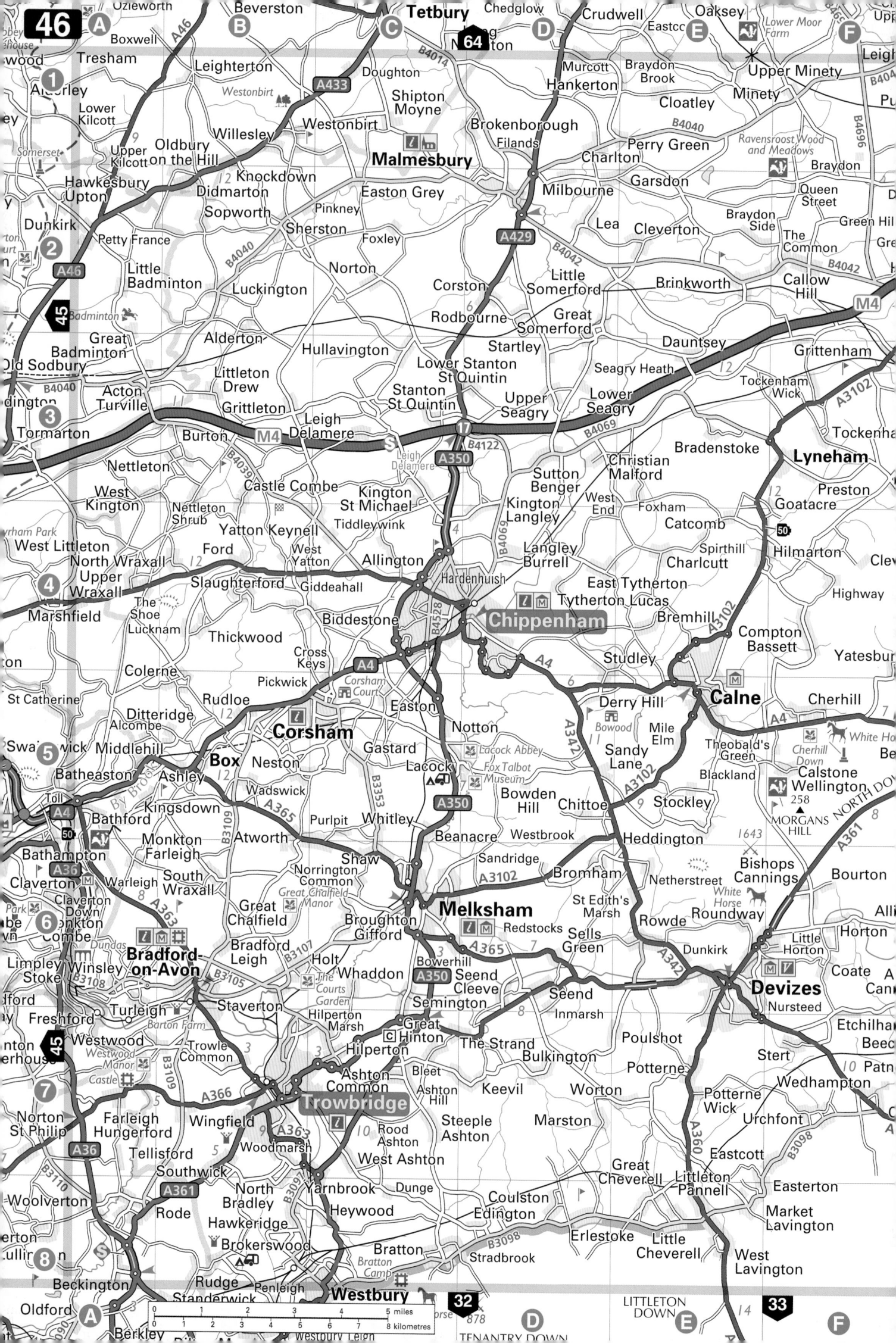

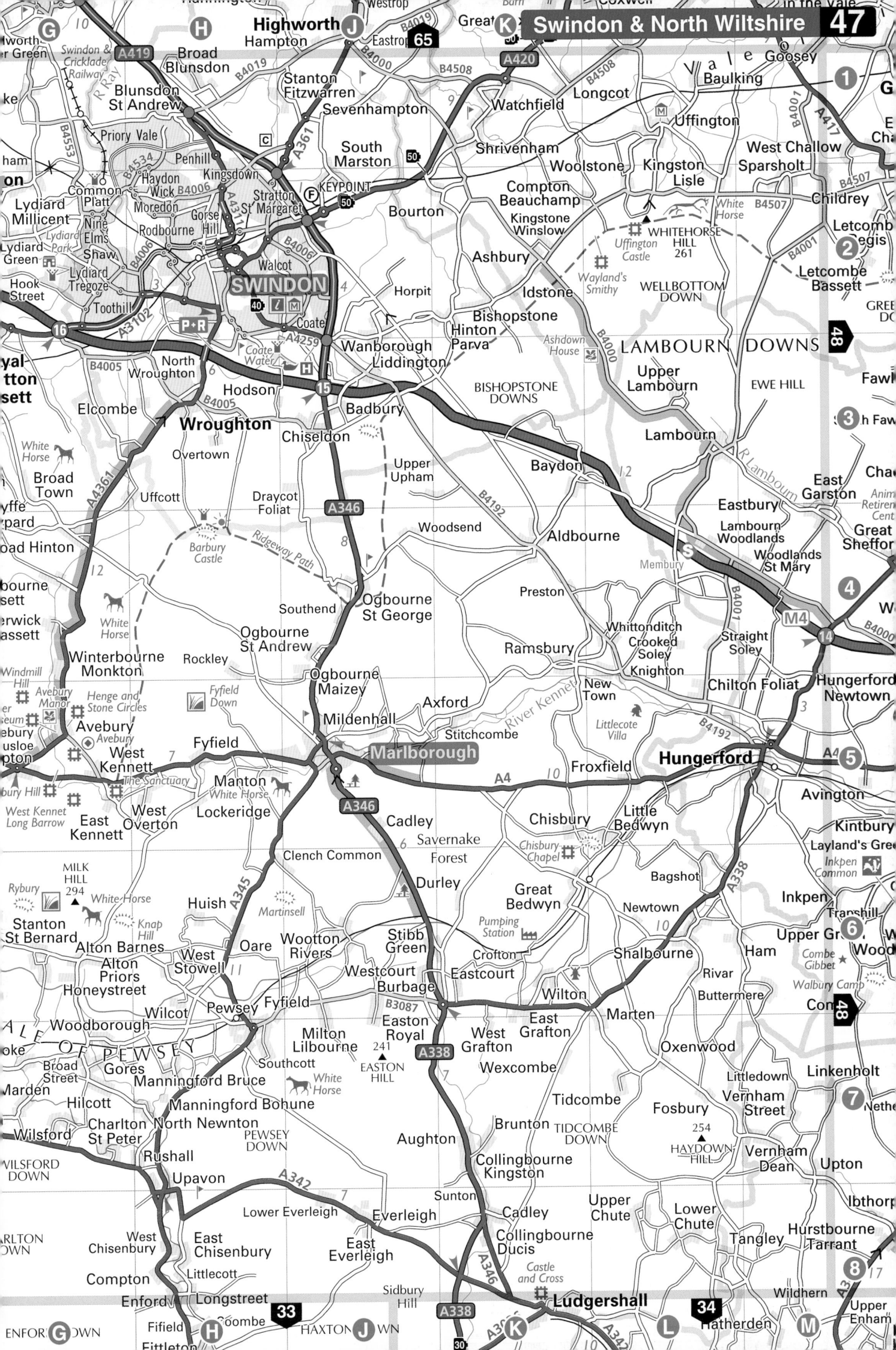

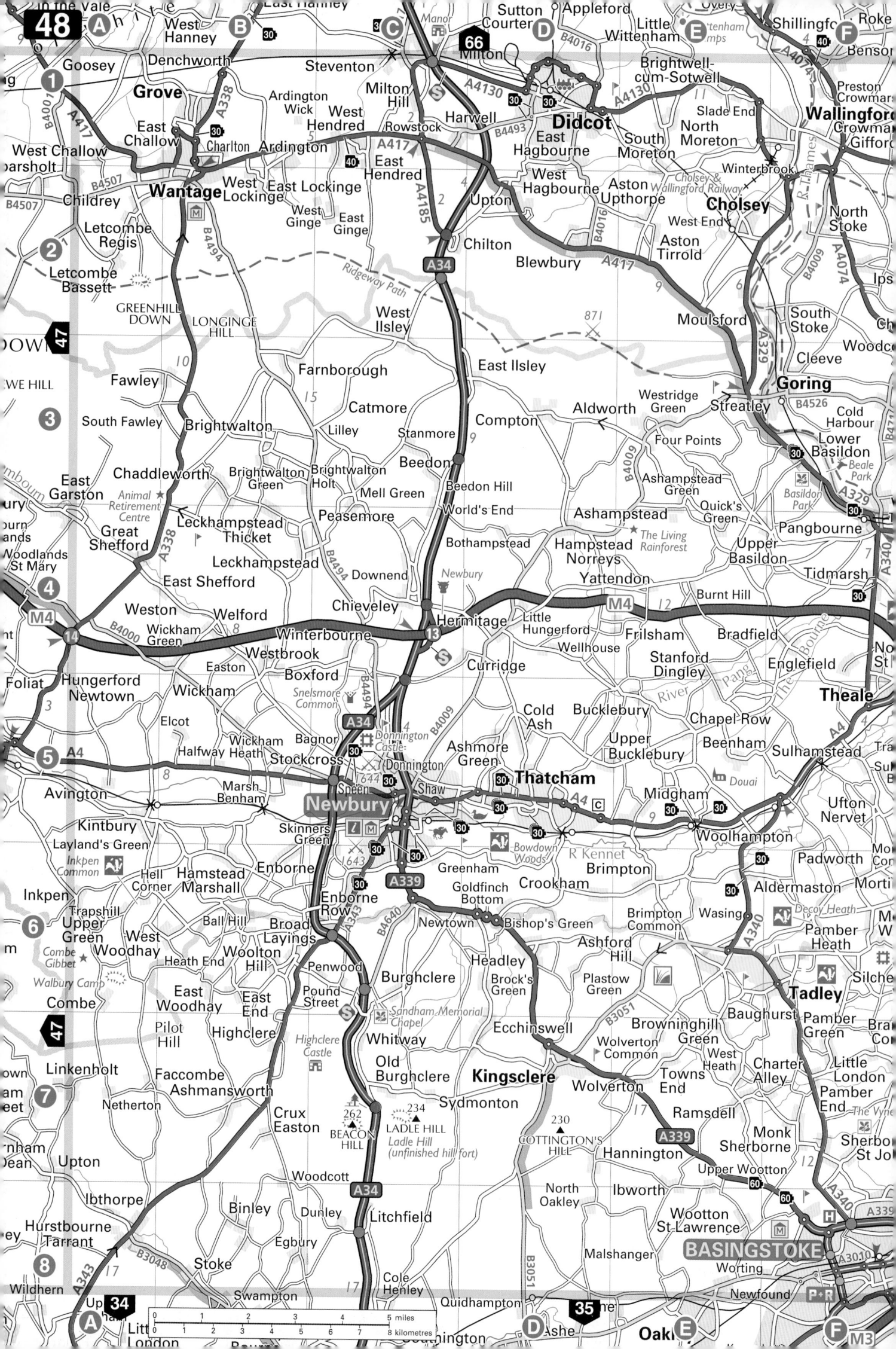

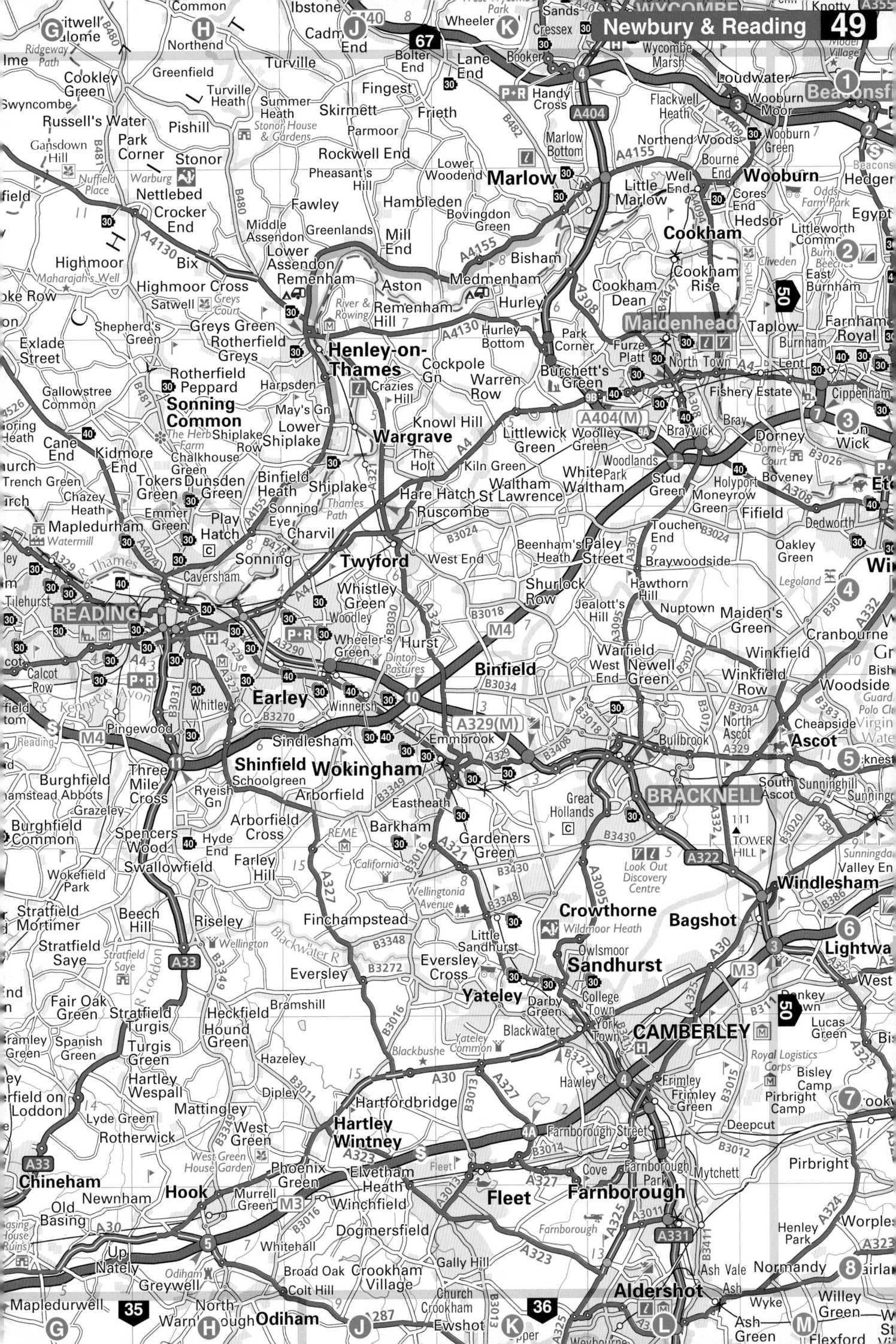

G H ley J Ashingdon
Halesville
Paglesham

71 Hawkwell 72 Great
Stambridge FOULNESS
ISLAND

A1245 B1013
Rayleigh Stroud Rochford Potton
Is
A129 Green R Roach
New
Thundersley A127 Barling
Daws Barling
A130 Heath
Thundersley Eastwood Little Great
A13 A1015 Prittlewell Wakering Wakering
Hadleigh A1159 C Bournes
Green
Leigh Westcliff Southchurch 5 North Shoebury
outh -on-Sea -on-Sea Shoeburyness
fleet Hadleigh Thorpe
Castle Bay
B1016 B1017

Leigh
Beck Canvey
Point **SOUTHEND-ON-SEA** Shoebury Ness

**Canvey
Island**

THAMES ESTUARY

Allhallows-on-Sea

St Mary's Allhallows
Hoo Isle of
Grain Grain
Cooling Lower Stoke
RSPB Middle Stoke Wallend
High Fenn Stoke Sheerness Minster
Halstow Street North
g Street Street West Marine
A228 Sharnal Minster Town East End
Street Mile
Hoo Town A250 Warden Point
St Werburgh Queenborough Halfway B2008
Broad Street Houses 30 Mud
Lower Upnor River Rushenden Row Warden
Upper Upnor Medway Eastchurch A2500 Leysdown-
Upnor Castle 15 on-Sea
The Historic A249 40
Dockyard, Chatham RSPB **ISLE OF SHEPPEY**
Fort Riverside Ham Elmley Isle of
Amherst Green Island Harty
Brompton Grange Lower Wetham The Swale
GILLINGHAM Rainham Green Lower Iwade
Luton East Halstow Sittingbourne & Kemsley
AM Rainham Upchurch Light Railway Conyer
Darland Kemsley
Otterham Howt Uplees
Capstone Rainham Quay Breach Green Murston
Hempstead Wigmore Newington Bobbing Luddenham
Moor Milton Court Oare Gra
Meresborough Street Lower Key St Regis **Sittingbourne** Broo
Medway Hartlip Chestnut Chalkwell Stre
Lidsing M2 Hartlip St Borden Teynham Faversham Goodnes
Bredhurst Guildstead Hill Danaway Bapchild A2 Deerton Stone Chapel
Lords Green Tunstall Rodmersham Street Davington
Wood Kemsley Chesley Oad Hearts Hill Lewson Hill B2040
Capel Street St Delight Rodmersham Street
Dunn Stockbury Stiff Street Green Ospringe Preston
I Hill Street Silver Bredgar Rawling Lynsted Whitehill Boughto
Westfield South Street Street North Hickmans Green
Sole Green Bexon Erriottwood Painter's Street Crouch
and Barn A249 Swanton Street Milstead Dungate M2 Forstal Selling
Boxley Bicknor Doddington Newnham Sheldwich
White Horse Hogben's
Kent Wood Wormshill Seed Eastling Hill
Sandling Event Centre Thurnham Hucking Frinsted Wichling Tong D Sheldwich
39 Broad Ringlestone Throwley Lees
P+R Street Throwley Badlesmere
Ware **Bearsted** Maidstone Payden Forstal
Grove Sutton Hollingbourne West Street Tong North
Green Street Street Green Street Shottenden
Willington Eyhorne Woodside Leaveland
Shepway Street Green Warren Stalisfield Chilha
Otham Leeds Harrietsham Street Lenham Green
Otham Hole Leeds Stocker's
Boughton Langley Broomfield Leadingcross Charing Hill Challock
Green Cock Five Wents Green Hill Molash
St Kingswood Platts Heath Sandway
Boughton Chart Chart Liverton Street Len Medmer
Monchelsea Sutton G H J K Head L A251 M

1

2

3

4

5

6

7

8

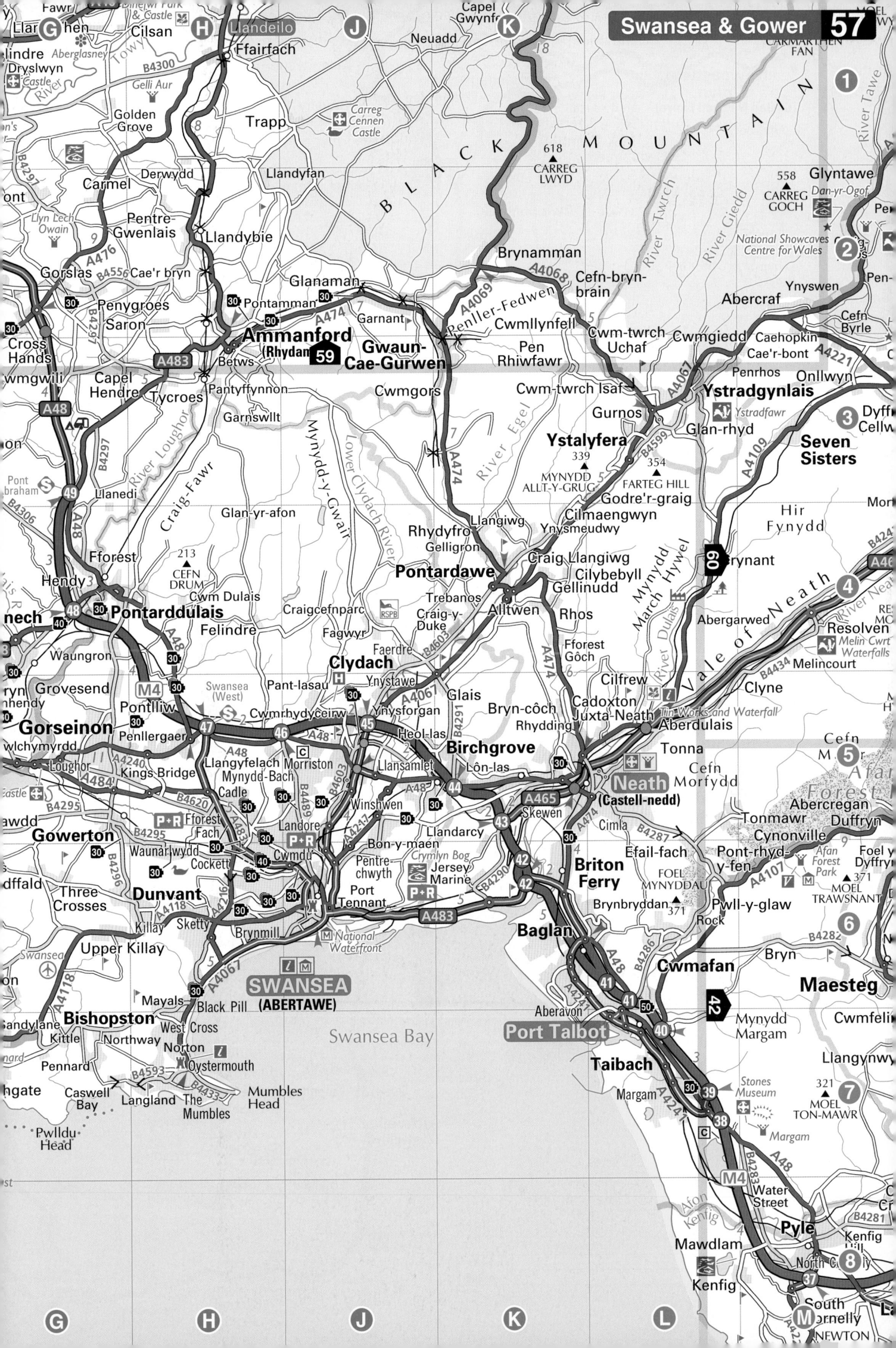

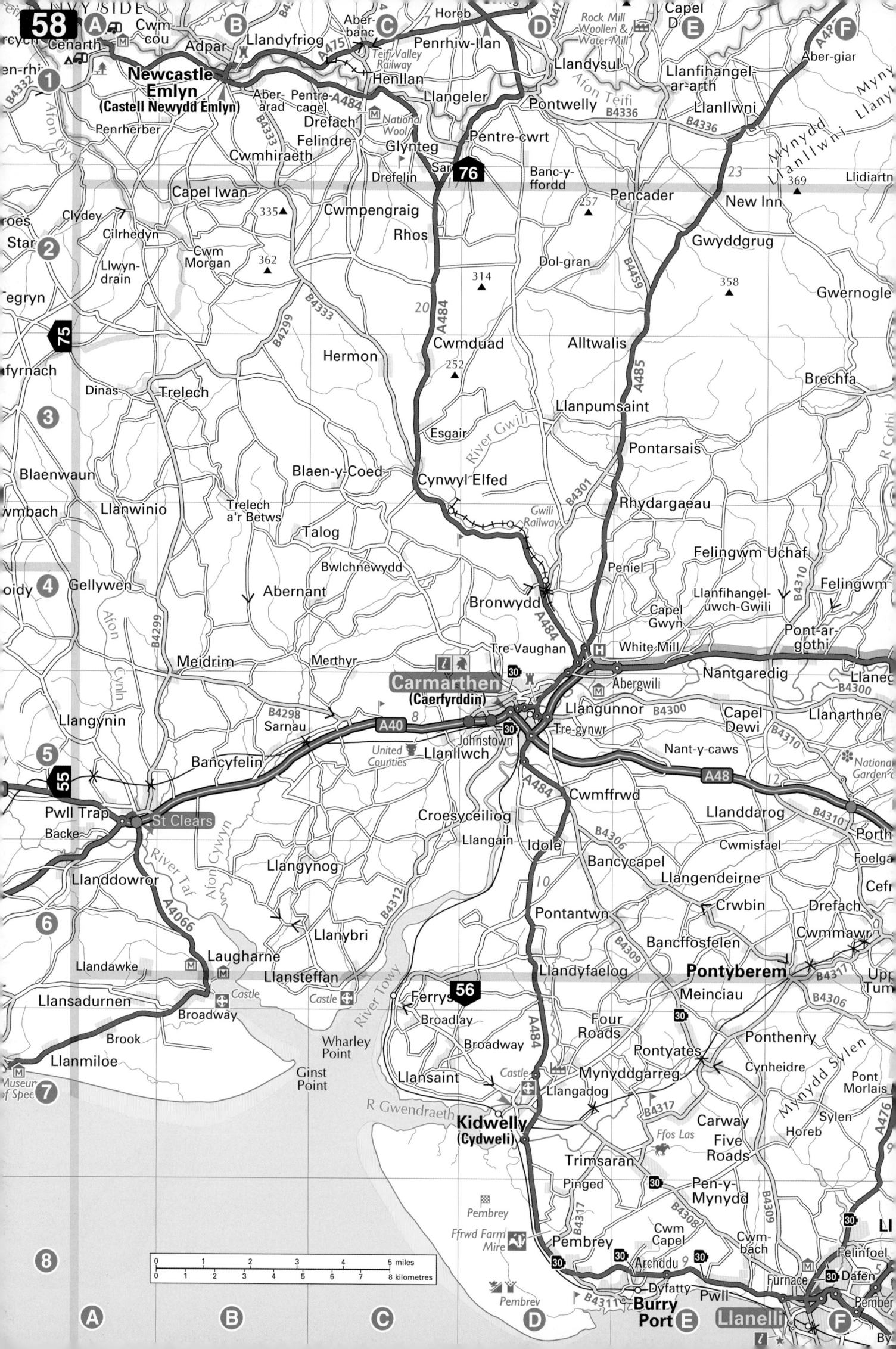

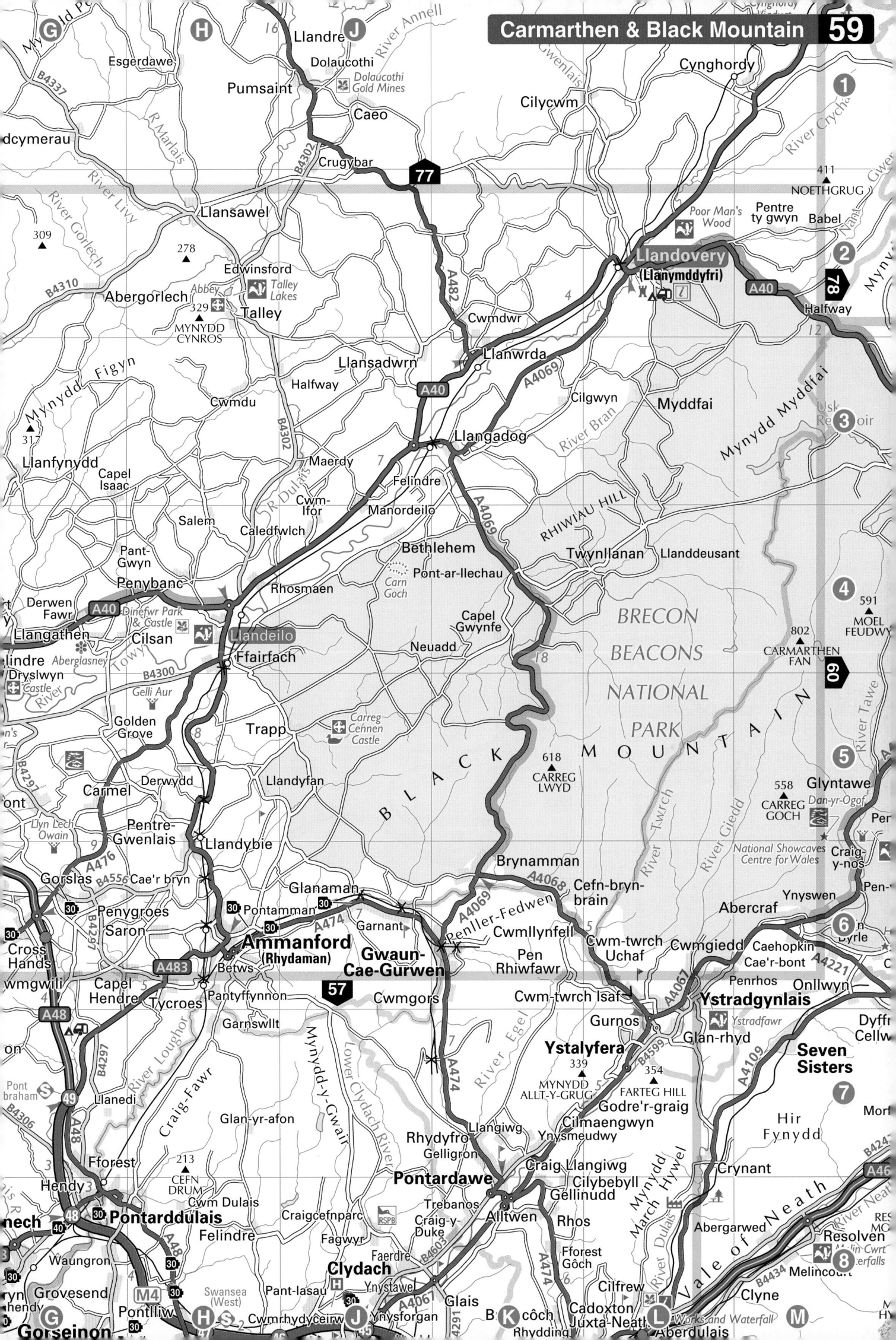

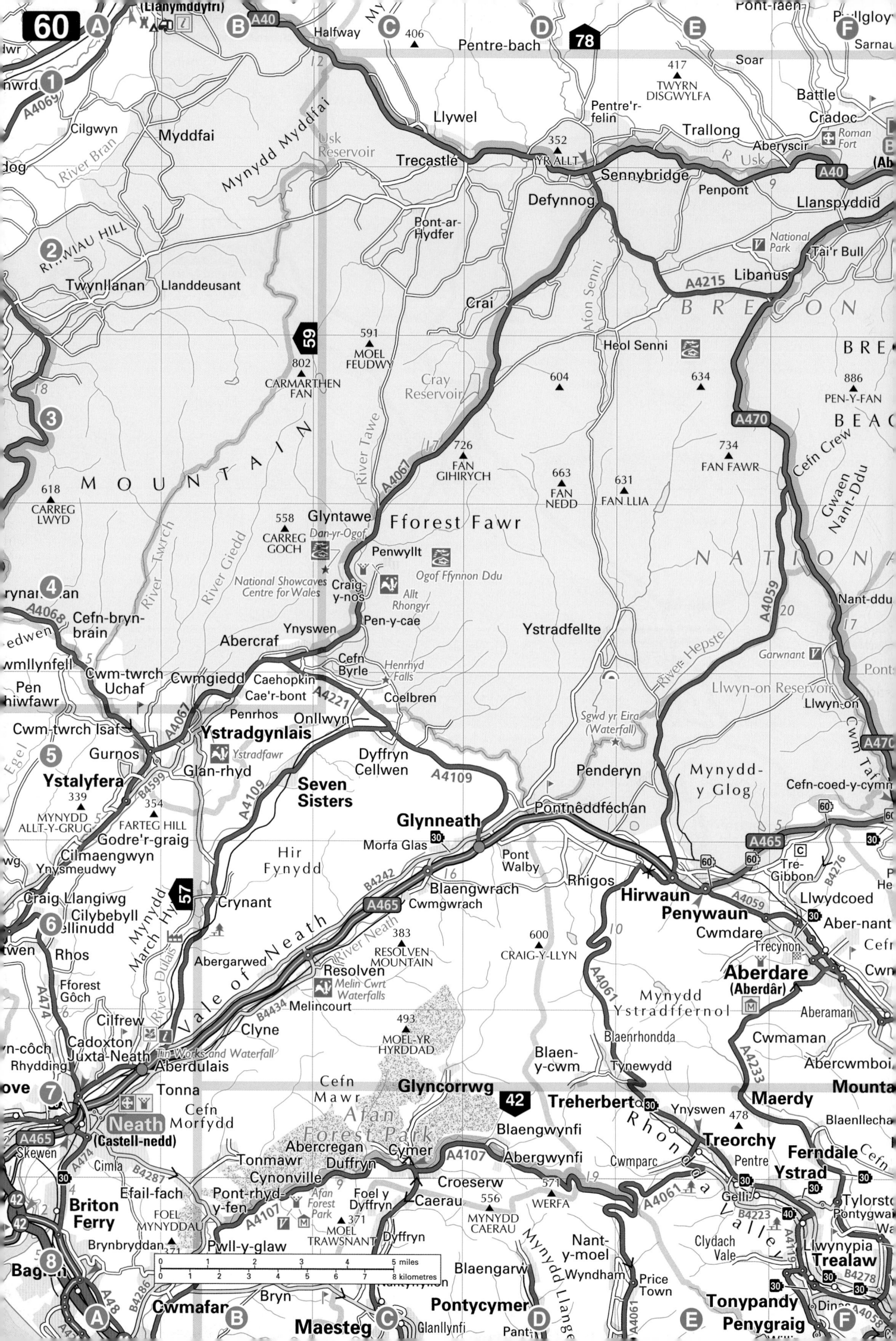

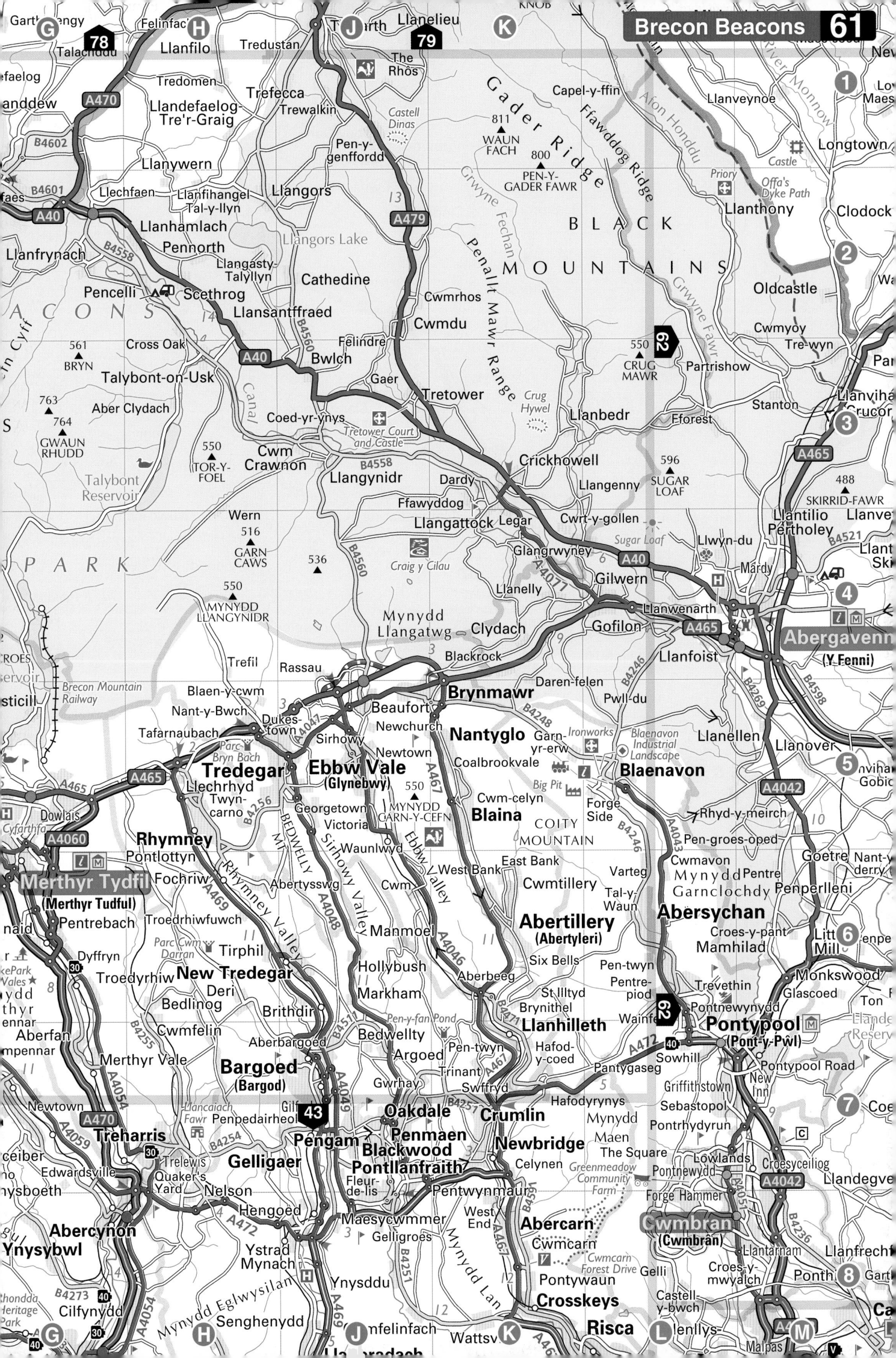

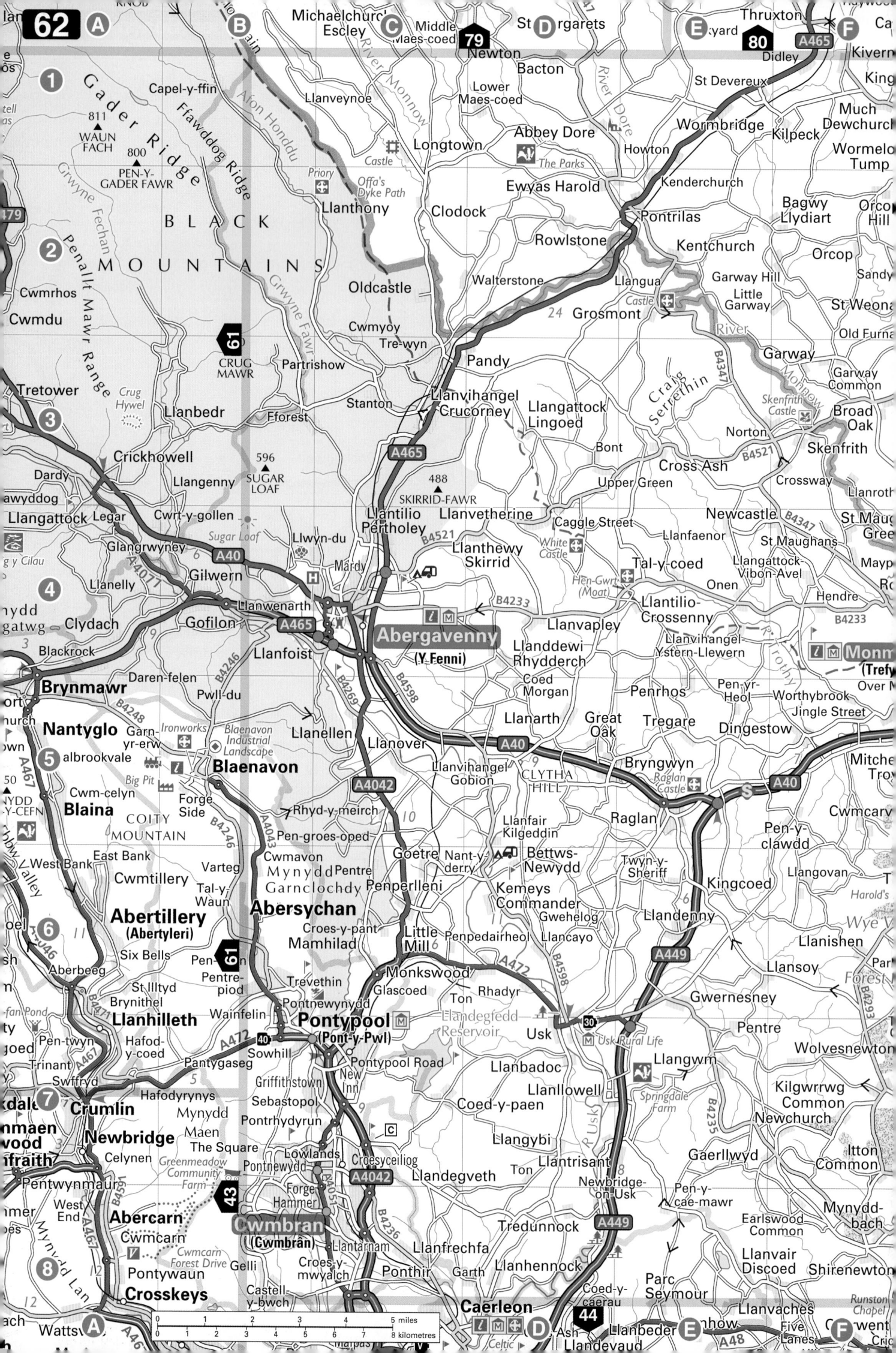

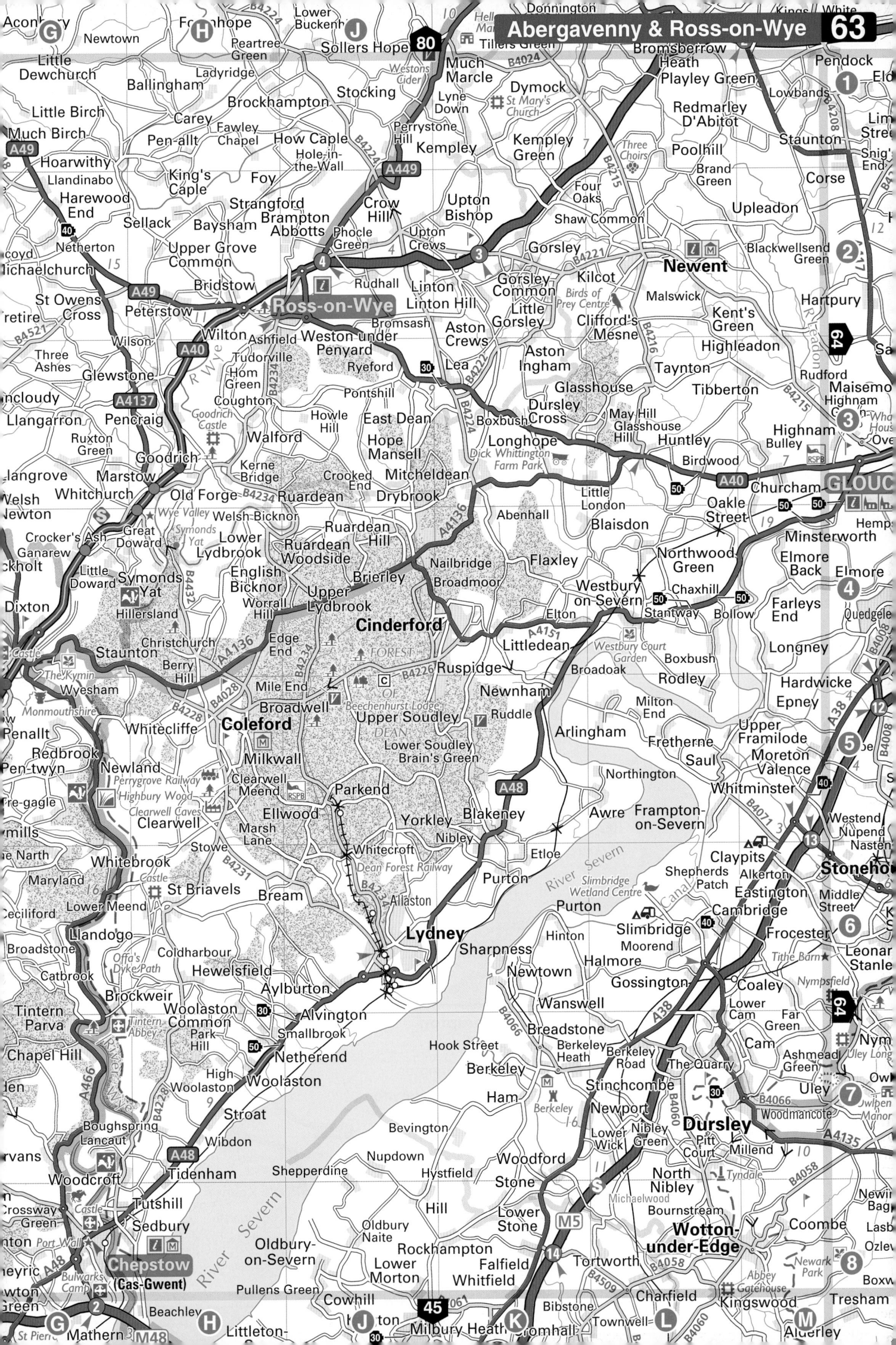

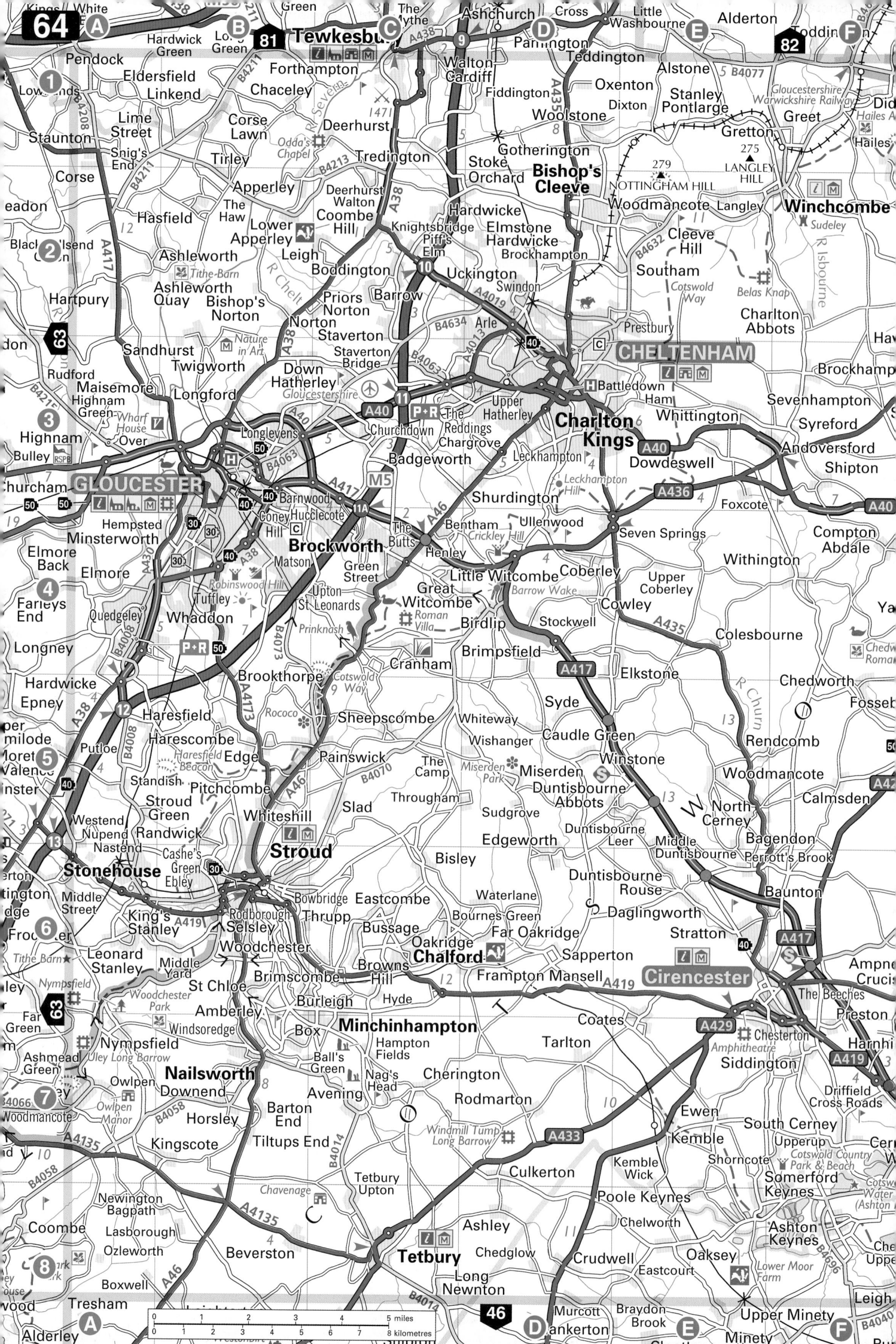

Snowshill
Cotswold Lavender
Batsford
Lemington
Welford
Children's Farm
Compton
Wigginton
Swerford
1
Taddington
nor
Cotswold
82
alconry
Centre
Four Shire
Stone
Barton-on-
the-Heath
Kitebrook
Great
Rollright
Bourton-on-the-Hill
Moreton-
in-Marsh
Little
Rollright
Rollright
Stones
Dunthrop
Heythrop
Cutsdean
Bourton
Downs
A424
Little
Compton
Salford
Over
Norton
B4026
A361
Ford
Longborough
Chastleton
30
Chipping
Norton
A44
Temple
Guiting
Condicote
A429
Evenlode
Chastleton
House
Adlestrop
Daylesford
The
Common
B4450
Dean
Enstone
66
eton
Cotswold
Donnington
Broadwell
Cornwell
Churchill
Chadlington
Taston
Fulwe
B4077
Barton
Stow-on-
the-Wold
Oddington
Maugersbury
Kingham
Sarsden
Spelsbury
Greenend
Chilson
B4022
arlbur
3
Naunton
Upper Swell
Lower Swell
Icomb
Bledington
Foscot
Lyneham
A361
Ascott-under-
Wychwood
Wychwood
Fawl
Notgrove
Upper
Slaughter
50
Wyck
Rissington
Foxholes
Bruern
Abbey
Ascott
Earl
Shipton-under-
Wychwood
Finstock
azleton
Lower Slaughter
Bourton-on-
the-Water
Miniatures
Model Village
Westcote
Nether
Westcote
Milton-under-
Wychwood
Langley
Ramsden
Cold
Aston
A429
Clapton-on-
the-Hill
Little
Rissington
Upper
Rissington
Idbury
Fifield
Leafield
B4022
Whiteoak
Green
Delly
End
4
North Leig
Turkdean
Motor & Toy
Great
Rissington
Fullbrook
Hill
Crawley
Hailey
Nev
Yatt
Northleach
Farmington
HABBER
GALLOWS HILL
Fordwells
Asthall
Leigh
Minster
Lovell Hall
World of
Mechanical Music
Sherborne
A40
Great
Barrington
Taynton
Fulbrook
Swinbrook
Minster
Lovell
Witney
Eastington
Windrush
Little
Barrington
Upton
Burford
Asthall
Charterville
Allotments
B4047
Cogges
30
Coln St Dennis
Westwell
Signet
60
8
A40
Curbridge
Ducklington
5
Calcot
B4425
Aldsworth
Holwell
Cotswold
Wildlife
Park
Shilton
B4020
Brize
Norton
Lew
High
Cog
Coln
Rogers
Winson
Carterton
Brize
Norton
Yelford
Ablington
R Leach
Eastleach
Turville
Eastleach
Martin
Kencot
B4477
Alvescot
Black
Bourton
Aston
Bright
npto
6
Arlington
Bibury
Filkins
Broadwell
Cote
arnsley
Coln
St Aldwyns
Hatherop
Broughton
Poggs
Bampton
B4449
Quenington
Southrop
Langford
Little
Clanfield
Clanfield
Weald
Shi
Chimney
Ampney
St Mary
Fairford
Park
Fairford
Little Faringdon
Grafton
Radcot
Carswell
Marsh
Duxord
66
oney
ter
Poulton
Milton End
A417
Lechlade
on Thames
B4449
Thrup
Hinton Waldrist
Sout
Poulton
Priory
field
Meysey
Hampton
Whelford
Fairford
Inglesham
Kelmscott
Thames Path
Buckland
7
Dunfield
Cotswold Water Park
(Fairford/Lechlade)
Buscot
Eaton
Hastings
Pusey
Marston
Meysey
Kempsford
R Cole
Buscot
Park
Faringdon
Hatford
Charney
Bassett
Down
Ampney
Upper
Inglesham
Badbury Hill
A417
Stanford
in the Vale
Latton
Castle
Eaton
Hannington
Wick
Coleshill
Great
Coxwell Barn
Littleworth
50
50
lade
Calcutt
A419
Hannington
Westrop
Great Coxwell
Little
Coxwell
Fernham
Shellingford
8
Highworth
Hampton
Eastrop
B4019
50
50
A420
Goosey
elworth
Green
Swindon &
Cricklade
Railway
Broad
Blunsdon
Stanton
Fitzwarren
47
B4508
Longcot
Baulking
Blunsdon
St Andrew

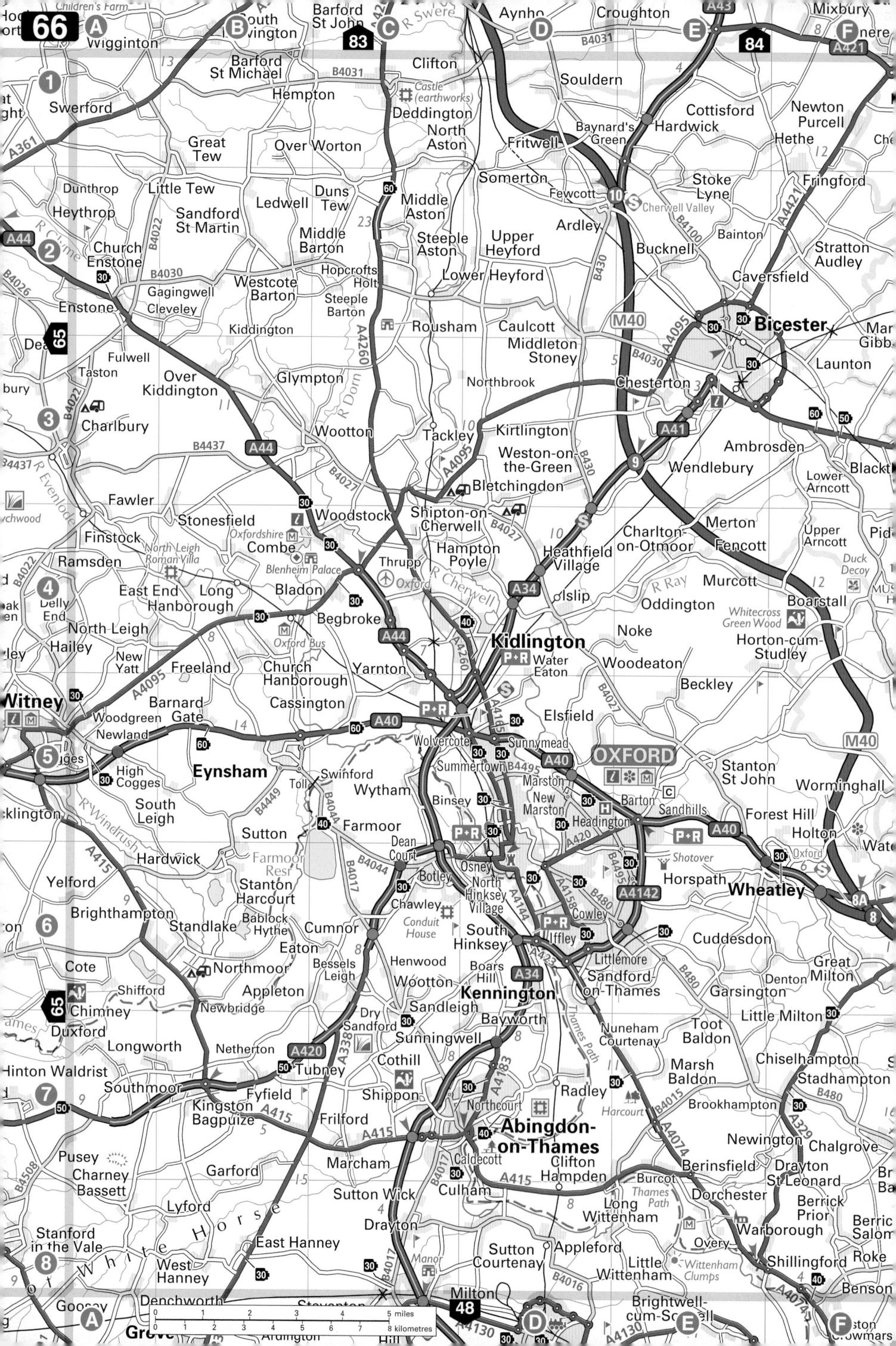

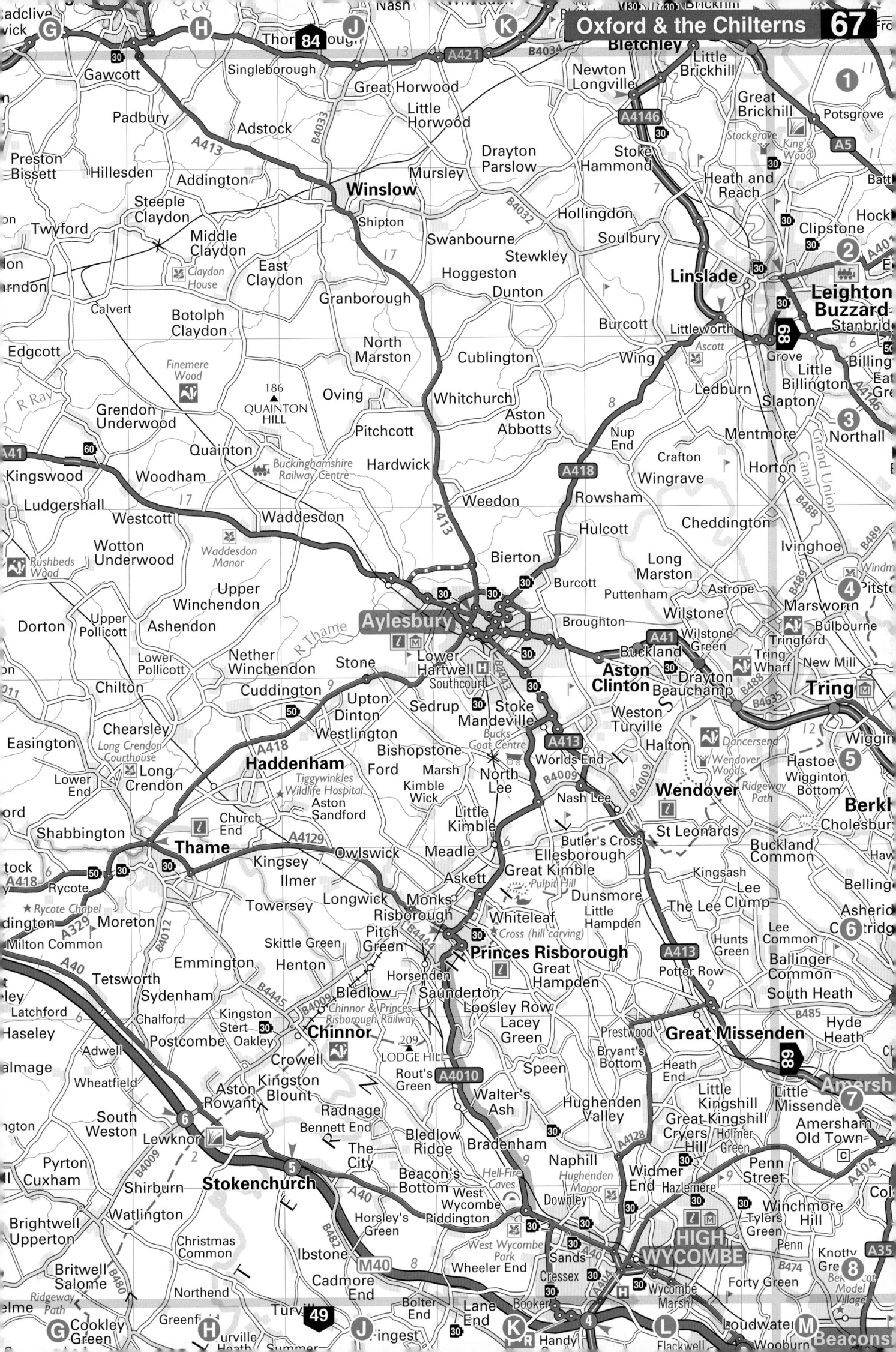

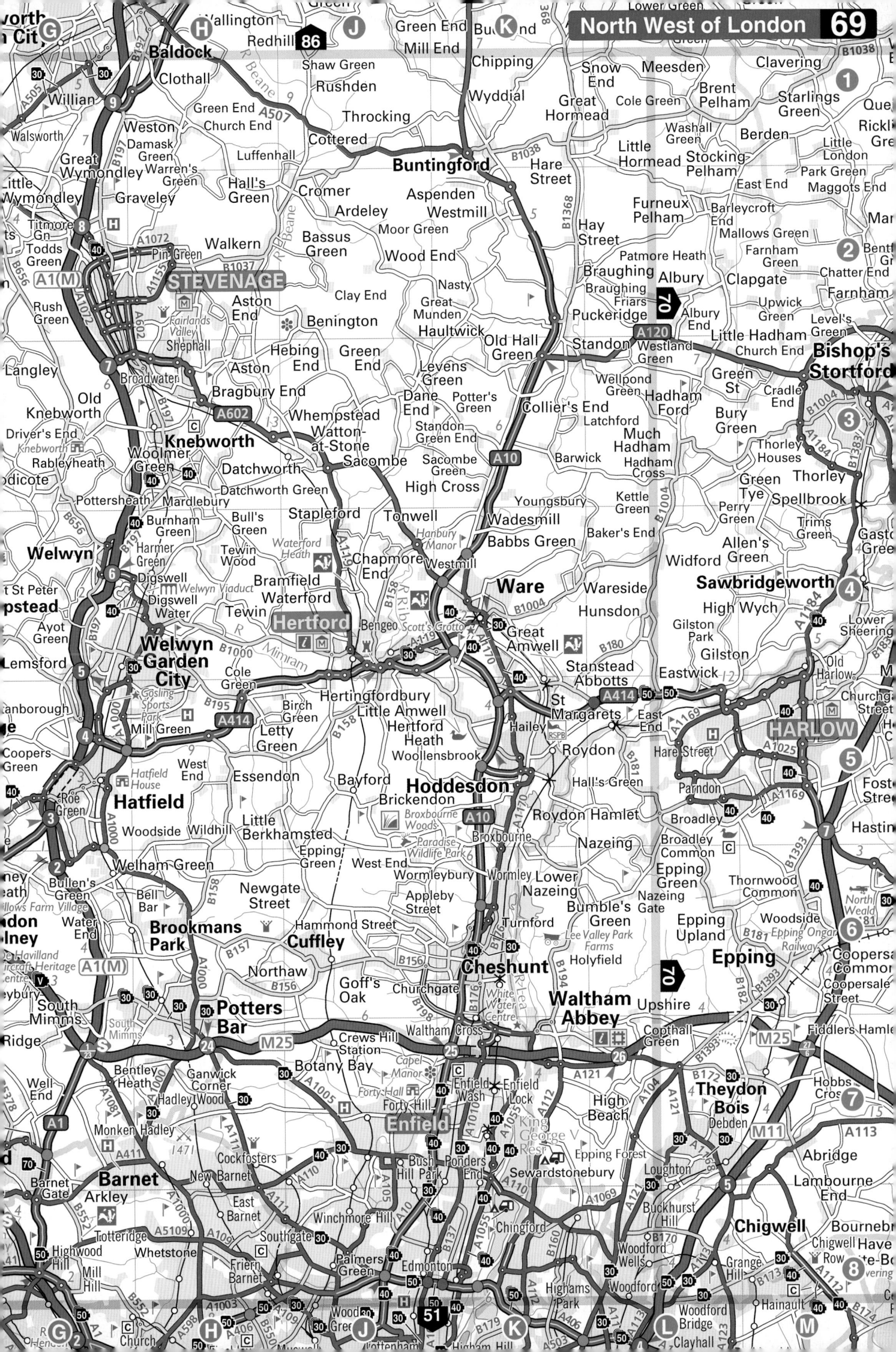

A · B · C · 87 · D · E · 88 · F

Newport
Howlett End
Lower Green
Roas Gree
Stickling Green
Wicken Bonhunt
Debden
Fampf
Hill End
Chipping
Snow End
Meesden
Lower Green
Clavering
Rickling
Widdington
Debden Green
Thaxted
Wyddial
Great Hormead
Cole Green
Brent Pelham
Starlings Green
Quendon
Hamperden End
Cutler's Green
ntingford
Washall Green
Berden
Rickling Green
Ugley
Woodend Green
Bardfield End Gree
Aspenden
Little Hormead
Stocking Pelham
Little London
Ugley Green
Henham
Broxted
Monk Street
Sibley's Green
Westmill Green
Hare Street
69
Furneux Pelham
Park Green
Maggots End
Manuden
Pledgdon Green
Brick End
Tilty
Duton Hill
d Er
Hay Street
Barleycroft End
Mallows Green
Bentfield Green
Elsenham
Fuller's End
Gaunt's End
Molehill Green
Great Easton
Nasty
Patmore Heath
Farnham Green
Chatter End
Tye Green
Linds
Great Munden
Braughing
Albury
Clapgate
Upwick Green
Farnham
Stansted Mountfitchet
Burton End
Bamber's Green
Great Dunmow
Haultwick
Braughing Friars
Puckeridge
Albury End
Level's Green
Birchanger
Stansted
A120
Smith's Green
Old Hall Green
Standon
Westland Green
Little Hadham
Church End
Bishop's Stortford
8A
Takeley
Little Canfield
Levens Green
Wellpond Green
Hadham Ford
Green St
Cradle End
Birchanger Green
Takeley St
Brewers End
Hope End Green
Barnsto
Collier's End
Latchford
Much Hadham
Bury Green
Thorley Houses
Great Hallingbury
Hatfield Forest
Great Canfield
Philpot End
Wellstye Green
Stan Green End
Barwick
Hadham Cross
Thorley
Little Hallingbury
Hatfield Broad Oak
Taverners Green
Sacombe Green
Youngsbury
Kettle Green
Green Tye
Spellbrook
Wright's Green
Broad Street
Aythorpe Roding
High Roding
Bishop's Green
igh Cross
Wadesmill
Baker's End
Perry Green
Trims Green
Gaston Green
M11
Hatfield Heath
Roundbush Gn
White Roding
THE RODING
Babbs Green
Widford
Allen's Green
Ardley End
High Ea
Westmill
Ware
Wareside
Hunsdon
Sawbridgeworth
High Wych
Lower Sheering
Sheering
Newman's End
A1060
Leaden Roding
Clatterfor
End
Great Amwell
Gilston Park
Gilston
Old Harlow
Matching Tye
Manwood Green
Nether Street
Margaret Roding
Goo East
St Margarets
Stanstead Abbotts
Eastwick
A414
East End
Churchgate Street
HARLOW
Hobbs Cross
Matching
Matching Green
Abbess Roding
Beauchamp Roding
Farm End
Hailey
Roydon
Hare Street
Threshers Bush
Little Laver
Birds Green
Pepper's Green
Boyto Cros
Hoddesdon
Hall's Green
Parndon
Foster Street
High Laver
Norwood End
Miller's Green
Shellow Bowells
Broxbourne
Nazeing
Broadley
Broadley Common
Magdalen Laver
Fyfield
Willingale
Cooksmill Green
Wormley Lower Nazeing
Epping Green
Nazeing Gate
Hastingwood
Moreton
Radley Green
Turnford
Bumble's Green
Thornwood Common
Tyler's Green
Bobbingworth
Shelley
Norton Mandeville
Norton Heath
Epping Upland
Woodside
North Weald
Bovinger
High Ongar
A414
Cheshunt
Holyfield
Epping
Epping Ongar Railway
North Weald Bassett
Wooden Church
Greensted
Chipping Ongar
Blackmore
Waltham Abbey
Upshire
Coopersale Common
Toot Hill
Marden Ash
Paslow Wood Common
Mill Green
Copthall Green
Coopersale Street
Stondon Massey
M25
Fiddlers Hamlet
Stanford Rivers
Hare Street
Doddinghurst
Hook End
Fryerning
High Beach
Theydon Bois
Hobbs Cross
Stapleford Tawney
Nuclear Bunker
Kelvedon Hatch
Wyatt's Green
Heybridge
Enfield
Enfield Lock
Debden
Passingford Bridge
Fox Hatch
Swallows Cross
King George V Res
Epping Forest
Abridge
A113
Navestock
Navestock Side
Crow Green
Pilgrims Hatch
Mountnessing
Sewardstonebury
Loughton
Lambourne End
Sabine's Green
Wattons Green
Coxtie Green
BRENTWOOD
Chingford
Buckhurst Hill
Chigwell
Bournebridge
Chigwell Row
Havering-atte-Bower
Noak Hill
South Weald
Brook Street
Ingra
Woodford Wells
Grange Hill
Havering
Stapleford Abbotts
Harold Hill
Woodford
Hainault
Collier Row
Gidea
Little Warley
Higham Hill
Clayhall

0 1 2 3 4 5 miles
0 1 2 3 4 5 6 7 8 kilometres

G H J K

Duck End
Howe Street
Sible Hedingham 88
Maplestead
Little Maplestead
Bures
Wormingford

Finchingfield
Brickkiln Green
Whiteash Green
Boose's Green
Mount Bures
Countess Cross
Colne Engaine
White Colne
Wakes Colne
Fordham
Little Horkesley

Bridge End
Waltham's Cross
Wethersfield
Blackmore End
Halstead
Earls Colne
Chappel
Swan Street
Rose Green
Fordstreet
Gallows Green
Fordham Heath
Eight Ash Green

Great Bardfield
Oxen End
Shalford
Shalford Green
Church End
Jasper's Green
High Garrett
Gosfield
Beazley End
Greenstead Green
Burton's Green
Great Tey
Aldham
Seven Star Green
Marks Tey
Beacon End
Stanway

Duck End
Bardfield Saling
Great Saling
Bocking Churchstreet
Stisted
Tumbler's Green
Marks Hall
Coggeshall
Little Tey
Pott's Green
Copford Green
Stanway
Colchester Zoo

Stebbing
Blake End
Duckend Green
Rayne
Braintree
Bocking
Bradwell
Pattiswick
Broad Green
Surrex
Langley Green
Eastorpe
Heckfordbridge
Layer-de-la-Haye

Crow's Green
Panfield
Bartholomew Green
Tye Green
Perry Green
Cressing
Feering
Gore Pit
Messing
Smythe's Green
Birch
Craxe Green

Gransmore Green
Bannister Green
Molehill Green
Great Notley
Black Notley
Hawbush Green
Silver End
Kelvedon
Inworth
Hardy's Green
Birch Green
Layer Breton

Felsted
Cock Green
Coblers Green
Willows Green
Young's End
Row Green
The Green
White Notley
Cressing Temple
Rivenhall End
Tiptree Heath
Tiptree
Layer Marney

North End
Hartford End
Little Leighs
Great Leighs
Rank's Green
Faulkbourne
Chipping Hill
Little Braxted
Paternoster Heath

Howe Street
Church End
Chatham Green
Gambles Green
Flack's Green
Terling
Fairstead
Witham
Great Braxted
Great Totham
Oxley Green
Tolleshunt Knights
Salcott-cum-Virley

Great Waltham
Broad's Green
Little Waltham
Russell Green
Wickham Bishops
Great Totham
Little Totham
Tolleshunt D'Arcy

Chignall Smealy
Broomfield
P+R
Hatfield Peverel
Broad Street Green
Tolleshunt Major
Tollesbury

Chignall St James
Boreham
Little Baddow
Nounsley
Langford
Heybridge
Goldhanger

Springfield
Ulting Wick
Museum of Power
Heybridge Basin
River Blackwater

Writtle
CHELMSFORD
Woodham Walter
Maldon
Northey Is
Osea Is
St Lawrence

Widford
P+R
Elm Green
Danbury
Runsell Green
Woodham Mortimer
Ramsey Island
St Lawrence

Great Baddow
Sandon
Howe Green
Horne Row
Gay Bowers
Hazeleigh
Rudley Green
Mundon Hill
Maylandsea

Galleywood
Butt's Green
Bicknacre
Cock Clarks
Purleigh
Roundbush
Steeple

Margaretting
Margaretting Tye
East Hanningfield
Howegreen
Farther Howegreen
Latchingdon
Mayland

West Hanningfield
Chapel Row
Woodham Ferrers
Stow Maries
Cold Norton
Althorne

Stock
Coalhill
Hanningfield Reservoir
RHS Hyde Hall
Tropical Wings
Rettendon
South Woodham Ferrers
North Fambridge
Bridgemarsh Island
Creeksea
Burnham

Ramsden Heath
South Hanningfield
Downham
Marsh Farm
South Fambridge
Canewdon

Ramsden Bellhouse
Billericay
South Green
Runwell
Battlesbridge
Hullbridge
Ashingdon
Halesville
Paglesham

Great Burstead
Wickford
Shotgate
Rawreth
Hockley
Hawkwell
Ballards Gore
Great Stambridge

Crays Hill
Nevendon
North Benfleet
Rayleigh
Stroud Green
Rochford

A1017 A131 A120 A12 A130 A414 A132 A127 A129 A138 A1016 A1060

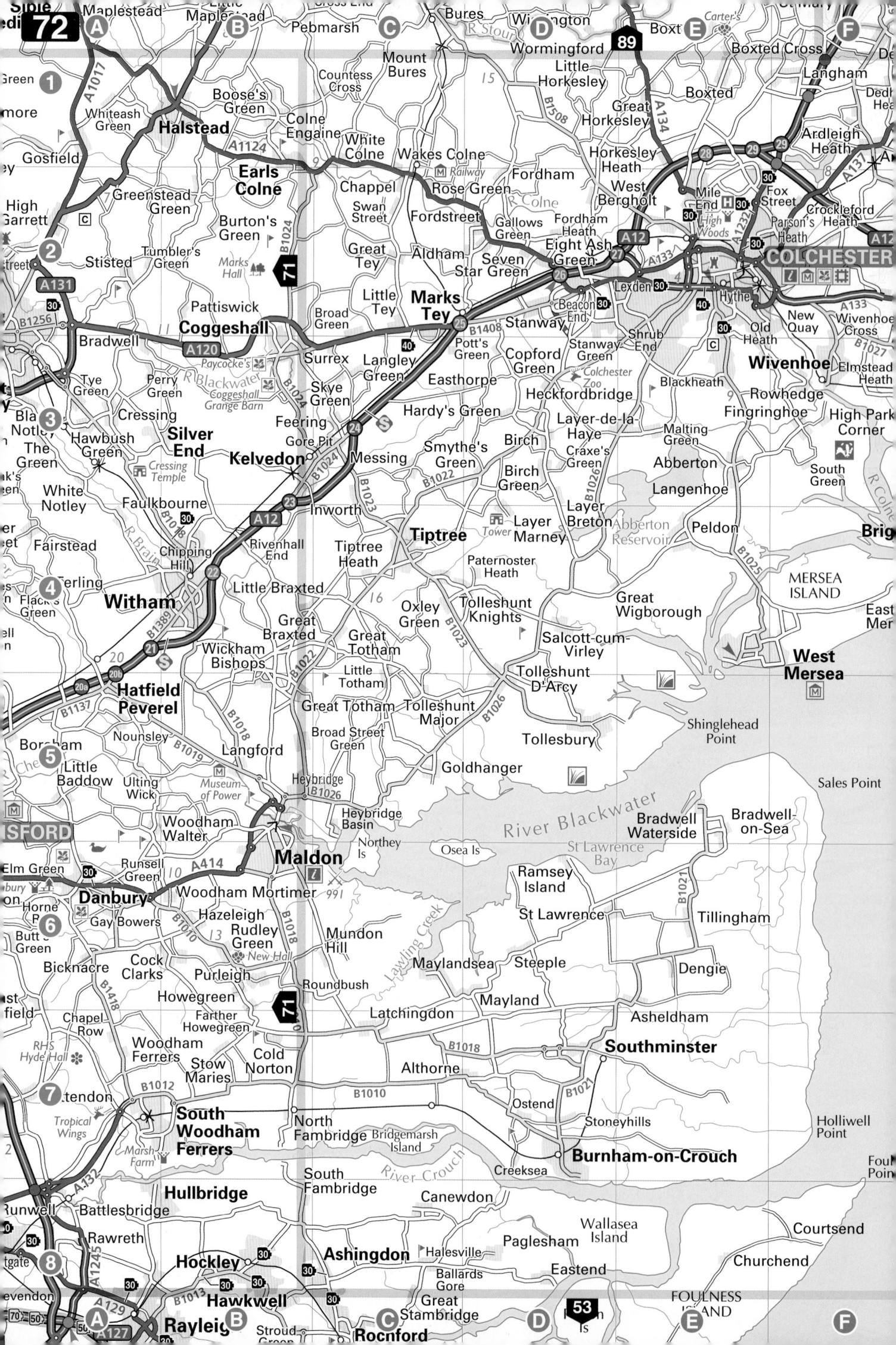

Brantham

Cattawade
Mistley Towers
Mistley
New Mistley

Holbrook R
River Stour
90
Wrabness
Parkeston Quay
Parkeston

Street
Shotley Gate
International
Ferry
Terminal
The
Redoubt
Bath Side
Harwich
Harbour
Dovercourt
Harwich

Landguard Fort
Landguard
Point

tford M
dge-Cottage
nningtree
ford
Little
Bromley
Mistley
Heath

Bradfield
B1352
Ramsey
Upper
Dovercourt
30

Bradfield Heath
A120

Horsleycross
Street
Wix

Wix
Green
Stones
Green
Great
Oakley
Little
Oakley

Horsley
Cross
19
Tendring
Heath

Great
Bromley
Little
Bentley
Tendring Green
Goose
Green
B1414
17
Beaumont

Pennyhole
Bay

Hoek van Holland
Esbjerg

Hare Green
A133
Tendring
B1035
Thorpe
Green
Thorpe-
le-Soken

Horsey
Island
Tower
The Naze

ating
Green
Frating
ead Row
Great
Bentley
16
C
Weeley
B1033

Kirby
le Soken
B1034
Walton on
the Naze

rd
Aingers
Green
Weeley
Heath
B1441
B1414
Kirby Cross
B1033
Frinton-on-Sea

Thorrington
A133
Cook's
Green

Samson's
Corner
Little Clacton
B1442
Great
Holland
B1032

Hurst
Green
B1027
30
Great
Clacton
30
30
Holland-
on-Sea

St Osyth
Rush
Green
30
CLACTON-ON-SEA

Jaywick
30

Colne Point

0   1   2   3   4   5 miles
0   1   2   3   4   5   6   7   8 kilometres

Rosslare Harbour

STRUMBLE HEAD

Carregwa

Pen Brush

Llanwnda

Pwll Deri

Ocean

Trefasser

Goodwick

Pembrokeshire
Coast Path

Manorowen

St Nicholas

Panteg

Scledd

A4219

Ynys
Daullyn

Granston

Jordanston

A40

Carreg Sampson

Abercastle

Llangloffan

Porthgain

Trefin

Mathry

Castle
Morris

Letterston

Abereiddy

Llanrhian

16

A487

Llangloffan
Fen

B4331

Berea

Square &
Compass

Welsh
Hook

Croes-goch

Treffynnon

Tretio

B4330

ST DAVID'S HEAD

Treleddyd-fawr

Carnhedryn

Treglemais

Cerbyd

River Solva

Llandeloy

15

Rhodiad-
y-brenin

Caer
Farchell

Tancredston

Pont-yr-hafod

Wolf's
Castle

Whitesands
Bay

Whitchurch

Middle Mill

Treffgarne
Owen

Hayscastle

Hayscastle
Cross

RAMSEY
ISLAND

Bishop's
Palace

St Davids
(Tyddewi)

Nine
Wells

Solva

A487

Treffgarne

RSPB

Ramsey Sound

St David's Peninsula
Heritage Coast

Pen-y-cwn

54

178
DUDWELL
MT

Lewestin

Newgale

16

Roch

Wolfsdale

PEMBROKESHIRE
COAST

Roch Gate

A40

Simpson
Cross

Camrose

NATIONAL PARK

Rickets Head

Nolton Haven

Nolton

A487

Keeston

Pembrokeshire
County

Tangiers

Western Cleddau

St Brides Bay
Heritage Coast

Pelcomb Cross

Pelcomb

Druidston

Lambston

Pelcomb
Bridge

Glanafon

Sutton

0 1 2 3 4 5 miles
0 1 2 3 4 5 6 7 8 kilometres

St Brides Bay

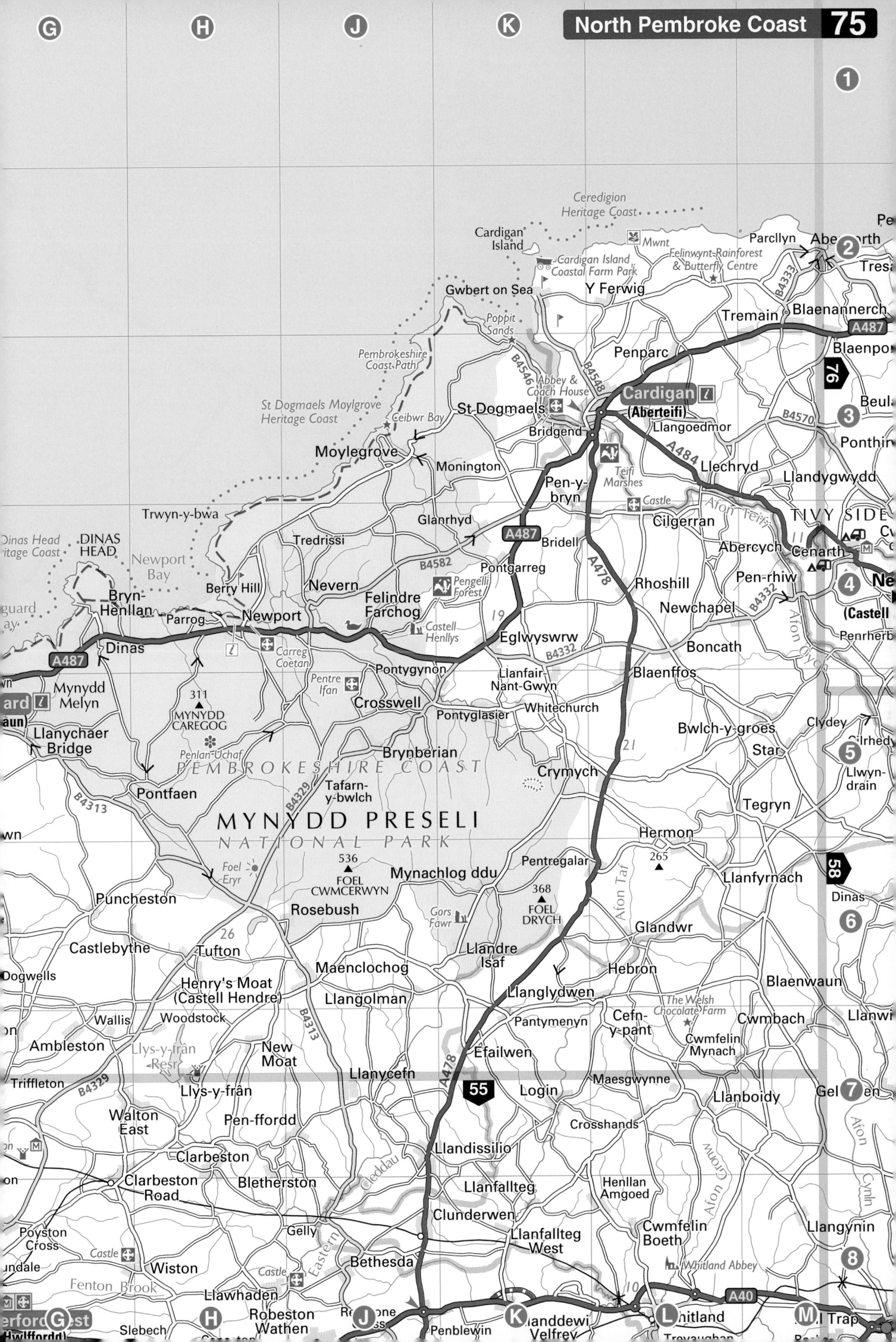

G   H   J   K

1

Ceredigion
Heritage Coast

Cardigan
Island

Mwnt
Felinwynt Rainforest
& Butterfly Centre

Parcllyn

Abe   rth

2

Tres

Cardigan Island
Coastal Farm Park

Y Ferwig

Tremain

Blaenannerch

A487

Gwbert on Sea

Penparc

Blaenpo

Poppit
Sands

76

Pembrokeshire
Coast Path

Cardigan
(Aberteifi)

Beul

St Dogmaels
Moylgrove
Heritage Coast

Abbey &
Coach House

St Dogmaels

Llangoedmor

B4570

3

Ponthir

A484

Ceibwr Bay

Bridgend

Teifi
Marshes

Llechryd

Llandygwydd

Moylegrove

Pen-y-
bryn

Castle

Afon Teifi

TIVY SIDE

Monington

Cilgerran

Abercych

Cenarth

Trwyn-y-bwa

Glanrhyd

A487

Bridell

Rhoshill

Pen-rhiw

B4332

4

Ne

Tredrissi

Pontgarreg

A478

Newchapel

(Castell

Dinas Head
eritage Coast

DINAS
HEAD

Newport
Bay

Berry Hill

Nevern

Pengelli
Forest

19

Eglwyswrw

Boncath

Penrherb

Bryn-
Henllan

Parrog

Newport

Felindre
Farchog

Castell
Henllys

B4332

Blaenffos

Clydey

irhed

5

Dinas

Carreg
Coetan

Pontygynon

Llanfair-
Nant-Gwyn

Whitechurch

Bwlch-y-groes

Star

Llwyn-
drain

A487

guard

Mynydd
Melyn

311

Pentre
Ifan

Crosswell

Pontyglasier

21

Tegryn

58

Llanychaer
Bridge

MYNYDD
CAREGOG

Brynberian

Hermon

265

Llanfyrnach

Dinas

Penlan-Uchaf

PEMBROKESHIRE   COAST

Crymych

6

B4313

Pontfaen

Tafarn-
y-bwlch

Foel
Eryr

536

Pentregalar

MYNYDD PRESELI
NATIONAL PARK

FOEL
CWMCERWYN

Mynachlog ddu

368

Glandwr

Blaenwaun

Puncheston

Rosebush

Gors
Fawr

FOEL
DRYCH

Afon Taf

Hebron

The Welsh
Chocolate Farm

Cwmbach

Llanwi

Castlebythe

Tufton

Maenclochog

Llandre
Isaf

Llanglydwen

Cefn-
y-pant

Dogwells

Henry's Moat
(Castell Hendre)

Llangolman

Pantymenyn

Cwmfelin
Mynach

Wallis

Woodstock

B4313

Ambleston

Llys-y-frân
Resr

New
Moat

Efailwen

Maesgwynne

Llanboidy

Gel   en

7

Triffleton

B4329

Llanycefn

A478

Login

Walton
East

Pen-ffordd

55

Crosshands

Clarbeston

Llandissilio

Henllan
Amgoed

Cwmfelin
Boeth

Llangynin

Clarbeston
Road

Bletherston

Llanfallteg

Poyston
Cross

Castle

Gelly

Clunderwen

Llanfallteg
West

8

ndale

Castle

Wiston

Bethesda

Llanddewi
Velfrey

Whitland Abbey

A40

Fenton Brook

Llawhaden

Penblewin

hitland

l Trap

erford   G est
wlfford

Slebech

H

Robeston
Wathen

R   ne
ss

J

K

anddewi
Velfrey

L

Treyaughan

M

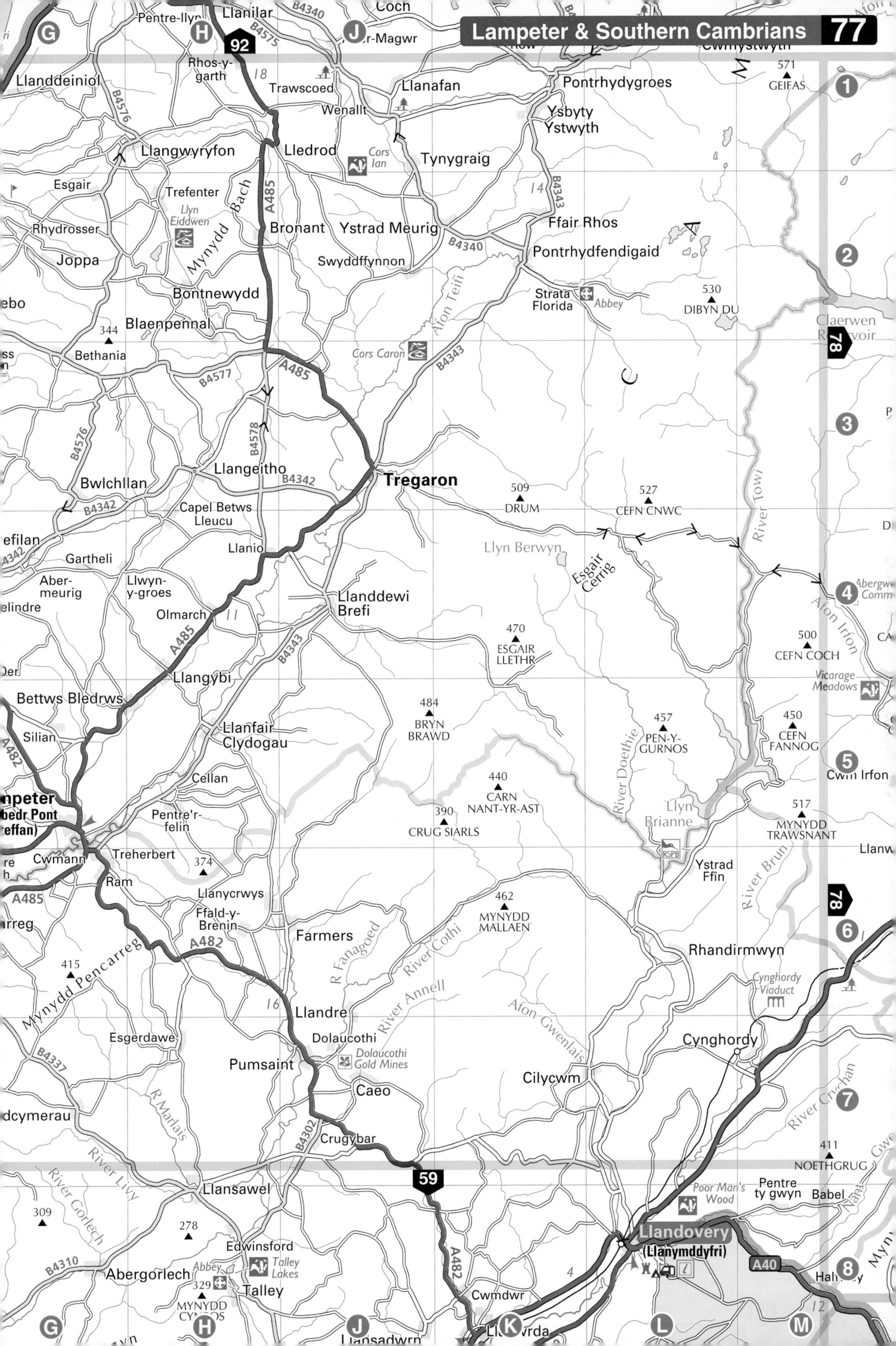

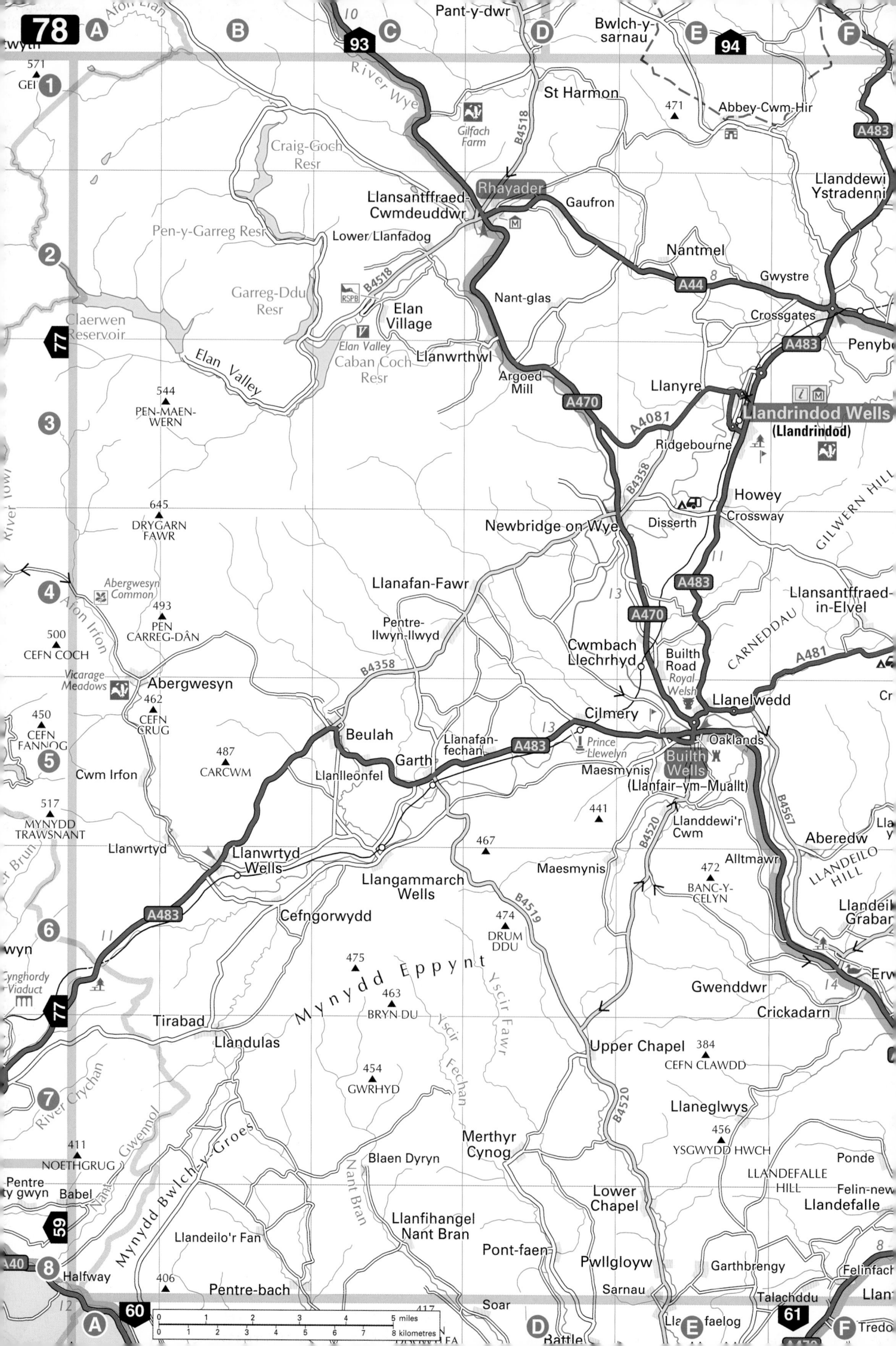

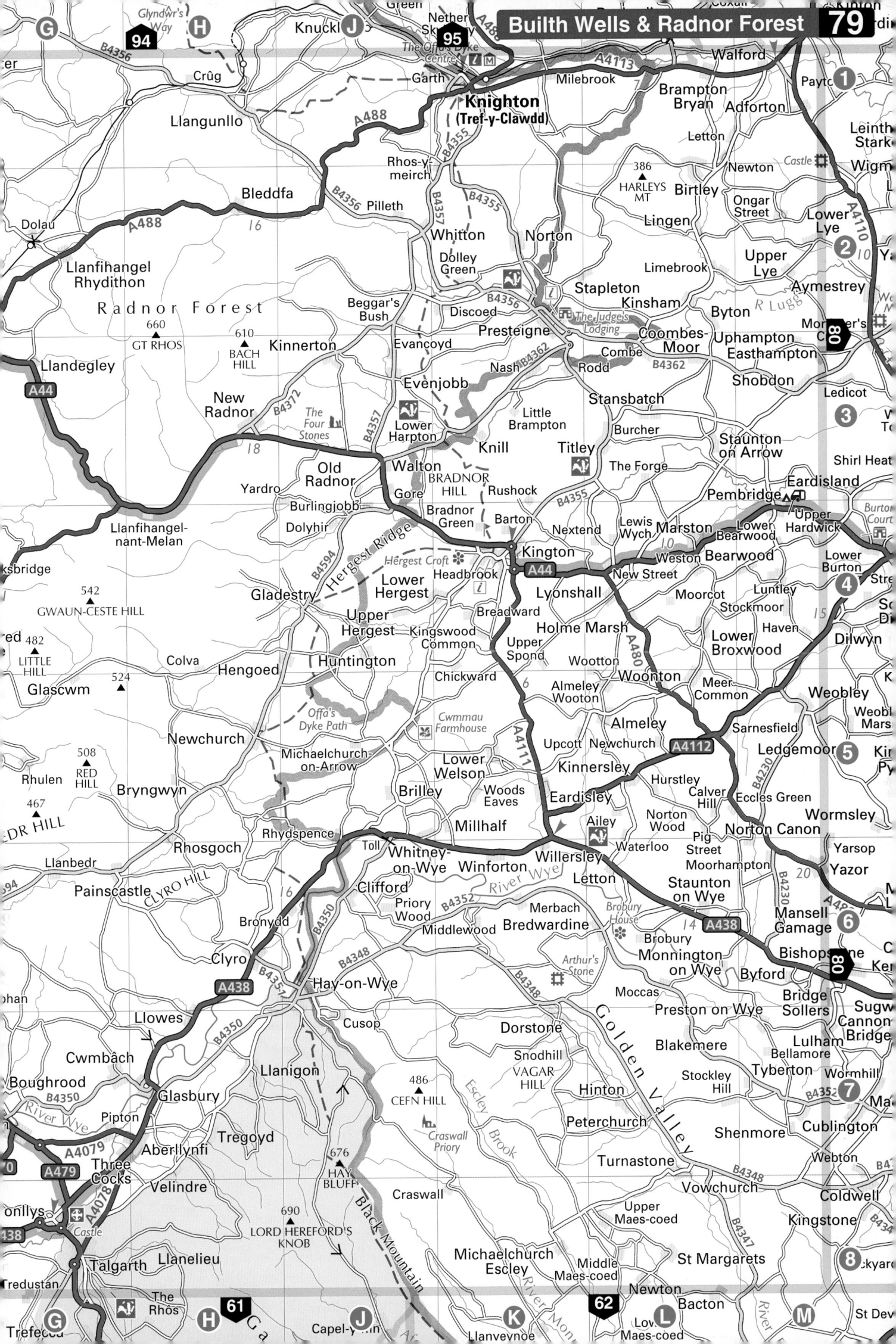

95 A | B Forest Geology Trail | C | D 96 | E | F

1
Kinton
Avardine
River Te...
Knowbury
Hints
Dudnill
Bransley
Burrington
Ludford
Ludlow
Caynham
Knowl
Coreley
Bay...
Overton
Ashford Carbonell
Whitton
Milson
Paytoe
Pipe Aston
Ashford Bowdler
Greete
Nash
Bickley
Neen Sollars
Mamb...
Elton
Middleton
Little Hereford
Bleathwood
Boraston
Knighton on Teme
Bay...
A456

2
Leinthall Starkes
Richards Castle
Woofferton
Brimfield Cross
Burford
Newnham
Rochford
Castle
Wigmore
Oreleton Common
Comberton
Wyson
Berrington
Tenbury Wells
Upper Rochford
Lin...
A4110
Leinthall Earls
Ashley Moor
Brimfield
Berrington Green
Kyrewood
Hanley Or...
Lower Lye
Croft Ambrey
B4362
Orleton
Stony Cross
Callows Grave
Hanley Child
Hanley William
79
Upper Lye
Croft Castle
A49
Middleton on the Hill
St Michaels
Hanley Child
St...
Aymestrey
Water Mill
Bircher
Ashton
Miles Hope
Kyre Park
Bank Street
Broadheath
Upper Stoke Sapey
B4203

3
Yarpole
Moreton Eye
The Hundred
Woonton
Leysters
Kyre Green
Bliss
Sweet Green
Mortimer's Cross
1461
Lugg Green
Luston
Berrington Hall
Grafton
Bockleton
Wolferlow
Ledicot
Aston
Eyton
Kimbolton
Whyle
Collington
Kingsland
The Broad
Stockton
Grantsfield
Hatfield
Thornbury
Old Church
Tedstone Wafer
West Town
Cobnash
Leominster
Pudleston
Edvin Loach
Sandy Cross

4
Shirl Heath
Lawton
Cholstrey
Ebnall
Steen's Bridge
A44
Docklow
Grendon Green
Edwyn Ralph
Bredenbury
Brockhar... Estate
Eardisland
R Arrow
Baron's Cross
Stretford
Bromyard Downs
Monkland
A44
Burton Court
Wall End
Newtown
Humber
Marston Stannett
Bromyard
Upper Hardwick
Ivington Green
Ivington
Stoke Prior
Risbury

5
Lower Burton
Brierley
Wharton
Risbury
Hegdon Hill
Munderfield Row
Stanford Bishop
Sollers Dilwyn
Aulden
Marlbrook
Bowley Town
Pencombe
Stoke Cross
Munderfield Stocks
Dilwyn
Birley
Upper Hill
Newton
Bowley
Little Cowarne
Hope under Dinmore
Maund Bryan
Ullingswick
Stoke Lacy
Bishop's Frome
Weobley
Knapton Green
Bush Bank
Queenswood
Bodenham
England's Gate
A417
Panks Bridge
Evesb...
Westhope
Bodenham Moor
Pool Head
Upper Town
Felton
Moreton Jeffries
Much Cowarne
Halmond Frome

6
Ledgemoor
King's Pyon
Highway
Urdimarsh
The Vauld
Walker's Green
Preston Wynne
Hillhampton
Burley Gate
Five Bridges
Fr...
Wormsley
Canon Pyon
Wellington
Marden
Ocle Pychard
Lower Egleton
Castle Frome
Yarsop
Yazor
Wellington Marsh
Franklands Gate
A465
Newtown
Upper Egleton
Stretton Grandison
Mansell Lacy
Tillington Common
Portway
Sutton St Nicholas
Westhide
Monkhide
Brinsop
Tillington
Moreton on Lugg
Sutton Marsh
Withington Marsh
Withington
A4103
Yarkhill
Canon Frome

7
Garnage
Credenhill
Kenchester
Burghill
Upper Lyde
Pipe and Lyde
Marsh Nunnington
Shucknall
Lower Town
Swinmore Common
Bishopstone
Stretton Sugwas
A49
Holmer
Shelwick
White Stone
Weston Beggard
Ashperton
Bridge Sollers
Sugwas Pool
Huntington
Westfields
Hagley
Munsley
Cannon Bridge
Swainshill
King's Acre
A465
Lugwardine
Trumpet
Lulham
Upper Breinton
A438
Bartestree
Stoke Edith
Tarrington
Bellamore
Wormhill
Eaton Bishop
Breinton
Hereford
Tupsley
Dormington
Perton
Durlow Common
Waller's Gre...
Madley
Ruckhall
Warham
Blackmarstone
Hampton Bishop
Clouds
Putley Green
A4172

8
79
Clehonger
Belmont
Lower Bullingham
Rotherwas Chapel
Checkley
Putley
Little Marcl...
Kingstone
Webton
Goose Pool
Grafton
Dinedor
Mordiford
Aylton
Coldwell
B4349
Bullinghope
Portway
B4224
Woolhope
Allensmore
Cobhall Common
Twyford Common
Dinedor
Holme Lacy
Kynaston
Rushall
Hungerstone
Haywood
Callow
Aconbury
Lower Buckenhill
Much Marcle
Thruxton
Cockyard
Kivernoll
A465
Newtown
Peartree Green
Sollers Hope
Tillers Gre...
Didley
Ladyridge
Westons Cider
Hellens Manor
B4024

A Devere | B | C | D 63 | E Brockhampton | F Dym...

Scale: 0 1 2 3 4 5 miles / 0 1 2 3 4 5 6 7 8 kilometres

Wyre Forest Bank
Callow Hill
Lye Head
Gorst Hill
Bliss Gate
Heightington
Rock
Greenway
Pensax
Abberley
Dunley
Abberley Common
Abberley
Noutard's Green
Astley
Comhampton
Frog Pool
Elms Green
Redmarley
Great Witley
WOODBURY HILL
Witley Court
Stanford Bridge
Shelsley Walsh
Shelsley Beauchamp
Clifton upon Teme
Martley
Hill Side
Ockeridge
Wichenford
Sinton Green
Moseley
Shoulton
Berrow Green
Horsham
Wants Green
Hallow
Collins Green
Knightwick
Lulsley
Broad Green
Lower Broadheath
Upper Broadheath
Broadwas
Ravenhills Green
Leigh Court Barn
Leigh
Rushwick
Alfrick
Brockamin
Bransford
Alfrick Pound
Smith End Green
Leigh Sinton
Upper Wick
Lower Wick
Longley Green
Storridge
Bowling Green
Powick
Pole Elm
Greenhill
Stifford's Bridge
Cradley
West Malvern
Mathon
Lower Howsell
Upper Howsell
Newland
Deblin's Green
Callow End
Kempsey
Draycott
Ham Green
Great Malvern
Guarlford
Malvern Link
Madresfield
Clifton
Rhydd
Newbridge Green
Colwall
South End
Storeyard Green
Upper Wyche
Lower Wyche
Three Counties
Malvern Wells
Hanley Swan
Hanley Castle
Gilbert's End
Severn Stoke
High Green
Birch Green
Wellington Heath
Eastnor
Little Malvern
Upper Welland
Hook Bank
Upton-upon-Severn
Ryall
Welland
Newbridge Green
Longdon Heath
Hollybush
Castlemorton Common
Castlemorton
Longdon
Queenhill
Uckinghall
Ripple
Chandlers Cross
Camer's Green
Rye Street
Birts Street
Sledge Green
Berrow
White End
Kings Green
Bromsberrow
Bromsberrow Heath
Broom's Green
Playley Green
Pendock
Hardwick Green
Long Green
Eldersfield
Lowbands
Linkenum
Chaceley
Forthampton
Tewkesbury
Bushley
Bushley Green
Slades Green
Shuthonger
Puckrup
Church End
Twyning Green
Bredon
Bredon's Hardwick
Ashchurch
The Mythe
Walton Cardiff

Stourport-on-Severn
Areley Kings
Astley Cross
Chadwick
Lincomb
Crossway Green
The Burf
Comhampton
Sytchampton
Northampton
Shrawley
Sankyn's Green
Holt Fleet
Uphampton
Ombersley
Hadley
Holt
Holt Heath
Sinton
Salwarpe
Chatley
Grimley
Sinton
Oakall Green
Hawford
Hawford Dovecote
Ladywood
Fernhill Heath
Hindlip
Hallow Heath
Northwick
Worcester
Rainbow Hill
Elgar
Henwick
St Johns
Newtown
Cherry Orchard
Whittington
Norton
Hatfield
Littleworth
Green Street
Stoulton
Stonehall
Napleton
Pirton
Kerswell Green
Wadborough
Ramsden
Besford
Defford
Dunstall Common
Earl's Croome
Holly Green
The Grove
Strensham (northbound)
Naunton
Upper Strensham
Strensham (southbound)
Hill End
Westmancote
Bredon Barn
Bredon's Norton
Lower Westmancote
Overbury
Kemerton
Kinsham
Beckford
Conderton
Pamington
Teddington
Oxenton

Ribbesford
Summerfield
Wilden
Upper Milton
Charlton
Torton
Hartlebury
Waresley
Titton
Norchard
Acton
Cutnall Green
Dunhampton
Doverdale
Oldfield
Droitwich
Shenstone
Chaddesley Corbett
Cakebole
Rushock
Purshull Green
Cooksey Green
Elmley Lovett
Bryan's Green
Elmbridge
Upton Warren
Broad Alley
Hampton Lovett
Rashwood
Woodcote Green
Park Gate
Dodford
Lickey End
Blackwell
Burcot
Bromsgrove
Sidemoor
Finstall
Tardebigge
Rock Hill
Aston Fields
Stoke Prior
Stoke Heath
Stoke Pound
Banks Green
Woodgate
Webbs of Wychbold
Wychbold
Astwood
Hanbury Hall
Hanbury
Gallows Green
Harbours Hill
Sharpway Gate
Lower Bentley
Mount Pleasant
Woolmere Green
Gooseholl Green
Broughton Green
Bradley Green
Stock Green
Huddington
Phepson
Himbleton
Earls Common
Stock Wood
Sale Green
Martin Hussingtree
Oddingley
Tibberton
Crowle Green
Warndon
Trotshill
Crowle
Broughton Hackett
Grafton Flyford
The Bourne
Dormston
Spetchley
Churchill
Upton Snodsbury
North Piddle
Flyford Flavell
White Ladies Aston
Naunton Beauchamp
Abberton
Bishampton
Peopleton
Throckmorton
Pinvin
Hawbridge
Drakes Broughton
Wadborough
Pershore
Upper Moor
Lower Moor
Wyre Piddle
Fladbury
Charlton
Cropthorne
Wick
Pensham
Little Comberton
Birlingham
Great Comberton
Woodmancote
Eckington
Elmley Castle
Bredon Hill
Ashton under Hill
Grafton
Conderton
Beckford
Silk Mill
The Priory
Bredon Barn

A B C D E F

1

Lickey Rock
Barnt Green
Weatheroak Hill
Tanner's Green
Four Ashes
Danley Green
Fen End

M42
98
Hopwood Park
Forshaw Heath
Terry's Green
Dwood
Chadwick End
A4141
A417

Staple Hill
Apes Dale
Withybed Green
Portway
Wood End
Green
Hockley Heath
Chessetts Wood
Baddesley Clinton

Sidemoor
Lickey End
Burcot
Linthurst
Blackwell
Alvechurch
Rowney Green
Heath Gn
Branson's Cross
Aspley Heath
Tanworth in Arden
Kemps Green
Kingswood
Lapworth
Kingswood Brook
Baddesley Clinton
Wroxall
Haps Knob

Rock Hill
Aston Fields
Finstall
Broad Green
Beoley
Holt End
Trap's Green
Danzey Green
M40
Lowsonford
Turner's Green
Rowington

2
Tardebigge
Stoke Pound
Banks Green
Foxlydiate
Webheath
A435
A4023
A4189
Ullenhall
Outhill
Henley-in-Arden
Buckley Green
Kite Green
Preston Bagot
Holywell
Shrewley
Little Shrewley

Avoncroft
Woodgate
Upper Bentley
Headless Cross
REDDITCH
Mappleborough Green
Oldberrow
Beaudesert
Preston Green
High Cross
Lye Green
Pinley Green
Hampton

Harbours Hill
Lower Bentley
Callow Hill
Walkwood
Crabbs Cross
Green Lane
A4189
Studley Common
Wootton Wawen
Shelfield
Langley
Langley Green
Lower Norton
Norton Lindsey

Hanbury
Toolmere Green
Mount Pleasant
Ham Green
Hunt End
Studley
Thomas Town
Spernall
Wootton Wawen
Claverdon

81
Mere Green
Bradley Green
Broughton Green
Astwood Bank
Littleworth
Feckenham
Edgiock
Shurnock
Sambourne
Ridgeway
New End
Coughton
Coughton Court
Shelfield Green
Great Alne
Little Alne
Aston Cantlow
Mary Arden's Farm
Edstone
Bearley Cross
Bearley
Pigeon Green
Heath End
Snitterfield
Pathlow
Wilmcote
A46

3
Phepson
Earls Common
Huddington
Stock Green
Holberrow Green
Bouts
Cladswell
Cookhill
Arrow
Alcester
King's Coughton
Kinwarton Dovecote
Upton
Walcot
Haselor
Bishopton
Alveston
Tiddington
Hamp

4
Grafton Flyford
The Bourne
Dormston
Inkberrow
A422
Abbots Morton
Weethley
Oversley Green
Exhall
Red Hill
Temple Grafton
A46
Billesley
Shottery
Anne Hathaway's Cottage
Stratford-upon-Avon
Tiddington

North Piddle
Kington
Flyford Flavell
Goom's Hill
Wood Bevington
Ragley Hall
Wixford
Ardens Grafton
Cranhill
Binton
Luddington
Butterfly Farm

5
Abberton
Naunton Beauchamp
Church Lench
Rous Lench
Iron Cross
Dunnington
Broom
Bidford-on-Avon
Welford-on-Avon
Weston-on-Avon
Clifford Chambers
Atherstone on Stour
Preston on Stour
Willicote
Alderm

Peopleton
Bishampton
Ab Lench
Atch Lench
Salford Priors
B439
Barton
Dorsington
Long Marston
Wimpstone
Lower Quinton
Crimscote

Pinvin
Throckmorton
Harvington
Norton
Abbot's Salford
Marlcliff
Cleeve Prior
North Littleton
Pebworth
Broad Marston
Upper Quinton
Admington
Newbold on Stour

6
Upper Moor
Lower Moor
A44
Lenchwick
Offenham
Middle Littleton
Honeybourne
Mickleton
Kiftsgate Court
Hidcote Bartrim
Armscote

Wyre Piddle
Fladbury
Chadbury
Evesham
Tithe Barn
South Littleton
B4632
Hidcote Manor Garden
Blackwell
Ilmington

Wick
Charlton
Cropthorne
Bengeworth
Badsey
Aldington
Bretforton
The Fleece Inn
Vale of Evesham
Aston-sub-Edge
Hidcote Boyce
Darlingscott

7
Pensham
Little Comberton
Hampton
Bricklehampton
Netherton
Hinton Green
Wickhamford
Weston-sub-Edge
Chipping Campden
Ebrington
Charingworth
A429

81
Great Comberton
Elmley Castle
Hinton on the Green
Murcot
Willersey
Saintbury
Cotswold Way
Broad Campden
Stretton on Fosse

Bredon Hill
Kersoe
Ashton under Hill
Grafton
Childswickham
Aston Somerville
Wormington
Broadway
Broadway Tower
Chipping Campden
Blockley
Paxford
Draycott
Tidmin

8
Beckford
Conderton
Sedgeberrow
Dumbleton
Buckland
Laverton
Rectory
Cotswold Lavender
Aston Magna
Lower Lemington

Overbury
Kemerton
Silk Mill
A46
Great Washbourne
Alderton
Stanton
Snowshill
Snowshill Manor
Batsford
Dorn

Aston Cross
Little Washbourne
Alstone
Toddington
Wormington
Stanway
Broadway
Blockley
Cotswold Falconry Centre
Moreton-in-Marsh

Teddington
Oxenton
Stanford Dixton
Didbrook
Stanway
Warwickshire Railway
65
Bourton-on-the-Hill
Bourton Downs
Sezincote
Four Shire Stone

0 1 2 3 4 5 miles
0 1 2 3 4 5 6 7 8 kilometres

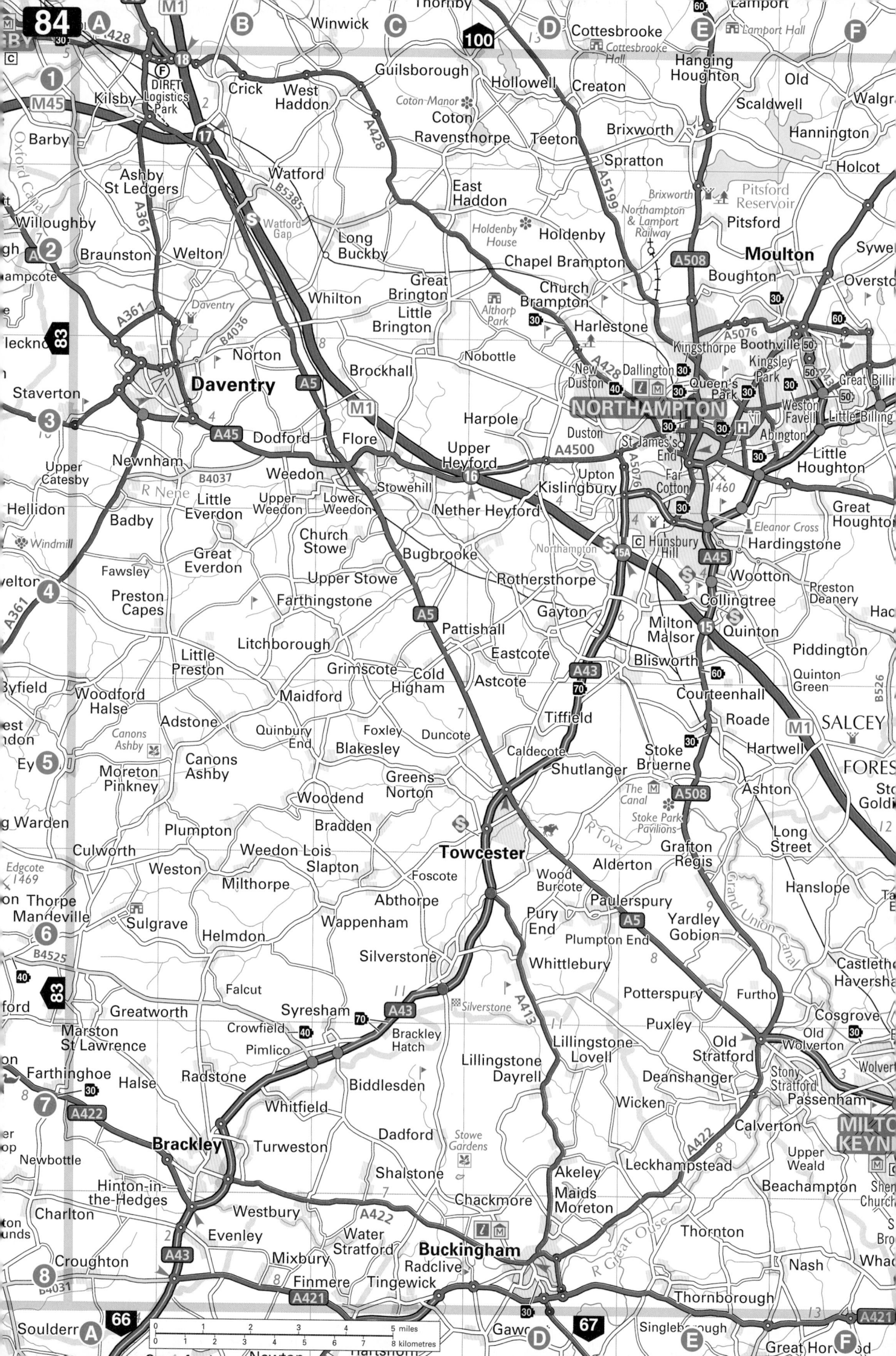

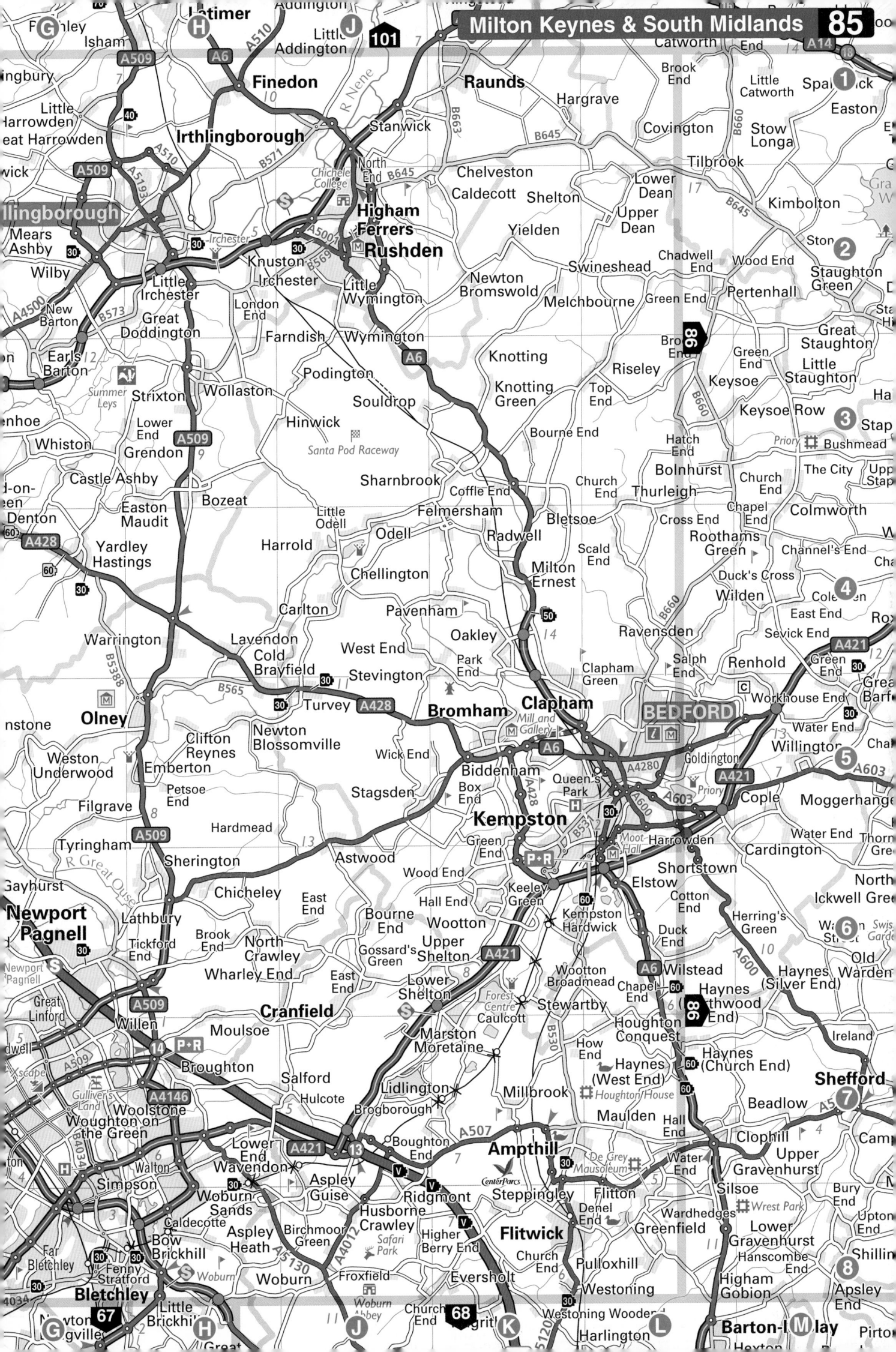

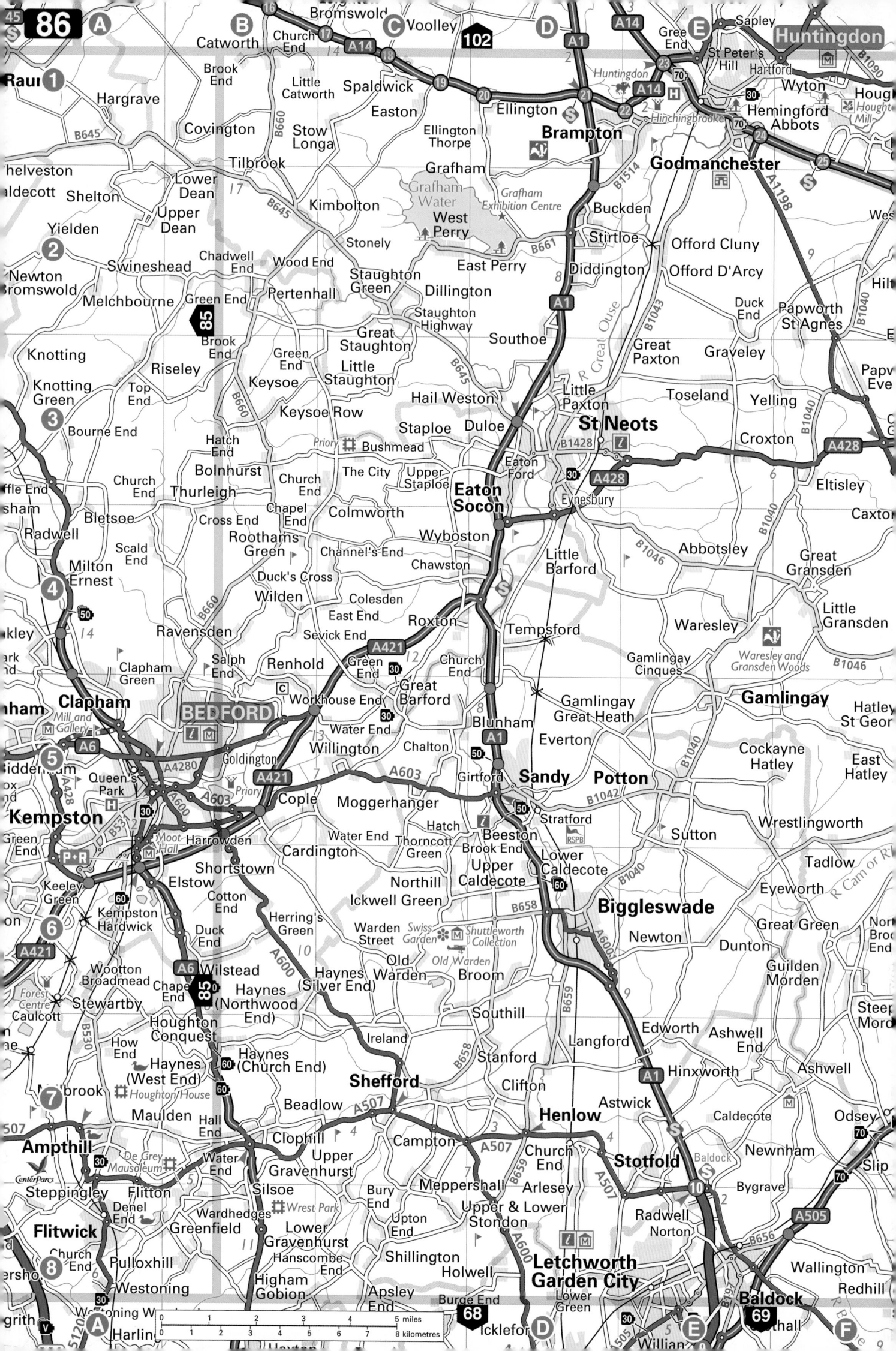

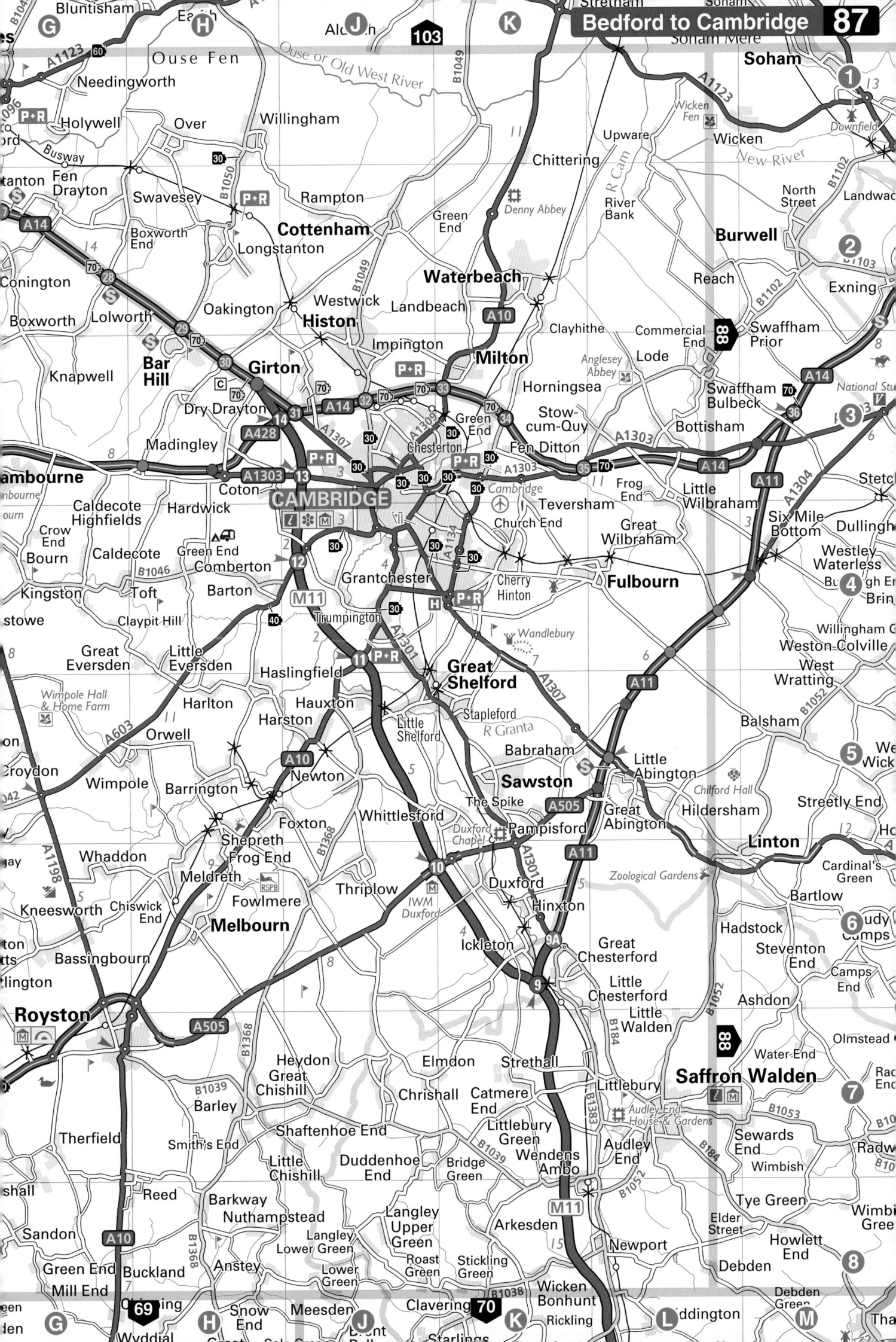

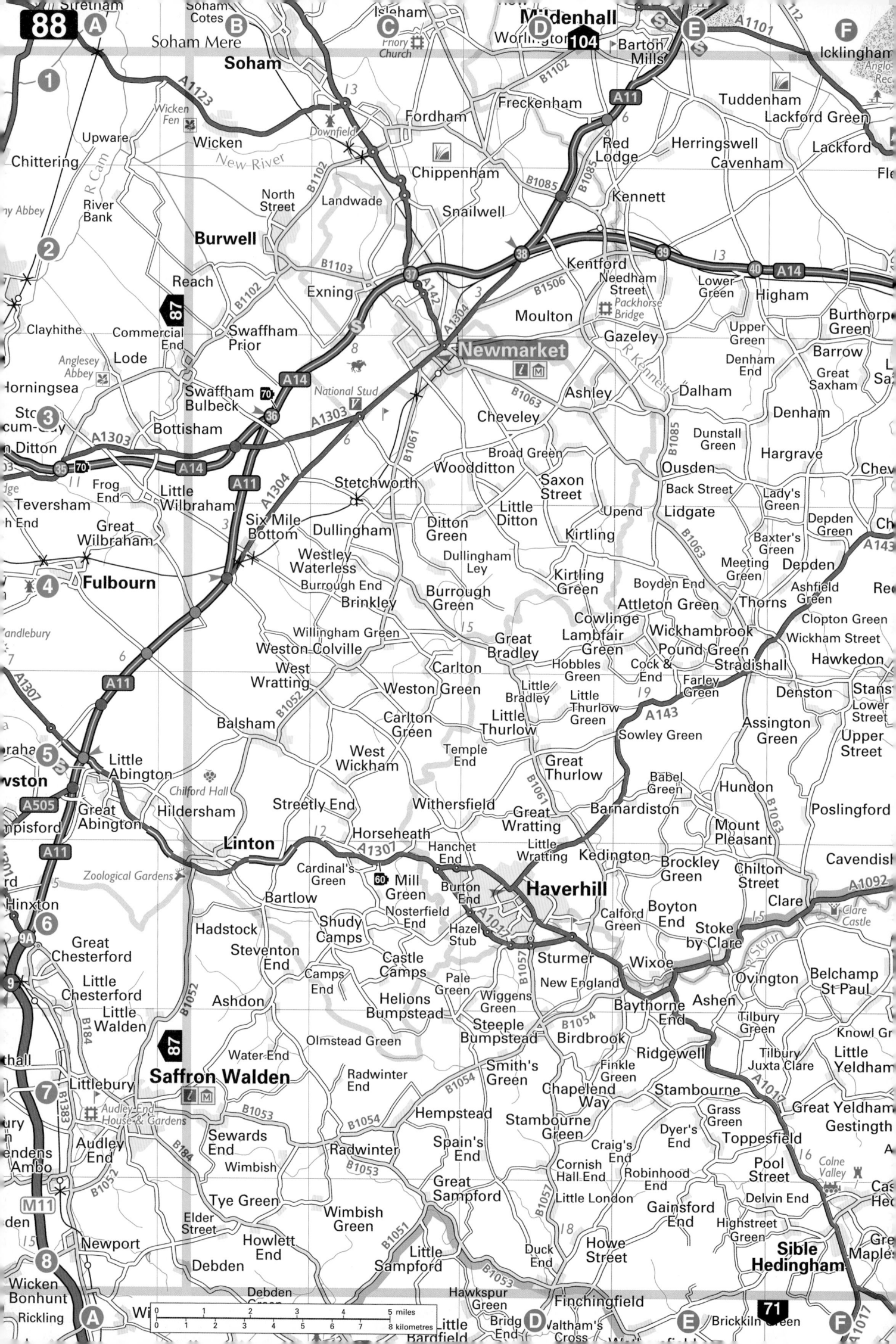

G H J 105 K

Thornham Parv
Thornham Magna
Ixworth Thorpe
Bardw
Stanton
Wattisfield
Allwood Green
Mill Street
1

Troston
Bangrove
Upthorpe
Walsham le Willows
Cranmer Green
Gislingham
Wickham Street
Thornham Magna

Brockley
Ampton
Wyken
West Street
Langham
Badwell Ash
Long Thurlow
Crowland
Four Ashes
Badwell Green
Westhorpe
Finningham
Wyverstone Street
Wickham Skeith
Wickham Green

Ingham
Great Livermere
Ixworth
Hunston
Stowlangtoft
Great Ashfield
Earl's Green
Wyverstone
Cotton
Brockford

Timworth
Upper Town
Grimstone End
Stanton Street
Hunston Green
Bacton Green
Cow Green
Ford's Green
Canhams Green
Bacton
Mendlesham

Timworth Green
Conyer's Green
Pakenham
Thurston
Great Green
Norton
Norton Little Green
Bacton Green
Brown Street
Mendlesham Green

Fornham St Martin
Great Barton
Cattishall
Battlies Green
Thurston Planch
Tostock
Elmswell
Base Green
Haughley Green
Dagworth
Gipping
Middlewood Green

Bury St Edmunds
Blackthorpe
Beyton Gn
Kingshall Street
Beyton
Broadgrass Gn
Broadgrass Green
Wetherden
Old Newton
Saxham Street
3

Horringer
Rushbrooke
Rougham Green
Hessett
Woolpit
Haughley
Harleston
Stowupland
Forward Green
Earl Stonham

High Green
Nowton
Sicklesmere
Bradfield St George
Drinkstone
Woolpit Green
Borley Green
Clopton Green
Onehouse
Stowmarket
Creeting St Mary

Pinford End
Little Welnetham
Maypole Green
Drinkstone Green
Rattlesden
Buxhall Fen Street
Buxhall
Great Finborough
Combs
Needham Market
4

Hawstead
Hawstead Green
Bradfield Combust
Gedding
Poystreet Green
Mill Green
Combs Ford
Moats Tye
Battisford Tye
Battisford
Ringshall
Barking

Mickley Green
Great Welnetham
Hoggards Green
Oldhall Green
Felsham
Hightown Green
Brettenham
Battisford Tye
Charles Tye
Barking Tye
Lower Street

Melon Green
Stanningfield
Cross Green
Great Green
Thorpe Green
Cooks Green
Cross Green
Bird Street
Ringshall Stocks
Baylham

Harrow Green
Windsor Green
Cockfield
Thorpe Morieux
Hitcham Causeway
Wattisham
Great Bricett
Upper Street
5

Lawshall
Lawshall Green
Shimpling Street
Preston
Hitcham Street
Hitcham
Nedging Tye
Greenstreet Green
Offton

Cross Green
Audley End
Giffords Hall
Alpheton
Guildhall
Kettlebaston
Bildeston
Nedging
Naughton
Somersham
Little Blakenham

Boxted
Shimpling
Lavenham
Little Hall
Brent Eleigh
Monks Eleigh
Ash Street
Flowton

Bridge Street
Stanstead
Kentwell Hall & Gardens
Swingleton Green
Chelsworth
Semer
Whatfield
Elmsett
Bramford

Glemsford
Melford Hall
Little Waldingfield
Milden
Lindsey Tye
Aldham
Sproughton

Long Melford
Acton
Rose Green
Lindsey
St James's Chapel
Stone Street
Burstall
6

Liston
Newman's Green
Great Waldingfield
Kersey Tye
Kersey
Hintlesham
Duke Street
Washbrook

Borley
Chilton
Mill Green
Wicker Street Green
Kersey Upland
Coram Street
Hadleigh
Chattisham
Copdock

Sudbury
Ballingdon
Cornard Tye
Newton
Edwardstone
Groton
Horners Green
Calais Street
Hadleigh Heath
Bower House Tye
Polstead Heath
Layham
Coles Green

Bulmer
Great Cornard
Boxford
Stone Street
Whitestreet Green
Raydon
Great Wenham
Little Wenham
7

Bulmer Tye
Middleton
Little Cornard
Hagmore Green
Assington
Polstead
Shelley
Lower Raydon
Capel St Mary

Great Henny
Rose Green
Leavenheath
Stoke-by-Nayland
Holton St Mary
Bentley

Wickham St Paul
Henny Street
Twinstead
Dorking Tye
Honey Tye
Thorington Street
Higham
Stratford St Mary
East Bergholt
East End

Alphamstone
Lamarsh
Nayland
Boxted
Flatford Mill & Bridge Cottage
8

Little Maplestead
Cross End
Bures
Wissington
Wormingford
Boxted Cross
Dedham
Mistley

Pebmarsh
Mount Bures
Countess Cross
Little Horkesley
Lan am
Mar gtree

Boose's
G H J 72 K L M

A B C D E F

Stanton
Wattisfield
Mellis
Yaxley
Denham
Stradbroke
Denham Green

1 Wyken
Upthorpe
Walsham le Willows
Randle Street
Allwood Green
Mill Street
Thornham Parva
Braiseworth
Eye
106
Horham
Wootten Green

West Street
Langham
Cranmer Green
Gislingham
Thornham Magna
Stoke Ash
Standwell Green
Redlingfield Green
Occold
Athelington Street
Stanway Green
Coal St

Badwell Ash
Hunston
Four Ashes
Badwell Green
Westhorpe
Wickham Street
Wickham Green
Thorndon
Redlingfield
Dublin
Southolt
Fingal Street
Worli

Stowlangtoft
Great Ashfield
Finningham
Wickham Skeith
Thwaite
Rishangles
Bedingfield
Bedfield

2 Stanton Street
Hunston Green
Wyverstone Street
Cotton
Brockford Street
Hestley Green
Bedingfield Green
Kenton
Monk Soham
Bedfield Little Gree
Post Mill

Norton Little Green
Norton
Bacton Green
Cow Green
Ford's Green
Canhams Green
Mendlesham
Brockford Green
Park Green
Wetheringsett
Blacksmith's Green
Aspall
Earl Soham

Elmswell
Haughley Green
Ward Green
Brown Street
Mendlesham Green
Wetherup Street
Debenham
Fen Street
Ashfield cum Thorpe

Broadgrass Gn
Haughley
Wetherden
Gipping
Middlewood Green
Mickfield
Winston
Cretingham

3 Woolpit
Woolpit Green
Borley Green
Old Newton
Saxham Street
Little Stonham
Mill Green
A1120

Harleston
Dagworth
Stowupland
A14
A1308
Stonham Aspal
Mid Suffolk
Suffolk Owl Sanctuary
Pettaugh
Framsden
Fri

Clopton Green
Onehouse
Stowmarket
Forward Green
Earl Stonham
Crowfield Green
Helmingham Hall
Monewden

Rattlesden
Buxhall Fen Street
R. Gipping
Creeting St Mary
Crowfield
Helmingham
Gosbeck
Otley
Leth

Poystreet Green
Buxhall
Great Finborough
Combs Ford
Combs
Needham Market
Needham Lake
Crowfield
Gosbeck
Otley
Otley Green
Clopton Corner
Charsfiel
Dallin

4 Hightown Green
Battisford Tye
Battisford
Ringshall
Barking
Hemingstone
Ashbocking
Clopton

Brettenham
Cross Green
Bird Street
Charles Tye
Barking Tye
Lower Street
Barham
Swilland
Clopton

Cooks Green
cham Causeway
Ringshall Stocks
Great Bricett
Baylham
Bells Cross
Grundisburgh
Burgh

itcham Street
Hitcham
Nedging Tye
Greenstreet Green
Offton
Upper Street
Great Blakenham
Henley
Witnesham
Hasketon

5 Bildeston
Naughton
Somersham
Little Blakenham
Claydon
Akenham
Tuddenham
Culpho
Boot Street
Great Bealing

Monks Eleigh
Nedging
Ash Street
Whatfield
Elmsett
Flowton
Bramford
Whitton
Westerfield
Playford
Little Bealings

Chelsworth
Semer
Lindsey Tye
Aldham
Sproughton
Burstall
Castle Hill
Rushmere St Andrew
Kesgrave

Rose Gn
Lindsey
Stone Street
A1071
RSPB
Hintlesham
Duke Street
Washbrook
Whight's Corner
Chantry
IPSWICH
Suffolk

6 St James's Chapel
Kersey Tye
Kersey
Coram Street
Copdock
Belstead

Wicker Street Green
Kersey Upland
Hadleigh
Chattisham
Coles Green
Wherstead
Nacton
A12

Horners Green
Hadleigh Heath
Bower House Tye
Polstead Heath
Layham
Great Wenham
Little Wenham
Freston
Woolverstone
Levington

7 Calais Street
Whitestreet Green
Raydon
Capel St Mary
Tattingstone White Horse
Tattingstone
Pin Mill

R. Box
B1068
Polstead
Shelley
Lower Raydon
Holton St Mary
Bentley
East End
Holbrook
Chelmondiston
Erwarton

Stoke-by-Nayland
Higham
Stratford St Mary
East Bergholt
Brantham
Upper Street
Stutton
Shotley Street

8 Boxted
Carter's
Dedham
Cattawade
Alton Water
Lower Holbrook
Shotl

Boxted Cross
Langham
Flatford Mill & Bridge Cottage
Mistley Towers
Mistley
Holbrook Bay
River Stour
International Ferry Terminal

A B Dedham
C ningtree
Wrabness
D w Mistley
E Parkeston
73
Parkston
F

Holbrook Bay
River Orwell

G H B1117 J 107 K B1387

Huntingfield Walpole Bramfield Tington

1

Suffolk Coast

B1125 Dunwich
Grey Friars

Laxfield Heveningham Darsham

ndish Street Ubbeston Green Owl's Green High Street Westleton Minsmere RSPB Dunwich Heath

Goddard's Corner Peasenhall A1120 Sibton Yoxford Middleton

pole en Capon's Green Badingham Middleton Moor B1122 2

Dennington Bruisyard North Green A12 Theberton Eastbridge

xtead ad Brabling Green B1120 Bruisyard Street Rendham Kelsale East Green Poplar Street

Castle Shawsgate Cransford Carlton Saxmundham Leiston Abbey

ham Swefling B1119 Sternfield B1119 Knodishall Sizewell

North Green Great Glemham Benhall Street Benhall Green Coldfair Green Leiston 3

Mill Green B1116 Stratford St Andrew 50 Friday Street Friston Knodishall Common Aldringham Thorpe Ness

Parham Kettleburgh Silverlace Green Farnham Snape Knodishall Common B1353 Thorpeness

Easton Hacheston Gromford B1122 RSPB

Marlesford Little Glemham Snape Street A1094 4

Lower Hacheston Snape Maltings Aldeburgh

Wickham Market Campsea Ash Blaxhall B1069 Iken River Alde Aldeburgh Bay

Pettistree Tunstall High Street

Upper Ufford 10 Rendlesham B1078 Sudbourne 5

Ufford Chillesford

Lower Ufford A1152 Friday Street Butley Castle Orford

Melton Eyke Bromeswell B1084 12 Butley High Corner Orford Ness

Woodbridge Capel Green Capel St Andrew 6

Sutton Hoo B1083 RSPB Orfordness-Havergate

sham Sutton Boyton Suffolk Heritage Coast

ham Waldringfield Shottisham River Ore

Newbourne Hemley Hollesley North Weir Point

Kirton Ramsholt B1083 Shingle Street Hollesley Bay 7

Falkenham Alderton Bawdsey

59 Trimley St Mary River Deben Felixstowe Ferry

Old Felixstowe

Walton Landguard Fort

61 Felixstowe 8

G Landguard H J K L M

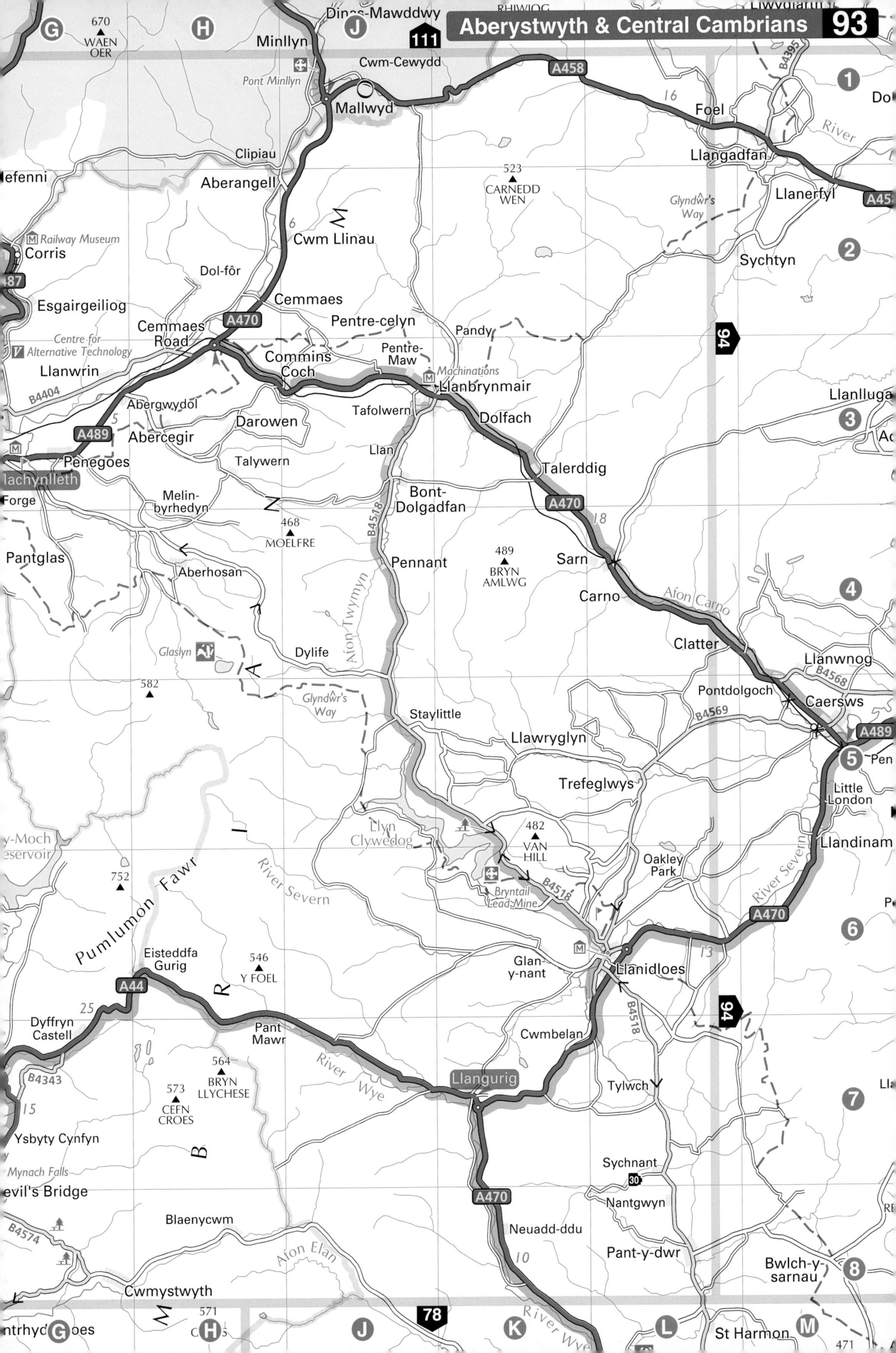

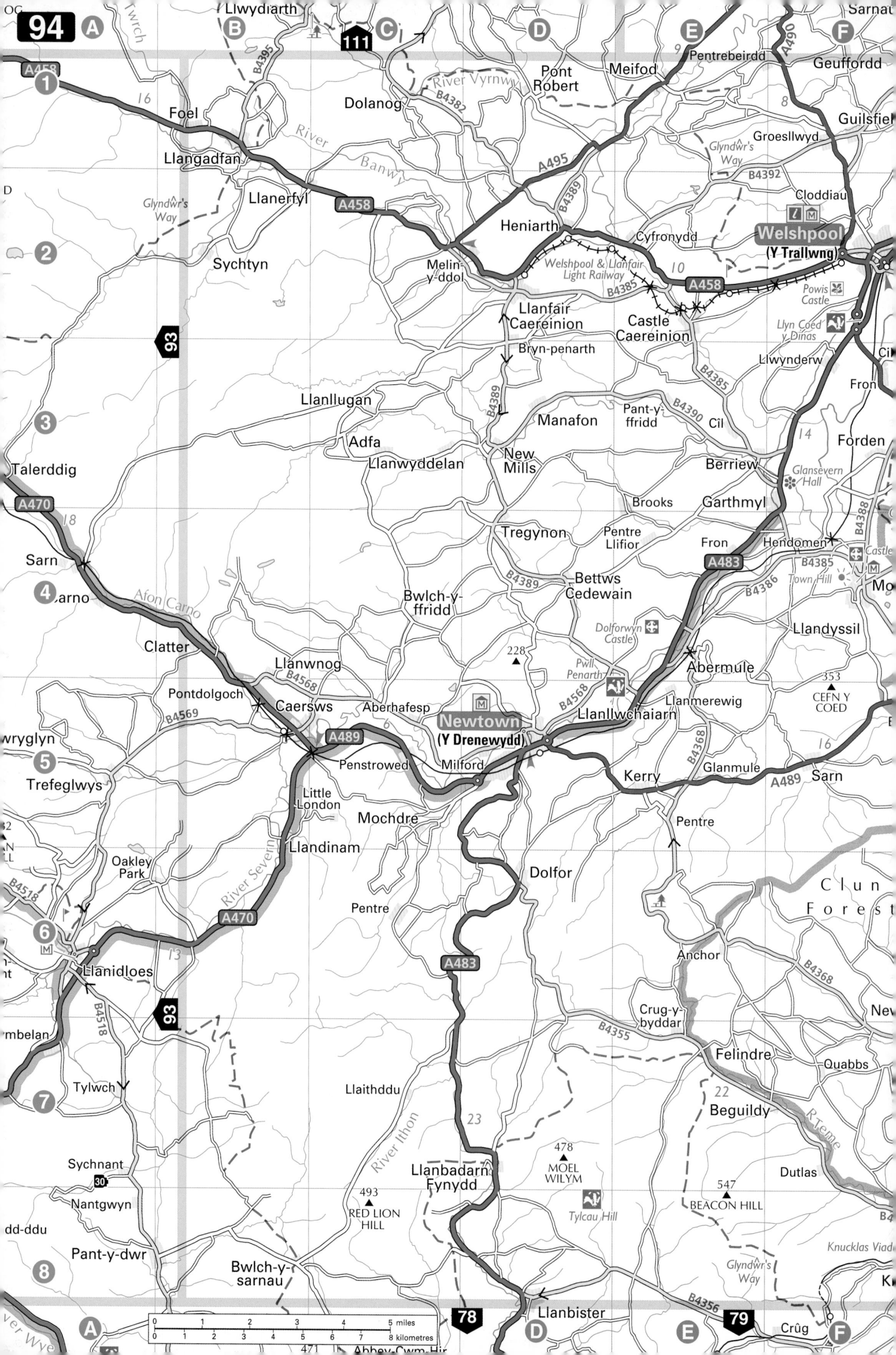

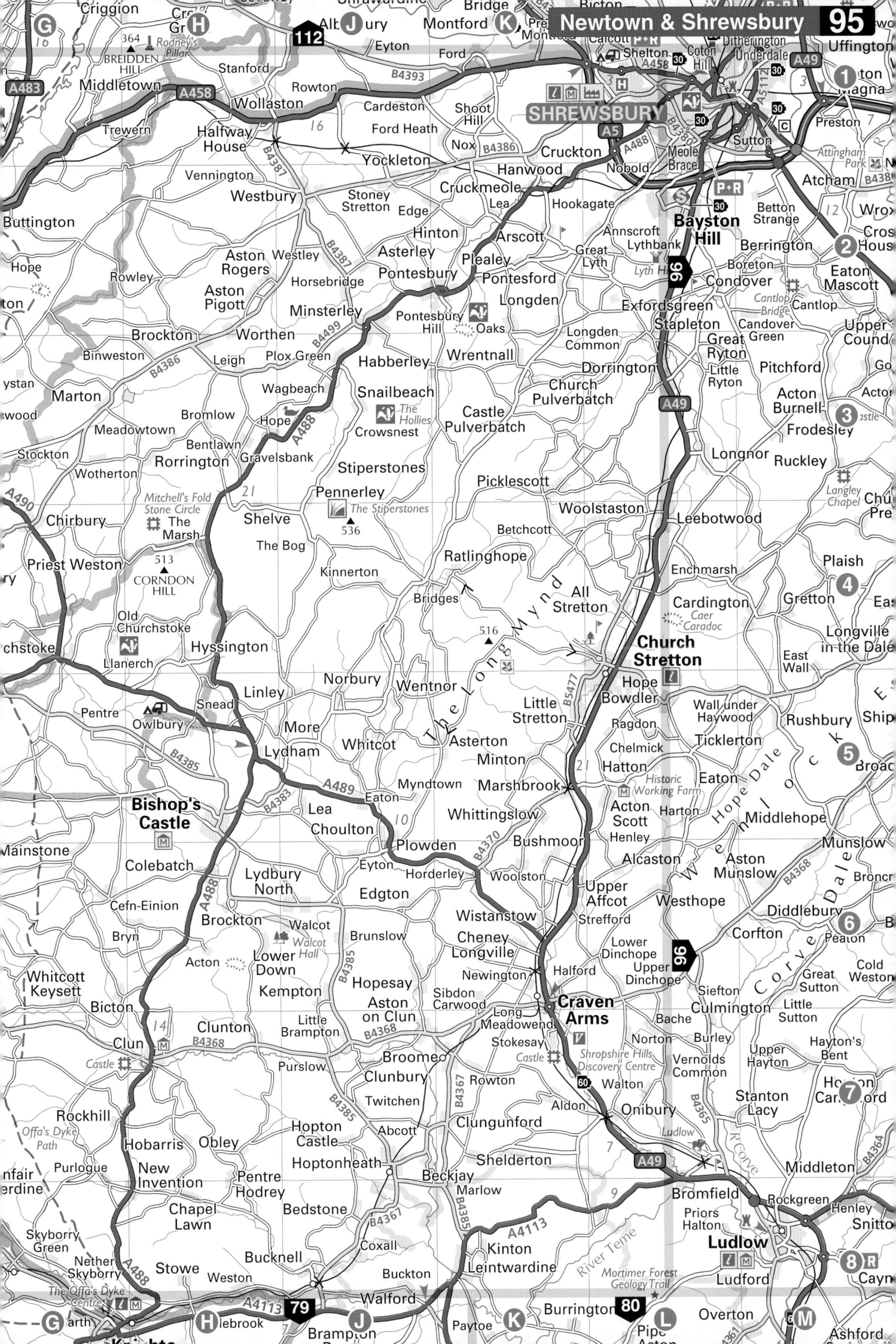

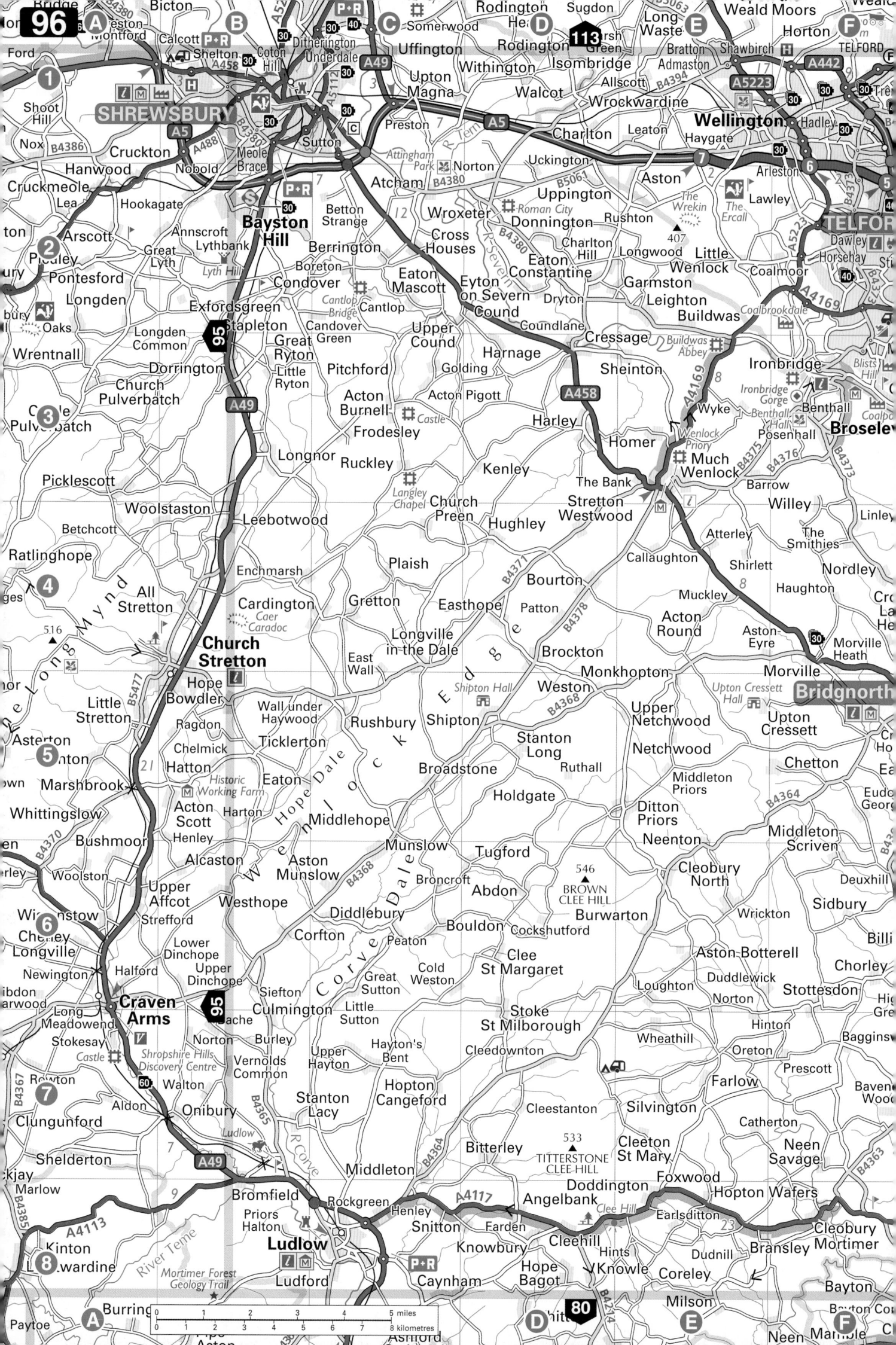

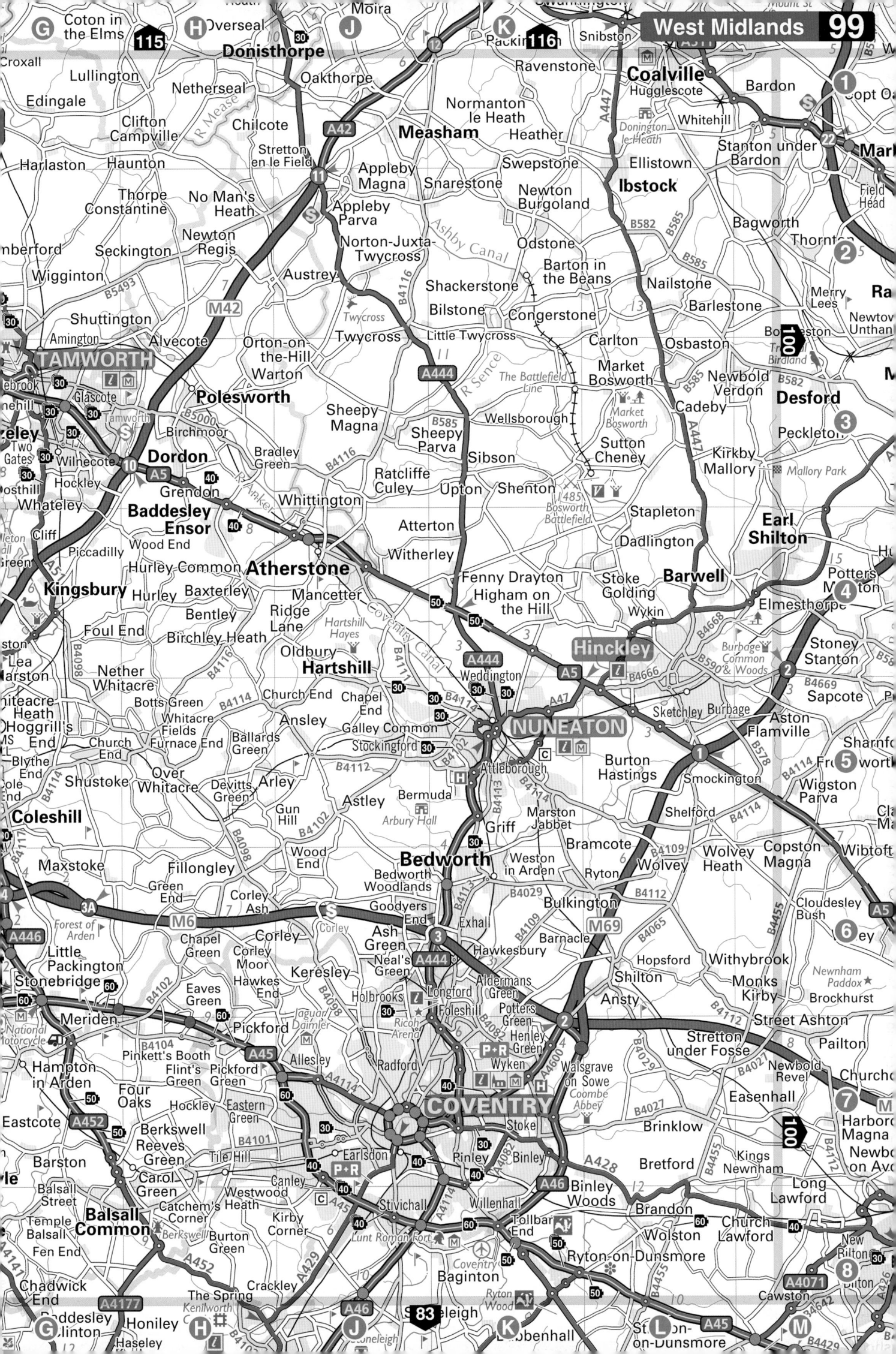

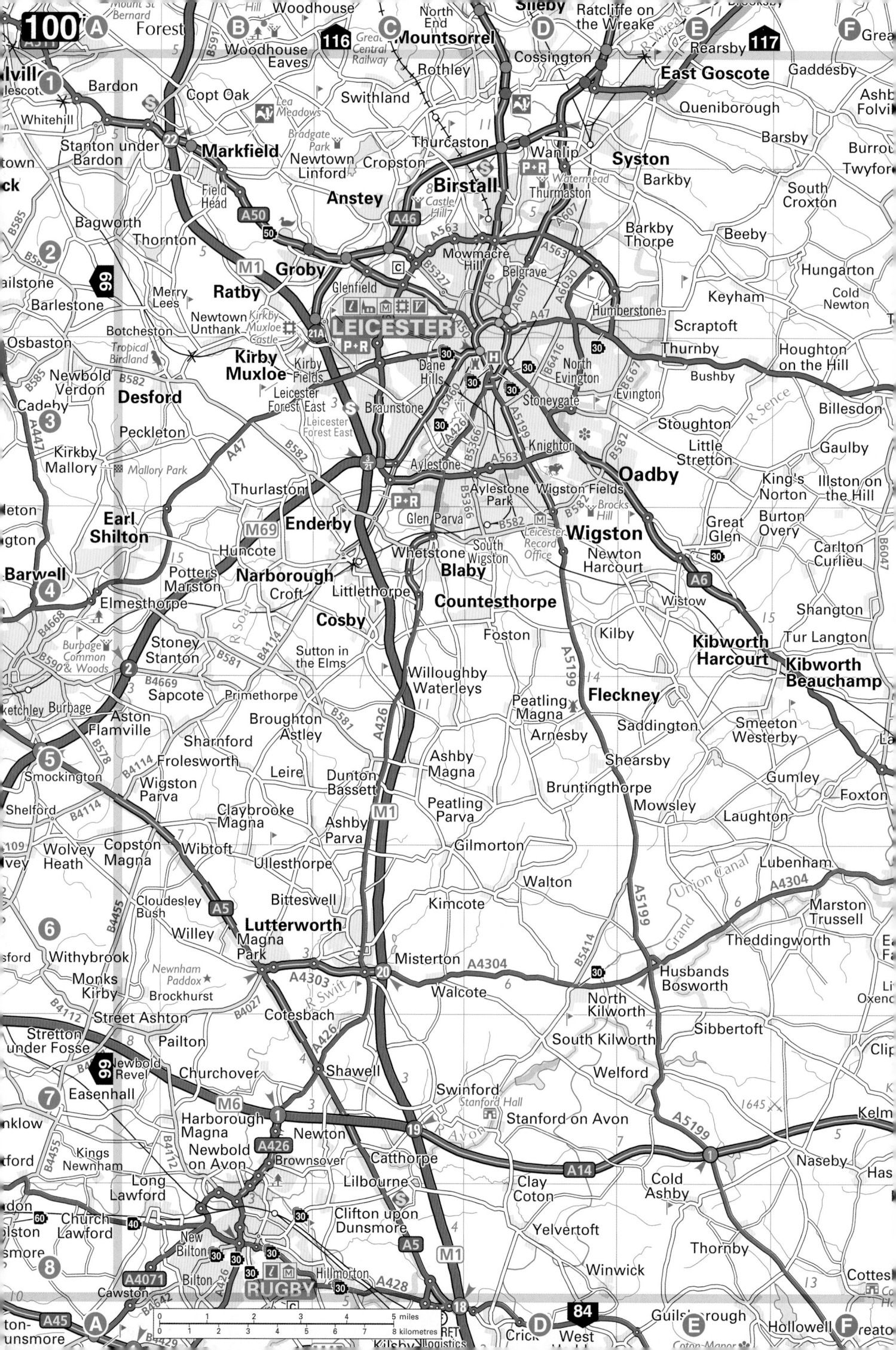

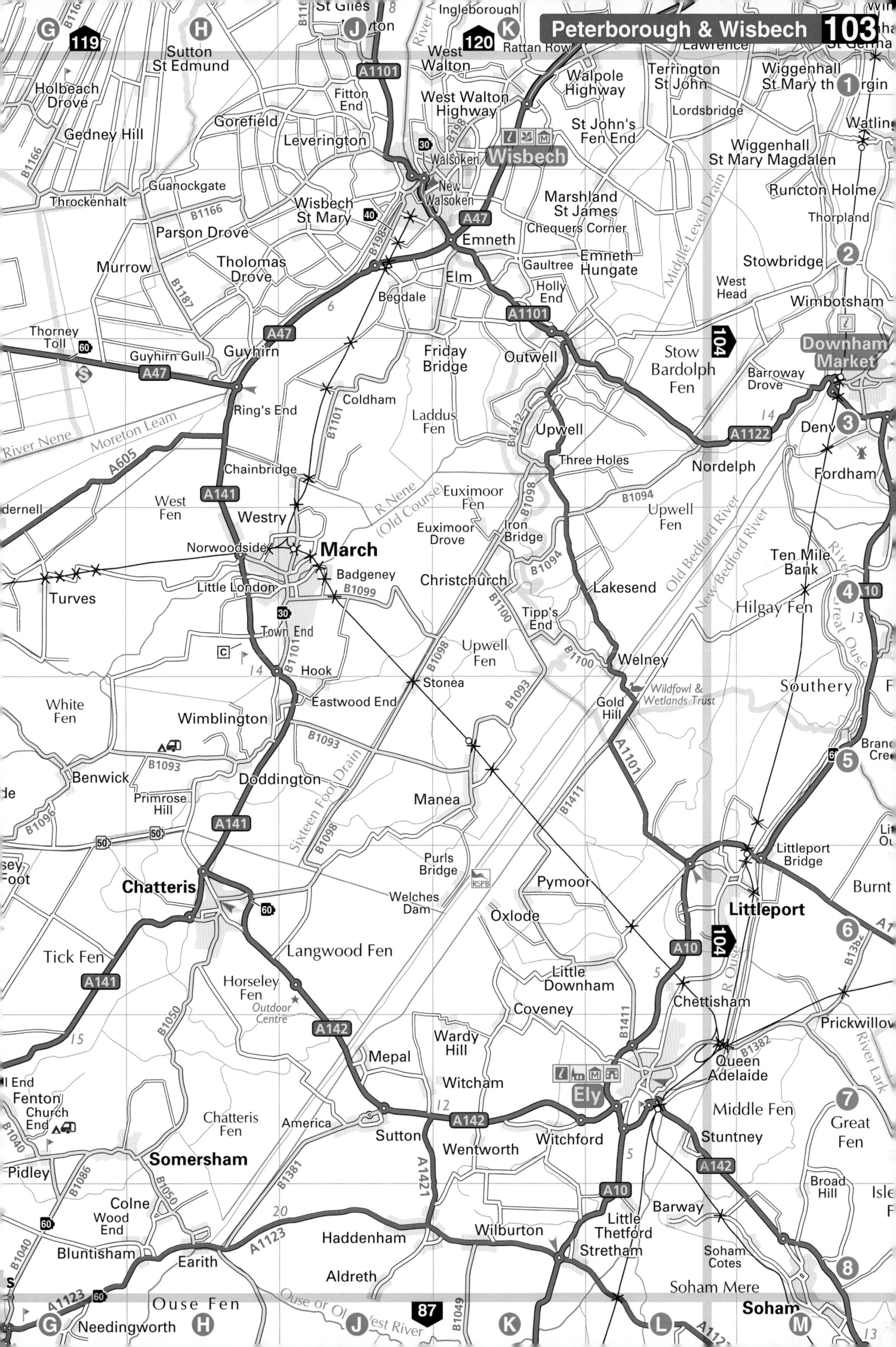

G 119
H
J
K 120
1

Sutton St Edmund
Holbeach Drove
Gedney Hill
B1166
St Giles
ton
Ingleborough
West Walton
Rattan Row
Walpole Highway
Terrington St John
Lawrence
Wiggenhall St Mary th' rgin
Watlin

Gorefield
Fitton End
Leverington
West Walton Highway
Walsoken
New Walsoken
Wisbech
St John's Fen End
Wiggenhall St Mary Magdalen
Lordsbridge

Throckenhalt
Guanockgate
Wisbech St Mary
B1166
B1187
Parson Drove
Tholomas Drove
Murrow
B1101
Begdale
Elm
Emneth
Marshland St James
Chequers Corner
Emneth Hungate
Gaultree
Holly End
Runcton Holme
Thorpland
Stowbridge
West Head
Wimbotsham
2

Thorney Toll
Guyhirn Gull
Guyhirn
A47
Ring's End
Coldham
Friday Bridge
Laddus Fen
Outwell
Stow Bardolph Fen
104
Barroway Drove
Downham Market
3
Denv
Fordham

River Nene
Moreton Leam
A605
A141
West Fen
Westry
Chainbridge
Norwoodside
March
Little London
Badgeney
B1099
Euximoor Fen
Euximoor Drove
Iron Bridge
Upwell
Three Holes
Nordelph
A1122
A1101
B1412
B1094
Upwell Fen
B1098
Christchurch
Lakesend
Ten Mile Bank
Hilgay Fen
Southery
4 10

Turves
Town End
30
C
14
Hook
Eastwood End
Stonea
B1098
Upwell Fen
Tipp's End
B1100
B1093
Welney
Gold Hill
Wildfowl & Wetlands Trust
5

White Fen
Wimblington
B1093
B1096
Benwick
Primrose Hill
Doddington
A141
Sixteen Foot Drain
B1098
Manea
B1411
B1093
Littleport Bridge
6

Chatteris
50
50
60
Langwood Fen
Horseley Fen Outdoor Centre
A142
Purls Bridge
Welches Dam
RSPB
Pymoor
Oxlode
Little Downham
A10 104
Littleport
Burnt

Tick Fen
A141
B1050
Mepal
Wardy Hill
Witcham
Coveney
B1411
Chettisham
Prickwillow
Great Fen
7

sey Foot
15
Fenton Church End
Chatteris Fen
America
Sutton
Wentworth
Witchford
Ely
Queen Adelaide
Middle Fen
Stuntney
A142

Pidley
B1040 B1086
Somersham
B1381
A1421
A142
A10
Little Thetford
Stretham
Barway
Broad Hill
Isle

Colne Wood End
Bluntisham
Haddenham
Aldreth
Wilburton
Soham Cotes
8

S
A1123
60
Needingworth
Ouse Fen
Ouse or Ol West River
87
A1049
Soham Mere
Soham
A112

G
H
J
K
L A12
M

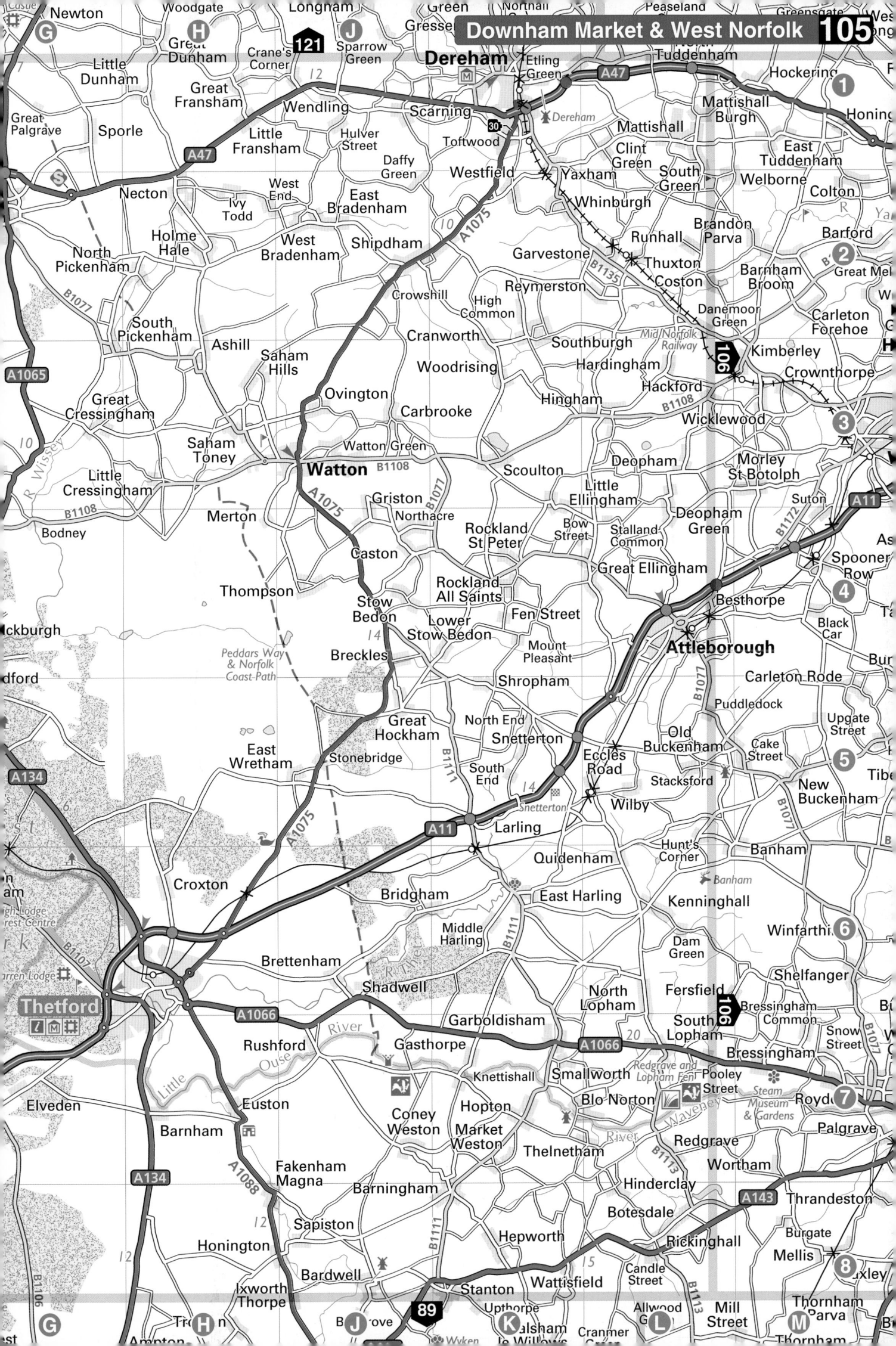

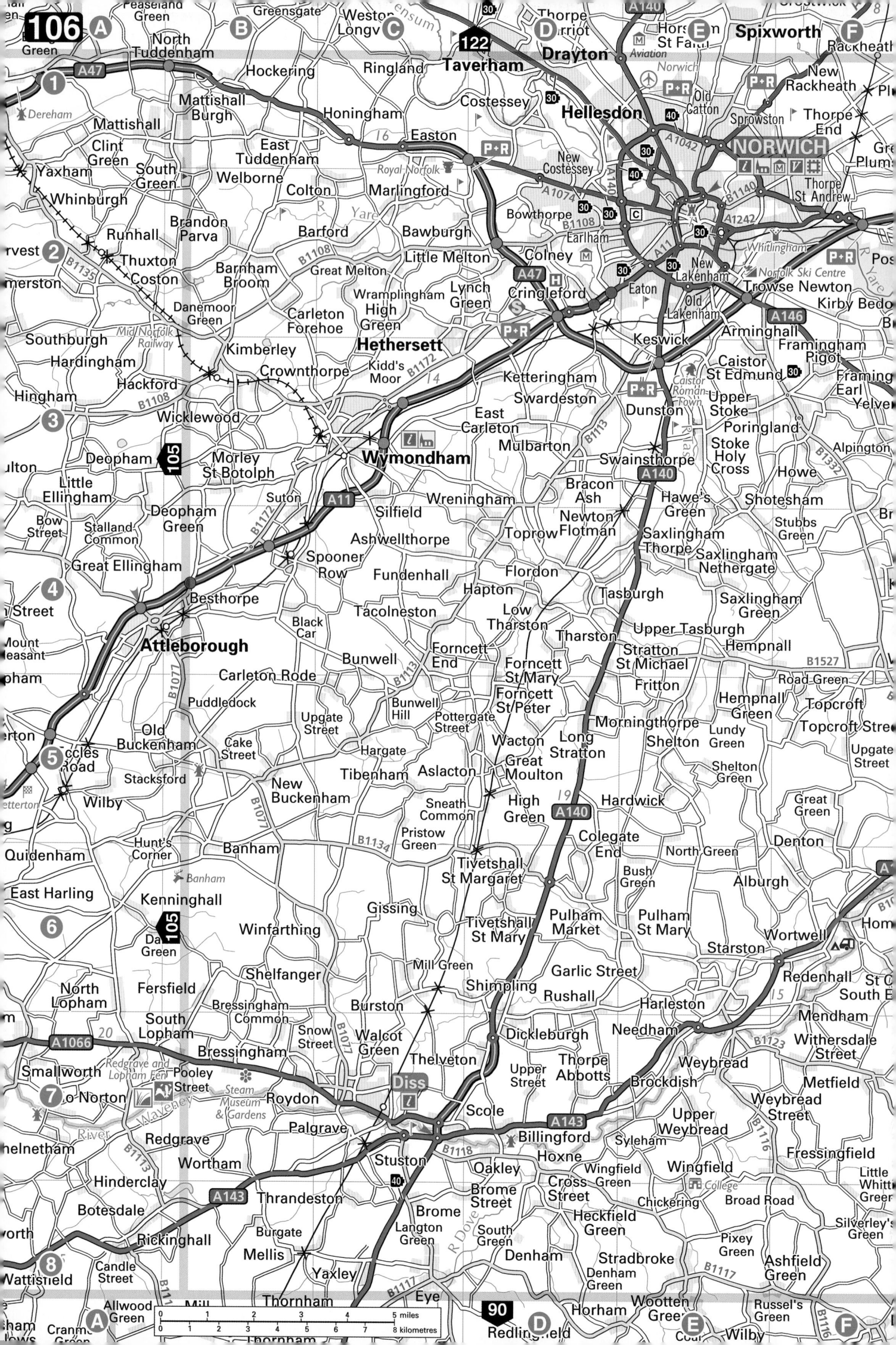

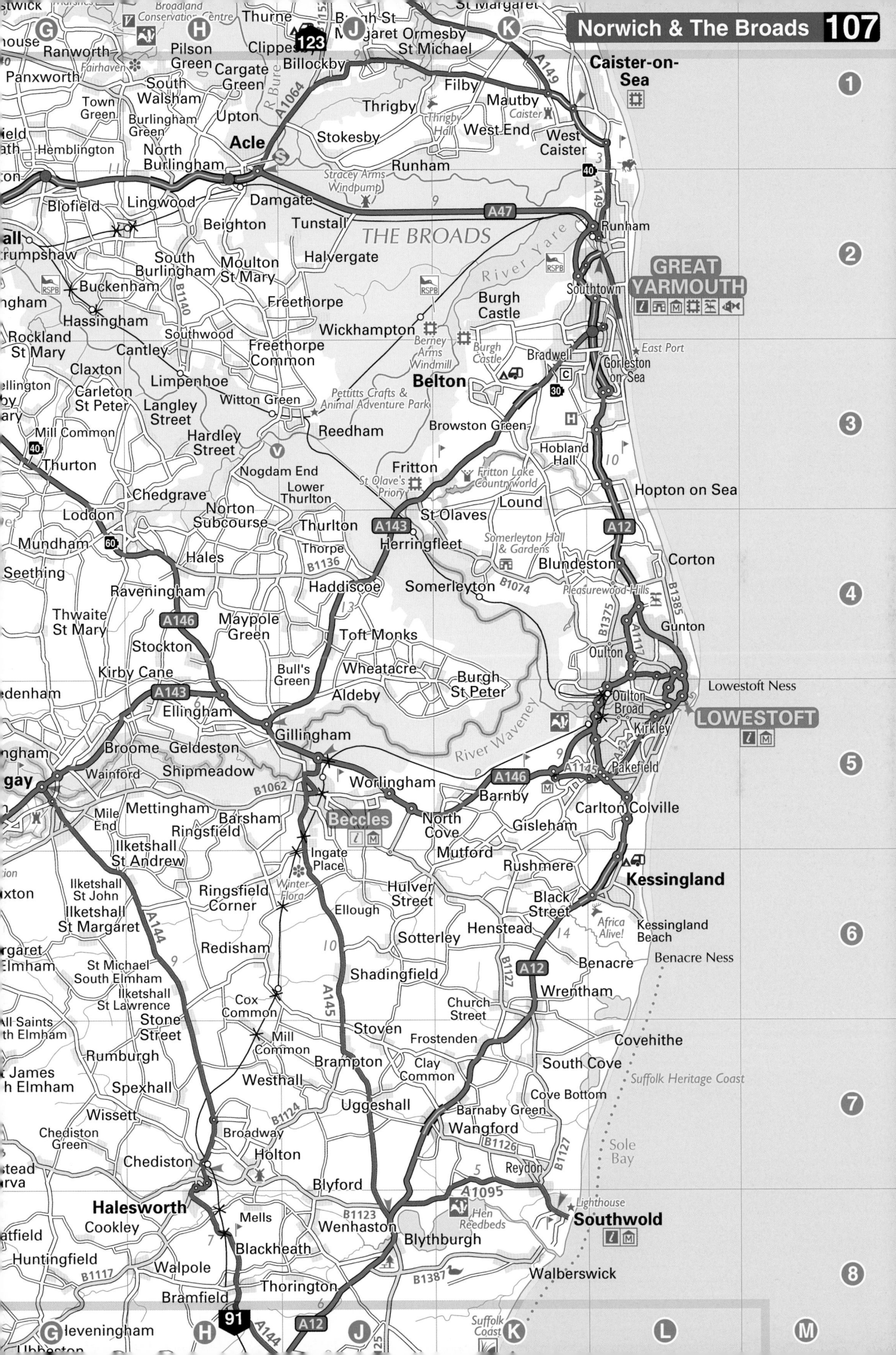

A B C D E F

1

2

C A E R N A R F O N

B A Y

3

Lleyn Heritage
Coast

Trwyn y
Grolech

564
YR EIFL

Tref

Carreg Ddu

Porth
Nefyn

Morfa
Nefyn

Pistyll

Llithfa

Llwy

B4417

Porth Dinllaen
Groesffordd

Nefyn

Edern

Fron B43

Bodfuan

4

Porth Ysgaden

Rhos-y-llan

Tudweiliog

Dinas

371
Carn
Fadrun

LLEYN

A497

Llanno

Porth
Colman

Bryn-
mawr

Llaniestyn

Garnfadryn

B4415

Efailnev

Denio

Pen-y-graig

B4417

14

Rhyd-y-clafdy

Llannor

Meyllteyrn

Penrhos

A499

Llanbedrog

Llangwnnadl

5

Sarn

Botwnnog

Mynytho

B4413

B4413

Trwyn Llanbedro

Bryncroes

Nanhoron

Rhydlios

Rhoshirwaun

Llandegwning

St Tudwal's
Road

Porthoer

Plas yn
Rhiw

Llangian

Anelog

Penycaerau

B4413

Y Rhiw

Abersoch

Aberdaron

Llanengan

Sarn Bach

6

Uwchmynydd

Llanfaelrhys

Porth
Ysgo

Porth Neigwl
or
Hell's Mouth

Bwlchtocyn

Marchros

St Tudwal's
Island East

St Tudwal's
Island West

Aberdaron
Bay

Porth
Ceiriad

Bardsey Sound

Lleyn Heritage
Coast

St Mary's

7

Ynys Enlli

BARDSEY ISLAND

8

A B C D E F

G
H
J
125
Groeslon
Moel Tryfan
Fron
Carmel
Cilgwyn
Nantlle
B4418
698
MYNYDD MAWR
Slateworks
Parc Glynllifon
13
18
Cwellyn
pass
1085
V
SNOWDON
Yr Wyddfa
Llyn Llydaw
12
1

Penygroes
Talysarn
Rhyd-Ddu
A4085
747
YR
ARAN
Glanaber
Llyn Gwynant
A498
Nant Gwynant

Pontlyfni
Llanllyfni
Aberdesach
Nebo
Tai'n Lôn
655
Crafnwyn and Beddgelert
Welsh Highland Railway
Beddgelert
Sygun Copper Mine
Rhiwbryfd
2

nnog-fawr
n-gôch
Capeluchaf
Nasareth
19
Pant Glas
782
MOEL HEBOG
Nantmor
770
Tan-y-grisiau
Tan-y-Gri
Reservo

522
GYRN-DDU
A487
Llanfihangel-y-pennant
552
MOEL DDU
110
Croesor
MOELWYN MAWR
711
MOELWYN BACH
Tan-y-Gri
Reservo
3
Rhyd-y-sarn

Llanaelhaearn
PENINSULA
Bryncir
Garn-Dolbenmaen
A498
A4085
Rhyd
Ffestiniog Railway
Tan-y-Bwlch

Glan-Dwyfach
Dolbenmaen
Afon Glaslyn
8
B4410
Llanfrothen
Plas Tan y Bwlch
Maentwrog
Gellilydan

St Cybi's Well
Golan
Prenteg
7
Garreg
A487
4
Penrhyndeudraeth
5
4

Pencaenewydd
Llangybi
Rhoslan
Penmorfa
Afon Dwyfawr
Wern
Tremadog
3
Toll
Gwaith Powdwr
Llandecwyn

Y Ffor
B4354
Llanarmon
Pentrefelin
A497
Porthmadog
Minffordd
Portmeirion
Afon Dwyfawr
9
Bryn-bwbach

Penarth Fawr
Medieval House
Llanystumdwy
Chwilog
13
Criccieth
Castle
Morfa Bychan
Borth-y-Gest
Ffestiniog Railway
Talsarnau
624
MOEL YSGYFARNOGOD
Llantrawsty

erch
Pen-ychain
Traeth Bach
Llanfihangel-y-traethau
Trawsf

eli
Harlech Point
Tremadog Bay
Morfa Harlech
A496
SNOWDONIA
5

Harlech
B4573
NATIONAL
720
RHINOG FAWR

Harlech Castle
Llanfair
PARK
Llandanwg
Pentre Gwynfryn
6
754
Y LLETHR

Llanbedr
Shell Island
Morfa Dyffryn
11
589
MOELFRE
750
DIFFWYS

Coed Ystumgwern
Llanenddwyn
Afon Ysgethin

Dyffryn Ardudwy
Burial Chamber
Cors-y-Gedol
110
Tal-y-bont

Llanddwywe
7
Bontddu
RSPB

Llanaber
Caerdeon
Penmaenpoo
A496
Cutiau
10
A493

Barmouth
Afon Mawddach
8

Barmouth Bridge
Barmouth Bay
Fairbourne Steam Railway
Fairbourne
Arthog

G
H
J
92
K
L
M

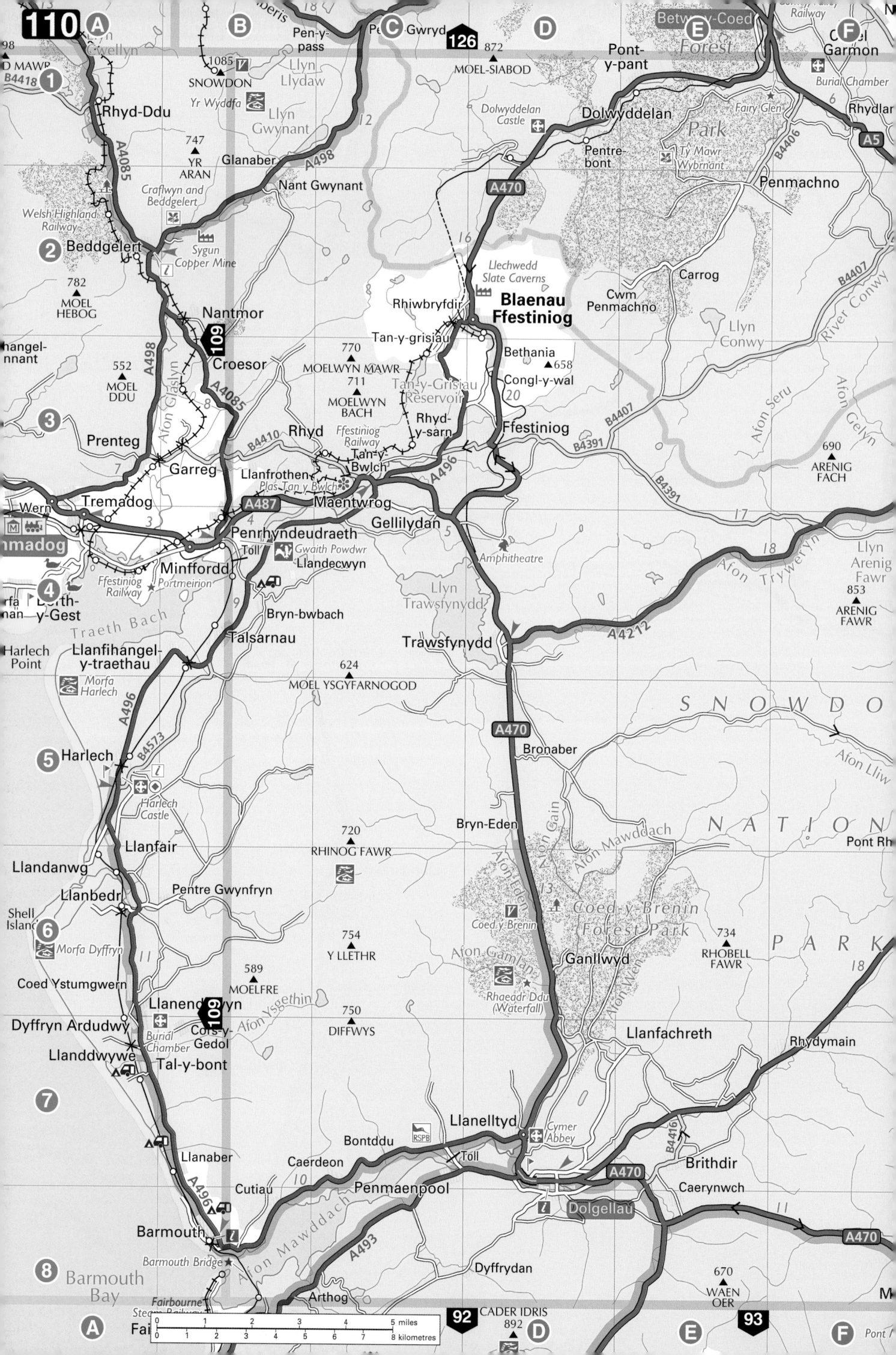

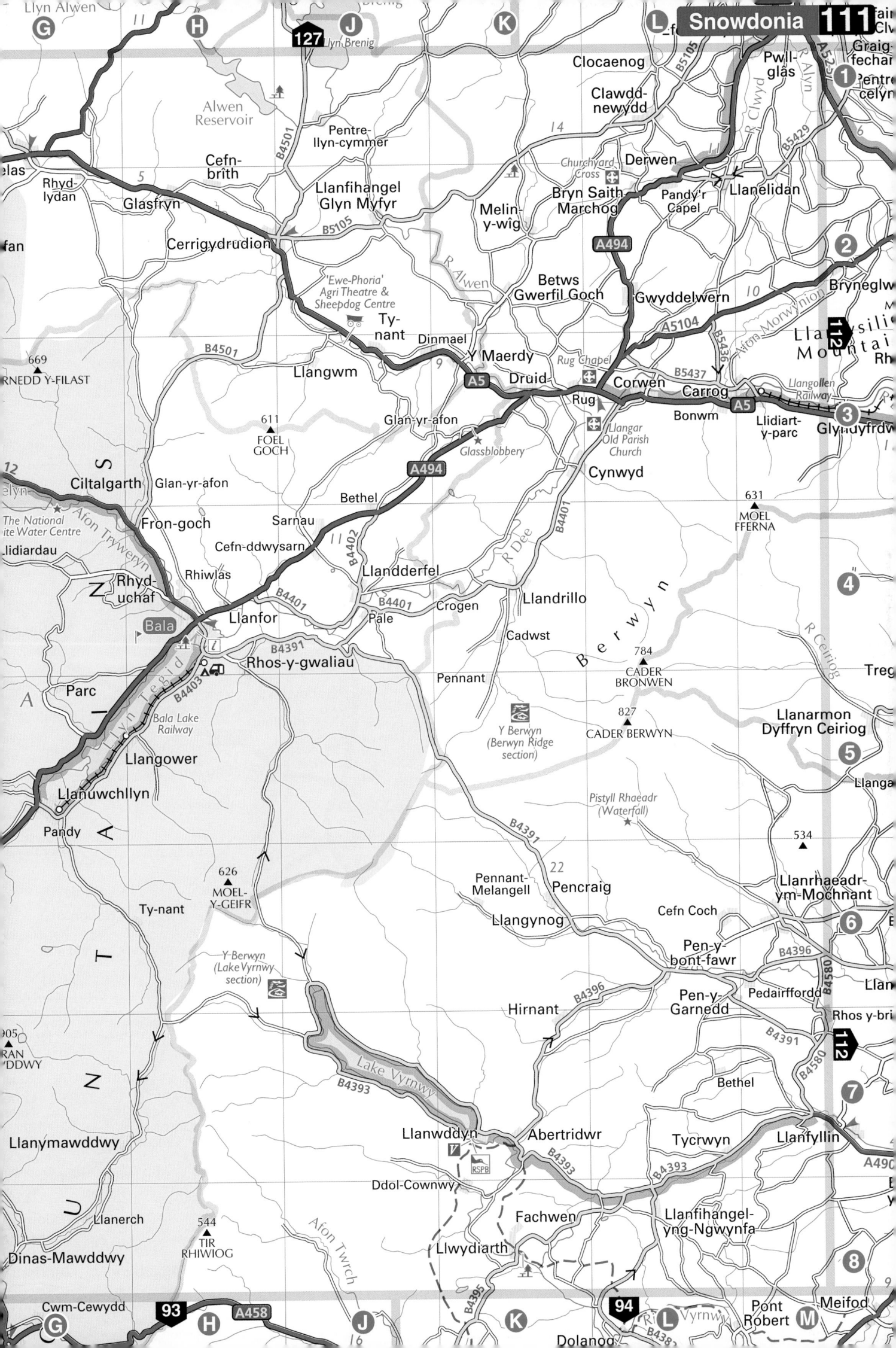

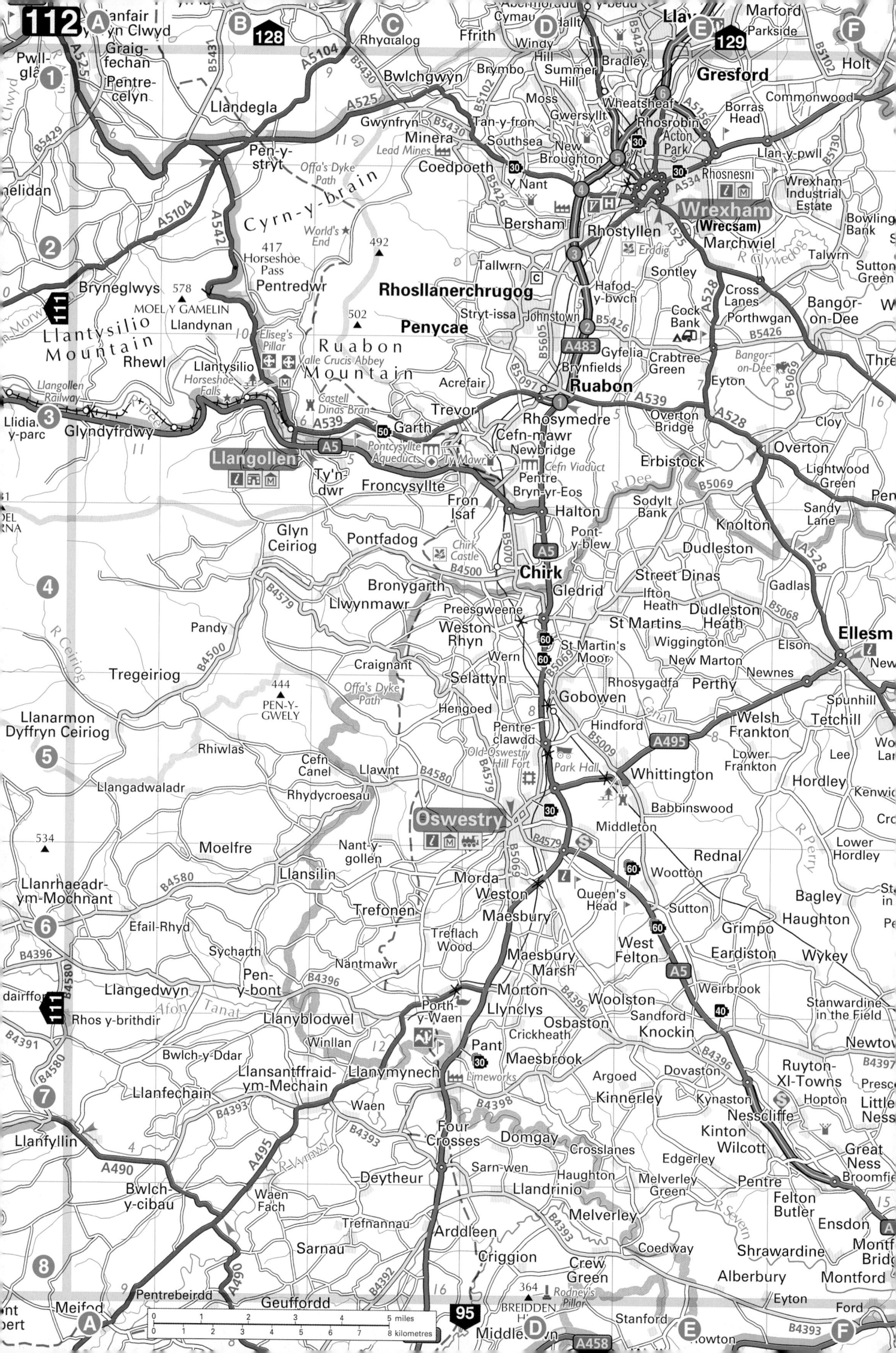

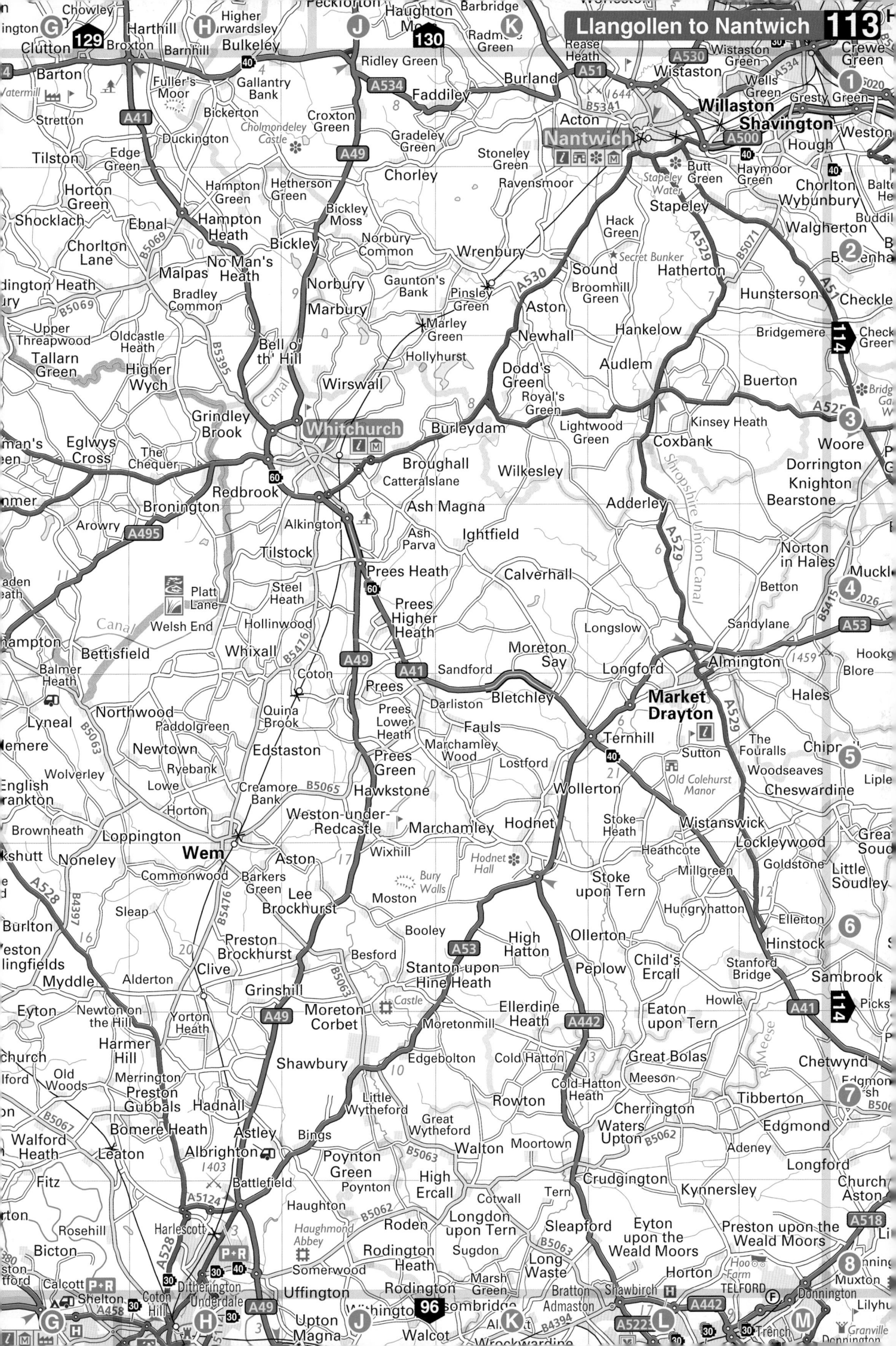

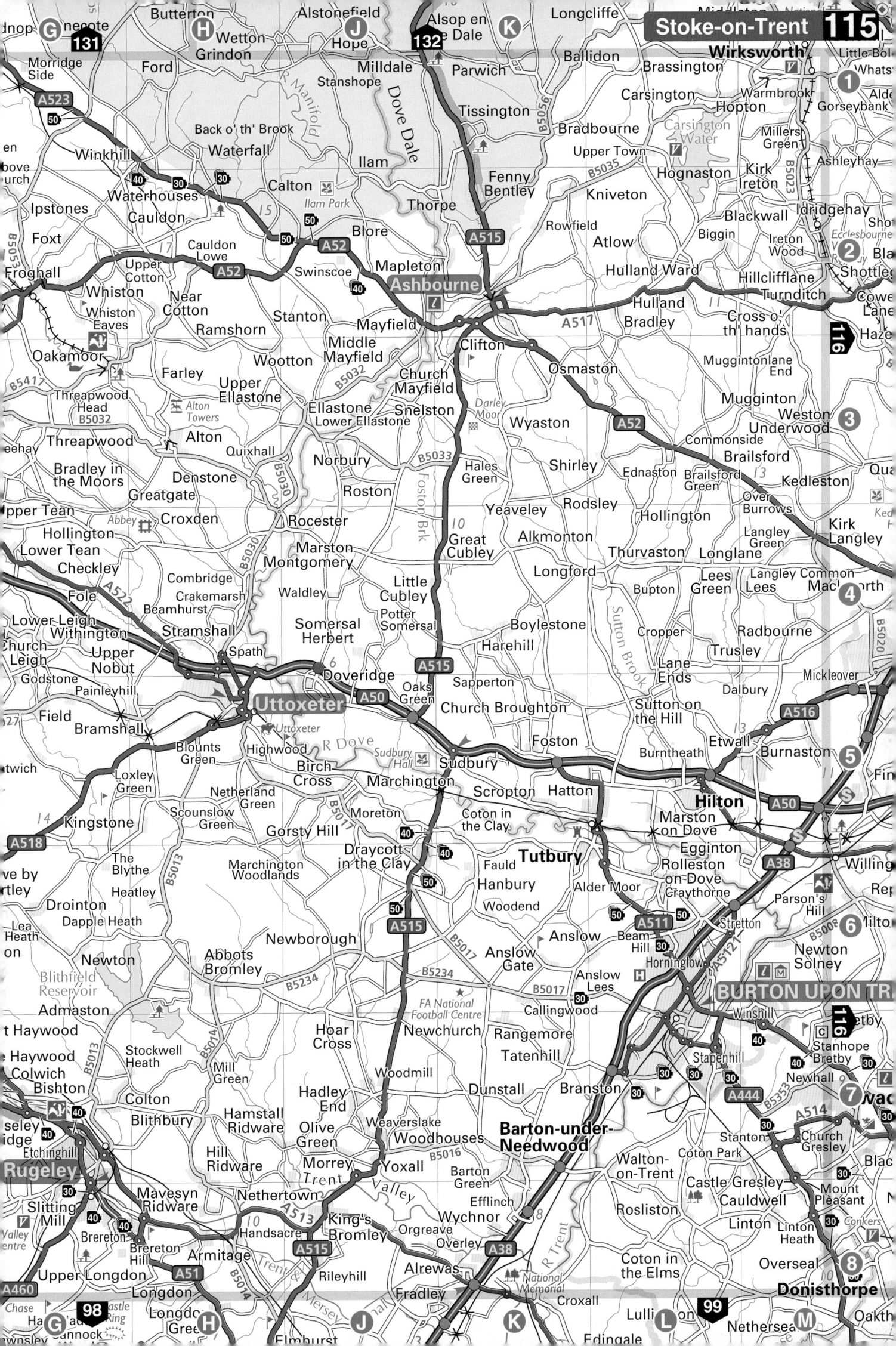

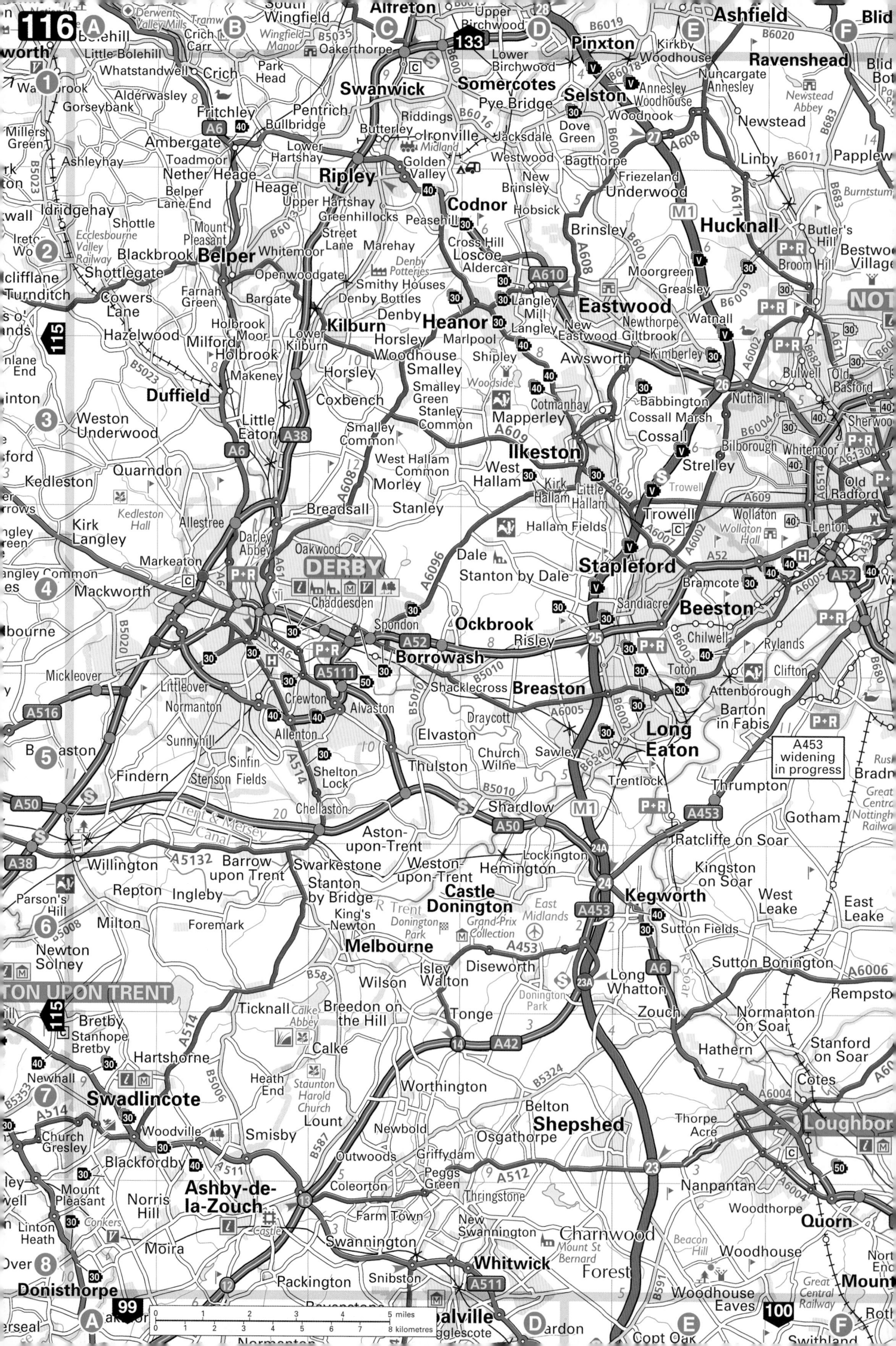

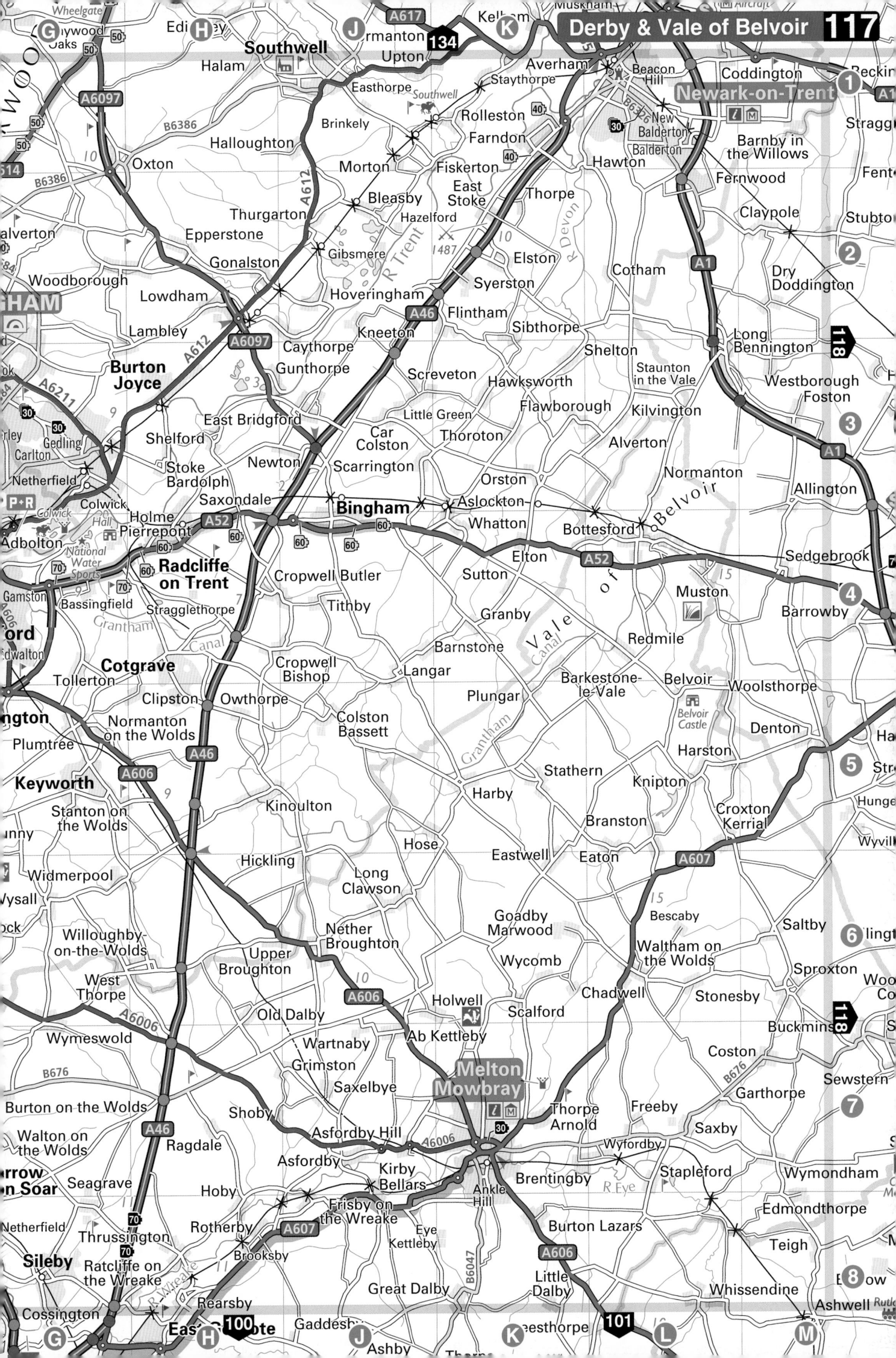

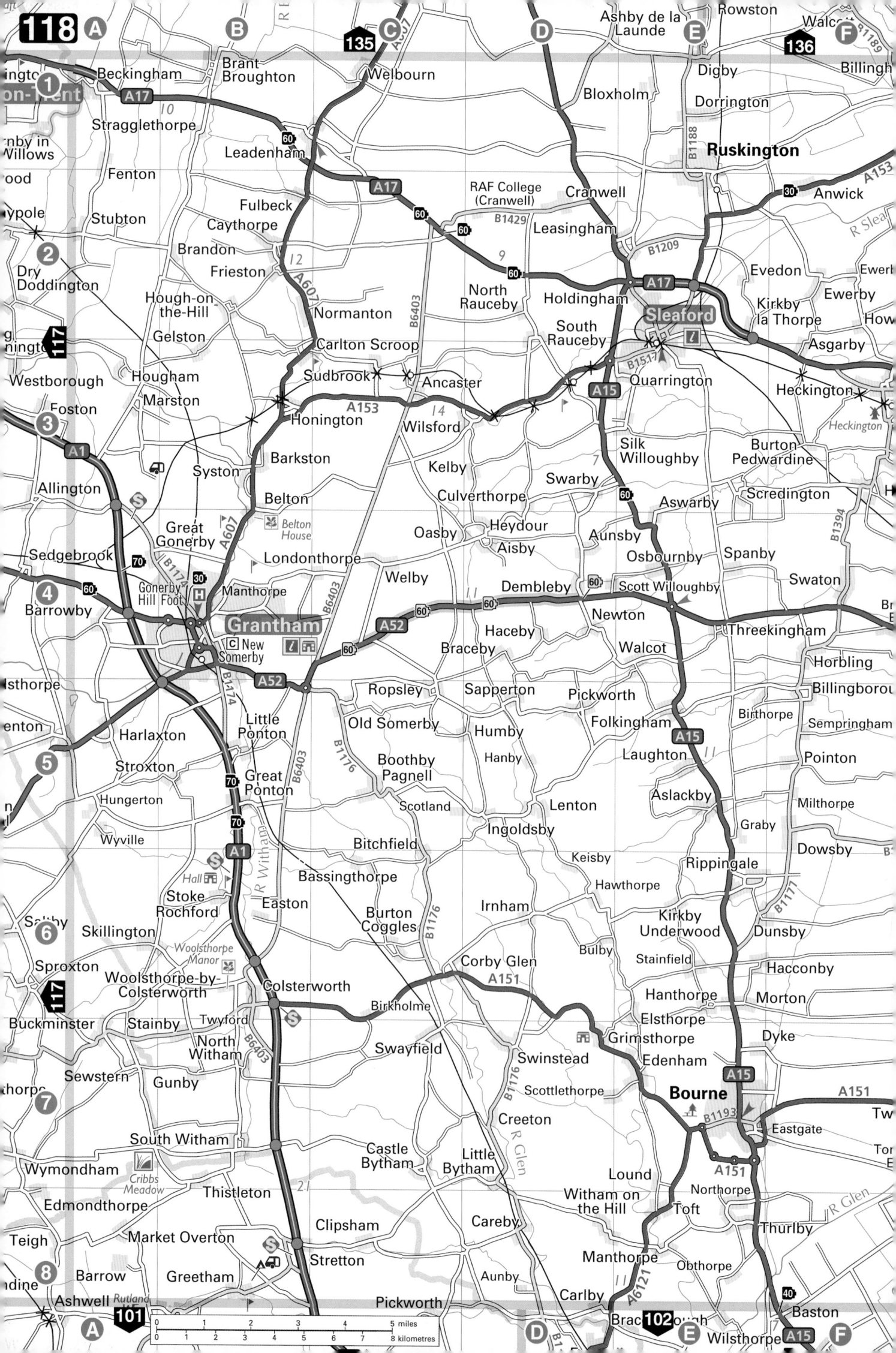

A · B · C · D · E · F

137

1 · 2 · 3 · 4 · 5 · 6 · 7 · 8

Friskney

Friskney Eaudike

Wrangle Common

23

40 Wrangle Lowgate

Wrangle

Hurn's End

asgate

gton End

119

THE WASH

ch ew

Dawsmere

Gedney Drove End

B1359

utton

119

pelgate

Little London

★Butterfly & Falconry Park

Long Sutton

60

60

Sutton Bridge

sses

Walpole Cross Keys

Terrington St Clement

Little London

The Wash

Clenchwarton

African Violet Centre

West Lynn

A17

11

Tydd Gote

Tydd St Mary

Walpole St Andrew

Hay Green

Tilney All Saints

A47

Tilney High End

Walpole St Peter

Four Gotes

Ingleborough

River Nene

8

St John's Highway

West Walton

Rattan Row

Tilney St Lawrence

Saddle Bow

West Winch

Wiggenhall St Germans

wton

Tydd St Giles

A110

103

Fitton

West Walton

0 1 2 3 4 5 miles
0 1 2 3 4 5 6 7 8 kilometres

Wiggenhall St Mary the Virgin

D

Holme Dunes

Holme n the Se

Old Hunstanton

Hunstanton

Ringstead

A149

Heacham

40 Norfolk Lavender

Sedgeford

Snettisham

Park Farm

RSPB

Southgate

Shernb

Ingoldisthorpe

12

B1440

Dersingham

Doddshill

Dersingham Bog

Wolferton

Sandringha West New

A149

B1439

Babingley River

Castle Rising

North Wootton

Castle

B1440

Congham

A148

Roydon

South Wootton

A148

A149

Gaywood

30 H

Pott Row

B1153

Fairstead

C

Bawsey

B1145

Gayton

King's Lynn

Brow-of-the-Hill

Ashwicke

Fair Green

East Winch

A47

A10

North Runcton

Middleton

West Bilne

Blackborough End

Setchey

Pentney

E · **104** · **F**

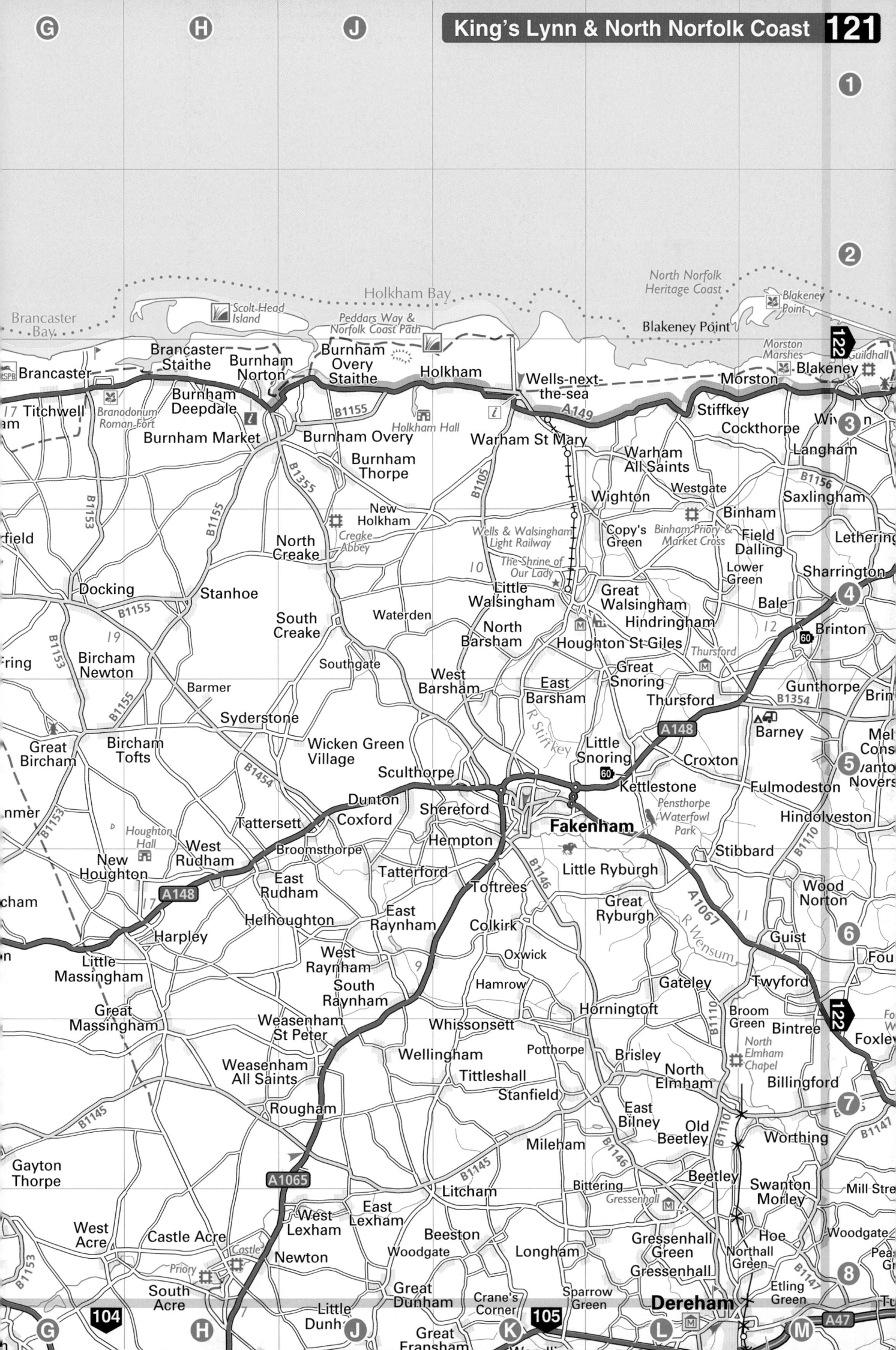

1

2

3

4

Mundesley
w Mill
Paston
B1159
Bacton
horpe
Walcott
Pollard
Street
pe   Ridlington
Witton
Ridlington
Street
Happisburgh

5

Whimpwell Green
Crostwight
ll
Happisburgh
ning   Common
Eccles on Sea
Lessingham   Hempstead
iggate
East   B1159   Ingham
Ruston   Corner   Sea Palling
ead
Ingham
Stalham   Waxham

6

Dilham 50
Calthorpe
Stalham   Street
Green
burgh
Low   Hickling
Street   A149
Barton   60   Sutton   Hickling Green
Turf   Hickling   Horsey Corner
Pennygate   Wood   Heath   Hill Common   Horsey
gate   Street   7   Hickling
Barton   Broad   Horsey Windpump
Broad   60
t   Neatishead   Catfield   Catfield
gate   Common
Irstead   Sharp   Potter   West   East
Green   Heigham   Somerton   Somerton

7

Threehammer
Common   Ludham   Martham   Winterton-on-Sea
loveton   BeWILDerwood
Johnson's   Cess   Hemsby
A1062   Street   Bastwick   Hole
oper   R Thurne   Hemsby   Newport
reet   Horning   Repps   Ormesby
Upper Street   Broad   Ormesby   Scratby
stwick   Rollesby   St Margaret
Bure   Broadland   Ormesby   California
Marshes   Conservation Centre   Thurne   Burgh St   St Michael
house   B1152   Margaret

8

Ranworth   Pilson   Cargate   Clippesby   Billockby   107   Caister-on-
Pan rth   Green   Green   Filby   Sea L   M
Fairhaven   South
Walsham   J   K   Mauthy
064

A   B   C   D   E   F

1

2

3

4

5

6

7

8

The Skerries

North Anglesey
Heritage Coast

Wylfa
Head

Cemlyn
Bay

Cemaes

CARMEL HEAD

Hen
Borth

Tregele

Llanfairynghornwy

Llanfechel

Holyhead
Bay

Swtan Folk

Church
Bay

Llanrhyddlad

Llanfflewyn

Dublin

Llanfaethlu

Llan

Dublin
Dún Laoghaire
(Apr-Sept)

Porth
Tywynmawr

Llanddeusant

North Stack

Llanfwrog

Llynnon Mill

Stryd-y-
Facsen

Elim

Gogarth
Bay

Breakwater

Holyhead

(Caergybi)

Llanfachraeth

Pen-llyn

Llaingoch

Holyhead Mountain
Hut Circles

Llanfigael

Llyn
Llywena

South Stack

RSPB

Ellins
Tower

Penrhos Feilw

Penrhos

Llanynghenedl

Presaddfe

Holyhead Mountain
Heritage Coast

Kingsland

A5

Valley

A5025

Bodedern

B5109

Penrhyn Mawr

Trefignath

A55

Caergeiliog

Bryngw

Trearddur Bay

B4545

HOLY ISLAND

Four Mile
Bridge

Llanfihangel
yn Nhowyn

Llechylched

Llanfair-yn-Neubwll

Capel Gwyn

A4080

Rhoscolyn

RSPB

Plas
Cymyran

Rhoscolyn
Head

Cymyran
Bay

Ty Newydd

Pencar

Llanfaelog

Rhosneigr

A4080

Bryn Du

Ty
Croes

Barclodiad
y Gawres

Porth Trecastell

Aberffraw

Anglesey
Circuit

Llan

Aberffraw
Bay

Aberffraw Bay
Heritage Coast

Malltrae

Llanddwyn

C A E R N A R F O N

B A Y

A B C D E F

1

2

Dulas Bay

V Seawatch Centre
Moelfre
Llanallgo
Marian-glas

125

3
Benllech
Red Wharf Bay
gongl
Red Wharf Bay
rgoch
Pentraeth
Llanddona
Glan-yr-afon
Caim
Penmon Priory
Toll
Penmon
Puffin Island
Black Point

GREAT ORMES HEAD

Great Orme
Heritage Coast

Conwy Bay

Llandudno

Llanrhos

4
A5025
B5109
oscefnhir
Llangoed
B5109
Llanfaes
Gaol
Beaumaris
Beaumaris Castle
Llansadwrn
Courthouse
Llandegfan

Dwygyfylchi
Penmaenmawr
Penmaenan
Capelulo
Henryd

Deganwy
Conwy
Conwy Castle
Tywyn
A546 B5115 A47
RSPB
16A
17
18
S

Llanfairfechan
Garizim
A55
15A
15 14
Nant-y-pandy
Gorddinog
SNOWDONIA
610
TAL-Y-FAN
Rowen
Ty'n-y-Groes

5
lanfa
P G
Menai Bridge
(Porthaethwy)
Bangor
Anglesey Column
Bryn
Celli Ddu
Britannia Bridge
Penrhos garnedd
14
13
12
Penrhyn
Llandygai
Tal-y-bont
Abergwyngregyn
Coedydd Aber
Afon Aber
Afon Anafon
Aber Falls
B5106
Caerhun
Castell

NATIONAL
Llanbedr-y-Cennin
Tal-y-Bont
Dolgarrog
Pont Dolgarrog

6
Y Felinheli
Capel-y-graig
9 10
A55
11
Waen-wen
Pentir
Rhyd-y-groes
Glasinfryn
Llanllechid
Rachub
Bethesda
Gerlan
MOEL WINION
580
757
Y DROSGL
942
FOEL-FRAS
Afon Dulyn
PARK
Llyn Eigiau
Trefriw Woollen Mills
Bethel
Seion
Llanddeiniolen
Waen-pentir
Sling
Ogwen Bank
Afon Caseg
Trefriw
Llanrhychwyn
Maenar
Vale of Conwy

7
Saron
Rhiwlas
Penisarwaun
Rhiwen
A4244
Mynydd Llandygai
Deiniolen
Clwt-y-bont
Gallt-y-foel
A5
12
1062
CARNEDD LLEWELYN
1044
CARNEDD DAFYDD
Llyn Cowlyd
Llyn Crafnant
Llanrug
Pont-rug
Caeathro
Cwm-y-glo
Brynrefail
Dinorwic
923
National Slate
ELIDIR FAWR
Llyn Padarn
Llanberis Lake Railway
Padarn
Pont Pen-y-benglog
946
Y GARN
Llyn Ogwen
917
Y TRYFAN
National Mountain Centre
(Plas y Brenin)
Capel Curig
The Ugly House
(Ty Hyll)
Gwydir

8
Groeslon
442
Llanberis
Electric Mountain
Waunfawr
Betws Garmon
726
MOEL EILIO
Snowdon Mountain Railway
National Slate
Dolbadarn Castle
Llyn Peris
Nant Peris
Gwastadnant
1001
GLYDER FAWR
994
GLYDER-FACH
Pass of Llanberis
A4086
18
Pen-y-pass
Pen-y-Gwryd
A4086
Pont Cyfyng
A5
6
Swallow Falls
(Rhaeadr Ewynnol)
Betws-y-Coed
Forest

ostryfan
Rhosgadfan
Penyffridd
Moel
Fron
gwyn
Nantlle
B4418
698
MYNYDD MAW
Llyn
Cwellyn
1085
Yr Wyddfa
872
MOEL-SIABOD
110
Pont-y-pant

A B C D E F

0   1   2   3   4   5 miles
0 1 2 3 4 5 6 7 8 kilometres

G   H   J

1

2

128

e Ormes Head

Penrhyn Bay

Rhôs-on-Sea

andrillo-n-Rhos

Colwyn Bay (Bae Colwyn)

Mochdre

dudno ction

Old Colwyn

Llanelian-yn-Rhôs

Bryn-y-Maen

ffraid nwy

Llysfaen

Rhyd-y-foel

Llanddulas

Abergele

Pensarn

A547

Dolwen

Betws-yn-Rhos

Dawn

Trofarth

Llanfair Talhaiarn

River Elwy

Hafodunos

Llangernyw

Llansannan

Tan-y-fron

Rhydgaled

Pandy Tudur

Bylchau

Waen

Nantglyn

Gwytherin

Afon Aled

Llyn Aled

Gors Maen Llwyd

Archaeological Trail

Llyn Brenig

ntre-arn-y-fedw

elin-coed

Nebo

Capel armon

MOEL SEISIOG 467

MOEL LLYN 448

Llyn Alwen

Mynydd Hiraethog

Llyn Brenig

Abergele Roads

Kinmel Bay

Kinmel Bay

Towyn

St George

Glascoed

Pentre Isaf

Groesffordd Marli

Llannefydd

Cefn Berain

Rhyl

Miniature Railway

Bodelwyddan

Bodelwyddan Castle

Pengwern

Castle

Henllan

Groes

Y Gyffylliog

Pentre Saron

Peniel

Prion

Pant-pastynog

Green

Fron

Denbigh Friary

Denbigh (Dinbych)

Castle

Kilford

Brook House

Llwyn

Prestatyn

Gronant

Llanasa

Gwaenysgor

Meliden

Trelawnyd

Dyserth

Cwm

Rhuddlan

Offa's Dyke

Rhuallt

St Asaph

Tremeirchion

Graig

Sodom

Trefnant

Bodfari

Pentre Llanrhaeadr

Pentre

Llandyrnog

Llanynys

Afon-v

Caerwys

Picton

Axton

Tregloga

Berth

Walwe

Pen-

Waen

lang

Llandyrnog

Ru (Rh

Llanfwrog

Bontuchel

Ruthin Gaol

Efenecht

Clocaenog

Clawdd-

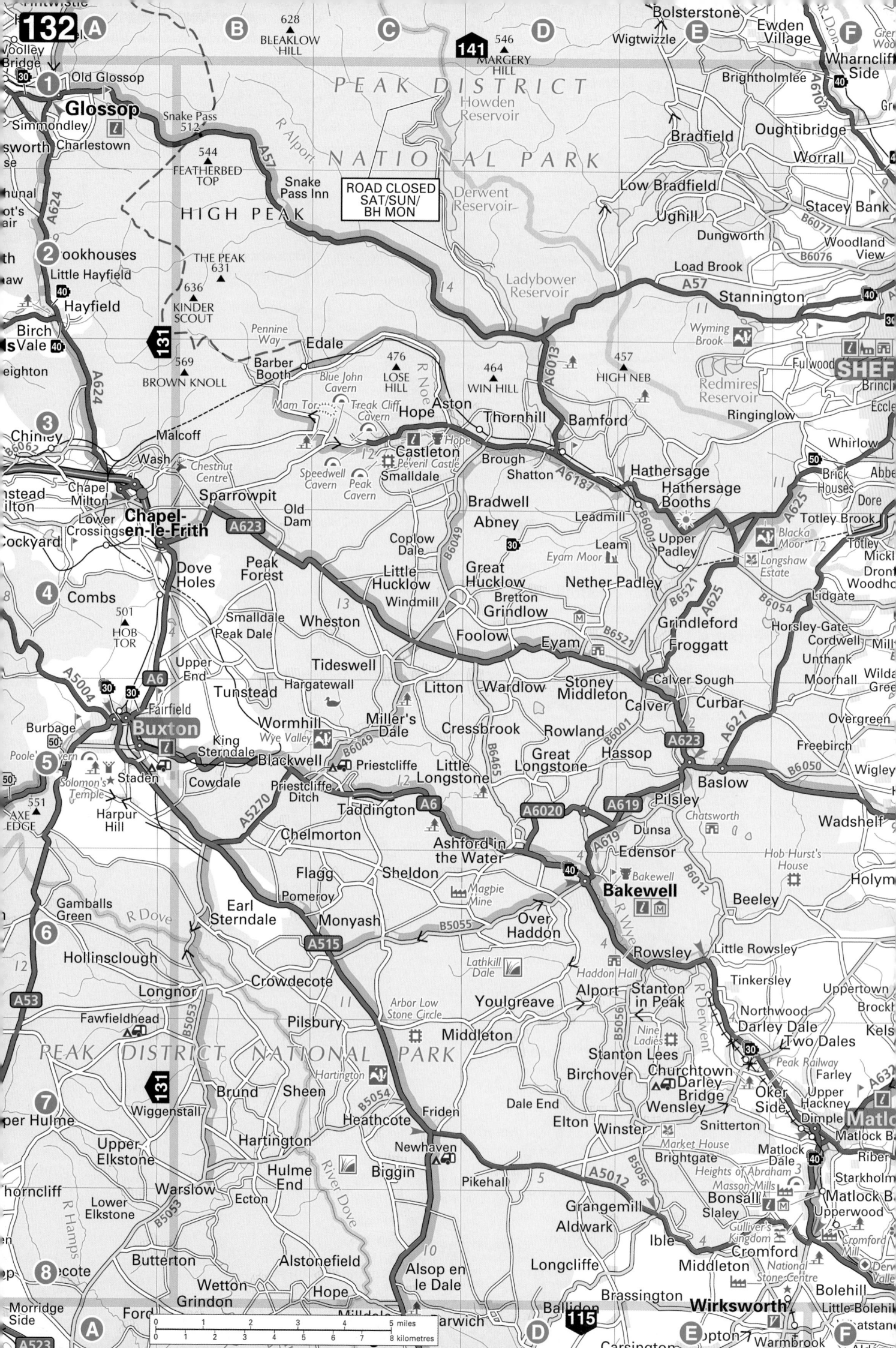

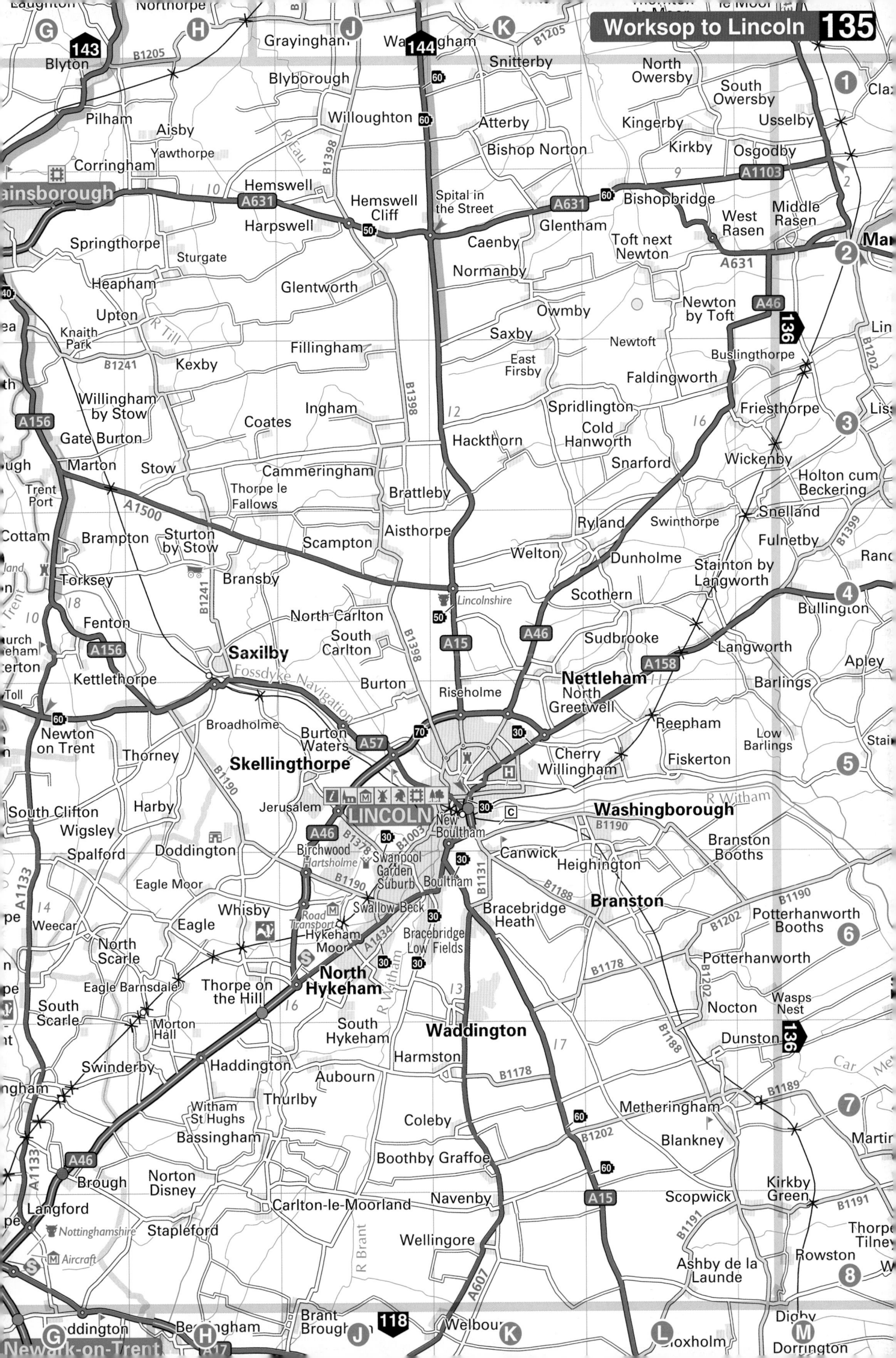

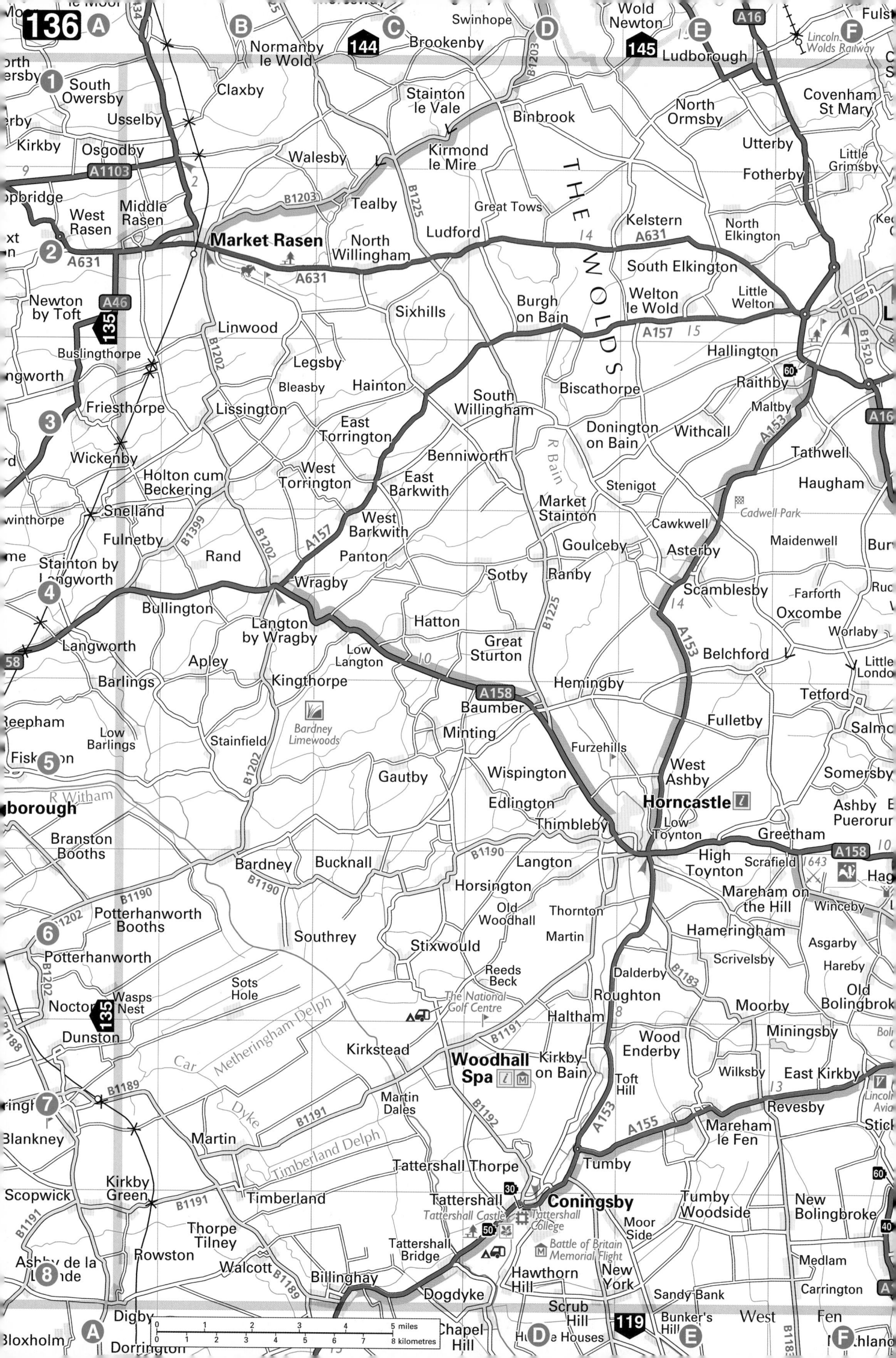

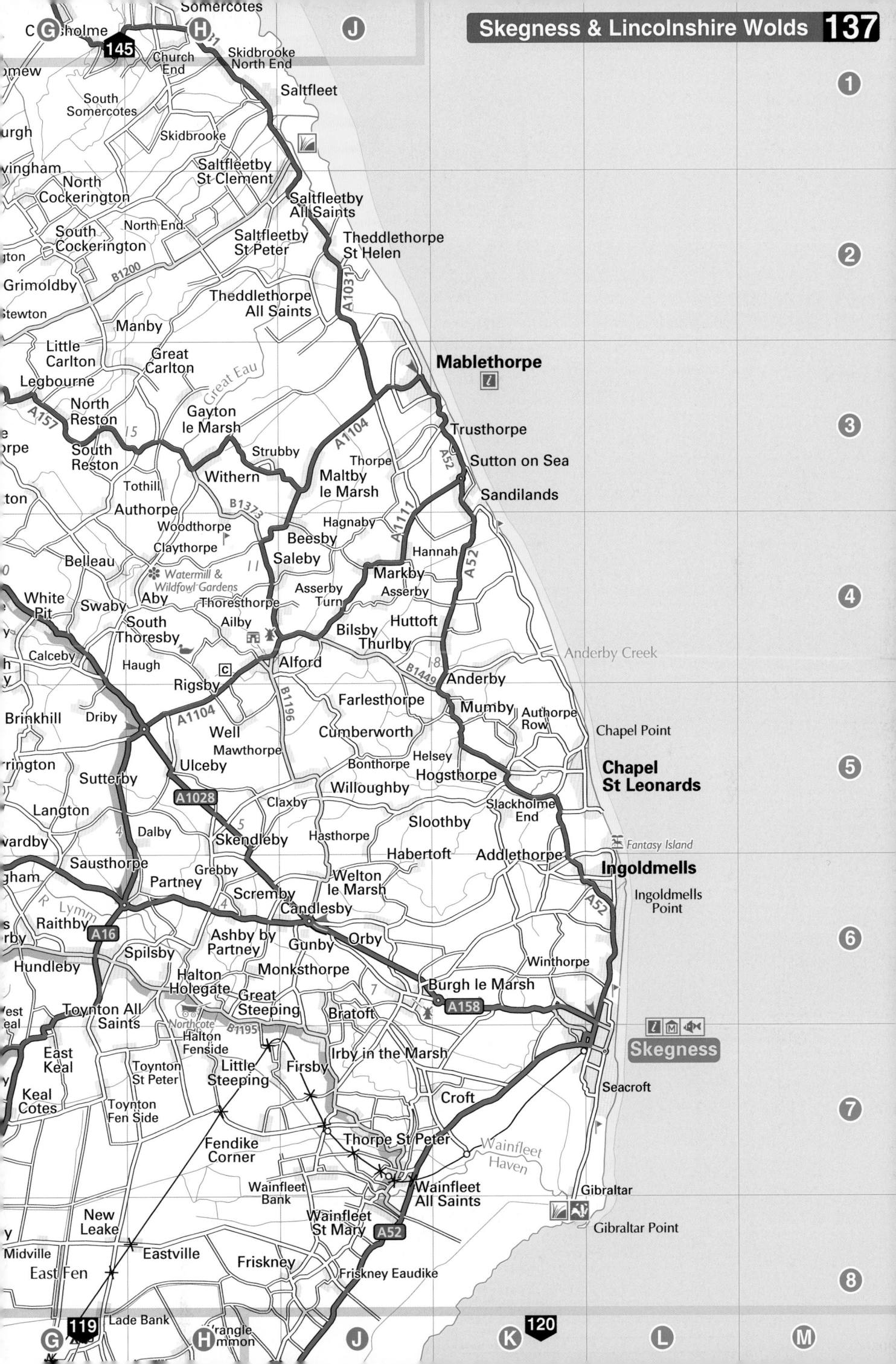

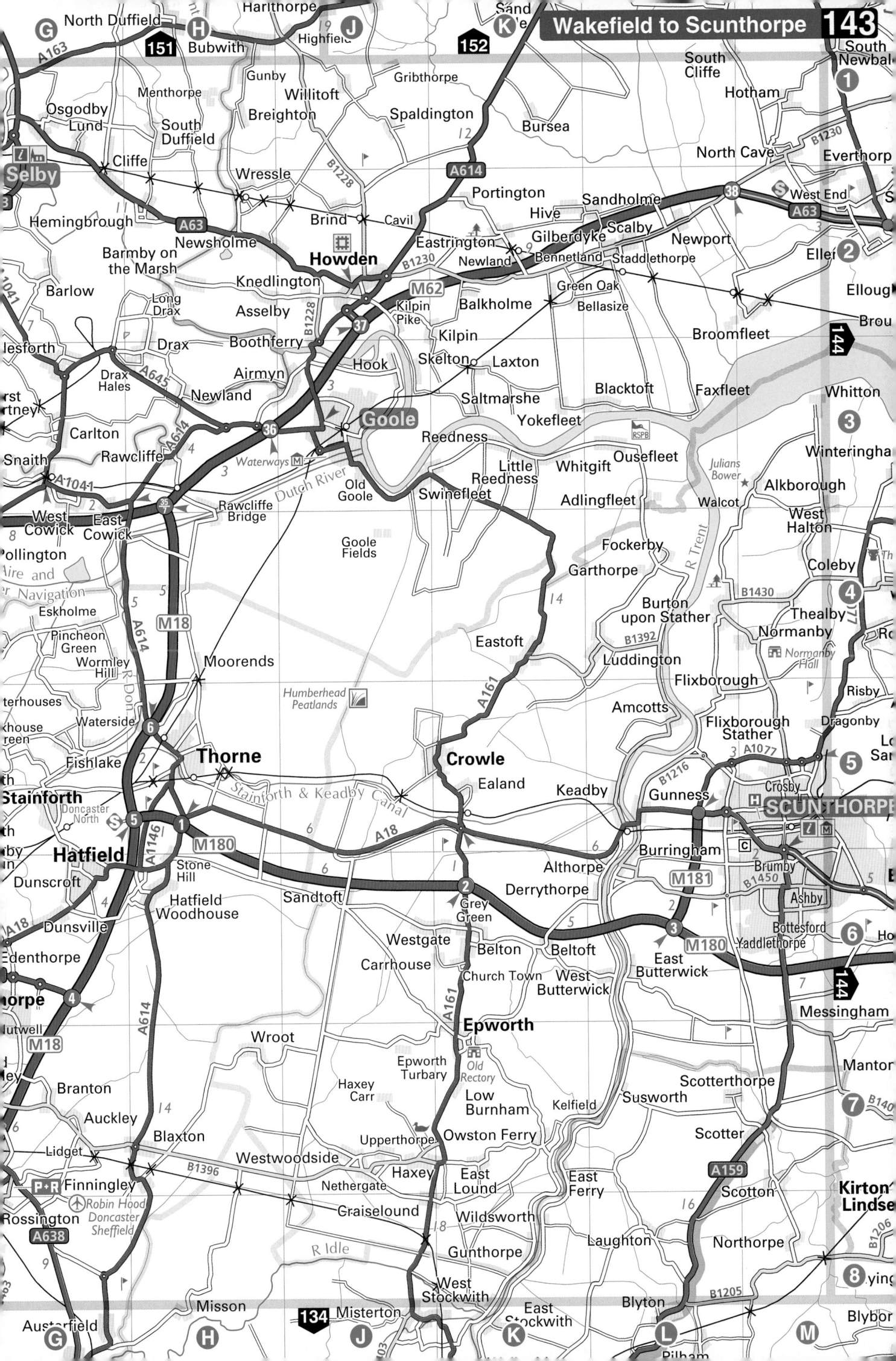

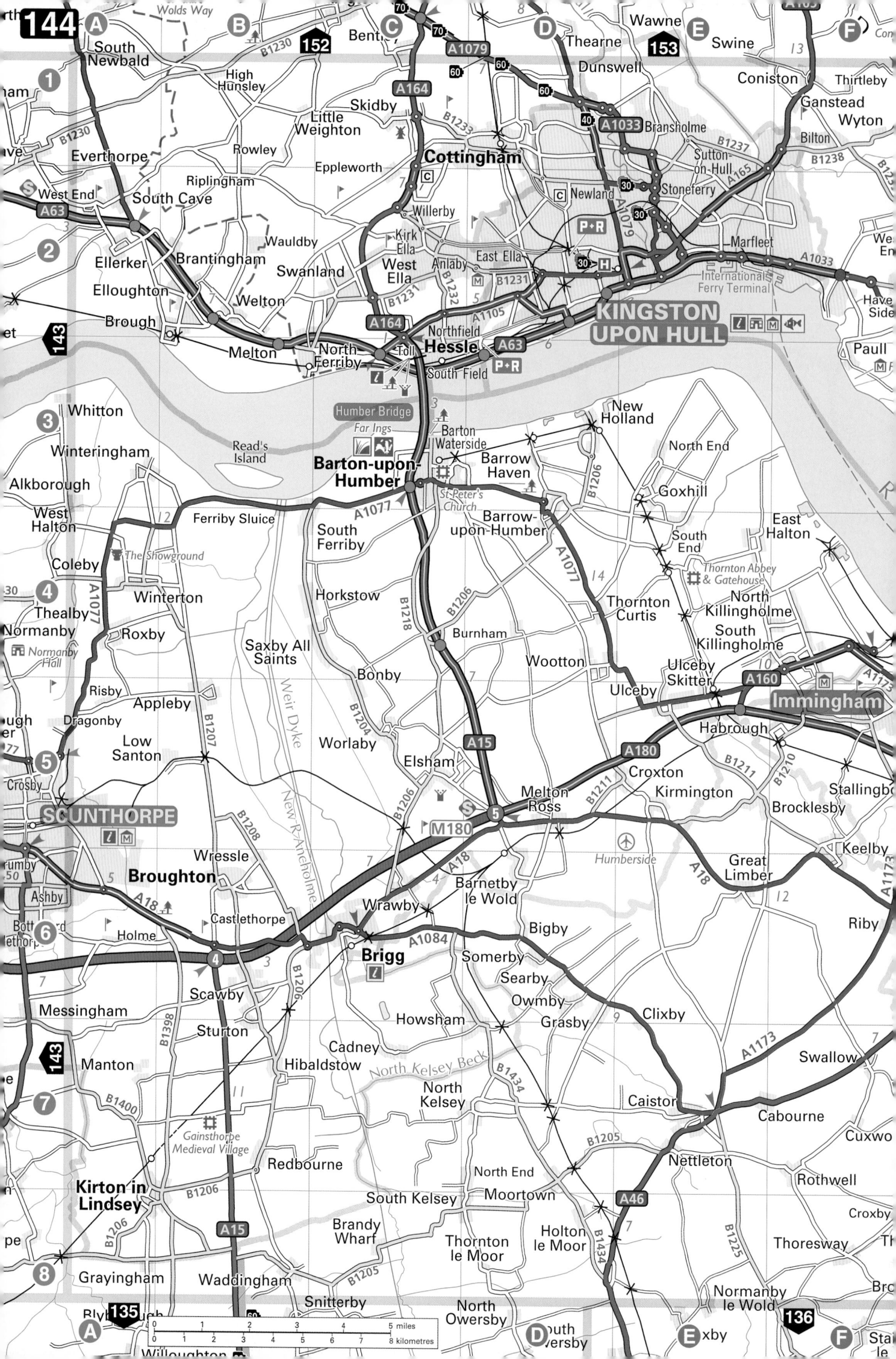

G B1238 B1242 **153** **H** Newton

Garton

Grimston

Flinto

oatley

Fitling

Humbleton

Hilston

1

Owstwick

ey

Danthorpe

North
End

Tunstall

E

2

Elstronwick

Burton
Pidsea

Roos

Waxholme

B1362

West
End

Rimswell

B1242

Owthorne

R

End

on

S

B1362

S

East End

B1362

Withernsea

Thorngumbald

A1033

Burstwick

Halsham

16

Keyingham

Hollym

Ryehill

4

3

Ottringham

Winestead

A1033

Holmpton

Patrington

Out
Newton

Patrington
Haven

Welwick

B1445

Easington

Sunk
Island

Weeton

Skeffling

South End

4

Spurn
Heritage Coast

Kilnsea

R

HUMBER

mingham
ck

Spurn Heritage Coast

5

GRIMSBY

SPURN HEAD

A180

B1210

aling

West Marsh

S

A180

Great
Coates

A1136

Little
Coates

Old
Clee

Cleethorpes

Rotterdam (Europoort)
Zeebrugge

6

lesby

6

Nunsthorpe

C

A46

Thrunscoe

The Jungle

A46

H

A16

A1098

Scartho

Pleasure
Island

50

Bradley

B1203

Humberston

Laceby

50

B1219

by upon
umber

Waltham

New Waltham

Holton
le Clay

A1031

Barnoldby
le Beck

Waltham
Windmill

RSPB

Brigsley

North
End

Tetney
Lock

7

Beelsby

A18

Ashby cum
Fenby

Tetney

North
Cotes

Hatcliffe

Waithe

Marshchapel

West
Ravendale

Grainsby

North
Thoresby

West
End

Eskham

Donna
Nook

Grainthorpe

by

East
Ravendale

B1201

Churchthorpe

29

North
Somercotes

hope

Wold
Newton

A16

15

Fulstow

Lincolnshire
Wolds Railway

Conisholme

A1031

8

B1203

Ludborough

136

Covenham
St Bartholomew

Church
End

Skidbrooke
North End

G

H

orth

J ham
St Mary

K

South
Somercotes

L

Saltf **M**

A   B   Haverigg Point C   Askam in Furness D   Marton E   Swarthmoor   nal F F

Pennington
Lindal in Furness
South Lakes Animal Park
Conishead
A590

1

Sandscale Haws

155

Great Urswick
Little Urswick
Brow End
Bardsea

North Walney

156

Dalton-in-Furness
Scales
Baycliff

BARROW-IN-FURNESS
Hawcoat   Newton   Stainton with Adgarley   13

2

North Scale
Furness Abbey   Bow Bridge   Dendron   Watermill   Aldingham
Gleaston
Vickerstown   Roose   Leece
A590   Barrow Island   30   Newbiggin
A5087

ISLE OF WALNEY   Biggar   Roosebeck

Rampside
Roa Island

3

Sheep Island   Piel Castle   Foulney Island
Piel Island

Hilpsford Point   Piel Bar
South Walney

4

Douglas

5

6

Fleetwood
Rossall Point

Cleveleys

7

Tho

Little Bispham
Norbreck
Bispha

A584   B5124
Warbre

North Shore   Foohi

8

| 0 | 1 | 2 | 3 | 4 | 5 miles |
| 0 | 1 | 2 | 3 | 4 | 5 | 6 | 7 | 8 kilometres |

BLACKPOOL
138

A   B   C   D   E   F

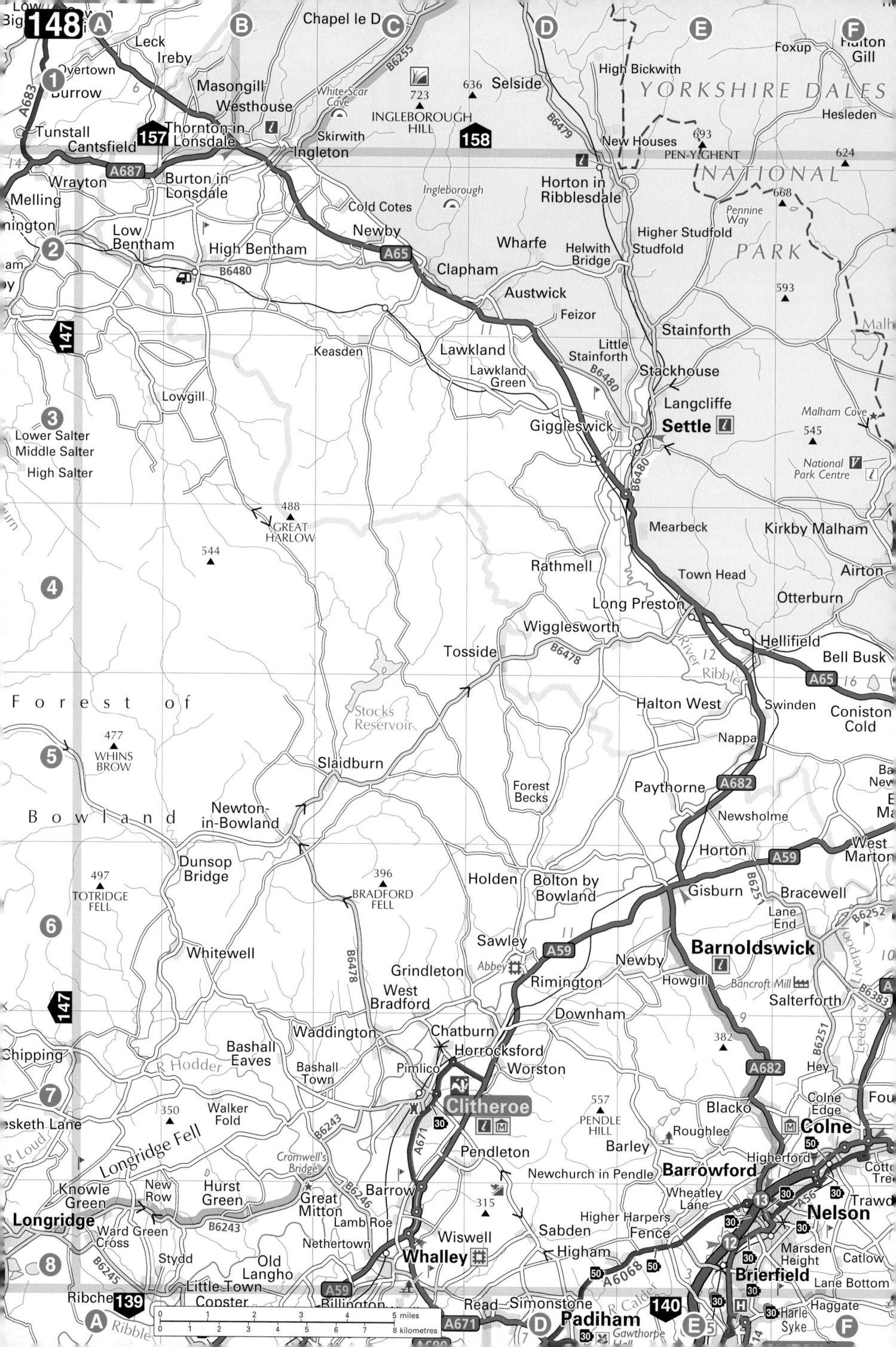

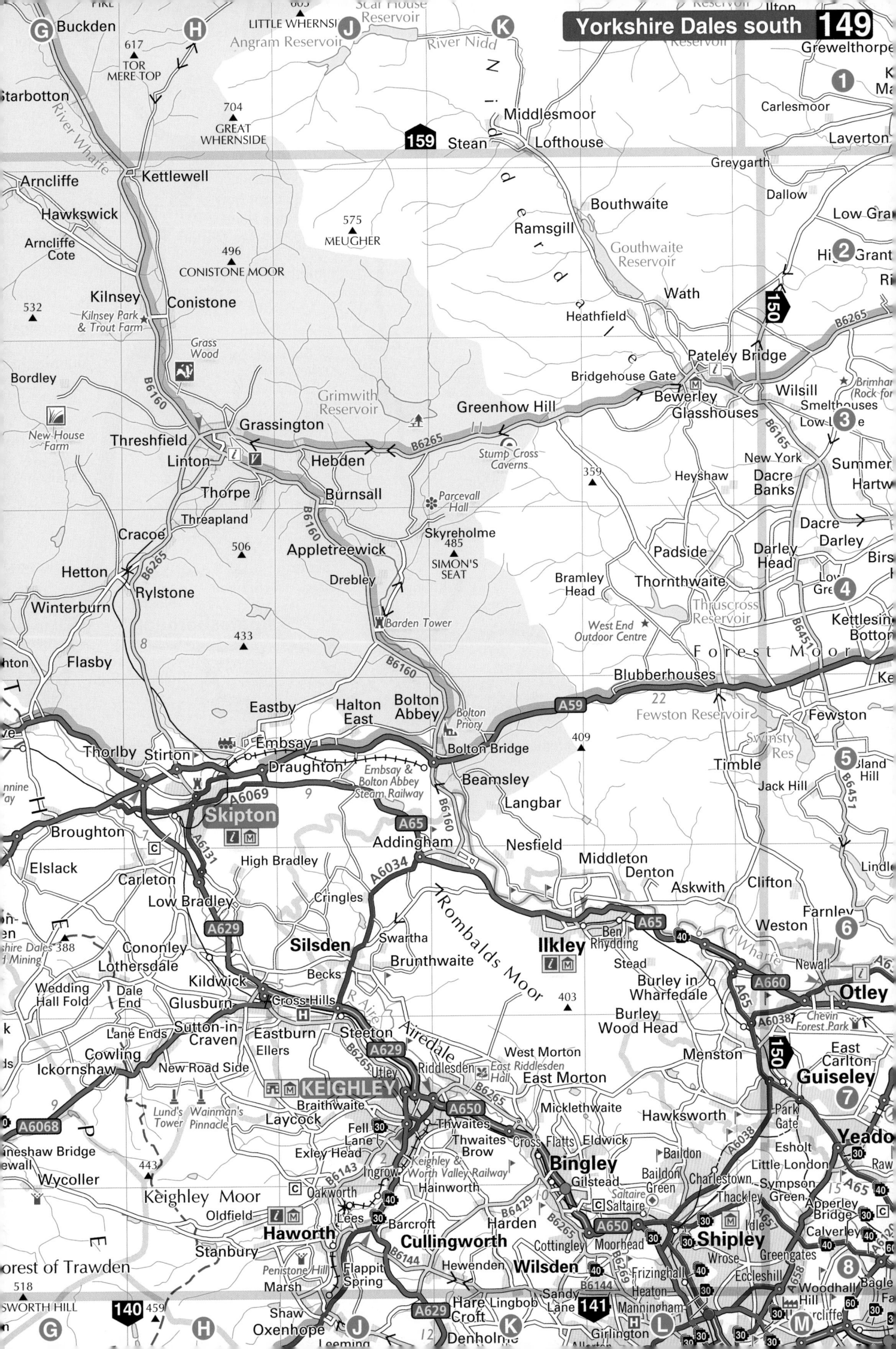

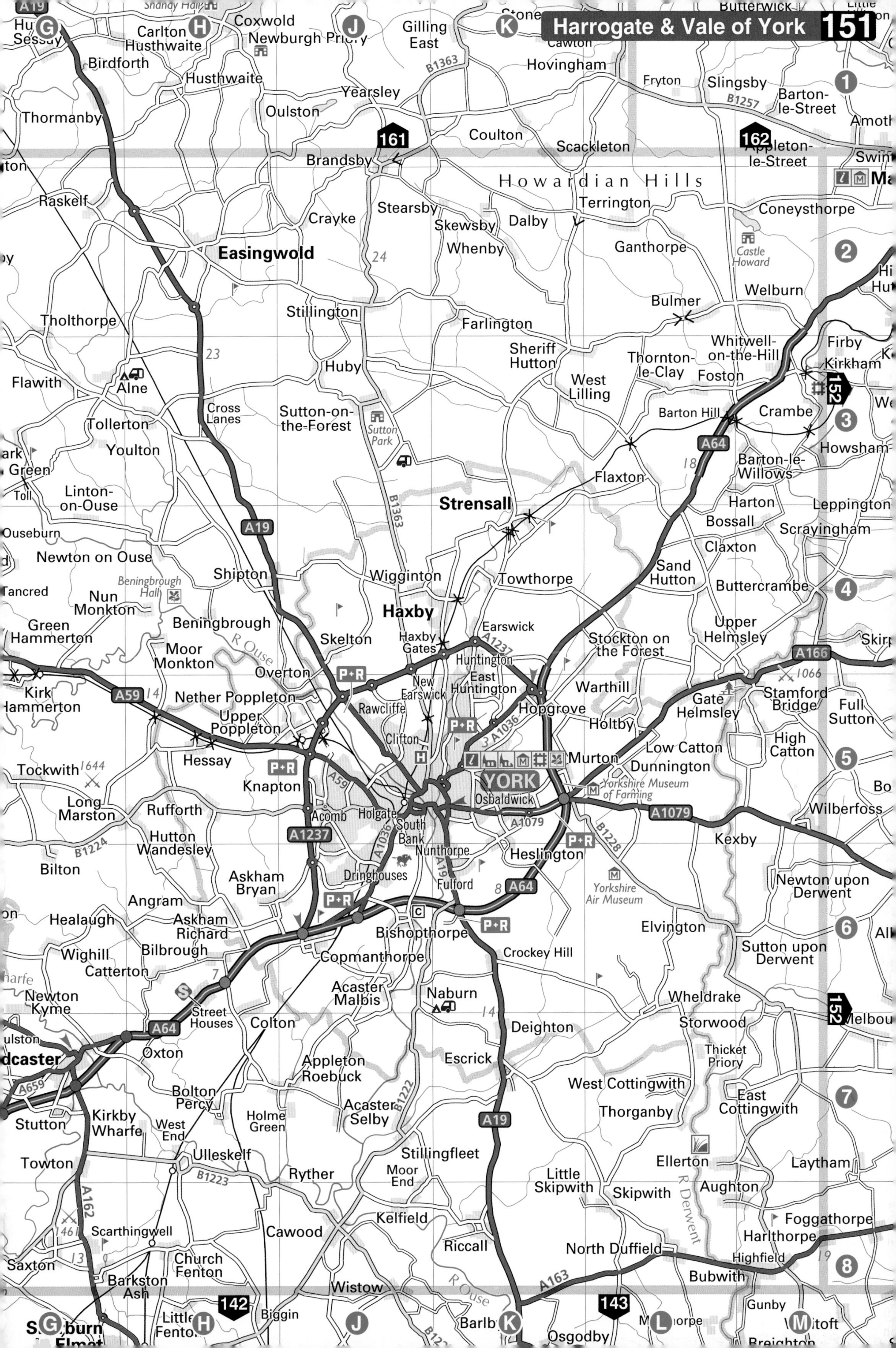
Carlton Husthwaite
Coxwold
Newburgh Priory
Gilling East
Hovingham
Fryton
Slingsby
Barton-le-Street
Birdforth
Husthwaite
Yearsley
Oulston
Thormanby
161
Coulton
Scackleton
162
Appleton-le-Street
Brandsby
Howardian Hills
Raskelf
Crayke
Stearsby
Skewsby
Dalby
Terrington
Coneysthorpe
Easingwold
Whenby
Ganthorpe
Castle Howard
Welburn
Bulmer
Tholthorpe
Stillington
Farlington
Sheriff Hutton
Thornton-le-Clay
Whitwell-on-the-Hill
Foston
Firby
Kirkham
152
Flawith
Alne
Huby
West Lilling
Barton Hill
Crambe
Cross Lanes
Sutton-on-the-Forest
Sutton Park
Tollerton
Youlton
A64
Howsham
Barton-le-Willows
Flaxton
Linton-on-Ouse
Strensall
Harton
Leppington
Bossall
Scrayingham
Ouseburn
A19
B1363
Newton on Ouse
Claxton
Sand Hutton
Shipton
Wigginton
Towthorpe
Buttercrambe
Beningbrough Hall
Nun Monkton
Haxby
Earswick
Upper Helmsley
Green Hammerton
Beningbrough
Skelton
Haxby Gates
Stockton on the Forest
Moor Monkton
R Ouse
A1237
Huntington
Overton
P+R
East Huntington
New Earswick
Warthill
A166
Kirk Hammerton
A59
Nether Poppleton
Rawcliffe
Gate Helmsley
Stamford Bridge
Full Sutton
Upper Poppleton
A1036
Hopgrove
Holtby
Clifton
Tockwith
Hessay
Murton
Low Catton
High Catton
Knapton
YORK
Dunnington
Long Marston
Osbaldwick
Yorkshire Museum of Farming
Rufforth
Acomb
Holgate
South Bank
A1079
Wilberfoss
Hutton Wandesley
Nunthorpe
Heslington
B1228
Kexby
Bilton
B1224
Askham Bryan
Dringhouses
Fulford
Yorkshire Air Museum
Newton upon Derwent
Angram
Healaugh
Askham Richard
Bishopthorpe
Elvington
Crockey Hill
Sutton upon Derwent
Wighill
Bilbrough
Catterton
Copmanthorpe
Acaster Malbis
Naburn
Wheldrake
Newton Kyme
Street Houses
Colton
Deighton
Storwood
Thicket Priory
Tadcaster
Oxton
Appleton Roebuck
Escrick
West Cottingwith
East Cottingwith
A659
Bolton Percy
Acaster Selby
B1222
Thorganby
Stutton
Kirkby Wharfe
West End
Holme Green
Towton
Ulleskelf
Stillingfleet
Ellerton
Laytham
B1223
Ryther
Moor End
Little Skipwith
Skipwith
R Derwent
Aughton
A162
Scarthingwell
Cawood
Kelfield
Foggathorpe
Harlthorpe
Saxton
Church Fenton
Riccall
North Duffield
Highfield
Bubwith
Barkston Ash
A163
Wistow
142
Biggin
143
Gunby
Little Fenton
Barlby
Osgodby
Sherburn in Elmet
Menthorpe
Wressle
Breighton

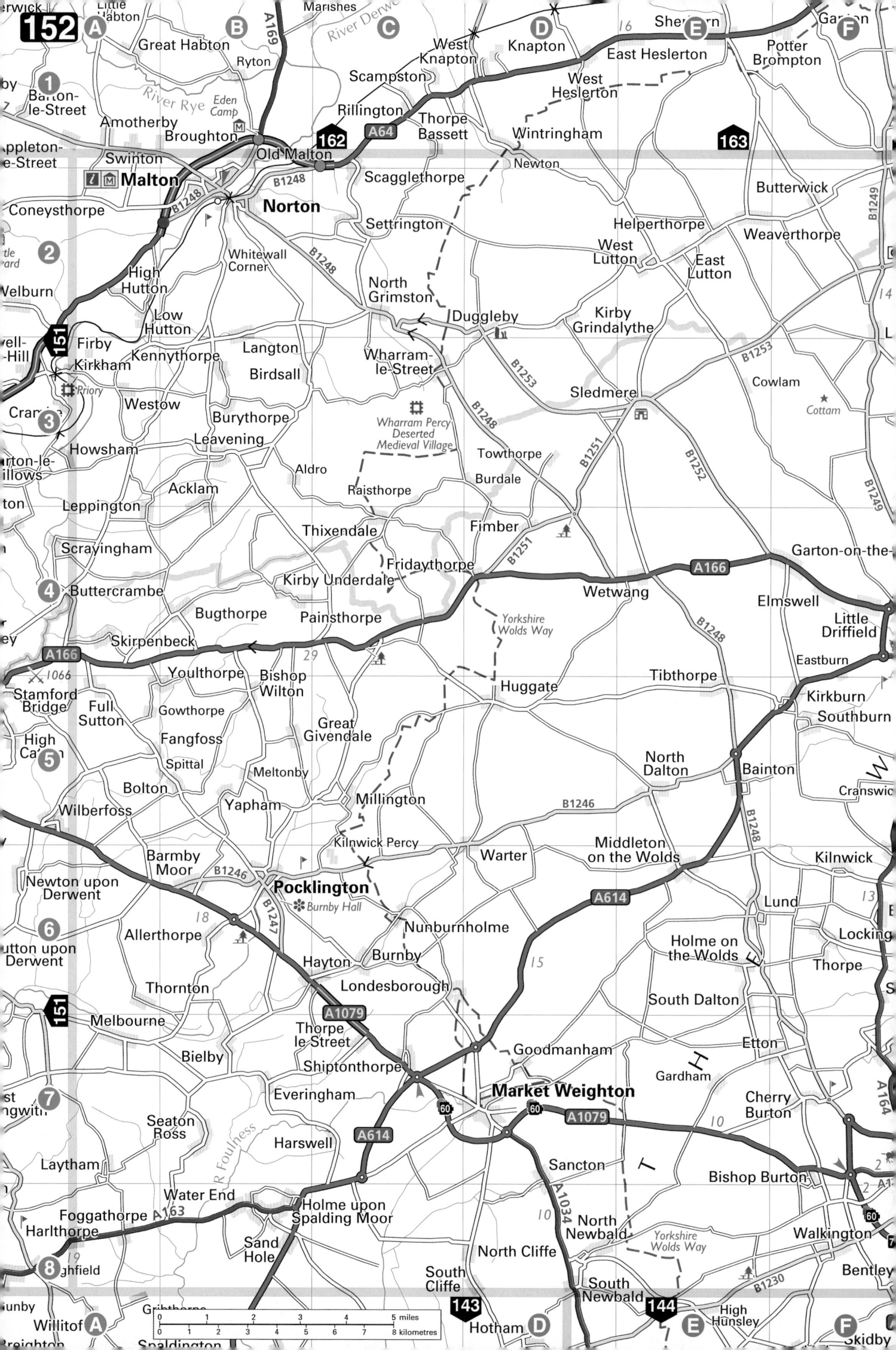

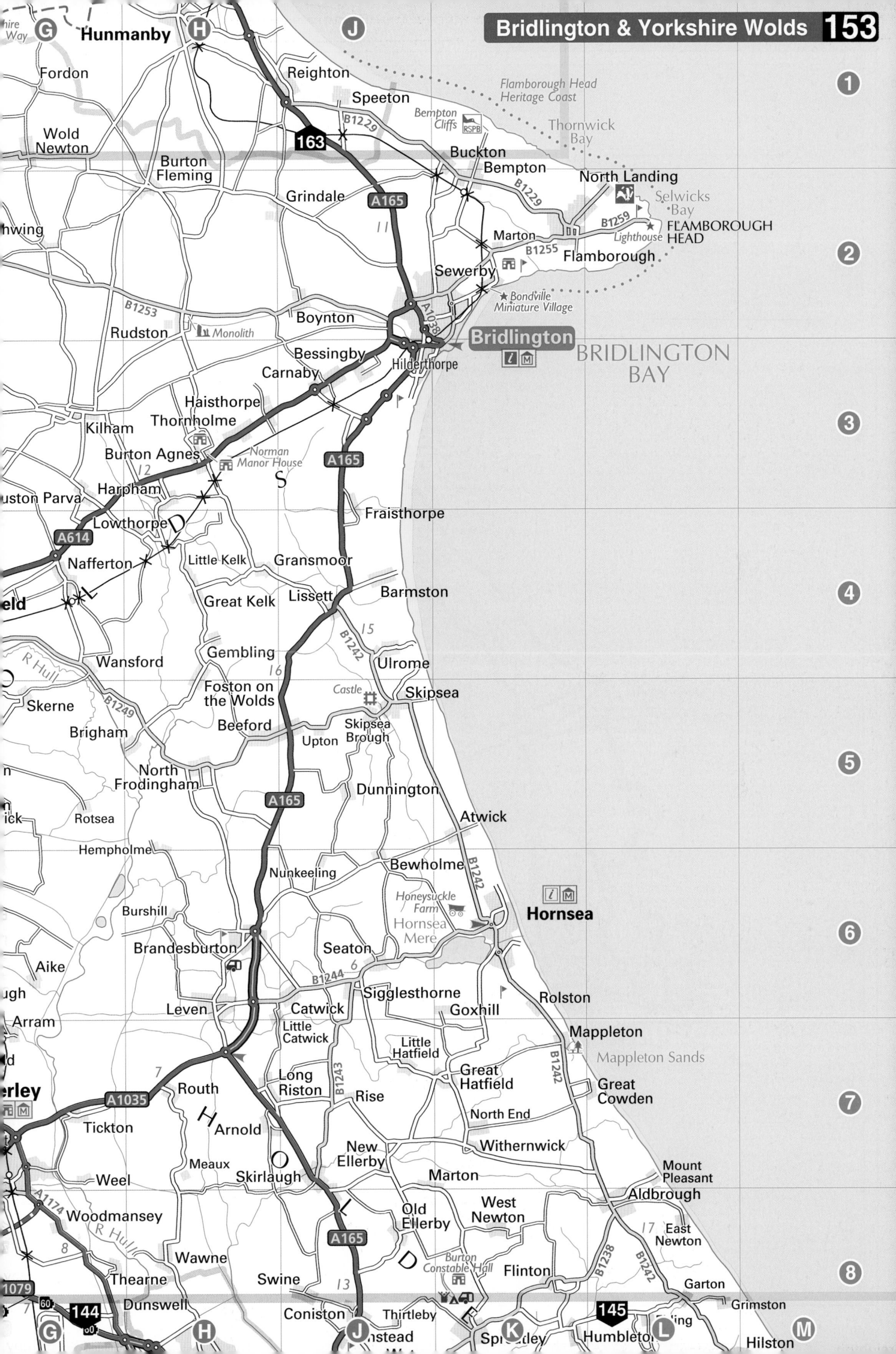

G
H
J

Hunmanby

Fordon

Reighton

Speeton

Flamborough Head
Heritage Coast

Thornwick
Bay

B1229

Bempton
Cliffs
RSPB

Wold
Newton

Burton
Fleming

Buckton

Bempton

North Landing

163

A165

Grindale

B1229

Selwicks
Bay

FLAMBOROUGH
HEAD

Marton

B1259

Flamborough

B1255

Lighthouse

B1253

Sewerby

Rudston

Monolith

Boynton

Bondville
Miniature Village

A1038

Bessingby

Bridlington

BRIDLINGTON
BAY

Carnaby

Hilderthorpe

Haisthorpe

Thornholme

Kilham

Norman
Manor House

Burton Agnes

A165

S

Harpham

12

uston Parva

Fraisthorpe

Lowthorpe

D

A614

Nafferton

Little Kelk

Gransmoor

Barmston

field

Great Kelk

Lissett

R Hull

Wansford

Gembling

B1242

15

16

Ulrome

Foston on
the Wolds

Castle

Skipsea

Skerne

B1249

Beeford

Upton

Skipsea
Brough

Brigham

North
Frodingham

A165

Dunnington

Rotsea

ick

Atwick

Hempholme

Nunkeeling

Bewholme

B1242

Burshill

Honeysuckle
Farm

Hornsea
Mere

Hornsea

Aike

Brandesburton

Seaton

ugh

B1244

6

Rolston

Leven

Catwick

Sigglesthorne

Goxhill

Arram

Little
Catwick

Mappleton

Mappleton Sands

7

A1035

Routh

Long
Riston

B1243

Rise

Little
Hatfield

Great
Hatfield

Great
Cowden

erley

H

Tickton

Arnold

O

North End

A1174

Weel

Meaux

Skirlaugh

L

New
Ellerby

Marton

Withernwick

Mount
Pleasant

Aldbrough

Woodmansey

Wawne

D

Old
Ellerby

West
Newton

B1238

B1242

17

East
Newton

A165

R Hull

8

Thearne

Swine

13

Burton
Constable Hall

Flinton

Garton

1079

144

Dunswell

Coniston

Thirtleby

145

Humbleton

Grimston

60

Hilston

G
H
J
K
L
M

1
2
3
4
5
6
7
8

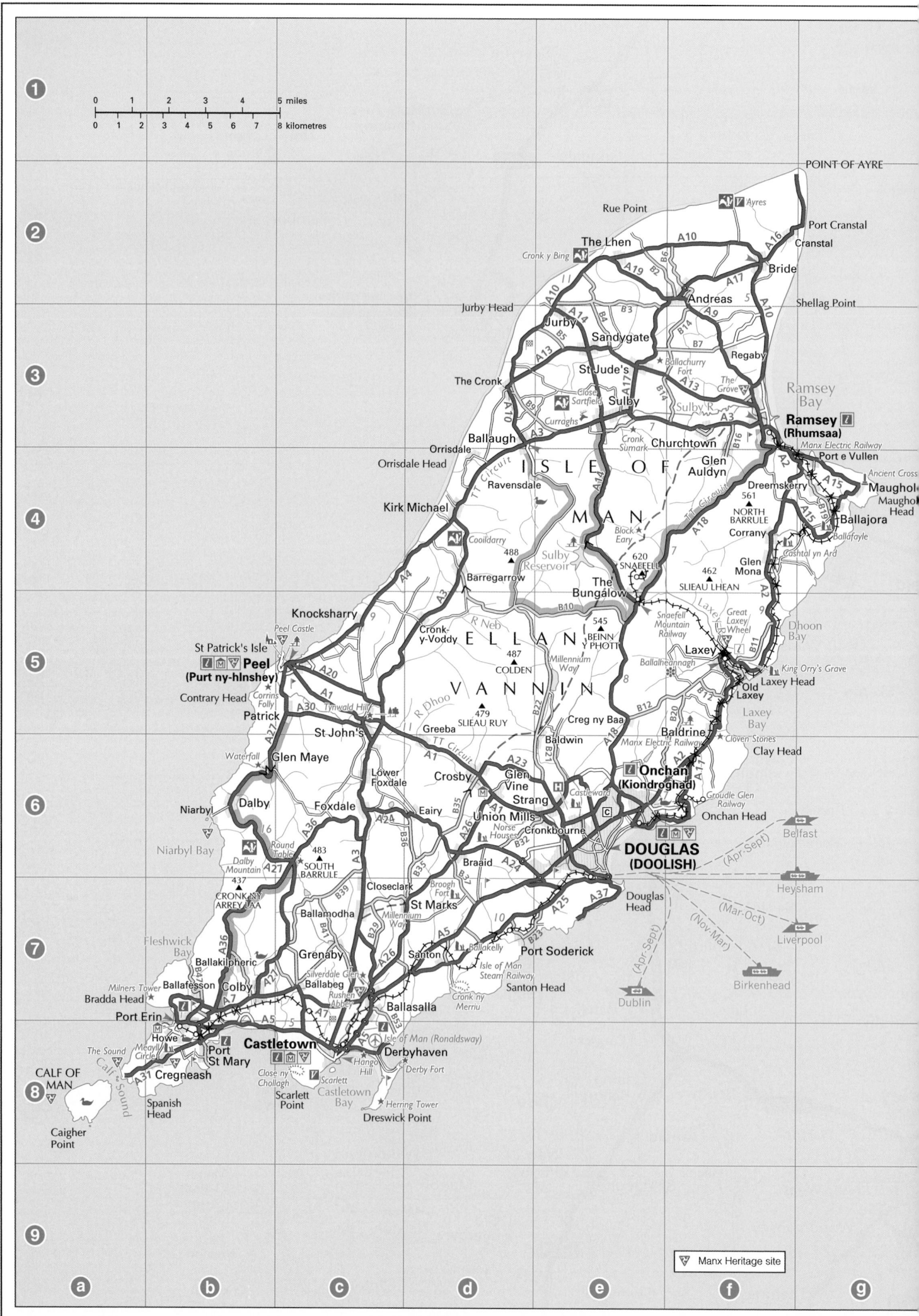

POINT OF AYRE

Ayres

Rue Point

Port Cranstal
Cranstal

The Lhen

A10

A19   B2   B6   Bride

Cronk y Bing   A19   Andreas   A17   Shellag Point

Jurby Head   A10   Jurby   A14   Sandygate   A9   5   A10   Regaby

A13   St Jude's   Ballachurry Fort   B14   B7   Ramsey Bay

The Cronk   A13   A3   The Grove   Ramsey (Rhumsaa)

A10   Close Sartfield   Sulby   Sulby R.   B16   Port e Vullen

Ballaugh   A3   Curraghs   Churchtown   A2   Ancient Cross

Orrisdale   Cronk Sumark   Glen Auldyn   Dreemskerry   Maughol

Orrisdale Head   Ravensdale   Block Eary   A18   NORTH BARRULE 561   Corrany   A15   Ballajora   Maughol Head

Kirk Michael   Cooildarry   488   620 SNAEFELL   SLIEAU LHEAN 462   Glen Mona   Cashtal yn Ard   Ballafayle

Barregarrow   Sulby Reservoir   The Bungalow   B10   Snaefell Mountain Railway   Great Laxey Wheel   A2   Dhoon Bay

Knocksharry   9   ELLAN   545 BEINN y PHOTT   Ballaheannagh   Laxey   B11   King Orry's Grave

St Patrick's Isle   Peel Castle   Cronk-y-Voddy   487 COLDEN   Millennium Way   Old Laxey   Laxey Head

Peel (Purt ny-hInshey)   A20   VANNIN   479 SLIEAU RUY   B22   Creg ny Baa   A18   B12   B20   Laxey Bay

Contrary Head   Corrins Folly   A30 Tynwald Hill   R Dhoo   Baldwin   Manx Electric Railway   Cloven Stones   Clay Head

Patrick   A1   St John's   Greeba   TT Circuit   A23   Glen Vine   Castleward   Onchan (Kiondroghad)   Groudle Glen Railway

Waterfall   Glen Maye   Lower Foxdale   Crosby   Strang   A1   Onchan Head

Niarbyl   Dalby   Foxdale   Eairy   A26   Union Mills   Norse Houses   B32   Cronkbourne   DOUGLAS (DOOLISH)   Belfast (Apr–Sept)

Niarbyl Bay   Round Table   483 SOUTH BARRULE   A24   B35   B36   Braaid   A24   Douglas Head   Heysham (Mar–Oct)

Dalby Mountain   A27   Closeclark   Brough Fort   St Marks   10   A25   A37   Liverpool (Nov–Mar)

437 CRONK NY ARREY LAA   B39   Ballamodha   Millennium Way   A5   Ballakelly   Port Soderick   (Apr–Sept)

Fleshwick Bay   A36   B41   Grenaby   B29   A26   Santon   Isle of Man Steam Railway   Santon Head   Birkenhead

Ballakilpheric   A27   Ballabeg   Silverdale Glen   Cronk ny Merriu   Dublin

Milners Tower   Ballafesson   Colby   7   Rushen Abbey   Ballasalla   B53   Isle of Man (Ronaldsway)

Bradda Head   A5   5   A7

Port Erin   Howe   Meayll Circle   Port St Mary   Castletown   Derbyhaven   Derby Fort

The Sound   Cregneash   Close ny Chollagh   Scarlett   Hango Hill

CALF OF MAN   A31   Scarlett Point   Castletown Bay   Herring Tower

Spanish Head   Dreswick Point

Caigher Point

Manx Heritage site

Scale: 0 1 2 3 4 5 miles / 0 1 2 3 4 5 6 7 8 kilometres

ISLE OF MAN

L A K E   D I S T R I C T

PILLAR

Egremont

St Bees

G

H

J

Wilton

164

K

HAYCOCK

L

Wasdale
Head

KIRK
FELL

GREAT
BLE

899

1

Thornhill

Carleton

Coulderton

Middletown

Haile

River Bleng

691

SEATALLAN

978

964

SCAF

2

Nethertown

Blackbeck

Calder Bridge

Ponsonby

R Irt

SCAFELL

PIK

Beckermet

Braystones

Calder

B5343

Wellington

Nether
Wasdale

Burnmoor
Tarn

R Mite

Boot

156

Hardknott
Fort

Har
P

Cross

Gosforth

Santon

Santon Bridge

Eskdale
Green

Beckfoot

E S K D A L E

652

HARTE
FELL

3

Seascale

Hallsenna Moor

Drigg

Holmrook

Muncaster
Mill

Ravenglass and Eskdale
Railway

River Esk

Devoke
Water

L A K E   D I S T R I C T

Hall
Dunnerdale

13

Saltcoats

Ravenglass

Roman
Bath
House

Muncaster

A595

N A T I O N A L

Ul ia

4

Broad Oak

Newbiggin

Waberthwaite

573

WHITFELL

P A R K

Broughton
Mills

Corney

Loganbeck

Beckfoot

Lower
Hawthwaite

Hycemoor

Selker Bay

Swinside
Stone Circle

Duddon
Bridge

5

Bro

Hyton

Bootle

Lady
Hall

Foxfie

Annaside

600

BLACK
COMBE

Hallthwaites

A595

Arnaby

Bridge End

Gutterby Spa

Whitbeck

The Green

A5093

The Hill

Sand Side

6

Souterga

Whicham

156

Silecroft

8

Kirksanton

Millom

Steel Green

Borwick
Rails

RSPB

Haverigg

Haverigg
Point

Askam
in Furness

7

Sandscale Haws

South
Anim

North Walney

146

Dalt
in-F

BARROW-
IN-FURNESS

590

Hawcoat

H

C

Furness
Abbey

8

North Scale

Vickerstown

M

row
Island

30

0   1   2   3   4   5 miles
0 1 2 3 4 5 6 7 8 kilometres

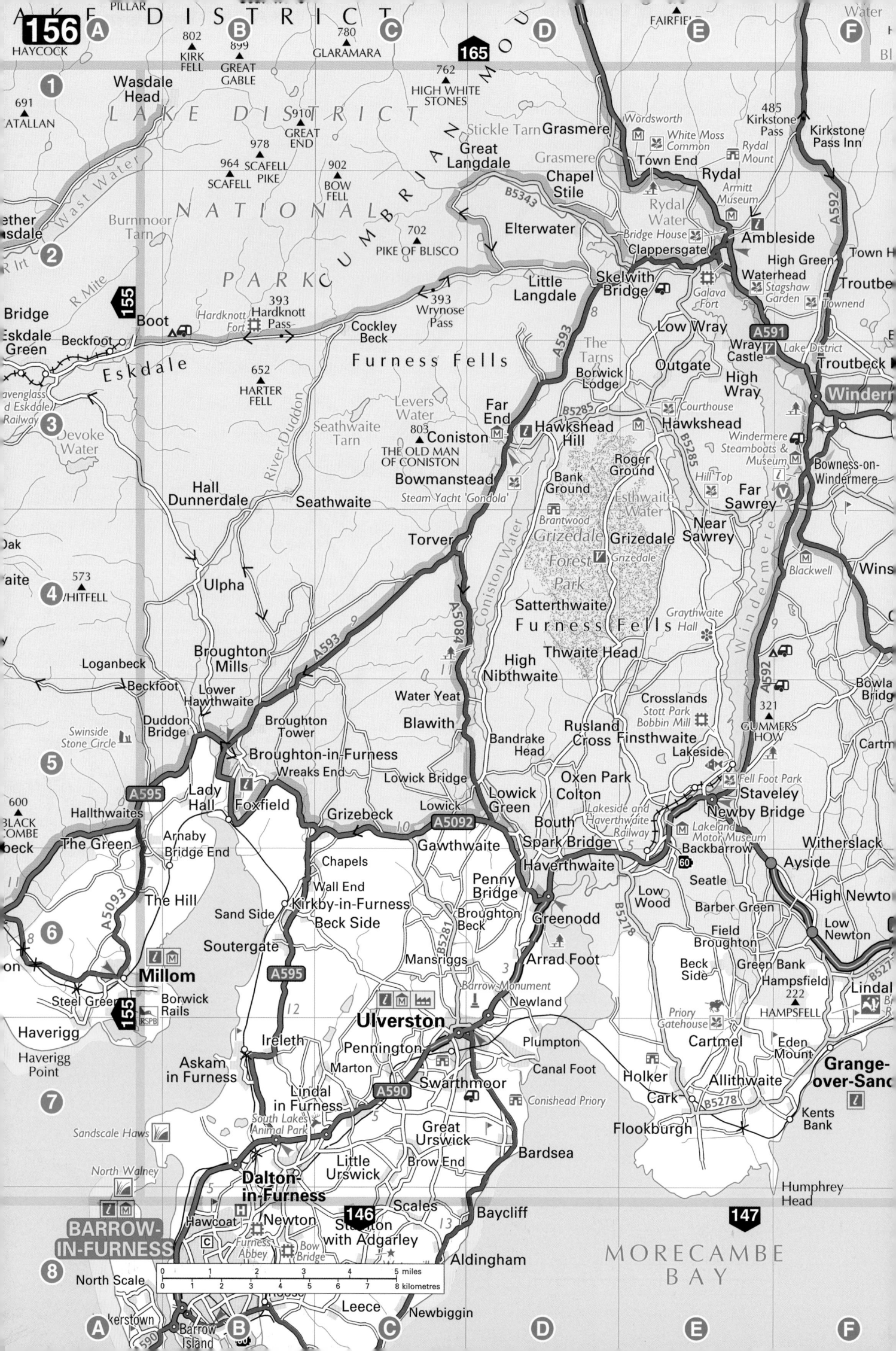

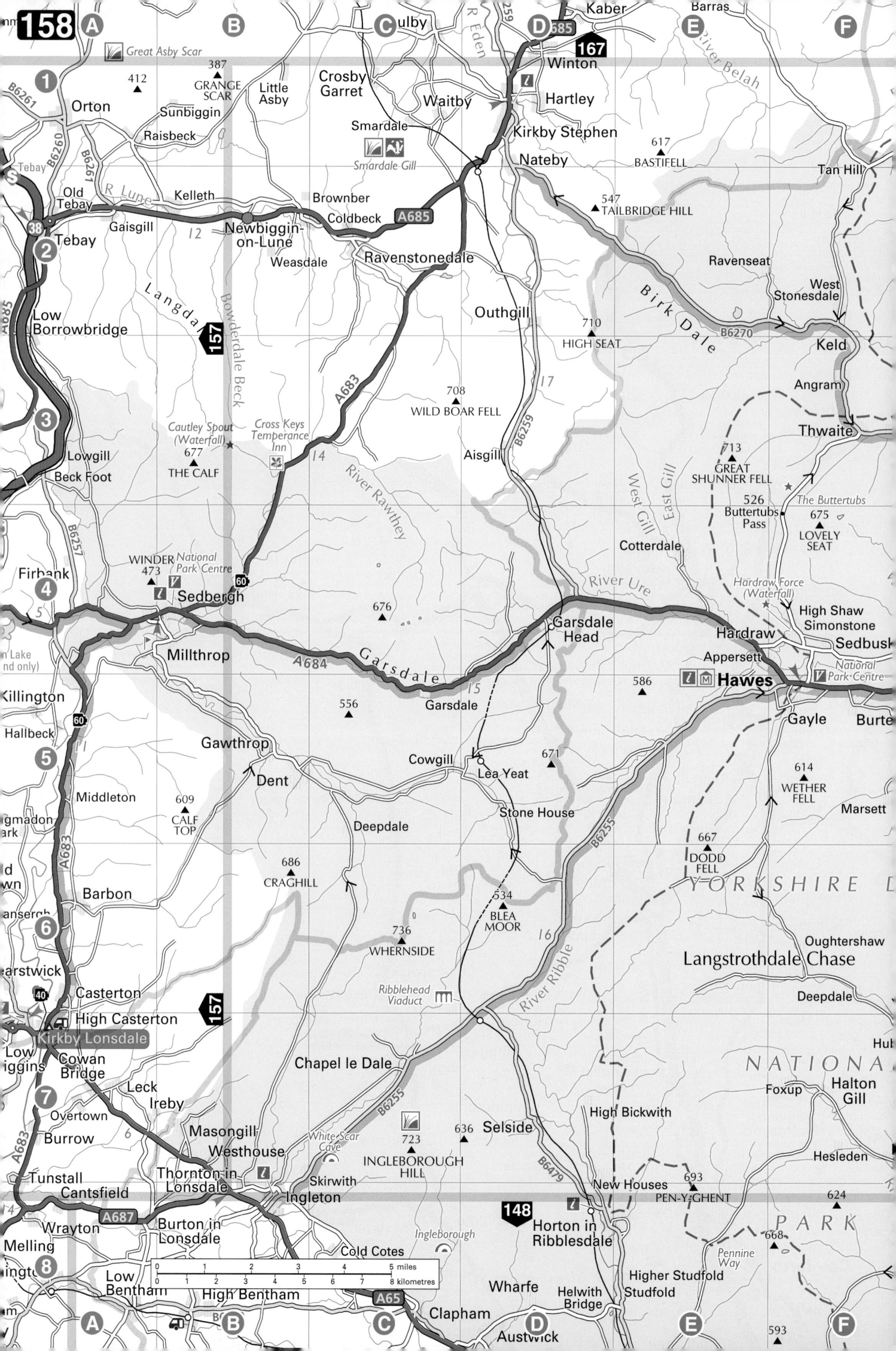

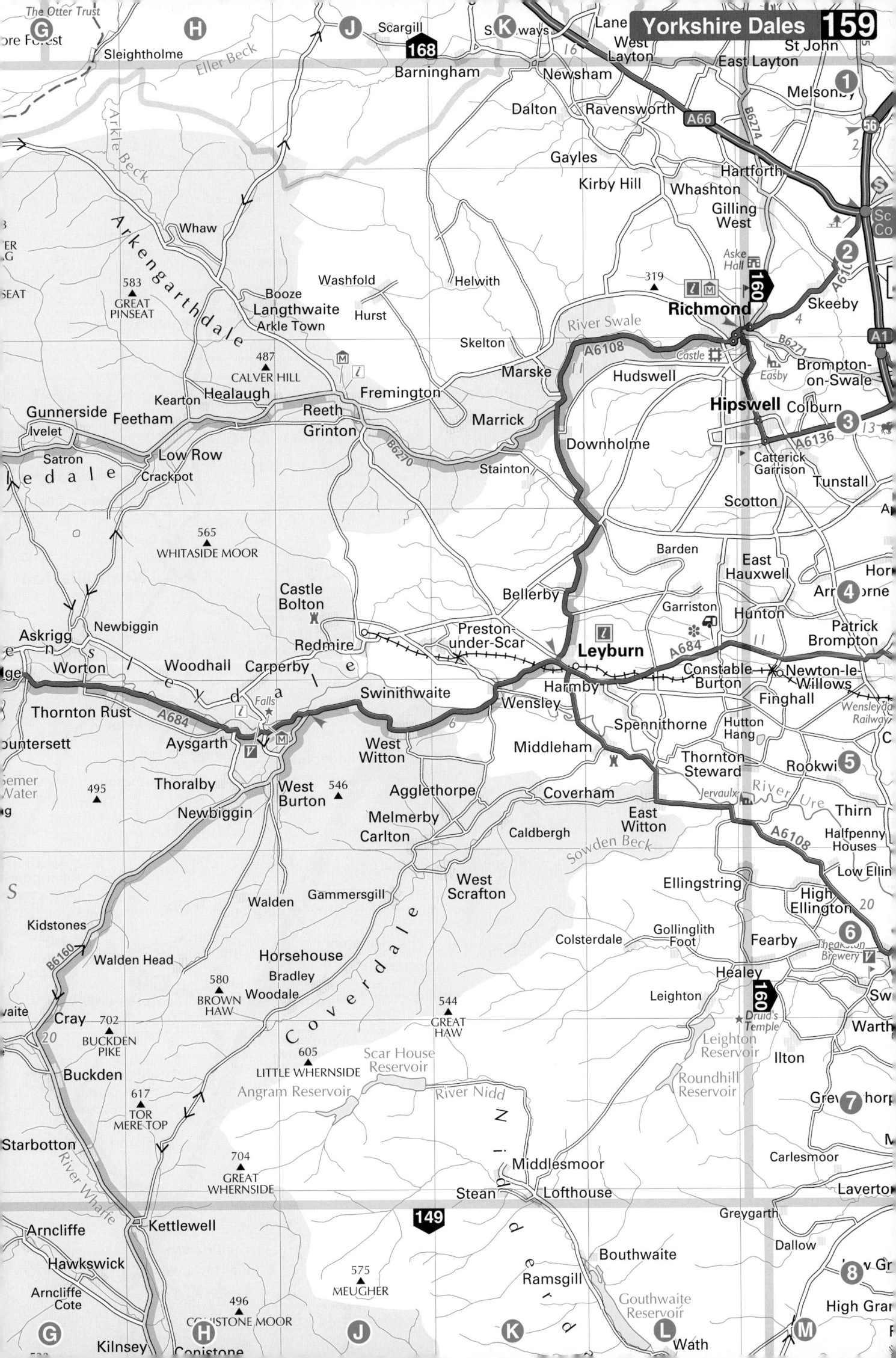

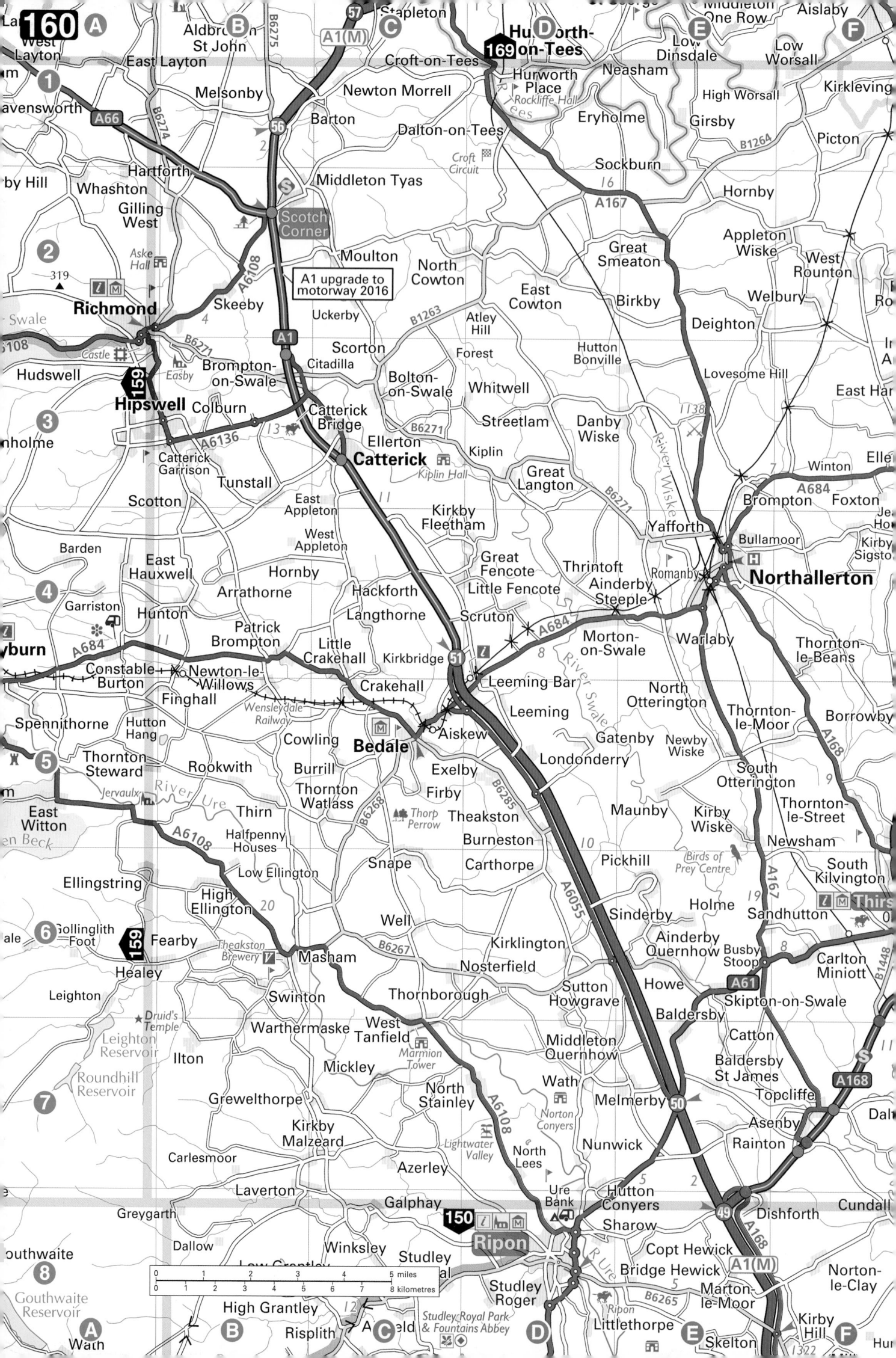

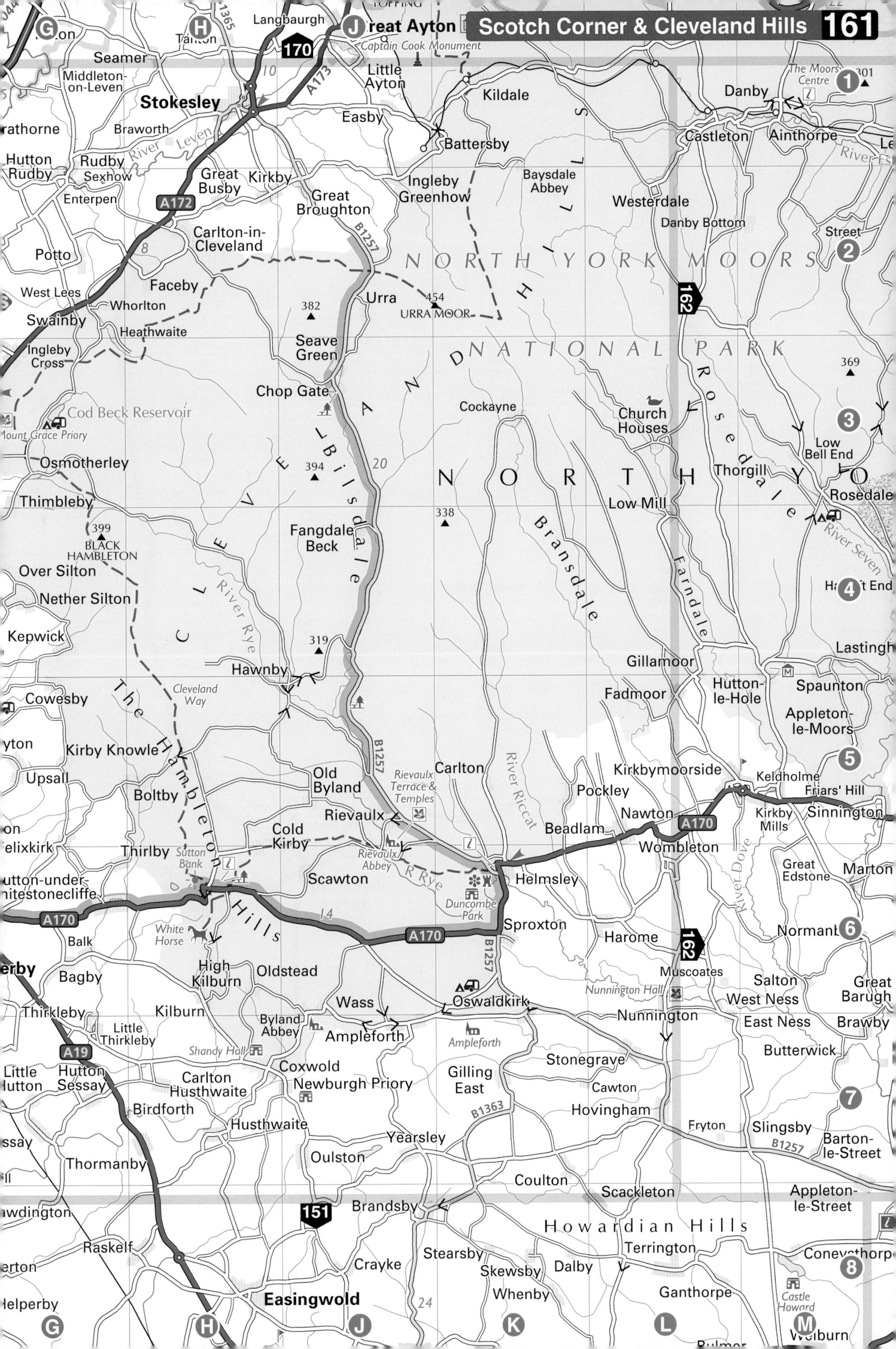

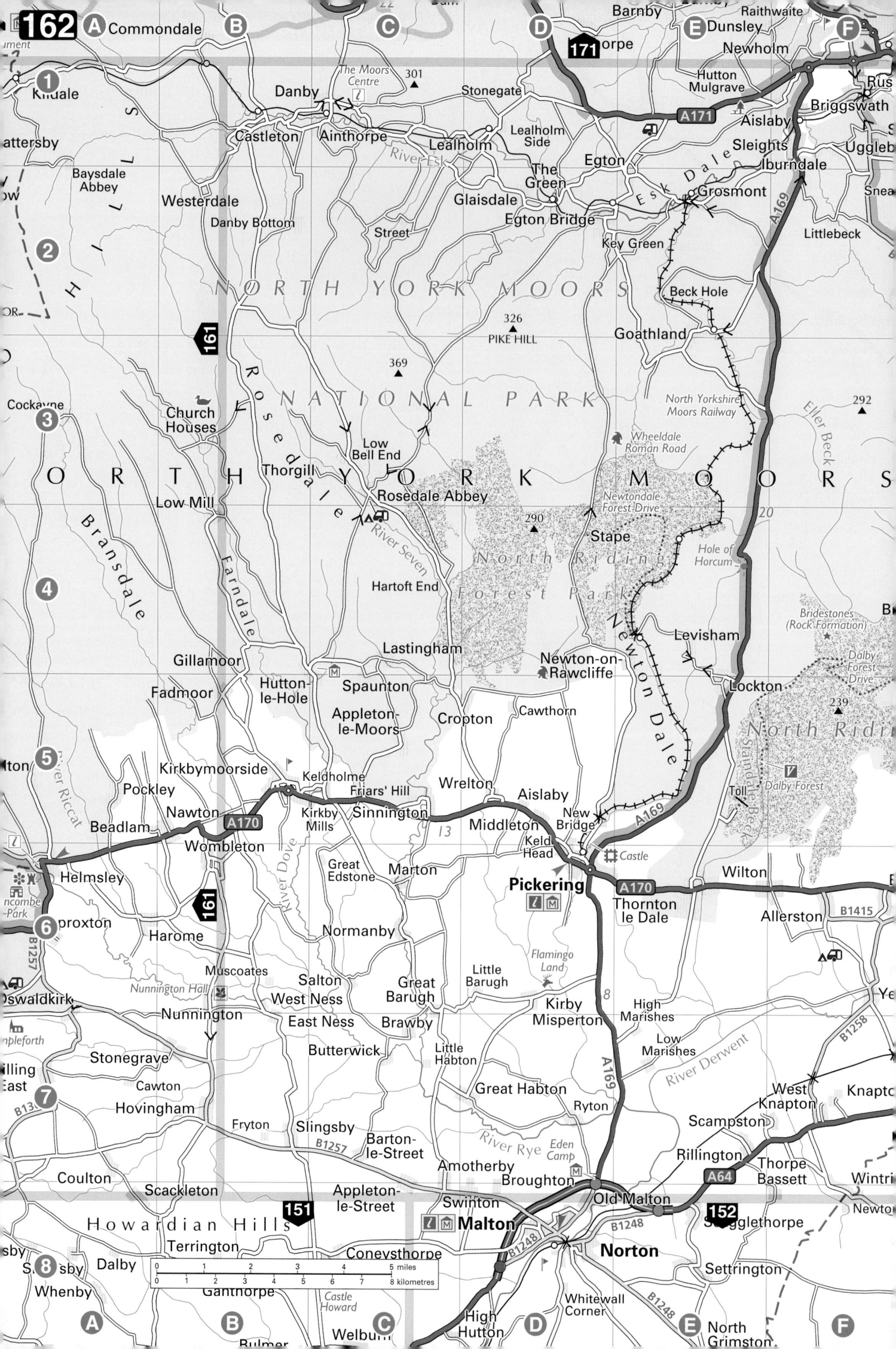

G H J

1
2
3
4
5
6
7
8

by
G
ick
Bay
insacre
High Hawsker
sker
ow
Raw
Fylingthorpe
171
20

Ness Point or
North Cheek
Robin Hood's Bay
Robin
Hood's Bay
Old Peak or
South Cheek
Ravenscar

Staintondale
Shire Horse Centre
Cloughton
Newlands
Hayburn
Wyke
Harwood
Dale
Cloughton
Wyke
Cloughton
Cromer Point
A165
Burniston
Broxa
Silpho
Suffield
Cleveland Way
Langdale
End
Hackness
Newby
Scarborough
Castle
Scalby
Everley
H
Hatherleigh
Deep Sea Trawler
orest Park
River Derwent
Sea Cut
Falsgrave
C
Oliver's Mount
A171
A170
West
Ayton
East Ayton
P+R
A165
Bee Dale
Eastfield
P+R
Osgodby
Cayton
Bay
Sawdon
Irton
Crossgates
B1261
High
Killerby
The
Wyke
Hutton
Buscel
Seamer
Cayton
7
Ruston
Wykeham
7
Filey Brigg
Snainton
17
Lebberston
Brompton-
by-Sawdon
A64
Gristhorpe
A1039
Filey
B1261
R-Hertford
Folkton
A1039
Muston
e
C
Willerby
West
Flotmanby
Filey Bay
Staxton
Flixton
7
16
Sherburn
Ganton
Yorkshire
Wolds Way
Hunmanby
Flamborough Head
Heritage Coast
East Heslerton
Potter
Brompton
Fordon
Reighton
n
Speeton
Foxholes
Wold
Newton
153
Burton
Fleming
Bempton
Cliffs
RSPB
Buckton
Bempton
B1249
Butterwick
Grindale
A165
B1229
Helperthorpe
Weaverthorpe
Thwing
Octon
C
ton
East
utton
lton
B12
Bondvil

G H J K L M

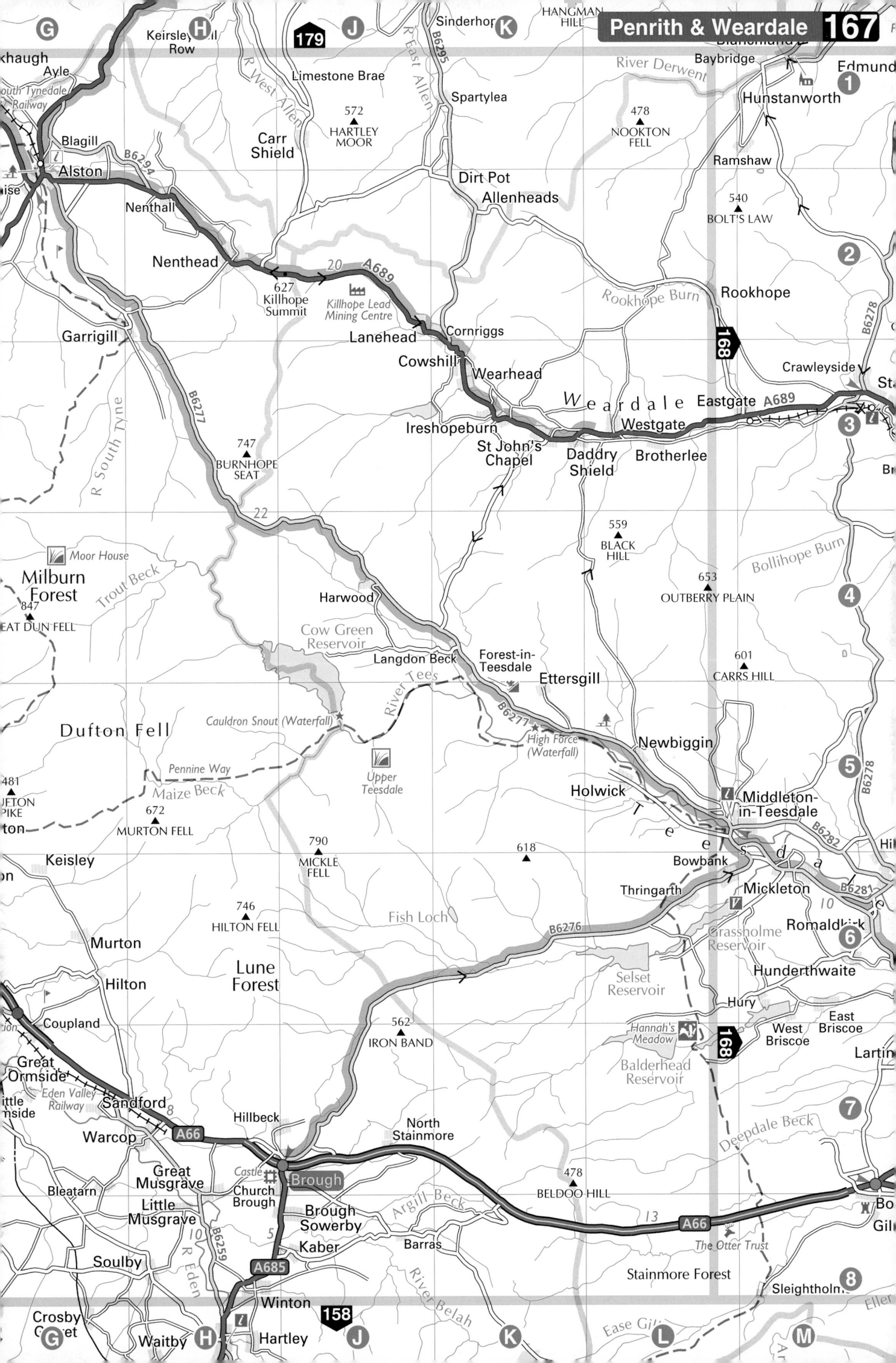

G
H
J
179
K
HANGMAN HILL
Sinderhope
Biantomura

River Derwent
Baybridge
Edmund
1

Keirsley Row
Limestone Brae
R West Allen
R East Allen
B6295
Hunstanworth

Ayle
khaugh
outh Tynedale Railway
572 ▲ HARTLEY MOOR
Spartylea
478 ▲ NOOKTON FELL
Ramshaw

Blagill
Alston
Carr Shield
540 ▲ BOLT'S LAW
2

Nenthall
Dirt Pot
Allenheads

Nenthead
A689
20
Rookhope Burn
Rookhope

Garrigill
B6294
627 Killhope Summit
Killhope Lead Mining Centre
Lanehead
Cornriggs
Cowshill
Wearhead
Weardale
Eastgate A689
Westgate
168
Crawleyside
St
3

B6277
747 ▲ BURNHOPE SEAT
22
Ireshopeburn
St John's Chapel
Daddry Shield
Brotherlee
B6278

Milburn Forest
Moor House
R South Tyne
Trout Beck
Harwood
559 ▲ BLACK HILL
653 ▲ OUTBERRY PLAIN
Bollihope Burn
4

847 ▲ EAT DUN FELL
Cow Green Reservoir
Langdon Beck
Forest-in-Teesdale
Ettersgill
601 ▲ CARRS HILL

Dufton Fell
Cauldron Snout (Waterfall) ★
River Tees
B6277
High Force (Waterfall) ★
Newbiggin
B6278
5

481 ▲ UFTON PIKE
ton
Pennine Way
Maize Beck
672 ▲ MURTON FELL
Upper Teesdale
Holwick
T
e
e
Middleton-in-Teesdale
B6282

Keisley
790 ▲ MICKLE FELL
618 ▲
Bowbank
s
d
a
Mickleton
B6281
10

Murton
746 ▲ HILTON FELL
Fish Loch
Thringarth
Grassholme Reservoir
Romaldkirk
6

Hilton
Lune Forest
B6276
Selset Reservoir
Hunderthwaite

Coupland
562 ▲ IRON BAND
Hannah's Meadow
168
Hury
West Briscoe
East Briscoe
Lartin

Great Ormside
Eden Valley Railway
Sandford 8
Balderhead Reservoir
Deepdale Beck
7

ittle nside
Warcop
A66
Hillbeck
North Stainmore
478 ▲ BELDOO HILL
Bo
Gil

Bleatarn
Great Musgrave
Castle
Church Brough
Brough
Brough Sowerby
Kaber
Argill Beck
13 A66
The Otter Trust
8

Little Musgrave
B6259
Barras
Stainmore Forest
Sleightholm

Soulby
R Eden
10
5
A685
Winton
158

Crosby
Waitby
Hartley
River Belah
Ease Gill
Eller
M

G
H
J
K
L

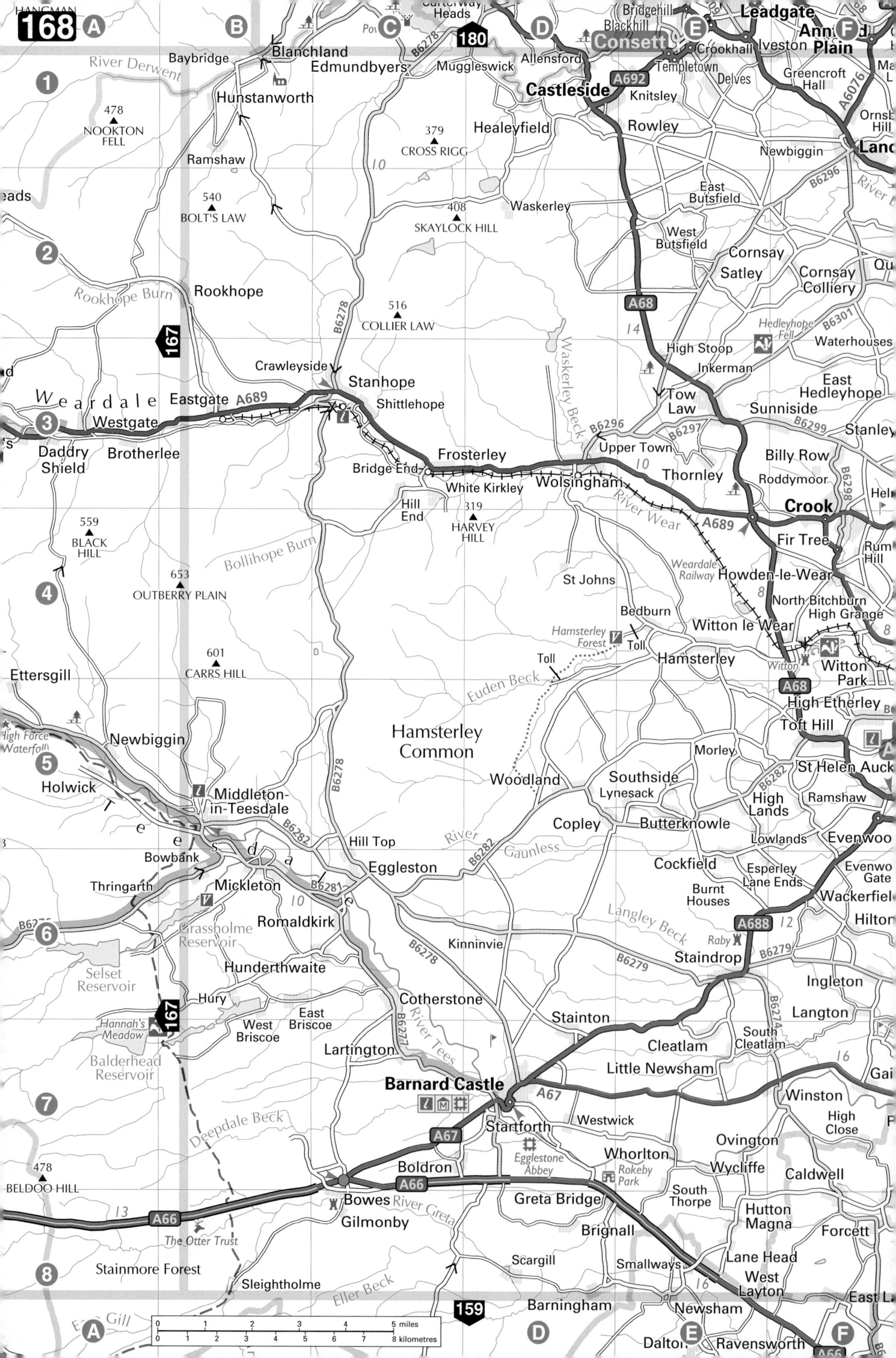

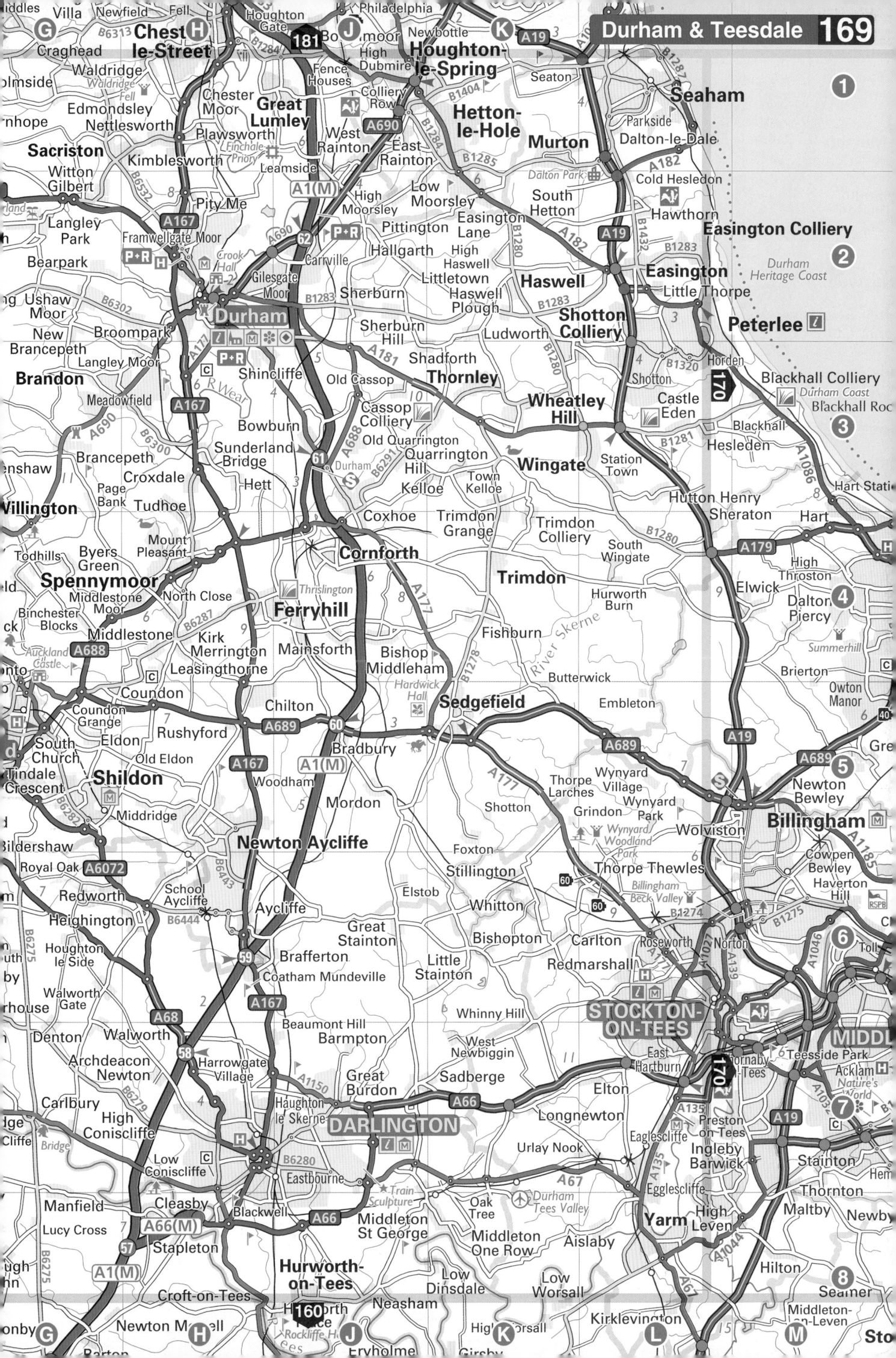

1
2
3
4
5
6
7
8

Brotton
Hummersea Scar
Carlin How
Skinningrove
Upton
Boulby
Staithes
Loftus
Heritage Centre
Dalehouse
Port Mulgrave
Easington
Liverton Mines
Hinderwell
Runswick Bay
North Yorkshire and Cleveland Heritage Coast
Roxby
Newton Mulgrave
Runswick
Handale
Borrowby
Kettleness
Goldsborough
Ellerby
Overdale Wyke
B1266
Scaling
A174
Lythe
Gerrick
Sandend
Sandsend Wyke
Mickleby
West Barnby
East Barnby
Scaling Dam
Raithwaite
Whitby
Dunsley
Abbey
Saltwick Bay
Ugthorpe
Newholm
The Moors Centre
301
162
Hutton Mulgrave
Ruswarp
St Eacre
Stone
A171
Briggswath
Aislaby

G   H   J   K   L   M

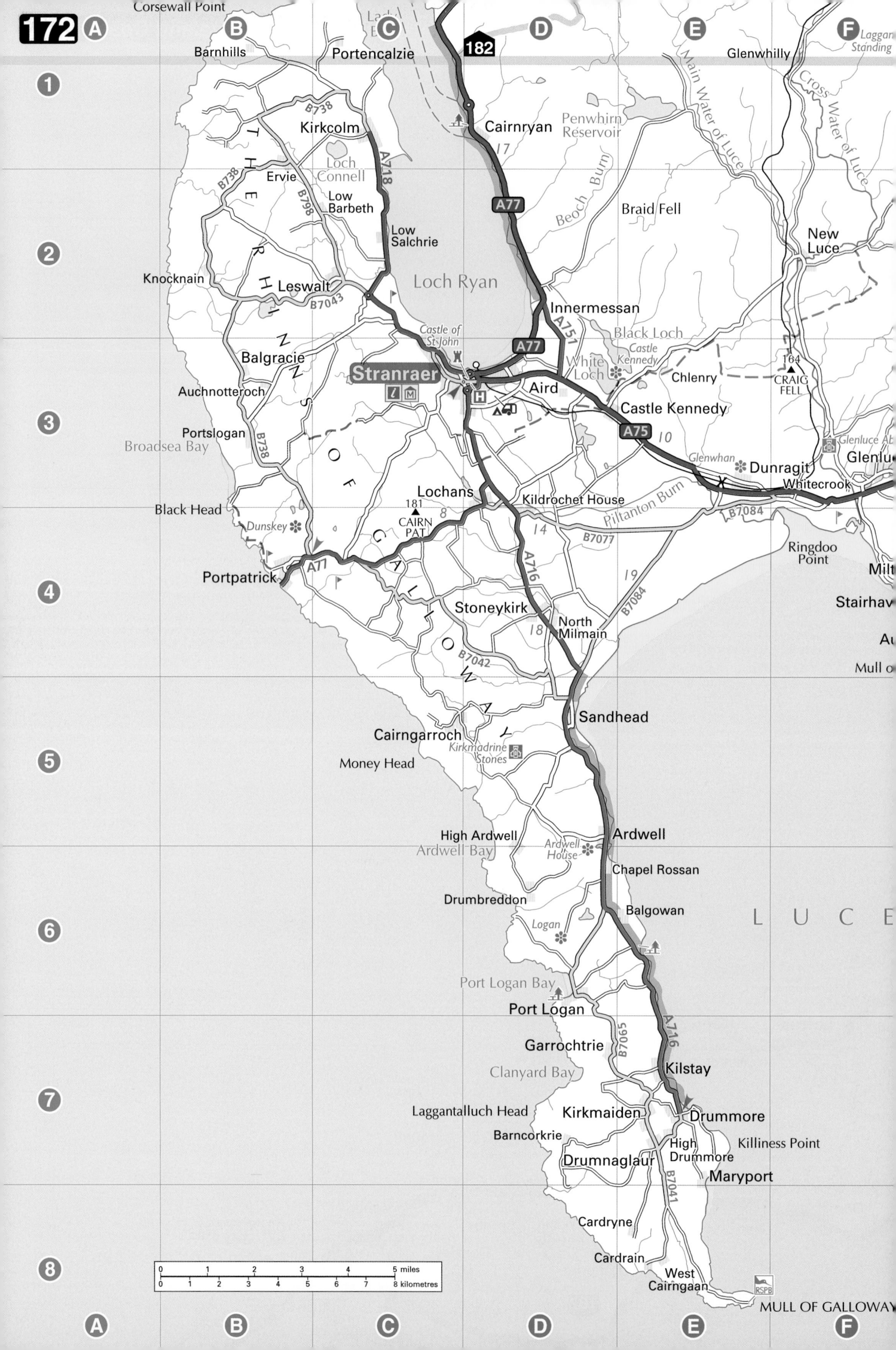

Corsewall Point

Ⓑ

Portencalzie

Ⓒ

Ⓓ

182

Ⓔ

Ⓕ Laggan Standing

Ⓐ

Barnhills

Glenwhilly

①

Kirkcolm

B738

Cairnryan

Penwhirn Reservoir

A77

Braid Fell

New Luce

②

Ervie

Loch Connell

Low Barbeth

A718

Low Salchrie

Loch Ryan

Innermessan

Black Loch

Knocknain

Leswalt

B7043

B798

Castle Kennedy

White Loch

Chlenry

CRAIG FELL

164

③

Balgracie

Castle of St John

Stranraer

A77

A751

Aird

Castle Kennedy

Glenluce Ab

Auchnotteroch

A75

10

Glenwhan

Dunragit

Glenlu

Portslogan

Broadsea Bay

B738

Lochans

181

CAIRN PAT

8

Kildrochet House

Piltanton Burn

Whitecrook

B7084

Black Head

Dunskey

A71

14

B7077

Ringdoo Point

④

Portpatrick

A71

A716

19

B7084

Stairhav

Stoneykirk

18

North Milmain

Mull o

B7042

⑤

Cairngarroch

Kirkmadrine Stones

Sandhead

Money Head

High Ardwell

Ardwell Bay

Ardwell House

Ardwell

Chapel Rossan

L U C E

⑥

Drumbreddon

Logan

Balgowan

Port Logan Bay

Port Logan

⑦

Garrochtrie

Clanyard Bay

B7065

A716

Kilstay

Laggantalluch Head

Kirkmaiden

Drummore

Barncorkrie

High Drummore

Killiness Point

Drumnaglaur

Maryport

B7041

Cardryne

Cardrain

⑧

West Cairngaan

RSPB

MULL OF GALLOWAY

Ⓐ   Ⓑ   Ⓒ   Ⓓ   Ⓔ   Ⓕ

0 1 2 3 4 5 miles
0 1 2 3 4 5 6 7 8 kilometres

G   H   183   J   K

1

River Bladnoch   Knowe

Black Burn

271
RTFIELD
FELL

G A L L O W A Y

184
URRALL
FELL

Carseriggan

Challoch   R Cree   Minnigaff

710
CAIRNSMORE
OF FLEET

Barfad

214
CULVENNAN
FELL

i M   **Newton Stewart**   Creebridge   Kirroughtree

2

Loch Ronald

Tarf   Water

B733   Shennanton   15   B735   Kirkcowan

A75   Craighlaw

A714   Palnure   A75

174 Baltersan

Causeway End   7   Gem Rock

3

Dernaglar Loch   A75

B733   R Bladnoch

Clugston   B7052   Torhouse Stone Circle   B733   Wigtown   18   Creetown   Kirkmabreck

Fell Loch   Bladnoch   Kirwaugh   Carsluith

CAIR

4

Castle Loch   T H E   Cairnholy Chambered Cair
Carsluith Castle

Mochrum Loch   Water of Malzie   B7005   M A C H A R S   Braehead   Orchardton Bay   Ravenshall Point

g   B7005   Culshabbin   Kirkinner   B7004

Auchenmalg Bay   Chapel Finian (ruin)   Barrachan   Whauphill   Culscadden

A747   13   Elrig   12   B7085   Little Airies   A746   Wig

5

Druchtag Motte   Sorbie   B7052   Garlieston

Mochrum   Drumtrodden Cup & Ring   Pouton   Cruggleton Bay

Drumtrodden Standing Stones   Drummoddie   Broughton Mains   B7004   B7063

B A Y   Port William   Big Balcraig   **174**   Priory

6

'Wren's Egg' Standing Stones   B7021

Barsalloch Fort   Monreith   Whithorn Story   V

Barsalloch Point   Rispain Camp   Whithorn   Portyerrock

Point of Leg   A747   10   A746   Isle of Whithorn

7

St Ninian's Cave   B7004

Kidsdale   St Ninian's Chapel (ruin)

Cutcloy

BURROW HEAD

8

G   H   J   K   L   M

G H J K 1

Crocketford

Auche Loch Loch

Lochobe Loch

Mossdale

Airds of Kells

A713

185

Knockvennie Smithy

Milton

Drumcoltran Tower

Beeswing

Loch Roan

Kirkpatrick Durham

Springholm

Kirkgunzeon

Kinhar

Loch Ken

Walbutt

Old Bridge of Urr

334 LOTUS HILL

Glensone Burn

Woodhall Loch

Laurieston

B795

Crossmichael

Hardgate

Redcastle

A711

430 CUIL HILL

2

Glenlochar

Clarebrand

B795

B794

14

Townhead of Greenlaw

Haugh of Urr

Threave Castle

Hillowton

A745

Edingham

176

Longwood

A75

Castle Douglas

Little Knox

Dalbeattie

3

Bridge of Dee

Threave Garden

Carlingwark Loch

6

Gelston

B793

8

Rhonehouse

B736

Barlochan

Palnackie

Caulkerbush

Craigley

Barnbarroch

Fairgirth

Ringford

A711

River Dee

A762

Airieland

343 SCREEL HILL

Orchardton Tower

Drumburn

RSPB

Fleet

15

B727

390 BENGAIRN

Kippford or Scaur

Mote of Mark

Sandyhills

Tongland

Colvend

Rockcliffe

A75

Twynholm

Little Sypland

East Stewartry Coast

Portling

4

Compstonend

Wildlife Park

Whinnie Liggate

Castlehill Point

A755

Kirkchrist

Auchencairn

Auchencairn Bay

MacLellan's Castle

Kirkcudbright

Culnaightrie

Heston Island

orgue

Mutehill

Balcary

Balcary Point

B727

Dundrennan

Rascarrel

5

Orroland

Abbey

A711

Dundrennan Abbey

mangan

Ross

Balmae

Netherlaw

Abbey Head

6

Little Ross

7

8

G H J K L M

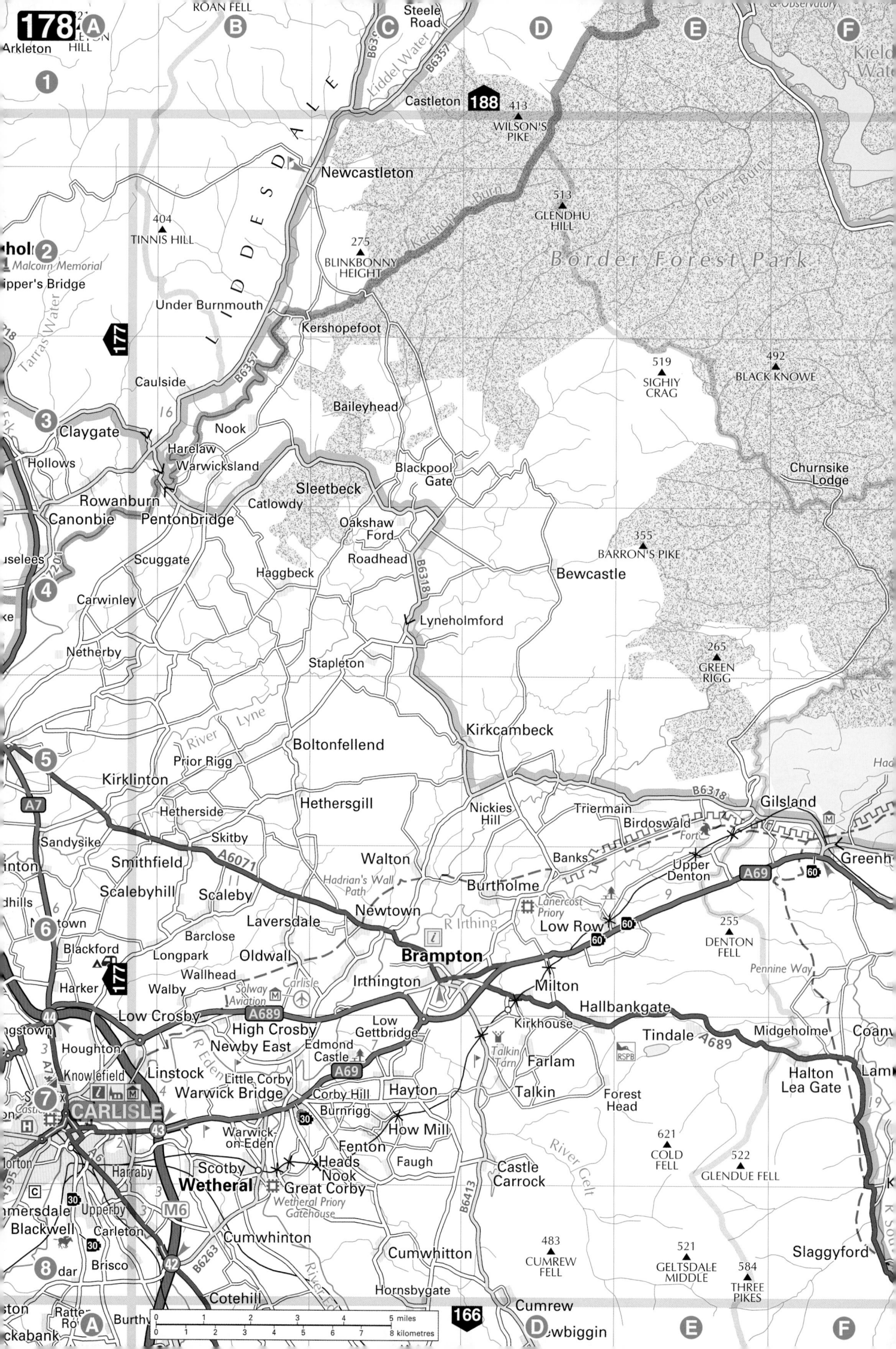

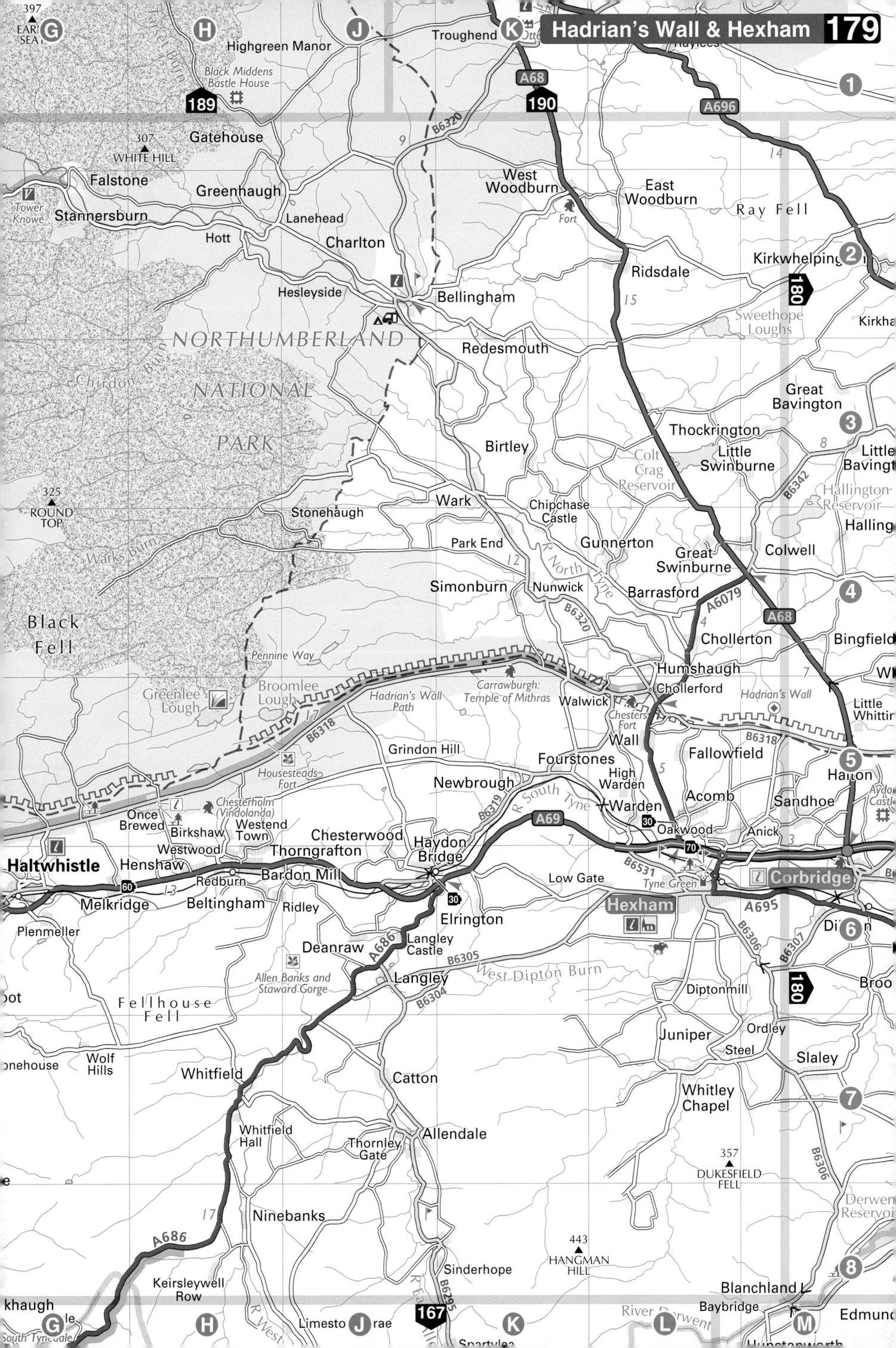

G   H   J   K

1
2
3
4
5
6
7
8

A1068
Ellington
Lynemouth
inton
A189
191 Beacon Point
Woodhorn
A197
ngton
Woodhorn Demesne
Hirst H M
North Seaton
30 **Newbiggin-by-the-Sea**
Wansbeck Riverside
epwash
Stakeford
North Seaton Colliery
Guide Post
llington
West Sleekburn
otland te
Bomarsund
30
East Sleekburn
7
Cambois
North Blyth
B1331
A193 C
Cowpen
Blyth
East Hartford
A189
Bebside
30
Newsham
A192
New Delaval
A1061
Shankhouse
A192
New Hartley
A193
Seaton Sluice
ington
East Cramlington
A190
Seaton
Hartley
B1326
Seaton Delaval
C
St Mary's Lighthouse
Seghill
Holywell
B1325
A192
Annitsford
9
A1148
Dudley
30
Burradon
ide pen
Camperdown
Earsdon
B1322
Monkseaton
Whitley Bay ⓘ
A1056
Shiremoor
Murton
Cullercoats
Killingworth
Backworth
A193
B1317
A191
H
Forest Hall
New York
Tynemouth
A189
A191
A19
C
ⓘ
Tynemouth Priory & Castle
Rising Sun
4
🚢 Amsterdam (IJmuiden)
Longbenton
4
North Shields
south osforth
A1058
5
Willington Quay
A187
SOUTH SHIELDS ⓘ M
Jesmond
50
Wallsend
Int. Ferry Terminal
Westoe
A183
40
Heaton
A187 M
Toll
Tyne Tunnel
Harton
Marsden Bay
Jarrow
A185
Marsden
Souter Lighthouse
Walker
B1313
Hebburn
H
A1300
Souter Point
Byker
Monkton
C
Whitburn
Felling
4
30
Cleadon
A183
40 A184
Wardley
A194
West Boldon
B1299
Souter Point
GATESHEAD
50
Boldon Colliery
A1018
30
Whitburn Bay
C
Low Fell
A167
A184
East Boldon
A184
Seaburn
ey
H
B1288
Bowes Railway & Museum
A194(M)
A19
Fulwell
Roker
A1290
Castletown
Southwick
Monkwearmouth
Springwell
A195
Wildfowl & Wetlands Trust
C
ⓘ M
North
Usworth
65
A1231
South Hylton
SUNDERLAND
BIRTLEY
Portobello
Penshaw Monument
Pennywell
A183
H
Hendon
30
WASHINGTON
S
Offerton
B1405
Ouston
64
Washington
A195
High Newport
Grangetown
Perkinsville
Fatfield
A183
2
New Silksworth
Tunstall
Durham Heritage Coast
River Wear
Penshaw
Herrington
Ryhope
3
Shiney Row
New Herrington
A1018
Pelton Fell
A183
Philadelphia
6
lton
63
Houghton Gate
Newbottle
A19
3
Chester-le-Street
Bournmoor
High Dumbire
Houghton-le-Sprin
169
Chester
H
J
Colliery
Seaton
K
Seaham
B1404

G   H   J   K   L   M

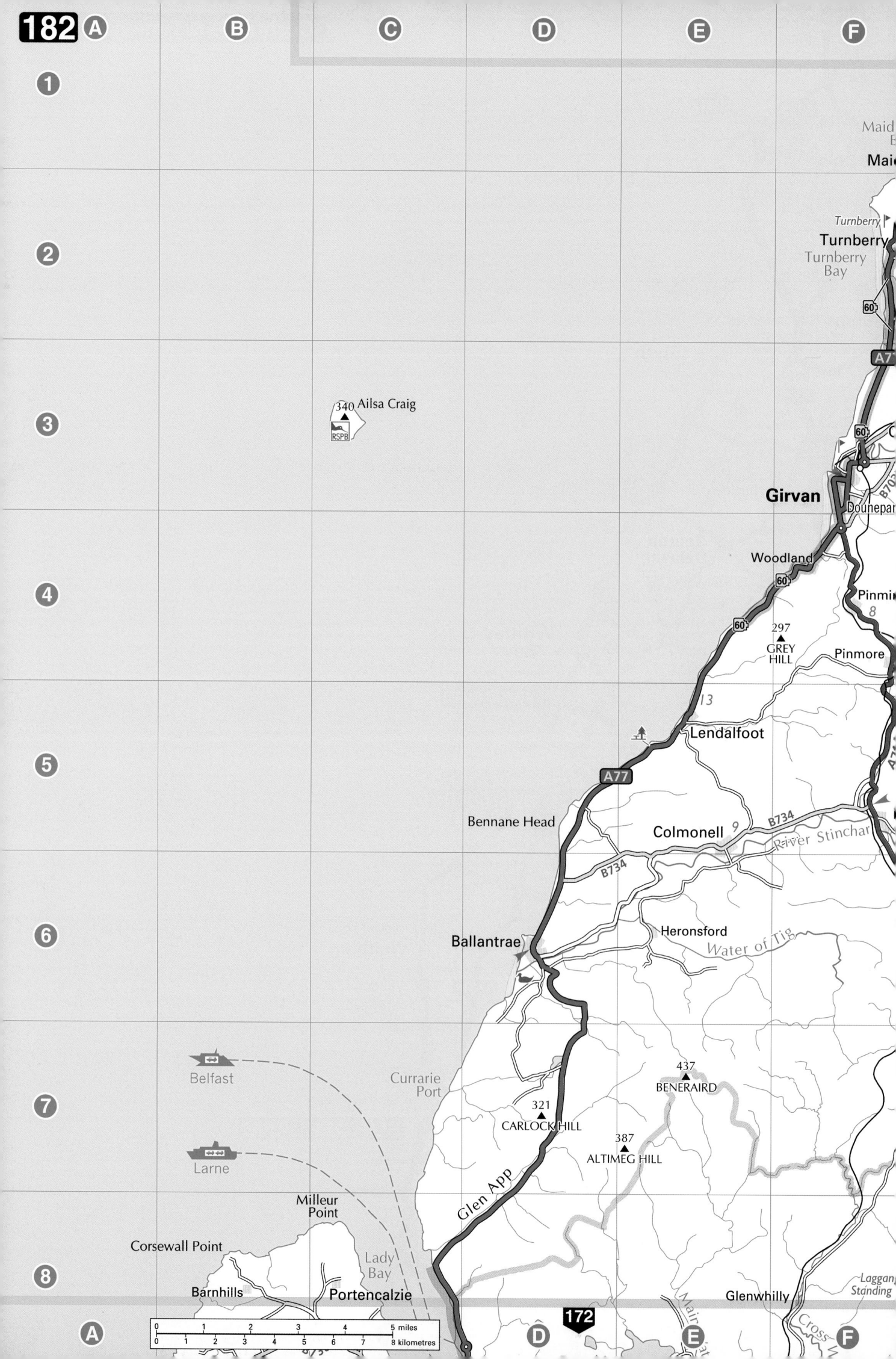

340 Ailsa Craig
RSPB

Maid
Mai

Turnberry
Turnberry
Turnberry Bay

60

A7

60

Girvan
Dounepar

Woodland
60

60
Pinmi
8

297
GREY
HILL

Pinmore

13

Lendalfoot

A77

Bennane Head

Colmonell
9
B734
River Stinchar

B734

Heronsford
Water of Tig

Ballantrae

437
BENERAIRD

Belfast

Currarie
Port

321
CARLOCK HILL

Larne

387
ALTIMEG HILL

Glen App

Milleur
Point

Corsewall Point

*Lady
Bay*

Laggan
Standing

Barnhills   **Portencalzie**

Glenwhilly

0   1   2   3   4   5 miles
0   1   2   3   4   5   6   7   8 kilometres

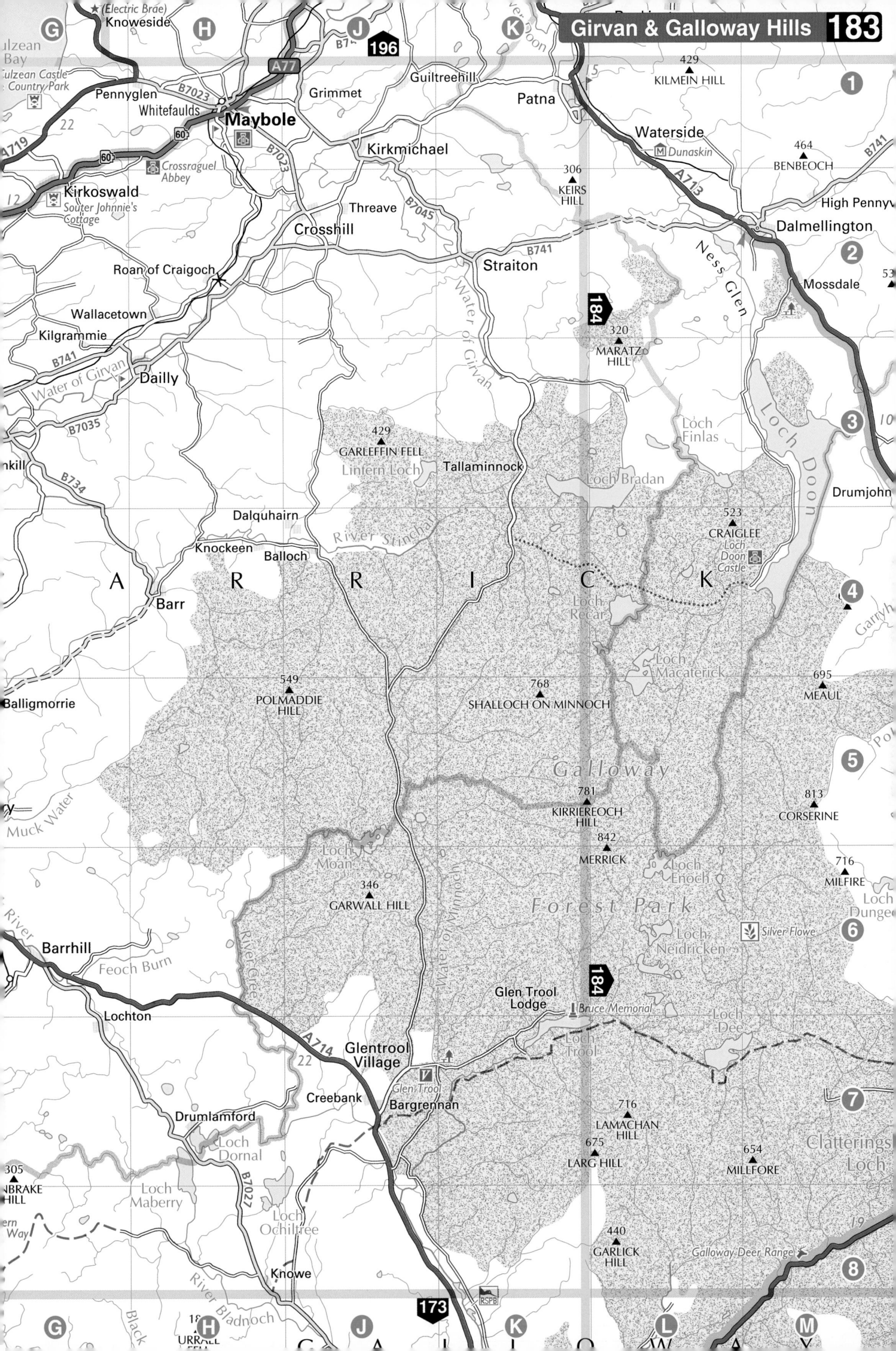

G
H
J
196
K
Girvan & Galloway Hills
183

★ (Electric Brae)
Knoweside

ulzean
Bay

ulzean Castle
 Country Park

Pennyglen
Whitefaulds

Maybole

Kirkoswald

Souter Johnnie's
Cottage

Crossraguel
Abbey

Kirkmichael

Threave

Crosshill

Roan of Craigoch

Wallacetown

Kilgrammie

Dailly

Water of Girvan

Dalquhairn

Knockeen
Balloch

A   R   R   I   C   K

Barr

Balligmorrie

549
▲ POLMADDIE
HILL

B7023

A77

B7023

B741

B7045

B741

Grimmet

Guiltreehill

Patna

KILMEIN HILL
429
▲

Waterside
Ⓜ Dunaskin

306
▲ KEIRS
HILL

464
▲ BENBEOCH

High Pennyv

Dalmellington

Mossdale
53

Ness Glen

184
320
▲ MARATZ
HILL

Loch
Finlas

Loch Bradan

Loch
Doon

Drumjohn

523.
CRAIGLEE
▲
Loch
Doon
Castle

Garleffin Fell
429
▲ GARLEFFIN FELL

Lintern Loch

Tallaminnock

River Stinchar

Loch Recar

Loch Macaterik

695
▲
MEAUL

Straiton

Water of Girvan

Galloway

768
▲
SHALLOCH ON MINNOCH

813
▲
CORSERINE

Muck Water

Barrhill

Feoch Burn

Lochton

A714

Drumlamford

Loch
Dornal

B7027

305
NBRAKE
HILL

Loch
Maberry

Loch
Ochiltree

Knowe

River Bladnoch

173

RSPB

781
▲
KIRRIEREOCH
HILL

842
▲
MERRICK

Loch
Enoch

716
▲
MILFIRE

Loch
Dunge

Loch
Moan

346
▲ GARWALL HILL

Water of Minnoch

Forest Park

Loch
Neidricken

Loch
Neidricken

Silver Flowe

184

Glen Trool
Lodge

Bruce Memorial

Loch
Dee

River Cree

Glentrool
Village

Glen Trool

Bargrennan

Creebank

Loch
Trool

716
▲
LAMACHAN
HILL

675
▲
LARG HILL

654
▲
MILLFORE

Clatterings
Loch

440
▲
GARLICK
HILL

Galloway Deer Range

G
H
J
K
L
M

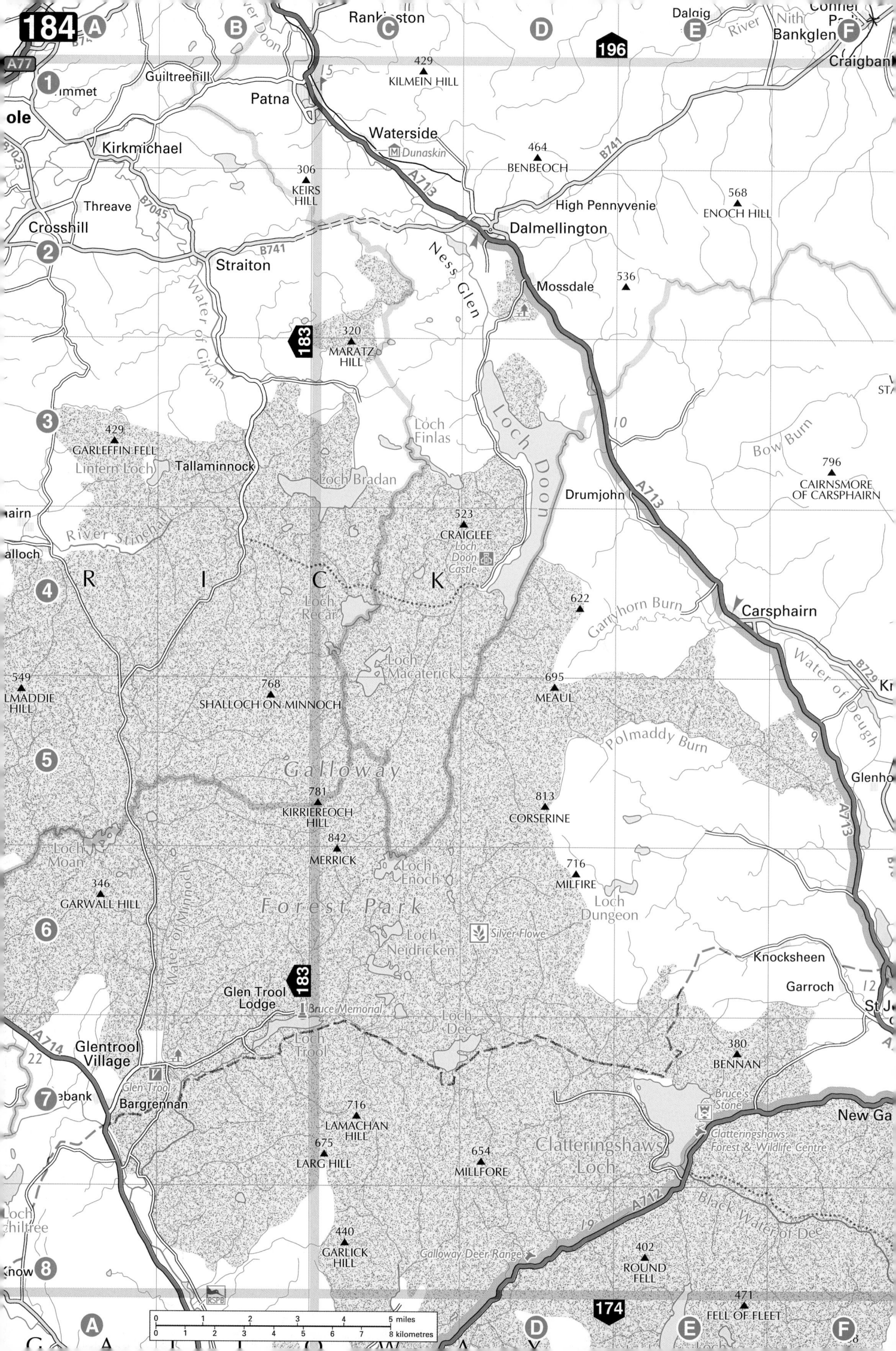

A **B** **C** **D** **E** **F**

A77

1

ole

Guiltreehill
Kimmet
Kirkmichael
Patna
429
KILMEIN HILL

Waterside
Dunaskin
464
BENBEOCH
High Pennyvenie
568
ENOCH HILL

2

Threave
Crosshill
B7045
B7023
Straiton
B741
306
KEIRS HILL
A713
Dalmellington
Mossdale
536

River Doon
Rankieston

196

B741

3

183
320
MARATZ HILL
Loch Finlas
Loch Doon
Drumjohn
Bow Burn
796
CAIRNSMORE OF CARSPHAIRN

Ness Glen

4

429
GARLEFFIN FELL
Linfern Loch
Tallaminnock
Loch Bradan
Loch Recar
523
CRAIGLEE
Loch Doon Castle
622
A713
Carsphairn
B729
Kr

River Stinchar
airn
alloch
R **I** **C** **K**

Garryhorn Burn

5

549
LMADDIE HILL
768
SHALLOCH ON MINNOCH
Loch Macaterick
Galloway
695
MEAUL
Polmaddy Burn
Water of Deugh
Glenho

6

781
KIRRIEREOCH HILL
842
MERRICK
Loch Enoch
813
CORSERINE
716
MILFIRE
Loch Dungeon

346
GARWALL HILL
Forest Park
Loch Neldricken
Silver Flowe
Knocksheen
Garroch
St J

Loch Moan
Water of Minnoch

7

A714
Glentrool Village
183
Glen Trool Lodge
Bruce Memorial
Loch Trool
Loch Dee
380
BENNAN
Bruce's Stone
New Ga

ebank
Bargrennan
Glen Trool
V
716
LAMACHAN HILL
Clatteringshaws Loch
Clatteringshaws Forest & Wildlife Centre

8

Loch hiltree
know
675
LARG HILL
654
MILLFORE
440
GARLICK HILL
Galloway Deer Range
402
ROUND FELL
471
FELL OF FLEET

RSPB
A712
Black Water of Dee

174

0	1	2	3	4	5 miles
0	1 2 3 4	5 6	7	8 kilometres	

A **B** **C** **D** **E** **F**

G

G H J

197
Kirkconnel
Kelloholm

A76
Newtown
Sanquhar
Ulzieside
Mennock

Kello Water

594
HARE HILL

Blackcraig

700
BLACKCRAIG

Euchan Water

450
CLOUD HILL
Polgown

478

475
COUNTAM

554
CAIRNKINNA HILL
Cleuch-head

Enterkinfoot

598
COLT HILL

Big Carlae

Old Auchenbrack
Auchenhessnane

Shinnel Water

Scaur Water

Benbuie

532
CORNHARROW HILL

337
BENNAN

Water of Ken

Southern Upland Way

15

Stenhouse
Tynron

B729
Moniaive
Kirkland

385
WETHER HILL

Black Water

Glencrosh
Craigneston

A702
13

431
BOGRIE HILL
Sundaywell

Skelston
Snade

Loch Urr

Loch Howie

Bogue

B7075

Balmaclellan

A712

281
LARGLEAR HILL

Ironmacannie

Corsock

Knockvennie Smithy

B794

175
Kirkpatrick

GREEN LOWTHER
725
LOWTHER HILL

Nether Fi nd

B797

Enterkin Burn

Lowther Hills

17

691
BALLENCI LAW

Durisdeermill
Durisdeer

Gateslack
East Morton

186
A76
A702

River Nith

23

Drumlanrig

Morton Loc
Morton Castle

Carronbridge
Tibbers

Burnhead
Penpont

Thornhill
Closeburnmill

B731
Keir Mill
Closeburn

Cample
Park

Kirkpatrick

Maxwelton

Keir Hills

Claughrie Burn

ligh dgirth
Blackwood
Auldgirth
Lag
Dalsw

Dunscore
Throughgate

A76
15

B729
17

Stepford

176
Holyw

392
SKEOCH HILL
Drumpark

Twelve Apos
Newbri

Te les
7

Shawhead

Cargen

A75
Eastlands
Crocketford
Lochfoot

A711

Milton

L M

Lochrutton Loch

Milton Loch

Lochober Loch

G H J K L M
Springholm

1
2
3
4
5
6
7
8

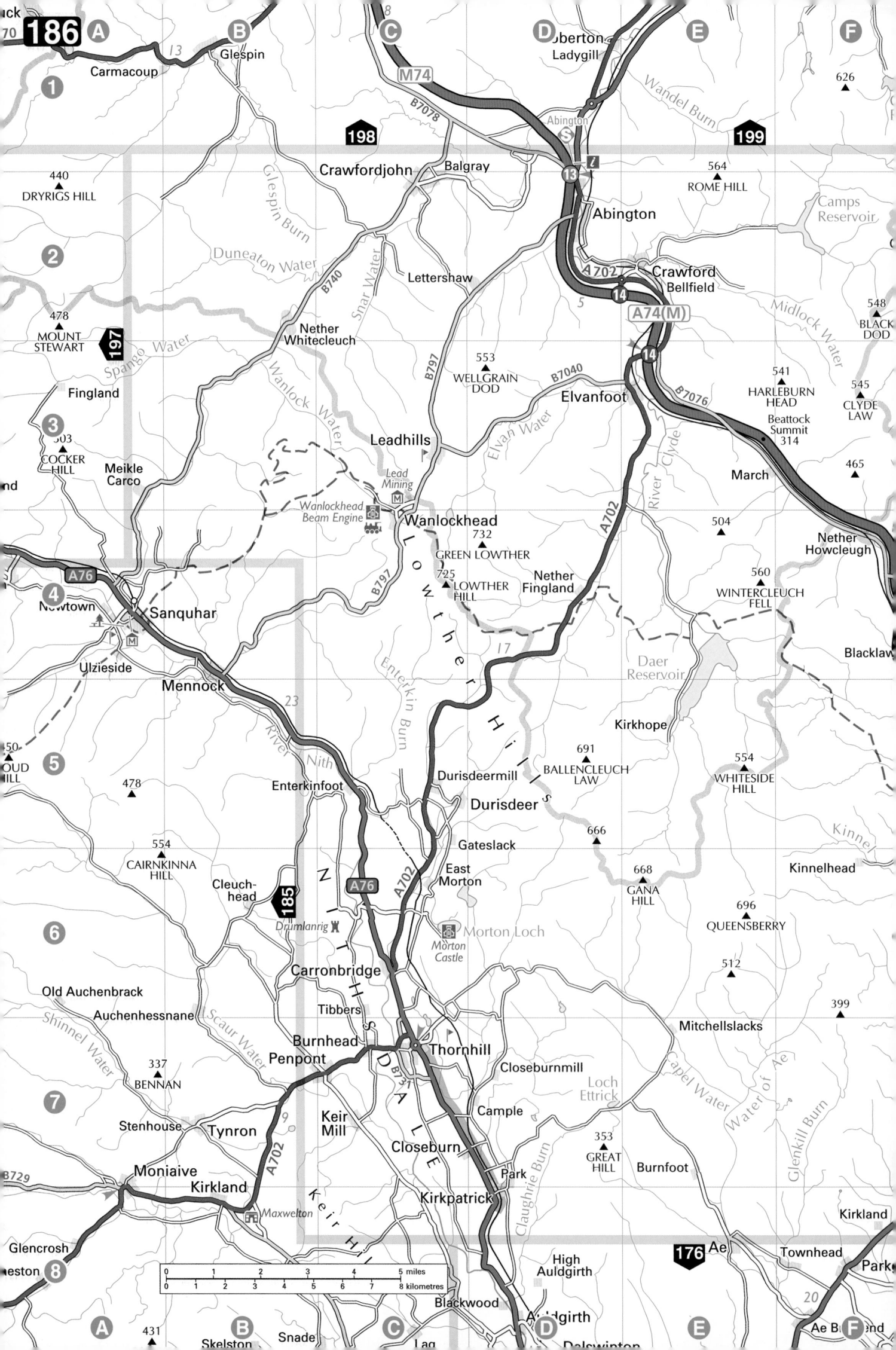

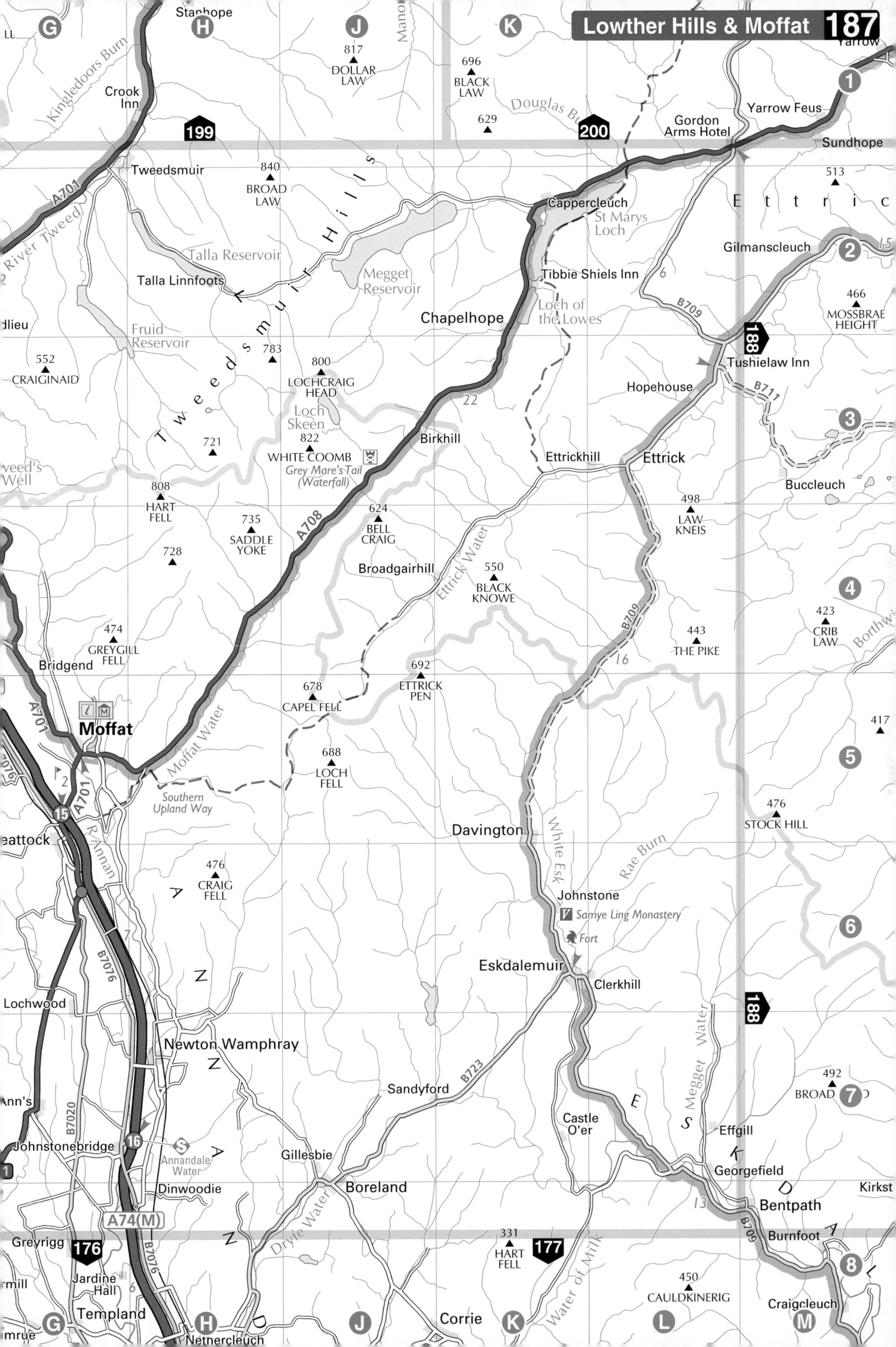

G   H   J   K

Stanhope
817 DOLLAR LAW
696 BLACK LAW
629
200
Yarrow
1
Yarrow Feus
Gordon Arms Hotel
Sundhope
Crook Inn
199
513
E t t r i c
River Tweed
A701
Tweedsmuir
840 BROAD LAW
Cappercleuch
St Marys Loch
Gilmanscleuch
2
Talla Reservoir
Megget Reservoir
Tibbie Shiels Inn
B709
466 MOSSBRAE HEIGHT
Talla Linnfoots
Chapelhope
Loch of the Lowes
188
Tushielaw Inn
B711
Fruid Reservoir
783
Lochcraig Head 800
Hopehouse
3
veed's Well
dlieu
552 CRAIGINAID
721
Loch Skeen
822 WHITE COOMB
Grey Mare's Tail (Waterfall)
Birkhill
22
6
Ettrickhill
Ettrick
Buccleuch
808 HART FELL
624 BELL CRAIG
498 LAW KNEIS
735 SADDLE YOKE
Broadgairhill
Ettrick Water
550 BLACK KNOWE
B709
443 THE PIKE
423 CRIB LAW
4
728
474 GREYGILL FELL
692 ETTRICK PEN
16
417
Bridgend
678 CAPEL FELL
5
Moffat
688 LOCH FELL
476 STOCK HILL
Southern Upland Way
Moffat Water
Davington
White Esk
Rae Burn
476 CRAIG FELL
Johnstone
Samye Ling Monastery
6
15
A701
R Annan
Fort
B7076
Eskdalemuir
Clerkhill
188
Lochwood
A701
Newton Wamphray
E
492 BROAD
7
B7020
B7076
Sandyford
B723
S
Megget Water
K
Effgill
Johnstonebridge
16
Annandale Water
Castle O'er
Georgefield
Kirkst
Ann's
B7020
Gillesbie
Boreland
13
Bentpath
B709
Greyrigg
176
A74(M)
Dinwoodie
Dryfe Water
Burnfoot
A
331 HART FELL
177
450 CAULDKINERIG
8
Jardine Hall
Templand
Nethercleuch
Corrie
Water of Milk
Craigcleuch

G   H   J   K   L   M

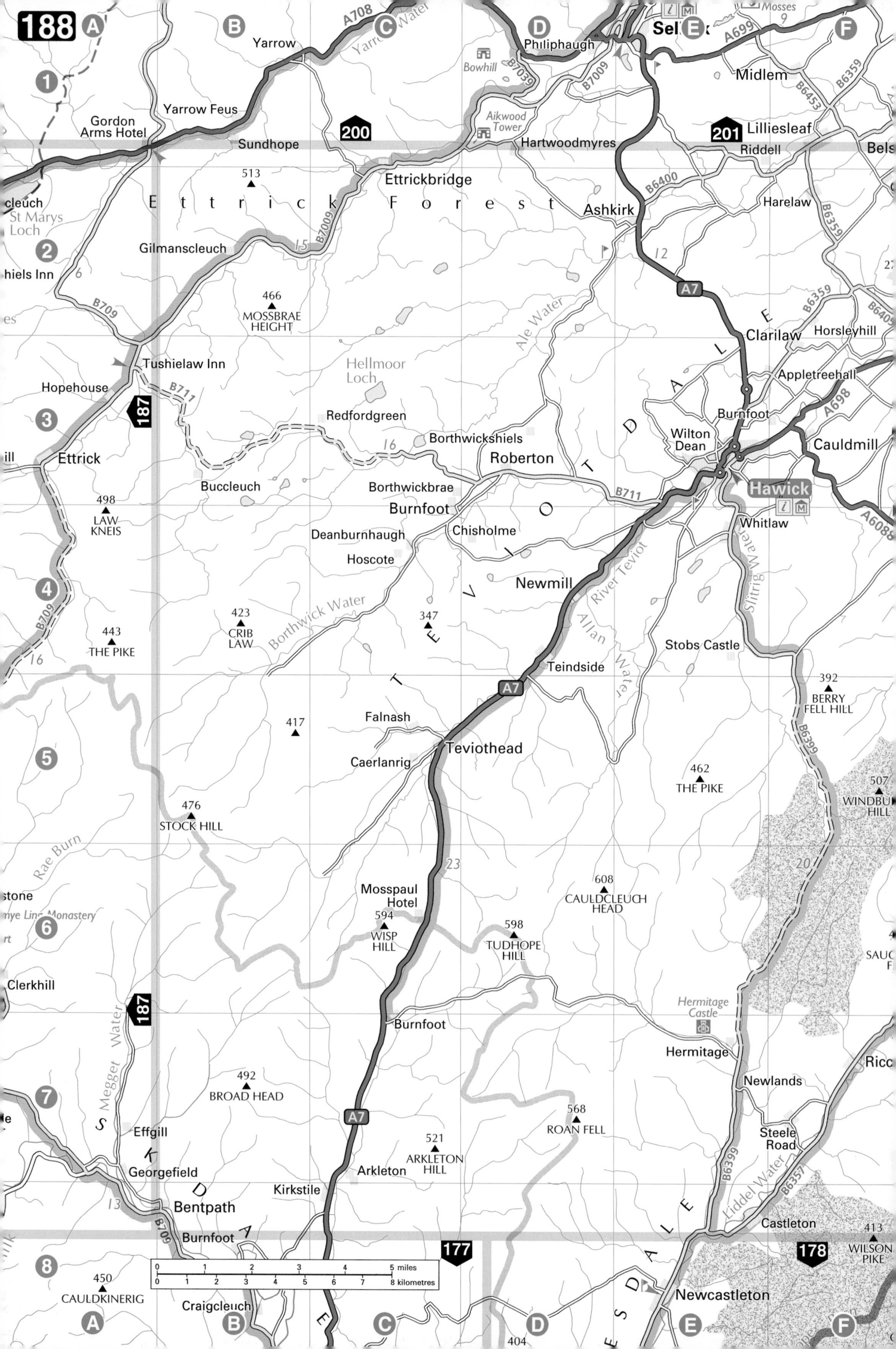

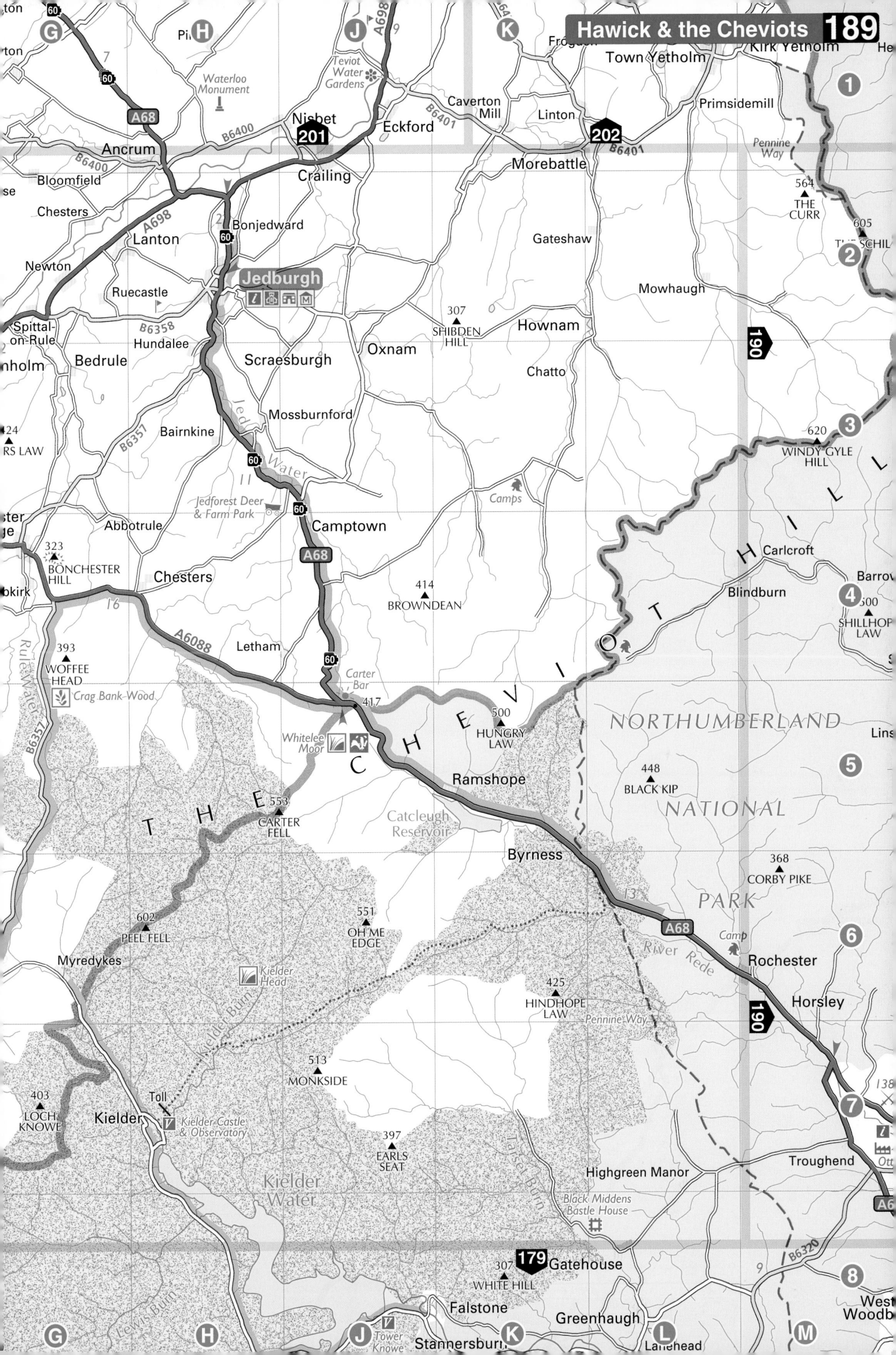

205

Muasdale

Glenacardoch
Point

Belloch

Barr Water

Glenbarr

MacAlister Clan

BEINN AN TUIRC
454

Cleongart

319

BÖRD
MOR
408

Bellochantuy Bay

Bellochantuy

N

Sado

194

SGREADAN
HILL
396

Ugadale

Tangy Loch

Glen Lussa

Peninver

Ardnac
Bay

Kilkenzie

A83

Kilmichael

B842

Machrihanish
Bay

Campbeltown

i

Machrihanish

Campbeltown

Campbeltown
Loch

B842

Island Da

Drumlemble

B843

6

Kilkerran

Kildalloig

Earadale Point

BEINN GHUILEAN
352

Achinhoan

THE
STATE
385

K

CNOC
MOY
446

Conie Glen

Glen Kerran

10

Ru

Dalsmeran

Glen Breakevie

B842

Strone Glen

Cattadale

Polliwilline Bay

BEINN NA LICE

Macharioch

428

Carskey

Southend

MULL
OF
KINTYRE

Dunaverty

Borgadalemore Point

Carskey Bay

Sanda Sound

Sheep Island

Sanda Island

G Carradale

B879

Carradale House

Carradale
Point

Carradale
Bay

dell
ay

K I L B R A N N A N

H Imachar

H Balliekine

J

792
BEINN
NUIS

K

Glen Rosa

Merkland Point

Brodick Castle, Garden
& Country Club

Brodick
Bay

1

Iorsa Water

A R R A N

Brodick

Strathwhillan

Corriegills

Auchagallon
Stone Circle

Machrie
Bay

Machrie

Tormore

Machrie Moor
Stone Circles

B880

512
A'CHRUACH

A841

Clauchlands Point

Margnaheglish

2

Moss Farm Road
Stone Circle

Balmichael

503
BEINN BHREAC

Balmichael

Lamlash

Lamlash
Bay

Holy Island

Torbeg

Shiskine

Cordon

194 Brown Head

Blackwaterfoot

Drumadoon
Bay

Kilpatrick

Kilpatrick Dun

Glen Scorrodale

Carn Ban

Auchencairn

Kingscross
Knockenkelly

Whiting Bay

Whiting
Bay

3

Glen Ashdale

Largymore

Corriecravie

Kilmory Water

Largybeg

Dippen Head

Torr a' Chaisteal Fort

Sliddery

Dippen

Kilmory

Lagg

Bennan

Torrylin
Cairn

Kildonan

4

Bennan Head

Pladda

195

5

6

7

340 Ailsa Craig

RSPB

8

G   H   J   K   L   M

Loch Ciàran
Loch Garasdale

A B R C **206** D E Cock of Arran F

1

Crossaig

247 ▲
CRUACH MHIC GOUGAIN

264 ▲
CNOC-AN T- SAMHLAIDH

Rhunahaorine

Cour Bay

Cour

Lochranza ⌂ Castle
Catacol
V
Glen Chalmadale 8

A841

2

Grogport
Barmollack

Pirnmill

Penrioch

North Arran

Glen Catacol

Loch Tanna

834 ▲
CAISTEAL ABHAIL

205

38

354 ▲
CRUACH NAN GABHAR

Whitefarland

715 ▲
BEINN BHARRAIN

Glen Iorsa

874
GOATFELL

3

ale

Water

B842

39

B879

Carradale

Imachar

Balliekine

792 ▲
BEINN NUIS

Glen Rosa

Bridgend
Dippen
Carradale House

Iorsa Water

A R R A N

Br

Carradale Point

Carradale Bay

Auchagallon Stone Circle

Machrie

4

319 ▲

454 ▲
BEINN AN TUIRC

Torrisdale

512 ▲
A'CHRUACH

408 ▲
BÒRD MÒR

Machrie Bay

Machrie Moor Stone Circles

B880

192

Saddell

Tormore

Moss Farm Road Stone Circle

Balmichael V

503 ▲
BEINN BHREAC

Saddell Bay

Balmichael

5

396 ▲
SGREADAN HILL

Ugadale

Torbeg

Shiskine

Glen Scorrodale

Blackwaterfoot

Carn Ban

Drumadoon Bay

Kilpatrick

Kilpatrick Dun

Glen Lussa

Brown Head

Ardnacross Bay

193

B842

Peninver

Corriecravie

Sliddery

Kilmory Water

6

Kilm ael

i

Campbeltown

Torr a' Chaisteal Fort

Kilmory

Lagg

Bennan

Campbeltown Loch

Island Davarr

Torrylin Cairn

Kilkerran

Kildalloig

Bennan Head

7

352 ▲
BEINN GHUILEAN

Achinhoan

Glen Kerran

Ru Stafnish

8

0 1 2 3 4 5 miles
0 1 2 3 4 5 6 7 8 kilometres

A B C D E F

Polliwilline Bay

G

H

J

207

K

Garroch Head

Ga___ty

Garroch Head

Little Cumbrae Island

Fairlie Ro__

__cko

B780

1

Drakemyre

Blackshaw

Munnoch

B780

B781

B780

B714

A737

Dalgarven Mill

Dalry

High

Portencross

Farland Head

B7048

Hunterston Power Station

12

West Kilbride

C

L

U

B780

Dalgarven

7

N

Seamill

B7047

A78

B780

A78

Kilwinning

2

B778

A738

A737

A78

30

30

B78_

Ardrossan

A738

Stevenston

Horse Isle

B780

Ardeer

nnox

Saltcoats

196

B779

Irvine

Maritime

Corrie

3

30

Merkland Point

V

4

Fulla

__dick Castle, Garden Country Club

Irvine Bay

Ga

Brodick Bay

F I R T H

Strathwhillan

Corriegills

O F

Clauchlands Point

C L Y D E

Baras

Margnaheglish

(Mar-Oct)

__sh

Lamlash Bay

Holy Island

Troon

Cordon

Larne

Royal

__chencairn

Kingscross

Knockenkelly

5

4

(May-Sept)

Whiting Bay

Pr

__iting Bay

V

Whiting Bay

Ashdale

Largymore

Ne

Largybeg

6

Ayr Bay

Dippen

Dippen Head

i

M

A

Kildonan

196

__da

Heads of Ayr

Heads of Ayr

Doonfo_

Burns Cotta

Fisherton

A719

7

Robe

Bir

Dunure

Culroy

Drumshang

Croy Brae (Electric Brae)

Knoweside

8

Culzean Bay

Culzean Castle & Country __k

182

Pennyglen

Whitefaulas

G

H

J

K

L

M

A7

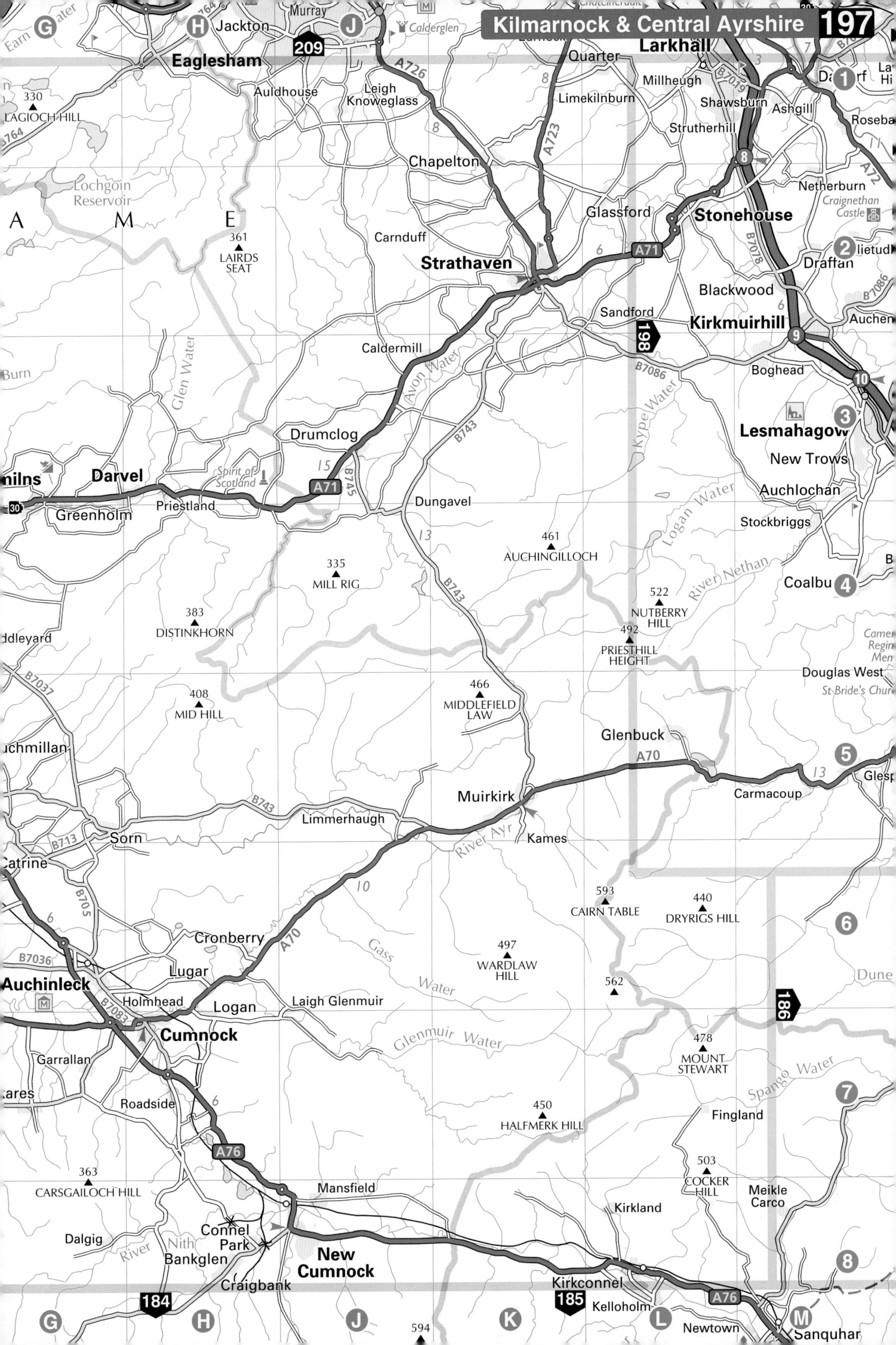

G   H Jackton   J   Calderglen   Larkhall   1

Eaglesham
Murray
209
A726
Quarter
Millheugh
Shawsburn   Ashgill   Roseba
Dalserf   La
Hi

Auldhouse
Leigh Knoweglass
Limekilnburn
Strutherhill
8
A72

330
LAGIOCH HILL
B764
A   M   E
8
Chapelton
A723
Struther hill
8
Netherburn
Craignethan Castle

361
LAIRDS SEAT
Carnduff
Glassford
A71
A726
Stonehouse
2   lietud
Draffan
B7078

Strathaven
6
Blackwood
B7086
Auchen

Lochgoin Reservoir
Caldermill
Sandford
Kirkmuirhill
9

198
Boghead
10

Drumclog
B743
Lesmahagow
3

A71
15
B745
New Trows

Darvel
Priestland
Dungavel
Auchlochan
ilns
30
Greenholm
13
Stockbriggs
461
AUCHINGILLOCH
Logan Water
Coalbu   4

335
MILL RIG
B743
522
NUTBERRY HILL
River Nethan

383
DISTINKHORN
492
PRIESTHILL HEIGHT
Camer Regin Men

ddleyard
B7037
Douglas West
St Bride's Chur

408
MID HILL
466
MIDDLEFIELD LAW

uchmillan
Glenbuck
A70
5
Glesp

B743
Carmacoup
13

Sorn
Limmerhaugh
Muirkirk
B713
Kames

Catrine
593
CAIRN TABLE
440
DRYRIGS HILL
6

Cronberry
A70
10
River Ayr
Gass
497
WARDLAW HILL
Dune

B7036
Lugar
Logan
Laigh Glenmuir
Water
562
186

Auchinleck
Holmhead
B7083
478
MOUNT STEWART

Cumnock
Glenmuir Water
Garrallan
Roadside
6
450
HALFMERK HILL
Fingland
7

ares
363
CARSGAILOCH HILL
A76
503
COCKER HILL
Meikle Carco

Mansfield
Kirkland

Dalgig
Connel Park
New Cumnock
Kirkconnel
185
A76
8

Bankglen
River Nith
Craigbank
Kelloholm
Newtown
Sanquhar

184
G   H   J   594   K   185   L   M

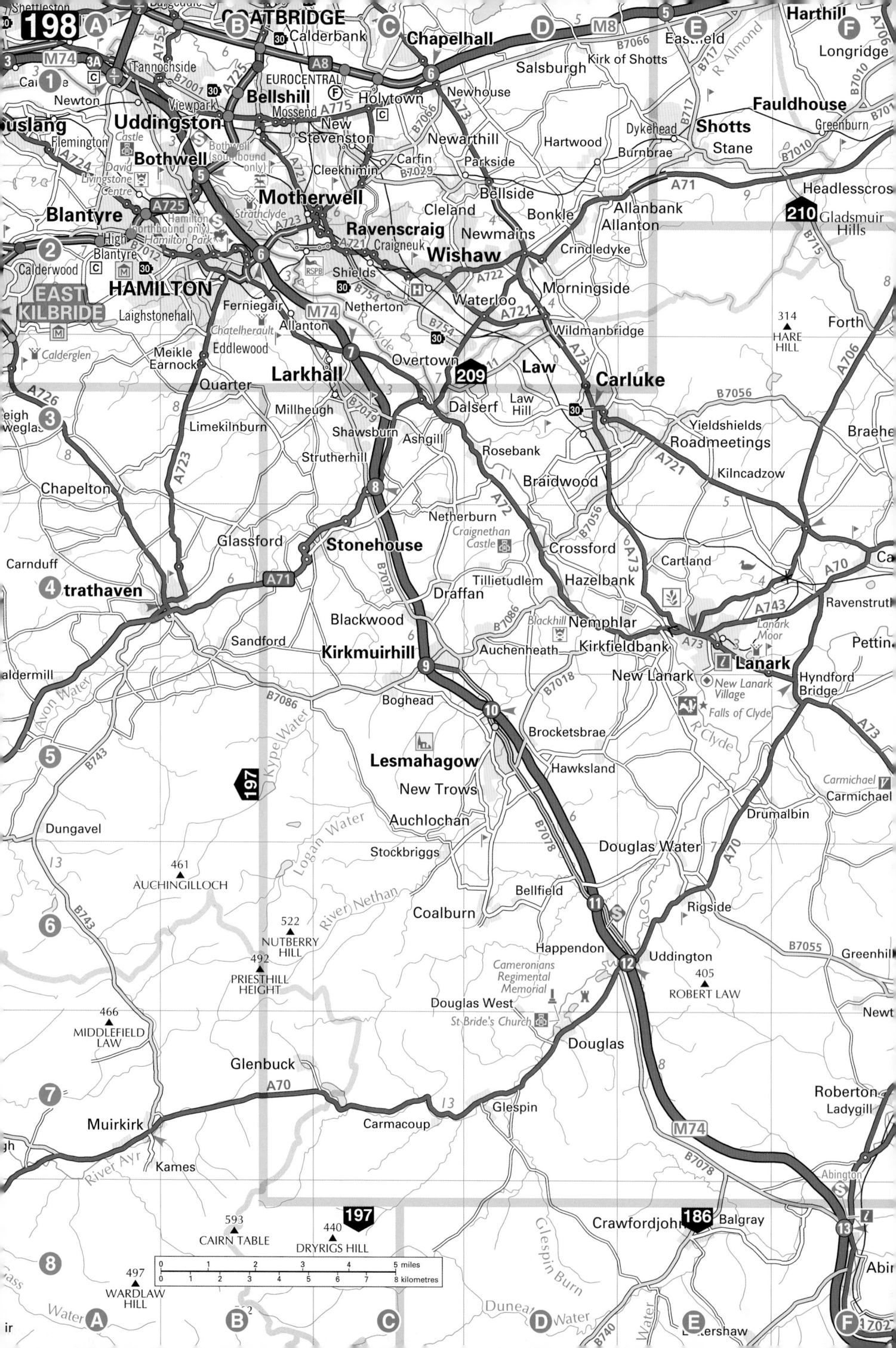

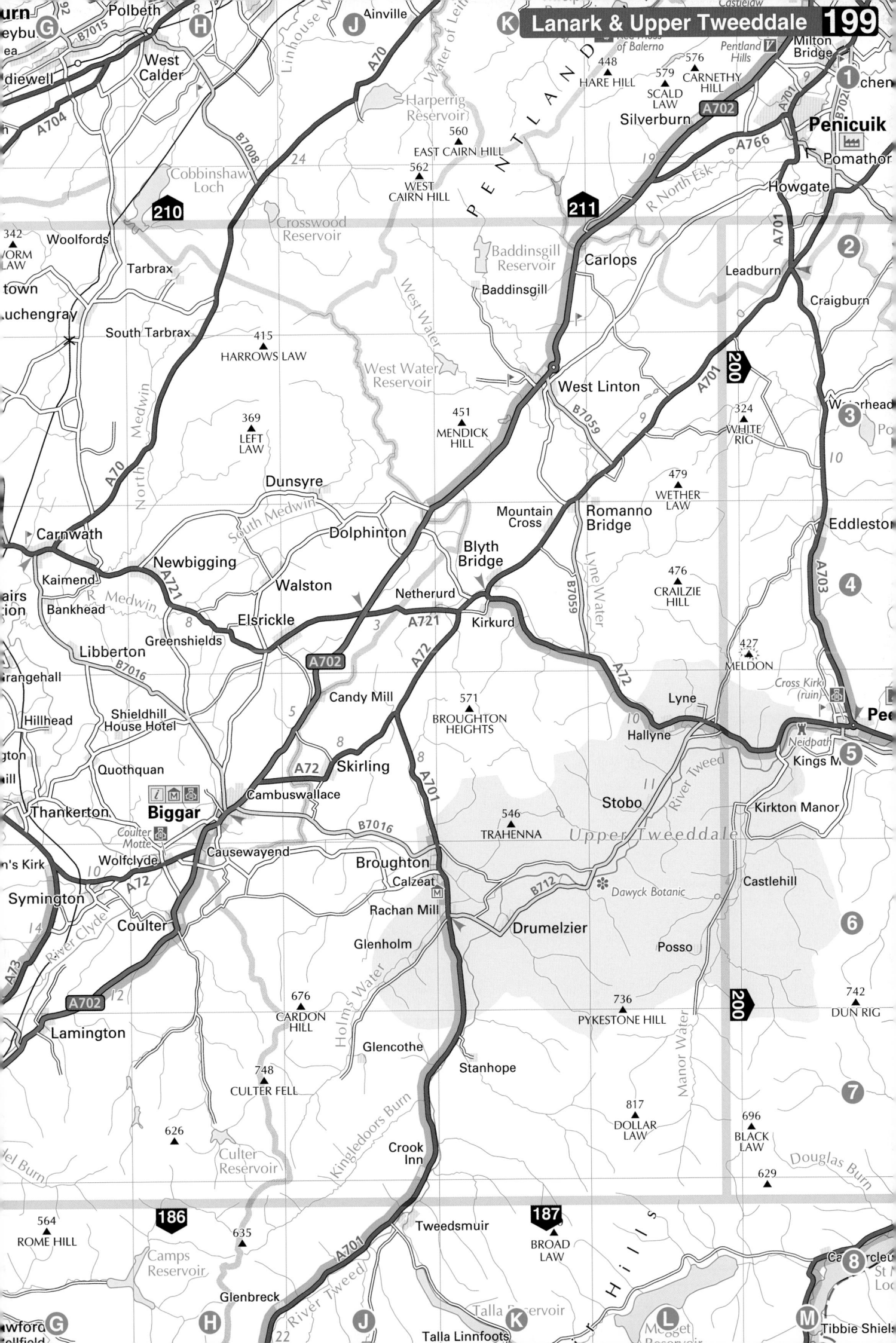

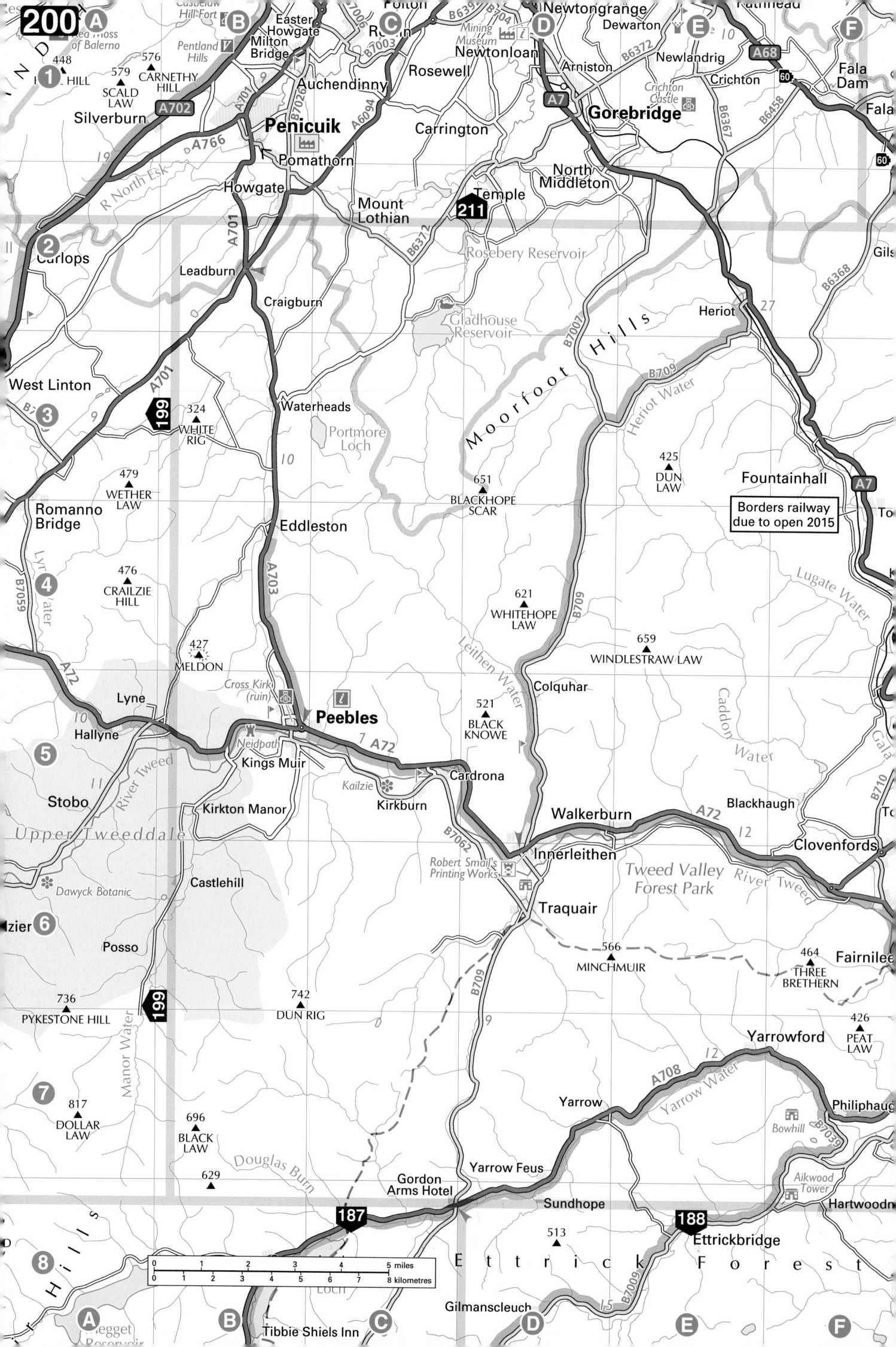

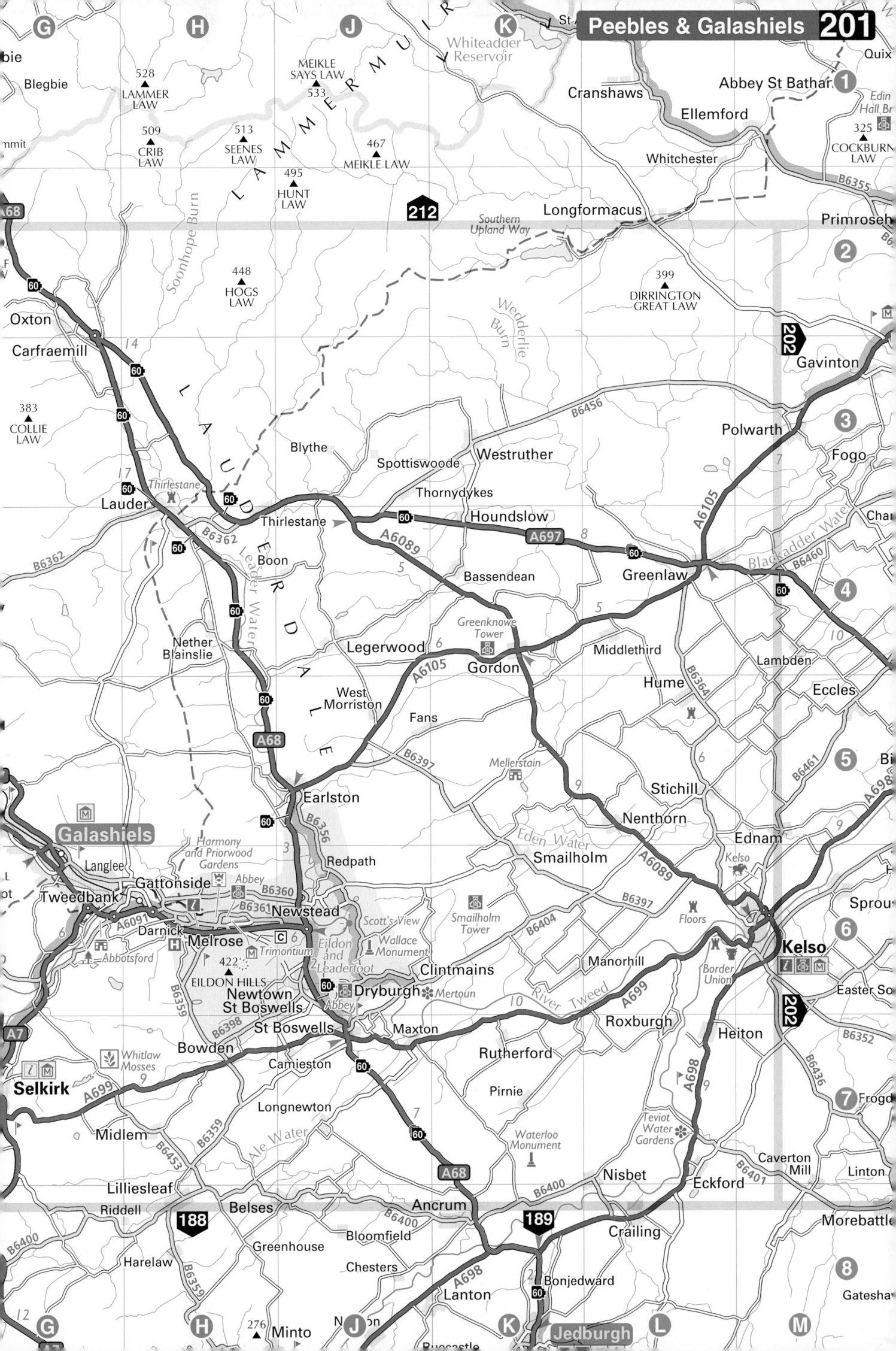

G   H   J   K   St

1

Quix

Whiteadder
Reservoir

Blegbie

Cranshaws
Abbey St Bathar...

Ellemford

528
LAMMER
LAW

MEIKLE
SAYS LAW

533

Whitchester

Edin
Hall Br

325
COCKBURN
LAW

509
CRIB
LAW

513
SEENES
LAW

467
MEIKLE
LAW

Longformacus

Primroseh

B6355

mmit

A68

495
HUNT
LAW

212

Southern
Upland Way

2

60

448
HOGS
LAW

Wedderlie
Burn

399
DIRRINGTON
GREAT LAW

202

Oxton

Carfraemill

Gavinton

60

14

A6105

Polwarth

3

Fogo

383
COLLIE
LAW

17

60

Thirlestane

Blythe

Spottiswoode

Westruther

7

60

Lauder

B6362

60

Thirlestane

A6089

Thornydykes

Houndslow

Blackadder Water

Cha

B6460

60

Boon

5

A697

8

60

Greenlaw

4

B6362

Nether
Blainslie

60

Bassendean

B6364

10

Greenknowe
Tower

Middlethird

Lambden

Legerwood

6

A6105

Gordon

Hume

Eccles

West
Morriston

60

Fans

5

B6461

5

Mellerstain

Stichill

Bi

A68

B6397

Nenthorn

Ednam

A698

Galashiels

Earlston

Eden Water

60

B6356

Smailholm

A6089

Kelso

Langlee

Harmony
and Priorwood
Gardens

3

Redpath

Kelso

6

Gattonside

Abbey

B6360

Newstead

B6404

Border
Union

Sprou

Tweedbank

A6091

Darnick

B6361

Smailholm
Tower

Floors

Kelso

Melrose

C 6

Scott's View

Wallace
Monument

Clintmains

Manorhill

202

Easter So

Abbotsford

Trimontium

Eildon
and
Leaderfoot

Mertoun

Heiton

B6352

422

60

Dryburgh

River Tweed

A699

Roxburgh

B6436

EILDON HILLS

Newtown
St Boswells

Abbey

Maxton

10

Rutherford

A698

7

B6359

St Boswells

Rutherford

Pirnie

Frogd

A7

Bowden

Camieston

60

Waterloo
Monument

Teviot
Water
Gardens

Whitlaw
Mosses

9

Longnewton

7

Caverton
Mill

Selkirk

A699

60

Nisbet

Eckford

B6401

Linton

Midlem

A68

B6400

188

Belses

Ancrum

189

Crailing

Morebattle

Lilliesleaf

B6453

Greenhouse

B6400

Riddell

Bloomfield

Chesters

A698

60

Bonjedward

8

B6400

Harelaw

B6359

A698

Lanton

Gatesha

12

G   H   **J** Nton   **K**   **Jedburgh**   L   M

276
Minto

Buccastle

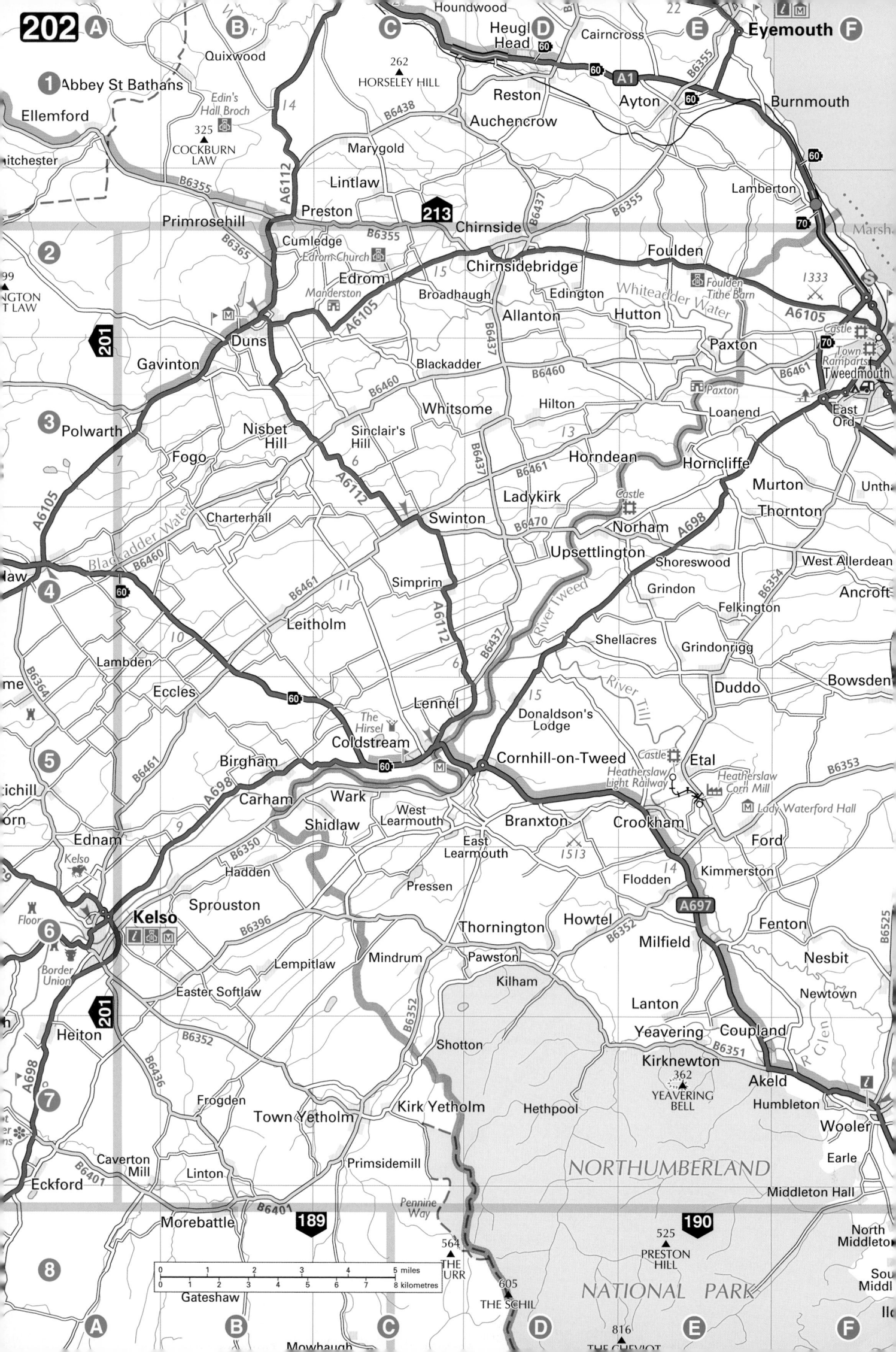

G   H   J

1
2
3
4
5
6
7
8

vs Bay

humberland
ge Coast

luds
lead
erston

Cheswick

CAUSEWAY
FLOODED
AT HIGH TIDE

Goswick

HOLY ISLAND

Haggerston

Holy
Island

Beal

Lindisfarne
Castle
Lindisfarne
Priory

Fenham

Castle Point

Guile Point

West
Kyloe

6353

owick

Fenwick

Longstone
Lighthouse

FARNE
ISLANDS

Buckton

Smeafield   Elwick

Staple
Sound

Detchant

Ross

North Northumberland
Heritage Coast

Holburn

Low
Middleton

Budle
Bay

Bamburgh

Inner
Sound

St Cuthbert's
Cave

Middleton

Easington

B1342

Bamburgh

Hetton
Steads

Belford

Waren
Mill

Budle

B1340

North
Hazelrigg

Outchester

Spindlestone   Burton

New
Shoreston

Seahouses

B6349

Bradford

South
Hazelrigg

Bellshill

Elford

North Sunderland

East
Horton

Warenton

Lucker

60
Adderstone

Chatton

Warenford

Newham

Beadnell

Swinhoe

Newstead

Chathill   Tughall

Beadnell
Bay

Wild Cattle
Park

Ros
Castle

Ellingham

Preston

Newton-by-the-Sea

newtown

Chillingham

190

Hepburn

267
CATERAN
HILL

Brownieside

North
Charlton

West
Ditchburn

South
Charlton

Preston
Pele Tower

191   Brunton

Doxford

Fallodon

Christon
Bank

Embleton &
Newton Links

Embleton

Embleton
Bay

Old Bewick

B6346 Harehope

Dunstan
Steads

Dunstanburgh Castle

Dunstan

G   H   J   K   L   M

River Till
A1
B1341
B6348
B347
B1339
B1340
15
60
9
14

A B C D 214 E F

1

Rudha
Bholsa

36
SGAR
BREA

Nave Island

Ardnave
Point

Gortantaoid
Point

Bunnahabha

2

Ton Mhòr

Kilnave

316
GUIR-
BHEINN

Eilean Mòr

Sanaigmore

Loch Gruinart

Finlaggan

Rudha Lamanais

Loch
Gòrr

Lecht Gruinart

RSPB

Loch
Finlaggan

Kiells

3

Saligo Bay

Loch
Gorm

B8018

B8017

Gruinart

Gleann Mòr

Ballygrant

8

Coul Point

Sunderland

B8018

A846

Ba
L

Machir
Bay

Kilchoman

A847

Bruichladdich

Loch
Indaal

Bridgend

Gartachossan

4

Kilchiaran Bay

ISLAY

Bowmore

3

Kilennan Burn

15
M

Port
Charlotte

ISLAY

Lossit Bay

RHINNS OF

231
BEINN TART A'MHILL

River Laggan

Duich R.

A846

B8016

454
BEINN URARA
Loch

5

Nereabolls

Rudha na
Faing

Portnahaven

A847

Port Wemyss

Glenegedale

Orsay

RHINNS
POINT

Laggan

Islay

Bay

346
BEINN SHOLUM

6

Rudha Mòr

Kintra

7

MAOL BUIDHE
165

THE OA

Lower
Killeyan

Risabus

Port
Ellen

A846

Arc
Lagav

Laphroaig

3

Texa

Kilnaughton Bay

RSPB

Kinnabus

American
Monument

Loch
Kinnabus

MULL
OF OA

Rudha nan Leacan

8

0   1   2   3   4   5 miles
0   1   2   3   4   5   6   7   8 kilometres

A B C D E F

G H J K

1

506
▲
SCRINADLE

398
▲
BEINN
TARSUINN

Danna
Island

St Cormac's
Chapel

Jura Forest

784
▲
BEINN
AN OIR

Loch a'
Chnuic Bhric

734
▲

Paps of Jura

Kilmory Knap
Chapel

Kilmory

Kilmory Bay

2

24

Knockrome

Ardfernal

Point of Knap

Jura

JURA

206

560
▲
GLASS BHEINN

Feolin Ferry

Keils

Small
Isles

Coulaghailtro

3

Kilberry
Sculptured
Stones

529
▲
DUBHA
BHEINN

Craighouse

A846

Kilberry

342
▲
BRAT
BHEINN

Rudha na Gaillich

Kilberry Head

213
▲
CRUACH A

Cabrach

Keppoch Point

Tiretigan

Am Fraoch
Eilean

Rudha na Tràille

4

Brosdale
Island

Loch Stornoway

NAM
ANN

Ard

McArthur's
Head

Port Askaig · Kennacraig

We

5

GEIR

Rudha Liath

Ronan Poir

Ardtalla

Claggain
Bay

Kinerarach

Tarbert

Kintour

Ardmore
Point

GIGHA

Rhunahaorine
Point

6

Kildalton
Cross

Port Ellen · Kennacraig

Ardminish

Rhunahaorine

Eilean
a' Chuirn

Achamore

38

194

Tayinloan

7

Rudha na
Gainmhich

Cara

A83

8

Muasdale

Glenacardoch
Point

Belloch

Glenbarr

G H J K L M

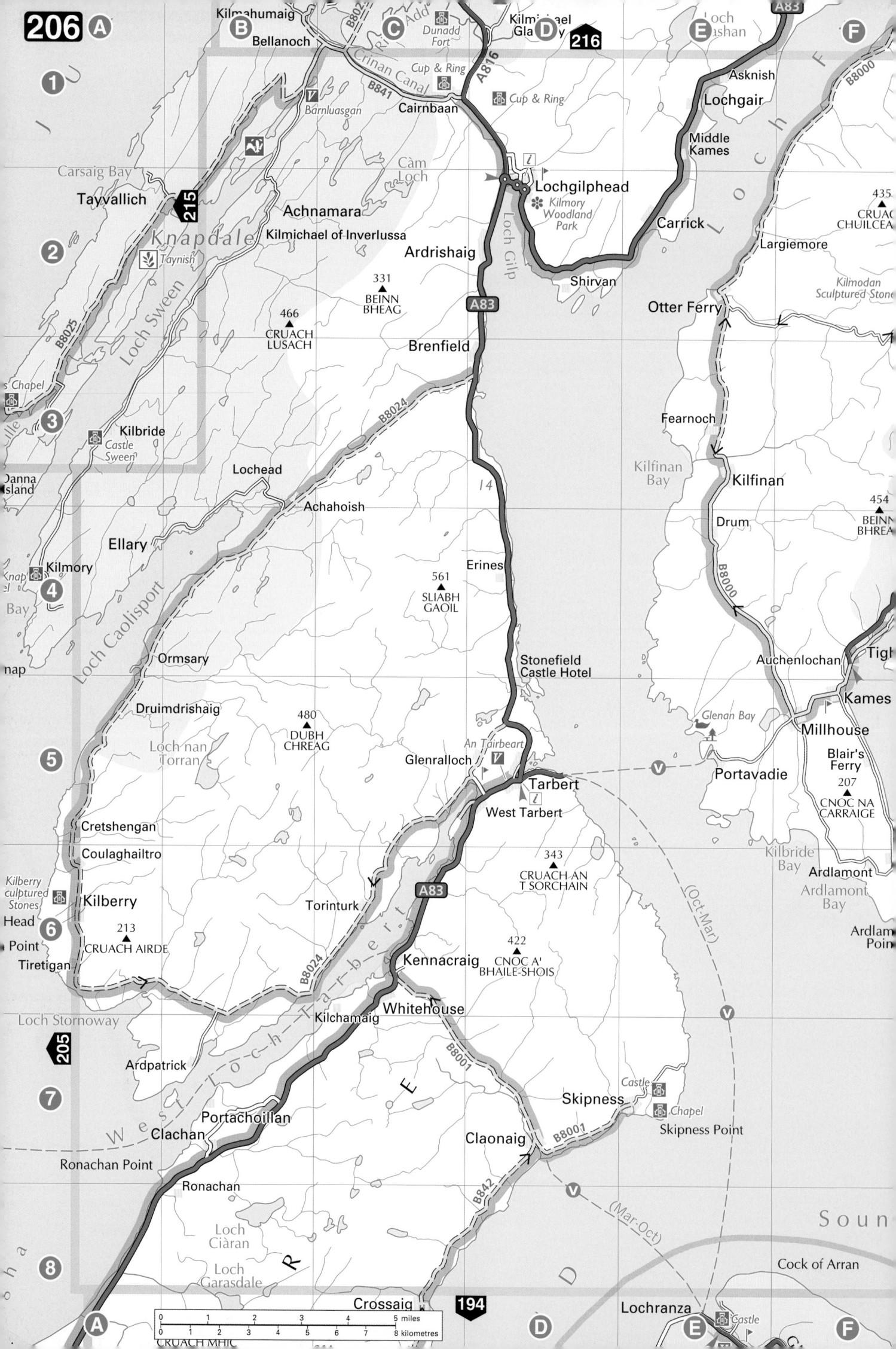

A   B   C   D   E   F

1

Kilmahumaig
Bellanoch
B802
Kilmichael
Gla y
Loch
ashan

Dunadd
Fort
Crinan Canal
B841
Cup & Ring
A816
216
A83
B8000
Asknish
Lochgair
Middle
Kames

Barnluasgan
Cairnbaan
Cup & Ring
Càm
Loch
i
Lochgilphead
Kilmory
Woodland
Park
Carrick

Carsaig Bay
215
Tayvallich
Achnamara
Kilmichael of Inverlussa
Knapdale
Taynish
Ardrishaig
Loch Gilp
Shirvan
Otter Ferry
435
CRUAC
CHUILCEA
Largiemore
Kilmodan
Sculptured Stone

2

331
BEINN
BHEAG
A83
Erines
Loch Sween
B8025

466
CRUACH
LUSACH
Brenfield
B8024
14
Fearnoch
Kilfinan
Bay
Kilfinan

3

Chapel
Kilbride
Castle
Sween
Lochead
Achahoish
Drum
454
BEINN
BHREA

4

Ellary
Kilmory
Knap
el
Bay
561
SLIABH
GAOIL
B8000

5

Ormsary
Loch Caolisport
Stonefield
Castle Hotel
Auchenlochan
Tigh
Glenan Bay
Kames

Druimdrishaig
480
DUBH
CHREAG
An Tairbeart
Glenralloch
V
V
Portavadie
Millhouse
Blair's
Ferry
207
CNOC NA
CARRAIGE

6

Cretshengan
Coulaghailtro
Tarbert
West Tarbert
Kilbride
Bay
Ardlamont
Ardlamont
Bay
Ardla
Poin

Kilberry
culptured
Stones
Kilberry
Loch nan
Torran
213
CRUACH AIRDE
Torinturk
A83
343
CRUACH AN
T SORCHAIN
Ardlam
Poin

Head
Point
Tiretigan
Kennacraig
422
CNOC A'
BHAILE-SHOIS
West Loch Tarbert
B8024

7

205
Loch Stornoway
Kilchamaig
Whitehouse
B8001
Skipness
Castle
(Oct-Mar)
V
V
Ardpatrick
Chapel

8

Portachoillan
Clachan
Claonaig
Skipness Point
B8001
E
Ronachan Point
B842
Ronachan
Loch
Ciàran
V
(Mar-Oct)
S o u n
Loch
Garasdale
R
Cock of Arran

A   B   C   D   E   F

Crossaig
194
Lochranza
Castle

0 1 2 3 4 5 miles
0 1 2 3 4 5 6 7 8 kilometres

CRUACH MHIC

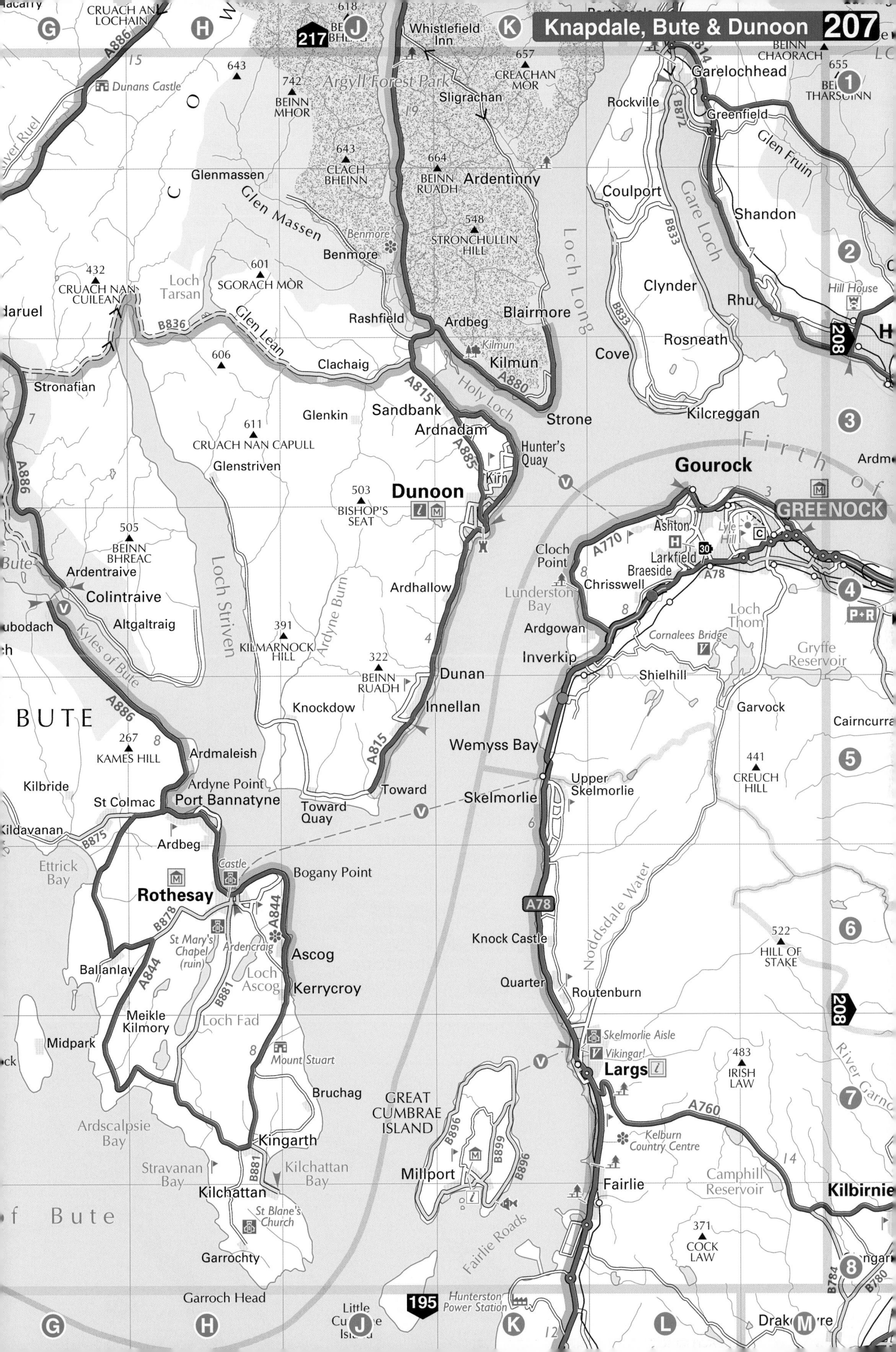

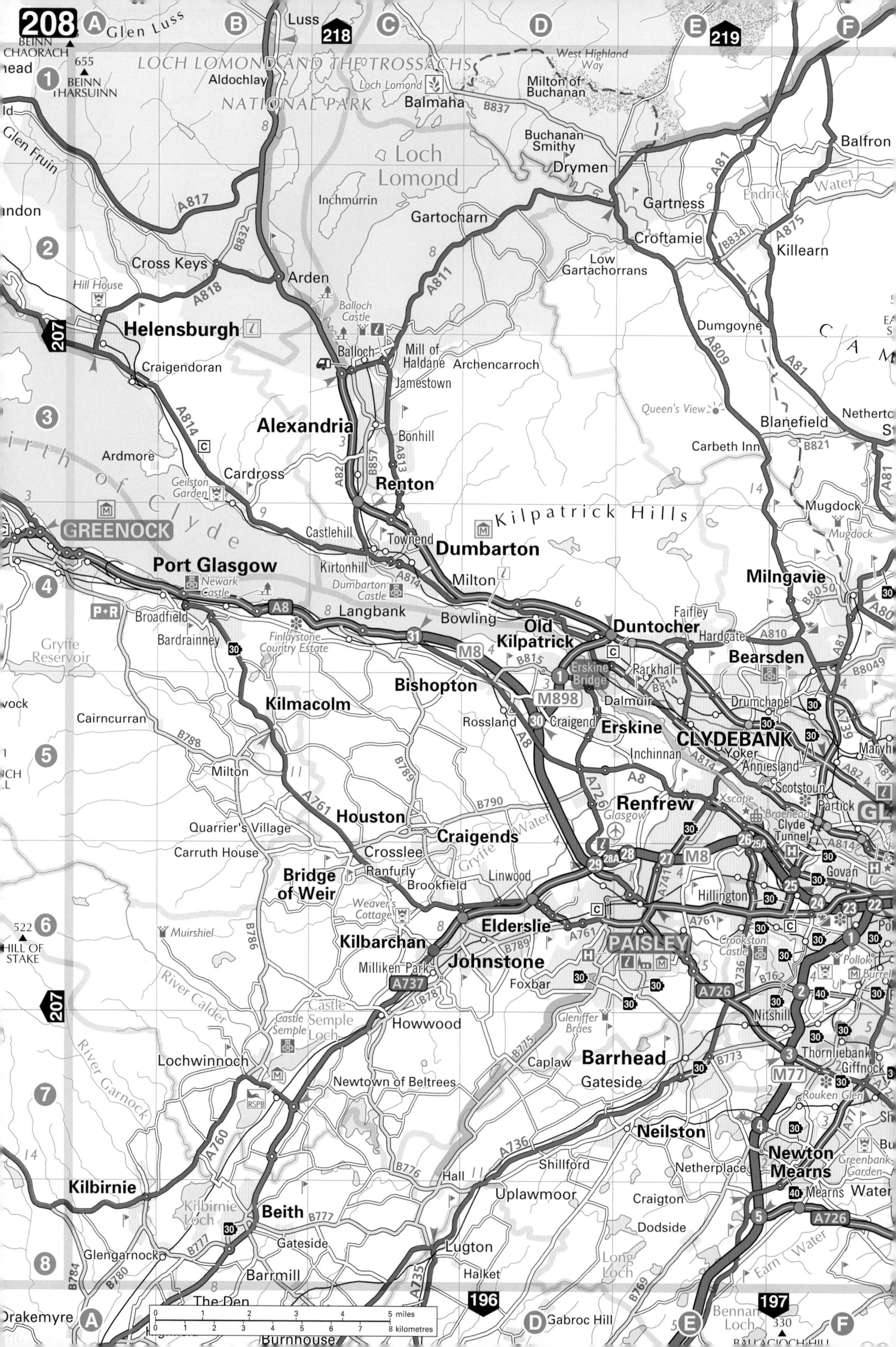

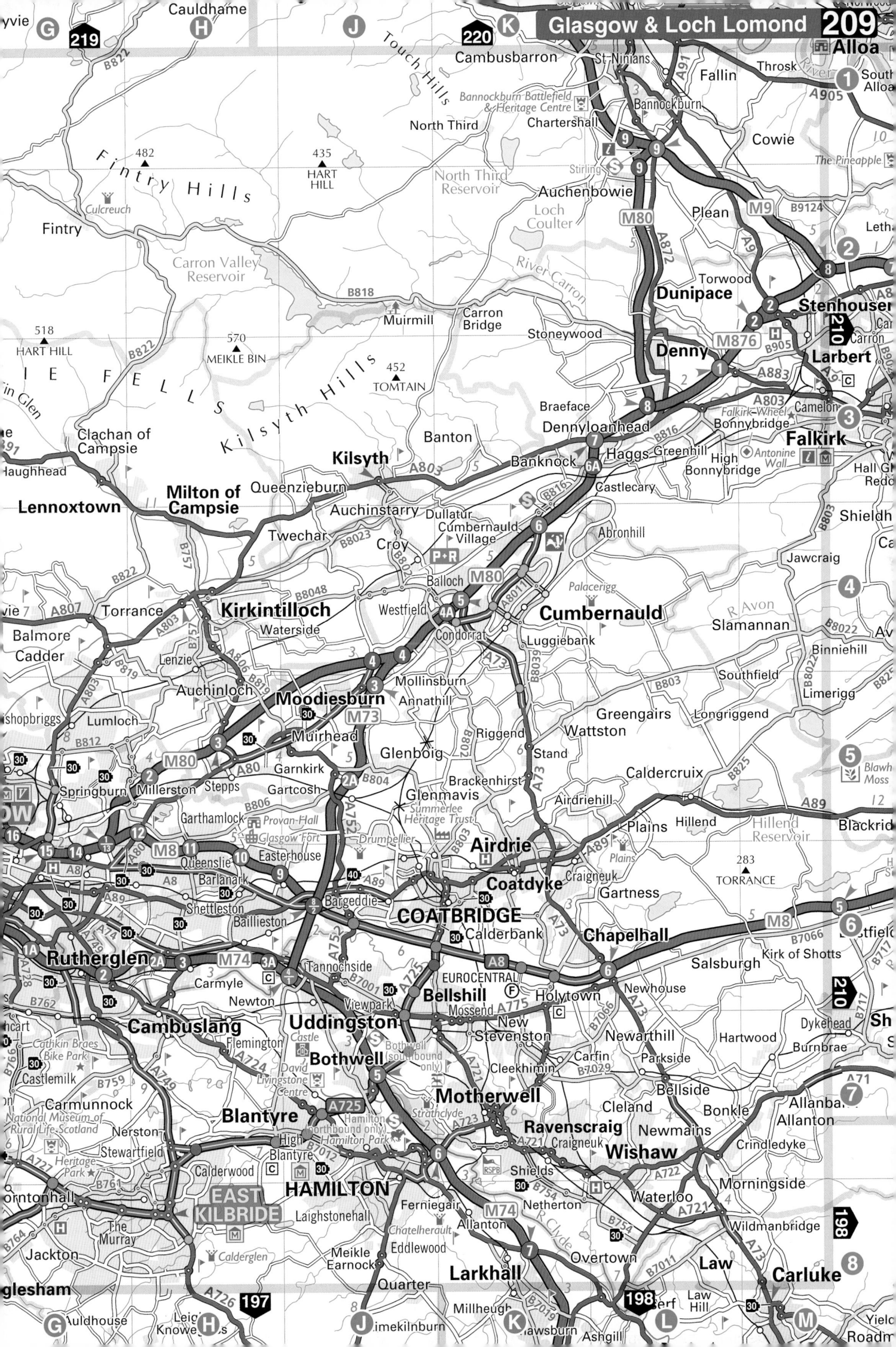

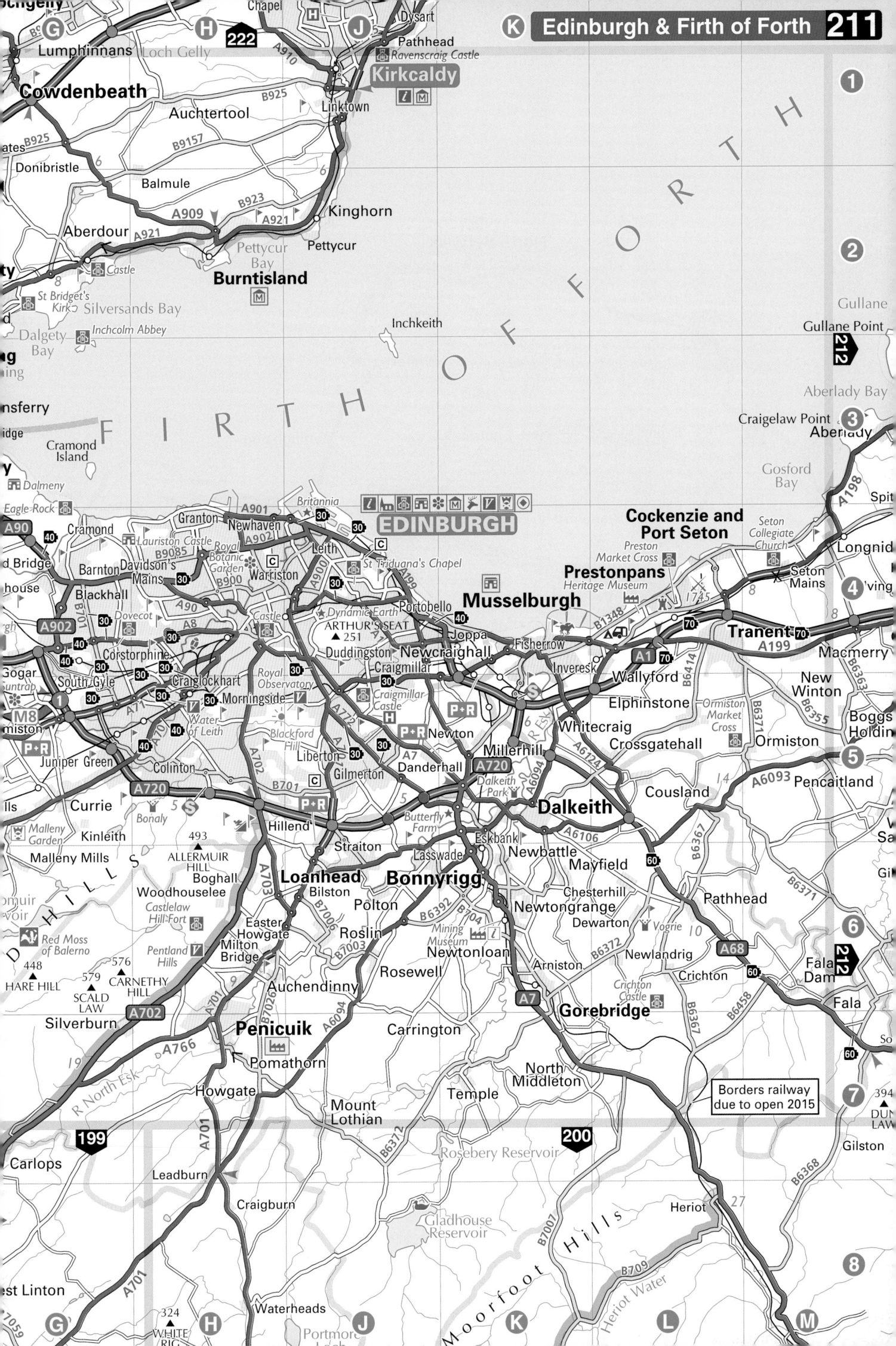

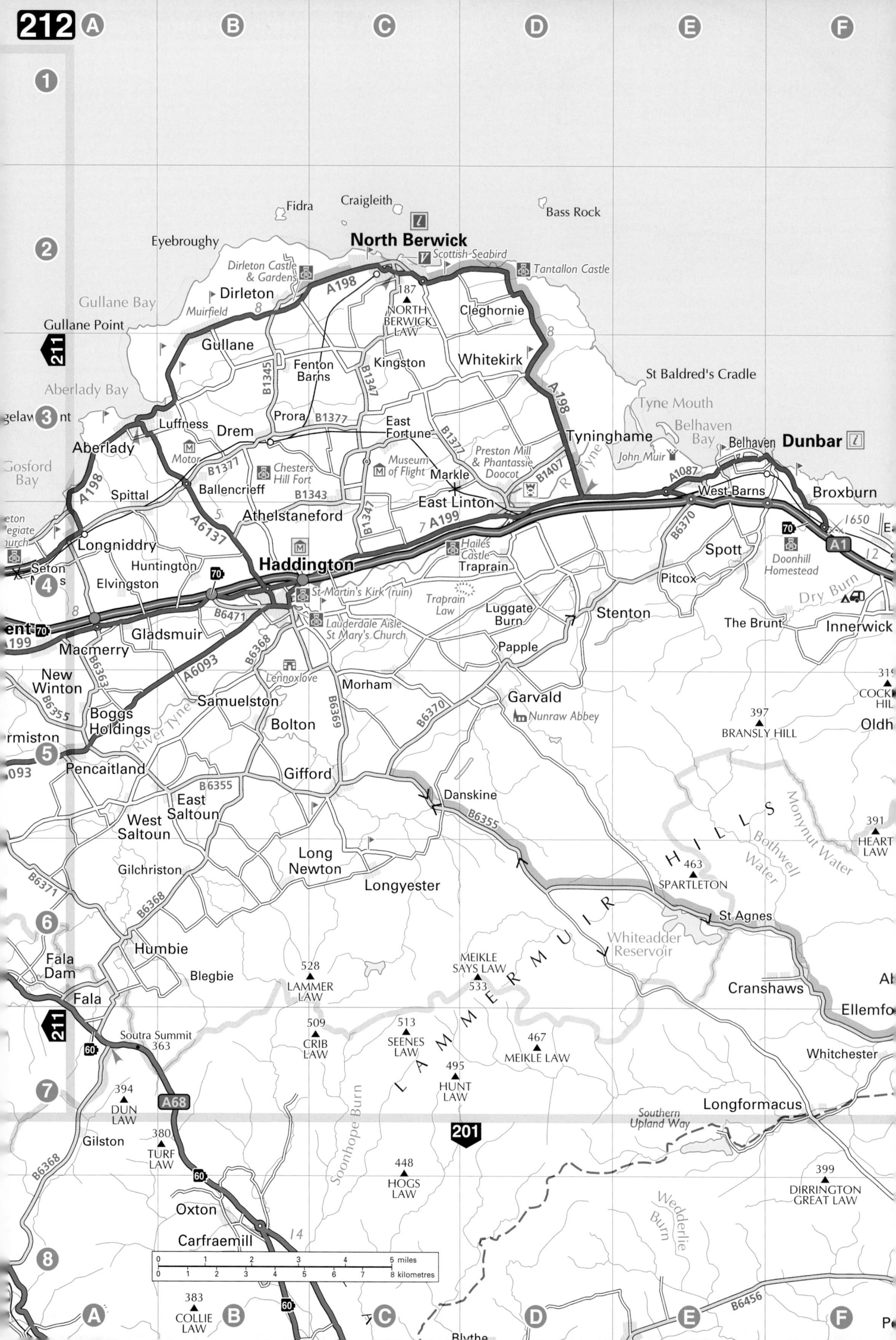

G H J

1
2
3
4
5
6
7
8

ess

Chapel Point

Thorntonloch
60
owhill

Reed
Point
Dunglass   Cove
Collegiate   60
Church   Cockburnspath

ks

Pease
Bay

Siccar
Point

Fast Castle Head

A1107

Pease Dean

Ecclaw

196
BROWN
RIG

Coldingham
Loch

ST ABB'S HEAD

St Abbs

Coldingham
Bay

60   Grantshouse

Southern
Upland Way   Butterdean

Eye Water

Quixwood

Bathans

Edin's
Hall Broch

325
COCKBURN
LAW

B6355

Primrosehill

Houndwood

Heugh
Head   60

262
HORSELEY HILL

B6438

Auchencrow

Marygold

Lintlaw

Preston

Coldingham

B6438

A1107   22

Cairncross

Reston

Ayton   60

60   A1

Eyemouth

Burnmouth

60

Lamberton

B6437

B6355

Chirnside

202

Foulden

70

Marshall Meadows Bay

Cumledge

Edrom Church

Chirnsidebridge

North Northumberlan
Heritage Coast

B6365

Edrom

Manderston

Broadhaugh

Edington

Allanton

Hutton

Whiteadder Water

Foulden
Tithe Barn

1333

A6105

S

Berwick-upo

A6112

15

A6105

Duns

Gavinton

Paxton

Castle
Town
Ramparts
70

Barracks

H

Blackadder

B6437

B6460

Whitsome

Hilton

13

Paxton

Loanend

East
Ord

Tweedmouth

Spittal

Huds
Head

Nisbet
Hill

Sinclair's
Hill

G H J K L M

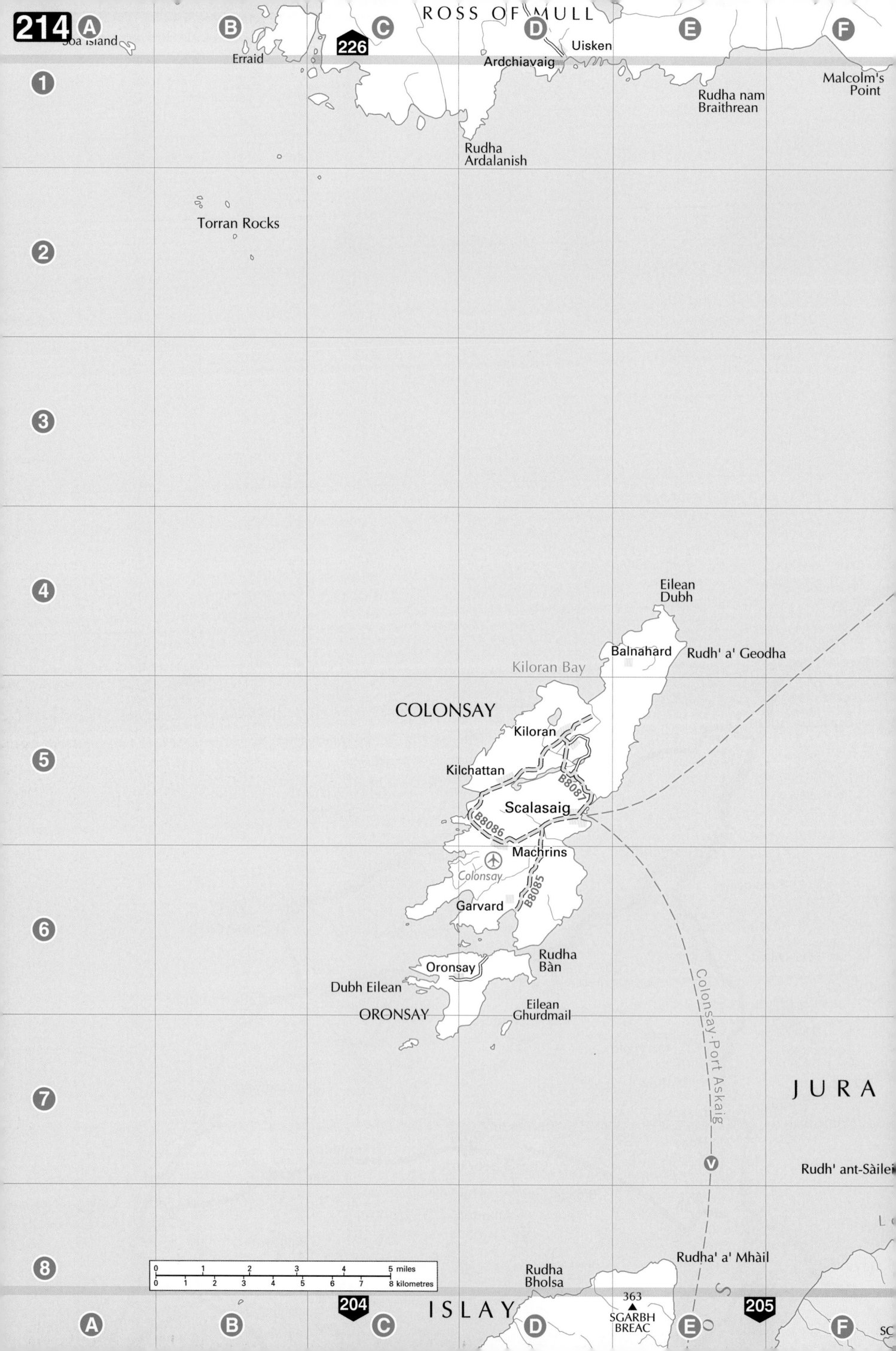

A B C D E F

ROSS OF MULL

Soa Island

Erraid

Uisken

Ardchiavaig

Rudha nam
Braithrean

Malcolm's
Point

Rudha
Ardalanish

Torran Rocks

Eilean
Dubh

Balnahard   Rudh' a' Geodha

Kiloran Bay

COLONSAY

Kiloran

Kilchattan

B8087

Scalasaig

B8086

Machrins

Colonsay

B8085

Garvard

Rudha
Bàn

Oronsay

Dubh Eilean

ORONSAY

Eilean
Ghurdmail

Colonsay-Port Askaig

JURA

Rudh' ant-Sàilei

V

Rudha' a' Mhàil

Rudha
Bholsa

363
▲
SGARBH
BREAC

ISLAY

0	1	2	3	4	5 miles
0	1	2	3	4	5	6	7	8 kilometres

A B C D E F

SC

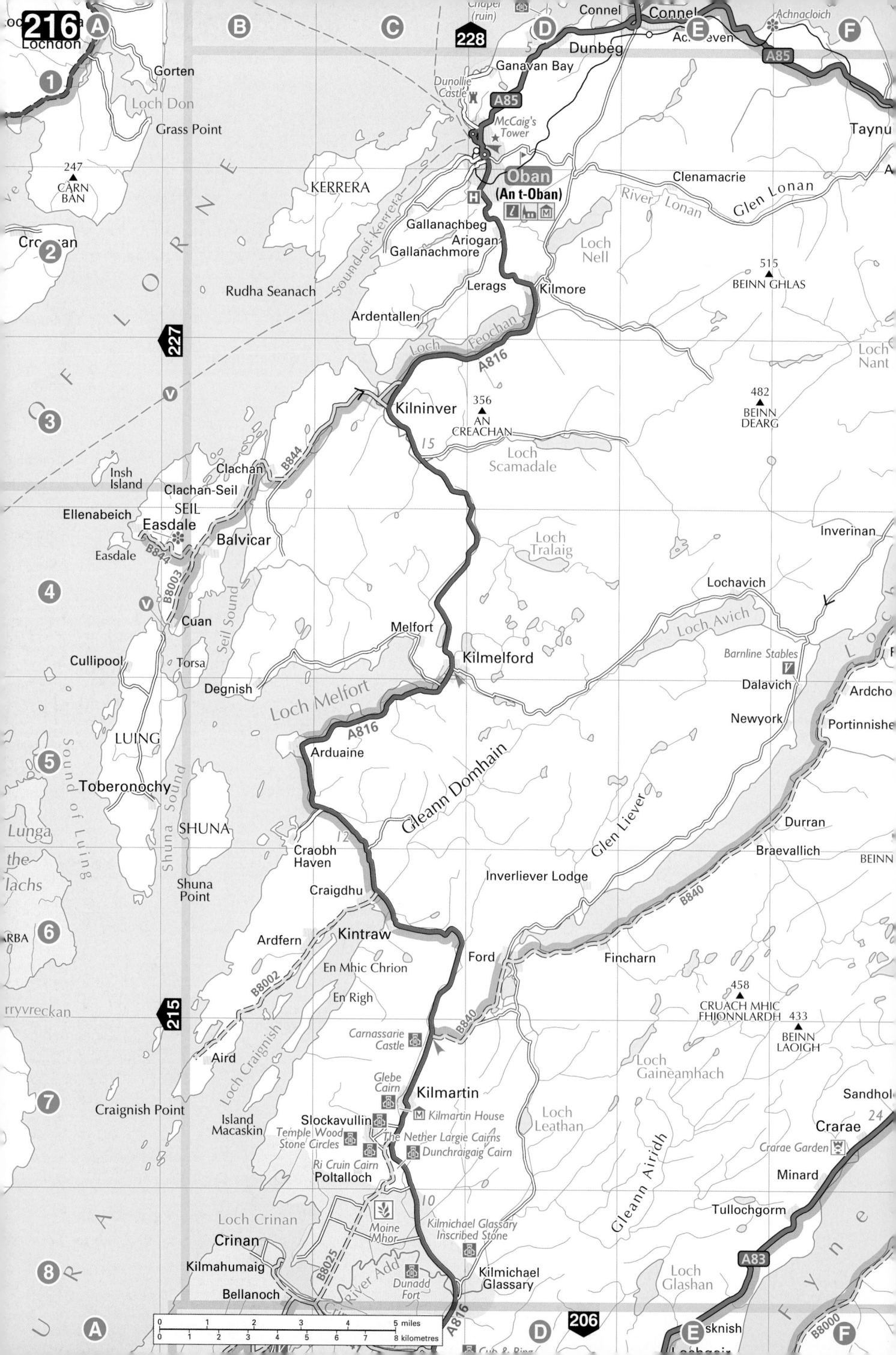

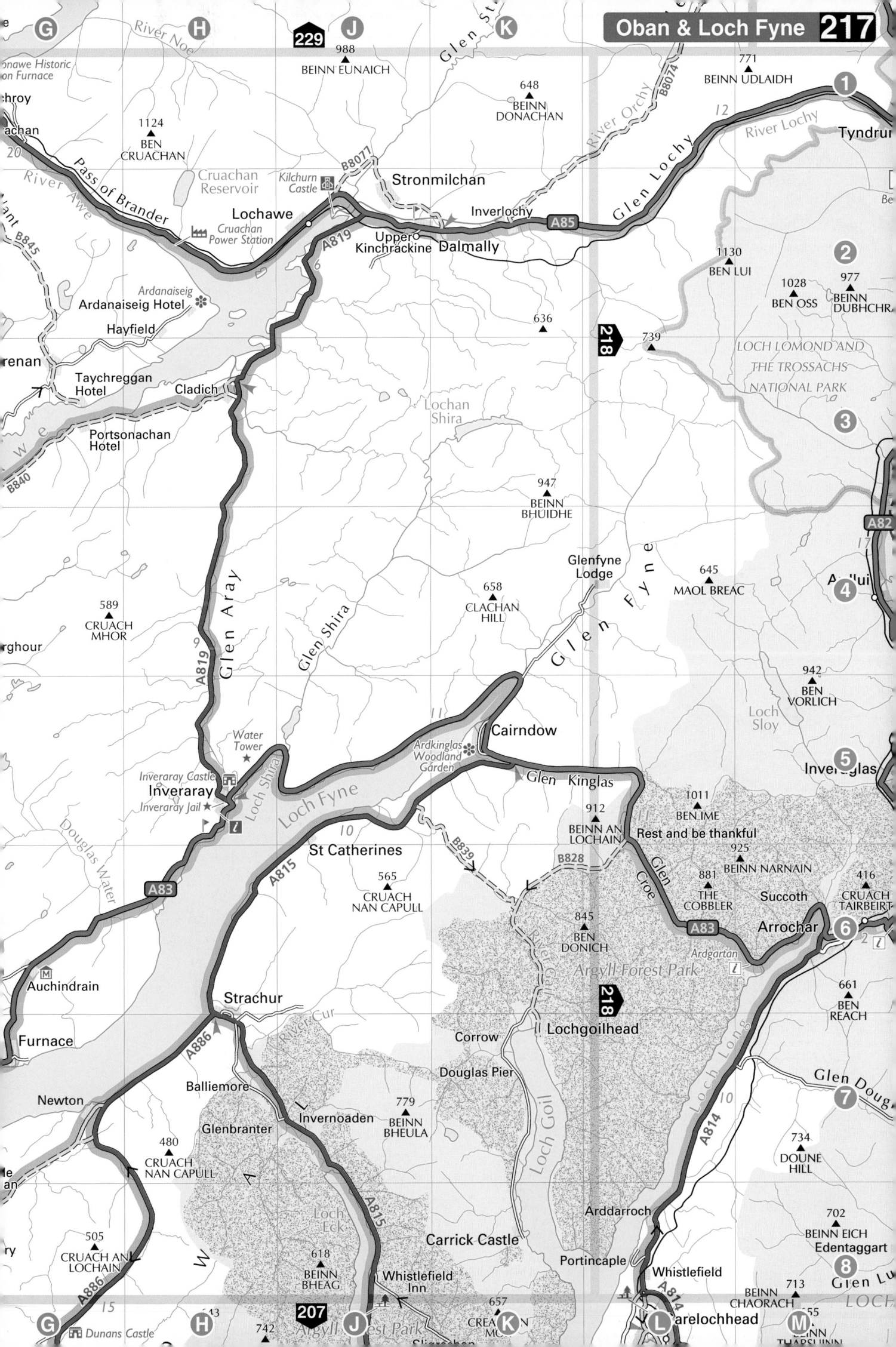

G   H   **229**   J   **988**   K

BEINN EUNAICH

onawe Historic
on Furnace

648
BEINN
DONACHAN

771
BEINN UDLAIDH

River Noe

Glen Stae

River Orchy

B8074

River Lochy

Glen Lochy

Tyndrum

1

chroy
achan

1124
BEN
CRUACHAN

B8077

Cruachan
Reservoir

Kilchurn
Castle

Stronmilchan

Inverlochy

A85

Glen Lochy

12

River Lochy

2

River Awe

Pass of Brander

Lochawe

Cruachan
Power Station

B845

Upper
Kinchrackine   Dalmally

A819

6

636

218

739

1130
BEN LUI

1028
BEN OSS

977
BEINN
DUBHCHRA

LOCH LOMOND AND
THE TROSSACHS
NATIONAL PARK

3

Ardanaiseig
Ardanaiseig Hotel

Hayfield

renan

Taychreggan
Hotel

Cladich

Portsonachan
Hotel

B840

Lochan
Shira

947
BEINN
BHUIDHE

Glenfyne
Lodge

645
MAOL BREAC

A82

4

A'llui

589
CRUACH
MHOR

rghour

A819

Glen Aray

Glen Shira

658
CLACHAN
HILL

Glen Fyne

942
BEN
VORLICH

Loch
Sloy

5

Inveglas

Water
Tower

Cairndow

Ardkinglas
Woodland
Garden

Glen   Kinglas

1011
BEN IME

912
BEINN AN
LOCHAIN

Rest and be thankful

925
BEINN NARNAIN

881
THE
COBBLER

416
CRUACH
TAIRBEIRT

Inveraray Castle

Inveraray

Inveraray Jail

Loch Shira

Loch Fyne

St Catherines

10

B839

B828

Glen

Croe

Succoth

Arrochar

6

2

Douglas Water

A83

A815

565
CRUACH
NAN CAPULL

845
BEN
DONICH

A83

Ardgartan

661
BEN
REACH

Auchindrain

Strachur

Argyll Forest Park

River Gail

7

Furnace

A886

River Cur

Corrow

Douglas Pier

218

Lochgoilhead

Arddarroch

Loch Long

10

A814

Glen Doug

Newton

Balliemore

Invernoaden

779
BEINN
BHEULA

734
DOUNE
HILL

Edentaggart

Glenbranter

480
CRUACH
NAN CAPULL

A815

A

Loch Goil

702
BEINN EICH

505
CRUACH AN
LOCHAIN

ry

A886

15

Loch
Eck

W

Carrick Castle

Portincaple

Whistlefield

8

BEINN
CHAORACH

713

Glen Lu

Dunans Castle

742

618
BEINN
BHEAG

Whistlefield
Inn

207

657
CREA
MO

Whistlefield

A814

arelochhead

55

G   H   J   K   L   M

Argyll est Park   Slizachen   BEINN
THARS INN

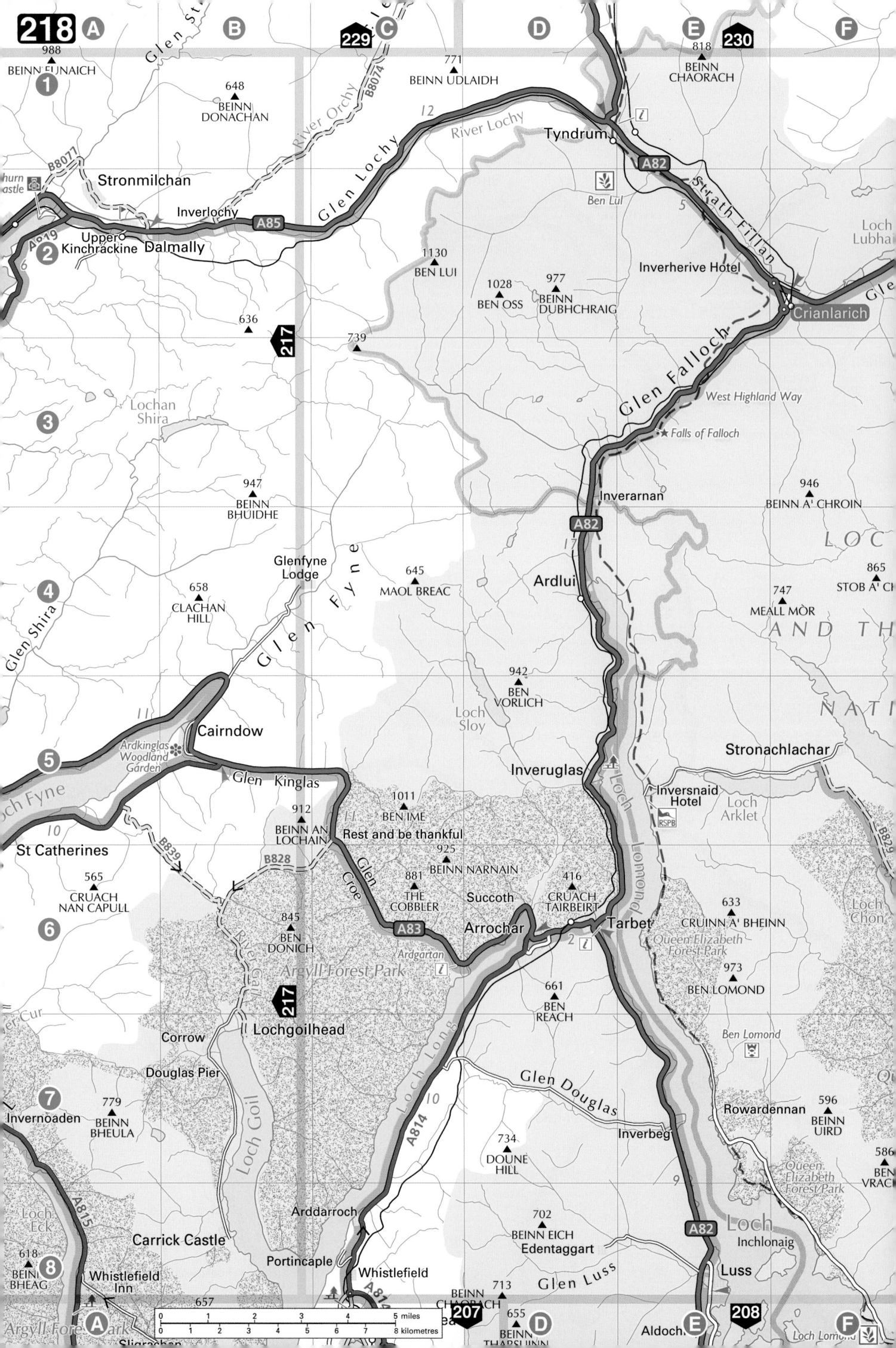

G 230 H J Finlarig 231

Killin

IEATHAICH 37

Falls of Dochart ★

Breadalbane Folklore Centre

B R E A D

Auchlyne

River Dochart

Dochart

A85

A85 5

778 ▲ MEALL AN FHIODHAIN

Lochearnhead

Balquhidder Auchtubh

Craigruie

Loch Voil

Kingshouse Hotel

Loch Doine

OMOND

Ballimore Strathyre

T R O S S A C H S

818 ▲ BENVANE

Strathyre Forest

671 ▲ MEALL CALA

Queen Elizabeth Forest Park

14

Ardchullarie More

A L   P A R K

876 ▲ BEN LEDI

Glen Finglas Reservoir

Falls of Leny ★

Kilmahog

Katrine

SS Sir Walter Scott

The Trossachs

Trossachs Pier

Coilantogle

Brig o'Turk

10 A821

729 ▲ BEN VENUE

700 ▲ BEINN BHREAC

Loch Achray

Queen Elizabeth Forest Park

Lendrick

Loch Drunkie

Menteith Hills

427 ▲ BEINN DEARG

Altskeith Hotel

7

A821

Milton

Queen Elizabeth Forest Park

chard

Loch Ard

Aberfoyle

Scottish Wool Centre

4 A81

Inchmahome Priory

Port of Menteith

Ruskie

Goodie Water

Lake of Menteith

abeth Park

Duchtay Water

208 ▲ ELRIG

Cunninghame Graham Memorial

Gartmore

Dalmary

Dykehead

Flanders Moss

River

Forth

B8034

CREAG UCHDAG 879 ▲ 1

682 ▲ RUADH MHEALL

Loch Lednock

Inve

Glen L

2

Glen Beich

671 ▲ SRÒN MHÒR

Dalveich

St Fillans

A85

River Earn

A84

220

Glen Vorlich

Ardvorlich

Loch Earn

3

985 ▲ BEN VORLICH

975 ▲ STUC A' CHROIN

Dalchruin

Glen

4

630 ▲ MEALL ODHAR

Loch Lubnaig

5

Kilmahog Woollen Mill

Callander (Calasraid)

i

Rob Roy and Trossachs

V

Upper Drumbane

A81

6

A84

Drumvaich 8

Burn of Cambus

6

B822

B8032

Buchany

Loch Venachar

Doun

220

Deanston

Doune Castle

Thornhill

B826

Meldrum

A873

air Dr

7

B8031

B822

A811

Arnprior

B8037

Kippen

19

Cauldhame

Gargunnock

B822

8

Touch Hill

West Highland Way

G Milto Buchanan

H

J

209

K

L

M

B835

A811

Buchlyvie

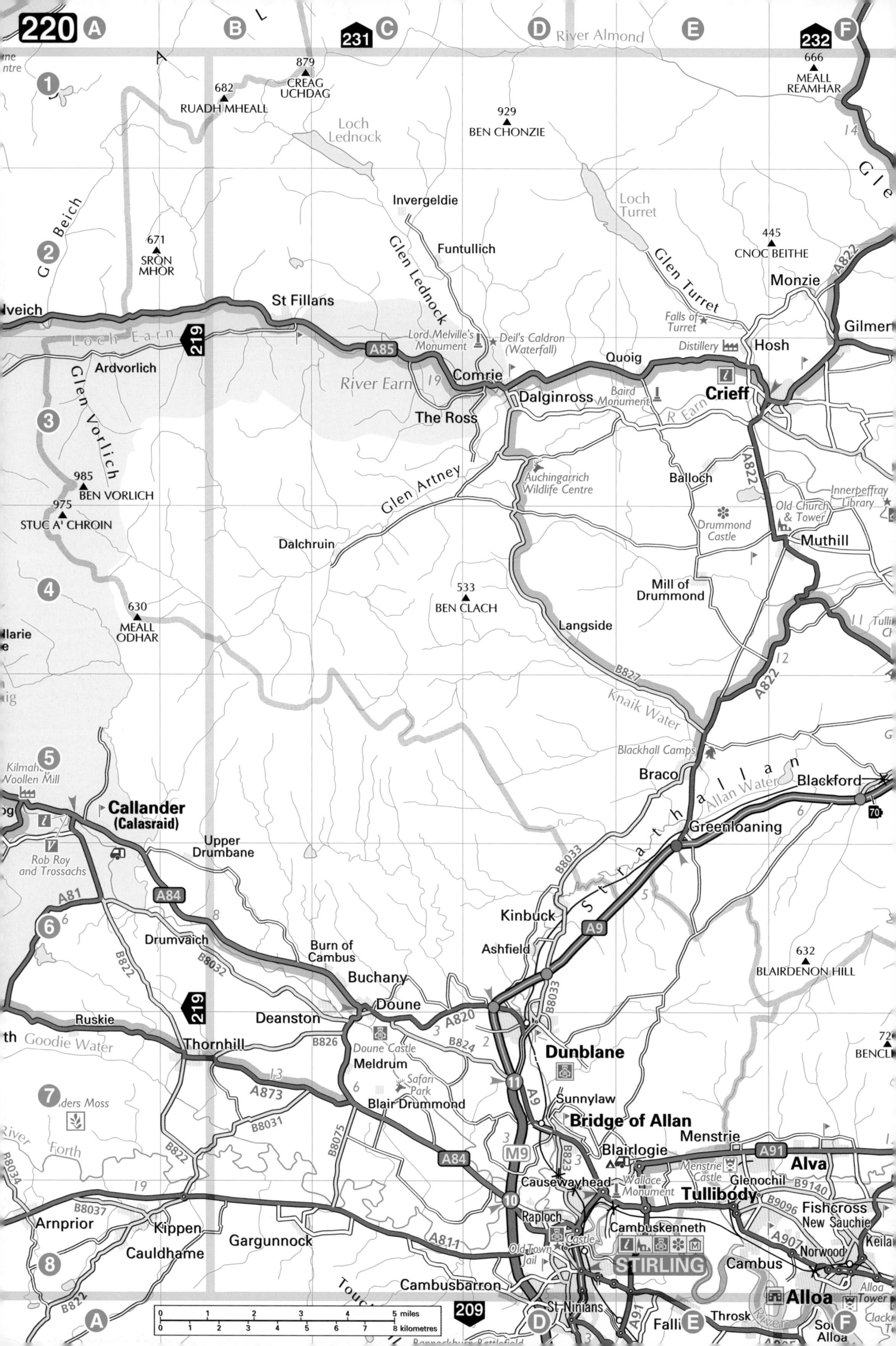

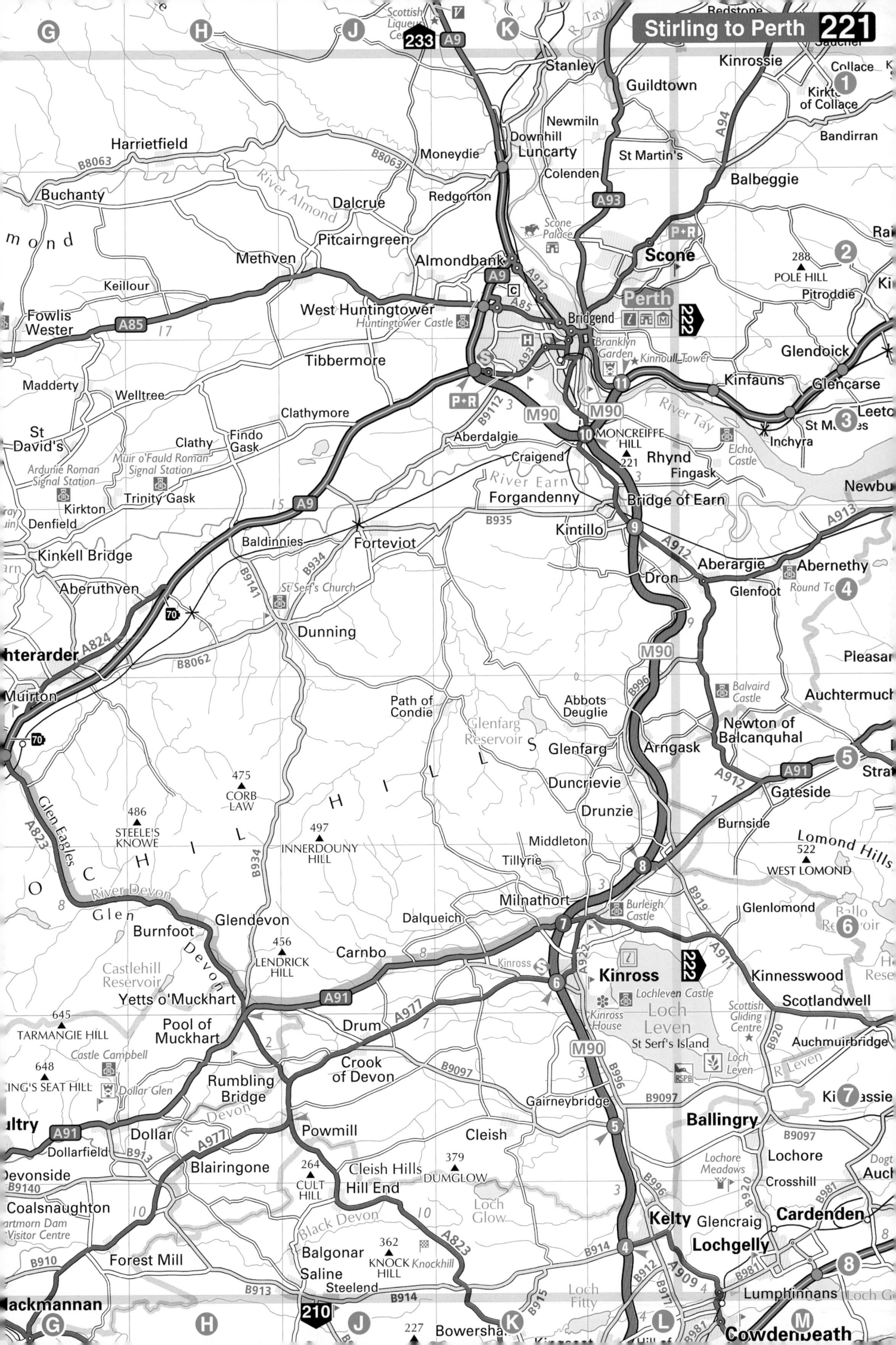

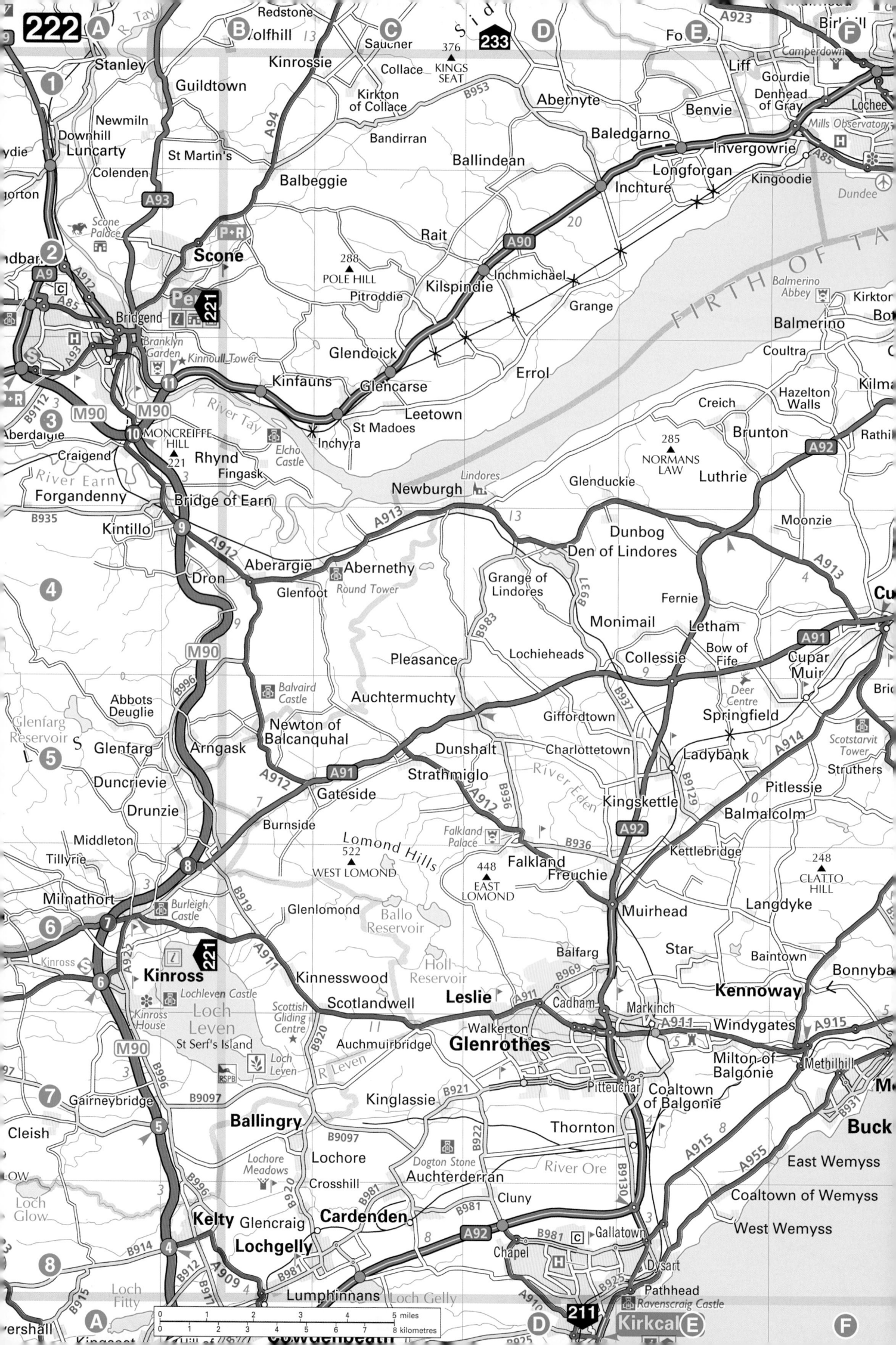

G H **234** J **K**noustie

1

Barry
West Haven
Carnoustie
Monifieth
Broughty Ferry
BUDDON NESS

Whitfield
Douglas and-Angus
Baldovie
B961
A92
B962
A930
B960
B959
Claypotts Castle
Barnhill

DUNDEE
North Carr Lightship
HM Frigate 'Unicorn'
A92 Tay Bridge

2

Newport-on-Tay
Tayport
Tentsmuir Point

Wormit
A946
A914

3

ST ANDREWS BAY

cklawhill
13
A919
Leuchars
RAF Leuchars
Balmullo
Tentsmuir Point

A914
10
13
Guardbridge

rae
irsie
A914
River Eden
Kincaple
A91
St Andrews
Castle
St Andrews

4

Strathkinness
Botanic Garden
Brownhills
A917
10
Boarhills

mback
B939
Blebocraigs
Craigtoun
Denhead

5

Pitscottie
Cameron Reservoir
A915
Kingsbarns
Balcomie Links
FIFE NESS

Ceres
Baldinnie
B940
12
Radernie
Dunino
Crail

thie
Peat Inn
New Gilston
B941
Lathones
Kingsmuir
B940
Scotland's Secret Bunker
B940
B9171

Woodside
Largoward
Lochty
Carnbee
B9131
Easter Pitkierie
A917

6

Upper Largo
A915
Arncroach
Kellie Castle
Wester Pitkierie
B9171
Kilrenny
Cellardyke

Lundin Mill
Colinsburgh
B942
Newton of Balcormo
Fisheries
Anstruther

Lower Largo
Drumeldrie
6
B941
B942
Kilconquhar
6
Pittenweem

Lundin Links
A917
St Monans

Largo Bay
Earlsferry
Elie

7

Isle of May

8

G H J K L M

A B C D E F

1

2

3

Gris
Clabhach

Hogh Bay   Bally

Bagh a Chaisteil
(Castlebay)   Totrona

4   Coll

Feall   Ac
Bay   Arileod
Calgary Point   Uig
(Mar-Oct)   Crossapol
Gunna   Bay   Rudh
RSPB   Loch Breachacha Fàsach

5

Rudha Port   Caoles   Rudha Dubh
Bhiosd   Clachan   B8069
Mor   Ruaig
Balephetrish   B8068
Loch   Bay
Haugh   Bhasapoll
Bay   Gott
Ballevullin Cornoigmore   Kenovay   Bay

6   Kilkenneth   Tiree

Moss   Heylipoll   B8065   Scarinish
Middleton   B8065
Barrapoll   Crossapoll
Hynish Bay   TIREE
Loch a   B8067 Balemartine
Phuill
Mannel
Rinn
7   Thorbhais   Hynish
Balephuil
Bay

8

0   1   2   3   4   5 miles
0   1   2   3   4   5   6   7   8 kilometres

A B C D E F

A B C D E F

1

Arinagour

COLL

Eilean
Ornsay

Ardmore Point

Sorne
Point

Quinish Point

Glengorm Castle

Tobermo

2

Caliach Point

Dervaig

292 ▲
'S AIRDE
BEINN

Achnadrish House

5

B8073

6

Calgary

SPEIN

Loch Fris

Calgary Bay

225

Treshnish Point

Ensay

342 ▲
CÀRN MÒR

3

Rudh' a' Chaoil

Burg

Fanmore

390 ▲
CNOC AN DÀ CHINN

Fladda

Ballygown

★ Eas Fors (Waterfall)

Loch Tuath

Lunga

19

Oskamull

NA

4

TRESHNISH
ISLES

Gometra

ULVA

Eorsa

Bac Mòr or Dutchmans Cap

Loch

Bac Beag

Little Colonsay

Inch Kenneth

B8035 17

5

🌿 Staffa

Inchkenneth Chapel 🏛
(ruin)

Balnahard

Fingal's Cave

*Loch na Keal,
Isle of Mull*

225

519 ▲
BEIN NA
SREINE

6

491 ▲
CREACH BHEINN

★ *Fossil Tree*

🏛 Burg

Loch Scridain

Pennycro

Rudha nan Cearc

7

🏛

IONA

Iona Abbey
& Nunnery 🏛

Kintra

Loch na Lathaich

14

Baile Mór

🏛

MacLean's Cross 🏛

V Fionnphort
(Mar-
Oct)

Sound of Iona

Aridhglas

6

A849

Bunessan

376 ▲
CRUACHAN
MIN

St Columba
Exhibition
Centre 🏛

Loch Assapol

8

Soa Island

ROSS OF MULL

Uisken

Malcolm's
Point

Erraid

Ardchiavaig

214

Rudha nam
Braithrean

G   H   J   237   K   L

GEÀRR CHREAG

Ardnastang

Liddesdale

Aràslighish

Oronsay

Carna

1

A884

Lochuisge

Auliston
Point

571 ▲ BEINN
LADAIN

522 ▲ MEALL A' CHOISE

20

Calve
Island

Drimnin

Loch
Teacuis

Glen Dubh

2

437 ▲ BEINN
BHUIDHE

738 ▲ BEINN MHEADHOIN

B849

550 ▲ SÌTHEAN NA RAPLAICH

Loch
Arienas

Acharn

Gleann Geal

228

A848

Claggan

Larachbeg

339 ▲ MEALL DAMH

3

10

Fuinary

A884

Rannoch River

en Aros

Loch
Aline

Achranich

Loch
Téarnait

Aros

Lochaline

464 ▲ GLAIS
BHEINN

514 ▲ AN
SLEAGHOCH

Glenaros House

Salen

Fishnish
Point

4

Fishnish Pier

A849

Killiechronan

B8035

2

v

Rudha an
Ridire

Gruline

Macquarie
Mausoleum

408 ▲ BEINN
NAN LUS

Glen Forsa

11

Scallastle Bay

Bernera
Island

Kilchera

Loch Bà

591 ▲ BEINN A' GHRÀIG

ISLE

636 ▲ BEINN
MHEADHON

Altcreich

i

v

966 ▲ BEN
MORE

OF

766 ▲ DUN DA
GHAOITHE

Craignure

Duart
Bay   Duart
Point

5

704 ▲ CRUACHAN
DEARG

MULL

Torosay

Duart

Lochdonhead

Lochdon

Gorten

17   A849

Strathcoil

Glen More

Grass Point

Loch Don

6

247 ▲ CARN
BÀN

Loch Fuaran

717 ▲ BEN
BUIE

698 ▲ BEN CREACH

Loch Spelve

Croggan

216

Pennyghael

503 ▲ BEINN NA
CROISE

Lochbuie

Loch
Uisg

Rudha Seanach

7

Leidle Water

Carsaig

337 ▲ MAOL
BÀN

NN
GACH

Rudha
Dubh

Loch Buie

377 ▲ DRUIM
FADA

Colonsay · Oban

v

Clachan

B844

Insh
Island

SEIL

8

Clachan-Seil

G   H   215   J   K   L   Ellenabeich   Easdale   M   Balvicar

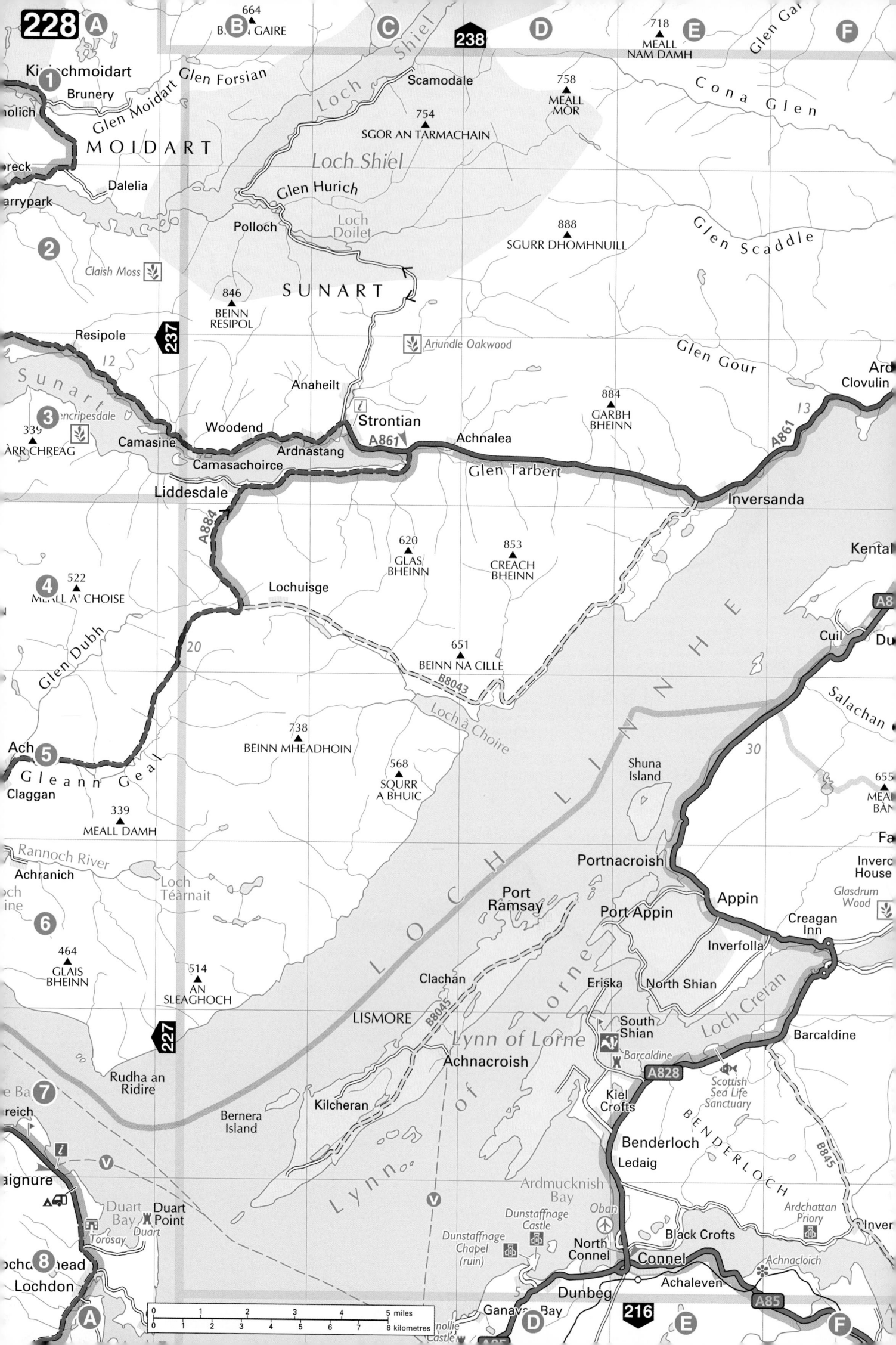

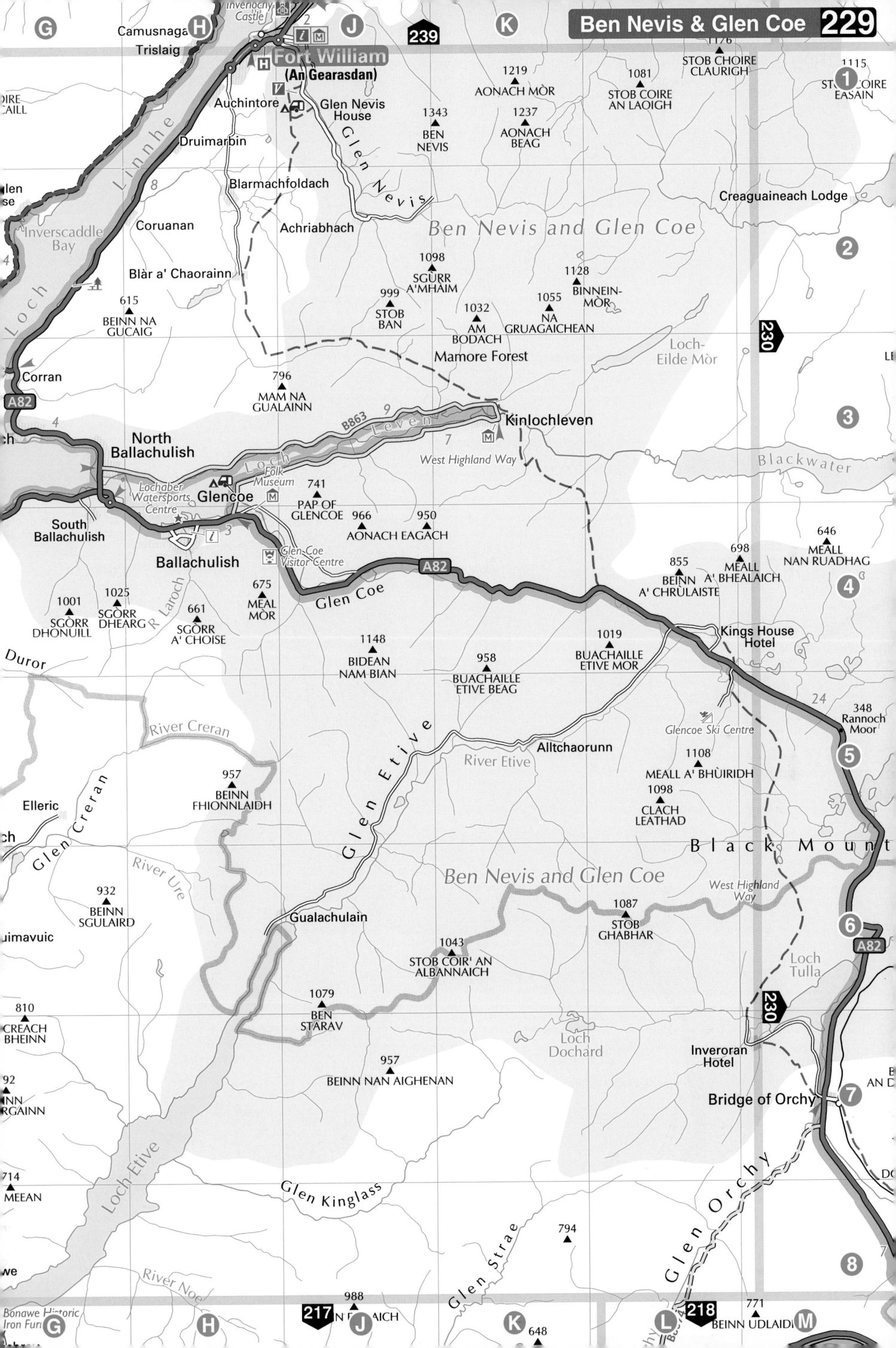

G H J K

Camusnagaul
Trislaig

239

1176
STOB CHOIRE
CLAURIGH

1115
ST COIRE
EASAIN

1

Inverlochy
Castle

Fort William
(An Gearasdan)

1219
AONACH MÒR

1081
STOB COIRE
AN LAOIGH

Auchintore

Glen Nevis
House

1343
BEN
NEVIS

1237
AONACH
BEAG

Druimarbin

Blarmachfoldach

Creaguaineach Lodge

2

COIRE
CAILL

Coruanan

Achriabhach

Ben Nevis and Glen Coe

Glen

Nevis

1098
SGÙRR
A'MHAIM

1128
BINNEIN-
MÒR

Inverscaddle
Bay

Blàr a' Chaorainn

999
STOB
BAN

1032
AM
BODACH

1055
NA
GRUAGAICHEAN

615
BEINN NA
GUCAIG

Glen
e

Loch-
Eilde Mòr

230

Corran

796
MAM NA
GUALAINN

Mamore Forest

A82

4

North
Ballachulish

B863

Loch Leven

7

Kinlochleven

West Highland Way

3

Blackwater

Lochaber
Watersports
Centre

Folk
Museum

South
Ballachulish

Glencoe

741
PAP OF
GLENCOE

966
AONACH EAGACH

950

Ballachulish

Glen-Coe
Visitor Centre

Glen Coe

A82

855
BEINN
A' CHRÙLAISTE

698
MEALL
A' BHEALAICH

646
MEALL
NAN RUADHAG

4

1001
SGORR
DHONUILL

1025
SGORR
DHEARG

661
SGORR
A' CHOISE

R Laroch

675
MEAL
MÒR

1019
BUACHAILLE
ETIVE MOR

Kings House
Hotel

Duror

River Creran

1148
BIDEAN
NAM BIAN

958
BUACHAILLE
ETIVE BEAG

Glencoe Ski Centre

348
Rannoch
Moor

24

5

Elleric

Glen Creran

River Ure

957
BEINN
FHIONNLAIDH

Glen Etive

River Etive

Alltchaorunn

1108
MEALL A' BHÙIRIDH

1098
CLACH
LEATHAD

B l a c k   M o u n t

uimavuic

932
BEINN
SGULAIRD

Ben Nevis and Glen Coe

West Highland Way

6

A82

Gualachulain

1087
STOB
GHABHAR

Loch
Tulla

810
CREACH
BHEINN

1043
STOB COIR' AN
ALBANNAICH

230

92
NN
RGAINN

1079
BEN
STARAV

Loch
Dochard

Inveroran
Hotel

7
B
AN D

Loch Etive

957
BEINN NAN AIGHENAN

Bridge of Orchy

714
MEEAN

Glen Kinglass

Glen Orchy

we

Bonawe Historic
Iron Furn

River Noe

Glen Strae

794

8

G H

River N...

988
N ... AICH

217

218

J

K

648

L

771
BEINN UDLAIDH

M

A   B   C   240   D   E   F

1176
▲
STOB CHOIRE
CLAURIGH

1046
▲
CHNO
DEARG
240

Loch
Gulbin

1101
▲
BEINN
EIBHINN

1145
▲
BEN
ALDER

108'
▲
1
TOB COIRE
N LAOIGH

1115
▲
STOB COIRE
EASAIN

Creaguaineach Lodge

Glen Ossian

844
▲
MEALL A'BHEALAICH

en Coe
2

Loch Ossian

952
▲
SGÒR
GAIBHRE

Loch
Eilde Mòr

229

Corrour
Station

626
▲
SRON A
CHLAONAID

906
▲
LEUM UILLEIM

864
▲
BEINN PHARIAGAIN

3

R Ericht

Blackwater   Reservoir

646
▲
MEALL
NAN RUADHAG

Rannoch
Station

Dunan
B846

Bridge
of Ericht

Finnar

698
▲
MEALL
A' BHEALAICH

855
▲
INN
ULAISTE
4
A'

738
▲
A' CHRUACH

Loch
Laidon

Loch
Eigheach

Bridge
of Gaur

Kings House
Hotel

Glencoe Ski Centre

24

348
Rannoch
Moor

R a n n o c h

M o o r

1108
▲
5
MEALL A' BHÙIRIDH

1098
▲
CLACH
LEATHAD

Loch Bà

931
▲
MEALL
BUIDHE

B l a c k   M o u n t

Water of Tulla

Loch an
Daimh

West Highland
Way

087
▲
OB
BHAR
6

A82

Loch
Tulla

1079
▲
BEINN
A' CHREACHAIN

229

Inveroran
Hotel

996
▲
BEINN
AN DÒTHAIDH

953
▲
BEINN
MHANACH

Loch
Lyon

BE

1038
▲
MEALL
GHAORDIE

7

Bridge of Orchy

1074
▲
BEN
DORAIN

1076
▲
BEINN HEASGARNICH

Glen Lochay

Glen Orchy

8

771
NN UDL

818
▲

218

937
▲
BEINN CHEATHAIC

219

B8074

River Lochay

Falls of

0   1   2   3   4   5 miles
0   1   2   3   4   5   6   7   8 kilometres

A   D   E   F

G   H   J   **241**   K

1

A' MHARCONAICH

1008
BEINN UDLAMAIN

991
SGAIRNEACH MHOR

Dalnaspidal

Loch Garry

Glen Garry

Dalnacardoch

A9

Loch Con

Loch Errochty

491
CRAIG BHAGAILTEACH

2

Calvine   Bruar

Struan   Pitagowan

232   Old Struan   Blai

841
BEINN MHOLACH

Trinafour

B847

511
TORR DUBH

Glen Errochty

Tay Forest Park

3

Tressait   B8019

892
BEINN A' CHUALLAICH

7   B846

Loch Tummel   Queen's View

ichonan

16

Loch Rannoch

Kinloch Rannoch

Drumchastle

Dunalastair

R Tummel

Tummel Bridge

Foss

Daloist

Frenich

Tay Forest Park

13

Loch Tumm

Inverhadden

Tempar

Dunalastair Water

Carie

Tay Forest Park

Camghouran

Tay Forest Park

1081
SCHIEHALLION

780
MEALL TAIRNEACHAN

780
FARRAGON HILL

4

Loch Glassie

Loch Rannoch and Glen Lyon

1042
CÀRN MAIRG

Glengoulandie Deer Park

B846

14

745
MEALL A' MHÙIC

824
BEINN DEARG

1027
CÀRN GORM

Coshieville

Keltneyburn

Camserney   Dull

Menzies   W

Dewars

5

G

Glen Lyon

River Lyon

Bridge of Balgie

Fortingall

Tay Forest Park

Kenmore

A827

Croftmoraig Stone Circle

River Tay

924
MEALL A' CHOIRE LEITH

1116
MEALL GARBH

1000
MEALL GREIGH

Fearnan

Acharn

The Crannog Centre

232   E

6

780
MEALL LUAIDHE

1214
BEN LAWERS

Glen Quar

7

DIGHREAG

Lochan na Làirige

Leckbuie

713
BEINN BHREAC

River Quaich

Ben Lawers

Lawers

A827   25

Loch Tay

864
SRÒN A' CHAOINEIDH

802
MEALL NAM FUARAN

Moirlanich Longhouse

Milton Morenish

Morenish

Ardeonaig

River Almond

8

Killin

Finlarig

Breadalbane Folklore Centre

Dochart

G   H   **219**   J   K   **220**   L   M

879
CREAG UCHDAG

682

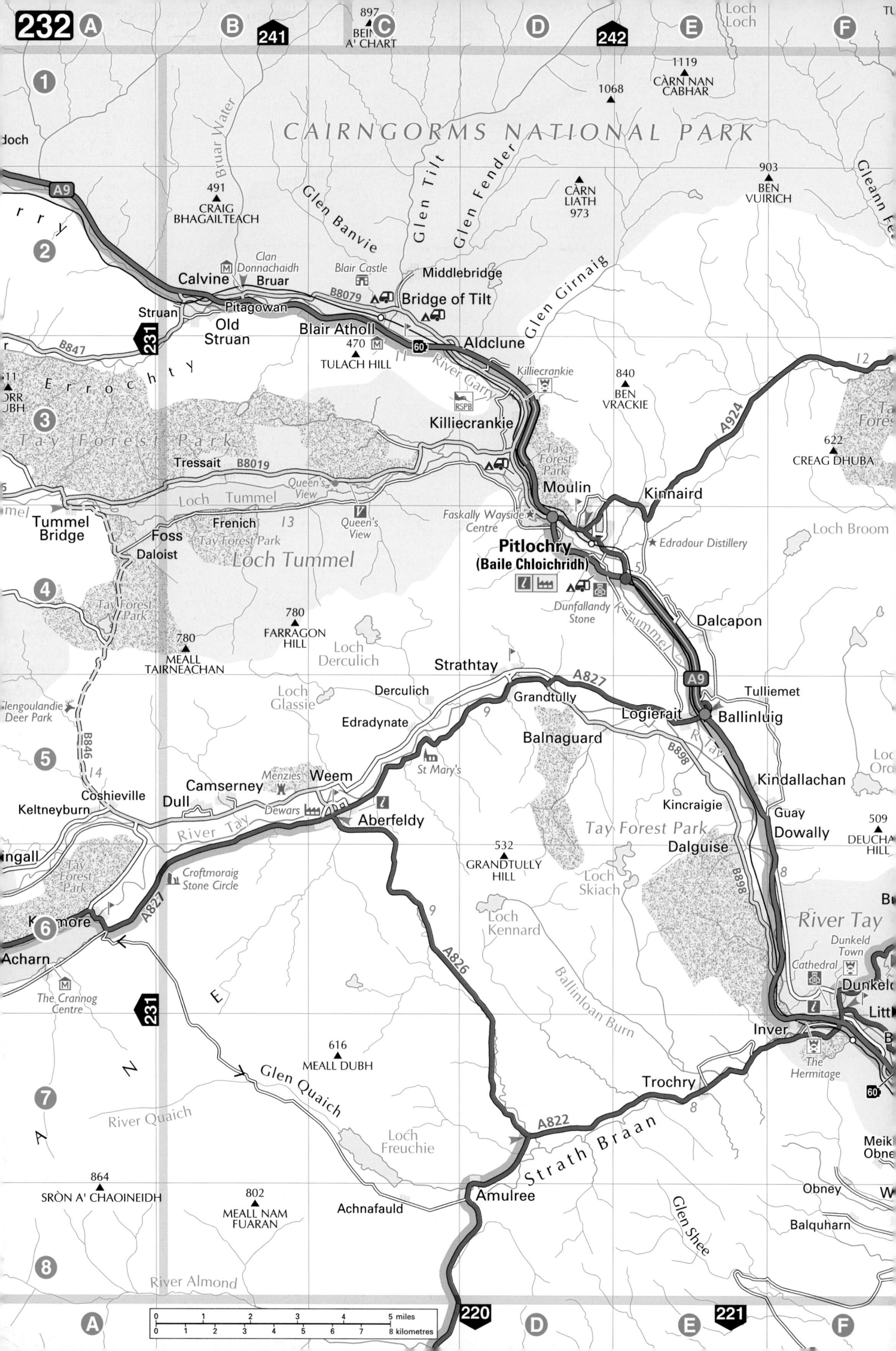

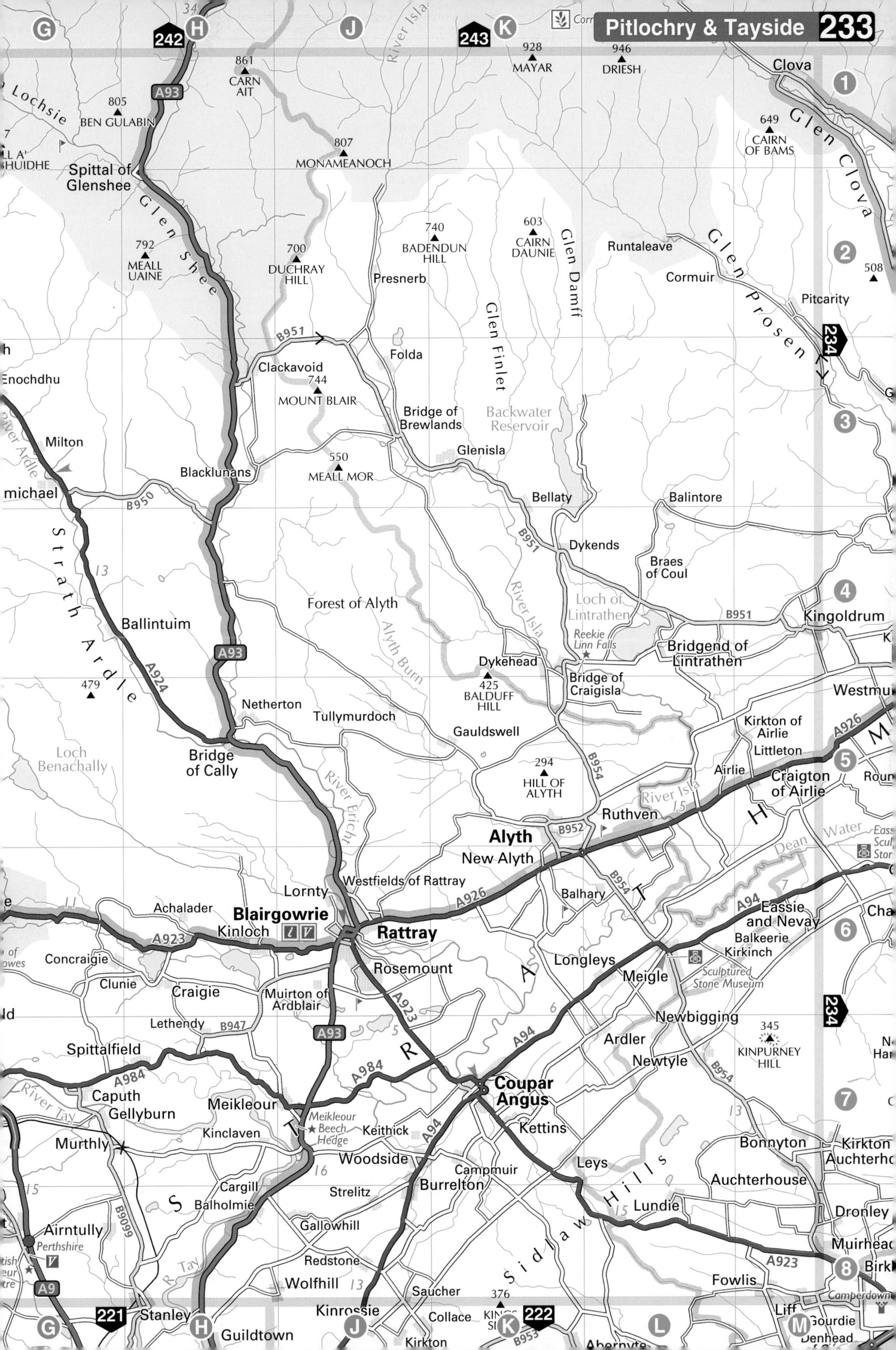

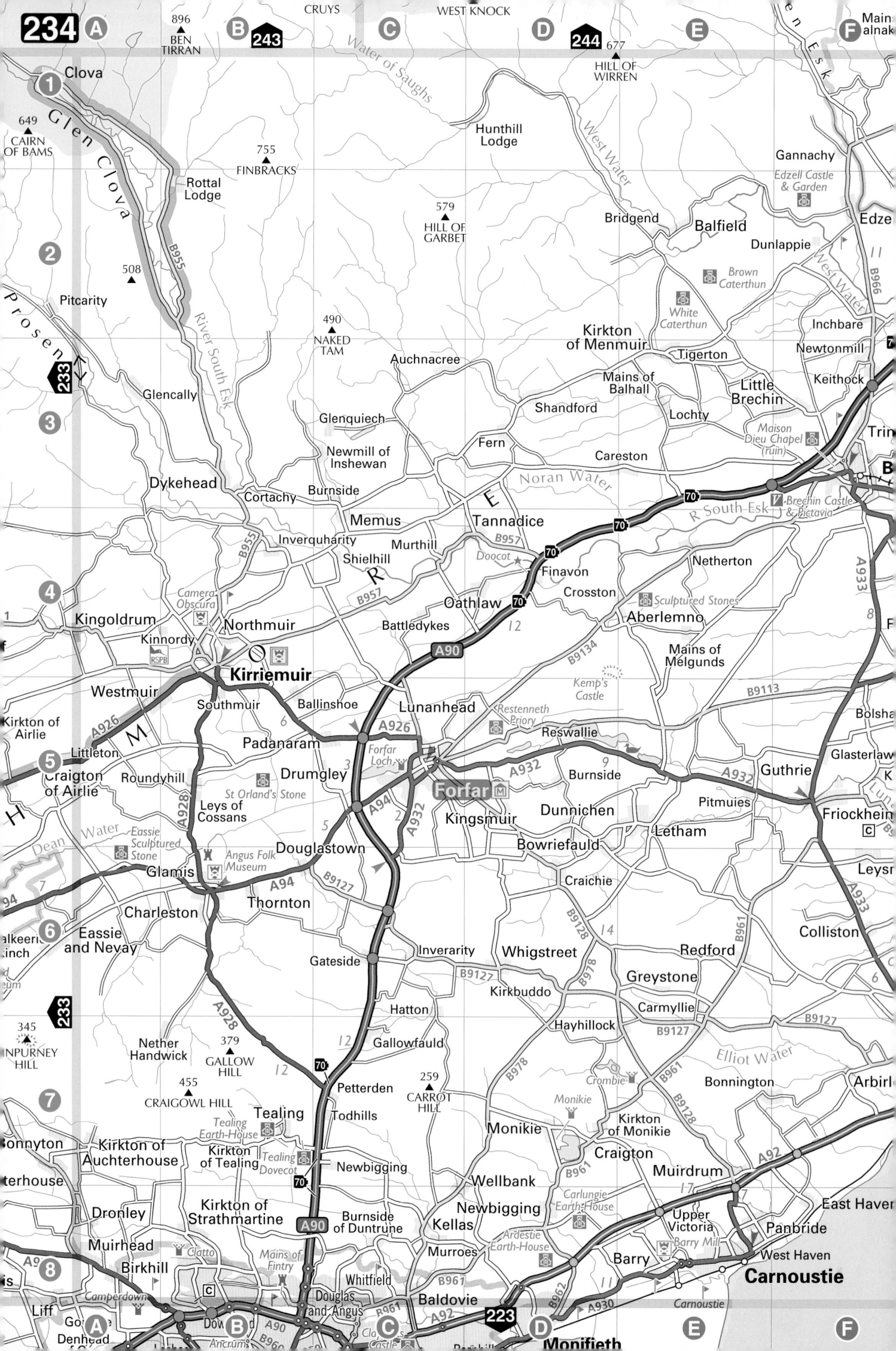

G | H | J | K | L | M

1
2
3
4
5
6
7
8

244
70
245

Pittarrow
edmyre
Inverbervie
Bervie Bay
Mains of Haulkerton
Laurencekirk
Gourdon
B9120
B9120
Redford
Benholm
50
Dykelands
Johnshaven
A937
13
North Esk
Marykirk
Bush
Craigo
Lochside
Milton Ness
Logie Pert
St Cyrus
Logie
Morphie
Hillside
House of Dun
A92
Dun
Montrose Air Station
Montrose
A935
9
Montrose Basin
Barnhead
Scurdie Ness
Maryton
Ferryden
Craig
A934
Usan
Westerton of Rossie
Braehead
Boddin Point
Lunan
Lunan Bay
Inverkeilor
Red Head
13
pelton
Cauldcots
A92
Marywell
Auchmithie
eans
Carlingheugh Bay
The Deil's Head
Arbroath

0   1   2   3   4   5 miles
0 1 2 3 4 5 6 7 8 kilometres

A Bhrideanach

MULLACH
MÒR

246

Rudha na Roinne

Kinloch

Loch
Scresort

570
▲
ORVAL

RÙM

810
▲
ASKIVAL

Harris
Bay

763
▲
SGÙRR NAN
GILLEAN

The Small Isles

Rudha nam
Meirleach

Sound of Rum

Bay of
Laig

Cleadale

Rudha an Fhasaidh

Laig

299
▲
AN
CRUACHAN

EIGG

Kildo

393
▲
AN SGÙRR

Sandavo

Sound of Eigg

Eilean
Chathastail

Eilean
nan Each

MUCK

Port Mor

Sanna Point

Sanna Bay

Sanna
Bay

Portuairk

Achnaha

Ardnamurchan
Point

Achosnich

MEAL

B8007

Eilean Mòr

Bagh a Chaisteil
(Castlebay)
Loch Baghasdail
(Lochboisdale)

Rudha
Mòr

Rudha
Sgor-innis

342
▲
BEINN
NA SEILG

Kil

Bousd

Sorisdale

225

Ormsaigmor

Cliad
Bay

COLL

B8072

Coll · Oban

oost

B8071

| 0 | 1 | 2 | 3 | 4 | 5 miles |
| 0 | 1 | 2 | 3 | 4 | 5 | 6 | 7 | 8 kilometres |

Ardmore Point

Arinagour

Sorne
P

226

A   B   C   D   E   F

Sleat

G   H   J   V   K   KNOYD

247

Ard
Thurinish

Point
of Sleat

Inverie
Bay

Rudha
Raonuill

Courteachan

Mallaigvaig

Mallaig
(Malaig)

547
CÀRN A'GHOBHAIR

Glasnacardoch Bay

Loch an
Nostaire

437
SGÙRR BHUIDHE

Beoraidbeg

Morar

Bracora

Bracorina

Tarbet

iesm

238 Swordland

Glenancross

Loch   Morar

B8008

A830

Lettermorar

Meoble

River Meoble

Bunacaimb

503
CÀRN A'
MHÀDAIDH-RUAIDH

MEITH

Eilean Ighe

Back of
Keppoch

600
SIDHEAN
MÒR

Luinga Mhòr

Arisaig

Loch nan Ceall

10

Rudh' Arisaig

Druimindarroch

Arisaig
House

Prince Charlie's
Cairn

Kinlochnanuagh

103
CRUACH
DOIRE

Loch nan Uamh

Polnish

Lochailort

Sound of Arisaig

Rudha
Choalais

Ardnish

Inverailort

Loch
Eilt

Loch Ailort

A861

877
ROIS-BHEINN

Smearisary

Glenuig

712

664
BEINN GAIRE

B8000

21

Eilean
Shona

Rudha Aird
Druimnich

Loch Moidart

Kinlochmoidart

Glen Forsian

Brunery

Glen Moidart

Loch

Ockle
Point

Morar, Moidart and
Ardnamurchan

Tioram

239
BEINN
BHREAC

Ardmolich

MOIDART

Imory

Ockle

Ardtoe

Shielfoot

Dalnabreck

Dalelia

Glen Hurich

356
BEINN
BHREAC

B8044

Kentra

Blain

Mingarrypark

228

Loc
Doil

Branault

Arevegaig

Polloch

ARDNAMURCHAN

437

Acharacle

Claish Moss

SUNAR

Loch
Mudle

A861

846
BEINN
RESIPOL

7

527
BEN
HIANT

Salen

Resipole

12

Anaheilt

Glenbeg

512
BEN
LAGA

B8007

Loch

Sunart

Glencripesdale

Woodend

Glenborrodale

Laga

339
GEÀRR CHREAG

Camasine

Ardnastang

Ardslignish

RSPB

Carna

Camasachoire

Auliston
Point

Oronsay

227

Liddesdale

A884

G   H   J   K   L   M

A **B** **C** **D** **E** **F**

1

2

3

4

5

6

7

8

BEINN NA
S...RAIG

Brochs

...lean Beag

248

Glen Shiel

FHUARA
...TERS

...lemo
Ornsay

Loch na Dal

Ornsay

Sandaig
Island

SOUND OF SLEAT

974
▲ BEINN
SGRITHEAL

773
▲ BEINN NAN CAORACH

Arnisdale

1011
▲ THE SADDLE

945
▲ SGURR
NA SGINE

Rudha
Buidhe

Loch Hourn

Glen Arnisdale

Rudh' Ard
Slisneach

Corran

614
▲

709
▲ DRUM
FADA

Kinloch
Hourn

247

Inverguseran

784
▲ BEINN NA
CAILLICH

Barrisdale
Bay

102
▲ SGUR
MHAO...

Airor

Glen Guseran

518
▲ DRUIM NA
CLUAIN-AIRIDHE

1019
▲ LADHAR
BHEINN

Knoydart

Sandaig

KNOYDART

940
▲ LUINNE BHEINN

Sandaig Bay

Inverie

Inverie
Bay

Loch an
Dubh-Lochain

1003
▲ SGURR MÒR

Rudha
Raonuill

M...igvaig

547
▲ CÀRN A'GHOBHAIR

854
▲ BEINN BHUIDHE

1039
▲ SGURR NA CICHE

Loch Nevis

Loch an
Nostaire

437
▲ SGURR BHUIDHE

Glen Dessarry

...raidbeg
...or
...ross

Bracora

Bracorina

Kylesmorar

Tarbet

723
▲ SGARR BREAC

859
▲ SGURR NAH-AIDE

Glen Pean

Swordland

Loch   Morar

Lettermorar

716
▲ AN STAC

949
▲ SGURR NAN COIREACHAN

964
▲ SGURR
THUILM

503
▲ CÀRN A'
MHÀDAIDH-RUAIDH

Meoble

710
▲ MEITH BHEINN

River Meoble

600
▲ SIDHEAN
MÒR

237

10

Prince Charlie's
Cairn

Loch Beoriad

633
▲

796
▲ SGURR
AN UTHA

Glen Finnan

Gleann Dubhlighe

Gleann Fionnlighe

Arisaig
House

Loch nan Uamh

Kinlochnanuagh

Polnish

Lochailort

Inverailort

Loch
Eilt

A830   14

Glenfinnan

Glenfinnan
Visitor Centre

Glenfinnan
Monument

Kinlocheil

Drimsallie

Ardnish

A861

877
▲ ROIS-BHEINN

882
▲ BEINN
ODHAR BHEAG

Garvan

...alais
...uig

Loch Ailort

712
▲

Loch Shiel

Glen Garvan

718
▲ MEALL
NAM DAMH

8

K...chmoi...
Brunery

664
▲ BEINN GAIRE

228

Scamodale

758
▲ MEAL...

Cona G...

0	1	2	3	4	5 miles

0	1	2	3	4	5	6	7	8 kilometres

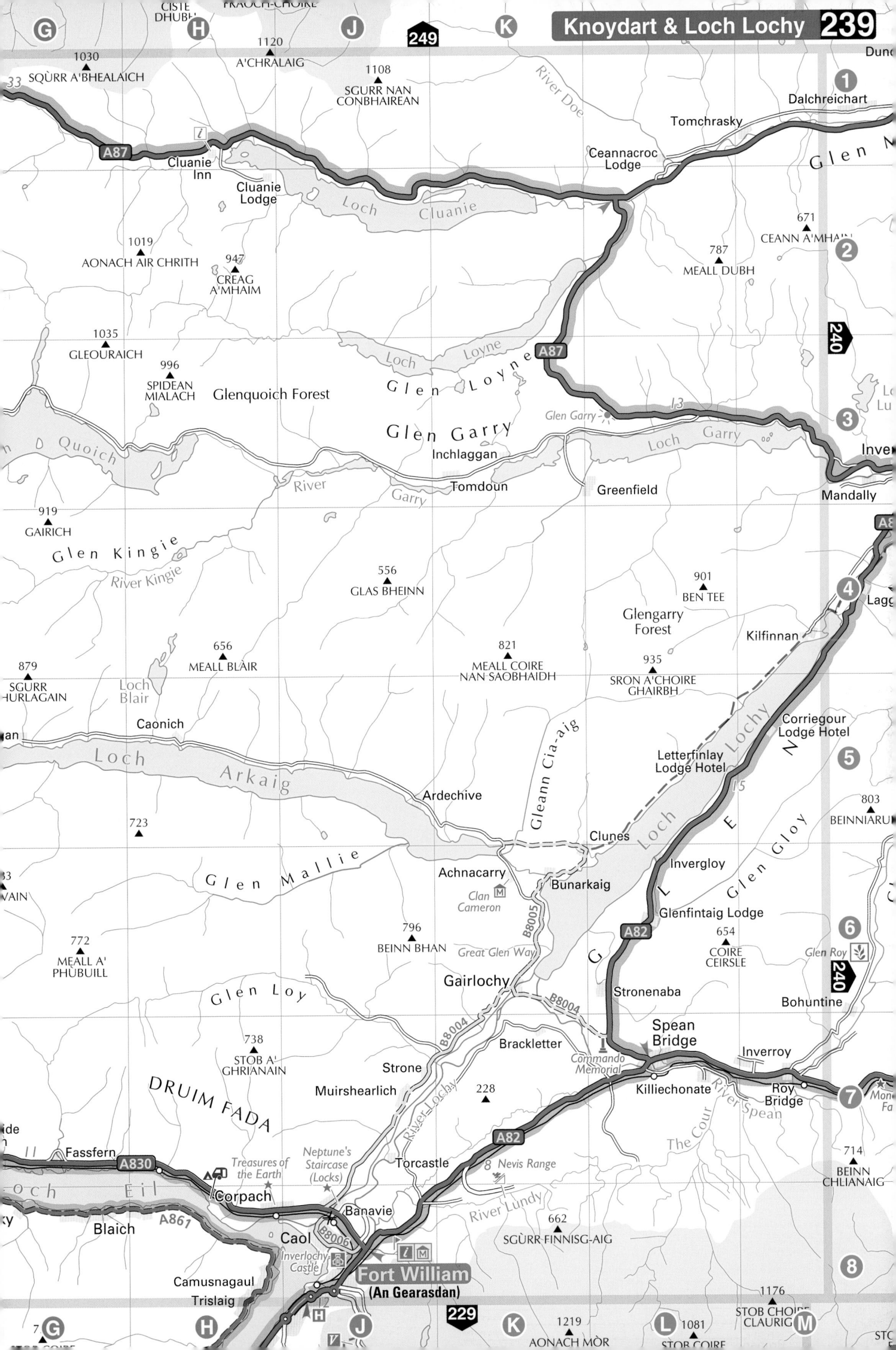

G H J 249 K

1

SQÙRR A'BHEALAICH 1030

A'CHRALAIG 1120

SGURR NAN CONBHAIREAN 1108

River Doe

Dalchreichart

Tomchrasky

Ceannacroc Lodge

Glen M

Dund

ℹ
A87
Cluanie Inn
Cluanie Lodge

Loch Cluanie

2
CEANN A'MHAIN 671

MEALL DUBH 787

AONACH AIR CHRITH 1019

CREAG A'MHAIM 947

Loch Loyne

Glen Loyne

A87

Glen Garry

3
Inver

Lo Lu

GLEOURAICH 1035

SPIDEAN MIALACH 996

Glenquoich Forest

Glen Garry

Inchlaggan

Tomdoun

Greenfield

Loch Garry

Mandally

A8

D Quoich

River

Garry

GAIRICH 919

Glen Kingie

River Kingie

GLAS BHEINN 556

BEN TEE 901

Glengarry Forest

Kilfinnan

Inve

4

Lagg

SGURR HURLAGAIN 879

MEALL BLAIR 656

Loch Blair

MEALL COIRE NAN SAOBHAIDH 821

SRON A'CHOIRE GHAIRBH 935

Corriegour Lodge Hotel

BEINNIARU 803

Caonich

Loch Arkaig

Ardechive

Gleann Cia-aig

Clunes

Letterfinlay Lodge Hotel

Loch Lochy

N

Glen Gloy

5

723

Glen Mallie

Achnacarry

Clan Cameron M

Bunarkaig

Invergloy

Glenfintaig Lodge

COIRE CEIRSLE 654

Glen Roy 🌿

6
240

VAIN 33

B8005

BEINN BHAN 796

Great Glen Way

G L E

Stronenaba

Bohuntine

MEALL A' PHÙBUILL 772

Glen Loy

STOB A' GHRIANAIN 738

Strone

Brackletter

Spean Bridge

Inverroy

Muirshearlich

228

Commando Memorial I

Killiechonate

Roy Bridge

River Spean

7
Mon Fa

DRUIM FADA

Fassfern
A830

River Lochy

Torcastle

A82

The Cour

BEINN CHLIANAIG 714

🏔 ⛴
Treasures of the Earth

Neptune's Staircase (Locks)

8 Nevis Range 🏔

River Lundy

Corpach

Blaich
A861

Banavie

SGÙRR FINNISG-AIG 662

STOB CHOIRE CLAURIG 1176

ky

Loch Eil

Caol
B8006

Inverlochy Castle

ℹ M

Fort William
(An Gearasdan)

Camusnagaul

Trislaig

7 G

H J 229 K
AONACH MÒR 1219

L
STOB COIRE 1081

M
⭐

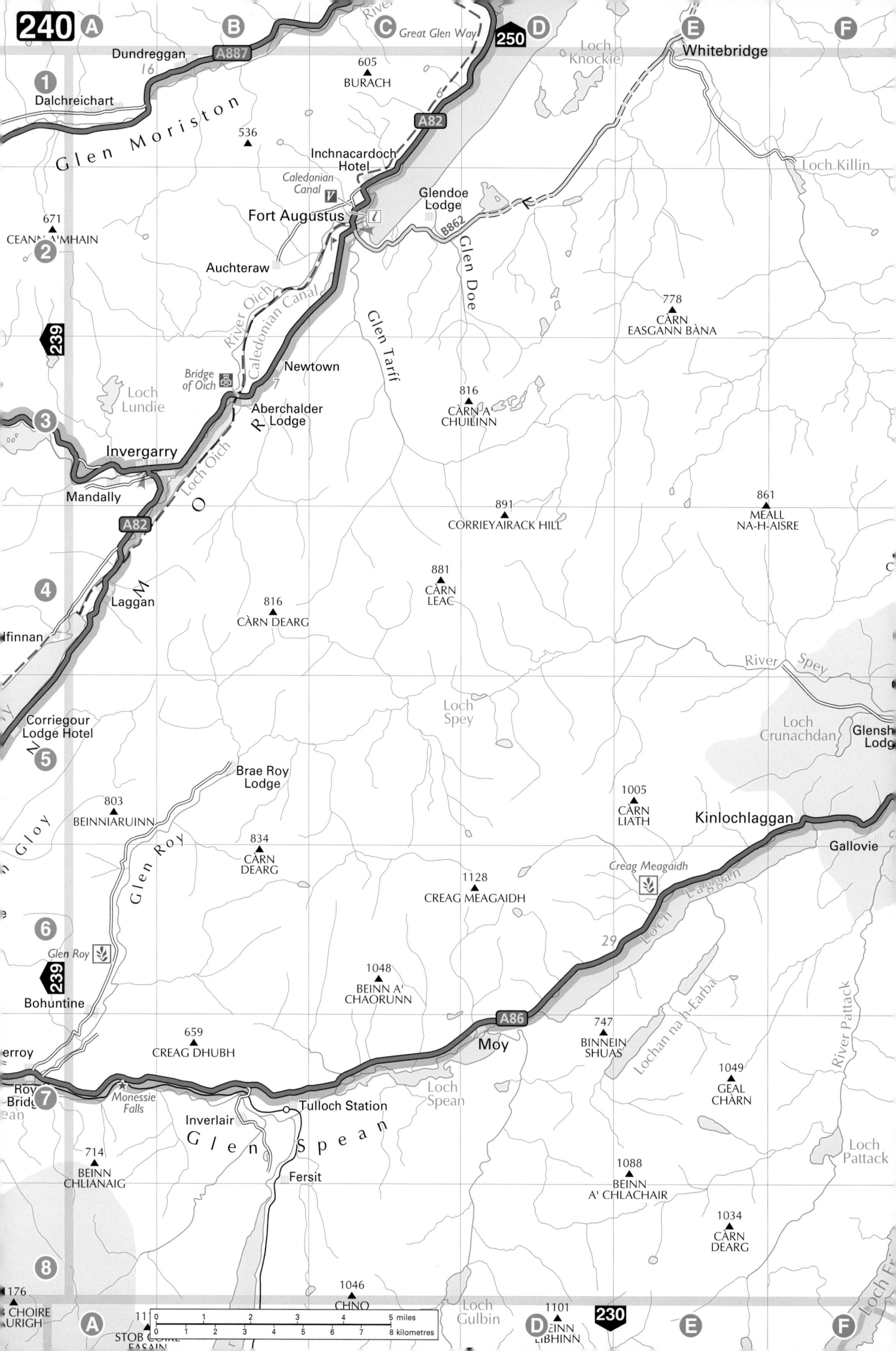

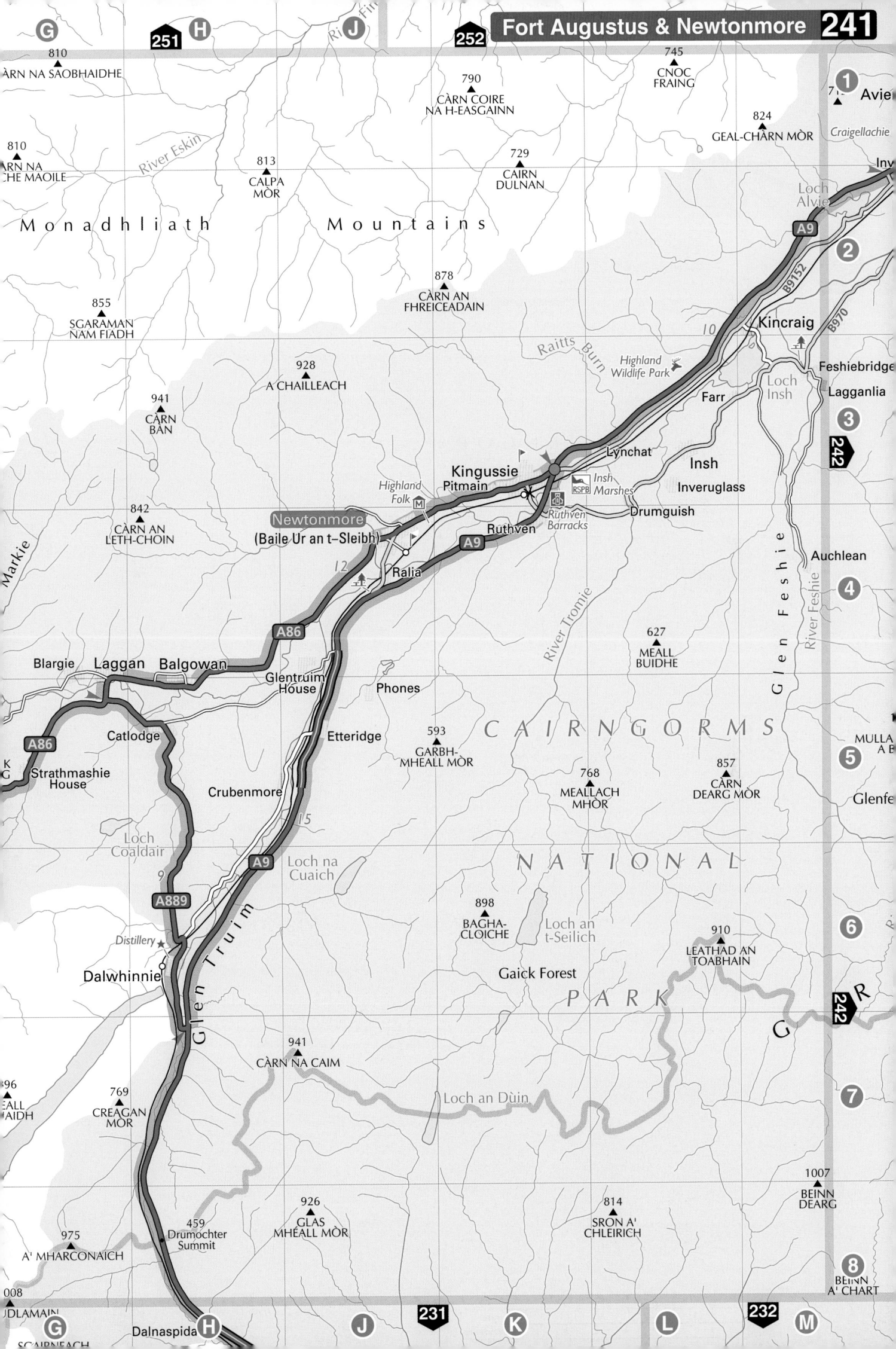

G **251** H **252**

810
ÀRN NA SAOBHAIDHE

790
CÀRN COIRE
NA H-EASGAINN

745
CNOC
FRAING

1
Avie

810
RN NA
CHE MAOILE

River Eskin

813
CALPA
MÒR

729
CAIRN
DULNAN

824
GEAL-CHÀRN MÒR

7
Inv

Loch
Alvie

A9

Craigellachie

2

B9152

Monadhliath   Mountains

855
SGARAMAN
NAM FIADH

878
CÀRN AN
FHREICEADAIN

Raitts Burn

Highland
Wildlife Park

10

Kincraig

B9970

Feshiebridge

Lagganlia

3

242

928
A CHAILLEACH

Loch
Insh

941
CÀRN
BÀN

Farr

Lynchat

Insh

Inveruglass

Auchlean

4

842
CÀRN AN
LETH-CHOIN

Highland
Folk
M

Kingussie
Pitmain

RSPB
Insh
Marshes

Drumguish

Glen Feshie

River Feshie

Newtonmore
(Baile Ur an t–Sleibh)

Ruthven
Barracks

Ruthven

12

Ralia

A9

River Tromie

627
MEALL
BUIDHE

C A I R N G O R M S

MULLA
A B

5

Glenfe

Blargie   Laggan   Balgowan

A86

Glentruim
House

Phones

593
GARBH-
MHEALL MÒR

768
MEALLACH
MHÒR

857
CÀRN
DEARG MÒR

Catlodge

Etteridge

A86
K
G

Strathmashie
House

Crubenmore

15

N A T I O N A L

Loch
Coaldair

A9

Loch na
Cuaich

898
BAGHA-
CLOICHE

Loch an
t-Seilich

910
LEATHAD AN
TOABHAIN

6

9

A889

Glen Truim

Gaick Forest

P A R K

R
G

242

Distillery

Dalwhinnie

941
CÀRN NA CAIM

Loch an Dùin

7

96
EALL
AIDH

769
CREAGAN
MÒR

1007
BEINN
DEARG

975
A' MHARCONAICH

926
GLAS
MHEALL MÒR

814
SRON A'
CHLEIRICH

459
Drumochter
Summit

8
BEINN
A' CHART

008
DLAMAIN

SCAIRNEACH

Dalnaspida   Dalnaspida

606
CÀRN
TUADHAN

1

824
CÀRN MÒR

712
Aviemore

River Spey
B970

821
GEAL CHÀRN

Straanruie

River Nethy

Craigellachie

803
CARN BHEADHAIR

Glenmore
Forest Park

809
MEALL A' BHUACHAILLE

Inverdruie
Coylumbridge

Glenmore 🅅

Reindeer
Centre

730
MAIM
SUIM

Loch
Alvie

Rothiemurchus 🅅

C A I R N G O R M S

Glen More

A9

2

Loch an
Eilean

Loch
Morlich

713
THE
BRUACH

Glenmore Lodge

241

B9152

Kincraig

B970

Rothiemurchus
Lodge

Cairngorm
Ski Area

N A T I O N A L

Feshiebridge

1245
CAIRN
GORM

Lagganlia

3

Loch
Insh

C A I R N G O R M

Lochan
Buidhe

1083
BEINN A
CHAORRUINN

1196
NORTH
TOP

117
BEN
AVO

1108
SGÒR AN
DUBH MÒR

1295
BRAERIACH

Lairig Ghru

M O U N T A I N S

1084
CÀRN
EÀS

Glen Feshie

Auchlean

Loch
Einich

1309
BEN
MACDHUI

P A R K

K 1177
SOUTH
TOP

4

River Feshie

1049
CÀRN
BAN MÒR

1293
CAIRN
TOUL

930
BEINN
BHREAC

Glen Derry

1017
MULLACH CLACH
A BHLÀIR

1157
BEINN
BHROTAIN

River Dee

Glen Lui

Quoich Water

M

O

5

Glenfeshie   Forest

813
SGÒR
MÒR

Glen Dee

Linn of Dee

Mar Lodge
Estate

Allanaquoich

Br

859
MORRC
HILL

River Eldart

Inverey

River Feshie

816
CARN
LIATH

6

R

A

M

P

I

A

N

Glen Ey

241

999
CARN
EALAR

1006
AN
SGARSOCH

919
CARN BHAC

886
SGOR
MOR

G

Tarf Water

93
TH
CAIRN

7

Gleann Mòr

Glenshe
Ski Are

Baddoch Burn

1007
BEINN
DEARG

River Tilt

1050
GLAS
TULAICHEAN

34

8

897
BEINN
A' CHART

Loch
Loch

Glen Lo

0   1   2   3   4   5 miles
0 1 2 3 4 5 6 7 8 kilometres

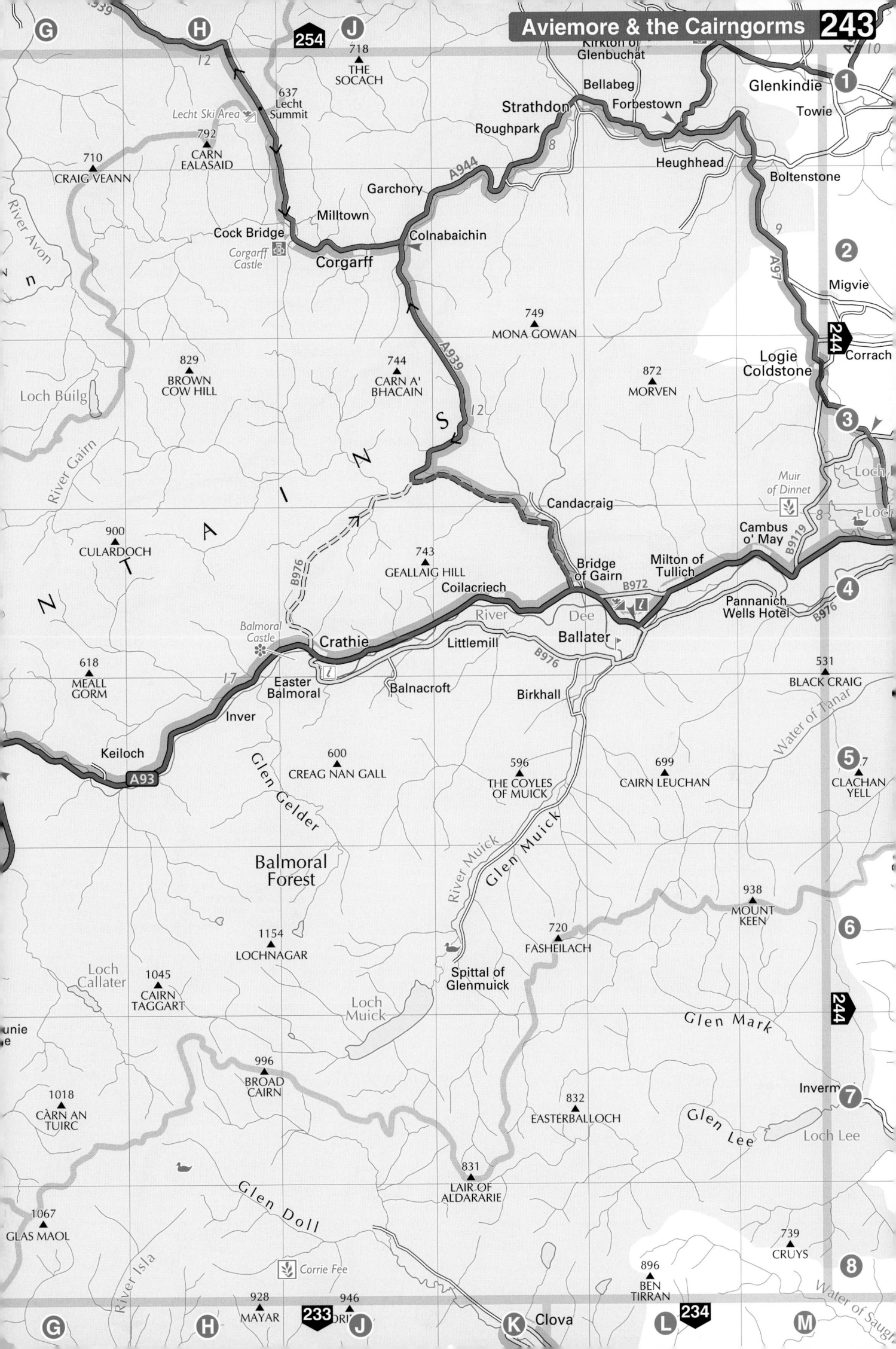

G **H** **J** 254 718 ▲ THE SOCACH

Kirkton of Glenbuchat

1 Glenkindie

Towie

637 Lecht Summit

Lecht Ski Area

Bellabeg

Forbestown

Strathdon

Roughpark

792 ▲ CARN EALASAID

710 ▲ CRAIG VEANN

Heughhead

Boltenstone

A944

8

Garchory

Milltown

Cock Bridge

Corgarff Castle

Corgarff

Colnabaichin

2 Migvie

9

A97

244 Corrach

829 ▲ BROWN COW HILL

744 ▲ CARN A' BHACAIN

749 ▲ MONA GOWAN

872 ▲ MORVEN

Logie Coldstone

Loch Buig

River Gairn

A939

12

3

Muir of Dinnet

Loch

Loch

Candacraig

900 ▲ CULARDOCH

743 ▲ GEALLAIG HILL

Coilacriech

Bridge of Gairn

B972

Milton of Tullich

Cambus o' May

B9119

618 ▲ MEALL GORM

B976

River Dee

Ballater

Pannanich Wells Hotel

B976

4

Balmoral Castle

Crathie

Littlemill

B976

531 ▲ BLACK CRAIG

Easter Balmoral

Balnacroft

Birkhall

Inver

600 ▲ CREAG NAN GALL

596 ▲ THE COYLES OF MUICK

699 ▲ CAIRN LEUCHAN

Water of Tanar

Keiloch

Glen Gelder

A93

5 7 CLACHAN YELL

Balmoral Forest

River Muick

Glen Muick

938 ▲ MOUNT KEEN

6

1154 ▲ LOCHNAGAR

720 ▲ FASHEILACH

Loch Callater

1045 ▲ CAIRN TAGGART

Loch Muick

Spittal of Glenmuick

244

Glen Mark

996 ▲ BROAD CAIRN

832 ▲ EASTERBALLOCH

Inverm

7

1018 ▲ CÀRN AN TUIRC

Glen Lee

Loch Lee

831 ▲ LAIR OF ALDARARIE

Glen Doll

739 ▲ CRUYS

1067 ▲ GLAS MAOL

Corrie Fee

896 ▲ BEN TIRRAN

8

River Isla

928 ▲ MAYAR

946 ▲ DRI..

233

J

K Clova

234

L

M

Water of Saugh

G **H**

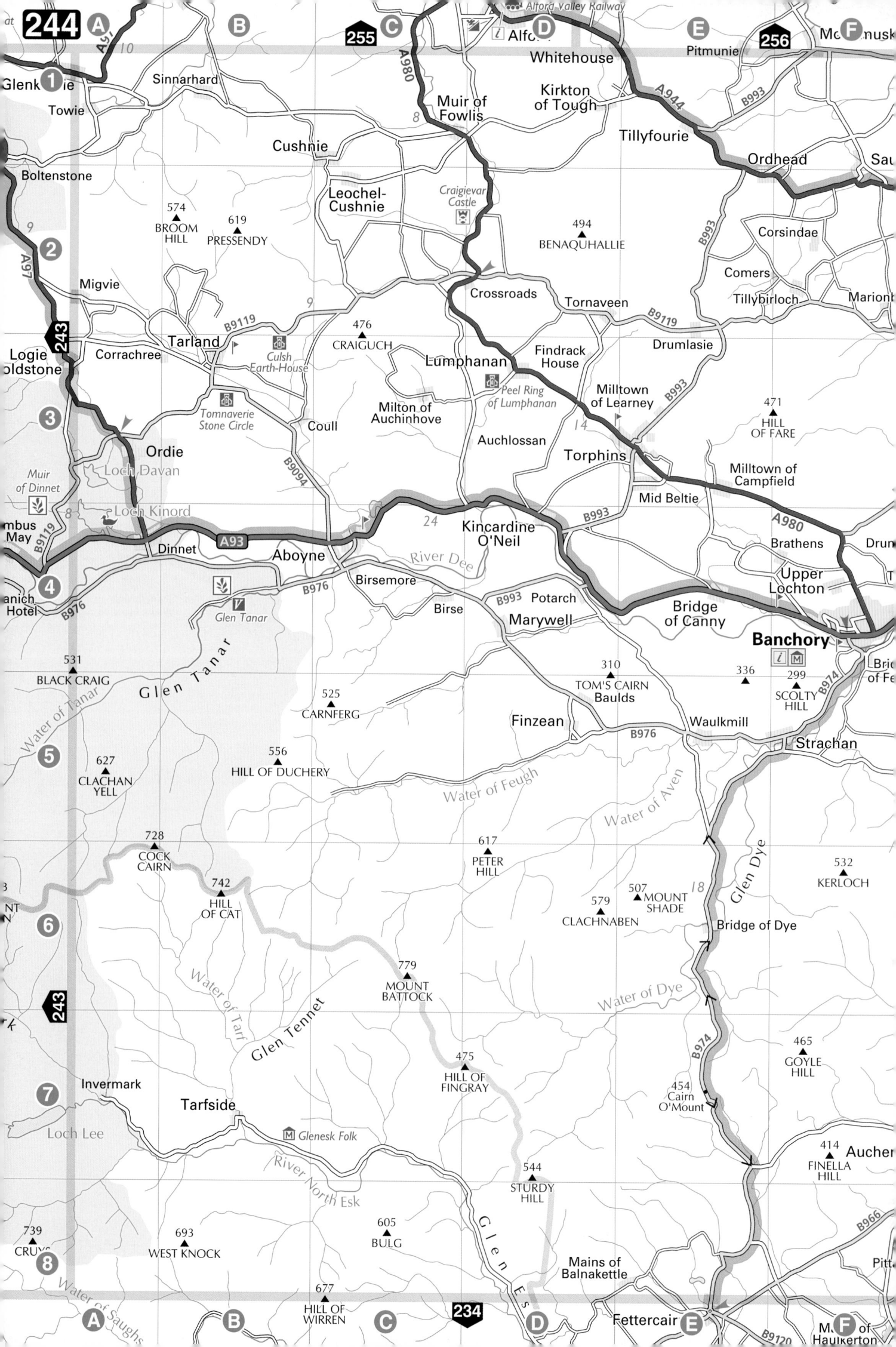

A B C D E F

1

HEALAVAL
BHEAG B

Harlosh

258

Os D

Colbost
Point

Dun
Beag

Bracadale

Loch Duagrich

Mu

368
▲
BEINN NA
BOINEID

Harlosh
Island

Coillore

Tarner
Island

Struan

Ullinish
Lodge Hotel

Loch Bracadale

Wiay

Idrigill
Point

Oronsay

Portnalong

Fiskavaig

439
▲
ROINEVAL

Loch Harport

B8009

Fernilea

2

Rudha nan Clach

Drynoch

369
▲
ARNAVAL

Carbost

23

A863

Merkadale

Talisker
Bay

Glen Dryno

369
▲
BEINN BHR

Talisker

Glen Eynort

3

447
▲
BEINN
BHREAC

Grula

Loch Eynort

97
▲
SGU
A' GHE

434
▲
AN CRUACHIN

4

Glenbrittle House

C u

Bualintur

SC
ALA

Loch Brittle

225
▲
CEANN NA BEINNE

5

Rudh' an Dùnain

Soay Soun

6

Rud
Aong

C
U
I
L
L
I
N

7

CANNA

210
▲
CÀRN A' GHAILL

Garrisdale Point

A'Chill

Canna
Harbour

Kilmory
Bay

Rudha
Shamhnan Insir

RÙM

Sanday

302
▲
MULLACH
MÒR

Sound of Canna

Rudha na
Roinne

Kinloch

Loch
Scresort

8

| 0 | 1 | 2 | 3 | 4 | 5 miles |
| 0 | 1 2 | 3 | 4 5 | 6 7 | 8 kilometres |

A Bhrideanach

236

570
▲
ORVAL

A B C D E F

Penifiler
412
BEN
TIANAVAIG
DÙN CAAN 444
259
Camusterrach
Culduie

Camastianavaig
Tianavaig
Bay
Oskaig
Rudha na' Leac
Toscaig
River
Toscaig
1

Ollach
B883
Clachan
310
BEINN NA LEAC
Eilean
Meadhonach
Eilean
Mòr
Caolas Mòr
2

Inverarish
The Braes
Eyre
Point
SCALPAY
CROWLIN ISLANDS
Port-an-Eo

444
BEN LEE
Peinchorran
Suisnish
Point
67
Longay
248
Drumb

Sconser
achan
Badicaul

773
GLAMAIG
A87
Dunan
Luib
Loch Ainort
17
Caolas Scalpay
27
Pabay
Kyle of Loch
(Caol Loch Ailse)
3

I S L E   O F
564
GLAS BHEIN
MHÒRN
Corry
Broadford
Bay
Waterloo
Lower
Breakish
Skye Bridge
Kyleakin

S K Y E
965
N GILLEAN
732
BEINN NA
CAILLICH
Broadford
9
A87

The Cuillin Hills
708
BEINN
DEORG MHÒR
B8083
i
Harrapool
Skulamus
Upper
Breakish
4
732
SGURR N
COINNIC

Hills
927
BLAVEN
Torrin
14
A851
Ky

94
ARS
INN
Loch na
Crèitheach
605
BEN ASLAK

Loch
oruisk
Kirkibost
B8083
Loch
Slapin
300
BEINN
NAN CARN
Heast
561
BEINN NA
SEAMRAIG
5

344
BEN
MEABOST
Suisnish
Rudha
Suisnish
Drumfearn
Loch na Dal

Loch
Scavaig
Elgol
Loch Eishort
Duisdalemore
Isleornsay
Ornsay
Sandaig
Island

chlach
lach
Glasnakille
298
SGÒRACH
BREAC
6

DAY
Strathaird
Point
Tokavaig
Ord River
Teangue
17
SOUND OF SLEAT
Rudh' Ard
Slisneach

Tarskavaig
Achnacloich
Loch nam
Uamph
Knock
238
Inverguser

Tarskavaig Bay
Ferrindonald
Knock
Bay

Kilmore
7
Glen
Airor

Kilbeg
518
DRUIM NA
CLUAIN-AIRIDHE

Clan Donald
V
A851
Ardvasar
Armadale
Sandaig

Aird of
Sleat
Calligarry
V
8

Ard
Thurinish
237
Sandaig Bay

G
H
J
Point
of Sleat
K
L
Rudha
Raonuill
M
Inverie
Bay

A87
Glen Varragill
9

SOUND

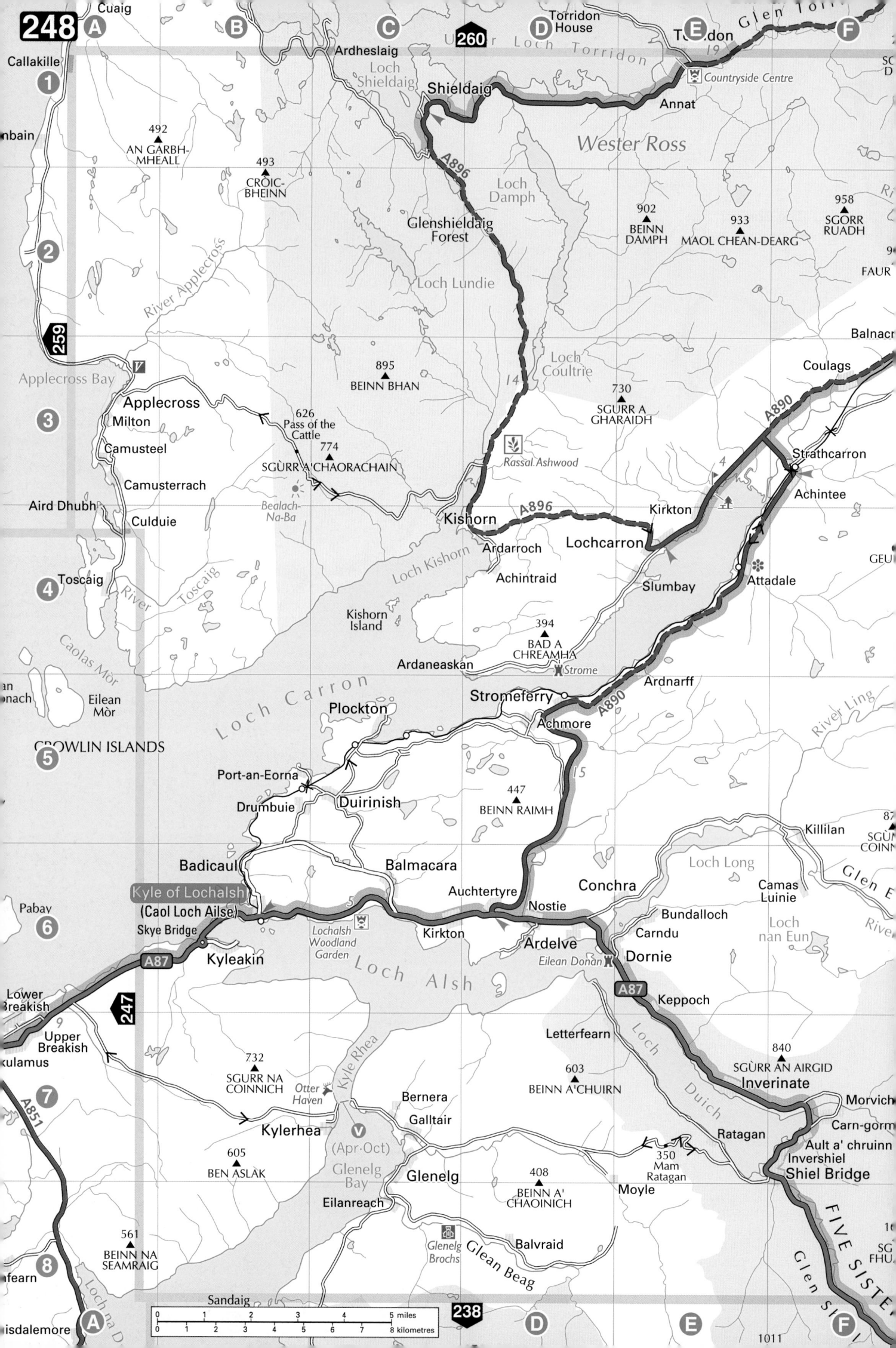

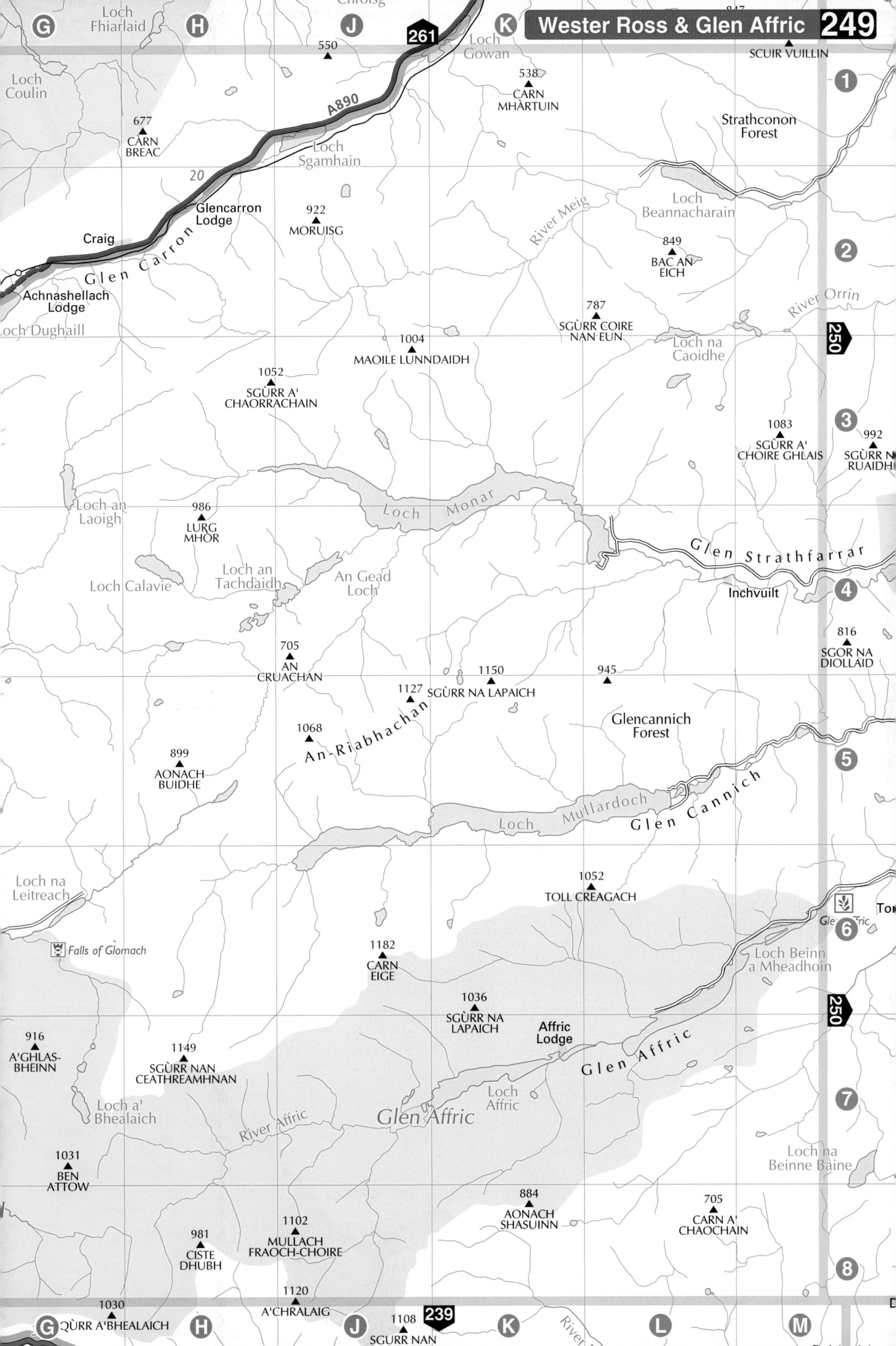

Loch Fhiarlaid

Loch Coulin

550

Loch Gowan

SCUIR VUILLIN

1

538
CARN
MHÀRTUIN

Strathconon
Forest

677
CARN
BREAC

A890

20

Loch
Sgamhain

Loch
Beannacharain

River Meig

Glencarron
Lodge

922
MORUISG

2

Craig

Glen Carron

849
BAC AN
EICH

River Orrin

Achnashellach
Lodge

och Dughaill

787
SGÙRR COIRE
NAN EUN

Loch na
Caoidhe

250

1004
MAOILE LUNNDAIDH

1083
SGÙRR A'
CHOIRE GHLAIS

992
SGÙRR N
RUAIDH

3

1052
SGÙRR A'
CHAORRACHAIN

Loch Monar

Glen Strathfarrar

Loch an
Laoigh

986
LURG
MHOR

Loch Calavie

Loch an
Tachdaidh

An Gead
Loch

Inchvuilt

4

816
SGOR NA
DIOLLAID

705
AN
CRUACHAN

1150
SGÙRR NA LAPAICH

945

1127

1068

An-Riabhachan

Glencannich
Forest

899
AONACH
BUIDHE

5

Loch Mullardoch

Glen Cannich

Loch na
Leitreach

1052
TOLL CREAGACH

To

Gle   ric

6

Falls of Glomach

Loch Beinn
a Mheadhoin

1182
CARN
EIGE

250

1036
SGÙRR NA
LAPAICH

Affric
Lodge

Glen Affric

916
A'GHLAS-
BHEINN

1149
SGÙRR NAN
CEATHREAMHNAN

Loch a'
Bhealaich

River Affric

Glen Affric

Loch
Affric

7

Loch na
Beinne Bàine

1031
BEN
ATTOW

884
AONACH
SHASUINN

705
CARN A'
CHAOCHAIN

1102
MULLACH
FRAOCH-CHOIRE

981
CISTE
DHUBH

8

1120
A'CHRALAIG

1030
QÙRR A'BHEALAICH

1108
SGURR NAN

239

River

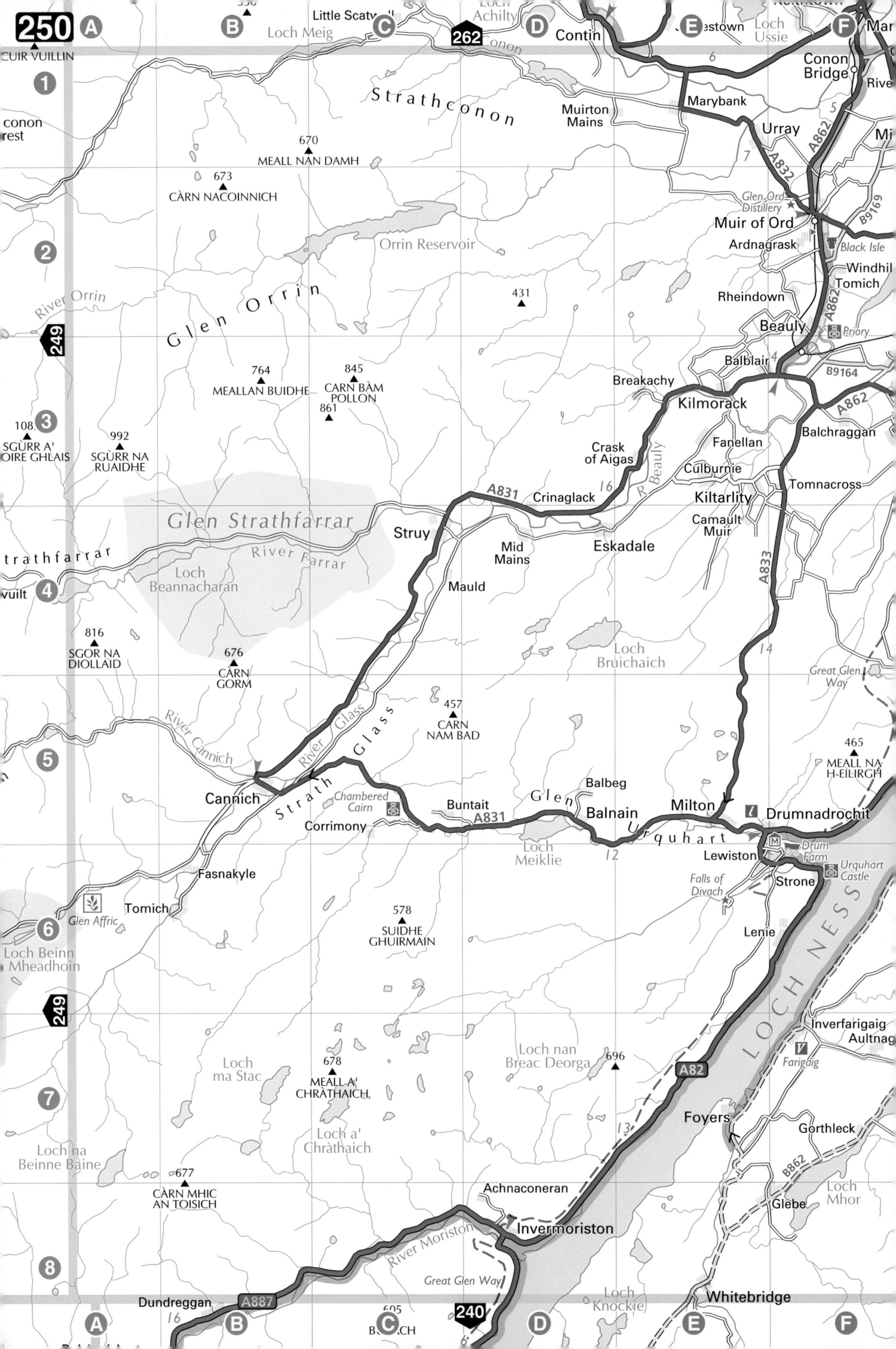

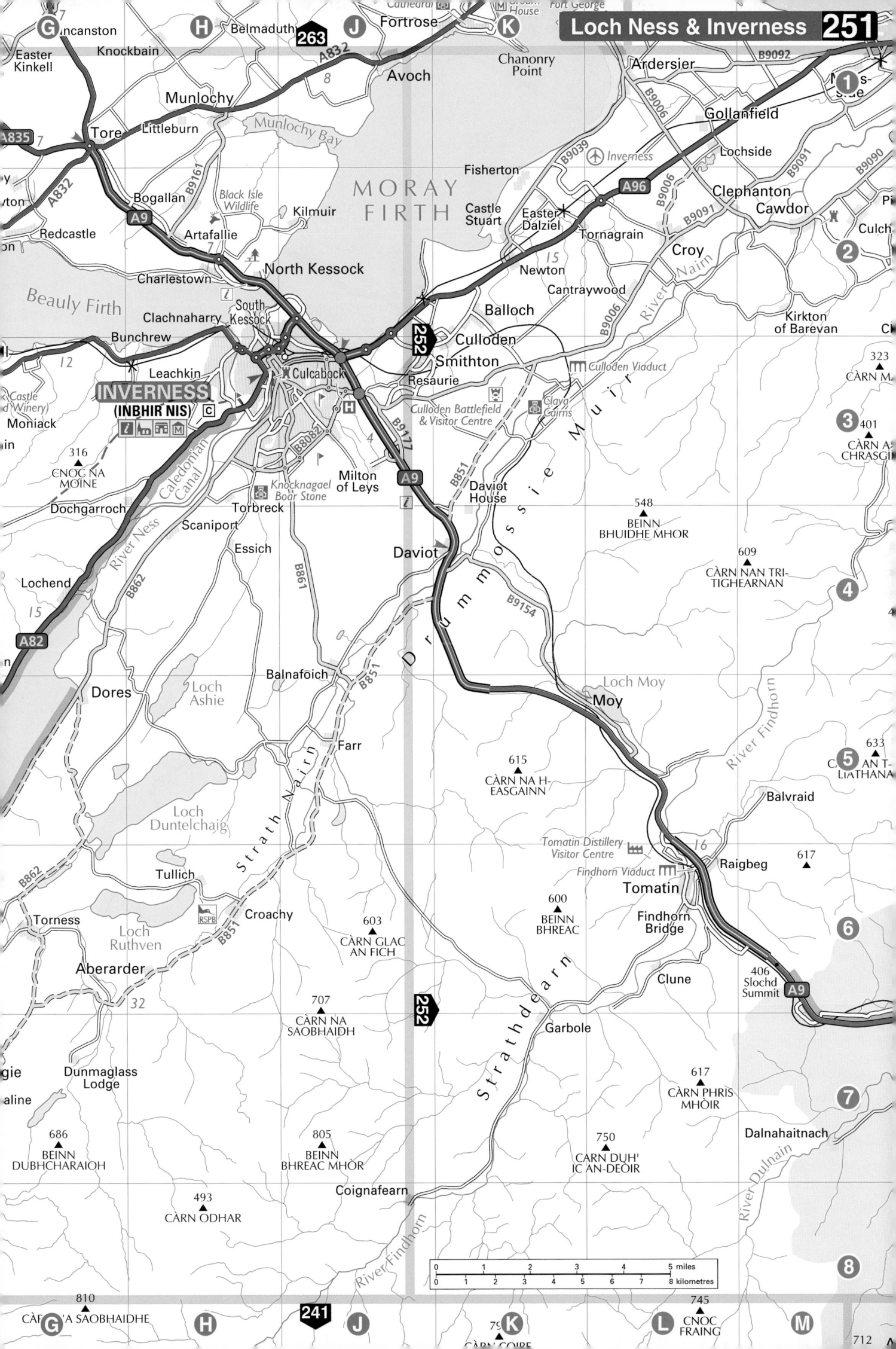

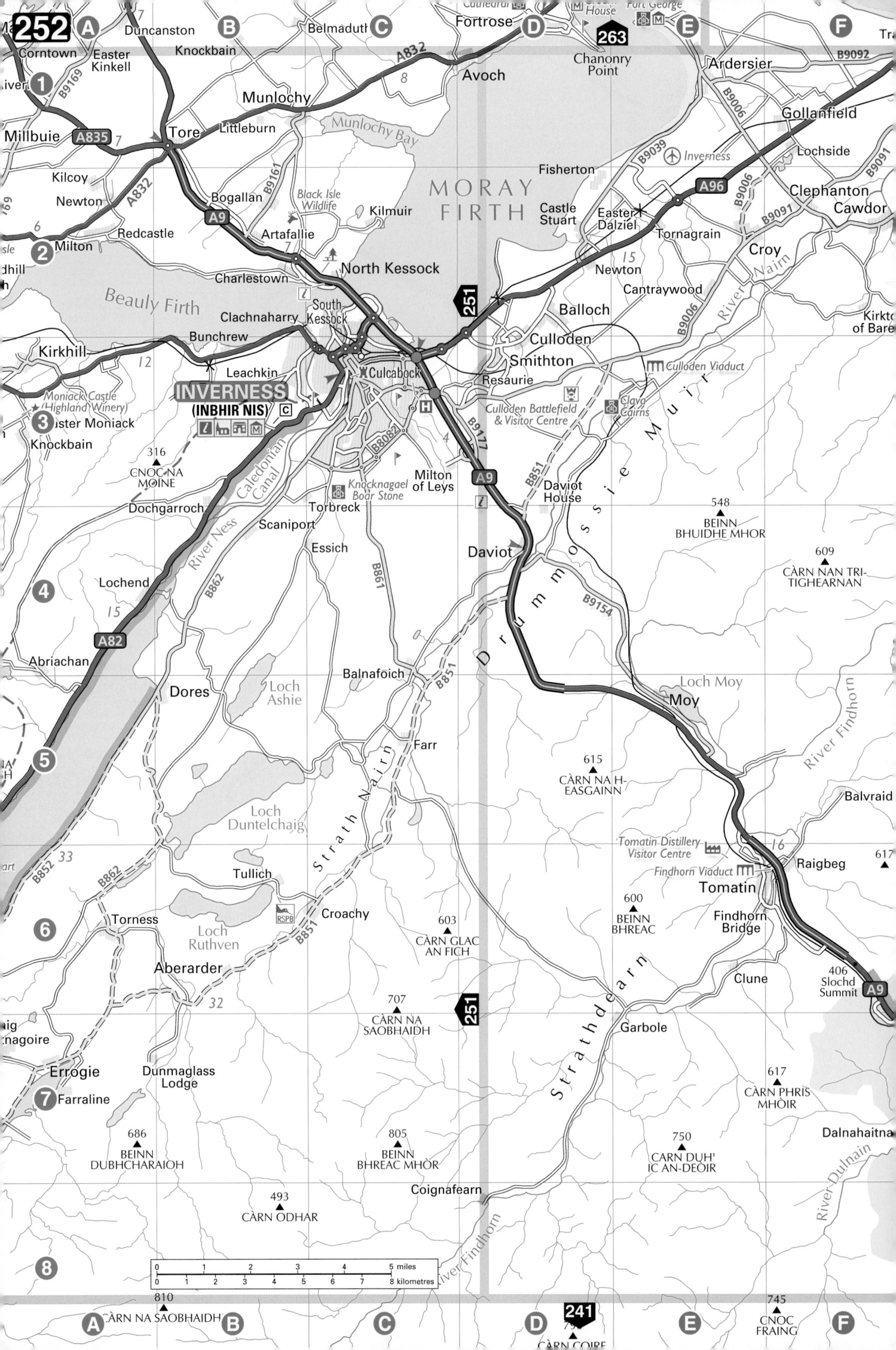

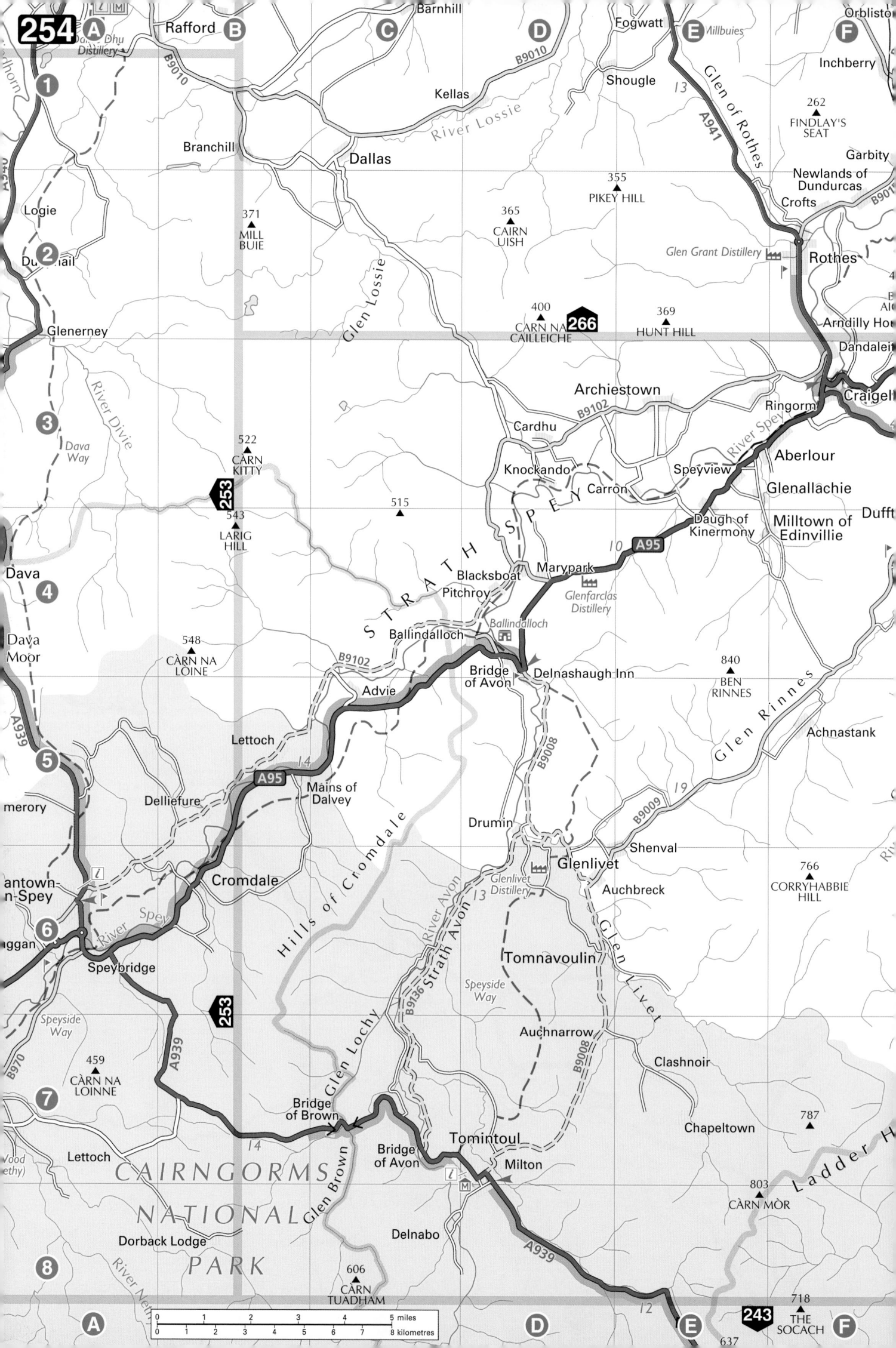

G quish
WHITEASH HILL
MILLSTONE HILL
H
J
K LURG HILL
1

A96
429
Glenbarry
250
THIEF'S HILL
Forgie
Berryhillock
KNOCK HILL
20
271
WETHER HILL
Lootcherbrae

Sound Muir
Aultmore Forgieside
Grange Crossroads
Bracobrae
Knock
Drumnagorrach

chroisk
Upper Mulben
Rumbach
Newmill
Davoch of Grange
Farmtown
Bridge of Marnoch
2

9103
Mulben
B9017
Strath Isla
A95
River Isla

Deanshaugh
Tauchers
Rosarie
Fife Keith
Strathisla Distillery
Keith
Rothiemay
Inverkeith

A95
Hill of Towie
B9014
365
MEIKLE BALLOCH
Bogniebrae
Forgue

338
HILL OF TOWIE
Keith and Dufftown Railway
A96
267
Ruthven
A97
12
3

372
KNOCKAN
gieknockater
B9115
Drummuir
Cairnie
River Deveron
B9022
B901

Glenfiddich Distillery
B9014
A920
Nordic Ski Centre
Castle
Affleck
Drumblade
256

Balvenie Castle
Haugh of Glass
14
Huntly
Strath Bogie
Brideswell
4

rktown Mortlach
Auchindoun Castle
Bridgend
Kirkstile
A96
Thomastown

A941
Culdrain
Hillhead
Bainshole

503
525
Kirkney
Gartly
419 WICHACH HILL
466 HILL OF FOUDLAN
Glens of Foudlan
5

Bridgend
440 CRANSMILL HILL
A97
Leith Hall
Largie

18
564
Mains of Lesmoir
TAP O' NOTH
Kennethmont
B9002
Picardy Symbol Stone
Dunnideer
Insch

571 ROUND HILL
Cabrach
Belhinnie
A941
Rhynie
Cottown
Clatt
Duncanstone
6

Aldivalloch
Aldunie
B9002
St Mary's Kirk (Ruin)
A97
Leslie
256
B992

722 THE BUCK
5
484 MIRE OF MIDGATES
Lethenty
7

629 HILL OF THREE STONES
Lumsden
475 BRUX HILL
CORREEN HILLS

enyon
632 CREAG AN EUNAN
Mossat
A944
Tullynessle
Keig

Belnacraig
Kildrummy Castle
Kildrummy
Milltown
Scotsmill
Bridge of Alford
Montgarrie
Alford Valley Railway

Glenbuchat Castle
A97
Haughton House
Alford
8

Kirkton of Glenbuchat
243
Bellabeg
G
H
244
Glenkindie
J
Sinnarhard
K
A96
L
Whitehouse
M Kirkton

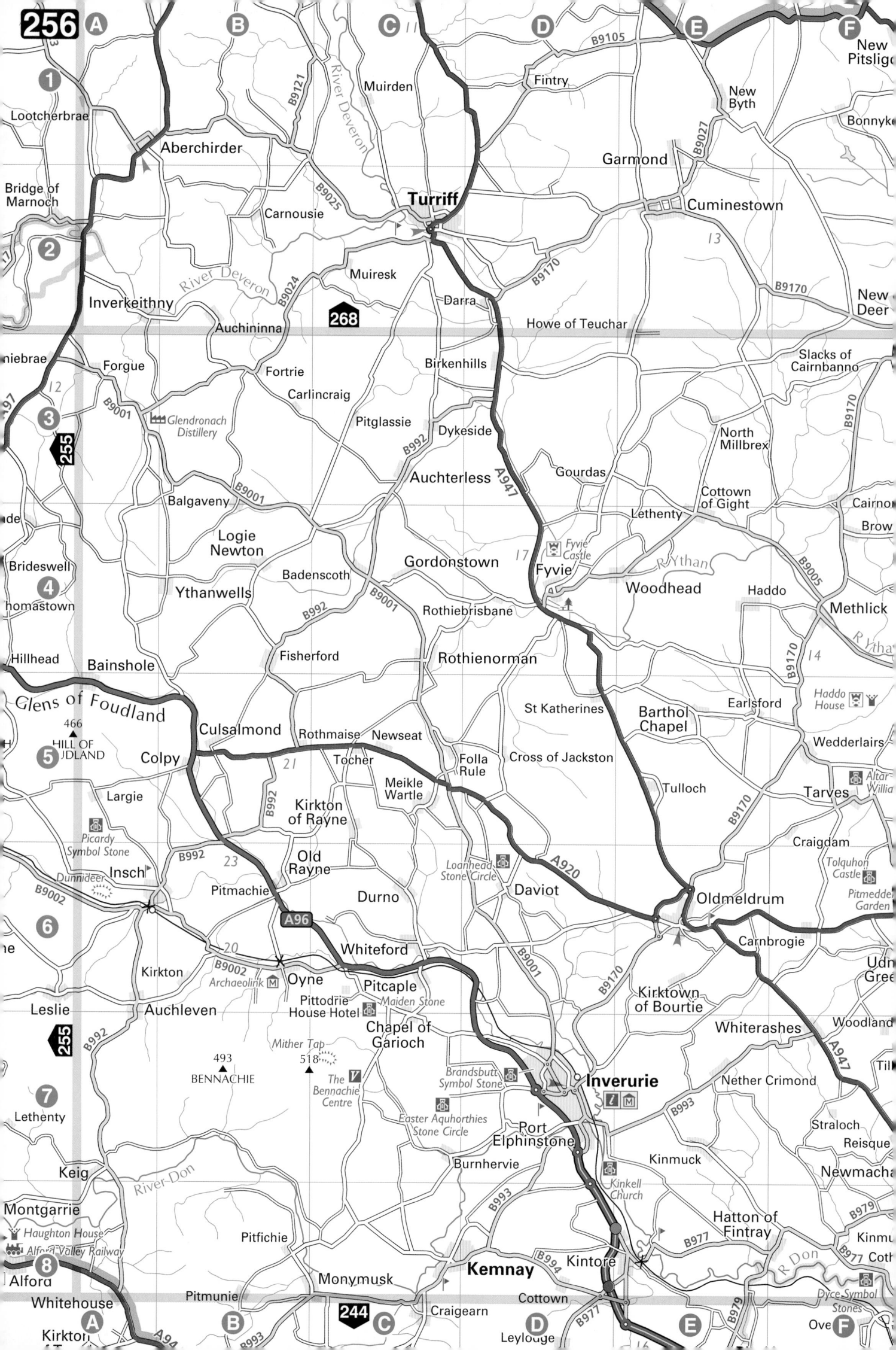

WAUGHTON HILL
G B9093
H
Strichen
J
Crimond
K Blackhill
60
Strathbeg

New Leeds
B9093
A952
18

Leys
Backfolds
Kirktown
St Fergus

Denhead
Rora
60
A90

Fetterangus

A981 A950
6
Deer Abbey
Dunshillock
River Ugie

Maud
B9106
Aden
Mintlaw
269
Longside
Inverugie
Buchanhaven
Peterhead
M

Blackhill of Clackriach
Old Deer
A950
Inverquhomery
9
Peterhead
H

B9029
B9029

Drymuir
Bulwark
Stuartfield
Inverquhomery
Hillhead of Cocklaw
Burnhaven
Peterhead Bay

Nethermuir
Millbreck
Nether Kinmundy
Buchan Ness

B9030
Clola
Blackhill
Stirling
Boddam

uchnagatt
12
Kinnadie
Kinknockie
Lendrum Terrace

Inkhorn
Coldwells
Ardallie
Longhaven

A948
A952
Hatton
A90
Auchiries
Bullers of Buchan

Arthrath
Muirtack
14
17
North Haven

Ythanbank
Birness
Bogbrae
Chapel Hill
Slains
Cruden Bay

uchedly
Artrochie
A975
Bay of Cruden

Kinharrachie
Whinnyfold
The Skares

Ellon P+R
B9005
Kirkton of Logie Buchan
Kirktown of Slains

Esslemont
A920
10
Collieston

tmedden
Logierieve
B9000
32
Forvie

ousieside
B9000

Udny Station
A90
Newburgh

Cultercullen
Foveran

A975

Delfrigs

Causeyend
B9979

Whitecairns
B999
Belhelvie
Balmedie
Balmedie
B977

B999
B977

Potterton
245
G
H Bla og
J
K
L
M

0 1 2 3 4 5 miles
0 1 2 3 4 5 6 7 8 kilometres

A   B   C   D   E   F

1

2

3

4

5

6

7

8

Fladda-chùain

Rudha Hu

The Little Minch

Tairbeart
(Tarbert)
(V)

Lùb Score

Borneskitaig

Kilmuir

Kilva

Balgown

Lir

(V)

Loch nam Madadh
(Lochmaddy)

Waternish Point

Totscore

Idrigill

Ascrib
Islands

Uig Bay

Earlish

Loch Snizort

283
▲
BEN
GEARY

Geary

A87

Trumpan

Gillen

Hallin

16

Ardmore
Point

DUNVEGAN
HEAD

Isay

Mingay

Stein

Lusta

214
▲
BEN
DIUBAIG

Greshornish
House
Hotel

Loch Greshornish

Ki

Loch Snizore

Loch
Bay

Boreraig

Claigan

Bay

327
▲
BEINN
BHREAC

Treaslane

Flashader

22

Loch Pooltiel

Uig

Upperglen

A850

Loch Dunvegan

Oisgill Bay

Feriniquarrie

Totaig

Edinbane

Bernisdale

A850

Milovaig

Glendale

Colbost

B884

Waterstein

Lephin

Colbost Croft

M

M

Toy

Skinidin

Dunvegan

i

Dunvegan

ISLE OF

Giant Angus MacAskill

A864

Kilmuir

Neist
Point

Lonmore

Caroy River

265
▲
BEN
AKETIL

271
▲
CRUACHAN BEINN
A' CHEARCAILL

Moonen Bay

Roskhill

SKYE

Ramasaig

469
▲
HEALAVAL
MORE

Roag

Orbost

Vatten

Glen Ose

Hoe Rape

488
▲
HEALAVAL
BHEAG

Harlosh

Loch Caroy

A863

Ose

Dun
Beag

Hoe Point

368
▲

246

Harlosh Island

Colbost
Point

Tarner
Island

Bracadale

| 0 | 1 | 2 | 3 | 4 | 5 miles |
| 0 | 1 | 2 | 3 | 4 | 5 | 6 | 7 | 8 kilometres |

Troдday

North Duntulm

Kilmaluag

seum Life

Flodigarry

Eilean Flodigarry

Poldorais

542 ▲
MEAL NA SUIREAMACH

Digg

Staffin Bay

Staffin Island

Brogaig

Stenscholl

Staffin

464 ▲
BIODA BUIDHE

Trotternish

Kilt Rock Waterfall

Ellishader

Maligar

Valtos

Marishader

Rudha nam Brathairean

River Conon

611 ▲
BEINN EDRA

Garros

Culnaknock

Loch a' Bhràige

Rudha na Fearn

Lealt

Òb Chuaig

Tote

A855

608 ▲
CREAG A' LAIN

einlich

nisdal

RONA

uaig

451 ▲
BEINN A' SGÀ

Callakille

River Romesdal

esdal

Old Man of Storr
719 ▲
THE STORR

Lonbain

S O U N D   O F   R A A S A Y

I N N E R   S O U N D

Kensaleyre

River Haulton

Eilean Tigh

Loch Leathan

16

Loch Fada

Eilean Fladday

B8036

Carbost

Borve

Manish Point

Loch Arnish

Torran

Drumuie

Arnish

Glengrasco

312 ▲

Brochel

Torvaig

Portree

Seafield

RAASAY

417 ▲
BEINN NA GRÉINE

Penifiler

412 ▲
BEN TIANAVAIG

Milton

Camu

Glenmore

Aird Dhu'

Glenvarragill

444 °

247 DÙN CAAN

A87

Mugeary

Camastianav

Tianavaig

Oskaig

Rudha na' Leac

Toscaig

Ap

Applecross Bay

260

248

247

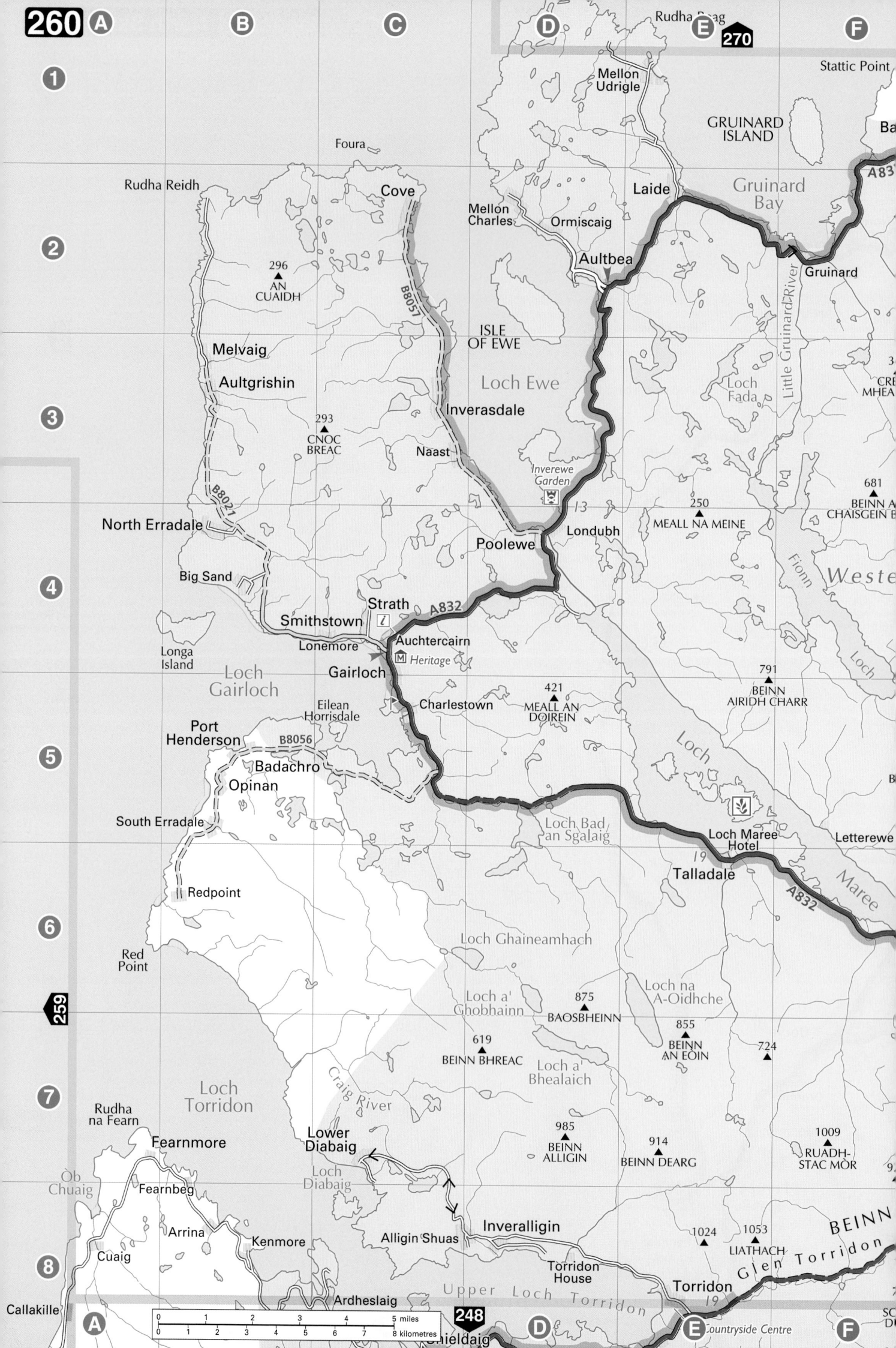

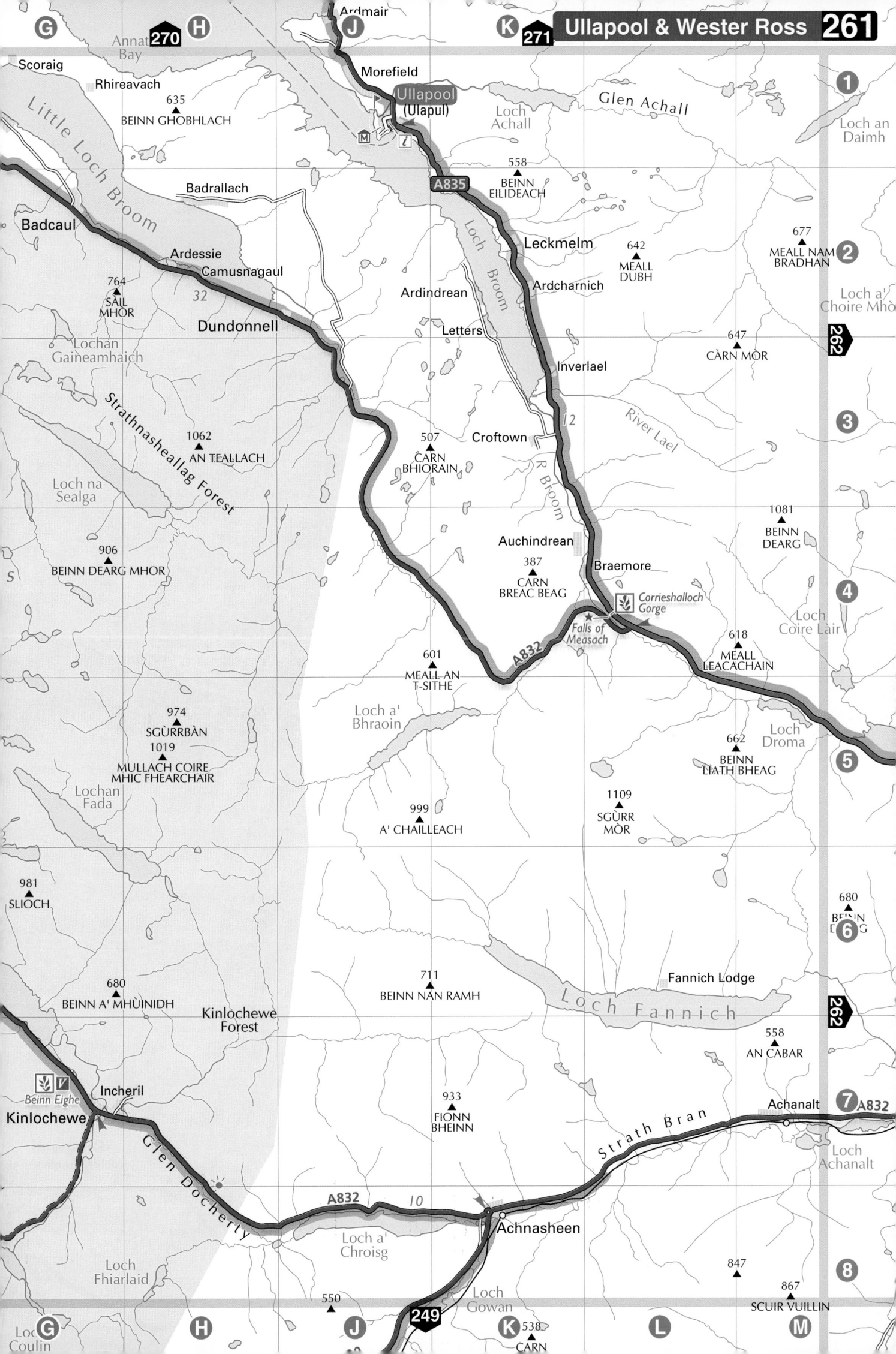

G 270 H J K 271

Ardmair

Scoraig
Annat Bay
Rhireavach
635
BEINN GHOBHLACH

Morefield
Ullapool
(Ulapul)

Glen Achall
Loch Achall

Loch an Daimh

1

Badcaul
Ardessie
Camusnagaul
32
Dundonnell

Badrallach

A835

558
BEINN EILIDEACH

Leckmelm

Ardcharnich

642
MEALL DUBH

677
MEALL NAM BRADHAN

2

Loch a' Choire Mhò

764
SÀIL MHOR

Lochan Gaineamhaich

Ardindrean

Letters

Inverlael

647
CÀRN MÒR

262

Loch Broom

Strathnasheallag Forest

1062
AN TEALLACH

507
CÀRN BHIORAIN

Croftown

R Broom

River Lael

12

3

Loch na Sealga

906
BEINN DEARG MHOR

S

1081
BEINN DEARG

Auchindrean

387
CÀRN BREAC BEAG

Braemore

Corrieshalloch Gorge

4

Loch Coire Làir

974
SGÙRRBÀN

1019
MULLACH COIRE MHIC FHEARCHAIR

Lochan Fada

601
MEALL AN T-SITHE

A832

Falls of Measach

618
MEALL LEACACHAIN

981
SLIOCH

Loch a' Bhraoin

662
BEINN LIATH BHEAG

Loch Droma

5

680
BEINN DEARG

6

680
BEINN A' MHÙINIDH

Kinlochewe Forest

999
A' CHAILLEACH

1109
SGÙRR MÒR

711
BEINN NAN RAMH

Fannich Lodge

Loch Fannich

262

Beinn Eighe
Incheril

Kinlochewe

Glen Docherty

933
FIONN BHEINN

558
AN CABAR

Achanalt

7 A832

Loch Achanalt

Loch Coulin

A832

10

Loch a' Chroisg

Strath Bran

Achnasheen

847

8

Loch Fhiarlaid

249

Loch Gowan

867
SCUIR VUILLIN

G H J K L M

538
CÀRN

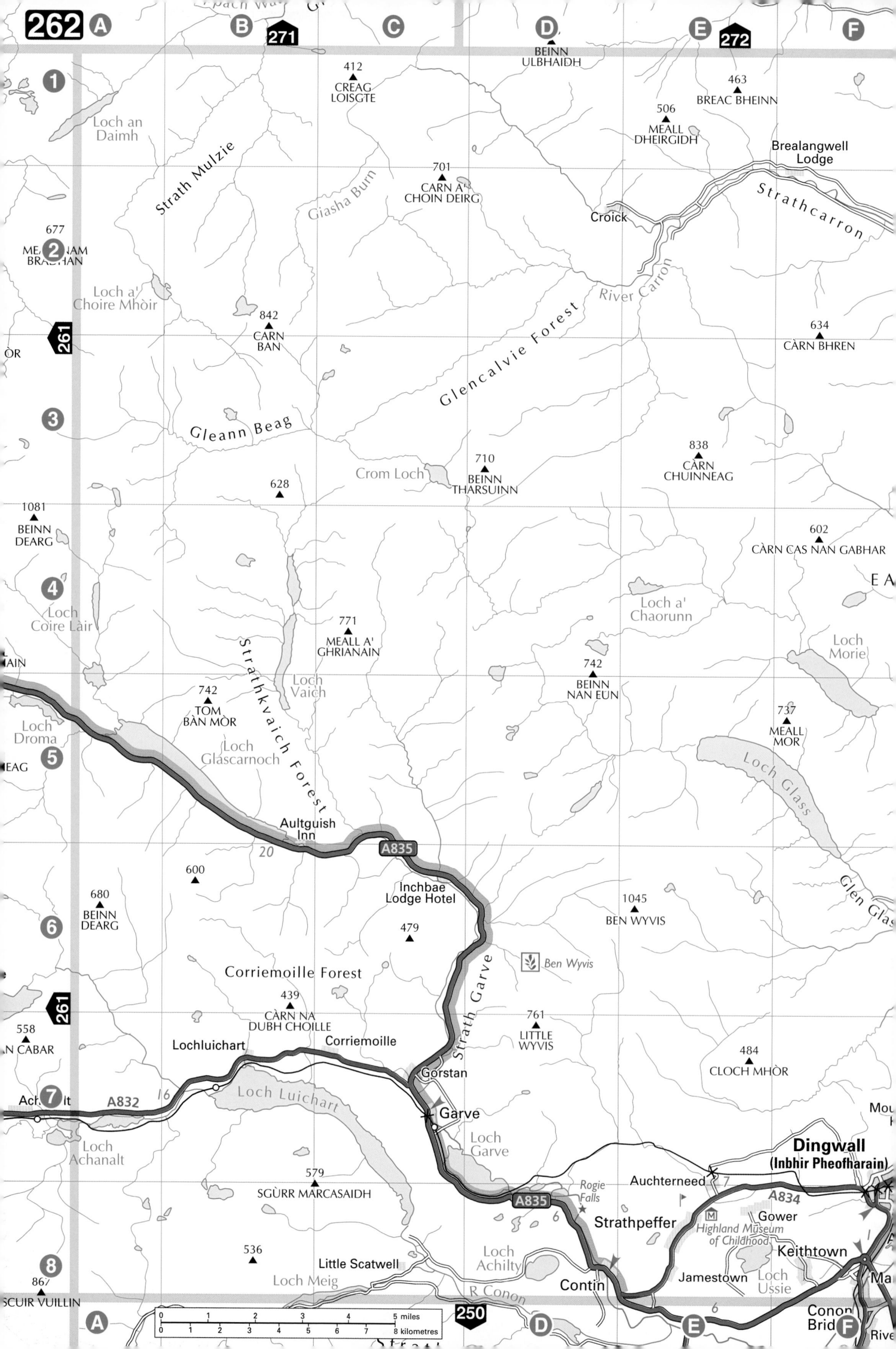

G 272 H J 273 K

1

Sleasdairidh
BEINN
DONUILL 349
Cambusavie
Platform
Loch Fleet

Badninish
Skelbo
Skelbo Street
Fourpenny
Embo

River Evelix
Achvaich
Birichin
Embo Street
Pitgrudy

Rearquhar
Astle
Evelix
A949
Camore
Royal Dornoch
Dornoch

Kyle of Sutherland
A836
Bonar Bridge
Loch Migdale
A949
Spinningdale 10
Clashmore
A9
3
Historylinks

Lower ledfield
Ardgay
Kincardine
Upper Ardchronie
A836

2
Whiteface
Dornoch Firth 6
Cuthill
264

Struie Hill
Ferrytown
Ardmore
Cambuscurrie Bay
Ferry Point
Innis Mhor

Edderton
A836
Glenmorangie Distillery
Morangie

BEINN CLACH AN FHEADAIN 477
19
Aultnamain Inn
284
Tain
(Baile Dhubhthaich)
Inver

3

ROSS
BEINN THARSUINN 692
CNOC AN T-SABHAIL 379
Toulv
Lochslin
Loch Eye
Hill of Fearn
Rh e

4
B9165

Rusdale
B9176
Newfield 6
Fearn
Tullich
B9166

Ardross
Ballchraggan
Arabella
Shandwick
Bal
Shan

River Alness
Achandunie
Kildary
Ankerville

Millcraig
Rhicullen
Tomich
A9 8
Milton
Pitcalnie
Nigg
B9175

5

CNOC CEISLEIN 523
Moultavie
Achnagarron
Delny
Kilmuir
Barbaraville
Nigg Bay

Alness
(Alanais)
Dalmore
Balintraid
Saltburn
Nigg Ferry

Invergordon
(Jun-Sept) V
Cromarty

6

Evanton
B817
2
Cromarty Firth
Balblair
Resolis
Cromarty Bay
Hugh Miller's Cottage
Newton

Teanord
5
Clanland & Seapoint
Udale Bay
RSPB
Allerton
Navity
264

Cullicudden
Jemimaville
B9163
Upper Eathie

Brae

7

Findon Mains
A9
B9169
Raddery
Whiteness Head

BLACK ISLE
B9160
A832 10

Culbokie
MOUNT EAGLE 255
Killen
RSPB
Rosemarkie
Nai
(Inbhir N

Duncanston
Cathedral
Groam House
Fort George
Tradespark

Easter Kinkell
Belmaduthy
Fortrose
Chanonry Point
Ard sier

Knockbain
A832
8
Avoch
252
Moss-side

G 251 H J K L M

1
2
3
4
5
6
7
8

1

2

3

4

5

Branderburgh

Stotfield

Lossiemouth

B9040

Burghead
Well

Hopeman   Burnside

Burghead

B9012   Duffus   St Peter's Kirk
& Parish Cross

Cummingston

6

Loch
Spynie

B9013   Roseisle   Duffus
Castle

B9012

B9135

Burghead Bay   College of
Roseisle

A941   Spynie
Palace   B9103

Stonewells

Kin
on

Lochill

Findhorn   Hempriggs   Quarrywood   Viewfield

B9089   Calcots

Bishopmill   Innesmill

B9011   Newton   Elgin

Findhorn
Bay   Kinloss   Coltfield   A96   Urquhart

Glen Moray
Distillery   7   The
Lochs

incorth
House   Alves   New Elgin   Lhanbryde

266   Linkwood   9

Grange Hall   Kilbuiack   12   A96

eno's Stone   Muir of
Miltonduff   Mosstodlo

ow   **Forres**   Crofts
of Dippl

Califer   Clackmarras

Pluscarden   Longmorn   B9103

Rafford   Barnhill   Orbliston

Dallas Dhu
Distillery   Fogwatt   Millbuies   8

B9010   Inchberry

B9010

Shougle   Glen

Kellas

262

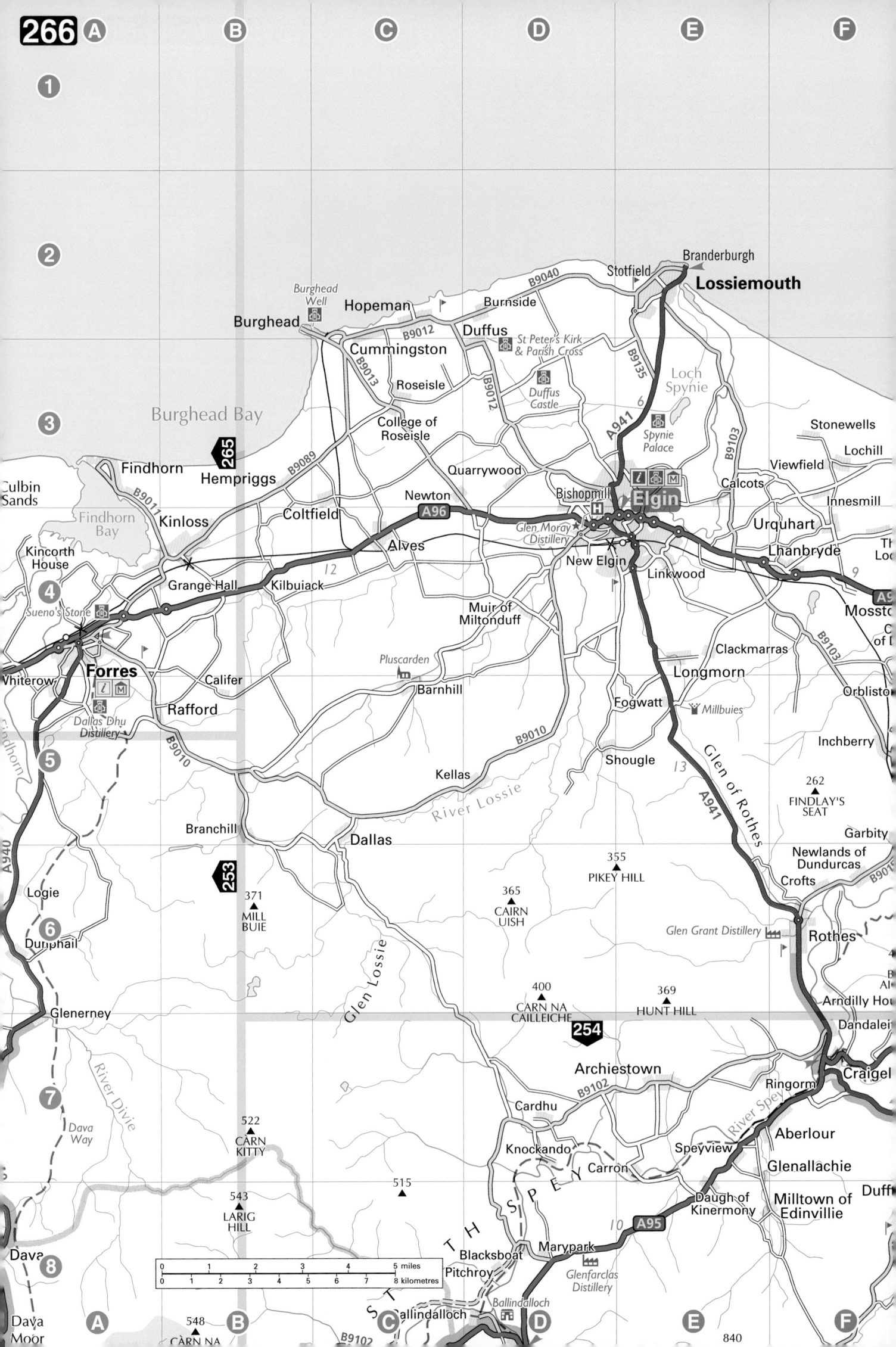

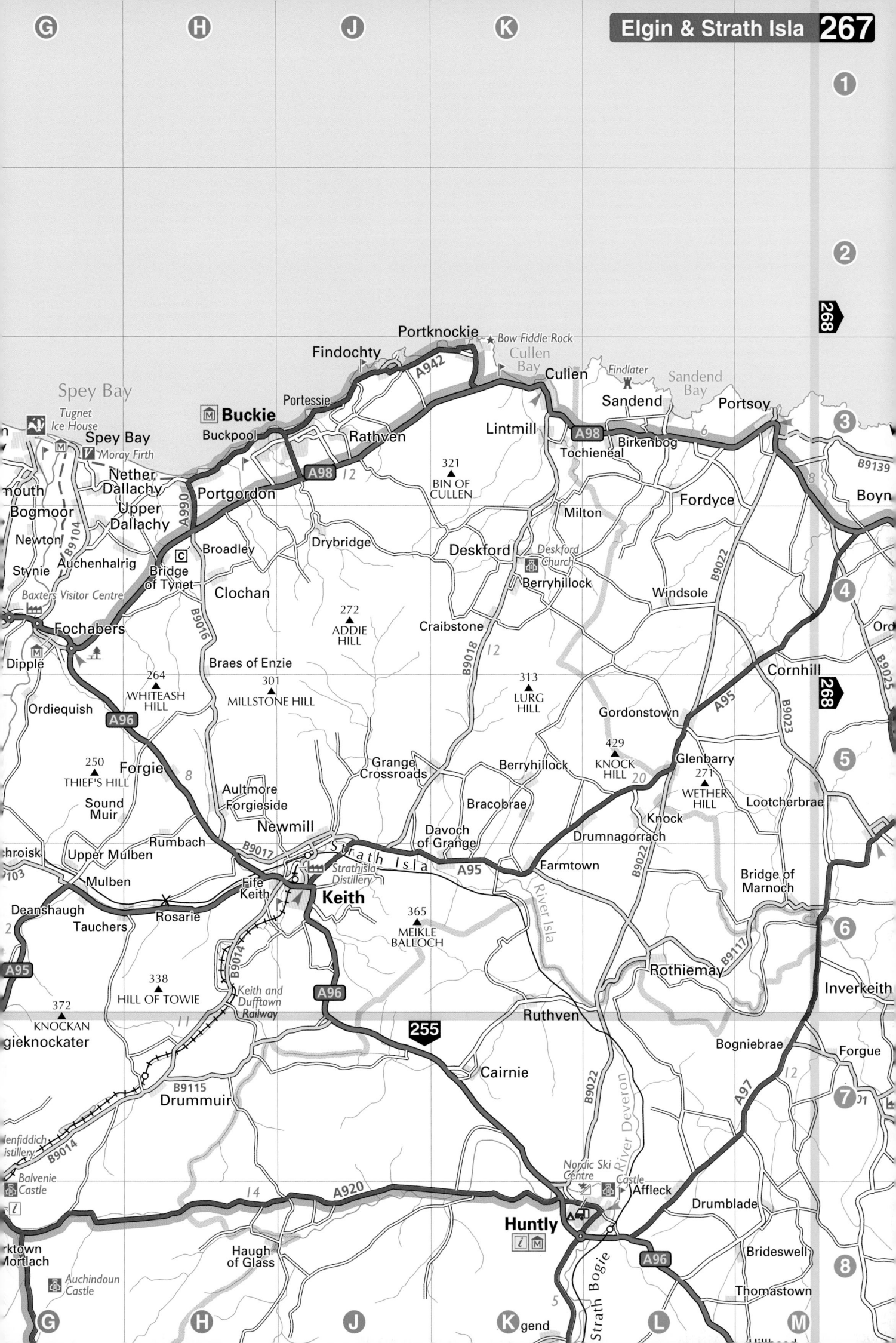

G   H   J   K

1

2

268

Portknockie
Findochty   ★ Bow Fiddle Rock
A942   Cullen Bay
Portessie   Cullen   Findlater   Sandend Bay
Buckie   Lintmill   Sandend   Portsoy
Buckpool   Rathven   A98   Birkenbog   6
Spey Bay   321   Tochieneal   8
Tugnet   Spey Bay   BIN OF   Milton   Fordyce   B9139
Ice House   Moray Firth   A98   /2   CULLEN   Boyn
Nether   Portgordon   Drybridge   Deskford   3
Dallachy   A990   Deskford   Church   Windsole
mouth   Upper   Broadley   Berryhillock   B9022
Bogmoor   Dallachy   Clochan   Craibstone   Cornhill   4
Newton   Auchenhalrig   C   272   B9018   /2   A95   268
Stynie   Bridge   ADDIE   313   B9025
Baxters Visitor Centre   of Tynet   HILL   LURG   Gordonstown
Fochabers   B9016   264   Braes of Enzie   HILL   429   Glenbarry   5
Dipple   WHITEASH   301   Grange   KNOCK   271   B9023
HILL   MILLSTONE HILL   Crossroads   Berryhillock   HILL   20   WETHER   Lootcherbrae
Ordiequish   A96   Berryhillock   HILL   Knock
Forgie   8   Aultmore   Bracobrae   Drumnagorrach   Bridge of
250   Forgieside   Davoch   Marnoch
THIEF'S HILL   Newmill   of Grange   Farmtown   B9022
Sound   B9017   Strath Isla   A95   B9117
Muir   Rumbach   Strathisla   6
chroisk   Upper Mulben   Distillery   River Isla   Rothiemay
9703   Mulben   Fife   365   Inverkeith
Deanshaugh   Keith   **Keith**   MEIKLE   B9022
Tauchers   Rosarie   BALLOCH   7
A95   338   Ruthven   Bogniebrae   Forgue
HILL OF TOWIE   Keith and   255   /2   B901
372   Dufftown   Cairnie   A97   7
KNOCKAN   Railway   A96   B9022   River Deveron
gieknockater   B9115   Nordic Ski   Drumblade
Drummuir   Centre   A920   Castle   Affleck
lenfiddich   /4   Brideswell
istillery   B9014   Haugh   Huntly   A96   8
Balvenie   of Glass   Thomastown
Castle   Auchindoun   Strath Bogie   5
ktown   Castle
Mortlach

G   H   J   K   L   M

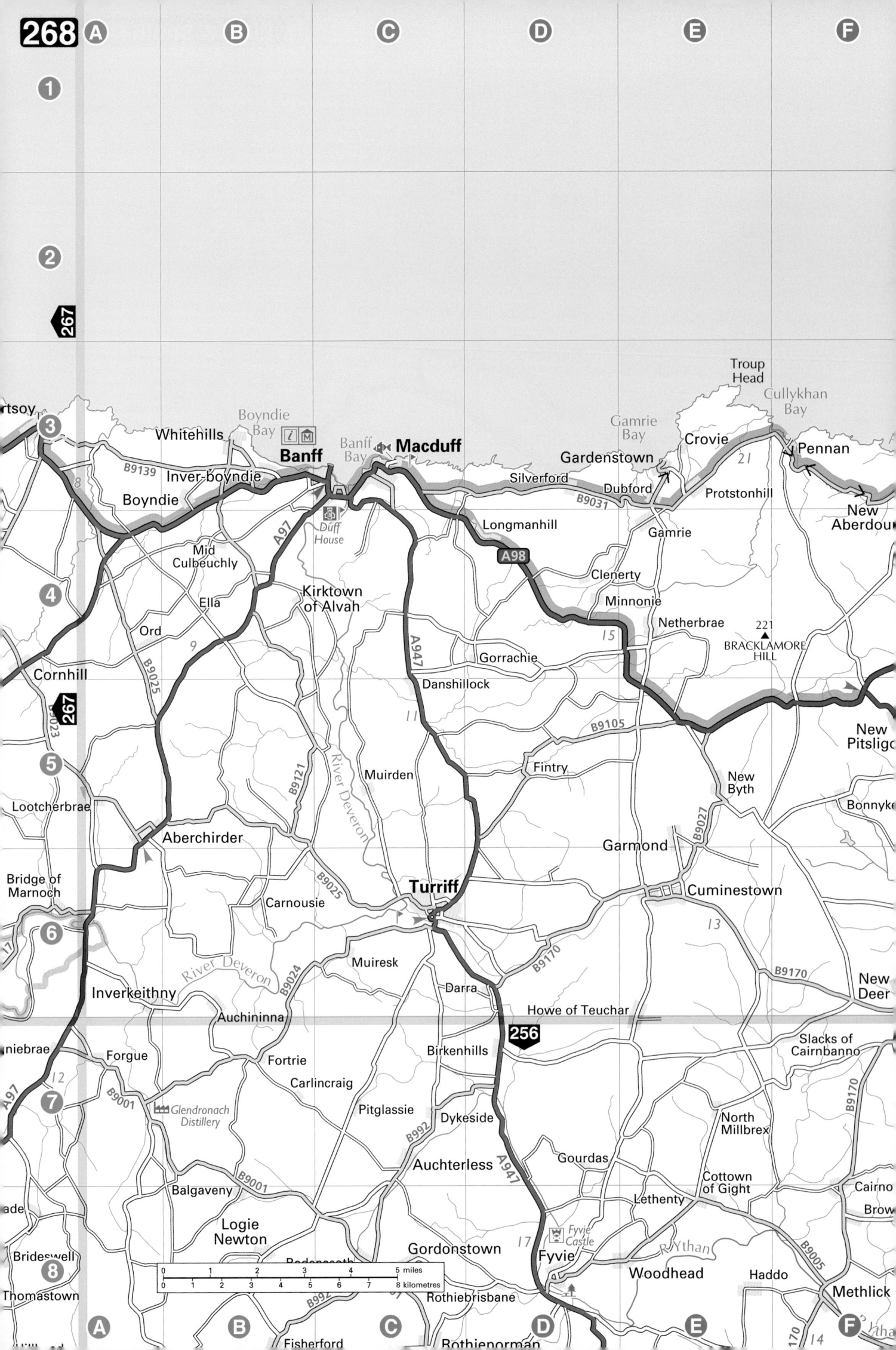

G　　　　H　　　　J　　　　K

1

2

3

Rosehearty
Pittulie
Peathill
Craigiefold
Coburby
Mid Ardlaw
B9031
B9032
A98
10
A981
12

Sandhaven
Castle Lighthouse & Museum
Kinnaird Head
Fraserburgh ℹ️
Fraserburgh Bay
Kirktown
Pitblae
Percyhorner
60
A90
Memsie
Memsie Cairn
60
Rathen
Newburgh
234 ▲ WAUGHTON HILL
A952
12
60

Maggie's Hoosie
Cairnbulg
Inverallochy
Whitelinks Bay
St Combs
B9033
Crofts of Savoch
Lonmay
Loch of Strathbeg
RSPB
Rattray Head

4

5

6

7

8

Strichen
New Leeds
B9093
B9093
Leys
Denhead
Fetterangus
A950
A981
Maud
B9106
B9029
B9028
B9029
Deer Abbey
Dunshillock
Old Deer
Blackhill of Clackriach
Aden
Mintlaw
257
Stuartfield
Millbreck
Clola
Drymuir
Bulwark
Nethermuir
B9030
Kinnadie
Auchnagatt
12
Inkhorn
Coldwells
A948
Arthrat
Muirtack
A952
14

Crimond
Blackhill
60
18
Kirktown
Backfolds
Rora
St Fergus
A90
60

River Ugie
Inverugie
Buchanhaven
H
Peterhead
A950
9
Inverquhomery
Nether Kinmundy
Hillhead of Cocklaw
Blackhill
Stirling
Longhaven
A90
Auchiries
Bullers of Buchan
North Haven
Slains
Cruden Bay
Longside
Longhaven
Buchan Ness
Boddam
Peterhead
M
Peterhead Bay
A982
Burnhaven
Lendrum Terrace
Kinknockie
Ardallie
Hatton

L　　　　M

Ⓐ   Ⓑ   Ⓒ   Ⓓ   Ⓔ   Ⓕ

1

Point of Stoer

Old Man of Stoer

OLDANY ISLAND

Eddrach Bay

Culkein Drumbeg

Culkein

Clashnessie Bay

Oldany

Drumbeg

2

Achnacarnin

Clashmore

Clashnessie

Nedd

Loch Poll

Stoer

Clachtoll

B869

Loch Beannac

Bay of Clachtoll

Rhicarn

3

Achmelvich Bay

A837

Achmelvich

Baddidarrach

ℹ

Lochinver

Soyea Island

Loch Inver

Strathan

Assyr

Inverkirkaig

4

Rhu Coigach

River Kirkaig

Fionn Loch

Eilean Mòr

Enard Bay

Rubha Mòr

Reiff

Achnahaird

5

Altandhu

Loch Sionasc

Eilean Mullagrach

Loch Osgaig

Isle Ristol

612

Polbain

STAC POLLAIDH

Glas-leac Mòr

Badentarbet

SUMMER ISLES

769

CUL BE

6

Achiltibuie

Loch Lurgainn

Tanera Beg

Badentarbat Bay

Polglass

Ⓥ Steornabhagh (Stornoway)

Tanera Mòr

🏔 Ben Mor Coigach

Glas-leac Beag

Horse Island

Horse Sound

C O I G A C H

652

BEN MORE COIGACH

Achduart

7

Priest Island

Eilean Dubh

Culnacraig

Strathcanai

Greenstone Point

Leac Dhonn

Isle Martin

A835

Cailleach Head

Strath

8

Rudha Beag

Ardmair

Ⓐ ellon urigle

0   1   2   3   4   5 miles
0   1   2   3   4   5   6   7   8 kilometres

261 ▽

Scoraig

Annat Bay

Mo Id Ullapo

Ⓐ   Ⓓ Rhireavach   Ⓔ   Ⓕ

635

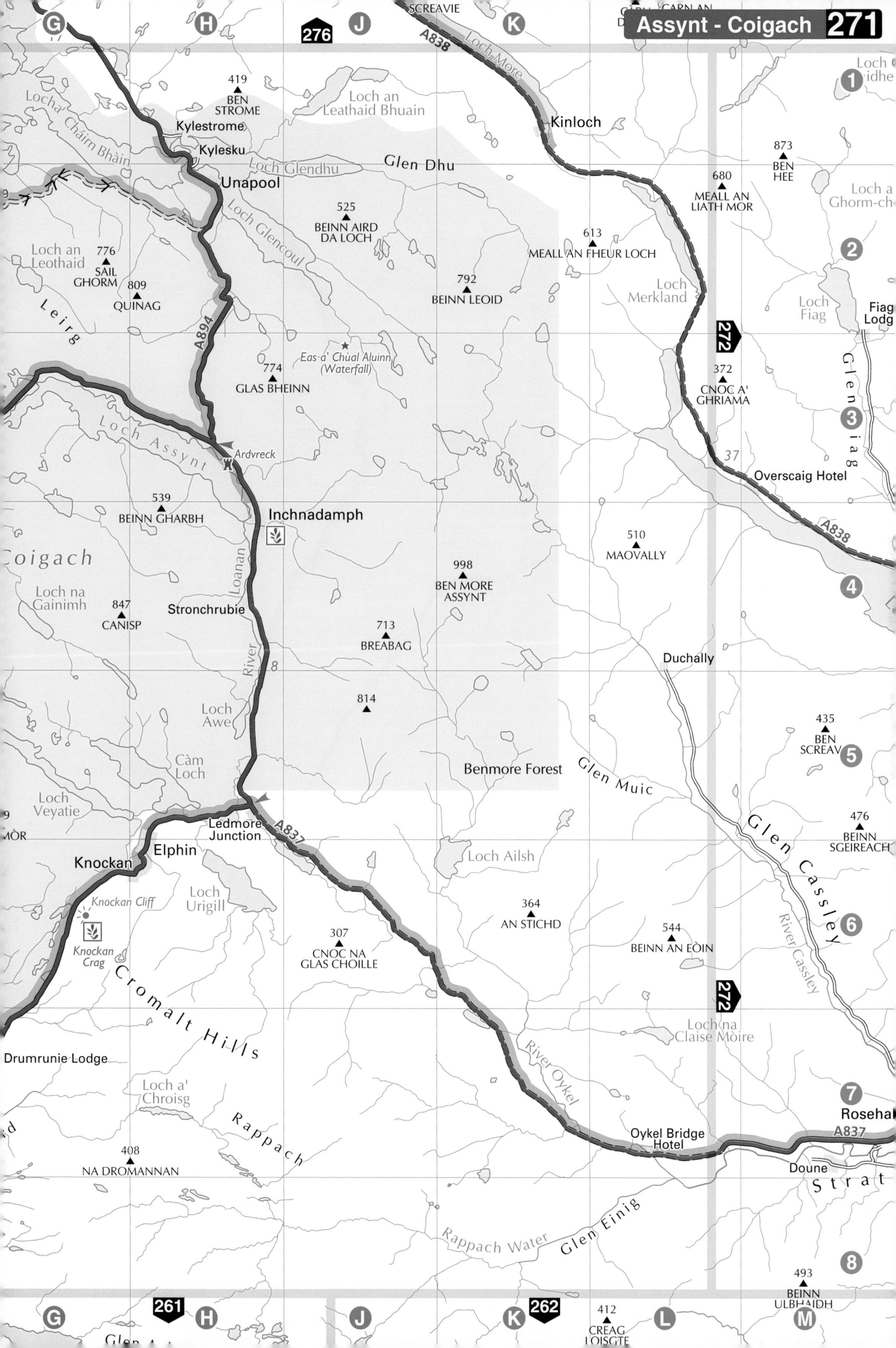

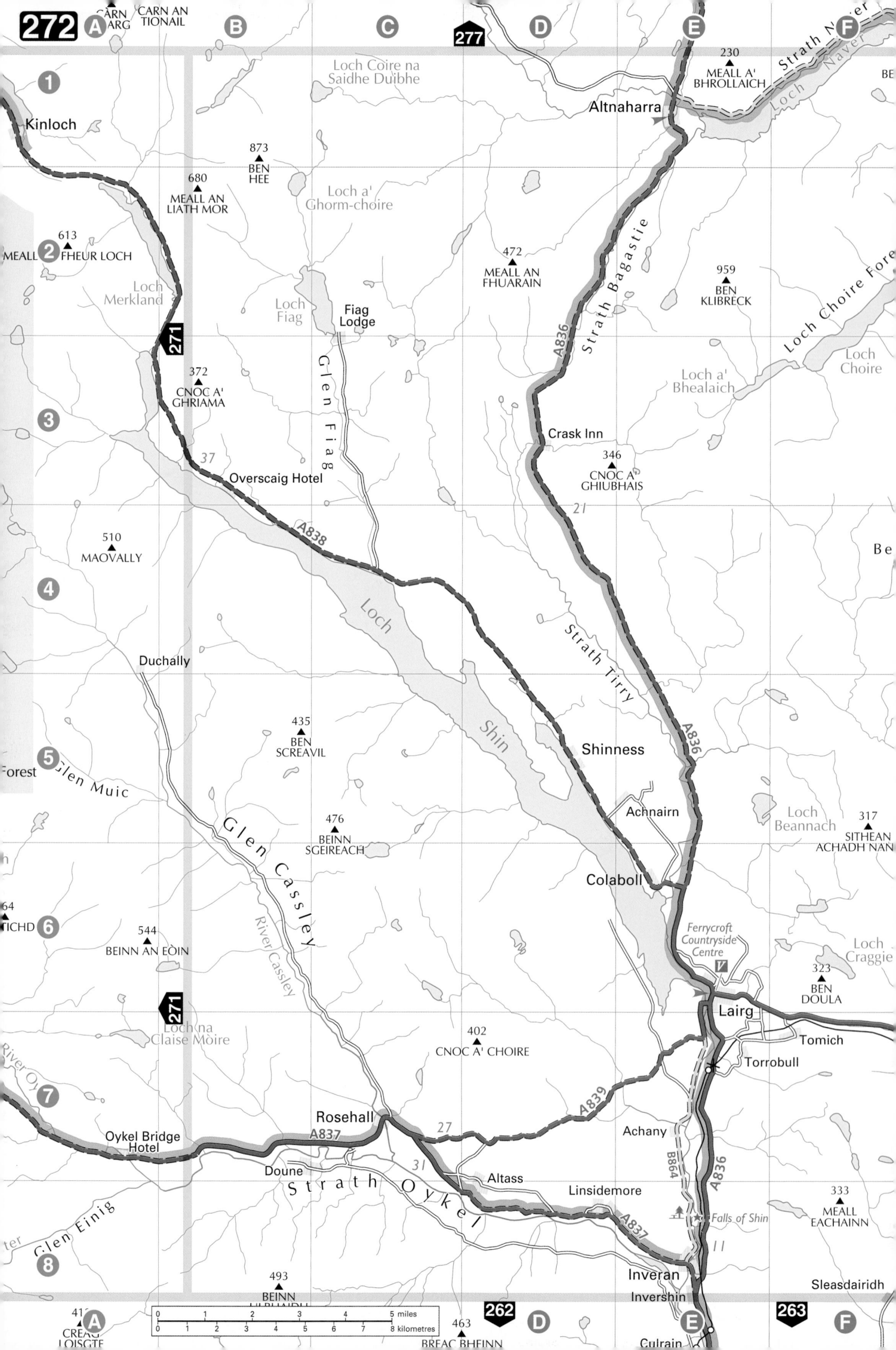

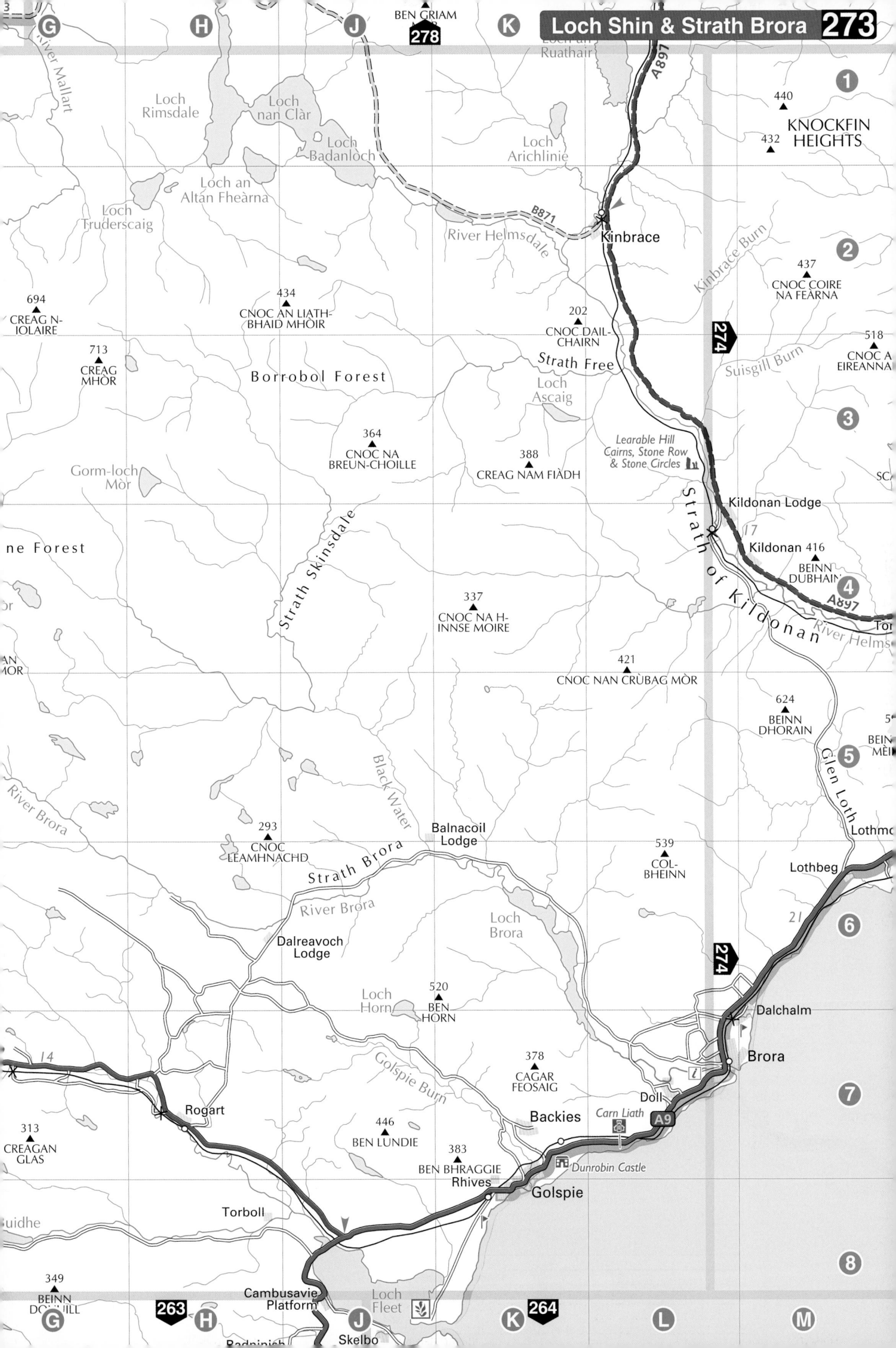

G   H   J   K   L   M

BEN GRIAM **278**

1

440 ▲

KNOCKFIN
HEIGHTS

432 ▲

Loch an
Ruathair

Loch
Rimsdale

Loch nan Clàr

Loch
Badanloch

Loch an
Altán Fheàrna

Loch
Arichlinie

A897

2

437 ▲
CNOC COIRE
NA FEÀRNA

Loch
Truderscaig

River Helmsdale

B871

Kinbrace

Kinbrace Burn

274

Suisgill Burn

518 ▲
CNOC A
EIREANNA

694 ▲
CREAG N-
IOLAIRE

434 ▲
CNOC AN LIATH-
BHAID MHÒIR

202 ▲
CNOC DAIL-
CHAIRN

Strath Free

3

713 ▲
CREAG
MHÒR

Borrobol Forest

Loch
Ascaig

Learable Hill
Cairns, Stone Row
& Stone Circles

SC

364 ▲
CNOC NA
BREUN-CHOILLE

388 ▲
CREAG NAM FIÀDH

Kildonan Lodge

Gorm-loch
Mòr

17

Kildonan 416 ▲

BEINN
DUBHAIN

4

ne Forest

Strath Skinsdale

337 ▲
CNOC NA H-
INNSE MOIRE

A897

Tor

River Helms

421 ▲
CNOC NAN CRÙBAG MÒR

624 ▲
BEINN
DHORAIN

BEIN
MÈI

5

5

River Brora

293 ▲
CNOC
LEAMHNACHD

Black Water

Balnacoil
Lodge

539 ▲
COL-
BHEINN

Glen Loth

Lothmo

Lothbeg

Strath Brora

River Brora

Loch
Brora

21

6

Dalreavoch
Lodge

Loch
Horn

520 ▲
BEN
HORN

274

Dalchalm

Brora

7

313 ▲
CREAGAN
GLAS

Rogart

Golspie Burn

378 ▲
CAGAR
FEOSAIG

Doll

Carn Liath

A9

14

Backies

446 ▲
BEN LUNDIE

Carn Liath

383 ▲
BEN BHRAGGIE
Rhives

Dunrobin Castle

Golspie

uidhe

Torboll

349 ▲
BEINN
DO HILL

263

Cambusavie
Platform

Loch
Fleet

264

Skelbo

G   H   J   K   L   M

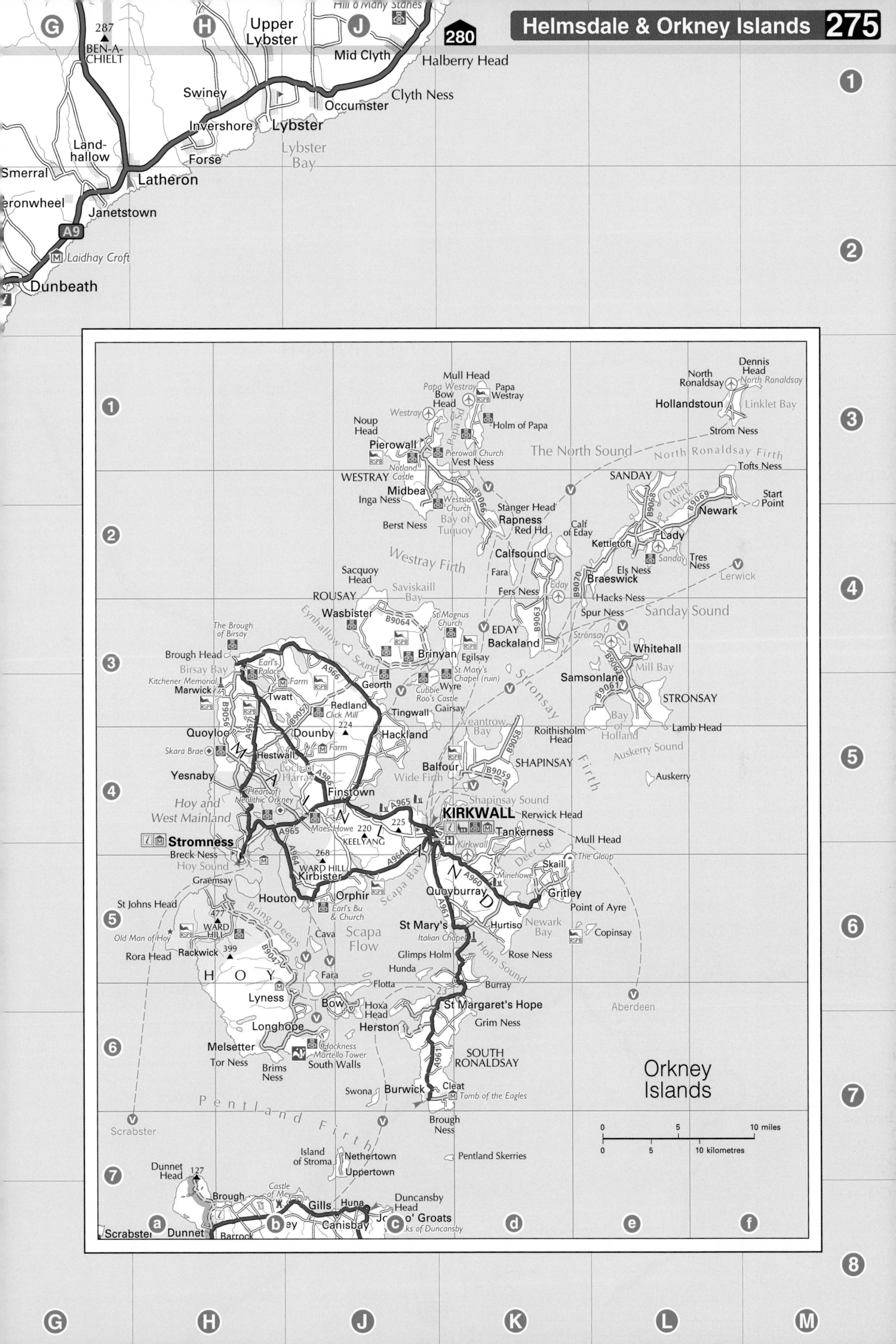

Orkney Islands

G · H · J · K · L · M

0   5   10 miles
0   5   10 kilometres

BEN-A-CHIELT 287

Upper Lybster
Mid Clyth
Hill o' Many Stanes
280
Halberry Head
Swiney
Clyth Ness
Occumster
Invershore
Lybster
Forse
Lybster Bay
Land-hallow
Smerral
eronwheel
Latheron
Janetstown
A9
Laidhay Croft
Dunbeath

Mull Head
Papa Westray
Bow Head
Papa Westray
RSPB
North Ronaldsay
Dennis Head
North Ronaldsay
Hollandstoun
Linklet Bay
Noup Head
Westray
Holm of Papa
The North Sound
North Ronaldsay Firth
Strom Ness
Pierowall
RSPB
Pierowall Church
Vest Ness
Tofts Ness
WESTRAY
Notland Castle
SANDAY
Midbea
Westside Church
Stanger Head
Otters Wick
Newark
Start Point
Inga Ness
B9066
Rapness
Red Hd
B9069
Berst Ness
Bay of Tuquoy
Red Hd
Calf of Eday
Kettletoft
Lady
Tres Ness
Sacquoy Head
Westray Firth
Calfsound
Sanday
Els Ness
Lerwick
Saviskaill Bay
Fara
Braeswick
Hacks Ness
ROUSAY
St Magnus Church
Fers Ness
B9070
Spur Ness
Sanday Sound
Wasbister
B9064
Egilsay
Eday
Stronsay
Whitehall
The Brough of Birsay
RSPB
Brinyan
EDAY
Mill Bay
Brough Head
A966
Georth
Cubbie Roo's Castle
Backaland
B9061
Samsonlane
Birsay Bay
Earl's Palace
Farm
Wyre
St Mary's Chapel (ruin)
STRONSAY
Kitchener Memorial
Twatt
Redland
Tingwall
Gairsay
Stronsay Firth
Marwick
RSPB
B9057
Click Mill
Hackland
Veantrow Bay
Roithisholm Head
Bay of Holland
Quayloo
224
Dounby
Wide Firth
B9058
Lamb Head
Skara Brae
Farm
MAINLAND
Balfour
SHAPINSAY
B9059
Auskerry Sound
Hestwall
Loch of Harray
Auskerry
Yesnaby
A986
Finstown
Shapinsay Sound
Heart of Neolithic Orkney
A965
225
Rerwick Head
Hoy and West Mainland
Maes Howe 220
KIRKWALL
Tankerness
Mull Head
Stromness
KEELYANG
Kirkwall
Deer Sd
Skaill
The Gloup
Breck Ness
268
A964
Minehowe
Gritley
Hoy Sound
WARD HILL
Kirbister
A960
Point of Ayre
Graemsay
Houton
Orphir
Scapa Bay
Quoyburray
St Johns Head
Earl's Bu & Church
Newark Bay
Copinsay
477
St Mary's
Hurtiso
RSPB
WARD HILL
A961
Italian Chapel
Rose Ness
Old Man of Hoy
Cava
Scapa Flow
Glimps Holm
Holm Sound
Rackwick
399
Fara
Hunda
Aberdeen
Rora Head
B9067
Flotta
Burray
HOY
Bow
23
Burray
Lyness
Hoxa Head
St Margaret's Hope
Longhope
Herston
Grim Ness
Melsetter
Hackness Martello Tower
SOUTH RONALDSAY
Tor Ness
Brims Ness
South Walls
Swona
Burwick
Cleat
Tomb of the Eagles
A961
Brough Ness
Pentland Firth
Scrabster
Island of Stroma
Nethertown
Pentland Skerries
Uppertown
Dunnet Head 127
Brough
Castle of Mey
Gills
Huna
Duncansby Head
Scrabster
Dunnet
ey
Barrock
Canisbay
John o' Groats
ks of Duncansby

G · H · J · K · L · M

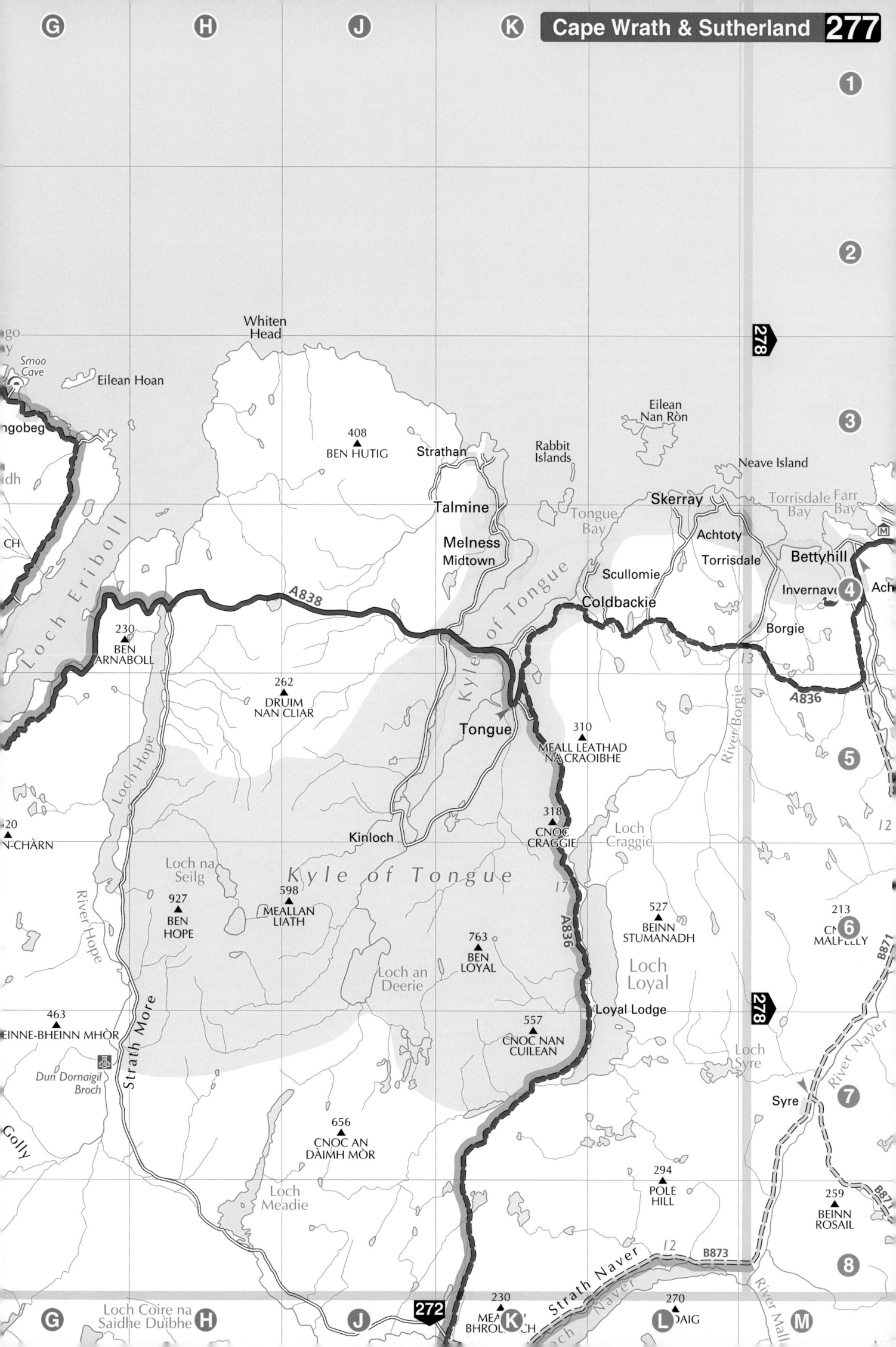

1

2

278

3

Whiten
Head

Smoo
Cave

go

Eilean Hoan

ngobeg

408
▲
BEN HUTIG

Strathan

Rabbit
Islands

Eilean
Nan Ròn

Neave Island

CH

dh

Skerray

Torrisdale Farr
Bay   Bay

Talmine

Tongue
Bay

Achtoty

Melness

Midtown

Torrisdale

Bettyhill

A838

Scullomie

Invernave

Ach

Coldbackie

4

230
▲
BEN
ARNABOLL

Kyle of Tongue

Borgie

River/Borgie

13

A836

Loch Eriboll

262
▲
DRUIM
NAN CLIAR

310
▲
MEALL LEATHAD
NA CRAOIBHE

Tongue

5

12

20
▲
N-CHÀRN

Loch Hope

Kinloch

318
▲
CNOC
CRAGGIE

Loch
Craggie

Kyle of Tongue

17

Loch na
Seilg

598
▲
MEALLAN
LIATH

527
▲
BEINN
STUMANADH

213
▲
CN
MALPELLY

6

927
▲
BEN
HOPE

763
▲
BEN
LOYAL

A836

Loch
Loyal

B871

River Hope

Loch an
Deerie

278

463
▲
EINNE-BHEINN MHÒR

Loyal Lodge

Strath More

557
▲
CNOC NAN
CUILEAN

Loch
Syre

River Naver

Dun Dornaigil
Broch

Syre

7

Golly

656
▲
CNOC AN
DÀIMH MÒR

294
▲
POLE
HILL

259
▲
BEINN
ROSAIL

B871

Loch
Meadie

Strath Naver

12

B873

8

272

230
▲
MEA
BHROL CH

270
▲
AIG

River Mall

Saidhe Duibhe

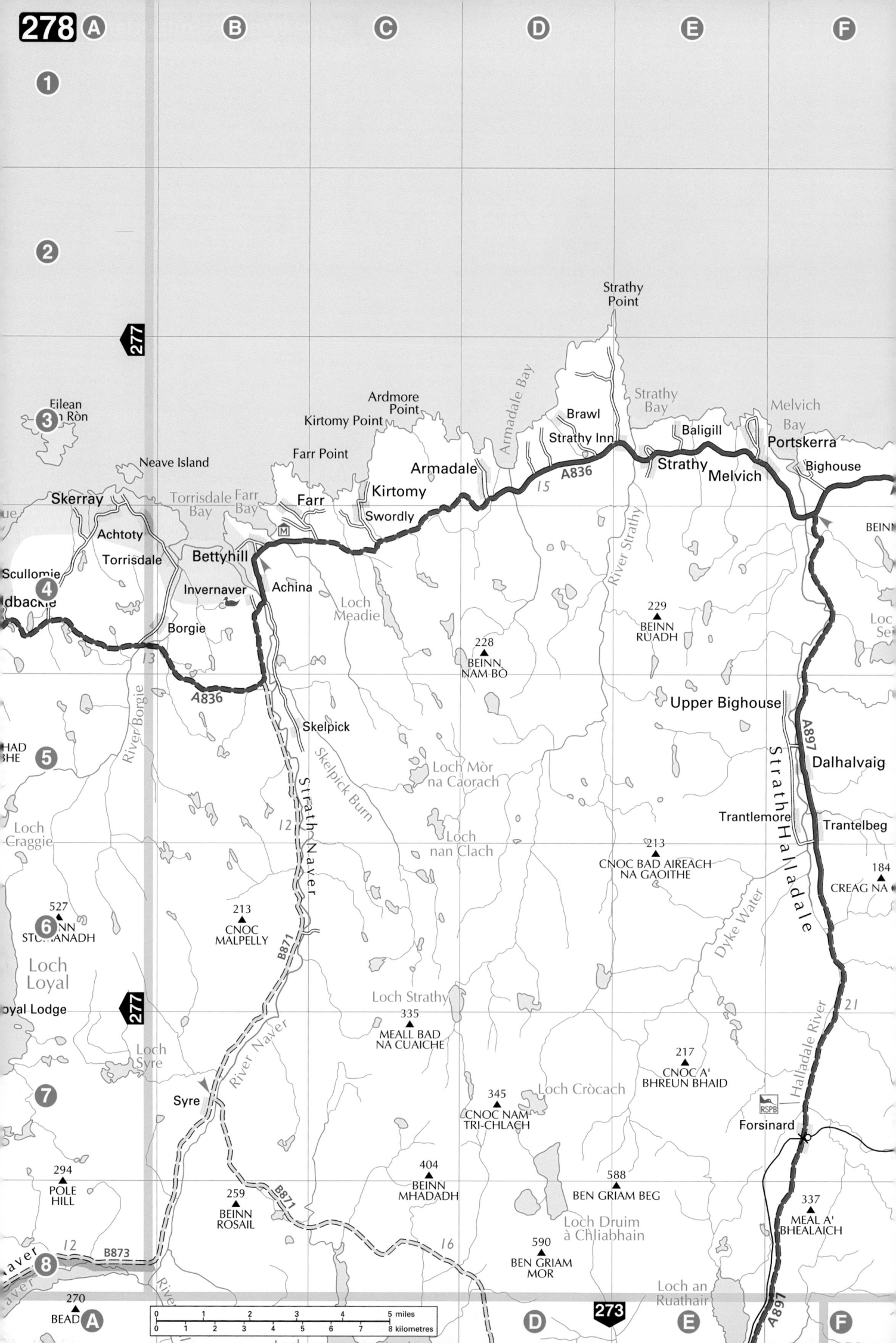

A   B   C   D   E   F

1

2

277

3

Eilean
n Ròn

Neave Island

Skerray

Achtoty

Torrisdale

Scullomie

dbackie

4

Torrisdale
Bay

Farr
Bay

Bettyhill

Invernaver

Borgie

Achina

Farr Point

Farr

Swordly

Kirtomy

Kirtomy Point

Ardmore
Point

Armadale

Armadale Bay

Strathy Inn

Brawl

Strathy
Point

Strathy
Bay

Baligill

Strathy

Melvich

Portskerra

Bighouse

Melvich
Bay

BEIN

A836   15

River Strathy

Loch
Meadie

BEINN
NAM BO   228

BEINN
RUADH   229

Loc
Se

Upper Bighouse

HAD
BHE

5

River Borgie

A836   13

Skelpick

Skelpick Burn

Strath Naver   12

Loch Mòr
na Caorach

Loch nan Clach

CNOC BAD AIREACH
NA GAOITHE   213

Strath Halladale

A897

Dalhalvaig

Trantlemore

Trantelbeg

Dyke Water

CREAG NA   184

Loch
Craggie

6

NN
STO ANADH   527

CNOC
MALPELLY   213

B871

CNOC A'
BHREUN BHAID   217

Loch
Loyal

277

Loch Strathy

MEALL BAD
NA CUAICHE   335

Halladale River   21

yal Lodge

Loch
Syre

7

Syre

River Naver

CNOC NAM
TRI-CHLACH   345

Loch Cròcach

RSPB

Forsinard

POLE
HILL   294

BEINN
ROSAIL   259

B871

BEINN
MHADADH   404

BEN GRIAM BEG   588

Loch Druim
à Chliabhain

MEAL A'
BHEALAICH   337

12   B873

8

aver

River

16

BEN GRIAM
MOR   590

Loch an
Ruathair

A897

BEAD   270

A

273

D   E   F

G H J K **1**

DUNNET HEAD ▲ 127

Stromness
V

Briga Head

▲ 121
DUNNET
HILL

Brough _i_

St John's
Loch

Brims Ness

Holborn
Head

St Mary's
Chapel (ruin)

Crosskirk

West Dunnet

2

Dunnet

Scrabster

Thurso
Bay

_i_ M

Thurso

Dunnet
Bay

Castlehill

Dunnet

A836

A836

Murkle

280

Castletown

16

Bridge of Forss

Skiall

Achreamie

Lythmore

B874

5

Olrig
House

Tain

3

Sandside
Bay

Upper
Dounreay

Cnoc Freiceadain
Long Cairns

Glengolly

A9

Weydale

B876

Isauld

Forss Water

Shebster

Westfield

Hilliclay

Reay

Achvarasdal

Loch
Calder

Sordale

Bower

242
▲ BEINN
RATHA

Broubster

Knockdee

4 Halcro

Roadside

Loch
Scarmclate

Shurrery

B874

Clayock

Gillock

B870

Halkirk

Georgemas
Junction
Station

290
▲ BEIN NAM
BAD MHÒR

Loch
Scye

Shurrery
Lodge

Scotscalder
Station

Loch
Watten

21

243
▲ CNOC AN
OARAIN BHÀIN

Dorrery

Harpsdale

176
▲ SPITTAL
HILL

B870

5

Watten

Loch
Shurrery

Olgrinmore

160
▲ BRAIGH FÉITH HEMIGAL

132
▲ DRUIM A'
CHRACAIRNIE

River Thurso

Spittal

Mybster

Loch of
Toftingall

Loch Tuim
Ghlais

Loch
Caluim

Westerdale

Strath Beg

23

6

203
▲ CNOC PREAS
A'MHADAIDH

200
▲ CNOC BEUL
NA FAIRE

136
▲ BEINN CHÀITEAG

280

Altnabreac Station

Loch
More

A9

Loch
Ruard

Achavanich

Loch
Stemster

7 BALL▲
HI

275
▲ NOC
GALL

Loch an
Thulachan

Loch
Sand

Loch
Rangag

248
▲ STEMSTER HILL

Rumsdale Water

Strathmore Water

Dalnawillan Lodge

226
▲ COIRE
NA BEINN

Glutt Water

348
▲ BEN
ALISKY

287
▲ BEN-A-
CHIELT

8

G H **274** J K CNOCAN L M Swiney

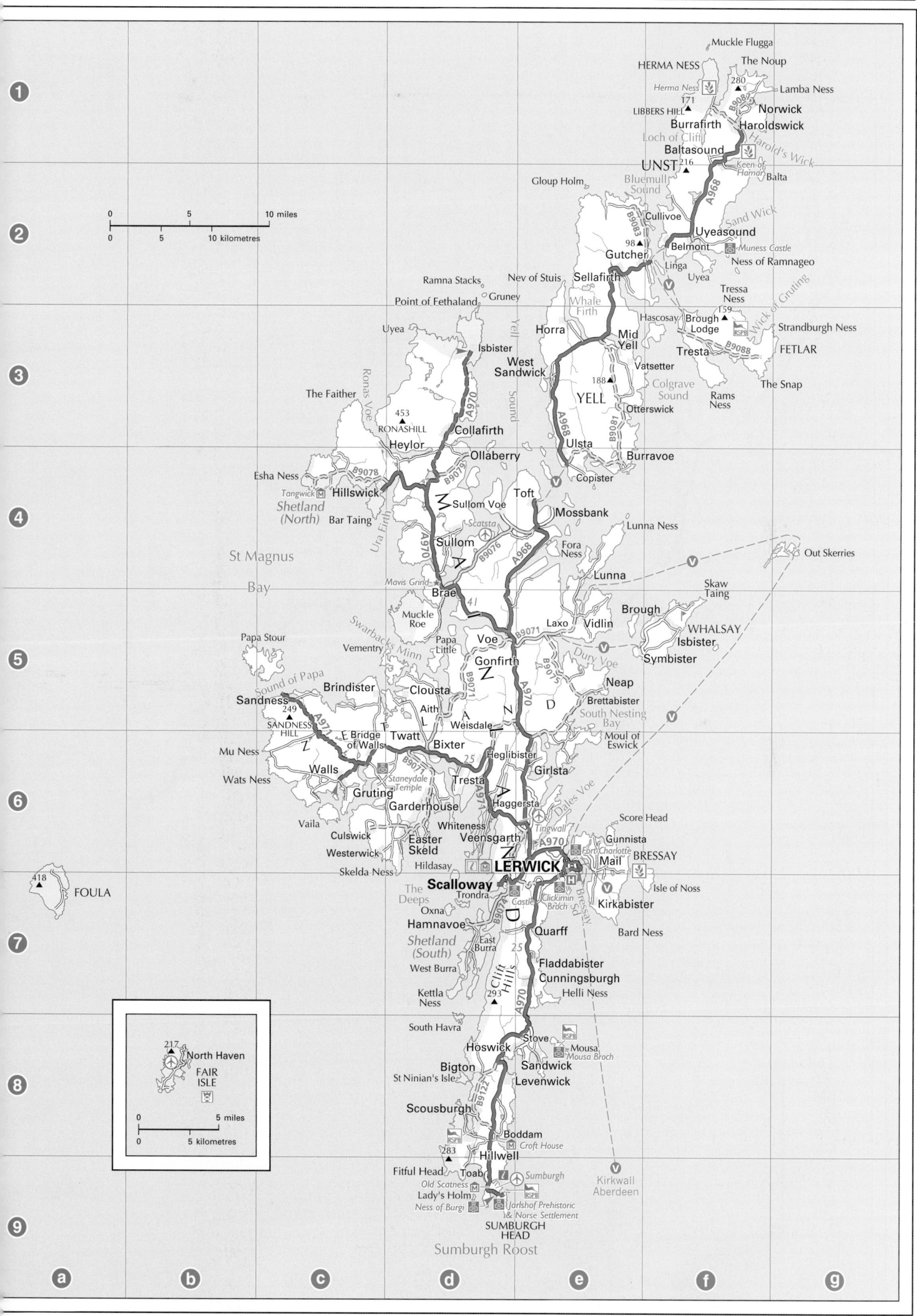

Muckle Flugga
The Noup
HERMA NESS
Herma Ness
171
LIBBERS HILL
280
Lamba Ness
Norwick
Burrafirth
Haroldswick
Loch of Cliff
Baltasound
UNST
216
Keen of Haman
Balta
Gloup Holm
Bluemull Sound
Sand Wick

Ramna Stacks
Nev of Stuis
Gruney
Point of Fethaland
Cullivoe
B9083
A968
Uyeasound
Belmont
Muness Castle
Gutcher
Linga
Ness of Ramnageo
Uyea
Sellafirth
Tressa Ness
Whale Firth
Hascosay
159
Brough Lodge
Uyea
Horra
B9083
RSPB
Strandburgh Ness
Mid Yell
Tresta
B9088
FETLAR
West Sandwick
Vatsetter
The Snap
YELL
188
Colgrave Sound
Otterswick
Rams Ness
A968
B9081
The Faither
Ronas Voe
RONASHILL 453
Collafirth
Ulsta
Burravoe
Heylor
Ollaberry
Copister
Esha Ness
B9078
B9079
Tangwick
Hillswick
A970
Sullom Voe
Toft
Mossbank
Lunna Ness
Shetland (North)
Bar Taing
Scatsta
Sullom
B9076
A968
Fora Ness
Lunna
St Magnus
Ura Firth
Skaw Taing
Out Skerries
Bay
Mavis Grind
Brae
41
Muckle Roe
Laxo
Vidlin
Brough
WHALSAY
Papa Stour
Swarbacks Minn
Papa Little
Voe
B9071
Isbister
Vementry
Gonfirth
Symbister
Sound of Papa
Brindister
Clousta
Neap
Brettabister
Sandness
249
Aith
Weisdale
South Nesting Bay
SANDNESS HILL
Moul of Eswick
Mu Ness
B9071
Bridge of Walls
Twatt
Bixter
Wats Ness
Walls
Heglibister
Girlsta
Gruting
Staneydale Temple
Tresta
Haggersta
Garderhouse
Score Head
Vaila
Whiteness
Tingwall
Gunnista
Culswick
Veensgarth
A970
Mail
BRESSAY
Westerwick
Easter Skeld
Hildasay
Fort Charlotte
LERWICK
Isle of Noss
Skelda Ness
Scalloway
Castle
Clickimin Broch
Kirkabister
The Deeps
Trondra
Oxna
Quarff
Bard Ness
Hamnavoe
East Burra
Fladdabister
Shetland (South)
25
Cunningsburgh
West Burra
Clift Hills
Helli Ness
Kettla Ness
293
A970
South Havra
Stove
RSPB
Mousa
Hoswick
Mousa Broch
Bigton
Sandwick
St Ninian's Isle
Levenwick
Scousburgh
B9122
Boddam
Croft House
RSPB
283
Hillwell
Fitful Head
Toab
Old Scatness
Sumburgh
Kirkwall
Aberdeen
Lady's Holm
RSPB
Ness of Burgi
Jarlshof Prehistoric & Norse Settlement
SUMBURGH HEAD
Sumburgh Roost

217
North Haven
FAIR ISLE
FOULA
418

0   5   10 miles
0   5   10 kilometres

0   5 miles
0   5 kilometres

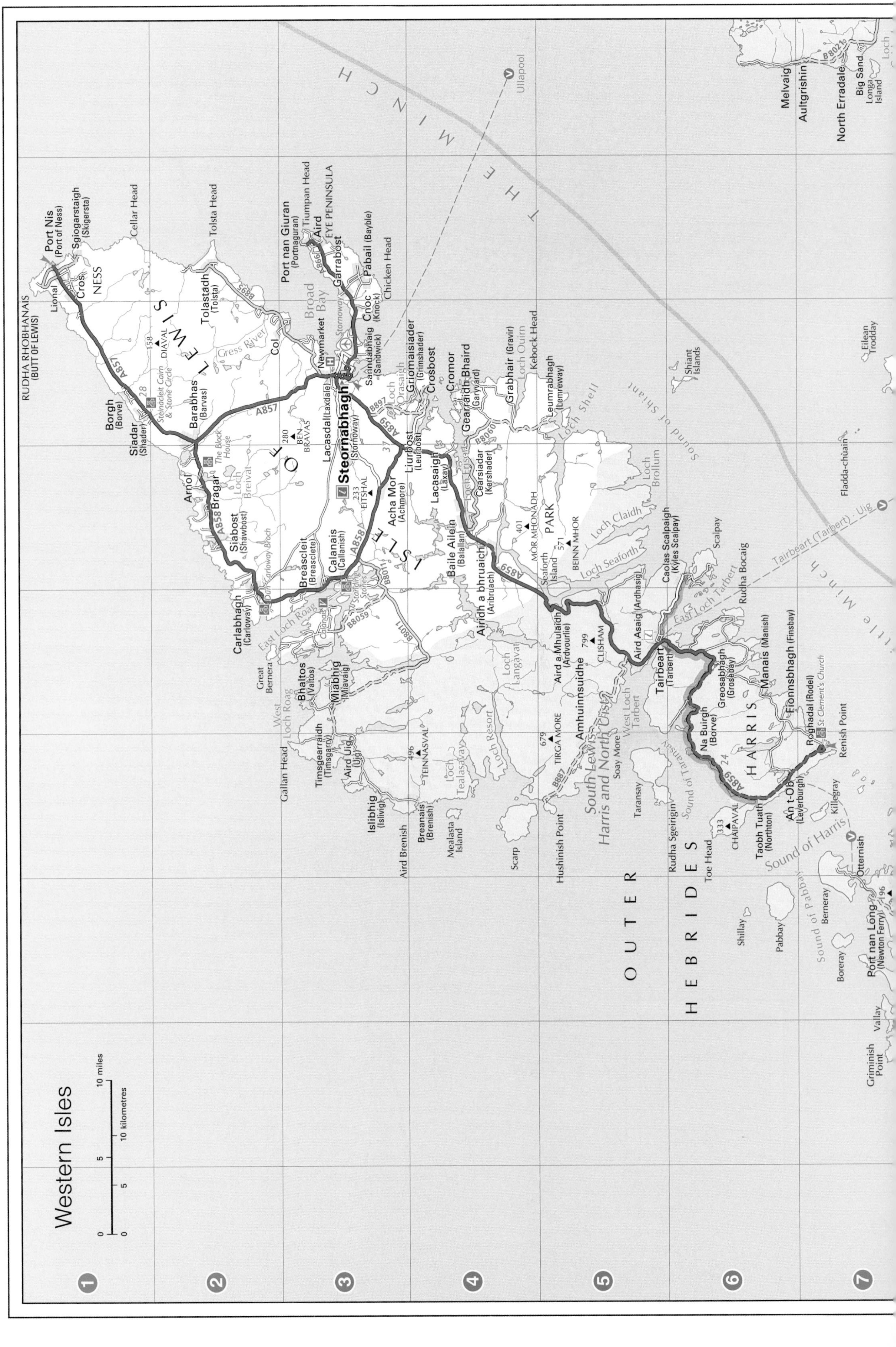

Western Isles

THE MINCH

Ullapool

OUTER HEBRIDES

LEWIS

RUDHA RHOBHANAIS
(BUTT OF LEWIS)

Port Nis
(Port of Ness)
Sgiogarstaigh
(Skigersta)
Lional
Cros
NESS
Cellar Head

Tolastadh
(Tolsta)
Tolsta Head

A857

158
DIAVAL
Steinacleit Cairn
& Stone Circle

Gress River

Col

Port nan Giuran
(Portnaguran)
Tiumpan Head
Aird
EYE PENINSULA
Garrabost
Pabail
(Bayble)
Chicken Head

Borgh
(Borve)
Siadar
(Shader)
28
Barabhas
(Barvas)

280
BEN
BRAVAS
A857

Lacasdall (Laxdale)
Newmarket
Sandabhaig
(Sandwick)
Croc
(Knock)

Arnol
A858
Bragar
Siabost
(Shawbost)
The Black
House
Loch
Breival

Steornabhagh
A859
B897

Griomaisiader
(Grimshader)
Crosbost
Cromor
Gearraidh Bhaird
(Garyrd)

233
EITSHAL

Liurbost
(Leurbost)
37
Lacasaigh
(Laxay)

Grabhair (Gravir)
Loch Ouirm
Kebock Head

Breascleit
(Breasclete)
Calanais
(Callanish)
Acha Mor
(Achmore)

Cearsiadar
(Kershader)

Leumrabhagh
(Lemreway)

Carlabhagh
(Carloway)
East Loch Roag
Dun Carloway Broch

B8011
Callanish
Standing
Stones
B8059

Baile Ailein
(Balallan)
Airidh a bhruaich
(Aribruach)

401
MOR MHONADH
571
Seaforth
Island
BEINN MHOR

PARK

Loch Shell

Loch
Brollum

Shiant
Islands

Sound of Shiant

Great
Bernera
Bhaltos
(Valtos)
Miabhig
(Miavaig)

West Loch Roag

Loch Resort

Loch Seaforth

A859
Aird a Mhulaidh
(Ardvourlie)
CLISHAM

Caolas Scalpaigh
(Kyles Scalpay)
Scalpay

Rudha Bocaig

Eilean
Trodday

Gallan Head
Timsgearraidh
(Timsgarry)
Aird Uig
(Uig)

496
TEINNASVAL

Loch
Langavat

Amhuinnsuidhe
799

Aird Asaig
(Ardhasig)

Tairbeart
East Loch Tarbert

Fladda-chùain

Tairbeart (Tarbert) / Uig

Islibhig
(Islivig)

Breanais
(Brenish)
Mealasta
Island

Loch
Tealasvay

679
TIRGA MORE
B887

Soay More
Soay Beg

Tairbeart
(Tarbert)

Greosabhagh
(Grosebay)

Manais
(Manish)

Fionnsbhagh
(Finsbay)

Little Minch

Aird Brenish

Scarp

Hushinish Point

South Lewis,
Harris and North Uist

Taransay

West Loch
Tarbert

Sound of Taransay

Na Buirgh
(Borve)
24
A859

St. Clement's Church
Roghadal
(Rodel)

Rudha Sgeirigin

Toe Head

333
CHAIPAVAL

An t-Ob
(Leverburgh)

Taobh Tuath
(Northton)

Killegray

Renish Point

OUTER

HEBRIDES

Rudha Sgeirigin

Shillay
Pabbay

Berneray
Boreray

Sound of Pabbay

Port nan Long
(Newton Ferry)
196

Otternish

Sound of Harris

Griminish
Point
Valay

Melvaig
Aultgrishin
North Erradale

Big Sand
Longa
Island

B8021

10 miles
10 kilometres
5
5
0
0

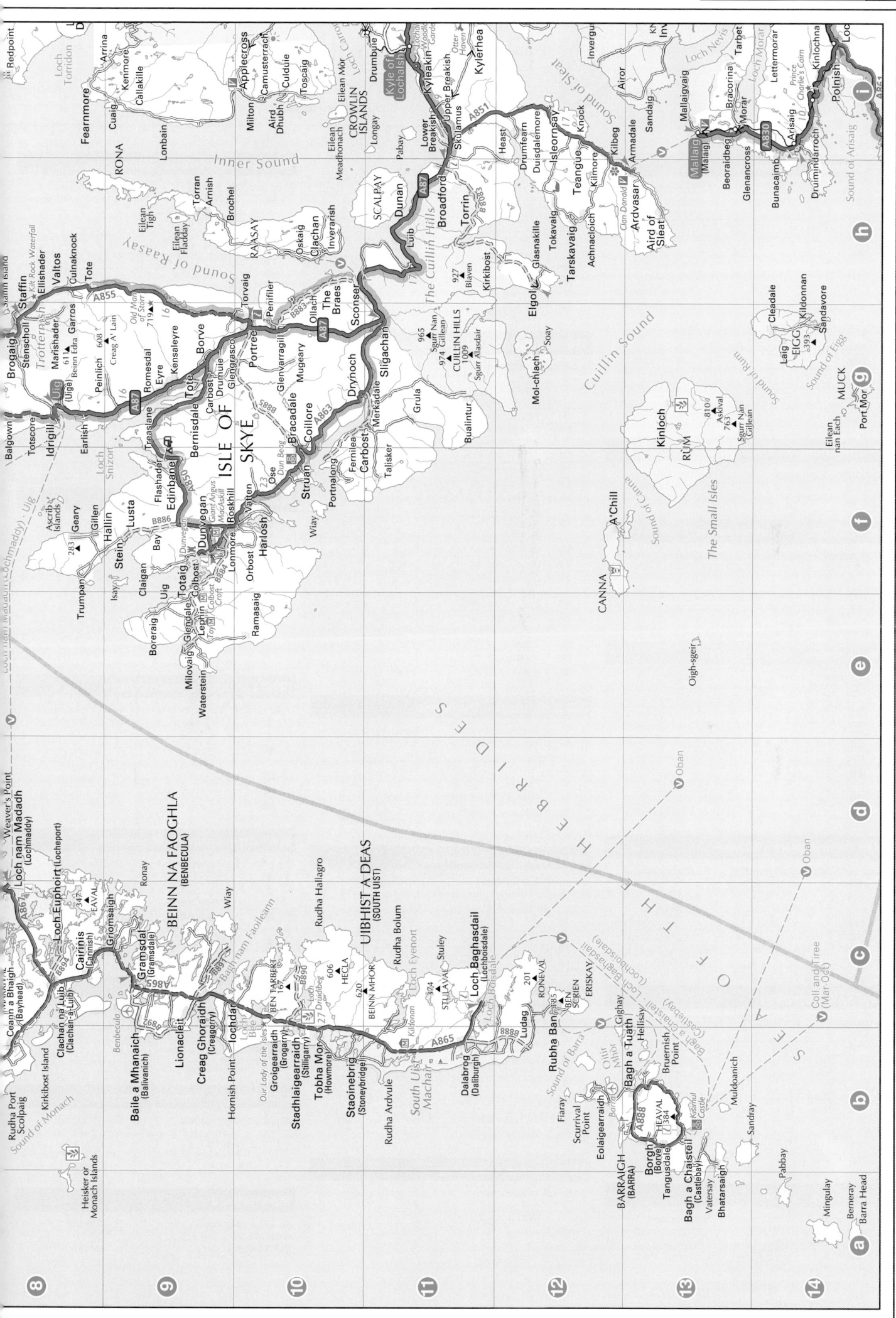

Restricted junctions

Motorway and Primary Route junctions which have access or exit restrictions are shown on the map pages thus:

M1 London - Leeds

Junction	Northbound	Southbound
2	Access only from A1 (northbound)	Exit only to A1 (southbound)
4	Access only from A41 (northbound)	Exit only to A41 (southbound)
6A	Access only from M25 (no link from A405)	Exit only to M25 (no link from A405)
7	Access only from A414	Exit only to A414
17	Exit only to M45	Access only from M45
19	Exit only to M6 (northbound)	Access only from M6
21A	Exit only, no access	Access only, no exit
23A	Access only from A42	No restriction
24A	Access only, no exit	Exit only, no access
35A	Exit only, no access	Access only, no exit
43	Exit only to M621	Access only from M621
48	Exit only to A1(M) (northbound)	Access only from A1(M) (southbound)

M2 Rochester - Faversham

Junction	Westbound	Eastbound
1	No exit to A2 (eastbound)	No access from A2 (westbound)

M3 Sunbury - Southampton

Junction	Northeastbound	Southwestbound
8	Access only from A303, no exit	Exit only to A303, no access
10	Exit only, no access	Access only, no exit
14	Access from M27 only, no exit	No access to M27 (westbound)

M4 London - South Wales

Junction	Westbound	Eastbound
1	Access only from A4 (westbound)	Exit only to A4 (eastbound)
21	Exit only to M48	Access only from M48
23	Access only from M48	Exit only to M48
25	Exit only, no access	Access only, no exit
25A	Exit only, no access	Access only, no exit
29	Exit only to A48(M)	Access only from A48(M)
38	Exit only, no access	No restriction
39	Access only, no exit	No access or exit

M5 Birmingham - Exeter

Junction	Northeastbound	Southwestbound
10	Access only, no exit	Exit only, no access
11A	Access only from A417 (westbound)	Exit only to A417 (eastbound)
18A	Exit only to M49	Access only from M49
18	Exit only, no access	Access only, no exit
29	No restriction	Access only from A30 (westbound)

M6 Toll Motorway

Junction	Northwestbound	Southeastbound
T1	Access only, no exit	No access or exit
T2	No access or exit	Exit only, no access
T3	Staggered junction, follow signs - access only from A38 (northbound)	Staggered junction, follow signs - access only from A38 (southbound)
T5	Access only, no exit	Exit only to A5148 (northbound), no access
T7	Exit only, no access	Access only, no exit
T8	Exit only, no access	Access only, no exit

M6 Rugby - Carlisle

Junction	Northbound	Southbound
3A	Exit only to M6 Toll	Access only from M6 Toll
4A	Access only from M42 (southbound)	Exit only to M42
5	Exit only, no access	Access only, no exit
10A	Exit only to M54	Access only from M54
11A	Access only from M6 Toll	Exit only to M6 Toll

	with M56	No restriction	Access only from M56 (eastbound)
(jct 20A)			
20		Access only, no exit	No restriction
24		Access only, no exit	Exit only, no access
25		Exit only, no access	Access only, no exit
29		No direct access, use adjacent slip road to jct 29A	No direct exit, use adjacent slip road from jct 29A
29A		Access only, no exit	Exit only, no access
30		Access only from M61	Exit only to M61
31A		Exit only, no access	Access only, no exit
45		Exit only, no access	Access only, no exit

M8 Edinburgh - Bishopton

Junction	Westbound	Eastbound
8	No access from M73 (southbound) or from A8 (eastbound) & A89	No exit to M73 (northbound) or to A8 (westbound) & A89
9	Access only, no exit	Exit only, no access
13	Access only from M80 (southbound)	Exit only to M80 (northbound)
14	Access only, no exit	Exit only, no access
16	Exit only to A804	Access only from A879
17	Exit only to A82	No restriction
18	Access only from A82 (eastbound)	Exit only to A814
19	No access from A814 (westbound)	Exit only to A814 (westbound)
20	Exit only, no access	Access only, no exit
21	Access only, no exit	Exit only to A8
22	Exit only to M77 (southbound)	Access only from M77 (northbound)
23	Exit only to B768	Access only from B768
25	No access or exit from or to A8	No access or exit from or to A8
25A	Exit only, no access	Access only, no exit
28	Exit only, no access	Access only, no exit
28A	Exit only to A737	Access only from A737

M9 Edinburgh - Dunblane

Junction	Northwestbound	Southeastbound
1A	Exit only to M9 spur	Access only from M9 spur
2	Access only, no exit	Exit only, no access
3	Exit only, no access	Access only, no exit
6	Access only, no exit	Exit only to A905
8	Exit only to M876 (southwestbound)	Access only from M876 (northeastbound)

M11 London - Cambridge

Junction	Northbound	Southbound
4	Access only from A406 (eastbound)	Exit only to A406
5	Exit only, no access	Access only, no exit
9	Exit only to A11	Access only from A11
13	Exit only, no access	Access only, no exit
14	Exit only, no access	Access only, no exit

M20 Swanley - Folkestone

Junction	Northwestbound	Southeastbound
2	Staggered junction; follow signs - access only	Staggered junction; follow signs - exit only
3	Exit only to M26 (westbound)	Access only from M26 (eastbound)
5	Access only from A20	For access follow signs - exit only to A20
6	No restriction	For exit follow signs
11A	Access only, no exit	Exit only, no access

M23 Hooley - Crawley

Junction	Northbound	Southbound
7	Exit only to A23 (northbound)	Access only from A23 (southbound)
10A	Access only, no exit	Exit only, no access

M25 London Orbital Motorway

Junction	Clockwise	Anticlockwise
1B	No direct access, use slip road to Jct 2. Exit only	Access only, no exit
5	No exit to M26 (eastbound)	No access from M26
19	Exit only, no access	Access only, no exit
21	Access only from M1 (southbound). Exit only to M1 (northbound)	Access only from M1 (southbound). Exit only to M1 (northbound)
31	No exit (use slip road via jct 30), access only	No access (use slip road via jct 30), exit only

M26 Sevenoaks - Wrotham

Junction	Westbound	Eastbound
with M25 (jct 5)	Exit only to clockwise M25 (westbound)	Access only from anticlockwise M25 (eastbound)
with M20 (jct 3)	Access only from M20 (northwestbound)	Exit only to M20 (southeastbound)

M27 Cadnam - Portsmouth

Junction	Westbound	Eastbound
4	Staggered junction; follow signs - access only from M3 (southbound). Exit only to M3 (northbound)	Staggered junction; follow signs - access only from M3 (southbound). Exit only to M3 (northbound)
10	Exit only, no access	Access only, no exit
12	Staggered junction; follow signs - exit only to M275 (southbound)	Staggered junction; follow signs - access only from M275 (northbound)

M40 London - Birmingham

Junction	Northwestbound	Southeastbound
3	Exit only, no access	Access only, no exit
7	Exit only, no access	Access only, no exit
8	Exit only to M40/A40	Access only from M40/A40
13	Exit only, no access	Access only, no exit
14	Access only, no exit	Exit only, no access
16	Access only, no exit	Exit only, no access

M42 Bromsgrove - Measham

Junction	Northeastbound	Southwestbound
1	Access only, no exit	Exit only, no access
7	Exit only to M6 (northwestbound)	Access only from M6 (northwestbound)
7A	Exit only to M6 (southeastbound)	No access or exit
8	Access only from M6 (southeastbound)	Exit only to M6 (northwestbound)

M45 Coventry - M1

Junction	Westbound	Eastbound
Dunchurch (unnumbered)	Access only from A45	Exit only, no access
with M1 (jct 17)	Access only from M1 (northbound)	Exit only to M1 (southbound)

M53 Mersey Tunnel - Chester

Junction	Northbound	Southbound
11	Access only from M56 (westbound). Exit only to M56 (eastbound)	Access only from M56 (westbound). Exit only to M56 (eastbound)

M54 Telford

Junction	Westbound	Eastbound
with M6 (jct 10A)	Access only from M6 (northbound)	Exit only to M6 (southbound)

M56 North Cheshire

Junction	Westbound	Eastbound
1	Access only from M60 (westbound)	Exit only to M60 (eastbound) & A34 (northbound)
2	Exit only, no access	Access only, no exit
3	Access only, no exit	Exit only, no access
4	Exit only, no access	Access only, no exit
7	Exit only, no access	No restriction
8	Access only, no exit	No access or exit
15	Exit only to M53	Access only from M53
16	No access or exit	No restriction

M57 Liverpool Outer Ring Road

Junction	Northwestbound	Southeastbound
3	Access only, no exit	Exit only, no access
5	Access only from A580 (westbound)	Exit only, no access

M58 Liverpool - Wigan

Junction	Westbound	Eastbound
1	Exit only, no access	Access only, no exit

M60 Manchester Orbital

Junction	Clockwise	Anticlockwise
2	Access only, no exit	Exit only, no access
3	No access from M56	Access only from A34 (northbound)
4	Access only from A34 (northbound). Exit only to M56	Access only from M56 (eastbound). Exit only to A34 (southbound)
5	Access and exit only from and to A5103 (northbound)	Access and exit only from and to A5103 (southbound)
7	No direct access, use slip road to jct 8. Exit only to A56	Access only from A56. No exit - use jct 8
14	Access from A580 (eastbound)	Exit only to A580 (westbound)
16	Access only, no exit	Exit only, no access
20	Exit only, no access	Access only, no exit
22	No restriction	Exit only, no access
25	Exit only, no access	No restriction
26	No restriction	Exit only, no access
27	Access only, no exit	Exit only, no access

M61 Manchester - Preston

Junction	Northwestbound	Southeastbound
3	No access or exit	Exit only, no access
with M6 (jct 30)	Exit only to M6 (northbound)	Access only from M6 (southbound)

M62 Liverpool - Kingston upon Hull

Junction	Westbound	Eastbound
23	Access only, no exit	Exit only, no access
32A	No access to A1(M) (southbound)	No restriction

M65 Preston - Colne

Junction	Northeastbound	Southwestbound
9	Exit only, no access	Access only, no exit
11	Access only, no exit	Exit only, no access

M66 Bury

Junction	Northbound	Southbound
with A56	Exit only to A56 (northbound)	Access only from A56 (southbound)
1	Exit only, no access	Access only, no exit

M67 Hyde Bypass

Junction	Westbound	Eastbound
1	Access only, no exit	Exit only, no access
2	Exit only, no access	Access only, no exit
3	Exit only, no access	No restriction

M69 Coventry - Leicester

Junction	Northbound	Southbound
2	Access only, no exit	Exit only, no access

M73 East of Glasgow

Junction	Northbound	Southbound
2	No access from or exit to A89. No access from M8 (eastbound)	No access from or exit to A89. No exit to M8 (westbound)
3	Exit only to A80 (northeastbound)	Access only from A80 (southwestbound)

M74 and A74(M) Glasgow - Gretna

Junction	Northbound	Southbound
3	Exit only, no access	Access only, no exit
3A	Access only, no exit	Exit only, no access
7	Access only, no exit	Exit only, no access
9	No access or exit	Exit only, no access
10	No restrictions	Access only, no exit
11	Access only, no exit	Exit only, no access
12	Exit only, no access	Access only, no exit
18	Exit only, no access	Access only, no exit

M77 South of Glasgow

Junction	Northbound	Southbound
with M8 (jct 22)	No exit to M8 (westbound)	No access from M8 (eastbound)
4	Access only, no exit	Exit only, no access
6	Access only, no exit	Exit only, no access
7	Access only, no exit	No restriction

M80 Glasgow - Stirling

Junction	Northbound	Southbound
4A	Exit only, no access	Access only, no exit
6A	Access only, no exit	Exit only, no access
8	Exit only to M876 (northeastbound)	Access only from M876 (southwestbound)

M90 Forth Road Bridge - Perth

Junction	Northbound	Southbound
2A	Exit only to A92 (eastbound)	Access only from A92 (westbound)
7	Access only, no exit	Exit only, no access
8	Exit only, no access	Access only, no exit
10	No access from A912. No exit to A912 (southbound)	No access from A912 (northbound). No exit to A912

M180 Doncaster - Grimsby

Junction	Westbound	Eastbound
1	Access only, no exit	Exit only, no access

M606 Bradford Spur

Junction	Northbound	Southbound
2	Exit only, no access	No restriction

M621 Leeds - M1

Junction	Clockwise	Anticlockwise
2A	Access only, no exit	Exit only, no access
4	No exit or access	No restriction
5	Access only, no exit	Exit only, no access
6	Exit only, no access	Access only, no exit
with M1 (jct 43)	Exit only to M1 (southbound)	Access only from M1 (northbound)

M876 Bonnybridge - Kincardine Bridge

Junction	Northeastbound	Southwestbound
with M80 (jct 5)	Access only from M80 (northeastbound)	Exit only to M80 (southwestbound)
with M9 (jct 8)	Exit only to M9 (eastbound)	Access only from M9 (westbound)

A1(M) South Mimms - Baldock

Junction	Northbound	Southbound
2	Exit only, no access	Access only, no exit
3	No restriction	Exit only, no access
5	Access only, no exit	No access or exit

A1(M) Pontefract - Bedale

Junction	Northbound	Southbound
41	No access to M62 (eastbound)	No restriction
43	Access only from M1 (northbound)	Exit only to M1 (southbound)

A1(M) Scotch Corner - Newcastle upon Tyne

Junction	Northbound	Southbound
57	Exit only to A66(M) (eastbound)	Access only from A66(M) (westbound)
65	No access Exit only to A194(M) & A1 (northbound)	No exit Access only from A194(M) & A1 (southbound)

A3(M) Horndean - Havant

Junction	Northbound	Southbound
1	Access only from A3	Exit only to A3
4	Exit only, no access	Access only, no exit

A48(M) Cardiff Spur

Junction	Westbound	Eastbound
29	Access only from M4 (westbound)	Exit only to M4 (eastbound)
29A	Exit only to A48 (westbound)	Access only from A48 (eastbound)

A66(M) Darlington Spur

Junction	Westbound	Eastbound
with A1(M) (jct 57)	Exit only to A1(M) (southbound)	Access only from A1(M) (northbound)

A194(M) Newcastle upon Tyne

Junction	Northbound	Southbound
with A1(M) (jct 65)	Access only from A1(M) (northbound)	Exit only to A1(M) (southbound)

A12 M25 - Ipswich

Junction	Northeastbound	Southwestbound
13	Access only, no exit	No restriction
14	Exit only, no access	Access only, no exit
20A	Exit only, no access	Access only, no exit
20B	Access only, no exit	Exit only, no access
21	No restriction	Access only, no exit
23	Exit only, no access	Access only, no exit
24	Access only, no exit	Exit only, no access
27	Exit only, no access	Access only, no exit
Dedham & Stratford St Mary (unnumbered)	Exit only	Access only

A14 M1 - Felixstowe

Junction	Westbound	Eastbound
with M1/M6 (jct19)	Exit only to M6 and M1 (northbound)	Access only from M6 and M1 (southbound)
4	Exit only, no access	Access only, no exit
31	Access only from A1307	Exit only to A1307
34	Access only, no exit	Exit only, no access
36	Exit only to A11, access only from A1303	Access only from A11
38	Access only from A11	Exit only to A11
39	Exit only, no access	Access only, no exit
61	Access only, no exit	Exit only, no access

A55 Holyhead - Chester

Junction	Westbound	Eastbound
8A	Exit only, no access	Access only, no exit
23A	Access only, no exit	Exit only, no access
24A	Exit only, no access	No access or exit
33A	Exit only, no access	No access or exit
33B	Exit only, no access	Access only, no exit
37	Exit only to A5104	Access only from A5104

Index to place names

This index lists places appearing in the main-map section of the atlas in alphabetical order. The reference following each name gives the atlas page number and grid reference of the square in which the place appears. The map shows counties, unitary authorities and administrative areas, together with a list of the abbreviated name forms used in the index.

Scotland

Abers	**Aberdeenshire**
Ag & B	**Argyll and Bute**
Angus	**Angus**
Border	**Scottish Borders**
C Aber	**City of Aberdeen**
C Dund	**City of Dundee**
C Edin	**City of Edinburgh**
C Glas	**City of Glasgow**
Clacks	**Clackmannanshire (1)**
D & G	**Dumfries & Galloway**
E Ayrs	**East Ayrshire**
E Duns	**East Dunbartonshire (2)**
E Loth	**East Lothian**
E Rens	**East Renfrewshire (3)**
Falk	**Falkirk**
Fife	**Fife**
Highld	**Highland**
Inver	**Inverclyde (4)**
Mdloth	**Midlothian (5)**
Moray	**Moray**
N Ayrs	**North Ayrshire**
N Lans	**North Lanarkshire (6)**
Ork	**Orkney Islands**
P & K	**Perth & Kinross**
Rens	**Renfrewshire (7)**
S Ayrs	**South Ayrshire**
Shet	**Shetland Islands**
S Lans	**South Lanarkshire**
Stirlg	**Stirling**
W Duns	**West Dunbartonshire (8)**
W Isls	**Western Isles** **(Na h-Eileanan an Iar)**
W Loth	**West Lothian**

Wales

Blae G	**Blaenau Gwent (9)**
Brdgnd	**Bridgend (10)**
Caerph	**Caerphilly (11)**
Cardif	**Cardiff**
Carmth	**Carmarthenshire**
Cerdgn	**Ceredigion**
Conwy	**Conwy**
Denbgs	**Denbighshire**
Flints	**Flintshire**
Gwynd	**Gwynedd**
IoA	**Isle of Anglesey**
Mons	**Monmouthshire**
Myr Td	**Merthyr Tydfil (12)**
Neath	**Neath Port Talbot (13)**
Newpt	**Newport (14)**
Pembks	**Pembrokeshire**
Powys	**Powys**
Rhondd	**Rhondda Cynon Taff (15)**
Swans	**Swansea**
Torfn	**Torfaen (16)**
V Glam	**Vale of Glamorgan (17)**
Wrexhm	**Wrexham**

Channel Islands & Isle of Man

Guern	**Guernsey**
Jersey	**Jersey**
IoM	**Isle of Man**

England

BaNES	**Bath & N E Somerset (18)**
Barns	**Barnsley (19)**
Bed	**Bedford**
Birm	**Birmingham**
Bl w D	**Blackburn with Darwen (20)**
Bmouth	**Bournemouth**
Bolton	**Bolton (21)**
Bpool	**Blackpool**
Br & H	**Brighton & Hove (22)**
Br For	**Bracknell Forest (23)**
Bristl	**City of Bristol**
Bucks	**Buckinghamshire**
Bury	**Bury (24)**
C Beds	**Central Bedfordshire**
C Brad	**City of Bradford**
C Derb	**City of Derby**
C KuH	**City of Kingston upon Hull**
C Leic	**City of Leicester**
C Nott	**City of Nottingham**
C Pete	**City of Peterborough**
C Plym	**City of Plymouth**
C Port	**City of Portsmouth**
C Sotn	**City of Southampton**
C Stke	**City of Stoke-on-Trent**
C York	**City of York**
Calder	**Calderdale (25)**
Cambs	**Cambridgeshire**
Ches E	**Cheshire East**
Ches W	**Cheshire West and Chester**
Cnwll	**Cornwall**
Covtry	**Coventry**
Cumb	**Cumbria**
Darltn	**Darlington (26)**
Derbys	**Derbyshire**
Devon	**Devon**
Donc	**Doncaster (27)**
Dorset	**Dorset**
Dudley	**Dudley (28)**
Dur	**Durham**
E R Yk	**East Riding of Yorkshire**
E Susx	**East Sussex**
Essex	**Essex**
Gatesd	**Gateshead (29)**
Gloucs	**Gloucestershire**
Gt Lon	**Greater London**
Halton	**Halton (30)**
Hants	**Hampshire**
Hartpl	**Hartlepool (31)**
Herefs	**Herefordshire**
Herts	**Hertfordshire**
IoS	**Isles of Scilly**
IoW	**Isle of Wight**
Kent	**Kent**
Kirk	**Kirklees (32)**
Knows	**Knowsley (33)**
Lancs	**Lancashire**
Leeds	**Leeds**
Leics	**Leicestershire**
Lincs	**Lincolnshire**
Lpool	**Liverpool**
Luton	**Luton**
M Keyn	**Milton Keynes**

Manch	**Manchester**
Medway	**Medway**
Middsb	**Middlesbrough**
NE Lin	**North East Lincolnshire**
N Linc	**North Lincolnshire**
N Som	**North Somerset (34)**
N Tyne	**North Tyneside (35)**
N u Ty	**Newcastle upon Tyne**
N York	**North Yorkshire**
Nhants	**Northamptonshire**
Norfk	**Norfolk**
Notts	**Nottinghamshire**
Nthumb	**Northumberland**
Oldham	**Oldham (36)**
Oxon	**Oxfordshire**
Poole	**Poole**
R & Cl	**Redcar & Cleveland**
Readg	**Reading**
Rochdl	**Rochdale (37)**
Rothm	**Rotherham (38)**
Rutlnd	**Rutland**
S Glos	**South Gloucestershire (39)**
S on T	**Stockton-on-Tees (40)**
S Tyne	**South Tyneside (41)**
Salfd	**Salford (42)**
Sandw	**Sandwell (43)**
Sefton	**Sefton (44)**
Sheff	**Sheffield**
Shrops	**Shropshire**
Slough	**Slough (45)**
Solhll	**Solihull (46)**
Somset	**Somerset**
St Hel	**St Helens (47)**
Staffs	**Staffordshire**
Sthend	**Southend-on-Sea**
Stockp	**Stockport (48)**
Suffk	**Suffolk**
Sundld	**Sunderland**
Surrey	**Surrey**
Swindn	**Swindon**
Tamesd	**Tameside (49)**
Thurr	**Thurrock (50)**
Torbay	**Torbay**
Traffd	**Trafford (51)**
W & M	**Windsor and Maidenhead (5**
W Berk	**West Berkshire**
W Susx	**West Sussex**
Wakefd	**Wakefield (53)**
Warrtn	**Warrington (54)**
Warwks	**Warwickshire**
Wigan	**Wigan (55)**
Wilts	**Wiltshire**
Wirral	**Wirral (56)**
Wokham	**Wokingham (57)**
Wolves	**Wolverhampton (58)**
Worcs	**Worcestershire**
Wrekin	**Telford & Wrekin (59)**
Wsall	**Walsall (60)**

ORKNEY ISLANDS

SHETLAND ISLANDS

WESTERN ISLES (Na h-Eileanan an Iar)

HIGHLAND

MORAY

S C O T L A N D

Aberdeen

ABERDEENSHIRE

ANGUS

PERTH & KINROSS

Dundee

ARGYLL & BUTE

STIRLING

FIFE

1

8
4 2
Glasgow
7
3

FALK

W LOTH

6

Edinburgh

E LOTH

5

NORTH AYRSHIRE

S LANS

E AYRS

SCOTTISH BORDERS

S AYRS

DUMFRIES & GALLOWAY

NORTHUMBERLAND

Newcastle upon Tyne
35
41
29
Sunderland

CUMBRIA

DURHAM

31
26 40 R & CL
Middlesbrough

IoM

NORTH YORKSHIRE

Bradford
Blackpool
LANCASHIRE
25
Leeds
York
EAST RIDING OF YORKSHIRE
Kingston upon Hull

20
53
32
N LINC
N E LIN
21 24 37
36
44 55
47 42 19 27
Liverpool 33 54 51 Manchester
56 30 48 38
Sheffield

IoA

CONWY

FLINTS

CHES W

CHES E

DERBYS

NOTTS

LINCOLNSHIRE

DENBGS

WREXHAM

Stoke-on-Trent

Derby

Nottingham

GWYNEDD

STAFFS

59

LEICS

RUTLAND

Peterborough

NORFOLK

SHROPSHIRE

58 60
28 43
46

Birmingham
Coventry

NHANTS

Milton Keynes

BED

CAMBS

SUFFOLK

POWYS

CERDGN

WORCS

WARWKS

BEDS Luton

HERTS

ESSEX

PEMBKS

CARMTH

HEREFS

GLOUCS

OXON

BUCKS

GREATER LONDON

Southend-on-Sea

12 9
13 16 MONS
15 11
10 14
Swansea Cardiff
17

39
Bristol
34 18

Swindon

Reading
W BERK
52 45
57 23

50
MEDWAY

W A L E S   E N G L A N D

WILTSHIRE

SURREY

KENT

SOMERSET

HAMPSHIRE

W SUSX

E SUSX

22

DEVON

DORSET

Southampton
Portsmouth
Bournemouth
Poole
IoW

CORNWALL

Torbay

Plymouth

CHANNEL ISLANDS

Guernsey

Jersey

IoS

A

Abbas Combe Somset 32 B6
Abberley Worcs 81 H2
Abberley Common Worcs 81 G2
Abberton Essex 72 E3
Abberton Worcs 82 A4
Abberwick Nthumb 191 G3
Abbess Roding Essex 70 E5
Abbey Devon 29 L8
Abbey-Cwm-Hir Powys 78 E1
Abbeydale Sheff 132 F3
Abbey Dore Herefs 62 D1
Abbey Green Staffs 131 J8
Abbey Hill Somset 30 D7
Abbey St Bathans Border 213 G6
Abbeystead Lancs 147 L5
Abbey Town Cumb 177 G8
Abbey Village Lancs 139 J3
Abbey Wood Gt Lon 52 A3
Abbotrule Border 189 G4
Abbots Bickington Devon 27 G8
Abbots Bromley Staffs 115 H6
Abbotsbury Dorset 16 A5
Abbot's Chair Derbys 131 K2
Abbots Deuglie P & K 221 K5
Abbotsham Devon 27 G5
Abbotskerswell Devon 8 C1
Abbots Langley Herts 68 E6
Abbotsleigh Devon 8 B5
Abbots Leigh N Som 45 G4
Abbotsley Cambs 86 E4
Abbots Morton Worcs 82 B4
Abbots Ripton Cambs 102 E7
Abbot's Salford Warwks 82 C5
Abbotstone Hants 35 H4
Abbotswood Hants 34 D6
Abbots Worthy Hants 35 G4
Abbotts Ann Hants 34 D2
Abbott Street Dorset 17 J3
Abcott Shrops 95 J7
Abdon Shrops 96 D6
Abenhall Gloucs 63 K4
Aberaeron Cerdgn 76 E3
Aberaman Rhondd 60 F7
Aberangell Gwynd 93 J2
Aber-arad Carmth 76 B7
Aberarder Highld 251 H6
Aberargie P & K 222 B4
Aberarth Cerdgn 76 E3
Aberavon Neath 57 K7
Aber-banc Cerdgn 76 C7
Aberbargoed Caerph 61 J7
Aberbeeg Blae G 61 K6
Abercanaid Myr Td 61 G6
Abercarn Caerph 43 K3
Abercastle Pembks 74 D5
Abercegir Powys 93 H3
Aberchalder Lodge Highld 240 B3
Aberchirder Abers 268 A5
Aber Clydach Powys 61 H3
Abercraf Powys 59 M6
Abercregan Neath 42 C2
Abercwmboi Rhondd 60 F7
Abercych Pembks 75 M4
Abercynon Rhondd 43 G3
Aberdalgie P & K 221 K3
Aberdare Rhondd 60 F6
Aberdaron Gwynd 108 C6
Aberdeen C Aber 245 L2
Aberdeen Crematorium
  C Aber 245 K2
Aberdesach Gwynd 109 G1
Aberdour Fife 211 G2
Aberdulais Neath 57 L5
Aberdyfi Gwynd 92 D4
Aberedw Powys 78 F6
Abereiddy Pembks 74 C6
Abererch Gwynd 109 G4
Aberfan Myr Td 61 G7
Aberfeldy P & K 232 C5
Aberffraw IoA 124 F6
Aberffrwd Cerdgn 92 E7
Aberford Leeds 150 F8
Aberfoyle Stirlg 219 H7
Abergarw Brdgnd 42 D5
Abergarwed Neath 60 B6
Abergavenny Mons 62 C4
Abergele Conwy 127 J4
Aber-giar Carmth 76 F7
Abergorlech Carmth 59 G2
Abergwesyn Powys 78 A4
Abergwili Carmth 58 D5
Abergwydol Powys 93 G3
Abergwynfi Neath 42 D3
Abergwyngregyn Gwynd 126 C5
Abergynolwyn Gwynd 92 C5
Aberhafesp Powys 94 C5
Aberhosan Powys 93 H4

Aberkenfig Brdgnd 42 D5
Aberlady E Loth 212 A3
Aberlemno Angus 234 E4
Aberllefenni Gwynd 93 G2
Aberllynfi Powys 79 H7
Aberlour Moray 254 E3
Aber-Magwr Cerdgn 92 E8
Aber-meurig Cerdgn 77 G4
Abermorddu Flints 129 G8
Abermule Powys 94 E4
Abernant Carmth 58 C4
Aber-nant Rhondd 60 F6
Abernethy P & K 222 C4
Abernyte P & K 222 D1
Aberporth Cerdgn 76 A5
Abersoch Gwynd 108 E6
Abersychan Torfn 62 B6
Aberthin V Glam 42 F6
Abertillery Blae G 61 K6
Abertridwr Caerph 43 H4
Abertridwr Powys 111 K7
Abertysswg Caerph 61 H6
Aberuthven P & K 221 H4
Aberyscir Powys 60 F1
Aberystwyth Cerdgn 92 C7
Aberystwyth Crematorium
  Cerdgn 92 D6
Abingdon-on-Thames Oxon 66 C7
Abinger Common Surrey 37 H2
Abinger Hammer Surrey 37 H2
Abington Nhants 84 F3
Abington S Lans 186 D2
Abington Pigotts Cambs 86 F6
Abingworth W Susx 21 J3
Ab Kettleby Leics 117 J7
Ab Lench Worcs 82 B5
Ablington Gloucs 65 G5
Ablington Wilts 33 K2
Abney Derbys 132 D4
Above Church Staffs 115 G2
Aboyne Abers 244 C4
Abram Wigan 139 J7
Abriachan Highld 250 F4
Abridge Essex 70 C7
Abronhill N Lans 209 L4
Abson S Glos 45 L4
Abthorpe Nhants 84 C6
Aby Lincs 137 H4
Acaster Malbis C York 151 J6
Acaster Selby N York 151 J7
Accrington Lancs 139 M2
Accrington Crematorium
  Lancs 140 A2
Acha Ag & B 224 F4
Achahoish Ag & B 206 B3
Achalader P & K 233 H6
Achaleven Ag & B 228 E8
Acha Mor W Isls 282 f3
Achanalt Highld 261 M7
Achandunie Highld 263 H5
Achany Highld 272 E7
Acharacle Highld 237 K7
Acharn Highld 227 K2
Acharn P & K 231 L6
Achavanich Highld 279 L7
Achduart Highld 270 D7
Achfary Highld 276 D8
A'Chill Highld 246 C7
Achiltibuie Highld 270 D6
Achina Highld 278 B4
Achinhoan Ag & B 192 F5
Achintee Highld 248 F3
Achintraid Highld 248 D4
Achmelvich Highld 270 E3
Achmore Highld 248 D5
Achmore W Isls 282 f3
Achnacarnin Highld 270 D2
Achnacarry Highld 239 K6
Achnacloich Highld 247 J6
Achnaconeran Highld 250 D8
Achnacroish Ag & B 228 C7
Achnadrish House Ag & B 226 F2
Achnafauld P & K 232 C2
Achnagarron Highld 263 J6
Achnaha Highld 236 F6
Achnahaird Highld 270 D6
Achnairn Highld 272 E5
Achnalea Highld 228 C3
Achnamara Ag & B 206 B2
Achnasheen Highld 261 K8
Achnashellach Lodge Highld 249 G2
Achnastank Moray 254 F5
Achosnich Highld 236 E7
Achranich Highld 227 K3
Achreamie Highld 279 H3
Achriabhach Highld 229 J2
Achriesgill Highld 276 D5
Achtoty Highld 277 M4
Achurch Nhants 102 A6
Achvaich Highld 263 J1

Achvarasdal Highld 279 H3
Ackergill Highld 280 E5
Acklam Middsb 170 C7
Acklam N York 152 B3
Ackleton Shrops 97 H4
Acklington Nthumb 191 J6
Ackton Wakefd 142 C4
Ackworth Moor Top Wakefd 142 C4
Acle Norfk 107 H1
Acock's Green Birm 98 E4
Acol Kent 41 J2
Acomb C York 151 J5
Acomb Nthumb 179 L5
Acombe Somset 30 B8
Aconbury Herefs 80 C8
Acre Lancs 140 B3
Acrefair Wrexhm 112 D3
Acton Ches E 113 K1
Acton Dorset 17 J7
Acton Gt Lon 51 G3
Acton Shrops 95 H6
Acton Staffs 114 C3
Acton Suffk 89 H6
Acton Worcs 81 J2
Acton Beauchamp Herefs 80 F5
Acton Bridge Ches W 130 B4
Acton Burnell Shrops 96 C3
Acton Green Herefs 81 G5
Acton Park Wrexhm 112 C3
Acton Pigott Shrops 96 C3
Acton Round Shrops 96 E4
Acton Scott Shrops 95 L5
Acton Trussell Staffs 114 E7
Acton Turville S Glos 46 A3
Adbaston Staffs 114 B6
Adber Dorset 31 K6
Adbolton Notts 117 G4
Adderbury Oxon 83 L8
Adderley Shrops 113 L3
Adderstone Nthumb 203 J7
Addiewell W Loth 210 C6
Addingham C Brad 149 K6
Addington Bucks 67 H2
Addington Gt Lon 51 K6
Addington Kent 52 E7
Addiscombe Gt Lon 51 J5
Addlestone Surrey 50 D6
Addlestonemoor Surrey 50 D6
Addlethorpe Lincs 137 K6
Adeney Wrekin 113 M7
Adeyfield Herts 68 D5
Adfa Powys 94 C3
Adforton Herefs 79 M1
Adisham Kent 41 H4
Adlestrop Gloucs 65 K2
Adlingfleet E R Yk 143 L3
Adlington Ches E 131 H4
Adlington Lancs 139 J5
Admaston Staffs 115 G7
Admaston Wrekin 96 E1
Admington Warwks 82 E6
Adpar Cerdgn 76 B7
Adsborough Somset 30 D5
Adscombe Somset 30 B3
Adstock Bucks 67 H1
Adstone Nhants 84 B5
Adswood Stockp 131 H2
Adversane W Susx 37 G6
Advie Highld 254 C5
Adwalton Leeds 141 K2
Adwell Oxon 67 G7
Adwick Le Street Donc 142 E6
Adwick upon Dearne Donc 142 D7
Ae D & G 176 C1
Ae Bridgend D & G 176 D2
Affetside Bury 139 M5
Affleck Abers 255 L4
Affpuddle Dorset 16 F4
Affric Lodge Highld 249 K7
Afon-wen Flints 128 D5
Afton Devon 8 C2
Afton IoW 18 E6
Agecroft Crematorium Salfd 140 B7
Agglethorpe N York 159 K5
Aigburth Lpool 129 J2
Aike E R Yk 153 G6
Aiketgate Cumb 166 B1
Aikhead Cumb 165 H1
Aikton Cumb 177 J8
Ailby Lincs 137 H4
Ailey Herefs 79 L5
Ailsworth C Pete 102 C4
Ainderby Quernhow N York 160 E6
Ainderby Steeple N York 160 E4
Aingers Green Essex 73 G3
Ainsdale Sefton 138 C5
Ainsdale-on-Sea Sefton 138 C5
Ainstable Cumb 166 C2
Ainsworth Bury 139 M5
Ainthorpe N York 162 C1

Aintree Sefton 138 D4
Ainville W Loth 210 F6
Aird Ag & B 216 B1
Aird D & G 172 D2
Aird W Isls 282 h3
Aird a Mhulaidh W Isls 282 e4
Aird Asaig W Isls 282 e5
Aird Dhubh Highld 248 D4
Airdeny Ag & B 216 F1
Aird of Kinloch Ag & B 227 G5
Aird of Sleat Highld 247 J7
Airdrie N Lans 209 K6
Airdriehill N Lans 209 K5
Airds of Kells D & G 175 J3
Aird Uig W Isls 282 d3
Airidh a bhruaich W Isls 282 f4
Airieland D & G 175 J3
Airlie Angus 233 M5
Airmyn E R Yk 143 J3
Airntully P & K 233 G8
Airor Highld 247 M7
Airth Falk 210 B2
Airton N York 148 E6
Aisby Lincs 118 D4
Aisby Lincs 135 H1
Aisgill Cumb 158 D2
Aish Devon 7 K3
Aish Devon 8 C3
Aisholt Somset 30 B4
Aiskew N York 160 C5
Aislaby N York 162 D1
Aislaby N York 162 F1
Aislaby S on T 169 L8
Aisthorpe Lincs 135 J4
Aith Shet 281 d5
Akeld Nthumb 202 E7
Akeley Bucks 84 D7
Akenham Suffk 90 D5
Albaston Cnwll 12 A8
Alberbury Shrops 112 E8
Albourne W Susx 22 C4
Albourne Green W Susx 22 C4
Albrighton Shrops 97 H3
Albrighton Shrops 113 H7
Alburgh Norfk 106 F6
Albury Herts 70 C3
Albury Oxon 67 G7
Albury Surrey 37 G2
Albury End Herts 70 B2
Albury Heath Surrey 37 G2
Alby Hill Norfk 122 D6
Alcaig Highld 263 G8
Alcaston Shrops 95 L6
Alcester Warwks 82 C4
Alcester Lane End Birm 98 D7
Alciston E Susx 23 H7
Alcombe Somset 29 H2
Alcombe Wilts 46 A6
Alconbury Cambs 102 D8
Alconbury Weston Cambs 102 D7
Aldborough N York 150 F3
Aldborough Norfk 122 D5
Aldbourne Wilts 47 K4
Aldbrough E R Yk 153 L8
Aldbrough St John N York 169 G8
Aldbury Herts 68 B4
Aldcliffe Lancs 147 J4
Aldclune P & K 232 D3
Aldeburgh Suffk 91 K4
Aldeby Norfk 107 J5
Aldenham Herts 68 F7
Alderbury Wilts 33 L5
Aldercar Derbys 116 D2
Alderford Norfk 122 C7
Alderholt Dorset 33 K8
Alderley Gloucs 45 M1
Alderley Edge Ches E 131 H4
Aldermans Green Covtry 99 K6
Aldermaston W Berk 48 E5
Alderminster Warwks 82 F5
Alder Moor Staffs 115 L6
Aldersey Green Ches W 129 K8
Aldershot Hants 36 C1
Alderton Gloucs 82 B8
Alderton Nhants 84 D5
Alderton Shrops 113 H6
Alderton Suffk 91 H7
Alderton Wilts 46 B3
Alderwasley Derbys 116 A1
Aldfield N York 150 C2
Aldford Ches W 129 K7
Aldgate Rutlnd 101 L3
Aldham Essex 72 D2
Aldham Suffk 90 B6
Aldingbourne W Susx 20 F5
Aldingham Cumb 146 E2
Aldington Kent 40 E8
Aldington Worcs 82 C6
Aldington Corner Kent 40 E7
Aldivalloch Moray 255 G6

Aldochlay Ag & B........208 B1
Aldon Shrops........95 K7
Aldoth Cumb........164 F1
Aldreth Cambs........103 J8
Aldridge Wsall........98 D3
Aldringham Suffk........91 K3
Aldro N York........152 B3
Aldsworth Gloucs........65 H5
Aldsworth W Susx........20 C5
Aldunie Moray........255 G6
Aldwark Derbys........132 E8
Aldwark N York........151 G3
Aldwick W Susx........20 E7
Aldwincle Nhants........101 M7
Aldworth W Berk........48 E3
Alexandria W Duns........208 C3
Aley Somset........30 B3
Alfardisworthy Devon........26 E8
Alfington Devon........14 D3
Alfold Surrey........36 F4
Alfold Bars W Susx........36 F4
Alfold Crossways Surrey........36 F4
Alford Abers........255 M8
Alford Lincs........137 H4
Alford Somset........31 K4
Alford Crematorium Lincs........137 H4
Alfreton Derbys........133 H8
Alfrick Worcs........81 H4
Alfrick Pound Worcs........81 G5
Alfriston E Susx........23 H6
Algarkirk Lincs........119 J4
Alhampton Somset........31 K4
Alkborough N Linc........143 M3
Alkerton Gloucs........63 M6
Alkerton Oxon........83 J6
Alkham Kent........41 H6
Alkington Shrops........113 K4
Alkmonton Derbys........115 K4
Allaleigh Devon........8 B4
Allanaquoich Abers........242 F5
Allanbank N Lans........209 M7
Allanton Border........202 D2
Allanton N Lans........209 M7
Allanton S Lans........209 K8
Allaston Gloucs........63 J6
Allbrook Hants........34 F6
All Cannings Wilts........46 F4
Allendale Nthumb........179 J7
Allen End Warwks........98 F4
Allenheads Nthumb........167 K2
Allensford Dur........168 D1
Allen's Green Herts........70 C4
Allensmore Herefs........80 B8
Allenton C Derb........116 B5
Aller Devon........28 D5
Aller Somset........30 F5
Allerby Cumb........164 E3
Allercombe Devon........14 B4
Allerford Somset........28 F2
Allerston N York........162 F6
Allerthorpe E R Yk........152 B6
Allerton C Brad........141 H1
Allerton Highld........263 K6
Allerton Lpool........129 J2
Allerton Bywater Leeds........142 C2
Allerton Mauleverer N York........150 F4
Allesley Covtry........99 J7
Allestree C Derb........116 B4
Allet Common Cnwll........4 C5
Allexton Leics........101 H3
Allgreave Ches E........131 J6
Allhallows Medway........53 H3
Allhallows-on-Sea Medway........53 H3
Alligin Shuas Highld........260 D8
Allimore Green Staffs........114 D7
Allington Dorset........15 K4
Allington Kent........53 G7
Allington Lincs........117 M3
Allington Wilts........33 L3
Allington Wilts........46 C4
Allington Wilts........46 F6
Allithwaite Cumb........156 E7
Alloa Clacks........220 F8
Allonby Cumb........164 E2
Allostock Ches W........130 E5
Alloway S Ayrs........196 C7
Allowenshay Somset........30 F8
All Saints South Elmham Suffk........107 G7
Allscott Shrops........97 G4
Allscott Wrekin........96 E1
All Stretton Shrops........95 L4
Alltami Flints........129 G6
Alltchaorunn Highld........229 K5
Alltmawr Powys........78 F6
Alltwalis Carmth........58 E3
Alltwen Neath........57 K4
Alltyblaca Cerdgn........76 F6
Allweston Dorset........31 L8
Allwood Green Suffk........90 B1
Almeley Herefs........79 L5

Almeley Wooton Herefs........79 L5
Almer Dorset........17 H3
Almholme Donc........142 F6
Almington Staffs........113 M4
Almodington W Susx........20 D7
Almondbank P & K........221 J2
Almondbury Kirk........141 J5
Almondsbury S Glos........45 J2
Alne N York........151 L5
Alness Highld........263 H6
Alnham Nthumb........190 E4
Alnmouth Nthumb........191 J4
Alnwick Nthumb........191 H4
Alperton Gt Lon........50 F2
Alphamstone Essex........89 H8
Alpheton Suffk........89 H5
Alphington Devon........13 L4
Alpington Norfk........106 F3
Alport Derbys........132 D6
Alpraham Ches E........130 B7
Alresford Essex........72 F3
Alrewas Staffs........115 K8
Alsager Ches E........130 F8
Alsagers Bank Staffs........114 C2
Alsop en le Dale Derbys........132 C8
Alston Cumb........167 G2
Alston Devon........15 G2
Alstone Gloucs........82 A8
Alstone Somset........30 D2
Alstonefield Staffs........132 C8
Alston Sutton Somset........44 E8
Alswear Devon........28 C6
Alt Oldham........140 E7
Altandhu Highld........270 C5
Altarnun Cnwll........11 J6
Altass Highld........272 D8
Altcreich Ag & B........227 K5
Altgaltraig Ag & B........207 G4
Altham Lancs........140 A1
Althorne Essex........72 D7
Althorpe N Linc........143 L6
Altnabreac Station Highld........279 H7
Altnaharra Highld........272 E1
Altofts Wakefd........142 B3
Alton Derbys........133 G6
Alton Hants........35 L3
Alton Staffs........115 H4
Alton Wilts........33 K2
Alton Barnes Wilts........47 G6
Alton Pancras Dorset........16 D2
Alton Priors Wilts........47 G6
Altrincham Traffd........130 E2
Altrincham Crematorium Traffd........130 E2
Altskeith Hotel Stirlg........219 G6
Alva Clacks........220 F7
Alvanley Ches W........129 L5
Alvaston C Derb........116 C5
Alvechurch Worcs........82 B1
Alvecote Warwks........99 H3
Alvediston Wilts........33 G6
Alveley Shrops........97 G6
Alverdiscott Devon........27 J4
Alverstoke Hants........19 K4
Alverstone IoW........19 K6
Alverthorpe Wakefd........141 M3
Alverton Notts........117 L3
Alves Moray........266 C4
Alvescot Oxon........65 K6
Alveston S Glos........45 J1
Alveston Warwks........82 F4
Alvingham Lincs........137 G2
Alvington Gloucs........63 J7
Alwalton C Pete........102 C4
Alwinton Nthumb........190 C5
Alwoodley Leeds........150 C7
Alwoodley Gates Leeds........150 D7
Alyth P & K........233 L7
Ambergate Derbys........116 B1
Amber Hill Lincs........119 H2
Amberley Gloucs........64 B6
Amberley W Susx........21 H4
Amber Row Derbys........133 G8
Amberstone E Susx........23 K5
Amble Nthumb........191 K5
Amblecote Dudley........97 K6
Ambler Thorn C Brad........141 H2
Ambleside Cumb........156 E2
Ambleston Pembks........75 G7
Ambrosden Oxon........66 F3
Amcotts N Linc........143 L5
America Cambs........103 J7
Amersham Bucks........68 B7
Amersham Common Bucks........68 B7
Amersham Old Town Bucks........68 B7
Amersham on the Hill Bucks........68 B7
Amerton Staffs........114 F6
Amesbury Wilts........33 K3
Amhuinnsuidhe W Isls........282 d5
Amington Staffs........99 G3

Amisfield Town D & G........176 D2
Amlwch IoA........125 H1
Ammanford Carmth........59 H6
Amotherby N York........162 C7
Ampfield Hants........34 E6
Ampleforth N York........161 J7
Ampney Crucis Gloucs........64 F6
Ampney St Mary Gloucs........65 G6
Ampney St Peter Gloucs........65 G6
Amport Hants........34 C2
Ampthill C Beds........85 K7
Ampton Suffk........89 H1
Amroth Pembks........55 K5
Amulree P & K........232 D8
Amwell Herts........68 F4
Anaheilt Highld........228 C3
Ancaster Lincs........118 C3
Anchor Shrops........94 E6
Ancroft Nthumb........202 F4
Ancrum Border........189 H1
Ancton W Susx........21 G6
Anderby Lincs........137 K4
Andersea Somset........30 E4
Andersfield Somset........30 C4
Anderson Dorset........17 G3
Anderton Ches W........130 C4
Anderton Cnwll........6 E4
Andover Hants........34 C1
Andoversford Gloucs........64 F3
Andreas IoM........154 f2
Anelog Gwynd........108 B6
Anerley Gt Lon........51 L3
Anfield Lpool........129 J1
Anfield Crematorium Lpool........129 J1
Angarrack Cnwll........2 F3
Angarrick Cnwll........3 K4
Angelbank Shrops........96 D8
Angersleigh Somset........30 B7
Angerton Cumb........177 H7
Angle Pembks........54 D6
Anglesey IoA........125 G3
Angmering W Susx........21 H6
Angram N York........151 H6
Angram N York........158 F3
Angrouse Cnwll........3 H7
Anick Nthumb........179 L5
Ankerville Highld........264 C5
Ankle Hill Leics........117 K7
Anlaby E R Yk........144 C2
Anmer Norfk........121 G5
Anmore Hants........19 L1
Annan D & G........177 G5
Annaside Cumb........155 K5
Annat Highld........248 E1
Annathill N Lans........209 J3
Anna Valley Hants........34 D2
Annbank S Ayrs........196 E6
Annesley Notts........116 E1
Annesley Woodhouse Notts........116 E1
Annfield Plain Dur........180 E8
Anniesland C Glas........208 F5
Annitsford N Tyne........181 G4
Annscroft Shrops........95 L2
Ansdell Lancs........138 D2
Ansford Somset........31 L4
Ansley Warwks........99 J5
Anslow Staffs........115 L6
Anslow Gate Staffs........115 K6
Anslow Lees Staffs........115 K6
Ansteadbrook Surrey........36 D4
Anstey Hants........35 L3
Anstey Herts........87 H8
Anstey Leics........100 C2
Anstruther Fife........223 K6
Ansty W Susx........37 L6
Ansty Warwks........99 L6
Ansty Wilts........33 G5
Ansty Cross Dorset........16 E2
Anthill Common Hants........19 L1
Anthonys Surrey........50 C6
Anthorn Cumb........177 G7
Antingham Norfk........122 E5
An t-Ob W Isls........282 d6
Anton's Gowt Lincs........119 J2
Antony Cnwll........6 D4
Antrobus Ches W........130 C4
Anvil Corner Devon........11 M2
Anvil Green Kent........40 E5
Anwick Lincs........118 F2
Anwoth D & G........174 F4
Aperfield Gt Lon........51 L7
Apes Dale Worcs........82 A1
Apethorpe Nhants........102 A4
Apeton Staffs........114 D7
Apley Lincs........136 B5
Apperknowle Derbys........133 H4
Apperley Gloucs........64 B2
Apperley Bridge C Brad........150 B8
Apperley Dene Nthumb........180 C7
Appersett N York........158 E4

Appin Ag & B........228 E6
Appleby N Linc........144 B5
Appleby-in-Westmorland Cumb........166 F6
Appleby Magna Leics........99 J2
Appleby Parva Leics........99 J2
Appleby Street Herts........69 J6
Applecross Highld........248 A3
Appledore Devon........27 H5
Appledore Devon........29 K7
Appledore Kent........25 H2
Appledore Heath Kent........25 H1
Appleford Oxon........66 D8
Applegarth Town D & G........176 F2
Applehaigh Wakefd........142 A5
Appleshaw Hants........34 C1
Applethwaite Cumb........165 J5
Appleton Halton........129 M2
Appleton Oxon........66 C6
Appleton Warrtn........130 B3
Appleton-le-Moors N York........162 C5
Appleton-le-Street N York........162 C7
Appleton Roebuck N York........151 J7
Appleton Thorn Warrtn........130 C3
Appleton Wiske N York........160 F2
Appletreehall Border........188 F3
Appletreewick N York........149 J4
Appley Somset........29 K6
Appley Bridge Lancs........139 G6
Apse Heath IoW........19 J7
Apsley End C Beds........86 C8
Apuldram W Susx........20 D6
Arabella Highld........264 C5
Arbirlot Angus........234 F7
Arboll Highld........264 D3
Arborfield Wokham........49 H5
Arborfield Cross Wokham........49 J5
Arbourthorne Sheff........133 G3
Arbroath Angus........235 G7
Arbuthnott Abers........245 H8
Arcadia Kent........39 L6
Archddu Carmth........56 E4
Archdeacon Newton Darltn........169 H7
Archencarroch W Duns........208 C3
Archiestown Moray........254 E3
Archirondel Jersey........9 f2
Arclid Green Ches E........130 F7
Ardallie Abers........257 J4
Ardanaiseig Hotel Ag & B........217 H2
Ardaneaskan Highld........248 D4
Ardarroch Highld........248 D4
Ardbeg Ag & B........204 F7
Ardbeg Ag & B........207 H5
Ardbeg Ag & B........207 K2
Ardcharnich Highld........261 K2
Ardchiavaig Ag & B........214 D1
Ardchonnel Ag & B........216 F5
Ardchullarie More Stirlg........219 K4
Arddarroch Ag & B........218 C8
Arddleen Powys........112 C8
Ardechive Highld........239 J5
Ardeer N Ayrs........196 B3
Ardeley Herts........69 J2
Ardelve Highld........248 D6
Arden Ag & B........208 B2
Ardens Grafton Warwks........82 D4
Ardentallen Ag & B........216 C2
Ardentinny Ag & B........207 K2
Ardentraive Ag & B........207 G4
Ardeonaig Stirlg........231 J8
Ardersier Highld........252 E1
Ardessie Highld........261 H2
Ardfern Ag & B........216 C6
Ardfernal Ag & B........205 J2
Ardgay Highld........263 G2
Ardgour Highld........229 G3
Ardgowan Inver........207 L4
Ardhallow Ag & B........207 K4
Ardhasig W Isls........282 e5
Ardheslaig Highld........260 C8
Ardindrean Highld........261 K2
Ardingly W Susx........38 A7
Ardington Oxon........48 B1
Ardington Wick Oxon........48 B1
Ardlamont Ag & B........206 F4
Ardleigh Essex........72 F1
Ardleigh Heath Essex........72 F1
Ardler P & K........233 L7
Ardley Oxon........66 D2
Ardley End Essex........70 D4
Ardlui Ag & B........218 D4
Ardlussa Ag & B........215 J6
Ardmair Highld........270 F8
Ardmaleish Ag & B........207 H5
Ardminish Ag & B........205 L6
Ardmolich Highld........237 K6
Ardmore Ag & B........208 A3
Ardmore Highld........263 J3
Ardnadam Ag & B........207 K3
Ardnagrask Highld........250 F2

Ardnarff Highld	248	E4
Ardnastang Highld	228	B3
Ardpatrick Ag & B	206	B7
Ardrishaig Ag & B	206	D2
Ardross Highld	263	H5
Ardrossan N Ayrs	195	L3
Ardsley Barns	142	B6
Ardsley East Leeds	141	M3
Ardslignish Highld	237	H8
Ardtalla Ag & B	205	G5
Ardtoe Highld	237	J6
Arduaine Ag & B	216	B5
Ardullie Highld	263	G7
Ardvasar Highld	247	K7
Ardvorlich P & K	219	K3
Ardvourlie W Isls	282	e5
Ardwell D & G	172	D5
Ardwick Manch	140	C8
Areley Kings Worcs	81	H1
Arevegaig Highld	237	J7
Arford Hants	36	B3
Argoed Caerph	61	J7
Argoed Shrops	112	E7
Argoed Mill Powys	78	D3
Argos Hill E Susx	23	J2
Aribruach W Isls	282	f4
Aridhglas Ag & B	226	C7
Arileod Ag & B	224	F4
Arinagour Ag & B	225	G4
Ariogan Ag & B	216	D2
Arisaig Highld	237	J3
Arisaig House Highld	237	K4
Arkendale N York	150	E4
Arkesden Essex	87	K8
Arkholme Lancs	147	L2
Arkleby Cumb	164	F3
Arkleton D & G	188	C7
Arkle Town N York	159	H2
Arkley Gt Lon	69	G7
Arksey Donc	142	F6
Arkwright Town Derbys	133	H5
Arle Gloucs	64	D2
Arlecdon Cumb	164	D7
Arlescote Warwks	83	J5
Arlesey C Beds	86	D7
Arleston Wrekin	96	F1
Arley Ches E	130	C3
Arley Warwks	99	H5
Arlingham Gloucs	63	L5
Arlington Devon	27	L3
Arlington E Susx	23	J5
Arlington Gloucs	65	G5
Arlington Beccott Devon	27	L3
Armadale Highld	247	K7
Armadale Highld	278	D3
Armadale W Loth	210	B5
Armaside Cumb	164	F5
Armathwaite Cumb	166	C2
Arminghall Norfk	106	E3
Armitage Staffs	115	H8
Armitage Bridge Kirk	141	H5
Armley Leeds	141	L1
Armscote Warwks	82	F6
Armshead Staffs	114	E2
Armston Nhants	102	B6
Armthorpe Donc	143	G6
Arnabost Ag & B	225	G4
Arnaby Cumb	156	A5
Arncliffe N York	149	G2
Arncliffe Cote N York	149	G2
Arncroach Fife	223	J6
Arndilly House Moray	266	F6
Arne Dorset	17	J5
Arnesby Leics	100	D5
Arngask P & K	221	L5
Arnisdale Highld	238	D2
Arnish Highld	259	K7
Arniston Mdloth	211	K6
Arnol W Isls	282	f2
Arnold E R Yk	153	H7
Arnold Notts	117	G2
Arnprior Stirlg	219	K8
Arnside Cumb	157	G7
Aros Ag & B	227	G3
Arowry Wrexhm	113	G4
Arrad Foot Cumb	156	D6
Arram E R Yk	153	G7
Arran N Ayrs	194	E4
Arrathorne N York	160	B4
Arreton IoW	19	J6
Arrina Highld	260	B8
Arrington Cambs	87	G5
Arrochar Ag & B	218	D6
Arrow Warwks	82	C4
Arrowfield Top Worcs	98	C8
Arscott Shrops	95	K2
Artafallie Highld	251	H2
Arthington Leeds	150	C6
Arthingworth Nhants	101	G7
Arthog Gwynd	110	C8
Arthrath Abers	257	H4
Arthursdale Leeds	150	E8
Artrochie Abers	257	J5
Arundel W Susx	21	G5
Asby Cumb	164	E6
Ascog Ag & B	207	J3
Ascot W & M	50	A5
Ascott Warwks	83	H8
Ascott Earl Oxon	65	L3
Ascott-under-Wychwood Oxon	65	L3
Asenby N York	160	F7
Asfordby Leics	117	J7
Asfordby Hill Leics	117	J7
Asgarby Lincs	118	F3
Asgarby Lincs	136	F6
Ash Devon	8	C1
Ash Devon	12	C1
Ash Dorset	32	E8
Ash Kent	41	J4
Ash Kent	52	D6
Ash Somset	30	D6
Ash Somset	31	G6
Ash Surrey	36	D1
Ashampstead W Berk	48	E4
Ashampstead Green W Berk	48	E3
Ashbocking Suffk	90	E4
Ashbourne Derbys	115	K2
Ashbrittle Somset	29	J6
Ashburnham Place E Susx	24	C4
Ashburton Devon	13	H8
Ashbury Devon	12	C3
Ashbury Oxon	47	K2
Ashby N Linc	143	M6
Ashby by Partney Lincs	137	H6
Ashby cum Fenby NE Lin	145	H7
Ashby de la Launde Lincs	135	L8
Ashby-de-la-Zouch Leics	116	B8
Ashby Folville Leics	100	F1
Ashby Magna Leics	100	C5
Ashby Parva Leics	100	C5
Ashby Puerorum Lincs	136	F5
Ashby St Ledgers Nhants	84	B2
Ashby St Mary Norfk	107	G3
Ashchurch Gloucs	81	L8
Ashcombe Devon	13	L6
Ashcombe N Som	44	C6
Ashcott Somset	31	G3
Ashdon Essex	88	B6
Ashe Hants	35	H1
Asheldham Essex	72	E6
Ashen Essex	88	B6
Ashendon Bucks	67	H4
Asheridge Bucks	68	B6
Ashfield Hants	34	E7
Ashfield Herefs	63	H2
Ashfield Stirlg	220	D6
Ashfield cum Thorpe Suffk	90	F3
Ashfield Green Suffk	88	F4
Ashfield Green Suffk	106	F8
Ashfold Crossways W Susx	37	K5
Ashford Devon	7	K5
Ashford Devon	27	J4
Ashford Kent	40	D6
Ashford Surrey	50	D4
Ashford Bowdler Shrops	80	C1
Ashford Carbonell Shrops	80	C1
Ashford Hill Hants	48	E6
Ashford in the Water Derbys	132	D5
Ashgill S Lans	198	C3
Ash Green Surrey	36	D1
Ash Green Warwks	99	J6
Ashill Devon	29	K8
Ashill Norfk	105	H3
Ashill Somset	30	D7
Ashingdon Essex	72	C8
Ashington Nthumb	181	G1
Ashington Poole	17	K3
Ashington Somset	31	J6
Ashington W Susx	21	K4
Ashkirk Border	188	E2
Ashlett Hants	19	J3
Ashleworth Gloucs	64	A2
Ashleworth Quay Gloucs	64	B2
Ashley Cambs	88	D3
Ashley Ches E	130	F3
Ashley Devon	28	B8
Ashley Dorset	18	A3
Ashley Gloucs	64	D8
Ashley Hants	18	C4
Ashley Hants	34	E4
Ashley Kent	41	J5
Ashley Nhants	101	H5
Ashley Staffs	114	B4
Ashley Wilts	46	B5
Ashley Green Bucks	68	B6
Ashleyhay Derbys	115	M1
Ashley Heath Dorset	17	M2
Ashley Moor Herefs	80	B2
Ash Magna Shrops	113	J4
Ashmansworth Hants	48	B7
Ashmansworthy Devon	26	F7
Ashmead Green Gloucs	63	M7
Ashmill Devon	11	M3
Ash Mill Devon	28	D6
Ashmore Dorset	32	E7
Ashmore Green W Berk	48	D5
Ashorne Warwks	83	G4
Ashover Derbys	133	G7
Ashover Hay Derbys	133	G7
Ashow Warwks	83	H1
Ash Parva Shrops	113	J4
Ashperton Herefs	80	D7
Ashprington Devon	8	B3
Ash Priors Somset	29	L5
Ashreigney Devon	27	L8
Ash Street Suffk	89	K6
Ashtead Surrey	50	F7
Ash Thomas Devon	29	H8
Ashton C Pete	102	B2
Ashton Ches W	129	L6
Ashton Cnwll	2	F5
Ashton Devon	13	K5
Ashton Hants	35	H7
Ashton Herefs	80	C2
Ashton Inver	207	L4
Ashton Nhants	84	E5
Ashton Nhants	102	B5
Ashton Somset	30	F1
Ashton Common Wilts	46	C7
Ashton Hill Wilts	46	C7
Ashton-in-Makerfield Wigan	139	H7
Ashton Keynes Wilts	64	F8
Ashton under Hill Worcs	82	A7
Ashton-under-Lyne Tamesd	140	E7
Ashton upon Mersey Traffd	130	F1
Ashurst Hants	18	E2
Ashurst Kent	38	D5
Ashurst Lancs	138	F6
Ashurst W Susx	21	L4
Ashurstwood W Susx	38	B6
Ash Vale Surrey	49	L8
Ashwater Devon	11	M4
Ashwell Herts	86	F7
Ashwell Rutlnd	101	J1
Ashwell Somset	30	E7
Ashwell End Herts	86	E7
Ashwellthorpe Norfk	106	C4
Ashwick Somset	31	K1
Ashwicken Norfk	120	F7
Ashwood Staffs	97	K5
Askam in Furness Cumb	156	B7
Askern Donc	142	F5
Askerswell Dorset	15	M4
Askham Cumb	166	C6
Askham Notts	134	E5
Askham Bryan C York	151	H6
Askham Richard C York	151	H6
Asknish Ag & B	206	E1
Askrigg N York	159	G4
Askwith N York	149	L6
Aslackby Lincs	118	E5
Aslacton Norfk	106	D5
Aslockton Notts	117	K3
Asney Somset	31	G3
Aspall Suffk	90	E2
Aspatria Cumb	164	F2
Aspenden Herts	69	K2
Aspenshaw Derbys	131	K2
Asperton Lincs	119	J4
Aspley Staffs	114	C5
Aspley Guise C Beds	85	J8
Aspley Heath C Beds	85	H8
Aspley Heath Warwks	82	C1
Aspull Wigan	139	J6
Aspull Common Wigan	139	J8
Asselby E R Yk	143	H2
Asserby Lincs	137	J4
Asserby Turn Lincs	137	J4
Assington Suffk	89	J7
Assington Green Suffk	88	F5
Astbury Ches E	131	G2
Astcote Nhants	84	D4
Asterby Lincs	136	E4
Asterley Shrops	95	J2
Asterton Shrops	95	K5
Asthall Oxon	65	L5
Asthall Leigh Oxon	65	L4
Astle Highld	263	K2
Astley Shrops	113	H7
Astley Warwks	99	J5
Astley Wigan	139	L7
Astley Worcs	81	H2
Astley Abbots Shrops	96	F4
Astley Bridge Bolton	139	L5
Astley Cross Worcs	81	J1
Astley Green Wigan	139	L7
Aston Birm	98	D5
Aston Ches E	113	K2
Aston Ches W	130	A4
Aston Derbys	132	D3
Aston Flints	129	G6
Aston Herefs	80	B3
Aston Herts	69	H3
Aston Oxon	65	M6
Aston Rothm	133	J3
Aston Shrops	97	H5
Aston Shrops	113	H6
Aston Staffs	114	B3
Aston Staffs	114	D6
Aston Wokham	49	J2
Aston Wrekin	96	E1
Aston Abbotts Bucks	67	K3
Aston Botterell Shrops	96	E6
Aston-by-Stone Staffs	114	E5
Aston Cantlow Warwks	82	D3
Aston Clinton Bucks	67	L4
Aston Crews Herefs	63	K3
Aston Cross Gloucs	81	L8
Aston End Herts	69	H3
Aston-Eyre Shrops	96	E4
Aston Fields Worcs	81	M2
Aston Flamville Leics	100	A5
Aston Heath Ches W	130	A4
Aston Ingham Herefs	63	K3
Aston juxta Mondrum Ches E	130	C8
Aston le Walls Nhants	83	L5
Aston Magna Gloucs	82	E8
Aston Munslow Shrops	96	C6
Aston on Clun Shrops	95	J7
Aston Pigott Shrops	95	H2
Aston Rogers Shrops	95	H2
Aston Rowant Oxon	67	H7
Aston Sandford Bucks	67	J5
Aston Somerville Worcs	82	B7
Aston-sub-Edge Gloucs	82	D7
Aston Tirrold Oxon	48	E2
Aston-upon-Trent Derbys	116	C5
Aston Upthorpe Oxon	48	E2
Astrop Nhants	83	L7
Astrope Herts	67	L4
Astwick C Beds	86	E7
Astwith Derbys	133	J6
Astwood M Keyn	85	J5
Astwood Worcs	81	L2
Astwood Bank Worcs	82	B3
Astwood Crematorium Worcs	81	K4
Aswarby Lincs	118	E4
Aswardby Lincs	137	G5
Atcham Shrops	96	C2
Atch Lench Worcs	82	B4
Athelhampton Dorset	16	E4
Athelington Suffk	90	F1
Athelney Somset	30	E5
Athelstaneford E Loth	212	C4
Atherfield Green IoW	19	G7
Atherington Devon	27	L6
Atherington W Susx	21	G6
Atherstone Somset	30	F7
Atherstone Warwks	99	J3
Atherstone on Stour Warwks	82	F5
Atherton Wigan	139	K7
Atley Hill N York	160	D2
Atlow Derbys	115	L2
Attadale Highld	248	E4
Attenborough Notts	116	E4
Atterby Lincs	135	K1
Attercliffe Sheff	133	G2
Atterley Shrops	96	E4
Atterton Leics	99	K4
Attleborough Norfk	105	L4
Attleborough Warwks	99	K5
Attlebridge Norfk	122	C8
Attleton Green Suffk	88	E4
Atwick E R Yk	153	K5
Atworth Wilts	46	B6
Auberrow Herefs	80	C6
Aubourn Lincs	135	J7
Auchbreck Moray	254	D6
Auchedly Abers	257	G5
Auchenblae Abers	244	F7
Auchenbowie Stirlg	209	L2
Auchencairn D & G	175	K4
Auchencairn D & G	176	C3
Auchencairn N Ayrs	195	G5
Auchencrow Border	213	J7
Auchendinny Mdloth	211	H6
Auchengray S Lans	199	G2
Auchenhalrig Moray	267	H4
Auchenheath S Lans	198	D3
Auchenhessnane D & G	185	K4
Auchenlochan Ag & B	206	F4
Auchenmade N Ayrs	196	C2
Auchenmalg D & G	173	G4
Auchentiber N Ayrs	196	D2
Auchindrain Ag & B	217	G6
Auchindrean Highld	261	K6
Auchininna Abers	268	B6
Auchinleck E Ayrs	197	G6

Name	County	Page	Grid
Auchinloch	N Lans	209	H5
Auchinstarry	N Lans	209	J4
Auchintore	Highld	229	H1
Auchiries	Abers	257	K4
Auchlean	Highld	241	M4
Auchlee	Abers	245	K4
Auchleven	Abers	256	A6
Auchlochan	S Lans	198	D5
Auchlossan	Abers	244	D3
Auchlyne	Stirlg	219	H1
Auchmillan	E Ayrs	197	G5
Auchmithie	Angus	235	G6
Auchmuirbridge	Fife	222	C7
Auchnacree	Angus	234	C3
Auchnagatt	Abers	257	G3
Auchnarrow	Moray	254	D7
Auchnotteroch	D & G	172	B3
Auchroisk	Moray	267	G6
Auchterarder	P & K	221	G4
Auchteraw	Highld	240	B2
Auchterblair	Highld	253	H7
Auchtercairn	Highld	260	C4
Auchterderran	Fife	222	C8
Auchterhouse	Angus	233	M7
Auchterless	Abers	256	C4
Auchtermuchty	Fife	222	D5
Auchterneed	Highld	262	E7
Auchtertool	Fife	211	H1
Auchtertyre	Highld	248	D6
Auchtubh	Stirlg	219	J3
Auckengill	Highld	280	E3
Auckley	Donc	143	G7
Audenshaw	Tamesd	140	D8
Audlem	Ches E	113	L3
Audley	Staffs	114	C2
Audley End	Essex	87	L7
Audley End	Essex	89	G7
Audley End	Suffk	89	G4
Audmore	Staffs	114	C7
Audnam	Dudley	97	K6
Aughertree	Cumb	165	H3
Aughton	E R Yk	151	L8
Aughton	Lancs	138	E6
Aughton	Lancs	147	L1
Aughton	Rothm	133	J2
Aughton	Wilts	47	K7
Aughton Park	Lancs	138	E6
Auldearn	Highld	253	H1
Aulden	Herefs	80	B4
Auldgirth	D & G	176	B2
Auldhouse	S Lans	197	J1
Ault a' chruinn	Highld	248	F7
Aultbea	Highld	260	D2
Aultgrishin	Highld	260	B3
Aultguish Inn	Highld	262	B6
Ault Hucknall	Derbys	133	J6
Aultmore	Moray	267	H5
Aultnagoire	Highld	250	F7
Aultnamain Inn	Highld	263	J4
Aunby	Lincs	118	D8
Aunk	Devon	14	B3
Aunsby	Lincs	118	D4
Aust	S Glos	45	H1
Austendike	Lincs	119	J7
Austerfield	Donc	134	D1
Austerlands	Oldham	140	E6
Austhorpe	Leeds	142	B3
Austonley	Kirk	141	H6
Austrey	Warwks	99	J2
Austwick	N York	148	D2
Authorpe	Lincs	137	G3
Authorpe Row	Lincs	137	K5
Avebury	Wilts	47	G5
Avebury Trusloe	Wilts	47	G5
Aveley	Thurr	52	C3
Avening	Gloucs	64	C7
Averham	Notts	117	K1
Aveton Gifford	Devon	7	K5
Aviemore	Highld	242	B1
Avington	W Berk	48	A5
Avoch	Highld	251	J1
Avon	Hants	18	A4
Avonbridge	Falk	210	B4
Avon Dassett	Warwks	83	K5
Avonmouth	Bristl	45	G3
Avonwick	Devon	7	K3
Awbridge	Hants	34	D6
Awkley	S Glos	45	H2
Awliscombe	Devon	14	D2
Awre	Gloucs	63	L5
Awsworth	Notts	116	E3
Axborough	Worcs	97	J7
Axbridge	Somset	44	E8
Axford	Hants	35	J4
Axford	Wilts	47	K5
Axminster	Devon	15	G3
Axmouth	Devon	14	F4
Axton	Flints	128	D4
Aycliffe	Dur	169	H6
Aydon	Nthumb	180	B5
Aylburton	Gloucs	63	J6
Ayle	Nthumb	167	G1
Aylesbeare	Devon	14	B4
Aylesbury	Bucks	67	K4
Aylesby	NE Lin	145	G6
Aylesford	Kent	52	F7
Aylesham	Kent	41	H5
Aylestone	C Leic	100	C3
Aylestone Park	C Leic	100	D3
Aylmerton	Norfk	122	D4
Aylsham	Norfk	122	D6
Aylton	Herefs	80	F7
Aylworth	Gloucs	65	J3
Aymestrey	Herefs	80	A2
Aynho	Nhants	83	L8
Ayot Green	Herts	69	G4
Ayot St Lawrence	Herts	69	G4
Ayot St Peter	Herts	69	G4
Ayr	S Ayrs	196	C6
Aysgarth	N York	159	H5
Ayshford	Devon	29	J7
Ayside	Cumb	156	F6
Ayston	Rutlnd	101	J3
Aythorpe Roding	Essex	70	E4
Ayton	Border	213	K6
Azerley	N York	160	C7

B

Name	County	Page	Grid
Babbacombe	Torbay	8	D2
Babbington	Notts	116	E3
Babbinswood	Shrops	112	E5
Babbs Green	Herts	69	K4
Babcary	Somset	31	J5
Babel	Carmth	59	M2
Babel Green	Suffk	88	E5
Babell	Flints	128	E5
Babeny	Devon	12	F7
Bablock Hythe	Oxon	66	B6
Babraham	Cambs	87	K5
Babworth	Notts	134	D3
Bachau	IoA	125	H3
Bache	Shrops	95	L1
Bacheldre	Powys	94	F5
Bachelor's Bump	E Susx	24	F5
Backaland	Ork	275	d3
Backbarrow	Cumb	156	E5
Backe	Carmth	58	A5
Backfolds	Abers	269	J5
Backford	Ches W	129	J5
Backford Cross	Ches W	129	J5
Backies	Highld	273	K7
Back of Keppoch	Highld	237	J3
Back o' th' Brook	Staffs	115	H1
Back Street	Suffk	88	E3
Backwell	N Som	44	F5
Backworth	N Tyne	181	H4
Bacon's End	Solhll	98	F6
Baconsthorpe	Norfk	122	C4
Bacton	Herefs	62	D1
Bacton	Norfk	123	G5
Bacton	Suffk	90	C2
Bacton Green	Suffk	90	B2
Bacup	Lancs	140	C3
Badachro	Highld	260	C5
Badbury	Swindn	47	J3
Badby	Nhants	84	A3
Badcall	Highld	276	B7
Badcall	Highld	276	C5
Badcaul	Highld	261	G2
Baddeley Edge	C Stke	114	E1
Baddeley Green	C Stke	114	E1
Baddesley Clinton	Warwks	82	F1
Baddesley Ensor	Warwks	99	H4
Baddidarrach	Highld	270	E3
Baddinsgill	Border	199	K2
Badenscoth	Abers	256	C4
Badentarbet	Highld	270	D6
Badenyon	Abers	255	G7
Badgall	Cnwll	11	J5
Badgeney	Cambs	103	J4
Badger	Shrops	97	H3
Badger's Cross	Cnwll	2	D4
Badgers Mount	Kent	52	B6
Badgeworth	Gloucs	64	C3
Badgworth	Somset	44	E8
Badharlick	Cnwll	11	J5
Badicaul	Highld	248	B6
Badingham	Suffk	91	G2
Badlesmere	Kent	40	D4
Badlieu	Border	187	G2
Badlipster	Highld	280	B6
Badluarach	Highld	261	G1
Badninish	Highld	263	K1
Badrallach	Highld	261	H2
Badsey	Worcs	82	C6
Badshot Lea	Surrey	36	C1
Badsworth	Wakefd	142	D5
Badwell Ash	Suffk	89	K2
Badwell Green	Suffk	89	K2
Bagber	Dorset	32	C8
Bagby	N York	161	G6
Bag Enderby	Lincs	136	F5
Bagendon	Gloucs	64	E5
Bagginswood	Shrops	96	F7
Baggrow	Cumb	165	G2
Bagh a Chaisteil	W Isls	283	b13
Bagham	Kent	40	E4
Bagh a Tuath	W Isls	283	b13
Bagillt	Flints	128	F4
Baginton	Warwks	99	K8
Baglan	Neath	57	K6
Bagley	Leeds	141	K1
Bagley	Shrops	112	F6
Bagley	Somset	31	G2
Bagmore	Hants	35	K2
Bagnall	Staffs	114	E1
Bagnor	W Berk	48	C5
Bagshot	Surrey	49	M6
Bagshot	Wilts	47	L6
Bagstone	S Glos	45	K2
Bagthorpe	Notts	116	D1
Bagworth	Leics	99	M2
Bagwy Llydiart	Herefs	62	F2
Baildon	C Brad	149	L7
Baildon Green	C Brad	149	L7
Baile Ailein	W Isls	282	f4
Baile a Mhanaich	W Isls	283	c9
Baile Mor	Ag & B	226	B7
Bailey Green	Hants	35	K5
Baileyhead	Cumb	178	C3
Bailiff Bridge	Calder	141	J3
Baillieston	C Glas	209	H6
Bailrigg	Lancs	147	J4
Bainbridge	N York	159	G4
Bainshole	Abers	256	A5
Bainton	C Pete	102	B2
Bainton	E R Yk	152	E5
Bainton	Oxon	66	E2
Baintown	Fife	222	F6
Bairnkine	Border	189	H3
Baker's End	Herts	69	L4
Baker Street	Thurr	52	D3
Bakewell	Derbys	132	D6
Bala	Gwynd	111	H4
Balallan	W Isls	282	f4
Balbeg	Highld	250	D5
Balbeggie	P & K	222	B1
Balblair	Highld	250	E3
Balblair	Highld	263	J6
Balby	Donc	142	E7
Balcary	D & G	175	K5
Balchraggan	Highld	250	F3
Balchreick	Highld	276	B4
Balcombe	W Susx	37	M5
Balcombe Lane	W Susx	37	M4
Balcomie Links	Fife	223	L5
Baldersby	N York	160	E7
Baldersby St James	N York	160	E7
Balderstone	Lancs	139	J1
Balderstone	Rochdl	140	D5
Balderton	Notts	117	L1
Baldhu	Cnwll	4	C6
Baldinnie	Fife	223	G5
Baldinnies	P & K	221	J4
Baldock	Herts	86	E8
Baldovie	C Dund	234	C8
Baldrine	IoM	154	f5
Baldslow	E Susx	24	E4
Baldwin	IoM	154	e6
Baldwinholme	Cumb	177	K8
Baldwin's Gate	Staffs	114	B3
Baldwin's Hill	W Susx	38	B5
Bale	Norfk	121	M4
Baledgarno	P & K	222	D1
Balemartine	Ag & B	224	C7
Balerno	C Edin	211	G5
Balfarg	Fife	222	D6
Balfield	Angus	234	E2
Balfour	Ork	275	d4
Balfron	Stirlg	208	F1
Balgaveny	Abers	256	B4
Balgonar	Fife	221	J8
Balgowan	D & G	172	E5
Balgowan	Highld	241	H4
Balgown	Highld	258	F3
Balgracie	D & G	172	B3
Balgray	S Lans	186	C2
Balham	Gt Lon	51	H4
Balhary	P & K	233	L6
Balholmie	P & K	233	H8
Baligill	Highld	278	E3
Balintore	Angus	233	L4
Balintore	Highld	264	D5
Balintraid	Highld	263	K5
Balivanich	W Isls	283	c9
Balk	N York	161	G6
Balkeerie	Angus	233	M6
Balkholme	E R Yk	143	K2
Ballabeg	IoM	154	c7
Ballachulish	Highld	229	H4
Ballafesson	IoM	154	b7
Ballajora	IoM	154	g4
Ballakilpheric	IoM	154	b7
Ballamodha	IoM	154	c7
Ballanlay	Ag & B	207	G6
Ballantrae	S Ayrs	182	D6
Ballards Gore	Essex	72	C8
Ballards Green	Warwks	99	H5
Ballasalla	IoM	154	c7
Ballater	Abers	243	L4
Ballaugh	IoM	154	d3
Ballchraggan	Highld	263	K5
Ballencrieff	E Loth	212	B3
Ballevullin	Ag & B	224	B6
Ball Green	C Stke	114	D1
Ball Haye Green	Staffs	131	K8
Ball Hill	Hants	48	B6
Ballidon	Derbys	115	K1
Balliekine	N Ayrs	194	D3
Balliemore	Ag & B	217	H7
Balligmorrie	S Ayrs	183	G5
Ballimore	Stirlg	219	H4
Ballindalloch	Moray	254	D4
Ballindean	P & K	222	D2
Ballingdon	Suffk	89	H7
Ballinger Common	Bucks	67	M6
Ballingham	Herefs	63	H1
Ballingry	Fife	222	B7
Ballinluig	P & K	232	E5
Ballinshoe	Angus	234	B5
Ballintuim	P & K	233	G4
Balloch	Highld	252	D2
Balloch	N Lans	209	K4
Balloch	P & K	220	E3
Balloch	S Ayrs	183	J4
Balloch	W Duns	208	C3
Balls Cross	W Susx	36	E5
Balls Green	E Susx	38	D6
Ball's Green	Gloucs	64	B7
Ballygown	Ag & B	226	E4
Ballygrant	Ag & B	204	F3
Ballyhaugh	Ag & B	224	F4
Balmacara	Highld	248	C6
Balmaclellan	D & G	185	G7
Balmae	D & G	175	H6
Balmaha	Stirlg	208	C1
Balmalcolm	Fife	222	E5
Balmangan	D & G	175	G5
Balmedie	Abers	257	H8
Balmer Heath	Shrops	113	G4
Balmerino	Fife	222	F2
Balmerlawn	Hants	18	D3
Balmichael	N Ayrs	194	E5
Balmore	E Duns	209	G4
Balmuchy	Highld	264	D4
Balmule	Fife	211	H2
Balmullo	Fife	223	G3
Balnacoil Lodge	Highld	273	J5
Balnacra	Highld	248	F3
Balnacroft	Abers	243	J5
Balnafoich	Highld	251	J4
Balnaguard	P & K	232	D5
Balnahard	Ag & B	214	E4
Balnahard	Ag & B	226	E5
Balnain	Highld	250	D5
Balnakeil	Highld	276	F3
Balne	N York	142	F4
Balquharn	P & K	232	F8
Balquhidder	Stirlg	219	H3
Balsall Common	Solhll	99	G8
Balsall Heath	Birm	98	D6
Balsall Street	Solhll	99	G8
Balscote	Oxon	83	J6
Balsham	Cambs	88	B5
Baltasound	Shet	281	f1
Balterley	Staffs	114	B2
Balterley Green	Staffs	114	B2
Balterley Heath	Staffs	114	B2
Baltersan	D & G	174	C3
Baltonsborough	Somset	31	J4
Balvicar	Ag & B	216	B4
Balvraid	Highld	248	D8
Balvraid	Highld	252	F5
Balwest	Cnwll	2	F5
Bamber Bridge	Lancs	139	H3
Bamber's Green	Essex	70	E3
Bamburgh	Nthumb	203	K6
Bamford	Derbys	132	D3
Bamford	Rochdl	140	C5
Bampton	Cumb	166	C7
Bampton	Devon	29	G6
Bampton	Oxon	65	L6
Bampton Grange	Cumb	166	C7
Banavie	Highld	239	J8
Banbury	Oxon	83	K7
Banbury Crematorium	Oxon	83	K6
Bancffosfelen	Carmth	58	E6
Banchory	Abers	244	F4

Place	Page	Grid
Banchory-Devenick Abers	245	K3
Bancycapel Carmth	58	D6
Bancyfelin Carmth	58	B5
Banc-y-ffordd Carmth	76	D7
Bandirran P & K	222	C1
Bandrake Head Cumb	156	D5
Banff Abers	268	C3
Bangor Gwynd	125	K5
Bangor Crematorium Gwynd	125	L5
Bangor-on-Dee Wrexhm	112	F2
Bangors Cnwll	11	H3
Bangor's Green Lancs	138	D6
Bangrove Suffk	89	J1
Banham Norfk	106	B6
Bank Hants	18	D2
Bankend D & G	176	D5
Bankfoot P & K	233	C4
Bankglen E Ayrs	197	H8
Bank Ground Cumb	156	D3
Bankhead C Aber	245	K2
Bankhead S Lans	199	G4
Bank Newton N York	148	F5
Banknock Falk	209	K3
Banks Cumb	178	D6
Banks Lancs	138	E4
Banks Green Worcs	82	A2
Bankshill D & G	177	G3
Bank Street Worcs	80	E3
Bank Top Calder	141	H3
Bank Top Lancs	139	G6
Banningham Norfk	122	E5
Bannister Green Essex	71	G2
Bannockburn Stirlg	209	L1
Banstead Surrey	51	H7
Bantham Devon	7	K6
Banton N Lans	209	K3
Banwell N Som	44	E7
Bapchild Kent	40	B3
Bapton Wilts	33	G3
Barabhas W Isls	282	g2
Barassie S Ayrs	196	C4
Barbaraville Highld	263	K5
Barber Booth Derbys	132	B3
Barber Green Cumb	156	F6
Barbieston S Ayrs	196	E6
Barbon Cumb	157	K6
Barbridge Ches E	130	B8
Barbrook Devon	28	C2
Barby Nhants	84	A1
Barcaldine Ag & B	228	F7
Barcheston Warwks	83	G7
Barclose Cumb	178	B6
Barcombe E Susx	22	F4
Barcombe Cross E Susx	23	G4
Barcroft C Brad	149	J8
Barden N York	159	L4
Barden Park Kent	38	F4
Bardfield End Green Essex	70	F1
Bardfield Saling Essex	71	G2
Bardney Lincs	136	B6
Bardon Leics	99	M1
Bardon Mill Nthumb	179	H6
Bardowie E Duns	209	G4
Bardown E Susx	39	G7
Bardrainney Inver	208	B4
Bardsea Cumb	156	D7
Bardsey Leeds	150	E7
Bardsey Island Gwynd	108	A7
Bardsley Oldham	140	D7
Bardwell Suffk	105	J8
Bare Lancs	147	J3
Bareppa Cnwll	3	K5
Barfad D & G	173	J2
Barford Norfk	106	C2
Barford Warwks	83	G3
Barford St John Oxon	83	K8
Barford St Martin Wilts	33	J4
Barford St Michael Oxon	83	K8
Barfrestone Kent	41	H5
Bargate Derbys	116	B2
Bargeddie N Lans	209	J6
Bargoed Caerph	61	J7
Bargrennan D & G	183	J7
Barham Cambs	102	C8
Barham Kent	41	G5
Barham Suffk	90	D5
Barham Crematorium Kent	41	H5
Bar Hill Cambs	87	H3
Barholm Lincs	102	B1
Barkby Leics	100	E2
Barkby Thorpe Leics	100	E2
Barkers Green Shrops	113	H6
Barkestone-le-Vale Leics	117	K4
Barkham Wokham	49	J5
Barking Gt Lon	51	L2
Barking Suffk	90	C4
Barkingside Gt Lon	51	L1
Barking Tye Suffk	90	C5
Barkisland Calder	141	G4
Barkla Shop Cnwll	4	B5
Barkston Lincs	118	B3
Barkston Ash N York	151	G8
Barkway Herts	87	H8
Barlanark C Glas	209	H6
Barlaston Staffs	114	D4
Barlavington W Susx	21	G4
Barlborough Derbys	133	J4
Barlby N York	143	G1
Barlestone Leics	99	L2
Barley Herts	87	H7
Barley Lancs	148	E7
Barleycroft End Herts	70	B2
Barley Hole Rothm	142	B8
Barleythorpe Rutlnd	101	J2
Barling Essex	53	K1
Barlings Lincs	135	M5
Barlochan D & G	175	K3
Barlow Derbys	133	G5
Barlow Gatesd	180	E6
Barlow N York	143	G2
Barmby Moor E R Yk	152	B6
Barmby on the Marsh E R Yk	143	H2
Barmer Norfk	121	H5
Barming Heath Kent	39	J2
Barmollack Ag & B	194	C2
Barmouth Gwynd	109	L8
Barmpton Darltn	169	J7
Barmston E R Yk	153	J4
Barnaby Green Suffk	107	K7
Barnacarry Ag & B	216	F8
Barnack C Pete	102	B2
Barnacle Warwks	99	K6
Barnard Castle Dur	168	D7
Barnard Gate Oxon	66	B5
Barnardiston Suffk	88	E5
Barnbarroch D & G	175	L3
Barnburgh Donc	142	D7
Barnby Suffk	107	K5
Barnby Dun Donc	142	F6
Barnby in the Willows Notts	117	M1
Barnby Moor Notts	134	D3
Barncorkrie D & G	172	D7
Barnehurst Gt Lon	52	B4
Barnes Gt Lon	51	G4
Barnes Street Kent	39	G4
Barnet Gt Lon	69	H7
Barnetby le Wold N Linc	144	D6
Barnet Gate Gt Lon	69	G8
Barney Norfk	121	M5
Barnham Suffk	105	H7
Barnham W Susx	20	F6
Barnham Broom Norfk	106	B2
Barnhead Angus	235	G4
Barnhill C Dund	223	H1
Barnhill Ches W	113	H1
Barnhill Moray	266	C5
Barnhills D & G	182	B8
Barningham Dur	168	D8
Barningham Suffk	105	K8
Barnoldby le Beck NE Lin	145	G7
Barnoldswick Lancs	148	F6
Barnsdale Bar Donc	142	D5
Barns Green W Susx	37	H5
Barnsley Barns	142	A6
Barnsley Gloucs	65	G6
Barnsley Crematorium Barns	142	B6
Barnsole Kent	41	J4
Barnstaple Devon	27	K4
Barnston Essex	70	F3
Barnston Wirral	129	G3
Barnstone Notts	117	J4
Barnt Green Worcs	98	C8
Barnton C Edin	211	G4
Barnton Ches W	130	C5
Barnwell All Saints Nhants	102	A6
Barnwell St Andrew Nhants	102	A6
Barnwood Gloucs	64	B3
Baron's Cross Herefs	80	A4
Baronwood Cumb	166	C2
Barr S Ayrs	183	H4
Barra W Isls	283	b13
Barrachan D & G	173	J5
Barraigh W Isls	283	b13
Barrapoll Ag & B	224	B6
Barras Cumb	167	J8
Barrasford Nthumb	179	L4
Barregarrow IoM	154	d4
Barrets Green Ches E	130	B7
Barrhead E Rens	208	E7
Barrhill S Ayrs	183	G6
Barrington Cambs	87	H5
Barrington Somset	30	F7
Barripper Cnwll	3	G3
Barrmill N Ayrs	196	D1
Barrock Highld	280	C2
Barrow Gloucs	64	C2
Barrow Lancs	148	C8
Barrow Rutlnd	118	A3
Barrow Shrops	96	E3
Barrow Somset	32	B4
Barrow Suffk	88	F3
Barroway Drove Norfk	104	B3
Barrow Bridge Bolton	139	K5
Barrow Burn Nthumb	190	B4
Barrowby Lincs	118	A4
Barrowden Rutlnd	101	L3
Barrowford Lancs	148	E7
Barrow Gurney N Som	45	G5
Barrow Haven N Linc	144	D3
Barrow Hill Derbys	133	H4
Barrow-in-Furness Cumb	146	D2
Barrow Island Cumb	146	D2
Barrow Nook Lancs	138	F7
Barrow's Green Ches E	130	D8
Barrow Street Wilts	32	D5
Barrow-upon-Humber N Linc	144	D4
Barrow upon Soar Leics	116	E8
Barrow upon Trent Derbys	116	B6
Barrow Vale BaNES	45	J7
Barry Angus	234	E8
Barry V Glam	43	H7
Barry Island V Glam	43	H8
Barsby Leics	100	F1
Barsham Suffk	107	H5
Barston Solhll	99	G7
Bartestree Herefs	80	D7
Barthol Chapel Abers	256	E5
Bartholomew Green Essex	71	H3
Barthomley Ches E	114	B1
Bartley Hants	18	D1
Bartley Green Birm	98	C7
Bartlow Cambs	88	B6
Barton Cambs	87	H4
Barton Ches W	113	G1
Barton Gloucs	65	G2
Barton Herefs	79	K4
Barton Lancs	138	D6
Barton Lancs	147	K8
Barton N York	160	C1
Barton Oxon	66	E5
Barton Torbay	8	D2
Barton Warwks	82	D5
Barton Bendish Norfk	104	E2
Barton End Gloucs	64	B7
Barton Green Staffs	115	K7
Barton Hartshorn Bucks	66	F1
Barton Hill N York	151	L3
Barton in Fabis Notts	116	E5
Barton in the Beans Leics	99	L2
Barton-le-Clay C Beds	68	D1
Barton-le-Street N York	162	C7
Barton-le-Willows N York	151	M3
Barton Mills Suffk	104	E8
Barton-on-Sea Hants	18	C5
Barton-on-the-Heath Warwks	83	G8
Barton St David Somset	31	J4
Barton Seagrave Nhants	101	J7
Barton Stacey Hants	34	F3
Barton Town Devon	28	B3
Barton Turf Norfk	123	G7
Barton-under-Needwood Staffs	115	K7
Barton-upon-Humber N Linc	144	C3
Barton upon Irwell Salfd	140	A8
Barton Waterside N Linc	144	C3
Barugh Barns	141	M6
Barugh Green Barns	141	M6
Barvas W Isls	282	g2
Barway Cambs	103	L8
Barwell Leics	99	L4
Barwick Devon	12	E1
Barwick Herts	69	K3
Barwick Somset	31	J8
Barwick in Elmet Leeds	150	F8
Baschurch Shrops	112	F7
Bascote Warwks	83	J3
Bascote Heath Warwks	83	J3
Base Green Suffk	89	L3
Basford Green Staffs	114	F1
Bashall Eaves Lancs	148	B7
Bashall Town Lancs	148	C7
Bashley Hants	18	C4
Basildon Essex	52	F1
Basildon & District Crematorium Essex	53	G2
Basingstoke Hants	48	F8
Basingstoke Crematorium Hants	35	H2
Baslow Derbys	132	E5
Bason Bridge Somset	30	E2
Bassaleg Newpt	44	B2
Bassendean Border	201	K4
Bassenthwaite Cumb	165	H4
Bassett C Sotn	34	F7
Bassingbourn Cambs	87	G6
Bassingfield Notts	117	G4
Bassingham Lincs	135	H7
Bassingthorpe Lincs	118	C6
Bassus Green Herts	69	J2
Basted Kent	38	F2
Baston Lincs	102	C1
Bastwick Norfk	123	J8
Batch Somset	44	C7
Batchworth Herts	68	D8
Batchworth Heath Herts	68	D8
Batcombe Dorset	16	B2
Batcombe Somset	31	M3
Bate Heath Ches E	130	D4
Batford Herts	68	F4
Bath BaNES	45	L6
Bathampton BaNES	45	M5
Bathealton Somset	29	K6
Batheaston BaNES	45	M5
Bathford BaNES	46	A5
Bathgate W Loth	210	C5
Bathley Notts	134	F7
Bathpool Cnwll	11	K7
Bathpool Somset	30	C6
Bath Side Essex	73	K1
Bathville W Loth	210	B5
Bathway Somset	45	H8
Batley Kirk	141	K3
Batsford Gloucs	82	E8
Batson Devon	7	L7
Battersby N York	161	K1
Battersea Gt Lon	51	H4
Battisborough Cross Devon	7	H5
Battisford Suffk	90	C4
Battisford Tye Suffk	89	L4
Battle E Susx	24	D6
Battle Powys	60	F1
Battleborough Somset	30	E1
Battledown Gloucs	64	D3
Battledykes Angus	234	C4
Battlefield Shrops	113	H8
Battlesbridge Essex	71	J8
Battlesden C Beds	68	B2
Battleton Somset	29	K6
Battlies Green Suffk	89	H2
Battramsley Cross Hants	18	E4
Batt's Corner Hants	36	B3
Baughton Worcs	81	K6
Baughurst Hants	48	E7
Baulds Abers	244	D5
Baulking Oxon	47	L1
Baumber Lincs	136	D5
Baunton Gloucs	64	E6
Baveney Wood Shrops	96	F7
Baverstock Wilts	33	J4
Bawburgh Norfk	106	D2
Bawdeswell Norfk	122	A7
Bawdrip Somset	30	E3
Bawdsey Suffk	91	H7
Bawsey Norfk	120	E7
Bawtry Donc	134	C1
Baxenden Lancs	140	A2
Baxterley Warwks	99	H4
Baxter's Green Suffk	88	E4
Bay Highld	258	D6
Bayble W Isls	282	h3
Baybridge Hants	35	H6
Baybridge Nthumb	168	B1
Baycliff Cumb	156	F2
Baydon Wilts	47	K6
Bayford Herts	69	J5
Bayford Somset	32	B5
Bayhead W Isls	283	b8
Bay Horse Lancs	147	K5
Bayley's Hill Kent	38	D3
Baylham Suffk	90	C5
Baynard's Green Oxon	66	E1
Baysdale Abbey N York	161	K2
Baysham Herefs	63	H2
Bayston Hill Shrops	96	B2
Baythorne End Essex	88	E6
Bayton Worcs	96	F8
Bayton Common Worcs	81	G1
Bayworth Oxon	66	D6
Beach S Glos	45	L5
Beachampton Bucks	84	E7
Beachamwell Norfk	104	E2
Beachley Gloucs	45	H1
Beacon Devon	14	E2
Beacon End Essex	72	D2
Beacon Hill E Susx	38	D7
Beacon Hill Kent	39	K6
Beacon Hill Notts	117	L1
Beacon Hill Surrey	36	C3
Beacon's Bottom Bucks	67	J8
Beaconsfield Bucks	50	B1
Beadlam N York	161	L5
Beadlow C Beds	86	C7
Beadnell Nthumb	203	L7
Beaford Devon	27	K7
Beal N York	142	D4
Beal Nthumb	203	H4
Bealbury Cnwll	6	D2
Bealsmill Cnwll	11	L7
Beam Hill Staffs	115	L6
Beamhurst Staffs	115	H4

Place	County	Page	Grid
Beaminster	Dorset	15	L2
Beamish	Dur	180	F8
Beamsley	N York	149	K5
Bean	Kent	52	C4
Beanacre	Wilts	46	C5
Beanley	Nthumb	190	F3
Beardon	Devon	12	C5
Beardwood	Bl w D	139	K2
Beare	Devon	14	A2
Beare Green	Surrey	37	J2
Bearley	Warwks	82	E3
Bearley Cross	Warwks	82	E3
Bearpark	Dur	169	G2
Bearsden	E Duns	208	F4
Bearsted	Kent	39	K2
Bearstone	Shrops	114	A4
Bearwood	Birm	98	C6
Bearwood	Herefs	79	M4
Bearwood	Poole	17	L3
Beattock	D & G	187	G6
Beauchamp Roding	Essex	70	E5
Beauchief	Sheff	132	F3
Beaudesert	Warwks	82	E2
Beaufort	Blae G	61	J5
Beaulieu	Hants	18	E5
Beaulieu Road Station	Hants	18	E2
Beauly	Highld	250	F2
Beaumaris	IoA	126	B4
Beaumont	Cumb	177	K7
Beaumont	Essex	73	H2
Beaumont	Jersey	9	c3
Beaumont Hill	Darltn	169	G2
Beausale	Warwks	82	F1
Beauworth	Hants	35	J5
Beaworthy	Devon	12	B3
Beazley End	Essex	71	H1
Bebington	Wirral	129	H3
Bebside	Nthumb	181	G3
Beccles	Suffk	107	J5
Becconsall	Lancs	138	F3
Beckbury	Shrops	97	H3
Beckenham	Gt Lon	51	K5
Beckenham Crematorium Gt Lon		51	K5
Beckermet	Cumb	155	J1
Beckett End	Norfk	104	F4
Beckfoot	Cumb	155	L3
Beckfoot	Cumb	156	B5
Beck Foot	Cumb	157	K3
Beckfoot	Cumb	164	E1
Beckford	Worcs	82	A8
Beckhampton	Wilts	47	G5
Beck Hole	N York	162	E2
Beckingham	Lincs	118	A1
Beckingham	Notts	134	F2
Beckington	Somset	46	A8
Beckjay	Shrops	95	J7
Beckley	E Susx	24	F3
Beckley	Hants	18	C4
Beckley	Oxon	66	E5
Beck Row	Suffk	104	D7
Becks	C Brad	149	J6
Beck Side	Cumb	156	B6
Beck Side	Cumb	156	E6
Beckton	Gt Lon	51	L3
Beckwithshaw	N York	150	C5
Becontree	Gt Lon	52	A2
Becquet Vincent	Jersey	9	d2
Bedale	N York	160	C5
Bedburn	Dur	168	E4
Bedchester	Dorset	32	E7
Beddau	Rhondd	43	G4
Beddgelert	Gwynd	109	L2
Beddingham	E Susx	23	G5
Beddington	Gt Lon	51	H5
Beddington Corner	Gt Lon	51	H5
Bedfield	Suffk	90	F2
Bedfield Little Green	Suffk	90	F2
Bedford	Bed	85	L5
Bedford Crematorium	Bed	86	B5
Bedgebury Cross	Kent	39	H6
Bedham	W Susx	36	F4
Bedhampton	Hants	20	A5
Bedingfield	Suffk	90	E2
Bedingfield Green	Suffk	90	E2
Bedlam	N York	150	C3
Bedlington	Nthumb	181	G3
Bedlinog	Myr Td	61	H6
Bedminster	Bristl	45	H5
Bedminster Down	Bristl	45	H5
Bedmond	Herts	68	E6
Bednall	Staffs	114	F7
Bedrule	Border	189	G3
Bedstone	Shrops	95	J8
Bedwas	Caerph	43	J4
Bedwellty	Caerph	61	J7
Bedworth	Warwks	99	K6
Bedworth Woodlands	Warwks	99	K6
Beeby	Leics	100	F1
Beech	Hants	35	L3
Beech	Staffs	114	D4
Beech Hill	W Berk	49	G6
Beechingstoke	Wilts	47	G7
Beedon	W Berk	48	C3
Beedon Hill	W Berk	48	C3
Beeford	E R Yk	153	H5
Beeley	Derbys	132	E6
Beelsby	NE Lin	145	G7
Beenham	Berks	48	E5
Beenham's Heath	W & M	49	K4
Beeny	Cnwll	11	G4
Beer	Devon	14	F5
Beer	Somset	30	F4
Beercrocombe	Somset	30	D6
Beer Hackett	Dorset	31	K8
Beesands	Devon	8	B6
Beesby	Lincs	137	J4
Beeson	Devon	8	B6
Beeston	C Beds	86	D5
Beeston	Ches W	129	M7
Beeston	Leeds	141	L2
Beeston	Norfk	121	K8
Beeston	Notts	116	E4
Beeston Regis	Norfk	122	D3
Beeswing	D & G	176	A5
Beetham	Cumb	157	H6
Beetham	Somset	30	D8
Beetley	Norfk	121	L8
Began	Cardif	43	K5
Begbroke	Oxon	66	C4
Begdale	Cambs	103	J2
Beggarington Hill	Leeds	141	L3
Beggar's Bush	Powys	79	J2
Beguildy	Powys	94	F7
Beighton	Norfk	107	H2
Beighton	Sheff	133	J3
Beinn Na Faoghla	W Isls	283	c9
Beith	N Ayrs	208	B8
Bekesbourne	Kent	41	G4
Bekesbourne Hill	Kent	41	G4
Belaugh	Norfk	122	F7
Belbroughton	Worcs	97	L7
Belchalwell	Dorset	16	F1
Belchalwell Street	Dorset	16	F1
Belchamp Otten	Essex	88	F6
Belchamp St Paul	Essex	88	F6
Belchamp Walter	Essex	89	G7
Belchford	Lincs	136	E4
Belford	Nthumb	203	H6
Belgrave	C Leic	100	D2
Belhaven	E Loth	212	E3
Belhelvie	Abers	257	H8
Belhinnie	Abers	255	J6
Bellabeg	Abers	243	K1
Bellamore	Herefs	79	M7
Bellanoch	Ag & B	216	B8
Bellasize	E R Yk	143	K2
Bellaty	Angus	233	K3
Bell Bar	Herts	69	H6
Bell Busk	N York	148	F4
Belleau	Lincs	137	G4
Bell End	Worcs	97	L7
Bellerby	N York	159	K4
Bellever	Devon	12	F7
Belle Vue	Cumb	177	L7
Belle Vue	Wakefd	142	A4
Bellfield	S Lans	186	E2
Bellfield	S Lans	198	D6
Bell Heath	Worcs	97	L7
Bell Hill	Hants	35	M6
Bellingdon	Bucks	68	B6
Bellingham	Nthumb	179	J2
Belloch	Ag & B	192	D1
Bellochantuy	Ag & B	192	D2
Bell o' th' Hill	Ches W	113	L2
Bellows Cross	Dorset	33	J8
Bells Cross	Suffk	90	D5
Bellshill	N Lans	209	H6
Bellshill	Nthumb	203	J7
Bellside	N Lans	209	L7
Bellsquarry	W Loth	210	D6
Bells Yew Green	E Susx	38	F6
Belluton	BaNES	45	J6
Belmaduthy	Highld	263	H8
Belmesthorpe	Rutlnd	102	A2
Belmont	Bl w D	139	K4
Belmont	Gt Lon	51	H6
Belmont	S Ayrs	196	C7
Belmont	Shet	281	f2
Belnacraig	Abers	255	H8
Belowda	Cnwll	4	F3
Belper	Derbys	116	B2
Belper Lane End	Derbys	116	B2
Belph	Derbys	133	L4
Belsay	Nthumb	180	D3
Belses	Border	201	J8
Belsford	Devon	7	L3
Belsize	Herts	68	D7
Belstead	Suffk	90	D7
Belstone	Devon	12	E4
Belthorn	Lancs	139	L3
Beltinge	Kent	41	G2
Beltingham	Nthumb	179	H6
Beltoft	N Linc	143	K6
Belton	Leics	116	D7
Belton	Lincs	118	B3
Belton	N Linc	143	K6
Belton	Norfk	107	K5
Belton	Rutlnd	101	H3
Beltring	Kent	39	H4
Belvedere	Gt Lon	52	B3
Belvoir	Leics	117	L5
Bembridge	IoW	19	L6
Bemerton	Wilts	33	K5
Bempton	E R Yk	153	K2
Benacre	Suffk	107	K6
Benbecula	W Isls	283	c9
Benbuie	D & G	185	H4
Benderloch	Ag & B	228	D7
Benenden	Kent	39	K6
Benfieldside	Dur	180	D8
Bengates	Norfk	122	F6
Bengeo	Herts	69	J4
Bengeworth	Worcs	82	B6
Benhall Green	Suffk	91	J3
Benhall Street	Suffk	91	H3
Benholm	Abers	235	K2
Beningbrough	N York	151	H4
Benington	Herts	69	J2
Benington	Lincs	119	L2
Benington Sea End	Lincs	119	L2
Benllech	IoA	125	J3
Benmore	Ag & B	207	J2
Bennacott	Cnwll	11	K4
Bennan	N Ayrs	193	K4
Bennet Head	Cumb	166	B6
Bennetland	E R Yk	143	L2
Bennett End	Bucks	67	J7
Benniworth	Lincs	136	D3
Benover	Kent	39	H4
Ben Rhydding	C Brad	149	L6
Benslie	N Ayrs	196	C2
Benson	Oxon	66	F8
Bentfield Green	Essex	70	D2
Benthall	Shrops	96	F3
Bentham	Gloucs	64	C4
Benthoul	C Aber	245	H3
Bentlawn	Shrops	95	H3
Bentley	Donc	142	E6
Bentley	E R Yk	152	F6
Bentley	Hants	36	A2
Bentley	Suffk	90	D7
Bentley	Warwks	99	H4
Bentley Crematorium	Essex	70	E2
Bentley Heath	Herts	69	H7
Bentley Heath	Solhll	98	F8
Benton	Devon	28	B4
Bentpath	D & G	188	B8
Bentwichen	Devon	28	C4
Bentworth	Hants	35	K3
Benvie	Angus	222	E1
Benville	Dorset	15	M2
Benwick	Cambs	103	G5
Beoley	Worcs	82	C1
Beoraidbeg	Highld	237	K2
Bepton	W Susx	20	D3
Berden	Essex	70	C1
Bere Alston	Devon	6	E2
Bere Ferrers	Devon	6	E2
Berepper	Cnwll	3	G6
Bere Regis	Dorset	17	G4
Bergh Apton	Norfk	106	F3
Berhill	Somset	31	G4
Berinsfield	Oxon	66	E7
Berkeley	Gloucs	63	K7
Berkeley Heath	Gloucs	63	K7
Berkeley Road	Gloucs	63	L7
Berkhamsted	Herts	68	C5
Berkley	Somset	32	D1
Berkswell	Solhll	99	H1
Bermondsey	Gt Lon	51	J3
Bermuda	Warwks	99	K5
Bernera	Highld	248	C7
Bernisdale	Highld	258	F6
Berrick Prior	Oxon	66	F8
Berrick Salome	Oxon	66	F8
Berriedale	Highld	274	F3
Berrier	Cumb	165	L3
Berriew	Powys	94	E3
Berrington	Nthumb	202	F4
Berrington	Shrops	96	C2
Berrington	Worcs	80	D2
Berrington Green	Worcs	80	D2
Berrow	Somset	44	C8
Berrow	Worcs	81	H8
Berrow Green	Worcs	81	H3
Berry Brow	Kirk	141	H5
Berry Cross	Devon	27	H7
Berry Down Cross	Devon	27	K2
Berry Hill	Gloucs	63	H4
Berry Hill	Pembks	75	H4
Berryhillock	Moray	267	K4
Berryhillock	Moray	267	K4
Berrynarbor	Devon	27	K2
Berry Pomeroy	Devon	8	B3
Berry's Green	Gt Lon	51	L7
Bersham	Wrexhm	112	D2
Berthengam	Flints	128	D4
Berwick	E Susx	23	H6
Berwick Bassett	Wilts	47	G4
Berwick Hill	Nthumb	180	E4
Berwick St James	Wilts	33	J3
Berwick St John	Wilts	32	F6
Berwick St Leonard	Wilts	32	F4
Berwick-upon-Tweed	Nthumb	202	F3
Bescaby	Leics	117	L6
Bescar	Lancs	138	E5
Besford	Shrops	113	J6
Besford	Worcs	81	L6
Bessacarr	Donc	142	F7
Bessels Leigh	Oxon	66	C6
Besses o' th' Barn	Bury	140	B6
Bessingby	E R Yk	153	J3
Bessingham	Norfk	122	D4
Bestbeech Hill	E Susx	38	F7
Besthorpe	Norfk	106	B4
Besthorpe	Notts	135	G6
Bestwood Village	Notts	116	F2
Beswick	E R Yk	152	F6
Betchcott	Shrops	95	K4
Betchworth	Surrey	37	K1
Bethania	Cerdgn	77	G3
Bethania	Gwynd	110	D3
Bethel	Gwynd	111	J4
Bethel	Gwynd	125	J6
Bethel	IoA	125	G5
Bethel	Powys	111	L7
Bethersden	Kent	40	B7
Bethesda	Gwynd	126	C6
Bethesda	Pembks	55	J3
Bethlehem	Carmth	59	J4
Bethnal Green	Gt Lon	51	K2
Betley	Staffs	114	B2
Betsham	Kent	52	D4
Betteshanger	Kent	41	J5
Bettiscombe	Dorset	15	J3
Bettisfield	Wrexhm	113	G4
Betton	Shrops	113	M4
Betton Strange	Shrops	96	C2
Bettws	Newpt	44	C1
Bettws Bledrws	Cerdgn	77	H5
Bettws Cedewain	Powys	94	D4
Bettws Evan	Cerdgn	76	B5
Bettws-Newydd	Mons	62	D6
Bettyhill	Highld	278	B4
Betws	Brdgnd	42	D4
Betws	Carmth	59	H6
Betws Garmon	Gwynd	125	K8
Betws Gwerfil Goch	Denbgs	111	K2
Betws-y-Coed	Conwy	126	F8
Betws-yn-Rhos	Conwy	127	H5
Beulah	Cerdgn	76	B6
Beulah	Powys	78	C5
Bevendean	Br & H	22	E6
Bevercotes	Notts	134	D5
Beverley	E R Yk	153	G7
Beverston	Gloucs	64	B8
Bevington	Gloucs	63	K7
Bewaldeth	Cumb	165	H4
Bewcastle	Cumb	178	D4
Bewdley	Worcs	97	H8
Bewerley	N York	149	L3
Bewholme	E R Yk	153	J6
Bewlbridge	Kent	39	H6
Bexhill	E Susx	24	D5
Bexley	Gt Lon	52	B4
Bexleyheath	Gt Lon	52	A4
Bexleyhill	W Susx	36	D6
Bexon	Kent	53	J7
Bexwell	Norfk	104	C3
Beyton	Suffk	89	J3
Beyton Green	Suffk	89	J3
Bhaltos	W Isls	282	e3
Bhatarsaigh	W Isls	283	b13
Bibstone	S Glos	45	K1
Bibury	Gloucs	65	G5
Bicester	Oxon	66	E3
Bickenhill	Solhll	99	G7
Bicker	Lincs	119	H4
Bicker Bar	Lincs	119	H4
Bicker Gauntlet	Lincs	119	H4
Bickershaw	Wigan	139	J7
Bickerstaffe	Lancs	138	F7
Bickerton	Ches E	113	H1
Bickerton	Devon	8	B7
Bickerton	N York	151	G5
Bickerton	Nthumb	190	E6
Bickford	Staffs	114	D8

Place	County	Page	Grid
Bickington	Devon	13	J8
Bickington	Devon	27	J4
Bickleigh	Devon	7	G2
Bickleigh	Devon	13	M1
Bickleton	Devon	27	J5
Bickley	Ches W	113	J2
Bickley	Gt Lon	51	L5
Bickley	N York	163	G4
Bickley	Worcs	80	E1
Bickley Moss	Ches W	113	J2
Bicknacre	Essex	71	J6
Bicknoller	Somset	29	K3
Bicknor	Kent	53	J7
Bickton	Hants	33	K8
Bicton	Herefs	80	B2
Bicton	Shrops	95	G6
Bicton	Shrops	113	G8
Bidborough	Kent	38	E5
Bidden	Hants	35	L1
Biddenden	Kent	39	L5
Biddenden Green	Kent	39	M5
Biddenham	Bed	85	K5
Biddestone	Wilts	46	B4
Biddisham	Somset	44	D8
Biddlesden	Bucks	84	C7
Biddlestone	Nthumb	190	D6
Biddulph	Staffs	131	H7
Biddulph Moor	Staffs	131	H8
Bideford	Devon	27	H5
Bidford-on-Avon	Warwks	82	D5
Bidston	Wirral	129	G2
Bielby	E R Yk	152	B7
Bieldside	C Aber	245	K3
Bierley	IoW	19	H8
Bierton	Bucks	67	K4
Big Balcraig	D & G	173	K6
Bigbury	Devon	7	K5
Bigbury-on-Sea	Devon	7	J6
Bigby	Lincs	144	D6
Big Carlae	D & G	185	G3
Biggar	Cumb	146	D3
Biggar	S Lans	199	H5
Biggin	Derbys	115	L2
Biggin	Derbys	132	C7
Biggin	N York	142	E1
Biggin Hill	Gt Lon	51	L7
Biggleswade	C Beds	86	D6
Bigholms	D & G	177	K3
Bighouse	Highld	278	F3
Bighton	Hants	35	J4
Biglands	Cumb	177	H8
Bignor	W Susx	21	G4
Bigrigg	Cumb	164	D8
Big Sand	Highld	260	B4
Bigton	Shet	281	d8
Bilborough	C Nott	116	E3
Bilbrook	Somset	29	J3
Bilbrook	Staffs	97	K3
Bilbrough	N York	151	H6
Bilbster	Highld	280	C5
Bildershaw	Dur	169	G6
Bildeston	Suffk	89	K5
Billacott	Cnwll	11	J4
Billericay	Essex	71	G8
Billesdon	Leics	100	F3
Billesley	Warwks	82	D4
Billingborough	Lincs	118	F5
Billinge	St Hel	139	G7
Billingford	Norfk	106	D7
Billingford	Norfk	121	M7
Billingham	S on T	170	B6
Billinghay	Lincs	136	C8
Billingley	Barns	142	C6
Billingshurst	W Susx	37	G5
Billingsley	Shrops	97	G6
Billington	C Beds	68	B3
Billington	Lancs	148	C8
Billington	Staffs	114	D7
Billockby	Norfk	107	J1
Billy Row	Dur	168	F3
Bilsborrow	Lancs	147	K7
Bilsby	Lincs	137	J4
Bilsham	W Susx	21	G6
Bilsington	Kent	40	D8
Bilsthorpe	Notts	134	C7
Bilsthorpe Moor	Notts	134	C7
Bilston	Mdloth	211	J6
Bilston	Wolves	98	B4
Bilstone	Leics	99	K2
Bilting	Kent	40	D5
Bilton	E R Yk	144	F1
Bilton	N York	150	D4
Bilton	N York	151	G6
Bilton	Nthumb	191	J4
Bilton	Warwks	100	B8
Bilton Banks	Nthumb	191	J4
Binbrook	Lincs	136	D1
Binchester Blocks	Dur	169	G4
Bincombe	Dorset	16	D5
Binegar	Somset	31	K1

Place	County	Page	Grid
Bines Green	W Susx	21	L3
Binfield	Br For	49	K4
Binfield Heath	Oxon	49	H3
Bingfield	Nthumb	180	A4
Bingham	Notts	117	J3
Bingham's Melcombe	Dorset	16	E2
Bingley	C Brad	149	K7
Bings	Shrops	113	J7
Binham	Norfk	121	L4
Binley	Covtry	99	K7
Binley	Hants	48	B8
Binley Woods	Warwks	99	L7
Binnegar	Dorset	17	G5
Binniehill	Falk	209	M4
Binscombe	Surrey	36	E2
Binsey	Oxon	66	C5
Binstead	IoW	19	K5
Binsted	Hants	36	A3
Binsted	W Susx	21	G5
Binton	Warwks	82	D4
Bintree	Norfk	121	M7
Binweston	Shrops	95	H3
Birch	Essex	72	D3
Birch	Rochdl	140	C6
Bircham Newton	Norfk	121	G5
Bircham Tofts	Norfk	121	G5
Birchanger	Essex	70	D3
Birch Cross	Staffs	115	J5
Birchencliffe	Kirk	141	H4
Bircher	Herefs	80	B2
Birchfield	Birm	98	D5
Birch Green	Essex	72	D3
Birch Green	Herts	69	J5
Birch Green	Worcs	81	K6
Birchgrove	Cardif	43	J5
Birchgrove	Swans	57	K5
Birchgrove	W Susx	38	B7
Birch Heath	Ches W	130	A7
Birch Hill	Ches W	129	M5
Birchington	Kent	41	J2
Birchley Heath	Warwks	99	H4
Birchmoor	Warwks	99	H3
Birchmoor Green	C Beds	85	J8
Birchover	Derbys	132	E7
Birch Vale	Derbys	131	K2
Birchwood	Lincs	135	J6
Birch Wood	Somset	30	C8
Bircotes	Notts	134	C2
Birdbrook	Essex	88	E7
Birdforth	N York	161	G7
Birdham	W Susx	20	D6
Birdingbury	Warwks	83	K2
Birdlip	Gloucs	64	D4
Birdoswald	Cumb	178	E5
Birdsall	N York	152	B3
Birds Edge	Kirk	141	K6
Birds Green	Essex	70	E5
Birdsgreen	Shrops	97	H6
Birdsmoorgate	Dorset	15	J3
Bird Street	Suffk	89	K5
Birdwell	Barns	142	A7
Birdwood	Gloucs	63	L3
Birgham	Border	202	B5
Birichin	Highld	263	K2
Birkacre	Lancs	139	H5
Birkby	N York	160	D2
Birkdale	Sefton	138	C5
Birkenbog	Abers	267	L3
Birkenhead	Wirral	129	H2
Birkenhills	Abers	256	D3
Birkenshaw	Kirk	141	K2
Birkhall	Abers	243	K5
Birkhill	Angus	234	A8
Birkhill	D & G	187	J3
Birkholme	Lincs	118	C6
Birkin	N York	142	E2
Birks	Leeds	141	L2
Birkshaw	Nthumb	179	H5
Birley	Herefs	80	B4
Birley Carr	Sheff	133	G1
Birling	Kent	52	E6
Birling	Nthumb	191	K5
Birling Gap	E Susx	23	J8
Birlingham	Worcs	81	L6
Birmingham	Birm	98	D6
Birnam	P & K	232	F7
Birness	Abers	257	H5
Birse	Abers	244	C4
Birsemore	Abers	244	C4
Birstall	Kirk	141	K3
Birstall	Leics	100	D2
Birstwith	N York	150	B4
Birthorpe	Lincs	118	C5
Birtley	Gatesd	181	G7
Birtley	Herefs	79	L2
Birtley	Nthumb	179	K3
Birtley Crematorium	Gatesd	181	G7
Birts Street	Worcs	81	H7
Bisbrooke	Rutlnd	101	J3

Place	County	Page	Grid
Biscathorpe	Lincs	136	D3
Biscovey	Cnwll	5	H4
Bisham	W & M	49	K2
Bishampton	Worcs	82	A5
Bish Mill	Devon	28	C6
Bishop Auckland	Dur	169	G5
Bishopbridge	Lincs	135	L2
Bishopbriggs	E Duns	209	G5
Bishop Burton	E R Yk	152	F7
Bishop Middleham	Dur	169	J4
Bishopmill	Moray	266	E3
Bishop Monkton	N York	150	D3
Bishop Norton	Lincs	135	K1
Bishopsbourne	Kent	41	G5
Bishops Cannings	Wilts	46	F6
Bishop's Castle	Shrops	95	H5
Bishop's Caundle	Dorset	32	B8
Bishop's Cleeve	Gloucs	64	D2
Bishop's Frome	Herefs	80	F5
Bishops Gate	Surrey	50	B5
Bishop's Green	Essex	70	F3
Bishop's Green	Hants	48	D6
Bishops Hull	Somset	30	B6
Bishop's Itchington	Warwks	83	J4
Bishops Lydeard	Somset	29	M5
Bishop's Norton	Gloucs	64	B2
Bishop's Nympton	Devon	28	D6
Bishop's Offley	Staffs	114	D5
Bishop's Stortford	Herts	70	C3
Bishop's Sutton	Hants	35	J4
Bishop's Tachbrook	Warwks	83	H3
Bishop's Tawton	Devon	27	K5
Bishopsteignton	Devon	13	L7
Bishopstoke	Hants	34	F7
Bishopston	Swans	57	G7
Bishopstone	Bucks	67	J5
Bishopstone	E Susx	23	G7
Bishopstone	Herefs	80	A6
Bishopstone	Kent	41	G2
Bishopstone	Swindn	47	K2
Bishopstone	Wilts	33	J5
Bishopstrow	Wilts	32	E2
Bishop Sutton	BaNES	45	H7
Bishop's Waltham	Hants	35	H7
Bishopswood	Somset	30	C8
Bishop's Wood	Staffs	97	J2
Bishopsworth	Bristl	45	H5
Bishop Thornton	N York	150	C3
Bishopthorpe	C York	151	J6
Bishopton	Darltn	169	K6
Bishopton	Rens	208	D5
Bishopton	Warwks	82	E4
Bishop Wilton	E R Yk	152	B5
Bishton	Newpt	44	D2
Bishton	Staffs	115	G7
Bisley	Gloucs	64	C6
Bisley	Surrey	50	B7
Bisley Camp	Surrey	50	B7
Bispham	Bpool	146	F7
Bispham Green	Lancs	138	F5
Bissoe	Cnwll	3	K3
Bisterne	Hants	18	A3
Bitchet Green	Kent	38	E3
Bitchfield	Lincs	118	C6
Bittadon	Devon	27	K3
Bittaford	Devon	7	K3
Bittering	Norfk	121	K8
Bitterley	Shrops	96	D7
Bitterne	C Sotn	34	F8
Bitteswell	Leics	100	C6
Bitton	S Glos	45	K5
Bix	Oxon	49	H2
Bixter	Shet	281	d6
Blaby	Leics	100	C4
Blackadder	Border	202	C3
Blackawton	Devon	8	B4
Blackborough	Devon	14	C1
Blackborough End	Norfk	120	E8
Black Bourton	Oxon	65	L6
Blackboys	E Susx	23	J3
Blackbrook	Derbys	116	B2
Blackbrook	St Hel	139	G8
Blackbrook	Staffs	114	B4
Blackbrook	Surrey	37	J2
Blackburn	Abers	245	J1
Blackburn	Bl w D	139	K2
Blackburn	Rothm	133	H1
Blackburn	W Loth	210	C6
Black Callerton	N u Ty	180	E5
Black Car	Norfk	106	B4
Black Corner	W Susx	37	L3
Blackcraig	E Ayrs	185	G1
Black Crofts	Ag & B	228	C6
Black Cross	Cnwll	4	E3
Blackden Heath	Ches E	130	F5
Blackdog	Abers	245	L1
Black Dog	Devon	13	J1
Blackdown	Devon	12	C6
Blackdown	Dorset	15	J2

Place	County	Page	Grid
Blackdyke	Cumb	176	F8
Blacker	Barns	142	A5
Blacker Hill	Barns	142	B7
Blackfen	Gt Lon	51	M4
Blackfield	Hants	19	G3
Blackford	Cumb	177	L6
Blackford	P & K	220	F3
Blackford	Somset	30	F2
Blackford	Somset	31	L5
Blackfordby	Leics	116	B7
Blackgang	IoW	19	H8
Blackhall	C Edin	211	G4
Blackhall	Dur	170	B3
Blackhall Colliery	Dur	170	B3
Blackhall Mill	Gatesd	180	C3
Blackhaugh	Border	200	F5
Blackheath	Essex	72	E3
Blackheath	Gt Lon	51	K4
Blackheath	Sandw	98	B6
Blackheath	Suffk	107	J8
Blackheath	Surrey	36	F2
Black Heddon	Nthumb	180	C4
Blackhill	Abers	257	K3
Blackhill	Abers	269	K5
Blackhill	Dur	180	D8
Blackhill of Clackriach	Abers	269	G4
Blackhorse	Devon	14	A4
Blackjack	Lincs	119	H4
Blackland	Wilts	46	E5
Black Lane Ends	Lancs	149	G7
Blacklaw	D & G	186	F4
Blackley	Manch	140	C7
Blackley Crematorium	Manch	140	C7
Blacklunans	P & K	233	H3
Blackmarstone	Herefs	80	C7
Blackmill	Brdgnd	42	E4
Blackmoor	Hants	36	A4
Black Moor	Leeds	150	D7
Blackmoor	N Som	44	F6
Blackmoorfoot	Kirk	141	H5
Blackmore	Essex	70	F6
Blackmore End	Essex	71	H1
Blackmore End	Herts	68	F4
Blackness	Falk	210	E3
Blacknest	Hants	36	A3
Blacknest	W & M	50	B5
Black Notley	Essex	71	J3
Blacko	Lancs	148	E7
Black Pill	Swans	57	H6
Blackpool	Bpool	146	F8
Blackpool	Devon	8	C5
Blackpool	Devon	13	J7
Blackpool Gate	Cumb	178	C3
Blackridge	W Loth	210	A5
Blackrock	Cnwll	3	G4
Blackrock	Mons	61	K4
Blackrod	Bolton	139	J6
Blacksboat	Moray	254	D4
Blackshaw	D & G	176	D5
Blackshaw Head	Calder	140	D4
Blacksmith's Green	Suffk	90	D2
Blacksnape	Bl w D	139	L3
Blackstone	W Susx	22	C4
Black Street	Suffk	107	K6
Black Tar	Pembks	55	G5
Blackthorn	Oxon	66	F3
Blackthorpe	Suffk	89	H3
Blacktoft	E R Yk	143	L3
Blacktop	C Aber	245	J3
Black Torrington	Devon	12	B2
Blackwall	Derbys	115	L2
Blackwater	Cnwll	4	B5
Blackwater	Hants	49	K7
Blackwater	IoW	19	H6
Blackwater	Somset	30	C7
Blackwaterfoot	N Ayrs	194	D6
Blackwell	Cumb	177	L8
Blackwell	Darltn	169	H8
Blackwell	Derbys	132	C5
Blackwell	Derbys	133	J7
Blackwell	Warwks	82	F6
Blackwell	Worcs	82	A1
Blackwellsend Green	Gloucs	63	M2
Blackwood	Caerph	43	J2
Blackwood	D & G	176	B2
Blackwood	S Lans	198	C4
Blackwood Hill	Staffs	131	H8
Blacon	Ches W	129	J6
Bladbean	Kent	41	G6
Bladnoch	D & G	174	C4
Bladon	Oxon	66	C4
Bladon	Somset	30	F6
Blaenannerch	Cerdgn	75	M2
Blaenau Ffestiniog	Gwynd	110	D2
Blaenavon	Torfn	61	L6
Blaen Dyryn	Powys	78	C7
Blaenffos	Pembks	75	L5
Blaengarw	Brdgnd	42	D3
Blaengeuffordd	Cerdgn	92	E7
Blaengwrach	Neath	60	C6

Blaengwynfi Neath 42 D2
Blaenllechau Rhondd 42 F2
Blaenpennal Cerdgn 77 H2
Blaenplwyf Cerdgn 92 C8
Blaenporth Cerdgn 76 A5
Blaenrhondda Rhondd 60 D7
Blaenwaun Carmth 75 M6
Blaen-y-Coed Carmth 58 C3
Blaen-y-cwm Blae G 61 H5
Blaenycwm Cerdgn 93 H8
Blaen-y-cwm Rhondd 60 D7
Blagdon N Som 45 G7
Blagdon Somset 30 B7
Blagdon Torbay 8 C3
Blagdon Hill Somset 30 B7
Blagill Cumb 167 G1
Blaguegate Lancs 138 F6
Blaich Highld 239 G8
Blain Highld 237 K6
Blaina Blae G 61 K5
Blair Atholl P & K 232 C2
Blair Drummond Stirlg 220 C7
Blairgowrie P & K 233 J6
Blairhall Fife 210 C2
Blairingone P & K 221 H7
Blairlogie Stirlg 220 E7
Blairmore Ag & B 207 K2
Blairmore Highld 276 B4
Blair's Ferry Ag & B 206 F5
Blaisdon Gloucs 63 K4
Blakebrook Worcs 97 J8
Blakedown Worcs 97 K8
Blake End Essex 71 H3
Blakeley Lane Staffs 114 F2
Blakemere Ches W 130 A5
Blakemere Herefs 79 L3
Blakemore Devon 7 M3
Blakenall Heath Wsall 98 C3
Blakeney Gloucs 63 K5
Blakeney Norfk 122 A3
Blakenhall Ches E 114 A2
Blakenhall Wolves 97 K4
Blakeshall Worcs 97 J7
Blakesley Nhants 84 C5
Blanchland Nthumb 168 B1
Blandford Camp Dorset 17 H1
Blandford Forum Dorset 17 G1
Blandford St Mary Dorset 17 G2
Bland Hill N York 150 B5
Blanefield Stirlg 208 F3
Blankney Lincs 135 L7
Blantyre S Lans 209 J7
Blar a' Chaorainn Highld 229 H2
Blargie Highld 241 G4
Blarmachfoldach Highld 229 H2
Blashford Hants 18 A2
Blaston Leics 101 H4
Blatherwycke Nhants 101 L4
Blawith Cumb 156 C5
Blawquhairn D & G 184 F6
Blaxhall Suffk 91 J4
Blaxton Donc 143 H7
Blaydon Gatesd 180 F6
Bleadney Somset 31 H2
Bleadon N Som 44 C7
Bleak Street Somset 32 C4
Blean Kent 40 F3
Bleasby Lincs 136 B3
Bleasby Notts 117 J2
Bleasdale Lancs 147 L6
Bleatarn Cumb 167 G2
Bleathwood Herefs 80 D1
Blebocraigs Fife 223 G4
Bleddfa Powys 79 H2
Bledington Gloucs 65 K3
Bledlow Bucks 67 J6
Bledlow Ridge Bucks 67 J7
Bleet Wilts 46 C7
Blegbie E Loth 212 E4
Blencarn Cumb 166 E4
Blencogo Cumb 165 G1
Blendworth Hants 35 L8
Blennerhasset Cumb 165 G2
Bletchingdon Oxon 66 D3
Bletchingley Surrey 37 M1
Bletchley M Keyn 85 G8
Bletchley Shrops 113 K5
Bletherston Pembks 55 H3
Bletsoe Bed 85 K4
Blewbury Oxon 48 D2
Blickling Norfk 122 D6
Blidworth Notts 134 B8
Blidworth Bottoms Notts 117 G1
Blindburn Nthumb 189 L4
Blindcrake Cumb 164 F4
Blindley Heath Surrey 38 A4
Blisland Cnwll 10 F8
Blissford Hants 33 L8
Bliss Gate Worcs 81 G1
Blisworth Nhants 84 D4

Blithbury Staffs 115 H7
Blitterlees Cumb 176 F8
Blockley Gloucs 82 E8
Blofield Norfk 107 G2
Blofield Heath Norfk 107 G1
Blo Norton Norfk 105 K7
Bloomfield Border 189 G2
Blore Staffs 114 A4
Blore Staffs 115 J2
Blounce Hants 35 L2
Blounts Green Staffs 115 H5
Blowick Sefton 138 D4
Bloxham Oxon 83 K8
Bloxholm Lincs 118 E1
Bloxworth Dorset 17 G4
Blubberhouses N York 149 L5
Blue Anchor Cnwll 4 E3
Blue Anchor Somset 29 J2
Blue Bell Hill Kent 52 F6
Blundellsands Sefton 138 C7
Blundeston Suffk 107 L4
Blunham C Beds 86 C5
Blunsdon St Andrew Swindn 47 H1
Bluntington Worcs 97 J8
Bluntisham Cambs 103 H8
Blunts Cnwll 6 C2
Blunts Green Warwks 82 D2
Blurton C Stke 114 D3
Blyborough Lincs 135 J1
Blyford Suffk 107 J8
Blymhill Staffs 97 H1
Blymhill Lawn Staffs 97 J1
Blyth Notts 134 C2
Blyth Nthumb 181 H3
Blyth Bridge Border 199 K4
Blythburgh Suffk 107 J8
Blyth Crematorium Nthumb 181 H3
Blythe Border 201 J3
Blythe Bridge Staffs 114 F3
Blythe End Warwks 99 G5
Blythe Marsh Staffs 114 F3
Blyton Lincs 135 G1
Boarhills Fife 223 K4
Boarhunt Hants 19 K2
Boarley Kent 53 G7
Boarsgreave Lancs 140 C4
Boarshead E Susx 38 C6
Boar's Head Wigan 139 H6
Boars Hill Oxon 66 D6
Boarstall Bucks 66 F4
Boasley Cross Devon 12 C4
Boath Highld 263 G5
Boat of Garten Highld 253 H7
Bobbing Kent 53 J6
Bobbington Staffs 97 H5
Bobbingworth Essex 70 D6
Bocaddon Cnwll 5 L3
Bocking Essex 71 J2
Bocking Churchstreet Essex 71 J2
Bockleton Worcs 80 D3
Boconnoc Cnwll 5 K3
Boddam Abers 257 L3
Boddam Shet 281 d8
Boddington Gloucs 64 C2
Bodedern IoA 124 F4
Bodelwyddan Denbgs 127 K4
Bodenham Herefs 80 C5
Bodenham Wilts 33 L5
Bodenham Moor Herefs 80 D5
Bodewryd IoA 125 G2
Bodfari Denbgs 128 C5
Bodffordd IoA 125 G4
Bodfuan Gwynd 108 E4
Bodham Norfk 122 C3
Bodiam E Susx 24 E2
Bodicote Oxon 83 K7
Bodieve Cnwll 10 D7
Bodinnick Cnwll 5 K4
Bodle Street Green E Susx 23 L4
Bodmin Cnwll 5 H2
Bodney Norfk 105 G4
Bodorgan IoA 125 G6
Bodsham Kent 40 E6
Bodwen Cnwll 5 H3
Bodymoor Heath Warwks 99 G4
Bogallan Highld 251 H2
Bogbrae Abers 257 J4
Bogend S Ayrs 196 D4
Boggs Holdings E Loth 212 A5
Boghall Mdloth 211 H6
Boghall W Loth 210 C5
Boghead S Lans 198 D5
Bogmoor Moray 267 G4
Bogmuir Abers 235 G1
Bogniebrae Abers 255 M3
Bognor Regis W Susx 20 F7
Bogroy Highld 253 G7
Bogue D & G 185 G6
Bohetherick Cnwll 6 E1

Bohortha Cnwll 3 L4
Bohuntine Highld 240 A6
Bojewyan Cnwll 2 B4
Bokiddick Cnwll 5 H2
Bolam Dur 169 G6
Bolam Nthumb 180 D2
Bolberry Devon 7 K7
Bold Heath St Hel 129 M2
Boldmere Birm 98 E4
Boldon Colliery S Tyne 181 J6
Boldre Hants 18 E4
Boldron Dur 168 C7
Bole Notts 134 F2
Bolehill Derbys 132 F8
Bole Hill Derbys 133 G5
Bolenowe Cnwll 3 H3
Bolham Devon 29 G7
Bolham Water Devon 29 L8
Bolingey Cnwll 4 C4
Bollington Ches E 131 J4
Bollington Cross Ches E 131 H4
Bollow Gloucs 63 L4
Bolney W Susx 37 L6
Bolnhurst Bed 86 B3
Bolshan Angus 234 F5
Bolsover Derbys 133 J5
Bolster Moor Kirk 141 G6
Bolsterstone Sheff 141 L8
Boltby N York 161 H5
Boltenstone Abers 243 M2
Bolter End Bucks 67 J8
Bolton Bolton 139 L6
Bolton Cumb 166 E6
Bolton E Loth 212 B5
Bolton E R Yk 152 B5
Bolton Nthumb 191 G3
Bolton Abbey N York 149 K5
Bolton Bridge N York 149 K5
Bolton by Bowland Lancs 148 D6
Boltonfellend Cumb 178 B5
Boltongate Cumb 165 H3
Bolton le Sands Lancs 147 J2
Bolton Low Houses Cumb 165 H2
Bolton New Houses Cumb 165 H2
Bolton-on-Swale N York 160 C3
Bolton Percy N York 151 H7
Bolton Town End Lancs 147 J2
Bolton Upon Dearne Barns 142 C7
Bolventor Cnwll 11 H7
Bomarsund Nthumb 181 G2
Bomere Heath Shrops 113 G7
Bonar Bridge Highld 263 G2
Bonawe Ag & B 228 F8
Bonby N Linc 144 C5
Boncath Pembks 75 L4
Bonchester Bridge Border 189 G4
Bonchurch IoW 19 K8
Bondleigh Devon 12 F2
Bonds Lancs 147 J6
Bonehill Devon 13 G7
Bonehill Staffs 99 G3
Bo'ness Falk 210 D3
Boney Hay Staffs 98 D2
Bonhill W Duns 208 C3
Boningale Shrops 97 J3
Bonjedward Border 189 H2
Bonkle N Lans 209 M7
Bonnington Angus 234 F7
Bonnington Kent 40 D8
Bonnybank Fife 222 F6
Bonnybridge Falk 209 L3
Bonnykelly Abers 268 F5
Bonnyrigg Mdloth 211 J6
Bonnyton Angus 233 M7
Bonsall Derbys 132 E8
Bonshaw Tower D & G 177 H4
Bont Mons 62 D3
Bontddu Gwynd 110 C7
Bont-Dolgadfan Powys 93 J3
Bont-goch or Elerch Cerdgn 92 E6
Bonthorpe Lincs 137 J5
Bontnewydd Cerdgn 77 H2
Bontnewydd Gwynd 125 J7
Bontuchel Denbgs 128 C8
Bonvilston V Glam 43 G7
Bonwm Denbgs 111 L3
Bon-y-maen Swans 57 J6
Boode Devon 27 J3
Booker Bucks 49 K1
Booley Shrops 113 J6
Boon Border 201 J4
Boon Hill Staffs 114 C2
Boorley Green Hants 35 G8
Boosbeck R & Cl 170 F7
Boose's Green Essex 71 K1
Boot Cumb 155 M3
Booth Calder 141 G2
Boothby Graffoe Lincs 135 K7
Boothby Pagnell Lincs 118 C5
Boothferry E R Yk 143 J3

Booth Green Ches E 131 H3
Boothstown Salfd 139 L7
Booth Town Calder 141 G2
Boothville Nhants 84 F2
Bootle Cumb 155 K5
Bootle Sefton 138 D8
Boots Green Ches W 130 E5
Boot Street Suffk 90 F5
Booze N York 159 L2
Boraston Shrops 80 E1
Bordeaux Guern 9 k2
Borden Kent 53 J6
Borden W Susx 36 B5
Border Cumb 177 G8
Borders Crematorium Border 201 H6
Bordley N York 149 G3
Bordon Camp Hants 36 B4
Boreham Essex 71 J5
Boreham Wilts 32 E2
Boreham Street E Susx 24 C5
Borehamwood Herts 69 G7
Boreland D & G 187 J8
Boreraig Highld 258 B6
Boreton Shrops 96 C2
Borgh W Isls 282 g1
Borgh W Isls 283 b13
Borgie Highld 278 B4
Borgue D & G 175 G5
Borgue Highld 274 F3
Borley Essex 89 G6
Borley Green Essex 89 G6
Borley Green Suffk 89 K3
Borneskitaig Highld 258 F2
Borness D & G 174 F5
Boroughbridge N York 150 E3
Borough Green Kent 38 F2
Borras Head Wrexhm 112 E1
Borrowash Derbys 116 C4
Borrowby N York 160 F5
Borrowby N York 171 H7
Borrowstoun Falk 210 D3
Borstal Medway 52 F5
Borth Cerdgn 92 D5
Borthwickbrae Border 188 C3
Borthwickshiels Border 188 D3
Borth-y-Gest Gwynd 109 K4
Borve Highld 259 G7
Borve W Isls 282 d6
Borve W Isls 282 g1
Borve W Isls 283 b13
Borwick Lancs 147 K1
Borwick Lodge Cumb 156 E3
Borwick Rails Cumb 156 A6
Bosavern Cnwll 2 B5
Bosbury Herefs 80 F6
Boscarne Cnwll 5 H1
Boscastle Cnwll 10 F4
Boscombe Bmouth 17 M4
Boscombe Wilts 33 L3
Boscoppa Cnwll 5 H4
Bosham W Susx 20 C6
Bosham Hoe W Susx 20 D6
Bosherston Pembks 54 F7
Boskednan Cnwll 2 C4
Boskenna Cnwll 2 C6
Bosley Ches E 131 H6
Bosoughan Cnwll 4 E3
Bossall N York 151 M4
Bossiney Cnwll 10 F5
Bossingham Kent 40 F5
Bossington Somset 28 F1
Bostock Green Ches W 130 C6
Boston Lincs 119 K3
Boston Crematorium Lincs 119 K3
Boston Spa Leeds 150 F6
Boswarthan Cnwll 2 C4
Boswinger Cnwll 5 G6
Botallack Cnwll 2 B4
Botany Bay Gt Lon 69 J7
Botcheston Leics 100 B2
Botesdale Suffk 105 L8
Bothal Nthumb 180 F2
Bothampstead W Berk 48 D4
Bothamsall Notts 134 D5
Bothel Cumb 165 G3
Bothenhampton Dorset 15 L4
Bothwell S Lans 209 J7
Botley Bucks 68 B6
Botley Hants 35 G8
Botley Oxon 66 C6
Botolph Claydon Bucks 67 H2
Botolphs W Susx 21 L5
Botolph's Bridge Kent 40 F8
Bottesford Leics 117 L4
Bottesford N Linc 143 M6
Bottisham Cambs 87 L3
Bottomcraig Fife 222 F2
Bottom of Hutton Lancs 138 F2
Bottom o' th' Moor Bolton 139 K5
Bottoms Calder 140 D3

Bottoms Cnwll 2 B6
Botts Green Warwks 99 H5
Botusfleming Cnwll 6 E3
Botwnnog Gwynd 108 D5
Bough Beech Kent 38 D4
Boughrood Powys 79 G7
Boughspring Gloucs 63 H7
Boughton Nhants 84 E2
Boughton Norfk 104 D3
Boughton Notts 134 D6
Boughton Aluph Kent 40 D6
Boughton End C Beds 85 J7
Boughton Green Kent 39 J3
Boughton Malherbe Kent 39 M3
Boughton Monchelsea Kent 39 J3
Boughton Street Kent 40 D3
Boulby R & Cl 171 H7
Boulder Clough Calder 140 F3
Bouldnor IoW 18 F5
Bouldon Shrops 96 C6
Boulmer Nthumb 191 K3
Boulston Pembks 55 G4
Boultham Lincs 135 J6
Bourn Cambs 87 G4
Bourne Lincs 118 E7
Bournebridge Essex 70 D8
Bournebrook Birm 98 D6
Bourne End Bed 85 K3
Bourne End Bucks 49 L2
Bourne End C Beds 85 J6
Bourne End Herts 68 C6
Bournemouth Bmouth 17 L4
Bournemouth Crematorium
    Bmouth 17 M4
Bournes Green Gloucs 64 C6
Bournes Green Sthend 53 K2
Bournheath Worcs 98 B8
Bournmoor Dur 181 H8
Bournstream Gloucs 63 L8
Bournville Birm 98 D7
Bourton Dorset 32 C4
Bourton N Som 44 D6
Bourton Oxon 47 K2
Bourton Shrops 96 D4
Bourton Wilts 46 F6
Bourton on Dunsmore
    Warwks 83 K1
Bourton-on-the-Hill Gloucs 65 J1
Bourton-on-the-Water Gloucs 65 H3
Bousd Ag & B 225 H3
Boustead Hill Cumb 177 J7
Bouth Cumb 156 D5
Bouthwaite N York 149 L2
Bouts Worcs 82 B3
Boveney Bucks 50 B3
Boveridge Dorset 33 J7
Bovey Tracey Devon 13 J7
Bovingdon Herts 68 C6
Bovingdon Green Bucks 49 K2
Bovinger Essex 70 D6
Bovington Dorset 16 F5
Bovington Camp Dorset 16 F5
Bow Cnwll 177 K7
Bow Devon 8 B3
Bow Devon 13 G2
Bow Gt Lon 51 K2
Bow Ork 275 c6
Bowbank Dur 168 B6
Bow Brickhill M Keyn 85 H8
Bowbridge Gloucs 64 B6
Bowburn Dur 169 J3
Bowcombe IoW 19 H6
Bowd Devon 14 D4
Bowden Border 201 H7
Bowden Devon 8 C5
Bowden Hill Wilts 46 D5
Bowdon Traffd 130 E2
Bower Highld 280 B4
Bower Ashton Bristl 45 H4
Bowerchalke Wilts 33 H6
Bowerhill Wilts 46 C6
Bower Hinton Somset 31 G7
Bower House Tye Suffk 89 K7
Bowermadden Highld 280 B3
Bowers Staffs 114 C4
Bowers Gifford Essex 53 G1
Bowershall Fife 210 E1
Bower's Row Leeds 142 B2
Bowes Dur 168 C7
Bowgreave Lancs 147 K7
Bowhouse D & G 176 D5
Bowithick Cnwll 11 H6
Bowker's Green Lancs 138 E6
Bowland Border 200 F5
Bowland Bridge Cumb 156 F5
Bowley Herefs 80 C5
Bowley Town Herefs 80 C5
Bowlhead Green Surrey 36 D3
Bowling C Brad 141 J2
Bowling W Duns 208 D4

Bowling Bank Wrexhm 112 F2
Bowling Green Worcs 81 H5
Bowmanstead Cumb 156 D3
Bowmore Ag & B 204 D4
Bowness-on-Solway Cumb 177 H6
Bowness-on-Windermere
    Cumb 156 F3
Bow of Fife Fife 222 E4
Bowriefauld Angus 234 D6
Bowscale Cumb 165 K4
Bowsden Nthumb 202 F5
Bowston Cumb 157 H3
Bow Street Cerdgn 92 D6
Bow Street Norfk 105 L4
Bowthorpe Norfk 106 D2
Box Gloucs 64 B7
Box Wilts 46 B5
Boxbush Gloucs 63 K3
Boxbush Gloucs 63 L4
Box End Bed 85 K5
Boxford Suffk 89 K7
Boxford W Berk 48 B4
Boxgrove W Susx 20 E5
Box Hill Surrey 51 G8
Boxley Kent 53 G7
Boxmoor Herts 68 D6
Box's Shop Cnwll 11 H2
Boxted Essex 72 E1
Boxted Essex 89 K8
Boxted Suffk 89 G5
Boxted Cross Essex 72 E1
Boxwell Gloucs 64 A8
Boxworth Cambs 87 G2
Boxworth End Cambs 87 G2
Boyden End Suffk 88 E4
Boyden Gate Kent 41 H2
Boylestone Derbys 115 K4
Boyndie Abers 268 B3
Boyndlie Abers 269 G4
Boynton E R Yk 153 J2
Boysack Angus 234 F5
Boys Hill Dorset 16 C1
Boythorpe Derbys 133 G5
Boyton Cnwll 11 L4
Boyton Suffk 91 J6
Boyton Wilts 32 F3
Boyton Cross Essex 70 F5
Boyton End Suffk 88 E6
Bozeat Nhants 85 H3
Braaid IoM 154 d6
Brabling Green Suffk 91 G2
Brabourne Kent 40 E7
Brabourne Lees Kent 40 E7
Brabstermire Highld 280 D2
Bracadale Highld 246 E1
Braceborough Lincs 102 B1
Bracebridge Heath Lincs 135 K6
Bracebridge Low Fields Lincs 135 J6
Braceby Lincs 118 D4
Bracewell Lancs 148 F6
Brackenfield Derbys 133 G7
Brackenhirst N Lans 209 K5
Brackenthwaite Cumb 165 J1
Brackenthwaite N York 150 C5
Bracklesham W Susx 20 C7
Brackletter Highld 239 K7
Brackley Nhants 84 B7
Brackley Hatch Nhants 84 C7
Bracknell Br For 49 L5
Braco P & K 220 E5
Bracobrae Moray 267 K5
Bracon Ash Norfk 106 D3
Bracora Highld 237 L2
Bracorina Highld 237 L2
Bradaford Devon 11 M4
Bradbourne Derbys 115 K1
Bradbury Dur 169 J5
Bradden Nhants 84 C5
Braddock Cnwll 5 K2
Bradeley C Stke 114 D1
Bradenham Bucks 67 K7
Bradenstoke Wilts 46 E3
Bradfield Devon 14 B1
Bradfield Essex 73 H1
Bradfield Norfk 122 F5
Bradfield Sheff 132 E1
Bradfield W Berk 48 F4
Bradfield Combust Suffk 89 H4
Bradfield Green Ches E 130 D7
Bradfield Heath Essex 73 H1
Bradfield St Clare Suffk 89 H4
Bradfield St George Suffk 89 H3
Bradford C Brad 141 J1
Bradford Cnwll 11 G4
Bradford Devon 12 A1
Bradford Nthumb 180 C3
Bradford Nthumb 203 J6
Bradford Abbas Dorset 31 K8
Bradford Leigh Wilts 46 B6
Bradford-on-Avon Wilts 46 B6

Bradford-on-Tone Somset 30 B6
Bradford Peverell Dorset 16 C4
Bradiford Devon 27 K4
Brading IoW 19 K6
Bradley Derbys 115 L2
Bradley Hants 35 K3
Bradley Kirk 141 J4
Bradley N York 159 J6
Bradley NE Lin 145 G6
Bradley Staffs 114 D7
Bradley Wolves 98 B4
Bradley Worcs 82 A3
Bradley Wrexhm 112 E1
Bradley Common Ches W 113 H2
Bradley Green Somset 30 C3
Bradley Green Warwks 99 H3
Bradley Green Worcs 82 A3
Bradley in the Moors Staffs 115 H3
Bradley Stoke S Glos 45 J3
Bradmore Notts 117 G5
Bradney Somset 30 E3
Bradninch Devon 14 A2
Bradninch Devon 27 L4
Bradnop Staffs 131 K8
Bradnor Green Herefs 79 K4
Bradpole Dorset 15 L4
Bradshaw Bolton 139 L5
Bradshaw Calder 141 G2
Bradshaw Kirk 141 G5
Bradstone Devon 11 M6
Bradwall Green Ches E 130 E7
Bradwell Derbys 132 C3
Bradwell Devon 27 J2
Bradwell Essex 71 K3
Bradwell M Keyn 85 G7
Bradwell Norfk 107 K3
Bradwell Crematorium Staffs 114 D2
Bradwell-on-Sea Essex 72 E5
Bradwell Waterside Essex 72 E5
Bradworthy Devon 26 E8
Brae Highld 263 H7
Brae Shet 281 d4
Braeface Falk 209 K3
Braehead Angus 235 H5
Braehead D & G 173 K4
Braehead S Lans 198 F3
Braemar Abers 243 G5
Braemore Highld 261 L4
Braemore Highld 274 E2
Brae Roy Lodge Highld 240 B5
Braeside Inver 207 L4
Braes of Coul Angus 233 L4
Braes of Enzie Moray 267 H4
Braeswick Ork 275 e2
Braevallich Ag & B 216 E5
Brafferton Darltn 169 H6
Brafferton N York 150 F2
Brafield-on-the-Green Nhants 84 F3
Bragar W Isls 282 f2
Bragbury End Herts 69 H3
Braidwood S Lans 198 D3
Brailsford Derbys 115 L3
Brailsford Green Derbys 115 L3
Brain's Green Gloucs 63 K5
Braintree Essex 71 J2
Braiseworth Suffk 90 D1
Braishfield Hants 34 E6
Braithwaite C Brad 149 J7
Braithwaite Cumb 165 H6
Braithwell Donc 133 K1
Braken Hill Wakefd 142 C4
Bramber W Susx 21 L5
Brambridge Hants 35 G6
Bramcote Notts 116 E4
Bramcote Warwks 99 L5
Bramcote Crematorium Notts 116 E4
Bramdean Hants 35 J5
Bramerton Norfk 106 F2
Bramfield Herts 69 H4
Bramfield Suffk 107 H8
Bramford Suffk 90 D6
Bramhall Stockp 131 H3
Bramham Leeds 150 F7
Bramhope Leeds 150 C7
Bramley Hants 49 G7
Bramley Leeds 141 K1
Bramley Rothm 133 K1
Bramley Surrey 36 F2
Bramley Corner Hants 48 F7
Bramley Green Hants 49 G7
Bramley Head N York 149 L4
Bramling Kent 41 H4
Brampford Speke Devon 13 L3
Brampton Cambs 86 E1
Brampton Cumb 166 F6
Brampton Cumb 178 C6
Brampton Lincs 135 G4
Brampton Norfk 122 E6
Brampton Rothm 142 C7
Brampton Suffk 107 J7

Brampton Abbotts Herefs 63 J2
Brampton Ash Nhants 101 H6
Brampton Bryan Herefs 79 L1
Brampton-en-le-Morthen
    Rothm 133 J2
Bramshall Staffs 115 H5
Bramshaw Hants 34 C4
Bramshill Hants 49 H6
Bramshott Hants 36 C4
Bramwell Somset 31 G5
Branault Highld 237 G6
Brancaster Norfk 121 G3
Brancaster Staithe Norfk 121 H3
Brancepeth Dur 169 G3
Branchill Moray 266 C5
Brand End Lincs 119 L3
Branderburgh Moray 266 E2
Brandesburton E R Yk 153 H6
Brandeston Suffk 90 F3
Brand Green Gloucs 63 L2
Brandis Corner Devon 12 A2
Brandiston Norfk 122 C7
Brandon Dur 169 G3
Brandon Lincs 118 B2
Brandon Nthumb 190 F3
Brandon Suffk 104 F6
Brandon Warwks 99 L8
Brandon Bank Norfk 104 C5
Brandon Creek Norfk 104 C5
Brandon Parva Norfk 106 B2
Brandsby N York 151 J1
Brandy Wharf Lincs 144 C8
Brane Cnwll 2 B5
Bran End Essex 71 G2
Branksome Poole 17 L4
Branksome Park Poole 17 L4
Bransbury Hants 34 F2
Bransby Lincs 135 G4
Branscombe Devon 14 E5
Bransford Worcs 81 H5
Bransgore Hants 18 B4
Bransholme C KuH 144 E1
Bransley Shrops 96 E8
Branson's Cross Worcs 82 C1
Branston Leics 117 L7
Branston Lincs 135 K6
Branston Staffs 115 L7
Branston Booths Lincs 135 L6
Branstone IoW 19 J7
Brant Broughton Lincs 118 B1
Brantham Suffk 90 D8
Branthwaite Cumb 164 E5
Branthwaite Cumb 165 J1
Brantingham E R Yk 144 B2
Branton Donc 143 G7
Branton Nthumb 190 F3
Branton Green N York 150 F3
Branxton Nthumb 202 D5
Brassey Green Ches W 129 M7
Brassington Derbys 115 L1
Brasted Kent 38 D2
Brasted Chart Kent 51 M8
Brathens Abers 244 F4
Bratoft Lincs 137 J6
Brattleby Lincs 135 J3
Bratton Somset 29 G2
Bratton Wilts 46 C8
Bratton Wrekin 96 E1
Bratton Clovelly Devon 12 B4
Bratton Fleming Devon 27 M3
Bratton Seymour Somset 31 L5
Braughing Herts 69 K2
Braughing Friars Herts 70 J3
Braunston Nhants 84 A2
Braunston Rutlnd 101 H2
Braunstone Leics 100 C4
Braunton Devon 27 J4
Brawby N York 162 C7
Brawl Highld 278 D3
Braworth N York 161 H1
Bray W & M 49 L3
Braybrooke Nhants 101 G6
Braydon Wilts 46 F1
Braydon Brook Wilts 64 C5
Braydon Side Wilts 46 E2
Brayford Devon 28 B4
Bray's Hill E Susx 24 B4
Bray Shop Cnwll 11 L7
Braystones Cumb 155 H2
Braythorn N York 150 C6
Brayton N York 142 F2
Braywick W & M 49 L3
Braywoodside W & M. 49 L4
Brazacott Cnwll 11 L4
Breach Kent 41 G6
Breach Kent 53 H6
Breachwood Green Herts 68 F3
Breaden Heath Shrops 113 G4
Breadsall Derbys 116 B4
Breadstone Gloucs 63 L7

Breadward Herefs 79 K4
Breage Cnwll 3 G5
Breakachy Highld 250 E3
Breakspear Crematorium
  Gt Lon 50 D1
Brealangwell Lodge Highld .. 262 F1
Bream Gloucs 63 J6
Breamore Hants 33 L7
Brean Somset 44 C7
Breanais W Isls 282 d4
Breascleit W Isls 282 f3
Breasclete W Isls 282 f3
Breaston Derbys 116 D5
Brechfa Carmth 58 F3
Brechin Angus 234 F3
Breckles Norfk 105 J4
Brecon Powys 61 G2
Bredbury Stockp 131 H2
Brede E Susx 24 E4
Bredenbury Herefs 80 E4
Bredfield Suffk 91 G4
Bredgar Kent 53 J7
Bredhurst Kent 53 G6
Bredon Worcs 81 L7
Bredon's Hardwick Worcs 81 L8
Bredon's Norton Worcs 81 L7
Bredwardine Herefs 79 L6
Breedon on the Hill Leics 116 C7
Breich W Loth 210 C7
Breightmet Bolton 139 L6
Breighton E R Yk 143 H1
Breinton Herefs 80 B7
Bremhill Wilts 46 E4
Bremridge Devon 28 B5
Brenchley Kent 39 H5
Brendon Devon 11 L1
Brendon Devon 28 D1
Brendon Hill Somset 29 J4
Brenfield Ag & B 206 D3
Brenish W Isls 282 d4
Brenkley N u Ty 180 F4
Brent Eleigh Suffk 89 J3
Brentford Gt Lon 50 F3
Brentingby Leics 117 K7
Brent Knoll Somset 30 E1
Brent Mill Devon 7 K3
Brent Pelham Herts 70 B1
Brentwood Essex 70 E8
Brenzett Kent 25 J2
Brenzett Green Kent 25 J2
Brereton Staffs 115 G8
Brereton Green Ches E 130 F6
Brereton Heath Ches E 130 F6
Brereton Hill Staffs 115 G8
Bressay Shet 281 e6
Bressingham Norfk 106 B7
Bressingham Common Norfk .. 106 B7
Bretby Derbys 116 A7
Bretby Crematorium Derbys ... 115 M7
Bretford Warwks 99 L7
Bretforton Worcs 82 C4
Bretherton Lancs 138 F4
Brettabister Shet 281 e5
Brettenham Norfk 105 J6
Brettenham Suffk 89 K4
Bretton Derbys 132 D4
Bretton Flints 129 H7
Brewers End Essex 70 E4
Brewer Street Surrey 51 J8
Brewood Staffs 97 K2
Briantspuddle Dorset 16 F4
Brick End Essex 70 E2
Brickendon Herts 69 J5
Bricket Wood Herts 68 E6
Brick Houses Sheff 132 F3
Brickkiln Green Essex 71 H1
Bricklehampton Worcs 82 A6
Bride IoM 154 f2
Bridekirk Cumb 164 F4
Bridell Pembks 75 L4
Bridestowe Devon 12 C5
Brideswell Abers 255 M4
Bridford Devon 13 J5
Bridge Kent 41 G4
Bridge End Cumb 156 A6
Bridge End Cumb 165 L1
Bridge End Devon 7 K5
Bridge End Dur 168 C3
Bridge End Essex 71 G1
Bridge End Lincs 118 F4
Bridgefoot Cumb 164 E5
Bridge Green Essex 87 K7
Bridgehampton Somset 31 J6
Bridge Hewick N York 150 D2
Bridgehill Dur 180 D8
Bridgehouse Gate N York 149 L3
Bridgemary Hants 19 K3
Bridgemere Ches E 113 M2

Bridgend Abers 255 K4
Bridgend Ag & B 194 B3
Bridgend Ag & B 204 E4
Bridgend Angus 234 E2
Bridgend Brdgnd 42 D5
Bridgend Cerdgn 75 L3
Bridgend Cumb 165 L7
Bridgend D & G 187 G4
Bridgend Devon 7 G5
Bridgend Fife 223 G5
Bridgend Moray 255 H5
Bridgend P & K 221 L2
Bridgend W Loth 210 D4
Bridgend of Lintrathen Angus .. 233 L4
Bridge of Alford Abers 255 L8
Bridge of Allan Stirlg 220 D7
Bridge of Avon Moray 254 C7
Bridge of Avon Moray 254 D4
Bridge of Balgie P & K 231 G6
Bridge of Brewlands Angus 233 J3
Bridge of Brown Highld 254 C7
Bridge of Cally P & K 233 H5
Bridge of Canny Abers 244 E4
Bridge of Craigisla Angus 233 J4
Bridge of Dee D & G 175 J3
Bridge of Don C Aber 245 L2
Bridge of Dulsie Highld 253 H3
Bridge of Dye Abers 244 E6
Bridge of Earn P & K 221 L3
Bridge of Ericht P & K 230 F4
Bridge of Feugh Abers 244 F4
Bridge of Forss Highld 279 J3
Bridge of Gairn Abers 243 K4
Bridge of Gaur P & K 230 F4
Bridge of Marnoch Abers 267 M6
Bridge of Orchy Ag & B 230 B7
Bridge of Tilt P & K 232 C2
Bridge of Tynet Moray 267 H4
Bridge of Walls Shet 281 c6
Bridge of Weir Rens 208 C4
Bridge Reeve Devon 28 B8
Bridgerule Devon 11 K2
Bridges Shrops 95 J4
Bridge Sollers Herefs 80 A6
Bridge Street Suffk 89 H5
Bridgetown Cnwll 11 L5
Bridgetown Somset 29 G4
Bridge Trafford Ches W 129 K5
Bridge Yate S Glos 45 K4
Bridgham Norfk 105 J6
Bridgnorth Shrops 97 G5
Bridgwater Somset 30 D3
Bridlington E R Yk 153 K3
Bridport Dorset 15 K4
Bridstow Herefs 63 H2
Brierfield Lancs 148 E8
Brierley Barns 142 B5
Brierley Gloucs 63 J4
Brierley Herefs 80 C4
Brierley Hill Dudley 97 L6
Brierton Hartpl 170 B5
Briery Cumb 165 J6
Brigg N Linc 144 C6
Briggate Norfk 123 G6
Briggswath N York 162 F1
Brigham Cumb 164 E4
Brigham Cumb 165 J6
Brigham E R Yk 153 H5
Brighouse Calder 141 J3
Brighstone IoW 19 G7
Brightgate Derbys 132 E7
Brighthampton Oxon 66 A6
Brightholmlee Sheff 132 F1
Brightley Devon 12 E3
Brightling E Susx 24 C3
Brightlingsea Essex 73 G4
Brighton Br & H 22 D6
Brighton Cnwll 4 E4
Brighton le Sands Sefton 138 C7
Brightons Falk 210 B3
Brightwalton W Berk 48 B3
Brightwalton Green W Berk 48 B3
Brightwalton Holt W Berk 48 B3
Brightwell Suffk 90 F6
Brightwell Baldwin Oxon 67 G8
Brightwell-cum-Sotwell Oxon 48 E1
Brightwell Upperton Oxon 67 G8
Brignall Dur 168 D8
Brig o'Turk Stirlg 219 J6
Brigsley NE Lin 145 H7
Brigsteer Cumb 157 G5
Brigstock Nhants 101 L6
Brill Bucks 67 G4
Brill Cnwll 3 J5
Brilley Herefs 79 J5
Brimfield Herefs 80 C2
Brimfield Cross Herefs 80 C2
Brimington Derbys 133 H5
Brimley Devon 13 J7
Brimpsfield Gloucs 64 D4

Brimpton W Berk 48 E6
Brimpton Common W Berk 48 E6
Brimscombe Gloucs 64 C6
Brimstage Wirral 129 G3
Brind E R Yk 143 J2
Brindham Somset 31 H3
Brindister Shet 281 c5
Brindle Lancs 139 J5
Brineton Staffs 97 H1
Bringhurst Leics 101 J5
Bringsty Common Herefs 81 G4
Brington Cambs 102 B8
Briningham Norfk 122 A5
Brinkely Notts 117 J1
Brinkhill Lincs 137 G5
Brinkley Cambs 88 C4
Brinklow Warwks 99 L7
Brinkworth Wilts 46 E2
Brinscall Lancs 139 J3
Brinscombe Somset 44 E8
Brinsea N Som 44 F6
Brinsley Notts 116 D2
Brinsop Herefs 80 B6
Brinsworth Rothm 133 H2
Brinton Norfk 122 A4
Brinyan Ork 275 c3
Brisco Cumb 178 A8
Brisley Norfk 121 L7
Brislington Bristl 45 J5
Brissenden Green Kent 40 B7
Bristol Bristl 45 H4
Briston Norfk 122 B5
Brisworthy Devon 7 G2
Britannia Lancs 140 C3
Britford Wilts 33 L5
Brithdir Caerph 61 J6
Brithdir Gwynd 110 E7
British Legion Village Kent 52 F7
Briton Ferry Neath 57 K6
Britwell Salome Oxon 67 G8
Brixham Torbay 8 D4
Brixton Devon 7 G4
Brixton Gt Lon 51 J4
Brixton Deverill Wilts 32 E3
Brixworth Nhants 84 E1
Brize Norton Oxon 65 L5
Broad Alley Worcs 81 K2
Broad Blunsdon Swindn 47 H1
Broadbottom Tamesd 131 K1
Broadbridge W Susx 20 D6
Broadbridge Heath W Susx 37 H4
Broad Campden Gloucs 82 E7
Broad Carr Calder 141 H4
Broad Chalke Wilts 33 H5
Broad Clough Lancs 140 C3
Broadclyst Devon 14 A3
Broadfield Inver 208 B4
Broadfield Pembks 55 K6
Broadford Highld 247 K4
Broad Ford Kent 39 H5
Broadford Bridge W Susx 37 G6
Broadgairhill Border 187 K4
Broadgrass Green Suffk 89 K3
Broad Green Cambs 88 D3
Broad Green Essex 72 C2
Broad Green Worcs 81 H4
Broad Green Worcs 82 A1
Broadhaugh Border 202 D2
Broad Haven Pembks 54 D4
Broadheath Traffd 130 E2
Broadheath Worcs 80 F2
Broadhembury Devon 14 C2
Broadhempston Devon 8 B2
Broad Hill Cambs 104 B8
Broad Hinton Wilts 47 G4
Broadholme Lincs 135 H5
Broadland Row E Susx 24 F3
Broadlay Carmth 56 C3
Broad Layings Hants 48 B6
Broadley Essex 70 B5
Broadley Lancs 140 C4
Broadley Moray 267 H4
Broadley Common Essex 70 B5
Broad Marston Worcs 82 D6
Broadmayne Dorset 16 D5
Broad Meadow Staffs 114 C2
Broadmere Hants 35 J2
Broadmoor Gloucs 63 J4
Broadmoor Pembks 55 J5
Broadnymett Devon 13 G2
Broad Oak Cumb 155 K4
Broadoak Dorset 15 K3
Broad Oak E Susx 23 K3
Broad Oak E Susx 24 E3
Broadoak Gloucs 63 K4
Broad Oak Hants 49 H8
Broad Oak Herefs 62 F3
Broad Oak Kent 41 G3
Broad Oak St Hel 139 G8

Broadoak Wrexhm 129 J7
Broad Road Suffk 106 F8
Broad's Green Essex 71 G4
Broadstairs Kent 41 L2
Broadstone Mons 63 G6
Broadstone Poole 17 K3
Broadstone Shrops 96 C5
Broad Street E Susx 24 F4
Broad Street Essex 70 E4
Broad Street Kent 39 L2
Broad Street Kent 40 F7
Broad Street Medway 53 G4
Broad Street Wilts 47 G7
Broad Street Green Essex 71 L5
Broad Town Wilts 47 G3
Broadwas Worcs 81 H4
Broadwater Herts 69 H3
Broadwater W Susx 21 K6
Broadwaters Worcs 97 J7
Broadway Carmth 56 B3
Broadway Carmth 56 C3
Broadway Pembks 54 E4
Broadway Somset 30 D7
Broadway Suffk 107 H7
Broadway Worcs 82 C7
Broadwell Gloucs 63 H5
Broadwell Gloucs 65 J2
Broadwell Oxon 65 K6
Broadwell Warwks 83 K2
Broadwey Dorset 16 C6
Broadwindsor Dorset 15 K2
Broadwood Kelly Devon 12 E2
Broadwoodwidger Devon 12 A5
Brobury Herefs 79 L6
Brochel Highld 259 K7
Brochroy Ag & B 216 F1
Brock Lancs 147 K7
Brockamin Worcs 81 H4
Brockbridge Hants 35 J7
Brockdish Norfk 106 E7
Brockencote Worcs 97 K8
Brockenhurst Hants 18 D3
Brocketsbrae S Lans 198 D5
Brockford Green Suffk 90 D2
Brockford Street Suffk 90 D2
Brockhall Nhants 84 C3
Brockham Surrey 37 J1
Brockhampton Gloucs 64 D2
Brockhampton Gloucs 64 F3
Brockhampton Hants 20 B5
Brockhampton Herefs 63 H1
Brockhampton Green Dorset 16 D2
Brockholes Kirk 141 J5
Brockhurst Derbys 133 G6
Brockhurst Warwks 100 A6
Brocklebank Cumb 165 J2
Brocklesby Lincs 144 E5
Brockley N Som 44 F5
Brockley Suffk 89 G1
Brockley Green Suffk 88 E6
Brockley Green Suffk 89 G4
Brockleymoor Cumb 166 C3
Brockmoor Dudley 97 K5
Brockscombe Devon 12 B4
Brock's Green Hants 48 D6
Brockton Shrops 95 H3
Brockton Shrops 95 H6
Brockton Shrops 96 D4
Brockton Shrops 97 G3
Brockton Staffs 114 C5
Brockweir Gloucs 63 G6
Brockwood Park Hants 35 K5
Brockworth Gloucs 64 C4
Brocton Cnwll 5 G1
Brocton Staffs 114 F7
Brodick N Ayrs 195 G4
Brodie Moray 264 F8
Brodsworth Donc 142 D6
Brogaig Highld 259 H3
Brogborough C Beds 85 J7
Brokenborough Wilts 46 D1
Broken Cross Ches E 131 H5
Broken Cross Ches W 130 D5
Brokerswood Wilts 46 B8
Bromborough Wirral 129 H3
Brome Suffk 106 C8
Brome Street Suffk 106 C8
Bromeswell Suffk 91 G5
Bromfield Cumb 165 G1
Bromfield Shrops 96 B8
Bromham Bed 85 K5
Bromham Wilts 46 D6
Bromley Barns 141 M7
Bromley Dudley 97 K5
Bromley Gt Lon 51 K4
Bromley Shrops 97 G4
Bromley Common Gt Lon 51 L5
Bromley Cross Essex 72 E2
Bromley Green Kent 40 C8
Bromlow Shrops 95 H3

Place	County	Page	Grid
Brompton Medway		53	G5
Brompton N York		160	E3
Brompton-by-Sawdon N York		163	G6
Brompton-on-Swale N York		160	B3
Brompton Ralph Somset		29	K4
Brompton Regis Somset		29	G4
Bromsash Herefs		63	J2
Bromsberrow Gloucs		81	G8
Bromsberrow Heath Gloucs		81	G8
Bromsgrove Worcs		81	M1
Bromstead Heath Staffs		114	B8
Bromyard Herefs		80	F4
Bromyard Downs Herefs		80	F4
Bronaber Gwynd		110	D5
Bronant Cerdgn		77	H2
Broncroft Shrops		96	C6
Brongest Cerdgn		76	B6
Bronington Wrexhm		113	H3
Bronllys Powys		79	H8
Bronwydd Carmth		58	D4
Bronydd Powys		79	J6
Bronygarth Shrops		112	C4
Bron-y-Nant Crematorium Conwy		127	G4
Brook Carmth		56	A3
Brook Hants		34	C8
Brook Hants		34	D5
Brook IoW		18	F6
Brook Kent		40	E6
Brook Surrey		36	D3
Brook Surrey		37	G2
Brooke Norfk		106	F3
Brooke Rutlnd		101	J2
Brookenby Lincs		145	G8
Brook End Bed		86	B3
Brook End C Beds		86	D5
Brook End Cambs		86	B1
Brook End M Keyn		85	H6
Brookfield Rens		208	C6
Brookhampton Oxon		66	F7
Brookhampton Somset		31	K5
Brook Hill Hants		34	C7
Brook House Denbgs		128	C6
Brookhouse Lancs		147	K3
Brookhouse Rothm		133	K2
Brookhouse Green Ches E		130	F7
Brookhouses Derbys		131	K2
Brookland Kent		25	J2
Brooklands Traffd		130	F2
Brookmans Park Herts		69	H6
Brooks Powys		94	E3
Brooksby Leics		117	H8
Brooks End Kent		41	J2
Brooks Green W Susx		37	H6
Brook Street Essex		70	E8
Brook Street Kent		40	B8
Brook Street Suffk		89	G5
Brook Street W Susx		22	D2
Brookthorpe Gloucs		64	B4
Brookville Norfk		104	E4
Brookwood Surrey		50	B7
Broom C Beds		86	D6
Broom Rothm		133	J1
Broom Warwks		82	C4
Broome Norfk		107	G5
Broome Shrops		95	K7
Broome Worcs		97	K7
Broomedge Warrtn		130	D3
Broome Park Nthumb		191	G4
Broomer's Corner W Susx		21	K3
Broomershill W Susx		21	H3
Broomfield Essex		71	H5
Broomfield Kent		39	L3
Broomfield Kent		41	G2
Broomfield Somset		30	B4
Broomfields Shrops		112	F7
Broomfleet E R Yk		143	M2
Broom Green Norfk		121	L6
Broomhall W & M		50	B5
Broomhaugh Nthumb		180	B6
Broom Hill Barns		142	C7
Broom Hill Dorset		17	K2
Broom Hill Notts		116	F2
Broomhill Nthumb		191	K6
Broom Hill Worcs		97	L8
Broomhill Green Ches E		113	K2
Broomley Nthumb		180	C6
Broompark Dur		169	H2
Broom's Green Gloucs		81	G8
Broomsthorpe Norfk		121	J6
Broom Street Kent		40	D3
Brora Highld		274	B7
Broseley Shrops		96	F3
Brotherhouse Bar Lincs		119	J8
Brotherlee Dur		167	L3
Brothertoft Lincs		119	J2
Brotherton N York		142	D3
Brotton R & Cl		170	F6
Broubster Highld		279	J4
Brough Cumb		167	J7
Brough Derbys		132	D3
Brough E R Yk		144	B2
Brough Highld		280	B2
Brough Notts		135	G7
Brough Shet		281	f5
Broughall Shrops		113	J3
Brough Lodge Shet		281	f3
Brough Sowerby Cumb		167	J8
Broughton Border		199	K6
Broughton Bucks		67	K4
Broughton Cambs		102	F7
Broughton Flints		129	H7
Broughton Hants		34	C1
Broughton Lancs		139	G1
Broughton M Keyn		85	H7
Broughton N Linc		144	B6
Broughton N York		149	G5
Broughton N York		162	D8
Broughton Nhants		101	H8
Broughton Oxon		83	K7
Broughton Salfd		140	B7
Broughton Staffs		114	B5
Broughton V Glam		42	D7
Broughton Astley Leics		100	C5
Broughton Beck Cumb		156	C6
Broughton Gifford Wilts		46	C6
Broughton Green Worcs		81	M3
Broughton Hackett Worcs		81	L4
Broughton-in-Furness Cumb		156	B5
Broughton Mains D & G		174	C6
Broughton Mills Cumb		156	B4
Broughton Moor Cumb		164	E4
Broughton Poggs Oxon		65	K6
Broughton Tower Cumb		156	B5
Broughty Ferry C Dund		223	H1
Brow End Cumb		156	C7
Brownber Cumb		158	B2
Brown Candover Hants		35	J3
Brown Edge Lancs		138	D5
Brown Edge Staffs		114	E1
Brown Heath Ches W		129	K6
Brownheath Shrops		113	G5
Brownhill Abers		256	F4
Brownhills Fife		223	J4
Brownhills Wsall		98	D2
Brownieside Nthumb		191	H2
Browninghill Green Hants		48	E7
Brown Lees Staffs		131	G8
Brownlow Heath Ches E		131	G7
Brownrigg Cumb		164	D6
Brownrigg Cumb		177	G8
Brownsea Island Dorset		17	K5
Brown's Green Birm		98	D5
Brownsham Devon		26	E5
Browns Hill Gloucs		64	C6
Brownsover Warwks		100	B7
Brownston Devon		7	K4
Brown Street Suffk		90	C3
Brow-of-the-Hill Norfk		120	E7
Browston Green Norfk		107	K3
Broxa N York		163	G4
Broxbourne Herts		69	K5
Broxburn E Loth		212	F3
Broxburn W Loth		210	E4
Broxfield Nthumb		191	J3
Broxted Essex		70	E2
Broxton Ches W		113	H1
Broyle Side E Susx		23	G4
Bruan Highld		280	D8
Bruar P & K		232	B2
Brucefield Highld		264	E3
Bruchag Ag & B		207	J7
Bruera Ches W		129	K7
Bruern Abbey Oxon		65	K3
Bruichladdich Ag & B		204	C4
Bruisyard Suffk		91	H2
Bruisyard Street Suffk		91	H2
Brumby N Linc		143	M6
Brund Staffs		132	B7
Brundall Norfk		107	G2
Brundish Suffk		91	G1
Brundish Street Suffk		91	G1
Brunery Highld		237	L6
Brunnion Cnwll		2	D4
Brunslow Shrops		95	J6
Brunswick Village N u Ty		180	F4
Bruntcliffe Leeds		141	L2
Brunthwaite C Brad		149	J6
Bruntingthorpe Leics		100	D5
Brunton Fife		222	F4
Brunton Nthumb		191	J1
Brunton Wilts		47	K7
Brushford Devon		12	F1
Brushford Somset		29	G4
Bruton Somset		31	L4
Bryan's Green Worcs		81	K2
Bryanston Dorset		17	G1
Bryant's Bottom Bucks		67	L7
Brydekirk D & G		177	G5
Bryher IoS		10	b2
Brymbo Wrexhm		112	D1
Brympton Somset		31	H7
Bryn Carmth		57	G3
Bryn Ches W		130	B5
Bryn Neath		42	B3
Bryn Shrops		95	H6
Bryn Wigan		139	H7
Brynamman Carmth		59	K6
Brynberian Pembks		75	J5
Brynbryddan Neath		57	L6
Bryn-bwbach Gwynd		110	B4
Bryncae Rhondd		42	F5
Bryncethin Brdgnd		42	D5
Bryncir Gwynd		109	H3
Bryn-coch Neath		57	K5
Bryncroes Gwynd		108	C5
Bryncrug Gwynd		92	D3
Bryn Du IoA		124	F5
Bryn-Eden Gwynd		110	D5
Bryneglwys Denbgs		112	A2
Brynfields Wrexhm		112	D3
Brynford Flints		128	E5
Bryn Gates Wigan		139	J7
Bryn Golau Rhondd		42	F4
Bryngwran IoA		124	F4
Bryngwyn Mons		62	D5
Bryngwyn Powys		79	H5
Bryn-Henllan Pembks		75	G4
Brynhoffnant Cerdgn		76	B3
Bryning Lancs		138	E2
Brynithel Blae G		61	K6
Brynmawr Blae G		61	J5
Bryn-mawr Gwynd		108	C5
Brynmenyn Brdgnd		42	D5
Brynmill Swans		57	H6
Brynna Rhondd		42	F5
Bryn-penarth Powys		94	D3
Brynrefail Gwynd		125	K7
Brynrefail IoA		125	H2
Brynsadler Rhondd		42	F5
Bryn Saith Marchog Denbgs		111	L2
Brynsiencyn IoA		125	H6
Brynteg IoA		125	J3
Bryn-y-bal Flints		128	F6
Bryn-y-Maen Conwy		127	G4
Bryn-yr-Eos Wrexhm		112	D3
Bualintur Highld		246	F4
Buarth-draw Flints		128	E4
Bubbenhall Warwks		83	J1
Bubwith E R Yk		151	M8
Buccleuch Border		188	B3
Buchanan Smithy Stirlg		208	D1
Buchanhaven Abers		269	L6
Buchanty P & K		221	G2
Buchany Stirlg		220	C6
Buchlyvie Stirlg		219	J8
Buckabank Cumb		165	L1
Buckden Cambs		86	D2
Buckden N York		159	G7
Buckenham Norfk		107	G2
Buckerell Devon		14	D3
Buckfast Devon		7	L2
Buckfastleigh Devon		7	L2
Buckhaven Fife		222	F7
Buckholt Mons		63	G4
Buckhorn Devon		11	M3
Buckhorn Weston Dorset		32	C6
Buckhurst Hill Essex		69	L8
Buckie Moray		267	J3
Buckingham Bucks		84	D8
Buckland Bucks		67	L4
Buckland Devon		7	K6
Buckland Gloucs		82	C8
Buckland Hants		18	E4
Buckland Herts		87	G8
Buckland Kent		41	J6
Buckland Oxon		65	M7
Buckland Surrey		37	K1
Buckland Brewer Devon		27	G6
Buckland Common Bucks		68	A5
Buckland Dinham Somset		32	C1
Buckland Filleigh Devon		12	B1
Buckland in the Moor Devon		13	G7
Buckland Monachorum Devon		6	F1
Buckland Newton Dorset		16	D2
Buckland Ripers Dorset		16	C5
Buckland St Mary Somset		30	C8
Buckland-Tout-Saints Devon		7	L5
Bucklebury W Berk		48	E5
Bucklers Hard Hants		18	E4
Bucklesham Suffk		90	F6
Buckley Flints		129	G7
Buckley Green Warwks		82	E2
Bucklow Hill Ches E		130	E3
Buckminster Leics		118	A7
Bucknall C Stke		114	E2
Bucknall Lincs		136	C6
Bucknell Oxon		66	E2
Bucknell Shrops		95	J8
Buckpool Moray		267	H…
Bucksburn C Aber		245	K…
Buck's Cross Devon		26	F…
Bucks Green W Susx		37	H…
Buckshaw Village Lancs		139	H…
Bucks Hill Herts		68	B…
Bucks Horn Oak Hants		36	M…
Buck's Mills Devon		26	F…
Buckton E R Yk		153	K…
Buckton Herefs		95	J…
Buckton Nthumb		203	H…
Buckworth Cambs		102	C…
Budby Notts		134	C…
Buddileigh Staffs		114	A…
Bude Cnwll		11	H…
Budge's Shop Cnwll		6	F…
Budlake Devon		14	A…
Budle Nthumb		203	H…
Budleigh Salterton Devon		14	B…
Budlett's Common E Susx		23	G…
Budock Water Cnwll		3	K…
Buerton Ches E		113	L…
Bugbrooke Nhants		84	D…
Bugford Devon		8	A…
Buglawton Ches E		131	G…
Bugle Cnwll		5	G…
Bugley Dorset		32	C…
Bugthorpe E R Yk		152	B…
Buildwas Shrops		96	F…
Builth Road Powys		78	D…
Builth Wells Powys		78	D…
Bulbourne Herts		68	A…
Bulbridge Wilts		33	J…
Bulby Lincs		118	C…
Bulford Wilts		33	L…
Bulford Camp Wilts		33	L…
Bulkeley Ches E		113	J…
Bulkington Warwks		99	K…
Bulkington Wilts		46	D…
Bulkworthy Devon		27	G…
Bullamoor N York		160	F…
Bull Bay IoA		125	F…
Bullbridge Derbys		116	B…
Bullbrook Br For		49	L…
Bullen's Green Herts		69	H…
Bulley Gloucs		63	M…
Bullgill Cumb		164	E…
Bullinghope Herefs		80	C…
Bullington Hants		35	H…
Bullington Lincs		136	A…
Bullockstone Kent		41	G…
Bull's Green Herts		69	H…
Bull's Green Norfk		107	J…
Bulmer Essex		89	J…
Bulmer N York		151	J…
Bulmer Tye Essex		89	G…
Bulphan Thurr		52	D…
Bulstone Devon		14	E…
Bulstrode Herts		68	C…
Bulverhythe E Susx		24	D…
Bulwark Abers		257	G…
Bulwell C Nott		116	F…
Bulwick Nhants		101	J…
Bumble's Green Essex		69	L…
Bunacaimb Highld		237	J…
Bunarkaig Highld		239	K…
Bunbury Ches E		130	A…
Bunbury Heath Ches E		130	A…
Bunchrew Highld		251	H…
Buncton W Susx		21	K…
Bundalloch Highld		238	E…
Bunessan Ag & B		226	D…
Bungay Suffk		107	G…
Bunker's Hill Lincs		119	J…
Bunnahabhain Ag & B		204	F…
Bunny Notts		117	G…
Buntait Highld		250	C…
Buntingford Herts		69	K…
Bunwell Norfk		106	C…
Bunwell Hill Norfk		106	C…
Bupton Derbys		115	K…
Burbage Derbys		131	K…
Burbage Leics		99	L…
Burbage Wilts		47	K…
Burcher Herefs		79	J…
Burchett's Green E Susx		39	G…
Burchett's Green W & M		49	L…
Burcombe Wilts		33	J…
Burcot Oxon		66	E…
Burcot Worcs		82	A…
Burcote Shrops		97	K…
Burcott Bucks		67	K…
Burcott Bucks		67	L…
Burdale N York		152	D…
Bures Essex		89	H…
Burford Oxon		65	K…
Burford Shrops		80	D…
Burg Ag & B		226	C…
Burgate Suffk		106	B…
Burgates Hants		36	A…

Burge End - Caldecotte 299

Burge End Herts 68 F1
Burgess Hill W Susx 22 E3
Burgh Suffk 90 F5
Burgh by Sands Cumb 177 K7
Burgh Castle Norfk 107 K2
Burghclere Hants 48 C6
Burghead Moray 266 C2
Burghfield W Berk 49 G5
Burghfield Common W Berk 49 G5
Burgh Heath Surrey 51 H7
Burgh Hill E Susx 24 C2
Burghill Herefs 80 B6
Burgh Island Devon 7 J6
Burgh le Marsh Lincs 137 J6
Burgh next Aylsham Norfk 122 E6
Burgh on Bain Lincs 136 D2
Burgh St Margaret Norfk 123 J8
Burgh St Peter Norfk 107 K5
Burghwallis Donc 142 E5
Burham Kent 52 F6
Buriton Hants 20 B3
Burland Ches E 113 K1
Burlawn Cnwll 10 D8
Burleigh Gloucs 64 C6
Burlescombe Devon 29 K7
Burleston Dorset 16 E4
Burlestone Devon 8 B5
Burley Hants 18 C3
Burley Rutlnd 101 J1
Burley Shrops 96 B7
Burleydam Ches E 113 K3
Burley Gate Herefs 80 E6
Burley in Wharfedale C Brad 149 L6
Burley Lawn Hants 18 C3
Burley Street Hants 18 B3
Burley Wood Head C Brad 149 L7
Burlingham Green Norfk 107 H1
Burlingjobb Powys 79 J4
Burlington Shrops 97 H1
Burlton Shrops 113 G6
Burmarsh Kent 25 L1
Burmington Warwks 83 G7
Burn N York 142 F2
Burnage Manch 131 G1
Burnaston Derbys 115 M5
Burnbanks Cumb 166 C7
Burnbrae N Lans 210 A7
Burnby E R Yk 152 C6
Burn Cross Sheff 142 A8
Burndell W Susx 21 G6
Burnden Bolton 139 L6
Burnedge Rochdl 140 D5
Burneside Cumb 157 H3
Burneston N York 160 D5
Burnett BaNES 45 K6
Burnfoot Border 188 C4
Burnfoot Border 188 F3
Burnfoot D & G 177 K1
Burnfoot D & G 186 E7
Burnfoot D & G 188 C6
Burnfoot P & K 221 H6
Burnham Bucks 50 A3
Burnham N Linc 144 D4
Burnham Deepdale Norfk 121 H3
Burnham Green Herts 69 H4
Burnham Market Norfk 121 H3
Burnham Norton Norfk 121 H3
Burnham-on-Crouch Essex 72 D7
Burnham-on-Sea Somset 30 D1
Burnham Overy Norfk 121 J3
Burnham Overy Staithe Norfk 121 J3
Burnham Thorpe Norfk 121 J3
Burnhaven Abers 257 L3
Burnhead D & G 186 C7
Burnhervie Abers 256 C7
Burnhill Green Staffs 97 H3
Burnhope Dur 169 G1
Burnhouse N Ayrs 196 D1
Burniston N York 163 H4
Burnley Lancs 140 C1
Burnley Crematorium Lancs 140 B2
Burnmouth Border 213 L6
Burn Naze Lancs 147 G7
Burn of Cambus Stirlg 220 C6
Burnopfield Dur 180 E7
Burnrigg Cumb 178 C7
Burnsall N York 149 J3
Burnside Angus 234 C3
Burnside Angus 234 D5
Burnside Fife 222 B5
Burnside Moray 266 D2
Burnside W Loth 210 E4
Burnside of Duntrune Angus 234 C8
Burntcommon Surrey 50 D8
Burntheath Derbys 115 L5
Burnt Heath Essex 72 F2
Burnt Hill W Berk 48 E4
Burnthouse Cnwll 3 K4
Burnt Houses Dur 168 E6
Burntisland Fife 211 H2
Burnt Oak E Susx 23 H2
Burntwood Staffs 98 D2
Burntwood Green Staffs 98 D2
Burnt Yates N York 150 C4
Burnworthy Somset 30 B7
Burpham Surrey 50 C8
Burpham W Susx 21 H5
Burradon N Tyne 181 G4
Burradon Nthumb 190 D5
Burrafirth Shet 281 f1
Burras Cnwll 3 H4
Burraton Cnwll 6 E2
Burravoe Shet 281 e4
Burrells Cumb 166 F7
Burrelton P & K 233 J7
Burridge Devon 15 H2
Burridge Devon 27 K4
Burridge Hants 19 J2
Burrill N York 160 C5
Burringham N Linc 143 L6
Burrington Devon 27 L7
Burrington Herefs 80 B1
Burrington N Som 44 F7
Burrough End Cambs 88 C4
Burrough Green Cambs 88 C4
Burrough on the Hill Leics 101 G1
Burrow Lancs 157 K7
Burrow Somset 29 G2
Burrow Bridge Somset 30 E5
Burrowhill Surrey 50 B6
Burrows Cross Surrey 37 G2
Burry Swans 56 E6
Burry Green Swans 56 E6
Burry Port Carmth 56 E5
Burscough Lancs 138 E5
Burscough Bridge Lancs 138 F5
Bursea E R Yk 143 K1
Burshill E R Yk 153 H6
Bursledon Hants 19 H2
Burslem C Stke 114 D2
Burstall Suffk 90 C6
Burstock Dorset 15 K2
Burston Norfk 106 C6
Burston Staffs 114 E5
Burstow Surrey 37 M3
Burstwick E R Yk 145 G2
Burtersett N York 158 F5
Burtholme Cumb 178 D6
Burthorpe Green Suffk 88 F2
Burthwaite Cumb 165 M1
Burthy Cnwll 4 E4
Burtle Hill Somset 30 F2
Burtoft Lincs 119 J4
Burton Ches W 129 H5
Burton Ches W 129 L7
Burton Dorset 16 D4
Burton Dorset 18 B5
Burton Lincs 135 J5
Burton Nthumb 203 K6
Burton Pembks 55 G5
Burton Somset 30 B2
Burton Somset 31 H8
Burton Wilts 32 D4
Burton Wilts 46 B3
Burton Agnes E R Yk 153 H3
Burton Bradstock Dorset 15 L5
Burton Coggles Lincs 118 C6
Burton Dassett Warwks 83 J5
Burton End Essex 70 D2
Burton End Suffk 88 D6
Burton Fleming E R Yk 153 H2
Burton Green Warwks 99 H8
Burton Green Wrexhm 129 H7
Burton Hastings Warwks 99 L5
Burton-in-Kendal Cumb 157 H7
Burton in Lonsdale N York 148 A2
Burton Joyce Notts 117 H3
Burton Latimer Nhants 101 K8
Burton Lazars Leics 117 K8
Burton Leonard N York 150 D3
Burton on the Wolds Leics 117 G7
Burton Overy Leics 100 E4
Burton Pedwardine Lincs 118 F3
Burton Pidsea E R Yk 145 H2
Burton Salmon N York 142 D2
Burton's Green Essex 71 K2
Burton upon Stather N Linc 143 L4
Burton upon Trent Staffs 115 L6
Burton Waters Lincs 135 J5
Burtonwood Warrtn 130 A1
Burwardsley Ches W 129 L8
Burwarton Shrops 96 E6
Burwash E Susx 24 B2
Burwash Common E Susx 23 L3
Burwash Weald E Susx 23 L3
Burwell Cambs 88 B2
Burwell Lincs 137 G4
Burwen IoA 125 G1
Burwick Ork 275 c6
Bury Bury 140 B5
Bury Cambs 102 F6
Bury Somset 29 G5
Bury W Susx 21 G4
Bury End C Beds 86 C8
Bury Green Herts 70 C3
Bury St Edmunds Suffk 89 G2
Burythorpe N York 152 B3
Busby E Rens 208 F7
Busby Stoop N York 160 E6
Buscot Oxon 65 J7
Bush Abers 235 J2
Bush Cnwll 11 J1
Bush Bank Herefs 80 B5
Bushbury Wolves 97 L3
Bushbury Crematorium Wolves 97 L3
Bushby Leics 100 E3
Bushey Herts 68 E8
Bushey Heath Herts 68 F8
Bush Green Norfk 106 E6
Bush Green Suffk 89 H4
Bush Hill Park Gt Lon 69 J7
Bushley Worcs 81 K8
Bushley Green Worcs 81 K8
Bushmead Bed 86 C3
Bushmoor Shrops 95 K6
Bushton Wilts 46 F3
Busk Cumb 166 E2
Buslingthorpe Lincs 135 M3
Bussage Gloucs 64 C6
Bussex Somset 30 E4
Butcher's Cross E Susx 23 J2
Butcombe N Som 45 G6
Bute Ag & B 207 G5
Butleigh Somset 31 H4
Butleigh Wootton Somset 31 H4
Butler's Cross Bucks 67 K5
Butler's Hill Notts 116 F2
Butlers Marston Warwks 83 H5
Butley Suffk 91 J5
Butley High Corner Suffk 91 J5
Buttercrambe N York 151 M4
Butterdean Border 213 H6
Butterknowle Dur 168 E5
Butterleigh Devon 14 A1
Butterley Derbys 116 C1
Buttermere Cumb 165 G7
Buttermere Wilts 47 M6
Butters Green Staffs 114 C2
Buttershaw C Brad 141 H2
Butterstone P & K 233 G6
Butterton Staffs 114 C3
Butterton Staffs 131 L8
Butterwick Dur 169 K5
Butterwick Lincs 119 L3
Butterwick N York 152 F2
Butterwick N York 162 C7
Butt Green Ches E 113 L1
Buttington Powys 95 G2
Buttonbridge Shrops 97 G7
Buttonoak Shrops 97 G7
Buttsash Hants 19 G2
Buttsbear Cross Cnwll 11 K2
Butt's Green Essex 71 J6
Buxhall Suffk 89 K4
Buxhall Fen Street Suffk 89 K3
Buxted E Susx 23 H3
Buxton Derbys 131 L5
Buxton Norfk 122 E7
Buxton Heath Norfk 122 D7
Bwlch Powys 61 J3
Bwlchgwyn Wrexhm 112 C1
Bwlchllan Cerdgn 77 G3
Bwlchnewydd Carmth 58 C4
Bwlchtocyn Gwynd 108 E6
Bwlch-y-cibau Powys 112 B8
Bwlch-y-Ddar Powys 112 B7
Bwlchyfadfa Cerdgn 76 D5
Bwlch-y-ffridd Powys 94 C4
Bwlch-y-groes Pembks 75 M5
Bwlchymyrdd Swans 57 G5
Bwlch-y-sarnau Powys 94 B8
Byermoor Gatesd 180 F7
Byers Green Dur 169 G4
Byfield Nhants 83 M4
Byfleet Surrey 50 D6
Byford Herefs 79 M6
Bygrave Herts 86 F7
Byker N u Ty 181 G6
Byland Abbey N York 161 J6
Bylchau Conwy 127 K7
Byley Ches W 130 E6
Bynea Carmth 57 G5
Byrness Nthumb 189 K5
Bystock Devon 14 B6
Bythorn Cambs 102 B8
Byton Herefs 79 L2
Bywell Nthumb 180 C6
Byworth W Susx 36 E6

C

Cabbacott Devon 27 G6
Cabourne Lincs 144 E7
Cabrach Ag & B 205 H3
Cabrach Moray 255 H6
Cabus Lancs 147 J6
Cackle Street E Susx 23 G2
Cackle Street E Susx 24 C3
Cackle Street E Susx 24 E3
Cadbury Devon 13 L2
Cadbury Barton Devon 28 B7
Cadder E Duns 209 G4
Caddington C Beds 68 D3
Caddonfoot Border 200 F6
Cadeby Donc 142 E7
Cadeby Leics 99 L3
Cadeleigh Devon 13 L1
Cade Street E Susx 23 K3
Cadgwith Cnwll 3 J8
Cadham Fife 222 D6
Cadishead Salfd 130 D1
Cadle Swans 57 H5
Cadley Lancs 139 G2
Cadley Wilts 47 J5
Cadley Wilts 47 K8
Cadmore End Bucks 67 J8
Cadnam Hants 34 C8
Cadney N Linc 144 C7
Cadole Flints 128 E7
Cadoxton V Glam 43 H7
Cadoxton Juxta-Neath Neath 57 L5
Cadwst Denbgs 111 K4
Caeathro Gwynd 125 J7
Caehopkin Powys 59 M6
Caenby Lincs 135 K2
Caeo Carmth 77 J7
Caerau Brdgnd 42 C3
Caerau Cardif 43 H6
Cae'r-bont Powys 59 M6
Cae'r bryn Carmth 59 H6
Caerdeon Gwynd 110 C7
Caer Farchell Pembks 74 C6
Caergeiliog IoA 124 E4
Caergwrle Flints 129 G8
Caerhun Conwy 126 F5
Caerlanrig Border 188 C5
Caerleon Newpt 44 D1
Caernarfon Gwynd 125 H7
Caerphilly Caerph 43 J4
Caersws Powys 94 B5
Caerwedros Cerdgn 76 C4
Caerwent Mons 44 F1
Caerwys Flints 128 D5
Caerynwch Gwynd 110 E8
Caggle Street Mons 62 D4
Caim IoA 126 C3
Cairinis W Isls 283 c8
Cairnbaan Ag & B 206 C1
Cairnbulg Abers 269 J3
Cairncross Border 213 K6
Cairncurran Inver 208 A5
Cairndow Ag & B 217 K5
Cairneyhill Fife 210 D2
Cairngarroch D & G 172 C5
Cairnie Abers 255 K3
Cairnorrie Abers 256 F3
Cairnryan D & G 172 D1
Cairnty Moray 267 G5
Caister-on-Sea Norfk 107 L1
Caistor Lincs 144 E7
Caistor St Edmund Norfk 106 E3
Cakebole Worcs 81 K1
Cake Street Norfk 106 B5
Calais Street Suffk 89 K7
Calanais W Isls 282 f3
Calbourne IoW 19 G6
Calceby Lincs 137 G4
Calcot Flints 128 E5
Calcot Gloucs 65 G5
Calcot W Berk 49 G4
Calcot Row W Berk 49 G4
Calcots Moray 266 E3
Calcott Kent 95 K1
Calcott Shrops 95 K1
Calcutt N York 150 E4
Calcutt Wilts 65 G8
Caldbeck Cumb 165 K3
Caldbergh N York 159 K5
Caldecote Cambs 87 G4
Caldecote Cambs 102 C5
Caldecote Herts 86 E7
Caldecote Nhants 84 D5
Caldecote Highfields Cambs 87 G3
Caldecott Nhants 85 K2
Caldecott Oxon 66 D7
Caldecott Rutlnd 101 J4
Caldecotte M Keyn 85 H8

Calder Cumb 155 J2
Calderbank N Lans 209 K6
Calder Bridge Cumb 155 J2
Calderbrook Rochdl 140 E4
Caldercruix N Lans 209 L5
Calder Grove Wakefd 141 M4
Caldermill S Lans 197 J3
Caldermore Rochdl 140 D4
Calder Vale Lancs 147 K6
Calderwood S Lans 209 H7
Caldey Island Pembks 55 K7
Caldicot Mons 44 F1
Caldmore Wsall 98 C4
Caldwell N York 168 F8
Caldy Wirral 128 F3
Caledfwlch Carmth 59 J4
Calenick Cnwll 4 D6
Calf of Man IoM 154 a8
Calford Green Suffk 88 D6
Calfsound Ork 275 d2
Calgary Ag & B 226 D2
Califer Moray 265 H8
California Falk 210 B4
California Norfk 123 M4
California Cross Devon 7 K4
Calke Derbys 116 B7
Callakille Highld 259 M5
Callander Stirlg 219 K5
Callanish W Isls 282 f3
Callaughton Shrops 96 E4
Callestick Cnwll 4 C5
Calligarry Highld 247 K7
Callington Cnwll 6 D1
Callingwood Staffs 115 K6
Callow Herefs 80 C8
Callow End Worcs 81 J5
Callow Hill Wilts 46 F2
Callow Hill Worcs 82 B2
Callow Hill Worcs 97 G8
Callows Grave Worcs 80 C2
Calmore Hants 34 D7
Calmsden Gloucs 64 F5
Calne Wilts 46 E5
Calow Derbys 133 H5
Calshot Hants 19 H3
Calstock Cnwll 6 E1
Calstone Wellington Wilts 46 F4
Calthorpe Norfk 122 D5
Calthorpe Street Norfk 123 H6
Calthwaite Cumb 166 B3
Calton N York 148 F4
Calton Staffs 115 H2
Calveley Ches E 130 B7
Calver Derbys 132 E5
Calverhall Shrops 113 K4
Calver Hill Herefs 79 L5
Calverleigh Devon 29 G8
Calverley Leeds 150 B8
Calver Sough Derbys 132 E5
Calvert Bucks 67 G2
Calverton M Keyn 84 F7
Calverton Notts 117 G2
Calvine P & K 232 B2
Calvo Cumb 176 F8
Calzeat Border 199 K6
Cam Gloucs 63 M7
Camasachoirce Highld 228 B3
Camasine Highld 237 L8
Camas Luinie Highld 248 F6
Camastianavaig Highld 247 L1
Camault Muir Highld 250 E4
Camber E Susx 25 H3
Camberley Surrey 49 L6
Camberwell Gt Lon 51 J4
Camblesforth N York 143 G3
Cambo Nthumb 180 B2
Cambois Nthumb 181 H2
Camborne Cnwll 3 G4
Cambourne Cambs 87 G3
Cambridge Cambs 87 J3
Cambridge Gloucs 63 L6
Cambridge City Crematorium
     Cambs 87 H3
Cambrose Cnwll 4 A5
Cambus Clacks 220 E8
Cambusavie Platform Highld 263 L1
Cambusbarron Stirlg 220 D8
Cambuskenneth Stirlg 220 D8
Cambuslang S Lans 209 H7
Cambus o' May Abers 243 M4
Cambuswallace S Lans 199 H5
Camden Town Gt Lon 51 H2
Cameley BaNES 45 J7
Camelford Cnwll 10 F6
Camelon Falk 209 M3
Camerory Highld 253 K5
Camer's Green Worcs 81 H8
Camerton BaNES 45 K7
Camerton Cumb 164 D4
Camghouran P & K 231 G4

Camieston Border 201 J7
Cammachmore Abers 245 K4
Cammeringham Lincs 135 J3
Camore Highld 263 L2
Campbeltown Ag & B 192 E4
Camperdown N Tyne 181 G4
Cample D & G 186 D7
Campmuir P & K 233 K7
Camps W Loth 210 E5
Campsall Donc 142 E5
Campsea Ash Suffk 91 H4
Camps End Cambs 88 C6
Campton C Beds 86 C7
Camptown Border 189 J4
Camrose Pembks 54 F3
Camserney P & K 232 B5
Camusnagaul Highld 239 H8
Camusnagaul Highld 261 H2
Camusteel Highld 248 A3
Camusterrach Highld 248 A3
Canada Hants 34 C7
Canal Foot Cumb 156 D7
Canaston Bridge Pembks 55 H4
Candacraig Abers 243 K4
Candlesby Lincs 137 H6
Candle Street Suffk 105 L8
Candover Green Shrops 96 C2
Candy Mill Border 199 J5
Cane End Oxon 49 G3
Canewdon Essex 72 C8
Canford Bottom Dorset 17 K3
Canford Cliffs Poole 17 L5
Canford Crematorium Bristl 45 H3
Canford Heath Poole 17 K4
Canford Magna Poole 17 K3
Canhams Green Suffk 90 C2
Canisbay Highld 280 D2
Canklow Rothm 133 H2
Canley Covtry 99 J7
Canley Crematorium Covtry 99 J8
Cann Dorset 32 E6
Canna Highld 246 B7
Cannich Highld 250 B3
Cannington Somset 30 C3
Canning Town Gt Lon 51 L3
Cannock Staffs 98 B2
Cannock Wood Staffs 98 D1
Cannon Bridge Herefs 80 A7
Canonbie D & G 177 L4
Canon Frome Herefs 80 F6
Canon Pyon Herefs 80 B5
Canons Ashby Nhants 84 B5
Canonstown Cnwll 2 E4
Canterbury Kent 40 F4
Cantley Norfk 107 H3
Cantlop Shrops 96 C2
Canton Cardif 43 J6
Cantraywood Highld 252 E2
Cantsfield Lancs 147 M1
Canvey Island Essex 53 G2
Canwick Lincs 135 K6
Canworthy Water Cnwll 11 J4
Caol Highld 239 J8
Caolas Scalpaigh W Isls 282 f6
Caoles Ag & B 224 D5
Caonich Highld 239 H5
Capel Kent 39 G4
Capel Surrey 37 J3
Capel Bangor Cerdgn 92 E7
Capel Betws Lleucu Cerdgn 77 M4
Capel Coch IoA 125 H3
Capel Curig Conwy 126 E8
Capel Cynon Cerdgn 76 C5
Capel Dewi Carmth 58 E5
Capel Dewi Cerdgn 76 E6
Capel-Dewi Cerdgn 92 D7
Capel Garmon Conwy 127 G8
Capel Green Suffk 91 J5
Capel Gwyn Carmth 58 E4
Capel Gwyn IoA 124 F4
Capel Gwynfe Carmth 59 K4
Capel Hendre Carmth 59 G6
Capel Isaac Carmth 59 G3
Capel Iwan Carmth 58 B2
Capel le Ferne Kent 41 H7
Capelles Guern 9 J2
Capel Llanilltern Cardif 43 H5
Capel Mawr IoA 125 G5
Capel Parc IoA 124 F3
Capel St Andrew Suffk 91 J5
Capel St Mary Suffk 90 C7
Capel Seion Cerdgn 92 D7
Capel Trisant Cerdgn 92 F8
Capeluchaf Gwynd 109 H2
Capelulo Conwy 126 E4
Capel-y-ffin Powys 61 L1
Capel-y-graig Gwynd 125 K6
Capenhurst Ches W 129 J5
Capernwray Lancs 147 K2
Capheaton Nthumb 180 C3

Caplaw E Rens 208 D7
Capon's Green Suffk 91 G2
Cappercleuch Border 187 K2
Capstone Medway 53 G6
Capton Devon 8 C4
Capton Somset 29 K3
Caputh P & K 233 G7
Caradon Town Cnwll 11 K8
Carbeth Inn Stirlg 208 E3
Carbis Cnwll 5 G3
Carbis Bay Cnwll 2 E3
Carbost Highld 246 E2
Carbost Highld 259 G7
Carbrook Sheff 133 G2
Carbrooke Norfk 105 J3
Carburton Notts 134 C5
Carclaze Cnwll 5 H4
Car Colston Notts 117 J3
Carcroft Donc 142 E6
Cardenden Fife 222 C8
Cardeston Shrops 95 J1
Cardewlees Cumb 177 K8
Cardhu Moray 254 D3
Cardiff Cardif 43 J6
Cardigan Cerdgn 75 L3
Cardinal's Green Cambs 88 C6
Cardington Bed 86 B5
Cardington Shrops 96 C4
Cardinham Cnwll 5 J1
Cardrain D & G 172 E8
Cardrona Border 200 C5
Cardross Ag & B 208 B3
Cardross Crematorium
     Ag & B 208 B3
Cardryne D & G 172 E8
Cardurnock Cumb 177 G7
Careby Lincs 118 D8
Careston Angus 234 E3
Carew Pembks 55 H6
Carew Cheriton Pembks 55 H6
Carew Newton Pembks 55 H6
Carey Herefs 63 H1
Carfin N Lans 209 K7
Carfraemill Border 201 G2
Cargate Green Norfk 107 H1
Cargenbridge D & G 176 C4
Cargill P & K 233 H8
Cargo Cumb 177 L7
Cargreen Cnwll 6 E2
Cargurrel Cnwll 3 M4
Carham Nthumb 202 B5
Carhampton Somset 29 H2
Carharrack Cnwll 3 J3
Carie P & K 231 H4
Carinish W Isls 283 c8
Carisbrooke IoW 19 H6
Cark Cumb 156 E7
Carkeel Cnwll 6 E3
Carlabhagh W Isls 282 e2
Carland Cross Cnwll 4 D4
Carlbury Darltn 169 G7
Carlby Lincs 102 A1
Carlcroft Nthumb 190 B4
Carlecotes Barns 141 J7
Carleen Cnwll 3 G5
Carlesmoor N York 160 B7
Carleton Cumb 155 J1
Carleton Cumb 166 C5
Carleton Cumb 178 A8
Carleton Lancs 146 F7
Carleton N York 149 H6
Carleton Wakefd 142 D4
Carleton Crematorium Bpool 146 F7
Carleton Forehoe Norfk 106 B2
Carleton Rode Norfk 106 C5
Carleton St Peter Norfk 107 G3
Carlidnack Cnwll 3 K5
Carlincraig Abers 256 B3
Carlingcott BaNES 45 K7
Carlin How R & Cl 171 G6
Carlisle Cumb 177 L7
Carlisle Crematorium Cumb 177 L8
Carloggas Cnwll 4 E2
Carlops Border 199 K2
Carloway W Isls 282 e2
Carlton Barns 142 B5
Carlton Bed 85 J4
Carlton Cambs 88 C4
Carlton Leeds 142 A2
Carlton Leics 99 L2
Carlton N York 143 G3
Carlton N York 159 J5
Carlton N York 161 K5
Carlton Notts 117 G3
Carlton S on T 169 K6
Carlton Suffk 91 J2
Carlton Colville Suffk 107 K5
Carlton Curlieu Leics 100 F4
Carlton Green Cambs 88 C5
Carlton Husthwaite N York 161 H7

Carlton-in-Cleveland N York 161 H2
Carlton in Lindrick Notts 134 B3
Carlton-le-Moorland Lincs 135 H8
Carlton Miniott N York 160 F6
Carlton-on-Trent Notts 134 F7
Carlton Scroop Lincs 118 B7
Carluke S Lans 198 D3
Carlyon Bay Cnwll 5 H4
Carmacoup S Lans 198 C7
Carmarthen Carmth 58 D3
Carmel Carmth 59 G5
Carmel Flints 128 E4
Carmel Gwynd 125 J3
Carmichael S Lans 198 F5
Carmountside Crematorium
     C Stke 114 D7
Carmunnock C Glas 209 G7
Carmyle C Glas 209 H6
Carmyllie Angus 234 E6
Carnaby E R Yk 153 J3
Carnbee Fife 223 J6
Carnbo P & K 221 J6
Carn Brea Cnwll 3 H3
Carnbrogie Abers 256 F6
Carndu Highld 248 F6
Carnduff S Lans 197 J2
Carne Cnwll 3 K6
Carne Cnwll 4 E7
Carne Cnwll 4 F3
Carnell E Ayrs 196 F4
Carnewas Cnwll 4 D1
Carnforth Lancs 147 K2
Carn-gorm Highld 248 F7
Carnhedryn Pembks 74 C6
Carnhell Green Cnwll 3 G4
Carnie Abers 245 H2
Carnkie Cnwll 3 H3
Carnkie Cnwll 3 H4
Carnkiet Cnwll 4 C4
Carno Powys 93 L4
Carnock Fife 210 D1
Carnon Downs Cnwll 3 K3
Carnousie Abers 268 B6
Carnoustie Angus 234 E8
Carnsmerry Cnwll 5 G3
Carnwath S Lans 199 G4
Carnyorth Cnwll 2 B4
Carol Green Solhll 99 H7
Carpalla Cnwll 4 F4
Carperby N York 159 H5
Carr Rothm 133 K2
Carradale Ag & B 194 C3
Carrbridge Highld 253 G7
Carrbrook Tamesd 140 E7
Carrefour Jersey 9 c2
Carreglefn IoA 125 G2
Carr Gate Wakefd 141 M3
Carrhouse N Linc 143 K6
Carrick Ag & B 206 E2
Carrick Castle Ag & B 217 K8
Carriden Falk 210 D3
Carrington Lincs 136 F8
Carrington Mdloth 211 K6
Carrington Traffd 130 E1
Carrog Conwy 110 E2
Carrog Denbgs 111 L3
Carron Falk 210 A3
Carron Moray 254 E3
Carronbridge D & G 186 C6
Carron Bridge Stirlg 209 K2
Carronshore Falk 210 A2
Carrow Hill Mons 44 E1
Carr Shield Nthumb 167 J1
Carrutherstown D & G 176 E4
Carruth House Inver 208 B6
Carr Vale Derbys 133 J5
Carrville Dur 169 J2
Carsaig Ag & B 227 G8
Carseriggan D & G 173 H1
Carsethorn D & G 176 C7
Carshalton Gt Lon 51 H6
Carsington Derbys 115 L2
Carskey Ag & B 192 D6
Carsluith D & G 174 D4
Carsphairn D & G 184 E4
Carstairs S Lans 198 F4
Carstairs Junction S Lans 198 F4
Carswell Marsh Oxon 65 L7
Carter's Clay Hants 34 C6
Carters Green Essex 70 D5
Carterton Oxon 65 L5
Carterway Heads Nthumb 180 C8
Carthew Cnwll 5 G4
Carthorpe N York 160 D6
Cartington Nthumb 190 E5
Cartland S Lans 198 E4
Cartledge Derbys 132 F4
Cartmel Cumb 156 E7
Cartmel Fell Cumb 156 F5
Carway Carmth 56 E3

Carwinley Cumb 177 L4
Cashe's Green Gloucs 64 B6
Cashmoor Dorset 33 G8
Cassington Oxon 66 C5
Cassop Colliery Dur 169 K3
Castallack Cnwll 2 C6
Castel Guern 9 j3
Castell Conwy 126 F6
Castell-y-bwch Torfn 62 B8
Casterton Cumb 157 K6
Castle Cnwll 5 J3
Castle Acre Norfk 121 H8
Castle Ashby Nhants 85 G3
Castlebay W Isls 283 b13
Castle Bolton N York 159 J4
Castle Bromwich Solhll 98 F5
Castle Bytham Lincs 118 C7
Castlebythe Pembks 75 H6
Castle Caereinion Powys 94 E2
Castle Camps Cambs 88 C6
Castle Carrock Cumb 178 D7
Castlecary Falk 209 L3
Castle Cary Somset 31 L4
Castle Combe Wilts 46 B3
Castle Donington Leics 116 D6
Castle Douglas D & G 175 J2
Castle Eaton Swindn 65 H7
Castle Eden Dur 169 L3
Castle End C Pete 102 C2
Castleford Wakefd 142 C3
Castle Frome Herefs 80 F6
Castle Gate Cnwll 2 D4
Castle Green Cumb 157 H4
Castle Green Surrey 50 B6
Castle Gresley Derbys 115 M7
Castle Hedingham Essex 88 F8
Castlehill Border 200 B6
Castlehill Highld 280 B3
Castle Hill Kent 39 H5
Castle Hill Suffk 90 D6
Castlehill W Duns 208 C4
Castle Kennedy D & G 172 D3
Castle Lachlan Ag & B 217 G8
Castlemartin Pembks 54 E7
Castlemilk C Glas 209 G6
Castle Morris Pembks 74 E6
Castlemorton Worcs 81 H7
Castlemorton Common Worcs 81 H7
Castle O'er D & G 187 K7
Castle Pulverbatch Shrops 95 K3
Castle Rising Norfk 120 E6
Castleside Dur 168 D1
Castle Stuart Highld 252 D2
Castlethorpe M Keyn 84 F6
Castlethorpe N Linc 144 B6
Castleton Border 188 E4
Castleton Derbys 132 C3
Castleton N York 162 B1
Castleton Newpt 43 L5
Castleton Rochdl 140 C5
Castletown Dorset 16 D7
Castletown Highld 280 A3
Castletown IoM 154 c8
Castletown Sundld 181 J7
Castley N York 150 C6
Caston Norfk 105 J4
Castor C Pete 102 C4
Caswell Bay Swans 57 G7
Catacol N Ayrs 194 E1
Cat and Fiddle Derbys 131 K5
Catbrain S Glos 45 H3
Catbrook Mons 63 G6
Catch Flints 128 F5
Catchall Cnwll 2 C5
Catchem's Corner Solhll 99 H8
Catchgate Dur 180 E8
Catcliffe Rothm 133 H2
Catcomb Wilts 46 E4
Catcott Somset 30 F3
Catcott Burtle Somset 30 F2
Caterham Surrey 51 J7
Catfield Norfk 123 H7
Catfield Common Norfk 123 H7
Catford Gt Lon 51 K4
Catforth Lancs 138 F1
Cathcart C Glas 209 G7
Cathedine Powys 61 J2
Catherine-de-Barnes Solhll 98 F7
Catherine Slack C Brad 141 G2
Catherington Hants 35 L4
Catherston Leweston Dorset 15 J4
Catherton Shrops 96 E7
Catisfield Hants 19 J2
Catley Herefs 80 F6
Catley Lane Head Rochdl 140 C4
Catlodge Highld 241 H5
Catlow Lancs 148 F8
Catlowdy Cumb 178 B3
Catmere End Essex 87 K7
Catmore W Berk 48 C3

Caton Devon 13 H8
Caton Lancs 147 K3
Caton Green Lancs 147 L3
Cator Court Devon 13 G7
Catrine E Ayrs 197 G6
Cat's Ash Newpt 44 B1
Catsfield E Susx 24 C4
Catsfield Stream E Susx 24 C4
Catsgore Somset 31 H5
Catsham Somset 31 J4
Catshill Worcs 98 B8
Catstree Shrops 97 G4
Cattadale Ag & B 192 D6
Cattal N York 150 F5
Cattawade Suffk 90 C8
Catterall Lancs 147 K7
Catteralslane Shrops 113 J3
Catterick N York 160 C3
Catterick Bridge N York 160 B3
Catterick Garrison N York 160 B3
Catterlen Cumb 166 B4
Catterline Abers 245 J7
Catterton N York 151 H6
Catteshall Surrey 36 E2
Catthorpe Leics 100 C7
Cattishall Suffk 89 H2
Cattistock Dorset 16 B3
Catton N York 160 E7
Catton Nthumb 179 J7
Catwick E R Yk 153 J6
Catworth Cambs 86 B1
Caudle Green Gloucs 64 D5
Caulcott C Beds 85 K6
Caulcott Oxon 66 D2
Cauldcots Angus 235 G6
Cauldhame Stirlg 219 L8
Cauldmill Border 188 F3
Cauldon Staffs 115 H2
Cauldon Lowe Staffs 115 H2
Cauldwell Derbys 115 L8
Caulkerbush D & G 176 B2
Caulside D & G 178 B3
Caundle Marsh Dorset 31 L8
Caunsall Worcs 97 J7
Caunton Notts 134 E7
Causeway Hants 35 M6
Causeway End Cumb 157 G5
Causeway End D & G 173 K3
Causeway End Essex 71 G3
Causewayend S Lans 199 H6
Causewayhead Cumb 176 F8
Causewayhead Stirlg 220 D8
Causeyend Abers 257 H7
Causey Park Nthumb 191 H7
Causey Park Bridge Nthumb 191 H7
Cavendish Suffk 88 F6
Cavenham Suffk 88 F1
Caversfield Oxon 66 E2
Caversham Readg 49 H4
Caverswall Staffs 114 F3
Caverton Mill Border 202 A7
Cavil E R Yk 143 J2
Cawdor Highld 252 F2
Cawkwell Lincs 136 E4
Cawood N York 151 J8
Cawsand Cnwll 6 E5
Cawston Norfk 122 C6
Cawston Warwks 100 A8
Cawthorn N York 162 D5
Cawthorne Barns 141 L6
Cawton N York 161 K7
Caxton Cambs 86 F3
Caxton End Cambs 87 G4
Caxton Gibbet Cambs 86 F3
Caynham Shrops 80 D1
Caythorpe Lincs 118 B2
Caythorpe Notts 117 J2
Cayton N York 163 J6
Ceann a Bhaigh W Isls 283 b8
Ceannacroc Lodge Highld 239 L1
Cearsiadar W Isls 282 f4
Ceciliford Mons 63 G6
Cefn Newpt 44 B1
Cefn Berain Conwy 127 K6
Cefn-brith Conwy 111 H2
Cefn-bryn-brain Carmth 59 K6
Cefn Byrle Powys 60 C5
Cefn Canel Powys 112 C5
Cefn Coch Powys 111 L6
Cefn-coed-y-cymmer Myr Td 60 F5
Cefn Cribwr Brdgnd 42 C5
Cefn Cross Brdgnd 42 C5
Cefn-ddwysarn Gwynd 111 J4
Cefn-Einion Shrops 95 G6
Cefneithin Carmth 59 G6
Cefngorwydd Powys 78 B6
Cefn-mawr Wrexhm 112 D3
Cefnpennar Rhondd 61 G2
Cefn-y-bedd Flints 129 H8
Cefn-y-pant Carmth 75 L7

Ceint IoA 125 J4
Cellan Cerdgn 77 H5
Cellardyke Fife 223 K6
Cellarhead Staffs 114 F2
Celleron Cumb 166 C5
Celynen Caerph 43 K3
Cemaes IoA 124 F1
Cemmaes Powys 93 H2
Cemmaes Road Powys 93 H3
Cenarth Cerdgn 76 A7
Cerbyd Pembks 74 D6
Ceres Fife 223 G5
Cerne Abbas Dorset 16 C2
Cerney Wick Gloucs 65 G7
Cerrigceinwen IoA 125 G5
Cerrigydrudion Conwy 111 J2
Cess Norfk 123 J7
Ceunant Gwynd 125 J7
Chaceley Gloucs 64 B1
Chacewater Cnwll 4 B6
Chackmore Bucks 84 D8
Chacombe Nhants 83 L6
Chadbury Worcs 82 B6
Chadderton Oldham 140 D6
Chadderton Fold Oldham 140 D6
Chaddesden C Derb 116 C4
Chaddesley Corbett Worcs 97 K8
Chaddlehanger Devon 12 B7
Chaddleworth W Berk 48 B3
Chadlington Oxon 65 M3
Chadshunt Warwks 83 H4
Chadwell Leics 117 K6
Chadwell Shrops 114 A8
Chadwell End Bed 86 B2
Chadwell Heath Gt Lon 52 A1
Chadwell St Mary Thurr 52 E3
Chadwick Worcs 81 J2
Chadwick End Solhll 82 F1
Chadwick Green St Hel 139 G7
Chaffcombe Somset 15 H1
Chafford Hundred Thurr 52 D3
Chagford Devon 13 G5
Chailey E Susx 22 F3
Chainbridge Cambs 103 J3
Chainhurst Kent 39 J4
Chalbury Dorset 17 K1
Chalbury Common Dorset 17 K2
Chaldon Surrey 51 J7
Chaldon Herring Dorset see East Chaldon
Chale IoW 19 H8
Chale Green IoW 19 H7
Chalfont Common Bucks 68 C8
Chalfont St Giles Bucks 68 C8
Chalfont St Peter Bucks 50 C1
Chalford Gloucs 64 C6
Chalford Oxon 67 H7
Chalford Wilts 32 E1
Chalgrave C Beds 68 C2
Chalgrove Oxon 66 F7
Chalk Kent 52 E4
Chalk End Essex 70 F5
Chalkhouse Green Oxon 49 H3
Chalkway Somset 15 J1
Chalkwell Kent 53 J6
Challaborough Devon 7 J6
Challacombe Devon 28 B3
Challoch D & G 173 K2
Challock Kent 40 C5
Chalmington Dorset 16 B2
Chalton C Beds 68 C2
Chalton C Beds 86 C5
Chalton Hants 20 B4
Chalvey Slough 50 B3
Chalvington E Susx 23 H5
Chambers Green Kent 40 B6
Chandler's Cross Herts 68 D7
Chandlers Cross Worcs 81 H7
Chandler's Ford Hants 34 F7
Channel's End Bed 86 C4
Chanterlands Crematorium
　C KuH 144 D2
Chantry Somset 32 B2
Chantry Suffk 90 D6
Chapel Cumb 165 H4
Chapel Fife 222 D8
Chapel Allerton Leeds 150 D8
Chapel Allerton Somset 30 F1
Chapel Amble Cnwll 10 D7
Chapel Brampton Nhants 84 E2
Chapelbridge Cambs 102 F4
Chapel Choriton Staffs 114 C4
Chapel Cross E Susx 23 K3
Chapel End Bed 86 B4
Chapel End C Beds 85 L6
Chapel End Cambs 102 C6
Chapel End Warwks 99 J5
Chapelend Way Essex 88 E7
Chapel-en-le-Frith Derbys 131 L3
Chapel Field Bury 140 B6
Chapelgate Lincs 119 L6
Chapel Green Warwks 83 L3

Chapel Green Warwks 99 H6
Chapel Haddlesey N York 142 F3
Chapelhall N Lans 209 K6
Chapel Hill Abers 257 K4
Chapel Hill Lincs 119 G1
Chapel Hill Mons 63 G7
Chapel Hill N York 150 D6
Chapelhope Border 187 K2
Chapelknowe D & G 177 K4
Chapel Lawn Shrops 95 H8
Chapel le Dale N York 158 C7
Chapel Leigh Somset 29 L5
Chapel Milton Derbys 131 L3
Chapel of Garioch Abers 256 C7
Chapel Rossan D & G 172 D6
Chapel Row E Susx 23 L5
Chapel Row Essex 71 J7
Chapel Row W Berk 48 E5
Chapels Cumb 156 B6
Chapel St Leonards Lincs 137 K5
Chapel Stile Cumb 156 D2
Chapelton Angus 234 F6
Chapelton Devon 27 K5
Chapelton S Lans 197 K1
Chapeltown Bl w D 139 L4
Chapel Town Cnwll 4 E4
Chapeltown Moray 254 E7
Chapeltown Sheff 142 A8
Chapmanslade Wilts 32 D1
Chapmans Well Devon 11 L4
Chapmore End Herts 69 J4
Chappel Essex 72 C2
Charaton Cnwll 6 B1
Chard Somset 15 H1
Chard Junction Somset 15 H2
Chardleigh Green Somset 30 D8
Chardstock Devon 15 G2
Charfield S Glos 63 L8
Chargrove Gloucs 64 D3
Charing Kent 40 B5
Charing Crematorium Kent 40 B5
Charing Heath Kent 40 B5
Charing Hill Kent 40 B5
Charingworth Gloucs 82 E7
Charlbury Oxon 66 A3
Charlcombe BaNES 45 L5
Charlcutt Wilts 46 E4
Charlecote Warwks 83 G4
Charlemont Sandw 98 C4
Charles Devon 28 B4
Charleshill Surrey 36 D2
Charleston Angus 234 B6
Charlestown C Aber 245 L3
Charlestown C Brad 149 L8
Charlestown Calder 140 E4
Charlestown Cnwll 5 H4
Charlestown Derbys 131 L1
Charlestown Dorset 16 C6
Charlestown Fife 210 E2
Charlestown Highld 251 H2
Charlestown Highld 260 C5
Charlestown Salfd 140 B7
Charles Tye Suffk 89 L5
Charlesworth Derbys 131 K1
Charlinch Somset 30 C3
Charlottetown Fife 222 E5
Charlton Gt Lon 51 L3
Charlton Hants 34 D2
Charlton Herts 68 F2
Charlton Nhants 83 M8
Charlton Nthumb 179 J2
Charlton Oxon 48 B1
Charlton Somset 30 D5
Charlton Somset 31 K2
Charlton Somset 31 K8
Charlton Surrey 50 D5
Charlton W Susx 20 E4
Charlton Wilts 32 F6
Charlton Wilts 46 D1
Charlton Worcs 81 J1
Charlton Worcs 82 B6
Charlton Wrekin 96 D1
Charlton Abbots Gloucs 64 F2
Charlton Adam Somset 31 J5
Charlton All Saints Wilts 33 L6
Charlton Down Dorset 16 C4
Charlton Hill Shrops 96 D2
Charlton Horethorne Somset 31 L6
Charlton Kings Gloucs 64 D3
Charlton Mackrell Somset 31 H5
Charlton Marshall Dorset 17 H2
Charlton Musgrove Somset 32 B5
Charlton-on-Otmoor Oxon 66 E4
Charlton on the Hill Dorset 17 H2
Charlton St Peter Wilts 47 G7
Charlwood Hants 35 K4
Charlwood Surrey 37 K3
Charminster Dorset 16 C4
Charmouth Dorset 15 H4
Charndon Bucks 67 G2

Charney Bassett Oxon 66 A8
Charnock Green Lancs 139 H4
Charnock Richard Lancs 139 H4
Charnock Richard
   Crematorium Lancs 139 H4
Charsfield Suffk 90 F4
Chart Corner Kent...................... 39 K3
Charter Alley Hants.................... 48 E7
Charterhall Border 202 B4
Charterhouse Somset 45 G7
Chartershall Stirlg 209 L1
Charterville Allotments Oxon 65 L5
Chartham Kent............................ 40 E4
Chartham Hatch Kent................. 40 E4
Chart Hill Kent........................... 39 K3
Chartridge Bucks 68 B6
Chart Sutton Kent...................... 39 K3
Chartway Street Kent 39 L3
Charvil Wokham 49 J4
Charwelton Nhants 83 M4
Chase Terrace Staffs 98 D2
Chasetown Staffs 98 D2
Chastleton Oxon 65 K1
Chasty Devon 11 L2
Chatburn Lancs 148 D7
Chatcull Staffs 114 B4
Chatham Caerph 43 K4
Chatham Medway 53 G5
Chatham Green Essex 71 H4
Chathill Nthumb...................... 203 K7
Chatley Worcs 81 J3
Chattenden Medway 53 G4
Chatter End Essex 70 C2
Chatteris Cambs 103 H6
Chatterton Lancs 140 B4
Chattisham Suffk 90 C6
Chatto Border 189 K3
Chatton Nthumb...................... 203 G7
Chaul End C Beds 68 D3
Chawleigh Devon 28 C8
Chawley Oxon 66 C6
Chawston Bed 86 C4
Chawton Hants........................... 35 L3
Chaxhill Gloucs 63 L4
Chazey Heath Oxon 49 G3
Cheadle Staffs 115 G3
Cheadle Stockp 131 G2
Cheadle Heath Stockp 131 G2
Cheadle Hulme Stockp 131 G2
Cheam Gt Lon 51 H6
Cheapside W & M 50 B5
Chearsley Bucks 67 H5
Chebsey Staffs 114 D6
Checkendon Oxon 49 G2
Checkley Ches E 114 A2
Checkley Herefs 80 E7
Checkley Staffs 115 H5
Checkley Green Ches E 114 A2
Chedburgh Suffk 88 F4
Cheddar Somset 44 F4
Cheddington Bucks 68 A4
Cheddleton Staffs 114 F1
Cheddleton Heath Staffs 114 F1
Cheddon Fitzpaine Somset........ 30 C5
Chedglow Wilts 64 D8
Chedgrave Norfk 107 H3
Chedington Dorset 15 L2
Chediston Suffk 107 G7
Chediston Green Suffk 107 G7
Chedworth Gloucs 64 F5
Chedzoy Somset 30 C3
Cheeseman's Green Kent 40 D7
Cheetham Hill Manch 140 C7
Cheldon Devon 28 C8
Chelford Ches E 130 F5
Chellaston C Derb 116 C1
Chellington Bed 85 J4
Chelmarsh Shrops 97 G5
Chelmick Shrops 95 L5
Chelmondiston Suffk 90 E7
Chelmorton Derbys 132 B5
Chelmsford Essex 71 H5
Chelmsford Crematorium
   Essex 71 G6
Chelmsley Wood Solhll............. 98 F6
Chelsea Gt Lon 51 H3
Chelsfield Gt Lon 52 A6
Chelsham Surrey 51 K7
Chelston Somset 29 L6
Chelsworth Suffk 89 K5
Cheltenham Gloucs 64 D3
Cheltenham Crematorium
   Gloucs 64 E3
Chelveston Nhants 85 K1
Chelvey N Som 44 F5
Chelwood BaNES........................ 45 J6
Chelwood Common E Susx 38 B7
Chelwood Gate E Susx 38 B7
Chelworth Wilts......................... 64 E8
Chelworth Lower Green Wilts ... 65 G8

Chelworth Upper Green Wilts... 65 G8
Cheney Longville Shrops 95 K6
Chenies Bucks 68 C7
Chepstow Mons 63 G8
Chequerbent Bolton................. 139 K6
Chequers Corner Norfk........... 103 K2
Cherhill Wilts............................. 46 F5
Cherington Gloucs 64 C7
Cherington Warwks 83 G7
Cheriton Devon 28 C2
Cheriton Hants.......................... 35 J5
Cheriton Kent............................ 41 G7
Cheriton Swans 56 E6
Cheriton Bishop Devon............. 13 H4
Cheriton Fitzpaine Devon......... 13 K2
Cheriton or Stackpole Elidor
   Pembks 55 G7
Cherrington Wrekin 113 L7
Cherry Burton E R Yk............... 152 F7
Cherry Hinton Cambs................ 87 K4
Cherry Orchard Worcs 81 K4
Cherry Willingham Lincs 135 L5
Chertsey Surrey 50 D5
Cheselbourne Dorset 16 E3
Chesham Bucks 68 B6
Chesham Bury 140 B5
Chesham Bois Bucks 68 B7
Cheshunt Herts 69 K6
Chesley Kent 53 J6
Cheslyn Hay Staffs 98 B2
Chessetts Wood Warwks 99 G8
Chessington Gt Lon 50 F6
Chester Ches W 129 J6
Chesterblade Somset 31 L3
Chester Crematorium Ches W . 129 J6
Chesterfield Derbys 133 G5
Chesterfield Staffs 98 E2
Chesterfield Crematorium
   Derbys 133 H5
Chesterhill Mdloth 211 L6
Chester-le-Street Dur............... 181 G8
Chester Moor Dur.................... 169 H1
Chesters Border 189 G2
Chesters Border 189 H4
Chesterton Cambs 87 K3
Chesterton Cambs 102 C4
Chesterton Gloucs 64 E7
Chesterton Oxon 66 E3
Chesterton Shrops 97 H4
Chesterton Staffs 114 C2
Chesterton Green Warwks 83 H4
Chesterwood Nthumb 179 J6
Chestfield Kent.......................... 40 F2
Chestnut Street Kent 53 J6
Cheston Devon 7 K3
Cheswardine Shrops 114 A5
Cheswick Nthumb.................... 203 G4
Cheswick Green Solhll............... 98 E8
Chetnole Dorset 16 B1
Chettiscombe Devon 29 H7
Chettisham Cambs 103 L6
Chettle Dorset 32 F8
Chetton Shrops 96 F5
Chetwode Bucks 66 F1
Chetwynd Wrekin 114 A7
Chetwynd Aston Wrekin 114 B8
Cheveley Cambs 88 D3
Chevening Kent.......................... 52 A7
Chevington Suffk 88 F3
Chevithorne Devon 29 H7
Chew Magna BaNES................... 45 H6
Chew Moor Bolton.................... 139 K6
Chew Stoke BaNES.................... 45 H6
Chewton Keynsham BaNES 45 K5
Chewton Mendip Somset 45 H8
Chichacott Devon 12 E3
Chicheley M Keyn 85 H6
Chichester W Susx..................... 20 E6
Chichester Crematorium
   W Susx 20 E5
Chickerell Dorset....................... 16 C6
Chickering Suffk 106 G2
Chicklade Wilts.......................... 32 F4
Chickward Herefs 79 K4
Chidden Hants........................... 35 K7
Chiddingfold Surrey 36 E4
Chiddingly E Susx 23 J4
Chiddingstone Kent................... 38 D4
Chiddingstone Causeway
   Kent 38 E4
Chideock Dorset......................... 15 K4
Chidham W Susx........................ 20 C6
Chidswell Kirk 141 K3
Chieveley W Berk 48 C4
Chignall St James Essex 71 G5
Chignall Smealy Essex 71 G5
Chigwell Essex 70 B4
Chigwell Row Essex 70 C8
Chilbolton Hants....................... 34 C2

Chilcomb Hants......................... 35 G5
Chilcombe Dorset 15 M4
Chilcompton Somset 45 J8
Chilcote Leics 99 H1
Childer Thornton Ches W........ 129 J4
Child Okeford Dorset 32 D8
Childrey Oxon 48 A2
Child's Ercall Shrops 113 L6
Childswickham Worcs 82 C7
Childwall Lpool 129 K2
Childwick Bury Herts 68 F5
Childwick Green Herts 68 F5
Chilfrome Dorset....................... 16 B3
Chilgrove W Susx...................... 20 D4
Chilham Kent............................. 40 E4
Chilla Devon 12 B2
Chillaton Devon 12 B6
Chillenden Kent......................... 41 J4
Chillerton IoW........................... 19 H6
Chillesford Suffk 91 J5
Chillingham Nthumb............... 203 H6
Chillington Devon 8 B6
Chillington Somset 30 F8
Chilmark Wilts 33 G4
Chilmington Green Kent........... 40 C7
Chilson Oxon 65 L3
Chilsworthy Cnwll..................... 12 A8
Chilsworthy Devon 11 L1
Chiltern Green C Beds 68 E3
Chilterns Crematorium Bucks .. 68 B7
Chilthorne Domer Somset........ 31 H7
Chilton Bucks 67 G5
Chilton Devon 13 K2
Chilton Dur.............................. 169 H5
Chilton Kent 41 J6
Chilton Oxon 48 C2
Chilton Suffk 89 H6
Chilton Candover Hants............ 35 J3
Chilton Cantelo Somset 31 J6
Chilton Foliat Wilts 47 L5
Chilton Polden Somset 30 E3
Chilton Street Suffk 88 E6
Chilton Trinity Somset.............. 30 D3
Chilwell Notts 116 E4
Chilworth Hants........................ 34 E7
Chilworth Surrey 36 F2
Chimney Oxon 65 M7
Chineham Hants........................ 49 G7
Chingford Gt Lon 69 K8
Chinley Derbys 131 L3
Chinnor Oxon 67 J6
Chipchase Castle Nthumb 179 K4
Chipnall Shrops 114 A5
Chippenham Cambs 88 D1
Chippenham Wilts..................... 46 D4
Chipperfield Herts 68 D6
Chipping Herts 69 K1
Chipping Lancs 147 M7
Chipping Campden Gloucs 82 E7
Chipping Hill Essex 71 K4
Chipping Norton Oxon 65 L2
Chipping Ongar Essex 70 E6
Chipping Sodbury S Glos 45 L3
Chipping Warden Nhants 83 L5
Chipstable Somset 29 J5
Chipstead Kent.......................... 38 D2
Chipstead Surrey 51 H7
Chirbury Shrops 95 G4
Chirk Wrexhm 112 D4
Chirnside Border 202 D2
Chirnsidebridge Border 202 C2
Chirton Wilts 47 G7
Chisbury Wilts 47 K5
Chiselborough Somset 31 G7
Chiseldon Swindn...................... 47 J3
Chiselhampton Oxon 66 E7
Chisholme Border 188 D4
Chislehampton Oxon 66 E7
Chisholme Border 188 D4
Chislehurst Gt Lon 51 L5
Chislet Kent............................... 41 H2
Chisley Calder 140 F2
Chiswell Green Herts 68 E6
Chiswick Gt Lon 51 G3
Chiswick End Cambs 87 H6
Chisworth Derbys 131 K2
Chitcombe E Susx 24 E3
Chithurst W Susx...................... 36 C5
Chittering Cambs 87 K1
Chitterne Wilts 33 G2
Chittlehamholt Devon 28 B6
Chittlehampton Devon.............. 27 L5
Chittoe Wilts 46 D5
Chivelstone Devon 8 A7
Chivenor Devon......................... 27 J4
Chlenry D & G............................172 E3
Chobham Surrey 50 B6
Cholderton Wilts 34 B2
Cholesbury Bucks 68 B5
Chollerford Nthumb................ 179 L5
Chollerton Nthumb.................. 179 L4
Cholmondeston Ches E 130 C7

Cholsey Oxon 48 E2
Cholstrey Herefs 80 B3
Chop Gate N York 161 J3
Choppington Nthumb............. 181 G2
Chopwell Gatesd 180 D7
Chorley Ches E 113 L1
Chorley Lancs 139 H4
Chorley Shrops 96 F6
Chorley Staffs 98 D1
Chorleywood Herts 68 C7
Chorleywood West Herts 68 C7
Chorlton Ches E 114 A2
Chorlton-cum-Hardy Manch ... 130 F1
Chorlton Lane Ches W 113 G2
Choulton Shrops 95 J5
Chowley Ches W....................... 129 L8
Chrishall Essex 87 J7
Chrisswell Inver 207 L5
Christchurch Cambs 103 K4
Christchurch Dorset 18 B5
Christchurch Gloucs 63 H4
Christchurch Newpt 44 D1
Christian Malford Wilts 46 D3
Christleton Ches W 129 K6
Christmas Common Oxon 67 H8
Christon N Som 44 D7
Christon Bank Nthumb 191 J7
Christow Devon 13 J5
Christ's Hospital W Susx........... 37 H5
Chuck Hatch E Susx 38 C3
Chudleigh Devon 13 K6
Chudleigh Knighton Devon....... 13 K7
Chulmleigh Devon 28 B8
Chunal Derbys 131 K2
Church Lancs 139 L2
Churcham Gloucs 63 M3
Church Aston Wrekin 114 A8
Church Brampton Nhants 84 D2
Church Brough Cumb 167 J7
Church Broughton Derbys 115 K5
Church Cove Cnwll....................... 3 H8
Church Crookham Hants........... 49 L8
Churchdown Gloucs 64 C3
Church Eaton Staffs 114 C8
Church End Bed 85 L3
Church End Bed 86 C3
Church End Bucks 67 H5
Church End C Beds 68 C3
Church End C Beds 68 C3
Church End C Beds 85 J8
Church End C Beds 85 K8
Church End C Beds 86 D4
Church End C Beds 86 D7
Church End Cambs 87 K4
Church End Cambs 102 B8
Church End Cambs 102 E6
Church End Cambs 103 H5
Church End Essex 70 F3
Church End Essex 71 H2
Church End Essex 71 H4
Churchend Essex 72 E8
Church End Gloucs 81 K8
Church End Gt Lon 51 H1
Church End Herts 68 C3
Church End Herts 69 H1
Church End Herts 70 C3
Church End Lincs 119 H5
Church End Lincs 145 L2
Church End Warwks 99 H5
Church End Warwks 99 H5
Church Enstone Oxon 66 A2
Church Fenton N York 151 K4
Churchfield Sandw.................... 98 C5
Churchgate Herts 69 K6
Churchgate Street Essex 70 C5
Church Green Devon 14 D3
Church Gresley Derbys 115 M3
Church Hanborough Oxon 66 B4
Church Hill Staffs 98 C1
Church Houses N York 161 L3
Churchill Devon 15 G2
Churchill Devon 27 L3
Churchill N Som 44 E7
Churchill Oxon 65 K2
Churchill Worcs 81 L4
Churchill Worcs 97 K7
Churchinford Somset 30 C4
Church Knowle Dorset 17 H6
Church Laneham Notts............ 135 G4
Church Langton Leics 100 F5
Church Lawford Warwks 99 M8
Church Lawton Ches E 130 F8
Church Leigh Staffs 115 G4
Church Lench Worcs 82 B5
Church Mayfield Staffs 115 J3
Church Minshull Ches E 130 C7
Church Norton W Susx 20 E7
Churchover Warwks 100 B7
Church Preen Shrops 96 C4
Church Pulverbatch Shrops 95 K3

Churchstanton Somset............30 B7
Churchstoke Powys.............95 G4
Churchstow Devon...............7 K5
Church Stowe Nhants...........84 C4
Church Street Essex............88 F6
Church Street Kent.............52 F4
Church Street Suffk...........107 K6
Church Stretton Shrops........95 L4
Churchthorpe Lincs...........145 J8
Churchtown Bpool.............146 F7
Churchtown Cnwll..............10 F7
Churchtown Derbys............132 E7
Churchtown Devon..............28 B2
Churchtown IoM...............154 f3
Churchtown Lancs.............147 J7
Church Town N Linc...........143 K6
Churchtown Sefton............138 D4
Church Village Rhondd.........43 G4
Church Warsop Notts..........133 L6
Church Wilne Derbys..........116 D5
Churnsike Lodge Nthumb.......178 F3
Churston Ferrers Torbay........8 D4
Churt Surrey..................36 C3
Churton Ches W...............129 K8
Churwell Leeds...............141 L2
Chwilog Gwynd................109 H4
Chyandour Cnwll................2 D5
Chyanvounder Cnwll.............3 G6
Chyeowling Cnwll...............3 K3
Chyvarloe Cnwll................3 G6
Cil Powys.....................94 E3
Cilcain Flints...............128 E6
Cilcennin Cerdgn..............76 F3
Cilcewydd Powys...............94 F3
Cilfrew Neath.................57 L5
Cilfynydd Rhondd..............43 H3
Cilgerran Pembks..............75 L4
Cilgwyn Carmth................59 K3
Cilgwyn Gwynd................109 J1
Ciliau-Aeron Cerdgn...........76 F4
Cilmaengwyn Neath.............57 K4
Cilmery Powys.................78 D5
Cilrhedyn Pembks..............58 A2
Cilsan Carmth.................59 H4
Ciltalgarth Gwynd............111 G3
Cilycwm Carmth................77 L7
Cimla Neath...................57 L5
Cinderford Gloucs.............63 K4
Cinder Hill Wolves............97 L4
Cippenham Slough..............50 B3
Cirencester Gloucs............64 F6
Citadilla N York.............160 B3
City Gt Lon...................51 J3
City V Glam...................42 F6
City Dulas IoA...............125 H2
City of London Crematorium
   Gt Lon.....................51 L2
Clabhach Ag & B..............224 F3
Clachaig Ag & B..............207 J3
Clachan Ag & B...............206 B7
Clachan Ag & B...............216 B3
Clachan Ag & B...............228 D6
Clachan Highld...............247 H1
Clachan-a-Luib W Isls........283 c8
Clachan Mor Ag & B...........224 C5
Clachan na Luib W Isls.......283 c8
Clachan of Campsie E Duns....209 G3
Clachan-Seil Ag & B..........216 B3
Clachnaharry Highld..........251 H2
Clachtoll Highld.............270 D3
Clackavoid P & K.............233 H3
Clackmannan Clacks...........210 B1
Clackmarras Moray............266 E4
Clacton-on-Sea Essex..........73 J4
Cladich Ag & B...............217 H3
Cladswell Worcs...............82 C3
Claggan Highld...............227 K3
Claigan Highld...............258 C6
Clandown BaNES................45 K7
Clanfield Hants...............35 L7
Clanfield Oxon................65 L6
Clannaborough Devon...........13 H2
Clanville Hants...............34 D1
Clanville Somset..............31 K4
Claonaig Ag & B..............206 D7
Clapgate Dorset...............17 K2
Clapgate Herts................70 C2
Clapham Bed...................85 K5
Clapham Devon.................13 L5
Clapham Gt Lon................51 H4
Clapham N York...............148 C2
Clapham W Susx................21 J5
Clapham Green Bed.............85 K4
Clap Hill Kent................40 D7
Clappersgate Cumb............156 E2
Clapton Somset................15 J1
Clapton Somset................45 J8
Clapton-in-Gordano N Som......44 F4
Clapton-on-the-Hill Gloucs....65 H3
Clapworthy Devon..............28 B6

Clarach Cerdgn................92 D6
Claravale Gatesd.............180 E6
Clarbeston Pembks.............55 H3
Clarbeston Road Pembks........55 G3
Clarborough Notts............134 E3
Clare Suffk...................88 F6
Clarebrand D & G.............175 J2
Clarencefield D & G..........176 E5
Clarewood Nthumb.............180 B5
Clarilaw Border..............188 F3
Clark's Green Surrey..........37 J3
Clarkston E Rens.............208 F7
Clashmore Highld.............263 K6
Clashmore Highld.............270 D2
Clashnessie Highld...........270 E2
Clashnoir Moray..............254 E7
Clathy P & K.................221 H3
Clathymore P & K.............221 H3
Clatt Abers..................255 L6
Clatter Powys.................94 B4
Clatterford End Essex.........70 F4
Clatworthy Somset.............29 J4
Claughton Lancs..............147 K7
Claughton Lancs..............147 L3
Claughton Wirral.............129 G2
Clavelshay Somset.............30 C4
Claverdon Warwks..............82 E2
Claverham N Som...............44 F5
Clavering Essex...............70 C1
Claverley Shrops..............97 H5
Claverton BaNES...............46 A6
Claverton Down BaNES..........45 M6
Clawdd-coch V Glam............43 G6
Clawdd-newydd Denbgs.........111 L1
Clawthorpe Cumb..............157 H7
Clawton Devon.................11 L3
Claxby Lincs.................136 B1
Claxby Lincs.................137 H5
Claxton N York...............151 L4
Claxton Norfk................107 G3
Claybrooke Magna Leics.......100 B5
Clay Common Suffk............107 K7
Clay Coton Nhants............100 D8
Clay Cross Derbys............133 H7
Claydon Oxon..................83 K5
Claydon Suffk.................90 D5
Clay End Herts................69 J2
Claygate D & G...............177 L3
Claygate Kent.................39 H4
Claygate Surrey...............50 F6
Claygate Cross Kent...........38 F2
Clayhall Gt Lon...............51 L1
Clayhanger Devon..............29 J6
Clayhanger Wsall..............98 D3
Clayhidon Devon...............29 L7
Clayhill E Susx...............24 F3
Clayhill Hants................18 D2
Clayhithe Cambs...............87 K2
Clayock Highld...............279 L1
Claypit Hill Cambs............87 G4
Claypits Gloucs...............63 M6
Claypole Lincs...............117 M2
Claythorpe Lincs.............137 H4
Clayton C Brad...............141 H2
Clayton Donc.................142 C6
Clayton W Susx................22 D4
Clayton Green Lancs..........139 H3
Clayton-le-Moors Lancs.......139 M2
Clayton-le-Woods Lancs.......139 H3
Clayton West Kirk............141 L5
Clayworth Notts..............134 E2
Cleadale Highld..............236 F3
Cleadon S Tyne...............181 J6
Clearbrook Devon...............7 G2
Clearwell Gloucs..............63 H5
Clearwell Meend Gloucs........63 H5
Cleasby N York...............169 H8
Cleat Ork....................275 c6
Cleatlam Dur.................168 E7
Cleator Cumb.................164 D7
Cleator Moor Cumb............164 D7
Cleckheaton Kirk.............141 J3
Cleedownton Shrops............96 D7
Cleehill Shrops...............96 D8
Cleekhimin N Lans............209 K7
Clee St Margaret Shrops.......96 D7
Cleestanton Shrops............96 D7
Cleethorpes NE Lin...........145 J6
Cleeton St Mary Shrops........96 E7
Cleeve N Som..................44 F4
Cleeve Oxon...................48 F3
Cleeve Hill Gloucs............64 E2
Cleeve Prior Worcs............82 C5
Cleghornie E Loth............212 D2
Clehonger Herefs..............80 B7
Cleish P & K.................221 K7
Cleland N Lans...............209 L7
Clement's End C Beds..........68 C4
Clement Street Kent...........52 B5
Clenamacrie Ag & B...........216 E4

Clench Common Wilts...........47 H6
Clenchwarton Norfk...........120 D7
Clenerty Abers...............268 D4
Clent Worcs...................97 L7
Cleobury Mortimer Shrops......96 F8
Cleobury North Shrops.........96 E6
Cleongart Ag & B.............192 D2
Clephanton Highld............252 F2
Clerkhill D & G..............187 L6
Cleuch-head D & G............185 K3
Clevancy Wilts................46 F4
Clevedon N Som................44 E5
Cleveley Oxon.................66 B2
Cleveleys Lancs..............146 F7
Cleverton Wilts...............46 E2
Clewer Somset.................31 G1
Cley next the Sea Norfk......122 M4
Cliburn Cumb.................166 E5
Cliddesden Hants..............35 K1
Cliff Warwks..................99 G4
Cliffe Lancs.................139 L1
Cliffe Medway.................52 F4
Cliffe N York................143 G2
Cliffe N York................169 G7
Cliff End E Susx..............25 G4
Cliffe Woods Medway...........52 F4
Clifford Herefs...............79 J6
Clifford Leeds...............150 F7
Clifford Chambers Warwks......82 E5
Clifford's Mesne Gloucs.......63 K2
Cliffsend Kent................41 K2
Clifton Bristl...............45 H4
Clifton C Beds................86 D7
Clifton C Nott...............116 F4
Clifton C York...............151 J5
Clifton Calder...............141 J3
Clifton Cumb.................166 C5
Clifton Derbys...............115 K3
Clifton Devon.................27 L3
Clifton Donc.................142 E8
Clifton Lancs................138 F2
Clifton N York...............150 B6
Clifton Nthumb...............180 F2
Clifton Oxon..................66 C1
Clifton Salfd...............140 A7
Clifton Worcs.................81 J6
Clifton Campville Staffs......99 H1
Clifton Hampden Oxon..........66 C7
Clifton Reynes M Keyn.........85 H5
Clifton upon Dunsmore
   Warwks....................100 C8
Clifton upon Teme Worcs.......81 G3
Cliftonville Kent.............41 L1
Climping W Susx...............21 G6
Clink Somset..................32 C1
Clint N York.................150 C4
Clinterty C Aber.............245 J1
Clint Green Norfk............105 L1
Clintmains Border............201 L6
Clipiau Gwynd.................93 H1
Clippesby Norfk..............123 J8
Clipsham Rutlnd..............118 C8
Clipston Nhants..............100 F7
Clipston Notts...............117 H5
Clipstone C Beds..............68 B2
Clipstone Notts..............134 B7
Clitheroe Lancs..............148 C7
Clive Shrops.................113 H6
Clixby Lincs.................144 E7
Cloatley Wilts................46 E1
Clocaenog Denbgs.............111 L1
Clochan Moray................267 H4
Clock Face St Hel............129 M2
Cloddiau Powys................94 F2
Clodock Herefs................62 C2
Cloford Somset................32 B2
Clola Abers..................257 J3
Clophill C Beds...............86 B7
Clopton Nhants...............102 B7
Clopton Suffk.................90 F4
Clopton Corner Suffk..........90 F4
Clopton Green Suffk...........88 F4
Clopton Green Suffk...........89 K3
Clos du Valle Guern............9 k1
Closeburn D & G..............186 D7
Closeburnmill D & G..........186 D7
Closeclark IoM...............154 c7
Closworth Somset..............16 A1
Clothall Herts................69 H1
Clotton Ches W...............129 M6
Cloudesley Bush Warwks.......100 A6
Clouds Herefs.................80 D7
Clough Oldham................140 E6
Clough Foot Calder...........140 D3
Clough Head Calder...........141 H4
Cloughton N York.............163 H4
Cloughton Newlands N York....163 H4
Clousta Shet.................281 d5
Clova Angus..................233 M1
Clovelly Devon................26 E6

Clovenfords Border...........200 F6
Clovulin Highld..............228 F3
Clow Bridge Lancs............140 B2
Clowne Derbys................133 K4
Clows Top Worcs...............81 G1
Cloy Wrexhm..................112 F3
Cluanie Inn Highld...........239 H1
Cluanie Lodge Highld.........239 H2
Clubworthy Cnwll..............11 K4
Clugston D & G...............173 J3
Clun Shrops...................95 H7
Clunas Highld................253 G2
Clunbury Shrops...............95 J7
Clunderwen Carmth.............55 J3
Clune Highld.................252 E6
Clunes Highld................239 K6
Clungunford Shrops............95 K7
Clunie P & K.................233 H6
Clunton Shrops................95 H7
Cluny Fife...................222 D8
Clutton BaNES.................45 J7
Clutton Ches W...............113 G1
Clutton Hill BaNES............45 J7
Clwt-y-bont Gwynd............125 K7
Clydach Mons..................61 K4
Clydach Swans.................57 J4
Clydach Vale Rhondd...........42 E3
Clydebank W Duns.............208 E5
Clydebank Crematorium
   W Duns....................208 E4
Clydey Pembks.................75 M5
Clyffe Pypard Wilts...........47 G3
Clynder Ag & B...............207 L2
Clyne Neath...................60 B7
Clynnog-fawr Gwynd...........109 G2
Clyro Powys...................79 H6
Clyst Honiton Devon...........14 A4
Clyst Hydon Devon.............14 B2
Clyst St George Devon.........14 A5
Clyst St Lawrence Devon.......14 B3
Clyst St Mary Devon...........14 A4
Cnoc W Isls..................282 g3
Cnwch Coch Cerdgn.............92 E8
Coad's Green Cnwll............11 K7
Coal Aston Derbys............133 G4
Coalbrookvale Blae G..........61 K5
Coalburn S Lans..............198 D6
Coalburns Gatesd.............180 D6
Coaley Gloucs.................63 M6
Coalhill Essex................71 J7
Coalmoor Wrekin...............96 F2
Coalpit Heath S Glos..........45 K3
Coal Pool Wsall...............98 C3
Coalport Wrekin...............96 F3
Coalsnaughton Clacks.........221 G8
Coal Street Suffk.............90 F1
Coaltown of Balgonie Fife....222 E7
Coaltown of Wemyss Fife......222 E8
Coalville Leics...............99 L1
Coanwood Nthumb..............178 F7
Coat Somset...................31 G6
Coatbridge N Lans............209 J6
Coatdyke N Lans..............209 K6
Coate Swindn..................47 J2
Coate Wilts...................46 F6
Coates Cambs.................102 F4
Coates Gloucs.................64 E7
Coates Lincs.................135 H3
Coates Notts.................135 G3
Coates W Susx.................21 G3
Coatham R & Cl...............170 E5
Coatham Mundeville Darltn....169 H6
Cobbaton Devon................27 L5
Coberley Gloucs...............64 D4
Cobhall Common Herefs.........80 B8
Cobham Kent...................52 E6
Cobham Surrey.................50 E7
Coblers Green Essex...........71 G3
Cobley Dorset.................33 H6
Cobnash Herefs................80 B3
Cobo Guern.....................9 j2
Cobridge C Stke..............114 D2
Coburby Abers................269 G3
Cock Alley Derbys............133 H5
Cockayne N York..............161 K3
Cockayne Hatley C Beds........86 F5
Cock Bank Wrexhm.............112 E2
Cock Bevington Warwks.........82 C5
Cock Bridge Abers............243 J2
Cockburnspath Border.........213 G5
Cock Clarks Essex.............71 K6
Cock & End Suffk..............88 E4
Cockenzie and Port Seton
   E Loth....................211 L4
Cocker Bar Lancs.............139 G3
Cocker Brook Lancs...........139 L3
Cockerham Lancs..............147 J5
Cockermouth Cumb.............164 F4
Cockernhoe Herts..............68 E2
Cockersdale Leeds............141 K2

Cockett Swans 57 H6
Cockfield Dur 168 E6
Cockfield Suffk 89 H4
Cockfosters Gt Lon 69 H7
Cock Green Essex 71 G3
Cocking W Susx 20 E3
Cocking Causeway W Susx ... 20 E3
Cockington Torbay 8 D2
Cocklake Somset 31 G1
Cockley Beck Cumb 156 C2
Cockley Cley Norfk 104 F3
Cock Marling E Susx 24 F3
Cockpole Green Wokham 49 J3
Cocks Cnwll 4 C4
Cockshutford Shrops 96 D6
Cockshutt Shrops 113 G5
Cock Street Kent 39 K3
Cockthorpe Norfk 121 L3
Cockwells Cnwll 2 E4
Cockwood Devon 14 A6
Cockwood Somset 30 B2
Cockyard Derbys 131 L4
Cockyard Herefs 80 A8
Coddenham Suffk 90 D4
Coddington Ches W 129 K8
Coddington Herefs 81 G6
Coddington Notts 117 L1
Codford St Mary Wilts 33 G3
Codford St Peter Wilts 33 G3
Codicote Herts 69 G3
Codmore Hill W Susx 21 H3
Codnor Derbys 116 C2
Codrington S Glos 45 L3
Codsall Staffs 97 K3
Codsall Wood Staffs 97 J2
Coedely Rhondd 42 F4
Coedkernew Newpt 44 B2
Coed Morgan Mons 62 D5
Coedpoeth Wrexhm 112 D1
Coed Talon Flints 129 C6
Coedway Powys 112 E8
Coed-y-Bryn Cerdgn 76 C6
Coed-y-caerau Newpt 44 D1
Coed-y-paen Mons 62 C7
Coed-yr-ynys Powys 61 J3
Coed Ystumgwern Gwynd ... 109 K6
Coelbren Powys 60 C5
Coffinswell Devon 8 D1
Coffle End Bed 85 K3
Cofton Devon 13 M6
Cofton Hackett Worcs 98 C8
Cogan V Glam 43 J7
Cogenhoe Nhants 84 F3
Cogges Oxon 65 M5
Coggeshall Essex 71 K3
Coggin's Mill E Susx 23 K2
Coignafearn Highld 251 J8
Coilacriech Abers 243 K4
Coilantogle Stirlg 219 K5
Coillore Highld 246 E1
Coity Brdgnd 42 D5
Col W Isls 282 g3
Colaboll Highld 272 E6
Colan Cnwll 4 C5
Colaton Raleigh Devon 14 C5
Colbost Highld 258 C7
Colburn N York 160 B3
Colby Cumb 166 F6
Colby IoM 154 b7
Colby Norfk 122 E5
Colchester Essex 72 E2
Colchester Crematorium
  Essex 72 E3
Cold Ash W Berk 48 D5
Cold Ashby Nhants 100 E8
Cold Ashton S Glos 45 L4
Cold Aston Gloucs 65 H3
Coldbackie Highld 277 M4
Coldbeck Cumb 158 C2
Cold Blow Pembks 55 J4
Cold Brayfield M Keyn 85 H5
Cold Cotes N York 148 C2
Coldean Br & H 22 E5
Coldeast Devon 13 J7
Colden Calder 140 E2
Colden Common Hants 35 G6
Coldfair Green Suffk 91 K3
Coldham Cambs 103 J3
Cold Hanworth Lincs 135 L3
Coldharbour Cnwll 4 B5
Coldharbour Devon 29 J8
Coldharbour Gloucs 63 H6
Cold Harbour Herts 68 F4
Coldharbour Oxon 48 F3
Coldharbour Surrey 37 H2
Cold Harbour Wilts 32 E2
Cold Hatton Wrekin 113 K7
Cold Hatton Heath Wrekin .. 113 K7
Cold Hesledon Dur 169 L2
Cold Hiendley Wakefd 142 B5

Cold Higham Nhants 84 C4
Coldingham Border 213 K6
Cold Kirby N York 161 H6
Coldmeece Staffs 114 D5
Cold Newton Leics 100 F2
Cold Northcott Cnwll 11 H5
Cold Norton Essex 71 K7
Cold Overton Leics 101 H2
Coldred Kent 41 J4
Coldridge Devon 13 G1
Coldstream Border 202 C5
Coldwaltham W Susx 21 H3
Coldwell Herefs 80 A3
Coldwells Abers 257 H4
Cold Weston Shrops 96 C6
Cole Somset 31 L4
Colebatch Shrops 95 H6
Colebrook C Plym 7 G3
Colebrook Devon 14 B2
Colebrooke Devon 13 H3
Coleby Lincs 135 K7
Coleby N Linc 143 M4
Cole End Warwks 99 G5
Coleford Devon 13 H2
Coleford Gloucs 63 H6
Coleford Somset 31 L1
Coleford Water Somset 29 L4
Colegate End Norfk 106 D6
Cole Green Herts 69 H5
Cole Green Herts 70 B1
Cole Henley Hants 34 F1
Colehill Dorset 17 K2
Coleman Green Herts 69 G4
Coleman's Hatch E Susx 38 C6
Colemere Shrops 113 G5
Colemore Hants 35 L5
Colemore Green Shrops 97 G4
Colenden P & K 221 K1
Coleorton Leics 116 C8
Colerne Wilts 46 B5
Colesbourne Gloucs 64 E4
Cole's Cross Devon 8 A5
Coles Cross Dorset 15 J2
Colesden Bed 86 C4
Coles Green Suffk 90 C7
Coleshill Bucks 68 B8
Coleshill Oxon 65 K8
Coleshill Warwks 99 G5
Colestocks Devon 14 C3
Coley BaNES 45 H7
Colgate W Susx 37 K4
Colinsburgh Fife 223 H6
Colinton C Edin 211 H5
Colintraive Ag & B 207 G4
Colkirk Norfk 121 K6
Coll Ag & B 225 G4
Collace P & K 222 C1
Collafirth Shet 281 d3
Collaton Devon 7 L7
Collaton St Mary Torbay 8 C3
College of Roseisle Moray 266 C3
College Town Br For 49 K6
Collessie Fife 222 D4
Colleton Mills Devon 28 B7
Collier Row Gt Lon 52 B1
Collier's End Herts 69 K3
Collier's Green E Susx 24 E3
Colliers Green Kent 39 J5
Collier Street Kent 39 H4
Colliery Row Sundld 169 J1
Collieston Abers 257 J6
Collin D & G 176 D4
Collingbourne Ducis Wilts 47 K8
Collingbourne Kingston Wilts .. 47 K7
Collingham Leeds 150 E6
Collingham Notts 135 G7
Collington Herefs 80 F3
Collingtree Nhants 84 E4
Collins Green Warrtn 130 A1
Collins Green Worcs 81 G4
Colliston Angus 234 F6
Colliton Devon 14 C2
Collyweston Nhants 101 M3
Colmonell S Ayrs 182 E5
Colmworth Bed 86 C4
Colnabaichin Abers 243 J4
Colnbrook Slough 50 C3
Colne Cambs 103 H8
Colne Lancs 148 F7
Colne Bridge Kirk 141 J4
Colne Edge Lancs 148 F7
Colne Engaine Essex 71 K1
Colney Norfk 106 D2
Colney Heath Herts 69 G6
Colney Street Herts 68 F6
Coln Rogers Gloucs 65 G5
Coln St Aldwyns Gloucs 65 H6
Coln St Dennis Gloucs 65 G5
Colonsay Ag & B 214 D5
Colpy Abers 256 B5

Colquhar Border 200 D5
Colquite Cnwll 10 E8
Colscott Devon 26 F7
Colsterdale N York 159 L6
Colsterworth Lincs 118 B6
Colston Bassett Notts 117 J5
Coltfield Moray 266 C3
Colt Hill Hants 49 H8
Coltishall Norfk 122 F7
Colton Cumb 156 D5
Colton Leeds 142 B1
Colton N York 151 H6
Colton Norfk 106 C2
Colton Staffs 115 G7
Colt's Hill Kent 39 G4
Columbjohn Devon 13 M3
Colva Powys 79 H4
Colvend D & G 175 L4
Colwall Herefs 81 H6
Colwell Nthumb 179 M4
Colwich Staffs 115 G7
Colwick Notts 117 G3
Colwinston V Glam 42 E6
Colworth W Susx 20 F6
Colwyn Bay Conwy 127 G4
Colyford Devon 14 F4
Colyton Devon 14 F4
Combe Devon 7 L7
Combe Herefs 79 L3
Combe Oxon 66 B4
Combe W Berk 48 A6
Combe Almer Dorset 17 J3
Combe Common Surrey 36 E4
Combe Down BaNES 45 M6
Combe Fishacre Devon 8 C2
Combe Florey Somset 29 L4
Combe Hay BaNES 45 L7
Combe Martin Devon 27 K2
Combe Raleigh Devon 14 E2
Comberbach Ches W 130 C4
Comberford Staffs 99 G2
Comberton Cambs 87 H4
Comberton Herefs 80 C2
Combe St Nicholas Somset ... 30 D8
Combpyne Devon 15 G4
Combridge Staffs 115 H4
Combrook Warwks 83 H5
Combs Derbys 131 L4
Combs Suffk 90 B4
Combs Ford Suffk 90 B4
Combwich Somset 30 C2
Comers Abers 244 F2
Comhampton Worcs 81 J2
Commercial End Cambs 87 L3
Commins Coch Powys 93 H3
Commondale N York 170 F8
Common Edge Bpool 138 C1
Common End Cumb 164 D6
Common Moor Cnwll 6 A1
Common Platt Wilts 47 G2
Commonside Ches W 130 A5
Commonside Derbys 115 L3
Common Side Derbys 133 G4
Commonwood Shrops 113 H6
Commonwood Wrexhm 112 F1
Compass Somset 30 D4
Compstall Stockp 131 J2
Compstonend D & G 175 G4
Compton Devon 8 C2
Compton Hants 34 D5
Compton Hants 34 F5
Compton Staffs 97 J6
Compton Surrey 36 E2
Compton W Berk 48 D3
Compton W Susx 20 C4
Compton Wilts 47 H8
Compton Abbas Dorset 32 E7
Compton Abdale Gloucs 64 F4
Compton Bassett Wilts 46 F4
Compton Beauchamp Oxon ... 47 K2
Compton Bishop Somset 44 B7
Compton Chamberlayne Wilts .. 33 H5
Compton Dando BaNES 45 J6
Compton Dundon Somset 31 H4
Compton Durville Somset 30 F7
Compton Greenfield S Glos 45 H3
Compton Martin BaNES 45 G7
Compton Pauncefoot Somset ... 31 L5
Compton Valence Dorset 16 B4
Compton Verney Warwks 83 H5
Comrie Fife 210 D1
Comrie P & K 220 D3
Conaglen House Highld 229 G2
Conchra Highld 248 E6
Concraigie P & K 233 G6
Conder Green Lancs 147 J4
Conderton Worcs 81 M7
Condicote Gloucs 65 H2
Condorrat N Lans 209 K4

Condover Shrops 96 B2
Coney Hill Gloucs 64 B3
Coneyhurst Common W Susx .. 37 H6
Coneysthorpe N York 151 M2
Coneythorpe N York 150 E4
Coney Weston Suffk 105 J7
Conford Hants 36 M3
Congdon's Shop Cnwll 11 K7
Congerstone Leics 99 K2
Congham Norfk 120 F6
Congleton Ches E 131 G7
Congl-y-wal Gwynd 110 D3
Congresbury N Som 44 C6
Congreve Staffs 97 K1
Conheath D & G 176 C5
Conicavel Moray 253 J1
Coningsby Lincs 136 D8
Conington Cambs 87 G3
Conington Cambs 102 D6
Conisbrough Donc 142 D8
Conisholme Lincs 145 K8
Coniston Cumb 156 D3
Coniston E R Yk 144 F1
Coniston Cold N York 148 F5
Conistone N York 149 H2
Connah's Quay Flints 129 G6
Connel Ag & B 228 E8
Connel Park E Ayrs 197 H8
Connor Downs Cnwll 2 F3
Conon Bridge Highld 250 F2
Cononley N York 149 H6
Consall Staffs 114 F2
Consett Dur 180 D8
Constable Burton N York 159 L4
Constable Lee Lancs 140 B3
Constantine Cnwll 3 J5
Constantine Bay Cnwll 10 B7
Contin Highld 262 D8
Conwy Conwy 126 F4
Conyer Kent 40 C2
Conyer's Green Suffk 89 H2
Cooden E Susx 24 C6
Cookbury Devon 12 A2
Cookbury Wick Devon 11 M2
Cookham W & M 49 L2
Cookham Dean W & M 49 L2
Cookham Rise W & M 49 L2
Cookhill Worcs 82 C3
Cookley Suffk 107 G8
Cookley Worcs 97 J7
Cookley Green Oxon 49 G1
Cookney Abers 245 J5
Cooksbridge E Susx 22 F4
Cooksey Green Worcs 81 L1
Cook's Green Essex 73 J3
Cooks Green Suffk 89 K4
Cookshill Staffs 114 E3
Cooksland Cnwll 5 J1
Cooksmill Green Essex 70 F6
Cookson Green Ches W 130 B5
Coolham W Susx 37 H6
Cooling Medway 53 G4
Cooling Street Medway 52 F4
Coombe Cnwll 3 L3
Coombe Cnwll 3 L6
Coombe Cnwll 4 F4
Coombe Devon 13 J6
Coombe Devon 13 L3
Coombe Devon 14 C4
Coombe Gloucs 63 M8
Coombe Hants 35 K6
Coombe Wilts 33 K1
Coombe Bissett Wilts 33 K5
Coombe Cellars Devon 13 L8
Coombe Cross Hants 35 K6
Coombe Hill Gloucs 64 C3
Coombe Keynes Dorset 17 G6
Coombe Pafford Torbay 8 D2
Coombes W Susx 21 L5
Coombes-Moor Herefs 79 L3
Coombe Street Somset 32 C4
Coombeswood Dudley 98 B6
Coopersale Common Essex 70 C6
Coopersale Street Essex 70 C6
Cooper's Corner Kent 38 D3
Coopers Green E Susx 23 J3
Coopers Green Herts 69 G5
Cooper Street Kent 41 L3
Cooper Turning Bolton 139 J6
Cootham W Susx 21 J4
Copdock Suffk 90 D6
Copford Green Essex 72 D3
Copgrove N York 150 D3
Copister Shet 281 e4
Cople Bed 86 C4
Copley Calder 141 G3
Copley Dur 168 D5
Copley Tamesd 140 E8
Coplow Dale Derbys 132 C4
Copmanthorpe C York 151 J6

Copmere End Staffs 114 C5
Copp Lancs 147 H7
Coppathorne Cnwll 11 H3
Coppenhall Staffs 114 E7
Coppenhall Moss Ches E 130 D8
Copperhouse Cnwll 2 F3
Coppicegate Shrops 97 G7
Coppingford Cambs 102 D7
Coppins Corner Kent 40 B5
Copplestone Devon 13 H2
Coppull Lancs 139 H5
Coppull Moor Lancs 139 H5
Copsale W Susx 37 J6
Copster Green Lancs 139 K1
Copston Magna Warwks 99 M5
Cop Street Kent 41 J3
Copthall Green Essex 70 B3
Copt Heath Solhll 98 F7
Copt Hewick N York 150 D2
Copthorne Cnwll 11 K4
Copthorne W Susx 37 M3
Copt Oak Leics 100 B1
Copy's Green Norfk 121 L4
Copythorne Hants 34 C8
Coram Street Suffk 89 K6
Corbets Tey Gt Lon 52 C2
Corbiere Jersey 9 a3
Corbridge Nthumb 180 B6
Corby Nhants 101 K5
Corby Glen Lincs 118 C6
Corby Hill Cumb 178 B7
Cordon N Ayrs 195 G5
Cordwell Derbys 132 F4
Coreley Shrops 96 E8
Cores End Bucks 49 L2
Corfe Somset 30 C7
Corfe Castle Dorset 17 J6
Corfe Mullen Dorset 17 J3
Corfton Shrops 96 B6
Corgarff Abers 243 J2
Corhampton Hants 35 J6
Corks Pond Kent 39 G5
Corley Warwks 99 J6
Corley Ash Warwks 99 J6
Corley Moor Warwks 99 H6
Cormuir Angus 233 L2
Cornard Tye Suffk 89 H7
Corndon Devon 13 G5
Corner Row Lancs 138 E1
Corney Cumb 155 K4
Cornforth Dur 169 J4
Cornhill Abers 267 M4
Cornhill-on-Tweed Nthumb 202 D5
Cornholme Calder 140 D3
Cornish Hall End Essex 88 D7
Cornoigmore Ag & B 224 C6
Cornriggs Dur 167 K2
Cornsay Dur 168 F2
Cornsay Colliery Dur 168 F2
Corntown Highld 262 F8
Corntown V Glam 42 D6
Cornwell Oxon 65 K2
Cornwood Devon 7 H3
Cornworthy Devon 8 B4
Corpach Highld 239 H8
Corpusty Norfk 122 C5
Corrachree Abers 244 B3
Corran Highld 229 G3
Corran Highld 238 D2
Corrany IoM 154 f4
Corrie D & G 177 G2
Corrie N Ayrs 195 G4
Corriecravie N Ayrs 193 J4
Corriegills N Ayrs 195 G4
Corriegour Lodge Hotel
    Highld 239 M5
Corriemoille Highld 262 C7
Corrimony Highld 250 C5
Corringham Lincs 135 H2
Corringham Thurr 52 F2
Corris Gwynd 93 G2
Corris Uchaf Gwynd 92 F2
Corrow Ag & B 217 K7
Corry Highld 247 K4
Corscombe Devon 12 E3
Corscombe Dorset 15 L2
Corse Gloucs 64 A2
Corse Lawn Gloucs 64 B1
Corsham Wilts 46 C5
Corsindae Abers 244 F2
Corsley Wilts 32 D2
Corsley Heath Wilts 32 D2
Corsock D & G 185 J7
Corston BaNES 45 K6
Corston Wilts 46 D2
Corstorphine C Edin 211 G4
Cors-y-Gedol Gwynd 109 L7
Cortachy Angus 234 B3
Corton Suffk 107 L4
Corton Wilts 32 F3

Corton Denham Somset 31 K6
Coruanan Highld 229 H2
Corwen Denbgs 111 L3
Coryates Dorset 16 B5
Coryton Devon 12 B6
Coryton Thurr 52 F2
Cosby Leics 100 C4
Coseley Dudley 97 L4
Cosford Shrops 97 H4
Cosgrove Nhants 84 F6
Cosham C Port 19 L3
Cosheston Pembks 55 G6
Cossall Notts 116 E3
Cossall Marsh Notts 116 E3
Costessey Norfk 106 D1
Costock Notts 116 F6
Coston Leics 117 M7
Coston Norfk 106 B2
Cote Oxon 65 M6
Cote Somset 30 E2
Cotebrook Ches W 130 B6
Cotehill Cumb 166 B1
Cotes Cumb 157 G5
Cotes Leics 116 F7
Cotes Staffs 114 C4
Cotesbach Leics 100 C7
Cotes Heath Staffs 114 C4
Cotford St Luke Somset 30 A5
Cotgrave Notts 117 H4
Cothal Abers 256 F8
Cotham Notts 117 L2
Cothelstone Somset 30 B4
Cotherstone Dur 168 C6
Cothill Oxon 66 C7
Cotleigh Devon 14 E2
Cotmanhay Derbys 116 D3
Coton Cambs 87 H3
Coton Nhants 84 D1
Coton Shrops 113 J4
Coton Staffs 98 F2
Coton Staffs 114 C7
Coton Staffs 114 F5
Coton Clanford Staffs 114 D7
Coton Hayes Staffs 114 F5
Coton Hill Shrops 96 B3
Coton in the Clay Staffs 115 K5
Coton in the Elms Derbys 115 L8
Coton Park Derbys 115 M7
Cott Devon 8 B3
Cottage End Hants 34 E2
Cottam Lancs 139 G1
Cottam Notts 135 G4
Cottenham Cambs 87 J2
Cotterdale N York 158 E4
Cottered Herts 69 J1
Cotteridge Birm 98 D7
Cotterstock Nhants 102 A5
Cottesbrooke Nhants 100 F8
Cottesmore Rutlnd 101 K1
Cottingham E R Yk 144 D1
Cottingham Nhants 101 J5
Cottingley C Brad 149 K8
Cottingley Hall Crematorium
    Leeds 141 L2
Cottisford Oxon 66 E1
Cotton Suffk 90 C2
Cotton End Bed 86 B6
Cotton Tree Lancs 148 F7
Cottown Abers 255 K6
Cottown Abers 256 D8
Cottown of Gight Abers 256 E2
Cotts Devon 6 E2
Cotwall Wrekin 113 K8
Cotwalton Staffs 114 E4
Couch's Mill Cnwll 5 K3
Coughton Herefs 63 H3
Coughton Warwks 82 C3
Coulaghailtro Ag & B 206 A6
Coulags Highld 248 F3
Coulderton Cumb 155 H1
Coull Abers 244 B3
Coulport Ag & B 207 L2
Coulsdon Gt Lon 51 J7
Coulston Wilts 46 D8
Coulter S Lans 199 H6
Coultershaw Bridge W Susx 21 G3
Coultings Somset 30 C3
Coulton N York 161 K7
Coultra Fife 222 F3
Cound Shrops 96 D2
Coundlane Shrops 96 D2
Coundon Dur 169 G5
Coundon Grange Dur 169 G5
Countersett N York 159 G5
Countess Wilts 33 K2
Countess Cross Essex 72 C1
Countess Wear Devon 13 M5

Countesthorpe Leics 100 D4
Countisbury Devon 28 C1
Coupar Angus P & K 233 K7
Coup Green Lancs 139 H2
Coupland Cumb 167 G3
Coupland Nthumb 202 E7
Cour Ag & B 194 C2
Courteachan Highld 237 K1
Courteenhall Nhants 84 E4
Court Henry Carmth 59 G4
Courtsend Essex 72 F8
Courtway Somset 30 B4
Cousland Mdloth 211 L5
Cousley Wood E Susx 39 G6
Cove Ag & B 207 L3
Cove Border 213 G4
Cove Devon 29 G7
Cove Hants 49 L7
Cove Highld 260 C2
Cove Bay C Aber 245 L3
Cove Bottom Suffk 107 K7
Covehithe Suffk 107 L7
Coven Staffs 97 K2
Coveney Cambs 103 K7
Covenham St Bartholomew
    Lincs 136 F1
Covenham St Mary Lincs 136 F1
Coven Heath Staffs 97 K2
Coventry Covtry 99 J7
Coverack Cnwll 3 K7
Coverack Bridges Cnwll 3 H5
Coverham N York 159 K5
Covington Cambs 85 L1
Covington S Lans 199 G5
Cowan Bridge Lancs 157 K7
Cowbeech E Susx 23 K4
Cowbit Lincs 119 H7
Cowbridge V Glam 42 F6
Cowdale Derbys 132 B5
Cowden Kent 38 C5
Cowdenbeath Fife 211 G1
Cowden Pound Kent 38 C5
Cowden Station Kent 38 D5
Cowers Lane Derbys 116 A2
Cowes IoW 19 H4
Cowesby N York 161 G6
Cowesfield Green Wilts 34 B6
Cowfold W Susx 37 K6
Cowgill Cumb 158 C5
Cow Green Suffk 90 C2
Cowhill S Glos 45 J1
Cowie Stirlg 209 M1
Cowlam E R Yk 152 E3
Cowley Devon 13 L3
Cowley Gloucs 64 D4
Cowley Gt Lon 50 D3
Cowley Oxon 66 D6
Cowling Lancs 139 J4
Cowling N York 149 H7
Cowling N York 160 C5
Cowlinge Suffk 88 E4
Cowmes Kirk 141 J4
Cowpe Lancs 140 C4
Cowpen Nthumb 181 H3
Cowpen Bewley S on T 170 B5
Cowplain Hants 19 M2
Cowshill Dur 167 K3
Cowslip Green N Som 44 F6
Cowthorpe N York 150 F5
Coxall Herefs 95 J8
Coxbank Ches E 113 L3
Coxbench Derbys 116 C3
Coxbridge Somset 31 J3
Cox Common Suffk 107 H7
Coxford Cnwll 11 H3
Coxford Norfk 121 J5
Coxgreen Staffs 97 K6
Coxheath Kent 39 J3
Coxhoe Dur 169 J3
Coxley Somset 31 H2
Coxley Wakefd 141 L4
Coxley Wick Somset 31 H2
Coxpark Cnwll 12 A8
Coxtie Green Essex 70 E7
Coxwold N York 161 H7
Coychurch Brdgnd 42 E6
Coychurch Crematorium
    Brdgnd 42 D5
Coylton S Ayrs 196 E7
Coylumbridge Highld 242 B1
Coytrahen Brdgnd 42 D4
Crabbs Cross Worcs 82 B2
Crab Orchard Dorset 17 L1
Crabtree W Susx 37 K6
Crabtree Green Wrexhm 112 E3
Crackenthorpe Cumb 166 F6
Crackington Haven Cnwll 11 H3
Crackley Staffs 114 C2
Crackley Warwks 99 J8

Crackleybank Shrops 97 G1
Crackpot N York 159 H3
Cracoe N York 149 H4
Craddock Devon 29 K8
Cradle End Herts 70 C3
Cradley Dudley 97 L6
Cradley Herefs 81 G6
Cradley Heath Sandw 97 L6
Cradoc Powys 60 F1
Crafthole Cnwll 6 D4
Crafton Bucks 67 L3
Crag Foot Lancs 157 G7
Craggan Highld 253 K6
Cragg Hill Leeds 150 B8
Craghead Dur 180 F8
Crai Powys 60 D2
Craibstone Moray 267 K4
Craichie Angus 234 D6
Craig Angus 235 H4
Craig Highld 249 H2
Craigbank E Ayrs 197 H8
Craigburn Border 200 B2
Craigcefnparc Swans 57 J4
Craigcleuch D & G 177 K2
Craigdam Abers 256 F5
Craigdhu Ag & B 216 C6
Craigearn Abers 245 G1
Craigellachie Moray 254 F3
Craigend P & K 221 K3
Craigend Rens 208 D5
Craigendoran Ag & B 208 A3
Craigends Rens 208 C6
Craighlaw D & G 173 H3
Craighouse Ag & B 205 H3
Craigie P & K 233 H6
Craigie S Ayrs 196 E4
Craigiefold Abers 269 G3
Craigley D & G 175 J3
Craig Llangiwg Neath 57 K4
Craiglockhart C Edin 211 H5
Craigmillar C Edin 211 J4
Craignant Shrops 112 C4
Craigneston D & G 185 J5
Craigneuk N Lans 209 K6
Craigneuk N Lans 209 K7
Craignure Ag & B 227 L5
Craigo Angus 235 H3
Craig Penllyn V Glam 42 E6
Craigrothie Fife 222 F5
Craigruie Stirlg 219 H3
Craig's End Essex 88 E7
Craigton Angus 234 D7
Craigton C Aber 245 J3
Craigton E Rens 208 E8
Craigton Crematorium C Glas 208 E6
Craigton of Airlie Angus 233 M5
Craig-y-Duke Neath 57 K4
Craig-y-nos Powys 60 C4
Crail Fife 223 L5
Crailing Border 189 J1
Craiselound N Linc 143 J8
Crakehall N York 160 C5
Crakehill N York 160 F7
Crakemarsh Staffs 115 H4
Crambe N York 151 M3
Cramlington Nthumb 181 G3
Cramond C Edin 211 G4
Cramond Bridge C Edin 211 G4
Crampmoor Hants 34 E6
Cranage Ches E 130 E6
Cranberry Staffs 114 C4
Cranborne Dorset 33 H8
Cranbourne Br For 50 A4
Cranbrook Kent 39 J6
Cranbrook Common Kent 39 K5
Crane Moor Barns 141 M7
Crane's Corner Norfk 105 J1
Cranfield C Beds 85 J6
Cranford Devon 26 F6
Cranford Gt Lon 50 E4
Cranford St Andrew Nhants 101 K7
Cranford St John Nhants 101 K8
Cranham Gloucs 64 C4
Cranham Gt Lon 52 C2
Cranhill Warwks 82 D4
Crank St Hel 139 G7
Cranleigh Surrey 37 G3
Cranmer Green Suffk 89 L1
Cranmore IoW 18 F5
Cranmore Somset 31 L2
Cranoe Leics 101 G4
Cransford Suffk 91 H2
Cranshaws Border 212 F6
Cranstal IoM 154 f2
Cranswick E R Yk 152 F5
Crantock Cnwll 4 C3
Cranwell Lincs 118 D2
Cranwich Norfk 104 F4
Cranworth Norfk 105 K3
Craobh Haven Ag & B 216 B5

Crapstone Devon ... 6 F1
Crarae Ag & B ... 216 F7
Crask Inn Highld ... 272 D3
Crask of Aigas Highld ... 250 E3
Craster Nthumb ... 191 K2
Craswall Herefs ... 79 K8
Crateford Staffs ... 97 K2
Cratfield Suffk ... 107 G8
Crathes Abers ... 245 G4
Crathie Abers ... 243 J4
Crathie Highld ... 241 G5
Crathorne N York ... 161 G1
Craven Arms Shrops ... 95 K6
Crawcrook Gatesd ... 180 D6
Crawford Lancs ... 139 G7
Crawford S Lans ... 186 E2
Crawfordjohn S Lans ... 186 C2
Crawley Hants ... 34 F4
Crawley Oxon ... 65 M4
Crawley W Susx ... 37 L4
Crawley Down W Susx ... 38 A6
Crawleyside Dur ... 168 C3
Crawshawbooth Lancs ... 140 B3
Crawton Abers ... 245 J7
Craxe's Green Essex ... 72 D3
Cray N York ... 159 G6
Crayford Gt Lon ... 52 B4
Crayke N York ... 151 J2
Craymere Beck Norfk ... 122 B5
Crays Hill Essex ... 71 H8
Cray's Pond Oxon ... 48 F3
Craythorne Staffs ... 115 L6
Craze Lowman Devon ... 29 H8
Crazies Hill Wokham ... 49 J3
Creacombe Devon ... 28 E7
Creagan Inn Ag & B ... 228 F6
Creag Ghoraidh W Isls ... 283 c9
Creagorry W Isls ... 283 c9
Creaguaineach Lodge Highld ... 230 B2
Creamore Bank Shrops ... 113 H5
Creaton Nhants ... 84 D1
Creca D & G ... 177 H5
Credenhill Herefs ... 80 B6
Crediton Devon ... 13 J3
Creebank D & G ... 183 J7
Creebridge D & G ... 173 K2
Creech Dorset ... 17 H6
Creech Heathfield Somset ... 30 D5
Creech St Michael Somset ... 30 C6
Creed Cnwll ... 4 F5
Creekmouth Gt Lon ... 51 M3
Creeksea Essex ... 72 D7
Creeting St Mary Suffk ... 90 C4
Creeton Lincs ... 118 D7
Creetown D & G ... 174 D3
Cregneash IoM ... 154 b8
Creg ny Baa IoM ... 154 e5
Cregrina Powys ... 79 G5
Creich Fife ... 222 E3
Creigiau Cardif ... 43 G5
Cremyll Cnwll ... 6 E4
Cressage Shrops ... 96 D3
Cressbrook Derbys ... 132 C5
Cresselly Pembks ... 55 H5
Cressex Bucks ... 67 K8
Cressing Essex ... 71 J3
Cresswell Nthumb ... 191 K4
Cresswell Pembks ... 55 H5
Cresswell Staffs ... 114 F4
Creswell Derbys ... 133 K5
Creswell Green Staffs ... 98 D1
Cretingham Suffk ... 90 F3
Cretshengan Ag & B ... 206 A5
Crewe Ches E ... 130 D8
Crewe Ches W ... 112 F1
Crewe Crematorium Ches E ... 130 D8
Crewe Green Ches E ... 130 E8
Crew Green Powys ... 112 D8
Crewkerne Somset ... 15 K1
Crews Hill Station Gt Lon ... 69 J7
Crewton C Derb ... 116 C5
Crianlarich Stirlg ... 218 F2
Cribyn Cerdgn ... 76 F5
Criccieth Gwynd ... 109 J4
Crich Derbys ... 116 B1
Crich Carr Derbys ... 116 B1
Crichton Mdloth ... 211 L6
Crick Mons ... 44 F1
Crick Nhants ... 84 B1
Crickadarn Powys ... 78 F6
Cricket St Thomas Somset ... 15 J1
Crickheath Shrops ... 112 D7
Crickhowell Powys ... 61 K3
Cricklade Wilts ... 65 G8
Cricklewood Gt Lon ... 51 G2
Cridling Stubbs N York ... 142 E3
Crieff P & K ... 220 F3
Criggan Cnwll ... 5 G3
Criggion Powys ... 112 D8
Crigglestone Wakefd ... 141 M4

Crimble Rochdl ... 140 C5
Crimond Abers ... 269 K5
Crimplesham Norfk ... 104 C3
Crimscote Warwks ... 82 F5
Crinaglack Highld ... 250 D4
Crinan Ag & B ... 216 B8
Crindledyke N Lans ... 209 L7
Cringleford Norfk ... 106 D2
Cringles C Brad ... 149 J6
Crinow Pembks ... 55 K4
Cripplesease Cnwll ... 2 D4
Cripplestyle Dorset ... 33 J8
Cripp's Corner E Susx ... 24 D3
Croachy Highld ... 251 H3
Croanford Cnwll ... 10 E8
Crockenhill Kent ... 52 B5
Crocker End Oxon ... 49 H2
Crockerhill W Susx ... 20 F5
Crockernwell Devon ... 13 H4
Crocker's Ash Herefs ... 63 G4
Crockerton Wilts ... 32 E2
Crocketford D & G ... 185 K8
Crockey Hill C York ... 151 K6
Crockham Hill Kent ... 38 C3
Crockhurst Street Kent ... 39 G4
Crockleford Heath Essex ... 72 F2
Crock Street Somset ... 30 D8
Croeserw Neath ... 42 C3
Croes-goch Pembks ... 74 D6
Croes-lan Cerdgn ... 76 C6
Croesor Gwynd ... 110 B3
Croesyceiliog Carmth ... 58 D5
Croesyceiliog Torfn ... 62 C7
Croes-y-mwyalch Torfn ... 62 C8
Croes-y-pant Mons ... 62 C6
Croft Leics ... 100 B4
Croft Lincs ... 137 J7
Croft Warrtn ... 130 C1
Croftamie Stirlg ... 208 E2
Croft Mitchell Cnwll ... 3 H4
Crofton Cumb ... 165 J1
Crofton Wakefd ... 142 B4
Crofton Wilts ... 47 K6
Croft-on-Tees N York ... 160 D1
Croftown Highld ... 261 K3
Crofts Moray ... 266 F6
Crofts Bank Traffd ... 139 M8
Crofts of Dipple Moray ... 267 G4
Crofts of Savoch Abers ... 269 J4
Crofty Swans ... 56 F6
Crogen Gwynd ... 111 K4
Croggan Ag & B ... 227 K7
Croglin Cumb ... 166 D1
Croick Highld ... 262 D2
Cromarty Highld ... 264 B6
Crombie Fife ... 210 E2
Cromdale Highld ... 253 L6
Cromer Herts ... 69 J2
Cromer Norfk ... 122 E3
Cromford Derbys ... 132 F8
Cromhall S Glos ... 45 K1
Cromhall Common S Glos ... 45 K1
Cromor W Isls ... 282 g4
Crompton Fold Oldham ... 140 E6
Cromwell Notts ... 134 F7
Cronberry E Ayrs ... 197 H6
Crondall Hants ... 36 B1
Cronkbourne IoM ... 154 e6
Cronk-y-Voddy IoM ... 154 d5
Cronton Knows ... 129 L2
Crook Cumb ... 157 G4
Crook Dur ... 168 F4
Crookdake Cumb ... 165 G2
Crooke Wigan ... 139 H6
Crooked End Gloucs ... 63 J3
Crookedholm E Ayrs ... 196 E3
Crooked Soley Wilts ... 47 L4
Crookes Sheff ... 132 F2
Crookhall Dur ... 180 D8
Crookham Nthumb ... 202 E5
Crookham W Berk ... 48 D6
Crookham Village Hants ... 49 J8
Crooklands Cumb ... 157 H6
Crook of Devon P & K ... 221 J7
Cropper Derbys ... 115 L4
Cropredy Oxon ... 83 L6
Cropston Leics ... 100 C1
Cropthorne Worcs ... 82 B6
Cropton N York ... 162 D5
Cropwell Bishop Notts ... 117 H4
Cropwell Butler Notts ... 117 J4
Cros W Isls ... 282 h1
Crosbost W Isls ... 282 g4
Crosby Cumb ... 164 E3
Crosby IoM ... 154 d6
Crosby N Linc ... 143 M5
Crosby Sefton ... 138 C8
Crosby Garret Cumb ... 158 C1
Crosby Ravensworth Cumb ... 166 E7

Crosby Villa Cumb ... 164 E3
Croscombe Somset ... 31 K2
Crosemere Shrops ... 113 G5
Crosland Edge Kirk ... 141 H5
Crosland Hill Kirk ... 141 H5
Cross Somset ... 44 E8
Crossaig Ag & B ... 194 C1
Crossapoll Ag & B ... 224 C6
Cross Ash Mons ... 62 E3
Cross-at-Hand Kent ... 39 K4
Crossbush W Susx ... 21 H5
Crosscanonby Cumb ... 164 E3
Cross Coombe Cnwll ... 4 B4
Crossdale Street Norfk ... 122 E4
Cross End Bed ... 85 L4
Cross End Essex ... 89 G8
Crossens Sefton ... 138 D4
Cross Flatts C Brad ... 149 K7
Crossford Fife ... 210 E2
Crossford S Lans ... 198 D4
Crossgate Cnwll ... 11 L5
Crossgate Lincs ... 119 H6
Crossgate Staffs ... 114 E4
Crossgatehall E Loth ... 211 L5
Crossgates E Ayrs ... 196 D2
Crossgates Fife ... 210 F1
Cross Gates Leeds ... 142 B1
Crossgates N York ... 163 J6
Crossgates Powys ... 78 F2
Crossgill Lancs ... 147 L3
Cross Green Devon ... 11 M5
Cross Green Leeds ... 141 M2
Cross Green Staffs ... 97 K2
Cross Green Suffk ... 89 G4
Cross Green Suffk ... 89 H4
Cross Green Suffk ... 89 K4
Crosshands Carmth ... 55 L2
Cross Hands Carmth ... 59 G6
Crosshands E Ayrs ... 196 F5
Cross Hands Pembks ... 55 H4
Cross Hill Derbys ... 116 C2
Crosshill Fife ... 222 B7
Crosshill S Ayrs ... 183 J2
Cross Hills N York ... 149 H6
Crosshouse E Ayrs ... 196 D3
Cross Houses Shrops ... 96 C2
Cross Houses Shrops ... 96 F5
Cross in Hand E Susx ... 23 J3
Cross Inn Cerdgn ... 76 D4
Cross Inn Cerdgn ... 77 G2
Cross Inn Pembks ... 55 J5
Cross Inn Rhondd ... 43 G5
Cross Keys Ag & B ... 208 B2
Crosskeys Caerph ... 43 K3
Cross Keys Wilts ... 46 C5
Crosskirk Highld ... 279 H2
Crosslands Cumb ... 156 E5
Cross Lane IoW ... 19 H5
Cross Lane Head Shrops ... 97 G4
Cross Lanes Cnwll ... 3 H6
Cross Lanes Cnwll ... 4 C6
Cross Lanes N York ... 151 H3
Crosslanes Shrops ... 112 E7
Cross Lanes Wrexhm ... 112 E2
Crosslee Rens ... 208 C6
Crossley Kirk ... 141 K3
Crossmichael D & G ... 175 J2
Cross Oak Powys ... 61 H2
Cross of Jackston Abers ... 256 D5
Cross o' th' hands Derbys ... 115 M2
Crosspost W Susx ... 37 L6
Crossroads Abers ... 244 D2
Crossroads Abers ... 245 G5
Cross Street Suffk ... 106 D8
Crosston Angus ... 234 E4
Cross Town Ches E ... 130 E4
Crossway Mons ... 62 F3
Crossway Powys ... 78 E4
Crossway Green Mons ... 63 G8
Crossway Green Worcs ... 81 J2
Crossways Dorset ... 16 E5
Crosswell Pembks ... 75 J5
Crosthwaite Cumb ... 156 F4
Croston Lancs ... 138 F4
Crostwick Norfk ... 122 E8
Crostwight Norfk ... 123 G5
Crouch Kent ... 38 F2
Crouch Kent ... 40 D4
Crouch End Gt Lon ... 51 J1
Croucheston Wilts ... 33 J6
Crouch Hill Dorset ... 32 B8
Crough House Green Kent ... 38 C4
Croughton Nhants ... 84 A8
Crovie Abers ... 268 E3
Crow Hants ... 18 B3
Crowan Cnwll ... 3 G4
Crowborough E Susx ... 38 D7
Crowborough Town E Susx ... 38 D7
Crowcombe Somset ... 29 L3
Crowdecote Derbys ... 132 B6

Crowden Derbys ... 141 G7
Crowden Devon ... 12 C3
Crowdhill Hants ... 35 G6
Crowdleham Kent ... 52 C7
Crow Edge Barns ... 141 J6
Crowell Oxon ... 67 H7
Crow End Cambs ... 87 G4
Crowfield Nhants ... 84 B3
Crowfield Suffk ... 90 D4
Crowfield Green Suffk ... 90 D4
Crowgate Street Norfk ... 123 G7
Crow Green Essex ... 70 E7
Crowhill E Loth ... 213 G5
Crow Hill Herefs ... 63 J2
Crowhole Derbys ... 133 G4
Crowhurst E Susx ... 24 D5
Crowhurst Surrey ... 38 B4
Crowhurst Lane End Surrey ... 38 B4
Crowland Lincs ... 102 E3
Crowland Suffk ... 89 K1
Crowlas Cnwll ... 2 E4
Crowle N Linc ... 143 K5
Crowle Worcs ... 81 J4
Crowle Green Worcs ... 81 J4
Crowmarsh Gifford Oxon ... 48 F1
Crown Corner Suffk ... 90 F1
Crownhill C Plym ... 6 F3
Crownhill Crematorium
  M Keyn ... 84 F7
Crownpits Surrey ... 36 F2
Crownthorpe Norfk ... 106 B3
Crowntown Cnwll ... 3 G5
Crows-an-Wra Cnwll ... 2 B5
Crow's Green Essex ... 71 G3
Crowshill Norfk ... 105 J2
Crow's Nest Cnwll ... 6 B1
Crowsnest Shrops ... 95 J3
Crowthorne Wokham ... 49 K6
Crowton Ches W ... 130 B5
Croxall Staffs ... 99 G1
Croxby Lincs ... 144 F8
Croxdale Dur ... 169 H3
Croxden Staffs ... 115 H4
Croxley Green Herts ... 68 D7
Croxteth Lpool ... 138 E8
Croxton Cambs ... 86 E3
Croxton N Linc ... 144 E5
Croxton Norfk ... 105 H6
Croxton Norfk ... 121 G5
Croxton Staffs ... 114 B5
Croxtonbank Staffs ... 114 B5
Croxton Green Ches E ... 113 J1
Croxton Kerrial Leics ... 117 J2
Croy Highld ... 252 E2
Croy N Lans ... 209 J4
Croyde Devon ... 27 H3
Croyde Bay Devon ... 27 K3
Croydon Cambs ... 87 G5
Croydon Gt Lon ... 51 J6
Croydon Crematorium Gt Lon ... 51 J5
Crubenmore Highld ... 241 G6
Cruckmeole Shrops ... 95 K2
Cruckton Shrops ... 95 K1
Cruden Bay Abers ... 257 K4
Crudgington Wrekin ... 113 K8
Crudwell Wilts ... 64 D8
Cruft Devon ... 12 C3
Crug Powys ... 79 H1
Crugmeer Cnwll ... 10 C7
Crugybar Carmth ... 77 J7
Crug-y-byddar Powys ... 94 E7
Crumlin Caerph ... 43 K2
Crumplehorn Cnwll ... 5 L7
Crumpsall Manch ... 140 C7
Crundale Kent ... 40 E5
Crundale Pembks ... 54 F3
Crunwear Pembks ... 55 L5
Cruwys Morchard Devon ... 28 F8
Crux Easton Hants ... 48 B7
Cruxton Dorset ... 16 B3
Crwbin Carmth ... 58 E6
Cryers Hill Bucks ... 67 L7
Crymych Pembks ... 55 L5
Crynant Neath ... 60 B7
Crystal Palace Gt Lon ... 51 J5
Cuaig Highld ... 260 A8
Cuan Ag & B ... 215 L2
Cubbington Warwks ... 83 J2
Cubert Cnwll ... 4 C3
Cubley Barns ... 141 K7
Cublington Bucks ... 67 K3
Cublington Herefs ... 79 M7
Cuckfield W Susx ... 22 D2
Cucklington Somset ... 32 C5
Cuckney Notts ... 133 L5
Cuckoo Bridge Lincs ... 119 G6
Cuckoo's Corner Hants ... 35 M3
Cuckoo's Nest Ches W ... 129 J7
Cuddesdon Oxon ... 66 F6
Cuddington Bucks ... 67 H5

Cuddington - Dean 307

Cuddington Ches W 130 B5
Cuddington Heath Ches W 113 G2
Cuddy Hill Lancs 147 J8
Cudham Gt Lon 51 L7
Cudliptown Devon 12 C6
Cudnell Bmouth 17 L3
Cudworth Barns 142 B6
Cudworth Somset 30 F8
Cuerdley Cross Warrtn 130 A2
Cufaude Hants 49 G7
Cuffley Herts 69 J6
Cuil Highld 228 F4
Culbokie Highld 263 G7
Culbone Somset 28 E1
Culburnie Highld 250 E3
Culcabock Highld 251 J3
Culcharry Highld 253 G2
Culcheth Warrtn 130 C1
Culdrain Abers 255 K5
Culduie Highld 248 A4
Culford Suffk 89 G1
Culgaith Cumb 166 E5
Culham Oxon 66 D8
Culkein Highld 270 D2
Culkein Drumbeg Highld 270 F1
Culkerton Gloucs 64 D7
Cullen Moray 267 K3
Cullercoats N Tyne 181 J4
Cullerlie Abers 245 G3
Cullicudden Highld 263 H7
Cullingworth C Brad 149 J8
Cullipool Ag & B 215 L2
Cullivoe Shet 281 e2
Culloden Highld 252 D3
Cullompton Devon 14 B1
Culm Davy Devon 29 L7
Culmington Shrops 96 B7
Culmstock Devon 29 K8
Culnacraig Highld 270 E7
Culnaightrie D & G 175 J5
Culnaknock Highld 259 J4
Culpho Suffk 90 F5
Culrain Highld 263 G1
Culross Fife 210 C2
Culroy S Ayrs 196 C8
Culsalmond Abers 256 B5
Culscadden D & G 174 D5
Culshabbin D & G 173 H4
Culswick Shet 281 c6
Cultercullen Abers 257 G7
Cults C Aber 245 K3
Culverstone Green Kent 52 D6
Culverthorpe Lincs 118 D3
Culworth Nhants 84 A6
Cumbernauld N Lans 209 K4
Cumbernauld Village N Lans 209 K4
Cumberworth Lincs 137 J5
Cumdivock Cumb 165 K1
Cuminestown Abers 268 E6
Cumledge Border 202 B2
Cummersdale Cumb 177 L8
Cummertrees D & G 176 F5
Cummingston Moray 266 C2
Cumnock E Ayrs 197 H7
Cumnor Oxon 66 C6
Cumrew Cumb 178 D8
Cumrue D & G 176 E2
Cumwhinton Cumb 178 B8
Cumwhitton Cumb 178 C8
Cundall N York 150 F1
Cunninghamhead N Ayrs 196 D3
Cunningsburgh Shet 281 e7
Cupar Fife 222 F4
Cupar Muir Fife 222 F4
Curbar Derbys 132 E5
Curbridge Hants 19 J1
Curbridge Oxon 65 M5
Curdridge Hants 35 H8
Curdworth Warwks 98 F5
Curland Somset 30 C7
Curridge W Berk 48 C4
Currie C Edin 211 G5
Curry Mallet Somset 30 E6
Curry Rivel Somset 30 F6
Curteis Corner Kent 39 L5
Curtisden Green Kent 39 J5
Curtisknowle Devon 7 L4
Cury Cnwll 3 H6
Cushnie Abers 244 C1
Cushuish Somset 30 B5
Cusop Herefs 79 J7
Cutcloy D & G 174 C7
Cutcombe Somset 29 G3
Cutgate Rochdl 140 C5
Cuthill Highld 263 K2
Cutiau Gwynd 110 B8
Cutler's Green Essex 70 E1
Cutmadoc Cnwll 5 J2
Cutmere Cnwll 6 C3
Cutnall Green Worcs 81 K2
Cutsdean Gloucs 65 G1
Cutsyke Wakefd 142 C3
Cutthorpe Derbys 133 G5
Cuttivett Cnwll 6 D2
Cuxham Oxon 67 G8
Cuxton Medway 52 F5
Cuxwold Lincs 144 F7
Cwm Blae G 61 J6
Cwm Denbgs 128 C4
Cwmafan Neath 57 L6
Cwmaman Rhondd 60 F7
Cwmann Carmth 77 G6
Cwmavon Torfn 62 B6
Cwm-bach Carmth 56 E4
Cwmbach Carmth 75 M7
Cwmbach Powys 79 G7
Cwmbach Rhondd 60 F6
Cwmbach Llechrhyd Powys 78 E4
Cwmbelan Powys 93 K7
Cwmbran Torfn 62 C8
Cwmbrwyno Cerdgn 92 F7
Cwm Capel Carmth 56 E4
Cwmcarn Caerph 43 K3
Cwmcarvan Mons 62 F5
Cwm-celyn Blae G 61 K5
Cwm-Cewydd Gwynd 93 J1
Cwm-cou Cerdgn 76 B6
Cwm Crawnon Powys 61 J3
Cwmdare Rhondd 60 F6
Cwmdu Carmth 59 H3
Cwmdu Powys 61 J2
Cwmdu Swans 57 H6
Cwmduad Carmth 58 C3
Cwm Dulais Swans 57 H4
Cwmdwr Carmth 59 K2
Cwmfelin Brdgnd 42 C4
Cwmfelin Myr Td 61 H6
Cwmfelin Boeth Carmth 55 L3
Cwmfelinfach Caerph 43 J3
Cwmfelin Mynach Carmth 75 L7
Cwmffrwd Carmth 58 D5
Cwmgiedd Powys 59 L6
Cwmgorse Carmth 57 K3
Cwmgwili Carmth 57 G3
Cwmgwrach Neath 60 C6
Cwmhiraeth Carmth 76 C7
Cwm-Ifor Carmth 59 J4
Cwm Irfon Powys 78 A5
Cwmisfael Carmth 58 F5
Cwm Llinau Powys 93 J2
Cwmllynfell Neath 59 K6
Cwmmawr Carmth 58 F6
Cwm Morgan Carmth 58 B2
Cwmparc Rhondd 42 E3
Cwmpengraig Carmth 58 C2
Cwm Penmachno Conwy 110 E2
Cwmpennar Rhondd 61 G7
Cwmrhos Powys 61 J2
Cwmrhydyceirw Swans 57 J5
Cwmsychbant Cerdgn 76 E6
Cwmtillery Blae G 61 K6
Cwm-twrch Isaf Powys 57 L3
Cwm-twrch Uchaf Powys 59 L6
Cwm-y-glo Carmth 59 G6
Cwm-y-glo Gwynd 125 K7
Cwmyoy Mons 62 C3
Cwmystwyth Cerdgn 93 G8
Cwrt Gwynd 92 E3
Cwrt-newydd Cerdgn 76 E5
Cwrt-y-gollen Powys 61 K4
Cyfronydd Powys 94 E2
Cylibebyll Neath 57 K4
Cymau Flints 129 G8
Cymer Neath 42 C3
Cymmer Rhondd 42 F3
Cynghordy Carmth 77 M7
Cynheidre Carmth 56 E3
Cynonville Neath 42 C3
Cynwyd Denbgs 111 K3
Cynwyl Elfed Carmth 58 C3

D

Daccombe Devon 8 D1
Dacre Cumb 166 B5
Dacre N York 150 B4
Dacre Banks N York 150 B3
Daddry Shield Dur 167 K3
Dadford Bucks 84 C7
Dadlington Leics 99 L4
Dafen Carmth 56 F4
Daffy Green Norfk 105 J2
Dagenham Gt Lon 52 B2
Daglingworth Gloucs 64 E6
Dagnall Bucks 68 C4
Dagworth Suffk 89 L3
Dailly S Ayrs 183 H3
Dainton Devon 8 C2
Dairsie Fife 223 G4
Daisy Hill Bolton 139 K6
Daisy Hill Leeds 141 L2
Dalabrog W Isls 283 b11
Dalavich Ag & B 216 F5
Dalbeattie D & G 175 L3
Dalbury Derbys 115 M5
Dalby IoM 154 b6
Dalby Lincs 137 H5
Dalby N York 151 K2
Dalcapon P & K 232 E4
Dalchalm Highld 274 B6
Dalchreichart Highld 240 A1
Dalchruin P & K 220 C4
Dalcrue P & K 221 J2
Dalderby Lincs 136 E6
Dalditch Devon 14 B6
Daldowie Crematorium C Glas 209 H6
Dale Cumb 166 D2
Dale Derbys 116 D4
Dale Pembks 54 C5
Dale Bottom Cumb 165 J6
Dale End Derbys 132 D7
Dale End N York 149 G6
Dale Hill E Susx 39 H7
Dalehouse N York 171 H7
Dalelia Highld 237 L6
Dalgarven N Ayrs 196 B2
Dalgety Bay Fife 211 G2
Dalgig E Ayrs 197 G8
Dalginross P & K 220 D3
Dalguise P & K 232 E6
Dalhalvaig Highld 278 F5
Dalham Suffk 88 E3
Daliburgh W Isls 283 b11
Dalkeith Mdloth 211 K5
Dallas Moray 266 C5
Dallinghoo Suffk 91 G4
Dallington E Susx 24 B3
Dallington Nhants 84 E3
Dallow N York 150 B2
Dalmally Ag & B 217 K2
Dalmary Stirlg 219 H8
Dalmellington E Ayrs 184 D2
Dalmeny C Edin 210 F3
Dalmore Highld 263 H6
Dalmuir W Duns 208 E5
Dalnabreck Highld 237 K6
Dalnacardoch P & K 231 K1
Dalnahaitnach Highld 252 F7
Dalnaspidal P & K 231 J1
Dalnawillan Lodge Highld 279 H8
Daloist P & K 231 L4
Dalqueich P & K 221 K6
Dalquhairn S Ayrs 183 J4
Dalreavoch Lodge Highld 273 H6
Dalry N Ayrs 196 B1
Dalrymple E Ayrs 196 D8
Dalserf S Lans 198 C3
Dalsmeran Ag & B 192 D5
Dalston Cumb 165 L1
Dalston Gt Lon 51 J2
Dalswinton D & G 176 B2
Dalton Cumb 157 H7
Dalton D & G 176 F4
Dalton Lancs 139 G6
Dalton N York 159 K1
Dalton N York 160 F7
Dalton Nthumb 180 D4
Dalton Rothm 133 J1
Dalton-in-Furness Cumb 156 B7
Dalton-le-Dale Dur 169 L1
Dalton Magna Rothm 133 J1
Dalton-on-Tees N York 160 D1
Dalton Parva Rothm 133 J1
Dalton Piercy Hartpl 170 B4
Dalveich Stirlg 219 K2
Dalwhinnie Highld 241 H6
Dalwood Devon 14 F3
Damask Green Herts 69 H1
Damerham Hants 33 J7
Damgate Norfk 107 H2
Dam Green Norfk 105 L6
Danaway Kent 53 J6
Danbury Essex 71 J6
Danby N York 162 C1
Danby Bottom N York 162 B2
Danby Wiske N York 160 E3
Dandaleith Moray 254 F3
Danderhall Mdloth 211 J5
Danebridge Ches E 131 J6
Dane End Herts 69 J3
Danegate E Susx 38 E6
Danehill E Susx 22 F2
Dane Hills C Leic 100 C3
Danemoor Green Norfk 105 L2
Danesford Shrops 97 G5
Danesmoor Derbys 133 H7
Dane Street Kent 40 D5
Daniel's Water Kent 40 C7
Danshillock Abers 268 C5
Danskine E Loth 212 C5
Danthorpe E R Yk 145 H1
Danzey Green Warwks 82 D2
Dapple Heath Staffs 115 G6
Darby Green Hants 49 K7
Darcy Lever Bolton 139 L6
Dardy Powys 61 K3
Daren-felen Mons 61 K4
Darenth Kent 52 C5
Daresbury Halton 130 B3
Darfield Barns 142 C6
Darfoulds Notts 133 L4
Dargate Kent 40 E3
Darite Cnwll 6 B1
Darland Medway 53 G6
Darland Wrexhm 129 J8
Darlaston Wsall 98 B4
Darlaston Green Wsall 98 B4
Darley N York 150 B4
Darley Abbey C Derb 116 B4
Darley Bridge Derbys 132 E7
Darley Dale Derbys 132 E7
Darley Green Solhll 98 F8
Darleyhall Herts 68 F3
Darley Head N York 150 B4
Darlingscott Warwks 82 F6
Darlington Darltn 169 H7
Darlington Crematorium Darltn 169 H7
Darliston Shrops 113 J5
Darlton Notts 134 F5
Darnford Staffs 98 E2
Darnick Border 201 H6
Darowen Powys 93 H3
Darra Abers 268 D6
Darracott Devon 26 D7
Darracott Devon 27 H3
Darras Hall Nthumb 180 E5
Darrington Wakefd 142 D4
Darsham Suffk 91 K1
Darshill Somset 31 K2
Dartford Kent 52 B4
Dartington Devon 8 B2
Dartmeet Devon 12 F7
Dartmouth Devon 8 C4
Darton Barns 141 M5
Darvel E Ayrs 197 H3
Darwell Hole E Susx 24 C3
Darwen Bl w D 139 K3
Datchet W & M 50 C3
Datchworth Herts 69 H3
Datchworth Green Herts 69 H3
Daubhill Bolton 139 L6
Daugh of Kinermony Moray 254 E3
Dauntsey Wilts 46 E3
Dava Highld 253 J4
Davenham Ches W 130 C5
Davenport Stockp 131 H2
Davenport Green Ches E 131 G4
Davenport Green Traffd 130 F2
Daventry Nhants 84 B3
Davidson's Mains C Edin 211 H4
Davidstow Cnwll 11 G5
David Street Kent 52 E6
Davington D & G 187 K5
Davington Hill Kent 40 D3
Daviot Abers 256 D6
Daviot Highld 252 D4
Daviot House Highld 252 D4
Davis's Town E Susx 23 J4
Davoch of Grange Moray 267 K6
Davyhulme Traffd 139 M8
Daw End Wsall 98 C3
Dawesgreen Surrey 37 K2
Dawley Wrekin 96 F2
Dawlish Devon 13 M7
Dawlish Warren Devon 14 A7
Dawn Conwy 127 G5
Daws Green Somset 30 B6
Daws Heath Essex 53 H1
Daw's House Cnwll 11 K6
Dawsmere Lincs 120 A5
Daybrook Notts 116 F3
Day Green Ches E 130 F8
Dayhills Staffs 114 F5
Dayhouse Bank Worcs 98 B7
Daylesford Gloucs 65 K2
Ddol Flints 128 D5
Ddol-Cownwy Powys 111 K8
Deal Kent 41 L5
Dean Cumb 164 E5
Dean Devon 7 L2
Dean Devon 27 L2
Dean Devon 28 C1
Dean Dorset 33 G7
Dean Hants 34 F4
Dean Hants 35 H7
Dean Lancs 140 C3
Dean Oxon 65 M3
Dean Somset 31 L2

Dean Bottom Kent...... 52 C5
Deanburnhaugh Border 188 C4
Deancombe Devon 7 L2
Dean Court Oxon 66 C6
Deane Bolton 139 K6
Deane Hants 35 H1
Dean End Dorset 33 G7
Dean Head Barns 141 L7
Deanhead Kirk 141 G4
Deanland Dorset 33 G7
Deanlane End W Susx 20 B4
Dean Prior Devon 7 L2
Deanraw Nthumb 179 J6
Dean Row Ches E 131 G3
Deans W Loth 210 D5
Deanscales Cumb 164 E5
Deanshanger Nhants 84 E7
Deanshaugh Moray 267 G6
Deanston Stirlg 220 C6
Dean Street Kent 39 J3
Dearham Cumb 164 E3
Dearnley Rochdl 140 D4
Debach Suffk 90 F4
Debden Essex 70 C7
Debden Essex 87 L8
Debden Green Essex 70 E1
Debenham Suffk 90 E3
Deblin's Green Worcs 81 J5
Dechmont W Loth 210 D5
Dechmont Road W Loth 210 D5
Deddington Oxon 66 C1
Dedham Essex 90 C8
Dedham Heath Essex 72 F1
Dedworth W & M 50 B4
Deene Nhants 101 L5
Deenethorpe Nhants 101 L5
Deepcar Sheff 141 L8
Deepcut Surrey 49 L7
Deepdale Cumb 158 C5
Deepdale N York 158 F6
Deeping Gate C Pete 102 C2
Deeping St James Lincs 102 D2
Deeping St Nicholas Lincs 119 H8
Deerhurst Gloucs 64 C1
Deerhurst Walton Gloucs 64 C2
Deerton Street Kent 40 C3
Defford Worcs 81 L6
Defynnog Powys 60 D2
Deganwy Conwy 126 F4
Degnish Ag & B 216 B5
Deighton C York 151 K7
Deighton N York 160 E2
Deiniolen Gwynd 125 K7
Delabole Cnwll 10 F6
Delamere Ches W 130 A6
Delfrigs Abers 257 H7
Delley Devon 27 K6
Delliefure Highld 253 L5
Dell Quay W Susx 20 D6
Delly End Oxon 65 M4
Delnabo Moray 254 C8
Delnashaugh Inn Moray 254 D4
Delny Highld 263 K5
Delph Oldham 140 E6
Delves Dur 168 E1
Delvin End Essex 88 F8
Dembleby Lincs 118 D4
Demelza Cnwll 5 G2
Denaby Donc 142 D7
Denaby Main Donc 142 D7
Denbies Surrey 37 H1
Denbigh Denbgs 128 C6
Denbrae Fife 222 F3
Denbury Devon 8 B1
Denby Derbys 116 C2
Denby Bottles Derbys 116 C2
Denby Dale Kirk 141 K6
Denchworth Oxon 48 A1
Dendron Cumb 146 D2
Denel End C Beds 85 K8
Denfield P & K 221 G4
Denford Nhants 101 L8
Dengie Essex 72 E6
Denham Bucks 50 D2
Denham Suffk 88 E3
Denham Suffk 106 D8
Denham End Suffk 88 F3
Denham Green Bucks 50 D1
Denham Green Suffk 106 D8
Denhead Abers 269 J5
Denhead Fife 223 H4
Denhead of Gray C Dund 222 F1
Denholm Border 189 G3
Denholme C Brad 141 G1
Denholme Clough C Brad 141 G1
Denio Gwynd 108 F4
Denmead Hants 19 L1
Denmore C Aber 245 L1
Denne Park W Susx 37 J5
Dennington Suffk 91 G2

Denny Falk 209 L3
Dennyloanhead Falk 209 L3
Den of Lindores Fife 222 D4
Denshaw Oldham 140 E5
Denside Abers 245 H4
Densole Kent 41 G7
Denston Suffk 88 F5
Denstone Staffs 115 H3
Denstroude Kent 40 E3
Dent Cumb 158 B5
Denton Cambs 102 C6
Denton Darltn 169 G7
Denton E Susx 23 G6
Denton Kent 41 G6
Denton Kent 52 E4
Denton Lincs 117 M5
Denton N York 149 L6
Denton Nhants 85 G4
Denton Norfk 106 F5
Denton Oxon 66 E6
Denton Tamesd 131 H1
Denver Norfk 104 C3
Denwick Nthumb 191 J3
Deopham Norfk 105 L3
Deopham Green Norfk 105 L4
Depden Suffk 88 F4
Depden Green Suffk 88 F4
Deptford Gt Lon 51 K3
Deptford Wilts 33 H4
Derby C Derb 116 B4
Derby Devon 27 K4
Derbyhaven IoM 154 c8
Derculich P & K 232 C5
Dereham Norfk 105 K1
Deri Caerph 61 H6
Derril Devon 11 K2
Derringstone Kent 41 G5
Derrington Staffs 114 D7
Derriton Devon 11 L2
Derry Hill Wilts 46 D5
Derrythorpe N Linc 143 L6
Dersingham Norfk 120 F5
Dervaig Ag & B 226 E2
Derwen Denbgs 111 L2
Derwen Fawr Carmth 59 G4
Derwenlas Powys 92 F4
Derwydd Carmth 59 H5
Desborough Nhants 101 H6
Desford Leics 100 B3
Deskford Moray 267 K4
Detchant Nthumb 203 H6
Detling Kent 53 G7
Deuxhill Shrops 96 F6
Devauden Mons 62 F7
Devil's Bridge Cerdgn 92 F8
Devitts Green Warwks 99 H5
Devizes Wilts 46 E6
Devonport C Plym 6 E4
Devonside Clacks 221 G7
Devoran Cnwll 3 K3
Dewarton Mdloth 211 L6
Dewlish Dorset 16 E3
Dewsbury Kirk 141 K3
Dewsbury Moor Kirk 141 K3
Dewsbury Moor
    Crematorium Kirk 141 K3
Deytheur Powys 112 C8
Dial N Som 45 G5
Dial Green W Susx 36 D5
Dial Post W Susx 21 K3
Dibberford Dorset 15 K2
Dibden Hants 18 F2
Dibden Purlieu Hants 18 F2
Dickens Heath Solhll 98 E8
Dickleburgh Norfk 106 D7
Didbrook Gloucs 64 F1
Didcot Oxon 48 D1
Diddington Cambs 86 D2
Diddlebury Shrops 96 C6
Didley Herefs 62 F1
Didling W Susx 20 D3
Didmarton Gloucs 46 B2
Didsbury Manch 131 G1
Didworthy Devon 7 K2
Digby Lincs 135 M8
Digg Highld 259 H3
Diggle Oldham 140 F6
Digmoor Lancs 139 G6
Digswell Herts 69 H4
Digswell Water Herts 69 H4
Dihewyd Cerdgn 76 E4
Dilham Norfk 123 G6
Dilhorne Staffs 114 F3
Dill Hall Lancs 139 M2
Dillington Cambs 86 C2
Dilston Nthumb 180 A6
Dilton Wilts 32 E1
Dilton Marsh Wilts 32 D1
Dilwyn Herefs 80 A4
Dimple Bolton 139 L4

Dimple Derbys 132 F7
Dinas Carmth 58 A3
Dinas Cnwll 10 C7
Dinas Gwynd 108 D4
Dinas Pembks 75 G4
Dinas Rhondd 42 F3
Dinas Dinlle Gwynd 125 H8
Dinas-Mawddwy Gwynd 111 G8
Dinas Powys V Glam 43 J7
Dinder Somset 31 J2
Dinedor Herefs 80 C7
Dingestow Mons 62 F5
Dingle Lpool 129 J2
Dingleden Kent 39 K7
Dingley Nhants 101 G6
Dingwall Highld 262 F8
Dinmael Conwy 111 J3
Dinnet Abers 244 A4
Dinnington N u Ty 180 F4
Dinnington Rothm 133 K3
Dinnington Somset 30 F8
Dinorwic Gwynd 125 L7
Dinton Bucks 67 J5
Dinton Wilts 33 H4
Dinwoodie D & G 187 H8
Dinworthy Devon 26 E7
Dipford Somset 30 B6
Dippen Ag & B 194 B3
Dippen N Ayrs 195 G6
Dippenhall Surrey 36 B2
Dippermill Devon 12 B1
Dippertown Devon 12 B5
Dipple Moray 267 G4
Dipple S Ayrs 182 F2
Diptford Devon 7 L3
Dipton Dur 180 E8
Diptonmill Nthumb 179 L6
Dirleton E Loth 212 B2
Dirt Pot Nthumb 167 K2
Discoed Powys 79 K2
Diseworth Leics 116 D6
Dishforth N York 160 E8
Disley Ches E 131 J3
Diss Norfk 106 C7
Disserth Powys 78 E4
Distington Cumb 164 D6
Distington Hall Crematorium
    Cumb 164 D6
Ditchampton Wilts 33 J4
Ditcheat Somset 31 K4
Ditchingham Norfk 107 G5
Ditchling E Susx 22 E4
Ditherington Shrops 113 H8
Ditteridge Wilts 46 B5
Dittisham Devon 8 C4
Ditton Kent 52 F7
Ditton Green Cambs 88 D4
Ditton Priors Shrops 96 E5
Dixton Gloucs 64 E1
Dixton Mons 63 G4
Dizzard Cnwll 11 H3
Dobcross Oldham 140 F6
Dobwalls Cnwll 5 L2
Doccombe Devon 13 H5
Dochgarroch Highld 251 H3
Dockenfield Surrey 36 B3
Docker Lancs 157 J7
Docking Norfk 121 G4
Docklow Herefs 80 D4
Dockray Cumb 165 J1
Dockray Cumb 165 L6
Dodbrooke Devon 7 L6
Doddinghurst Essex 70 E7
Doddington Cambs 103 H5
Doddington Kent 40 B4
Doddington Lincs 135 H5
Doddington Nthumb 202 F6
Doddington Shrops 96 E8
Doddiscombsleigh Devon 13 K5
Dodd's Green Ches E 113 K3
Doddshill Norfk 120 F5
Doddy Cross Cnwll 6 C2
Dodford Nhants 84 B3
Dodford Worcs 97 L8
Dodington S Glos 45 L3
Dodington Somset 30 A3
Dodleston Ches W 129 J7
Dodscott Devon 27 K7
Dodside E Rens 208 E8
Dod's Leigh Staffs 115 G4
Dodworth Barns 141 M6
Dodworth Bottom Barns 141 M7
Dodworth Green Barns 141 M6
Doe Bank Birm 98 E4
Doe Lea Derbys 133 J6
Dogdyke Lincs 136 D8
Dogley Lane Kirk 141 J5
Dogmersfield Hants 49 J8
Dogridge Wilts 47 G2

Dogsthorpe C Pete 102 D3
Dog Village Devon 14 A3
Dolanog Powys 94 C2
Dolau Powys 79 J3
Dolaucothi Carmth 77 J1
Dolbenmaen Gwynd 109 J3
Doley Staffs 114 A5
Dolfach Powys 93 K3
Dol-for Powys 93 H2
Dolfor Powys 94 D6
Dolgarrog Conwy 126 H2
Dolgellau Gwynd 110 D7
Dolgoch Gwynd 92 F3
Dol-gran Carmth 58 G7
Doll Highld 273 K7
Dollar Clacks 221 G7
Dollarfield Clacks 221 G7
Dolley Green Powys 79 K2
Dollwen Cerdgn 92 E7
Dolphin Flints 128 E5
Dolphinholme Lancs 147 K5
Dolphinton S Lans 199 J4
Dolton Devon 27 K8
Dolwen Conwy 127 H5
Dolwyddelan Conwy 110 D1
Dolybont Cerdgn 92 D5
Dolyhir Powys 79 J4
Domgay Powys 112 D2
Donaldson's Lodge Nthumb 202 D5
Doncaster Donc 142 F7
Doncaster Carr Donc 142 F7
Donhead St Andrew Wilts 32 F6
Donhead St Mary Wilts 32 F6
Donibristle Fife 211 G1
Doniford Somset 29 K3
Donington Lincs 119 H4
Donington on Bain Lincs 136 D3
Donington Southing Lincs 119 G5
Donisthorpe Leics 99 J1
Donkey Street Kent 25 L1
Donkey Town Surrey 50 B6
Donnington Gloucs 65 G2
Donnington Herefs 81 G8
Donnington Shrops 96 D2
Donnington W Berk 48 C6
Donnington W Susx 20 D6
Donnington Wrekin 113 M8
Donnington Wood Wrekin 97 G1
Donyatt Somset 30 E8
Doomsday Green W Susx 37 J3
Doonfoot S Ayrs 196 C7
Dorback Lodge Highld 253 L8
Dorchester Dorset 16 D4
Dorchester Oxon 66 D1
Dordon Warwks 99 H3
Dore Sheff 132 F3
Dores Highld 251 G5
Dorking Surrey 37 J1
Dorking Tye Suffk 89 J7
Dormans Land Surrey 38 B5
Dormans Park Surrey 38 B5
Dormington Herefs 80 D7
Dormston Worcs 82 A4
Dorn Gloucs 82 F8
Dorney Bucks 50 B4
Dornie Highld 248 D6
Dornoch Highld 264 B2
Dornock D & G 177 H5
Dorrery Highld 279 H3
Dorridge Solhll 98 F8
Dorrington Lincs 118 E1
Dorrington Shrops 96 B3
Dorrington Shrops 114 A3
Dorsington Warwks 82 D5
Dorstone Herefs 79 K7
Dorton Bucks 67 G4
Dosthill Staffs 99 G3
Dothan IoA 124 F5
Dottery Dorset 15 L4
Doublebois Cnwll 5 L2
Doughton Gloucs 46 C1
Doulting Somset 31 L4
Dounby Ork 275 b4
Doune Highld 272 B7
Doune Stirlg 220 C6
Dounepark S Ayrs 182 F3
Dounie Highld 263 G2
Dousland Devon 7 G1
Dovaston Shrops 112 E7
Dove Green Notts 116 D1
Dove Holes Derbys 131 L4

Dovenby Cumb 164 E4
Dover Kent 41 K7
Dover Wigan 139 J7
Dovercourt Essex 73 K1
Doverdale Worcs 81 K2
Doveridge Derbys 115 J3
Doversgreen Surrey 37 L1
Dowally P & K 232 F5
Dowbridge Lancs 138 E2
Dowdeswell Gloucs 64 C3
Dowlais Myr Td 61 G5
Dowland Devon 12 D1
Dowlish Ford Somset 30 E8
Dowlish Wake Somset 30 E8
Down Ampney Gloucs 65 G7
Downderry Cnwll 6 C4
Downe Gt Lon 51 L6
Downend Gloucs 64 B7
Downend IoW 19 J6
Downend S Glos 45 K3
Downend W Berk 48 C4
Downfield C Dund 223 G1
Downgate Cnwll 11 K8
Downgate Cnwll 11 L8
Downham Essex 71 H7
Downham Gt Lon 51 K4
Downham Lancs 148 D7
Downham Market Norfk 104 C3
Down Hatherley Gloucs 64 C3
Downhead Somset 31 J6
Downhead Somset 32 A2
Downhill Cnwll 4 D1
Downhill P & K 221 K1
Downholland Cross Lancs 138 D6
Downholme N York 159 K3
Downicarey Devon 11 M4
Downies Abers 245 K4
Downing Flints 128 D4
Downley Bucks 67 K8
Down St Mary Devon 13 H7
Downs Crematorium Br & H 22 E6
Downside Somset 31 K2
Downside Somset 31 L1
Downside Surrey 50 E7
Down Thomas Devon 6 F5
Downton Hants 18 D5
Downton Wilts 33 L6
Dowsby Lincs 118 F5
Dowsdale Lincs 102 F2
Doxey Staffs 114 D6
Doxford Nthumb 191 H2
Doynton S Glos 45 L4
Draethen Caerph 43 K4
Draffan S Lans 198 C4
Dragonby N Linc 143 M5
Dragons Green W Susx 37 H6
Drakeholes Notts 134 E2
Drakelow Worcs 97 J7
Drakemyre N Ayrs 196 E1
Drakes Broughton Worcs 81 L5
Drakewalls Cnwll 12 B8
Draughton N York 149 J5
Draughton Nhants 101 K2
Drax N York 143 H3
Drax Hales N York 143 H3
Draycote Warwks 83 K1
Draycot Foliat Swindn 47 J3
Draycott Derbys 116 D5
Draycott Gloucs 82 E8
Draycott Shrops 97 H5
Draycott Somset 31 G1
Draycott Somset 31 J6
Draycott Worcs 81 K5
Draycott in the Clay Staffs 115 J6
Draycott in the Moors Staffs 114 E3
Drayford Devon 28 D8
Drayton C Port 19 L3
Drayton Leics 101 H5
Drayton Lincs 119 H4
Drayton Norfk 106 D1
Drayton Oxon 66 C8
Drayton Oxon 83 K7
Drayton Somset 30 F6
Drayton Worcs 97 K8
Drayton Bassett Staffs 99 G3
Drayton Beauchamp Bucks 67 L5
Drayton Parslow Bucks 67 K2
Drayton St Leonard Oxon 66 E7
Drebley N York 149 J4
Dreemskerry IoM 154 g4
Dreen Hill Pembks 54 F4
Drefach Carmth 58 F6
Drefach Carmth 76 C7
Drefach Carmth 76 F6
Drefelin Carmth 76 C7
Dreghorn N Ayrs 196 C3
Drellingore Kent 41 H7
Drem E Loth 212 B3
Dresden C Stke 114 E3
Drewsteignton Devon 13 H4

Driby Lincs 137 G5
Driffield E R Yk 152 F4
Driffield Gloucs 65 G7
Driffield Cross Roads Gloucs 64 F7
Drift Cnwll 2 C5
Drigg Cumb 155 K3
Drighlington Leeds 141 K2
Drimnin Highld 227 G2
Drimpton Dorset 15 K2
Drimsallie Highld 238 F7
Dringhouses C York 151 J6
Drinkstone Suffk 89 J3
Drinkstone Green Suffk 89 J3
Drive End Dorset 16 B1
Drointon Staffs 115 G6
Droitwich Worcs 81 K3
Dron P & K 221 L4
Dronfield Derbys 133 G4
Dronfield Woodhouse Derbys 133 G4
Drongan E Ayrs 196 E7
Dronley Angus 234 A8
Droop Dorset 16 E1
Dropping Well Rothm 133 H1
Droxford Hants 35 J7
Droylsden Tamesd 140 D8
Druid Denbgs 111 K3
Druidston Pembks 54 E3
Druimarbin Highld 229 H1
Druimavuic Ag & B 229 G6
Druimdrishaig Ag & B 206 A5
Druimindarroch Highld 237 K4
Drum Ag & B 206 E4
Drum P & K 221 J7
Drumalbin S Lans 198 F5
Drumbeg Highld 270 F2
Drumblade Abers 255 M4
Drumbreddon D & G 172 D6
Drumbuie Highld 248 B5
Drumburgh Cumb 177 J7
Drumburn D & G 175 L4
Drumchapel C Glas 208 E5
Drumchastle P & K 231 J4
Drumclog S Lans 197 J3
Drumeldrie Fife 223 G6
Drumelzier Border 199 K6
Drumfearn Highld 247 L5
Drumfrennie Abers 244 F4
Drumgley Angus 234 C5
Drumguish Highld 241 L3
Drumin Moray 254 D5
Drumjohn D & G 184 E3
Drumlamford S Ayrs 183 H7
Drumlasie Abers 244 E2
Drumleaning Cumb 177 J8
Drumlemble Ag & B 192 D4
Drumlithie Abers 245 H7
Drummoddie D & G 173 K6
Drummore D & G 172 E7
Drummuir Moray 255 H3
Drumnadrochit Highld 250 E5
Drumnaglaur D & G 172 E7
Drumnagorrach Moray 267 L5
Drumpark D & G 185 L7
Drumrunie Lodge Highld 271 G7
Drumshang S Ayrs 195 L8
Drumuie Highld 259 G2
Drumuillie Highld 253 H7
Drumvaich Stirlg 220 B6
Drunzie P & K 221 L5
Druridge Nthumb 191 K7
Drury Flints 129 G6
Drybeck Cumb 166 F7
Drybridge Moray 267 J4
Drybridge N Ayrs 196 D4
Drybrook Gloucs 63 J4
Dryburgh Border 201 J6
Dry Doddington Lincs 117 M2
Dry Drayton Cambs 87 H3
Drymen Stirlg 208 E1
Drymuir Abers 257 G3
Drynoch Highld 246 F2
Dry Sandford Oxon 66 C7
Dryslwyn Carmth 59 G5
Dry Street Essex 52 E2
Dryton Shrops 96 D2
Dubford Abers 268 E3
Dublin Suffk 90 E1
Duchally Highld 271 L4
Duck End Bed 85 L6
Duck End Cambs 86 F2
Duck End Essex 71 G2
Duck End Essex 88 D8
Duckend Green Essex 71 H3
Duckington Ches W 113 H1
Ducklington Oxon 65 M5
Duck's Cross Bed 86 C4
Duddenhoe End Essex 87 J7
Duddington Nhants 101 L3

Duddlestone Somset 30 C6
Duddleswell E Susx 38 C7
Duddlewick Shrops 96 F6
Duddo Nthumb 202 E4
Duddon Ches W 129 L6
Duddon Bridge Cumb 156 B5
Duddon Common Ches W 129 M6
Dudleston Shrops 112 E4
Dudleston Heath Shrops 112 E4
Dudley Dudley 97 L5
Dudley N Tyne 181 G4
Dudley Hill C Brad 141 J2
Dudley Port Sandw 98 B2
Dudnill Shrops 96 E8
Dudsbury Dorset 17 L3
Dudswell Herts 68 B5
Duffield Derbys 116 B3
Duffryn Neath 42 C3
Dufftown Moray 255 G4
Duffus Moray 266 D3
Dufton Cumb 166 F5
Duggleby N York 152 D2
Duirinish Highld 248 C5
Duisdalemore Highld 247 L6
Duisky Highld 239 G8
Dukestown Blae G 61 J5
Duke Street Suffk 90 C6
Dukinfield Tamesd 140 E8
Dukinfield Crematorium
Tamesd 140 E8
Dulas IoA 125 H2
Dulcote Somset 31 J4
Dulford Devon 14 C2
Dull P & K 232 B5
Dullatur N Lans 209 K4
Dullingham Cambs 88 C4
Dullingham Ley Cambs 88 C4
Dulnain Bridge Highld 253 J6
Duloe Bed 86 D3
Duloe Cnwll 5 M3
Dulverton Somset 29 G5
Dulwich Gt Lon 51 J4
Dumbarton W Duns 208 C4
Dumbleton Gloucs 82 B8
Dumfries D & G 176 C4
Dumgoyne Stirlg 208 E2
Dummer Hants 35 J2
Dumpton Kent 41 L2
Dun Angus 235 G3
Dunalastair P & K 231 K4
Dunan Ag & B 207 J5
Dunan Highld 247 J3
Dunan P & K 230 E4
Dunaverty Ag & B 192 E6
Dunball Somset 30 D3
Dunbar E Loth 212 E3
Dunbeath Highld 275 G2
Dunbeg Ag & B 228 D8
Dunblane Stirlg 220 D7
Dunbog Fife 222 D4
Dunbridge Hants 34 D5
Duncanston Highld 263 G8
Duncanstone Abers 255 L6
Dunchideock Devon 13 K5
Dunchurch Warwks 83 L1
Duncote Nhants 84 C5
Duncow D & G 176 C2
Duncrievie P & K 221 L5
Duncton W Susx 20 F3
Dundee C Dund 223 G1
Dundee Crematorium C Dund 222 F1
Dundon Somset 31 G4
Dundonald S Ayrs 196 D4
Dundonnell Highld 261 J2
Dundraw Cumb 165 H1
Dundreggan Highld 240 B1
Dundrennan D & G 175 J5
Dundry N Som 45 H5
Dunecht Abers 245 G2
Dunfermline Fife 210 E2
Dunfermline Crematorium
Fife 210 F2
Dunfield Gloucs 65 H7
Dunford Bridge Barns 141 J7
Dungate Kent 40 B3
Dungavel S Lans 197 L3
Dunge Wilts 46 C8
Dungworth Sheff 132 E2
Dunham Notts 135 G5
Dunham-on-the-Hill Ches W 129 L6
Dunhampstead Worcs 81 L3
Dunhampton Worcs 81 J2
Dunham Town Traffd 130 E2
Dunham Woodhouses Traffd 130 E2
Dunholme Lincs 135 L4
Dunino Fife 223 J5
Dunipace Falk 209 L2
Dunkeld P & K 232 F6
Dunkerton BaNES 45 L7
Dunkeswell Devon 14 D1

Dunkeswick N York 150 D6
Dunkirk Ches W 129 J5
Dunkirk Kent 40 E3
Dunkirk S Glos 46 A2
Dunkirk Wilts 46 E6
Dunk's Green Kent 38 F3
Dunlappie Angus 234 F2
Dunley Hants 48 C8
Dunley Worcs 81 H2
Dunlop E Ayrs 196 E1
Dunmaglass Highld 251 G7
Dunmere Cnwll 5 H1
Dunmore Falk 210 A1
Dunnet Highld 280 B2
Dunnichen Angus 234 D5
Dunning P & K 221 J4
Dunnington C York 151 L5
Dunnington E R Yk 153 J5
Dunnington Warwks 82 C4
Dunnockshaw Lancs 140 B2
Dunn Street Kent 53 G6
Dunoon Ag & B 207 K4
Dunphail Moray 253 J2
Dunragit D & G 172 E3
Duns Border 202 B2
Dunsa Derbys 132 E5
Dunsby Lincs 118 E6
Dunscar Bolton 139 L5
Dunscore D & G 185 L6
Dunscroft Donc 143 G6
Dunsdale R & Cl 170 E6
Dunsden Green Oxon 49 H3
Dunsdon Devon 11 K1
Dunsfold Surrey 36 F4
Dunsford Devon 13 J5
Dunshalt Fife 222 D5
Dunshillock Abers 269 H6
Dunsill Notts 133 J7
Dunsley N York 171 K8
Dunsley Staffs 97 J6
Dunsmore Bucks 67 L6
Dunsop Bridge Lancs 148 B6
Dunstable C Beds 68 C3
Dunstall Staffs 115 K7
Dunstall Common Worcs 81 K6
Dunstall Green Suffk 88 E3
Dunstan Nthumb 191 K2
Dunstan Steads Nthumb 191 J2
Dunster Somset 29 H2
Duns Tew Oxon 66 C2
Dunston Gatesd 180 F6
Dunston Lincs 135 L7
Dunston Norfk 106 E3
Dunston Staffs 114 E8
Dunstone Devon 7 H4
Dunstone Devon 13 G7
Dunston Heath Staffs 114 E8
Dunsville Donc 143 G6
Dunswell E R Yk 144 D1
Dunsyre S Lans 199 J3
Dunterton Devon 11 M6
Dunthrop Oxon 65 M2
Duntisbourne Abbots Gloucs 64 E5
Duntisbourne Leer Gloucs 64 E5
Duntisbourne Rouse Gloucs 64 E6
Duntish Dorset 16 D2
Duntocher W Duns 208 E4
Dunton Bucks 67 K2
Dunton C Beds 86 E6
Dunton Norfk 121 J5
Dunton Bassett Leics 100 C5
Dunton Green Kent 38 D2
Dunton Wayletts Essex 52 E1
Duntulm Highld 259 G2
Dunure S Ayrs 195 L7
Dunvant Swans 57 G6
Dunvegan Highld 258 C7
Dunwich Suffk 91 L1
Dunwood Staffs 131 J8
Durdar Cumb 177 L8
Durgan Cnwll 3 K5
Durham Dur 169 H2
Durham Crematorium Dur 169 H3
Durisdeer D & G 186 C5
Durisdeermill D & G 186 C5
Durkar Wakefd 141 M4
Durleigh Somset 30 C4
Durley Hants 35 G7
Durley Wilts 47 K6
Durley Street Hants 35 H7
Durlock Kent 41 J2
Durlock Kent 41 J4
Durlow Common Herefs 80 E7
Durn Rochdl 140 E4
Durness Highld 276 F3
Durno Abers 256 C6
Duror Highld 228 F4
Durran Ag & B 216 F5
Durrington W Susx 21 J6
Durrington Wilts 33 K2

Durris Abers	245	G4	
Dursley Gloucs	63	M7	
Dursley Cross Gloucs	63	K3	
Durston Somset	30	D5	
Durweston Dorset	17	G1	
Duston Nhants	84	D3	
Duthil Highld	253	H6	
Dutlas Powys	94	F7	
Duton Hill Essex	70	F2	
Dutson Cnwll	11	L5	
Dutton Ches W	130	B4	
Duxford Cambs	87	K6	
Duxford Oxon	66	A7	
Dwygyfylchi Conwy	126	E4	
Dwyran IoA	125	H6	
Dyce C Aber	245	K1	
Dyer's End Essex	88	E7	
Dyfatty Carmth	56	E5	
Dyffrydan Gwynd	110	D8	
Dyffryn Brdgnd	42	C3	
Dyffryn Myr Td	61	G6	
Dyffryn V Glam	43	H7	
Dyffryn Ardudwy Gwynd	109	K7	
Dyffryn Castell Cerdgn	93	G7	
Dyffryn Cellwen Neath	60	C5	
Dyke Lincs	118	E7	
Dyke Moray	264	F8	
Dykehead Angus	233	K4	
Dykehead Angus	234	B3	
Dykehead N Lans	210	A7	
Dykehead Stirlg	219	K7	
Dykelands Abers	235	H2	
Dykends Angus	233	K4	
Dykeside Abers	256	C3	
Dylife Powys	93	J4	
Dymchurch Kent	25	L1	
Dymock Gloucs	63	K1	
Dyrham S Glos	45	L4	
Dysart Fife	222	E8	
Dyserth Denbgs	128	C4	

E

Eachway Worcs	98	C8	
Eachwick Nthumb	180	D4	
Eagland Hill Lancs	147	H6	
Eagle Lincs	135	H6	
Eagle Barnsdale Lincs	135	H6	
Eagle Moor Lincs	135	H6	
Eaglescliffe S on T	169	L7	
Eaglesfield Cumb	164	E5	
Eaglesfield D & G	177	H4	
Eaglesham E Rens	208	F8	
Eagley Bolton	139	L5	
Eairy IoM	154	d6	
Eakring Notts	134	D7	
Ealand N Linc	143	K5	
Ealing Gt Lon	50	F3	
Eals Nthumb	178	F7	
Eamont Bridge Cumb	166	C5	
Earby Lancs	148	F6	
Earcroft Bl w D	139	K3	
Eardington Shrops	97	G5	
Eardisland Herefs	80	A4	
Eardisley Herefs	79	K5	
Eardiston Shrops	112	E6	
Eardiston Worcs	80	F2	
Earith Cambs	103	H8	
Earle Nthumb	202	F7	
Earlestown St Hel	130	B1	
Earley Wokham	49	H4	
Earlham Norfk	106	D2	
Earlham Crematorium Norfk	106	E2	
Earlish Highld	258	F4	
Earls Barton Nhants	85	G3	
Earls Colne Essex	71	L1	
Earls Common Worcs	81	M3	
Earl's Croome Worcs	81	K6	
Earlsditton Shrops	96	E8	
Earlsdon Covtry	99	J7	
Earl's Down E Susx	23	L3	
Earlsferry Fife	223	H7	
Earlsfield Gt Lon	51	H4	
Earlsford Abers	256	E5	
Earl's Green Suffk	90	B2	
Earlsheaton Kirk	141	L3	
Earl Shilton Leics	100	A4	
Earl Soham Suffk	90	F3	
Earl Sterndale Derbys	132	B6	
Earlston Border	201	J5	
Earlston E Ayrs	196	D4	
Earl Stonham Suffk	90	D3	
Earlswood Surrey	37	L1	
Earlswood Warwks	98	E8	
Earlswood Common Mons	62	F8	
Earnley W Susx	20	D7	
Earnshaw Bridge Lancs	139	G3	
Earsdon N Tyne	181	H4	
Earsdon Nthumb	191	J7	

Earsham Norfk	107	G5	
Earswick C York	151	K4	
Eartham W Susx	20	F5	
Earthcott S Glos	45	K2	
Easby N York	161	J1	
Easdale Ag & B	215	L1	
Easebourne W Susx	36	D6	
Easenhall Warwks	100	A7	
Eashing Surrey	36	E2	
Easington Bucks	67	G5	
Easington Dur	169	L2	
Easington E R Yk	145	K4	
Easington Nthumb	203	J6	
Easington Oxon	67	G7	
Easington R & Cl	171	H7	
Easington Colliery Dur	169	L2	
Easington Lane Sundld	169	K2	
Easingwold N York	151	H2	
Easole Street Kent	41	H5	
Eassie and Nevay Angus	233	M6	
East Aberthaw V Glam	42	F8	
East Allington Devon	7	M5	
East Anstey Devon	28	F5	
East Anton Hants	34	E1	
East Appleton N York	160	C3	
East Ashey IoW	19	K6	
East Ashling W Susx	20	D5	
East Aston Hants	34	F2	
East Ayton N York	163	H5	
East Balsdon Cnwll	11	K3	
East Bank Blae G	61	K6	
East Barkwith Lincs	136	C3	
East Barming Kent	39	H4	
East Barnby N York	171	J8	
East Barnet Gt Lon	69	H8	
East Barns E Loth	212	F4	
East Barsham Norfk	121	K5	
East Beckham Norfk	122	D4	
East Bedfont Gt Lon	50	D4	
East Bergholt Suffk	90	C8	
East Bierley Kirk	141	J2	
East Bilney Norfk	121	L7	
East Blatchington E Susx	23	H7	
East Bloxworth Dorset	17	H4	
East Boldon S Tyne	181	J6	
East Boldre Hants	18	F4	
East Bolton Nthumb	191	G3	
Eastbourne Darltn	169	J7	
Eastbourne E Susx	23	K7	
Eastbourne Crematorium			
E Susx	23	L6	
East Bower Somset	30	D3	
East Bradenham Norfk	105	J2	
East Brent Somset	44	D8	
Eastbridge Suffk	91	K2	
East Bridgford Notts	117	J3	
East Briscoe Dur	168	B6	
Eastbrook V Glam	43	J7	
East Buckland Devon	28	B4	
East Budleigh Devon	14	C5	
Eastburn C Brad	149	J7	
Eastburn E R Yk	152	F4	
East Burnham Bucks	50	B2	
East Burton Dorset	16	F5	
Eastbury Herts	68	E8	
Eastbury W Berk	47	M3	
East Butsfield Dur	168	E2	
East Butterwick N Linc	143	L6	
Eastby N York	149	J5	
East Calder W Loth	210	E5	
East Carleton Norfk	106	D3	
East Carlton Leeds	150	B7	
East Carlton Nhants	101	H5	
East Chaldon (Chaldon			
Herring) Dorset	16	F6	
East Challow Oxon	48	A1	
East Charleton Devon	7	L6	
East Chelborough Dorset	16	A2	
East Chiltington E Susx	22	F4	
East Chinnock Somset	31	H8	
East Chisenbury Wilts	47	H8	
East Cholderton Hants	34	C2	
Eastchurch Kent	53	L5	
East Clandon Surrey	50	D8	
East Claydon Bucks	67	H2	
East Clevedon N Som	44	E5	
East Coker Somset	31	J8	
Eastcombe Gloucs	64	C6	
Eastcombe Somset	29	L4	
East Compton Somset	31	K3	
East Cornworthy Devon	8	C4	
East Cote Cumb	176	F7	
Eastcote Gt Lon	50	E1	
Eastcote Nhants	84	D4	
Eastcote Solhll	99	G7	
Eastcott Cnwll	26	D7	
Eastcott Wilts	46	F7	
East Cottingwith E R Yk	151	L6	
Eastcourt Wilts	47	K6	
Eastcourt Wilts	64	E8	

East Cowes IoW	19	H4	
East Cowick E R Yk	143	G4	
East Cowton N York	160	D2	
East Cramlington Nthumb	181	G4	
East Cranmore Somset	31	L2	
East Creech Dorset	17	H6	
East Curthwaite Cumb	165	K1	
East Dean E Susx	23	J7	
East Dean Gloucs	63	K3	
East Dean Hants	34	C5	
East Dean W Susx	20	E4	
East Devon Crematorium			
Devon	14	B3	
Eastdown Devon	8	B5	
East Down Devon	27	L3	
East Drayton Notts	134	F4	
East Dulwich Gt Lon	51	J4	
East Dundry N Som	45	H5	
East Ella C KuH	144	D2	
East End Bed	86	C4	
East End C Beds	85	J5	
East End E R Yk	145	G2	
East End E R Yk	145	H2	
East End Essex	70	B5	
Eastend Essex	72	D8	
East End Hants	18	E4	
East End Hants	48	B6	
East End Herts	70	C2	
East End Kent	39	L6	
East End Kent	53	L4	
East End M Keyn	85	J6	
East End N Som	44	F5	
East End Oxon	66	B4	
East End Somset	31	L2	
East End Suffk	90	C8	
Easter Balmoral Abers	243	J5	
Easter Compton S Glos	45	H3	
Easter Dalziel Highld	252	E2	
Eastergate W Susx	20	F6	
Easterhouse C Glas	209	J6	
Easter Howgate Mdloth	211	H6	
Easter Kinkell Highld	263	G8	
Easter Moniack Highld	250	F3	
Eastern Green Covtry	99	H7	
Easter Ord Abers	245	J3	
Easter Pitkierie Fife	223	K6	
Easter Skeld Shet	281	d6	
Easter Softlaw Border	202	B6	
Easterton Wilts	46	F8	
Eastertown Somset	44	D8	
East Everleigh Wilts	47	J8	
East Farleigh Kent	39	J3	
East Farndon Nhants	100	F6	
East Ferry Lincs	143	K7	
Eastfield N Lans	210	A6	
Eastfield N York	163	J6	
East Firsby Lincs	135	K3	
East Fortune E Loth	212	C3	
East Garforth Leeds	142	C1	
East Garston W Berk	47	M4	
Eastgate Dur	168	B3	
Eastgate Lincs	118	F7	
Eastgate Norfk	122	C2	
East Ginge Oxon	48	C2	
East Goscote Leics	100	E1	
East Grafton Wilts	47	K6	
East Green Suffk	91	J2	
East Grimstead Wilts	34	B5	
East Grinstead W Susx	38	B5	
East Guldeford E Susx	25	H3	
East Haddon Nhants	84	C2	
East Hagbourne Oxon	48	D1	
East Halton N Linc	144	E4	
East Ham Gt Lon	51	L2	
Eastham Wirral	129	H4	
Eastham Ferry Wirral	129	J3	
Easthampstead Park			
Crematorium Br For	49	K5	
Easthampton Herefs	80	A3	
East Hanney Oxon	66	B8	
East Hanningfield Essex	71	J6	
East Hardwick Wakefd	142	D4	
East Harling Norfk	105	K6	
East Harlsey N York	160	F3	
East Harnham Wilts	33	K5	
East Harptree BaNES	45	H7	
East Hartburn S on T	169	L7	
East Hartford Nthumb	181	G3	
East Harting W Susx	20	C3	
East Hatch Wilts	32	F5	
East Hatley Cambs	86	F5	
East Hauxwell N York	159	L4	
East Haven Angus	234	F8	
Eastheath Wokham	49	J5	
East Heckington Lincs	119	G3	
East Hedleyhope Dur	168	F3	
East Helmsdale Highld	274	D5	
East Hendred Oxon	48	C1	
East Heslerton N York	163	G7	
East Hewish N Som	44	E6	

East Hoathly E Susx	23	H4	
East Holme Dorset	17	H5	
Easthope Shrops	96	D4	
Easthorpe Essex	72	C3	
Easthorpe Notts	117	J1	
East Horrington Somset	31	J2	
East Horsley Surrey	50	D8	
East Horton Nthumb	203	G7	
East Howe Bmouth	17	L3	
East Huntington C York	151	K5	
East Huntspill Somset	30	C2	
East Hyde C Beds	68	D2	
East Ilkerton Devon	28	C2	
East Ilsley W Berk	48	C3	
Eastington Devon	13	H1	
Eastington Gloucs	63	M6	
Eastington Gloucs	65	H4	
East Keal Lincs	137	G7	
East Kennett Wilts	47	G5	
East Keswick Leeds	150	E7	
East Kilbride S Lans	209	H8	
East Kimber Devon	12	C3	
East Kirkby Lincs	136	F5	
East Knighton Dorset	16	F5	
East Knowstone Devon	28	E6	
East Knoyle Wilts	32	E5	
East Lambrook Somset	31	G7	
East Lancashire Crematorium			
Bury	140	A6	
East Langdon Kent	41	K4	
East Langton Leics	100	F5	
East Lavant W Susx	20	D5	
East Lavington W Susx	20	F4	
East Layton N York	159	L1	
Eastleach Martin Gloucs	65	J6	
Eastleach Turville Gloucs	65	J6	
East Leake Notts	116	F6	
East Learmouth Nthumb	202	D5	
East Leigh Devon	7	M4	
East Leigh Devon	7	L3	
East Leigh Devon	13	G2	
Eastleigh Devon	27	J5	
Eastleigh Hants	34	F7	
East Lexham Norfk	121	J1	
Eastling Kent	40	F4	
East Linton E Loth	212	C3	
East Liss Hants	36	A5	
East Lockinge Oxon	48	B2	
East London Crematorium			
Gt Lon	51	L2	
East Lound N Linc	143	K7	
East Lulworth Dorset	17	G6	
East Lutton N York	152	F2	
East Lydeard Somset	30	B5	
East Lydford Somset	31	J4	
East Malling Kent	39	H2	
East Malling Heath Kent	39	H2	
East Marden W Susx	20	C4	
East Markham Notts	134	E5	
East Martin Hants	33	J7	
East Marton N York	148	F5	
East Meon Hants	35	L4	
East Mere Devon	29	H7	
East Mersea Essex	72	F4	
East Molesey Surrey	50	F5	
Eastmoor Norfk	104	E3	
East Morden Dorset	17	H4	
East Morton C Brad	149	K7	
East Morton D & G	186	D3	
East Ness N York	152	B7	
East Newton E R Yk	153	L8	
Eastney C Port	19	L4	
Eastnor Herefs	81	G7	
East Norton Leics	101	G3	
Eastoft N Linc	143	K4	
East Ogwell Devon	13	J8	
Easton Cambs	86	C1	
Easton Cumb	177	J7	
Easton Devon	13	G5	
Easton Dorset	16	D8	
Easton Hants	35	G4	
Easton Lincs	118	B6	
Easton Norfk	106	C1	
Easton Somset	31	J2	
Easton Suffk	91	G3	
Easton W Berk	48	B4	
Easton Wilts	46	C5	
Easton Grey Wilts	46	C2	
Easton-in-Gordano N Som	45	G4	
Easton Maudit Nhants	85	H3	
Easton-on-the-Hill Nhants	101	M3	
Easton Royal Wilts	47	J7	
East Orchard Dorset	32	D7	
East Ord Nthumb	202	F3	
East Panson Devon	11	L4	
East Parley Dorset	17	M3	
East Peckham Kent	39	G4	
East Pennar Pembks	54	G7	
East Pennard Somset	31	J4	

East Perry Cambs 86 C2
East Portlemouth Devon 7 L7
East Prawle Devon 8 A7
East Preston W Susx 21 J6
East Pulham Dorset 16 D1
East Putford Devon 26 F7
East Quantoxhead Somset 29 L2
East Rainham Medway 53 H5
East Rainton Sundld 169 J1
East Ravendale NE Lin 145 G7
East Raynham Norfk 121 J6
Eastrea Cambs 102 F4
East Riding Crematorium
E R Yk 152 F2
Eastriggs D & G 177 H5
East Rigton Leeds 150 E7
Eastrington E R Yk 143 K2
East Rolstone N Som 44 E6
Eastrop Swindn 65 J8
East Rounton N York 160 F2
East Rudham Norfk 121 H6
East Runton Norfk 122 D3
East Ruston Norfk 123 G6
Eastry Kent 41 J4
East Saltoun E Loth 212 B5
Eastshaw W Susx 36 C6
East Sheen Gt Lon 51 G4
East Shefford W Berk 48 A4
East Sleekburn Nthumb 181 G2
East Somerton Norfk 123 K7
East Stockwith Lincs 134 F1
East Stoke Dorset 17 G5
East Stoke Notts 117 K2
East Stour Dorset 32 D6
East Stourmouth Kent 41 H3
East Stowford Devon 27 L5
East Stratton Hants 35 H3
East Studdal Kent 41 J5
East Sutton Kent 39 L3
East Taphouse Cnwll 5 L2
East-the-Water Devon 27 H5
East Thirston Nthumb 191 J6
East Tilbury Thurr 52 E3
East Tisted Hants 35 L4
East Torrington Lincs 136 B3
East Tuddenham Norfk 106 B1
East Tytherley Hants 34 C5
East Tytherton Wilts 46 D2
East Village Devon 13 K2
Eastville Bristl 45 J4
Eastville Lincs 137 H8
East Wall Shrops 96 C4
East Walton Norfk 121 G8
East Water Somset 31 J1
East Week Devon 12 F4
Eastwell Leics 117 K6
East Wellow Hants 34 C6
East Wemyss Fife 222 F7
East Whitburn W Loth 210 C6
Eastwick Herts 70 B5
East Wickham Gt Lon 51 M3
East Williamston Pembks 55 J6
East Winch Norfk 120 F8
East Winterslow Wilts 34 B4
East Wittering W Susx 20 C7
East Witton N York 159 L5
Eastwood Notts 116 D2
Eastwood Sthend 53 H2
East Woodburn Nthumb 179 L2
Eastwood End Cambs 103 J5
East Woodhay Hants 48 B6
East Woodlands Somset 32 C2
East Worldham Hants 35 M3
East Wretham Norfk 105 J5
East Youlstone Devon 26 D7
Eathorpe Warwks 83 J2
Eaton Ches E 131 G6
Eaton Ches W 130 B7
Eaton Leics 117 L5
Eaton Norfk 106 E2
Eaton Notts 134 E4
Eaton Oxon 66 C6
Eaton Shrops 95 J5
Eaton Shrops 96 B5
Eaton Bishop Herefs 80 B7
Eaton Bray C Beds 68 B3
Eaton Constantine Shrops 96 D2
Eaton Ford Cambs 86 D3
Eaton Green C Beds 68 B3
Eaton Hastings Oxon 65 K2
Eaton Mascott Shrops 96 C2
Eaton Socon Cambs 86 D3
Eaton upon Tern Shrops 113 L7
Eaves Brow Warrtn 130 C1
Eaves Green Solhll 99 H6
Ebberston N York 162 F6
Ebbesborne Wake Wilts 33 G6
Ebbw Vale Blae G 61 J5
Ebchester Dur 180 D7
Ebdon N Som 44 D6

Ebford Devon 14 A5
Ebley Gloucs 64 B6
Ebnal Ches W 113 H2
Ebnall Herefs 80 B3
Ebrington Gloucs 82 E7
Ebsworthy Devon 12 C4
Ecchinswell Hants 48 D7
Ecclaw Border 213 G5
Ecclefechan D & G 177 G4
Eccles Border 202 B5
Eccles Kent 52 F6
Eccles Salfd 140 A8
Ecclesall Sheff 132 F3
Eccles Crematorium Salfd 139 M8
Ecclesfield Sheff 133 G1
Eccles Green Herefs 79 L5
Eccleshall Staffs 114 C5
Eccleshill C Brad 149 M8
Ecclesmachan W Loth 210 E4
Eccles on Sea Norfk 123 H5
Eccles Road Norfk 105 L5
Eccleston Ches W 129 J7
Eccleston Lancs 139 G4
Eccleston St Hel 138 F8
Eccleston Green Lancs 139 G4
Echt Abers 245 G2
Eckford Border 201 L7
Eckington Derbys 133 H4
Eckington Worcs 81 L7
Ecton Nhants 84 F3
Ecton Staffs 132 B8
Edale Derbys 132 B3
Eday Ork 275 d3
Edburton W Susx 22 C5
Edderside Cumb 164 E2
Edderton Highld 263 J3
Eddington Kent 41 G2
Eddleston Border 200 B4
Eddlewood S Lans 209 J8
Edenbridge Kent 38 C4
Edenfield Lancs 140 B4
Edenhall Cumb 166 D4
Edenham Lincs 118 E7
Eden Mount Cumb 156 F7
Eden Park Gt Lon 51 K5
Edensor Derbys 132 E5
Edentaggart Ag & B 218 D8
Edenthorpe Donc 143 G6
Edern Gwynd 108 E4
Edgarley Somset 31 H3
Edgbaston Birm 98 D6
Edgcombe Cnwll 3 J4
Edgcott Bucks 67 G3
Edgcott Somset 28 E3
Edge Gloucs 64 B5
Edge Shrops 95 K2
Edgebolton Shrops 113 J7
Edge End Gloucs 63 H4
Edgefield Norfk 122 B5
Edgefield Green Norfk 122 B4
Edgefold Bolton 139 L6
Edge Green Ches W 113 H1
Edgehill Warwks 83 J5
Edgerley Shrops 112 E7
Edgerton Kirk 141 H4
Edgeside Lancs 140 C3
Edgeworth Gloucs 64 D6
Edgeworthy Devon 28 E8
Edginswell Torbay 8 C2
Edgiock Worcs 82 B3
Edgmond Wrekin 114 A7
Edgmond Marsh Wrekin 114 A7
Edgton Shrops 95 J6
Edgware Gt Lon 51 G1
Edgworth Bl w D 139 L4
Edinbane Highld 258 E6
Edinburgh C Edin 211 J4
Edingale Staffs 99 G1
Edingham D & G 175 L2
Edingley Notts 134 D8
Edingthorpe Norfk 123 G5
Edingthorpe Green Norfk 122 F5
Edington Border 202 D2
Edington Nthumb 180 E2
Edington Somset 30 F3
Edington Wilts 46 D8
Edington Burtle Somset 30 F2
Edingworth Somset 44 D8
Edistone Devon 26 D6
Edithmead Somset 30 E1
Edith Weston Rutlnd 101 K2
Edlesborough Bucks 68 B3
Edlingham Nthumb 191 G4
Edlington Lincs 136 D5
Edmond Castle Cumb 178 C7
Edmondsham Dorset 33 J8
Edmondsley Dur 169 G1
Edmondthorpe Leics 117 M8
Edmonton Cnwll 10 D8
Edmonton Gt Lon 69 J8

Edmundbyers Dur 168 C1
Ednam Border 202 A5
Ednaston Derbys 115 L3
Edradynate P & K 232 C5
Edrom Border 202 C2
Edstaston Shrops 113 H5
Edstone Warwks 82 E3
Edvin Loach Herefs 80 F3
Edwalton Notts 117 G4
Edwardstone Suffk 89 J6
Edwardsville Myr Td 43 G2
Edwinsford Carmth 59 H2
Edwinstowe Notts 134 C6
Edworth C Beds 86 E7
Edwyn Ralph Herefs 80 F4
Edzell Angus 234 F2
Edzell Woods Abers 234 F2
Efail-fach Neath 57 L6
Efail Isaf Rhondd 43 H5
Efailnewydd Gwynd 108 F4
Efail-Rhyd Powys 112 A6
Efailwen Carmth 75 K7
Efenechtyd Denbgs 128 D8
Effgill D & G 187 L7
Effingham Surrey 50 E8
Efflinch Staffs 115 K8
Efford Devon 13 K2
Efford Crematorium C Plym 6 F3
Egbury Hants 48 B8
Egdean W Susx 21 G3
Egerton Bolton 139 L5
Egerton Kent 40 B6
Egerton Forstal Kent 40 A6
Eggborough N York 142 E3
Eggbuckland C Plym 6 F3
Eggesford Devon 28 B8
Eggington C Beds 68 B2
Egginton Derbys 115 M6
Egglescliffe S on T 169 L7
Eggleston Dur 168 C6
Egham Surrey 50 C5
Egham Wick Surrey 50 B5
Egleton Rutlnd 101 J2
Eglingham Nthumb 191 G2
Egloshayle Cnwll 10 D8
Egloskerry Cnwll 11 K5
Eglwysbach Conwy 126 F5
Eglwys-Brewis V Glam 42 F7
Eglwys Cross Wrexhm 113 G3
Eglwys Fach Cerdgn 92 F4
Eglwyswrw Pembks 75 K4
Egmanton Notts 134 E6
Egremont Cumb 164 D8
Egremont Wirral 129 H1
Egton N York 162 E2
Egton Bridge N York 162 D2
Egypt Bucks 50 B2
Egypt Hants 34 F3
Eigg Highld 236 F3
Eight Ash Green Essex 72 D2
Eilanreach Highld 248 C8
Eilean Reach Highld 248 C8
Eisteddfa Gurig Cerdgn 93 H6
Elan Village Powys 78 C2
Elberton S Glos 45 J1
Elbridge W Susx 20 F6
Elburton C Plym 7 G4
Elcombe Swindn 47 H3
Elcot W Berk 48 B5
Eldernell Cambs 103 G4
Eldersfield Worcs 64 A1
Elderslie Rens 208 D6
Elder Street Essex 88 B8
Eldon Dur 169 G5
Eldwick C Brad 149 L4
Elfhill Abers 245 H6
Elford Nthumb 203 A6
Elford Staffs 98 F1
Elgin Moray 266 E4
Elgol Highld 247 H6
Elham Kent 41 G6
Elie Fife 223 J7
Elilaw Nthumb 190 D4
Elim IoA 124 F3
Eling Hants 18 F1
Elkesley Notts 134 D4
Elkstone Gloucs 64 D4
Ella Abers 268 B4
Ellacombe Torbay 8 D2
Elland Calder 141 H4
Elland Lower Edge Calder 141 H4
Ellary Ag & B 206 A4
Ellastone Staffs 115 J3
Ellel Lancs 147 J4
Ellemford Border 212 D4
Ellenabeich Ag & B 215 L1
Ellenborough Cumb 164 D3
Ellenbrook Salfd 139 L7
Ellenhall Staffs 114 C6
Ellen's Green Surrey 37 G4
Ellerbeck N York 160 F3

Ellerby N York 171 J7
Ellerdine Heath Wrekin 113 K7
Ellerhayes Devon 14 A2
Elleric Ag & B 229 G5
Ellerker E R Yk 144 A2
Ellers N York 149 H7
Ellerton E R Yk 151 L7
Ellerton N York 160 C3
Ellerton Shrops 113 M6
Ellesborough Bucks 67 K6
Ellesmere Shrops 112 F4
Ellesmere Port Ches W 129 J4
Ellingham Hants 18 A2
Ellingham Norfk 107 H5
Ellingham Nthumb 203 K8
Ellingstring N York 159 M6
Ellington Cambs 86 D1
Ellington Nthumb 191 K7
Ellington Thorpe Cambs 86 D1
Elliots Green Somset 32 D2
Ellisfield Hants 35 K2
Ellishader Highld 259 H3
Ellistown Leics 99 L1
Ellon Abers 257 H5
Ellonby Cumb 166 A4
Ellough Suffk 107 J6
Elloughton E R Yk 144 B2
Ellwood Gloucs 63 H5
Elm Cambs 103 K2
Elmbridge Worcs 81 K2
Elmdon Essex 87 J7
Elmdon Solhll 98 F6
Elmdon Heath Solhll 98 F7
Elmer W Susx 21 G6
Elmers End Gt Lon 51 K5
Elmer's Green Lancs 139 G6
Elmesthorpe Leics 100 A4
Elm Green Essex 71 J6
Elmhurst Staffs 98 E1
Elmley Castle Worcs 82 A7
Elmley Lovett Worcs 81 K1
Elmore Gloucs 64 A4
Elmore Back Gloucs 63 M4
Elm Park Gt Lon 52 B2
Elmscott Devon 26 D6
Elmsett Suffk 90 C6
Elms Green Worcs 81 G2
Elmstead Heath Essex 72 F3
Elmstead Market Essex 72 F2
Elmstead Row Essex 72 F3
Elmsted Kent 40 F6
Elmstone Kent 41 H3
Elmstone Hardwicke Gloucs 64 D2
Elmswell E R Yk 152 F4
Elmswell Suffk 89 K2
Elmton Derbys 133 K5
Elphin Highld 271 H6
Elphinstone E Loth 211 L5
Elrick Abers 245 H2
Elrig D & G 173 J5
Elrington Nthumb 179 K6
Elsdon Nthumb 190 C7
Elsecar Barns 142 B7
Elsenham Essex 70 D2
Elsfield Oxon 66 D5
Elsham N Linc 144 C5
Elsing Norfk 122 B8
Elslack N York 149 G6
Elson Hants 19 K3
Elson Shrops 112 F4
Elsrickle S Lans 199 J4
Elstead Surrey 36 D2
Elsted W Susx 20 D3
Elsthorpe Lincs 118 E6
Elstob Dur 169 J6
Elston Lancs 139 J1
Elston Notts 117 K2
Elston Wilts 33 J2
Elstone Devon 28 B7
Elstow Bed 85 L6
Elstree Herts 68 F8
Elstronwick E R Yk 145 G1
Elswick Lancs 147 H8
Elswick N u Ty 180 F6
Elsworth Cambs 87 G3
Elterwater Cumb 156 D2
Eltham Gt Lon 51 L4
Eltham Crematorium Gt Lon 51 L4
Eltisley Cambs 86 F3
Elton Bury 140 B5
Elton Cambs 102 B4
Elton Ches W 129 K4
Elton Derbys 132 D7
Elton Gloucs 63 K4
Elton Herefs 80 B1
Elton Notts 117 K4
Elton S on T 169 L7
Elton Green Ches W 129 K5
Eltringham Nthumb 180 C6
Elvanfoot S Lans 186 E3

Place	County	Page	Grid
Elvaston	Derbys	116	C5
Elveden	Suffk	105	G7
Elvetham Heath	Hants	49	K7
Elvingston	E Loth	212	A4
Elvington	C York	151	L6
Elvington	Kent	41	J5
Elwell	Devon	28	B4
Elwick	Hartpl	170	B4
Elwick	Nthumb	203	J5
Elworth	Ches E	130	E7
Elworthy	Somset	29	K4
Ely	Cambs	103	L7
Ely	Cardif	43	J6
Emberton	M Keyn	85	H5
Embleton	Cumb	165	G4
Embleton	Dur	169	L5
Embleton	Nthumb	191	J2
Embo	Highld	264	C1
Emborough	Somset	31	K1
Embo Street	Highld	264	C2
Embsay	N York	149	H5
Emery Down	Hants	18	D2
Emley	Kirk	141	K5
Emley Moor	Kirk	141	K5
Emmbrook	Wokham	49	J5
Emmer Green	Readg	49	H4
Emmett Carr	Derbys	133	J4
Emmington	Oxon	67	H6
Emneth	Norfk	103	K2
Emneth Hungate	Norfk	103	K2
Empingham	Rutlnd	101	L2
Empshott	Hants	35	M4
Empshott Green	Hants	35	M5
Emstrey Crematorium	Shrops	96	C1
Emsworth	Hants	20	B5
Enborne	W Berk	48	B6
Enborne Row	W Berk	48	C6
Enchmarsh	Shrops	96	B4
Enderby	Leics	100	C3
Endmoor	Cumb	157	H5
Endon	Staffs	114	E1
Endon Bank	Staffs	114	E1
Enfield	Gt Lon	69	K7
Enfield Crematorium	Gt Lon	69	K7
Enfield Lock	Gt Lon	69	K7
Enfield Wash	Gt Lon	69	K7
Enford	Wilts	47	H8
Engine Common	S Glos	45	K2
England's Gate	Herefs	80	D5
Englefield	W Berk	48	F4
Englefield Green	Surrey	50	C4
Engleseabrook	Ches E	114	H4
English Bicknor	Gloucs	63	H4
Englishcombe	BaNES	45	L6
English Frankton	Shrops	113	G5
Engollan	Cnwll	10	B8
Enham-Alamein	Hants	34	D1
Enmore	Somset	30	C4
Enmore Green	Dorset	32	E6
Ennerdale Bridge	Cumb	164	E7
Enniscaven	Cnwll	4	F3
Enochdhu	P & K	233	G3
Ensay	Ag & B	226	D3
Ensbury	Bmouth	17	L3
Ensdon	Shrops	112	F8
Ensis	Devon	27	K5
Enson	Staffs	114	E6
Enstone	Oxon	66	A2
Enterkinfoot	D & G	186	C5
Enterpen	N York	161	G2
Enville	Staffs	97	J6
Eolaigearraidh	W Isls	283	b12
Epney	Gloucs	63	M5
Epperstone	Notts	117	H2
Epping	Essex	70	C6
Epping Green	Essex	70	B6
Epping Green	Herts	69	J5
Epping Upland	Essex	70	C6
Eppleby	N York	168	F8
Eppleworth	E R Yk	144	C2
Epsom	Surrey	51	G6
Epwell	Oxon	83	H7
Epworth	N Linc	143	K7
Epworth Turbary	N Linc	143	J7
Erbistock	Wrexhm	112	E3
Erdington	Birm	98	E5
Eridge Green	E Susx	38	E6
Eridge Station	E Susx	38	E6
Erines	Ag & B	206	D4
Eriska	Ag & B	228	D6
Eriswell	Suffk	104	E7
Erith	Gt Lon	52	B3
Erlestoke	Wilts	46	D8
Ermington	Devon	7	J4
Erpingham	Norfk	122	D5
Erriottwood	Kent	40	B3
Errogie	Highld	250	F7
Errol	P & K	222	D3
Erskine	Rens	208	D5
Ervie	D & G	172	B1
Erwarton	Suffk	90	F8
Erwood	Powys	78	F6
Eryholme	N York	160	D1
Eryrys	Denbgs	128	E8
Escalls	Cnwll	2	B5
Escomb	Dur	168	F4
Escott	Somset	29	K3
Escrick	N York	151	K7
Esgair	Carmth	58	C3
Esgair	Cerdgn	77	G2
Esgairgeiliog	Powys	93	G2
Esgerdawe	Carmth	77	H7
Esgyryn	Conwy	126	F4
Esh	Dur	169	G2
Esher	Surrey	50	E6
Esholt	C Brad	150	A7
Eshott	Nthumb	191	J6
Eshton	N York	149	G5
Esh Winning	Dur	169	G2
Eskadale	Highld	250	D4
Eskbank	Mdloth	211	K5
Eskdale Green	Cumb	155	L3
Eskdalemuir	D & G	187	K6
Eskham	Lincs	145	K8
Eskholme	Donc	143	G4
Esperley Lane Ends	Dur	168	E6
Esprick	Lancs	147	H8
Essendine	Rutlnd	102	A1
Essendon	Herts	69	H5
Essich	Highld	251	H4
Essington	Staffs	98	B3
Esslemont	Abers	257	G6
Eston	R & Cl	170	D7
Etal	Nthumb	202	E5
Etchilhampton	Wilts	46	F7
Etchingham	E Susx	24	C2
Etchinghill	Kent	41	G7
Etchinghill	Staffs	115	G7
Etchingwood	E Susx	23	H3
Etling Green	Norfk	105	K1
Etloe	Gloucs	63	K6
Eton	W & M	50	B3
Eton Wick	W & M	50	B3
Etruria	C Stke	114	D2
Etteridge	Highld	241	J5
Ettersgill	Dur	167	K5
Ettiley Heath	Ches E	130	E7
Ettingshall	Wolves	97	L4
Ettington	Warwks	83	G5
Etton	C Pete	102	C2
Etton	E R Yk	152	F7
Ettrick	Border	187	L3
Ettrickbridge	Border	188	C1
Ettrickhill	Border	187	L3
Etwall	Derbys	115	M5
Eudon George	Shrops	96	F5
Euston	Suffk	105	H7
Euximoor Drove	Cambs	103	K4
Euxton	Lancs	139	H4
Evancoyd	Powys	79	J3
Evanton	Highld	263	G6
Evedon	Lincs	118	E2
Evelith	Shrops	97	G2
Evelix	Highld	263	L2
Evenjobb	Powys	79	J3
Evenley	Nhants	84	B8
Evenlode	Gloucs	65	J1
Evenwood	Dur	168	F5
Evenwood Gate	Dur	168	F6
Evercreech	Somset	31	L3
Everingham	E R Yk	152	B7
Everleigh	Wilts	47	J8
Everley	N York	163	H5
Eversholt	C Beds	85	K8
Evershot	Dorset	16	A2
Eversley	Hants	49	J6
Eversley Cross	Hants	49	J6
Everthorpe	E R Yk	144	A2
Everton	C Beds	86	D5
Everton	Hants	18	D5
Everton	Lpool	129	H1
Everton	Notts	134	D2
Evertown	D & G	177	K4
Evesbatch	Herefs	80	F5
Evesham	Worcs	82	B6
Evington	C Leic	100	D3
Ewden Village	Sheff	141	L8
Ewell	Surrey	51	G6
Ewell Minnis	Kent	41	H6
Ewelme	Oxon	48	F1
Ewen	Gloucs	64	E7
Ewenny	V Glam	42	D6
Ewerby	Lincs	118	F2
Ewerby Thorpe	Lincs	118	F2
Ewhurst	Surrey	37	G3
Ewhurst Green	E Susx	24	E2
Ewhurst Green	Surrey	37	G3
Ewloe	Flints	129	G6
Ewloe Green	Flints	129	G6
Ewood	Bl w D	139	K3
Ewood Bridge	Lancs	140	B4
Eworthy	Devon	12	B4
Ewshot	Hants	36	B1
Ewyas Harold	Herefs	62	D2
Exbourne	Devon	12	E2
Exbridge	Somset	29	G6
Exbury	Hants	19	G4
Exceat	E Susx	23	H7
Exelby	N York	160	D5
Exeter	Devon	13	L4
Exeter & Devon Crematorium	Devon	13	L4
Exford	Somset	28	E3
Exfordsgreen	Shrops	95	L2
Exhall	Warwks	82	D4
Exhall	Warwks	99	K6
Exlade Street	Oxon	49	G3
Exley Head	C Brad	149	J7
Exminster	Devon	13	M5
Exmouth	Devon	14	A6
Exning	Suffk	88	C2
Exted	Kent	41	G6
Exton	Devon	14	A5
Exton	Hants	35	J6
Exton	Rutlnd	101	K1
Exton	Somset	29	G4
Exwick	Devon	13	L4
Eyam	Derbys	132	D4
Eydon	Nhants	83	M5
Eye	C Pete	102	E3
Eye	Herefs	80	C2
Eye	Suffk	106	C8
Eye Green	C Pete	102	E3
Eye Kettleby	Leics	117	K8
Eyemouth	Border	213	L6
Eyeworth	C Beds	86	E6
Eyhorne Street	Kent	39	L2
Eyke	Suffk	91	H5
Eynesbury	Cambs	86	D3
Eynsford	Kent	52	C6
Eynsham	Oxon	66	B5
Eype	Dorset	15	K4
Eyre	Highld	259	G6
Eythorne	Kent	41	J6
Eyton	Herefs	80	B3
Eyton	Shrops	95	J6
Eyton	Shrops	112	F8
Eyton	Shrops	113	G7
Eyton	Wrexhm	112	E3
Eyton on Severn	Shrops	96	D2
Eyton upon the Weald Moors	Wrekin	113	L8

F

Place	County	Page	Grid
Faccombe	Hants	48	A7
Faceby	N York	161	H2
Fachwen	Powys	111	K8
Facit	Lancs	140	D4
Fackley	Notts	133	J7
Faddiley	Ches E	113	K1
Fadmoor	N York	161	L5
Faerdre	Swans	57	J4
Fagwyr	Swans	57	J4
Faifley	W Duns	208	E4
Failand	N Som	45	G4
Failford	S Ayrs	196	F5
Failsworth	Oldham	140	D7
Fairbourne	Gwynd	92	D1
Fairburn	N York	142	D2
Fairfield	Derbys	131	L5
Fairfield	Kent	25	H2
Fairfield	Worcs	97	L8
Fairford	Gloucs	65	H6
Fairford Park	Gloucs	65	H6
Fairgirth	D & G	175	L3
Fair Green	Norfk	120	E8
Fairhaven	Lancs	138	C2
Fairlands	Surrey	50	B8
Fairlie	N Ayrs	207	L8
Fairlight	E Susx	24	F5
Fairmile	Devon	14	C3
Fairmile	Surrey	50	E6
Fairnilee	Border	200	F6
Fair Oak	Hants	35	G7
Fairoak	Staffs	114	B5
Fair Oak Green	Hants	49	G6
Fairseat	Kent	52	D6
Fairstead	Essex	71	J4
Fairstead	Norfk	120	E7
Fairstead	Norfk	122	F6
Fairwarp	E Susx	23	G2
Fairwater	Cardif	43	J6
Fairy Cross	Devon	27	G6
Fakenham	Norfk	121	K5
Fakenham Magna	Suffk	105	H8
Fala	Mdloth	211	M6
Fala Dam	Mdloth	211	M6
Falcut	Nhants	84	B6
Faldingworth	Lincs	135	L3
Faldouet	Jersey	9	f2
Falfield	S Glos	63	K8
Falkenham	Suffk	91	G7
Falkirk	Falk	210	A3
Falkirk Crematorium	Falk	210	A3
Falkland	Fife	222	F6
Fallburn	S Lans	199	G5
Fallgate	Derbys	133	G7
Fallin	Stirlg	209	L1
Fallodon	Nthumb	191	J6
Fallowfield	Manch	131	H3
Fallowfield	Nthumb	179	L5
Falls of Blarghour	Ag & B	216	F4
Falmer	E Susx	22	F5
Falmouth	Cnwll	3	K4
Falnash	Border	188	C5
Falsgrave	N York	163	J5
Falstone	Nthumb	179	J4
Fanagmore	Highld	276	B6
Fancott	C Beds	68	C2
Fanellan	Highld	250	D4
Fangdale Beck	N York	161	J3
Fangfoss	E R Yk	152	A5
Fanmore	Ag & B	226	E3
Fannich Lodge	Highld	261	J3
Fans	Border	201	J5
Far Bletchley	M Keyn	85	G8
Farcet	Cambs	102	D4
Far Cotton	Nhants	84	E3
Farden	Shrops	96	D8
Fareham	Hants	19	K2
Far End	Cumb	156	D2
Farewell	Staffs	98	D1
Far Forest	Worcs	97	J7
Farforth	Lincs	136	F4
Far Green	Gloucs	63	M7
Faringdon	Oxon	65	L3
Farington	Lancs	139	G3
Farlam	Cumb	178	D7
Farleigh	N Som	45	G5
Farleigh	Surrey	51	K7
Farleigh Hungerford	Somset	46	A7
Farleigh Wallop	Hants	35	J2
Farlesthorpe	Lincs	137	J5
Farleton	Cumb	157	H6
Farleton	Lancs	147	L2
Farley	Derbys	132	F7
Farley	Staffs	115	H4
Farley	Wilts	34	B5
Farley Green	Suffk	88	E4
Farley Green	Surrey	37	G3
Farley Hill	Wokham	49	H6
Farleys End	Gloucs	63	M5
Farlington	C Port	19	M3
Farlington	N York	151	K2
Farlow	Shrops	96	E7
Farmborough	BaNES	45	K7
Farmbridge End	Essex	70	F5
Farmcote	Gloucs	64	F1
Farmcote	Shrops	97	G5
Farmers	Carmth	77	J6
Farmington	Gloucs	65	H4
Farmoor	Oxon	66	C5
Far Moor	Wigan	139	G4
Farms Common	Cnwll	3	H4
Farm Town	Leics	116	C8
Farmtown	Moray	267	K6
Farnah Green	Derbys	116	B2
Farnborough	Gt Lon	51	L6
Farnborough	Hants	49	L7
Farnborough	W Berk	48	B3
Farnborough	Warwks	83	K5
Farnborough Park	Hants	49	L7
Farnborough Street	Hants	49	L7
Farncombe	Surrey	36	E2
Farndish	Bed	85	H3
Farndon	Ches W	112	F1
Farndon	Notts	117	K1
Farnell	Angus	235	G3
Farnham	Dorset	33	G7
Farnham	Essex	70	C2
Farnham	N York	150	E4
Farnham	Suffk	91	H3
Farnham	Surrey	36	B2
Farnham Common	Bucks	50	B2
Farnham Green	Essex	70	C2
Farnham Royal	Bucks	50	B2
Farningham	Kent	52	C5
Farnley	Leeds	141	L1
Farnley	N York	150	B6
Farnley Tyas	Kirk	141	J5
Farnsfield	Notts	134	C8
Farnworth	Bolton	139	L6
Farnworth	Halton	129	L2
Far Oakridge	Gloucs	64	D6
Farr	Highld	241	L3
Farr	Highld	251	J5
Farr	Highld	278	B4
Farraline	Highld	251	G7

Farringdon Devon ... 14 B4
Farrington Gurney BaNES ... 45 J7
Far Sawrey Cumb ... 156 E4
Farsley Leeds ... 141 K1
Farther Howegreen Essex ... 71 K6
Farthing Green Kent ... 39 K4
Farthinghoe Nhants ... 83 M7
Farthingloe Kent ... 41 J7
Farthingstone Nhants ... 84 B4
Farthing Street Gt Lon ... 51 L6
Fartown Kirk ... 141 J4
Fartown Leeds ... 141 K1
Farway Devon ... 14 E4
Fasnacloich Ag & B ... 229 G6
Fasnakyle Highld ... 250 B6
Fassfern Highld ... 239 G7
Fatfield Sundld ... 181 H8
Faugh Cumb ... 178 D4
Fauld Staffs ... 115 K6
Fauldhouse W Loth ... 210 B6
Faulkbourne Essex ... 71 J4
Faulkland Somset ... 45 L8
Fauls Shrops ... 113 K5
Faversham Kent ... 40 D3
Fawdington N York ... 150 F1
Fawdon N u Ty ... 180 F5
Fawdon Nthumb ... 190 E3
Fawfieldhead Staffs ... 131 L7
Fawkham Green Kent ... 52 C6
Fawler Oxon ... 66 A4
Fawley Bucks ... 49 J2
Fawley Hants ... 19 G3
Fawley W Berk ... 48 B3
Fawley Chapel Herefs ... 63 H1
Fawnog Flints ... 128 F6
Fawsley Nhants ... 84 A4
Faxfleet E R Yk ... 143 L3
Faygate W Susx ... 37 K4
Fazakerley Lpool ... 138 D8
Fazeley Staffs ... 99 G3
Fearby N York ... 160 B6
Fearn Highld ... 264 C4
Fearnan P & K ... 231 K6
Fearnbeg Highld ... 260 B6
Fearnhead Warrtn ... 130 C2
Fearnmore Highld ... 260 A7
Fearnoch Ag & B ... 206 E3
Featherstone Staffs ... 97 L2
Featherstone Wakefd ... 142 C3
Feckenham Worcs ... 82 B3
Feering Essex ... 72 C3
Feetham N York ... 159 H3
Feizor N York ... 148 D2
Felbridge Surrey ... 38 B5
Felbrigg Norfk ... 122 E4
Felcourt Surrey ... 38 B5
Felden Herts ... 68 D6
Felindre Carmth ... 59 G4
Felindre Carmth ... 59 K3
Felindre Carmth ... 76 C7
Felindre Cerdgn ... 77 G4
Felindre Powys ... 61 J2
Felindre Powys ... 94 B4
Felindre Swans ... 57 H4
Felindre Farchog Pembks ... 75 J4
Felin Fach Cerdgn ... 76 F4
Felinfach Powys ... 78 F8
Felinfoel Carmth ... 56 F4
Felingwm Isaf Carmth ... 58 F4
Felingwm Uchaf Carmth ... 58 F4
Felin-newydd Powys ... 78 F4
Felixkirk N York ... 161 G5
Felixstowe Suffk ... 91 G8
Felixstowe Ferry Suffk ... 91 H7
Felkington Nthumb ... 202 E4
Felkirk Wakefd ... 142 B5
Felling Gatesd ... 181 G6
Fell Lane C Brad ... 149 J7
Fell Side Cumb ... 165 L3
Felmersham Bed ... 85 K4
Felmingham Norfk ... 122 E5
Felpham W Susx ... 20 F7
Felsham Suffk ... 89 J4
Felsted Essex ... 71 G3
Feltham Gt Lon ... 50 E4
Felthamhill Surrey ... 50 E4
Felthorpe Norfk ... 122 D7
Felton Herefs ... 80 D5
Felton N Som ... 45 G6
Felton Nthumb ... 191 H6
Felton Butler Shrops ... 112 F8
Feltwell Norfk ... 104 E5
Fenay Bridge Kirk ... 141 J4
Fence Lancs ... 148 K4
Fence Rothm ... 133 J3
Fence Houses Sundld ... 169 J1
Fencott Oxon ... 66 E4
Fendike Corner Lincs ... 137 K7
Fen Ditton Cambs ... 87 K3
Fen Drayton Cambs ... 87 G2

Fen End Lincs ... 119 H7
Fen End Solhll ... 99 G8
Fenham Nthumb ... 203 H5
Feniscliffe Bl w D ... 139 K2
Feniscowles Bl w D ... 139 K3
Feniton Devon ... 14 D3
Fenland Crematorium Cambs ... 103 H4
Fenn Green Shrops ... 97 H6
Fenn Street Medway ... 53 G4
Fenny Bentley Derbys ... 115 K2
Fenny Bridges Devon ... 14 D3
Fenny Compton Warwks ... 83 K5
Fenny Drayton Leics ... 99 K4
Fenny Stratford M Keyn ... 85 G8
Fenrother Nthumb ... 191 H7
Fenstanton Cambs ... 87 G2
Fenstead End Suffk ... 88 F5
Fen Street Norfk ... 105 K4
Fen Street Suffk ... 90 E3
Fenton C Stke ... 114 D3
Fenton Cambs ... 103 G7
Fenton Cumb ... 178 C7
Fenton Lincs ... 118 A1
Fenton Lincs ... 135 G4
Fenton Notts ... 134 F3
Fenton Nthumb ... 202 F6
Fenton Barns E Loth ... 212 B3
Fenwick Donc ... 142 F4
Fenwick E Ayrs ... 196 F2
Fenwick Nthumb ... 180 C4
Fenwick Nthumb ... 203 H5
Feock Cnwll ... 3 L3
Feolin Ferry Ag & B ... 205 G3
Fergushill N Ayrs ... 196 C2
Feriniquarrie Highld ... 258 B6
Fermain Bay Guern ... 9 k3
Fern Angus ... 234 D3
Ferndale Rhondd ... 42 F2
Ferndown Dorset ... 17 L3
Fernham Oxon ... 65 L8
Fernhill Heath Worcs ... 81 K3
Fernhurst W Susx ... 36 D5
Fernie Fife ... 222 E4
Ferniegair S Lans ... 209 K8
Fernilea Highld ... 246 E2
Fernilee Derbys ... 131 K4
Fernwood Notts ... 117 L2
Ferrensby N York ... 150 E4
Ferriby Sluice N Linc ... 144 B4
Ferrindonald Highld ... 247 L7
Ferring W Susx ... 21 J4
Ferrybridge Wakefd ... 142 D3
Ferryden Angus ... 235 H4
Ferryhill Dur ... 169 H4
Ferry Point Highld ... 263 K3
Ferryside Carmth ... 56 C3
Ferrytown Highld ... 263 K2
Fersfield Norfk ... 106 B6
Fersit Highld ... 240 B7
Feshiebridge Highld ... 241 M3
Fetcham Surrey ... 50 F7
Fetlar Shet ... 281 f3
Fetterangus Abers ... 269 H6
Fettercairn Abers ... 235 G1
Fewcott Oxon ... 66 D2
Fewston N York ... 150 B5
Ffairfach Carmth ... 59 H4
Ffair Rhos Cerdgn ... 77 K2
Ffald-y-Brenin Carmth ... 77 H6
Ffawyddog Powys ... 61 K3
Ffestiniog Gwynd ... 110 D3
Ffordd-las Denbgs ... 128 D6
Fforest Carmth ... 57 G4
Fforest Mons ... 62 B3
Fforest Fach Swans ... 57 H5
Fforest Goch Neath ... 57 K4
Ffostrasol Cerdgn ... 76 C5
Ffrith Flints ... 129 G3
Ffynnonddewi Cerdgn ... 76 C4
Ffynnongroyw Flints ... 128 D3
Ffynnon-Oer Cerdgn ... 76 F4
Fiag Lodge Highld ... 272 C2
Ficklesole Surrey ... 51 K6
Fiddington Gloucs ... 64 D1
Fiddington Somset ... 30 B4
Fiddleford Dorset ... 32 D8
Fiddlers Green Cnwll ... 4 D4
Fiddlers Hamlet Essex ... 70 C6
Field Staffs ... 115 G5
Field Broughton Cumb ... 156 E6
Field Dalling Norfk ... 121 M4
Fieldhead Cumb ... 166 B3
Field Head Leics ... 100 B3
Fifehead Magdalen Dorset ... 32 C6
Fifehead Neville Dorset ... 32 C8
Fifehead St Quintin Dorset ... 16 E1
Fife Keith Moray ... 267 H6
Fifield Oxon ... 65 K3
Fifield W & M ... 49 L4

Fifield Wilts ... 33 K1
Figheldean Wilts ... 33 K2
Filands Wilts ... 46 D1
Filby Norfk ... 107 K1
Filey N York ... 163 L6
Filgrave M Keyn ... 85 G5
Filkins Oxon ... 65 K6
Filleigh Devon ... 28 B5
Filleigh Devon ... 28 C8
Fillingham Lincs ... 135 J3
Fillongley Warwks ... 99 H6
Filmore Hill Hants ... 35 K5
Filton S Glos ... 45 J3
Fimber E R Yk ... 152 D4
Finavon Angus ... 234 D4
Fincham Norfk ... 104 D2
Finchampstead Wokham ... 49 J6
Fincharn Ag & B ... 216 D6
Finchdean Hants ... 20 B4
Finchingfield Essex ... 88 D8
Finchley Gt Lon ... 51 H1
Findern Derbys ... 116 A5
Findhorn Moray ... 265 G7
Findhorn Bridge Highld ... 252 E6
Findochty Moray ... 267 J3
Findo Gask P & K ... 221 H3
Findon Abers ... 245 L4
Findon W Susx ... 21 J5
Findon Mains Highld ... 263 G7
Findrack House Abers ... 244 D3
Finedon Nhants ... 85 H1
Fineshade Nhants ... 101 L4
Fingal Street Suffk ... 90 F1
Fingask P & K ... 222 B3
Fingest Bucks ... 49 J1
Finghall N York ... 160 B5
Fingland Cumb ... 177 H7
Fingland D & G ... 197 L7
Finglesham Kent ... 41 K4
Finglinshaw Barns ... 141 M7
Finlarig Stirlg ... 231 G8
Finmere Oxon ... 84 C8
Finnart P & K ... 230 F4
Finningham Suffk ... 90 C2
Finningley Donc ... 143 H7
Finsbay W Isls ... 282 e6
Finstall Worcs ... 82 A1
Finsthwaite Cumb ... 156 E5
Finstock Oxon ... 66 A4
Finstown Ork ... 275 c4
Fintry Abers ... 268 D5
Fintry Stirlg ... 209 G2
Finzean Abers ... 244 D5
Fionnphort Ag & B ... 226 B7
Fionnsbhagh W Isls ... 282 e6
Firbank Cumb ... 157 K4
Firbeck Rothm ... 133 L2
Firby N York ... 152 A3
Firby N York ... 160 C5
Firgrove Rochdl ... 140 D5
Firle E Susx ... 23 G6
Firsby Lincs ... 137 H7
Firsdown Wilts ... 34 B4
Fir Tree Dur ... 168 F4
Fishbourne IoW ... 19 J5
Fishbourne W Susx ... 20 D6
Fishburn Dur ... 169 K4
Fishcross Clacks ... 220 F8
Fisher W Susx ... 20 E6
Fisherford Abers ... 256 B4
Fisherrow E Loth ... 211 K4
Fisher's Pond Hants ... 35 G6
Fisher's Row Lancs ... 147 H6
Fisherstreet W Susx ... 36 E4
Fisherton Highld ... 252 D2
Fisherton S Ayrs ... 196 B6
Fisherton de la Mere Wilts ... 33 G3
Fisherwick Staffs ... 98 F2
Fishery Estate W & M ... 49 L3
Fishguard Pembks ... 74 F5
Fishlake Donc ... 143 G5
Fishleigh Devon ... 12 D2
Fishmere End Lincs ... 119 J4
Fishnish Pier Ag & B ... 227 J4
Fishpond Bottom Dorset ... 15 J3
Fishponds Bristl ... 45 J4
Fishtoft Lincs ... 119 K3
Fishtoft Drove Lincs ... 119 K2
Fishwick Lancs ... 139 H2
Fiskavaig Highld ... 246 D2
Fiskerton Lincs ... 135 L5
Fiskerton Notts ... 117 K1
Fitling E R Yk ... 145 H1
Fittleton Wilts ... 33 K1
Fittleworth W Susx ... 21 G3
Fitton End Cambs ... 103 J1
Fitz Shrops ... 113 G7
Fitzhead Somset ... 29 L5

Fitzroy Somset ... 30 B5
Fitzwilliam Wakefd ... 142 C5
Five Ash Down E Susx ... 23 H3
Five Ashes E Susx ... 23 J2
Five Bells Somset ... 29 K2
Five Bridges Herefs ... 80 F6
Fivecrosses Ches W ... 129 M4
Fivehead Somset ... 30 E6
Fivelanes Cnwll ... 11 J6
Five Lanes Mons ... 44 F1
Five Oak Green Kent ... 39 G4
Five Oaks Jersey ... 9 e3
Five Oaks W Susx ... 37 G5
Five Roads Carmth ... 56 E4
Five Wents Kent ... 39 K3
Flack's Green Essex ... 71 J4
Flackwell Heath Bucks ... 49 L1
Fladbury Worcs ... 82 A6
Fladdabister Shet ... 281 e7
Flagg Derbys ... 132 C6
Flamborough E R Yk ... 153 K2
Flamstead Herts ... 68 D4
Flansham W Susx ... 20 F6
Flanshaw Wakefd ... 141 M4
Flappit Spring C Brad ... 149 J8
Flasby N York ... 149 G4
Flash Staffs ... 131 K6
Flashader Highld ... 258 E6
Flaunden Herts ... 68 C7
Flawborough Notts ... 117 K3
Flawith N York ... 151 G3
Flax Bourton N Som ... 45 G5
Flaxby N York ... 150 E4
Flaxley Gloucs ... 63 K4
Flaxmere Ches W ... 130 A5
Flaxpool Somset ... 29 L4
Flaxton N York ... 151 L3
Fleckney Leics ... 100 E5
Flecknoe Warwks ... 83 M3
Fledborough Notts ... 134 F5
Fleet Dorset ... 16 C6
Fleet Hants ... 20 B6
Fleet Hants ... 49 K8
Fleet Lincs ... 119 L6
Fleetend Hants ... 19 H3
Fleet Hargate Lincs ... 119 L6
Fleetwood Lancs ... 146 F6
Flemingston V Glam ... 42 F7
Flemington S Lans ... 209 H7
Flempton Suffk ... 89 G1
Fletcher Green Kent ... 38 E3
Fletchersbridge Cnwll ... 5 J2
Fletchertown Cumb ... 165 G2
Fletching E Susx ... 23 G3
Fleur-de-lis Caerph ... 43 J3
Flexbury Cnwll ... 11 J1
Flexford Surrey ... 36 D1
Flimby Cumb ... 164 D4
Flimwell E Susx ... 39 H7
Flint Flints ... 128 F5
Flintham Notts ... 117 K2
Flint Mountain Flints ... 128 F5
Flinton E R Yk ... 153 K8
Flint's Green Solhll ... 99 H7
Flishinghurst Kent ... 39 J6
Flitcham Norfk ... 120 F6
Flitton C Beds ... 85 L8
Flitwick C Beds ... 85 K8
Flixborough N Linc ... 143 L5
Flixborough Stather N Linc ... 143 L5
Flixton N York ... 163 J6
Flixton Suffk ... 107 G6
Flixton Traffd ... 130 E1
Flockton Kirk ... 141 K5
Flockton Green Kirk ... 141 L5
Flodden Nthumb ... 202 E6
Flodigarry Highld ... 259 H2
Flookburgh Cumb ... 156 E7
Flordon Norfk ... 106 D4
Flore Nhants ... 84 C3
Flotterton Nthumb ... 190 E5
Flowers Green E Susx ... 23 L5
Flowton Suffk ... 90 C6
Flushdyke Wakefd ... 141 L3
Flushing Cnwll ... 3 K4
Fluxton Devon ... 14 C4
Flyford Flavell Worcs ... 82 A4
Fobbing Thurr ... 52 F2
Fochabers Moray ... 267 G4
Fochriw Caerph ... 61 H6
Fockerby N Linc ... 143 L4
Foddington Somset ... 31 J5
Foel Powys ... 94 B1
Foelgastell Carmth ... 59 G6
Foel y Dyffryn Brdgnd ... 42 C3
Foggathorpe E R Yk ... 152 A8
Fogo Border ... 202 B3
Fogwatt Moray ... 266 E5
Foindle Highld ... 276 B6
Folda Angus ... 233 J3

Fole Staffs 115 G4
Foleshill Covtry 99 K7
Folke Dorset 31 L8
Folkestone Kent 41 H8
Folkingham Lincs 118 E5
Folkington E Susx 23 J6
Folksworth Cambs 102 C5
Folkton N York 163 J6
Folla Rule Abers 256 C5
Follifoot N York 150 D5
Folly Gate Devon 12 D3
Folly Hill Surrey 36 B1
Fonmon V Glam 43 G8
Fonthill Bishop Wilts 32 F4
Fonthill Gifford Wilts 32 F4
Fontmell Magna Dorset 32 E7
Fontmell Parva Dorset 32 D7
Fontwell W Susx 20 F5
Font-y-gary V Glam 43 G8
Foolow Derbys 132 D4
Foots Cray Gt Lon 52 A5
Forbestown Abers 243 L1
Forcett N York 168 F8
Ford Ag & B 216 D6
Ford Bucks 67 J5
Ford Derbys 133 H4
Ford Devon 7 J5
Ford Devon 8 B6
Ford Devon 27 G6
Ford Gloucs 65 G1
Ford Nthumb 202 E5
Ford Shrops 95 K1
Ford Somset 29 K5
Ford Somset 45 H8
Ford Staffs 115 H1
Ford W Susx 21 G6
Ford Wilts 33 L4
Ford Wilts 46 B4
Forda Devon 12 D4
Fordcombe Kent 38 E5
Fordell Fife 211 G1
Forden Powys 94 F3
Ford End Essex 71 G4
Forder Green Devon 8 B2
Ford Green Lancs 147 J6
Fordham Cambs 88 C1
Fordham Essex 72 D2
Fordham Norfk 104 C3
Fordham Heath Essex 72 C2
Ford Heath Shrops 95 K1
Fordingbridge Hants 33 K8
Fordon E R Yk 163 J7
Fordoun Abers 245 G8
Ford's Green Suffk 90 C2
Fordstreet Essex 72 D2
Ford Street Somset 29 L7
Fordton Devon 13 J3
Fordwells Oxon 65 L4
Fordwich Kent 41 G3
Fordyce Abers 267 L3
Forebridge Staffs 114 E7
Foremark Derbys 116 B6
Forest Guern 9 j4
Forest N York 160 C3
Forest Becks Lancs 148 D5
Forestburn Gate Nthumb 190 F7
Forest Chapel Ches E 131 J5
Forest Gate Gt Lon 51 L2
Forest Green Surrey 37 H3
Forest Hall N Tyne 181 G5
Forest Head Cumb 178 D7
Forest Hill Gt Lon 51 K4
Forest Hill Oxon 66 E5
Forest-in-Teesdale Dur 167 K4
Forest Lane Head N York 150 D4
Forest Mill Clacks 221 G8
Forest Park Crematorium
   Gt Lon 70 C8
Forest Row E Susx 38 C6
Forest Side IoW 19 H5
Forestside W Susx 20 C4
Forest Town Notts 133 L7
Forfar Angus 234 C5
Forgandenny P & K 221 K3
Forge Powys 93 G3
Forge Hammer Torfn 62 B7
Forge Side Torfn 61 L5
Forgie Moray 267 H5
Forgieside Moray 267 H5
Forgue Abers 256 A3
Forhill Worcs 98 D8
Formby Sefton 138 C6
Forncett End Norfk 106 C4
Forncett St Mary Norfk 106 D4
Forncett St Peter Norfk 106 D5
Fornham All Saints Suffk 89 G2
Fornham St Martin Suffk 89 G2
Fornighty Highld 253 H2
Forres Moray 265 G8
Forsbrook Staffs 114 F3

Forse Highld 275 H1
Forshaw Heath Warwks 98 E8
Forsinard Highld 278 F7
Forston Dorset 16 C3
Fort Augustus Highld 240 C2
Forteviot P & K 221 J4
Forth S Lans 198 F2
Forthampton Gloucs 64 B1
Fort Hommet Guern 9 i2
Fortingall P & K 231 K6
Fort le Marchant Guern 9 k1
Forton Hants 34 F2
Forton Lancs 147 J5
Forton Shrops 113 G8
Forton Somset 15 H1
Forton Staffs 114 B7
Fortrie Abers 256 B3
Fortrose Highld 263 K8
Fortuneswell Dorset 16 D7
Fort William Highld 239 J8
Forty Green Bucks 50 A1
Forty Hill Gt Lon 69 J7
Forward Green Suffk 90 C3
Fosbury Wilts 47 L7
Foscot Oxon 65 K3
Foscote Nhants 84 C6
Fosdyke Lincs 119 K5
Fosdyke Bridge Lincs 119 K5
Foss P & K 231 L4
Fossebridge Gloucs 65 G5
Foss-y-ffin Cerdgn 76 E3
Fosterhouses Donc 143 G5
Foster Street Essex 70 C5
Foston Derbys 115 K5
Foston Leics 100 D4
Foston Lincs 117 M3
Foston N York 151 L3
Foston on the Wolds E R Yk 153 H4
Fotherby Lincs 136 F2
Fothergill Cumb 164 D4
Fotheringhay Nhants 102 B5
Foula Shet 281 a7
Foulbridge Cumb 165 M1
Foulby Wakefd 142 B4
Foulden Border 202 E2
Foulden Norfk 104 F4
Foul End Warwks 99 H4
Foul Mile E Susx 23 K4
Foulness Island Essex 53 L1
Foulon Vale Crematorium
   Guern 9 j3
Foulridge Lancs 148 F7
Foulsham Norfk 122 A6
Fountainhall Border 200 F3
Four Ashes Solhll 98 F8
Four Ashes Staffs 97 H6
Four Ashes Staffs 97 L2
Four Ashes Suffk 89 K1
Four Cabots Guern 9 j3
Four Crosses Powys 112 C7
Four Crosses Staffs 98 B2
Four Elms Kent 38 C4
Four Foot Somset 31 J4
Four Forks Somset 30 C3
Four Gates Bolton 139 J6
Four Gotes Cambs 120 A8
Four Lane End Barns 141 L7
Four Lane Ends Ches W 130 A7
Four Lanes Cnwll 3 H3
Fourlanes End Ches E 130 F7
Four Marks Hants 35 K4
Four Mile Bridge IoA 124 E4
Four Oaks Birm 98 E4
Four Oaks E Susx 24 F2
Four Oaks Gloucs 63 K2
Four Oaks Solhll 99 H7
Fourpenny Highld 264 C1
Four Points W Berk 48 E3
Four Roads Carmth 56 E3
Four Shire Stone Warwks 65 K1
Fourstones Nthumb 179 K5
Four Throws Kent 39 J7
Four Wents Kent 38 F3
Fovant Wilts 33 H5
Foveran Abers 257 H7
Fowey Cnwll 5 H5
Fowley Common Warrtn 139 K8
Fowlhall Kent 39 H4
Fowlis Angus 233 M8
Fowlis Wester P & K 221 J3
Fowlmere Cambs 87 J6
Fownhope Herefs 80 D8
Foxbar Rens 208 D6
Foxcombe Devon 12 C5
Foxcote Gloucs 64 E3
Foxcote Somset 45 L7
Foxdale IoM 154 c6
Foxearth Essex 89 G6
Foxendown Kent 52 E5

Foxfield Cumb 156 B5
Foxham Wilts 46 E3
Fox Hatch Essex 70 E7
Foxhills Hants 18 E1
Foxhole Cnwll 4 F5
Foxholes N York 163 H8
Foxhunt Green E Susx 23 J4
Foxley Nhants 84 C5
Foxley Norfk 122 A7
Foxley Wilts 46 C2
Foxlydiate Worcs 82 B2
Fox Street Essex 72 F2
Foxt Staffs 115 G2
Foxton Cambs 87 H5
Foxton Dur 169 K5
Foxton Leics 100 F5
Foxton N York 160 E5
Foxup N York 158 F7
Foxwist Green Ches W 130 C6
Foxwood Shrops 96 E8
Foy Herefs 63 J7
Foyers Highld 250 E7
Foynesfield Highld 253 G1
Fraddam Cnwll 2 F4
Fraddon Cnwll 4 E5
Fradley Staffs 98 F1
Fradswell Staffs 114 F5
Fraisthorpe E R Yk 153 J3
Framfield E Susx 23 H3
Framingham Earl Norfk 106 F3
Framingham Pigot Norfk 106 F3
Framlingham Suffk 91 G3
Frampton Dorset 16 B4
Frampton Lincs 119 K4
Frampton Cotterell S Glos 45 K3
Frampton Mansell Gloucs 64 D6
Frampton-on-Severn Gloucs 63 L5
Frampton West End Lincs 119 J3
Framsden Suffk 90 E3
Framwellgate Moor Dur 169 H2
Franche Worcs 97 J7
Frandley Ches W 130 C4
Frankaborough Devon 11 M4
Frankby Wirral 129 F2
Frankfort Norfk 122 F6
Frankley Worcs 98 C7
Franklands Gate Herefs 80 C6
Frankley Worcs 98 C7
Franksbridge Powys 78 F4
Frankton Warwks 83 K1
Frant E Susx 38 F6
Fraserburgh Abers 269 J3
Frating Essex 73 G3
Frating Green Essex 73 G2
Fratton C Port 19 L4
Freathy Cnwll 6 D4
Freckenham Suffk 88 D1
Freckleton Lancs 138 E2
Freebirch Derbys 132 F5
Freeby Leics 117 L7
Freefolk Hants 35 G1
Freehay Staffs 115 G3
Freeland Oxon 66 B4
Freethorpe Norfk 107 H2
Freethorpe Common Norfk 107 H2
Freiston Lincs 119 L3
Fremington Devon 27 J4
Fremington N York 159 J3
Frenchay S Glos 45 J3
Frenchbeer Devon 12 F5
French Street Kent 51 M8
Frenich P & K 232 B1
Frensham Surrey 36 C3
Freshfield Sefton 138 C6
Freshford Wilts 46 A7
Freshwater IoW 18 E6
Freshwater Bay IoW 18 E6
Freshwater East Pembks 55 G7
Fressingfield Suffk 106 F7
Freston Suffk 90 E7
Freswick Highld 280 E3
Fretherne Gloucs 63 L5
Frettenham Norfk 122 F8
Freuchie Fife 222 D6
Freystrop Pembks 54 F4
Friar Park Sandw 98 C4
Friar's Gate E Susx 38 D6
Friars' Hill N York 162 C5
Friar Waddon Dorset 16 C5
Friday Bridge Cambs 103 K2
Friday Street Suffk 90 F3
Friday Street Suffk 91 H5
Friday Street Suffk 91 J3
Friday Street Surrey 37 H2
Fridaythorpe E R Yk 152 D4
Friden Derbys 132 C7
Friendly Calder 141 G3
Friern Barnet Gt Lon 69 H8
Friesthorpe Lincs 135 M3
Frieston Lincs 118 B2
Frieth Bucks 49 J1

Friezeland Notts 116 D2
Frilford Oxon 66 B7
Frilsham W Berk 48 E4
Frimley Surrey 49 L7
Frimley Green Surrey 49 L7
Frindsbury Medway 52 F5
Fring Norfk 121 G4
Fringford Oxon 66 F1
Frinsted Kent 40 A4
Frinton-on-Sea Essex 73 K3
Friockheim Angus 234 D1
Friog Gwynd 92 D1
Frisby on the Wreake Leics 117 J7
Friskney Lincs 137 J6
Friskney Eaudike Lincs 137 J6
Friston E Susx 23 J7
Friston Suffk 91 J3
Fritchley Derbys 116 B1
Fritham Hants 34 B8
Frith Bank Lincs 119 K3
Frith Common Worcs 80 F7
Frithelstock Devon 27 H7
Frithelstock Stone Devon 27 H7
Frithend Hants 36 B3
Frithsden Herts 68 C5
Frithville Lincs 119 K2
Frittenden Kent 39 K5
Frittiscombe Devon 8 B6
Fritton Norfk 106 E5
Fritton Norfk 107 K3
Fritwell Oxon 66 D1
Frizinghall C Brad 149 L8
Frizington Cumb 164 D7
Frocester Gloucs 63 M6
Frodesley Shrops 96 C3
Frodsham Ches W 130 M4
Frogden Border 202 B7
Frog End Cambs 87 H6
Frog End Cambs 87 L3
Froggatt Derbys 132 E4
Froghall Staffs 115 G2
Frogham Hants 33 L8
Frogham Kent 41 H5
Frogmore Devon 7 M6
Frognall Lincs 102 D2
Frogpool Cnwll 3 J3
Frog Pool Worcs 81 J2
Frogwell Cnwll 6 C1
Frolesworth Leics 100 B5
Frome Somset 32 C1
Frome St Quintin Dorset 16 B2
Fromes Hill Herefs 80 F6
Fron Denbgs 128 C6
Fron Gwynd 108 C3
Fron Gwynd 109 J1
Fron Powys 94 E4
Fron Powys 94 F3
Froncysyllte Denbgs 112 C3
Fron-goch Gwynd 111 H4
Fron Isaf Wrexhm 112 C3
Frostenden Suffk 107 K7
Frosterley Dur 168 C3
Froxfield C Beds 85 J8
Froxfield Wilts 47 L5
Froxfield Green Hants 35 L5
Fryern Hill Hants 34 F6
Fryerning Essex 70 F7
Fryton N York 162 B7
Fuinary Highld 227 J3
Fulbeck Lincs 118 B2
Fulbourn Cambs 87 L4
Fulbrook Oxon 65 L4
Fulflood Hants 35 G5
Fulford C York 151 K6
Fulford Somset 30 B5
Fulford Staffs 114 F4
Fulham Gt Lon 51 H4
Fulking W Susx 22 C5
Fullaford Devon 28 B3
Fullarton N Ayrs 196 C5
Fuller's End Essex 70 D2
Fuller's Moor Ches W 113 H1
Fuller Street Essex 71 H4
Fuller Street Kent 38 C2
Fullerton Hants 34 E5
Fulletby Lincs 136 E5
Fullready Warwks 83 G6
Full Sutton E R Yk 152 A5
Fullwood E Ayrs 196 E1
Fulmer Bucks 50 C3
Fulmodeston Norfk 121 M5
Fulnetby Lincs 136 B4
Fulney Lincs 119 J6
Fulstone Kirk 141 J6
Fulstow Lincs 145 L4
Fulwell Oxon 66 A3
Fulwell Sundld 181 J7
Fulwood Lancs 139 H2
Fulwood Notts 133 J8
Fulwood Sheff 132 F3

Fulwood Somset 30 B6
Fundenhall Norfk 106 C4
Funtington W Susx 20 C5
Funtley Hants 19 J2
Funtullich P & K 220 C2
Furley Devon 15 G2
Furnace Ag & B 217 G7
Furnace Carmth 56 F4
Furnace Cerdgn 92 E4
Furnace End Warwks 99 H5
Furner's Green E Susx 22 F2
Furness Vale Derbys 131 K3
Furneux Pelham Herts 70 B2
Further Quarter Kent 39 M5
Furtho Nhants 84 E6
Furzehill Devon 28 C2
Furzehill Dorset 17 K2
Furzehills Lincs 136 E5
Furzeley Corner Hants 19 L2
Furze Platt W & M 49 L3
Furzley Hants 34 C7
Fyfett Somset 30 C7
Fyfield Essex 70 E5
Fyfield Hants 34 C2
Fyfield Oxon 66 B7
Fyfield Wilts 47 H5
Fyfield Wilts 47 H6
Fyfield Bavant Wilts 33 H6
Fylingthorpe N York 163 G2
Fyning W Susx 36 B6
Fyvie Abers 256 D4

G

Gabroc Hill E Ayrs 196 E1
Gaddesby Leics 100 F1
Gaddesden Row Herts 68 D4
Gadfa IoA 125 H2
Gadgirth S Ayrs 196 E4
Gadlas Shrops 112 E4
Gaer Powys 61 J3
Gaer-llwyd Mons 62 F7
Gaerwen IoA 125 H5
Gagingwell Oxon 66 B2
Gailes N Ayrs 196 C4
Gailey Staffs 97 K1
Gainford Dur 168 F7
Gainsborough Lincs 135 G2
Gainsford End Essex 88 E8
Gairloch Highld 260 U4
Gairlochy Highld 239 K6
Gairneybridge P & K 221 L7
Gaisgill Cumb 157 K2
Gaitsgill Cumb 165 L1
Galashiels Border 201 G6
Galgate Lancs 147 J5
Galhampton Somset 31 K5
Gallanachbeg Ag & B 216 C2
Gallanachmore Ag & B 216 C2
Gallantry Bank Ches E 113 H1
Gallatown Fife 222 E8
Galley Common Warwks 99 J5
Galleywood Essex 71 H6
Gallovie Highld 240 F5
Gallowfauld Angus 234 C7
Gallowhill P & K 233 J4
Gallows Green Essex 72 D2
Gallows Green Worcs 81 L3
Gallowstree Common Oxon 49 G3
Galltair Highld 248 C7
Gallt-y-foel Gwynd 125 K7
Gally Hill Hants 49 K8
Gallypot Street E Susx 38 D6
Galmpton Devon 7 J4
Galmpton Torbay 8 D4
Galphay N York 150 C1
Galston E Ayrs 196 F4
Gamballs Green Staffs 131 L6
Gamblesby Cumb 166 E3
Gambles Green Essex 71 J4
Gamelsby Cumb 177 H8
Gamesley Derbys 131 K1
Gamlingay Cambs 86 E5
Gamlingay Cinques Cambs 86 E4
Gamlingay Great Heath
   Cambs 86 E5
Gammersgill N York 159 J6
Gamrie Abers 268 E4
Gamston Notts 117 G4
Gamston Notts 134 E4
Ganarew Herefs 63 G4
Ganavan Bay Ag & B 216 D1
Gang Cnwll 6 C1
Ganllwyd Gwynd 110 D6
Gannachy Angus 234 F1
Ganstead E R Yk 144 F1
Ganthorpe N York 151 L2
Ganton N York 163 H7
Ganwick Corner Herts 69 H7

Gappah Devon 13 K7
Garbity Moray 266 F5
Garboldisham Norfk 105 K7
Garbole Highld 252 E7
Garchory Abers 243 J2
Garden City Flints 129 H6
Gardeners Green Wokham 49 K5
Gardenstown Abers 268 E3
Garden Village Sheff 141 L8
Garderhouse Shet 281 d6
Gardham E R Yk 152 E7
Gare Hill Somset 32 C3
Garelochhead Ag & B 207 L1
Garford Oxon 66 B7
Garforth Leeds 142 B1
Gargrave N York 149 G5
Gargunnock Stirlg 220 B8
Garizim Conwy 126 D4
Garlic Street Norfk 106 E6
Garlieston D & G 174 D5
Garlinge Kent 41 K2
Garlinge Green Kent 40 F5
Garlogie Abers 245 H2
Garmond Abers 268 E5
Garmouth Moray 267 G3
Garmston Shrops 96 E2
Garnant Carmth 59 J6
Garn-Dolbenmaen Gwynd 109 J3
Garnett Bridge Cumb 157 H3
Garnfadryn Gwynd 108 E5
Garnkirk N Lans 209 H5
Garnswllt Swans 57 H5
Garn-yr-erw Torfn 61 K5
Garrabost W Isls 282 h3
Garrallan E Ayrs 197 G7
Garras Cnwll 3 H6
Garreg Gwynd 109 L3
Garrigill Cumb 167 H2
Garriston N York 159 L4
Garroch D & G 184 F6
Garrochtrie D & G 172 D7
Garrochty Ag & B 207 H8
Garros Highld 259 H4
Garsdale Cumb 158 C5
Garsdale Head Cumb 158 D4
Garsdon Wilts 46 D2
Garshall Green Staffs 114 F5
Garsington Oxon 66 E6
Garstang Lancs 147 J6
Garston Herts 68 E7
Garston Lpool 129 J3
Gartachossan Ag & B 204 E4
Gartcosh N Lans 209 J5
Garth Brdgnd 42 C4
Garth Mons 62 D4
Garth Powys 78 C5
Garth Powys 79 J1
Garth Wrexhm 112 C3
Garthamlock C Glas 209 H5
Garthbrengy Powys 78 E8
Gartheli Cerdgn 77 G4
Garthmyl Powys 94 F3
Garthorpe Leics 117 L7
Garthorpe N Linc 143 L4
Garth Penrhyncoch Cerdgn 92 E6
Garth Row Cumb 157 H3
Garths Cumb 157 H5
Gartly Abers 255 K5
Gartmore Stirlg 219 H7
Gartness N Lans 209 K6
Gartness Stirlg 208 E2
Gartocharn W Duns 208 D2
Garton E R Yk 145 H1
Garton-on-the-Wolds E R Yk 152 F4
Gartymore Highld 274 D5
Garvald E Loth 212 D5
Garvan Highld 238 F8
Garvard Ag & B 214 D6
Garve Highld 262 C7
Garvellachs Ag & B 215 J2
Garvestone Norfk 105 L2
Garvock Inver 207 L5
Garway Herefs 62 F3
Garway Common Herefs 62 F3
Garway Hill Herefs 62 F2
Garyvard W Isls 282 g4
Gasper Wilts 32 C4
Gastard Wilts 46 C5
Gasthorpe Norfk 105 K7
Gaston Green Essex 70 D4
Gatcombe IoW 19 H6
Gatebeck Cumb 157 J5
Gate Burton Lincs 135 G3
Gateford Notts 134 B3
Gateforth N York 142 E2
Gatehead E Ayrs 196 D4
Gate Helmsley N York 151 L5
Gatehouse Nthumb 179 H1
Gatehouse of Fleet D & G 174 F4
Gateley Norfk 121 L6

Gatenby N York 160 D5
Gatesgarth Cumb 165 G7
Gateshaw Border 189 L2
Gateshead Gatesd 181 G6
Gates Heath Ches W 129 L7
Gateside Angus 234 C6
Gateside E Rens 208 E7
Gateside Fife 222 B5
Gateside Fife 208 B8
Gateslack D & G 186 C5
Gathurst Wigan 139 G6
Gatley Stockp 131 G2
Gatton Surrey 51 H8
Gattonside Border 201 H6
Gaufron Powys 78 D2
Gaulby Leics 100 F3
Gauldry Fife 222 F2
Gauldswell P & K 233 K5
Gaulkthorn Lancs 139 M3
Gaultree Norfk 103 K2
Gaunton's Bank Ches E 113 J2
Gaunt's Common Dorset 17 K2
Gaunt's End Essex 70 E2
Gautby Lincs 136 C5
Gavinton Border 202 B3
Gawber Barns 141 M6
Gawcott Bucks 67 G1
Gawsworth Ches E 131 H5
Gawthorpe Wakefd 141 L3
Gawthrop Cumb 158 B5
Gawthwaite Cumb 156 C5
Gay Bowers Essex 71 J6
Gaydon Warwks 83 J4
Gayhurst M Keyn 85 G6
Gayle N York 158 F5
Gayles N York 159 L1
Gay Street W Susx 21 J3
Gayton Nhants 84 D4
Gayton Norfk 120 F7
Gayton Staffs 114 F6
Gayton Wirral 129 G4
Gayton le Marsh Lincs 137 H3
Gayton Thorpe Norfk 121 G7
Gaywood Norfk 120 E7
Gazeley Suffk 88 E2
Gear Cnwll 3 J6
Gearraidh Bhaird W Isls 282 g4
Geary Highld 258 D4
Gedding Suffk 89 J4
Geddington Nhants 101 K6
Gedling Notts 117 G3
Gedney Lincs 119 L6
Gedney Broadgate Lincs 119 L7
Gedney Drove End Lincs 120 A5
Gedney Dyke Lincs 119 L6
Gedney Hill Lincs 103 G1
Gee Cross Tamesd 131 J1
Geeston Rutlnd 101 L3
Geldeston Norfk 107 H5
Gelli Rhondd 42 E3
Gelli Torfn 62 B8
Gellifor Denbgs 128 D7
Gelligaer Caerph 43 H2
Gelligroes Caerph 43 J3
Gelligron Neath 57 K4
Gellilydan Gwynd 110 L2
Gellinudd Neath 57 K4
Gelly Pembks 55 J3
Gellyburn P & K 233 G7
Gellywen Carmth 58 A4
Gelston D & G 175 J3
Gelston Lincs 118 B3
Gembling E R Yk 153 H4
Gentleshaw Staffs 98 D1
Georgefield D & G 187 L7
George Green Bucks 50 C3
Georgeham Devon 27 H3
Georgemas Junction Station
   Highld 279 L4
George Nympton Devon 28 B6
Georgetown Blae G 61 J5
Georgia Cnwll 2 D4
Georth Ork 275 c3
Gerlan Gwynd 126 C6
Germansweek Devon 12 B4
Germoe Cnwll 2 F5
Gerrans Cnwll 3 M4
Gerrards Cross Bucks 50 C1
Gerrick R & Cl 171 G8
Gestingthorpe Essex 89 G7
Geuffordd Powys 112 B8
Gib Hill Ches W 130 C4
Gibraltar Lincs 137 K7
Gibsmere Notts 117 J2
Giddeahall Wilts 46 B4
Giddy Green Dorset 16 F5
Gidea Park Gt Lon 52 B1
Gidleigh Devon 12 F5
Giffnock E Rens 208 F7
Gifford E Loth 212 C5

Giffordtown Fife 222 E5
Giggleswick N York 148 D3
Gigha Ag & B 205 L6
Gilberdyke E R Yk 143 L2
Gilbert's End Worcs 81 J6
Gilbert Street Hants 35 K4
Gilchriston E Loth 212 B6
Gilcrux Cumb 164 F3
Gildersome Leeds 141 K2
Gildingwells Rothm 133 L3
Gilesgate Moor Dur 169 J2
Gileston V Glam 42 F8
Gilfach Caerph 43 J2
Gilfach Goch Brdgnd 42 E4
Gilfachrheda Cerdgn 76 D3
Gilgarran Cumb 164 D6
Gill Cumb 166 B5
Gillamoor N York 162 B4
Gillan Cnwll 3 K6
Gillen Highld 258 D5
Gillesbie D & G 187 J7
Gilling East N York 161 K7
Gillingham Dorset 32 D5
Gillingham Medway 53 G5
Gillingham Norfk 107 H5
Gilling West N York 160 B2
Gillock Highld 280 B4
Gillow Heath Staffs 131 H7
Gills Highld 280 D2
Gill's Green Kent 39 J7
Gilmanscleuch Border 188 B2
Gilmerton C Edin 211 J5
Gilmerton P & K 220 F2
Gilmonby Dur 168 C8
Gilmorton Leics 100 C6
Gilroes Crematorium C Leic 100 C2
Gilsland Nthumb 178 E5
Gilson Warwks 99 G5
Gilstead C Brad 149 L7
Gilston Border 200 F2
Gilston Herts 70 C4
Gilston Park Herts 70 B4
Giltbrook Notts 116 E2
Gilwern Mons 61 L4
Gimingham Norfk 122 F4
Ginclough Ches E 131 J4
Gingers Green E Susx 23 K5
Gipping Suffk 90 C3
Gipsey Bridge Lincs 119 J2
Girdle Toll N Ayrs 196 C3
Girlington C Brad 141 H1
Girlsta Shet 281 e6
Girsby N York 160 E1
Girtford C Beds 86 D5
Girthon D & G 174 F4
Girton Cambs 87 J3
Girton Notts 135 G6
Girvan S Ayrs 182 F3
Gisburn Lancs 148 E6
Gisleham Suffk 107 K5
Gislingham Suffk 90 C1
Gissing Norfk 106 C6
Gittisham Devon 14 D3
Gladestry Powys 79 J4
Gladsmuir E Loth 212 A4
Glais Swans 57 K5
Glaisdale N York 162 D2
Glamis Angus 234 B6
Glanaber Gwynd 110 B1
Glanafon Pembks 54 F3
Glanaman Carmth 59 J6
Glandford Norfk 122 A3
Glan-Duar Carmth 76 F6
Glandwr Pembks 75 L6
Glan-Dwyfach Gwynd 109 J3
Glandyfi Cerdgn 92 F4
Glangrwyney Powys 61 K4
Glanllynfi Brdgnd 42 C3
Glanmule Powys 94 E5
Glanrhyd Pembks 75 K4
Glan-rhyd Powys 57 L3
Glanton Nthumb 190 F3
Glanton Pike Nthumb 190 F3
Glanvilles Wootton Dorset 16 C1
Glan-y-don Flints 128 E4
Glan-y-llyn Rhondd 43 H5
Glan-y-nant Powys 93 K6
Glan-yr-afon Gwynd 111 H3
Glan-yr-afon Gwynd 111 K3
Glan-yr-afon IoA 126 B4
Glan-yr-afon Swans 57 H4
Glapthorn Nhants 101 M5
Glapwell Derbys 133 J6
Glasbury Powys 79 H7
Glascoed Denbgs 127 K5
Glascoed Mons 62 C6
Glascote Staffs 99 G3
Glascwm Powys 79 G5
Glasfryn Conwy 111 H2
Glasgow C Glas 209 G6

Glasinfryn Gwynd.................. 125 K6
Glasnacardoch Bay Highld 237 K2
Glasnakille Highld 247 H6
Glaspwll Powys 92 F4
Glassenbury Kent.................... 39 J6
Glassford S Lans 197 L2
Glass Houghton Wakefd 142 C3
Glasshouse Gloucs 63 L3
Glasshouse Hill Gloucs 63 L3
Glasshouses N York................ 149 L3
Glasson Cumb...................... 177 H6
Glasson Lancs....................... 147 J4
Glassonby Cumb.................... 166 D3
Glasterlaw Angus 234 F5
Glaston Rutlnd...................... 101 K3
Glastonbury Somset................ 31 H3
Glatton Cambs...................... 102 C6
Glazebrook Warrtn 130 D1
Glazebury Warrtn 139 K8
Glazeley Shrops 96 F5
Gleadless Sheff..................... 133 G3
Gleadsmoss Ches E................ 130 F6
Gleaston Cumb...................... 146 E2
Glebe Highld 250 F8
Gledhow Leeds 150 D8
Gledpark D & G 175 G5
Gledrid Shrops 112 D4
Glemsford Suffk 89 G5
Glenallachie Moray 254 E3
Glenancross Highld 237 K2
Glenaros House Ag & B 227 G4
Glen Auldyn IoM 154 f4
Glenbarr Ag & B 192 D1
Glenbarry Abers 267 L5
Glenbeg Highld 237 H8
Glenbervie Abers 245 G7
Glenboig N Lans 209 J5
Glenborrodale Highld 237 H8
Glenbranter Ag & B................ 217 J7
Glenbreck Border 187 G2
Glenbrittle House Highld 246 F4
Glenbuck E Ayrs 198 B7
Glencally Angus 234 A3
Glencaple D & G 176 C5
Glencarron Lodge Highld 249 H2
Glencarse P & K 222 C3
Glen Clunie Lodge Abers 242 F7
Glencoe Highld 229 H4
Glencothe Border.................. 199 J7
Glencraig Fife 222 B8
Glencrosh D & G 185 J5
Glendale Highld 258 B6
Glendaruel Ag & B 206 F2
Glendevon P & K 221 H6
Glendoe Lodge Highld 240 C2
Glendoick P & K 222 C3
Glenduckie Fife 222 D3
Glenegedale Ag & B 204 E6
Glenelg Highld 248 C7
Glenerney Moray 253 K2
Glenfarg P & K 221 L5
Glenfield Leics 100 C2
Glenfinnan Highld 238 E7
Glenfintaig Lodge Highld 239 L6
Glenfoot P & K 222 B4
Glenfyne Lodge Ag & B 218 B4
Glengarnock N Ayrs 208 B8
Glengolly Highld 279 K3
Glengorm Castle Ag & B 226 E1
Glengrasco Highld 259 G7
Glenholm Border................... 199 J6
Glenhoul D & G 184 F5
Glenisla Angus 233 K3
Glenkin Ag & B 207 J3
Glenkindie Abers 243 M1
Glenlivet Moray 254 D6
Glenlochar D & G 175 J2
Glenlomond P & K 222 B6
Glenluce D & G 172 F3
Glenmassen Ag & B 207 H2
Glenmavis N Lans 209 K5
Glen Maye IoM 154 b6
Glen Mona IoM 154 f4
Glenmore Highld 259 G8
Glenmore Lodge Highld 242 C2
Glen Nevis House Highld 229 J1
Glenochil Clacks 220 F8
Glen Parva Leics 100 C4
Glenquiech Angus 234 C3
Glenralloch Ag & B 206 D5
Glenridding Cumb.................. 165 L7
Glenrothes Fife 222 D7
Glenshero Lodge Highld 240 F5
Glenstriven Ag & B 207 H3
Glentham Lincs 135 K2
Glen Trool Lodge D & G 183 K7
Glentrool Village D & G 183 J7
Glentruim House Highld 241 J4
Glentworth Lincs 135 J2
Glenuig Highld 237 K5

Glenvarragill Highld 259 H8
Glen Vine IoM 154 d6
Glenwhilly D & G 182 F8
Glespin S Lans 198 D7
Glewstone Herefs 63 H3
Glinton C Pete...................... 102 C2
Glooston Leics 101 G4
Glossop Derbys 131 L1
Gloster Hill Nthumb 191 K5
Gloucester Gloucs 64 B3
Gloucester Crematorium
  Gloucs 64 B4
Glusburn N York.................... 149 H6
Glutt Lodge Highld 274 D1
Gluvian Cnwll 4 F2
Glympton Oxon 66 B3
Glynarthen Cerdgn 76 B5
Glyn Ceiriog Wrexhm 112 B4
Glyncorrwg Neath 60 C7
Glynde E Susx........................ 23 G5
Glyndebourne E Susx 23 G5
Glyndyfrdwy Denbgs 112 A3
Glynneath Neath 60 D5
Glynn Valley Crematorium
  Cnwll 5 J2
Glyntaff Rhondd 43 H4
Glyntaff Crematorium
  Rhondd 43 H4
Glyntawe Powys 60 C4
Glynteg Carmth 76 C7
Gnosall Staffs 114 C7
Gnosall Heath Staffs 114 C7
Goadby Leics 101 G4
Goadby Marwood Leics 117 K6
Goatacre Wilts 46 F4
Goatham Green E Susx 24 E3
Goathill Dorset...................... 31 L7
Goathland N York.................. 162 E2
Goathurst Somset................... 30 C4
Goathurst Common Kent 38 D3
Goat Lees Kent 40 D6
Gobowen Shrops 112 D5
Godalming Surrey 36 E2
Goddard's Corner Suffk 91 G2
Goddard's Green Kent 39 K6
Godford Cross Devon 14 D2
Godington Oxon 66 F2
Godley Tamesd 140 E8
Godmanchester Cambs 86 E1
Godmanstone Dorset.............. 16 C3
Godmersham Kent 40 D5
Godney Somset...................... 31 H2
Godolphin Cross Cnwll 2 F5
Godre'r-graig Neath 57 L3
Godshill Hants 33 L7
Godshill IoW 19 J7
Godstone Staffs 115 G5
Godstone Surrey 51 K8
Godsworthy Devon 12 C7
Godwinscroft Hants 18 B4
Goetre Mons 62 C6
Goff's Oak Herts 69 J6
Gofilon Mons 61 L4
Gogar C Edin 211 G4
Goginan Cerdgn 92 E7
Golan Gwynd 109 J3
Golant Cnwll 5 K4
Golberdon Cnwll 11 L8
Golborne Wigan 139 J8
Golcar Kirk 141 H4
Goldcliff Newpt 44 D2
Golden Cross E Susx 23 J5
Golden Green Kent 39 G4
Golden Grove Carmth 59 G5
Goldenhill C Stke 114 D1
Golden Hill Pembks 55 G6
Golden Pot Hants 35 L2
Golden Valley Derbys 116 C1
Golders Green Gt Lon 51 H2
Golders Green Crematorium
  Gt Lon 51 H1
Goldfinch Bottom W Berk 48 D6
Goldhanger Essex 72 C5
Gold Hill Cambs.................... 103 L5
Gold Hill Dorset..................... 32 D8
Golding Shrops 96 C3
Goldington Bed 86 B5
Goldsborough N York............. 150 E4
Goldsborough N York............. 171 J7
Golds Green Sandw 98 C5
Goldsithney Cnwll 2 E5
Goldstone Kent 41 J3
Goldstone Shrops 113 M6
Goldsworth Park Surrey 50 C7
Goldthorpe Barns 142 C7
Goldworthy Devon 27 G6
Golford Kent 39 K6
Golford Green Kent 39 K6
Gollanfield Highld 252 F1
Gollinglith Foot N York........... 159 L6

Golly Wrexhm 129 H7
Golsoncott Somset 29 J3
Golspie Highld 273 K8
Gomeldon Wilts 33 L4
Gomersal Kirk 141 K3
Gomshall Surrey 37 G1
Gonalston Notts 117 H2
Gonerby Hill Foot Lincs 118 B4
Gonfirth Shet...................... 281 d5
Goodameavy Devon 7 G2
Good Easter Essex 70 F5
Gooderstone Norfk 104 F3
Goodleigh Devon 27 L4
Goodmanham E R Yk............. 152 D7
Goodmayes Gt Lon 51 M2
Goodnestone Kent 40 D3
Goodnestone Kent 41 H4
Goodrich Herefs 63 H3
Goodrington Torbay 8 D3
Goodshaw Lancs 140 B3
Goodshaw Fold Lancs 140 B2
Goodstone Devon 13 H8
Goodwick Pembks 74 F4
Goodworth Clatford Hants 34 D2
Goodyers End Warwks 99 J6
Goole E R Yk........................ 143 J3
Goole Fields E R Yk............... 143 J4
Goom's Hill Worcs 82 B4
Goonbell Cnwll 4 B5
Goonhavern Cnwll 4 C4
Goonvrea Cnwll 4 B5
Goosecruives Abers 245 G7
Gooseford Devon 12 C7
Goose Green Essex 73 H2
Goose Green Kent 39 G3
Goose Green Kent 39 L6
Goose Green S Glos 45 K4
Goose Green W Susx 21 J3
Goose Green Wigan 139 H7
Gooseham Cnwll 26 D7
Gooseham Mill Cnwll 26 D7
Goosehill Green Worcs 81 L3
Goose Pool Herefs 80 B7
Goosey Oxon 47 M1
Goosnargh Lancs 147 L8
Goostrey Ches E 130 F5
Gorddinog Conwy 126 D5
Gordon Border...................... 201 K4
Gordon Arms Hotel Border 200 C8
Gordonstown Abers 256 C4
Gordonstown Abers 267 L5
Gore Powys 79 J3
Gorebridge Mdloth 211 K6
Gorefield Cambs................... 103 J1
Gore Pit Essex 72 C3
Gores Wilts 47 G7
Gore Street Kent 41 J2
Gorey Jersey 9 f3
Goring Oxon 48 F3
Goring-by-Sea W Susx 21 J6
Goring Heath Oxon 49 G3
Gorleston on Sea Norfk 107 L3
Gornal Wood Crematorium
  Dudley 97 K5
Gorrachie Abers 268 D4
Gorran Churchtown Cnwll 5 G6
Gorran Haven Cnwll 5 G6
Gorran High Lanes Cnwll 5 G6
Gorrig Cerdgn 76 D6
Gors Cerdgn 92 D7
Gorsedd Flints 128 E4
Gorse Hill Swindn 47 H2
Gorseinon Swans 57 G5
Gorseybank Derbys 115 M1
Gorsgoch Cerdgn 76 E5
Gorslas Carmth 59 G6
Gorsley Gloucs 63 K2
Gorsley Common Herefs 63 K2
Gorstage Ches W................... 130 B5
Gorstan Highld 262 C7
Gorstella Ches W................... 129 H7
Gorst Hill Worcs 97 G8
Gorsty Hill Staffs 115 H6
Gorten Ag & B 227 L6
Gorthleck Highld 250 F7
Gorton Manch 140 C8
Gosbeck Suffk 90 D4
Gosberton Lincs 119 H5
Gosberton Clough Lincs 119 G5
Gosfield Essex 71 J1
Gosford Devon 14 C3
Gosforth Cumb...................... 155 J2
Gosforth N u Ty 180 F5
Gosling Street Somset............ 31 J4
Gosmore Herts 68 F2
Gospel End Staffs 97 K4
Gospel Green W Susx 36 M4
Gosport Hants 19 K4
Gossard's Green C Beds 85 J6
Gossington Gloucs 63 L6

Goswick Nthumb 203 K5
Gotham Notts 116 F5
Gotherington Gloucs 64 C1
Gotton Somset 30 C5
Goudhurst Kent 39 K5
Goulceby Lincs 136 E5
Gourdas Abers 256 D5
Gourdie C Dund 222 F2
Gourdon Abers 235 K2
Gourock Inver 207 K4
Govan C Glas 208 F5
Goveton Devon 7 J6
Gowdall E R Yk..................... 143 G2
Gower Highld 262 E4
Gowerton Swans 57 G5
Gowkhall Fife 210 E1
Gowthorpe E R Yk................. 152 A5
Goxhill E R Yk...................... 153 J6
Goxhill N Linc 144 E4
Grabhair W Isls 282 g4
Graby Lincs 118 E5
Grade Cnwll 3 H8
Gradeley Green Ches E........... 113 K1
Graffham W Susx 20 F3
Grafham Cambs 86 D2
Grafham Surrey 36 G3
Grafton Herefs 80 C7
Grafton N York..................... 150 F3
Grafton Oxon 65 K7
Grafton Shrops 113 G6
Grafton Worcs 80 D3
Grafton Worcs 82 A7
Grafton Flyford Worcs 81 M4
Grafton Regis Nhants 84 E6
Grafton Underwood Nhants 101 K7
Grafty Green Kent 39 L4
Graianrhyd Denbgs 128 F8
Graig Conwy 126 F5
Graig Denbgs 128 C5
Graig-fechan Denbgs 112 A7
Grain Medway 53 H5
Grains Bar Oldham 140 E6
Grainsby Lincs 145 H7
Grainthorpe Lincs 145 K5
Grampound Cnwll 4 E5
Grampound Road Cnwll 4 E5
Gramsdal W Isls 283 c9
Gramsdale W Isls 283 c9
Granborough Bucks 67 J2
Granby Notts 117 J4
Grandborough Warwks 83 L2
Grand Chemins Jersey 9 e3
Grandes Rocques Guern 9 a1
Grandtully P & K 232 D5
Grange Cumb 165 H2
Grange Medway 53 G5
Grange P & K 222 D2
Grange Wirral 128 F2
Grange Crossroads Moray 267 K5
Grange Hall Moray 265 H4
Grangehall S Lans 199 G6
Grange Hill Essex 70 C8
Grangemill Derbys 132 E8
Grange Moor Kirk 141 K4
Grangemouth Falk 210 B3
Grange of Lindores Fife.......... 222 D4
Grange-over-Sands Cumb....... 156 F7
Grangepans Falk 210 D3
Grangetown R & Cl............... 170 D6
Grangetown Sundld 181 K8
Grange Villa Dur................... 180 F8
Gransmoor E R Yk................. 153 J4
Gransmore Green Essex 71 G3
Granston Pembks 74 E5
Grantchester Cambs 87 J4
Grantham Lincs 118 C4
Grantham Crematorium Lincs ... 118 B4
Granton C Edin 211 H4
Grantown-on-Spey Highld 253 K6
Grantsfield Herefs 80 C3
Grantshouse Border 213 H6
Grappenhall Warrtn 130 C2
Grasby Lincs 144 D6
Grasmere Cumb 156 D1
Grasscroft Oldham 140 E6
Grassendale Lpool 129 H3
Grassgarth Cumb.................. 165 K3
Grass Green Essex 88 C2
Grassington N York............... 149 H3
Grassmoor Derbys 133 H6
Grassthorpe Notts 134 F6
Grateley Hants 34 C2
Gratwich Staffs 115 G5
Graveley Cambs 86 D3
Graveley Herts 69 G2
Gravelly Hill Birm 98 E4
Gravelsbank Shrops 95 H3
Graveney Kent 40 E3
Gravesend Kent 52 E5
Gravir W Isls 282 g4

Grayingham Lincs 144 A8
Grayrigg Cumb. 157 J3
Grays Thurr 52 D3
Grayshott Hants 36 C4
Grayson Green Cumb. 164 C5
Grayswood Surrey 36 C4
Graythorpe Hartpl. 170 C5
Grazeley Wokham 49 G5
Greasbrough Rothm 142 C8
Greasby Wirral 128 F2
Greasley Notts 116 E2
Great Abington Cambs 87 L5
Great Addington Nhants 101 L8
Great Alne Warwks 82 D3
Great Altcar Lancs 138 C6
Great Amwell Herts 69 K4
Great Asby Cumb. 166 F8
Great Ashfield Suffk 89 K2
Great Ayton N York 170 D8
Great Baddow Essex 71 H6
Great Badminton S Glos. 46 A2
Great Bardfield Essex 71 G1
Great Barford Bed 86 C5
Great Barr Sandw 98 D4
Great Barrington Gloucs 65 J4
Great Barrow Ches W 129 L6
Great Barton Suffk 89 H2
Great Barugh N York 162 C6
Great Bavington Nthumb. 180 B3
Great Bealings Suffk 90 F5
Great Bedwyn Wilts 47 K6
Great Bentley Essex 73 G3
Great Billing Nhants 84 F3
Great Bircham Norfk 121 G5
Great Blakenham Suffk 90 D5
Great Blencow Cumb. 166 B4
Great Bolas Wrekin 113 J3
Great Bookham Surrey 50 E8
Great Bosullow Cnwll 2 C4
Great Bourton Oxon 83 K6
Great Bowden Leics 101 K5
Great Bradley Suffk 88 D4
Great Braxted Essex 72 B4
Great Bricett Suffk 90 B5
Great Brickhill Bucks 67 L1
Great Bridgeford Staffs 114 D6
Great Brington Nhants 84 C2
Great Bromley Essex 73 G2
Great Broughton Cumb. 164 E4
Great Broughton N York 161 J2
Great Budworth Ches W 130 C4
Great Burdon Darltn 169 J7
Great Burstead Essex 71 G8
Great Busby N York 161 H2
Great Canfield Essex 70 E3
Great Carlton Lincs 137 H5
Great Casterton Rutlnd 101 M2
Great Chalfield Wilts 46 B6
Great Chart Kent 40 C7
Great Chatwell Staffs 114 B8
Great Chell C Stke 114 D1
Great Chesterford Essex 87 K6
Great Cheverell Wilts 46 E8
Great Chishill Cambs 87 J7
Great Clacton Essex 73 J4
Great Cliffe Wakefd 141 M4
Great Clifton Cumb 164 D5
Great Coates NE Lin 145 G6
Great Comberton Worcs 81 L6
Great Comp Kent 39 G2
Great Corby Cumb. 178 B7
Great Cornard Suffk 89 H7
Great Cowden E R Yk. 153 L7
Great Coxwell Oxon 65 K8
Great Cransley Nhants 101 H8
Great Cressingham Norfk 105 G3
Great Crosthwaite Cumb. 165 J6
Great Cubley Derbys 115 K4
Great Cumbrae Island N Ayrs ... 207 L4
Great Dalby Leics 117 K8
Great Doddington Nhants 85 H2
Great Doward Herefs 63 G4
Great Dunham Norfk 121 H8
Great Dunmow Essex 70 F3
Great Durnford Wilts 33 K3
Great Easton Essex 70 F2
Great Easton Leics 101 J5
Great Eccleston Lancs 147 H7
Great Edstone N York 162 C6
Great Ellingham Norfk 105 L4
Great Elm Somset 32 C1
Great Everdon Nhants 84 B4
Great Eversden Cambs 87 H4
Great Fencote N York 160 D4
Greatfield Wilts 47 H3
Great Finborough Suffk 89 K4
Greatford Lincs 102 B1
Great Fransham Norfk 105 H1
Great Gaddesden Herts 68 C5
Greatgate Staffs 115 G3
Great Gidding Cambs 102 C6
Great Givendale E R Yk. 152 B5
Great Glemham Suffk 91 H3
Great Glen Leics 100 E4
Great Gonerby Lincs 118 B4
Great Gransden Cambs 86 F4
Great Green Cambs 86 F6
Great Green Norfk 106 F5
Great Green Suffk 89 J2
Great Green Suffk 89 J4
Great Habton N York 162 D7
Great Hale Lincs 118 F3
Great Hallingbury Essex 70 D3
Greatham Hants 36 A5
Greatham Hartpl. 170 C5
Greatham W Susx 21 H4
Great Hampden Bucks 67 K6
Great Harrowden Nhants 85 G1
Great Harwood Lancs 139 L1
Great Haseley Oxon 66 F6
Great Hatfield E R Yk. 153 K7
Great Haywood Staffs 114 F7
Great Heck N York 142 F3
Great Henny Essex 89 H7
Great Hinton Wilts 46 C7
Great Hockham Norfk 105 J5
Great Holland Essex 73 J3
Great Hollands Br For. 49 L5
Great Horkesley Essex 72 E1
Great Hormead Herts 69 L1
Great Horton C Brad 141 J2
Great Horwood Bucks 67 J1
Great Houghton Barns 142 C6
Great Houghton Nhants 84 F3
Great Hucklow Derbys 132 D4
Great Kelk E R Yk. 153 H4
Great Kimble Bucks 67 K6
Great Kingshill Bucks 67 L7
Great Langdale Cumb. 156 D2
Great Langton N York 160 D3
Great Leighs Essex 71 H4
Great Limber Lincs 144 E6
Great Linford M Keyn 85 G6
Great Livermere Suffk 89 H1
Great Longstone Derbys 132 D5
Great Lumley Dur 169 J1
Great Lyth Shrops 95 L2
Great Malvern Worcs 81 H6
Great Maplestead Essex 89 G8
Great Marton Bpool 138 C1
Great Massingham Norfk 121 H7
Great Melton Norfk 106 C2
Great Meols Wirral 128 F2
Great Milton Oxon 66 F6
Great Missenden Bucks 67 L6
Great Mitton Lancs 148 C8
Great Mongeham Kent 41 K5
Great Moulton Norfk 106 D5
Great Munden Herts 69 K2
Great Musgrave Cumb. 167 H7
Great Ness Shrops 112 F7
Great Notley Essex 71 H3
Great Oak Mons 62 D5
Great Oakley Essex 73 J2
Great Oakley Nhants 101 J6
Great Offley Herts 68 F2
Great Ormside Cumb. 167 G7
Great Orton Cumb 177 K7
Great Ouseburn N York 150 F3
Great Oxendon Nhants 100 F6
Great Oxney Green Essex 71 G6
Great Palgrave Norfk 105 G1
Great Pattenden Kent 39 J4
Great Paxton Cambs 86 E2
Great Plumpton Lancs 138 D1
Great Plumstead Norfk 106 F2
Great Ponton Lincs 118 B5
Great Potheridge Devon 27 J7
Great Preston Leeds 142 B2
Great Purston Nhants 83 M7
Great Raveley Cambs 102 E7
Great Rissington Gloucs 65 J4
Great Rollright Oxon 65 L1
Great Rudbaxton Pembks 54 F3
Great Ryburgh Norfk 121 L6
Great Ryle Nthumb. 190 E4
Great Ryton Shrops 96 B3
Great Saling Essex 71 G2
Great Salkeld Cumb. 166 D3
Great Sampford Essex 88 C8
Great Saredon Staffs 98 B2
Great Saughall Ches W 129 H5
Great Saxham Suffk 88 F3
Great Shefford W Berk 48 A4
Great Shelford Cambs 87 J5
Great Smeaton N York 160 E2
Great Snoring Norfk 121 L4
Great Somerford Wilts 46 D2
Great Soudley Shrops 114 A5
Great Stainton Darltn 169 J6
Great Stambridge Essex 53 J1
Great Staughton Cambs 86 C2
Great Steeping Lincs 137 H6
Great Stoke S Glos. 45 J3
Great Stonar Kent 41 K3
Greatstone-on-Sea Kent 25 K3
Great Strickland Cumb. 166 D6
Great Stukeley Cambs 102 E8
Great Sturton Lincs 136 D4
Great Sutton Ches W 129 J4
Great Sutton Shrops 96 C6
Great Swinburne Nthumb. ... 179 L4
Great Tew Oxon 66 B1
Great Tey Essex 72 C2
Great Thurlow Suffk 88 D5
Great Torrington Devon 27 J7
Great Tosson Nthumb 190 E6
Great Totham Essex 72 B5
Great Totham Essex 72 C4
Great Tows Lincs 136 D2
Great Urswick Cumb. 156 C7
Great Wakering Essex 53 K2
Great Waldingfield Suffk 89 J6
Great Walsingham Norfk 121 L4
Great Waltham Essex 71 G4
Great Warford Ches E 130 F4
Great Warley Essex 52 C1
Great Washbourne Gloucs 82 A8
Great Weeke Devon 13 G5
Great Welnetham Suffk 89 H3
Great Weldon Nhants 101 K5
Great Wenham Suffk 90 C7
Great Whittington Nthumb ... 180 B5
Great Wigborough Essex 72 D4
Great Wilbraham Cambs 87 L4
Great Wishford Wilts 33 J4
Great Witchingham Norfk ... 122 C7
Great Witcombe Gloucs 64 D4
Great Witley Worcs 81 H2
Great Wolford Warwks 82 F8
Greatworth Nhants 84 A6
Great Wratting Suffk 88 D5
Great Wymondley Herts 69 G2
Great Wyrley Staffs 98 C2
Great Wytheford Shrops 113 J7
Great Yarmouth Norfk 107 L2
Great Yarmouth
  Crematorium Norfk 107 K3
Great Yeldham Essex 88 F7
Grebby Lincs 137 H6
Greeba IoM 154 d6
Green Denbgs 128 C6
Green Bank Cumb. 156 E6
Greenburn W Loth 210 B7
Greencroft Hall Dur 168 F1
Green Cross Surrey 36 C3
Green Down Somset 45 H8
Green End Bed 85 K5
Green End Bed 86 B2
Green End Bed 86 B3
Green End Bed 86 C5
Green End Cambs 87 H4
Green End Cambs 87 K2
Green End Cambs 87 K3
Green End Cambs 102 D6
Green End Cambs 102 E8
Green End Herts 69 H1
Green End Herts 69 J3
Green End Herts 87 G8
Greenend Oxon 65 L3
Green End Warwks 99 H6
Greenfield Ag & B. 207 L1
Greenfield C Beds 85 L8
Greenfield Flints 128 E4
Greenfield Highld 239 L3
Greenfield Oldham 140 F7
Greenfield Oxon 49 H1
Greenford Gt Lon 50 F3
Greengairs N Lans 209 L5
Greengates C Brad 150 B8
Greengill Cumb. 164 F3
Greenhalgh Lancs 147 H8
Greenham Somset 29 K6
Greenham W Berk 48 C6
Green Hammerton N York 151 G4
Greenhaugh Nthumb 179 J2
Green Head Cumb 165 L1
Greenhead Nthumb 178 F6
Green Heath Staffs 98 C1
Greenheys Salfd 139 L7
Greenhill D & G 176 F3
Greenhill Falk 209 L3
Greenhill Herefs 81 G5
Greenhill Kent 40 F2
Greenhill S Lans 198 F6
Green Hill Wilts 46 F2
Greenhillocks Derbys 116 C2
Greenhithe Kent 52 C4
Greenholm E Ayrs 197 G3
Greenholme Cumb 157 J2
Greenhouse Border 188 F2
Greenhow Hill N York 149 K3
Greenland Highld 280 B3
Greenland Sheff 133 H2
Greenlands Bucks 49 J2
Green Lane Devon 13 H7
Green Lane Worcs 82 C2
Greenlaw Border 201 L4
Greenlea D & G 176 D4
Greenloaning P & K 220 E5
Green Moor Barns 141 L7
Greenmount Bury 140 A5
Green Oak E R Yk. 143 K2
Greenock Inver 207 M4
Greenock Crematorium Inver ... 207 M4
Greenodd Cumb. 156 D6
Green Ore Somset 31 J1
Green Quarter Cumb. 157 G2
Greensgate Norfk 122 B8
Greenshields S Lans 199 H4
Greenside Gatesd 180 E6
Greenside Kirk 141 J4
Greens Norton Nhants 84 C5
Greenstead Green Essex 71 K2
Greensted Essex 70 D6
Green Street E Susx 24 D5
Green Street Gloucs 64 C4
Green Street Herts 69 G7
Green Street Herts 70 C3
Green Street Worcs 81 K5
Green Street Green Gt Lon 51 M6
Green Street Green Kent 52 C5
Greenstreet Green Suffk 90 B5
Green Tye Herts 70 C3
Greenway Gloucs 81 G8
Greenway Somset 30 D6
Greenway V Glam 43 G7
Greenway Worcs 81 G1
Greenwich Gt Lon 51 K3
Greet Gloucs 64 F1
Greete Shrops 80 D1
Greetham Lincs 136 F5
Greetham Rutlnd 118 B8
Greetland Calder 141 G3
Gregson Lane Lancs 139 J2
Greinton Somset 30 F4
Grenaby IoM 154 C7
Grendon Nhants 85 G3
Grendon Warwks 99 H3
Grendon Green Herefs 80 E4
Grendon Underwood Bucks 67 G3
Grenofen Devon 12 C8
Grenoside Sheff 133 G1
Grenoside Crematorium Sheff ... 132 F1
Greosabhagh W Isls 282 e6
Gresford Wrexhm 112 E1
Gresham Norfk 122 D4
Greshornish House Hotel
  Highld 258 E6
Gressenhall Norfk 121 L8
Gressenhall Green Norfk 121 L8
Gressingham Lancs 147 L2
Gresty Green Ches E 113 M1
Greta Bridge Dur 168 D8
Gretna D & G 177 L5
Gretna Green D & G 177 K5
Gretton Gloucs 64 E1
Gretton Nhants 101 K4
Gretton Shrops 96 E5
Grewelthorpe N York 160 C7
Grey Friars Suffk 91 L1
Greygarth N York 150 A1
Grey Green N Linc 143 K6
Greylake Somset 30 F4
Greyrigg D & G 176 E1
Greys Green Oxon 49 H2
Greysouthen Cumb. 164 C5
Greystoke Cumb. 166 B4
Greystone Angus 234 E6
Greywell Hants 35 L1
Gribb Dorset 15 J2
Gribthorpe E R Yk. 143 J1
Griff Warwks 99 K5
Griffithstown Torfn 62 C7
Griffydam Leics 116 C7
Griggs Green Hants 36 B4
Grimeford Village Lancs 139 J5
Grimesthorpe Sheff 133 G6
Grimethorpe Barns 142 C6
Grimley Worcs 81 J3
Grimmet S Ayrs 183 J7
Grimoldby Lincs 137 G2
Grimpo Shrops 112 E6
Grimsargh Lancs 139 H1
Grimsby NE Lin 145 H6
Grimsby Crematorium NE Lin ... 145 H6
Grimscote Nhants 84 C4
Grimscott Cnwll 11 J1
Grimshader W Isls 282 g4
Grimshaw Bl w D 139 L3

Grimshaw Green Lancs 139 G5
Grimsthorpe Lincs 118 D7
Grimston E R Yk 145 H1
Grimston Leics 117 J7
Grimston Norfk 120 F7
Grimstone Dorset 16 C4
Grimstone End Suffk 89 J2
Grinacombe Moor Devon 12 A4
Grindale E R Yk 153 J2
Grindle Shrops 97 G3
Grindleford Derbys 132 E4
Grindleton Lancs 148 D6
Grindley Brook Shrops 113 H3
Grindlow Derbys 132 D4
Grindon Nthumb 202 E4
Grindon S on T 169 K5
Grindon Staffs 115 H1
Grindon Hill Nthumb 179 J5
Grindonrigg Nthumb 202 E4
Gringley on the Hill Notts........ 134 E2
Grinsdale Cumb..................... 177 L7
Grinshill Shrops 113 H6
Grinton N York 159 J3
Griomaisiader W Isls 282 g4
Griomsaigh W Isls 283 c9
Grishipoll Ag & B 224 F2
Grisling Common E Susx 23 G3
Gristhorpe N York 163 K6
Griston Norfk 105 J4
Gritley Ork 275 d5
Grittenham Wilts 46 F2
Grittleton Wilts 46 B3
Grizebeck Cumb..................... 156 C5
Grizedale Cumb..................... 156 D4
Groby Leics 100 B2
Groes Conwy 127 K6
Groes-faen Rhondd 43 G5
Groesffordd Gwynd 108 D4
Groesffordd Marli Denbgs........ 127 K5
Groeslwyd Powys 94 F1
Groeslon Gwynd 125 H8
Groeslon Gwynd 125 J7
Groes-Wen Caerph 43 H4
Grogarry W Isls 283 c10
Grogport Ag & B 194 C2
Groigearraidh W Isls 283 c10
Gromford Suffk 91 J3
Gronant Flints 128 C3
Groombridge E Susx 38 E6
Grosebay W Isls 282 e6
Grosmont Mons 62 E2
Grosmont N York 162 E2
Groton Suffk 89 J7
Grotton Oldham 140 E6
Grouville Jersey 9 e3
Grove Bucks 67 M3
Grove Dorset 16 D8
Grove Kent 41 H3
Grove Notts 134 E4
Grove Oxon 48 B1
Grove Pembks 55 G6
Grove Green Kent 39 K2
Grovenhurst Kent 39 H5
Grove Park Gt Lon 51 L4
Grovesend S Glos 45 K1
Grovesend Swans 57 G5
Grubb Street Kent 52 C5
Gruinard Highld 260 F2
Gruinart Ag & B 204 D3
Grula Highld 246 E3
Gruline Ag & B 227 G4
Grumbla Cnwll 2 C5
Grundisburgh Suffk 90 F5
Gruting Shet 281 c6
Gualachulain Highld 229 J6
Guanockgate Lincs 103 H2
Guardbridge Fife 223 H3
Guarlford Worcs 81 J6
Guay P & K 232 F5
Guernsey Guern 9 j3
Guestling Green E Susx 24 F4
Guestling Thorn E Susx 24 F4
Guestwick Norfk 122 B6
Guide Bridge Tamesd 140 D8
Guide Post Nthumb 181 G2
Guilden Morden Cambs 86 F6
Guilden Sutton Ches W 129 K6
Guildford Surrey 36 F1
Guildford Crematorium Surrey 36 E2
Guildstead Kent 53 H6
Guildtown P & K 221 L1
Guilsborough Nhants 84 D1
Guilsfield Powys 94 F1
Guilton Kent 41 J4
Guiltreehill S Ayrs 183 J1
Guineaford Devon 27 K3
Guisborough R & Cl 170 E7
Guiseley Leeds 150 B7
Guist Norfk 121 M6
Guiting Power Gloucs 65 G2

Gullane E Loth...................... 212 B2
Gulling Green Suffk 89 G4
Gulval Cnwll 2 D5
Gulworthy Devon 12 B8
Gumfreston Pembks 55 J6
Gumley Leics 100 F5
Gummow's Shop Cnwll 4 E3
Gunby E R Yk 143 H1
Gunby Lincs 118 B7
Gunby Lincs 137 J6
Gundleton Hants 35 J4
Gun Green Kent 39 J7
Gun Hill E Susx 23 J4
Gun Hill Warwks 99 H5
Gunn Devon 27 L4
Gunnerside N York 159 G3
Gunnerton Nthumb 179 L4
Gunness N Linc 143 L5
Gunnislake Cnwll 12 B8
Gunnista Shet 281 e6
Gunthorpe C Pete 102 D3
Gunthorpe N Linc 143 K8
Gunthorpe Norfk 121 M4
Gunthorpe Notts 117 H3
Gunton Suffk 107 L4
Gunwalloe Cnwll 3 G6
Gupworthy Somset 29 H4
Gurnard IoW 19 H4
Gurnett Ches E 131 H5
Gurney Slade Somset 31 K1
Gurnos Powys 57 L3
Gushmere Kent 40 D4
Gussage All Saints Dorset.......... 33 G8
Gussage St Andrew Dorset 33 G8
Gussage St Michael Dorset......... 33 G8
Guston Kent 41 K6
Gutcher Shet 281 f2
Guthrie Angus 234 E5
Guyhirn Cambs 103 H3
Guyhirn Gull Cambs 103 H3
Guy's Marsh Dorset 32 D6
Guyzance Nthumb 191 J5
Gwaenysgor Flints 128 C3
Gwalchmai IoA 125 G4
Gwastadnant Gwynd 126 C3
Gwaun-Cae-Gurwen Carmth 59 J6
Gwbert on Sea Cerdgn 75 K2
Gwealavellan Cnwll 2 F3
Gweek Cnwll 3 H5
Gwehelog Mons 62 D6
Gwenddwr Powys 78 E6
Gwennap Cnwll 3 J3
Gwent Crematorium Mons 62 C7
Gwenter Cnwll 3 J7
Gwernaffield Flints 128 F6
Gwernesney Mons 62 E6
Gwernogle Carmth 58 F2
Gwernymynydd Flints 128 F7
Gwersyllt Wrexhm 112 D1
Gwespyr Flints 128 D3
Gwindra Cnwll 4 F4
Gwinear Cnwll 2 F4
Gwithian Cnwll 2 F3
Gwredog IoA 125 G3
Gwrhay Caerph 61 J7
Gwyddelwern Denbgs 111 L2
Gwyddgrug Carmth 58 E2
Gwynfryn Wrexhm 112 C1
Gwystre Powys 78 B2
Gwytherin Conwy 127 H7
Gyfelia Wrexhm 112 E3
Gyrn-goch Gwynd 109 G2

H

Habberley Shrops 95 K3
Habberley Worcs 97 H7
Habergham Lancs 140 B1
Habertoft Lincs 137 J6
Habin W Susx 36 B6
Habrough NE Lin 144 F5
Hacconby Lincs 118 E6
Haceby Lincs 118 D4
Hacheston Suffk 91 G3
Hackbridge Gt Lon 51 H5
Hackenthorpe Sheff 133 H3
Hackford Norfk 106 B3
Hackforth N York 160 C4
Hack Green Ches E 113 L2
Hackland Ork 275 C4
Hackleton Nhants 84 F4
Hacklinge Kent 41 K4
Hackman's Gate Worcs 97 K7
Hackness N York 163 H4
Hackness Somset 30 E2
Hackney Gt Lon 51 K2
Hackthorn Lincs 135 K3
Hackthorpe Cumb 166 D6
Hacton Gt Lon 52 C2

Hadden Border 202 B6
Haddenham Bucks 67 H5
Haddenham Cambs 103 J8
Haddington E Loth 212 B4
Haddington Lincs 135 H7
Haddiscoe Norfk 107 J4
Haddo Abers 256 E4
Haddon Cambs 102 C5
Hade Edge Kirk 141 J6
Hadfield Derbys 140 F8
Hadham Cross Herts 70 B3
Hadham Ford Herts 70 B3
Hadleigh Essex 53 H2
Hadleigh Suffk 89 L6
Hadleigh Heath Suffk 89 K7
Hadley Worcs 81 K2
Hadley Wrekin 96 F1
Hadley End Staffs 115 J7
Hadley Wood Gt Lon 69 H7
Hadlow Kent 39 G3
Hadlow Down E Susx 23 J2
Hadnall Shrops 113 H7
Hadstock Essex 88 B6
Hadzor Worcs 81 L3
Haffenden Quarter Kent 39 M5
Hafodunos Conwy 127 H6
Hafod-y-bwch Wrexhm 112 D2
Hafod-y-coed Blae G 61 K7
Hafodyrynys Caerph 61 K7
Haggate Lancs 140 C1
Haggbeck Cumb 178 B4
Haggersta Shet 281 d6
Haggerston Nthumb 203 G4
Haggington Hill Devon 27 K2
Haggs Falk 209 L3
Hagley Herefs 80 D7
Hagley Worcs 97 K7
Hagmore Green Suffk 89 J7
Hagnaby Lincs 136 F7
Hagnaby Lincs 137 J4
Hagworthingham Lincs 136 F6
Haigh Wigan 139 J6
Haighton Green Lancs 139 H1
Haile Cumb 155 J1
Hailes Gloucs 64 F1
Hailey Herts 69 K5
Hailey Oxon 48 F2
Hailey Oxon 65 M4
Hailsham E Susx 23 K5
Hail Weston Cambs 86 D3
Hainault Gt Lon 70 C8
Haine Kent 41 K2
Hainford Norfk 122 E7
Hainton Lincs 136 C3
Hainworth C Brad 149 J8
Haisthorpe E R Yk 153 H3
Hakin Pembks 54 E5
Halam Notts 117 H1
Halbeath Fife 210 F1
Halberton Devon 29 H8
Halcro Highld 280 B4
Hale Cumb 157 H7
Hale Halton 129 L3
Hale Hants 33 L1
Hale Somset 32 C5
Hale Surrey 36 C1
Hale Traffd 130 F2
Hale Bank Halton 129 L3
Halebarns Traffd 130 F3
Hale Green E Susx 23 J4
Hale Nook Lancs 147 G7
Hales Norfk 107 H4
Hales Staffs 113 M5
Halesgate Lincs 119 K6
Hales Green Derbys 115 K4
Halesowen Dudley 98 B6
Hales Place Kent 40 F3
Hale Street Kent 39 G3
Halesville Essex 72 C8
Halesworth Suffk 107 H7
Halewood Knows 129 K3
Halford Devon 13 J7
Halford Shrops 95 K6
Halford Warwks 83 G6
Halfpenny Cumb 157 H5
Halfpenny Green Staffs 97 J5
Halfpenny Houses N York 160 B5
Halfway Carmth 59 J3
Halfway Carmth 59 M2
Halfway Sheff 133 J3
Halfway W Berk 48 B5
Halfway Bridge W Susx 36 D6
Halfway House Shrops 95 H1
Halfway Houses Kent 53 K4
Halifax Calder 141 H4
Halket E Ayrs 208 D8
Halkirk Highld 279 K4
Halkyn Flints 128 F5
Hall E Rens 208 C8
Hallam Fields Derbys 116 D4

Halland E Susx 23 H4
Hallaton Leics 101 H4
Hallatrow BaNES 45 J7
Hallbankgate Cumb 178 D7
Hallbeck Cumb 157 K5
Hall Cliffe Wakefd 141 L4
Hall Cross Lancs 138 F2
Hall Dunnerdale Cumb 156 B3
Hallen S Glos 45 H3
Hall End Bed 85 K6
Hall End C Beds 86 B5
Hallfield Gate Derbys 133 H8
Hallgarth Dur 169 J2
Hall Glen Falk 210 B5
Hall Green Birm 98 E6
Hallin Highld 258 C5
Halling Medway 52 F6
Hallington Lincs 136 F3
Hallington Nthumb 180 B5
Halliwell Bolton 139 L5
Halloughton Notts 117 J1
Hallow Worcs 81 J3
Hallow Heath Worcs 81 J3
Hallsands Devon 8 B7
Hall's Green Essex 69 L5
Hall's Green Herts 69 K5
Hallthwaites Cumb 156 A5
Hallworthy Cnwll 11 H5
Hallyne Border 199 L5
Halmer End Staffs 114 B2
Halmond's Frome Herefs 80 F5
Halmore Gloucs 63 K6
Halnaker W Susx 20 E5
Halsall Lancs 138 D5
Halse Nhants 84 A7
Halse Somset 29 L5
Halsetown Cnwll 2 D3
Halsham E R Yk 145 H2
Halsinger Devon 27 J3
Halstead Essex 71 K1
Halstead Kent 52 A6
Halstead Leics 101 K3
Halstock Dorset 15 M1
Halsway Somset 29 L3
Haltcliff Bridge Cumb 165 L2
Haltemprice Crematorium
    E R Yk............................. 144 C2
Haltham Lincs 136 D7
Haltoft End Lincs 119 L3
Halton Bucks 67 L5
Halton Halton 129 M3
Halton Lancs 147 K3
Halton Leeds 142 A1
Halton Nthumb 180 B5
Halton Wrexhm 112 D3
Halton East N York 149 J5
Halton Fenside Lincs 137 H7
Halton Gill N York 158 F7
Halton Green Lancs 147 K3
Halton Holegate Lincs 137 H6
Halton Lea Gate Nthumb 178 F7
Halton Quay Cnwll 6 E2
Halton Shields Nthumb 180 B5
Halton West N York 148 F5
Haltwhistle Nthumb 179 G6
Halvergate Norfk 107 J2
Halwell Devon 8 A4
Halwill Devon 12 B3
Halwill Junction Devon 12 B3
Ham Devon 14 F2
Ham Gloucs 63 K7
Ham Gloucs 64 E3
Ham Gt Lon 50 E4
Ham Kent 41 K4
Ham Somset 30 D6
Ham Somset 31 L1
Ham Wilts 47 L6
Hambleden Bucks 49 J2
Hambledon Hants 35 K2
Hambledon Surrey 36 E3
Hamble-le-Rice Hants 19 H2
Hambleton Lancs 147 G7
Hambleton N York 142 G7
Hambleton Moss Side Lancs 147 G7
Hambridge Somset 30 E4
Hambrook S Glos 45 J3
Hambrook W Susx 20 C5
Ham Common Dorset 32 D5
Hameringham Lincs 136 F6
Hamerton Cambs 102 C7
Ham Green Herefs 81 H6
Ham Green Kent 25 C3
Ham Green Kent 53 H5
Ham Green N Som 45 G4
Ham Green Worcs 82 B3
Ham Hill Kent 52 F6
Hamilton S Lans 209 J7
Hamlet Dorset 16 B1
Hamlins E Susx 23 K5
Hammerpot W Susx 21 H5

Hammersmith Gt Lon	51	G3	
Hammerwich Staffs	98	D2	
Hammerwood E Susx	38	C5	
Hammond Street Herts	69	J6	
Hammoon Dorset	32	D7	
Hamnavoe Shet	281	d7	
Hampden Park E Susx	23	K6	
Hamperden End Essex	70	E1	
Hampnett Gloucs	65	G4	
Hampole Donc	142	D5	
Hampreston Dorset	17	L3	
Hampsfield Cumb	156	F6	
Hampson Green Lancs	147	J5	
Hampstead Gt Lon	51	H2	
Hampstead Norreys W Berk	48	D4	
Hampsthwaite N York	150	C4	
Hampton C Pete	102	D4	
Hampton Devon	15	G3	
Hampton Gt Lon	50	F5	
Hampton Kent	40	F2	
Hampton Shrops	97	C6	
Hampton Swindn	65	J8	
Hampton Worcs	82	B6	
Hampton Bishop Herefs	80	D7	
Hampton Fields Gloucs	64	C7	
Hampton Green Ches W	113	H2	
Hampton Heath Ches W	113	H2	
Hampton in Arden Solhll	99	G7	
Hampton Loade Shrops	97	G6	
Hampton Lovett Worcs	81	K2	
Hampton Lucy Warwks	83	G4	
Hampton Magna Warwks	83	G2	
Hampton on the Hill Warwks	82	F2	
Hampton Poyle Oxon	66	D4	
Hampton Wick Gt Lon	50	F5	
Hamptworth Wilts	34	B7	
Hamrow Norfk	121	K6	
Hamsey E Susx	22	F5	
Hamsey Green Surrey	51	K7	
Hamstall Ridware Staffs	115	H7	
Hamstead Birm	98	D5	
Hamstead IoW	18	F5	
Hamstead Marshall W Berk	48	B6	
Hamsterley Dur	168	E4	
Hamsterley Dur	180	D7	
Hamstreet Kent	40	C8	
Ham Street Somset	31	J4	
Hamwood N Som	44	D7	
Hamworthy Poole	17	K4	
Hanbury Staffs	115	K6	
Hanbury Worcs	81	M2	
Hanby Lincs	118	D5	
Hanchet End Suffk	88	C6	
Hanchurch Staffs	114	C3	
Handa Island Highld	276	A6	
Handale R & Cl	171	G7	
Hand and Pen Devon	14	B3	
Handbridge Ches W	129	J6	
Handcross W Susx	37	L5	
Handforth Ches E	131	G3	
Hand Green Ches W	130	A7	
Handley Ches W	129	L8	
Handley Derbys	133	G7	
Handley Green Essex	71	G6	
Handsacre Staffs	115	H8	
Handsworth Birm	98	D5	
Handsworth Sheff	133	H2	
Handy Cross Bucks	49	K1	
Hanford C Stke	114	D3	
Hanford Dorset	32	D8	
Hanging Heaton Kirk	141	L3	
Hanging Houghton Nhants	101	G8	
Hanging Langford Wilts	33	H3	
Hangleton Br & H	22	D6	
Hangleton W Susx	21	J6	
Hanham S Glos	45	J4	
Hankelow Ches E	113	L2	
Hankerton Wilts	46	E1	
Hankham E Susx	23	K6	
Hanley C Stke	114	D2	
Hanley Castle Worcs	81	J6	
Hanley Child Worcs	80	F2	
Hanley Swan Worcs	81	J6	
Hanley William Worcs	80	F2	
Hanlith N York	148	F3	
Hanmer Wrexhm	113	G3	
Hannaford Devon	27	L5	
Hannah Lincs	137	J4	
Hannington Hants	48	D7	
Hannington Nhants	84	F1	
Hannington Swindn	65	H8	
Hannington Wick Swindn	65	H8	
Hanscombe End C Beds	86	C8	
Hanslope M Keyn	84	F6	
Hanthorpe Lincs	118	E6	
Hanwell Gt Lon	50	F3	
Hanwell Oxon	83	K6	
Hanwood Shrops	95	K2	
Hanworth Gt Lon	50	E5	
Hanworth Norfk	122	D4	
Happendon S Lans	198	E6	
Happisburgh Norfk	123	H5	
Happisburgh Common Norfk	123	H5	
Hapsford Ches W	129	L5	
Hapton Lancs	140	B2	
Hapton Norfk	106	D4	
Harberton Devon	8	A3	
Harbertonford Devon	8	A4	
Harbledown Kent	40	F4	
Harborne Birm	98	C6	
Harborough Magna Warwks	100	B7	
Harbottle Nthumb	190	C5	
Harbourneford Devon	7	K2	
Harbours Hill Worcs	81	M2	
Harbridge Hants	18	A2	
Harbridge Green Hants	33	K8	
Harbury Warwks	83	J3	
Harby Leics	117	K5	
Harby Notts	135	H5	
Harcombe Devon	13	K6	
Harcombe Devon	14	D4	
Harcombe Bottom Devon	15	H3	
Harden C Brad	149	K8	
Harden Wsall	98	C3	
Hardenhuish Wilts	46	C4	
Hardgate Abers	245	H3	
Hardgate D & G	175	K2	
Hardgate N York	150	C3	
Hardgate W Duns	208	E4	
Hardham W Susx	21	H3	
Hardhorn Lancs	147	G8	
Hardingham Norfk	105	L3	
Hardingstone Nhants	84	E4	
Hardington Somset	45	L8	
Hardington Mandeville Somset	31	H8	
Hardington Marsh Somset	15	L1	
Hardington Moor Somset	31	H8	
Hardisworthy Devon	26	D6	
Hardley Hants	19	G3	
Hardley Street Norfk	107	H3	
Hardmead M Keyn	85	H5	
Hardraw N York	158	F4	
Hardsough Lancs	140	B4	
Hardstoft Derbys	133	J7	
Hardway Hants	19	K3	
Hardway Somset	32	B4	
Hardwick Bucks	67	K3	
Hardwick Cambs	87	H3	
Hardwick Nhants	85	G1	
Hardwick Norfk	106	E5	
Hardwick Oxon	66	A6	
Hardwick Oxon	66	E1	
Hardwick Rothm	133	K3	
Hardwick Wsall	98	D4	
Hardwicke Gloucs	64	A4	
Hardwicke Gloucs	64	C2	
Hardy's Green Essex	72	D3	
Harebeating E Susx	23	K5	
Hare Croft C Brad	149	K8	
Harefield Gt Lon	50	D1	
Hare Green Essex	73	G2	
Hare Hatch Wokham	49	J3	
Harehill Derbys	115	K4	
Harehills Leeds	141	M1	
Harehope Nthumb	191	G2	
Harelaw Border	188	F2	
Harelaw D & G	178	B3	
Harelaw Dur	180	E8	
Hareplain Kent	39	L5	
Haresceugh Cumb	166	E2	
Harescombe Gloucs	64	B5	
Haresfield Gloucs	64	A5	
Harestock Hants	34	F4	
Hare Street Essex	70	B5	
Hare Street Essex	70	D7	
Hare Street Herts	69	K1	
Harewood Leeds	150	D6	
Harewood End Herefs	63	G2	
Harford Devon	7	J3	
Hargate Norfk	106	C5	
Hargatewall Derbys	132	B4	
Hargrave Ches W	129	L7	
Hargrave Nhants	85	K1	
Hargrave Suffk	88	F3	
Harker Cumb	177	L6	
Harkstead Suffk	90	E8	
Harlaston Staffs	99	G1	
Harlaxton Lincs	118	A5	
Harlech Gwynd	109	K5	
Harlescott Shrops	113	H8	
Harlesden Gt Lon	51	G2	
Harlesthorpe Derbys	133	K4	
Harleston Devon	8	B6	
Harleston Norfk	106	E6	
Harleston Suffk	89	L3	
Harlestone Nhants	84	D2	
Harle Syke Lancs	140	C1	
Harley Rothm	142	B8	
Harley Shrops	96	D3	
Harlington C Beds	68	D3	
Harlington Donc	142	D7	
Harlington Gt Lon	50	E3	
Harlosh Highld	258	D8	
Harlow Essex	70	C5	
Harlow Hill Nthumb	180	C5	
Harlthorpe E R Yk	152	A8	
Harlton Cambs	87	H5	
Harman's Cross Dorset	17	J6	
Harmby N York	159	L5	
Harmer Green Herts	69	H4	
Harmer Hill Shrops	113	H7	
Harmondsworth Gt Lon	50	D3	
Harmston Lincs	135	K7	
Harnage Shrops	96	D3	
Harnham Nthumb	180	C3	
Harnhill Gloucs	64	F7	
Harold Hill Gt Lon	70	D8	
Haroldston West Pembks	54	D4	
Haroldswick Shet	281	f1	
Harold Wood Gt Lon	52	C1	
Harome N York	161	L6	
Harpenden Herts	68	E4	
Harpford Devon	14	C4	
Harpham E R Yk	153	H3	
Harpley Norfk	121	H6	
Harpley Worcs	80	F3	
Harpole Nhants	84	D3	
Harpsdale Highld	279	K5	
Harpsden Oxon	49	J3	
Harpswell Lincs	135	J2	
Harpurhey Manch	140	C7	
Harpur Hill Derbys	131	L5	
Harraby Cumb	177	M7	
Harracott Devon	27	K5	
Harrapool Highld	247	K4	
Harrietfield P & K	221	H1	
Harrietsham Kent	39	L3	
Harringay Gt Lon	51	J1	
Harrington Cumb	164	C5	
Harrington Lincs	137	G5	
Harrington Nhants	101	G7	
Harringworth Nhants	101	K4	
Harris W Isls	282	e6	
Harriseahead Staffs	131	G8	
Harriston Cumb	165	G2	
Harrogate N York	150	D5	
Harrogate Crematorium N York	150	D5	
Harrold Bed	85	J4	
Harrop Dale Oldham	140	F6	
Harrow Gt Lon	50	F1	
Harrowbarrow Cnwll	12	A8	
Harrowden Bed	85	L6	
Harrowgate Village Darltn	169	H7	
Harrow Green Suffk	89	H4	
Harrow on the Hill Gt Lon	50	F2	
Harrow Weald Gt Lon	50	F1	
Harston Cambs	87	J5	
Harston Leics	117	L5	
Harswell E R Yk	152	C7	
Hart Hartpl	170	B4	
Hartburn Nthumb	180	D2	
Hartest Suffk	89	G5	
Hartfield E Susx	38	D6	
Hartford Cambs	86	E1	
Hartford Ches W	130	C5	
Hartford Somset	29	G5	
Hartfordbridge Hants	49	J7	
Hartford End Essex	71	G3	
Hartforth N York	159	L2	
Hartgrove Dorset	32	D7	
Harthill Ches W	129	L8	
Harthill N Lans	210	B6	
Harthill Rothm	133	K3	
Hartington Derbys	132	C7	
Hartington Nthumb	180	B1	
Hartland Devon	26	D6	
Hartland Quay Devon	26	C6	
Hartlebury Worcs	81	J1	
Hartlepool Hartpl	170	C4	
Hartlepool Crematorium Hartpl	170	C4	
Hartley Cumb	158	D1	
Hartley Kent	39	J4	
Hartley Kent	52	D5	
Hartley Nthumb	181	H4	
Hartley Green Kent	52	D5	
Hartley Green Staffs	114	F5	
Hartley Wespall Hants	49	G7	
Hartley Wintney Hants	49	J7	
Hartlip Kent	53	H6	
Hartoft End N York	162	C4	
Harton N York	151	L3	
Harton S Tyne	181	J6	
Harton Shrops	96	B5	
Hartpury Gloucs	64	A2	
Hartshead Kirk	141	J3	
Hartshill C Stke	114	D2	
Hartshill Warwks	99	J4	
Hartshorne Derbys	116	B7	
Hartside Nthumb	190	D3	
Hartsop Cumb	165	L8	
Hart Station Hartpl	170	B3	
Hartswell Somset	29	K5	
Hartwell Nhants	84	F5	
Hartwith N York	150	B3	
Hartwood N Lans	209	M7	
Hartwoodmyres Border	188	D1	
Harvel Kent	52	E6	
Harvington Worcs	82	C5	
Harvington Worcs	97	K8	
Harwell Notts	134	D2	
Harwell Oxon	48	C1	
Harwich Essex	73	K1	
Harwood Bolton	139	L5	
Harwood Dur	167	J4	
Harwood Dale N York	163	H3	
Harwood Lee Bolton	139	L5	
Harwood Park Crematorium Herts	69	H3	
Harworth Notts	134	C2	
Hasbury Dudley	98	B6	
Hascombe Surrey	36	F3	
Haselbech Nhants	100	F7	
Haselbury Plucknett Somset	31	G8	
Haseley Warwks	82	F2	
Haseley Green Warwks	82	F1	
Haseley Knob Warwks	82	F1	
Haselor Warwks	82	D4	
Hasfield Gloucs	64	B2	
Hasguard Pembks	54	D5	
Haskayne Lancs	138	D6	
Hasketon Suffk	90	F5	
Hasland Derbys	133	H5	
Haslemere Surrey	36	D4	
Haslingden Lancs	140	B3	
Haslingfield Cambs	87	H5	
Haslington Ches E	130	E8	
Hassall Ches E	130	E8	
Hassall Green Ches E	130	F7	
Hassell Street Kent	40	F4	
Hassingham Norfk	107	H2	
Hassness Cumb	165	G7	
Hassocks W Susx	22	D4	
Hassop Derbys	132	D5	
Haste Hill Surrey	36	D4	
Haster Highld	280	D6	
Hasthorpe Lincs	137	J5	
Hastingleigh Kent	40	E6	
Hastings E Susx	24	E5	
Hastings Somset	30	D7	
Hastings Borough Crematorium E Susx	24	E5	
Hastingwood Essex	70	C5	
Hastoe Herts	68	A5	
Haswell Dur	169	K2	
Haswell Plough Dur	169	K2	
Hatch C Beds	86	D5	
Hatch Beauchamp Somset	30	D6	
Hatch End Bed	86	B3	
Hatch End Gt Lon	50	E1	
Hatchet Gate Hants	18	F3	
Hatching Green Herts	68	E4	
Hatchmere Ches W	130	A5	
Hatcliffe NE Lin	145	G7	
Hatfield Donc	143	G6	
Hatfield Herefs	80	E3	
Hatfield Herts	69	G5	
Hatfield Worcs	81	K5	
Hatfield Broad Oak Essex	70	E4	
Hatfield Heath Essex	70	D4	
Hatfield Peverel Essex	71	J5	
Hatfield Woodhouse Donc	143	H6	
Hatford Oxon	65	M8	
Hatherden Hants	34	D1	
Hatherleigh Devon	12	D2	
Hathern Leics	116	E7	
Hatherop Gloucs	65	H6	
Hathersage Derbys	132	E3	
Hathersage Booths Derbys	132	E3	
Hatherton Ches E	113	L2	
Hatherton Staffs	98	B1	
Hatley St George Cambs	86	F5	
Hatt Cnwll	6	D2	
Hattersley Tamesd	131	K1	
Hattingley Hants	35	K3	
Hatton Abers	257	K6	
Hatton Angus	234	C6	
Hatton Derbys	115	L5	
Hatton Gt Lon	50	E4	
Hatton Lincs	136	E4	
Hatton Shrops	95	L5	
Hatton Warrtn	130	B3	
Hatton Warwks	82	F2	
Hatton Heath Ches W	129	K7	
Hatton of Fintray Abers	256	F8	
Haugh E Ayrs	196	F6	

Haugh Lincs...... 137 H4
Haugh Rochdl...... 140 D5
Haugham Lincs...... 136 F3
Haughhead E Duns...... 209 G3
Haugh Head Nthumb...... 202 F7
Haughley Suffk...... 89 L3
Haughley Green Suffk...... 89 L2
Haugh of Glass Moray...... 255 H4
Haugh of Urr D & G...... 175 K2
Haughs of Kinnaird Angus...... 235 G4
Haughton Notts...... 134 D5
Haughton Powys...... 112 D7
Haughton Shrops...... 96 F4
Haughton Shrops...... 97 G2
Haughton Shrops...... 112 F6
Haughton Shrops...... 113 J8
Haughton Staffs...... 114 D7
Haughton Green Tamesd...... 131 J1
Haughton le Skerne Darltn...... 169 J7
Haughton Moss Ches E...... 130 B8
Haultwick Herts...... 69 J3
Haunton Staffs...... 99 G1
Hautes Croix Jersey...... 9 d1
Hauxton Cambs...... 87 J5
Havannah Ches E...... 131 G6
Havant Hants...... 20 B5
Havant Crematorium Hants...... 20 B5
Haven Herefs...... 79 M4
Haven Bank Lincs...... 119 H1
Haven Side E R Yk...... 144 F2
Havenstreet IoW...... 19 J5
Havercroft Wakefd...... 142 B5
Haverfordwest Pembks...... 54 F4
Haverhill Suffk...... 88 D6
Haverigg Cumb...... 155 L7
Havering-atte-Bower Gt Lon...... 70 D8
Haversham M Keyn...... 84 F6
Haverthwaite Cumb...... 156 E6
Haverton Hill S on T...... 170 C6
Havyat N Som...... 44 F6
Havyatt Somset...... 31 H3
Hawarden Flints...... 129 H6
Hawbridge Worcs...... 81 L5
Hawbush Green Essex...... 71 J3
Hawcoat Cumb...... 146 D2
Hawen Cerdgn...... 76 C6
Hawes N York...... 158 F5
Hawe's Green Norfk...... 106 E4
Hawford Worcs...... 81 J3
Hawick Border...... 188 E3
Hawkchurch Devon...... 15 H3
Hawkedon Suffk...... 88 F4
Hawkenbury Kent...... 39 K4
Hawkeridge Wilts...... 46 B8
Hawkerland Devon...... 14 C5
Hawkesbury S Glos...... 45 M2
Hawkesbury Warwks...... 99 K6
Hawkesbury Upton S Glos...... 45 M2
Hawkes End Covtry...... 99 J6
Hawk Green Stockp...... 131 J2
Hawkhill Nthumb...... 191 J4
Hawkhurst Kent...... 39 J7
Hawkhurst Common E Susx...... 23 L4
Hawkinge Kent...... 41 H7
Hawkinge Crematorium
   Kent...... 41 G7
Hawkley Hants...... 35 M5
Hawkley Wigan...... 139 H7
Hawkridge Somset...... 28 F5
Hawksdale Cumb...... 165 L1
Hawkshaw Bury...... 139 M5
Hawkshead Cumb...... 156 E3
Hawkshead Hill Cumb...... 156 D3
Hawksland S Lans...... 198 D5
Hawkspur Green Essex...... 71 G1
Hawkstone Shrops...... 113 J5
Hawkswick N York...... 149 G2
Hawksworth Leeds...... 149 L7
Hawksworth Notts...... 117 K3
Hawkwell Essex...... 53 J1
Hawkwell Nthumb...... 180 C4
Hawley Hants...... 49 L7
Hawley Kent...... 52 C4
Hawling Gloucs...... 64 F3
Hawnby N York...... 161 J5
Haworth C Brad...... 149 J8
Hawridge Bucks...... 68 B6
Hawstead Suffk...... 89 G3
Hawstead Green Suffk...... 89 H3
Hawthorn Dur...... 169 L2
Hawthorn Hants...... 35 K4
Hawthorn Rhondd...... 43 H4
Hawthorn Hill Br For...... 49 L4
Hawthorn Hill Lincs...... 136 D6
Hawthorpe Lincs...... 118 D6
Hawton Notts...... 117 L1
Haxby C York...... 151 K4
Haxby Gates C York...... 151 K4
Haxey N Linc...... 143 J7
Haxey Carr N Linc...... 143 J7

Haxted Surrey...... 38 C4
Haxton Wilts...... 33 K1
Hay Cnwll...... 4 F4
Hay Cnwll...... 10 D8
Haycombe Crematorium
   BaNES...... 45 L6
Haydock St Hel...... 139 H8
Haydon BaNES...... 45 K8
Haydon Dorset...... 31 L7
Haydon Somset...... 30 C6
Haydon Bridge Nthumb...... 179 J6
Haydon Wick Swindn...... 47 H2
Haye Cnwll...... 11 L8
Hayes Gt Lon...... 50 E3
Hayes Gt Lon...... 51 L5
Hayes End Gt Lon...... 50 D3
Hayfield Ag & B...... 217 K2
Hayfield Derbys...... 131 L2
Haygate Wrekin...... 96 E1
Hay Green Norfk...... 120 C7
Hayhillock Angus...... 234 E1
Hayle Cnwll...... 2 F4
Hayley Green Dudley...... 98 B6
Hayling Island Hants...... 20 B6
Haymoor Green Ches E...... 113 L2
Hayne Devon...... 13 H5
Hayne Devon...... 29 G7
Haynes (Church End) C Beds...... 86 B7
Haynes (Northwood End)
   C Beds...... 86 B6
Haynes (Silver End) C Beds...... 86 B6
Haynes (West End) C Beds...... 85 L7
Hay-on-Wye Powys...... 79 J6
Hayscastle Pembks...... 74 E7
Hayscastle Cross Pembks...... 74 E7
Haysden Kent...... 38 F4
Hay Street Herts...... 69 K2
Hayton Cumb...... 164 F2
Hayton Cumb...... 178 C7
Hayton E R Yk...... 152 C6
Hayton Notts...... 134 E3
Hayton's Bent Shrops...... 96 C7
Haytor Vale Devon...... 13 H7
Haytown Devon...... 26 F7
Haywards Heath W Susx...... 22 E2
Haywood Donc...... 142 F5
Haywood Herefs...... 80 B8
Haywood Oaks Notts...... 134 C8
Hazards Green E Susx...... 24 C5
Hazelbank S Lans...... 198 D4
Hazelbury Bryan Dorset...... 16 E1
Hazeleigh Essex...... 71 K6
Hazeley Hants...... 49 H7
Hazelford Notts...... 117 J2
Hazel Grove Stockp...... 131 J4
Hazelhurst Tamesd...... 140 E7
Hazelslade Staffs...... 98 C1
Hazel Street Kent...... 39 H5
Hazel Stub Suffk...... 88 D6
Hazelton Walls Fife...... 222 E3
Hazelwood Derbys...... 116 B2
Hazlemere Bucks...... 67 L8
Hazlerigg N u Ty...... 180 F4
Hazles Staffs...... 114 F2
Hazleton Gloucs...... 65 G3
Heacham Norfk...... 120 E4
Headbourne Worthy Hants...... 35 G4
Headbrook Herefs...... 79 K4
Headcorn Kent...... 39 L4
Headingley Leeds...... 150 C8
Headington Oxon...... 66 D5
Headlam Dur...... 168 F7
Headlesscross N Lans...... 210 B7
Headless Cross Worcs...... 82 B2
Headley Hants...... 36 B4
Headley Hants...... 48 D6
Headley Surrey...... 51 G8
Headley Down Hants...... 36 B4
Headley Heath Worcs...... 98 D8
Headon Devon...... 11 M2
Headon Notts...... 134 E4
Heads Nook Cumb...... 178 C7
Heage Derbys...... 116 B2
Healaugh N York...... 151 G6
Healaugh N York...... 159 H3
Heald Green Stockp...... 131 G3
Heale Devon...... 28 A2
Heale Somset...... 30 C6
Heale Somset...... 30 F5
Healey N York...... 160 B6
Healey Nthumb...... 180 B7
Healey Rochdl...... 140 D4
Healey Wakefd...... 141 L4
Healeyfield Dur...... 168 D1
Healing NE Lin...... 145 G5
Heamoor Cnwll...... 2 D5
Heanor Derbys...... 116 D2
Heanton Punchardon Devon...... 27 J4
Heapham Lincs...... 135 H2
Hearn Hants...... 36 B3

Heart of England
   Crematorium Warwks...... 99 K5
Hearts Delight Kent...... 53 J6
Heasley Mill Devon...... 28 C4
Heast Highld...... 247 K5
Heath Derbys...... 133 J6
Heath Wakefd...... 142 A4
Heath and Reach C Beds...... 68 A2
Heath Common W Susx...... 21 J4
Heathcote Derbys...... 132 C7
Heathcote Shrops...... 113 L6
Heath End Bucks...... 67 L7
Heath End Hants...... 48 B6
Heath End Leics...... 116 B7
Heath End Warwks...... 82 F3
Heather Leics...... 99 K1
Heathfield Devon...... 13 J7
Heathfield E Susx...... 23 K3
Heathfield N York...... 149 L2
Heathfield Somset...... 29 L5
Heathfield Village Oxon...... 66 D4
Heath Green Worcs...... 82 C1
Heath Hall D & G...... 176 C3
Heath Hayes & Wimblebury
   Staffs...... 98 C2
Heath Hill Shrops...... 97 H1
Heath House Somset...... 30 F2
Heathstock Devon...... 14 F2
Heathton Shrops...... 97 H5
Heath Town Wolves...... 97 L3
Heathwaite N York...... 161 G2
Heatley Staffs...... 115 H6
Heatley Warrtn...... 130 D2
Heaton Bolton...... 139 L6
Heaton C Brad...... 149 L8
Heaton Lancs...... 147 J4
Heaton N u Ty...... 181 G5
Heaton Staffs...... 131 J7
Heaton Chapel Stockp...... 131 H1
Heaton Mersey Stockp...... 131 G2
Heaton Norris Stockp...... 131 H2
Heaton's Bridge Lancs...... 138 E5
Heaverham Kent...... 52 C7
Heaviley Stockp...... 131 H2
Heavitree Devon...... 13 L4
Hebburn S Tyne...... 181 H6
Hebden N York...... 149 J3
Hebden Bridge Calder...... 140 F2
Hebden Green Ches W...... 130 C6
Hebing End Herts...... 69 J3
Hebron Carmth...... 75 L6
Hebron IoA...... 125 H3
Hebron Nthumb...... 191 J8
Heckfield Hants...... 49 H6
Heckfield Green Suffk...... 106 D8
Heckfordbridge Essex...... 72 D3
Heckington Lincs...... 118 F3
Heckmondwike Kirk...... 141 K3
Heddington Wilts...... 46 E5
Heddon-on-the-Wall Nthumb...... 180 D5
Hedenham Norfk...... 107 G5
Hedge End Hants...... 19 H1
Hedgerley Bucks...... 50 B2
Hedgerley Green Bucks...... 50 B2
Hedging Somset...... 30 D5
Hedley on the Hill Nthumb...... 180 C7
Hednesford Staffs...... 98 C1
Hedon E R Yk...... 145 F2
Hedsor Bucks...... 49 L2
Hegdon Hill Herefs...... 80 D4
Heglibister Shet...... 281 d6
Heighington Darltn...... 169 H6
Heighington Lincs...... 135 L6
Heightington Worcs...... 81 H1
Heiton Border...... 201 L7
Hele Devon...... 13 H8
Hele Devon...... 14 A2
Hele Devon...... 27 J2
Hele Somset...... 30 B6
Helebridge Cnwll...... 11 J2
Hele Lane Devon...... 28 D8
Helensburgh Ag & B...... 208 A3
Helenton S Ayrs...... 196 D5
Helford Cnwll...... 3 J6
Helford Passage Cnwll...... 3 J5
Helhoughton Norfk...... 121 J6
Helions Bumpstead Essex...... 88 C7
Hellaby Rothm...... 133 K1
Helland Cnwll...... 10 D8
Hellandbridge Cnwll...... 10 F8
Hell Corner W Berk...... 48 A6
Hellescott Cnwll...... 11 K5
Hellesdon Norfk...... 106 E1
Hellesveor Cnwll...... 2 D3
Hellidon Nhants...... 83 M4
Hellifield N York...... 148 E4
Hellingly E Susx...... 23 K5
Hellington Norfk...... 107 G3
Helm Nthumb...... 191 H7
Helmdon Nhants...... 84 B6

Helme Kirk...... 141 H5
Helmingham Suffk...... 90 E4
Helmington Row Dur...... 168 F3
Helmsdale Highld...... 274 D5
Helmshore Lancs...... 140 B3
Helmsley N York...... 161 K6
Helperby N York...... 150 F2
Helperthorpe N York...... 152 E2
Helpringham Lincs...... 118 F3
Helpston C Pete...... 102 C2
Helsby Ches W...... 129 L6
Helsey Lincs...... 137 K5
Helston Cnwll...... 3 G5
Helstone Cnwll...... 10 F6
Helton Cumb...... 166 C6
Helwith N York...... 159 K2
Helwith Bridge N York...... 148 D2
Hemblington Norfk...... 107 G1
Hembridge Somset...... 31 K3
Hemel Hempstead Herts...... 68 D5
Hemerdon Devon...... 7 H3
Hemingbrough N York...... 143 H2
Hemingby Lincs...... 136 D5
Hemingfield Barns...... 142 B7
Hemingford Abbots Cambs...... 86 F1
Hemingford Grey Cambs...... 86 F1
Hemingstone Suffk...... 90 E5
Hemington Leics...... 116 D6
Hemington Nhants...... 102 B6
Hemington Somset...... 45 J2
Hemley Suffk...... 91 G5
Hemlington Middsb...... 170 C7
Hempholme E R Yk...... 153 H5
Hempnall Norfk...... 106 E4
Hempnall Green Norfk...... 106 E5
Hempriggs Moray...... 266 B3
Hempstead Essex...... 88 C7
Hempstead Medway...... 53 G5
Hempstead Norfk...... 122 C4
Hempstead Norfk...... 123 H6
Hempsted Gloucs...... 64 B4
Hempton Norfk...... 121 K5
Hempton Oxon...... 66 C1
Hemsby Norfk...... 123 K8
Hemswell Lincs...... 135 J2
Hemswell Cliff Lincs...... 135 J2
Hemsworth Wakefd...... 142 C5
Hemyock Devon...... 29 L8
Henbury Bristl...... 45 H3
Henbury Ches E...... 131 H5
Hendham Devon...... 7 L5
Hendomen Powys...... 94 F4
Hendon Gt Lon...... 51 G1
Hendon Sundld...... 181 K7
Hendon Crematorium Gt Lon...... 51 G1
Hendra Cnwll...... 3 J4
Hendra Cnwll...... 10 E7
Hendre Brdgnd...... 42 E5
Hendre Flints...... 128 E6
Hendre Mons...... 62 F4
Hendy Carmth...... 57 J2
Heneglwys IoA...... 125 G4
Henfield W Susx...... 22 C4
Henford Devon...... 11 M4
Henghurst Kent...... 40 B8
Hengoed Caerph...... 43 J3
Hengoed Powys...... 79 J4
Hengoed Shrops...... 112 D5
Hengrave Suffk...... 89 G2
Henham Essex...... 70 E2
Heniarth Powys...... 94 D2
Henlade Somset...... 30 C6
Henley Dorset...... 16 D2
Henley Gloucs...... 64 C4
Henley Shrops...... 95 L5
Henley Shrops...... 96 C4
Henley Somset...... 30 F4
Henley Suffk...... 90 E5
Henley W Susx...... 36 D5
Henley Green Covtry...... 99 K7
Henley-in-Arden Warwks...... 82 E2
Henley-on-Thames Oxon...... 49 J2
Henley Park Surrey...... 50 B8
Henley's Down E Susx...... 24 D5
Henley Street Kent...... 52 E5
Henllan Cerdgn...... 76 C7
Henllan Denbgs...... 127 L6
Henllan Amgoed Carmth...... 55 L3
Henllys Torfn...... 44 B1
Henlow C Beds...... 86 D7
Hennock Devon...... 13 J6
Henny Street Essex...... 89 H7
Henryd Conwy...... 126 F5
Henry's Moat (Castell Hendre)
   Pembks...... 75 H6
Hensall N York...... 142 F3
Henshaw Nthumb...... 179 H6
Hensingham Cumb...... 164 C7
Henstead Suffk...... 107 K6
Hensting Hants...... 35 G6

Henstridge Somset ... 32 B7
Henstridge Ash Somset ... 32 B6
Henstridge Marsh Somset ... 32 B6
Henton Oxon ... 67 J6
Henton Somset ... 31 H2
Henwick Worcs ... 81 J4
Henwood Cnwll ... 11 K7
Henwood Oxon ... 66 C6
Heol-las Swans ... 57 J5
Heol Senni Powys ... 60 D2
Heol-y-Cyw Brdgnd ... 42 E5
Hepburn Nthumb ... 190 F1
Hepple Nthumb ... 190 E6
Hepscott Nthumb ... 180 F2
Heptonstall Calder ... 140 E2
Hepworth Kirk ... 141 J6
Hepworth Suffk ... 105 K8
Herbrandston Pembks ... 54 E5
Hereford Herefs ... 80 C7
Hereford Crematorium Herefs ... 80 C7
Hereson Kent ... 41 L2
Heribusta Highld ... 258 F3
Heriot Border ... 200 E2
Hermiston C Edin ... 211 G5
Hermitage Border ... 188 E7
Hermitage Dorset ... 16 C1
Hermitage W Berk ... 48 D4
Hermitage W Susx ... 20 B5
Hermit Hill Barns ... 141 M7
Hermon Carmth ... 58 C3
Hermon IoA ... 125 G6
Hermon Pembks ... 75 L6
Herne Kent ... 41 G2
Herne Bay Kent ... 41 G2
Herne Common Kent ... 41 G2
Herne Hill Gt Lon ... 51 J4
Herne Pound Kent ... 39 G3
Herner Devon ... 27 K5
Hernhill Kent ... 40 E3
Herodsfoot Cnwll ... 5 L3
Heronden Kent ... 41 J4
Herongate Essex ... 52 D1
Heronsford S Ayrs ... 182 E6
Heronsgate Herts ... 68 C8
Herriard Hants ... 35 K2
Herringfleet Suffk ... 107 K4
Herring's Green Bed ... 86 B6
Herringswell Suffk ... 88 E1
Herringthorpe Rothm ... 133 J1
Herrington Sundld ... 181 J8
Hersden Kent ... 41 G3
Hersham Cnwll ... 11 J1
Hersham Surrey ... 50 E6
Herstmonceux E Susx ... 23 L5
Herston Dorset ... 17 K6
Herston Ork ... 275 C6
Hertford Herts ... 69 J4
Hertford Heath Herts ... 69 K5
Hertingfordbury Herts ... 69 J5
Hesketh Bank Lancs ... 138 F3
Hesketh Lane Lancs ... 147 M7
Hesket Newmarket Cumb ... 165 K3
Heskin Green Lancs ... 139 G4
Hesleden Dur ... 170 B3
Hesleden N York ... 158 F7
Hesley Donc ... 134 C1
Hesleyside Nthumb ... 179 J2
Heslington C York ... 151 K5
Hessay C York ... 151 H5
Hessenford Cnwll ... 6 C3
Hessett Suffk ... 89 J3
Hessle E R Yk ... 144 C3
Hessle Wakefd ... 142 C4
Hest Bank Lancs ... 147 J3
Hestley Green Suffk ... 90 D2
Heston Gt Lon ... 50 E3
Hestwall Ork ... 275 b4
Heswall Wirral ... 129 G3
Hethe Oxon ... 66 E1
Hethersett Norfk ... 106 C2
Hethersgill Cumb ... 178 B5
Hetherside Cumb ... 178 B5
Hetherson Green Ches W ... 113 H2
Hethpool Nthumb ... 202 D7
Hett Dur ... 169 H3
Hetton N York ... 149 G4
Hetton-le-Hole Sundld ... 169 K1
Hetton Steads Nthumb ... 203 G6
Heugh Nthumb ... 180 D4
Heughhead Abers ... 243 L1
Heugh Head Border ... 213 J6
Heveningham Suffk ... 91 H1
Hever Kent ... 38 D4
Heversham Cumb ... 157 H6
Hevingham Norfk ... 122 D7
Hewas Water Cnwll ... 4 F5
Hewelsfield Gloucs ... 63 H6
Hewenden C Brad ... 149 K8
Hewish N Som ... 44 E6
Hewish Somset ... 15 K1

Hewood Dorset ... 15 H2
Hexham Nthumb ... 179 L6
Hextable Kent ... 52 B5
Hexthorpe Donc ... 142 F7
Hexton Herts ... 68 E1
Hexworthy Cnwll ... 11 L6
Hexworthy Devon ... 12 F8
Hey Lancs ... 148 F7
Heybridge Essex ... 70 D2
Heybridge Essex ... 71 L5
Heybridge Basin Essex ... 72 C5
Heybrook Bay Devon ... 6 F5
Heydon Cambs ... 87 J7
Heydon Norfk ... 122 C6
Heydour Lincs ... 118 D4
Heyhead Manch ... 131 G3
Hey Houses Lancs ... 138 D2
Heylipoll Ag & B ... 224 B6
Heylor Shet ... 281 d4
Heyrod Tamesd ... 140 E7
Heysham Lancs ... 147 H4
Heyshaw N York ... 149 L3
Heyshott W Susx ... 20 E3
Heyside Oldham ... 140 D6
Heytesbury Wilts ... 32 F2
Heythrop Oxon ... 65 M2
Heywood Rochdl ... 140 C5
Heywood Wilts ... 46 C8
Hibaldstow N Linc ... 144 B3
Hickleton Donc ... 142 D6
Hickling Norfk ... 123 J6
Hickling Notts ... 117 J6
Hickling Green Norfk ... 123 H6
Hickling Heath Norfk ... 123 H7
Hickmans Green Kent ... 40 E4
Hicks Forstal Kent ... 41 G3
Hickstead W Susx ... 22 D3
Hidcote Bartrim Gloucs ... 82 E6
Hidcote Boyce Gloucs ... 82 E6
High Ackworth Wakefd ... 142 C4
Higham Barns ... 141 M6
Higham Derbys ... 133 H7
Higham Kent ... 38 F4
Higham Kent ... 52 F5
Higham Lancs ... 148 E8
Higham Suffk ... 88 E2
Higham Suffk ... 89 L8
Higham Dykes Nthumb ... 180 D4
Higham Ferrers Nhants ... 85 J2
Higham Gobion C Beds ... 86 C8
Higham Hill Gt Lon ... 51 K1
Higham on the Hill Leics ... 99 K4
Highampton Devon ... 12 C2
Highams Park Gt Lon ... 69 K8
High Angerton Nthumb ... 180 D2
High Ardwell D & G ... 172 D5
High Auldgirth D & G ... 176 B1
High Bankhill Cumb ... 166 D2
High Beach Essex ... 69 L7
High Bentham N York ... 148 B2
High Bewaldeth Cumb ... 165 H4
High Bickington Devon ... 27 L6
High Bickwith N York ... 158 D7
High Biggins Cumb ... 157 K7
High Blantyre S Lans ... 209 H7
High Bonnybridge Falk ... 209 L3
High Borrans Cumb ... 156 F3
High Bradley N York ... 149 H6
High Bray Devon ... 28 B4
Highbridge Hants ... 34 F6
Highbridge Somset ... 30 D2
Highbrook W Susx ... 38 A7
High Brooms Kent ... 38 F5
High Bullen Devon ... 27 J6
Highburton Kirk ... 141 J5
Highbury Gt Lon ... 51 J2
Highbury Somset ... 31 M1
High Buston Nthumb ... 191 J4
High Callerton Nthumb ... 180 L5
High Casterton Cumb ... 157 K7
High Catton E R Yk ... 151 M5
Highclere Hants ... 48 B7
Highcliffe Dorset ... 18 C5
High Close Dur ... 168 F7
High Cogges Oxon ... 66 A5
High Common Norfk ... 105 K2
High Coniscliffe Darltn ... 169 G7
High Crosby Cumb ... 178 B6
High Cross Cnwll ... 3 J5
High Cross E Ayrs ... 196 D2
High Cross Hants ... 35 L5
High Cross Herts ... 69 K3
Highcross Lancs ... 147 G8
High Cross W Susx ... 22 C4
High Cross Warwks ... 82 C2
High Drummore D & G ... 172 E7
High Dubmire Sundld ... 169 J1
High Easter Essex ... 70 F4
High Eggborough N York ... 142 F5
High Ellington N York ... 160 B6

Higher Alham Somset ... 31 L3
Higher Ansty Dorset ... 16 E2
Higher Ballam Lancs ... 138 D2
Higher Bartle Lancs ... 139 G1
Higher Berry End C Beds ... 85 J8
Higher Bockhampton Dorset ... 16 D4
Higher Brixham Torbay ... 8 D4
Higher Burrowton Devon ... 14 B3
Higher Burwardsley Ches W ... 129 M8
High Ercall Wrekin ... 113 K8
Higher Chillington Somset ... 15 J1
Higher Clovelly Devon ... 26 E6
Highercombe Somset ... 28 F5
Higher Coombe Dorset ... 15 M4
Higher Disley Ches E ... 131 J3
Higher Folds Wigan ... 139 K7
Higherford Lancs ... 148 F7
Higher Gabwell Devon ... 8 D1
Higher Halstock Leigh Dorset ... 15 L1
Higher Harpers Lancs ... 148 E8
Higher Heysham Lancs ... 147 H4
Higher Hurdsfield Ches E ... 131 J5
Higher Irlam Salfd ... 130 E1
Higher Kingcombe Dorset ... 15 M3
Higher Kinnerton Flints ... 129 H7
Higher Marston Ches W ... 130 C4
Higher Muddiford Devon ... 27 K3
Higher Nyland Dorset ... 32 B6
Higher Ogden Rochdl ... 140 E5
Higher Pentire Cnwll ... 3 G6
Higher Penwortham Lancs ... 139 G2
Higher Prestacott Devon ... 11 M4
Higher Studfold N York ... 148 E2
Higher Town Cnwll ... 4 C6
Higher Town Cnwll ... 5 G3
Higher Town IoS ... 10 C2
Higher Tregantle Cnwll ... 6 D4
Higher Walton Lancs ... 139 H2
Higher Walton Warrtn ... 130 B3
Higher Wambrook Somset ... 15 G2
Higher Waterston Dorset ... 16 D3
Higher Whatcombe Dorset ... 17 G2
Higher Wheelton Lancs ... 139 J3
Higher Whitley Ches W ... 130 B4
Higher Wincham Ches W ... 130 D4
Higher Wraxhall Dorset ... 16 A2
Higher Wych Ches W ... 113 H3
High Etherley Dur ... 168 F5
High Ferry Lincs ... 119 K2
Highfield E R Yk ... 151 M8
Highfield Gatesd ... 180 E7
Highfield N Ayrs ... 196 C1
Highfields Donc ... 142 E6
High Flats Kirk ... 141 K6
High Garrett Essex ... 71 J2
Highgate E Susx ... 38 C6
Highgate Gt Lon ... 51 H2
Highgate Kent ... 39 J7
High Grange Dur ... 168 F4
High Grantley N York ... 150 B2
High Green Cumb ... 156 F2
High Green Kirk ... 141 K5
High Green Norfk ... 106 C2
High Green Norfk ... 106 D5
High Green Sheff ... 142 A8
High Green Shrops ... 96 F6
High Green Suffk ... 89 G3
High Green Worcs ... 81 K6
Highgreen Manor Nthumb ... 189 L7
High Halden Kent ... 40 A7
High Halstow Medway ... 53 G4
High Ham Somset ... 30 F4
High Harrington Cumb ... 164 D5
High Harrogate N York ... 150 D5
High Haswell Dur ... 169 K2
High Hatton Shrops ... 113 K6
High Hauxley Nthumb ... 191 K5
High Hawsker N York ... 163 H5
High Hesket Cumb ... 166 B2
High Hoyland Barns ... 141 L5
High Hunsley E R Yk ... 144 B1
High Hurstwood E Susx ... 23 H2
High Hutton N York ... 152 A2
High Ireby Cumb ... 165 H3
High Kelling Norfk ... 122 C3
High Kilburn N York ... 161 H6
High Killerby N York ... 163 J6
High Knipe Cumb ... 166 C6
High Lands Dur ... 168 E5
Highlane Ches E ... 131 H6
Highlane Derbys ... 133 H3
High Lane Stockp ... 131 J3
High Lanes Cnwll ... 2 F4
High Laver Essex ... 70 D5
Highlaws Cumb ... 164 F1
Highleadon Gloucs ... 63 M2
High Legh Ches E ... 130 D3
Highleigh W Susx ... 20 D7
High Leven S on T ... 170 B8
Highley Shrops ... 97 G6

High Littleton BaNES ... 45 J7
High Lorton Cumb ... 165 G5
High Marishes N York ... 162 E7
High Marnham Notts ... 134 F5
High Melton Donc ... 142 D7
High Mickley Nthumb ... 180 C6
Highmoor Cumb ... 165 J1
Highmoor Oxon ... 49 H2
Highmoor Cross Oxon ... 49 H2
Highmoor Hill Mons ... 44 F1
High Moorsley Sundld ... 169 J2
Highnam Gloucs ... 64 A3
Highnam Green Gloucs ... 64 A3
High Newport Sundld ... 181 J8
High Newton Cumb ... 156 F6
High Nibthwaite Cumb ... 156 D5
High Offley Staffs ... 114 B6
High Ongar Essex ... 70 E6
High Onn Staffs ... 114 C8
High Park Corner Essex ... 72 F3
High Pennyvenie E Ayrs ... 184 D2
High Post Wilts ... 33 K4
Highridge N Som ... 45 H5
High Roding Essex ... 70 F4
High Row Cumb ... 165 K3
High Row Cumb ... 165 L6
High Salter Lancs ... 147 M3
High Salvington W Susx ... 21 K5
High Scales Cumb ... 165 G2
High Seaton Cumb ... 164 D4
High Shaw N York ... 158 F4
High Side Cumb ... 165 H4
High Spen Gatesd ... 180 E7
Highstead Kent ... 41 G2
Highsted Kent ... 40 B3
High Stoop Dur ... 168 E3
High Street Cnwll ... 5 G4
High Street Kent ... 39 J7
Highstreet Kent ... 40 E3
High Street Suffk ... 91 J1
High Street Suffk ... 91 K4
Highstreet Green Essex ... 88 F8
Highstreet Green Surrey ... 36 E4
Hightae D & G ... 176 E3
Highter's Heath Birm ... 98 E7
High Throston Hartpl ... 170 C4
Hightown Ches E ... 131 G7
Hightown Hants ... 18 B3
Hightown Sefton ... 138 C7
High Town Staffs ... 98 C1
Hightown Green Suffk ... 89 K4
High Toynton Lincs ... 136 E5
High Trewhitt Nthumb ... 190 E5
High Urpeth Dur ... 181 G8
High Valleyfield Fife ... 210 D2
High Warden Nthumb ... 179 L5
Highway Herefs ... 80 B5
Highway Wilts ... 46 F4
Highweek Devon ... 13 K8
High Westwood Dur ... 180 D7
Highwood Staffs ... 115 H5
Highwood Hill Gt Lon ... 69 G8
High Woolaston Gloucs ... 63 H7
High Worsall N York ... 160 F1
Highworth Swindn ... 65 J8
High Wray Cumb ... 156 E3
High Wych Herts ... 70 C4
High Wycombe Bucks ... 67 L8
Hilborough Norfk ... 105 G3
Hilcote Derbys ... 133 J8
Hilcott Wilts ... 47 G7
Hildenborough Kent ... 38 E4
Hilden Park Kent ... 38 F4
Hildersham Cambs ... 87 L5
Hilderstone Staffs ... 114 E4
Hilderthorpe E R Yk ... 153 J3
Hilfield Dorset ... 16 C2
Hilgay Norfk ... 104 C4
Hill S Glos ... 63 J8
Hill Warwks ... 83 K2
Hillam N York ... 142 D2
Hillbeck Cumb ... 168 C3
Hillborough Kent ... 41 G2
Hill Brow Hants ... 36 B5
Hillbutts Dorset ... 17 K2
Hill Chorlton Staffs ... 114 B4
Hillclifflane Derbys ... 115 M2
Hill Common Norfk ... 123 H7
Hill Common Somset ... 29 L5
Hill Deverill Wilts ... 32 E3
Hilldyke Lincs ... 119 K2
Hill End Dur ... 168 C3
Hillend Fife ... 210 F2
Hill End Fife ... 221 H2
Hill End Gloucs ... 81 K7
Hillend Mdloth ... 211 H5
Hillend N Lans ... 209 L5
Hillend Swans ... 56 D6
Hillersland Gloucs ... 63 H4
Hillerton Devon ... 13 G3

Hillesden Bucks	67	G1
Hillesley Gloucs	45	M1
Hillfarrance Somset	29	L6
Hill Green Kent	53	H6
Hillgrove W Susx	36	D5
Hillhampton Herefs	80	D6
Hillhead Abers	255	M4
Hillhead Devon	8	D4
Hill Head Hants	19	J3
Hillhead S Lans	199	G5
Hillhead of Cocklaw Abers	257	K3
Hilliard's Cross Staffs	98	F1
Hilliclay Highld	279	L1
Hillingdon Gt Lon	50	D2
Hillington C Glas	208	E6
Hillington Norfk	120	F6
Hillis Corner IoW	19	H5
Hillmorton Warwks	100	C8
Hillock Vale Lancs	140	A2
Hill of Beath Fife	210	F1
Hill of Fearn Highld	264	C4
Hillowton D & G	175	J2
Hillpool Worcs	97	K8
Hillpound Hants	35	J7
Hill Ridware Staffs	115	H8
Hillside Abers	245	K4
Hillside Angus	235	H3
Hillside Devon	7	K3
Hill Side Kirk	141	J4
Hill Side Worcs	81	H3
Hills Town Derbys	133	J5
Hillstreet Hants	34	D7
Hillswick Shet	281	C4
Hill Top Dur	168	C6
Hill Top Hants	18	F3
Hill Top Kirk	141	J4
Hill Top Rothm	133	H1
Hill Top Sandw	98	C5
Hill Top Wakefd	142	A4
Hillwell Shet	281	d8
Hilmarton Wilts	46	E4
Hilperton Wilts	46	C7
Hilperton Marsh Wilts	46	C7
Hilsea C Port	19	L3
Hilston E R Yk	145	H1
Hiltingbury Hants	34	F6
Hilton Border	202	D3
Hilton Cambs	86	F2
Hilton Cumb	167	G6
Hilton Derbys	115	L5
Hilton Dorset	16	E2
Hilton Dur	168	F6
Hilton Highld	264	D4
Hilton S on T	170	B8
Hilton Shrops	97	H4
Himbleton Worcs	81	L3
Himley Staffs	97	K5
Hincaster Cumb	157	H5
Hinchley Wood Surrey	50	F6
Hinckley Leics	99	L4
Hinderclay Suffk	105	L8
Hinderwell N York	171	J7
Hindford Shrops	112	E5
Hindhead Surrey	36	C4
Hindle Fold Lancs	139	L1
Hindley Nthumb	180	C7
Hindley Wigan	139	J6
Hindley Green Wigan	139	J7
Hindlip Worcs	81	K3
Hindolveston Norfk	122	A5
Hindon Wilts	32	F4
Hindringham Norfk	121	L3
Hingham Norfk	105	L3
Hinksford Staffs	97	J5
Hinstock Shrops	113	M6
Hintlesham Suffk	90	C6
Hinton Gloucs	63	K6
Hinton Hants	18	C4
Hinton Herefs	79	L7
Hinton S Glos	45	L4
Hinton Shrops	95	K2
Hinton Shrops	96	E7
Hinton Admiral Hants	18	C4
Hinton Ampner Hants	35	J5
Hinton Blewett BaNES	45	H7
Hinton Charterhouse BaNES	45	M7
Hinton Green Worcs	82	B7
Hinton-in-the-Hedges Nhants	84	A7
Hinton Marsh Hants	35	J5
Hinton Martell Dorset	17	K2
Hinton on the Green Worcs	82	B7
Hinton Parva Swindn	47	K2
Hinton St George Somset	30	F8
Hinton St Mary Dorset	32	C7
Hinton Waldrist Oxon	66	A7
Hints Shrops	96	E8
Hints Staffs	98	F3
Hinwick Bed	85	J3
Hinxhill Kent	40	D6
Hinxton Cambs	87	K6
Hinxworth Herts	86	E7
Hipperholme Calder	141	H3
Hipsburn Nthumb	191	J4
Hipswell N York	160	B3
Hirn Abers	245	G3
Hirnant Powys	111	K7
Hirst Nthumb	181	G2
Hirst Courtney N York	142	F3
Hirwaen Denbgs	128	D3
Hirwaun Rhondd	60	E6
Hiscott Devon	27	K5
Histon Cambs	87	J3
Hitcham Suffk	89	K5
Hitcham Causeway Suffk	89	K5
Hitcham Street Suffk	89	K5
Hitchin Herts	68	F1
Hither Green Gt Lon	51	K4
Hittisleigh Devon	13	G3
Hive E R Yk	143	K2
Hixon Staffs	114	F6
Hoaden Kent	41	J3
Hoar Cross Staffs	115	J7
Hoarwithy Herefs	63	G1
Hoath Kent	41	G2
Hoathly Kent	39	G6
Hobarris Shrops	95	H7
Hobbles Green Suffk	88	D4
Hobbs Cross Essex	70	C7
Hobbs Cross Essex	70	D5
Hobkirk Border	189	G4
Hobland Hall Norfk	107	K3
Hobsick Notts	116	D2
Hobson Dur	180	E7
Hoby Leics	117	H8
Hoccombe Somset	29	K5
Hockering Norfk	106	B1
Hockerton Notts	134	E8
Hockley Ches E	131	J3
Hockley Covtry	99	H7
Hockley Essex	71	K4
Hockley Staffs	99	G3
Hockley Heath Solhll	82	E1
Hockliffe C Beds	68	B2
Hockwold cum Wilton Norfk	104	E6
Hockworthy Devon	29	J7
Hoddesdon Herts	69	K5
Hoddlesden Bl w D	139	L3
Hoddom Cross D & G	177	G4
Hoddom Mains D & G	177	G4
Hodgehill Ches E	131	G5
Hodgeston Pembks	55	H7
Hodnet Shrops	113	K6
Hodsock Notts	134	C3
Hodsoll Street Kent	52	D6
Hodson Swindn	47	H3
Hodthorpe Derbys	133	L4
Hoe Hants	35	H7
Hoe Norfk	121	M8
Hoe Gate Hants	35	K8
Hoff Cumb	166	F7
Hogben's Hill Kent	40	D4
Hoggards Green Suffk	89	H4
Hoggeston Bucks	67	K2
Hoggrill's End Warwks	99	G5
Hog Hill E Susx	25	G4
Hoghton Lancs	139	J2
Hoghton Bottoms Lancs	139	J2
Hognaston Derbys	115	L2
Hogsthorpe Lincs	137	K5
Holbeach Lincs	119	K6
Holbeach Bank Lincs	119	K6
Holbeach Clough Lincs	119	K6
Holbeach Drove Lincs	103	G1
Holbeach Hurn Lincs	119	L6
Holbeach St Johns Lincs	119	K7
Holbeach St Mark's Lincs	119	L5
Holbeach St Matthew Lincs	119	L5
Holbeck Notts	133	L4
Holbeck Woodhouse Notts	133	L5
Holberrow Green Worcs	82	B3
Holbeton Devon	7	J5
Holborn Gt Lon	51	J3
Holborough Kent	52	F6
Holbrook Derbys	116	B3
Holbrook Sheff	133	J3
Holbrook Suffk	90	E7
Holbrook Moor Derbys	116	B3
Holbrooks Covtry	99	J6
Holburn Nthumb	203	G6
Holbury Hants	19	G3
Holcombe Devon	13	M7
Holcombe Somset	31	L1
Holcombe Rogus Devon	29	J7
Holcot Nhants	84	F1
Holden Lancs	148	D6
Holdenby Nhants	84	D2
Holden Gate Calder	140	D3
Holder's Green Essex	70	F1
Holdgate Shrops	96	D5
Holdingham Lincs	118	E2
Holditch Dorset	15	H2
Holdsworth Calder	141	G2
Holehouse Derbys	131	K1
Hole-in-the-Wall Herefs	63	J2
Holemoor Devon	12	A2
Hole Street W Susx	21	K4
Holford Somset	29	L3
Holgate C York	151	J5
Holker Cumb	156	E7
Holkham Norfk	121	K3
Hollacombe Devon	11	M2
Holland Fen Lincs	119	H2
Holland Lees Lancs	139	G6
Holland-on-Sea Essex	73	J4
Hollandstoun Ork	275	f1
Hollee D & G	177	J5
Hollesley Suffk	91	H6
Hollicombe Torbay	8	D2
Hollingbourne Kent	39	L2
Hollingbury Br & H	22	D5
Hollingdon Bucks	67	L2
Hollingthorpe Leeds	142	B2
Hollington Derbys	115	L4
Hollington Staffs	115	G4
Hollingworth Tamesd	140	F8
Hollinlane Ches E	131	G3
Hollins Bury	140	B6
Hollins Derbys	132	F5
Hollins Staffs	114	F2
Hollinsclough Staffs	131	L6
Hollins End Sheff	133	H3
Hollins Green Warrtn	130	D2
Hollins Lane Lancs	147	K5
Hollinswood Wrekin	96	F2
Hollinwood Shrops	113	H4
Hollinwood Crematorium Oldham	140	D7
Holllingrove E Susx	24	C3
Hollocombe Devon	27	L8
Holloway Derbys	132	F8
Holloway Gt Lon	51	J2
Holloway Wilts	32	E5
Hollowell Nhants	84	D1
Hollowmoor Heath Ches W	129	L6
Hollows D & G	177	L3
Hollybush Caerph	61	J6
Hollybush E Ayrs	196	D7
Hollybush Herefs	81	H7
Holly End Norfk	103	K2
Holly Green Worcs	81	K7
Hollyhurst Ches E	113	J3
Hollym E R Yk	145	J3
Hollywood Worcs	98	D7
Holmbridge Kirk	141	H6
Holmbury St Mary Surrey	37	H2
Holmbush Cnwll	5	H4
Holmcroft Staffs	114	E6
Holme Cambs	102	D6
Holme Cumb	157	H7
Holme Kirk	141	H6
Holme N Linc	144	A6
Holme N York	160	E6
Holme Notts	134	F7
Holme Chapel Lancs	140	C2
Holme Green N York	151	J7
Holme Hale Norfk	105	H2
Holme Lacy Herefs	80	D8
Holme Marsh Herefs	79	L4
Holme next the Sea Norfk	120	F3
Holme on the Wolds E R Yk	152	E6
Holme Pierrepont Notts	117	G4
Holmer Herefs	80	C6
Holmer Green Bucks	67	L7
Holme St Cuthbert Cumb	164	F1
Holmes Chapel Ches E	130	E6
Holmesfield Derbys	132	F4
Holmes Hill E Susx	23	J4
Holmeswood Lancs	138	E4
Holmethorpe Surrey	51	H8
Holme upon Spalding Moor E R Yk	152	B8
Holmewood Derbys	133	H6
Holmfield Calder	141	G2
Holmfirth Kirk	141	H6
Holmhead E Ayrs	197	H7
Holmpton E R Yk	145	K3
Holmrook Cumb	155	K3
Holmsford Bridge Crematorium N Ayrs	196	D3
Holmshurst E Susx	23	L2
Holmside Dur	169	G1
Holmwrangle Cumb	166	C1
Holne Devon	7	K1
Holnest Dorset	16	C1
Holnicote Somset	29	G2
Holsworthy Devon	11	L2
Holsworthy Beacon Devon	11	L1
Holt Dorset	17	K2
Holt Norfk	122	B4
Holt Wilts	46	B6
Holt Worcs	81	J3
Holt Wrexhm	112	F1
Holtby C York	151	L5
Holt End Worcs	82	C1
Holt Fleet Worcs	81	J3
Holt Green Lancs	138	E6
Holt Heath Dorset	17	L2
Holt Heath Worcs	81	J3
Holton Oxon	66	F5
Holton Somset	31	L5
Holton Suffk	107	H5
Holton cum Beckering Lincs	136	B3
Holton Heath Dorset	17	J4
Holton Hill E Susx	24	B2
Holton le Clay Lincs	145	H1
Holton le Moor Lincs	144	D4
Holton St Mary Suffk	90	C7
Holt Street Kent	41	H5
Holtye E Susx	38	C5
Holway Flints	128	E4
Holwell Dorset	32	B8
Holwell Herts	86	D3
Holwell Leics	117	J7
Holwell Oxon	65	K5
Holwick Dur	167	L5
Holworth Dorset	16	H3
Holybourne Hants	35	M3
Holy Cross Worcs	97	L7
Holyfield Essex	69	K6
Holyhead IoA	124	D3
Holy Island IoA	124	D3
Holy Island Nthumb	203	J5
Holymoorside Derbys	133	G6
Holyport W & M	49	J3
Holystone Nthumb	190	D5
Holytown N Lans	209	K6
Holytown Crematorium N Lans	209	K6
Holywell C Beds	68	C4
Holywell Cambs	87	G1
Holywell Cnwll	4	C3
Holywell Dorset	16	B2
Holywell Flints	128	E4
Holywell Nthumb	181	H4
Holywell Warwks	82	C1
Holywell Green Calder	141	G4
Holywell Lake Somset	29	K6
Holywell Row Suffk	104	E7
Holywood D & G	176	B3
Holywood Village D & G	176	C3
Homer Shrops	96	E3
Homer Green Sefton	138	D7
Homersfield Suffk	106	C4
Homescales Cumb	157	J5
Hom Green Herefs	63	H3
Homington Wilts	33	K5
Honeyborough Pembks	54	G5
Honeybourne Worcs	82	D6
Honeychurch Devon	12	E2
Honey Hill Kent	40	F3
Honeystreet Wilts	47	G6
Honey Tye Suffk	89	J8
Honiley Warwks	82	F1
Honing Norfk	123	G6
Honingham Norfk	106	C1
Honington Lincs	118	B3
Honington Suffk	105	H8
Honington Warwks	83	G6
Honiton Devon	14	E3
Honley Kirk	141	H5
Honnington Wrekin	114	A8
Honor Oak Crematorium Gt Lon	51	K4
Hoo Kent	41	J2
Hoobrook Worcs	97	J8
Hood Green Barns	141	M7
Hood Hill Rothm	142	B8
Hooe C Plym	6	F4
Hooe E Susx	24	C5
Hoo End Herts	68	F3
Hoo Green Ches E	130	D3
Hoohill Bpool	146	F8
Hook Cambs	103	J5
Hook Devon	15	G2
Hook E R Yk	143	J5
Hook Gt Lon	50	F6
Hook Hants	19	H4
Hook Hants	49	H8
Hook Pembks	55	G4
Hook Wilts	47	G2
Hookagate Shrops	95	K3
Hook Bank Worcs	81	J7
Hooke Dorset	15	M3
Hook End Essex	70	E7
Hookgate Staffs	114	A4
Hook Green Kent	39	G6
Hook Green Kent	52	D5
Hook Norton Oxon	83	H8
Hook Street Gloucs	63	K7
Hook Street Wilts	47	G2

Hookway Devon 13 K3
Hookwood Surrey 37 L2
Hooley Surrey 51 H7
Hooley Bridge Rochdl 140 C5
Hoo Meavy Devon 7 G2
Hoo St Werburgh Medway 53 G4
Hooton Ches W 129 J4
Hooton Levitt Rothm 133 K2
Hooton Pagnell Donc 142 D6
Hooton Roberts Rothm 142 D8
Hopcrofts Holt Oxon 66 C2
Hope Derbys 132 C3
Hope Devon 7 K6
Hope Flints 129 G7
Hope Powys 95 G2
Hope Shrops 95 H3
Hope Staffs 132 B8
Hope Bagot Shrops 96 C8
Hope Bowdler Shrops 95 L5
Hope End Green Essex 70 E3
Hopehouse Border 187 L3
Hopeman Moray 266 C2
Hope Mansell Herefs 63 J3
Hopesay Shrops 95 J6
Hopetown Wakefd 142 B3
Hope under Dinmore Herefs 80 C5
Hopgrove C York 151 K5
Hopperton N York 150 F4
Hop Pole Lincs 102 D1
Hopsford Warwks 99 L6
Hopstone Shrops 97 H4
Hopton Derbys 115 L1
Hopton Shrops 112 F7
Hopton Staffs 114 E6
Hopton Suffk 105 K7
Hopton Cangeford Shrops 96 C7
Hopton Castle Shrops 95 J7
Hoptonheath Shrops 95 J7
Hopton on Sea Norfk 107 L3
Hopton Wafers Shrops 96 E8
Hopwas Staffs 98 F3
Hopwood Rochdl 140 C6
Hopwood Worcs 98 C8
Horam E Susx 23 K4
Horbling Lincs 118 F4
Horbury Wakefd 141 L4
Horcott Gloucs 65 H7
Horden Dur 170 B3
Horderley Shrops 95 K6
Hordle Hants 18 D4
Hordley Shrops 112 F5
Horeb Carmth 56 F4
Horeb Cerdgn 76 D6
Horfield Bristl 45 H4
Horham Suffk 90 F1
Horkesley Heath Essex 72 E1
Horkstow N Linc 144 B4
Horley Oxon 83 K6
Horley Surrey 37 L2
Hornblotton Green Somset 31 K4
Hornby Lancs 147 L2
Hornby N York 160 B4
Hornby N York 160 E2
Horncastle Lincs 136 E6
Hornchurch Gt Lon 52 B2
Horncliffe Nthumb 202 E3
Horndean Border 202 D3
Horndean Hants 35 L8
Horndon Devon 12 C6
Horndon on the Hill Thurr 52 E2
Horne Surrey 38 A4
Horner Somset 28 F2
Horne Row Essex 71 J6
Horners Green Suffk 89 K7
Horney Common E Susx 23 G2
Horn Hill Bucks 68 C8
Horning Norfk 123 G8
Horninghold Leics 101 H4
Horninglow Staffs 115 L6
Horningsea Cambs 87 K3
Horningsham Wilts 32 D3
Horningtoft Norfk 121 K6
Horningtops Cnwll 6 B3
Hornsbury Somset 30 E8
Hornsby Cumb 166 C1
Hornsbygate Cumb 166 C1
Horns Cross Devon 27 G6
Horns Cross E Susx 24 E3
Hornsea E R Yk 153 K6
Hornsey Gt Lon 51 J1
Horn's Green Gt Lon 51 M7
Horn Street Kent 41 G8
Hornton Oxon 83 J6
Horpit Swindn 47 J2
Horra Shet 281 e3
Horrabridge Devon 7 G1
Horringer Suffk 89 G3
Horringford IoW 19 J6
Horrocks Fold Bolton 139 L5
Horrocksford Lancs 148 C7

Horsacott Devon 27 J4
Horsebridge Devon 12 A7
Horsebridge E Susx 23 K5
Horsebridge Hants 34 D5
Horsebridge Shrops 95 J2
Horsebridge Staffs 114 F1
Horsebrook Staffs 97 K3
Horsecastle N Som 44 E5
Horsedown Cnwll 3 G4
Horsegate Lincs 102 C2
Horsehay Wrekin 96 F2
Horseheath Cambs 88 C5
Horsehouse N York 159 J6
Horsell Surrey 50 C7
Horseman's Green Wrexhm 113 G3
Horsenden Bucks 67 J6
Horsey Norfk 123 J7
Horsey Somset 30 D3
Horsey Corner Norfk 123 J6
Horsford Norfk 122 D8
Horsforth Leeds 150 B8
Horsham W Susx 37 J5
Horsham Worcs 81 G4
Horsham St Faith Norfk 122 E8
Horsington Lincs 136 C6
Horsington Somset 32 B6
Horsley Derbys 116 C3
Horsley Gloucs 64 B7
Horsley Nthumb 180 D5
Horsley Nthumb 190 B6
Horsley Cross Essex 73 H2
Horsleycross Street Essex 73 G1
Horsley-Gate Derbys 132 F4
Horsleyhill Border 188 F2
Horsley's Green Bucks 67 J8
Horsley Woodhouse Derbys 116 C3
Horsmonden Kent 39 H5
Horspath Oxon 66 E6
Horstead Norfk 122 F7
Horsted Keynes W Susx 22 F2
Horton Bucks 68 A3
Horton Dorset 17 K1
Horton Lancs 148 E6
Horton Nhants 84 F4
Horton S Glos 45 M2
Horton Shrops 113 H5
Horton Somset 30 D7
Horton Staffs 131 J8
Horton Surrey 51 G6
Horton Swans 56 E7
Horton W & M 50 C4
Horton Wilts 46 F6
Horton Wrekin 113 L8
Horton Cross Somset 30 E7
Horton-cum-Studley Oxon 66 F4
Horton Green Ches W 113 G2
Horton Heath Hants 35 G7
Horton in Ribblesdale N York 148 D2
Horton Kirby Kent 52 C5
Horwich Bolton 139 J5
Horwich End Derbys 131 K3
Horwood Devon 27 J5
Hoscar Lancs 138 F5
Hoscote Border 188 C4
Hose Leics 117 J5
Hosey Hill Kent 51 M8
Hosh P & K 220 E3
Hoswick Shet 281 e8
Hotham E R Yk 143 M1
Hothfield Kent 40 C6
Hoton Leics 116 F7
Hott Nthumb 179 H2
Hough Ches E 113 M1
Hough Ches E 131 G4
Hougham Lincs 118 A3
Hough End Leeds 141 K1
Hough Green Halton 129 L2
Hough-on-the-Hill Lincs 118 B2
Houghton Cambs 86 F1
Houghton Cumb 177 L7
Houghton Hants 34 D4
Houghton Nthumb 180 D5
Houghton Pembks 55 G5
Houghton W Susx 21 H4
Houghton Conquest C Beds 85 L7
Houghton Gate Dur 181 H8
Houghton Green E Susx 25 C3
Houghton Green Warrtn 130 C1
Houghton le Side Darltn 169 G6
Houghton-le-Spring Sundld 169 H4
Houghton on the Hill Leics 100 E3
Houghton Regis C Beds 68 C2
Houghton St Giles Norfk 121 K4
Hound Green Hants 49 H1
Houndslow Border 201 K4
Houndsmoor Somset 29 L5
Houndwood Border 213 J6
Hounslow Gt Lon 50 F4
Househill Highld 253 G1
Houses Hill Kirk 141 K4

Housieside Abers 257 G6
Houston Rens 208 C5
Houstry Highld 275 G1
Houton Ork 275 b5
Hove Br & H 22 D6
Hove Edge Calder 141 H3
Hoveringham Notts 117 J2
Hoveton Norfk 122 F7
Hovingham N York 161 L7
Howbrook Barns 141 M8
How Caple Herefs 63 J1
Howden E R Yk 143 J2
Howden-le-Wear Dur 168 F4
Howe Highld 280 D1
Howe IoM 154 b8
Howe N York 160 E6
Howe Norfk 106 F3
Howe Bridge Wigan 139 K7
Howe Bridge Crematorium
   Wigan 139 K7
Howe Green Essex 71 H4
Howegreen Essex 71 K6
Howell Lincs 118 F2
How End C Beds 85 K7
Howe of Teuchar Abers 268 E6
Howes D & G 177 G5
Howe Street Essex 71 G4
Howe Street Essex 88 D8
Howey Powys 78 B4
Howgate Cumb 164 C6
Howgate Mdloth 211 H7
Howgill Lancs 148 E6
Howick Nthumb 191 K3
Howle Wrekin 113 M6
Howle Hill Herefs 63 J3
Howlett End Essex 88 B8
Howley Somset 15 G1
How Mill Cumb 178 C7
Howmore W Isls 283 b10
Hownam Border 189 L2
Howrigg Cumb 165 K1
Howsham N Linc 144 D6
Howsham N York 151 M3
Howtel Nthumb 202 D6
Howt Green Kent 53 J6
Howton Herefs 62 E1
Howtown Cumb 166 B6
Howwood Rens 208 C7
Hoxne Suffk 106 D7
Hoy Ork 275 b5
Hoylake Wirral 128 F2
Hoyland Common Barns 142 B7
Hoyland Nether Barns 142 B7
Hoyland Swaine Barns 141 L6
Hoyle W Susx 20 E3
Hoyle Mill Barns 142 A6
Hubberholme N York 159 G7
Hubberston Pembks 54 E5
Hubbert's Bridge Lincs 119 J3
Huby N York 150 C6
Huby N York 151 J3
Huccaby Devon 12 F8
Hucclecote Gloucs 64 C4
Hucking Kent 53 H7
Hucknall Notts 116 F2
Huddersfield Kirk 141 H4
Huddersfield Crematorium
   Kirk 141 J4
Huddington Worcs 81 L4
Hudnall Herts 68 C4
Hudswell N York 159 L3
Huggate E R Yk 152 D5
Hugglescote Leics 99 L1
Hughenden Valley Bucks 67 L7
Hughley Shrops 96 D4
Hugh Town IoS 10 c3
Huish Devon 27 J8
Huish Wilts 47 H6
Huish Champflower Somset 29 J5
Huish Episcopi Somset 31 G5
Hulcote C Beds 85 J7
Hulcott Bucks 67 K4
Huldon Devon 14 B6
Hulland Derbys 115 L2
Hulland Ward Derbys 115 L2
Hullavington Wilts 46 C3
Hullbridge Essex 71 K8
Hull, Kingston upon C KuH 144 D2
Hulme Manch 140 C8
Hulme Staffs 114 C6
Hulme Warrtn 130 B2
Hulme End Staffs 132 B7
Hulme Walfield Ches E 131 G6
Hulse Heath Ches E 130 E3
Hulton Lane Ends Bolton 139 K6
Hulverstone IoW 18 F6
Hulver Street Norfk 105 J1
Hulver Street Suffk 107 K6
Humber Devon 13 D1
Humber Herefs 80 C4

Humberston NE Lin 145 J6
Humberstone C Leic 100 E2
Humberton N York 150 F2
Humbie E Loth 212 A6
Humbleton E R Yk 145 G1
Humbleton Nthumb 202 F7
Humby Lincs 118 D5
Hume Border 201 L5
Humshaugh Nthumb 179 L4
Huna Highld 280 E2
Huncoat Lancs 140 A2
Huncote Leics 100 B4
Hundalee Border 189 L5
Hundall Derbys 133 H4
Hunderthwaite Dur 168 C6
Hundleby Lincs 137 G6
Hundle Houses Lincs 119 H1
Hundleton Pembks 54 F6
Hundon Suffk 88 E5
Hundred End Lancs 138 E3
Hundred House Powys 78 F4
Hungarton Leics 100 F2
Hungerford Hants 33 L8
Hungerford Somset 29 J3
Hungerford W Berk 47 M5
Hungerford Newtown W Berk 47 M4
Hunger Hill Bolton 139 K6
Hunger Hill Lancs 139 G5
Hungerstone Herefs 80 B8
Hungerton Lincs 118 A5
Hungryhatton Shrops 113 L6
Hunmanby N York 163 K7
Hunningham Warwks 83 J2
Hunnington Worcs 98 B7
Hunsbury Hill Nhants 84 E4
Hunsdon Herts 69 L4
Hunsingore N York 150 F5
Hunslet Leeds 141 M2
Hunsonby Cumb 166 D4
Hunstanton Norfk 120 E3
Hunstanworth Dur 168 B1
Hunsterson Ches E 113 M2
Hunston Suffk 89 K2
Hunston W Susx 20 D6
Hunston Green Suffk 89 K2
Hunstrete BaNES 45 J6
Hunsworth Kirk 141 J2
Hunt End Worcs 82 B2
Hunter's Inn Devon 28 B1
Hunter's Quay Ag & B 207 K3
Huntham Somset 30 E5
Hunthill Lodge Angus 234 D1
Huntingdon Cambs 86 E1
Huntingfield Suffk 107 G8
Huntingford Dorset 32 D5
Huntington C York 151 K4
Huntington Ches W 129 K6
Huntington E Loth 212 B4
Huntington Herefs 79 J3
Huntington Herefs 80 B6
Huntington Staffs 98 B1
Huntley Gloucs 63 L3
Huntly Abers 255 L4
Hunton Hants 35 G3
Hunton Kent 39 H3
Hunton N York 160 B4
Hunton Bridge Herts 68 D7
Hunt's Corner Norfk 105 L5
Huntscott Somset 29 G2
Hunt's Cross Lpool 129 K3
Hunts Green Bucks 67 L6
Hunts Green Warwks 98 F4
Huntsham Devon 29 H6
Huntshaw Devon 27 J6
Huntshaw Cross Devon 27 J6
Huntspill Somset 30 D2
Huntstile Somset 30 C4
Huntworth Somset 30 D4
Hunwick Dur 168 F4
Hunworth Norfk 122 B4
Hurcott Somset 30 F7
Hurdcott Wilts 33 L4
Hurdsfield Ches E 131 H5
Hurley W & M 49 G3
Hurley Warwks 99 H4
Hurley Bottom W & M 49 G2
Hurley Common Warwks 99 H4
Hurlford E Ayrs 196 E4
Hurliston Green Lancs 138 E5
Hurn Dorset 18 A4
Hurn's End Lincs 119 M2
Hursley Hants 34 F6
Hurst Dorset 16 F4
Hurst N York 159 J6
Hurst Somset 31 G7
Hurst Wokham 49 J4
Hurstbourne Priors Hants 34 F2
Hurstbourne Tarrant Hants 48 A2
Hurst Green E Susx 24 D4
Hurst Green Essex 73 G4

Hurst Green Lancs..............148 B8
Hurst Green Surrey..............51 K8
Hurst Hill Dudley..............97 L4
Hurstley Herefs..............79 L5
Hurstpierpoint W Susx..............22 D4
Hurst Wickham W Susx..............22 D4
Hurstwood Lancs..............140 C2
Hurtiso Ork..............275 d5
Hurtmore Surrey..............36 E2
Hurworth Burn Dur..............169 L4
Hurworth-on-Tees Darltn..............169 J8
Hurworth Place Darltn..............160 D1
Hury Dur..............168 B6
Husbands Bosworth Leics..............100 E6
Husborne Crawley C Beds..............85 J8
Husthwaite N York..............161 H7
Hutcherleigh Devon..............8 A5
Hutcliffe Wood Crematorium
    Sheff..............133 G3
Hut Green N York..............142 F3
Huthwaite Notts..............133 J7
Huttoft Lincs..............137 K4
Hutton Border..............202 E2
Hutton Cumb..............166 B5
Hutton E R Yk..............152 F5
Hutton Essex..............70 F8
Hutton Lancs..............139 G2
Hutton N Som..............44 D7
Hutton Bonville N York..............160 E3
Hutton Buscel N York..............163 H6
Hutton Conyers N York..............160 D7
Hutton Cranswick E R Yk..............153 G5
Hutton End Cumb..............166 B3
Hutton Hang N York..............159 L5
Hutton Henry Dur..............169 L3
Hutton-le-Hole N York..............162 B4
Hutton Lowcross R & Cl..............170 E7
Hutton Magna Dur..............168 E8
Hutton Mulgrave N York..............162 E1
Hutton Roof Cumb..............157 J7
Hutton Roof Cumb..............165 L4
Hutton Rudby N York..............161 G2
Hutton Sessay N York..............161 G7
Hutton Wandesley N York..............151 H5
Huxham Devon..............13 M3
Huxham Green Somset..............31 K4
Huxley Ches W..............129 L7
Huyton Knows..............129 K2
Hycemoor Cumb..............155 K5
Hyde Gloucs..............64 C6
Hyde Hants..............33 L8
Hyde Tamesd..............131 J1
Hyde End Wokham..............49 H5
Hyde Heath Bucks..............68 B7
Hyde Lea Staffs..............114 E7
Hydestile Surrey..............36 E3
Hykeham Moor Lincs..............135 J6
Hyndford Bridge S Lans..............198 F5
Hynish Ag & B..............224 C2
Hyssington Powys..............95 H4
Hystfield Gloucs..............63 K7
Hythe Essex..............72 E2
Hythe Hants..............19 G2
Hythe Kent..............41 G8
Hythe Somset..............44 F8
Hythe End W & M..............50 C4
Hyton Cumb..............155 K5

I

Ibberton Dorset..............16 F1
Ible Derbys..............132 E8
Ibsley Hants..............18 A2
Ibstock Leics..............99 L2
Ibstone Bucks..............67 J8
Ibthorpe Hants..............48 A8
Iburndale N York..............162 F1
Ibworth Hants..............48 E7
Icelton N Som..............44 D6
Ichrachan Ag & B..............217 G1
Ickburgh Norfk..............105 G4
Ickenham Gt Lon..............50 D2
Ickford Bucks..............66 F5
Ickham Kent..............41 H4
Ickleford Herts..............68 F1
Icklesham E Susx..............24 F4
Ickleton Cambs..............87 K6
Icklingham Suffk..............88 F1
Ickornshaw N York..............149 J3
Ickwell Green C Beds..............86 C6
Icomb Gloucs..............65 J3
Idbury Oxon..............65 K3
Iddesleigh Devon..............12 D1
Ide Devon..............13 L4
Ideford Devon..............13 K7
Ide Hill Kent..............38 D3
Iden E Susx..............25 G3
Iden Green Kent..............39 J6
Iden Green Kent..............39 K7

Idle C Brad..............149 M8
Idless Cnwll..............4 D5
Idlicote Warwks..............83 G6
Idmiston Wilts..............33 L3
Idole Carmth..............58 D5
Idridgehay Derbys..............115 M2
Idrigill Highld..............258 F4
Idstone Oxon..............47 K2
Iffley Oxon..............66 D6
Ifield W Susx..............37 K3
Ifold W Susx..............36 F4
Iford Bmouth..............18 A5
Iford E Susx..............22 F5
Ifton Mons..............44 F1
Ifton Heath Shrops..............112 E4
Ightfield Shrops..............113 K4
Ightham Kent..............38 F2
Iken Suffk..............91 J4
Ilam Staffs..............115 J2
Ilchester Somset..............31 H6
Ilderton Nthumb..............190 E4
Ilford Gt Lon..............51 L2
Ilford Somset..............30 E7
Ilfracombe Devon..............27 J2
Ilkeston Derbys..............116 D3
Ilketshall St Andrew Suffk..............107 H6
Ilketshall St John Suffk..............107 H6
Ilketshall St Lawrence Suffk..............107 H6
Ilketshall St Margaret Suffk..............107 G6
Ilkley C Brad..............149 K6
Illand Cnwll..............11 K7
Illey Dudley..............98 B7
Illidge Green Ches E..............130 F7
Illingworth Calder..............141 G2
Illogan Cnwll..............3 H2
Illston on the Hill Leics..............100 F3
Ilmer Bucks..............67 J6
Ilmington Warwks..............82 F6
Ilminster Somset..............30 E7
Ilsington Devon..............13 H7
Ilsington Dorset..............16 E4
Ilston Swans..............57 G6
Ilton N York..............160 B7
Ilton Somset..............30 E7
Imachar N Ayrs..............194 D3
Immingham NE Lin..............144 F5
Immingham Dock NE Lin..............145 G4
Impington Cambs..............87 J3
Ince Ches W..............129 K4
Ince Blundell Sefton..............138 C7
Ince-in-Makerfield Wigan..............139 J6
Inchbae Lodge Hotel Highld..............262 C6
Inchbare Angus..............234 F2
Inchberry Moray..............266 F5
Incheril Highld..............261 G7
Inchinnan Rens..............208 E5
Inchlaggan Highld..............239 K3
Inchmichael P & K..............222 D2
Inchnacardoch Hotel Highld..............240 C2
Inchnadamph Highld..............271 H4
Inchture P & K..............222 D2
Inchvuilt Highld..............249 L4
Inchyra P & K..............222 C3
Indian Queens Cnwll..............4 E3
Ingate Place Suffk..............107 J5
Ingatestone Essex..............70 F7
Ingbirchworth Barns..............141 K6
Ingerthorpe N York..............150 C3
Ingestre Staffs..............114 F6
Ingham Lincs..............135 J3
Ingham Norfk..............123 H6
Ingham Suffk..............89 G1
Ingham Corner Norfk..............123 H6
Ingleborough Norfk..............120 B8
Ingleby Derbys..............116 B6
Ingleby Arncliffe N York..............161 G3
Ingleby Barwick S on T..............170 B7
Ingleby Cross N York..............161 G3
Ingleby Greenhow N York..............161 J2
Ingleigh Green Devon..............12 E1
Inglesbatch BaNES..............45 L6
Inglesham Swindn..............65 J7
Ingleston D & G..............176 C6
Ingleton Dur..............168 F6
Ingleton N York..............158 B8
Inglewhite Lancs..............147 L7
Ingoe Nthumb..............180 C4
Ingol Lancs..............139 G1
Ingoldisthorpe Norfk..............120 F5
Ingoldmells Lincs..............137 K6
Ingoldsby Lincs..............118 D5
Ingram Nthumb..............190 E3
Ingrave Essex..............52 D1
Ingrow C Brad..............149 J7
Ings Cumb..............157 G3
Ingst S Glos..............45 H2
Ingthorpe Rutlnd..............101 M2
Ingworth Norfk..............122 D5
Inkberrow Worcs..............82 B4
Inkerman Dur..............168 E3

Inkhorn Abers..............257 G4
Inkpen W Berk..............48 A6
Inkstack Highld..............280 C2
Inmarsh Wilts..............46 D6
Innellan Ag & B..............207 J5
Innerleithen Border..............200 D6
Innerleven Fife..............222 F7
Innermessan D & G..............172 D2
Innerwick E Loth..............212 F4
Innesmill Moray..............266 F3
Insch Abers..............256 A6
Insh Highld..............241 L3
Inskip Lancs..............147 J8
Inskip Moss Side Lancs..............147 J8
Instow Devon..............27 H5
Insworke Cnwll..............6 E4
Intake Sheff..............133 H3
Inver Abers..............243 H5
Inver Highld..............264 D3
Inver P & K..............232 F7
Inverailort Highld..............238 B7
Inveralligin Highld..............260 D8
Inverallochy Abers..............269 J3
Inveran Highld..............272 E8
Inveraray Ag & B..............217 H5
Inverarish Highld..............247 H2
Inverarity Angus..............234 C6
Inverarnan Stirlg..............218 D3
Inverasdale Highld..............260 C3
Inverbeg Ag & B..............218 E7
Inverbervie Abers..............235 K1
Inver-boyndie Abers..............268 B3
Invercreran House Hotel
    Ag & B..............229 G6
Inverdruie Highld..............242 B1
Inveresk E Loth..............211 K5
Inveresragan Ag & B..............228 F8
Inverey Abers..............242 E5
Inverfarigaig Highld..............250 F7
Inverfolla Ag & B..............228 E6
Invergarry Highld..............240 A3
Invergeldie P & K..............220 C2
Invergloy Highld..............239 L6
Invergordon Highld..............263 J6
Invergowrie P & K..............222 F1
Inverguseran Highld..............238 B2
Inverhadden P & K..............231 J4
Inverherive Hotel Stirlg..............218 E2
Inverie Highld..............238 B3
Inverinan Ag & B..............216 F4
Inverinate Highld..............248 E1
Inverkeilor Angus..............235 G5
Inverkeithing Fife..............210 F2
Inverkeithny Abers..............268 A6
Inverkip Inver..............207 K4
Inverkirkaig Highld..............270 E4
Inverlael Highld..............261 K3
Inverlair Highld..............240 B7
Inverliever Lodge Ag & B..............216 D6
Inverlochy Ag & B..............217 K2
Invermark Angus..............244 A7
Invermoriston Highld..............250 D8
Invernaver Highld..............278 B4
Inverness Highld..............251 H3
Inverness Crematorium
    Highld..............251 H3
Invernoaden Ag & B..............217 J7
Inveroran Hotel Ag & B..............229 M7
Inverquharity Angus..............234 B4
Inverquhomery Abers..............257 J2
Inverroy Highld..............239 M7
Inversanda Highld..............228 E3
Invershiel Highld..............248 F7
Invershin Highld..............272 E8
Invershore Highld..............275 H1
Inversnaid Hotel Stirlg..............218 E5
Inverugie Abers..............269 L6
Inveruglas Ag & B..............218 D5
Inveruglass Highld..............241 L3
Inverurie Abers..............256 D7
Inwardleigh Devon..............12 D3
Inworth Essex..............72 C3
Iochdar W Isls..............283 b9
Iona Ag & B..............226 B7
Iping W Susx..............36 C6
Ipplepen Devon..............8 B2
Ipsden Oxon..............48 F2
Ipstones Staffs..............115 G2
Ipswich Suffk..............90 E6
Ipswich Crematorium Suffk..............90 E6
Irby Wirral..............128 F3
Irby in the Marsh Lincs..............137 J7
Irby upon Humber NE Lin..............145 G6
Irchester Nhants..............85 H2
Ireby Cumb..............165 H3
Ireby Lancs..............157 L7
Ireland C Beds..............86 C7
Ireleth Cumb..............156 B7
Ireshopeburn Dur..............167 K3
Ireton Wood Derbys..............115 M2

Irlam Salfd..............130 E1
Irnham Lincs..............118 D6
Iron Acton S Glos..............45 K2
Iron Bridge Cambs..............103 K4
Ironbridge Wrekin..............96 F3
Iron Cross Warwks..............82 C5
Ironmacannie D & G..............185 G2
Irons Bottom Surrey..............37 K2
Ironville Derbys..............116 D1
Irstead Norfk..............123 H7
Irthington Cumb..............178 C6
Irthlingborough Nhants..............85 J1
Irton N York..............163 H6
Irvine N Ayrs..............196 C3
Isauld Highld..............279 G3
Isbister Shet..............281 d3
Isbister Shet..............281 f5
Isfield E Susx..............23 G4
Isham Nhants..............101 J4
Isington Hants..............36 A2
Islandpool Worcs..............97 K7
Islay Ag & B..............204 E1
Isle Abbotts Somset..............30 E6
Isle Brewers Somset..............30 E6
Isleham Cambs..............104 C8
Isle of Dogs Gt Lon..............51 K3
Isle of Lewis W Isls..............282 f3
Isle of Man IoM..............154 e5
Isle of Mull Ag & B..............227 H5
Isle of Sheppey Kent..............40 C2
Isle of Skye Highld..............246 F1
Isle of Walney Cumb..............146 D3
Isle of Whithorn D & G..............174 D7
Isle of Wight IoW..............19 H4
Isle of Wight Crematorium
    IoW..............19 J5
Isleornsay Highld..............247 L6
Islesteps D & G..............176 C2
Islet Village Guern..............9 k2
Isleworth Gt Lon..............50 F4
Isley Walton Leics..............116 C6
Islibhig W Isls..............282 d3
Islington Gt Lon..............51 J2
Islington Crematorium Gt Lon..............51 H1
Islip Nhants..............101 L7
Islip Oxon..............66 D4
Islivig W Isls..............282 d3
Isombridge Wrekin..............96 E1
Istead Rise Kent..............52 D5
Itchen Abbas Hants..............35 H4
Itchen Stoke Hants..............35 H4
Itchingfield W Susx..............37 H5
Itchington S Glos..............45 K2
Itteringham Norfk..............122 C5
Itton Devon..............12 F3
Itton Mons..............62 F8
Itton Common Mons..............62 F8
Ivegill Cumb..............165 M2
Ivelet N York..............159 G3
Iver Bucks..............50 D3
Iver Heath Bucks..............50 C2
Iveston Dur..............168 E1
Ivinghoe Bucks..............68 B4
Ivinghoe Aston Bucks..............68 B3
Ivington Herefs..............80 B4
Ivington Green Herefs..............80 B4
Ivybridge Devon..............7 J4
Ivychurch Kent..............25 J2
Ivy Cross Dorset..............32 E6
Ivy Hatch Kent..............38 F3
Ivy Todd Norfk..............105 H2
Iwade Kent..............40 A2
Iwerne Courtney or Shroton
    Dorset..............32 E8
Iwerne Minster Dorset..............32 E8
Ixworth Suffk..............89 J1
Ixworth Thorpe Suffk..............89 J1

J

Jack Green Lancs..............139 J3
Jack Hill N York..............150 B5
Jack-in-the-Green Devon..............14 B3
Jack's Bush Hants..............34 C3
Jacksdale Notts..............116 D1
Jackson Bridge Kirk..............141 J6
Jackton S Lans..............209 G8
Jacobstow Cnwll..............11 H3
Jacobstowe Devon..............12 E2
Jacobs Well Surrey..............50 C8
Jameston Pembks..............55 H7
Jamestown Highld..............262 E8
Jamestown W Duns..............208 C3
Janetstown Highld..............275 G2
Janets-town Highld..............280 D6
Jardine Hall D & G..............176 E1
Jarrow S Tyne..............181 H6
Jarvis Brook E Susx..............38 C5
Jasper's Green Essex..............71 H2

Jawcraig - Kilmuir 325

Jawcraig Falk 209 M4
Jaywick Essex 73 H4
Jealott's Hill Br For 49 L4
Jeater Houses N York 160 F4
Jedburgh Border 189 H2
Jeffreyston Pembks 55 J5
Jemimaville Highld 263 K7
Jerbourg Guern 9 k4
Jersey Jersey 9 d2
Jersey Crematorium Jersey 9 d3
Jersey Marine Neath 57 K6
Jerusalem Lincs 135 J5
Jesmond N u Ty 181 G5
Jevington E Susx 23 J7
Jingle Street Mons 62 F5
Jockey End Herts 68 D4
Jodrell Bank Ches E 130 F5
Johnby Cumb 166 B4
John o' Groats Highld 280 E2
John's Cross E Susx 24 D3
Johnshaven Abers 235 K2
Johnson's Street Norfk 123 H8
Johnston Pembks 54 F5
Johnstone D & G 187 K6
Johnstone Rens 208 D6
Johnstonebridge D & G 187 G7
Johnstown Carmth 58 D5
Johnstown Wrexhm 112 D2
Joppa C Edin 211 K4
Joppa Cerdgn 77 G2
Joppa S Ayrs 196 E7
Jordans Bucks 50 B1
Jordanston Pembks 74 F5
Jordanthorpe Sheff 133 G3
Joyden's Wood Kent 52 B4
Jubilee Corner Kent 39 L4
Jump Barns 142 B7
Jumper's Town E Susx 38 C6
Juniper Nthumb 179 L7
Juniper Green C Edin 211 G5
Jura Ag & B 215 G7
Jurby IoM 154 e3
Jurston Devon 13 G5

K

Kaber Cumb 167 J8
Kaimend S Lans 199 G4
Kames Ag & B 206 F5
Kames E Ayrs 197 K5
Kea Cnwll 4 C6
Keadby N Linc 143 L5
Keal Cotes Lincs 137 G7
Kearby Town End N York 150 E6
Kearsley Bolton 139 M6
Kearsley Nthumb 180 B4
Kearsney Kent 41 J6
Kearstwick Cumb 157 K6
Kearton N York 159 H3
Keasden N York 148 C3
Keaton Devon 7 J4
Keckwick Halton 130 B3
Keddington Lincs 136 F2
Keddington Corner Lincs 137 G2
Kedington Suffk 88 E6
Kedleston Derbys 116 A3
Keelby Lincs 144 F5
Keele Staffs 114 C3
Keele University Staffs 114 C3
Keeley Green Bed 85 K6
Keelham C Brad 141 G1
Keeston Pembks 54 E3
Keevil Wilts 46 D7
Kegworth Leics 116 E6
Kehelland Cnwll 3 G3
Keig Abers 256 A7
Keighley C Brad 149 J7
Keighley Crematorium C Brad 149 J8
Keilarsbrae Clacks 220 F8
Keillour P & K 221 H2
Keiloch Abers 243 G5
Keils Ag & B 205 H3
Keinton Mandeville Somset 31 J5
Keir Mill D & G 186 C7
Keirsleywell Row Nthumb 179 H8
Keisby Lincs 118 D6
Keisley Cumb 167 G6
Keiss Highld 280 D4
Keith Moray 267 J6
Keithick P & K 233 J7
Keithock Angus 234 F3
Keithtown Highld 262 F8
Kelbrook Lancs 148 F7
Kelby Lincs 118 D3
Keld Cumb 166 D7
Keld N York 158 F2
Keld Head N York 162 D5
Keldholme N York 162 C5
Kelfield N Linc 143 L7
Kelfield N York 151 J8
Kelham Notts 134 F8
Kelhead D & G 176 F5
Kellacott Devon 12 A5
Kellamergh Lancs 138 E2
Kellas Angus 234 C8
Kellas Moray 266 D5
Kellaton Devon 8 B7
Kelleth Cumb 157 L2
Kelling Norfk 122 B3
Kellington N York 142 E3
Kelloe Dur 169 K3
Kelloholm D & G 185 J1
Kells Cumb 164 C7
Kelly Devon 11 M6
Kelly Bray Cnwll 11 L8
Kelmarsh Nhants 101 G7
Kelmscott Oxon 65 K7
Kelsale Suffk 91 J2
Kelsall Ches W 129 M6
Kelshall Herts 87 G7
Kelsick Cumb 165 G1
Kelso Border 201 M6
Kelstedge Derbys 133 G7
Kelstern Lincs 136 D2
Kelsterton Flints 129 G5
Kelston BaNES 45 K5
Keltneyburn P & K 231 L5
Kelton D & G 176 C5
Kelty Fife 221 L8
Kelvedon Essex 72 C3
Kelvedon Hatch Essex 70 E7
Kelynack Cnwll 2 B5
Kemacott Devon 28 B2
Kemback Fife 223 G4
Kemberton Shrops 97 G3
Kemble Gloucs 64 E7
Kemble Wick Gloucs 64 E7
Kemerton Worcs 81 L7
Kemeys Commander Mons 62 D6
Kemnay Abers 256 D8
Kempe's Corner Kent 40 D6
Kempley Gloucs 63 K1
Kempley Green Gloucs 63 K1
Kempsey Worcs 81 J5
Kempsford Gloucs 65 H7
Kemps Green Warwks 82 D1
Kempshott Hants 35 J1
Kempston Bed 85 K5
Kempston Hardwick Bed 85 K6
Kempton Shrops 95 J6
Kemp Town Br & H 22 E6
Kemsing Kent 52 C7
Kemsley Kent 40 B2
Kemsley Street Kent 53 H6
Kenardington Kent 25 H1
Kenchester Herefs 80 B6
Kencot Oxon 65 K6
Kendal Cumb 157 H4
Kenderchurch Herefs 62 E2
Kendleshire S Glos 45 K3
Kenfig Brdgnd 42 B5
Kenfig Hill Brdgnd 42 C5
Kenilworth Warwks 83 G1
Kenley Gt Lon 51 J7
Kenley Shrops 96 D3
Kenmore Highld 260 B8
Kenmore P & K 231 L6
Kenn Devon 13 L5
Kenn N Som 44 E5
Kennacraig Ag & B 206 C6
Kennards House Cnwll 11 K6
Kenneggy Cnwll 2 F5
Kennerleigh Devon 13 J1
Kennessee Green Sefton 138 D7
Kennet Clacks 210 B1
Kennethmont Abers 255 L6
Kennett Cambs 88 D2
Kennford Devon 13 L5
Kenninghall Norfk 105 L6
Kennington Kent 40 D6
Kennington Oxon 66 D6
Kennoway Fife 222 F6
Kenny Somset 30 D7
Kennyhill Suffk 104 D7
Kennythorpe N York 152 B3
Kenovay Ag & B 224 C6
Kensaleyre Highld 259 G6
Kensington Gt Lon 51 H3
Kensworth Common C Beds 68 C3
Kentallen Highld 228 F4
Kent and Sussex Crematorium Kent 38 F6
Kentchurch Herefs 62 E2
Kentford Suffk 88 E2
Kent Green Ches E 131 G8
Kentisbeare Devon 14 C1
Kentisbury Devon 27 L2
Kentisbury Ford Devon 27 L2
Kentish Town Gt Lon 51 H2
Kentmere Cumb 157 G2
Kenton Devon 13 M6
Kenton Gt Lon 50 F1
Kenton N u Ty 180 F5
Kenton Suffk 90 E2
Kenton Bankfoot N u Ty 180 F5
Kentra Highld 237 J6
Kents Bank Cumb 156 F7
Kent's Green Gloucs 63 L2
Kent's Oak Hants 34 D6
Kent Street E Susx 24 E4
Kent Street Kent 39 G2
Kenwick Shrops 112 F5
Kenwyn Cnwll 4 D5
Kenyon Warrtn 139 J8
Keoldale Highld 276 F3
Keppoch Highld 248 E6
Kepwick N York 161 G4
Keresley Covtry 99 J6
Kermincham Ches E 130 F6
Kernborough Devon 8 B6
Kerne Bridge Herefs 63 H3
Kerrera Ag & B 216 C2
Kerridge Ches E 131 J4
Kerridge-end Ches E 131 J4
Kerris Cnwll 2 C5
Kerry Powys 94 E5
Kerrycroy Ag & B 207 J6
Kersall Notts 134 E7
Kersbrook Devon 14 C6
Kerscott Devon 27 L5
Kersey Suffk 89 K6
Kersey Tye Suffk 89 K6
Kersey Upland Suffk 89 K6
Kershader W Isls 282 f4
Kershopefoot Cumb 178 B2
Kersoe Worcs 82 A7
Kerswell Devon 14 C2
Kerswell Green Worcs 81 K6
Kerthen Wood Cnwll 2 F4
Kesgrave Suffk 90 F6
Kessingland Suffk 107 L6
Kessingland Beach Suffk 107 L6
Kestle Cnwll 5 G5
Kestle Mill Cnwll 4 D3
Keston Gt Lon 51 L6
Keswick Cumb 165 J6
Keswick Norfk 106 E2
Ketsby Lincs 137 G4
Kettering Nhants 101 J7
Kettering Crematorium Nhants 101 J7
Ketteringham Norfk 106 D3
Kettins P & K 233 K7
Kettlebaston Suffk 89 K5
Kettlebridge Fife 222 E5
Kettlebrook Staffs 99 G3
Kettleburgh Suffk 91 G3
Kettle Green Herts 69 L3
Kettleholm D & G 176 F3
Kettleness N York 171 J7
Kettleshulme Ches E 131 K4
Kettlesing N York 150 B4
Kettlesing Bottom N York 150 B4
Kettlestone Norfk 121 L5
Kettlethorpe Lincs 135 G4
Kettletoft Ork 275 e2
Kettlewell N York 149 H2
Ketton Rutlnd 101 L3
Kew Gt Lon 50 F4
Kewstoke N Som 44 C6
Kexbrough Barns 141 M6
Kexby C York 151 L5
Kexby Lincs 135 H3
Key Green Ches E 131 H7
Key Green N York 162 D2
Keyham Leics 100 E2
Keyhaven Hants 18 D5
Keyingham E R Yk 145 H3
Keymer W Susx 22 D4
Keynsham BaNES 45 K5
Keysoe Bed 86 B3
Keysoe Row Bed 86 B3
Keyston Cambs 102 A8
Key Street Kent 53 J6
Keyworth Notts 117 G5
Kibbear Somset 30 B6
Kibblesworth Gatesd 181 G7
Kibworth Beauchamp Leics 100 F4
Kibworth Harcourt Leics 100 F4
Kidbrooke Gt Lon 51 L4
Kidburngill Cumb 164 E6
Kiddemore Green Staffs 97 J2
Kidderminster Worcs 97 J8
Kiddington Oxon 66 B3
Kidd's Moor Norfk 106 C3
Kidlington Oxon 66 D4
Kidmore End Oxon 49 G3
Kidsdale D & G 174 C7
Kidsgrove Staffs 131 G8
Kidstones N York 159 G6
Kidwelly Carmth 56 D3
Kiel Crofts Ag & B 228 D7
Kielder Nthumb 189 H7
Kiells Ag & B 204 F3
Kilbarchan Rens 208 C6
Kilbeg Highld 247 K7
Kilberry Ag & B 206 A6
Kilbirnie N Ayrs 208 A8
Kilbride Ag & B 207 G5
Kilbride Ag & B 215 L8
Kilbuiack Moray 266 B4
Kilburn Derbys 116 C2
Kilburn Gt Lon 51 H2
Kilburn N York 161 H6
Kilby Leics 100 D4
Kilchamaig Ag & B 206 C6
Kilchattan Ag & B 207 H8
Kilchattan Ag & B 214 D5
Kilcheran Ag & B 228 C7
Kilchoan Highld 236 F7
Kilchoman Ag & B 204 B4
Kilchrenan Ag & B 217 G3
Kilconquhar Fife 223 H6
Kilcot Gloucs 63 K2
Kilcoy Highld 251 G2
Kilcreggan Ag & B 207 L3
Kildale N York 161 K1
Kildalloig Ag & B 192 F4
Kildary Highld 263 K5
Kildavaig Ag & B 206 F6
Kildavanan Ag & B 207 G5
Kildonan Highld 274 B4
Kildonan N Ayrs 195 G6
Kildonan Lodge Highld 274 B4
Kildonnan Highld 236 F3
Kildrochet House D & G 172 D4
Kildrummy Abers 255 J8
Kildwick N York 149 H6
Kilfinan Ag & B 206 E3
Kilfinnan Highld 239 M4
Kilford Denbgs 128 C6
Kilgetty Pembks 55 K5
Kilgrammie S Ayrs 183 G3
Kilgwrrwg Common Mons 62 F7
Kilham E R Yk 153 G3
Kilham Nthumb 202 D6
Kilkenneth Ag & B 224 B6
Kilkenzie Ag & B 192 D3
Kilkerran Ag & B 192 E4
Kilkhampton Cnwll 26 D8
Killamarsh Derbys 133 J3
Killay Swans 57 H6
Killearn Stirlg 208 E2
Killen Highld 263 J8
Killerby Darltn 169 G6
Killerton Devon 14 A3
Killichonan P & K 231 G4
Killiechonate Highld 239 L7
Killiechronan Ag & B 227 G4
Killiecrankie P & K 232 D3
Killilan Highld 248 F5
Killimster Highld 280 D5
Killin Stirlg 231 G8
Killinghall N York 150 C4
Killington Cumb 157 K5
Killington Devon 28 B2
Killingworth N Tyne 181 G5
Killiow Cnwll 4 C6
Killochyett Border 200 F4
Kilmacolm Inver 208 B5
Kilmahog Stirlg 219 K5
Kilmahumaig Ag & B 216 B8
Kilmaluag Highld 259 G2
Kilmany Fife 222 F3
Kilmarnock E Ayrs 196 E3
Kilmartin Ag & B 216 C7
Kilmaurs E Ayrs 196 E3
Kilmelford Ag & B 216 C4
Kilmersdon Somset 45 K8
Kilmeston Hants 35 J5
Kilmichael Ag & B 192 E4
Kilmichael Glassary Ag & B 216 D8
Kilmichael of Inverlussa Ag & B 206 B2
Kilmington Devon 15 G3
Kilmington Wilts 32 C3
Kilmington Common Wilts 32 C4
Kilmington Street Wilts 32 C4
Kilmorack Highld 250 E3
Kilmore Ag & B 216 D2
Kilmore Highld 247 K7
Kilmory Ag & B 205 M2
Kilmory Highld 237 G6
Kilmory N Ayrs 193 K4
Kilmuir Highld 251 J2
Kilmuir Highld 258 D7

Kilmuir Highld 258 F3
Kilmuir Highld 263 K5
Kilmun Ag & B 207 K3
Kilnave Ag & B 204 D2
Kilncadzow S Lans 198 L3
Kilndown Kent 39 H6
Kiln Green Wokham 49 K3
Kilnhill Cumb 165 H4
Kilnhouses Ches W 130 C6
Kilnhurst Rothm 142 C8
Kilninver Ag & B 216 C3
Kiln Pit Hill Nthumb 180 C7
Kilnsea E R Yk 145 L4
Kilnsey N York 149 H2
Kilnwick E R Yk 152 F6
Kilnwick Percy E R Yk 152 C6
Kiloran Ag & B 214 D5
Kilpatrick N Ayrs 194 D5
Kilpeck Herefs 62 F1
Kilpin E R Yk 143 K2
Kilpin Pike E R Yk 143 J2
Kilrenny Fife 223 K6
Kilsby Nhants 84 A1
Kilspindie P & K 222 C2
Kilstay D & G 172 E7
Kilsyth N Lans 209 J3
Kiltarlity Highld 250 E3
Kilton R & Cl 171 G7
Kilton Thorpe R & Cl 171 G7
Kilvaxter Highld 258 F3
Kilve Somset 29 L2
Kilvington Notts 117 L3
Kilwinning N Ayrs 196 C3
Kimberley Norfk 106 B3
Kimberley Notts 116 E3
Kimberworth Rothm 133 H1
Kimblesworth Dur 169 H1
Kimble Wick Bucks 67 J5
Kimbolton Cambs 86 B2
Kimbolton Herefs 80 C3
Kimcote Leics 100 D6
Kimmeridge Dorset 17 H6
Kimmerston Nthumb 202 E6
Kimpton Hants 34 C2
Kimpton Herts 68 F3
Kimworthy Devon 26 E8
Kinbrace Highld 273 L2
Kinbuck Stirlg 220 D6
Kincaple Fife 223 H3
Kincardine Fife 210 B2
Kincardine Highld 263 G2
Kincardine O'Neil Abers 244 D4
Kinclaven P & K 233 H7
Kincorth C Aber 245 L3
Kincorth House Moray 265 G7
Kincraig Highld 241 M2
Kincraigie P & K 232 E5
Kindallachan P & K 232 E5
Kinerarach Ag & B 205 L5
Kineton Gloucs 65 G2
Kineton Warwks 83 H5
Kinfauns P & K 222 B3
Kingarth Ag & B 207 H7
Kingcausie Abers 245 J3
Kingcoed Mons 62 E6
Kingerby Lincs 135 L1
Kingford Devon 11 K2
Kingham Oxon 65 K2
Kingholm Quay D & G 176 C4
Kinghorn Fife 211 J2
Kinglassie Fife 222 C7
Kingoldrum Angus 233 M4
Kingoodie P & K 222 F1
King's Acre Herefs 80 B7
Kingsand Cnwll 6 E5
Kingsash Bucks 67 L6
Kingsbarns Fife 223 K5
Kingsbridge Devon 7 L6
Kingsbridge Somset 29 H3
Kings Bridge Swans 57 G5
King's Bromley Staffs 115 J8
Kingsburgh Highld 258 F5
Kingsbury Gt Lon 51 G1
Kingsbury Warwks 99 G4
Kingsbury Episcopi Somset 31 G6
King's Caple Herefs 63 H2
Kingsclere Hants 48 D7
King's Cliffe Nhants 101 M4
Kingscote Gloucs 64 B7
Kingscott Devon 27 K7
King's Coughton Warwks 82 C3
Kingscross N Ayrs 195 G5
Kingsdon Somset 31 H5
Kingsdown Kent 41 L5
Kingsdown Swindn 47 H1
Kingsdown Wilts 46 A5
Kingsdown Crematorium
  Swindn 47 H1
Kingseat Fife 210 F1
Kingsey Bucks 67 H6

Kingsfold W Susx 37 J4
Kingsford C Aber 245 J2
Kingsford E Ayrs 196 E2
Kingsford Worcs 97 J7
Kingsgate Kent 41 L1
Kings Green Gloucs 81 H8
Kingshall Street Suffk 89 J3
Kingsheanton Devon 27 K3
Kings Heath Birm 98 D7
Kings Hill Kent 39 H2
King's Hill Wsall 98 C4
Kings House Hotel Highld 229 L4
Kingshouse Hotel Stirlg 219 J3
Kingshurst Solhll 98 F5
Kingside Hill Cumb 177 G8
Kingskerswell Devon 8 C1
Kingskettle Fife 222 E6
Kingsland Dorset 15 K3
Kingsland Herefs 80 B3
Kingsland IoA 124 D3
Kings Langley Herts 68 D6
Kingsley Ches W 130 A5
Kingsley Hants 36 B3
Kingsley Staffs 115 G2
Kingsley Green W Susx 36 D5
Kingsley Park Nhants 84 E3
Kingslow Shrops 97 H4
King's Lynn Norfk 120 D7
Kings Meaburn Cumb 166 E6
Kingsmead Hants 35 J8
King's Mills Guern 9 i3
King's Moss St Hel 139 G7
Kingsmuir Angus 234 D5
Kings Muir Border 200 B5
Kingsmuir Fife 223 J5
Kings Newnham Warwks 99 M7
King's Newton Derbys 116 C6
Kingsnorth Kent 40 C7
King's Norton Birm 98 D7
King's Norton Leics 100 F4
Kings Nympton Devon 28 B7
King's Pyon Herefs 80 B5
Kings Ripton Cambs 102 F8
King's Somborne Hants 34 D4
King's Stag Dorset 32 B8
King's Stanley Gloucs 64 A6
King's Sutton Nhants 83 L8
Kingstanding Birm 98 D4
Kingsteignton Devon 13 K8
King Sterndale Derbys 132 B5
Kingsthorne Herefs 63 G5
Kingsthorpe Nhants 84 E3
Kingston Cambs 87 G4
Kingston Cnwll 11 L7
Kingston Devon 7 J5
Kingston Devon 14 C5
Kingston Dorset 16 E1
Kingston Dorset 17 J6
Kingston E Loth 212 C3
Kingston Hants 18 A3
Kingston IoW 19 H7
Kingston Kent 41 G5
Kingston W Susx 21 J6
Kingston Bagpuize Oxon 66 B7
Kingston Blount Oxon 67 H7
Kingston Deverill Wilts 32 D3
Kingstone Herefs 80 A8
Kingstone Somset 30 E8
Kingstone Staffs 115 H5
Kingstone Winslow Oxon 47 K2
Kingston Lisle Oxon 47 L2
Kingston near Lewes E Susx 22 F5
Kingston on Soar Notts 116 E6
Kingston on Spey Moray 267 G3
Kingston Russell Dorset 16 A4
Kingston St Mary Somset 30 B5
Kingston Seymour N Som 44 E5
Kingston Stert Oxon 67 H7
Kingston upon Hull C KuH 144 D2
Kingston upon Thames
  Gt Lon 50 F5
Kingston upon Thames
  Crematorium Gt Lon 51 G5
Kingstown Cumb 177 L7
King's Walden Herts 68 F2
Kingswear Devon 8 D4
Kingswells C Aber 245 J2
Kings Weston Bristl 45 G3
Kingswinford Dudley 97 K5
Kingswood Bucks 67 G3
Kingswood Gloucs 63 L8
Kingswood Kent 39 L3
Kingswood Powys 94 F3
Kingswood S Glos 45 J4
Kingswood Somset 29 K3
Kingswood Surrey 51 H7
Kingswood Warwks 82 E1
Kingswood Brook Warwks 82 E1
Kingswood Common Herefs 79 K4
Kingswood Common Staffs 97 J3

Kings Worthy Hants 35 G4
Kingthorpe Lincs 136 B4
Kington Herefs 79 K4
Kington S Glos 45 J1
Kington Worcs 82 A4
Kington Langley Wilts 46 D3
Kington Magna Dorset 32 C6
Kington St Michael Wilts 46 C3
Kingussie Highld 241 M3
Kinharrachie Abers 257 G5
Kinharvie D & G 176 B5
Kinkell Bridge P & K 221 G4
Kinknockie Abers 257 J3
Kinleith C Edin 211 G5
Kinlet Shrops 97 G7
Kinloch Highld 246 E8
Kinloch Highld 271 K1
Kinloch Highld 277 J5
Kinloch P & K 233 H6
Kinlochard Stirlg 219 G6
Kinlochbervie Highld 276 C5
Kinlocheil Highld 238 F7
Kinlochewe Highld 261 G7
Kinloch Hourn Highld 238 F2
Kinlochlaggan Highld 240 F5
Kinlochleven Highld 229 K3
Kinlochmoidart Highld 237 K6
Kinlochnanuagh Highld 237 L4
Kinloch Rannoch P & K 231 J4
Kinloss Moray 265 H7
Kinmel Bay Conwy 127 K4
Kinmuck Abers 256 E7
Kinmundy Abers 256 F8
Kinnabus Ag & B 204 D7
Kinnadie Abers 257 H3
Kinnaird P & K 232 E4
Kinneff Abers 245 J8
Kinnelhead D & G 186 F6
Kinnell Angus 234 F5
Kinnerley Shrops 112 E7
Kinnersley Herefs 79 L5
Kinnersley Worcs 81 K6
Kinnerton Powys 79 J3
Kinnerton Shrops 95 J4
Kinnerton Green Flints 129 H7
Kinnesswood P & K 222 B6
Kinninvie Dur 168 D6
Kinnordy Angus 234 B4
Kinoulton Notts 117 H5
Kinross P & K 221 K6
Kinrossie P & K 222 C1
Kinsbourne Green Herts 68 E4
Kinsey Heath Ches E 113 L3
Kinsham Herefs 79 L2
Kinsham Worcs 81 L8
Kinsley Wakefd 142 C5
Kinson Bmouth 17 L3
Kintbury W Berk 48 A5
Kintessack Moray 264 F7
Kintillo P & K 221 L4
Kinton Herefs 95 K8
Kinton Shrops 112 E7
Kintore Abers 256 E8
Kintour Ag & B 205 G6
Kintra Ag & B 204 D6
Kintra Ag & B 226 C7
Kintraw Ag & B 216 C6
Kinveachy Highld 253 G7
Kinver Staffs 97 J6
Kiplin N York 160 C3
Kippax Leeds 142 C2
Kippen Stirlg 219 L8
Kippford or Scaur D & G 175 L4
Kipping's Cross Kent 39 G5
Kirbister Ork 275 c5
Kirby Bedon Norfk 106 F2
Kirby Bellars Leics 117 J7
Kirby Cane Norfk 107 H5
Kirby Corner Covtry 99 J8
Kirby Cross Essex 73 J3
Kirby Fields Leics 100 B3
Kirby Grindalythe N York 152 D2
Kirby Hill N York 150 E2
Kirby Hill N York 159 L2
Kirby Knowle N York 161 G5
Kirby le Soken Essex 73 J3
Kirby Misperton N York 162 D6
Kirby Muxloe Leics 100 B3
Kirby Sigston N York 160 F4
Kirby Underdale E R Yk 152 B4
Kirby Wiske N York 160 E5
Kirdford W Susx 36 F5
Kirk Highld 280 C4
Kirkabister Shet 281 e7
Kirkandrews D & G 174 F5
Kirkandrews upon Eden
  Cumb 177 K7
Kirkbampton Cumb 177 J7
Kirkbean D & G 176 C7

Kirk Bramwith Donc 143 G5
Kirkbride Cumb 177 H7
Kirkbridge N York 160 C4
Kirkbuddo Angus 234 D6
Kirkburn Border 200 C5
Kirkburn E R Yk 152 F3
Kirkburton Kirk 141 K5
Kirkby Knows 138 E5
Kirkby Lincs 135 L1
Kirkby N York 161 G4
Kirkby Fleetham N York 160 D4
Kirkby Green Lincs 136 A8
Kirkby in Ashfield Notts 133 L8
Kirkby-in-Furness Cumb 156 D6
Kirkby la Thorpe Lincs 118 C3
Kirkby Lonsdale Cumb 157 K7
Kirkby Malham N York 148 F4
Kirkby Mallory Leics 99 M3
Kirkby Malzeard N York 160 C7
Kirkby Mills N York 162 C5
Kirkbymoorside N York 162 B5
Kirkby on Bain Lincs 136 D7
Kirkby Overblow N York 150 D6
Kirkby Stephen Cumb 158 D1
Kirkby Thore Cumb 166 E4
Kirkby Underwood Lincs 118 E4
Kirkby Wharf N York 151 H4
Kirkby Woodhouse Notts 116 E1
Kirkcaldy Fife 211 J1
Kirkcaldy Crematorium
  Fife 222 D8
Kirkcambeck Cumb 178 C5
Kirkchrist D & G 175 G4
Kirkcolm D & G 172 C1
Kirkconnel D & G 197 L8
Kirkconnell D & G 176 C5
Kirkcowan D & G 173 J3
Kirkcudbright D & G 175 H5
Kirkdale Lpool 129 H1
Kirk Deighton N York 150 F5
Kirk Ella E R Yk 144 C2
Kirkfieldbank S Lans 198 E4
Kirkgunzeon D & G 175 L2
Kirk Hallam Derbys 116 D3
Kirkham Lancs 138 E1
Kirkham N York 151 M3
Kirkhamgate Wakefd 141 L3
Kirk Hammerton N York 151 G5
Kirkharle Nthumb 180 B2
Kirkhaugh Nthumb 167 G1
Kirkheaton Kirk 141 J4
Kirkheaton Nthumb 180 B3
Kirkhill Highld 250 F3
Kirkhope S Lans 186 E5
Kirkhouse Cumb 178 D7
Kirkhouse Green Donc 143 G5
Kirkibost Highld 247 H5
Kirkinch P & K 233 L6
Kirkinner D & G 174 C4
Kirkintilloch E Duns 209 H4
Kirk Ireton Derbys 115 M2
Kirkland Cumb 164 E7
Kirkland Cumb 166 F4
Kirkland D & G 185 G5
Kirkland D & G 186 F8
Kirkland D & G 197 L8
Kirkland Guards Cumb 165 G3
Kirk Langley Derbys 115 M4
Kirkleatham R & Cl 170 E6
Kirklevington S on T 160 F1
Kirkley Suffk 107 L5
Kirklington N York 160 D6
Kirklington Notts 134 D8
Kirklinton Cumb 178 B5
Kirkliston C Edin 210 F4
Kirkmabreck D & G 174 D4
Kirkmaiden D & G 172 E7
Kirk Merrington Dur 169 H4
Kirk Michael IoM 154 d4
Kirkmichael P & K 233 G3
Kirkmichael S Ayrs 183 J1
Kirkmuirhill S Lans 198 C4
Kirknewton Nthumb 202 E6
Kirknewton W Loth 210 F5
Kirkney Abers 255 K5
Kirk of Shotts N Lans 209 M6
Kirkoswald Cumb 166 C2
Kirkoswald S Ayrs 183 G5
Kirkpatrick D & G 186 D8
Kirkpatrick Durham D & G 175 K1
Kirkpatrick-Fleming D & G 177 K3
Kirk Sandall Donc 142 F6
Kirksanton Cumb 155 L6
Kirk Smeaton N York 142 E6
Kirkstall Leeds 150 C8
Kirkstead Lincs 136 C7
Kirkstile Abers 255 L5
Kirkstile D & G 188 C8
Kirkstone Pass Inn Cumb 156 F1
Kirkstyle Highld 280 D2

Kirkthorpe Wakefd 142 B3
Kirkton Abers 256 B6
Kirkton D & G 176 C3
Kirkton Fife 222 F2
Kirkton Highld 248 C6
Kirkton Highld 248 E3
Kirkton P & K 221 G3
Kirkton Manor Border 200 B5
Kirkton of Airlie Angus 233 M5
Kirkton of Auchterhouse
Angus 234 A7
Kirkton of Barevan Highld 252 F2
Kirkton of Collace P & K 222 C1
Kirkton of Glenbuchat Abers 255 H8
Kirkton of Logie Buchan
Abers 257 H6
Kirkton of Menmuir Angus 234 E3
Kirkton of Monikie Angus 234 D7
Kirkton of Rayne Abers 256 C5
Kirkton of Skene Abers 245 H2
Kirkton of Strathmartine
Angus 234 B8
Kirkton of Tealing Angus 234 B7
Kirkton of Tough Abers 244 D1
Kirktown Abers 269 J3
Kirktown Abers 269 K6
Kirktown of Alvah Abers 268 B4
Kirktown of Bourtie Abers 256 E6
Kirktown of Fetteresso Abers 245 J6
Kirktown of Mortlach Moray 255 G4
Kirktown of Slains Abers 257 J6
Kirkurd Border 199 K4
Kirkwall Ork 275 c4
Kirkwhelpington Nthumb 180 B2
Kirk Yetholm Border 202 C7
Kirmington N Linc 144 B3
Kirmond le Mire Lincs 136 C1
Kirn Ag & B 207 K3
Kirriemuir Angus 234 B4
Kirstead Green Norfk 106 F4
Kirtlebridge D & G 177 H4
Kirtling Cambs 88 D4
Kirtling Green Cambs 88 D4
Kirtlington Oxon 66 D3
Kirtomy Highld 278 D1
Kirton Lincs 119 J4
Kirton Notts 134 D6
Kirton Suffk 91 G7
Kirton End Lincs 119 J3
Kirtonhill W Duns 208 C4
Kirton Holme Lincs 119 J3
Kirton in Lindsey N Linc 144 A8
Kirwaugh D & G 173 K4
Kishorn Highld 248 D4
Kislingbury Nhants 84 D3
Kitebrook Warwks 65 K1
Kite Green Warwks 82 E2
Kites Hardwick Warwks 83 L2
Kitleigh Cnwll 11 J3
Kitt Green Wigan 139 H6
Kittisford Somset 29 K6
Kittle Swans 57 G7
Kitt's Green Birm 98 F6
Kittybrewster C Aber 245 K2
Kitwood Hants 35 K4
Kivernoll Herefs 62 F1
Kiveton Park Rothm 133 K3
Knaith Lincs 135 G3
Knaith Park Lincs 135 G3
Knap Corner Dorset 32 D6
Knaphill Surrey 50 B7
Knapp Somset 30 D5
Knapp Hill Hants 34 E6
Knapthorpe Notts 134 E7
Knapton C York 151 J5
Knapton N York 162 F7
Knapton Norfk 122 F5
Knapton Green Herefs 80 B5
Knapwell Cambs 87 G3
Knaresborough N York 150 E4
Knarsdale Nthumb 178 F8
Knaven Abers 257 G3
Knayton N York 160 F5
Knebworth Herts 69 H3
Knedlington E R Yk 143 J2
Kneesall Notts 134 D6
Kneesworth Cambs 87 G6
Kneeton Notts 117 J2
Knelston Swans 56 E7
Knenhall Staffs 114 C6
Knettishall Suffk 105 K7
Knightacott Devon 28 B3
Knightcote Warwks 83 J4
Knightley Staffs 114 C6
Knightley Dale Staffs 114 C6
Knighton C Leic 100 D3
Knighton Devon 7 G5
Knighton Dorset 31 K8
Knighton Poole 17 L3
Knighton Powys 79 K1

Knighton Somset 30 B2
Knighton Staffs 114 A3
Knighton Staffs 114 B6
Knighton Wilts 47 L4
Knighton on Teme Worcs 80 E7
Knightsbridge Gloucs 64 C2
Knightsmill Cnwll 10 F6
Knightwick Worcs 81 G4
Knill Herefs 79 K3
Knipton Leics 117 L5
Knitsley Dur 168 E1
Kniveton Derbys 115 K2
Knock Cumb 166 F5
Knock Highld 247 L6
Knock Moray 267 L5
Knock W Isls 282 g3
Knockally Highld 274 F2
Knockan Highld 271 H6
Knockando Moray 254 D3
Knockbain Highld 250 F3
Knockbain Highld 263 H8
Knock Castle N Ayrs 207 K6
Knockdee Highld 279 L4
Knockdow Ag & B 207 J5
Knockdown Wilts 46 B1
Knockeen S Ayrs 183 H4
Knockenkelly N Ayrs 195 G5
Knockentiber E Ayrs 196 D3
Knockhall Kent 52 C4
Knockholt Kent 51 M7
Knockholt Pound Kent 52 A7
Knockin Shrops 112 E7
Knockinlaw E Ayrs 196 E3
Knockmill Kent 52 C6
Knocknain D & G 172 B2
Knockrome Ag & B 205 J2
Knocksharry IoM 154 c5
Knocksheen D & G 184 F6
Knodishall Suffk 91 K3
Knodishall Common Suffk 91 K3
Knole Somset 31 G6
Knole Park S Glos 45 H2
Knolls Green Ches E 130 F4
Knolton Wrexhm 112 E4
Knook Wilts 32 F3
Knossington Leics 101 H2
Knott End-on-Sea Lancs 147 G6
Knotting Bed 85 K3
Knotting Green Bed 85 K3
Knottingley Wakefd 142 D3
Knotty Ash Lpool 129 J1
Knotty Green Bucks 68 B8
Knowbury Shrops 96 D8
Knowe D & G 183 H8
Knowehead D & G 184 F5
Knoweside S Ayrs 195 L8
Knowle Bristl 45 J5
Knowle Devon 13 H2
Knowle Devon 14 B1
Knowle Devon 14 B6
Knowle Devon 27 J3
Knowle Shrops 96 D8
Knowle Solhll 98 F8
Knowle Somset 29 H2
Knowle Cross Devon 14 B3
Knowlefield Cumb 177 L7
Knowle Green Lancs 148 A8
Knowle Hill Surrey 50 C5
Knowle St Giles Somset 30 E8
Knowle Village Hants 19 J2
Knowle Wood Calder 140 D3
Knowl Green Essex 88 F7
Knowl Hill W & M 49 K3
Knowlton Dorset 17 K1
Knowlton Kent 41 J4
Knowsley Knows 138 E8
Knowstone Devon 28 E6
Knox N York 150 C4
Knox Bridge Kent 39 K5
Knucklas Powys 95 G8
Knuston Nhants 85 H2
Knutsford Ches E 130 E4
Knutton Staffs 114 C2
Krumlin Calder 141 G4
Kuggar Cnwll 3 J7
Kyleakin Highld 248 B6
Kyle of Lochalsh Highld 248 B6
Kylerhea Highld 248 C7
Kylesku Highld 271 H1
Kylesmorar Highld 238 C5
Kyles Scalpay W Isls 282 f6
Kylestrome Highld 271 H1
Kynaston Herefs 80 E8
Kynaston Shrops 112 E7
Kynnersley Wrekin 113 L8
Kyre Green Worcs 80 E3
Kyre Park Worcs 80 E3
Kyrewood Worcs 80 E2
Kyrle Somset 29 J6

L

La Bellieuse Guern 9 j3
Lacasaigh W Isls 282 f4
Lacasdal W Isls 282 g3
Laceby NE Lin 145 G6
Lacey Green Bucks 67 K7
Lach Dennis Ches W 130 D5
Lackenby R & Cl 170 D6
Lackford Suffk 88 F1
Lackford Green Suffk 88 F1
Lacock Wilts 46 C5
Ladbroke Warwks 83 K3
Ladderedge Staffs 114 F1
Laddingford Kent 39 H4
Lade Bank Lincs 119 L1
Ladock Cnwll 4 E5
Lady Ork 275 e2
Ladybank Fife 222 E5
Ladycross Cnwll 11 L5
Ladygill S Lans 198 F7
Lady Hall Cumb 156 B5
Ladykirk Border 202 D3
Ladyridge Herefs 63 H1
Lady's Green Suffk 88 E3
Ladywood Birm 98 D6
Ladywood Worcs 81 K3
La Fontenelle Guern 9 k1
La Fosse Guern 9 j4
Lag D & G 185 L5
Laga Highld 237 J8
Lagavulin Ag & B 204 F7
Lagg N Ayrs 193 K4
Laggan Highld 240 A4
Laggan Highld 241 G5
Lagganlia Highld 241 M3
La Greve Guern 9 k2
La Greve de Lecq Jersey 9 b1
La Hougue Bie Jersey 9 e3
La Houguette Guern 9 h3
Laid Highld 277 G4
Laide Highld 260 E2
Laig Highld 236 F3
Laigh Clunch E Ayrs 196 F2
Laigh Fenwick E Ayrs 196 F3
Laigh Glenmuir E Ayrs 197 J7
Laighstonehall S Lans 209 J8
Laindon Essex 52 E1
Lairg Highld 272 E6
Laisterdyke C Brad 141 J1
Laithes Cumb 166 B4
Lake Devon 12 C5
Lake Devon 27 K4
Lake IoW 19 K7
Lake Wilts 33 K3
Lakenheath Suffk 104 E6
Laker's Green Surrey 36 F4
Lakesend Norfk 103 L4
Lakeside Cumb 156 E5
Laleham Surrey 50 D5
Laleston Brdgnd 42 C5
Lamanva Cnwll 3 J5
Lamarsh Essex 89 H8
Lamas Norfk 122 E7
Lambden Border 202 A4
Lamberhurst Kent 39 H6
Lamberhurst Down Kent 39 G6
Lamberton Border 213 L7
Lambeth Gt Lon 51 J3
Lambeth Crematorium
Gt Lon 51 H4
Lambfair Green Suffk 88 E4
Lambley Notts 117 H2
Lambley Nthumb 178 F7
Lambourn W Berk 47 L3
Lambourne End Essex 70 C8
Lambourne Woodlands W Berk 47 L4
Lamb Roe Lancs 148 C8
Lambs Green W Susx 37 K3
Lambston Pembks 54 E3
Lamellion Cnwll 6 A2
Lamerton Devon 12 B7
Lamesley Gatesd 181 G7
Lamington S Lans 199 G7
Lamlash N Ayrs 195 G5
Lamonby Cumb 165 L3
Lamorick Cnwll 5 H2
Lamorna Cnwll 2 C6
Lamorran Cnwll 4 E6
Lampen Cnwll 5 L2
Lampeter Cerdgn 77 G5
Lampeter Velfrey Pembks 55 K4
Lamphey Pembks 55 G6
Lamplugh Cumb 164 E6
Lamport Nhants 101 G8
Lamyatt Somset 31 L4
Lana Devon 11 K1
Lana Devon 11 L3
Lanark S Lans 198 E4

Lancaster Lancs 147 J3
Lancaster & Morecambe
Crematorium Lancs 147 J3
Lancaut Gloucs 63 G7
Lanchester Dur 168 F1
Lancing W Susx 21 L6
L'Ancresse Guern 9 k1
Landbeach Cambs 87 K2
Landcross Devon 27 H6
Landerberry Abers 245 G3
Landford Wilts 34 B7
Land-hallow Highld 275 G2
Landican Crematorium Wirral 129 G3
Landimore Swans 56 E6
Landkey Devon 27 L4
Landore Swans 57 J5
Landrake Cnwll 6 C4
Landscove Devon 7 M2
Land's End Cnwll 2 A6
Landshipping Pembks 55 G4
Landue Cnwll 11 L6
Landulph Cnwll 6 E3
Landwade Suffk 88 C2
Lane Cnwll 4 D3
Laneast Cnwll 11 J6
Lane Bottom Lancs 140 C1
Lane End Bucks 49 K1
Lane End Cnwll 5 H1
Lane End Hants 35 H5
Lane End Kent 52 C4
Lane End Lancs 148 F6
Lane End Warrtn 130 D2
Lane End Wilts 32 D2
Lane Ends Derbys 115 L4
Lane Ends Lancs 140 B2
Lane Ends N York 149 H7
Lane Green Staffs 97 K3
Laneham Notts 134 F4
Lanehead Dur 167 J2
Lane Head Dur 168 E8
Lanehead Nthumb 179 H2
Lane Head Wigan 139 J8
Lane Head Wsall 98 B3
Lane Heads Lancs 147 H7
Laneshaw Bridge Lancs 149 G7
Lane Side Lancs 140 B3
Langaford Devon 12 A3
Langaller Somset 30 C5
Langar Notts 117 J4
Langbank Rens 208 C4
Langbar N York 149 K5
Langbaurgh N York 170 D8
Langcliffe N York 148 E3
Langdale End N York 163 G4
Langdon Cnwll 11 K5
Langdon Beck Dur 167 K4
Langdown Hants 19 G2
Langdyke Fife 222 E6
Langenhoe Essex 72 E3
Langford C Beds 86 D7
Langford Devon 14 B2
Langford Essex 71 K5
Langford N Som 44 F6
Langford Notts 135 G7
Langford Oxon 65 K6
Langford Budville Somset 29 K6
Langham Dorset 32 C5
Langham Essex 72 F1
Langham Norfk 121 M3
Langham Rutlnd 101 J1
Langham Suffk 89 K1
Langho Lancs 139 L1
Langholm D & G 177 L2
Langland Swans 57 H7
Langlee Border 201 G6
Langley Ches E 131 J5
Langley Derbys 116 D2
Langley Gloucs 64 E2
Langley Hants 19 G3
Langley Herts 69 G3
Langley Kent 39 K3
Langley Nthumb 179 J6
Langley Oxon 65 L4
Langley Rochdl 140 C6
Langley Slough 50 C3
Langley Somset 29 K5
Langley W Susx 36 B5
Langley Warwks 82 E3
Langley Burrell Wilts 46 D4
Langley Castle Nthumb 179 J6
Langley Common Derbys 115 M4
Langley Green Derbys 115 M4
Langley Green Essex 72 C3
Langley Green Warwks 82 E3
Langley Lower Green Essex 87 J8
Langley Marsh Somset 29 K5
Langley Mill Derbys 116 D2
Langley Moor Dur 169 H3
Langley Park Dur 169 G2
Langley Street Norfk 107 H3

Langley Upper Green Essex 87 J8
Langney E Susx 23 L6
Langold Notts 134 B2
Langore Cnwll 11 K5
Langport Somset 30 F5
Langrick Lincs 119 J2
Langridge BaNES 45 L5
Langridgeford Devon 27 K6
Langrigg Cumb 165 G2
Langrish Hants 35 L6
Langsett Barns 141 K7
Langside P & K 220 D4
Langstone Hants 20 B6
Langstone Newpt 44 D1
Langthorne N York 160 C4
Langthorpe N York 150 E2
Langthwaite N York 159 H2
Langtoft E R Yk 152 F3
Langtoft Lincs 102 C1
Langton Dur 168 F6
Langton Lincs 136 D6
Langton Lincs 137 G5
Langton N York 152 B2
Langton by Wragby Lincs 136 C4
Langton Green Kent 38 E5
Langton Green Suffk 106 C8
Langton Herring Dorset 16 B6
Langton Long Blandford
 Dorset 17 H2
Langton Matravers Dorset 17 K6
Langtree Devon 27 H7
Langtree Week Devon 27 H7
Langwathby Cumb 166 D4
Langwell House Highld 274 F3
Langwith Derbys 133 K5
Langwith Junction Derbys 133 K6
Langworth Lincs 135 L4
Lanivet Cnwll 5 H2
Lanjeth Cnwll 5 G4
Lank Cnwll 10 F7
Lanlivery Cnwll 5 J3
Lanner Cnwll 3 J3
Lanoy Cnwll 11 K7
Lanreath Cnwll 5 L3
Lansallos Cnwll 5 K4
Lanteglos Cnwll 10 F6
Lanteglos Highway Cnwll 5 K4
Lanton Border 189 G2
Lanton Nthumb 202 E6
La Passee Guern 9 j2
Lapford Devon 13 G1
Laphroaig Ag & B 204 F7
Lapley Staffs 97 K1
La Pulente Jersey 9 a3
Lapworth Warwks 82 E1
Larachbeg Highld 227 K3
Larbert Falk 209 M3
Larbreck Lancs 147 H7
Largie Abers 256 A5
Largiemore Ag & B 206 E2
Largoward Fife 223 H5
Largs N Ayrs 207 K7
Largybeg N Ayrs 195 G6
Largymore N Ayrs 195 G6
Larkbeare Devon 14 C3
Larkfield Inver 207 L4
Larkfield Kent 52 F7
Larkhall S Lans 198 C3
Larkhill Wilts 33 K2
Larling Norfk 105 K5
La Rocque Jersey 9 f4
La Rousaillerie Guern 9 j2
Lartington Dur 168 C7
Lasborough Gloucs 64 B8
Lasham Hants 35 K2
Lashbrook Devon 12 A1
Lashbrook Devon 12 B2
Lashenden Kent 39 L5
Lask Edge Staffs 131 H8
Lasswade Mdloth 211 J6
Lastingham N York 162 C4
Latcham Somset 31 G2
Latchford Herts 69 K3
Latchford Oxon 67 G6
Latchingdon Essex 72 C7
Latchley Cnwll 12 A7
Lately Common Warrtn 139 K8
Lathbury M Keyn 85 G6
Latheron Highld 275 G2
Latheronwheel Highld 275 G2
Lathones Fife 223 H5
Latimer Bucks 68 C7
Latteridge S Glos 45 K2
Lattiford Somset 32 B5
Latton Wilts 65 G7
Lauder Border 201 H4
Laugharne Carmth 56 B3
Laughterton Lincs 135 G4
Laughton E Susx 23 H4
Laughton Leics 100 E5

Laughton Lincs 118 E5
Laughton Lincs 143 L8
Laughton-en-le-Morthen
 Rothm 133 K2
Launcells Cnwll 11 J2
Launcells Cross Cnwll 11 K2
Launceston Cnwll 11 L5
Launton Oxon 66 F3
Laurencekirk Abers 235 H1
Laurieston D & G 175 H2
Laurieston Falk 210 B3
Lavendon M Keyn 85 H4
Lavenham Suffk 89 J5
Lavernock V Glam 43 J8
Laversdale Cumb 178 B6
Laverstock Wilts 33 L5
Laverstoke Hants 35 G1
Laverton Gloucs 82 C8
Laverton N York 160 B7
Laverton Somset 45 M8
La Villette Guern 9 j3
Lavister Wrexhm 129 J8
Law S Lans 209 L8
Lawers P & K 231 J7
Lawford Essex 73 G1
Lawford Somset 29 L4
Law Hill S Lans 209 L8
Lawhitton Cnwll 11 L6
Lawkland N York 148 D3
Lawkland Green N York 148 D3
Lawley Wrekin 96 F2
Lawnhead Staffs 114 C6
Lawns Wood Crematorium
 Leeds 150 C8
Lawrenny Pembks 55 G5
Lawshall Suffk 89 H4
Lawshall Green Suffk 89 H4
Lawton Herefs 80 B3
Laxay W Isls 282 f4
Laxdale W Isls 282 g3
Laxey IoM 154 f5
Laxfield Suffk 91 G1
Laxford Bridge Highld 276 C7
Laxo Shet 281 e5
Laxton E R Yk 143 K3
Laxton Nhants 101 L4
Laxton Notts 134 E6
Laycock C Brad 149 J7
Layer Breton Essex 72 D3
Layer-de-la-Haye Essex 72 D3
Layer Marney Essex 72 D4
Layham Suffk 89 L1
Layland's Green W Berk 48 A5
Laymore Dorset 15 J2
Layter's Green Bucks 50 C1
Laytham E R Yk 152 A1
Laythes Cumb 177 H7
Lazenby R & Cl 170 D6
Lazonby Cumb 166 D3
Lea Derbys 132 F8
Lea Herefs 63 K3
Lea Lincs 135 G2
Lea Shrops 95 J5
Lea Shrops 95 K4
Lea Wilts 46 D2
Leachkin Highld 251 H3
Leadburn Border 200 B2
Leadenham Lincs 118 B1
Leaden Roding Essex 70 E4
Leadgate Dur 180 D8
Leadgate Nthumb 180 D7
Leadhills S Lans 186 C3
Leadingcross Green Kent 39 M3
Leadmill Derbys 132 E4
Leafield Oxon 65 L4
Leagrave Luton 68 D2
Leahead Ches W 130 D6
Lea Heath Staffs 115 G6
Leake N York 160 F4
Leake Common Side Lincs 119 L1
Lealholm N York 162 D1
Lealholm Side N York 162 D1
Lealt Highld 259 H4
Leam Derbys 132 E4
Lea Marston Warwks 99 G5
Leamington Hastings Warwks 83 K2
Leamington Spa Warwks 83 H2
Leamside Dur 169 J1
Leap Cross E Susx 23 K5
Leasgill Cumb 157 H6
Leasingham Lincs 118 C3
Leasingthorne Dur 169 H4
Leatherhead Surrey 50 F7
Leathley N York 150 B6
Leaton Shrops 113 G4
Leaton Wrekin 96 E1
Lea Town Lancs 138 F2
Leaveland Kent 40 C4
Leavenheath Suffk 89 J7
Leavening N York 152 B3

Leaves Green Gt Lon 51 L6
Lea Yeat Cumb 158 D5
Lebberston N York 163 K6
Le Bigard Guern 9 i4
Le Bourg Guern 9 j4
Le Bourg Jersey 9 f4
Lechlade on Thames Gloucs 65 J7
Lecht Gruinart Ag & B 204 D3
Leck Lancs 157 K7
Leckbuie P & K 231 K7
Leckford Hants 34 E3
Leckhampstead Bucks 84 D7
Leckhampstead W Berk 48 B4
Leckhampstead Thicket
 W Berk 48 B4
Leckhampton Gloucs 64 D3
Leckmelm Highld 261 K2
Leckwith V Glam 43 J6
Leconfield E R Yk 152 F7
Ledaig Ag & B 228 E7
Ledburn Bucks 67 L3
Ledbury Herefs 81 G7
Leddington Gloucs 80 F8
Ledgemoor Herefs 80 A5
Ledicot Herefs 80 A3
Ledmore Junction Highld 271 H5
Ledsham Ches W 129 H5
Ledsham Leeds 142 C2
Ledston Leeds 142 C2
Ledstone Devon 7 L5
Ledston Luck Leeds 142 C2
Ledwell Oxon 66 B2
Lee Devon 27 H2
Lee Gt Lon 51 K4
Lee Hants 34 D7
Lee Shrops 112 F5
Leebotwood Shrops 96 B4
Lee Brockhurst Shrops 113 J6
Leece Cumb 146 E2
Lee Chapel Essex 52 E2
Lee Clump Bucks 67 M6
Lee Common Bucks 67 M6
Leeds Kent 39 K3
Leeds Leeds 141 L1
Leedstown Cnwll 2 F4
Lee Green Ches E 130 C7
Leek Staffs 131 K8
Leek Wootton Warwks 83 G2
Lee Mill Devon 7 H4
Leeming C Brad 141 G1
Leeming N York 160 D5
Leeming Bar N York 160 D4
Lee Moor Devon 7 H3
Lee-on-the-Solent Hants 19 J3
Lees C Brad 149 J8
Lees Derbys 115 L4
Lees Oldham 140 E6
Lees Green Derbys 115 L4
Leesthorpe Leics 101 H1
Lee Street Surrey 37 L2
Leeswood Flints 129 G7
Leetown P & K 222 C3
Leftwich Ches W 130 C5
Legar Powys 61 K4
Legbourne Lincs 137 G3
Legburthwaite Cumb 165 K6
Legerwood Border 201 J4
Le Gron Guern 9 i3
Legsby Lincs 136 B3
Le Haguais Jersey 9 e4
Le Hocq Jersey 9 e4
Leicester C Leic 100 D3
Leicester Forest East Leics 100 B3
Leigh Devon 28 C8
Leigh Dorset 16 B1
Leigh Gloucs 64 C2
Leigh Kent 38 E4
Leigh Shrops 95 H3
Leigh Surrey 37 K2
Leigh Wigan 139 K7
Leigh Wilts 64 F8
Leigh Worcs 81 H4
Leigh Beck Essex 53 H2
Leigh Delamere Wilts 46 C3
Leigh Green Kent 40 A8
Leigh Knoweglass S Lans 197 J1
Leighland Chapel Somset 29 J4
Leigh-on-Sea Sthend 53 H2
Leigh Park Dorset 17 K3
Leigh Sinton Worcs 81 H5
Leighswood Wsall 98 D3
Leighterton Gloucs 46 B1
Leighton N York 159 L6
Leighton Powys 94 F2
Leighton Shrops 96 E2
Leighton Somset 32 B2
Leighton Bromswold Cambs 102 C8
Leighton Buzzard C Beds 68 A2
Leigh upon Mendip Somset 31 M2
Leigh Woods N Som 45 H4

Leinthall Earls Herefs 80 B2
Leinthall Starkes Herefs 80 A1
Leintwardine Herefs 95 K8
Leire Leics 100 B5
Leiston Suffk 91 K3
Leith C Edin 211 J4
Leitholm Border 202 E6
Lelant Cnwll 2 F4
Lelley E R Yk 145 G1
Lem Hill Worcs 97 G8
Lempitlaw Border 202 E7
Lemreway W Isls 282 f5
Lemsford Herts 69 G4
Lenchwick Worcs 82 B5
Lendalfoot S Ayrs 182 E7
Lendrick Stirlg 219 J6
Lendrum Terrace Abers 257 K3
Lenham Kent 40 A5
Lenham Heath Kent 40 B5
Lenie Highld 250 F3
Lennel Border 202 C5
Lennox Plunton D & G 174 F4
Lennoxtown E Duns 209 G4
Lent Bucks 50 A3
Lenton C Nott 116 E4
Lenton Lincs 118 D5
Lenwade Norfk 122 C8
Lenzie E Duns 209 H4
Leochel-Cushnie Abers 244 C2
Leomansley Staffs 98 E2
Leominster Herefs 80 C3
Leonard Stanley Gloucs 64 A6
Leoville Jersey 9 b2
Lepe Hants 19 G4
Lephin Highld 258 B6
Leppington N York 152 A4
Lepton Kirk 141 K5
Lerags Ag & B 216 C2
L'Eree Guern 9 h3
Lerryn Cnwll 5 K3
Lerwick Shet 281 e6
Les Arquets Guern 9 h3
Lesbury Nthumb 191 J4
Les Hubits Guern 9 k3
Leslie Abers 255 M6
Leslie Fife 222 D6
Les Lohiers Guern 9 i3
Lesmahagow S Lans 198 C6
Les Murchez Guern 9 i4
Lesnewth Cnwll 11 G4
Les Nicolles Guern 9 j4
Les Quartiers Guern 9 j2
Les Quennevais Jersey 9 b3
Les Sages Guern 9 i3
Lessingham Norfk 123 H6
Lessonhall Cumb 165 H1
Lestowder Cnwll 3 K6
Les Villets Guern 9 i4
Leswalt D & G 172 C2
L'Etacq Jersey 9 a2
Letchmore Heath Herts 68 F7
Letchworth Garden City Herts 86 E8
Letcombe Bassett Oxon 48 A2
Letcombe Regis Oxon 48 A2
Letham Angus 234 D6
Letham Border 189 J4
Letham Falk 210 B2
Letham Fife 222 E4
Letham Grange Angus 235 G6
Lethendy P & K 233 H7
Lethenty Abers 256 M7
Lethenty Abers 256 E6
Letheringham Suffk 91 G4
Letheringsett Norfk 122 B4
Lettaford Devon 13 G6
Letterewe Highld 260 F5
Letterfearn Highld 248 D7
Letterfinlay Lodge Hotel
 Highld 239 L5
Lettermorar Highld 237 L3
Letters Highld 261 K2
Lettershaw S Lans 186 D2
Letterston Pembks 74 F6
Lettoch Highld 253 K7
Lettoch Highld 254 B6
Letton Herefs 79 L1
Letton Herefs 79 L6
Lett's Green Kent 51 M7
Letty Green Herts 69 H5
Letwell Rothm 133 L2
Leuchars Fife 223 H3
Leumrabhagh W Isls 282 g5
Leurbost W Isls 282 g4
Levalsa Meor Cnwll 5 G5
Levedale Staffs 114 D8
Level's Green Essex 70 C2
Leven E R Yk 153 H6
Leven Fife 222 F7
Levens Cumb 157 G2
Levens Green Herts 69 K3

Levenshulme Manch 131 G1
Levenwick Shet 281 d8
Leverburgh W Isls 282 d6
Leverington Cambs 103 J1
Leverstock Green Herts 68 D5
Leverton Lincs 119 L2
Le Villocq Guern 9 J2
Levington Suffk 90 F7
Levisham N York 162 G4
Lew Oxon 65 L6
Lewannick Cnwll 11 K6
Lewdown Devon 12 B5
Lewes E Susx 22 F5
Leweston Pembks 54 F2
Lewisham Gt Lon 51 K4
Lewisham Crematorium
Gt Lon 51 L4
Lewiston Highld 250 F6
Lewistown Brdgnd 42 E4
Lewis Wych Herefs 79 L4
Lewknor Oxon 67 H7
Leworthy Devon 11 L2
Leworthy Devon 28 B3
Lewson Street Kent 40 C3
Lewth Lancs 147 J8
Lewtrenchard Devon 12 B5
Lexden Essex 72 D2
Lexworthy Somset 30 C4
Ley Cnwll 5 K2
Leybourne Kent 52 E7
Leyburn N York 159 K4
Leycett Staffs 114 B2
Leygreen Herts 68 F2
Ley Hill Bucks 68 C6
Leyland Lancs 139 H3
Leyland Green St Hel 139 H7
Leylodge Abers 245 G1
Leys Abers 269 J5
Leys P & K 233 K7
Leysdown-on-Sea Kent 53 M5
Leysmill Angus 234 F6
Leys of Cossans Angus 234 B5
Leysters Herefs 80 D2
Leyton Gt Lon 51 K2
Leytonstone Gt Lon 51 K2
Lezant Cnwll 11 L6
Lezerea Cnwll 3 H4
Lhanbryde Moray 266 F4
Libanus Powys 60 F2
Libberton S Lans 199 G4
Liberton C Edin 211 J5
Lichfield Staffs 98 E2
Lickey Worcs 98 C8
Lickey End Worcs 81 M1
Lickey Rock Worcs 98 C8
Lickfold W Susx 36 D5
Liddaton Green Devon 12 B6
Liddesdale Highld 228 B3
Liddington Swindn 47 J3
Lidgate Derbys 132 F4
Lidgate Suffk 88 E4
Lidget Donc 143 G7
Lidgett Notts 134 C6
Lidham Hill E Susx 24 F4
Lidlington C Beds 85 K7
Lidsing Kent 53 G6
Liff Angus 222 F1
Lifford Birm 98 D7
Lifton Devon 11 M5
Liftondown Devon 11 M5
Lighthorne Warwks 83 H4
Lighthorne Heath Warwks 83 H4
Lightwater Surrey 50 B6
Lightwood C Stke 114 E4
Lightwood Green Ches E 113 L3
Lightwood Green Wrexhm 112 F3
Lilbourne Nhants 100 C8
Lilburn Tower Nthumb 190 H4
Lilleshall Wrekin 114 A8
Lilley Herts 68 E2
Lilley W Berk 48 C3
Lilliesleaf Border 201 H8
Lillingstone Dayrell Bucks 84 D7
Lillingstone Lovell Bucks 84 D7
Lillington Dorset 31 K8
Lilliput Poole 17 K5
Lilstock Somset 29 L2
Lilyhurst Shrops 97 G1
Limbrick Lancs 139 J4
Limbury Luton 68 D2
Limebrook Herefs 79 L2
Limefield Bury 140 B5
Limekilnburn S Lans 197 K1
Limekilns Fife 210 E2
Limerigg Falk 209 M5
Limerstone IoW 19 G7
Limestone Brae Nthumb 167 J4
Lime Street Worcs 64 A1
Limington Somset 31 J6
Limmerhaugh E Ayrs 197 J5

Limpenhoe Norfk 107 H3
Limpley Stoke Wilts 45 M6
Limpsfield Surrey 51 L8
Limpsfield Chart Surrey 51 L8
Linby Notts 116 F1
Linchmere W Susx 36 C5
Lincluden D & G 176 C3
Lincoln Lincs 135 K5
Lincoln Crematorium Lincs 135 K5
Lincomb Worcs 81 J2
Lincombe Devon 7 L6
Lincombe Devon 27 J2
Lindale Cumb 156 F6
Lindal in Furness Cumb 156 C7
Lindfield W Susx 22 E2
Lindford Hants 36 B4
Lindley Kirk 141 H4
Lindley N York 150 H6
Lindow End Ches E 130 F4
Lindridge Worcs 80 F2
Lindsell Essex 70 F2
Lindsey Suffk 89 K6
Lindsey Tye Suffk 89 K6
Liney Somset 30 E4
Linford Hants 18 B2
Linford Thurr 52 E3
Lingbob C Brad 149 K8
Lingdale R & Cl 170 F7
Lingen Herefs 79 L2
Lingfield Surrey 38 B4
Lingwood Norfk 107 G2
Linicro Highld 258 F3
Linkend Worcs 64 B1
Linkenholt Hants 48 A7
Linkhill Kent 24 E2
Linkinhorne Cnwll 11 L7
Linktown Fife 211 J1
Linkwood Moray 266 E4
Linley Shrops 95 J5
Linley Green Herefs 80 F4
Linleygreen Shrops 96 F4
Linlithgow W Loth 210 C4
Linshiels Nthumb 190 C5
Linsidemore Highld 272 D3
Linslade C Beds 67 M2
Linstead Parva Suffk 107 G7
Linstock Cumb 178 A7
Linthurst Worcs 82 B1
Linthwaite Kirk 141 H5
Lintlaw Border 213 H7
Lintmill Moray 267 K3
Linton Border 202 B7
Linton Cambs 88 B6
Linton Derbys 115 M8
Linton Herefs 63 K2
Linton Kent 39 J3
Linton Leeds 150 E6
Linton N York 149 H3
Linton Nthumb 191 K7
Linton Heath Derbys 115 M8
Linton Hill Herefs 63 K2
Linton-on-Ouse N York 151 G4
Linwood Hants 18 B2
Linwood Lincs 136 B2
Linwood Rens 208 D6
Lionacleit W Isls 283 c9
Lional W Isls 282 h1
Lions Green E Susx 23 J4
Liphook Hants 36 C4
Lipley Shrops 114 A5
Liscard Wirral 129 G1
Liscombe Somset 28 F4
Liskeard Cnwll 6 B2
Lismore Ag & B 228 C7
Liss Hants 36 A5
Lissett E R Yk 153 J4
Liss Forest Hants 36 A5
Lissington Lincs 136 B3
Liston Essex 89 G6
Lisvane Cardif 43 J5
Liswerry Newpt 44 D2
Litcham Norfk 121 J4
Litchard Brdgnd 42 D5
Litchborough Nhants 84 C4
Litchfield Hants 48 C8
Litherland Sefton 138 D8
Litlington Cambs 87 G6
Litlington E Susx 23 J7
Little Abington Cambs 87 L5
Little Addington Nhants 101 H4
Little Airies D & G 173 K5
Little Almshoe Herts 69 G2
Little Alne Warwks 82 D3
Little Altcar Sefton 138 C6
Little Amwell Herts 69 K5
Little Asby Cumb 158 B1
Little Aston Staffs 98 A5
Little Atherfield IoW 19 G7
Little Ayton N York 170 D8
Little Baddow Essex 71 J5

Little Badminton S Glos 46 A2
Little Bampton Cumb 177 J7
Little Bardfield Essex 71 G1
Little Barford Bed 86 D4
Little Barningham Norfk 122 C5
Little Barrington Gloucs 65 J4
Little Barrow Ches W 129 L5
Little Barugh N York 162 D6
Little Bavington Nthumb 180 B3
Little Bealings Suffk 90 F5
Littlebeck N York 162 F2
Little Bedwyn Wilts 47 L5
Little Bentley Essex 73 G2
Little Berkhamsted Herts 69 H5
Little Billing Nhants 84 F3
Little Billington C Beds 68 B3
Little Birch Herefs 63 G1
Little Bispham Bpool 146 F7
Little Blakenham Suffk 90 C5
Little Blencow Cumb 166 B4
Little Bloxwich Wsall 98 C3
Little Bognor W Susx 21 G3
Little Bolehill Derbys 116 A1
Little Bollington Ches E 130 E2
Little Bookham Surrey 50 E8
Littleborough Devon 28 E8
Littleborough Notts 135 G3
Littleborough Rochdl 140 D4
Littlebourne Kent 41 G4
Little Bourton Oxon 83 K6
Little Bowden Leics 101 G6
Little Bradley Suffk 88 D5
Little Brampton Herefs 79 K3
Little Brampton Shrops 95 J7
Little Braxted Essex 71 K4
Little Brechin Angus 234 F3
Littlebredy Dorset 16 B5
Little Brickhill M Keyn 67 L1
Little Bridgeford Staffs 114 D6
Little Brington Nhants 84 C3
Little Bromley Essex 73 G2
Little Broughton Cumb 164 E4
Little Budworth Ches W 130 B6
Little Burstead Essex 71 G8
Littlebury Essex 87 L7
Littlebury Green Essex 87 K7
Little Bytham Lincs 118 D7
Little Canfield Essex 70 E3
Little Carlton Lincs 137 G3
Little Carlton Notts 134 F8
Little Casterton Rutlnd 101 M2
Little Catwick E R Yk 153 H6
Little Catworth Cambs 86 B1
Little Cawthorpe Lincs 137 G3
Little Chalfont Bucks 68 C7
Little Chart Kent 40 B6
Little Chesterford Essex 87 L7
Little Cheveney Kent 39 H4
Little Cheverell Wilts 46 E8
Little Chishill Cambs 87 J7
Little Clacton Essex 73 H3
Little Clanfield Oxon 65 K6
Little Clifton Cumb 164 E5
Little Coates NE Lin 145 H6
Little Comberton Worcs 81 M6
Little Common E Susx 24 C5
Little Comp Kent 39 G2
Little Compton Warwks 65 K1
Little Corby Cumb 178 B7
Little Cornard Suffk 89 H7
Littlecott Wilts 47 H8
Little Cowarne Herefs 80 E5
Little Coxwell Oxon 65 L6
Little Crakehall N York 160 C4
Little Cransley Nhants 101 H8
Little Cressingham Norfk 105 H3
Little Crosby Sefton 138 C7
Little Crosthwaite Cumb 165 H5
Little Cubley Derbys 115 J4
Little Dalby Leics 117 K8
Littledean Gloucs 63 K4
Little Dewchurch Herefs 63 G1
Little Ditton Cambs 88 D3
Little Doward Herefs 63 G4
Littledown Hants 47 M7
Little Downham Cambs 103 L6
Little Driffield E R Yk 152 F4
Little Dunham Norfk 105 H1
Little Dunkeld P & K 232 F7
Little Dunmow Essex 71 G3
Little Durnford Wilts 33 K4
Little Easton Essex 70 F2
Little Eaton Derbys 116 B3
Little Ellingham Norfk 105 K3
Little Elm Somset 32 B2
Little Everdon Nhants 84 B4
Little Eversden Cambs 87 H4
Little Faringdon Oxon 65 J6
Little Fencote N York 160 D4

Little Fenton N York 142 E1
Little Fransham Norfk 105 H1
Little Gaddesden Herts 68 C4
Little Garway Herefs 62 F2
Little Gidding Cambs 102 C7
Little Glemham Suffk 91 H4
Little Gorsley Herefs 63 K2
Little Gransden Cambs 86 F4
Little Green Notts 117 J3
Little Green Somset 32 B1
Little Grimsby Lincs 136 F2
Little Gringley Notts 134 E3
Little Habton N York 162 G3
Little Hadham Herts 70 B3
Little Hale Lincs 118 F3
Little Hallam Derbys 116 D3
Little Hallingbury Essex 70 D4
Littleham Devon 14 B6
Littleham Devon 27 H6
Little Hampden Bucks 67 L6
Littlehampton W Susx 21 H6
Little Hanford Dorset 32 D8
Little Harrowden Nhants 85 G1
Little Haseley Oxon 66 F7
Little Hatfield E R Yk 153 J7
Little Hautbois Norfk 122 E7
Little Haven Pembks 54 D4
Littlehaven W Susx 37 J4
Little Hay Staffs 98 E3
Little Hayfield Derbys 131 K2
Little Haywood Staffs 115 G7
Little Heath Staffs 114 D8
Little Heath W Berk 49 G4
Littlehempston Devon 8 B2
Little Hereford Herefs 80 D2
Little Horkesley Essex 72 F1
Little Hormead Herts 69 L2
Little Horsted E Susx 23 G4
Little Horton C Brad 141 J2
Little Horton Wilts 46 F6
Little Horwood Bucks 67 J1
Little Houghton Barns 142 C6
Little Houghton Nhants 84 F3
Littlehoughton Nthumb 191 J3
Little Hucklow Derbys 132 C4
Little Hulton Salfd 139 L7
Little Hungerford W Berk 48 D4
Little Hutton N York 161 G7
Little Irchester Nhants 85 H2
Little Kelk E R Yk 153 H4
Little Keyford Somset 32 C2
Little Kimble Bucks 67 K5
Little Kineton Warwks 83 H5
Little Kingshill Bucks 67 L7
Little Knox D & G 175 K3
Little Langdale Cumb 156 D2
Little Langford Wilts 33 H4
Little Laver Essex 70 E5
Little Leigh Ches W 130 B4
Little Leighs Essex 71 H4
Little Lever Bolton 139 M6
Little Linford M Keyn 85 G6
Little Load Somset 31 G6
Little London Bucks 66 F4
Little London Cambs 103 J4
Little London E Susx 23 J3
Little London Essex 70 C1
Little London Essex 88 D8
Little London Gloucs 63 L3
Little London Hants 34 E1
Little London Hants 48 F7
Little London Leeds 150 B7
Little London Lincs 119 H7
Little London Lincs 119 M6
Little London Lincs 136 F5
Little London Norfk 120 C7
Little London Powys 94 C5
Little Longstone Derbys 132 D5
Little Madeley Staffs 114 B3
Little Malvern Worcs 81 H7
Little Mancot Flints 129 H6
Little Maplestead Essex 89 G8
Little Marcle Herefs 80 F7
Little Marland Devon 27 J8
Little Marlow Bucks 49 L2
Little Massingham Norfk 121 H6
Little Melton Norfk 106 D2
Littlemill Abers 243 K4
Littlemill Highld 253 H2
Little Mill Mons 62 C6
Little Milton Oxon 66 F7
Little Missenden Bucks 68 A7
Little Mongeham Kent 41 K5
Littlemoor Derbys 133 C7
Little Moor Somset 30 D4
Littlemore Oxon 66 D6
Little Musgrave Cumb 167 H8
Little Ness Shrops 112 F7
Little Neston Ches W 129 G4
Little Newcastle Pembks 75 G6

Little Newsham Dur 168 E7
Little Norton Somset 31 G7
Little Oakley Essex 73 J1
Little Oakley Nhants 101 K6
Little Odell Bed 85 J4
Little Offley Herts 68 E2
Little Ormside Cumb 167 G7
Little Orton Cumb 177 K7
Little Ouse Cambs 104 C5
Little Ouseburn N York 150 F4
Littleover C Derb 116 B5
Little Oxendon Nhants 100 F6
Little Packington Warwks 99 G6
Little Pattenden Kent 39 J4
Little Paxton Cambs 86 D3
Little Petherick Cnwll 10 C8
Little Plumpton Lancs 138 D1
Little Plumstead Norfk 107 G1
Little Ponton Lincs 118 B5
Littleport Cambs 104 B6
Littleport Bridge Cambs 104 B6
Little Posbrook Hants 19 J3
Little Potheridge Devon 27 J8
Little Preston Leeds 142 B2
Little Preston Nhants 84 B4
Littler Ches W 130 C6
Little Raveley Cambs 102 E7
Little Reedness E R Yk 143 K3
Little Ribston N York 150 E5
Little Rissington Gloucs 65 J3
Little Rollright Oxon 65 L1
Little Rowsley Derbys 132 E6
Little Ryburgh Norfk 121 L6
Little Ryle Nthumb 190 E4
Little Ryton Shrops 96 B3
Little Salkeld Cumb 166 D3
Little Sampford Essex 88 C8
Little Sandhurst Br For 49 K6
Little Saredon Staffs 97 L2
Little Saughall Ches W 129 J4
Little Saxham Suffk 88 F3
Little Scatwell Highld 262 C8
Little Shelford Cambs 87 J5
Little Shrewley Warwks 82 F2
Little Silver Devon 13 L1
Little Singleton Lancs 147 G7
Little Skipwith N York 151 K8
Little Smeaton N York 142 E4
Little Snoring Norfk 121 L5
Little Sodbury S Glos 45 M2
Little Sodbury End S Glos 45 L2
Little Somborne Hants 34 E4
Little Somerford Wilts 46 D2
Little Soudley Shrops 114 A6
Little Stainforth N York 148 E2
Little Stainton Darltn 169 K6
Little Stanney Ches W 129 J5
Little Staughton Bed 86 B3
Little Steeping Lincs 137 H7
Little Stoke Staffs 114 E5
Littlestone-on-Sea Kent 25 K2
Little Stonham Suffk 90 D3
Little Stretton Leics 100 E3
Little Stretton Shrops 95 K5
Little Strickland Cumb 166 D6
Little Stukeley Cambs 102 E8
Little Sugnall Staffs 114 C5
Little Sutton Ches W 129 J4
Little Sutton Shrops 96 C6
Little Swinburne Nthumb 179 M3
Little Sypland D & G 175 H4
Little Tew Oxon 66 A2
Little Tey Essex 72 C2
Little Thetford Cambs 103 L8
Little Thirkleby N York 161 G7
Little Thornage Norfk 122 B4
Little Thornton Lancs 147 G7
Little Thorpe Dur 169 L2
Littlethorpe Leics 100 C4
Littlethorpe N York 150 D2
Little Thurlow Suffk 88 D5
Little Thurlow Green Suffk 88 D5
Little Thurrock Thurr 52 D3
Littleton Angus 233 M5
Littleton BaNES 45 H6
Littleton Ches W 129 K6
Littleton D & G 175 G4
Littleton Dorset 17 H2
Littleton Hants 34 F4
Littleton Somset 31 H5
Littleton Surrey 36 E2
Littleton Surrey 50 D5
Littleton Drew Wilts 46 B3
Littleton-on-Severn S Glos 45 H4
Littleton Pannell Wilts 46 E8
Little Torrington Devon 27 J7
Little Totham Essex 72 C5
Little Town Cumb 165 H6
Littletown Dur 169 J2
Little Town Lancs 148 B8

Little Town Warrtn 130 C1
Little Twycross Leics 99 J2
Little Urswick Cumb 156 C7
Little Wakering Essex 53 K1
Little Walden Essex 87 L7
Little Waldingfield Suffk 89 J6
Little Walsingham Norfk 121 K4
Little Waltham Essex 71 H4
Little Warley Essex 52 D1
Little Washbourne Gloucs 82 A8
Little Weighton E R Yk 144 B1
Little Weldon Nhants 101 K5
Little Welnetham Suffk 89 H3
Little Welton Lincs 136 F2
Little Wenham Suffk 90 C7
Little Wenlock Wrekin 96 E2
Little Weston Somset 31 K5
Little Whitefield IoW 19 K5
Little Whittingham Green Suffk 106 F8
Little Whittington Nthumb 180 B5
Littlewick Green W & M 49 K3
Little Wilbraham Cambs 87 L3
Littlewindsor Dorset 15 K2
Little Witcombe Gloucs 64 C4
Little Witley Worcs 81 H3
Little Wittenham Oxon 66 E8
Little Wolford Warwks 83 G8
Littlewood Staffs 98 C2
Little Woodcote Gt Lon 51 H6
Littleworth Bucks 67 L3
Littleworth Oxon 65 L7
Littleworth Staffs 98 C1
Littleworth Staffs 114 E7
Littleworth W Susx 21 L3
Littleworth Worcs 81 K5
Littleworth Worcs 82 B3
Littleworth Common Bucks 50 B2
Little Wratting Suffk 88 D5
Little Wymington Bed 85 J2
Little Wymondley Herts 69 G2
Little Wyrley Staffs 98 C2
Little Wytheford Shrops 113 J7
Little Yeldham Essex 88 F7
Littley Green Essex 71 G4
Litton Derbys 132 C4
Litton N York 158 F7
Litton Somset 45 H8
Litton Cheney Dorset 15 M4
Liurbost W Isls 282 g4
Liverpool Lpool 129 H2
Liversedge Kirk 141 J3
Liverton Devon 13 J7
Liverton R & Cl 171 G7
Liverton Mines R & Cl 171 G7
Liverton Street Kent 39 L3
Livingston W Loth 210 E5
Livingston Village W Loth 210 D5
Lixwm Flints 128 E5
Lizard Cnwll 3 H8
Llaingoch IoA 124 D3
Llaithddu Powys 94 C7
Llan Powys 93 J3
Llanaber Gwynd 109 L7
Llanaelhaearn Gwynd 109 G3
Llanafan Cerdgn 77 J1
Llanafan-Fawr Powys 78 D4
Llanafan-fechan Powys 78 D5
Llanallgo IoA 125 J3
Llanarmon Gwynd 109 G4
Llanarmon Dyffryn Ceiriog Wrexhm 112 A5
Llanarmon-yn-Ial Denbgs 128 E8
Llanarth Cerdgn 76 D4
Llanarth Mons 62 D5
Llanarthne Carmth 58 F5
Llanasa Flints 128 D3
Llanbabo IoA 124 F2
Llanbadarn Fawr Cerdgn 92 D7
Llanbadarn Fynydd Powys 94 D7
Llanbadarn-y-garreg Powys 78 F5
Llanbadoc Mons 62 D7
Llanbadrig IoA 124 F1
Llanbeder Newpt 44 D1
Llanbedr Gwynd 109 K6
Llanbedr Powys 61 K3
Llanbedr Powys 79 G6
Llanbedr-Dyffryn-Clwyd Denbgs 128 D7
Llanbedrgoch IoA 125 J4
Llanbedrog Gwynd 108 F5
Llanbedr-y-Cennin Conwy 126 E6
Llanberis Gwynd 125 K7
Llanbethery V Glam 43 G7
Llanbister Powys 94 D8
Llanblethian V Glam 42 F7
Llanboidy Carmth 55 L2
Llanbradach Caerph 43 J4
Llanbrynmair Powys 93 K3
Llancadle V Glam 42 F8

Llancarfan V Glam 43 G7
Llancayo Mons 62 D6
Llancloudy Herefs 63 G3
Llancynfelyn Cerdgn 92 E5
Llandaff Cardif 43 J6
Llandanwg Gwynd 109 K6
Llandarcy Neath 57 K6
Llandawke Carmth 58 A6
Llanddaniel Fab IoA 125 J5
Llanddarog Carmth 58 F5
Llanddeiniol Cerdgn 77 G1
Llanddeiniolen Gwynd 125 K6
Llandderfel Gwynd 111 J4
Llanddeusant Carmth 59 L4
Llanddeusant IoA 124 F3
Llanddew Powys 61 G1
Llanddewi Swans 56 D7
Llanddewi Brefi Cerdgn 77 J4
Llanddewi'r Cwm Powys 78 E5
Llanddewi Rhydderch Mons 62 D4
Llanddewi Velfrey Pembks 55 K3
Llanddewi Ystradenni Powys 78 F2
Llanddoget Conwy 126 F7
Llanddona IoA 125 K4
Llanddowror Carmth 55 M4
Llanddulas Conwy 127 H4
Llanddwywe Gwynd 109 K7
Llanddyfnan IoA 125 J4
Llandecwyn Gwynd 110 B4
Llandefaelog Powys 60 F1
Llandefaelog-Tre'r-Graig Powys 61 H1
Llandefalle Powys 78 F8
Llandegfan IoA 125 K5
Llandegla Denbgs 112 B1
Llandegley Powys 79 G3
Llandegveth Mons 62 C8
Llandegwning Gwynd 108 D5
Llandeilo Carmth 59 H4
Llandeilo Graban Powys 78 F6
Llandeilo'r Fan Powys 59 B8
Llandeloy Pembks 74 D6
Llandenny Mons 62 E6
Llandevaud Newpt 44 E1
Llandevenny Mons 44 E2
Llandinabo Herefs 63 G2
Llandinam Powys 94 B5
Llandissilio Pembks 55 J3
Llandogo Mons 63 G6
Llandough V Glam 42 F7
Llandough V Glam 43 J7
Llandovery Carmth 59 L2
Llandow V Glam 42 E7
Llandre Carmth 77 J6
Llandre Cerdgn 92 D6
Llandre Isaf Pembks 75 K6
Llandrillo Denbgs 111 K4
Llandrillo-yn-Rhos Conwy 127 G4
Llandrindod Wells Powys 78 E3
Llandrinio Powys 112 D8
Llandudno Conwy 126 F3
Llandudno Junction Conwy 126 F4
Llandulas Powys 78 B7
Llandwrog Gwynd 125 H8
Llandybie Carmth 59 H6
Llandyfaelog Carmth 58 D6
Llandyfan Carmth 59 H5
Llandyfriog Cerdgn 76 B7
Llandyfrydog IoA 125 H3
Llandygai Gwynd 126 B5
Llandygwydd Cerdgn 75 M3
Llandynan Denbgs 112 B3
Llandyrnog Denbgs 128 D6
Llandyssil Powys 94 F4
Llandysul Cerdgn 76 D7
Llanedeyrn Cardif 43 K5
Llanedi Carmth 57 G3
Llaneglwys Powys 78 E7
Llanegryn Gwynd 92 D2
Llanegwad Carmth 58 F4
Llaneilian IoA 125 H1
Llanelian-yn-Rhôs Conwy 127 G4
Llanelidan Denbgs 111 L2
Llanelieu Powys 79 H8
Llanellen Mons 62 C5
Llanelli Carmth 56 F5
Llanelli Crematorium Carmth 56 F4
Llanelltyd Gwynd 110 D7
Llanelly Mons 61 K4
Llanelwedd Powys 78 E5
Llanenddwyn Gwynd 109 L6
Llanengan Gwynd 108 E6
Llanerch Gwynd 111 C8
Llanerch Powys 95 H4
Llanerchymedd IoA 125 G3
Llanerfyl Powys 94 B2
Llanfachraeth IoA 124 E3
Llanfachreth Gwynd 110 E7
Llanfaelog IoA 124 F5
Llanfaelrhys Gwynd 108 C6

Llanfaenor Mons 62 E4
Llanfaes IoA 126 B4
Llanfaes Powys 61 G2
Llanfaethlu IoA 124 E2
Llanfair Gwynd 109 K5
Llanfair Caereinion Powys 94 D2
Llanfair Clydogau Cerdgn 77 H5
Llanfair Dyffryn Clwyd Denbgs 128 D8
Llanfairfechan Conwy 126 B5
Llanfair Kilgeddin Mons 62 D5
Llanfair-Nant-Gwyn Pembks 75 K5
Llanfair P G IoA 125 J5
Llanfair Talhaiarn Conwy 127 J3
Llanfair Waterdine Shrops 94 H5
Llanfairynghornwy IoA 124 E1
Llanfair-yn-Neubwll IoA 124 E4
Llanfallteg Carmth 55 K3
Llanfallteg West Carmth 55 K3
Llanfarian Cerdgn 92 D7
Llanfechain Powys 112 B7
Llanfechell IoA 124 F1
Llanferres Denbgs 128 E7
Llanfflewyn IoA 124 F2
Llanfigael IoA 124 F3
Llanfihangel-ar-arth Carmth 76 D6
Llanfihangel Glyn Myfyr Conwy 111 J2
Llanfihangel Nant Bran Powys 78 C8
Llanfihangel-nant-Melan Powys 79 H4
Llanfihangel Rhydithon Powys 79 G2
Llanfihangel Rogiet Mons 44 F2
Llanfihangel Tal-y-llyn Powys 61 H2
Llanfihangel-uwch-Gwili Carmth 58 E4
Llanfihangel-y-Creuddyn Cerdgn 92 E8
Llanfihangel-yng-Ngwynfa Powys 111 L8
Llanfihangel yn Nhowyn IoA 124 E4
Llanfihangel-y-pennant Gwynd 92 E2
Llanfihangel-y-pennant Gwynd 109 J3
Llanfihangel-y-traethau Gwynd 109 L4
Llanfilo Powys 78 F8
Llanfoist Mons 62 B4
Llanfor Gwynd 111 H4
Llanfrechfa Torfn 62 C8
Llanfrothen Gwynd 110 B3
Llanfrynach Powys 61 G2
Llanfwrog Denbgs 128 D8
Llanfwrog IoA 124 E3
Llanfyllin Powys 112 A7
Llanfynydd Carmth 59 G3
Llanfynydd Flints 129 G8
Llanfyrnach Pembks 75 L4
Llangadfan Powys 94 B1
Llangadog Carmth 56 D3
Llangadog Carmth 59 K3
Llangadwaladr IoA 125 G6
Llangadwaladr Powys 112 B5
Llangaffo IoA 125 H6
Llangain Carmth 58 C5
Llangammarch Wells Powys 78 D5
Llangan V Glam 42 E6
Llangarron Herefs 63 G3
Llangasty-Talyllyn Powys 61 H2
Llangathen Carmth 59 G4
Llangattock Powys 61 K3
Llangattock Lingoed Mons 62 D3
Llangattock-Vibon-Avel Mons 62 F4
Llangedwyn Powys 112 B6
Llangefni IoA 125 H4
Llangeinor Brdgnd 42 D4
Llangeitho Cerdgn 77 H3
Llangeler Carmth 76 C4
Llangelynin Gwynd 92 C2
Llangendeirne Carmth 58 E6
Llangennech Carmth 57 G4
Llangennith Swans 56 D6
Llangenny Powys 61 K3
Llangernyw Conwy 127 H6
Llangian Gwynd 108 E6
Llangiwg Neath 57 K4
Llangloffan Pembks 74 E5
Llanglydwen Carmth 75 L6
Llangoed IoA 126 B4
Llangoedmor Cerdgn 75 L3
Llangollen Denbgs 112 B3
Llangolman Pembks 75 H2
Llangors Powys 61 H2
Llangovan Mons 62 F6
Llangower Gwynd 111 G5
Llangrannog Cerdgn 76 B4
Llangristiolus IoA 125 H5
Llangrove Herefs 63 G3

Llangua Mons 62 E2
Llangunllo Powys 79 H1
Llangunnor Carmth 58 D5
Llangurig Powys 93 K7
Llangwm Conwy 111 J3
Llangwm Mons 62 E7
Llangwm Pembks 55 G5
Llangwnnadl Gwynd 108 C5
Llangwyfan Denbgs 128 D6
Llangwyllog IoA 125 H4
Llangwyryfon Cerdgn 77 H1
Llangybi Cerdgn 77 H4
Llangybi Gwynd 109 G3
Llangybi Mons 62 D7
Llangyfelach Swans 57 H5
Llangynhafal Denbgs 128 D7
Llangynidr Powys 61 J3
Llangynin Carmth 55 M3
Llangynllo Cerdgn 76 C6
Llangynog Carmth 58 C6
Llangynog Powys 111 K6
Llangynwyd Brdgnd 42 C4
Llanhamlach Powys 61 H2
Llanharan Rhondd 42 F5
Llanharry Rhondd 42 F5
Llanhennock Mons 62 D8
Llanhilleth Blae G 61 K7
Llanidan IoA 125 J6
Llanidloes Powys 93 L6
Llaniestyn Gwynd 108 D5
Llanigon Powys 79 H7
Llanilar Cerdgn 92 D8
Llanilid Rhondd 42 E5
Llanina Cerdgn 76 D3
Llanio Cerdgn 77 H4
Llanishen Cardif 43 J5
Llanishen Mons 62 F6
Llanllechid Gwynd 126 C6
Llanlleonfel Powys 78 C5
Llanllowell Mons 62 D7
Llanllugan Powys 94 C3
Llanllwch Carmth 58 C5
Llanllwchaiarn Powys 94 D5
Llanllwni Carmth 76 E7
Llanllyfni Gwynd 109 H1
Llanmadoc Swans 56 D6
Llanmaes V Glam 42 E7
Llanmartin Newpt 44 E1
Llanmerewig Powys 94 E5
Llanmihangel V Glam 42 E7
Llanmiloe Carmth 55 M5
Llanmorlais Swans 56 F6
Llannefydd Conwy 127 K5
Llannon Carmth 56 F3
Llannor Gwynd 108 F4
Llanon Cerdgn 76 F2
Llanover Mons 62 C5
Llanpumsaint Carmth 58 D3
Llanraeadr-ym-Mochnant
  Powys 111 M6
Llanrhian Pembks 74 D6
Llanrhidian Swans 56 F6
Llanrhos Conwy 126 F4
Llanrhychwyn Conwy 126 F7
Llanrhyddlad IoA 124 F2
Llanrhystud Cerdgn 76 F1
Llanrothal Herefs 62 F3
Llanrug Gwynd 125 J7
Llanrumney Cardif 43 K5
Llanrwst Conwy 126 F7
Llansadurnen Carmth 56 A3
Llansadwrn Carmth 59 J3
Llansadwrn IoA 125 K4
Llansaint Carmth 56 C3
Llansamlet Swans 57 J5
Llansanffraid Glan Conwy
  Conwy 126 F4
Llansannan Conwy 127 J6
Llansannor V Glam 42 F6
Llansantffraed Powys 61 H2
Llansantffraed-Cwmdeuddwr
  Powys 78 D2
Llansantffraed-in-Elvel Powys 78 F4
Llansantffraid Cerdgn 76 F2
Llansantffraid-ym-Mechain
  Powys 112 C7
Llansawel Carmth 59 H2
Llansilin Powys 112 B6
Llansoy Mons 62 E6
Llanspyddid Powys 60 F2
Llanstadwell Pembks 54 F6
Llansteffan Carmth 56 C3
Llanstephan Powys 78 F6
Llantarnam Torfn 62 C8
Llanteg Pembks 55 L5
Llanthewy Skirrid Mons 62 D4
Llanthony Mons 62 B2
Llantilio-Crossenny Mons 62 E4
Llantilio Pertholey Mons 62 C4
Llantrisant IoA 124 F3

Llantrisant Mons 62 D7
Llantrisant Rhondd 43 G5
Llantrithyd V Glam 43 G7
Llantwit Fardre Rhondd 43 G4
Llantwit Major V Glam 42 F7
Llantysilio Denbgs 112 B3
Llanuwchllyn Gwynd 111 G5
Llanvaches Newpt 44 E1
Llanvair Discoed Mons 62 F8
Llanvapley Mons 62 D4
Llanvetherine Mons 62 D4
Llanveynoe Herefs 62 C1
Llanvihangel Crucorney Mons 62 C3
Llanvihangel Gobion Mons 62 D5
Llanvihangel-Ystern-Llewern
  Mons 62 E4
Llanwarne Herefs 63 G2
Llanwddyn Powys 111 K7
Llanwenarth Mons 62 B4
Llanwenog Cerdgn 76 F6
Llanwern Newpt 44 D2
Llanwinio Carmth 58 A4
Llanwnda Gwynd 125 H8
Llanwnda Pembks 74 F4
Llanwnnen Cerdgn 76 F6
Llanwnog Powys 94 B4
Llanwonno Rhondd 42 F3
Llanwrda Carmth 59 K3
Llanwrin Powys 93 G3
Llanwrthwl Powys 78 D3
Llanwrtyd Powys 78 B5
Llanwrtyd Wells Powys 78 B6
Llanwyddelan Powys 94 C3
Llanyblodwel Shrops 112 C7
Llanybri Carmth 58 B6
Llanybydder Carmth 76 F6
Llanycefn Pembks 55 J2
Llanychaer Bridge Pembks 75 G5
Llanycrwys Carmth 77 H6
Llanymawddwy Gwynd 111 G7
Llanymynech Powys 112 C7
Llanynghenedl IoA 124 E3
Llanynys Denbgs 128 C7
Llan-y-pwll Wrexhm 112 F1
Llanyre Powys 78 E3
Llanystumdwy Gwynd 109 H4
Llanywern Powys 61 H2
Llawhaden Pembks 55 H3
Llawnt Shrops 112 C5
Llawryglyn Powys 93 K5
Llay Wrexhm 129 H8
Llechcynfarwy IoA 125 G3
Llechfaen Powys 61 G2
Llechrhyd Caerph 61 H5
Llechryd Cerdgn 75 L3
Llechylched IoA 124 F4
Lledrod Cerdgn 77 H1
Llidiardau Gwynd 111 G4
Llidiartnenog Carmth 77 G7
Llidiart-y-parc Denbgs 111 M3
Llithfaen Gwynd 108 F3
Lloc Flints 128 D4
Llowes Powys 79 H7
Llwydcoed Rhondd 60 F6
Llwydcoed Crematorium
  Rhondd 60 F6
Llwydiarth Powys 111 K8
Llwyn Denbgs 128 C6
Llwyncelyn Cerdgn 76 E3
Llwyndafydd Cerdgn 76 C4
Llwynderw Powys 94 F3
Llwyn-drain Pembks 58 A2
Llwyn-du Mons 62 C4
Llwyndyrys Gwynd 108 F3
Llwyngwril Gwynd 92 D2
Llwynhendy Carmth 56 F5
Llwynmawr Wrexhm 112 C4
Llwyn-on Myr Td 60 F5
Llwyn-y-brain Carmth 55 L4
Llwyn-y-groes Cerdgn 77 G4
Llwynypia Rhondd 42 F3
Llynclys Shrops 112 D6
Llynfaes IoA 125 G4
Llyn-y-pandy Flints 128 E6
Llysfaen Conwy 127 H4
Llyswen Cerdgn 76 E3
Llyswen Powys 79 G7
Llysworney V Glam 42 E6
Llys-y-frân Pembks 55 H2
Llywel Powys 60 C1
Load Brook Sheff 132 E2
Loan Falk 210 C4
Loanend Nthumb 202 E3
Loanhead Mdloth 211 J6
Loaningfoot D & G 176 C7
Loans S Ayrs 196 C4
Lobb Devon 27 H3
Lobhillcross Devon 12 B5
Lochailort Highld 238 B7
Lochaline Highld 227 K3

Lochans D & G 172 D3
Locharbriggs D & G 176 C3
Lochavich Ag & B 216 E4
Lochawe Ag & B 217 J2
Loch Baghasdail W Isls 283 c11
Lochboisdale W Isls 283 c11
Lochbuie Ag & B 227 H7
Lochcarron Highld 248 E4
Lochdon Ag & B 227 L6
Lochdonhead Ag & B 227 L5
Lochead Ag & B 206 B3
Lochearnhead Stirlg 219 K2
Locheilside Station Highld 239 G7
Lochend Highld 251 G4
Locheport W Isls 283 c8
Loch Euphoirt W Isls 283 c8
Lochfoot D & G 176 B4
Lochgair Ag & B 206 E1
Lochgelly Fife 222 C8
Lochgilphead Ag & B 206 D2
Lochgoilhead Ag & B 217 K7
Lochieheads Fife 222 D4
Lochill Moray 266 F3
Lochindorb Lodge Highld 253 J4
Lochinver Highld 270 E4
Lochluichart Highld 262 B7
Lochmaben D & G 176 D2
Lochmaddy W Isls 283 d8
Loch Maree Hotel Highld 260 E6
Loch nam Madadh W Isls 283 d8
Lochore Fife 222 B7
Lochranza N Ayrs 194 E1
Lochside Abers 235 J3
Lochside D & G 176 C3
Lochside Highld 252 F1
Lochslin Highld 264 C6
Lochton S Ayrs 183 G7
Lochty Angus 234 E3
Lochty Fife 223 J5
Lochuisge Highld 228 B4
Lochwinnoch Rens 208 B7
Lochwood D & G 187 G6
Lockengate Cnwll 5 H3
Lockerbie D & G 176 F3
Lockeridge Wilts 47 H5
Lockerley Hants 34 C5
Locking N Som 44 D7
Locking Stumps Warrtn 130 C1
Lockington E R Yk 152 F6
Lockington Leics 116 D6
Lockleywood Shrops 113 M6
Locksbottom Gt Lon 51 L6
Locksgreen IoW 19 G5
Locks Heath Hants 19 H2
Lockton N York 162 E5
Loddington Leics 101 H3
Loddington Nhants 101 H7
Loddiswell Devon 7 L5
Loddon Norfk 107 G2
Lode Cambs 87 L3
Lode Heath Solhll 98 F7
Lodge Hill Crematorium Birm 98 C7
Lodsworth W Susx 36 D6
Lofthouse Leeds 142 A3
Lofthouse N York 159 K8
Lofthouse Gate Wakefd 142 A3
Loftus R & Cl 171 G7
Logan E Ayrs 197 H6
Loganbeck Cumb 156 D4
Loganlea W Loth 210 C6
Loggerheads Staffs 114 A4
Logie Angus 235 H3
Logie Fife 223 G3
Logie Moray 253 K2
Logie Coldstone Abers 243 M3
Logie Newton Abers 256 B4
Logie Pert Angus 235 G4
Logierait P & K 232 E5
Logieve Abers 257 G6
Login Carmth 55 L2
Lolworth Cambs 87 H2
Lonbain Highld 259 M6
Londesborough E R Yk 152 C6
London Gt Lon 51 H3
London Apprentice Cnwll 5 G5
London Beach Kent 39 M6
London Colney Herts 68 F6
Londonderry N York 160 D5
London End Nhants 85 J7
Londonthorpe Lincs 118 C4
Londubh Highld 260 D4
Lonemore Highld 260 C4
Long Ashton N Som 45 H5
Long Bank Worcs 97 H8
Long Bennington Lincs 117 J2
Longbenton N Tyne 181 G5
Longborough Gloucs 65 J1
Long Bredy Dorset 16 A4

Longbridge Birm 98 C7
Longbridge Warwks 83 G3
Longbridge Deverill Wilts 32 E3
Long Buckby Nhants 84 C2
Longburgh Cumb 177 J3
Longburton Dorset 31 L8
Long Cause Devon 8 B3
Long Clawson Leics 117 J6
Longcliffe Derbys 132 D8
Longcombe Devon 8 C3
Long Common Hants 35 G7
Long Compton Staffs 114 D7
Long Compton Warwks 83 G8
Longcot Oxon 47 K5
Long Crendon Bucks 67 G5
Long Crichel Dorset 17 J1
Longcroft Cumb 177 H7
Longcross Surrey 50 C6
Longden Shrops 95 K2
Longden Common Shrops 95 K2
Long Ditton Surrey 50 F5
Longdon Staffs 115 H8
Longdon Worcs 81 J7
Longdon Green Staffs 98 D9
Longdon Heath Worcs 81 J7
Longdon upon Tern Wrekin 113 K8
Longdown Devon 13 K4
Longdowns Cnwll 3 J4
Long Drax N York 143 H2
Long Duckmanton Derbys 133 J5
Long Eaton Derbys 116 E5
Longfield Kent 52 D5
Longford Covtry 99 K6
Longford Derbys 115 L4
Longford Gloucs 64 B3
Longford Gt Lon 50 D4
Longford Kent 38 D2
Longford Shrops 113 L5
Longford Wrekin 114 A7
Longforgan P & K 222 E1
Longformacus Border 212 F7
Longframlington Nthumb 191 G6
Long Green Ches W 129 L5
Long Green Worcs 81 J8
Longham Dorset 17 L3
Longham Norfk 121 L8
Long Hanborough Oxon 66 B4
Longhaven Abers 257 L4
Long Hedges Lincs 119 K2
Longhirst Nthumb 191 J8
Longhope Gloucs 63 K3
Longhope Ork 275 b6
Longhorsley Nthumb 191 H7
Longhoughton Nthumb 191 J3
Long Itchington Warwks 83 K2
Longlands Cumb 165 J3
Longlane Derbys 115 L4
Long Lawford Warwks 100 A8
Longlevens Gloucs 64 B3
Longley Calder 141 G3
Longley Kirk 141 J6
Longley Green Worcs 81 G5
Longleys P & K 233 L6
Long Load Somset 31 G6
Longmanhill Abers 268 D4
Long Marston Herts 67 L4
Long Marston N York 151 H5
Long Marston Warwks 82 E5
Long Marton Cumb 166 F5
Long Meadowend Shrops 95 K5
Long Melford Suffk 89 H6
Longmoor Camp Hants 36 B4
Longmorn Moray 266 E4
Longmoss Ches E 131 H5
Long Newnton Gloucs 64 C8
Longnewton Border 201 J7
Long Newton E Loth 212 B6
Longnewton S on T 169 K7
Longney Gloucs 63 M4
Longniddry E Loth 212 A4
Longnor Shrops 96 B3
Longnor Staffs 132 B6
Longparish Hants 34 F2
Longpark Cumb 178 A6
Long Preston N York 148 E4
Longridge Lancs 147 M8
Longridge Staffs 114 E8
Longridge W Loth 210 C6
Longriggend N Lans 209 L3
Long Riston E R Yk 153 H7
Longrock Cnwll 2 D5
Longsdon Staffs 114 F1
Longshaw Wigan 139 G7
Longside Abers 269 J6
Long Sight Oldham 140 D4
Longslow Shrops 113 L4
Longstanton Cambs 87 H2
Longstock Hants 34 D3
Longstone Pembks 55 K5
Longstowe Cambs 86 F4

Long Stratton Norfk ... 106 D5
Long Street M Keyn ... 84 F5
Longstreet Wilts ... 47 H8
Long Sutton Hants ... 35 M2
Long Sutton Lincs ... 119 M7
Long Sutton Somset ... 31 G6
Longthorpe C Pete ... 102 D4
Long Thurlow Suffk ... 89 K2
Longthwaite Cumb ... 166 B6
Longton C Stke ... 114 E3
Longton Lancs ... 138 F3
Longtown Cumb ... 177 L5
Longtown Herefs ... 62 C1
Longueville Jersey ... 9 e3
Longville in the Dale Shrops ... 96 C4
Long Waste Wrekin ... 113 K8
Long Whatton Leics ... 116 D6
Longwick Bucks ... 67 J6
Long Wittenham Oxon ... 66 E8
Longwitton Nthumb ... 180 C1
Longwood D & G ... 175 H3
Longwood Shrops ... 96 D2
Longworth Oxon ... 66 A7
Longyester E Loth ... 212 C6
Lon-las Swans ... 57 K5
Lonmay Abers ... 269 J4
Lonmore Highld ... 258 D7
Looe Cnwll ... 6 B4
Loose Kent ... 39 J3
Loosebeare Devon ... 13 G2
Loosegate Lincs ... 119 K6
Loosley Row Bucks ... 67 K7
Lootcherbrae Abers ... 268 A5
Lopcombe Corner Wilts ... 34 B4
Lopen Somset ... 30 F8
Loppington Shrops ... 113 G5
Lorbottle Nthumb ... 190 E5
Lordington W Susx ... 20 C5
Lordsbridge Norfk ... 104 B1
Lords Wood Medway ... 53 G6
Lornty P & K ... 233 J6
Loscoe Derbys ... 116 C2
Loscombe Dorset ... 15 L3
Lossiemouth Moray ... 266 E2
Lostford Shrops ... 113 K5
Lostock Gralam Ches W ... 130 D5
Lostock Green Ches W ... 130 D5
Lostock Hall Lancs ... 139 H3
Lostock Hall Fold Bolton ... 139 K6
Lostock Junction Bolton ... 139 K6
Lostwithiel Cnwll ... 5 J3
Lothbeg Highld ... 274 C6
Lothersdale N York ... 149 G6
Lothmore Highld ... 274 C6
Loudwater Bucks ... 49 L1
Loughborough Leics ... 116 F7
Loughborough Crematorium
  Leics ... 116 F7
Loughor Swans ... 57 G5
Loughton Essex ... 70 B7
Loughton M Keyn ... 85 G7
Loughton Shrops ... 96 E6
Lound Lincs ... 118 E7
Lound Notts ... 134 D2
Lound Suffk ... 107 K4
Lounston Devon ... 13 J7
Lount Leics ... 116 C7
Louth Lincs ... 136 F2
Love Clough Lancs ... 140 B2
Lovedean Hants ... 19 M1
Lover Wilts ... 34 B6
Loversall Donc ... 142 F8
Loves Green Essex ... 70 F6
Lovesome Hill N York ... 160 E4
Loveston Pembks ... 55 J5
Lovington Somset ... 31 K5
Low Ackworth Wakefd ... 142 C4
Low Angerton Nthumb ... 180 C2
Lowbands Gloucs ... 63 M1
Low Barbeth D & G ... 172 C2
Low Barlings Lincs ... 136 A5
Low Bell End N York ... 162 C3
Low Bentham N York ... 148 A2
Low Biggins Cumb ... 157 K7
Low Borrowbridge Cumb ... 157 K2
Low Bradfield Sheff ... 132 E2
Low Bradley N York ... 149 H6
Low Braithwaite Cumb ... 166 A2
Low Burnham N Linc ... 143 M7
Low Buston Nthumb ... 191 J5
Lowca Cumb ... 164 C6
Low Catton E R Yk ... 151 L5
Low Coniscliffe Darltn ... 169 H7
Low Crosby Cumb ... 178 B7
Lowdham Notts ... 117 H2
Lowe Shrops ... 113 H5
Lowe Hill Staffs ... 131 K8
Low Ellington N York ... 160 B6
Lower Aisholt Somset ... 30 B4

Lower Ansty Dorset ... 16 E2
Lower Apperley Gloucs ... 64 B2
Lower Arncott Oxon ... 66 F3
Lower Ashton Devon ... 13 K6
Lower Assendon Oxon ... 49 H2
Lower Ballam Lancs ... 138 D2
Lower Bartle Lancs ... 139 G1
Lower Basildon W Berk ... 48 F3
Lower Bearwood Herefs ... 79 M4
Lower Beeding W Susx ... 37 K5
Lower Benefield Nhants ... 101 L5
Lower Bentley Worcs ... 82 A2
Lower Beobridge Shrops ... 97 H5
Lower Birchwood Derbys ... 116 D1
Lower Boddington Nhants ... 83 L5
Lower Boscaswell Cnwll ... 2 B4
Lower Bourne Surrey ... 36 C2
Lower Brailes Warwks ... 83 H7
Lower Breakish Highld ... 247 L4
Lower Bredbury Stockp ... 131 H2
Lower Broadheath Worcs ... 81 J4
Lower Broxwood Herefs ... 79 L4
Lower Buckenhill Herefs ... 80 E8
Lower Bullingham Herefs ... 80 C7
Lower Burgate Hants ... 33 K7
Lower Burrowton Devon ... 14 B3
Lower Burton Herefs ... 80 A4
Lower Caldecote C Beds ... 86 D6
Lower Cam Gloucs ... 63 L7
Lower Canada N Som ... 44 D7
Lower Catesby Nhants ... 83 M3
Lower Chapel Powys ... 78 E8
Lower Chicksgrove Wilts ... 33 G5
Lower Chute Wilts ... 47 L8
Lower Clapton Gt Lon ... 51 K2
Lower Clent Worcs ... 97 L8
Lower Creedy Devon ... 13 K2
Lower Crossings Derbys ... 131 L4
Lower Cumberworth Kirk ... 141 K6
Lower Darwen Bl w D ... 139 K3
Lower Dean Bed ... 85 L2
Lower Denby Kirk ... 141 K6
Lower Diabaig Highld ... 260 C7
Lower Dicker E Susx ... 23 J5
Lower Dinchope Shrops ... 95 L6
Lower Down Shrops ... 95 H6
Lower Dunsforth N York ... 150 F3
Lower Egleton Herefs ... 80 E6
Lower Elkstone Staffs ... 131 L8
Lower Ellastone Staffs ... 115 J3
Lower End Bucks ... 67 G5
Lower End M Keyn ... 85 H7
Lower End Nhants ... 84 F3
Lower End Nhants ... 85 H3
Lower Everleigh Wilts ... 47 J8
Lower Exbury Hants ... 19 G4
Lower Eythorne Kent ... 41 J5
Lower Failand N Som ... 45 G4
Lower Farringdon Hants ... 35 L4
Lower Feltham Gt Lon ... 50 E4
Lower Fittleworth W Susx ... 21 G3
Lower Foxdale IoM ... 154 c6
Lower Frankton Shrops ... 112 E5
Lower Freystrop Pembks ... 54 F4
Lower Froyle Hants ... 36 A2
Lower Gabwell Devon ... 8 D1
Lower Gledfield Highld ... 263 G2
Lower Godney Somset ... 31 G2
Lower Gornal Dudley ... 97 L5
Lower Gravenhurst C Beds ... 86 C8
Lower Green Herts ... 86 D8
Lower Green Herts ... 87 J8
Lower Green Kent ... 38 E5
Lower Green Kent ... 39 G5
Lower Green Norfk ... 121 L4
Lower Green Staffs ... 97 K2
Lower Green Suffk ... 88 E2
Lower Hacheston Suffk ... 91 H4
Lower Halliford Surrey ... 50 E5
Lower Halstock Leigh Dorset ... 15 M1
Lower Halstow Kent ... 53 J5
Lower Hamworthy Poole ... 17 K4
Lower Hardres Kent ... 40 F5
Lower Harpton Herefs ... 79 K3
Lower Hartlip Kent ... 53 H6
Lower Hartshay Derbys ... 116 C1
Lower Hartwell Bucks ... 67 J4
Lower Hatton Staffs ... 114 C4
Lower Hawthwaite Cumb ... 156 B5
Lower Hergest Herefs ... 79 K4
Lower Heyford Oxon ... 66 C2
Lower Heysham Lancs ... 147 H4
Lower Higham Kent ... 52 H4
Lower Holbrook Suffk ... 90 E8
Lower Hordley Shrops ... 112 F5
Lower Horncroft W Susx ... 21 G3
Lowerhouse Lancs ... 140 B1
Lower Houses Kirk ... 141 J5
Lower Howsell Worcs ... 81 H5
Lower Irlam Salfd ... 130 D1

Lower Kilburn Derbys ... 116 C3
Lower Kilcott Gloucs ... 46 A1
Lower Killeyan Ag & B ... 204 D7
Lower Kingcombe Dorset ... 16 A3
Lower Kingswood Surrey ... 51 H8
Lower Kinnerton Ches W ... 129 H7
Lower Langford N Som ... 44 F6
Lower Largo Fife ... 223 G6
Lower Leigh Staffs ... 115 G4
Lower Lemington Gloucs ... 82 F8
Lower Llanfadog Powys ... 78 C2
Lower Lovacott Devon ... 27 J5
Lower Loxhore Devon ... 27 L3
Lower Lydbrook Gloucs ... 63 H4
Lower Lye Herefs ... 79 M2
Lower Machen Newpt ... 43 K4
Lower Maes-coed Herefs ... 62 D1
Lower Mannington Dorset ... 17 L2
Lower Marston Somset ... 32 C2
Lower Meend Gloucs ... 63 H4
Lower Merridge Somset ... 30 B4
Lower Middleton Cheney
  Nhants ... 83 L7
Lower Milton Somset ... 31 J2
Lower Moor Worcs ... 82 A6
Lower Morton S Glos ... 63 J8
Lower Nazeing Essex ... 69 K6
Lower Norton Warwks ... 82 F3
Lower Nyland Dorset ... 32 C6
Lower Penarth V Glam ... 43 J7
Lower Penn Staffs ... 97 K4
Lower Pennington Hants ... 18 E5
Lower Penwortham Lancs ... 139 G2
Lower Peover Ches E ... 130 E5
Lower Place Rochdl ... 140 D5
Lower Pollicott Bucks ... 67 H4
Lower Quinton Warwks ... 82 E6
Lower Rainham Medway ... 53 H5
Lower Raydon Suffk ... 90 B7
Lower Roadwater Somset ... 29 J3
Lower Salter Lancs ... 147 M3
Lower Seagry Wilts ... 46 D3
Lower Sheering Essex ... 70 C4
Lower Shelton C Beds ... 85 K6
Lower Shiplake Oxon ... 49 J3
Lower Shuckburgh Warwks ... 83 L3
Lower Slaughter Gloucs ... 65 H4
Lower Soothill Kirk ... 141 L3
Lower Soudley Gloucs ... 63 K5
Lower Standen Kent ... 41 H7
Lower Stanton St Quintin
  Wilts ... 46 D3
Lower Stoke Medway ... 53 H4
Lower Stone Gloucs ... 63 K8
Lower Stonnall Staffs ... 98 D3
Lower Stow Bedon Norfk ... 105 K4
Lower Street Dorset ... 17 G3
Lower Street E Susx ... 24 C5
Lower Street Norfk ... 122 F4
Lower Street Suffk ... 88 F5
Lower Street Suffk ... 90 D5
Lower Stretton Warrtn ... 130 C3
Lower Stroud Dorset ... 15 K3
Lower Sundon C Beds ... 68 D2
Lower Swanwick Hants ... 19 H2
Lower Swell Gloucs ... 65 H4
Lower Tadmarton Oxon ... 83 J7
Lower Tale Devon ... 14 C2
Lower Tean Staffs ... 115 G4
Lower Thurlton Norfk ... 107 J3
Lower Town Cnwll ... 3 G5
Lower Town Devon ... 13 G8
Lower Town Herefs ... 80 E6
Lower Town Pembks ... 74 F5
Lower Trebullett Cnwll ... 11 L7
Lower Treluswell Cnwll ... 3 K4
Lower Tysoe Warwks ... 83 H6
Lower Ufford Suffk ... 91 G5
Lower Upcott Devon ... 13 K6
Lower Upham Hants ... 35 H7
Lower Upnor Medway ... 53 G5
Lower Vexford Somset ... 29 L4
Lower Walton Warrtn ... 130 B3
Lower Waterston Dorset ... 16 E4
Lower Weare Somset ... 44 E8
Lower Weedon Nhants ... 84 C3
Lower Welson Herefs ... 79 K5
Lower Westmancote Worcs ... 81 L7
Lower Whatcombe Dorset ... 17 G2
Lower Whatley Somset ... 32 B2
Lower Whitley Ches W ... 130 B4
Lower Wick Gloucs ... 63 L7
Lower Wick Worcs ... 81 J5
Lower Wield Hants ... 35 K3
Lower Willingdon E Susx ... 23 K6
Lower Withington Ches E ... 130 F5
Lower Woodend Bucks ... 49 K2
Lower Woodford Wilts ... 33 K4
Lower Wraxhall Dorset ... 16 A2
Lower Wyche Worcs ... 81 H6

Lower Wyke C Brad ... 141 J3
Lowesby Leics ... 100 F2
Lowestoft Suffk ... 107 L5
Loweswater Cumb ... 164 F6
Low Fell Gatesd ... 181 G2
Lowfield Heath W Susx ... 37 L3
Low Gartachorrans Stirlg ... 208 D2
Low Gate Nthumb ... 179 L6
Low Gettbridge Cumb ... 178 C7
Lowgill Cumb ... 157 K3
Lowgill Lancs ... 148 A3
Low Grantley N York ... 150 B2
Low Green N York ... 150 B4
Low Habberley Worcs ... 97 J8
Low Ham Somset ... 30 F4
Low Harrogate N York ... 150 C5
Low Hawsker N York ... 163 G1
Low Hesket Cumb ... 166 B2
Low Hutton N York ... 152 A2
Lowick Cumb ... 156 D5
Lowick Nhants ... 101 L7
Lowick Nthumb ... 203 G5
Lowick Bridge Cumb ... 156 D5
Lowick Green Cumb ... 156 D5
Low Knipe Cumb ... 166 C6
Low Laithe N York ... 150 B3
Lowlands Dur ... 168 E5
Lowlands Torfn ... 62 C7
Low Langton Lincs ... 136 C3
Low Leighton Derbys ... 131 K3
Low Lorton Cumb ... 164 F5
Low Marishes N York ... 162 E7
Low Marnham Notts ... 134 D7
Low Middleton Nthumb ... 203 H6
Low Mill N York ... 161 L4
Low Moor C Brad ... 141 J2
Low Moorsley Sundld ... 169 J2
Low Moresby Cumb ... 164 C6
Low Newton Cumb ... 156 F6
Low Row Cumb ... 165 G2
Low Row Cumb ... 165 G2
Low Row Cumb ... 178 D6
Low Row N York ... 159 H3
Low Salchrie D & G ... 172 C2
Low Santon N Linc ... 144 B5
Lowsonford Warwks ... 82 E2
Low Street Norfk ... 123 G6
Low Street Thurr ... 52 E2
Low Tharston Norfk ... 106 D4
Lowther Cumb ... 166 D6
Lowther Castle Cumb ... 166 C6
Lowthorpe E R Yk ... 153 H4
Lowton Devon ... 12 F4
Lowton Somset ... 30 B7
Lowton Wigan ... 139 J8
Lowton Common Wigan ... 139 J8
Lowton St Mary's Wigan ... 139 J8
Low Torry Fife ... 210 D2
Low Toynton Lincs ... 136 E5
Low Valley Barns ... 142 B7
Low Wood Cumb ... 156 E6
Low Worsall N York ... 160 F1
Low Wray Cumb ... 156 E2
Loxbeare Devon ... 29 H3
Loxhill Surrey ... 36 F3
Loxhore Devon ... 27 L3
Loxhore Cott Devon ... 27 L3
Loxley Warwks ... 83 G4
Loxley Green Staffs ... 115 H5
Loxter Herefs ... 81 G7
Loxton N Som ... 44 D7
Loxwood W Susx ... 36 F4
Loyal Lodge Highld ... 277 L7
Lubenham Leics ... 100 F6
Lucasgate Lincs ... 119 M2
Lucas Green Surrey ... 50 B7
Luccombe Somset ... 29 G2
Luccombe Village IoW ... 19 K7
Lucker Nthumb ... 203 H4
Luckett Cnwll ... 11 M7
Lucking Street Essex ... 89 G8
Luckington Wilts ... 46 B2
Lucklawhill Fife ... 223 G4
Lucknam Wilts ... 46 B4
Luckwell Bridge Somset ... 28 F3
Lucton Herefs ... 80 B2
Lucy Cross N York ... 169 G8
Ludag W Isls ... 283 c12
Ludborough Lincs ... 145 H8
Ludbrook Devon ... 7 J4
Ludchurch Pembks ... 55 K4
Luddenden Calder ... 141 G3
Luddenden Foot Calder ... 140 F3
Luddenham Court Kent ... 40 C3
Luddesdown Kent ... 52 E5
Luddington N Linc ... 143 L4
Luddington Warwks ... 82 E5
Luddington in the Brook
  Nhants ... 102 C6
Ludford Lincs ... 136 D2

Ludford Shrops 96 C8
Ludgershall Bucks 67 G4
Ludgershall Wilts 34 B1
Ludgvan Cnwll 2 D4
Ludham Norfk 123 H7
Ludlow Shrops 96 C8
Ludney Somset 30 F8
Ludwell Wilts 32 F6
Ludworth Dur 169 K2
Luffenhall Herts 69 J1
Luffincott Devon 11 L4
Luffness E Loth 212 B3
Lugar E Ayrs 197 H6
Luggate Burn E Loth 212 D4
Lugg Green Herefs 80 B3
Luggiebank N Lans 209 K4
Lugton E Ayrs 208 C8
Lugwardine Herefs 80 D7
Luib Highld 247 J3
Luing Ag & B 215 L2
Lulham Herefs 80 A7
Lullington Derbys 99 H1
Lullington E Susx 23 J6
Lullington Somset 45 M8
Lulsgate Bottom N Som 45 G6
Lulsley Worcs 81 G4
Lulworth Camp Dorset 16 F6
Lumb Calder 140 F3
Lumb Lancs 140 C3
Lumbutts Calder 140 E3
Lumby N York 142 D2
Lumloch E Duns 209 H5
Lumphanan Abers 244 D3
Lumphinnans Fife 222 B8
Lumsden Abers 255 K7
Lunan Angus 235 H5
Lunanhead Angus 234 D5
Luncarty P & K 221 K1
Lund E R Yk 152 E6
Lund N York 143 G1
Lundie Angus 233 L8
Lundin Links Fife 223 G6
Lundin Mill Fife 223 G6
Lundy Devon 26 B2
Lundy Green Norfk 106 E5
Lunga Ag & B 215 K3
Lunna Shet 281 e4
Lunsford Kent 52 F7
Lunsford's Cross E Susx 24 C5
Lunt Sefton 138 D7
Luntley Herefs 79 M4
Luppitt Devon 14 E1
Lupridge Devon 7 L4
Lupset Wakefd 141 M4
Lupton Cumb 157 J6
Lurgashall W Susx 36 D5
Lurley Devon 29 G7
Lusby Lincs 136 F6
Luscombe Devon 8 B3
Luson Devon 7 H5
Luss Ag & B 218 E8
Lussagiven Ag & B 215 J7
Lusta Highld 258 D5
Lustleigh Devon 13 H6
Luston Herefs 80 B3
Luthermuir Abers 235 G2
Luthrie Fife 222 E3
Lutley Dudley 97 L6
Luton Devon 13 L7
Luton Devon 14 C2
Luton Luton 68 G3
Luton Medway 53 G5
Lutterworth Leics 100 C6
Lutton Devon 7 H3
Lutton Devon 7 K5
Lutton Lincs 119 M6
Lutton Nhants 102 C6
Luxborough Somset 29 H3
Luxulyan Cnwll 5 H2
Luzley Tamesd 140 E7
Lybster Highld 275 H1
Lydbury North Shrops 95 J6
Lydcott Devon 28 B4
Lydd Kent 25 K3
Lydden Kent 41 H6
Lydden Kent 41 K2
Lyddington Rutlnd 101 J4
Lydeard St Lawrence Somset 29 L4
Lyde Green Hants 49 H7
Lydford Devon 12 C5
Lydford on Fosse Somset 31 J5
Lydgate Calder 140 D3
Lydgate Rochdl 140 E4
Lydham Shrops 95 H5
Lydiard Green Wilts 47 G2
Lydiard Millicent Wilts 47 G2
Lydiard Tregoze Swindn 47 G2
Lydiate Sefton 138 D7
Lydiate Ash Worcs 98 B8
Lydlinch Dorset 32 B8

Lydney Gloucs 63 J6
Lydstep Pembks 55 J7
Lye Dudley 97 L6
Lye Cross N Som 44 F6
Lye Green Bucks 68 B6
Lye Green E Susx 38 D6
Lye Green Warwks 82 E2
Lye Head Worcs 97 G8
Lye's Green Wilts 32 D2
Lyford Oxon 66 B8
Lymbridge Green Kent 40 F6
Lyme Regis Dorset 15 H4
Lyminge Kent 40 F7
Lymington Hants 18 L4
Lyminster W Susx 21 H6
Lymm Warrtn 130 D2
Lympne Kent 40 F8
Lympsham Somset 44 C8
Lympstone Devon 14 A6
Lynbridge Devon 28 C1
Lynchat Highld 241 L3
Lynch Green Norfk 106 C2
Lyndhurst Hants 18 D2
Lyndon Rutlnd 101 K3
Lyndon Green Birm 98 F6
Lyne Border 199 L5
Lyne Surrey 50 C5
Lyneal Shrops 113 G5
Lyne Down Herefs 63 J1
Lyneham Devon 13 K6
Lyneham Oxon 65 K3
Lyneham Wilts 46 F3
Lyneholmford Cumb 178 C4
Lynemouth Nthumb 191 K7
Lyne of Skene Abers 245 G2
Lynesack Dur 168 E5
Lyness Ork 275 b6
Lyng Norfk 122 B7
Lyng Somset 30 E5
Lynmouth Devon 28 C1
Lynn Staffs 98 D3
Lynn Wrekin 114 B8
Lynsted Kent 40 B3
Lynstone Cnwll 11 H2
Lynton Devon 28 C1
Lyon's Gate Dorset 16 C2
Lyonshall Herefs 79 L4
Lytchett Matravers Dorset 17 J3
Lytchett Minster Dorset 17 J4
Lyth Highld 280 C4
Lytham Lancs 138 D2
Lytham St Anne's Lancs 138 D2
Lythbank Shrops 95 L2
Lythe N York 171 K8
Lythmore Highld 279 J3

M

Mabe Burnthouse Cnwll 3 J4
Mablethorpe Lincs 137 J3
Macclesfield Ches E 131 H5
Macclesfield Crematorium
  Ches E 131 H5
Macduff Abers 268 C3
Macharioch Ag & B 192 E6
Machen Caerph 43 K4
Machrie N Ayrs 194 D4
Machrihanish Ag & B 192 D4
Machrins Ag & B 214 D5
Machynlleth Powys 93 G3
Machynys Carmth 56 F5
Mackworth Derbys 116 A4
Macmerry E Loth 211 M4
Maddaford Devon 12 D4
Madderty P & K 221 G3
Maddington Wilts 33 J2
Maddiston Falk 210 B4
Madehurst W Susx 21 G5
Madeley Staffs 114 B3
Madeley Wrekin 96 F3
Madeley Heath Staffs 114 B2
Madford Devon 29 L8
Madingley Cambs 87 H3
Madley Herefs 80 A7
Madresfield Worcs 81 J5
Madron Cnwll 2 C5
Maenaddwyn IoA 125 H3
Maenan Conwy 126 F6
Maenclochog Pembks 75 J6
Maendy V Glam 42 F6
Maenporth Cnwll 3 K5
Maentwrog Gwynd 110 C3
Maen-y-groes Cerdgn 76 C3
Maer Cnwll 11 H1
Maer Staffs 114 B4
Maerdy Carmth 59 J3
Maerdy Rhondd 42 E2
Maesbrook Shrops 112 D7
Maesbury Shrops 112 D6

Maesbury Marsh Shrops 112 D6
Maes-glas Newpt 44 C2
Maesgwynne Carmth 55 L2
Maeshafn Denbgs 128 E7
Maesllyn Cerdgn 76 C6
Maesmynis Powys 78 D3
Maesmynis Powys 78 E5
Maesteg Brdgnd 42 C3
Maesybont Carmth 59 G5
Maesycwmmer Caerph 43 J3
Magdalen Laver Essex 70 D5
Maggieknockater Moray 254 F3
Maggots End Essex 70 C2
Maghull Sefton 138 D7
Magna Park Leics 100 B6
Magor Mons 44 E2
Maidenbower W Susx 37 L4
Maiden Bradley Wilts 32 D3
Maidencombe Torbay 8 D1
Maidenhayne Devon 15 G3
Maiden Head N Som 45 H5
Maidenhead W & M 49 L3
Maiden Law Dur 168 F1
Maiden Newton Dorset 16 B3
Maidens S Ayrs 182 F1
Maiden's Green Br For 49 L4
Maidenwell Lincs 136 F4
Maiden Wells Pembks 55 H7
Maidford Nhants 84 B5
Maids Moreton Bucks 84 D8
Maidstone Kent 39 J2
Maidwell Nhants 101 K3
Mail Shet 281 e6
Maindee Newpt 44 C1
Mainland Ork 275 C4
Mainland Shet 281 d6
Mainsforth Dur 169 J4
Mains of Balhall Angus 234 D3
Mains of Balnakettle Abers 244 E8
Mains of Dalvey Highld 254 B5
Mains of Haulkerton Abers 235 H1
Mains of Lesmoir Abers 255 J6
Mains of Melgunds Angus 234 E4
Mainsriddle D & G 176 B7
Mainstone Shrops 95 G6
Maisemore Gloucs 64 A3
Major's Green Worcs 98 E7
Makeney Derbys 116 B3
Malborough Devon 7 K7
Malcoff Derbys 131 L3
Malden Rushett Gt Lon 50 F6
Maldon Essex 71 K5
Malham N York 148 F3
Maligar Highld 259 H4
Mallaig Highld 237 K1
Mallaigvaig Highld 237 K1
Malleny Mills C Edin 211 G6
Mallows Green Essex 70 C2
Malltraeth IoA 125 G6
Mallwyd Gwynd 93 J1
Malmesbury Wilts 46 D2
Malmsmead Devon 28 D1
Malpas Ches W 113 H2
Malpas Cnwll 4 D6
Malpas Newpt 44 C1
Malshanger Hants 48 E8
Malswick Gloucs 63 L2
Maltby Lincs 136 F3
Maltby Rothm 133 K1
Maltby S on T 170 B8
Maltby le Marsh Lincs 137 J3
Malting Green Essex 72 E3
Maltman's Hill Kent 40 A6
Malton N York 152 B2
Malvern Link Worcs 81 H5
Malvern Wells Worcs 81 H6
Mamble Worcs 80 F1
Mamhilad Mons 62 C6
Manaccan Cnwll 3 J6
Manafon Powys 94 D3
Manais W Isls 282 e6
Manaton Devon 13 H6
Manby Lincs 137 G2
Mancetter Warwks 99 J4
Manchester Manch 140 C8
Mancot Flints 129 H6
Mandally Highld 240 A3
Manea Cambs 103 K5
Maney Birm 98 E4
Manfield N York 169 G8
Mangerton Dorset 15 L3
Mangotsfield S Glos 45 K4
Mangrove Green Herts 68 E2
Manhay Cnwll 3 H5
Manish W Isls 282 e6
Mankinholes Calder 140 E3
Manley Ches W 129 L5
Manmoel Caerph 61 J7
Mannel Ag & B 224 C7

Manningford Bohune Wilts 47 H7
Manningford Bruce Wilts 47 H7
Manningham C Brad 141 J1
Manning's Heath W Susx 37 K5
Mannington Dorset 17 L2
Manningtree Essex 73 G1
Mannofield C Aber 245 K3
Manorbier Pembks 55 H7
Manorbier Newton Pembks 55 H6
Manordeilo Carmth 59 J4
Manorhill Border 201 K6
Manorowen Pembks 74 F5
Manor Park Gt Lon 51 L2
Manor Park Crematorium
  Gt Lon 51 L2
Mansell Gamage Herefs 79 M6
Mansell Lacy Herefs 80 A6
Mansergh Cumb 157 K6
Mansfield E Ayrs 197 J8
Mansfield Notts 133 K7
Mansfield & District
  Crematorium Notts 133 K7
Mansfield Woodhouse Notts 133 K7
Mansriggs Cumb 156 D6
Manston Dorset 32 D7
Manston Kent 41 K2
Manston Leeds 142 B1
Manswood Dorset 17 J1
Manthorpe Lincs 118 B4
Manthorpe Lincs 118 E8
Manton N Linc 144 A7
Manton Notts 134 C4
Manton Rutlnd 101 J3
Manton Wilts 47 H5
Manuden Essex 70 C2
Manwood Green Essex 70 E4
Maperton Somset 31 L5
Maplebeck Notts 134 E7
Maple Cross Herts 68 C8
Mapledurham Oxon 49 G4
Mapledurwell Hants 49 G8
Maplehurst W Susx 37 J6
Maplescombe Kent 52 C6
Mapleton Derbys 115 K2
Mapleton Kent 38 C3
Mapperley Derbys 116 D3
Mapperley Park C Nott 117 G3
Mapperton Dorset 15 L3
Mappleborough Green
  Warwks 82 C2
Mappleton E R Yk 153 K7
Mapplewell Barns 141 M5
Mappowder Dorset 16 E2
Marazanvose Cnwll 4 C5
Marazion Cnwll 2 E5
Marbury Ches E 113 J2
March Cambs 103 J4
March S Lans 186 E3
Marcham Oxon 66 C4
Marchamley Shrops 113 K5
Marchamley Wood Shrops 113 K5
Marchington Staffs 115 J5
Marchington Woodlands
  Staffs 115 J6
Marchros Gwynd 108 E6
Marchwiel Wrexhm 112 E2
Marchwood Hants 18 F2
Marcross V Glam 42 D7
Marden Herefs 80 C6
Marden Kent 39 J4
Marden Wilts 47 G2
Marden Ash Essex 70 E6
Marden Beech Kent 39 J5
Mardens Hill E Susx 38 D7
Marden Thorn Kent 39 J5
Mardlebury Herts 69 H3
Mardy Mons 62 C4
Marefield Leics 101 G2
Mareham le Fen Lincs 136 E7
Mareham on the Hill Lincs 136 E6
Marehay Derbys 116 C2
Marehill W Susx 21 H3
Maresfield E Susx 23 G2
Marfleet C KuH 144 E2
Marford Wrexhm 129 H8
Margam Neath 57 L7
Margam Crematorium Neath 42 B4
Margaret Marsh Dorset 32 D7
Margaret Roding Essex 70 F5
Margaretting Essex 71 G6
Margaretting Tye Essex 71 G7
Margate Kent 41 K1
Margnaheglish N Ayrs 195 G4
Margrie D & G 174 F5
Margrove Park R & Cl 170 F7
Marham Norfk 104 D2
Marhamchurch Cnwll 11 J2
Marholm C Pete 102 C3
Marian-glas IoA 125 J3
Mariansleigh Devon 28 C6

Marine Town Kent 53 K4
Marionburgh Abers 244 F2
Marishader Highld 259 H4
Maristow Devon 6 F2
Marjoriebanks D & G 176 E2
Mark Somset 30 F1
Markbeech Kent 38 D5
Markby Lincs 137 J4
Mark Causeway Somset 30 E2
Mark Cross E Susx 38 F7
Markeaton C Derb 116 B4
Markeaton Crematorium
    C Derb 116 B4
Market Bosworth Leics 99 L3
Market Deeping Lincs 102 C2
Market Drayton Shrops 113 L5
Market Harborough Leics 100 F6
Market Lavington Wilts 46 E8
Market Overton Rutlnd 118 A8
Market Rasen Lincs 136 B2
Market Stainton Lincs 136 D4
Market Warsop Notts 133 L6
Market Weighton E R Yk 152 D7
Market Weston Suffk 105 K7
Markfield Leics 100 F6
Markham Caerph 61 J6
Markham Moor Notts 134 E5
Markinch Fife 222 E6
Markington N York 150 C3
Markle E Loth 212 C3
Marksbury BaNES 45 K6
Mark's Corner IoW 19 H5
Marks Tey Essex 72 C2
Markwell Cnwll 6 D3
Markyate Herts 68 D4
Marlborough Wilts 47 J5
Marlbrook Herefs 80 C4
Marlbrook Worcs 98 B8
Marlcliff Warwks 82 C5
Marldon Devon 8 C2
Marle Green E Susx 23 K4
Marlesford Suffk 91 H3
Marley Kent 41 G5
Marley Kent 41 K4
Marley Green Ches E 113 J2
Marley Hill Gatesd 180 F7
Marlingford Norfk 106 C2
Marloes Pembks 54 C5
Marlow Bucks 49 K2
Marlow Herefs 95 K8
Marlow Bottom Bucks 49 K1
Marlpit Hill Kent 38 C4
Marlpits E Susx 24 C4
Marlpits E Susx 38 C7
Marlpool Derbys 116 D3
Marnhull Dorset 32 C2
Marple Stockp 131 J2
Marple Bridge Stockp 131 J2
Marr Donc 142 E6
Marrick N York 159 K3
Marros Carmth 55 L5
Marsden Kirk 141 G5
Marsden S Tyne 181 K6
Marsden Height Lancs 148 F4
Marsett N York 158 F5
Marsh Bucks 67 K5
Marsh C Brad 149 J8
Marsh Devon 30 C8
Marshall's Heath Herts 68 F4
Marshalswick Herts 68 F5
Marsham Norfk 122 D6
Marsh Baldon Oxon 66 E7
Marsh Benham W Berk 48 B5
Marshborough Kent 41 J4
Marshbrook Shrops 95 K5
Marshchapel Lincs 145 K7
Marsh Farm Luton 68 D2
Marshfield Newpt 43 L5
Marshfield S Glos 45 M4
Marshgate Cnwll 11 G2
Marsh Gibbon Bucks 66 F3
Marsh Green Devon 14 B4
Marsh Green Kent 38 C4
Marsh Green Wrekin 113 K8
Marshland St James Norfk 103 L2
Marsh Lane Derbys 133 H4
Marsh Lane Gloucs 63 H5
Marshside Sefton 138 D4
Marsh Street Somset 29 H2
Marshwood Dorset 15 J3
Marske N York 159 K3
Marske-by-the-Sea R & Cl 170 E6
Marsland Green Wigan 139 K7
Marston Ches W 130 D5
Marston Herefs 79 C4
Marston Lincs 118 A3
Marston Oxon 66 D5
Marston Somset 30 F1
Marston Staffs 97 J1
Marston Staffs 114 E6
Marston Warwks 99 G4

Marston Wilts 46 D7
Marston Green Solhll 98 F6
Marston Jabbet Warwks 99 K5
Marston Magna Somset 31 K6
Marston Meysey Wilts 65 H7
Marston Montgomery Derbys . 115 G6
Marston Moretaine C Beds 85 K7
Marston on Dove Derbys 115 L5
Marston St Lawrence Nhants .. 83 M6
Marston Stannett Herefs 80 D4
Marston Trussell Nhants 100 F6
Marstow Herefs 63 H3
Marsworth Bucks 68 A4
Marten Wilts 47 L7
Marthall Ches E 130 F4
Martham Norfk 123 J7
Martin Hants 33 J7
Martin Kent 41 K6
Martin Lincs 136 B7
Martin Lincs 136 D6
Martindale Cumb 166 B6
Martin Dales Lincs 136 C7
Martin Drove End Hants 33 H6
Martinhoe Devon 28 B1
Martin Hussingtree Worcs 81 K3
Martinscroft Warrtn 130 C2
Martinstown Dorset 16 C5
Martlesham Suffk 90 F6
Martlesham Heath Suffk 90 F6
Martletwy Pembks 55 H5
Martley Worcs 81 H3
Martock Somset 31 G7
Marton Ches E 131 G6
Marton Ches W 130 C6
Marton Cumb 156 C7
Marton E R Yk 153 J7
Marton E R Yk 153 K2
Marton Lincs 135 G3
Marton Middsb 170 C7
Marton N York 150 F3
Marton N York 162 C6
Marton Shrops 95 G3
Marton Warwks 83 J2
Marton-le-Moor N York 150 E2
Martyr's Green Surrey 50 E7
Martyr Worthy Hants 35 G4
Marwick Ork 275 b3
Marwood Devon 27 K3
Marybank Highld 250 E1
Maryburgh Highld 262 F8
Maryculter Abers 245 J4
Marygold Border 213 H7
Maryhill C Glas 208 F5
Maryhill Crematorium C Glas . 208 F5
Marykirk Abers 235 H2
Maryland Mons 63 G6
Marylebone Gt Lon 51 H3
Marylebone Wigan 139 H6
Marypark Moray 254 D4
Maryport Cumb 164 D3
Maryport D & G 172 E7
Marystow Devon 12 B6
Mary Tavy Devon 12 C6
Maryton Angus 235 H4
Marywell Abers 244 D4
Marywell Abers 245 L4
Marywell Angus 235 G6
Masham N York 160 B6
Mashbury Essex 71 G5
Mason N u Ty 180 F4
Masongill N York 157 L7
Masonhill Crematorium
    S Ayrs 196 D7
Mastin Moor Derbys 133 J4
Matching Essex 70 D5
Matching Green Essex 70 D5
Matching Tye Essex 70 D5
Matfen Nthumb 180 C4
Matfield Kent 39 G5
Mathern Mons 45 G1
Mathon Herefs 81 G6
Mathry Pembks 74 E6
Matlask Norfk 122 C4
Matlock Derbys 132 F7
Matlock Bank Derbys 132 F7
Matlock Bath Derbys 132 F8
Matlock Dale Derbys 132 F7
Matson Gloucs 64 B4
Matterdale End Cumb 165 L6
Mattersey Notts 134 D2
Mattersey Thorpe Notts 134 D2
Mattingley Hants 49 H7
Mattishall Norfk 105 L1
Mattishall Burgh Norfk 105 L1
Mauchline E Ayrs 196 F5
Maud Abers 269 G6
Maufant Jersey 9 e2
Maugersbury Gloucs 65 J2
Maughold IoM 154 g4
Mauld Highld 250 C4

Maulden C Beds 85 L7
Maulds Meaburn Cumb 166 E7
Maunby N York 160 E5
Maund Bryan Herefs 80 D5
Maundown Somset 29 J5
Mautby Norfk 107 K1
Mavesyn Ridware Staffs 115 H8
Mavis Enderby Lincs 137 G6
Mawbray Cumb 164 E1
Mawdesley Lancs 139 G5
Mawdlam Brdgnd 42 B5
Mawgan Cnwll 3 H6
Mawgan Porth Cnwll 4 D2
Maw Green Ches E 130 D8
Mawla Cnwll 4 A5
Mawnan Cnwll 3 K5
Mawnan Smith Cnwll 3 K5
Mawsley Nhants 101 H8
Mawthorpe Lincs 137 J5
Maxey C Pete 102 C2
Maxstoke Warwks 99 G6
Maxted Street Kent 40 F6
Maxton Border 201 J7
Maxton Kent 41 J7
Maxwell Town D & G 176 C4
Maxworthy Cnwll 11 J4
Mayals Swans 57 H6
May Bank Staffs 114 D2
Maybole S Ayrs 183 H1
Maybury Surrey 50 C7
Mayes Green Surrey 37 H3
Mayfield E Susx 23 K2
Mayfield Mdloth 211 K6
Mayfield Staffs 115 J2
Mayford Surrey 50 C7
May Hill Gloucs 63 L3
Mayland Essex 72 D6
Maylandsea Essex 72 C6
Maynard's Green E Susx 23 K3
Maypole Birm 98 D7
Maypole Kent 41 G2
Maypole Mons 62 F4
Maypole Green Norfk 107 J4
Maypole Green Suffk 89 J3
Maypole Green Suffk 91 G2
May's Green Oxon 49 H3
May's Green Surrey 50 E7
Mead Devon 26 C7
Meadgate BaNES 45 K7
Meadle Bucks 67 K6
Meadowfield Dur 169 H3
Meadowtown Shrops 95 H3
Meadwell Devon 12 A6
Meaford Staffs 114 D4
Meal Bank Cumb 157 H4
Mealrigg Cumb 164 F2
Mealsgate Cumb 165 H2
Meanwood Leeds 150 C8
Mearbeck N York 148 E4
Meare Somset 31 G3
Meare Green Somset 30 D6
Meare Green Somset 30 E5
Mearns E Rens 208 F7
Mears Ashby Nhants 85 G2
Measham Leics 99 J1
Meashop Cumb 156 F6
Meaux E R Yk 153 H7
Meavy Devon 7 G2
Medbourne Leics 101 H5
Meddon Devon 26 D7
Meden Vale Notts 134 B5
Medlam Lincs 136 F8
Medlar Lancs 147 H8
Medmenham Bucks 49 K2
Medomsley Dur 180 D7
Medstead Hants 35 K3
Medway Crematorium Kent 53 G6
Meerbrook Staffs 131 K7
Meer Common Herefs 79 L5
Meesden Herts 70 B1
Meeson Wrekin 113 L7
Meeth Devon 12 D1
Meeting Green Suffk 88 E4
Meeting House Hill Norfk 122 F6
Meidrim Carmth 58 B5
Meifod Powys 94 E1
Meigle P & K 233 L6
Meikle Carco D & G 186 A3
Meikle Earnock S Lans 209 J8
Meikle Kilmory Ag & B 207 G6
Meikle Obney P & K 232 F7
Meikleour P & K 233 J7
Meikle Wartle Abers 256 C5
Meinciau Carmth 56 E3
Meir C Stke 114 E3
Meir Heath Staffs 114 E3
Melbourn Cambs 87 H6
Melbourne Derbys 116 C6
Melbourne E R Yk 152 A7
Melbur Cnwll 4 F4

Melbury Devon 26 F7
Melbury Abbas Dorset 32 E6
Melbury Bubb Dorset 16 B2
Melbury Osmond Dorset 16 A1
Melbury Sampford Dorset 16 A2
Melchbourne Bed 85 K2
Melcombe Bingham Dorset 16 E2
Meldon Devon 12 D4
Meldon Nthumb 180 D2
Meldon Park Nthumb 180 D2
Meldreth Cambs 87 H6
Meldrum Stirlg 220 C7
Melfort Ag & B 216 C4
Meliden Denbgs 128 C3
Melinau Pembks 55 K4
Melin-byrhedyn Powys 93 H4
Melincourt Neath 60 B6
Melin-y-coed Conwy 127 G5
Melin-y-ddol Powys 94 D7
Melin-y-wig Denbgs 111 K2
Melkinthorpe Cumb 166 D5
Melkridge Nthumb 179 K5
Melksham Wilts 46 C6
Mellangoose Cnwll 3 H5
Mell Green W Berk 48 C3
Mellguards Cumb 166 C6
Melling Lancs 147 M2
Melling Sefton 138 E7
Melling Mount Sefton 138 E7
Mellis Suffk 106 C7
Mellon Charles Highld 260 D2
Mellon Udrigle Highld 260 E1
Mellor Lancs 139 K2
Mellor Stockp 131 K3
Mellor Brook Lancs 139 J2
Mells Somset 32 B1
Mells Suffk 107 H8
Melmerby Cumb 166 E3
Melmerby N York 159 K5
Melmerby N York 160 E7
Melness Highld 277 K3
Melon Green Suffk 89 G4
Melplash Dorset 15 L3
Melrose Border 201 H6
Melsetter Ork 275 b6
Melsonby N York 160 B1
Meltham Kirk 141 H5
Meltham Mills Kirk 141 H5
Melton E R Yk 144 E2
Melton Suffk 91 G5
Meltonby E R Yk 152 B5
Melton Constable Norfk 122 A5
Melton Mowbray Leics 117 K7
Melton Ross N Linc 144 D5
Melvaig Highld 260 B3
Melverley Shrops 112 E8
Melverley Green Shrops 112 E8
Melvich Highld 278 E3
Membury Devon 15 G2
Memsie Abers 269 H4
Memus Angus 234 C4
Menabilly Cnwll 5 J4
Menagissey Cnwll 4 B5
Menai Bridge IoA 125 K5
Mendham Suffk 106 F4
Mendip Crematorium Somset .. 31 K2
Mendlesham Suffk 90 D2
Mendlesham Green Suffk 90 C3
Menheniot Cnwll 6 C3
Menithwood Worcs 81 G2
Mennock D & G 185 K2
Menston C Brad 149 L7
Menstrie Clacks 220 E7
Menthorpe N York 143 H1
Mentmore Bucks 67 M3
Meoble Highld 238 C2
Meole Brace Shrops 96 B1
Meonstoke Hants 35 J7
Meopham Kent 52 D5
Meopham Green Kent 52 D5
Meopham Station Kent 52 D5
Mepal Cambs 103 J7
Meppershall C Beds 86 C8
Merbach Herefs 79 K6
Mere Ches E 130 E3
Mere Wilts 32 D4
Mere Brow Lancs 138 E4
Mereclough Lancs 140 C3
Mere Green Birm 98 E4
Mere Green Worcs 81 L3
Mere Heath Ches W 130 C5
Meresborough Medway 53 G6
Mereworth Kent 39 G3
Meriden Solhll 99 G7
Merkadale Highld 246 E2
Merley Poole 17 K3
Merlin's Bridge Pembks 54 F4
Merrington Shrops 113 G7
Merrion Pembks 54 F7
Merriott Somset 31 G8

Merrivale Devon............ 12 D7
Merrow Surrey............ 36 F1
Merry Field Hill Dorset....... 17 K2
Merry Hill Herts............ 68 E8
Merryhill Wolves............ 97 K4
Merry Lees Leics............ 100 A2
Merrymeet Cnwll............ 6 B2
Mersea Island Essex............ 72 F4
Mersham Kent............ 40 D7
Merstham Surrey............ 51 H8
Merston W Susx............ 20 E6
Merstone IoW............ 19 J6
Merther Cnwll............ 4 D6
Merthyr Carmth............ 58 C5
Merthyr Cynog Powys............ 78 D7
Merthyr Dyfan V Glam............ 43 H7
Merthyr Mawr Brdgnd............ 42 D6
Merthyr Tydfil Myr Td............ 61 G6
Merthyr Vale Myr Td............ 61 G7
Merton Devon............ 27 J8
Merton Gt Lon............ 51 H5
Merton Norfk............ 105 H4
Merton Oxon............ 66 E3
Meshaw Devon............ 28 D7
Messing Essex............ 72 C3
Messingham N Linc............ 143 M6
Metfield Suffk............ 106 F7
Metherell Cnwll............ 6 E1
Metheringham Lincs............ 135 L7
Methil Fife............ 222 F7
Methilhill Fife............ 222 F7
Methley Leeds............ 142 B2
Methley Junction Leeds............ 142 B3
Methlick Abers............ 256 F4
Methven P & K............ 221 J2
Methwold Norfk............ 104 E4
Methwold Hythe Norfk............ 104 E4
Mettingham Suffk............ 107 H5
Metton Norfk............ 122 D4
Mevagissey Cnwll............ 5 G6
Mexborough Donc............ 142 D7
Mey Highld............ 280 C2
Meyllteyrn Gwynd............ 108 D5
Meysey Hampton Gloucs............ 65 G7
Miabhig W Isls............ 282 e3
Miavaig W Isls............ 282 e3
Michaelchurch Herefs............ 63 G2
Michaelchurch Escley Herefs....... 79 K8
Michaelchurch-on-Arrow
   Powys............ 79 J5
Michaelstone-y-Fedw Newpt....... 43 K5
Michaelston-le-Pit V Glam............ 43 J7
Michaelstow Cnwll............ 10 F6
Michelcombe Devon............ 7 K1
Micheldever Hants............ 35 G3
Micheldever Station Hants............ 35 G2
Michelmersh Hants............ 34 D5
Mickfield Suffk............ 90 D3
Micklebring Donc............ 133 K1
Mickleby N York............ 171 J8
Micklefield Leeds............ 142 C1
Micklefield Green Herts............ 68 D7
Mickleham Surrey............ 50 F8
Mickleover C Derb............ 116 A5
Micklethwaite C Brad............ 149 K7
Micklethwaite Cumb............ 165 J1
Mickleton Dur............ 168 B6
Mickleton Gloucs............ 82 E6
Mickletown Leeds............ 142 B2
Mickle Trafford Ches W............ 129 K5
Mickley Derbys............ 132 F4
Mickley N York............ 160 C7
Mickley Green Suffk............ 89 G4
Mickley Square Nthumb............ 180 C6
Mid Ardlaw Abers............ 269 H3
Midbea Ork............ 275 C2
Mid Beltie Abers............ 244 E3
Mid Bockhampton Dorset............ 18 B4
Mid Calder W Loth............ 210 E5
Mid Clyth Highld............ 280 C8
Mid Culbeuchly Abers............ 268 B4
Middle Assendon Oxon............ 49 H2
Middle Aston Oxon............ 66 C2
Middle Barton Oxon............ 66 B2
Middlebie D & G............ 177 H4
Middlebridge P & K............ 232 C2
Middle Chinnock Somset............ 31 G8
Middle Claydon Bucks............ 67 H2
Middlecliffe Barns............ 142 C6
Middlecott Devon............ 13 G5
Middleham N York............ 159 L5
Middle Handley Derbys............ 133 H4
Middle Harling Norfk............ 105 K6
Middlehill Cnwll............ 6 B1
Middlehill Wilts............ 46 B5
Middlehope Shrops............ 96 B5
Middle Kames Ag & B............ 206 E1
Middle Littleton Worcs............ 82 C6
Middle Madeley Staffs............ 114 B3

Middle Maes-coed Herefs............ 79 L8
Middlemarsh Dorset............ 16 C1
Middle Mayfield Staffs............ 115 J3
Middle Mill Pembks............ 74 C7
Middlemore Devon............ 12 C8
Middle Quarter Kent............ 40 A7
Middle Rasen Lincs............ 136 A2
Middle Rocombe Devon............ 8 D1
Middle Salter Lancs............ 147 M3
Middlesbrough Middsb............ 170 C6
Middlesceugh Cumb............ 165 L2
Middleshaw Cumb............ 157 J5
Middlesmoor N York............ 159 K7
Middle Stoford Somset............ 30 B6
Middle Stoke Medway............ 53 H4
Middlestone Dur............ 169 H4
Middlestone Moor Dur............ 169 H4
Middle Stoughton Somset............ 30 F1
Middlestown Wakefd............ 141 L4
Middle Street Gloucs............ 63 M6
Middle Taphouse Cnwll............ 5 K2
Middlethird Border............ 201 L6
Middleton Ag & B............ 224 B6
Middleton Cumb............ 157 K5
Middleton Derbys............ 132 D7
Middleton Derbys............ 132 E8
Middleton Essex............ 89 H7
Middleton Hants............ 34 F2
Middleton Herefs............ 80 D1
Middleton Lancs............ 147 H4
Middleton Leeds............ 141 M2
Middleton N York............ 149 L6
Middleton N York............ 162 D5
Middleton Nhants............ 101 J5
Middleton Norfk............ 120 E8
Middleton Nthumb............ 180 C2
Middleton Nthumb............ 203 H6
Middleton P & K............ 221 L6
Middleton Rochdl............ 140 C6
Middleton Shrops............ 96 C7
Middleton Shrops............ 112 D5
Middleton Suffk............ 91 K2
Middleton Swans............ 56 D7
Middleton Warwks............ 98 F4
Middleton Cheney Nhants............ 83 L7
Middleton Crematorium
   Rochdl............ 140 C6
Middleton Green Staffs............ 114 F4
Middleton Hall Nthumb............ 202 F8
Middleton-in-Teesdale Dur...... 168 B5
Middleton Moor Suffk............ 91 J2
Middleton One Row Darltn...... 169 K8
Middleton-on-Leven N York...... 161 G1
Middleton-on-Sea W Susx........ 20 F6
Middleton on the Hill Herefs...... 80 C2
Middleton on the Wolds
   E R Yk............ 152 E6
Middleton Park C Aber............ 245 K1
Middleton Priors Shrops............ 96 E5
Middleton Quernhow N York...... 160 E7
Middleton St George Darltn...... 169 K8
Middleton Scriven Shrops............ 96 F6
Middleton Stoney Oxon............ 66 D2
Middleton Tyas N York............ 160 B2
Middletown Cumb............ 155 H1
Middle Town IoS............ 10 b3
Middletown N Som............ 44 F4
Middletown Powys............ 95 H1
Middle Tysoe Warwks............ 83 H6
Middle Wallop Hants............ 34 C3
Middlewich Ches E............ 130 D6
Middle Winterslow Wilts............ 34 B4
Middlewood Cnwll............ 11 K7
Middlewood Herefs............ 79 K6
Middle Woodford Wilts............ 33 K4
Middlewood Green Suffk............ 90 C3
Middleyard E Ayrs............ 197 G4
Middle Yard Gloucs............ 64 B6
Middlezoy Somset............ 30 E4
Middridge Dur............ 169 H5
Midford BaNES............ 45 M6
Midge Hall Lancs............ 139 G3
Midgeholme Cumb............ 178 E7
Midgham W Berk............ 48 E5
Midgley Calder............ 140 F3
Midgley Wakefd............ 141 L5
Mid Holmwood Surrey............ 37 J2
Midhopestones Sheff............ 141 K7
Midhurst W Susx............ 36 C6
Mid Lavant W Susx............ 20 D5
Midlem Border............ 201 H7
Mid Mains Highld............ 250 D4
Midney Somset............ 31 H5
Midpark Ag & B............ 207 G2
Midsomer Norton BaNES............ 45 K8
Midtown Highld............ 277 K4
Midville Lincs............ 137 G8
Mid Warwickshire
   Crematorium Warwks............ 83 G3
Midway Ches E............ 131 H3

Mid Yell Shet............ 281 e3
Migvie Abers............ 244 A2
Milborne Port Somset............ 31 L7
Milborne St Andrew Dorset...... 16 F3
Milborne Wick Somset............ 31 L6
Milbourne Nthumb............ 180 D4
Milbourne Wilts............ 46 D2
Milburn Cumb............ 166 F5
Milbury Heath S Glos............ 45 K1
Milby N York............ 150 F2
Milcombe Oxon............ 83 K8
Milden Suffk............ 89 J6
Mildenhall Suffk............ 104 E8
Mildenhall Wilts............ 47 J5
Milebrook Powys............ 79 K1
Milebush Kent............ 39 J4
Mile Elm Wilts............ 46 E5
Mile End Essex............ 72 E2
Mile End Gloucs............ 63 H5
Mile End Suffk............ 107 G5
Mileham Norfk............ 121 K7
Mile Oak Br & H............ 22 C5
Mile Oak Kent............ 39 H4
Mile Oak Staffs............ 98 F5
Miles Hope Herefs............ 80 D2
Milesmark Fife............ 210 E1
Miles Platting Manch............ 140 C7
Mile Town Kent............ 53 K4
Milfield Nthumb............ 202 E6
Milford Derbys............ 116 B3
Milford Devon............ 26 D6
Milford Powys............ 94 D5
Milford Staffs............ 114 F7
Milford Surrey............ 36 E2
Milford Haven Pembks............ 54 E5
Milford on Sea Hants............ 18 D5
Milkwall Gloucs............ 63 H5
Millais Jersey............ 9 a1
Milland W Susx............ 36 B5
Milland Marsh W Susx............ 36 C5
Mill Bank Calder............ 140 F3
Millbeck Cumb............ 165 H5
Millbreck Abers............ 257 J3
Millbridge Surrey............ 36 C2
Millbrook C Beds............ 85 K7
Millbrook C Sotn............ 34 E8
Millbrook Cnwll............ 6 E4
Millbrook Jersey............ 9 c3
Millbrook Tamesd............ 140 E7
Mill Brow Stockp............ 131 J2
Millbuie Abers............ 245 H2
Millbuie Highld............ 250 F1
Millcombe Devon............ 8 B5
Mill Common Norfk............ 107 G3
Mill Common Suffk............ 107 H7
Millcorner E Susx............ 24 E3
Millcraig Highld............ 263 H5
Mill Cross Devon............ 7 L3
Milldale Staffs............ 115 J1
Mill End Bucks............ 49 J2
Mill End Cambs............ 103 G7
Millend Gloucs............ 63 L7
Mill End Herts............ 87 G8
Millerhill Mdloth............ 211 K5
Miller's Dale Derbys............ 132 C5
Millers Green Derbys............ 115 M1
Miller's Green Essex............ 70 E5
Millerston C Glas............ 209 H5
Millgate Lancs............ 140 D4
Mill Green Cambs............ 88 C6
Mill Green Essex............ 70 F4
Mill Green Herts............ 69 G5
Mill Green Lincs............ 119 H6
Mill Green Norfk............ 106 C6
Millgreen Shrops............ 113 L6
Mill Green Staffs............ 98 D3
Mill Green Staffs............ 115 H7
Mill Green Suffk............ 89 J6
Mill Green Suffk............ 89 K4
Mill Green Suffk............ 90 D3
Mill Green Suffk............ 91 H3
Millhalf Herefs............ 79 K5
Millhayes Devon............ 14 F2
Millhead Lancs............ 147 K2
Millheugh S Lans............ 198 B3
Mill Hill E Susx............ 23 L6
Mill Hill Gt Lon............ 69 G8
Millhouse Ag & B............ 206 F5
Millhouse Cumb............ 165 K3
Millhousebridge D & G............ 176 F2
Millhouse Green Barns............ 141 K7
Millhouses Barns............ 142 C6
Millhouses Sheff............ 133 G3
Milliken Park Rens............ 208 C6
Millin Cross Pembks............ 55 G4
Millington E R Yk............ 152 C5
Millmeece Staffs............ 114 C5
Millness Cumb............ 157 H6
Mill of Drummond P & K............ 220 E4
Mill of Haldane W Duns............ 208 C3

Millom Cumb............ 155 M6
Millook Cnwll............ 11 H3
Millpool Cnwll............ 2 F5
Millpool Cnwll............ 11 G8
Millport N Ayrs............ 207 K8
Mill Side Cumb............ 157 G6
Mill Street Kent............ 39 H2
Mill Street Norfk............ 122 B7
Mill Street Suffk............ 90 C1
Millthorpe Derbys............ 132 F4
Millthrop Cumb............ 157 L4
Milltimber C Aber............ 245 J3
Milltown Abers............ 243 J2
Milltown Abers............ 255 J8
Milltown Cnwll............ 5 J3
Milltown D & G............ 177 K4
Milltown Derbys............ 133 G7
Milltown Devon............ 27 K3
Milltown of Campfield Abers...... 244 E3
Milltown of Edinvillie Moray...... 254 F4
Milltown of Learney Abers...... 244 E3
Milnathort P & K............ 221 L6
Milngavie E Duns............ 208 F4
Milnrow Rochdl............ 140 D5
Milnthorpe Cumb............ 157 H6
Milnthorpe Wakefd............ 142 A4
Milovaig Highld............ 258 B6
Milson Shrops............ 80 E1
Milstead Kent............ 40 A3
Milston Wilts............ 33 L2
Milthorpe Lincs............ 118 F5
Milthorpe Nhants............ 84 B6
Milton C Stke............ 114 E2
Milton Cambs............ 87 K3
Milton Cumb............ 178 D6
Milton D & G............ 172 F4
Milton D & G............ 175 L1
Milton Derbys............ 116 A6
Milton Highld............ 248 A3
Milton Highld............ 250 E5
Milton Highld............ 251 G2
Milton Highld............ 263 K5
Milton Highld............ 280 D6
Milton Inver............ 208 B5
Milton Kent............ 52 E4
Milton Moray............ 254 D7
Milton Moray............ 267 K4
Milton N Som............ 44 D6
Milton Newpt............ 44 D1
Milton Notts............ 134 E5
Milton Oxon............ 66 C8
Milton Oxon............ 83 K8
Milton P & K............ 233 G3
Milton Pembks............ 55 H6
Milton Somset............ 31 G6
Milton Stirlg............ 219 H7
Milton W Duns............ 208 D4
Milton Abbas Dorset............ 16 F2
Milton Abbot Devon............ 12 A6
Milton Bridge Mdloth............ 211 H6
Milton Bryan C Beds............ 68 B1
Milton Clevedon Somset............ 31 L3
Milton Combe Devon............ 6 F2
Milton Common Oxon............ 67 G6
Milton Damerel Devon............ 27 G8
Milton End Gloucs............ 63 L5
Milton End Gloucs............ 65 H7
Milton Ernest Bed............ 85 K4
Milton Green Ches W............ 129 K7
Milton Hill Oxon............ 48 C1
Milton Keynes M Keyn............ 85 G7
Milton Lilbourne Wilts............ 47 J7
Milton Malsor Nhants............ 84 E4
Milton Morenish P & K............ 231 J7
Milton of Auchinhove Abers...... 244 C3
Milton of Balgonie Fife............ 222 E7
Milton of Buchanan Stirlg...... 208 D1
Milton of Campsie E Duns...... 209 H4
Milton of Leys Highld............ 251 J3
Milton of Murtle C Aber............ 245 J3
Milton of Tullich Abers............ 243 L4
Milton on Stour Dorset............ 32 D7
Milton Regis Kent............ 40 A2
Milton Street E Susx............ 23 J6
Milton-under-Wychwood
   Oxon............ 65 K3
Milverton Somset............ 29 L5
Milverton Warwks............ 83 H2
Milwich Staffs............ 114 F5
Milwr Flints............ 128 E5
Minard Ag & B............ 216 F7
Minchington Dorset............ 33 G7
Minchinhampton Gloucs............ 64 C7
Mindrum Nthumb............ 202 F6
Minehead Somset............ 29 H2
Minera Wrexhm............ 112 C1
Minety Wilts............ 46 F1
Minffordd Gwynd............ 109 L4
Mingarrypark Highld............ 237 K6
Miningsby Lincs............ 136 F6

Minions Cnwll...... 11 J8
Minishant S Ayrs...... 196 C8
Minllyn Gwynd...... 111 G8
Minnigaff D & G...... 173 K2
Minnis Bay Kent...... 41 J2
Minnonie Abers...... 268 D4
Minshull Vernon Ches E...... 130 D7
Minskip N York...... 150 E3
Minstead Hants...... 18 D2
Minsted W Susx...... 20 D3
Minster Kent...... 41 J2
Minster Kent...... 53 L4
Minsterley Shrops...... 95 J2
Minster Lovell Oxon...... 65 L5
Minsterworth Gloucs...... 63 M4
Minterne Magna Dorset...... 16 C2
Minterne Parva Dorset...... 16 C2
Minting Lincs...... 136 C5
Mintlaw Abers...... 269 J6
Mintlyn Crematorium Norfk...... 120 E7
Minto Border...... 188 F2
Minton Shrops...... 95 K5
Minwear Pembks...... 55 H4
Minworth Birm...... 98 F5
Mirehouse Cumb...... 164 C7
Mireland Highld...... 280 D4
Mirfield Kirk...... 141 K4
Miserden Gloucs...... 64 D5
Miskin Rhondd...... 43 G5
Miskin Rhondd...... 43 G5
Misson Notts...... 134 D1
Misterton Leics...... 100 C4
Misterton Notts...... 134 F1
Misterton Somset...... 15 K1
Mistley Essex...... 73 G1
Mistley Heath Essex...... 73 H1
Mitcham Gt Lon...... 51 H5
Mitcheldean Gloucs...... 63 K3
Mitchell Cnwll...... 4 D4
Mitchellslacks D & G...... 186 E1
Mitchel Troy Mons...... 62 F5
Mitford Nthumb...... 180 E2
Mithian Cnwll...... 4 B5
Mitton Staffs...... 114 D8
Mixbury Oxon...... 84 B8
Mixenden Calder...... 141 G2
Moats Tye Suffk...... 90 B4
Mobberley Ches E...... 130 F4
Mobberley Staffs...... 115 G3
Moccas Herefs...... 79 L6
Mochdre Conwy...... 127 G4
Mochdre Powys...... 94 C5
Mochrum D & G...... 173 J5
Mockbeggar Hants...... 18 B2
Mockbeggar Kent...... 39 H4
Mockerkin Cumb...... 164 E6
Modbury Devon...... 7 J4
Moddershall Staffs...... 114 E4
Moelfre IoA...... 125 J2
Moelfre Powys...... 112 B6
Moel Tryfan Gwynd...... 125 J8
Moffat D & G...... 187 G5
Moggerhanger C Beds...... 86 C5
Moira Leics...... 116 A8
Molash Kent...... 40 D5
Mol-chlach Highld...... 246 F6
Mold Flints...... 128 F7
Moldgreen Kirk...... 141 J4
Molehill Green Essex...... 70 E2
Molehill Green Essex...... 71 H3
Molescroft E R Yk...... 152 F7
Molesden Nthumb...... 180 E2
Molesworth Cambs...... 102 B8
Molland Devon...... 28 E5
Mollington Ches W...... 129 J5
Mollington Oxon...... 83 K5
Mollinsburn N Lans...... 209 J5
Monachty Cerdgn...... 76 F3
Mondynes Abers...... 245 G7
Monewden Suffk...... 90 F3
Moneydie P & K...... 221 J1
Moneyrow Green W & M...... 49 L3
Moniaive D & G...... 185 J5
Monifieth Angus...... 223 J1
Monikie Angus...... 234 D7
Monimail Fife...... 222 E4
Monington Pembks...... 75 K3
Monk Bretton Barns...... 142 B6
Monken Hadley Gt Lon...... 69 H7
Monk Fryston N York...... 142 D2
Monkhide Herefs...... 80 E6
Monkhill Cumb...... 177 K7
Monkhopton Shrops...... 96 E5
Monkland Herefs...... 80 B4
Monkleigh Devon...... 27 H6
Monknash V Glam...... 42 D7
Monkokehampton Devon...... 12 H2
Monkseaton N Tyne...... 181 J4
Monks Eleigh Suffk...... 89 K5
Monk's Gate W Susx...... 37 K5

Monks Heath Ches E...... 131 G5
Monk Sherborne Hants...... 48 F7
Monks Horton Kent...... 40 E7
Monksilver Somset...... 29 K3
Monks Kirby Warwks...... 100 A5
Monk Soham Suffk...... 90 F2
Monkspath Solhll...... 98 E8
Monks Risborough Bucks...... 67 K6
Monksthorpe Lincs...... 137 H6
Monk Street Essex...... 70 F2
Monkswood Mons...... 62 D6
Monkton Devon...... 14 E2
Monkton Kent...... 41 J2
Monkton S Ayrs...... 196 D5
Monkton S Tyne...... 181 H6
Monkton V Glam...... 42 D7
Monkton Combe BaNES...... 45 M6
Monkton Deverill Wilts...... 32 E3
Monkton Farleigh Wilts...... 46 A6
Monkton Heathfield Somset...... 30 C5
Monkton Up Wimborne
    Dorset...... 33 H8
Monkton Wyld Dorset...... 15 H3
Monkwearmouth Sundld...... 181 H6
Monkwood Hants...... 35 K5
Monmore Green Wolves...... 97 L4
Monmouth Mons...... 63 G4
Monnington on Wye Herefs...... 79 L6
Monreith D & G...... 173 J6
Montacute Somset...... 31 H7
Montcliffe Bolton...... 139 K5
Montford Shrops...... 112 F8
Montford Bridge Shrops...... 113 G8
Montgarrie Abers...... 255 L8
Montgomery Powys...... 94 F4
Monton Salfd...... 140 A7
Montrose Angus...... 235 H4
Mont Saint Guern...... 9 i3
Monxton Hants...... 34 C2
Monyash Derbys...... 132 C6
Monymusk Abers...... 256 C8
Monzie P & K...... 220 F2
Moodiesburn N Lans...... 209 J5
Moonzie Fife...... 222 F4
Moor Allerton Leeds...... 150 D8
Moorbath Dorset...... 15 K4
Moorby Lincs...... 136 E6
Moorcot Herefs...... 79 L4
Moor Crichel Dorset...... 17 K1
Moordown Bmouth...... 17 L4
Moore Halton...... 130 B3
Moor End C Beds...... 68 B3
Moor End Calder...... 141 G2
Moor End Devon...... 12 F1
Moorend Gloucs...... 63 L6
Moor End Lancs...... 147 G6
Moor End N York...... 151 J8
Moorends Donc...... 143 H4
Moorgreen Hants...... 35 G7
Moor Green Herts...... 69 J2
Moorgreen Notts...... 116 E2
Moorhall Derbys...... 132 F5
Moorhampton Herefs...... 79 M6
Moorhead C Brad...... 149 L8
Moor Head Leeds...... 141 K2
Moorhouse Cumb...... 177 H8
Moorhouse Cumb...... 177 K7
Moorhouse Donc...... 142 D5
Moorhouse Notts...... 134 E6
Moorhouse Bank Surrey...... 51 L8
Moorland Somset...... 30 E4
Moorlinch Somset...... 30 F3
Moor Monkton N York...... 151 H4
Moor Row Cumb...... 164 D7
Moor Row Cumb...... 165 H1
Moorsholm R & Cl...... 170 F7
Moorside Dorset...... 32 D7
Moor Side Lancs...... 138 E1
Moor Side Lancs...... 147 K8
Moorside Leeds...... 150 C8
Moor Side Lincs...... 136 E8
Moorside Oldham...... 140 E6
Moorstock Kent...... 40 E7
Moor Street Birm...... 98 C6
Moor Street Medway...... 53 H6
Moorswater Cnwll...... 5 M2
Moorthorpe Wakefd...... 142 C5
Moortown Devon...... 12 C7
Moortown Hants...... 18 A3
Moortown IoW...... 19 G7
Moortown Leeds...... 150 D7
Moortown Lincs...... 144 D7
Moortown Wrekin...... 113 K7
Morangie Highld...... 263 K6
Morar Highld...... 237 K2
Moray Crematorium
    Moray...... 267 H4
Morborne Cambs...... 102 C5
Morchard Bishop Devon...... 13 H1
Morcombelake Dorset...... 15 J4

Morcott Rutlnd...... 101 K3
Morda Shrops...... 112 D6
Morden Dorset...... 17 H3
Morden Gt Lon...... 51 H5
Mordiford Herefs...... 80 D7
Mordon Dur...... 169 J5
More Shrops...... 95 H5
Morebath Devon...... 29 G6
Morebattle Border...... 189 K1
Morecambe Lancs...... 147 H3
Moredon Swindn...... 47 H2
Morefield Highld...... 261 J1
Morehall Kent...... 41 G7
Moreleigh Devon...... 7 L4
Morenish P & K...... 231 H8
Moresby Parks Cumb...... 164 C6
Morestead Hants...... 35 G6
Moreton Dorset...... 16 F5
Moreton Essex...... 70 D5
Moreton Herefs...... 80 C2
Moreton Oxon...... 67 G6
Moreton Staffs...... 114 B8
Moreton Staffs...... 115 J5
Moreton Wirral...... 129 G2
Moreton Corbet Shrops...... 113 J6
Moretonhampstead
    Devon...... 13 H5
Moreton-in-Marsh Gloucs...... 65 J1
Moreton Jeffries Herefs...... 80 E5
Moretonmill Shrops...... 113 J7
Moreton Morrell Warwks...... 83 H4
Moreton on Lugg Herefs...... 80 C6
Moreton Paddox Warwks...... 83 H4
Moreton Pinkney Nhants...... 84 B5
Moreton Say Shrops...... 113 K4
Moreton Valence Gloucs...... 63 M5
Morfa Cerdgn...... 76 B4
Morfa Bychan Gwynd...... 109 K4
Morfa Dinlle Gwynd...... 125 H8
Morfa Glas Neath...... 60 C6
Morfa Nefyn Gwynd...... 108 E3
Morganstown Cardif...... 43 H5
Morgan's Vale Wilts...... 33 L6
Morham E Loth...... 212 C5
Moriah Cerdgn...... 92 D7
Morland Cumb...... 166 E6
Morley Ches E...... 130 F3
Morley Derbys...... 116 C3
Morley Dur...... 168 E5
Morley Leeds...... 141 L2
Morley Green Ches E...... 130 F3
Morley St Botolph Norfk...... 106 B3
Mornick Cnwll...... 11 L8
Morningside C Edin...... 211 H5
Morningside N Lans...... 209 L7
Morningthorpe Norfk...... 106 E5
Morpeth Nthumb...... 180 F2
Morphie Abers...... 235 H3
Morrey Staffs...... 115 J7
Morridge Side Staffs...... 115 G1
Morriston Swans...... 57 J5
Morston Norfk...... 121 M3
Mortehoe Devon...... 27 H2
Morthen Rothm...... 133 J2
Mortimer W Berk...... 49 G6
Mortimer Common W Berk...... 49 G6
Mortimer's Cross Herefs...... 80 A3
Mortimer West End Hants...... 48 F6
Mortlake Gt Lon...... 51 G4
Mortlake Crematorium
    Gt Lon...... 51 G4
Morton Cumb...... 166 B3
Morton Cumb...... 177 L7
Morton Derbys...... 133 H7
Morton IoW...... 19 K6
Morton Lincs...... 118 E6
Morton Lincs...... 134 F1
Morton Notts...... 117 J1
Morton Shrops...... 112 D6
Morton Hall Lincs...... 135 H7
Mortonhall Crematorium
    C Edin...... 211 J5
Morton-on-Swale N York...... 160 D4
Morton on the Hill Norfk...... 122 C8
Morton Tinmouth Dur...... 168 F6
Morvah Cnwll...... 2 B4
Morval Cnwll...... 6 B3
Morvich Highld...... 248 F7
Morville Shrops...... 96 F4
Morville Heath Shrops...... 96 F4
Morwenstow Cnwll...... 26 C7
Mosborough Sheff...... 133 H3
Moscow E Ayrs...... 196 F3
Mose Shrops...... 97 G5
Mosedale Cumb...... 165 K4
Moseley Birm...... 98 D6
Moseley Wolves...... 97 L4
Moseley Worcs...... 81 J3
Moses Gate Bolton...... 139 L6
Moss Ag & B...... 224 B6

Moss Donc...... 142 F5
Moss Wrexhm...... 112 D1
Mossat Abers...... 255 K7
Mossbank Shet...... 281 e4
Moss Bank St Hel...... 139 G8
Mossbay Cumb...... 164 C5
Mossblown S Ayrs...... 196 D6
Mossbrow Traffd...... 130 D2
Mossburnford Border...... 189 H3
Mossdale D & G...... 175 G2
Mossdale E Ayrs...... 184 D2
Moss Edge Lancs...... 147 H7
Moss End Ches E...... 130 D4
Mossend N Lans...... 209 K7
Mosser Mains Cumb...... 164 F5
Mossley Ches E...... 131 H7
Mossley Tamesd...... 140 E7
Mosspaul Hotel Border...... 188 C6
Moss Side Cumb...... 177 G8
Moss-side Highld...... 253 G1
Moss Side Lancs...... 138 D2
Moss Side Sefton...... 138 D2
Mosstodloch Moray...... 267 G4
Mossyard D & G...... 174 E4
Mossy Lea Lancs...... 139 G5
Mosterton Dorset...... 15 K2
Moston Manch...... 140 C7
Moston Shrops...... 113 J6
Moston Green Ches E...... 130 D7
Mostyn Flints...... 128 E3
Motcombe Dorset...... 32 E6
Mothecombe Devon...... 7 H5
Motherby Cumb...... 166 C5
Motherwell N Lans...... 209 K7
Motspur Park Gt Lon...... 51 G5
Mottingham Gt Lon...... 51 L4
Mottisfont Hants...... 34 C3
Mottistone IoW...... 18 F7
Mottram in Longdendale
    Tamesd...... 140 F8
Mottram St Andrew Ches E...... 131 G4
Mouilpied Guern...... 9 j3
Mouldsworth Ches W...... 129 L5
Moulin P & K...... 232 D3
Moulsecoomb Br & H...... 22 F5
Moulsford Oxon...... 48 E2
Moulsoe M Keyn...... 85 H7
Moultavie Highld...... 263 H5
Moulton Ches W...... 130 C5
Moulton Lincs...... 119 J3
Moulton N York...... 160 C2
Moulton Nhants...... 84 F2
Moulton Suffk...... 88 D2
Moulton V Glam...... 43 G7
Moulton Chapel Lincs...... 119 J7
Moulton St Mary Norfk...... 107 J3
Moulton Seas End Lincs...... 119 K6
Mount Cnwll...... 4 C4
Mount Cnwll...... 5 K1
Mount Kirk...... 141 H4
Mountain C Brad...... 141 G2
Mountain Ash Rhondd...... 61 G7
Mountain Cross Border...... 199 K4
Mountain Street Kent...... 40 E5
Mount Ambrose Cnwll...... 4 B6
Mount Bures Essex...... 89 H8
Mountfield E Susx...... 24 D3
Mountgerald House Highld...... 263 G6
Mount Hawke Cnwll...... 4 B5
Mount Hermon Cnwll...... 3 H7
Mountjoy Cnwll...... 4 E3
Mount Lothian Mdloth...... 200 C2
Mountnessing Essex...... 70 F7
Mounton Mons...... 63 G8
Mount Pleasant Ches E...... 131 H7
Mount Pleasant Derbys...... 115 M8
Mount Pleasant Derbys...... 116 B2
Mount Pleasant Dur...... 169 H4
Mount Pleasant E R Yk...... 153 H7
Mount Pleasant E Susx...... 23 G4
Mount Pleasant Norfk...... 105 K4
Mount Pleasant Suffk...... 88 E5
Mount Pleasant Worcs...... 82 D7
Mountsett Crematorium Dur...... 180 E7
Mountsorrel Leics...... 116 F8
Mount Sorrel Wilts...... 33 H6
Mount Tabor Calder...... 141 G4
Mousehill Surrey...... 36 E3
Mousehole Cnwll...... 2 D5
Mouswald D & G...... 176 E4
Mow Cop Ches E...... 131 G8
Mowhaugh Border...... 189 L2
Mowmacre Hill C Leic...... 100 D2
Mowsley Leics...... 100 E5
Moy Highld...... 240 D7
Moy Highld...... 252 E5
Moyle Highld...... 248 D7
Moylegrove Pembks...... 75 J3
Muasdale Ag & B...... 205 L8
Muchalls Abers...... 245 K5

Much Birch Herefs 63 G1
Much Cowarne Herefs 80 E6
Much Dewchurch Herefs 62 F1
Muchelney Somset 30 F6
Muchelney Ham Somset 31 G6
Much Hadham Herts 70 B3
Much Hoole Lancs 138 F3
Much Hoole Town Lancs 138 F3
Muchlarnick Cnwll 5 L3
Much Marcle Herefs 80 F8
Much Wenlock Shrops 96 E3
Muck Highld 236 E4
Mucking Thurr 52 E3
Muckingford Thurr 52 E3
Muckleford Dorset 16 C4
Mucklestone Staffs 114 A4
Muckley Shrops 96 E4
Muckton Lincs 137 G3
Muddiford Devon 27 K3
Muddles Green E Susx 23 J4
Mudeford Dorset 18 B5
Mudford Somset 31 J7
Mudford Sock Somset 31 J7
Mudgley Somset 31 G2
Mud Row Kent 53 M4
Mugdock Stirlg 208 F4
Mugeary Highld 246 F1
Mugginton Derbys 115 M3
Muggintonlane End Derbys ... 115 M3
Muggleswick Dur 168 D1
Muirden Abers 268 C5
Muirdrum Angus 234 E7
Muiresk Abers 268 C6
Muirhead Angus 233 M8
Muirhead Fife 222 D6
Muirhead N Lans 209 J5
Muirkirk E Ayrs 197 K5
Muirmill Stirlg 209 J2
Muir of Fowlis Abers 244 C1
Muir of Miltonduff Moray ... 266 C4
Muir of Ord Highld 250 F2
Muirshearlich Highld 239 J7
Muirtack Abers 257 J4
Muirton P & K 221 G5
Muirton Mains Highld 250 E1
Muirton of Ardblair P & K ... 233 J6
Muker N York 158 F3
Mulbarton Norfk 106 D3
Mulben Moray 267 G6
Mulfra Cnwll 2 C4
Mull Ag & B 227 H5
Mullacott Cross Devon 27 J2
Mullion Cnwll 3 H7
Mullion Cove Cnwll 3 H7
Mumby Lincs 137 K5
Munderfield Row Herefs 80 F5
Munderfield Stocks Herefs ... 80 F5
Mundesley Norfk 123 G4
Mundford Norfk 104 F4
Mundham Norfk 107 L2
Mundon Hill Essex 72 C6
Mundy Bois Kent 40 B6
Mungrisdale Cumb 165 L4
Munlochy Highld 251 H1
Munnoch N Ayrs 195 L1
Munsley Herefs 80 F7
Munslow Shrops 96 C6
Murchington Devon 13 G5
Murcot Worcs 82 C7
Murcott Oxon 66 E4
Murcott Wilts 46 D1
Murkle Highld 279 L3
Murlaggan Highld 239 G5
Murrell Green Hants 49 H7
Murroes Angus 234 C4
Murrow Cambs 103 H2
Mursley Bucks 67 K2
Murston Kent 40 B2
Murthill Angus 234 C4
Murthly P & K 233 G7
Murton C York 151 K5
Murton Cumb 167 G5
Murton Dur 169 K1
Murton N Tyne 181 H5
Murton Nthumb 202 F3
Musbury Devon 15 G4
Muscoates N York 162 B6
Musselburgh E Loth 211 K4
Muston Leics 117 L4
Muston N York 163 K6
Mustow Green Worcs 97 K8
Muswell Hill Gt Lon 51 H1
Mutehill D & G 175 H5
Mutford Suffk 107 K5
Muthill P & K 220 F4
Mutterton Devon 14 B2
Muxton Wrekin 114 A8
Mybster Highld 279 L3
Myddfai Carmth 59 L3
Myddle Shrops 113 G6

Mydroilyn Cerdgn 76 E4
Myerscough Lancs 147 H1
Mylor Cnwll 3 L4
Mylor Bridge Cnwll 3 K4
Mynachlog ddu Pembks 75 K6
Mydd-llan Flints 128 D3
Myndtown Shrops 95 J5
Mynydd-bach Mons 62 F8
Mynydd-Bach Swans 57 J5
Mynydd Buch Cerdgn 92 F7
Mynyddgarreg Carmth 56 D3
Mynydd Isa Flints 128 F7
Mynydd Llandygai Gwynd ... 126 B6
Mynytho Gwynd 108 E5
Myrebird Abers 245 G4
Myredykes Border 189 G6
Mytchett Surrey 49 L1
Mytholm Calder 140 E2
Mytholmroyd Calder 140 F3
Mythop Lancs 138 D1
Myton-on-Swale N York 150 F3

N

Naast Highld 260 C3
Nab's Head Lancs 139 J2
Na Buirgh W Isls 282 d6
Naburn C York 151 J6
Nab Wood Crematorium
   C Brad 149 L8
Naccolt Kent 40 D6
Nackington Kent 40 F4
Nacton Suffk 90 F7
Nafferton E R Yk 153 G4
Nag's Head Gloucs 64 C7
Nailbridge Gloucs 63 J4
Nailsbourne Somset 30 B5
Nailsea N Som 44 F5
Nailstone Leics 99 L2
Nailsworth Gloucs 64 B7
Nairn Highld 264 D8
Nalderswood Surrey 37 K2
Nancegollan Cnwll 3 G4
Nancledra Cnwll 2 D4
Nanhoron Gwynd 108 E5
Nannerch Flints 128 E5
Nanpantan Leics 116 E8
Nanpean Cnwll 4 F4
Nanquidno Cnwll 2 B5
Nanstallon Cnwll 5 H2
Nant-ddu Powys 60 F4
Nanternis Cerdgn 76 C4
Nantgaredig Carmth 58 F4
Nantgarw Rhondd 43 H4
Nant-glas Powys 78 D2
Nantglyn Denbgs 127 K7
Nantgwyn Powys 93 L8
Nant Gwynant Gwynd 110 B2
Nantile Gwynd 109 J1
Nantmawr Shrops 112 C6
Nantmel Powys 78 E2
Nantmor Gwynd 109 L2
Nant Peris Gwynd 126 B7
Nantwich Ches E 113 L1
Nant-y-Bwch Blae G 61 H5
Nant-y-caws Carmth 58 E5
Nant-y-derry Mons 62 C6
Nantyffyllon Brdgnd 42 C3
Nantyglo Blae G 61 K5
Nant-y-gollen Shrops 112 C5
Nant-y-moel Brdgnd 42 D3
Nant-y-pandy Conwy 126 D5
Naphill Bucks 67 K7
Napleton Worcs 81 K5
Nappa N York 148 E5
Napton on the Hill Warwks ... 83 L3
Narberth Pembks 55 J4
Narborough Leics 100 C4
Narborough Norfk 104 E1
Narkurs Cnwll 6 C4
Nasareth Gwynd 109 H2
Naseby Nhants 100 F7
Nash Bucks 84 F8
Nash Gt Lon 51 L6
Nash Herefs 79 K3
Nash Newpt 44 D2
Nash Shrops 80 E1
Nash End Worcs 97 H7
Nash Lee Bucks 67 K5
Nash's Green Hants 35 K2
Nash Street Kent 52 D5
Nassington Nhants 102 B4
Nastend Gloucs 64 A6
Nasty Herts 69 K3
Nateby Cumb 158 D1
Nateby Lancs 147 J7
Natland Cumb 157 H5
Naughton Suffk 89 L5
Naunton Gloucs 65 G2

Naunton Worcs 81 K7
Naunton Beauchamp Worcs ... 81 M5
Navenby Lincs 135 K8
Navestock Essex 70 D7
Navestock Side Essex 70 E7
Navidale House Hotel Highld ... 274 D5
Navity Highld 264 B7
Nawton N York 161 L5
Nayland Suffk 89 K8
Nazeing Essex 69 L6
Nazeing Gate Essex 69 L6
Neacroft Hants 18 B4
Neal's Green Warwks 99 J8
Near Cotton Staffs 115 H2
Near Sawrey Cumb 156 E3
Neasden Gt Lon 51 G2
Neasham Darltn 169 J8
Neath Neath 57 L5
Neatham Hants 35 M3
Neatishead Norfk 123 G7
Nebo Cerdgn 77 G2
Nebo Conwy 127 G8
Nebo Gwynd 109 H2
Nebo IoA 125 H2
Necton Norfk 105 H2
Nedd Highld 270 F2
Nedderton Nthumb 180 F2
Nedging Suffk 89 K5
Nedging Tye Suffk 89 L5
Needham Norfk 106 E7
Needham Market Suffk 90 C4
Needham Street Suffk 88 E2
Needingworth Cambs 87 G1
Neen Savage Shrops 96 F7
Neen Sollars Shrops 80 F1
Neenton Shrops 96 E6
Nefyn Gwynd 108 E3
Neilston E Rens 208 E7
Nelson Caerph 43 H3
Nelson Lancs 148 F8
Nemphlar S Lans 198 E4
Nempnett Thrubwell BaNES ... 45 G7
Nenthall Cumb 167 H2
Nenthead Cumb 167 H2
Nenthorn Border 201 L5
Neopardy Devon 13 J3
Nep Town W Susx 22 B4
Nercwys Flints 128 F7
Nereabolls Ag & B 204 C5
Nerston S Lans 209 H7
Nesbit Nthumb 202 F6
Nesfield N York 149 K6
Ness Ches W 129 G4
Nesscliffe Shrops 112 F7
Neston Ches W 129 G4
Neston Wilts 46 B5
Netchwood Shrops 96 E5
Nether Alderley Ches E 131 G4
Netheravon Wilts 33 K1
Nether Blainslie Border 201 H4
Netherbrae Abers 268 E4
Nether Broughton Leics 117 J6
Netherburn S Lans 198 C4
Netherbury Dorset 15 L3
Netherby Cumb 177 L4
Netherby N York 150 D6
Nether Cerne Dorset 16 C3
Nether Compton Dorset 31 K7
Nethercote Warwks 83 M2
Nethercott Devon 11 L3
Nethercott Devon 27 H3
Nether Crimond Abers 256 E7
Nether Dallachy Moray 267 G3
Netherend Gloucs 63 H7
Nether Exe Devon 13 L3
Netherfield E Susx 24 C3
Netherfield Leics 117 G8
Netherfield Notts 117 G3
Nether Fingland S Lans 186 D4
Nethergate N Linc 143 J7
Nethergate Norfk 122 B5
Netherhampton Wilts 33 K5
Nether Handley Derbys 133 H4
Nether Handwick Angus 234 C4
Nether Haugh Rothm 142 C8
Netherhay Dorset 15 J2
Nether Headon Notts 134 E4
Nether Heage Derbys 116 B2
Nether Heyford Nhants 84 C3
Nether Howcleugh S Lans ... 186 F4
Nether Kellet Lancs 147 K2
Nether Kinmundy Abers 257 K3
Netherland Green Staffs 115 H5
Nether Langwith Notts 133 K5
Netherlaw D & G 175 J6
Netherley Abers 245 J5
Nethermill D & G 176 D1
Nethermuir Abers 257 G3

Naunton Worcs 81 K7
Netherne-on-the-Hill Surrey ... 51 J7
Netheroyd Hill Kirk 141 H4
Nether Padley Derbys 132 E4
Netherplace E Rens 208 E7
Nether Poppleton C York 151 J5
Nether Row Cumb 165 K3
Netherseal Derbys 99 H1
Nether Silton N York 161 G4
Nether Skyborry Shrops 95 G8
Nether Stowey Somset 30 B3
Nether Street Essex 70 E5
Netherstreet Wilts 46 E6
Netherthong Kirk 141 H6
Netherthorpe Derbys 133 J5
Netherton Angus 234 E4
Netherton Devon 13 L8
Netherton Dudley 97 L5
Netherton Hants 48 A7
Netherton Herefs 63 G2
Netherton Kirk 141 H5
Netherton N Lans 209 K8
Netherton Nthumb 190 E4
Netherton Oxon 66 B7
Netherton P & K 233 H5
Netherton Shrops 97 G6
Netherton Stirlg 208 F3
Netherton Wakefd 141 L4
Netherton Worcs 82 A7
Nethertown Cumb 155 H1
Nethertown Highld 280 E1
Nethertown Lancs 148 C8
Nethertown Staffs 115 J8
Netherurd Border 199 J4
Nether Wallop Hants 34 C4
Nether Wasdale Cumb 155 L2
Nether Welton Cumb 165 K2
Nether Westcote Gloucs 65 J3
Nether Whitacre Warwks 99 G5
Nether Whitecleuch S Lans ... 186 B2
Nether Winchendon Bucks 67 H4
Netherwitton Nthumb 191 G8
Nethy Bridge Highld 253 J7
Netley Hants 19 G2
Netley Marsh Hants 34 D8
Nettlebed Oxon 49 G2
Nettlebridge Somset 31 L1
Nettlecombe Dorset 15 L3
Nettlecombe IoW 19 J8
Nettleden Herts 68 C5
Nettleham Lincs 135 K4
Nettlestead Kent 39 H3
Nettlestead Green Kent 39 H3
Nettlestone IoW 19 L5
Nettlesworth Dur 169 H1
Nettleton Lincs 144 E7
Nettleton Wilts 46 B3
Nettleton Shrub Wilts 46 B3
Netton Devon 7 G5
Netton Wilts 33 K3
Neuadd Carmth 59 K4
Neuadd-ddu Powys 93 K8
Nevendon Essex 53 G1
Nevern Pembks 75 J4
Nevill Holt Leics 101 H4
New Abbey D & G 176 C5
New Aberdour Abers 268 F3
New Addington Gt Lon 51 K6
Newall Leeds 150 B6
New Alresford Hants 35 J4
New Alyth P & K 233 K6
Newark C Pete 102 E3
Newark Ork 275 f2
Newark-on-Trent Notts 117 L1
New Arram E R Yk 153 G7
Newarthill N Lans 209 L7
New Ash Green Kent 52 D6
New Balderton Notts 117 L1
Newbarn Kent 40 F7
New Barn Kent 52 D5
New Barnet Gt Lon 69 H7
New Barton Nhants 85 G2
Newbattle Mdloth 211 K6
New Bewick Nthumb 190 F2
Newbie D & G 177 H6
Newbiggin Cumb 146 E3
Newbiggin Cumb 155 K4
Newbiggin Cumb 166 B5
Newbiggin Cumb 166 D1
Newbiggin Cumb 166 E5
Newbiggin Dur 167 L5
Newbiggin Dur 168 F1
Newbiggin N York 159 G4
Newbiggin N York 159 H5
Newbiggin-by-the-Sea
   Nthumb 181 H1
Newbigging Angus 233 L7
Newbigging Angus 234 C7
Newbigging Angus 234 D8
Newbigging S Lans 199 H4
Newbiggin-on-Lune Cumb ... 158 C2

New Bilton Warwks 100 B8
Newbold Derbys 133 G5
Newbold Leics 116 C7
Newbold on Avon Warwks 100 B7
Newbold on Stour Warwks 82 F6
Newbold Pacey Warwks 83 G4
Newbold Revel Warwks 99 M7
Newbold Verdon Leics 99 L3
New Bolingbroke Lincs 136 F8
Newborough C Pete 102 D2
Newborough IoA 125 G6
Newborough Staffs 115 J6
Newbottle Nhants 83 M7
Newbottle Sundld 181 H8
New Boultham Lincs 135 K5
Newbourne Suffk 91 G6
New Bradwell M Keyn 84 F7
New Brampton Derbys 133 G5
New Brancepeth Dur 169 G2
Newbridge C Edin 210 F4
Newbridge Caerph 43 K2
Newbridge Cerdgn 76 F3
Newbridge Cnwll 2 C5
Newbridge Cnwll 4 C6
Newbridge D & G 176 C3
Newbridge Hants 34 C7
Newbridge IoW 18 F6
New Bridge N York 162 D5
Newbridge Oxon 66 B6
Newbridge Wrexhm 112 D3
Newbridge Green Worcs 81 J7
Newbridge-on-Usk Mons 62 D8
Newbridge on Wye Powys 78 E4
New Brighton Flints 128 F6
New Brighton Wirral 129 G1
New Brinsley Notts 116 D2
New Brotton R & Cl 171 G6
Newbrough Nthumb 179 K5
New Broughton Wrexhm 112 D1
New Buckenham Norfk 106 B5
Newbuildings Devon 13 J2
Newburgh Abers 257 J6
Newburgh Abers 269 H4
Newburgh Fife 222 C3
Newburgh Lancs 138 F5
Newburgh Priory N York 161 J7
Newburn N u Ty 180 E6
New Bury Bolton 139 L6
Newbury Somset 32 B1
Newbury W Berk 48 C5
Newbury Wilts 32 D3
Newbury Park Gt Lon 51 L1
Newby Cumb 166 E6
Newby Lancs 148 E6
Newby N York 148 C2
Newby N York 163 J4
Newby N York 170 C8
Newby Bridge Cumb 156 E5
Newby Cross Cumb 177 L8
Newby East Cumb 178 B7
Newby Head Cumb 166 E6
New Byth Abers 268 E5
Newby West Cumb 177 L8
Newby Wiske N York 160 E5
Newcastle Mons 62 F4
Newcastle Shrops 95 G7
Newcastle Emlyn Carmth 76 B7
Newcastleton Border 178 C2
Newcastle-under-Lyme Staffs ... 114 D2
Newcastle upon Tyne N u Ty 181 G6
Newchapel Pembks 75 L4
Newchapel Staffs 131 G8
Newchapel Surrey 38 A5
Newchurch Blae G 61 J5
Newchurch Herefs 79 L5
Newchurch IoW 19 J6
Newchurch Kent 25 K1
Newchurch Mons 62 F7
Newchurch Powys 79 H5
Newchurch Staffs 115 J7
Newchurch in Pendle Lancs 148 E7
New Costessey Norfk 106 D2
New Cowper Cumb 164 F2
Newcraighall C Edin 211 K4
New Crofton Wakefd 142 B4
New Cross Cerdgn 92 D8
New Cross Gt Lon 51 K4
New Cross Somset 30 F7
New Cumnock E Ayrs 197 J8
New Cut E Susx 24 E4
New Deer Abers 268 F6
New Delaval Nthumb 181 H3
New Delph Oldham 140 F6
New Denham Bucks 50 D2
Newdigate Surrey 37 J3
New Duston Nhants 84 D3
New Earswick C York 151 K5
New Eastwood Notts 116 D2
New Edlington Donc 142 E7
New Elgin Moray 266 E4

New Ellerby E R Yk 153 J7
Newell Green Br For 49 L5
New Eltham Gt Lon 51 L4
New End Worcs 82 C3
Newenden Kent 24 F2
New England C Pete 102 D3
New England Essex 88 E6
Newent Gloucs 63 L2
New Farnley Leeds 141 L2
New Ferry Wirral 129 H3
Newfield Dur 169 G4
Newfield Dur 181 G8
Newfield Highld 264 B6
New Fletton C Pete 102 D4
Newfound Hants 48 E8
New Fryston Wakefd 142 C2
Newgale Pembks 54 D2
New Galloway D & G 185 G7
Newgate Norfk 122 A3
Newgate Street Herts 69 J6
New Gilston Fife 223 G5
New Grimsby IoS 10 b2
Newhall Ches E 113 K2
Newhall Derbys 115 M7
Newham Nthumb 203 K7
New Hartley Nthumb 181 H3
Newhaven C Edin 211 H4
Newhaven Derbys 132 C7
Newhaven E Susx 23 G7
New Haw Surrey 50 D6
New Hedges Pembks 55 K6
New Herrington Sundld 181 H8
Newhey Rochdl 140 E5
New Holkham Norfk 121 J4
New Holland N Linc 144 D3
Newholm N York 171 K8
New Houghton Derbys 133 K6
New Houghton Norfk 121 H6
Newhouse N Lans 209 L6
New Houses Suffk 91 F7
New Houses Wigan 139 H7
New Hutton Cumb 157 J4
New Hythe Kent 52 F7
Newick E Susx 22 F3
Newingreen Kent 40 F8
Newington Kent 41 G7
Newington Kent 53 J6
Newington Oxon 66 F7
Newington Shrops 95 K6
Newington Bagpath Gloucs 64 B8
New Inn Carmth 58 E2
New Inn Torfn 62 C7
New Invention Shrops 95 H8
New Lakenham Norfk 106 E2
New Lanark S Lans 198 E4
Newland C KuH 144 D2
Newland Cumb 156 D6
Newland E R Yk 143 K2
Newland Gloucs 63 H5
Newland N York 143 H3
Newland Oxon 66 A5
Newland Somset 28 E3
Newlandrig Mdloth 211 L6
Newlands Border 188 E7
Newlands Cumb 165 K3
Newlands Nthumb 180 D7
Newlands of Dundurcas
    Moray 266 F6
New Lane Lancs 138 E5
New Lane End Warrtn 130 C1
New Langholm D & G 177 K2
New Leake Lincs 137 G8
New Leeds Abers 269 H5
New Lodge Barns 142 A6
New Longton Lancs 139 G3
New Luce D & G 172 F2
Newlyn Cnwll 2 D5
Newlyn East Cnwll 4 D3
Newmachar Abers 256 F7
Newmains N Lans 209 L7
New Malden Gt Lon 51 G6
Newman's End Essex 70 D4
Newman's Green Suffk 89 H6
Newmarket Suffk 88 C3
Newmarket W Isls 282 g3
New Marske R & Cl 170 E6
New Marston Oxon 66 D5
New Marton Shrops 112 E4
New Mill Abers 245 H7
Newmill Border 188 D4
New Mill Cnwll 2 D4
New Mill Herts 68 A4
Newmill Kirk 141 J4
Newmill Moray 267 J5
Newmillerdam Wakefd 141 M4
Newmill of Inshewan Angus 234 C3
Newmills C Edin 211 L6
New Mills Cnwll 4 E4
New Mills Derbys 131 K3

Newmills Fife 210 D2
Newmills Mons 63 G5
New Mills Powys 94 D3
Newmiln P & K 221 L1
Newmilns E Ayrs 197 G3
New Milton Hants 18 C4
New Mistley Essex 73 H1
New Moat Pembks 75 H7
Newnes Shrops 112 F5
Newney Green Essex 71 G5
Newnham Gloucs 63 K5
Newnham Hants 49 H8
Newnham Herts 86 E7
Newnham Kent 40 B4
Newnham Nhants 84 B3
Newnham Worcs 80 E2
New Ollerton Notts 134 D6
New Oscott Birm 98 E4
New Pitsligo Abers 268 F5
New Polzeath Cnwll 10 C6
Newport Cnwll 11 L5
Newport Dorset 17 G4
Newport E R Yk 143 L2
Newport Essex 87 L8
Newport Gloucs 63 K7
Newport Highld 274 F3
Newport IoW 19 H6
Newport Newpt 44 C1
Newport Norfk 123 K8
Newport Pembks 75 H4
Newport Wrekin 114 A7
Newport-on-Tay Fife 223 G2
Newport Pagnell M Keyn 85 G6
Newpound Common W Susx 37 G5
New Prestwick S Ayrs 196 C6
New Quay Cerdgn 76 D3
Newquay Cnwll 4 D3
New Quay Essex 72 F2
New Rackheath Norfk 106 F1
New Radnor Powys 79 H3
New Rent Cumb 166 B3
New Ridley Nthumb 180 C7
New Road Side N York 149 H7
New Romney Kent 25 K2
New Rossington Donc 143 G8
New Row Cerdgn 92 F8
New Row Lancs 148 A8
New Sauchie Clacks 220 F8
Newsbank Ches E 131 G6
Newseat Abers 256 C5
Newsham Lancs 147 K8
Newsham N York 160 B5
Newsham N York 168 E8
Newsham Nthumb 181 H3
New Sharlston Wakefd 142 B4
Newsholme E R Yk 143 H2
Newsholme Lancs 148 E5
New Shoreston Nthumb 203 K6
New Silksworth Sundld 181 J8
New Skelton R & Cl 170 F7
Newsome Kirk 141 J5
New Somerby Lincs 118 B4
New Southgate
    Crematorium Gt Lon 69 H8
New Springs Wigan 139 J6
Newstead Border 201 H6
Newstead Notts 116 E1
Newstead Nthumb 203 J7
New Stevenston N Lans 209 K7
New Street Herefs 79 L4
New Swannington Leics 116 D8
Newthorpe N York 142 D1
Newthorpe Notts 116 E2
New Thundersley Essex 53 G1
Newtimber W Susx 22 D4
Newtoft Lincs 135 L2
Newton Ag & B 217 G7
Newton Border 189 G2
Newton Brdgnd 42 C6
Newton C Beds 86 E6
Newton Cambs 87 J5
Newton Cambs 119 M8
Newton Cardif 43 K6
Newton Ches W 129 J6
Newton Ches W 129 L7
Newton Ches W 129 M4
Newton Cumb 146 D2
Newton Derbys 133 J7
Newton Herefs 79 L1
Newton Herefs 79 L8
Newton Herefs 80 C4
Newton Highld 251 G2
Newton Highld 252 D2
Newton Highld 263 L6
Newton Highld 280 D6
Newton Lancs 147 G8
Newton Lancs 157 J7
Newton Lincs 118 D4
Newton Mdloth 211 K5
Newton Moray 266 C3

Newton Moray 267 G4
Newton N York 152 D1
Newton Nhants 101 J6
Newton Norfk 121 H8
Newton Notts 117 J3
Newton Nthumb 180 C6
Newton Nthumb 190 D5
Newton S Lans 198 F6
Newton S Lans 209 H6
Newton Sandw 98 C4
Newton Shrops 112 F4
Newton Somset 29 K3
Newton Staffs 115 G6
Newton Suffk 89 J7
Newton W Loth 210 E3
Newton Warwks 100 C7
Newton Wilts 34 B6
Newton Abbot Devon 13 K8
Newton Arlosh Cumb 177 G6
Newton Aycliffe Dur 169 H5
Newton Bewley Hartpl 170 B5
Newton Blossomville M Keyn 85 H5
Newton Bromswold Nhants 85 K8
Newton Burgoland Leics 99 K2
Newton-by-the-Sea Nthumb 203 L8
Newton by Toft Lincs 135 L4
Newton Ferrers Cnwll 6 C2
Newton Ferrers Devon 7 G5
Newton Ferry W Isls 282 C2
Newton Flotman Norfk 106 E4
Newtongrange Mdloth 211 K6
Newton Green Mons 45 G1
Newton Harcourt Leics 100 F4
Newton Heath Manch 140 C7
Newtonhill Abers 245 K5
Newton Hill Wakefd 141 M3
Newton-in-Bowland Lancs 148 B3
Newton Kyme N York 151 G4
Newton-le-Willows N York 160 B5
Newton-le-Willows St Hel 139 H8
Newtonloan Mdloth 211 K6
Newton Longville Bucks 67 K1
Newton Mearns E Rens 208 F7
Newtonmill Angus 234 F3
Newtonmore Highld 241 J4
Newton Morrell N York 160 C1
Newton Mountain Pembks 55 G5
Newton Mulgrave N York 171 H7
Newton of Balcanquhal P & K 222 E5
Newton of Balcormo Fife 223 J6
Newton on Ouse N York 151 H4
Newton-on-Rawcliffe N York 162 E4
Newton on the Hill Shrops 113 H7
Newton-on-the-Moor
    Nthumb 191 H5
Newton on Trent Lincs 135 L4
Newton Poppleford Devon 14 C5
Newton Purcell Oxon 66 F1
Newton Regis Warwks 99 H2
Newton Reigny Cumb 166 B4
Newton St Cyres Devon 13 K3
Newton St Faith Norfk 122 E8
Newton St Loe BaNES 45 L6
Newton St Petrock Devon 27 G4
Newton Solney Derbys 115 M6
Newton Stacey Hants 34 E3
Newton Stewart D & G 173 K2
Newton Tony Wilts 34 B3
Newton Tracey Devon 27 J5
Newton under Roseberry
    R & Cl 170 D8
Newton Underwood Nthumb 180 E2
Newton upon Derwent E R Yk 151 M6
Newton Valence Hants 35 L4
Newton Wamphray D & G 187 H7
Newton with Scales Lancs 138 F4
Newtown Blae G 61 J5
Newtown Ches W 129 M4
Newtown Cnwll 2 F5
Newtown Cnwll 11 K7
Newtown Cumb 164 E1
Newtown Cumb 166 C6
Newtown Cumb 177 L6
Newtown Cumb 178 C6
Newtown D & G 185 J1
Newtown Derbys 131 K3
Newtown Devon 14 C4
Newtown Devon 28 C6
Newtown Dorset 15 L2
New Town Dorset 17 K1
New Town Dorset 32 F7
New Town Dorset 33 G7
New Town E Susx 23 H3
Newtown Gloucs 63 K6
Newtown Hants 18 D8
Newtown Hants 35 J8
Newtown Hants 48 C6
Newtown Herefs 80 B4
Newtown Herefs 80 D4
Newtown Herefs 80 E6

Newtown Herefs 81 G7
Newtown Highld 240 B3
Newtown IoW 19 G5
Newtown Lancs 139 G4
New Town Nhants 101 L7
Newtown Nthumb 190 E6
Newtown Nthumb 202 F6
Newtown Nthumb 203 G8
Newtown Poole 17 K4
Newtown Powys 94 D5
Newtown Rhondd 61 G7
Newtown Shrops 112 F7
Newtown Shrops 113 H5
Newtown Somset 30 C8
Newtown Staffs 98 C3
Newtown Staffs 131 H7
Newtown Wigan 139 H6
Newtown Wilts 32 F5
New Town Wilts 47 L4
Newtown Wilts 47 L6
Newtown Worcs 81 K4
Newtown Worcs 98 B7
Newtown-in-St Martin Cnwll .. 3 J6
Newtown Linford Leics 100 B2
Newtown of Beltrees Rens .. 208 C7
Newtown St Boswells Border .. 201 J6
Newtown Unthank Leics 100 B3
New Tredegar Caerph 61 J6
New Trows S Lans 198 D5
New Tupton Derbys 133 H6
Newtyle Angus 233 L7
New Walsoken Cambs 103 K2
New Waltham NE Lin 145 H6
New Whittington Derbys 133 H4
New Winton E Loth 211 M5
New Yatt Oxon 66 A4
Newyears Green Gt Lon 50 D1
Newyork Ag & B 216 F5
New York Lincs 136 D8
New York N Tyne 181 H5
New York N York 150 B3
Nextend Herefs 79 L4
Neyland Pembks 54 F6
Niarbyl IoM 154 b6
Nibley Gloucs 63 K5
Nibley S Glos 45 K3
Nibley Green Gloucs 63 L7
Nicholashayne Devon 29 K7
Nicholaston Swans 56 F7
Nickies Hill Cumb 178 D5
Nidd N York 150 D4
Nigg C Aber 245 K2
Nigg Highld 264 C5
Nigg Ferry Highld 264 B6
Nimlet BaNES 45 L5
Ninebanks Nthumb 179 H4
Nine Elms Swindn 47 G2
Nine Wells Pembks 74 C7
Ninfield E Susx 24 C5
Ningwood IoW 18 F6
Nisbet Border 201 L8
Nisbet Hill Border 202 B3
Niton IoW 19 H8
Nitshill C Glas 208 C7
Noah's Ark Kent 52 C7
Noak Bridge Essex 52 E1
Noak Hill Gt Lon 70 D8
Noblethorpe Barns 141 L6
Nobold Shrops 95 L2
Nobottle Nhants 84 C3
Nocton Lincs 135 L6
Nogdam End Norfk 107 H3
Noke Oxon 66 E4
Nolton Pembks 54 E3
Nolton Haven Pembks 54 D3
No Man's Heath Ches W 113 H2
No Man's Heath Warwks 99 H2
No Man's Land Cnwll 6 B3
Nomansland Devon 28 E8
Nomansland Wilts 34 B7
Noneley Shrops 113 H6
Nonington Kent 41 H5
Nook Cumb 157 H6
Nook Cumb 178 B3
Norbiton Gt Lon 51 G5
Norbreck Bpool 146 F7
Norbridge Herefs 81 K6
Norbury Ches E 113 J2
Norbury Derbys 115 J3
Norbury Gt Lon 51 J5
Norbury Shrops 95 J3
Norbury Staffs 114 B6
Norbury Common Ches E 113 J2
Norbury Junction Staffs 114 B7
Norchard Worcs 81 J2
Norcott Brook Ches W 130 B4
Norcross Lancs 146 F7
Nordelph Norfk 103 L3
Norden Rochdl 140 C5
Nordley Shrops 96 F4

Norham Nthumb 202 D4
Norland Town Calder 141 G3
Norley Ches W 130 B5
Norleywood Hants 18 E4
Norlington E Susx 23 G4
Normanby Lincs 135 K2
Normanby N Linc 143 M4
Normanby N York 162 C6
Normanby R & Cl 170 D7
Normanby le Wold Lincs 136 B1
Norman Cross Cambs 102 D5
Normandy Surrey 50 B8
Norman's Bay E Susx 24 C6
Norman's Green Devon 14 C2
Normanton C Derb 116 B5
Normanton Leics 117 L3
Normanton Lincs 118 B2
Normanton Notts 134 E8
Normanton Rutlnd 101 K2
Normanton Wakefd 142 B3
Normanton Wilts 33 K3
Normanton le Heath Leics 99 K1
Normanton on Soar Notts 116 E7
Normanton on the Wolds
  Notts 117 G5
Normanton on Trent Notts .. 134 F6
Normoss Lancs 147 G8
Norney Surrey 36 D2
Norrington Common Wilts 46 C6
Norris Green Cnwll 6 E1
Norris Green Lpool 129 J1
Norris Hill Leics 116 B8
Norristhorpe Kirk 141 K3
Northacre Norfk 105 J4
Northall Bucks 68 B3
Northallerton N York 160 E4
Northall Green Norfk 121 M8
Northam C Sotn 19 G1
Northam Devon 27 H5
Northampton Nhants 84 E3
Northampton Worcs 81 J2
North Anston Rothm 133 K3
North Ascot Br For 49 M5
North Aston Oxon 66 C1
Northaw Herts 69 H6
Northay Somset 30 D8
North Baddesley Hants 34 E6
North Ballachulish Highld 229 G3
North Barrow Somset 31 K5
North Barsham Norfk 121 K4
North Benfleet Essex 53 G1
North Bersted W Susx 20 F6
North Berwick E Loth 212 C2
North Bitchburn Dur 168 F4
North Blyth Nthumb 181 H2
North Boarhunt Hants 19 K2
North Bockhampton Dorset .. 18 B4
Northborough C Pete 102 C2
Northbourne Kent 41 K5
North Bovey Devon 13 H6
North Bradley Wilts 46 B7
North Brentor Devon 12 C6
North Brewham Somset 32 B3
North Bridge Surrey 36 E3
Northbridge Street E Susx 24 D2
Northbrook Hants 35 G3
Northbrook Oxon 66 D3
North Brook End Cambs 86 F6
North Buckland Devon 27 H3
North Burlingham Norfk 107 H2
North Cadbury Somset 31 K5
North Carlton Lincs 135 J4
North Carlton Notts 134 B3
North Cave E R Yk 143 M1
North Cerney Gloucs 64 E5
North Chailey E Susx 22 F3
Northchapel W Susx 36 E5
North Charford Hants 33 L7
North Charlton Nthumb 191 H4
North Cheam Gt Lon 51 G6
North Cheriton Somset 31 M5
North Chideock Dorset 15 K4
Northchurch Herts 68 B5
North Cliffe E R Yk 152 D8
North Clifton Notts 135 G5
North Close Dur 169 H4
North Cockerington Lincs 137 G2
North Connel Ag & B 228 E8
North Cornelly Brdgnd 42 B5
North Corner Cnwll 3 K7
North Cotes Lincs 145 J7
Northcott Devon 11 L4
Northcott Devon 14 D1
Northcott Devon 29 K8
North Country Cnwll 4 A6
Northcourt Oxon 66 D7
North Cove Suffk 107 K5
North Cowton N York 160 D2
North Crawley M Keyn 85 H6
North Cray Gt Lon 52 A4

North Creake Norfk 121 J4
North Curry Somset 30 D6
North Dalton E R Yk 152 E5
North Deighton N York 150 E5
North Devon Crematorium
  Devon 27 K4
Northdown Kent 41 L1
North Duffield N York 151 L8
North Duntulm Highld 259 G2
North East Surrey
  Crematorium Gt Lon 51 G5
Northedge Derbys 133 G6
North Elham Kent 41 G6
North Elkington Lincs 136 E2
North Elmham Norfk 121 L7
North Elmsall Wakefd 142 D5
Northend Bucks 67 K6
North End C Port 19 L3
North End Cumb 177 K7
North End Dorset 32 D5
North End E R Yk 145 K7
North End E R Yk 153 K7
North End Essex 71 G3
North End Hants 33 J7
North End Hants 35 J5
North End Leics 116 F8
North End Lincs 119 H3
North End Lincs 137 H2
North End Lincs 145 J7
North End N Linc 144 E3
North End N Som 44 E5
North End Nhants 85 J2
North End Norfk 105 K5
North End Nthumb 191 G6
North End Sefton 138 C6
North End W Susx 21 G6
North End W Susx 21 J5
Northend Warwks 83 J5
Northenden Manch 131 G2
Northend Woods Bucks 49 L1
North Erradale Highld 260 B4
North Evington C Leic 100 D3
North Fambridge Essex 71 K7
North Ferriby E R Yk 144 B3
Northfield Birm 98 C7
Northfield C Aber 245 K2
Northfield E R Yk 144 F2
Northfields Lincs 102 A2
Northfleet Kent 52 D4
North Frodingham E R Yk 153 H5
North Gorley Hants 33 L8
North Green Norfk 106 E5
North Green Suffk 91 G3
North Green Suffk 91 J2
North Greetwell Lincs 135 K5
North Grimston N York 152 C2
North Halling Medway 52 F6
North Hayling Hants 20 B6
North Hazelrigg Nthumb 203 G6
North Heasley Devon 28 C4
North Heath W Susx 37 G6
North Hele Devon 29 H4
North Hill Cnwll 11 K7
North Hillingdon Gt Lon 50 D2
North Hinksey Village Oxon .. 66 D6
North Holmwood Surrey 37 J2
North Huish Devon 7 K3
North Hykeham Lincs 135 J6
Northiam E Susx 24 E2
Northill C Beds 86 C6
Northington Gloucs 63 L5
Northington Hants 35 H3
North Kelsey Lincs 144 D7
North Kessock Highld 251 H2
North Killingholme N Linc 144 F4
North Kilvington N York 160 F5
North Kilworth Leics 100 D6
North Kingston Hants 18 B3
North Kyme Lincs 118 F1
North Landing E R Yk 153 L2
Northlands Lincs 119 K1
Northleach Gloucs 65 G4
North Lee Bucks 67 K5
North Lees N York 160 D7
Northleigh Devon 14 E3
Northleigh Devon 27 L4
North Leigh Kent 40 F6
North Leigh Oxon 66 A4
North Leverton with
  Habblesthorpe Notts 134 F3
Northlew Devon 12 C3
North Littleton Worcs 82 C5
Northload Bridge Somset 31 H3
North Lopham Norfk 105 L6
North Luffenham Rutlnd 101 K3
North Marden W Susx 20 C4
North Marston Bucks 67 J3
North Middleton Mdloth 211 K7
North Middleton Nthumb 190 E1

North Millbrex Abers 256 E3
North Milmain D & G 172 D4
North Molton Devon 28 C5
Northmoor Oxon 66 B6
North Moreton Oxon 48 E1
Northmuir Angus 234 B4
North Mundham W Susx 20 E6
North Muskham Notts 134 F7
North Newbald E R Yk 152 D8
North Newington Oxon 83 K7
North Newnton Wilts 47 H7
North Newton Somset 30 D4
Northney Hants 20 B6
North Nibley Gloucs 63 L7
North Oakley Hants 48 D8
North Ockendon Gt Lon 52 C2
Northolt Gt Lon 50 E2
Northop Flints 128 F6
Northop Hall Flints 129 G6
North Ormesby Middsb 170 C6
North Ormsby Lincs 136 E1
Northorpe Kirk 141 K3
Northorpe Lincs 118 E8
Northorpe Lincs 119 G4
Northorpe Lincs 143 M8
North Otterington N York 160 E5
Northover Somset 31 H3
Northover Somset 31 H6
North Owersby Lincs 135 L1
Northowram Calder 141 H2
North Perrott Somset 15 L1
North Petherton Somset 30 D4
North Petherwin Cnwll 11 K5
North Pickenham Norfk 105 H2
North Piddle Worcs 81 M4
North Poorton Dorset 15 M3
Northport Dorset 17 H5
North Poulner Hants 18 B2
North Queensferry Fife 210 F3
North Radworthy Devon 28 C4
North Rauceby Lincs 118 D2
Northrepps Norfk 122 E4
North Reston Lincs 137 G3
North Rigton N York 150 C6
North Ripley Hants 18 B4
North Rode Ches E 131 H6
North Ronaldsay Ork 275 f1
North Row Cumb 165 H4
North Runcton Norfk 120 E8
North Scale Cumb 146 C2
North Scarle Lincs 135 G6
North Seaton Nthumb 181 H2
North Seaton Colliery
  Nthumb 181 H2
North Shian Ag & B 228 E6
North Shields N Tyne 181 J5
North Shoebury Sthend 53 K2
North Shore Bpool 146 F8
North Side C Pete 102 F3
North Side Cumb 164 C5
North Skelton R & Cl 170 F7
North Somercotes Lincs 145 L8
North Stainley N York 160 D7
North Stainmore Cumb 167 J7
North Stifford Thurr 52 D3
North Stoke BaNES 45 L5
North Stoke Oxon 48 F2
North Stoke W Susx 21 H5
North Street Cambs 88 B2
North Street Hants 33 K7
North Street Hants 35 K4
North Street Kent 40 D4
North Street Medway 53 H4
North Street W Berk 48 F4
North Sunderland Nthumb 203 K6
North Tamerton Cnwll 11 K3
North Tawton Devon 12 F2
North Third Stirlg 209 K1
North Thoresby Lincs 145 H8
North Togston Nthumb 191 K5
Northton W Isls 282 d6
North Town Devon 12 C1
North Town Somset 31 J2
North Town W & M 49 L3
North Tuddenham Norfk 122 A8
North Uist W Isls 283 b8
North Walbottle N u Ty 180 E5
North Walsham Norfk 122 F5
North Waltham Hants 35 H2
North Warnborough Hants 35 M1
Northway Somset 29 L5
Northway Swans 57 G7
North Weald Bassett Essex 70 D6
North Wheatley Notts 134 F2
North Whilborough Devon 8 C2
Northwich Ches W 130 C5
North Wick BaNES 45 H6
Northwick S Glos 45 H2
Northwick Somset 30 E1
Northwick Worcs 81 J4

Place	County	Page	Grid
North Widcombe	BaNES	45	H7
North Willingham	Lincs	136	C2
North Wingfield	Derbys	133	H6
North Witham	Lincs	118	B7
Northwold	Norfk	104	E4
Northwood	C Stke	114	D2
Northwood	Derbys	132	E6
Northwood	Gt Lon	50	E1
Northwood	IoW	19	H5
Northwood	Shrops	113	G5
Northwood Green	Gloucs	63	L4
North Wootton	Dorset	31	L7
North Wootton	Norfk	120	H6
North Wootton	Somset	31	J3
North Wraxall	Wilts	46	B4
North Wroughton	Swindn	47	H3
Norton	Donc	142	E5
Norton	E Susx	23	G7
Norton	Gloucs	64	B2
Norton	Halton	130	A3
Norton	Herts	86	E8
Norton	IoW	18	E6
Norton	Mons	62	F3
Norton	N Som	44	D6
Norton	N York	152	B2
Norton	Nhants	84	B3
Norton	Notts	133	L5
Norton	Powys	79	K2
Norton	S on T	170	B6
Norton	Sheff	133	G3
Norton	Shrops	95	L7
Norton	Shrops	96	D2
Norton	Shrops	96	E6
Norton	Shrops	97	J3
Norton	Suffk	89	J2
Norton	Swans	57	H7
Norton	W Susx	20	F5
Norton	Wilts	46	C2
Norton	Worcs	81	K5
Norton	Worcs	82	B5
Norton Bavant	Wilts	32	F2
Norton Bridge	Staffs	114	D5
Norton Canes	Staffs	98	C2
Norton Canon	Herefs	79	M6
Norton Corner	Norfk	122	B6
Norton Disney	Lincs	135	H7
Norton Ferris	Wilts	32	C4
Norton Fitzwarren	Somset	30	B5
Norton Green	IoW	18	E6
Norton Hawkfield	BaNES	45	H6
Norton Heath	Essex	70	F6
Norton in Hales	Shrops	113	M4
Norton in the Moors	C Stke	114	D1
Norton-Juxta-Twycross	Leics	99	J2
Norton-le-Clay	N York	150	F2
Norton Lindsey	Warwks	82	F3
Norton Little Green	Suffk	89	K2
Norton Malreward	BaNES	45	J6
Norton Mandeville	Essex	70	E6
Norton St Philip	Somset	45	M7
Norton Subcourse	Norfk	107	H4
Norton sub Hamdon	Somset	31	G7
Norton Wood	Herefs	79	L5
Norwell	Notts	134	F7
Norwell Woodhouse	Notts	134	E7
Norwich	Norfk	106	E2
Norwich (St Faith) Crematorium	Norfk	122	E8
Norwick	Shet	281	f1
Norwood	Clacks	220	F8
Norwood	Derbys	133	J3
Norwood	Kent	25	K1
Norwood End	Essex	70	E5
Norwood Green	Calder	141	H2
Norwood Green	Gt Lon	50	E4
Norwood Hill	Surrey	37	K2
Norwoodside	Cambs	103	H4
Noseley	Leics	101	G4
Noss Mayo	Devon	7	G5
Nosterfield	N York	160	C6
Nosterfield End	Cambs	88	C6
Nostie	Highld	248	D6
Notgrove	Gloucs	65	G3
Nottage	Brdgnd	42	B6
Notter	Cnwll	6	D3
Nottingham	C Nott	116	F4
Nottington	Dorset	16	C6
Notton	Wakefd	142	A5
Notton	Wilts	46	C5
Nounsley	Essex	71	J5
Noutard's Green	Worcs	81	J2
Nowton	Suffk	89	H3
Nox	Shrops	95	K1
Nuffield	Oxon	49	G2
Nunburnholme	E R Yk	152	C6
Nuncargate	Notts	116	E1
Nunclose	Cumb	166	C2
Nuneaton	Warwks	99	K5
Nuneham Courtenay	Oxon	66	E7
Nunhead	Gt Lon	51	K4
Nunkeeling	E R Yk	153	J6
Nun Monkton	N York	151	H4
Nunney	Somset	32	B2
Nunney Catch	Somset	32	B2
Nunnington	Herefs	80	D6
Nunnington	N York	161	L6
Nunsthorpe	NE Lin	145	H6
Nunthorpe	C York	151	J6
Nunthorpe	Middsb	170	C7
Nunthorpe Village	Middsb	170	D8
Nunton	Wilts	33	K5
Nunwick	N York	160	D7
Nunwick	Nthumb	179	K4
Nupdown	S Glos	63	J7
Nup End	Bucks	67	L3
Nupend	Gloucs	64	A5
Nuptown	Br For	49	L4
Nursling	Hants	34	E7
Nursted	Hants	36	A6
Nursteed	Wilts	46	F6
Nurton	Staffs	97	J3
Nutbourne	W Susx	20	C6
Nutbourne	W Susx	21	J3
Nutfield	Surrey	37	M1
Nuthall	Notts	116	E3
Nuthampstead	Herts	87	H8
Nuthurst	W Susx	37	J5
Nutley	E Susx	23	G2
Nutley	Hants	35	J2
Nuttall	Bury	140	B4
Nutwell	Donc	143	G7
Nybster	Highld	280	E3
Nyetimber	W Susx	20	E7
Nyewood	W Susx	36	B6
Nymet Rowland	Devon	13	G1
Nymet Tracey	Devon	13	G3
Nympsfield	Gloucs	64	A7
Nynehead	Somset	29	L6
Nythe	Somset	30	F4
Nyton	W Susx	20	F5

O

Place	County	Page	Grid
Oadby	Leics	100	D3
Oad Street	Kent	53	J6
Oakall Green	Worcs	81	J3
Oakamoor	Staffs	115	G3
Oakbank	W Loth	210	E5
Oak Cross	Devon	12	D3
Oakdale	Caerph	43	J2
Oake	Somset	29	L6
Oaken	Staffs	97	J3
Oakenclough	Lancs	147	K6
Oakenholt	Flints	129	G5
Oakengates	Wrekin	96	F1
Oakenshaw	Dur	169	G3
Oakenshaw	Kirk	141	J2
Oakerthorpe	Derbys	133	H8
Oakford	Cerdgn	76	E4
Oakford	Devon	29	G6
Oakfordbridge	Devon	29	G6
Oakgrove	Ches E	131	H6
Oakham	Rutlnd	101	J2
Oakhanger	Ches E	114	B1
Oakhanger	Hants	36	A4
Oakhill	Somset	31	K2
Oakhurst	Kent	38	E3
Oakington	Cambs	87	H2
Oaklands	Powys	78	E5
Oakle Street	Gloucs	63	M4
Oakley	Bed	85	K4
Oakley	Bucks	66	F4
Oakley	Fife	210	D1
Oakley	Hants	35	H1
Oakley	Oxon	67	H7
Oakley	Poole	17	K3
Oakley	Suffk	106	D7
Oakley Green	W & M	50	A4
Oakley Park	Powys	93	L6
Oakridge	Gloucs	64	C6
Oaks	Lancs	139	K1
Oaks	Shrops	95	K3
Oaksey	Wilts	64	E8
Oaks Green	Derbys	115	J5
Oakshaw Ford	Cumb	178	C4
Oakshott	Hants	35	M5
Oakthorpe	Leics	99	J1
Oak Tree	Darltn	169	K8
Oakwood	C Derb	116	C4
Oakwood	Nthumb	179	L5
Oakworth	C Brad	149	A7
Oare	Kent	40	C3
Oare	Somset	28	D2
Oare	Wilts	47	H6
Oasby	Lincs	118	D4
Oath	Somset	30	F5
Oathlaw	Angus	234	D2
Oatlands Park	Surrey	50	E6
Oban	Ag & B	216	D1
Obley	Shrops	95	H7
Obney	P & K	232	F8
Oborne	Dorset	31	L7
Obthorpe	Lincs	118	E8
Occold	Suffk	90	D1
Occumster	Highld	275	J1
Ochiltree	E Ayrs	196	F6
Ockbrook	Derbys	116	C4
Ocker Hill	Sandw	98	B4
Ockeridge	Worcs	81	H3
Ockham	Surrey	50	D7
Ockle	Highld	237	G6
Ockley	Surrey	37	H3
Ocle Pychard	Herefs	80	C6
Octon	E R Yk	153	G2
Odcombe	Somset	31	H7
Odd Down	BaNES	45	L6
Oddingley	Worcs	81	L3
Oddington	Gloucs	65	J2
Oddington	Oxon	66	E4
Odell	Bed	85	J4
Odham	Devon	12	C2
Odiham	Hants	49	H8
Odsal	C Brad	141	J2
Odsey	Cambs	86	F7
Odstock	Wilts	33	K5
Odstone	Leics	99	K2
Offchurch	Warwks	83	J2
Offenham	Worcs	82	C6
Offerton	Stockp	131	H2
Offerton	Sundld	181	J7
Offham	E Susx	22	F5
Offham	Kent	39	G2
Offham	W Susx	21	H5
Offleymarsh	Staffs	114	B5
Offord Cluny	Cambs	86	E2
Offord D'Arcy	Cambs	86	E2
Offton	Suffk	90	C5
Offwell	Devon	14	E3
Ogbourne Maizey	Wilts	47	J4
Ogbourne St Andrew	Wilts	47	J4
Ogbourne St George	Wilts	47	J4
Ogden	Calder	141	G2
Ogle	Nthumb	180	E3
Oglet	Lpool	129	K3
Ogmore	V Glam	42	D6
Ogmore-by-Sea	V Glam	42	C6
Ogmore Vale	Brdgnd	42	E4
Ogwen Bank	Gwynd	126	C6
Okeford Fitzpaine	Dorset	32	D8
Okehampton	Devon	12	E4
Oker Side	Derbys	132	E7
Okewood Hill	Surrey	37	H3
Olchard	Devon	13	K7
Old	Nhants	84	F1
Old Aberdeen	C Aber	245	L1
Old Alresford	Hants	35	J4
Oldany	Highld	270	E2
Old Auchenbrack	D & G	185	J3
Old Basford	C Nott	116	F3
Old Basing	Hants	49	G8
Old Beetley	Norfk	121	L7
Oldberrow	Warwks	82	D2
Old Bewick	Nthumb	190	F2
Old Bolingbroke	Lincs	136	F6
Old Bramhope	Leeds	150	B7
Old Brampton	Derbys	133	G5
Old Bridge of Urr	D & G	175	J1
Old Buckenham	Norfk	106	B5
Old Burghclere	Hants	48	C7
Oldbury	Kent	38	F2
Oldbury	Sandw	98	C5
Oldbury	Shrops	97	G5
Oldbury	Warwks	99	J4
Oldbury Naite	S Glos	63	J8
Oldbury-on-Severn	S Glos	63	J8
Oldbury on the Hill	Gloucs	46	B1
Old Byland	N York	161	J5
Old Cantley	Donc	143	G7
Old Cassop	Dur	169	J3
Old Castle	Brdgnd	42	D6
Oldcastle	Mons	62	C2
Oldcastle Heath	Ches W	113	G2
Old Catton	Norfk	106	E1
Old Churchstoke	Powys	95	G4
Old Clee	NE Lin	145	H6
Old Cleeve	Somset	29	J3
Old Clipstone	Notts	134	C6
Old Colwyn	Conwy	127	H4
Oldcotes	Notts	134	B2
Old Dailly	S Ayrs	183	G3
Old Dalby	Leics	117	H6
Old Dam	Derbys	132	B4
Old Deer	Abers	269	H6
Old Ditch	Somset	31	H1
Old Edlington	Donc	142	E8
Old Eldon	Dur	169	H5
Old Ellerby	E R Yk	153	J8
Old Felixstowe	Suffk	91	H8
Oldfield	C Brad	149	H8
Oldfield	Worcs	81	J2
Old Fletton	C Pete	102	D4
Oldford	Somset	32	C1
Old Forge	Herefs	63	H3
Old Furnace	Herefs	62	F2
Old Glossop	Derbys	131	L1
Old Goole	E R Yk	143	H3
Old Grimsby	IoS	10	b2
Old Hall Green	Herts	69	K3
Oldhall Green	Suffk	89	H4
Old Hall Street	Norfk	122	H6
Oldham	Oldham	140	D6
Oldhamstocks	E Loth	213	L6
Old Harlow	Essex	70	C5
Old Heath	Essex	72	E2
Old Hunstanton	Norfk	120	F3
Old Hurst	Cambs	102	F7
Old Hutton	Cumb	157	J5
Old Kea	Cnwll	4	D6
Old Kilpatrick	W Duns	208	D4
Old Knebworth	Herts	69	G3
Old Lakenham	Norfk	106	E2
Oldland	S Glos	45	K4
Old Langho	Lancs	148	B8
Old Laxey	IoM	154	f5
Old Leake	Lincs	119	L2
Old Malton	N York	152	B1
Oldmeldrum	Abers	256	E6
Oldmill	Cnwll	11	M7
Old Milverton	Warwks	83	G2
Oldmixon	N Som	44	C7
Old Newton	Suffk	90	B3
Old Quarrington	Dur	169	J3
Old Radford	C Nott	116	F3
Old Radnor	Powys	79	J3
Old Rayne	Abers	256	B6
Old Romney	Kent	25	J2
Old Shoreham	W Susx	22	B6
Oldshoremore	Highld	276	D3
Old Soar	Kent	38	F3
Old Sodbury	S Glos	45	L3
Old Somerby	Lincs	118	C5
Oldstead	N York	161	H6
Old Stratford	Nhants	84	E7
Old Struan	P & K	232	B2
Old Swarland	Nthumb	191	H6
Old Swinford	Dudley	97	K6
Old Tebay	Cumb	157	K2
Old Thirsk	N York	160	F6
Old Town	Calder	140	F2
Old Town	Cumb	157	J6
Old Town	Cumb	166	B2
Old Town	E Susx	23	K7
Old Town	IoS	10	c3
Old Trafford	Traffd	140	B8
Old Tupton	Derbys	133	H6
Oldwall	Cumb	178	B6
Old Warden	C Beds	86	C6
Oldways End	Somset	28	F6
Old Weston	Cambs	102	F7
Old Wick	Highld	280	E6
Old Windsor	W & M	50	C4
Old Wives Lees	Kent	40	E4
Old Woking	Surrey	50	C4
Old Wolverton	M Keyn	84	F7
Old Woodhall	Lincs	136	D6
Old Woods	Shrops	113	G6
Olgrinmore	Highld	279	K5
Olive Green	Staffs	115	J7
Oliver's Battery	Hants	34	F5
Ollaberry	Shet	281	d4
Ollach	Highld	247	J5
Ollerton	Ches E	130	F4
Ollerton	Notts	134	D6
Ollerton	Shrops	113	G6
Olmarch	Cerdgn	77	H4
Olmstead Green	Cambs	88	C7
Olney	M Keyn	85	H5
Olrig House	Highld	279	J3
Olton	Solhll	98	E7
Olveston	S Glos	45	J2
Ombersley	Worcs	81	J3
Ompton	Notts	134	C6
Once Brewed	Nthumb	179	H6
Onchan	IoM	154	e6
Onecote	Staffs	131	L8
Onehouse	Suffk	89	K3
Onen	Mons	62	E4
Ongar Street	Herefs	79	M2
Onibury	Shrops	95	L7
Onich	Highld	229	G2
Onllwyn	Neath	60	C5
Onneley	Staffs	114	B3
Onslow Green	Essex	71	G3
Onslow Village	Surrey	36	E1
Onston	Ches W	130	B5
Openwoodgate	Derbys	116	B2
Opinan	Highld	260	B5
Orbliston	Moray	266	F5

Orbost Highld....258 D7
Orby Lincs....137 J6
Orchard Portman Somset....30 C6
Orcheston Wilts....33 J2
Orcop Herefs....62 F2
Orcop Hill Herefs....62 F2
Ord Abers....268 A4
Ordhead Abers....244 E2
Ordie Abers....244 A3
Ordiequish Moray....267 G5
Ordley Nthumb....179 L7
Ordsall Notts....134 D4
Ore E Susx....24 F5
Oreleton Common Herefs....80 B2
Oreton Shrops....96 E7
Orford Suffk....91 K5
Orford Warrtn....130 B2
Organford Dorset....17 H4
Orgreave Staffs....115 J8
Orkney Islands Ork....275 C4
Orlestone Kent....40 C8
Orleton Herefs....80 B2
Orleton Worcs....81 G2
Orlingbury Nhants....85 G1
Ormathwaite Cumb....165 J5
Ormesby R & Cl....170 C5
Ormesby St Margaret Norfk....123 K8
Ormesby St Michael Norfk....123 K8
Ormiscaig Highld....260 D2
Ormiston E Loth....211 M5
Ormsaigmore Highld....236 F7
Ormsary Ag & B....206 A4
Ormskirk Lancs....138 E6
Ornsby Hill Dur....168 F1
Oronsay Ag & B....214 C6
Orphir Ork....275 b5
Orpington Gt Lon....51 M5
Orrell Sefton....138 D8
Orrell Wigan....139 G7
Orrell Post Wigan....139 G6
Orrisdale IoM....154 d4
Orroland D & G....175 J5
Orsett Thurr....52 D3
Orslow Staffs....114 C8
Orston Notts....117 K3
Orthwaite Cumb....165 H4
Ortner Lancs....147 K5
Orton Cumb....157 K1
Orton Nhants....101 H7
Orton Staffs....97 K4
Orton Longueville C Pete....102 D4
Orton-on-the-Hill Leics....99 J3
Orton Rigg Cumb....177 K8
Orton Waterville C Pete....102 C4
Orwell Cambs....87 H5
Osbaldeston Lancs....139 K1
Osbaldeston Green Lancs....139 K1
Osbaldwick C York....151 K5
Osbaston Leics....99 L3
Osbaston Shrops....112 D7
Osborne IoW....19 H5
Osbournby Lincs....118 E4
Oscroft Ches W....129 L6
Ose Highld....258 D6
Osgathorpe Leics....116 D7
Osgodby Lincs....135 M1
Osgodby N York....143 G1
Osgodby N York....163 J5
Oskaig Highld....247 H1
Oskamull Ag & B....226 E4
Osmaston Derbys....115 K3
Osmington Dorset....16 D6
Osmington Mills Dorset....16 D6
Osmondthorpe Leeds....142 A1
Osmotherley N York....161 G3
Osney Oxon....66 D6
Ospringe Kent....40 C3
Ossett Wakefd....141 L4
Ossington Notts....134 E6
Ostend Essex....72 D7
Osterley Gt Lon....50 F3
Oswaldkirk N York....161 K6
Oswaldtwistle Lancs....139 L2
Oswestry Shrops....112 D5
Otford Kent....52 B7
Otham Kent....39 K3
Otham Hole Kent....39 K3
Othery Somset....30 F4
Otley Leeds....150 B6
Otley Suffk....90 E4
Otley Green Suffk....90 E4
Otterbourne Hants....34 F6
Otterburn N York....148 F4
Otterburn Nthumb....190 C7
Otter Ferry Ag & B....206 C4
Otterham Cnwll....11 H4
Otterhampton Somset....30 C2
Otterham Quay Kent....53 H6
Otterham Station Cnwll....11 G5
Otternish W Isls....282 c7

Ottershaw Surrey....50 C6
Otterswick Shet....281 e3
Otterton Devon....14 C5
Otterwood Hants....18 F3
Ottery St Mary Devon....14 C3
Ottinge Kent....41 G6
Ottringham E R Yk....145 H3
Oughterby Cumb....177 J7
Oughtershaw N York....158 F6
Oughterside Cumb....164 F3
Oughtibridge Sheff....132 F1
Oughtrington Warrtn....130 D2
Oulston N York....161 J7
Oulton Cumb....177 H8
Oulton Leeds....142 B2
Oulton Norfk....122 C6
Oulton Staffs....114 B7
Oulton Staffs....114 E4
Oulton Suffk....107 L4
Oulton Broad Suffk....107 L5
Oulton Street Norfk....122 C6
Oundle Nhants....102 A5
Ounsdale Staffs....97 K5
Ousby Cumb....166 E4
Ousden Suffk....88 E3
Ousefleet E R Yk....143 L3
Ouston Dur....181 G8
Outchester Nthumb....203 J6
Out Elmstead Kent....41 G5
Outgate Cumb....156 E3
Outhgill Cumb....158 D2
Outhill Warwks....82 D2
Outlands Staffs....114 B5
Outlane Kirk....141 G4
Out Newton E R Yk....145 K3
Out Rawcliffe Lancs....147 H7
Outwell Norfk....103 K3
Outwick Hants....33 K7
Outwood Surrey....37 M2
Outwood Wakefd....142 A3
Outwood Gate Bury....140 B6
Outwoods Leics....116 C7
Outwoods Staffs....114 B7
Ouzlewell Green Leeds....142 A3
Ovenden Calder....141 G2
Over Cambs....87 H1
Over Ches W....130 C6
Over Gloucs....64 A4
Over S Glos....45 H2
Over Burrows Derbys....115 L4
Overbury Worcs....81 M7
Overcombe Dorset....16 D6
Over Compton Dorset....31 K7
Overdale Crematorium
  Bolton....139 K6
Over End Cambs....102 B5
Overgreen Derbys....132 F5
Over Green Warwks....98 F4
Over Haddon Derbys....132 D6
Over Kellet Lancs....147 K2
Over Kiddington Oxon....66 B3
Overleigh Somset....31 G4
Overley Staffs....115 J8
Over Monnow Mons....63 G4
Over Norton Oxon....65 L2
Over Peover Ches E....130 F5
Overpool Ches W....129 J4
Overscaig Hotel Highld....272 B3
Overseal Derbys....115 M8
Over Silton N York....161 G4
Oversland Kent....40 D4
Oversley Green Warwks....82 C4
Overstone Nhants....84 F2
Over Stowey Somset....30 B3
Overstrand Norfk....122 E4
Over Stratton Somset....31 G7
Overstreet Wilts....33 J3
Over Tabley Ches E....130 E4
Overthorpe Nhants....83 L7
Overton C Aber....245 J1
Overton Ches W....129 M4
Overton Hants....35 G1
Overton Lancs....147 H4
Overton N York....151 J5
Overton Shrops....80 C1
Overton Swans....56 E7
Overton Wakefd....141 L4
Overton Wrexhm....112 E3
Overton Bridge Wrexhm....112 E3
Overton Green Ches E....130 F7
Overtown Lancs....157 K7
Overtown N Lans....209 L8
Overtown Swindn....47 H3
Overtown Wakefd....142 A4
Over Wallop Hants....34 C3
Over Whitacre Warwks....99 H5
Over Woodhouse Derbys....133 J5
Over Worton Oxon....66 B2
Overy Oxon....66 E8
Oving Bucks....67 J3

Oving W Susx....20 E6
Ovingdean Br & H....22 E6
Ovingham Nthumb....180 D6
Ovington Dur....168 E7
Ovington Essex....88 F6
Ovington Hants....35 H4
Ovington Norfk....105 J3
Ovington Nthumb....180 C6
Ower Hants....19 H3
Ower Hants....34 D7
Owermoigne Dorset....16 E5
Owlbury Shrops....95 H5
Owlerton Sheff....133 G2
Owlpen Gloucs....64 A7
Owl's Green Suffk....91 G1
Owlsmoor Br For....49 K6
Owlswick Bucks....67 J6
Owmby Lincs....135 K2
Owmby Lincs....144 D6
Owslebury Hants....35 G6
Owston Donc....142 E5
Owston Leics....101 G2
Owston Ferry N Linc....143 K7
Owstwick E R Yk....145 H1
Owthorne E R Yk....145 J2
Owthorpe Notts....117 H5
Owton Manor Hartpl....170 C5
Oxborough Norfk....104 E3
Oxbridge Dorset....15 L3
Oxcombe Lincs....136 F4
Oxcroft Derbys....133 J5
Oxen End Essex....71 G1
Oxenholme Cumb....157 H5
Oxenhope C Brad....140 F1
Oxen Park Cumb....156 D5
Oxenpill Somset....31 G3
Oxenton Gloucs....64 D1
Oxenwood Wilts....47 L7
Oxford Oxon....66 D6
Oxford Crematorium Oxon....66 D6
Oxhey Herts....68 E8
Oxhill Dur....180 F8
Oxhill Warwks....83 H6
Oxley Wolves....97 K3
Oxley Green Essex....72 C4
Oxley's Green E Susx....24 C3
Oxlode Cambs....103 K6
Oxnam Border....189 J3
Oxnead Norfk....122 E6
Oxshott Surrey....50 F6
Oxshott Heath Surrey....50 E6
Oxspring Barns....141 L7
Oxted Surrey....51 K8
Oxton Border....201 G2
Oxton N York....151 H7
Oxton Notts....117 G1
Oxwich Swans....56 F7
Oxwich Green Swans....56 F7
Oxwick Norfk....121 K6
Oykel Bridge Hotel Highld....271 L7
Oyne Abers....256 B6
Oystermouth Swans....57 H7
Ozleworth Gloucs....64 A8

P

Pabail W Isls....282 h3
Packers Hill Dorset....16 D1
Packington Leics....116 B8
Packmoor C Stke....114 D1
Packmores Warwks....83 G2
Padanaram Angus....234 C5
Padbury Bucks....67 H1
Paddington Gt Lon....51 H3
Paddington Warrtn....130 C2
Paddlesworth Kent....41 G7
Paddlesworth Kent....52 E6
Paddock Wood Kent....39 G4
Paddolgreen Shrops....113 H5
Padfield Derbys....140 F8
Padgate Warrtn....130 C2
Padhams Green Essex....70 F7
Padiham Lancs....140 B1
Padside N York....149 L4
Padstow Cnwll....10 C7
Padworth W Berk....48 F5
Page Bank Dur....169 G4
Pagham W Susx....20 E7
Paglesham Essex....72 D6
Paignton Torbay....8 C3
Pailton Warwks....100 A7
Paine's Cross E Susx....23 K3
Painleyhill Staffs....115 G5
Painscastle Powys....79 G6
Painshawfield Nthumb....180 C6
Painsthorpe E R Yk....152 B4
Painswick Gloucs....64 C5
Painter's Forstal Kent....40 C3
Paisley Rens....208 E6

Paisley Woodside
  Crematorium Rens....208 D6
Pakefield Suffk....107 L5
Pakenham Suffk....89 J2
Pale Gwynd....111 J4
Pale Green Essex....88 D6
Palestine Hants....34 B3
Paley Street W & M....49 L4
Palfrey Wsall....98 C4
Palgrave Suffk....106 C7
Pallington Dorset....16 F4
Palmersbridge Cnwll....11 H7
Palmers Green Gt Lon....69 J8
Palmerston E Ayrs....196 F7
Palmerstown V Glam....43 H7
Palnackie D & G....175 K3
Palnure D & G....174 C2
Palterton Derbys....133 J6
Pamber End Hants....48 F7
Pamber Green Hants....48 F7
Pamber Heath Hants....48 F6
Pamington Gloucs....81 L8
Pamphill Dorset....17 K3
Pampisford Cambs....87 K5
Panborough Somset....31 G2
Panbride Angus....234 E8
Pancrasweek Devon....11 K2
Pancross V Glam....43 G7
Pandy Caerph....43 J4
Pandy Gwynd....92 D3
Pandy Gwynd....111 G5
Pandy Mons....62 C3
Pandy Powys....93 K3
Pandy Wrexhm....112 B4
Pandy'r Capel Denbgs....111 L2
Pandy Tudur Conwy....127 G6
Panfield Essex....71 H2
Pangbourne W Berk....48 F4
Pangdean W Susx....22 D5
Panks Bridge Herefs....80 E5
Pannal N York....150 D5
Pannal Ash N York....150 C5
Pannanich Wells Hotel Abers....243 L4
Pant Shrops....112 D7
Pantasaph Flints....128 E4
Panteg Pembks....74 F5
Pantersbridge Cnwll....5 K1
Pant-ffrwyth Brdgnd....42 E5
Pant Glas Gwynd....109 H2
Pantglas Powys....93 G4
Pant-Gwyn Carmth....59 G4
Pant-lasau Swans....57 J5
Pant Mawr Powys....93 J7
Panton Lincs....136 C4
Pant-pastynog Denbgs....128 B7
Pantperthog Gwynd....93 G3
Pant-y-dwr Powys....93 L8
Pant-y-ffridd Powys....94 E3
Pantyffynnon Carmth....57 H3
Pantygaseg Torfn....61 L7
Pant-y-gog Brdgnd....42 D3
Pantymenyn Carmth....75 K7
Pant-y-mwyn Flints....128 E6
Panxworth Norfk....107 G1
Papcastle Cumb....164 F4
Papigoe Highld....280 E6
Papple E Loth....212 D4
Papplewick Notts....116 F1
Papworth Everard Cambs....86 F3
Papworth St Agnes Cambs....86 F2
Par Cnwll....5 H4
Paramour Street Kent....41 J3
Parbold Lancs....139 G5
Parbrook Somset....31 J4
Parbrook W Susx....37 G6
Parc Gwynd....111 G5
Parc Gwyn Crematorium
  Pembks....55 K4
Parcllyn Cerdgn....75 M2
Parc Seymour Newpt....44 E1
Pardshaw Cumb....164 E5
Parham Suffk....91 G3
Park D & G....186 D7
Park Nthumb....178 F6
Park Bottom Cnwll....3 H3
Park Bridge Tamesd....140 E7
Park Corner E Susx....38 E6
Park Corner Oxon....49 G1
Park Corner W & M....49 K2
Park Crematorium Lancs....138 D2
Park End Bed....85 K4
Parkend Gloucs....63 J5
Park End Nthumb....179 K4
Parkers Green Kent....38 F4
Parkeston Essex....73 K1
Parkeston Quay Essex....90 F8
Park Farm Kent....40 D7
Parkgate Ches W....129 G4
Parkgate Cumb....165 H1
Parkgate D & G....176 D1

Parkgate E Susx	24 C4	Peak Dale Derbys	132 B4
Parkgate Essex	71 G1	Peak Forest Derbys	132 B4
Park Gate Hants	19 J2	Peak Hill Lincs	119 J8
Parkgate Kent	39 L6	Peakirk C Pete	102 D2
Parkgate Kent	52 B6	Pearson's Green Kent	39 H4
Park Gate Leeds	150 A7	Peartree Green Herefs	80 E8
Parkgate Surrey	37 K2	Peasedown St John BaNES	45 K7
Park Gate Worcs	81 L1	Peasehill Derbys	116 C2
Park Green Essex	70 C2	Peaseland Green Norfk	122 B8
Park Green Suffk	90 D2	Peasemore W Berk	48 C3
Parkgrove Crematorium Angus	234 F5	Peasenhall Suffk	91 H2
Parkhall W Duns	208 E4	Pease Pottage W Susx	37 L4
Parkham Devon	27 G6	Peaslake Surrey	37 G2
Parkham Ash Devon	26 F6	Peasley Cross St Hel	129 M1
Park Head Derbys	116 B1	Peasmarsh E Susx	25 G3
Park Hill Gloucs	63 H7	Peasmarsh Somset	30 E8
Parkhouse Mons	63 G6	Peasmarsh Surrey	36 E2
Parkmill Swans	57 G7	Peathill Abers	269 G3
Park Royal Gt Lon	51 G3	Peat Inn Fife	223 H5
Parkside Dur	169 L1	Peatling Magna Leics	100 D5
Parkside N Lans	209 L7	Peatling Parva Leics	100 D5
Parkside Wrexhm	129 J8	Peaton Shrops	96 C6
Parkstone Poole	17 K4	Pebmarsh Essex	89 G8
Park Street Herts	68 F6	Pebworth Worcs	82 D6
Park Street W Susx	37 H4	Pecket Well Calder	140 F2
Park Wood Crematorium Calder	141 H3	Peckforton Ches E	129 M8
Parley Green Dorset	17 M3	Peckham Gt Lon	51 J4
Parmoor Bucks	49 J1	Peckleton Leics	100 A3
Parndon Essex	70 B5	Pedairffordd Powys	111 M6
Parndon Wood Crematorium Essex	70 C5	Pedlinge Kent	40 F8
Parracombe Devon	28 B2	Pedmore Dudley	97 K7
Parrog Pembks	75 H4	Pedwell Somset	30 F4
Parsonby Cumb	164 F3	Peebles Border	200 B5
Parson Cross Sheff	133 G1	Peel IoM	154 c5
Parson Drove Cambs	103 H2	Peel Lancs	138 D2
Parson's Heath Essex	72 F2	Peel Common Hants	19 K3
Parson's Hill Derbys	116 A6	Peene Kent	41 F7
Partick C Glas	208 F5	Peening Quarter Kent	39 M7
Partington Traffd	130 D2	Peggs Green Leics	116 C7
Partney Lincs	137 H6	Pegsdon C Beds	68 E1
Parton Cumb	164 C6	Pegswood Nthumb	180 F7
Partridge Green W Susx	22 B3	Pegwell Kent	41 K3
Partrishow Powys	62 B3	Peinchorran Highld	247 H2
Parwich Derbys	115 K1	Peinlich Highld	259 G5
Paslow Wood Common Essex	70 E6	Pelcomb Pembks	54 F3
Passenham Nhants	84 F7	Pelcomb Bridge Pembks	54 F3
Passfield Hants	36 B4	Pelcomb Cross Pembks	54 F3
Passingford Bridge Essex	70 D7	Peldon Essex	72 E4
Paston C Pete	102 D3	Pell Green E Susx	39 G6
Paston Norfk	123 G4	Pelsall Wsall	98 C3
Pasturefields Staffs	114 F6	Pelsall Wood Wsall	98 C3
Patchacott Devon	12 B3	Pelton Dur	181 G8
Patcham Br & H	22 D5	Pelton Fell Dur	181 G8
Patchetts Green Herts	68 F7	Pelutho Cumb	164 F1
Patching W Susx	21 J5	Pelynt Cnwll	5 L4
Patchole Devon	27 L2	Pemberton Carmth	56 F5
Patchway S Glos	45 J3	Pemberton Wigan	139 H7
Pateley Bridge N York	149 L3	Pembles Cross Kent	39 M4
Paternoster Heath Essex	72 D4	Pembrey Carmth	56 D4
Pathe Somset	30 F5	Pembridge Herefs	79 M4
Pathead Fife	222 E8	Pembroke Pembks	55 G6
Pathead Mdloth	211 L6	Pembroke Dock Pembks	54 F6
Pathlow Warwks	82 E3	Pembury Kent	39 G5
Path of Condie P & K	221 K5	Pen-allt Herefs	63 H1
Patmore Heath Herts	70 B2	Penallt Mons	63 G5
Patna E Ayrs	183 K1	Penally Pembks	55 J7
Patney Wilts	47 G7	Penare Cnwll	5 L4
Patrick IoM	154 c5	Penarth V Glam	43 J7
Patrick Brompton N York	160 B4	Penblewin Pembks	55 J4
Patricroft Salfd	139 M8	Pen-bont Rhydybeddau Cerdgn	92 E6
Patrington E R Yk	145 J3	Penbryn Cerdgn	76 B5
Patrington Haven E R Yk	145 J3	Pencader Carmth	58 E2
Patrixbourne Kent	41 G4	Pencaenewydd Gwynd	109 G3
Patterdale Cumb	165 L7	Pencaitland E Loth	212 A5
Pattingham Staffs	97 J4	Pencarnisiog IoA	124 K3
Pattishall Nhants	84 C4	Pencarreg Carmth	76 F6
Pattiswick Green Essex	71 K2	Pencarrow Cnwll	10 F6
Patton Shrops	96 D4	Pencelli Powys	61 H2
Paul Cnwll	2 D5	Penclawdd Swans	57 G5
Paulerspury Nhants	84 D6	Pencoed Brdgnd	42 E5
Paull E R Yk	144 F3	Pencombe Herefs	80 E5
Paul's Dene Wilts	33 K4	Pencoyd Herefs	63 G2
Paulton BaNES	45 K7	Pencraig Herefs	63 H3
Paunton Herefs	80 F5	Pencraig Powys	111 K6
Pauperhaugh Nthumb	191 G6	Pendeen Cnwll	2 B4
Pave Lane Wrekin	114 B8	Penderyn Rhondd	60 D7
Pavenham Bed	85 K4	Pendine Carmth	55 L5
Pawlett Somset	30 D2	Pendlebury Salfd	140 B7
Pawston Nthumb	202 C6	Pendleton Lancs	148 D7
Paxford Gloucs	82 E7	Pendock Worcs	81 H8
Paxton Border	202 E3	Pendoggett Cnwll	10 E6
Payden Street Kent	40 B4	Pendomer Somset	31 H8
Payhembury Devon	14 C2	Pendoylan V Glam	43 G6
Paynter's Lane End Cnwll	3 H2	Pendre Brdgnd	42 D4
Paythorne Lancs	148 E5	Penegoes Powys	93 G3
Paytoe Herefs	80 A1	Penelewey Cnwll	3 K3
Peacehaven E Susx	22 F7	Pen-ffordd Pembks	55 J2
		Pengam Caerph	43 J2
		Pengam Cardif	43 K6

Penge Gt Lon	51 K5	Penrhyncoch Cerdgn	92 D6
Pengelly Cnwll	10 F6	Penrhyndeudraeth Gwynd	109 L4
Pengorffwysfa IoA	125 H1	Penrhyn-side Conwy	126 F3
Pengover Green Cnwll	6 B2	Penrice Swans	56 F7
Pen-groes-oped Mons	62 C5	Penrioch N Ayrs	194 D2
Pengwern Denbgs	127 K4	Penrith Cumb	166 C4
Penhale Cnwll	3 H7	Penrose Cnwll	10 B8
Penhale Cnwll	4 E3	Penruddock Cumb	166 A5
Penhale Cnwll	5 J3	Penryn Cnwll	3 K4
Penhale Cnwll	6 E4	Pensarn Conwy	127 J4
Penhallow Cnwll	4 C4	Pensax Worcs	81 G2
Penhalurick Cnwll	3 H3	Pensby Wirral	129 G3
Penhalvean Cnwll	3 H3	Penselwood Somset	32 C4
Penhill Swindn	47 H1	Pensford BaNES	45 J6
Penhow Newpt	44 E1	Pensham Worcs	81 L6
Penhurst E Susx	24 C4	Penshaw Sundld	181 H8
Peniarth Gwynd	92 D2	Penshurst Kent	38 E4
Penicuik Mdloth	211 H7	Penshurst Station Kent	38 E4
Peniel Carmth	58 D4	Pensilva Cnwll	11 K8
Peniel Denbgs	127 L7	Pensnett Dudley	97 K5
Penifiler Highld	259 H8	Penstone Devon	13 H3
Peninver Ag & B	192 F3	Penstrowed Powys	94 C5
Penisarwaun Gwynd	125 K7	Pentewan Cnwll	5 G5
Penistone Barns	141 K7	Pentir Gwynd	125 K6
Penjerrick Cnwll	3 K5	Pentire Cnwll	4 C3
Penketh Warrtn	130 A2	Pentlepoir Pembks	55 J5
Penkill S Ayrs	183 G3	Pentlow Essex	89 G6
Penkridge Staffs	97 L1	Pentlow Street Essex	89 G6
Penlean Cnwll	11 H3	Pentney Norfk	120 F8
Penleigh Wilts	32 E1	Pentonbridge Cumb	178 B3
Penley Wrexhm	112 F3	Penton Grafton Hants	34 D2
Penllergaer Swans	57 H5	Penton Mewsey Hants	34 D2
Pen-llyn IoA	124 F3	Pentraeth IoA	125 J4
Penllyn V Glam	42 E6	Pentre Denbgs	128 C7
Pen-lon IoA	125 G6	Pentre Flints	129 H6
Penmachno Conwy	110 E2	Pentre Mons	62 C6
Penmaen Caerph	43 J2	Pentre Mons	62 E7
Penmaen Swans	56 F7	Pentre Powys	94 C6
Penmaenan Conwy	126 E4	Pentre Powys	94 E5
Penmaenmawr Conwy	126 E4	Pentre Powys	95 G5
Penmaenpool Gwynd	110 C7	Pentre Rhondd	42 E2
Penmark V Glam	43 G7	Pentre Shrops	112 E7
Penmon IoA	126 C3	Pentre Wrexhm	112 D3
Penmorfa Gwynd	109 K3	Pentre Bach Cerdgn	77 G6
Penmount Crematorium Cnwll	4 D5	Pentre Bach Flints	128 F4
Penmynydd IoA	125 J5	Pentrebach Myr Td	61 G6
Penn Bucks	67 M8	Pentre-bach Powys	78 B8
Penn Wolves	97 K4	Pentrebeirdd Powys	94 E1
Pennal Gwynd	92 F3	Pentre Berw IoA	125 H5
Pennan Abers	268 F3	Pentre-bont Conwy	110 D1
Pennant Cerdgn	76 F3	Pentrebychan Crematorium Wrexhm	112 D2
Pennant Denbgs	111 K5	Pentre-cagel Carmth	76 C7
Pennant Powys	93 J4	Pentre-celyn Denbgs	112 A1
Pennant-Melangell Powys	111 K6	Pentre-celyn Powys	93 J2
Pennard Swans	57 G7	Pentre-chwyth Swans	57 J6
Pennerley Shrops	95 J3	Pentre-clawdd Shrops	112 D5
Pennicott Devon	13 K2	Pentre-cwrt Carmth	76 D7
Pennington Cumb	156 D7	Pentredwr Denbgs	112 B2
Pennington Hants	18 D4	Pentrefelin Gwynd	109 J4
Pennington Green Wigan	139 J6	Pentrefelin IoA	125 H1
Pennorth Powys	61 H2	Pentre Ffwrndan Flints	128 F5
Penn Street Bucks	68 A7	Pentrefoelas Conwy	111 G1
Pennsylvania S Glos	45 L4	Pentregalar Pembks	75 L6
Penny Bridge Cumb	156 D6	Pentregat Cerdgn	76 C5
Pennycross Ag & B	226 F7	Pentre-Gwenlais Carmth	59 H5
Pennygate Norfk	123 G7	Pentre Gwynfryn Gwynd	109 L6
Pennyghael Ag & B	227 G7	Pentre Halkyn Flints	128 E5
Pennyglen S Ayrs	183 H1	Pentre Hodrey Shrops	95 H7
Penny Green Derbys	133 L4	Pentre Isaf Conwy	127 K5
Penny Hill Lincs	119 K6	Pentre Llanrhaeadr Denbgs	128 C7
Pennymoor Devon	28 F8	Pentre Llifior Powys	94 E4
Pennywell Sundld	181 J7	Pentre-llwyn-llwyd Powys	78 C4
Penparc Cerdgn	75 L3	Pentre-llyn Cerdgn	92 D8
Penparcau Cerdgn	92 D7	Pentre-llyn-cymmer Conwy	111 J1
Penpedairheol Caerph	43 J2	Pentre-Maw Powys	93 J3
Penpedairheol Mons	62 C6	Pentre Meyrick V Glam	42 E6
Penperlleni Mons	62 C6	Pentre-piod Torfn	62 B6
Penpethy Cnwll	10 F5	Pentre-poeth Newpt	44 B2
Penpillick Cnwll	5 J4	Pentre'rbryn Cerdgn	76 D4
Penpol Cnwll	3 K3	Pentre'r-felin Cerdgn	77 H5
Penpoll Cnwll	5 K4	Pentre'r Felin Conwy	126 F6
Penponds Cnwll	3 G3	Pentre'r-felin Powys	60 D1
Penpont Cnwll	10 F7	Pentre Saron Denbgs	127 L7
Penpont D & G	186 C7	Pentre-tafarn-y-fedw Conwy	126 F7
Penpont Powys	60 D2	Pentre ty gwyn Carmth	59 M2
Penquit Devon	7 J4	Pentrich Derbys	116 C1
Penrest Cnwll	11 L7	Pentridge Dorset	33 H7
Penrherber Carmth	76 B7	Pen-twyn Caerph	61 K7
Pen-rhiw Pembks	75 M4	Pen-twyn Mons	63 G5
Penrhiwceiber Rhondd	43 G2	Pen-twyn Torfn	61 L6
Pen Rhiwfawr Neath	57 K3	Pentwynmaur Caerph	43 K2
Penrhiw-llan Cerdgn	76 C6	Pentyrch Cardif	43 H5
Penrhiw-pal Cerdgn	76 C6	Penwithick Cnwll	5 H4
Penrhos Gwynd	108 F5	Penwood Hants	34 D1
Penrhos IoA	124 D3	Penwyllt Powys	60 C2
Penrhos Mons	62 E5	Penybanc Carmth	59 H4
Penrhos Powys	59 L6	Penybont Powys	78 F2
Penrhos garnedd Gwynd	125 K5	Pen-y-bont Powys	112 D4
Penrhyn Bay Conwy	127 G3	Pen-y-bont-fawr Powys	111 L6

Pen-y-bryn Pembks 75 L4
Pen-y-cae Powys 60 C4
Penycae Wrexhm 112 D3
Pen-y-cae-mawr Mons 62 E8
Penycaerau Gwynd 108 C6
Pen-y-cefn Flints 128 D4
Pen-y-clawdd Mons 62 F5
Pen-y-coedcae Rhondd 43 G4
Pen-y-cwn Pembks 54 D2
Pen-y-fai Brdgnd 42 F4
Pen-y-felin Flints 128 D5
Penyffordd Flints 129 G7
Penyffridd Gwynd 125 J8
Pen-y-garn Cerdgn 92 D6
Pen-y-Garnedd Powys 111 L6
Pen-y-genffordd Powys 61 J1
Pen-y-graig Gwynd 108 C5
Penygraig Rhondd 42 F3
Penygroes Carmth 59 G6
Penygroes Gwynd 109 H1
Pen-y-Gwryd Gwynd 126 D8
Pen-y-lan V Glam 42 F6
Pen-y-Mynydd Carmth 56 E4
Penymynydd Flints 129 G7
Pen-y-pass Gwynd 126 C8
Pen-y-stryt Denbgs 112 E1
Penywaun Rhondd 60 F6
Penzance Cnwll 2 D5
Peopleton Worcs 81 L5
Peover Heath Ches E 130 F5
Peper Harow Surrey 36 D2
Peplow Shrops 113 K6
Pepper's Green Essex 70 F5
Pepperstock C Beds 68 D3
Perceton N Ayrs 196 C3
Percyhorner Abers 269 H3
Perelle Guern 9 I3
Perham Down Wilts 34 B1
Periton Somset 29 G2
Perivale Gt Lon 50 F2
Perkins Village Devon 14 B4
Perkinsville Dur 181 G8
Perlethorpe Notts 134 C5
Perranarworthal Cnwll 3 K3
Perranporth Cnwll 4 B3
Perranuthnoe Cnwll 2 E5
Perranwell Cnwll 3 K3
Perranwell Cnwll 4 C4
Perran Wharf Cnwll 3 K3
Perranzabuloe Cnwll 4 C4
Perrott's Brook Gloucs 64 E6
Perry Birm 98 D5
Perry Barr Birm 98 D5
Perry Barr Crematorium Birm 98 D5
Perry Green Essex 71 K3
Perry Green Herts 70 B4
Perry Green Wilts 46 E1
Perrystone Hill Herefs 63 J1
Perry Street Somset 15 H2
Pershall Staffs 114 C5
Pershore Worcs 81 L6
Pertenhall Bed 86 B2
Perth P & K 221 K3
Perth Crematorium P & K 221 K2
Perthy Shrops 112 E5
Perton Herefs 80 E7
Perton Staffs 97 J3
Pertwood Wilts 32 E4
Peterborough C Pete 102 D4
Peterborough Crematorium
   C Pete 102 D3
Peterchurch Herefs 79 L7
Peterculter C Aber 245 J3
Peterhead Abers 257 L2
Peterlee Dur 169 L2
Petersfield Hants 35 M6
Peter's Green Herts 68 F3
Petersham Gt Lon 50 F4
Peters Marland Devon 27 H8
Peterstone Wentlooge Newpt 43 L5
Peterston-super-Ely V Glam 43 G6
Peterstow Herefs 63 H2
Peter Tavy Devon 12 C7
Petham Kent 40 F5
Petherwin Gate Cnwll 11 K5
Petrockstow Devon 12 C1
Petsoe End M Keyn 85 H5
Pet Street Kent 40 E6
Pett E Susx 24 F4
Pettaugh Suffk 90 E3
Pett Bottom Kent 40 F6
Petterden Angus 234 C7
Pettinain S Lans 198 F4
Pettistree Suffk 91 G4
Petton Devon 29 H6
Petton Shrops 113 G6
Petts Wood Gt Lon 51 M5

Pettycur Fife 211 J2
Petty France S Glos 46 A2
Pettymuk Abers 257 G7
Petworth W Susx 36 E6
Pevensey E Susx 23 L6
Pevensey Bay E Susx 24 B6
Pewsey Wilts 47 H7
Pheasant's Hill Bucks 49 J2
Phepson Worcs 81 L3
Philadelphia Sundld 181 H8
Philham Devon 26 D6
Philiphaugh Border 200 F7
Phillack Cnwll 2 F3
Philleigh Cnwll 3 L3
Philpot End Essex 70 F3
Philpstoun W Loth 210 E4
Phocle Green Herefs 63 J2
Phoenix Green Hants 49 J7
Phones Highld 241 J5
Pibsbury Somset 31 G5
Pica Cumb 164 D6
Piccadilly Warwks 99 G4
Piccotts End Herts 68 D5
Pickburn Donc 142 E6
Pickering N York 162 D6
Picket Piece Hants 34 E2
Picket Post Hants 18 B2
Pickford Covtry 99 H7
Pickford Green Covtry 99 H7
Pickhill N York 160 E6
Picklescott Shrops 95 K3
Pickmere Ches E 130 D4
Pickney Somset 30 B5
Pickstock Wrekin 114 A6
Pickup Bank Bl w D 139 L3
Pickwell Devon 27 H3
Pickwell Leics 101 K1
Pickwick Wilts 46 B5
Pickworth Lincs 118 D5
Pickworth Rutlnd 101 L1
Picton Ches W 129 K5
Picton Flints 128 D3
Picton N York 160 F1
Piddinghoe E Susx 23 G6
Piddington Bucks 67 K8
Piddington Nhants 84 F4
Piddington Oxon 66 F4
Piddlehinton Dorset 16 D3
Piddletrenthide Dorset 16 D3
Pidley Cambs 103 G7
Piercebridge Darltn 169 G7
Pierowall Ork 275 C1
Piff's Elm Gloucs 64 C2
Pigdon Nthumb 180 E1
Pigeon Green Warwks 82 F3
Pig Oak Dorset 17 K2
Pig Street Herefs 79 L5
Pikehall Derbys 132 D7
Pilford Dorset 17 K2
Pilgrims Hatch Essex 70 E7
Pilham Lincs 135 H1
Pill N Som 45 G4
Pillaton Cnwll 6 D2
Pillatonmill Cnwll 6 D2
Pillerton Hersey Warwks 83 G5
Pillerton Priors Warwks 83 G5
Pilleth Powys 79 J2
Pilley Barns 142 A7
Pilley Hants 18 E4
Pilley Bailey Hants 18 E4
Pillgwenlly Newpt 44 C2
Pillhead Devon 27 H5
Pilling Lancs 147 H6
Pilling Lane Lancs 147 G6
Pilson Green Norfk 107 H1
Piltdown E Susx 23 G4
Pilton Devon 27 K4
Pilton Nhants 101 M6
Pilton Rutlnd 101 K1
Pilton Somset 31 K3
Pilton Green Swans 56 E7
Pimlico Lancs 148 C7
Pimlico Nhants 84 B7
Pimperne Dorset 17 H1
Pinchbeck Lincs 119 H6
Pinchbeck Bars Lincs 119 G6
Pinchbeck West Lincs 119 G6
Pincheon Green Donc 143 D4
Pinchinthorpe R & Cl 170 D7
Pincock Lancs 139 H4
Pinfold Lancs 138 E5
Pinford End Suffk 89 D7
Pinged Carmth 56 D4

Pingewood W Berk 49 G5
Pin Green Herts 69 H2
Pinhoe Devon 13 M4
Pinkett's Booth Covtry 99 H7
Pinkney Wilts 46 B2
Pinley Covtry 99 K7
Pinley Green Warwks 82 F2
Pin Mill Suffk 90 E7
Pinminnoch S Ayrs 182 F4
Pinmore S Ayrs 182 F4
Pinn Devon 14 C5
Pinner Gt Lon 50 E1
Pinner Green Gt Lon 50 E1
Pinsley Green Ches E 113 K2
Pinvin Worcs 81 M5
Pinxton Derbys 133 J8
Pipe and Lyde Herefs 80 C6
Pipe Aston Herefs 80 B1
Pipe Gate Shrops 114 A3
Pipehill Staffs 98 E2
Piperhill Highld 253 G2
Pipers Pool Cnwll 11 J6
Pipewell Nhants 101 J6
Pippacott Devon 27 J3
Pippin Street Lancs 139 H3
Pipton Powys 79 G7
Pirbright Surrey 50 B7
Pirbright Camp Surrey 50 B7
Pirnie Border 201 K7
Pirnmill N Ayrs 194 D2
Pirton Herts 68 F1
Pirton Worcs 81 K5
Pisgah Cerdgn 92 E7
Pishill Oxon 49 H1
Pistyll Gwynd 108 E3
Pitagowan P & K 232 B2
Pitblae Abers 269 H3
Pitcairngreen P & K 221 J2
Pitcalnie Highld 264 C5
Pitcaple Abers 256 C6
Pitcarity Angus 233 M2
Pitchcombe Gloucs 64 B5
Pitchcott Bucks 67 J3
Pitcher Row Lincs 119 J5
Pitchford Shrops 96 C3
Pitch Green Bucks 67 J6
Pitch Place Surrey 36 C3
Pitch Place Surrey 50 B8
Pitchroy Moray 254 D4
Pitcombe Somset 31 L4
Pitcot V Glam 42 D6
Pitcox E Loth 212 E4
Pitfichie Abers 256 B8
Pitglassie Abers 256 C5
Pitgrudy Highld 264 B2
Pitlessie Fife 222 E5
Pitlochry P & K 232 D4
Pitmachie Abers 256 B6
Pitmain Highld 241 K3
Pitmedden Abers 256 F6
Pitminster Somset 30 B7
Pitmuies Angus 234 E5
Pitmunie Abers 256 B8
Pitney Somset 31 G5
Pitroddie P & K 222 C2
Pitscottie Fife 223 G4
Pitsea Essex 52 F1
Pitses Oldham 140 E7
Pitsford Nhants 84 E2
Pitstone Bucks 68 B4
Pittarrow Abers 245 G8
Pitt Court Gloucs 63 L7
Pittenweem Fife 223 K6
Pitteuchar Fife 222 D7
Pittington Dur 169 J2
Pittodrie House Hotel Abers 256 C6
Pitton Wilts 34 B4
Pitt's Wood Kent 38 F3
Pittulie Abers 269 H3
Pityme Cnwll 10 C7
Pity Me Dur 169 H2
Pivington Kent 40 B6
Pixey Green Suffk 106 E8
Pixham Surrey 37 J1
Plains N Lans 209 L5
Plain Street Cnwll 10 D6
Plaish Shrops 96 C4
Plaistow Gt Lon 51 L2
Plaistow W Susx 36 F5
Plaitford Hants 34 C7
Plank Lane Wigan 139 J2
Plas Cymyran IoA 124 E4
Plastow Green Hants 48 D6
Platt Kent 39 G2
Platt Bridge Wigan 139 J2
Platt Lane Shrops 113 H4
Platts Heath Kent 39 L3

Plawsworth Dur 169 H1
Plaxtol Kent 38 F3
Playden E Susx 25 G3
Playford Suffk 90 F5
Play Hatch Oxon 49 H4
Playing Place Cnwll 4 C6
Playley Green Gloucs 63 M1
Pleasley Shrops 95 K2
Plean Stirlg 209 M2
Pleasance Fife 222 C4
Pleasington Bl w D 139 J2
Pleasington Crematorium
   Bl w D 139 K2
Pleasley Derbys 133 K6
Pleasleyhill Notts 133 K6
Pleck Dorset 32 B8
Pledgdon Green Essex 70 E2
Pledwick Wakefd 142 A4
Pleinheaume Guern 9 J2
Plemont Jersey 9 a1
Plemstall Ches W 129 K5
Plenmeller Nthumb 179 G6
Pleshey Essex 71 G4
Plockton Highld 248 C5
Plowden Shrops 95 J6
Plox Green Shrops 95 J3
Pluckley Kent 40 B6
Pluckley Station Kent 40 B6
Pluckley Thorne Kent 40 B6
Plucks Gutter Kent 41 J3
Plumbland Cumb 164 F3
Plumgarths Cumb 157 G4
Plumley Ches E 130 E5
Plumpton Cumb 156 D7
Plumpton Cumb 166 C3
Plumpton E Susx 22 E4
Plumpton Nhants 84 B5
Plumpton End Nhants 84 D6
Plumpton Green E Susx 22 E4
Plumpton Head Cumb 166 C4
Plumstead Gt Lon 51 L3
Plumstead Norfk 122 C4
Plumstead Green Norfk 122 C4
Plumtree Notts 117 G5
Plumtree Green Kent 39 K4
Plungar Leics 117 K5
Plurenden Kent 40 B7
Plush Dorset 16 D2
Plusha Cnwll 11 J6
Plushabridge Cnwll 11 K8
Plwmp Cerdgn 76 C5
Plymouth C Plym 6 F4
Plympton C Plym 7 G4
Plymstock C Plym 7 G4
Plymtree Devon 14 B2
Pockley N York 161 K5
Pocklington E R Yk 152 B6
Pode Hole Lincs 119 H7
Podimore Somset 31 J6
Podington Bed 85 J3
Podmore Staffs 114 B4
Point Clear Essex 73 G4
Pointon Lincs 118 F5
Pokesdown Bmouth 18 A5
Polbain Highld 270 C6
Polbathic Cnwll 6 C3
Polbeth W Loth 210 D6
Polbrock Cnwll 5 G1
Polebrook Nhants 102 B6
Pole Elm Worcs 81 J5
Polegate E Susx 23 K6
Pole Moor Kirk 141 G4
Polesworth Warwks 99 H3
Polgigga Cnwll 2 B6
Polglass Highld 270 D6
Polgooth Cnwll 5 G5
Polgown D & G 185 H2
Poling W Susx 21 H6
Poling Corner W Susx 21 H5
Polkerris Cnwll 5 J4
Pollard Street Norfk 123 G5
Pollington E R Yk 142 F4
Polloch Highld 228 B2
Pollokshaws C Glas 208 F6
Pollokshields C Glas 208 F6
Polmassick Cnwll 5 G5
Polmear Cnwll 5 J4
Polmont Falk 210 B3
Polnish Highld 237 L4
Polperro Cnwll 5 L5
Polruan Cnwll 5 K5
Polsham Somset 31 H2
Polstead Suffk 89 K7
Polstead Heath Suffk 89 K7
Poltalloch Ag & B 216 C7
Poltescoe Cnwll 3 J7
Poltimore Devon 13 M3
Polton Mdloth 211 J6
Polwarth Border 202 A3
Polyphant Cnwll 11 J6

Polzeath Cnwll.....10 C6
Pomathorn Mdloth.....211 H7
Pomeroy Derbys.....132 B6
Ponde Powys.....78 F7
Pondersbridge Cambs.....102 F5
Ponders End Gt Lon.....69 K7
Ponsanooth Cnwll.....3 J3
Ponsonby Cumb.....155 J2
Ponsongath Cnwll.....3 J7
Ponsworthy Devon.....13 G7
Pontac Jersey.....9 e4
Pontamman Carmth.....59 H6
Pontantwn Carmth.....58 E6
Pontardawe Neath.....57 K4
Pontarddulais Swans.....57 G4
Pont-ar-gothi Carmth.....58 F4
Pont-ar-Hydfer Powys.....60 C2
Pont-ar-llechau Carmth.....59 K4
Pontarsais Carmth.....58 E3
Pontblyddyn Flints.....129 G7
Pont Cyfyng Conwy.....126 E8
Pont Dolgarrog Conwy.....126 F6
Pontdolgoch Powys.....94 B5
Pont-Ebbw Newpt.....44 C2
Pontefract Wakefd.....142 C3
Pontefract Crematorium
  Wakefd.....142 C4
Ponteland Nthumb.....180 E4
Ponterwyd Cerdgn.....93 G7
Pontesbury Shrops.....95 K2
Pontesbury Hill Shrops.....95 K2
Pontesford Shrops.....95 K2
Pontfadog Wrexhm.....112 C4
Pontfaen Pembks.....75 H5
Pont-faen Powys.....78 D8
Pontgarreg Cerdgn.....76 B4
Pontgarreg Pembks.....75 K4
Ponthenry Carmth.....56 E3
Ponthir Torfn.....62 C8
Ponthirwaun Cerdgn.....76 A6
Pontllanfraith Caerph.....43 J3
Pontlliw Swans.....57 H5
Pontlottyn Caerph.....61 H6
Pontlyfni Gwynd.....109 H1
Pont Morlais Carmth.....56 F3
Pontneddfechan Neath.....60 D5
Pontnewydd Torfn.....62 B7
Pontnewynydd Torfn.....62 B6
Pont Pen-y-benglog Gwynd.....126 C7
Pontrhydfendigaid Cerdgn.....77 K2
Pont Rhyd-sarn Gwynd.....111 G6
Pont Rhyd-y-cyff Brdgnd.....42 C4
Pont-rhyd-y-fen Neath.....42 B3
Pontrhydygroes Cerdgn.....77 K1
Pontrhydyrun Torfn.....62 C7
Pontrilas Herefs.....62 E2
Pont Robert Powys.....94 D1
Pont-rug Gwynd.....125 J7
Ponts Green E Susx.....24 B4
Pontshaen Cerdgn.....76 D6
Pontshill Herefs.....63 J3
Pontsticill Myr Td.....61 G5
Pont Walby Neath.....60 D6
Pontwelly Carmth.....76 D7
Pontyates Carmth.....56 E3
Pontyberem Carmth.....58 F6
Pont-y-blew Wrexhm.....112 D4
Pontybodkin Flints.....129 G7
Pontyclun Rhondd.....42 F5
Pontycymer Brdgnd.....42 D3
Pontyglasier Pembks.....75 K5
Pontygwaith Rhondd.....42 F3
Pontygynon Pembks.....75 K5
Pont-y-pant Conwy.....110 E1
Pontypool Torfn.....62 B7
Pontypool Road Torfn.....62 C7
Pontypridd Rhondd.....43 G4
Pont-yr-hafod Pembks.....74 E7
Pont-yr-Rhyl Brdgnd.....42 D4
Pontywaun Caerph.....43 K3
Pool Cnwll.....3 H3
Pool IoS.....10 b2
Pool Leeds.....150 C6
Poole Poole.....17 K4
Poole Crematorium Poole.....17 K3
Poole Keynes Gloucs.....64 C8
Poolewe Highld.....260 D4
Pooley Bridge Cumb.....166 B6
Pooley Street Norfk.....105 L7
Poolfold Staffs.....131 H7
Pool Head Herefs.....80 D5
Poolhill Gloucs.....63 L1
Pool of Muckhart Clacks.....221 H7
Pool Quay Powys.....95 G1
Pool Street Essex.....88 F7
Pooting's Kent.....38 C3
Popham Hants.....35 H2
Poplar Gt Lon.....51 K3
Poplar Street Suffk.....91 K2
Porchfield IoW.....19 G5

Poringland Norfk.....106 F3
Porkellis Cnwll.....3 H4
Porlock Somset.....28 F2
Porlock Weir Somset.....28 F1
Portachoillan Ag & B.....206 B2
Port-an-Eorna Highld.....248 B5
Port Appin Ag & B.....228 D6
Port Askaig Ag & B.....205 G3
Portavadie Ag & B.....206 C5
Port Bannatyne Ag & B.....207 H5
Portbury N Som.....45 G4
Port Carlisle Cumb.....177 H6
Port Charlotte Ag & B.....204 C4
Portchester Hants.....19 K3
Portchester Crematorium
  Hants.....19 K2
Port Clarence S on T.....170 C6
Port Driseach Ag & B.....206 F4
Port Ellen Ag & B.....204 E7
Port Elphinstone Abers.....256 D7
Portencalzie D & G.....172 C8
Portencross N Ayrs.....195 K1
Port Erin IoM.....154 b8
Portesham Dorset.....16 B5
Portessie Moray.....267 J3
Port e Vullen IoM.....154 g4
Port Eynon Swans.....56 E7
Portfield Gate Pembks.....54 F4
Portgate Devon.....12 A5
Port Gaverne Cnwll.....10 D6
Port Glasgow Inver.....208 B4
Portgordon Moray.....267 J3
Portgower Highld.....274 D5
Porth Cnwll.....4 D2
Porth Rhondd.....42 F3
Porthallow Cnwll.....3 K6
Porthallow Cnwll.....5 L4
Porthcawl Brdgnd.....42 B6
Porthcothan Cnwll.....10 B8
Porthcurno Cnwll.....2 B6
Porth Dinllaen Gwynd.....108 D3
Port Henderson Highld.....260 B5
Porthgain Pembks.....74 D5
Porthgwarra Cnwll.....2 B6
Porthill Staffs.....114 D2
Porthkea Cnwll.....4 D6
Porthkerry V Glam.....43 G8
Porthleven Cnwll.....3 H5
Porthmadog Gwynd.....109 K4
Porthmeor Cnwll.....2 C4
Porth Navas Cnwll.....3 J5
Portholland Cnwll.....4 F6
Porthoustock Cnwll.....3 K6
Porthpean Cnwll.....5 H5
Porthtowan Cnwll.....4 A5
Porthwgan Wrexhm.....112 F2
Porthyrhyd Carmth.....58 F5
Porth-y-Waen Shrops.....112 C6
Portincaple Ag & B.....218 C8
Portinfer Jersey.....9 a1
Portington E R Yk.....143 K2
Portinnisherrich Ag & B.....216 F5
Portinscale Cumb.....165 H6
Port Isaac Cnwll.....10 D6
Portishead N Som.....44 F4
Portknockie Moray.....267 K3
Portlethen Abers.....245 K4
Portling D & G.....175 L4
Portloe Cnwll.....4 F7
Port Logan D & G.....172 D6
Portlooe Cnwll.....6 A4
Portmahomack Highld.....264 E3
Portmellon Cnwll.....5 G6
Port Mor Highld.....236 E4
Portmore Hants.....18 E4
Port Mulgrave N York.....171 J7
Portnacroish Ag & B.....228 E6
Portnaguran W Isls.....282 h3
Portnahaven Ag & B.....204 B6
Portnalong Highld.....246 D2
Port nan Giuran W Isls.....282 h3
Port nan Long W Isls.....282 c7
Port Nis W Isls.....282 h1
Portobello C Edin.....211 J4
Portobello Gatesd.....181 G7
Portobello Wolves.....98 B4
Port of Menteith Stirlg.....219 J7
Port of Ness W Isls.....282 h1
Porton Wilts.....33 L4
Portontown Devon.....12 A7
Portpatrick D & G.....172 B4
Port Quin Cnwll.....10 D6
Port Ramsay Ag & B.....228 D6
Portreath Cnwll.....3 G2
Portree Highld.....259 H7
Port St Mary IoM.....154 b8
Portscatho Cnwll.....3 M4
Portsea C Port.....19 L4
Portskerra Highld.....278 E3
Portskewett Mons.....45 G1

Portslade Br & H.....22 C6
Portslade-by-Sea Br & H.....22 C6
Portslogan D & G.....172 B3
Portsmouth C Port.....19 L4
Portsmouth Calder.....140 D3
Port Soderick IoM.....154 d7
Port Solent C Port.....19 L3
Portsonachan Hotel Ag & B.....217 G3
Portsoy Abers.....267 M3
Port Sunlight Wirral.....129 H3
Portswood C Sotn.....34 F8
Port Talbot Neath.....57 L7
Port Tennant Swans.....57 J6
Portuairk Highld.....236 E7
Portway Herefs.....80 B6
Portway Herefs.....80 C8
Portway Sandw.....98 B6
Portway Worcs.....82 C1
Port Wemyss Ag & B.....204 B6
Port William D & G.....173 J6
Portwrinkle Cnwll.....6 B6
Portyerrock D & G.....174 D7
Posbury Devon.....13 J3
Posenhall Shrops.....96 E3
Poslingford Suffk.....88 F5
Posso Border.....199 L6
Postbridge Devon.....12 F6
Postcombe Oxon.....67 H7
Post Green Dorset.....17 J4
Postling Kent.....40 F7
Postwick Norfk.....106 F2
Potarch Abers.....244 D4
Potsgrove C Beds.....68 B1
Potten End Herts.....68 C5
Potten Street Kent.....41 H2
Pottergate Street Norfk.....106 D5
Potterhanworth Lincs.....135 L6
Potterhanworth Booths Lincs.....135 M6
Potter Heigham Norfk.....123 H7
Potterne Wilts.....46 E7
Potterne Wick Wilts.....46 E7
Potter Row Bucks.....67 L6
Potters Bar Herts.....69 H6
Potters Brook Lancs.....147 J5
Potter's Cross Staffs.....97 J6
Potters Crouch Herts.....68 E6
Potter's Forstal Kent.....39 M4
Potters Green Covtry.....99 K7
Potter's Green E Susx.....23 H3
Potter's Green Herts.....69 K3
Pottersheath Herts.....69 G3
Potters Marston Leics.....100 B4
Potter Somersal Derbys.....115 J4
Potterspury Nhants.....84 E6
Potterton Abers.....257 H8
Potterton Leeds.....150 F8
Potthorpe Norfk.....121 L7
Pottle Street Wilts.....32 D3
Potto N York.....161 G2
Potton C Beds.....86 E5
Pott Row Norfk.....120 F7
Pott's Green Essex.....72 C3
Pott Shrigley Ches E.....131 J4
Poughill Cnwll.....11 J1
Poughill Devon.....13 K1
Poulner Hants.....18 B2
Poulshot Wilts.....46 E7
Poulton Gloucs.....65 G7
Poulton Wirral.....129 G2
Poulton-le-Fylde Lancs.....147 G2
Poulton Priory Gloucs.....65 G7
Pound Bank Worcs.....97 G8
Poundbury Dorset.....16 C4
Poundffald Swans.....57 G6
Poundgate E Susx.....38 D7
Pound Green E Susx.....23 H3
Pound Green Suffk.....88 E4
Pound Green Worcs.....97 G7
Pound Hill W Susx.....37 L3
Poundon Bucks.....66 F2
Poundsbridge Kent.....38 C5
Poundsgate Devon.....13 G8
Poundstock Cnwll.....11 H3
Pound Street Hants.....48 C6
Pounsley E Susx.....23 H3
Pouton D & G.....174 C5
Pouy Street Suffk.....91 H1
Povey Cross Surrey.....37 L3
Powburn Nthumb.....190 H4
Powderham Devon.....13 M5
Powerstock Dorset.....15 L3
Powfoot D & G.....176 F5
Pow Green Herefs.....81 G6
Powhill Cumb.....177 H7
Powick Worcs.....81 J5
Powmill P & K.....221 J7
Poxwell Dorset.....16 D6
Poyle Slough.....50 C4
Poynings W Susx.....22 C5

Poyntington Dorset.....31 L6
Poynton Ches E.....131 H3
Poynton Wrekin.....113 J8
Poynton Green Wrekin.....113 J7
Poyston Cross Pembks.....55 G3
Poystreet Green Suffk.....89 K4
Praa Sands Cnwll.....2 F5
Pratt's Bottom Gt Lon.....52 A6
Praze-an-Beeble Cnwll.....3 G4
Predannack Wollas Cnwll.....3 H7
Prees Shrops.....113 J5
Preesall Lancs.....147 G6
Prees Green Shrops.....113 J5
Preesgweene Shrops.....112 D4
Prees Heath Shrops.....113 J5
Prees Higher Heath Shrops.....113 J4
Prees Lower Heath Shrops.....113 J5
Prendwick Nthumb.....190 D6
Pren-gwyn Cerdgn.....76 D6
Prenteg Gwynd.....109 K3
Prenton Wirral.....129 G2
Prescot Knows.....129 L1
Prescott Devon.....29 K8
Prescott Shrops.....96 F7
Prescott Shrops.....112 F7
Presnerb Angus.....233 J7
Pressen Nthumb.....202 C6
Prestatyn Denbgs.....128 C3
Prestbury Ches E.....131 H4
Prestbury Gloucs.....64 C3
Presteigne Powys.....79 K2
Prestleigh Somset.....31 K3
Prestolee Bolton.....139 M6
Preston Border.....213 H7
Preston Br & H.....22 D6
Preston Devon.....13 H7
Preston Dorset.....16 D4
Preston E R Yk.....144 F2
Preston Gloucs.....64 F7
Preston Herts.....69 F2
Preston Kent.....40 D3
Preston Kent.....41 H3
Preston Lancs.....139 G2
Preston Nthumb.....203 K8
Preston Rutlnd.....101 J2
Preston Shrops.....96 C1
Preston Somset.....29 K4
Preston Suffk.....89 J5
Preston Torbay.....8 D3
Preston Wilts.....46 F3
Preston Wilts.....47 K4
Preston Bagot Warwks.....82 E2
Preston Bissett Bucks.....67 G1
Preston Bowyer Somset.....29 L5
Preston Brockhurst Shrops.....113 J6
Preston Brook Halton.....130 B4
Preston Candover Hants.....35 J2
Preston Capes Nhants.....84 B4
Preston Crematorium Lancs.....139 H1
Preston Crowmarsh Oxon.....48 F1
Preston Deanery Nhants.....84 F4
Preston Green Warwks.....82 E2
Preston Gubbals Shrops.....113 H7
Preston Montford Shrops.....113 J8
Preston on Stour Warwks.....82 F5
Preston on Tees S on T.....169 L7
Preston on the Hill Halton.....130 B3
Preston on Wye Herefs.....79 M7
Prestonpans E Loth.....211 L4
Preston Patrick Cumb.....157 H6
Preston Plucknett Somset.....31 H4
Preston Street Kent.....41 H4
Preston-under-Scar N York.....159 K4
Preston upon the Weald
  Moors Wrekin.....113 L8
Preston Wynne Herefs.....80 D6
Prestwich Bury.....140 B6
Prestwick Nthumb.....180 E4
Prestwick S Ayrs.....196 C6
Prestwood Bucks.....67 L7
Prestwood Staffs.....97 K6
Price Town Brdgnd.....42 E3
Prickwillow Cambs.....104 B7
Priddy Somset.....31 H1
Priestacott Devon.....12 B1
Priestcliffe Derbys.....132 C5
Priestcliffe Ditch Derbys.....132 C5
Priest Hutton Lancs.....157 H7
Priestland E Ayrs.....197 H3
Priestley Green Calder.....141 H3
Priest Weston Shrops.....95 H4
Priestwood Green Kent.....52 E6
Primethorpe Leics.....100 B5
Primrose Green Norfk.....122 B8
Primrose Hill Cambs.....103 H5
Primrose Hill Derbys.....133 J8
Primrose Hill Dudley.....97 L6
Primrose Hill Lancs.....138 E4
Primsidemill Border.....202 C7

Princes Gate Pembks...... 55 K4
Princes Risborough Bucks...... 67 K6
Princethorpe Warwks...... 83 J1
Princetown Devon...... 12 E7
Prinsted W Susx...... 20 C5
Prion Denbgs...... 128 C7
Prior Rigg Cumb...... 178 B5
Priors Halton Shrops...... 96 B8
Priors Hardwick Warwks...... 83 L4
Priorslee Wrekin...... 97 G1
Priors Marston Warwks...... 83 L4
Priors Norton Gloucs...... 64 C2
Priory Vale Swindn...... 47 H1
Priory Wood Herefs...... 79 J6
Prisk V Glam...... 42 F6
Priston BaNES...... 45 K7
Pristow Green Norfk...... 106 C5
Prittlewell Sthend...... 53 J2
Privett Hants...... 35 L5
Prixford Devon...... 27 K3
Probus Cnwll...... 4
Prora E Loth...... 212 B3
Prospect Cumb...... 164 F3
Prospidnick Cnwll...... 3 G5
Protstonhill Abers...... 268 C3
Prudhoe Nthumb...... 180 D6
Prussia Cove Cnwll...... 2 E5
Publow BaNES...... 45 J6
Puckeridge Herts...... 69 K2
Puckington Somset...... 30 E7
Pucklechurch S Glos...... 45 K4
Puckrup Gloucs...... 81 K7
Puddinglake Ches W...... 130 E5
Puddington Ches W...... 129 H5
Puddington Devon...... 28 E8
Puddledock Norfk...... 105 L5
Puddletown Dorset...... 16 E4
Pudleston Herefs...... 80 D3
Pudsey Leeds...... 141 K1
Pulborough W Susx...... 21 H3
Puleston Wrekin...... 114 A7
Pulford Ches W...... 129 J7
Pulham Dorset...... 16 D1
Pulham Market Norfk...... 106 D6
Pulham St Mary Norfk...... 106 E6
Pullens Green S Glos...... 63 J8
Pulloxhill C Beds...... 85 L8
Pumpherston W Loth...... 210 E5
Pumsaint Carmth...... 77 J7
Puncheston Pembks...... 75 G6
Puncknowle Dorset...... 15 M5
Punnett's Town E Susx...... 23 K3
Purbrook Hants...... 19 M2
Purfleet Thurr...... 52 C3
Puriton Somset...... 30 D3
Purleigh Essex...... 71 K6
Purley Gt Lon...... 51 J6
Purley W Berk...... 49 G4
Purlogue Shrops...... 95 G7
Purlpit Wilts...... 46 C5
Purls Bridge Cambs...... 103 K3
Purse Caundle Dorset...... 32 B7
Purshull Green Worcs...... 81 K1
Purslow Shrops...... 95 J7
Purston Jaglin Wakefd...... 142 C4
Purtington Somset...... 15 J1
Purton Gloucs...... 63 K6
Purton Gloucs...... 63 K6
Purton Wilts...... 47 G2
Purton Stoke Wilts...... 47 G1
Pury End Nhants...... 84 D6
Pusey Oxon...... 65 M7
Putley Herefs...... 80 E7
Putley Green Herefs...... 80 F7
Putloe Gloucs...... 64 A5
Putney Gt Lon...... 51 G4
Putney Vale Crematorium
Gt Lon...... 51 G4
Putsborough Devon...... 27 H3
Puttenham Herts...... 67 L4
Puttenham Surrey...... 36 D2
Puttock End Essex...... 89 G7
Putton Dorset...... 16 C6
Puxley Nhants...... 84 D4
Puxton N Som...... 44 E6
Pwll Carmth...... 56 E4
Pwllcrochan Pembks...... 54 F6
Pwll-du Mons...... 61 L5
Pwll-glâs Denbgs...... 111 M1
Pwllgloyw Powys...... 78 E8
Pwllheli Gwynd...... 108 F4
Pwllmeyric Mons...... 63 G8
Pwll Trap Carmth...... 58 A5
Pwll-y-glaw Neath...... 42 B3
Pydew Conwy...... 126 F4
Pye Bridge Derbys...... 116 D1
Pyecombe W Susx...... 22 D4
Pye Corner Newpt...... 44 D2
Pye Green Staffs...... 114 F8
Pyle Brdgnd...... 42 B5

Pyleigh Somset...... 29 L5
Pylle Somset...... 31 K3
Pymoor Cambs...... 103 K6
Pymore Dorset...... 15 L4
Pyrford Surrey...... 50 D7
Pyrton Oxon...... 67 G7
Pytchley Nhants...... 101 J8
Pyworthy Devon...... 11 K2

Q

Quabbs Shrops...... 94 F7
Quadring Lincs...... 119 H5
Quadring Eaudike Lincs...... 119 H5
Quainton Bucks...... 67 H3
Quaker's Yard Myr Td...... 43 H3
Quaking Houses Dur...... 180 F8
Quarley Hants...... 34 C2
Quarndon Derbys...... 116 B3
Quarr Hill IoW...... 19 K5
Quarrier's Village Inver...... 208 B5
Quarrington Lincs...... 118 E3
Quarrington Hill Dur...... 169 J3
Quarrybank Ches W...... 130 A6
Quarry Bank Dudley...... 97 L6
Quarrywood Moray...... 266 D3
Quarter N Ayrs...... 207 K6
Quarter S Lans...... 197 L1
Quatford Shrops...... 97 G5
Quatt Shrops...... 97 G5
Quebec Dur...... 168 F2
Quedgeley Gloucs...... 64 A4
Queen Adelaide Cambs...... 104 B7
Queenborough Kent...... 53 K4
Queen Camel Somset...... 31 K6
Queen Charlton BaNES...... 45 J5
Queen Dart Devon...... 28 E7
Queenhill Worcs...... 81 K7
Queen Oak Dorset...... 32 C4
Queen's Bower IoW...... 19 J6
Queensbury C Brad...... 141 H2
Queensferry Flints...... 129 H6
Queen's Head Shrops...... 112 E6
Queenslie C Glas...... 209 H6
Queen's Park Bed...... 85 L5
Queen's Park Nhants...... 84 E4
Queen Street Kent...... 39 H4
Queen Street Wilts...... 46 F2
Queenzieburn N Lans...... 209 J3
Quendon Essex...... 70 D1
Queniborough Leics...... 100 E1
Quenington Gloucs...... 65 H6
Quernmore Lancs...... 147 K4
Queslett Birm...... 98 D4
Quethiock Cnwll...... 6 C2
Quick's Green W Berk...... 48 E4
Quidenham Norfk...... 105 L6
Quidhampton Hants...... 35 G1
Quidhampton Wilts...... 33 K5
Quina Brook Shrops...... 113 H5
Quinbury End Nhants...... 84 B5
Quinton Dudley...... 98 C6
Quinton Nhants...... 84 E4
Quinton Green Nhants...... 84 F4
Quintrell Downs Cnwll...... 4 D3
Quixhall Staffs...... 115 H3
Quixwood Border...... 213 H6
Quoditch Devon...... 12 A3
Quoig P & K...... 220 B3
Quorn Leics...... 116 F8
Quothquan S Lans...... 199 G5
Quoyburray Ork...... 275 d5
Quoyloo Ork...... 275 b4

R

Raasay Highld...... 259 K8
Rabbit's Cross Kent...... 39 K4
Rableyheath Herts...... 69 G3
Raby Cumb...... 177 G3
Raby Wirral...... 129 H4
Rachan Mill Border...... 199 K6
Rachub Gwynd...... 126 C6
Rackenford Devon...... 28 E7
Rackham W Susx...... 21 H4
Rackheath Norfk...... 122 F8
Racks D & G...... 176 D4
Rackwick Ork...... 275 a5
Radbourne Derbys...... 115 M4
Radcliffe Bury...... 140 B6
Radcliffe Nthumb...... 191 K5
Radcliffe on Trent Notts...... 117 H4
Radclive Bucks...... 84 D8
Radcot Oxon...... 65 L7
Raddery Highld...... 263 J7
Raddington Somset...... 29 J5
Radernie Fife...... 223 H5

Radford Covtry...... 99 J7
Radford Semele Warwks...... 83 H2
Radlet Somset...... 30 B3
Radlett Herts...... 68 F7
Radley Devon...... 28 C6
Radley Oxon...... 66 D7
Radley Green Essex...... 70 F6
Radmore Green Ches E...... 130 B8
Radnage Bucks...... 67 J7
Radstock BaNES...... 45 K8
Radstone Nhants...... 84 B7
Radway Warwks...... 83 J5
Radwell Bed...... 85 K4
Radwell Herts...... 86 E8
Radwinter Essex...... 88 C7
Radwinter End Essex...... 88 C7
Radyr Cardif...... 43 H5
RAF College (Cranwell) Lincs...... 118 D2
Rafford Moray...... 265 H8
Ragdale Leics...... 117 H7
Ragdon Shrops...... 95 J3
Raginnis Cnwll...... 2 D6
Raglan Mons...... 62 E5
Ragnall Notts...... 134 F5
Raigbeg Highld...... 252 F6
Rainbow Hill Worcs...... 81 K4
Rainford St Hel...... 138 F7
Rainham Gt Lon...... 52 B3
Rainham Medway...... 53 H6
Rainhill St Hel...... 129 L2
Rainhill Stoops St Hel...... 129 L2
Rainow Ches E...... 131 J4
Rainsbrook Crematorium
Warwks...... 83 M1
Rainsough Bury...... 140 B7
Rainton N York...... 160 E7
Rainworth Notts...... 134 B8
Raisbeck Cumb...... 157 K1
Raise Cumb...... 167 G2
Raisthorpe N York...... 152 C3
Rait P & K...... 222 C2
Raithby Lincs...... 136 F3
Raithby Lincs...... 137 G6
Raithwaite N York...... 171 K8
Rake Hants...... 36 B5
Rakewood Rochdl...... 140 E5
Ralia Highld...... 241 J4
Ram Carmth...... 77 G6
Ramasaig Highld...... 258 B7
Rame Cnwll...... 3 J4
Rame Cnwll...... 6 E5
Ram Hill S Glos...... 45 K3
Ram Lane Kent...... 40 C6
Rampisham Dorset...... 16 A2
Rampside Cumb...... 146 E3
Rampton Cambs...... 87 J2
Rampton Notts...... 134 F4
Ramsbottom Bury...... 140 B4
Ramsbury Wilts...... 47 K4
Ramscraigs Highld...... 274 F3
Ramsdean Hants...... 35 L6
Ramsdell Hants...... 48 E7
Ramsden Oxon...... 65 M4
Ramsden Worcs...... 81 L6
Ramsden Bellhouse Essex...... 71 H8
Ramsden Heath Essex...... 71 H7
Ramsey Cambs...... 102 F6
Ramsey Essex...... 73 J1
Ramsey IoM...... 154 f3
Ramsey Forty Foot Cambs...... 102 F6
Ramsey Heights Cambs...... 102 E6
Ramsey Island Essex...... 72 D6
Ramsey Island Pembks...... 74 A7
Ramsey Mereside Cambs...... 102 F5
Ramsey St Mary's Cambs...... 102 E6
Ramsgate Kent...... 41 L2
Ramsgill N York...... 149 K2
Ramshaw Dur...... 168 B1
Ramshaw Dur...... 168 F5
Ramsholt Suffk...... 91 H7
Ramshope Nthumb...... 189 K5
Ramshorn Staffs...... 115 H3
Ramsley Devon...... 12 F4
Ramsnest Common Surrey...... 36 E4
Ranby Lincs...... 136 D4
Ranby Notts...... 134 C3
Rand Lincs...... 136 B4
Randalls Park Crematorium
Surrey...... 50 F7
Randwick Gloucs...... 64 B5
Ranfurly Rens...... 208 C6
Rangemore Staffs...... 115 K7
Rangeworthy S Glos...... 45 K2
Rankinston E Ayrs...... 196 E8
Ranksborough Rutlnd...... 101 H1
Rank's Green Essex...... 71 H3
Rannoch Station P & K...... 230 D4
Ranscombe Somset...... 29 G2
Ranskill Notts...... 134 C2
Ranton Staffs...... 114 D6

Ranton Green Staffs...... 114 D7
Ranworth Norfk...... 123 G8
Raploch Stirlg...... 220 D8
Rapness Ork...... 275 d2
Rapps Somset...... 30 E7
Rascarrel D & G...... 175 K5
Rashfield Ag & B...... 207 J2
Rashwood Worcs...... 81 L2
Raskelf N York...... 151 G2
Rassau Blae G...... 61 J5
Rastrick Calder...... 141 H3
Ratagan Highld...... 248 E7
Ratby Leics...... 100 B2
Ratcliffe Culey Leics...... 99 J3
Ratcliffe on Soar Notts...... 116 E6
Ratcliffe on the Wreake Leics...... 117 G8
Ratfyn Wilts...... 33 L2
Rathen Abers...... 269 J4
Rathillet Fife...... 222 F3
Rathmell N York...... 148 D4
Ratho C Edin...... 210 F5
Ratho Station C Edin...... 210 F4
Rathven Moray...... 267 J3
Ratlake Hants...... 34 E6
Ratley Warwks...... 83 J5
Ratling Kent...... 41 H4
Ratlinghope Shrops...... 95 K4
Rattan Row Norfk...... 120 B8
Rattar Highld...... 280 C2
Ratten Row Cumb...... 165 K3
Ratten Row Cumb...... 165 L1
Ratten Row Lancs...... 147 H7
Rattery Devon...... 7 J3
Rattlesden Suffk...... 89 K3
Ratton Village E Susx...... 23 K7
Rattray P & K...... 233 J6
Raughton Cumb...... 165 L1
Raughton Head Cumb...... 165 L2
Raunds Nhants...... 85 K1
Ravenfield Rothm...... 133 J1
Ravenglass Cumb...... 155 K3
Ravenhills Green Worcs...... 81 G4
Raveningham Norfk...... 107 H4
Ravenscar N York...... 163 H2
Ravenscraig N Lans...... 209 K7
Ravensdale IoM...... 154 e4
Ravensden Bed...... 86 B4
Ravenseat N York...... 158 E2
Ravenshead Notts...... 133 L8
Ravensmoor Ches E...... 113 K2
Ravensthorpe Kirk...... 141 K4
Ravensthorpe Nhants...... 84 C1
Ravenstone Leics...... 99 L1
Ravenstone M Keyn...... 85 G5
Ravenstonedale Cumb...... 158 C2
Ravenstruther S Lans...... 198 F4
Ravensworth N York...... 159 L1
Raw N York...... 163 G2
Rawcliffe C York...... 151 J5
Rawcliffe E R Yk...... 143 H3
Rawcliffe Bridge E R Yk...... 143 H3
Rawdon Leeds...... 150 B7
Rawdon Crematorium Leeds...... 150 B8
Rawling Street Kent...... 40 B3
Rawmarsh Rothm...... 142 C8
Rawnsley Staffs...... 98 C1
Rawreth Essex...... 71 J8
Rawridge Devon...... 14 E2
Rawtenstall Lancs...... 140 B3
Raydon Suffk...... 90 B7
Raylees Nthumb...... 190 C7
Rayleigh Essex...... 53 H1
Raymond's Hill Devon...... 15 H3
Rayne Essex...... 71 H3
Raynes Park Gt Lon...... 51 G5
Reach Cambs...... 88 B2
Read Lancs...... 140 A1
Reading Readg...... 49 H4
Reading Crematorium Readg...... 49 H4
Reading Street Kent...... 25 G1
Reading Street Kent...... 41 L2
Reagill Cumb...... 166 E7
Realwa Cnwll...... 2 F4
Rearquhar Highld...... 263 K1
Rearsby Leics...... 117 H8
Rease Heath Ches E...... 113 L1
Reay Highld...... 279 G3
Reculver Kent...... 41 H2
Red Ball Devon...... 29 K7
Redberth Pembks...... 55 J6
Redbourn Herts...... 68 E4
Redbourne N Linc...... 144 B7
Redbrook Gloucs...... 63 G5
Redbrook Wrexhm...... 113 H3
Redbrook Street Kent...... 40 B8
Redburn Highld...... 253 H2
Redburn Nthumb...... 179 H6
Redcar R & Cl...... 170 E6
Redcastle D & G...... 175 K2
Redcastle Highld...... 251 G2

Red Dial Cumb...... 165 H2
Redding Falk...... 210 B3
Reddingmuirhead Falk...... 210 B3
Reddish Stockp...... 131 H1
Redditch Worcs...... 82 B2
Redditch Crematorium Worcs...... 82 B2
Rede Suffk...... 88 F4
Redenhall Norfk...... 106 F6
Redenham Hants...... 34 C1
Redesmouth Nthumb...... 179 K3
Redford Abers...... 235 J2
Redford Angus...... 234 E6
Redford W Susx...... 36 C5
Redfordgreen Border...... 188 C3
Redgate Rhondd...... 42 F4
Redgorton P & K...... 221 K2
Redgrave Suffk...... 105 L7
Redhill Abers...... 245 H3
Red Hill Bmouth...... 17 L3
Redhill Herts...... 86 F8
Redhill N Som...... 45 G6
Redhill Surrey...... 37 L1
Red Hill Warwks...... 82 D4
Redisham Suffk...... 107 H6
Redland Bristl...... 45 H4
Redland Ork...... 275 c3
Redlingfield Suffk...... 90 E1
Redlingfield Green Suffk...... 90 E1
Red Lodge Suffk...... 88 D1
Red Lumb Rochdl...... 140 C4
Redlynch Somset...... 32 B4
Redlynch Wilts...... 33 L6
Redmain Cumb...... 164 F4
Redmarley Worcs...... 81 H2
Redmarley D'Abitot Gloucs...... 63 L1
Redmarshall S on T...... 169 K6
Redmile Leics...... 117 L4
Redmire N York...... 159 J4
Redmyre Abers...... 245 G8
Rednal Birm...... 98 C6
Rednal Shrops...... 112 E6
Redpath Border...... 201 J6
Redpoint Highld...... 260 B6
Red Post Cnwll...... 11 K2
Red Rock Wigan...... 139 H6
Red Roses Carmth...... 55 L4
Red Row Nthumb...... 191 K6
Redruth Cnwll...... 4 A6
Redstocks Wilts...... 46 D6
Redstone P & K...... 233 J8
Redstone Cross Pembks...... 55 J4
Red Street Staffs...... 114 C1
Redvales Bury...... 140 B6
Red Wharf Bay IoA...... 125 J3
Redwick Newpt...... 44 E2
Redwick S Glos...... 45 H2
Redworth Darltn...... 169 G6
Reed Herts...... 87 H8
Reedham Norfk...... 107 J3
Reedness E R Yk...... 143 K3
Reeds Beck Lincs...... 136 D6
Reeds Holme Lancs...... 140 B3
Reepham Lincs...... 135 L5
Reepham Norfk...... 122 B4
Reeth N York...... 159 J3
Reeves Green Solhll...... 99 H7
Regaby IoM...... 154 f3
Regil N Som...... 45 G6
Reiff Highld...... 270 C5
Reigate Surrey...... 37 L1
Reighton N York...... 163 L7
Reisque Abers...... 256 F7
Reiss Highld...... 280 D5
Rejerrah Cnwll...... 4 C4
Releath Cnwll...... 3 G4
Relubbus Cnwll...... 2 F4
Relugas Moray...... 253 J2
Remenham Wokham...... 49 J2
Remenham Hill Wokham...... 49 J2
Rempstone Notts...... 116 F6
Rendcomb Gloucs...... 64 E5
Rendham Suffk...... 91 H2
Rendlesham Suffk...... 91 H4
Renfrew Rens...... 208 E5
Renhold Bed...... 86 B5
Renishaw Derbys...... 133 J4
Rennington Nthumb...... 191 J3
Renton W Duns...... 208 C3
Renwick Cumb...... 166 E2
Repps Norfk...... 123 J8
Repton Derbys...... 116 A6
Resaurie Highld...... 251 J3
Rescassa Cnwll...... 5 G6
Rescorla Cnwll...... 5 G5
Resipole Highld...... 237 L7
Reskadinnick Cnwll...... 3 G3
Resolis Highld...... 263 J6
Resolven Neath...... 60 C6
Rest and be thankful Ag & B...... 218 C2
Reston Border...... 213 J6

Restronguet Cnwll...... 3 K4
Reswallie Angus...... 234 D5
Reterth Cnwll...... 4 F2
Retford Notts...... 134 D3
Retire Cnwll...... 5 G2
Rettendon Essex...... 71 J7
Retyn Cnwll...... 4 E3
Revesby Lincs...... 136 E7
Rew Devon...... 7 K7
Rew Devon...... 13 H8
Rewe Devon...... 13 M3
Rew Street IoW...... 19 H5
Rexon Devon...... 12 A5
Reydon Suffk...... 107 K7
Reymerston Norfk...... 105 L2
Reynalton Pembks...... 55 J5
Reynoldston Swans...... 56 E6
Rezare Cnwll...... 11 L7
Rhadyr Mons...... 62 D6
Rhandirmwyn Carmth...... 77 L6
Rhayader Powys...... 78 D2
Rheindown Highld...... 250 F2
Rhes-y-cae Flints...... 128 E5
Rhewl Denbgs...... 112 B3
Rhewl Denbgs...... 128 D7
Rhewl-fawr Flints...... 128 D3
Rhewl Mostyn Flints...... 128 D4
Rhicarn Highld...... 270 E3
Rhiconich Highld...... 276 D5
Rhicullen Highld...... 263 J5
Rhigos Rhondd...... 60 D6
Rhireavach Highld...... 261 G1
Rhives Highld...... 273 K7
Rhiwbina Cardif...... 43 J5
Rhiwbryfdir Gwynd...... 110 D2
Rhiwderyn Newpt...... 43 L4
Rhiwen Gwynd...... 125 K7
Rhiwinder Rhondd...... 42 F4
Rhiwlas Gwynd...... 111 H4
Rhiwlas Gwynd...... 125 K6
Rhiwlas Powys...... 112 B5
Rhiwsaeson Rhondd...... 43 G5
Rhode Somset...... 30 C4
Rhoden Green Kent...... 39 H4
Rhodesia Notts...... 133 L4
Rhodes Minnis Kent...... 40 F6
Rhodiad-y-brenin Pembks...... 74 C6
Rhonehouse D & G...... 175 J3
Rhoose V Glam...... 43 G8
Rhos Carmth...... 58 C2
Rhos Denbgs...... 128 D7
Rhos Neath...... 57 K4
Rhosbeirio IoA...... 125 G2
Rhoscefnhir IoA...... 125 J4
Rhoscolyn IoA...... 124 D4
Rhoscrowther Pembks...... 54 E6
Rhosesmor Flints...... 128 F6
Rhos-fawr Gwynd...... 109 G4
Rhosgadfan Gwynd...... 125 J8
Rhosgoch IoA...... 125 G2
Rhosgoch Powys...... 79 H5
Rhos Haminiog Cerdgn...... 76 F2
Rhoshill Pembks...... 75 L4
Rhoshirwaun Gwynd...... 108 C5
Rhoslan Gwynd...... 109 H3
Rhoslefain Gwynd...... 92 C2
Rhosllanerchrugog Wrexhm...... 112 D2
Rhôs Lligwy IoA...... 125 J2
Rhosmaen Carmth...... 59 H4
Rhosmeirch IoA...... 125 H4
Rhosneigr IoA...... 124 E5
Rhosnesni Wrexhm...... 112 E2
Rhôs-on-Sea Conwy...... 127 G4
Rhosrobin Wrexhm...... 112 E1
Rhossili Swans...... 56 D7
Rhostryfan Gwynd...... 125 J8
Rhostyllen Wrexhm...... 112 D2
Rhosybol IoA...... 125 G2
Rhos y-brithdir Powys...... 111 M7
Rhosygadfa Shrops...... 112 D4
Rhos-y-garth Cerdgn...... 77 H1
Rhos-y-gwaliau Gwynd...... 111 H4
Rhos-y-llan Gwynd...... 108 D4
Rhosymedre Wrexhm...... 112 D3
Rhos-y-meirch Powys...... 79 K1
Rhu Ag & B...... 207 M2
Rhuallt Denbgs...... 128 C5
Rhubodach Ag & B...... 207 G4
Rhuddall Heath Ches W...... 130 A7
Rhuddlan Cerdgn...... 76 F6
Rhuddlan Denbgs...... 127 L4
Rhulen Powys...... 79 G5
Rhunahaorine Ag & B...... 205 M6
Rhyd Gwynd...... 110 B3
Rhydargaeau Carmth...... 58 D4
Rhydcymerau Carmth...... 77 G7
Rhydd Worcs...... 81 J6
Rhyd-Ddu Gwynd...... 109 K1
Rhydding Neath...... 57 K5
Rhydgaled Conwy...... 127 K6

Rhydlanfair Conwy...... 110 F1
Rhydlewis Cerdgn...... 76 C5
Rhydlios Gwynd...... 108 C5
Rhyd-lydan Conwy...... 111 G2
Rhydowen Cerdgn...... 76 E6
Rhydrosser Cerdgn...... 77 G2
Rhydspence Herefs...... 79 J5
Rhydtalog Flints...... 128 F8
Rhyd-uchaf Gwynd...... 111 G4
Rhyd-y-clafdy Gwynd...... 108 E4
Rhydycroesau Shrops...... 112 C5
Rhydyfelin Cerdgn...... 92 D7
Rhydyfelin Rhondd...... 43 H4
Rhyd-y-foel Conwy...... 127 H4
Rhydyfro Neath...... 57 K4
Rhyd-y-groes Gwynd...... 125 K6
Rhydymain Gwynd...... 110 F7
Rhyd-y-meirch Mons...... 62 C5
Rhydymwyn Flints...... 128 E6
Rhyd y pennau Cerdgn...... 92 D6
Rhyd-yr-onnen Gwynd...... 92 D3
Rhyd-y-sarn Gwynd...... 110 C3
Rhyl Denbgs...... 127 K3
Rhymney Caerph...... 61 H5
Rhynd P & K...... 222 B3
Rhynie Abers...... 255 K6
Rhynie Highld...... 264 C4
Ribbesford Worcs...... 97 H8
Ribbleton Lancs...... 139 H2
Ribby Lancs...... 138 E2
Ribchester Lancs...... 139 K1
Riber Derbys...... 132 F7
Riby Lincs...... 144 F6
Riccall N York...... 151 K8
Riccarton Border...... 188 F7
Riccarton E Ayrs...... 196 E4
Richards Castle Herefs...... 80 C1
Richings Park Bucks...... 50 C3
Richmond Gt Lon...... 50 F4
Richmond N York...... 159 M2
Richmond Sheff...... 133 H3
Richmond Fort Guern...... 9 I2
Rich's Holford Somset...... 29 L4
Rickerscote Staffs...... 114 E7
Rickford N Som...... 44 F7
Rickham Devon...... 7 L7
Rickinghall Suffk...... 105 L8
Rickling Essex...... 70 D1
Rickling Green Essex...... 70 D1
Rickmansworth Herts...... 68 D8
Riddell Border...... 188 E1
Riddings Derbys...... 116 C1
Riddlecombe Devon...... 27 L8
Riddlesden C Brad...... 149 K7
Ridge BaNES...... 45 H4
Ridge Dorset...... 17 H5
Ridge Herts...... 69 G7
Ridge Wilts...... 33 G4
Ridgebourne Powys...... 78 E3
Ridge Green Surrey...... 37 L1
Ridge Lane Warwks...... 99 J4
Ridge Row Kent...... 41 G6
Ridgeway Derbys...... 133 H4
Ridgeway Worcs...... 82 B3
Ridgeway Cross Herefs...... 81 G5
Ridgewell Essex...... 88 E7
Ridgewood E Susx...... 23 H3
Ridgmont C Beds...... 85 J8
Riding Mill Nthumb...... 180 B6
Ridley Kent...... 52 D6
Ridley Nthumb...... 179 H6
Ridley Green Ches E...... 113 J1
Ridlington Norfk...... 123 G5
Ridlington Rutlnd...... 101 J3
Ridlington Street Norfk...... 123 G5
Ridsdale Nthumb...... 179 L2
Rievaulx N York...... 161 J5
Rigg D & G...... 177 J5
Riggend N Lans...... 209 K5
Righoul Highld...... 253 G2
Rigmadon Park Cumb...... 157 K5
Rigsby Lincs...... 137 H4
Rigside S Lans...... 198 E6
Riley Green Lancs...... 139 J3
Rileyhill Staffs...... 115 J8
Rilla Mill Cnwll...... 11 K7
Rillaton Cnwll...... 11 K7
Rillington N York...... 162 E7
Rimington Lancs...... 148 D6
Rimpton Somset...... 31 K6
Rimswell E R Yk...... 145 J2
Rinaston Pembks...... 75 G7
Rindleford Shrops...... 97 G4
Ringford D & G...... 175 H3
Ringinglow Sheff...... 132 F3
Ringland Norfk...... 106 C1
Ringles Cross E Susx...... 23 H3
Ringlestone Kent...... 39 L2
Ringley Bolton...... 139 M6
Ringmer E Susx...... 23 G5

Ringmore Devon...... 7 J5
Ringmore Devon...... 13 L8
Ring o'Bells Lancs...... 138 F5
Ringorm Moray...... 254 E3
Ring's End Cambs...... 103 H3
Ringsfield Suffk...... 107 H5
Ringsfield Corner Suffk...... 107 H6
Ringshall Herts...... 68 C4
Ringshall Suffk...... 90 B4
Ringshall Stocks Suffk...... 90 B4
Ringstead Nhants...... 101 L8
Ringstead Norfk...... 120 F3
Ringwood Hants...... 18 A3
Ringwould Kent...... 41 K6
Rinsey Cnwll...... 2 F5
Rinsey Croft Cnwll...... 2 F5
Ripe E Susx...... 23 H5
Ripley Derbys...... 116 C2
Ripley Hants...... 18 A4
Ripley N York...... 150 C4
Ripley Surrey...... 50 D7
Riplingham E R Yk...... 144 F3
Riplington Hants...... 35 K6
Ripon N York...... 150 D2
Rippingale Lincs...... 118 E6
Ripple Kent...... 41 K6
Ripple Worcs...... 81 K7
Ripponden Calder...... 140 F4
Risabus Ag & B...... 204 D7
Risbury Herefs...... 80 C4
Risby N Linc...... 144 A5
Risby Suffk...... 88 F2
Risca Caerph...... 43 K3
Rise E R Yk...... 153 J7
Riseden E Susx...... 38 F7
Riseden Kent...... 39 H6
Risegate Lincs...... 119 H5
Riseholme Lincs...... 135 K5
Risehow Cumb...... 164 D4
Riseley Bed...... 85 L3
Riseley Wokham...... 49 H6
Rishangles Suffk...... 90 E2
Rishton Lancs...... 139 L2
Rishworth Calder...... 140 F4
Rising Bridge Lancs...... 140 A3
Risley Derbys...... 116 D4
Risley Warrtn...... 130 C1
Risplith N York...... 150 B2
Rivar Wilts...... 47 L6
Rivenhall End Essex...... 71 K4
River Kent...... 41 J6
River W Susx...... 36 D6
River Bank Cambs...... 87 J2
Riverford Highld...... 250 F1
Riverhead Kent...... 38 D2
Rivers Corner Dorset...... 32 C8
Rivington Lancs...... 139 J3
Roachill Devon...... 28 E6
Roade Nhants...... 84 E5
Road Green Norfk...... 106 F4
Roadhead Cumb...... 178 C4
Roadmeetings S Lans...... 198 E3
Roadside E Ayrs...... 197 H7
Roadside Highld...... 279 J6
Roadwater Somset...... 29 J3
Roag Highld...... 258 D7
Roa Island Cumb...... 146 D3
Roan of Craigoch S Ayrs...... 183 H2
Roast Green Essex...... 87 J8
Roath Cardif...... 43 K6
Roberton Border...... 188 D3
Roberton S Lans...... 198 E4
Robertsbridge E Susx...... 24 D3
Roberttown Kirk...... 141 J3
Robeston Wathen Pembks...... 55 J4
Robgill Tower D & G...... 177 J2
Robin Hill Staffs...... 131 H8
Robin Hood Lancs...... 139 G5
Robin Hood Leeds...... 141 M2
Robin Hood Crematorium
    Solhll...... 98 E7
Robinhood End Essex...... 88 E7
Robin Hood's Bay N York...... 163 G2
Roborough Devon...... 6 F4
Roborough Devon...... 27 K7
Roby Knows...... 129 K2
Roby Mill Lancs...... 139 G6
Rocester Staffs...... 115 J4
Roch Pembks...... 54 E3
Rochdale Rochdl...... 140 D5
Rochdale Crematorium
    Rochdl...... 140 C5
Roche Cnwll...... 5 G3
Rochester Medway...... 52 F5
Rochester Nthumb...... 189 M6
Rochford Essex...... 53 J1
Rochford Worcs...... 80 E2
Roch Gate Pembks...... 54 E3
Rock Cnwll...... 10 C7
Rock Neath...... 57 L6

Rock - Rutherglen 347

Rock Nthumb 191 J2
Rock W Susx 21 K4
Rock Worcs 81 G1
Rockbeare Devon 14 B4
Rockbourne Hants 33 K7
Rockcliffe Cumb 177 K6
Rockcliffe D & G 175 L4
Rockcliffe Cross Cumb 177 K6
Rock End Staffs 131 H8
Rockend Torbay 8 D2
Rock Ferry Wirral 129 H2
Rockfield Highld 264 E3
Rockfield Mons 62 F4
Rockford Devon 28 D1
Rockford Hants 18 B2
Rockgreen Shrops 96 C8
Rockhampton S Glos 63 K8
Rockhead Cnwll 10 F5
Rockhill Shrops 95 G7
Rock Hill Worcs 81 L1
Rockingham Nhants 101 J5
Rockland All Saints Norfk 105 K4
Rockland St Mary Norfk 107 G3
Rockland St Peter Norfk 105 K4
Rockley Notts 134 E5
Rockley Wilts 47 H4
Rockliffe Lancs 140 C3
Rockville Ag & B 207 L1
Rockwell End Bucks 49 J1
Rockwell Green Somset 29 L6
Rodborough Gloucs 64 B6
Rodbourne Swindn 47 H2
Rodbourne Wilts 46 D2
Rodd Herefs 79 K3
Roddam Nthumb 190 E2
Rodden Dorset 16 B5
Roddymoor Dur 168 F3
Rode Somset 46 A8
Rode Heath Ches E 130 F8
Rode Heath Ches E 131 G6
Rodel W Isls 282 d7
Roden Wrekin 113 J8
Rodhuish Somset 29 J3
Rodington Wrekin 113 K8
Rodington Heath Wrekin 113 K8
Rodley Gloucs 63 L5
Rodley Leeds 150 B8
Rodmarton Gloucs 64 D7
Rodmell E Susx 22 F6
Rodmersham Kent 40 B3
Rodmersham Green Kent 40 B3
Rodney Stoke Somset 31 H1
Rodsley Derbys 115 K3
Rodway Somset 30 C3
Roecliffe N York 150 E3
Roe Cross Tamesd 140 E8
Roe Green Herts 69 G5
Roe Green Herts 87 G8
Roe Green Salfd 139 M7
Roehampton Gt Lon 51 G4
Roffey W Susx 37 J4
Rogart Highld 273 H7
Rogate W Susx 36 B6
Roger Ground Cumb 156 E3
Rogerstone Newpt 44 B2
Roghadal W Isls 282 d7
Rogiet Mons 44 F2
Roke Oxon 66 F8
Roker Sundld 181 K7
Rollesby Norfk 123 J8
Rolleston Leics 100 F3
Rolleston Notts 117 K1
Rolleston on Dove Staffs 115 L6
Rolston E R Yk 153 K6
Rolstone N Som 44 D6
Rolvenden Kent 39 L7
Rolvenden Layne Kent 39 L7
Romaldkirk Dur 168 C6
Romanby N York 160 E4
Romanno Bridge Border 199 K3
Romansleigh Devon 28 C6
Romden Castle Kent 40 A7
Romesdal Highld 258 F6
Romford Dorset 17 L1
Romford Gt Lon 52 B1
Romiley Stockp 131 J2
Romney Street Kent 52 C6
Romsey Hants 34 D6
Romsley Shrops 97 H6
Romsley Worcs 98 B7
Rona Highld 259 L5
Ronachan Ag & B 206 B8
Rood Ashton Wilts 46 C7
Rookhope Dur 167 L2
Rookley IoW 19 H6
Rookley Green IoW 19 H7
Rooks Bridge Somset 44 D8
Rooks Nest Somset 29 K4
Rookwith N York 160 B5
Roos E R Yk 145 H2
Roose Cumb 146 D2
Roosebeck Cumb 146 E2
Roothams Green Bed 86 B4
Ropley Hants 35 K4
Ropley Dean Hants 35 K4
Ropley Soke Hants 35 K4
Ropsley Lincs 118 C5
Rora Abers 269 K6
Rorrington Shrops 95 H3
Rosarie Moray 267 H6
Rose Cnwll 4 C4
Roseacre Lancs 147 H8
Rose Ash Devon 28 D6
Rosebank S Lans 198 D3
Rosebush Pembks 75 J6
Rosecare Cnwll 11 H3
Rosecliston Cnwll 4 D3
Rosedale Abbey N York 162 C3
Rose Green Essex 72 C2
Rose Green Suffk 89 J7
Rose Green Suffk 89 K6
Rose Green W Susx 20 E7
Rosehall Highld 272 C7
Rosehearty Abers 269 G3
Rose Hill E Susx 23 G4
Rose Hill Lancs 140 B2
Rosehill Shrops 113 G8
Roseisle Moray 266 C3
Roselands E Susx 23 K7
Rosemarket Pembks 54 F5
Rosemarkie Highld 263 K8
Rosemary Lane Devon 29 L7
Rosemount P & K 233 J6
Rosenannon Cnwll 4 F2
Rosenithon Cnwll 3 K6
Roser's Cross E Susx 23 J3
Rosevean Cnwll 5 H3
Rosevine Cnwll 3 M4
Rosewarne Cnwll 2 F4
Rosewell Mdloth 211 J6
Roseworth S on T 169 L6
Roseworthy Cnwll 3 G3
Rosgill Cumb 166 D7
Roskestal Cnwll 2 B6
Roskhill Highld 258 D7
Roskorwell Cnwll 3 K6
Rosley Cumb 165 K2
Roslin Mdloth 211 J6
Rosliston Derbys 115 L8
Rosneath Ag & B 207 L2
Ross D & G 175 G6
Ross Nthumb 203 J5
Rossett Wrexhm 129 J8
Rossett Green N York 150 D5
Rossington Donc 143 G8
Rossland Rens 208 D5
Ross-on-Wye Herefs 63 J2
Roster Highld 280 C8
Rostherne Ches E 130 E3
Rosthwaite Cumb 165 H7
Roston Derbys 115 J3
Rosudgeon Cnwll 2 E5
Rosyth Fife 210 F2
Rothbury Nthumb 190 F6
Rotherby Leics 117 H8
Rotherfield E Susx 38 E7
Rotherfield Greys Oxon 49 H3
Rotherfield Peppard Oxon 49 H3
Rotherham Rothm 133 H1
Rotherham Crematorium Rothm 133 J1
Rothersthorpe Nhants 84 D4
Rotherwick Hants 49 H7
Rothes Moray 266 F6
Rothesay Ag & B 207 H6
Rothiebrisbane Abers 256 D4
Rothiemay Moray 267 L6
Rothiemurchus Lodge Highld 242 C2
Rothienorman Abers 256 C4
Rothley Leics 100 D1
Rothley Nthumb 180 C1
Rothmaise Abers 256 B5
Rothwell Leeds 142 A2
Rothwell Lincs 144 F7
Rothwell Nhants 101 H7
Rotsea E R Yk 153 G5
Rottal Lodge Angus 234 B2
Rottingdean Br & H 22 F6
Rottington Cumb 164 C8
Roucan D & G 176 D3
Roucan Loch Crematorium D & G 176 D3
Roud IoW 19 H7
Rougham Norfk 121 H7
Rougham Green Suffk 89 H3
Rough Close Staffs 114 E4
Rough Common Kent 40 F3
Roughlee Lancs 148 E7
Roughpark Abers 243 K1
Roughton Lincs 136 D6
Roughton Norfk 122 E4
Roughton Shrops 97 G4
Roughway Kent 38 F3
Roundbush Essex 72 B6
Round Bush Herts 68 F7
Roundbush Green Essex 70 E4
Round Green Luton 68 E3
Roundham Somset 15 K1
Roundhay Leeds 150 D8
Rounds Green Sandw 98 C5
Round Street Kent 52 E5
Roundstreet Common W Susx 37 G5
Roundway Wilts 46 E6
Roundyhill Angus 234 B5
Rousay Ork 275 c3
Rousdon Devon 15 G4
Rousham Oxon 66 C2
Rous Lench Worcs 82 B4
Routenburn N Ayrs 207 K6
Routh E R Yk 153 H7
Rout's Green Bucks 67 J7
Row Cnwll 10 F7
Row Cumb 157 G5
Row Cumb 166 E4
Rowanburn D & G 177 L3
Rowardennan Stirlg 218 E7
Rowarth Derbys 131 K2
Row Ash Hants 35 H8
Rowberrow Somset 44 F7
Rowborough IoW 19 G6
Rowde Wilts 46 E6
Rowden Devon 12 F3
Rowen Conwy 126 E5
Rowfield Derbys 115 K2
Rowfoot Nthumb 178 F6
Rowford Somset 30 C5
Row Green Essex 71 H3
Rowhedge Essex 72 F3
Rowhook W Susx 37 H4
Rowington Warwks 82 F2
Rowland Derbys 132 D5
Rowland's Castle Hants 20 B5
Rowland's Gill Gatesd 180 E7
Rowledge Surrey 36 B2
Rowley Dur 168 E1
Rowley E R Yk 144 B1
Rowley Shrops 95 H2
Rowley Hill Kirk 141 J5
Rowley Regis Sandw 98 B6
Rowley Regis Crematorium Sandw 98 B6
Rowlstone Herefs 62 D2
Rowly Surrey 37 G3
Rowner Hants 19 K3
Rowney Green Worcs 82 B1
Rownhams Hants 34 E7
Rowrah Cumb 164 E7
Rowsham Bucks 67 K3
Rowsley Derbys 132 E6
Rows of Trees Ches E 131 G4
Rowstock Oxon 48 C1
Rowston Lincs 136 A8
Rowthorne Derbys 133 J6
Rowton Ches W 129 K6
Rowton Shrops 95 J1
Rowton Shrops 95 K7
Rowton Wrekin 113 K7
Row Town Surrey 50 D6
Roxburgh Border 201 L7
Roxby N Linc 144 A4
Roxby N York 171 H7
Roxton Bed 86 C4
Roxwell Essex 70 F5
Royal Leamington Spa Warwks 83 H2
Royal Oak Darltn 169 G6
Royal Oak Lancs 138 E7
Royal's Green Ches E 113 K3
Royal Tunbridge Wells Kent 38 F5
Royal Wootton Bassett Wilts 46 F3
Roy Bridge Highld 239 M7
Roydhouse Kirk 141 K5
Roydon Essex 69 L5
Roydon Norfk 106 C7
Roydon Norfk 120 F7
Roydon Hamlet Essex 69 L5
Royston Barns 142 B5
Royston Herts 87 G7
Royton Oldham 140 D6
Rozel Jersey 9 e2
Ruabon Wrexhm 112 D3
Ruaig Ag & B 224 D5
Ruan High Lanes Cnwll 4 E6
Ruan Lanihorne Cnwll 4 E6
Ruan Major Cnwll 3 H7
Ruan Minor Cnwll 3 J8
Ruardean Gloucs 63 J3
Ruardean Hill Gloucs 63 J4
Ruardean Woodside Gloucs 63 J4
Rubery Birm 98 C7
Rubha Ban W Isls 283 c12
Ruckcroft Cumb 166 C2
Ruckhall Herefs 80 B7
Ruckinge Kent 40 D8
Ruckland Lincs 136 F4
Ruckley Shrops 96 C3
Rudby N York 161 G1
Rudchester Nthumb 180 D5
Ruddington Notts 116 F5
Ruddle Gloucs 63 K5
Ruddlemoor Cnwll 5 G4
Rudford Gloucs 63 M3
Rudge Somset 46 B8
Rudgeway S Glos 45 J2
Rudgwick W Susx 37 G4
Rudhall Herefs 63 J2
Rudheath Ches W 130 D5
Rudheath Woods Ches E 130 E5
Rudley Green Essex 71 K6
Rudloe Wilts 46 B5
Rudry Caerph 43 K4
Rudston E R Yk 153 H2
Rudyard Staffs 131 J8
Ruecastle Border 189 G2
Rufford Lancs 138 F4
Rufforth C York 151 H5
Rug Denbgs 111 K3
Rugby Warwks 100 B8
Rugeley Staffs 115 G7
Ruishton Somset 30 C6
Ruislip Gt Lon 50 E2
Rùm Highld 236 D1
Rumbach Moray 267 H5
Rumbling Bridge P & K 221 J7
Rumburgh Suffk 107 G7
Rumby Hill Dur 168 F4
Rumford Cnwll 10 B8
Rumford Falk 210 B4
Rumney Cardif 43 K6
Rumwell Somset 30 B6
Runcorn Halton 129 L3
Runcton W Susx 20 E6
Runcton Holme Norfk 104 C2
Runfold Surrey 36 C2
Runhall Norfk 105 L2
Runham Norfk 107 J1
Runham Norfk 107 L2
Runnington Somset 29 L6
Runsell Green Essex 71 J6
Runshaw Moor Lancs 139 G4
Runswick N York 171 J7
Runtaleave Angus 233 L2
Runwell Essex 71 J8
Ruscombe Wokham 49 J4
Rushall Herefs 80 E8
Rushall Norfk 106 D6
Rushall Wilts 47 H7
Rushall Wsall 98 C3
Rushbrooke Suffk 89 H3
Rushbury Shrops 96 C5
Rushden Herts 69 J1
Rushden Nhants 85 J2
Rushenden Kent 53 K5
Rusher's Cross E Susx 38 F7
Rushford Devon 12 B7
Rushford Norfk 105 J7
Rush Green Essex 73 H4
Rush Green Gt Lon 52 B2
Rush Green Herts 69 G2
Rush Green Warrtn 130 D2
Rushlake Green E Susx 23 L3
Rushmere Suffk 107 K6
Rushmere St Andrew Suffk 90 E6
Rushmoor Surrey 36 C3
Rushock Herefs 79 K3
Rushock Worcs 81 K1
Rusholme Manch 131 G1
Rushton Ches W 130 B7
Rushton Nhants 101 J6
Rushton Shrops 96 D2
Rushton Spencer Staffs 131 J7
Rushwick Worcs 81 J4
Rushyford Dur 169 H5
Ruskie Stirlg 219 K7
Ruskington Lincs 118 E1
Rusland Cross Cumb 156 E5
Rusper W Susx 37 K3
Ruspidge Gloucs 63 K5
Russell Green Essex 71 H4
Russell's Water Oxon 49 H1
Russel's Green Suffk 90 F1
Russ Hill Surrey 37 K3
Rusthall Kent 38 E5
Rustington W Susx 21 H6
Ruston N York 163 G6
Ruston Parva E R Yk 153 G3
Ruswarp N York 162 F1
Ruthall Shrops 96 D5
Rutherford Border 201 K7
Rutherglen S Lans 209 G6

Ruthernbridge Cnwll......5 G2
Ruthin Denbgs......128 D8
Ruthrieston C Aber......245 K3
Ruthven Abers......267 K6
Ruthven Angus......233 L5
Ruthven Highld......241 K4
Ruthvoes Cnwll......4 F3
Ruthwaite Cumb......165 H3
Ruthwell D & G......176 E5
Ruxley Corner Gt Lon......52 A5
Ruxton Green Herefs......63 G3
Ruyton-XI-Towns Shrops......112 F7
Ryal Nthumb......180 B4
Ryall Dorset......15 J4
Ryall Worcs......81 K7
Ryarsh Kent......52 E7
Rycote Oxon......67 G6
Rydal Cumb......156 E2
Ryde IoW......19 K5
Rye E Susx......25 G3
Ryebank Shrops......113 H5
Ryeford Herefs......63 J3
Rye Foreign E Susx......25 G3
Rye Harbour E Susx......25 H3
Ryehill E R Yk......145 G3
Ryeish Green Wokham......49 H5
Rye Street Worcs......81 H8
Ryhall Rutlnd......102 A1
Ryhill Wakefd......142 B5
Ryhope Sundld......181 K8
Rylah Derbys......133 J6
Ryland Lincs......135 K4
Rylands Notts......116 F4
Rylstone N York......149 H4
Ryme Intrinseca Dorset......31 J8
Ryther N York......151 J7
Ryton Gatesd......180 E6
Ryton N York......162 D7
Ryton Shrops......97 G3
Ryton Warwks......99 L6
Ryton-on-Dunsmore Warwks......99 K8
Ryton Woodside Gatesd......180 E6

S

Sabden Lancs......148 D8
Sabine's Green Essex......70 E7
Sacombe Herts......69 J3
Sacombe Green Herts......69 J3
Sacriston Dur......169 G1
Sadberge Darltn......169 J2
Saddell Ag & B......194 B4
Saddington Leics......100 E5
Saddle Bow Norfk......120 D8
Saddlescombe W Susx......22 D5
Sadgill Cumb......157 G2
Saffron Walden Essex......87 L7
Sageston Pembks......55 H6
Saham Hills Norfk......105 H3
Saham Toney Norfk......105 H3
Saighton Ches W......129 K7
St Abbs Border......213 K5
St Agnes Border......212 F6
St Agnes Cnwll......4 B5
St Agnes IoS......10 b3
St Albans Herts......68 F5
St Allen Cnwll......4 D5
St Andrew Guern......9 j3
St Andrews Fife......223 J4
St Andrew's Major V Glam......43 H7
St Andrews Well Dorset......15 L4
St Anne's Lancs......138 C2
St Ann's D & G......187 G7
St Ann's Chapel Cnwll......12 A8
St Ann's Chapel Devon......7 J5
St Anthony Cnwll......3 K6
St Anthony's Hill E Susx......23 L7
St Arvans Mons......63 G7
St Asaph Denbgs......128 B5
St Athan V Glam......42 F8
St Aubin Jersey......9 c3
St Austell Cnwll......5 G4
St Bees Cumb......164 C8
St Blazey Cnwll......5 H4
St Blazey Gate Cnwll......5 H4
St Boswells Border......201 J7
St Brelade Jersey......9 b3
St Brelade's Bay Jersey......9 b3
St Breock Cnwll......10 D8
St Breward Cnwll......10 F7
St Briavels Gloucs......63 H6
St Brides Pembks......54 C5
St Bride's Major V Glam......42 D6
St Brides Netherwent Mons......44 E1
St Brides super-Ely V Glam......43 H6
St Brides Wentlooge Newpt......44 C3
St Budeaux C Plym......6 D5
Saintbury Gloucs......82 D7
St Buryan Cnwll......2 C6

St Catherine BaNES......45 M5
St Catherines Ag & B......217 J5
St Chloe Gloucs......64 B6
St Clears Carmth......58 A5
St Cleer Cnwll......6 A1
St Clement Cnwll......4 D6
St Clement Jersey......9 e4
St Clether Cnwll......11 H5
St Colmac Ag & B......207 G5
St Columb Major Cnwll......4 E2
St Columb Minor Cnwll......4 D2
St Columb Road Cnwll......4 E3
St Combs Abers......269 K4
St Cross South Elmham Suffk......106 F6
St Cyrus Abers......235 J2
St David's P & K......221 G3
St Davids Pembks......74 B7
St Day Cnwll......4 B5
St Decumans Somset......29 K2
St Dennis Cnwll......4 F3
St Devereux Herefs......62 E1
St Dogmaels Pembks......75 K3
St Dogwells Pembks......75 G6
St Dominick Cnwll......6 D1
St Donats V Glam......42 E8
St Edith's Marsh Wilts......46 E6
St Endellion Cnwll......10 D6
St Enoder Cnwll......4 E3
St Erme Cnwll......4 D5
St Erney Cnwll......6 D3
St Erth Cnwll......2 E4
St Erth Praze Cnwll......2 F4
St Ervan Cnwll......10 B8
St Eval Cnwll......4 E1
St Ewe Cnwll......5 G5
St Fagans Cardif......43 H6
St Fergus Abers......269 K6
St Fillans P & K......220 B2
St Florence Pembks......55 J6
St Gennys Cnwll......11 G3
St George Conwy......127 K4
St Georges N Som......44 D6
St George's V Glam......43 H6
St George's Hill Surrey......50 D6
St Germans Cnwll......6 D3
St Giles in the Wood Devon......27 J7
St Giles-on-the-Heath Devon......11 L4
St Gluvias Cnwll......3 K4
St Harmon Powys......78 D1
St Helen Auckland Dur......168 F5
St Helens Cumb......164 D4
St Helens E Susx......24 E5
St Helens IoW......19 L6
St Helens St Hel......139 G8
St Helens Crematorium St Hel......139 G8
St Helier Gt Lon......51 H5
St Helier Jersey......9 d3
St Hilary Cnwll......2 E5
St Hilary V Glam......42 F7
Saint Hill Devon......14 C1
Saint Hill W Susx......38 B6
St Illtyd Blae G......61 K6
St Ippollitts Herts......69 G2
St Ishmael's Pembks......54 D5
St Issey Cnwll......10 C8
St Ive Cnwll......6 C2
St Ive Cross Cnwll......6 C2
St Ives Cambs......87 G1
St Ives Cnwll......2 E3
St Ives Dorset......17 M2
St James Norfk......122 F7
St James's End Nhants......84 E3
St James South Elmham Suffk......107 G7
St Jidgey Cnwll......4 F1
St John Cnwll......6 E4
St John Jersey......9 c1
St Johns Dur......168 D4
St John's IoM......154 C5
St Johns Kent......38 E2
St Johns Surrey......50 C7
St Johns Worcs......81 J4
St John's Chapel Devon......27 J5
St John's Chapel Dur......167 K3
St John's Fen End Norfk......103 L1
St John's Highway Norfk......120 C8
St John's Kirk S Lans......199 G6
St John's Town of Dalry D & G......184 F6
St John's Wood Gt Lon......51 H2
St Jude's IoM......154 e3
St Just Cnwll......2 B5
St Just-in-Roseland Cnwll......3 L4
St Katherines Abers......256 D5
St Keverne Cnwll......3 K6
St Kew Cnwll......10 E7
St Kew Highway Cnwll......10 E7
St Keyne Cnwll......6 A3
St Lawrence Cnwll......5 H2
St Lawrence Essex......72 D6
St Lawrence IoW......19 J8
St Lawrence Jersey......9 c2

St Lawrence Kent......41 K2
St Leonards Bucks......67 M5
St Leonards Dorset......17 M2
St Leonards E Susx......24 E5
St Leonard's Street Kent......39 H2
St Levan Cnwll......2 B7
St Lythans V Glam......43 H7
St Mabyn Cnwll......10 E7
St Madoes P & K......222 C3
St Margarets Herefs......79 L8
St Margarets Herts......69 K5
St Margaret's at Cliffe Kent......41 K6
St Margaret's Bay Kent......41 K6
St Margaret's Hope Ork......275 c6
St Margaret South Elmham Suffk......107 G6
St Marks IoM......154 d7
St Martin Cnwll......3 J6
St Martin Cnwll......6 B4
St Martin Guern......9 j3
St Martin Jersey......9 e2
St Martin's IoS......10 c1
St Martin's P & K......221 L1
St Martins Shrops......112 D4
St Martin's Moor Shrops......112 D4
St Mary Jersey......9 c2
St Mary Bourne Hants......34 F1
St Marychurch Torbay......8 D2
St Mary Church V Glam......42 F7
St Mary Cray Gt Lon......52 A5
St Mary Hill V Glam......42 E6
St Mary in the Marsh Kent......25 K2
St Marylebone Crematorium Gt Lon......51 H1
St Mary's IoS......10 c3
St Mary's Ork......275 d5
St Mary's Bay Kent......25 K2
St Mary's Grove N Som......44 F5
St Mary's Hoo Medway......53 H4
St Maughans Mons......62 F4
St Maughans Green Mons......62 F4
St Mawes Cnwll......3 L4
St Mawgan Cnwll......4 E2
St Mellion Cnwll......6 D2
St Mellons Cardif......43 K5
St Merryn Cnwll......10 B7
St Mewan Cnwll......5 G4
St Michael Caerhays Cnwll......4 F6
St Michael Church Somset......30 D5
St Michael Penkevil Cnwll......4 D6
St Michaels Kent......39 M6
St Michaels Worcs......80 D2
St Michael's on Wyre Lancs......147 J7
St Michael South Elmham Suffk......107 G6
St Minver Cnwll......10 D7
St Monans Fife......223 J6
St Neot Cnwll......5 L1
St Neots Cambs......86 D3
St Nicholas Pembks......74 E5
St Nicholas V Glam......43 H6
St Nicholas at Wade Kent......41 J2
St Ninians Stirlg......209 L1
St Olaves Norfk......107 J3
St Osyth Essex......73 H4
St Ouen Jersey......9 b2
St Owens Cross Herefs......63 G2
St Pauls Cray Gt Lon......52 A5
St Paul's Walden Herts......69 G3
St Peter Jersey......9 b2
St Peter Port Guern......9 k3
St Peter's Guern......9 i3
St Peter's Kent......41 L2
St Peter's Hill Cambs......86 E1
St Petrox Pembks......55 G7
St Pinnock Cnwll......5 L2
St Quivox S Ayrs......196 D6
St Ruan Cnwll......3 J8
St Sampson Guern......9 k2
St Saviour Guern......9 i3
St Saviour Jersey......9 d3
St Stephen Cnwll......4 F4
St Stephens Cnwll......6 B5
St Stephens Cnwll......11 L5
St Teath Cnwll......10 F6
St Tudy Cnwll......10 F7
St Twynnells Pembks......54 F7
St Veep Cnwll......5 K4
St Vigeans Angus......235 G6
St Wenn Cnwll......5 G2
St Weonards Herefs......63 G2
St y-Nyll V Glam......43 H6
Salcombe Devon......7 L7
Salcombe Regis Devon......14 D5
Salcott-cum-Virley Essex......72 D4
Sale Traffd......130 F2
Saleby Lincs......137 J4
Sale Green Worcs......81 L4
Salehurst E Susx......24 D2
Salem Carmth......59 H4

Salem Cerdgn......92 E6
Salen Ag & B......227 H4
Salen Highld......237 K7
Salesbury Lancs......139 K1
Salford C Beds......85 H7
Salford Oxon......65 L2
Salford Salfd......140 B8
Salford Priors Warwks......82 C5
Salfords Surrey......37 L2
Salhouse Norfk......123 G8
Saline Fife......221 K5
Salisbury Wilts......33 K4
Salisbury Crematorium Wilts......33 K4
Salkeld Dykes Cumb......166 D3
Salle Norfk......122 C6
Salmonby Lincs......136 F5
Salperton Gloucs......65 G3
Salph End Bed......86 B5
Salsburgh N Lans......209 L6
Salt Staffs......114 F6
Salta Cumb......164 E2
Saltaire C Brad......149 L8
Saltash Cnwll......6 D4
Saltburn Highld......263 K6
Saltburn-by-the-Sea R & Cl......170 F6
Saltby Leics......117 M6
Salt Coates Cumb......177 G8
Saltcoats Cumb......155 K3
Saltcoats N Ayrs......195 L3
Saltcotes Lancs......138 D2
Saltdean Br & H......22 F6
Salterbeck Cumb......164 C5
Salterforth Lancs......148 F6
Salterswall Ches W......130 C6
Salterton Wilts......33 K4
Saltfleet Lincs......137 H1
Saltfleetby All Saints Lincs......137 H1
Saltfleetby St Clement Lincs......137 J1
Saltfleetby St Peter Lincs......137 H2
Saltford BaNES......45 K5
Salthouse Norfk......122 B3
Saltley Birm......98 C5
Saltmarsh Newpt......44 D2
Saltmarshe E R Yk......143 K3
Saltney Flints......129 J6
Salton N York......162 C6
Saltrens Devon......27 H6
Saltwell Crematorium Gatesd......181 G6
Saltwick Nthumb......180 E3
Saltwood Kent......40 F8
Salvington W Susx......21 K6
Salwarpe Worcs......81 K3
Salway Ash Dorset......15 K4
Sambourne Warwks......82 C3
Sambrook Wrekin......113 M6
Samlesbury Lancs......139 H2
Samlesbury Bottoms Lancs......139 J2
Sampford Arundel Somset......29 K7
Sampford Brett Somset......29 K3
Sampford Courtenay Devon......12 F2
Sampford Moor Somset......29 K7
Sampford Peverell Devon......29 J8
Sampford Spiney Devon......12 D8
Samsonlane Ork......275 e3
Samson's Corner Essex......73 G4
Samuelston E Loth......212 B5
Sanaigmore Ag & B......204 C2
Sancreed Cnwll......2 C5
Sancton E R Yk......152 D7
Sand Somset......31 G2
Sandaig Highld......247 M8
Sandale Cumb......165 H3
Sandal Magna Wakefd......142 A4
Sandavore Highld......236 F4
Sanday Ork......275 e2
Sandbach Ches E......130 C6
Sandbank Ag & B......207 K3
Sandbanks Poole......17 K5
Sandend Abers......267 L3
Sanderstead Gt Lon......51 J6
Sandford Cumb......167 G7
Sandford Devon......13 J2
Sandford Dorset......17 H5
Sandford Hants......18 B5
Sandford IoW......19 J7
Sandford N Som......44 E7
Sandford S Lans......197 L2
Sandford Shrops......112 C6
Sandford Shrops......113 J5
Sandford-on-Thames Oxon......66 D6
Sandford Orcas Dorset......31 K6
Sandford St Martin Oxon......66 C2
Sandgate Kent......41 G8
Sandhaven Abers......269 H3
Sandhead D & G......172 D6
Sandhill Rothm......142 C8
Sandhills Dorset......16 B3
Sandhills Dorset......31 L8
Sand Hills Leeds......150 F7
Sandhills Oxon......66 E5

Sandhills Surrey 36 D3
Sandhoe Nthumb 180 A5
Sandhole Ag & B. 216 F7
Sand Hole E R Yk 152 B8
Sandholme E R Yk 143 L2
Sandholme Lincs 119 K4
Sandhurst Br For. 49 K6
Sandhurst Gloucs 64 B2
Sandhurst Kent 39 K7
Sandhurst Cross Kent 24 K7
Sand Hutton N York 151 L4
Sandhutton N York 160 E6
Sandiacre Derbys 116 E4
Sandilands Lincs 137 K3
Sandiway Ches W. 130 B5
Sandleheath Hants 33 K7
Sandleigh Oxon 66 C6
Sandley Dorset 32 C6
Sandling Kent 53 G7
Sandlow Green Ches E. 130 F6
Sandness Shet 281 c5
Sandon Essex 71 H6
Sandon Herts 87 G8
Sandon Staffs 114 E5
Sandon Bank Staffs 114 E6
Sandown IoW 19 K6
Sandplace Cnwll 6 A3
Sandridge Herts 68 F5
Sandridge Wilts 46 D6
Sandringham Norfk 120 F5
Sands Bucks 67 K8
Sandsend N York 171 K8
Sand Side Cumb 156 B6
Sandside Cumb 157 G6
Sandtoft N Linc 143 J6
Sandway Kent 39 M3
Sandwich Kent 41 K4
Sandwick Cumb 166 A6
Sandwick Shet 281 e8
Sandwick W Isls 282 g3
Sandwith Cumb 164 C7
Sandwith Newtown Cumb 164 C7
Sandy C Beds 86 D5
Sandy Bank Lincs 136 E8
Sandycroft Flints 129 H6
Sandy Cross E Susx 23 K3
Sandy Cross Herefs 80 F4
Sandyford D & G 187 J7
Sandygate Devon 13 K7
Sandygate IoM 154 e3
Sandy Haven Pembks 54 D5
Sandyhills D & G 175 M4
Sandylands Lancs 147 H3
Sandy Lane C Brad 149 K8
Sandylane Staffs 113 M4
Sandylane Swans 57 G7
Sandy Lane Wilts 46 D5
Sandy Lane Wrexhm 112 F3
Sandy Park Devon 13 G5
Sandysike Cumb 177 L5
Sandyway Herefs 63 G2
Sangobeg Highld 277 G3
Sangomore Highld 276 F3
Sankey Bridges Warrtn 130 B2
Sankyn's Green Worcs 81 H2
Sanna Bay Highld 236 E6
Sanndabhaig W Isls 282 g3
Sannox N Ayrs 195 G2
Sanquhar D & G 185 K1
Santon Cumb 155 K2
Santon IoM 154 d7
Santon Bridge Cumb 155 K2
Santon Downham Suffk 105 G6
Sapcote Leics 100 B5
Sapey Common Herefs 81 G2
Sapiston Suffk 105 J8
Sapley Cambs 102 E8
Sapperton Derbys 115 K4
Sapperton Gloucs 64 D6
Sapperton Lincs 118 D5
Saracen's Head Lincs 119 K6
Sarclet Highld 280 D7
Sarisbury Hants 19 H2
Sarn Brdgnd 42 D5
Sarn Gwynd 108 D5
Sarn Powys 93 L4
Sarn Powys 94 F5
Sarnau Carmth 58 B5
Sarnau Cerdgn 76 B5
Sarnau Gwynd 111 J4
Sarnau Powys 78 A3
Sarnau Powys 112 C8
Sarn Bach Gwynd 108 E6
Sarnesfield Herefs 79 L5
Sarn-wen Powys 112 C7
Saron Carmth 59 H6
Saron Carmth 76 C7
Saron Gwynd 125 H7
Saron Gwynd 125 J6
Sarratt Herts 68 D7

Sarre Kent 41 H2
Sarsden Oxon 65 L3
Sarson Hants 34 C2
Satley Dur 168 E2
Satmar Kent 41 H7
Satron N York 159 G3
Satterleigh Devon 28 B6
Satterthwaite Cumb 156 D4
Satwell Oxon 49 H2
Sauchen Abers 244 F1
Saucher P & K 233 J8
Sauchieburn Abers 235 G2
Saul Gloucs 63 L5
Saundby Notts 134 F2
Saundersfoot Pembks 55 K6
Saunderton Bucks 67 J6
Saunton Devon 27 H3
Sausthorpe Lincs 137 G6
Saveock Cnwll 4 C6
Saverley Green Staffs 114 F4
Savile Town Kirk 141 K4
Sawbridge Warwks 83 L2
Sawbridgeworth Herts 70 C4
Sawdon N York 163 G5
Sawley Derbys 116 D5
Sawley Lancs 148 D6
Sawley N York 150 C2
Sawston Cambs 87 K5
Sawtry Cambs 102 D6
Saxby Leics 117 L7
Saxby Lincs 135 K3
Saxby All Saints N Linc 144 C4
Saxelbye Leics 117 J7
Saxham Street Suffk 90 C3
Saxilby Lincs 135 H4
Saxlingham Norfk 122 A4
Saxlingham Green Norfk 106 E4
Saxlingham Nethergate Norfk 106 E4
Saxlingham Thorpe Norfk 106 E4
Saxmundham Suffk 91 J3
Saxondale Notts 117 H3
Saxon Street Cambs 88 D3
Saxtead Suffk 91 G2
Saxtead Green Suffk 90 F2
Saxtead Little Green Suffk 90 F2
Saxthorpe Norfk 122 C5
Saxton N York 151 G8
Sayers Common W Susx 22 D4
Scackleton N York 161 L8
Scaftworth Notts 134 D2
Scagglethorpe N York 152 C1
Scalasaig Ag & B 214 D5
Scalby E R Yk 143 L2
Scalby N York 163 H4
Scald End Bed 85 L4
Scaldwell Nhants 84 E1
Scaleby Cumb 178 B6
Scalebyhill Cumb 178 B6
Scale Houses Cumb 166 E2
Scales Cumb 146 E2
Scales Cumb 165 K5
Scalesceugh Cumb 166 B1
Scalford Leics 117 K6
Scaling N York 171 H7
Scaling Dam R & Cl 171 H7
Scalloway Shet 281 d7
Scalpay Highld 247 J2
Scamblesby Lincs 136 E4
Scammonden Kirk 141 G4
Scamodale Highld 228 C1
Scampston N York 162 F7
Scampton Lincs 135 J4
Scaniport Highld 251 H4
Scapegoat Hill Kirk 141 G4
Scarba Ag & B 215 K3
Scarborough N York 163 J5
Scarcewater Cnwll 4 F4
Scarcliffe Derbys 133 K6
Scarcroft Leeds 150 E7
Scarfskerry Highld 280 C2
Scargill Dur 168 D8
Scarinish Ag & B 224 D6
Scarisbrick Lancs 138 D5
Scarness Cumb 165 H4
Scarning Norfk 105 J1
Scarrington Notts 117 J3
Scarth Hill Lancs 138 E6
Scarthingwell N York 151 G8
Scartho NE Lin 145 H6
Scawby N Linc 144 B6
Scawsby Donc 142 E6
Scawthorpe Donc 142 E6
Scawton N York 161 J6
Scayne's Hill W Susx 22 F3
Scethrog Powys 61 H2
Scholar Green Ches E 131 G8
Scholemoor Crematorium
   C Brad 141 H1
Scholes Kirk 141 H3
Scholes Kirk 141 J6

Scholes Leeds 150 E8
Scholes Rothm 142 B8
Scholes Wigan 139 J6
School Aycliffe Dur 169 H6
School Green C Brad 141 H1
School Green Ches W 130 C6
Schoolgreen Wokham 49 H5
School House Dorset 15 J2
Scissett Kirk 141 L5
Scleddau Pembks 74 F7
Scofton Notts 134 C4
Scole Norfk 106 C7
Sconser Highld 247 H2
Scone P & K 221 L2
Scoonie Fife 222 F6
Scopwick Lincs 135 M8
Scoraig Highld 261 G1
Scorborough E R Yk 152 F6
Scorrier Cnwll 4 B6
Scorriton Devon 7 K1
Scorton Lancs 147 K6
Scorton N York 160 C3
Sco Ruston Norfk 122 F7
Scotby Cumb 178 B7
Scotch Corner N York 160 B2
Scotforth Lancs 147 J4
Scot Hay Staffs 114 C2
Scothern Lincs 135 L4
Scotland Lincs 118 D3
Scotland Gate Nthumb 181 G2
Scotlandwell P & K 222 C7
Scot Lane End Bolton 139 J6
Scotscalder Station Highld 279 K5
Scotsdike Cumb 177 L4
Scot's Gap Nthumb 180 C2
Scotsmill Abers 255 L7
Scotstoun C Glas 208 F5
Scotswood N u Ty 180 F6
Scotter Lincs 143 M7
Scotterthorpe Lincs 143 L7
Scottlethorpe Lincs 118 D7
Scotton Lincs 143 M7
Scotton N York 150 D4
Scotton N York 160 B3
Scottow Norfk 122 F6
Scott Willoughby Lincs 118 D4
Scoulton Norfk 105 K3
Scounslow Green Staffs 115 H5
Scourie Highld 276 B7
Scourie More Highld 276 A7
Scousburgh Shet 281 d8
Scouthead Oldham 140 E6
Scrabster Highld 279 K2
Scraesburgh Border 189 J3
Scrafield Lincs 136 F6
Scrainwood Nthumb 190 D4
Scrane End Lincs 119 L3
Scraptoft Leics 100 E2
Scratby Norfk 123 K8
Scrayingham N York 151 M4
Scrays E Susx 24 D3
Scredington Lincs 118 E3
Scremby Lincs 137 H6
Scremerston Nthumb 202 F3
Screveton Notts 117 J3
Scrivelsby Lincs 136 E6
Scriven N York 150 E4
Scrooby Notts 134 C2
Scropton Derbys 115 K5
Scrub Hill Lincs 136 D8
Scruton N York 160 D4
Scuggate Cumb 178 B4
Scullomie Highld 277 L4
Sculthorpe Norfk 121 K5
Scunthorpe N Linc 143 M5
Scurlage Swans 56 E7
Sea Somset 30 E8
Seaborough Dorset 15 K2
Seabridge Staffs 114 C3
Seabrook Kent 41 G8
Seaburn Sundld 181 K6
Seacombe Wirral 129 H2
Seacroft Leeds 150 E8
Seacroft Lincs 137 L7
Seadyke Lincs 119 K4
Seafield Highld 259 H8
Seafield W Loth 210 D6
Seafield Crematorium C Edin 211 J4
Seaford E Susx 23 H7
Seaforth Sefton 138 C8
Seagrave Leics 117 G6
Seagry Heath Wilts 46 D3
Seaham Dur 169 L1
Seahouses Nthumb 203 L6
Seal Kent 38 D2
Sealand Flints 129 H6
Seale Surrey 36 D1
Seamer N York 163 J6
Seamer N York 170 C8
Seamill N Ayrs 195 K2

Sea Palling Norfk 123 J6
Searby Lincs 144 D6
Seasalter Kent 40 E2
Seascale Cumb 155 J2
Seathwaite Cumb 156 B3
Seathwaite Cumb 165 H8
Seatle Cumb 156 E6
Seatoller Cumb 165 H7
Seaton Cnwll 6 C4
Seaton Cumb 164 D4
Seaton Devon 14 F4
Seaton Dur 169 L1
Seaton E R Yk 153 J6
Seaton Kent 41 H4
Seaton Nthumb 181 H3
Seaton Rutlnd 101 K4
Seaton Burn N Tyne 181 G4
Seaton Carew Hartpl 170 C5
Seaton Delaval Nthumb 181 H4
Seaton Ross E R Yk 152 B7
Seaton Sluice Nthumb 181 H3
Seatown Dorset 15 K4
Seave Green N York 161 J3
Seaview IoW 19 L5
Seaville Cumb 177 G8
Seavington St Mary Somset 30 F7
Seavington St Michael Somset 30 F7
Sebastopol Torfn 62 C7
Sebergham Cumb 165 K2
Seckington Warwks 99 H2
Sedbergh Cumb 157 L4
Sedbury Gloucs 63 H8
Sedbusk N York 158 F4
Sedgeberrow Worcs 82 B7
Sedgebrook Lincs 117 M4
Sedge Fen Suffk 104 D6
Sedgefield Dur 169 K5
Sedgeford Norfk 120 F4
Sedgehill Wilts 32 E5
Sedgley Dudley 97 L4
Sedgley Park Bury 140 B7
Sedgwick Cumb 157 H5
Sedlescombe E Susx 24 E4
Sedrup Bucks 67 J5
Seed Kent 40 B4
Seend Wilts 46 D6
Seend Cleeve Wilts 46 D6
Seer Green Bucks 68 B3
Seething Norfk 107 G4
Sefton Sefton 138 D7
Sefton Town Sefton 138 D7
Seghill Nthumb 181 G4
Seighford Staffs 114 D6
Seion Gwynd 125 K6
Seisdon Staffs 97 J4
Seisiadar Highld 112 C5
Selattyn Shrops 112 C5
Selborne Hants 35 M4
Selby N York 142 F1
Selham W Susx 20 F3
Selhurst Gt Lon 51 J5
Selkirk Border 201 G7
Sellack Herefs 63 H2
Sellafirth Shet 281 e2
Sellan Cnwll 2 C5
Sellick's Green Somset 30 B7
Sellindge Kent 40 E7
Selling Kent 40 D4
Sells Green Wilts 46 D6
Selly Oak Birm 98 D7
Selmeston E Susx 23 H6
Selsdon Gt Lon 51 K6
Selsey Gloucs 64 B6
Selsey W Susx 20 D8
Selsfield Common W Susx 38 A6
Selside Cumb 157 H5
Selside N York 158 D7
Selsted Kent 41 H6
Selston Notts 116 D1
Selworthy Somset 29 G2
Semer Suffk 89 K6
Semington Wilts 46 C6
Semley Wilts 32 E5
Sempringham Lincs 118 F5
Send Surrey 50 C7
Send Marsh Surrey 50 D7
Senghenydd Caerph 43 H3
Sennen Cnwll 2 B5
Sennen Cove Cnwll 2 B6
Sennybridge Powys 60 D2
Serlby Notts 134 C2
Sessay N York 161 G7
Setchey Norfk 104 C1
Setley Hants 18 D3
Seton Mains E Loth 211 M4
Settle N York 148 E3
Settrington N York 152 C2
Seven Ash Somset 29 L4
Sevenhampton Gloucs 64 F3
Sevenhampton Swindn 47 J1
Seven Hills Crematorium Suffk 90 F7

Seven Kings Gt Lon 51 M2
Sevenoaks Kent 38 E2
Sevenoaks Weald Kent 38 E3
Seven Sisters Neath 60 B5
Seven Springs Gloucs 64 D4
Seven Star Green Essex 72 D2
Severn Beach S Glos 45 G2
Severn Stoke Worcs 81 K6
Sevick End Bed 86 B4
Sevington Kent 40 D7
Sewards End Essex 88 B7
Sewardstonebury Essex 69 K7
Sewell C Beds 68 C3
Sewerby E R Yk 153 K2
Seworgan Cnwll 3 H5
Sewstern Leics 118 A7
Sexhow N York 161 G2
Sezincote Gloucs 65 H4
Sgiogarstaigh W Isls 282 h1
Shabbington Bucks 67 G5
Shackerley Shrops 97 J2
Shackerstone Leics 99 K2
Shacklecross Derbys 116 C5
Shackleford Surrey 36 D2
Shade Calder 140 D3
Shader W Isls 282 g1
Shadforth Dur 169 J3
Shadingfield Suffk 107 J6
Shadoxhurst Kent 40 C7
Shadwell Leeds 150 D7
Shadwell Norfk 105 J6
Shaftenhoe End Herts 87 H7
Shaftesbury Dorset 32 E6
Shaftholme Donc 142 F6
Shafton Barns 142 B5
Shafton Two Gates Barns 142 B5
Shakerley Wigan 139 K7
Shalbourne Wilts 47 L6
Shalcombe IoW 18 F6
Shalden Hants 35 L3
Shalden Green Hants 35 L2
Shaldon Devon 13 L8
Shalfleet IoW 18 F6
Shalford Essex 71 H1
Shalford Surrey 36 F2
Shalford Green Essex 71 H2
Shallowford Staffs 114 D5
Shalmsford Street Kent 40 E4
Shalstone Bucks 84 C7
Shamley Green Surrey 36 F2
Shandford Angus 234 D3
Shandon Ag & B 207 L2
Shandwick Highld 264 D5
Shangton Leics 100 F4
Shankhouse Nthumb 181 G3
Shanklin IoW 19 K7
Shap Cumb 166 D7
Shapinsay Ork 275 d4
Shapwick Dorset 17 H2
Shapwick Somset 30 F3
Shard End Birm 98 F5
Shardlow Derbys 116 D5
Shareshill Staffs 97 L2
Sharlston Wakefd 142 B4
Sharlston Common Wakefd ... 142 B4
Sharman's Cross Solhll 98 E7
Sharnal Street Medway 53 G4
Sharnbrook Bed 85 K3
Sharneyford Lancs 140 C3
Sharnford Leics 100 B5
Sharnhill Green Dorset 16 D2
Sharoe Green Lancs 139 G1
Sharow N York 150 D2
Sharpenhoe C Beds 68 D1
Sharperton Nthumb 190 D5
Sharp Green Norfk 123 H7
Sharpness Gloucs 63 K6
Sharpthorne W Susx 38 B6
Sharptor Cnwll 11 J8
Sharpway Gate Worcs 81 L2
Sharrington Norfk 122 A4
Shatterford Worcs 97 H7
Shatterling Kent 41 J4
Shatton Derbys 132 D3
Shaugh Prior Devon 7 G2
Shave Cross Dorset 15 J3
Shavington Ches E 113 M1
Shaw C Brad 140 F1
Shaw Oldham 140 D6
Shaw Swindn 47 G2
Shaw W Berk 48 C5
Shaw Wilts 46 C6
Shawbirch Wrekin 113 L8
Shawbost W Isls 282 f2
Shawbury Shrops 113 J7
Shawclough Rochdl 140 D5
Shaw Common Gloucs 63 K2
Shawdon Hill Nthumb 190 F3
Shawell Leics 100 C7
Shawford Hants 34 F6

Shawforth Lancs 140 D4
Shaw Green Herts 69 J1
Shaw Green Lancs 139 G4
Shaw Green N York 150 C5
Shawhead D & G 185 L7
Shaw Mills N York 150 C3
Shawsburn S Lans 198 D2
Shear Cross Wilts 32 E3
Shearington D & G 176 D5
Shearsby Leics 100 D5
Shearston Somset 30 D5
Shebbear Devon 12 B1
Shebdon Staffs 114 B6
Shebster Highld 279 H3
Sheddens E Rens 208 F7
Shedfield Hants 35 H8
Sheen Staffs 132 B7
Sheepbridge Derbys 133 G5
Sheep Hill Dur 180 E7
Sheepridge Kirk 141 J4
Sheepscar Leeds 141 M1
Sheepscombe Gloucs 64 C5
Sheepstor Devon 7 G1
Sheepwash Devon 12 C2
Sheepwash Nthumb 181 G2
Sheepway N Som 45 G4
Sheepy Magna Leics 99 J3
Sheepy Parva Leics 99 J3
Sheering Essex 70 D4
Sheerness Kent 53 K4
Sheerwater Surrey 50 D6
Sheet Hants 36 A6
Sheffield Cnwll 2 D5
Sheffield Sheff 133 G4
Sheffield Bottom W Berk 49 G5
Sheffield City Road
  Crematorium Sheff 133 G3
Sheffield Green E Susx 22 F2
Shefford C Beds 86 C7
Sheigra Highld 276 B4
Sheinton Shrops 96 E3
Shelderton Shrops 95 K7
Sheldon Birm 98 F6
Sheldon Derbys 132 C6
Sheldon Devon 14 D1
Sheldwich Kent 40 D4
Sheldwich Lees Kent 40 D4
Shelf Calder 141 H2
Shelfanger Norfk 106 C6
Shelfield Warwks 82 D3
Shelfield Wsall 98 C3
Shelfield Green Warwks 82 D3
Shelford Notts 117 H3
Shelford Warwks 99 L5
Shellacres Nthumb 202 D4
Shelley Essex 70 E6
Shelley Kirk 141 K5
Shelley Suffk 89 L7
Shelley Far Bank Kirk 141 K5
Shellingford Oxon 65 L8
Shellow Bowells Essex 70 F5
Shelsley Beauchamp Worcs ... 81 G3
Shelsley Walsh Worcs 81 G3
Shelton Bed 85 K2
Shelton Norfk 106 E5
Shelton Notts 117 K3
Shelton Shrops 95 L1
Shelton Green Norfk 106 E5
Shelton Lock C Derb 116 C5
Shelton Under Harley Staffs .. 114 C4
Shelve Shrops 95 H4
Shelwick Herefs 80 C6
Shenfield Essex 70 F8
Shenington Oxon 83 J6
Shenley Herts 68 F7
Shenley Brook End M Keyn ... 85 G8
Shenleybury Herts 68 F6
Shenley Church End M Keyn ... 85 G7
Shenmore Herefs 79 M7
Shennanton D & G 173 J2
Shenstone Staffs 98 E3
Shenstone Worcs 97 J8
Shenstone Woodend Staffs ... 98 E3
Shenton Leics 99 K3
Shenval Moray 254 E6
Shepeau Stow Lincs 102 F1
Shephall Herts 69 H2
Shepherd's Bush Gt Lon 51 G3
Shepherd's Green Oxon 49 H2
Shepherds Patch Gloucs 63 L6
Shepherdswell Kent 41 H5
Shepley Kirk 141 J6
Shepperdine S Glos 63 J8
Shepperton Surrey 50 D5
Shepperton Green Surrey 50 D5
Shepreth Cambs 87 H5
Shepshed Leics 116 E7
Shepton Beauchamp Somset .. 30 F7
Shepton Mallet Somset 31 K2
Shepton Montague Somset ... 31 L4

Shepway Kent 39 J3
Sheraton Dur 170 B4
Sherborne Dorset 31 L7
Sherborne Gloucs 65 H4
Sherborne Somset 45 H7
Sherborne St John Hants 48 F7
Sherbourne Warwks 83 G3
Sherburn Dur 169 J2
Sherburn N York 163 G7
Sherburn Hill Dur 169 J2
Sherburn in Elmet N York 142 D1
Shere Surrey 37 G1
Shereford Norfk 121 K5
Sherfield English Hants 34 C6
Sherfield on Loddon Hants ... 49 G7
Sherfin Lancs 140 B3
Sherford Devon 8 A6
Sherford Dorset 17 H4
Sheriffhales Shrops 97 G1
Sheriff Hutton N York 151 K3
Sheringham Norfk 122 D3
Sherington M Keyn 85 H6
Shermanbury W Susx 22 B3
Shernborne Norfk 120 F5
Sherrington Wilts 33 G3
Sherston Wilts 46 B2
Sherwood C Nott 116 F3
Sherwood Forest
  Crematorium Notts 134 D6
Shetland Islands Shet 281 d6
Shettleston C Glas 209 H6
Shevington Wigan 139 H6
Shevington Moor Wigan 139 H5
Shevington Vale Wigan 139 G6
Sheviock Cnwll 6 D4
Shibden Head C Brad 141 H2
Shide IoW 19 H6
Shidlaw Nthumb 202 C5
Shiel Bridge Highld 248 F7
Shieldaig Highld 248 C1
Shieldhill D & G 176 D2
Shieldhill Falk 210 B4
Shieldhill House Hotel S Lans .. 199 G5
Shields N Lans 209 K7
Shielfoot Highld 237 J6
Shielhill Angus 234 C4
Shielhill Inver 207 L4
Shifford Oxon 66 A6
Shifnal Shrops 97 G2
Shilbottle Nthumb 191 J4
Shildon Dur 169 G5
Shillford E Rens 208 D7
Shillingford Devon 29 H6
Shillingford Oxon 66 E8
Shillingford Abbot Devon 13 L5
Shillingford St George Devon .. 13 L5
Shillingstone Dorset 32 D8
Shillington C Beds 86 C8
Shillmoor Nthumb 190 B4
Shilton Oxon 65 K5
Shilton Warwks 99 L6
Shimpling Norfk 106 D6
Shimpling Suffk 89 H5
Shimpling Street Suffk 89 H4
Shincliffe Dur 169 H3
Shiney Row Sundld 181 H8
Shinfield Wokham 49 H5
Shingay Cambs 86 F6
Shingle Street Suffk 91 J6
Shinnersbridge Devon 8 B2
Shinness Highld 272 D5
Shipbourne Kent 38 F3
Shipdham Norfk 105 J2
Shipham Somset 44 E7
Shiphay Torbay 8 D2
Shiplake Oxon 49 J3
Shiplake Row Oxon 49 H3
Shiplate N Som 44 D7
Shipley C Brad 149 L8
Shipley Derbys 116 D3
Shipley Shrops 97 H4
Shipley W Susx 37 H6
Shipley Bridge Surrey 37 M3
Shipley Hatch Kent 40 C7
Shipmeadow Suffk 107 H5
Shippea Hill Station Cambs ... 104 C6
Shippon Oxon 66 C7
Shipston-on-Stour Warwks ... 83 G7
Shipton Bucks 67 J2
Shipton Gloucs 64 F3
Shipton N York 151 H4
Shipton Shrops 96 D5
Shipton Bellinger Hants 34 B2
Shipton Gorge Dorset 15 L4
Shipton Green W Susx 20 C7
Shipton Moyne Gloucs 46 C1
Shipton-on-Cherwell Oxon 66 C4
Shiptonthorpe E R Yk 152 C7
Shipton-under-
  Wychwood Oxon 65 L3

Shirburn Oxon 67 G7
Shirdley Hill Lancs 138 D5
Shire Cumb 166 E1
Shirebrook Derbys 133 K6
Shiregreen Sheff 133 G1
Shirehampton Bristl 44 G4
Shiremoor N Tyne 181 H4
Shirenewton Mons 62 F8
Shire Oak Wsall 98 D3
Shireoaks Notts 133 L3
Shirkoak Kent 40 E7
Shirland Derbys 133 H8
Shirlett Shrops 96 E5
Shirley C Sotn 34 C6
Shirley Derbys 115 L3
Shirley Gt Lon 51 K6
Shirley Solhll 98 E7
Shirl Heath Herefs 80 A3
Shirrell Heath Hants 35 H8
Shirvan Ag & B 206 D2
Shirwell Devon 27 L3
Shiskine N Ayrs 194 E5
Shittlehope Dur 168 C3
Shobdon Herefs 79 M3
Shobley Hants 18 B2
Shobrooke Devon 13 K2
Shoby Leics 117 H7
Shocklach Ches W 113 G2
Shocklach Green Ches W 113 G2
Shoeburyness Sthend 53 K2
Sholden Kent 41 K5
Sholing C Sotn 19 G2
Shoot Hill Shrops 95 K1
Shop Cnwll 10 B7
Shop Cnwll 26 B7
Shopwyke W Susx 20 E6
Shore Rochdl 140 D4
Shoreditch Gt Lon 51 J2
Shoreditch Somset 30 C6
Shoreham Kent 52 B6
Shoreham-by-Sea W Susx 22 C6
Shoreswood Nthumb 202 E4
Shorley Hants 35 J5
Shorncote Gloucs 64 F7
Shorne Kent 52 E5
Shorta Cross Cnwll 6 B3
Shortbridge E Susx 23 G3
Shortfield Common Surrey 36 C2
Shortgate E Susx 23 H4
Short Heath Birm 98 E5
Shortheath Hants 36 A4
Short Heath Wsall 98 B3
Shortlanesend Cnwll 4 C5
Shortlees E Ayrs 196 E4
Shortstown Bed 86 B4
Shorwell IoW 19 G7
Shoscombe BaNES 45 L7
Shotesham Norfk 106 E4
Shotgate Essex 71 J8
Shotley Suffk 90 F8
Shotley Bridge Dur 180 D8
Shotleyfield Nthumb 180 C8
Shotley Gate Suffk 90 F8
Shotley Street Suffk 90 F8
Shottenden Kent 40 D4
Shottermill Surrey 36 C4
Shottery Warwks 82 E4
Shotteswell Warwks 83 K6
Shottisham Suffk 91 H6
Shottle Derbys 116 A2
Shottlegate Derbys 116 A2
Shotton Dur 169 K5
Shotton Dur 169 L3
Shotton Flints 129 H6
Shotton Nthumb 180 F3
Shotton Nthumb 202 C7
Shotton Colliery Dur 169 K3
Shotts N Lans 210 A7
Shotwick Ches W 129 H5
Shougle Moray 266 D5
Shouldham Norfk 104 D2
Shouldham Thorpe Norfk 104 D2
Shoulton Worcs 81 J3
Shover's Green E Susx 39 G7
Shraleybrook Staffs 114 B2
Shrawardine Shrops 112 F8
Shrawley Worcs 81 J2
Shreding Green Bucks 50 C3
Shrewley Warwks 82 F2
Shrewsbury Shrops 96 B1
Shrewton Wilts 33 J2
Shripney W Susx 20 F6
Shrivenham Oxon 47 K1
Shropham Norfk 105 K3
Shrub End Essex 72 D3
Shucknall Herefs 80 D6
Shudy Camps Cambs 88 C6
Shuna Ag & B 216 B5
Shurdington Gloucs 64 D3
Shurlock Row W & M 49 K4

Shurnock Worcs 82 B3
Shurrery Highld 279 J4
Shurrery Lodge Highld 279 J5
Shurton Somset 30 B2
Shustoke Warwks 99 G5
Shute Devon 13 L3
Shute Devon 14 F5
Shutford Oxon 83 J7
Shut Heath Staffs 114 D7
Shuthonger Gloucs 81 K8
Shutlanger Nhants 84 E5
Shutterton Devon 13 M6
Shutt Green Staffs 97 K2
Shuttington Warwks 99 H2
Shuttlewood Derbys 133 J5
Shuttleworth Bury 140 B4
Siabost W Isls 282 f2
Siadar W Isls 282 g1
Sibbertoft Nhants 100 E6
Sibdon Carwood Shrops 95 K6
Sibford Ferris Oxon 83 H7
Sibford Gower Oxon 83 H7
Sible Hedingham Essex 88 F8
Sibley's Green Essex 70 F2
Siblyback Cnwll 11 J8
Sibsey Lincs 119 K2
Sibsey Fenside Lincs 119 K1
Sibson Cambs 102 B4
Sibson Leics 99 K3
Sibster Highld 280 D5
Sibthorpe Notts 117 K2
Sibthorpe Notts 134 E5
Sibton Suffk 91 J2
Sicklesmere Suffk 89 H3
Sicklinghall N York 150 E6
Sidbrook Somset 30 C5
Sidbury Devon 14 D4
Sidbury Shrops 96 F6
Sid Cop Barns 142 B6
Sidcot N Som 44 E7
Sidcup Gt Lon 51 M4
Siddick Cumb 164 D4
Siddington Ches E 131 G5
Siddington Gloucs 64 C7
Sidemoor Worcs 81 L1
Sidestrand Norfk 122 F3
Sidford Devon 14 D4
Sidlesham W Susx 20 D7
Sidlesham Common W Susx 20 D6
Sidley E Susx 24 D5
Sidmouth Devon 14 D5
Siefton Shrops 96 K6
Sigford Devon 13 H7
Sigglesthorne E R Yk 153 J6
Sigingstone V Glam 42 E7
Signet Oxon 65 K5
Silchester Hants 48 F6
Sileby Leics 117 G8
Silecroft Cumb 155 L6
Silfield Norfk 106 C3
Silian Cerdgn 77 G5
Silkstead Hants 34 F6
Silkstone Barns 141 L6
Silkstone Common Barns 141 L6
Silk Willoughby Lincs 118 E3
Silloth Cumb 176 F8
Silpho N York 163 H4
Silsden C Brad 149 J6
Silsoe C Beds 86 B8
Silton Dorset 32 C5
Silverburn Mdloth 211 G7
Silverdale Lancs 157 G7
Silverdale Staffs 114 C2
Silver End Essex 71 K3
Silverford Abers 268 C3
Silvergate Norfk 122 D6
Silverlace Green Suffk 91 H3
Silverley's Green Suffk 106 F8
Silverstone Nhants 84 C4
Silver Street Kent 53 J7
Silver Street Somset 31 J4
Silverton Devon 13 M2
Silverwell Cnwll 4 B5
Silvington Shrops 96 E7
Simister Bury 140 C6
Simmondley Derbys 131 K1
Simonburn Nthumb 179 K4
Simonsbath Somset 28 D3
Simonsburrow Devon 29 L7
Simonstone Lancs 140 A1
Simonstone N York 158 F4
Simprim Border 202 C4
Simpson M Keyn 85 H8
Simpson Cross Pembks 54 E3
Sinclair's Hill Border 202 C3
Sinclairston E Ayrs 196 F7
Sinderby N York 160 E6
Sinderhope Nthumb 179 K8
Sinderland Green Traffd 130 E2
Sindlesham Wokham 49 J5

Sinfin C Derb 116 B5
Singleborough Bucks 67 J1
Single Street Gt Lon 51 L7
Singleton Kent 40 C7
Singleton Lancs 147 G8
Singleton W Susx 20 L4
Singlewell Kent 52 E5
Sinkhurst Green Kent 39 K5
Sinnarhard Abers 244 B1
Sinnington N York 162 C5
Sinton Worcs 81 J3
Sinton Worcs 81 J3
Sinton Green Worcs 81 J3
Sipson Gt Lon 50 D3
Sirhowy Blae G 61 J5
Sissinghurst Kent 39 K6
Siston S Glos 45 K4
Sitcott Devon 11 L4
Sithney Cnwll 3 G5
Sithney Common Cnwll 3 G5
Sithney Green Cnwll 3 G5
Sittingbourne Kent 40 B3
Six Ashes Shrops 97 H5
Six Bells Blae G 61 K6
Sixhills Lincs 136 C2
Six Mile Bottom Cambs 88 B4
Sixmile Cottages Kent 40 F6
Sixpenny Handley Dorset 33 G7
Six Rues Jersey 9 c2
Sizewell Suffk 91 L3
Skaill Ork 275 d5
Skares E Ayrs 197 G2
Skateraw Abers 245 K5
Skateraw E Loth 213 G4
Skeabost Highld 259 G7
Skeeby N York 160 B2
Skeffington Leics 101 G3
Skeffling E R Yk 145 K4
Skegby Notts 133 K7
Skegby Notts 134 F5
Skegness Lincs 137 L7
Skelbo Highld 264 B1
Skelbo Street Highld 264 B1
Skelbrooke Donc 142 D5
Skeldyke Lincs 119 K4
Skellingthorpe Lincs 135 J5
Skellorn Green Ches E 131 H3
Skellow Donc 142 E5
Skelmanthorpe Kirk 141 K5
Skelmersdale Lancs 138 F6
Skelmorlie N Ayrs 207 K5
Skelpick Highld 278 B6
Skelston D & G 185 K6
Skelton C York 151 J4
Skelton Cumb 166 B4
Skelton E R Yk 143 J3
Skelton N York 150 E2
Skelton N York 159 K3
Skelton R & Cl 170 F7
Skelwith Bridge Cumb 156 E2
Skendleby Lincs 137 H5
Skene House Abers 245 G2
Skenfrith Mons 62 F3
Skerne E R Yk 153 G5
Skerray Highld 277 L4
Skerricha Highld 276 C6
Skerton Lancs 147 J3
Sketchley Leics 99 L5
Sketty Swans 57 H6
Skewen Neath 57 K5
Skewsby N York 151 K2
Skeyton Norfk 122 E6
Skeyton Corner Norfk 122 E6
Skiall Highld 279 H3
Skidbrooke Lincs 137 H1
Skidbrooke North End Lincs 137 H1
Skidby E R Yk 144 C1
Skigersta W Isls 282 h1
Skilgate Somset 29 H5
Skillington Lincs 118 A6
Skinburness Cumb 176 F7
Skinflats Falk 210 B2
Skinidin Highld 258 C7
Skinners Green W Berk 48 C6
Skinningrove R & Cl 171 G6
Skipness Ag & B 206 B7
Skipper's Bridge D & G 177 L2
Skiprigg Cumb 165 L2
Skipsea E R Yk 153 J5
Skipsea Brough E R Yk 153 J5
Skipton N York 149 H5
Skipton-on-Swale N York 160 E6
Skipwith N York 151 L8
Skirlaugh E R Yk 153 J7
Skirling Border 199 J5
Skirmett Bucks 49 J1
Skirpenbeck E R Yk 152 A4
Skirwith Cumb 166 E4
Skirwith N York 158 C7
Skirza Highld 280 E3

Skitby Cumb 178 B5
Skittle Green Bucks 67 J6
Skokholm Island Pembks 54 B6
Skomer Island Pembks 54 B5
Skulamus Highld 247 L4
Skyborry Green Shrops 95 G8
Skye Green Essex 72 C3
Skye of Curr Highld 253 J6
Skyreholme N York 149 J4
Slack Calder 140 E2
Slackcote Oldham 140 E6
Slack Head Cumb 157 G6
Slackholme End Lincs 137 K5
Slacks of Cairnbanno Abers 256 F3
Slad Gloucs 64 C5
Slade Devon 14 D1
Slade Devon 27 J4
Slade Devon 28 E5
Slade End Oxon 48 E1
Slade Green Gt Lon 52 B4
Slade Heath Staffs 97 L2
Slade Hooton Rothm 133 K2
Sladesbridge Cnwll 10 E8
Slades Green Worcs 81 J8
Slaggyford Nthumb 178 F8
Slaidburn Lancs 148 C5
Slaithwaite Kirk 141 G5
Slaley Derbys 132 E8
Slaley Nthumb 180 A7
Slamannan Falk 209 M4
Slapton Bucks 68 B3
Slapton Devon 8 B6
Slapton Nhants 84 C6
Slattocks Rochdl 140 D6
Slaugham W Susx 37 L5
Slaughterford Wilts 46 B4
Slawston Leics 101 G4
Sleaford Hants 36 B3
Sleaford Lincs 118 E2
Sleagill Cumb 166 E6
Sleap Shrops 113 H6
Sleapford Wrekin 113 L8
Sleapshyde Herts 69 G5
Sleasdairidh Highld 272 F4
Slebech Pembks 55 H4
Sledge Green Worcs 81 J8
Sledmere E R Yk 152 E3
Sleetbeck Cumb 178 C3
Sleight Dorset 17 J3
Sleightholme Dur 168 B8
Sleights N York 162 F1
Slepe Dorset 17 H4
Slickly Highld 280 C3
Sliddery N Ayrs 193 J4
Sligachan Highld 247 G3
Sligrachan Ag & B 207 K1
Slimbridge Gloucs 63 L6
Slindon Staffs 114 C5
Slindon W Susx 20 F5
Slinfold W Susx 37 H4
Sling Gwynd 126 B6
Slingsby N York 162 B7
Slip End C Beds 68 D3
Slip End Herts 86 F7
Slipton Nhants 101 L7
Slitting Mill Staffs 115 G8
Slockavullin Ag & B 216 C7
Sloley Norfk 122 F6
Sloncombe Devon 13 H5
Sloothby Lincs 137 J5
Slough Slough 50 C3
Slough Crematorium Bucks 50 B3
Slough Green Somset 30 C7
Slough Green W Susx 37 L5
Slumbay Highld 248 E4
Slyfield Green Surrey 50 C8
Slyne Lancs 147 J3
Smailholm Border 201 K6
Smallbridge Rochdl 140 D5
Smallbrook Devon 13 K3
Smallbrook Gloucs 63 H7
Smallburgh Norfk 123 G6
Smalldale Derbys 132 B4
Smalldale Derbys 132 C3
Small Dole W Susx 22 C5
Smalley Derbys 116 C3
Smalley Common Derbys 116 C3
Smalley Green Derbys 116 C3
Smallfield Surrey 37 M2
Small Heath Birm 98 C6
Small Hythe Kent 25 G1
Smallridge Devon 15 G2
Smallthorne C Stke 114 D2
Smallways N York 168 A4
Smallwood Ches E 130 F7
Small Wood Hey Lancs 147 H6
Smallworth Norfk 105 K7
Smannell Hants 34 E1
Smardale Cumb 158 C1
Smarden Kent 39 L5

Smarden Bell Kent 39 L5
Smart's Hill Kent 38 E5
Smeafield Nthumb 203 H5
Smearisary Highld 237 J5
Smeatharpe Devon 30 B8
Smeeth Kent 40 E7
Smeeton Westerby Leics 100 E5
Smelthouses N York 150 B3
Smerral Highld 275 G2
Smestow Staffs 97 J5
Smethwick Sandw 98 C6
Smethwick Green Ches E 130 F7
Smisby Derbys 116 B7
Smitheclose IoW 19 J5
Smith End Green Worcs 81 H5
Smithfield Cumb 178 B6
Smith Green Lancs 147 J5
Smithies Barns 142 A6
Smithincott Devon 29 J8
Smith's End Herts 87 H7
Smith's Green Essex 70 E3
Smith's Green Essex 88 D7
Smithstown Highld 260 C4
Smithton Highld 252 D3
Smithy Bridge Rochdl 140 D5
Smithy Green Ches E 130 E5
Smithy Green Stockp 131 G3
Smithy Houses Derbys 116 C2
Smockington Leics 99 M5
Smoo Highld 277 G3
Smythe's Green Essex 72 D3
Snade D & G 185 L5
Snailbeach Shrops 95 J3
Snailwell Cambs 88 C2
Snainton N York 163 G6
Snaith E R Yk 143 G3
Snake Pass Inn Derbys 132 B2
Snape N York 160 C6
Snape Suffk 91 J3
Snape Green Lancs 138 D5
Snape Street Suffk 91 J4
Snaresbrook Gt Lon 51 L1
Snarestone Leics 99 K2
Snarford Lincs 135 L3
Snargate Kent 25 J2
Snave Kent 25 J1
Sneachill Worcs 81 L4
Snead Powys 95 H5
Sneath Common Norfk 106 D5
Sneaton N York 162 F1
Sneatonthorpe N York 162 F2
Snelland Lincs 135 M4
Snelson Ches E 130 F5
Snelston Derbys 115 J3
Snetterton Norfk 105 K5
Snettisham Norfk 120 F4
Snibston Leics 116 C8
Snig's End Gloucs 64 A1
Snitter Nthumb 190 E5
Snitterby Lincs 135 K1
Snitterfield Warwks 82 F3
Snitterton Derbys 132 E5
Snitton Shrops 96 D8
Snoadhill Kent 40 B6
Snodhill Herefs 79 K7
Snodland Kent 52 F6
Snoll Hatch Kent 39 G4
Snowden Hill Barns 141 L7
Snow End Herts 69 L1
Snowshill Gloucs 82 C8
Snow Street Norfk 106 B7
Soake Hants 19 L2
Soar Cardif 43 H5
Soar Devon 7 K7
Soar Powys 60 E1
Soay Highld 246 F6
Soberton Hants 35 J7
Soberton Heath Hants 35 J8
Sockbridge Cumb 166 C5
Sockburn Darltn 160 E1
Sodom Denbgs 128 C3
Sodylt Bank Shrops 112 E3
Soham Cambs 104 B8
Soham Cotes Cambs 104 B8
Solas W Isls 282 c7
Solbury Pembks 54 E4
Soldon Devon 26 E8
Soldon Cross Devon 26 E8
Soldridge Hants 35 K4
Sole Street Kent 40 E5
Sole Street Kent 52 E5
Solihull Solhll 98 F7
Sollers Dilwyn Herefs 80 A4
Sollers Hope Herefs 80 E8
Sollom Lancs 138 F4
Solva Pembks 74 C7
Solwaybank D & G 177 J3
Somerby Leics 101 G1
Somerby Lincs 144 D6
Somercotes Derbys 116 C1

Somerford Dorset 18 B5
Somerford Keynes Gloucs 64 E8
Somerley W Susx 20 D7
Somerleyton Suffk 107 K4
Somersal Herbert Derbys 115 J4
Somersby Lincs 136 F5
Somersham Cambs 103 G7
Somersham Suffk 90 C5
Somerton Oxon 66 D2
Somerton Somset 31 H5
Somerton Suffk 89 G4
Somerwood Shrops 113 J8
Sompting W Susx 21 K6
Sonning Wokham 49 J4
Sonning Common Oxon 49 H3
Sonning Eye Oxon 49 H4
Sontley Wrexhm 112 E2
Sopley Hants 18 B4
Sopworth Wilts 46 B2
Sorbie D & G 174 C5
Sordale Highld 279 L4
Sorisdale Ag & B 225 H3
Sorn E Ayrs 197 G5
Sortat Highld 280 C4
Sotby Lincs 136 D4
Sots Hole Lincs 136 B6
Sotterley Suffk 107 J6
Soughton Flints 128 F6
Soulbury Bucks 67 L2
Soulby Cumb 166 B5
Soulby Cumb 167 H8
Souldern Oxon 66 D1
Souldrop Bed 85 J3
Sound Ches E 113 K2
Sound Muir Moray 267 G5
Soundwell S Glos 45 J4
Sourton Devon 12 D4
Soutergate Cumb 156 B6
South Acre Norfk 121 H8
South Alkham Kent 41 H7
Southall Gt Lon 50 E3
South Allington Devon 8 B7
South Alloa Falk 210 A1
Southam Gloucs 64 E2
Southam Warwks 83 K3
South Ambersham W Susx 20 F3
Southampton C Sotn 19 G1
Southampton Crematorium
Hants 34 F7
South Anston Rothm 133 K3
South Ascot W & M 50 A5
South Ashford Kent 40 C7
South Baddesley Hants 18 E4
South Ballachulish Highld 229 G4
South Bank C York 151 J5
South Bank R & Cl 170 C6
South Barrow Somset 31 K5
South Beddington Gt Lon 51 H6
South Beer Cnwll 11 K4
South Benfleet Essex 53 G2
South Bersted W Susx 20 F6
South Bockhampton Dorset 18 B4
Southborough Gt Lon 51 L5
Southborough Kent 38 F5
Southbourne Bmouth 18 A5
Southbourne W Susx 20 C5
South Bowood Dorset 15 K3
South Bramwith Donc 143 G5
South Brent Devon 7 K3
South Brewham Somset 32 B4
South Bristol Crematorium
Bristl 45 H5
South Broomhill Nthumb 191 K6
Southburgh Norfk 105 K2
South Burlingham Norfk 107 H2
Southburn E R Yk 152 F5
South Cadbury Somset 31 K5
South Carlton Lincs 135 J4
South Carlton Notts 134 B3
South Cave E R Yk 144 A2
South Cerney Gloucs 64 F7
South Chailey E Susx 22 F4
South Chard Somset 15 H2
South Charlton Nthumb 191 H2
South Cheriton Somset 32 B6
South Church Dur 169 G5
Southchurch Sthend 53 J2
South Cleatlam Dur 168 E7
South Cliffe E R Yk 152 D8
South Clifton Notts 135 G5
South Cockerington Lincs 137 G2
South Cornelly Brdgnd 42 B5
Southcott Cnwll 11 H3
Southcott Devon 12 D4
Southcott Devon 13 H6
Southcott Devon 27 H7
Southcott Wilts 47 H7
Southcourt Bucks 67 K5
South Cove Suffk 107 K7
South Creake Norfk 121 J4

South Crosland Kirk 141 H5
South Croxton Leics 100 F2
South Dalton E R Yk 152 E6
South Darenth Kent 52 C5
South Duffield N York 143 H1
Southease E Susx 23 G6
South Elkington Lincs 136 E2
South Elmsall Wakefd 142 D5
Southend Ag & B 192 E6
South End E R Yk 145 K4
South End Hants 33 J7
South End Herefs 81 G6
South End N Linc 144 E4
South End Norfk 105 K5
Southend Wilts 47 J4
Southend Crematorium
Sthend 53 J2
Southend-on-Sea Sthend 53 J2
Southernby Cumb 165 L3
Southernden Kent 39 L4
Southerndown V Glam 42 D7
Southerness D & G 176 C7
South Erradale Highld 260 B5
Southerton Devon 14 C4
South Essex Crematorium
Gt Lon 52 C2
South Fambridge Essex 72 B8
South Fawley W Berk 48 A3
South Ferriby N Linc 144 B4
South Field E R Yk 144 C3
Southfield Falk 209 M4
Southfleet Kent 52 D5
Southford IoW 19 J7
Southgate Gt Lon 69 J8
Southgate Norfk 120 E5
Southgate Norfk 121 J4
Southgate Norfk 122 C6
Southgate Swans 57 G7
South Godstone Surrey 38 A4
South Gorley Hants 18 B2
South Gosforth N u Ty 181 G5
South Green Essex 71 G8
South Green Essex 72 F3
South Green Kent 53 J7
South Green Norfk 105 L1
South Green Suffk 106 D8
South Gyle C Edin 211 G4
South Hanningfield Essex 71 H7
South Harting W Susx 20 C3
South Hayling Hants 20 B6
South Hazelrigg Nthumb 203 G6
South Heath Bucks 67 M6
South Heighton E Susx 23 G6
South Hetton Dur 169 K2
South Hiendley Wakefd 142 B6
South Hill Cnwll 11 L8
South Hill Somset 31 G5
South Hinksey Oxon 66 D6
South Hole Devon 26 C6
South Holmwood Surrey 37 J2
South Hornchurch Gt Lon 52 B2
South Horrington Somset 31 J2
South Huish Devon 7 K6
South Hykeham Lincs 135 J6
South Hylton Sundld 181 J7
Southill C Beds 86 C6
Southington Hants 35 G1
South Kelsey Lincs 144 D8
South Kessock Highld 251 H2
South Killingholme N Linc 144 F4
South Kilvington N York 160 F6
South Kilworth Leics 100 D7
South Kirkby Wakefd 142 C5
South Knighton Devon 13 J8
South Kyme Lincs 119 G2
South Lanarkshire
Crematorium S Lans 209 H7
Southleigh Devon 14 E4
South Leigh Oxon 66 B5
South Leverton Notts 134 F3
South Littleton Worcs 82 C6
South London Crematorium
Gt Lon 51 H5
South Lopham Norfk 105 L7
South Luffenham Rutlnd 101 K3
South Malling E Susx 23 G5
South Marston Swindn 47 J2
South Merstham Surrey 51 H8
South Middleton Nthumb 190 E2
South Milford N York 142 D2
South Milton Devon 7 K6
South Mimms Herts 69 G6
Southminster Essex 72 D7
South Molton Devon 28 C5
South Moor Dur 180 F8
Southmoor Oxon 66 B7
South Moreton Oxon 48 E1
Southmuir Angus 234 B5
South Mundham W Susx 20 E6

South Muskham Notts 134 F8
South Newbald E R Yk 152 D8
South Newington Oxon 83 J8
South Newton Wilts 33 J4
South Normanton Derbys 133 J8
South Norwood Gt Lon 51 J5
South Nutfield Surrey 37 M1
South Ockendon Thurr 52 D2
Southoe Cambs 86 D2
Southolt Suffk 90 E2
South Ormsby Lincs 137 G4
Southorpe C Pete 102 B3
South Ossett Wakefd 141 L4
South Otterington N York 160 E5
Southover Dorset 16 B4
Southover E Susx 24 B2
South Owersby Lincs 135 L1
Southowram Calder 141 H3
South Park Surrey 37 K1
South Perrott Dorset 15 L1
South Petherton Somset 31 G7
South Petherwin Cnwll 11 K6
South Pickenham Norfk 105 G3
South Pill Cnwll 6 E3
South Pool Devon 7 M6
South Poorton Dorset 15 M3
Southport Sefton 138 D4
Southport Crematorium
Lancs 138 D5
South Queensferry C Edin 210 F3
South Radworthy Devon 28 C4
South Rauceby Lincs 118 D2
South Raynham Norfk 121 J6
South Reddish Stockp 131 H1
Southrepps Norfk 122 E4
South Reston Lincs 137 G3
Southrey Lincs 136 B6
South Ronaldsay Ork 275 c6
Southrop Gloucs 65 J6
Southrope Hants 35 K2
South Runcton Norfk 104 C2
South Scarle Notts 135 G7
Southsea C Port 19 L4
Southsea Wrexhm 112 D1
South Shian Ag & B 228 E7
South Shields S Tyne 181 J5
South Shields Crematorium
S Tyne 181 J6
South Shore Bpool 138 C1
Southside Dur 168 E5
South Somercotes Lincs 137 H1
South Stainley N York 150 D3
South Stifford Thurr 52 D3
South Stoke BaNES 45 L6
South Stoke Oxon 48 F2
South Stoke W Susx 21 H5
South Stour Kent 40 D7
South Street Kent 40 D4
South Street Kent 40 F2
South Street Kent 52 D6
South Tarbrax S Lans 199 H3
South Tawton Devon 12 F4
South Tehidy Cnwll 3 G3
South Thoresby Lincs 137 G4
South Thorpe Dur 168 E7
South Town Hants 35 K4
Southtown Norfk 107 L2
Southtown Somset 30 D7
South Uist W Isls 283 c10
Southwaite Cumb 166 B2
South Walsham Norfk 107 H1
Southwark Gt Lon 51 J3
South Warnborough Hants 35 L2
Southwater W Susx 37 J5
Southwater Street W Susx 37 J5
Southway Somset 31 H2
South Weald Essex 70 E8
Southwell Dorset 16 D8
Southwell Notts 117 J1
South West Middlesex
Crematorium Gt Lon 50 E4
South Weston Oxon 67 H7
South Wheatley Cnwll 11 J4
Southwick Hants 19 L2
Southwick Nhants 101 M5
Southwick Somset 30 E2
Southwick Sundld 181 J7
Southwick W Susx 22 C6
Southwick Wilts 46 B7
South Widcombe BaNES 45 H7
South Wigston Leics 100 D4
South Willesborough Kent 40 D7
South Willingham Lincs 136 C3
South Wingate Dur 169 L4
South Wingfield Derbys 133 G8
South Witham Lincs 118 B7
Southwold Suffk 107 K8
South Wonston Hants 34 F4
Southwood Norfk 107 H2
Southwood Somset 31 G4

South Woodham Ferrers
Essex 71 K7
South Wootton Norfk 120 E7
South Wraxall Wilts 46 B6
South Zeal Devon 12 F4
Sowerby Calder 141 G3
Sowerby N York 160 F6
Sowerby Bridge Calder 141 G4
Sowerby Row Cumb 165 L3
Sower Carr Lancs 147 G2
Sowerhill Somset 28 F6
Sowhill Torfn 62 B7
Sowley Green Suffk 88 E5
Sowood Calder 141 G4
Sowton Devon 6 C7
Sowton Devon 14 A4
Soyland Town Calder 140 F4
Spa Common Norfk 122 F5
Spain's End Essex 88 D7
Spalding Lincs 119 H7
Spaldington E R Yk 143 J1
Spaldwick Cambs 86 C1
Spalford Notts 135 G6
Spanby Lincs 118 E4
Spanish Green Hants 49 G7
Sparham Norfk 122 B7
Sparhamill Norfk 122 B7
Spark Bridge Cumb 156 D5
Sparket Cumb 166 B5
Sparkford Somset 31 K5
Sparkhill Birm 98 E6
Sparkwell Devon 7 H3
Sparrow Green Norfk 121 L8
Sparrowpit Derbys 132 B3
Sparrows Green E Susx 39 G4
Sparsholt Hants 34 F4
Sparsholt Oxon 47 M2
Spartylea Nthumb 167 K1
Spath Staffs 115 H4
Spaunton N York 162 C5
Spaxton Somset 30 C3
Spean Bridge Highld 239 L7
Spear Hill W Susx 21 K3
Spearywell Hants 34 D5
Speen Bucks 67 K7
Speen W Berk 48 E5
Speeton N York 163 L7
Speke Lpool 129 K3
Speldhurst Kent 38 E5
Spellbrook Herts 70 C4
Spelmonden Kent 39 H6
Spelsbury Oxon 65 M3
Spen Kirk 141 H3
Spencers Wood Wokham 49 H5
Spen Green Ches E 130 F7
Spennithorne N York 159 L5
Spennymoor Dur 169 H4
Spernall Warwks 82 C3
Spetchley Worcs 81 K4
Spetisbury Dorset 17 H2
Spexhall Suffk 107 H1
Spey Bay Moray 267 G3
Speybridge Highld 253 K6
Speyview Moray 254 E3
Spilsby Lincs 137 G7
Spindlestone Nthumb 203 J6
Spinkhill Derbys 133 J4
Spinningdale Highld 263 J2
Spion Kop Notts 133 L6
Spirthill Wilts 46 E4
Spital Wirral 129 H3
Spital Hill Donc 134 C1
Spital in the Street Lincs 135 K2
Spithurst E Susx 23 G4
Spittal E Loth 212 A4
Spittal E R Yk 152 B3
Spittal Highld 279 L5
Spittal Nthumb 202 F3
Spittal Pembks 55 G2
Spittalfield P & K 233 H7
Spittal of Glenmuick Abers 243 K6
Spittal of Glenshee P & K 233 H2
Spittal-on-Rule Border 189 G2
Spixworth Norfk 122 E7
Splatt Cnwll 10 C7
Splatt Cnwll 11 J5
Splatt Devon 12 E2
Splayne's Green E Susx 23 G4
Splottlands Cardif 43 K6
Spofforth N York 150 E5
Spondon C Derb 116 C4
Spon Green Flints 129 G7
Spooner Row Norfk 106 B4
Sporle Norfk 105 G1
Spott E Loth 212 E4
Spottiswoode Border 201 J3
Spratton Nhants 84 D1
Spreakley Surrey 36 B3
Spreyton Devon 13 G3
Spriddlestone Devon 7 G4

Spridlington Lincs ... 135 K3
Springburn C Glas ... 209 G5
Springfield D & G ... 177 K5
Springfield Essex ... 71 H5
Springfield Fife ... 222 H1
Springhill Staffs ... 98 B3
Springhill Staffs ... 98 D2
Springholm D & G ... 175 K1
Springside N Ayrs ... 196 B6
Springthorpe Lincs ... 135 H2
Spring Vale Barns ... 141 L7
Springwell Sundld ... 181 G7
Springwood Crematorium
Lpool ... 129 K3
Sproatley E R Yk ... 145 F1
Sproston Green Ches W ... 130 E6
Sprotbrough Donc ... 142 E7
Sproughton Suffk ... 90 D6
Sprouston Border ... 202 B6
Sprowston Norfk ... 106 E1
Sproxton Leics ... 117 M6
Sproxton N York ... 161 K6
Spunhill Shrops ... 112 F5
Spurstow Ches E ... 130 A8
Spyway Dorset ... 15 M4
Square & Compass Pembks ... 74 D6
Stableford Shrops ... 97 G4
Stableford Staffs ... 114 C4
Stacey Bank Sheff ... 132 F2
Stackhouse N York ... 148 E3
Stackpole Pembks ... 55 G7
Stacksteads Lancs ... 140 C3
Staddiscombe C Plym ... 7 G4
Staddlethorpe E R Yk ... 143 L2
Staden Derbys ... 131 L5
Stadhampton Oxon ... 66 F7
Stadhlaigearraidh W Isls ... 283 b10
Staffield Cumb ... 166 D2
Staffin Highld ... 259 H3
Stafford Staffs ... 114 E7
Stafford Crematorium Staffs ... 114 E6
Stagsden Bed ... 85 J5
Stainborough Barns ... 141 M7
Stainburn Cumb ... 164 D5
Stainburn N York ... 150 C6
Stainby Lincs ... 118 B7
Staincross Barns ... 141 M5
Staindrop Dur ... 168 E6
Staines-upon-Thames Surrey ... 50 D5
Stainfield Lincs ... 118 E6
Stainfield Lincs ... 136 B5
Stainforth Donc ... 143 G5
Stainforth N York ... 148 E2
Staining Lancs ... 147 G3
Stainland Calder ... 141 G4
Stainsacre N York ... 163 G1
Stainsby Derbys ... 133 J6
Stainton Cumb ... 157 H5
Stainton Cumb ... 166 C5
Stainton Cumb ... 177 L7
Stainton Donc ... 133 L1
Stainton Dur ... 168 D7
Stainton Middsb ... 170 B7
Stainton N York ... 159 K3
Stainton by Langworth
Lincs ... 135 L4
Staintondale N York ... 163 H3
Stainton le Vale Lincs ... 136 C1
Stainton with Adgarley
Cumb ... 146 E1
Stair Cumb ... 165 H6
Stair E Ayrs ... 196 E6
Stairfoot Barns ... 142 B6
Stairhaven D & G ... 172 F4
Staithes N York ... 171 H7
Stakeford Nthumb ... 181 G2
Stake Pool Lancs ... 147 H6
Stakes Hants ... 19 M2
Stalbridge Dorset ... 32 B7
Stalbridge Weston Dorset ... 32 B7
Stalham Norfk ... 123 H6
Stalham Green Norfk ... 123 H6
Stalisfield Green Kent ... 40 B5
Stalland Common Norfk ... 105 L4
Stallen Dorset ... 31 K7
Stallingborough NE Lin ... 145 G5
Stalling Busk N York ... 159 G5
Stallington Staffs ... 114 E4
Stalmine Lancs ... 147 G6
Stalmine Moss Side Lancs ... 147 G6
Stalybridge Tamesd ... 140 E8
Stambourne Essex ... 88 E7
Stambourne Green Essex ... 88 E7
Stamford Lincs ... 102 A2
Stamford Nthumb ... 191 J2
Stamford Bridge Ches W ... 129 K6
Stamford Bridge E R Yk ... 151 M5
Stamfordham Nthumb ... 180 C4
Stamford Hill Gt Lon ... 51 J2

Stanah Lancs ... 147 G7
Stanborough Herts ... 69 G5
Stanbridge C Beds ... 68 B2
Stanbridge Dorset ... 17 K2
Stanbury C Brad ... 149 H8
Stand Bury ... 140 B6
Stand N Lans ... 209 K5
Standburn Falk ... 210 B4
Standeford Staffs ... 97 K2
Standen Kent ... 39 L5
Standen Street Kent ... 39 K7
Standerwick Somset ... 32 D1
Standford Hants ... 36 B4
Standingstone Cumb ... 164 D4
Standish Gloucs ... 64 A5
Standish Wigan ... 139 H5
Standish Lower Ground Wigan ... 139 H6
Standlake Oxon ... 66 B6
Standon Hants ... 34 F5
Standon Herts ... 69 K3
Standon Staffs ... 114 C4
Standon Green End Herts ... 69 K3
Standwell Green Suffk ... 90 D1
Stane N Lans ... 210 A7
Stanfield Norfk ... 121 K7
Stanford C Beds ... 86 D7
Stanford Kent ... 40 F7
Stanford Shrops ... 95 H1
Stanford Bishop Herefs ... 80 F5
Stanford Bridge Worcs ... 81 G2
Stanford Bridge Wrekin ... 113 M6
Stanford Dingley W Berk ... 48 E4
Stanford in the Vale Oxon ... 65 M8
Stanford le Hope Thurr ... 52 E3
Stanford on Avon Nhants ... 100 D7
Stanford on Soar Notts ... 116 E7
Stanford on Teme Worcs ... 81 G2
Stanford Rivers Essex ... 70 D7
Stanfree Derbys ... 133 J5
Stanghow R & Cl ... 170 F7
Stanground C Pete ... 102 D4
Stanhill Lancs ... 139 L2
Stanhoe Norfk ... 121 H4
Stanhope Border ... 199 K7
Stanhope Dur ... 168 C3
Stanhope Kent ... 40 C7
Stanhope Bretby Derbys ... 115 M7
Stanion Nhants ... 101 K6
Stanklin Worcs ... 97 J8
Stanley Derbys ... 116 C3
Stanley Dur ... 180 F6
Stanley Notts ... 133 J7
Stanley P & K ... 221 K1
Stanley Shrops ... 97 G6
Stanley Staffs ... 114 E1
Stanley Wakefd ... 142 A3
Stanley Common Derbys ... 116 C3
Stanley Crook Dur ... 168 F3
Stanley Ferry Wakefd ... 142 A3
Stanley Gate Lancs ... 138 F6
Stanley Moor Staffs ... 114 E1
Stanley Pontlarge Gloucs ... 64 E1
Stanmer Br & H ... 22 E5
Stanmore Gt Lon ... 68 F8
Stanmore Hants ... 34 F5
Stanmore W Berk ... 48 C3
Stannersburn Nthumb ... 179 G2
Stanningfield Suffk ... 89 H4
Stanningley Leeds ... 141 K1
Stannington Nthumb ... 180 F3
Stannington Sheff ... 132 F2
Stannington Station Nthumb ... 180 F3
Stansbatch Herefs ... 79 L3
Stansfield Suffk ... 88 F5
Stanshope Staffs ... 115 J1
Stanstead Suffk ... 89 G5
Stanstead Abbotts Herts ... 69 K5
Stansted Kent ... 52 D6
Stansted Mountfitchet Essex ... 70 D2
Stanton Derbys ... 115 M7
Stanton Gloucs ... 82 C8
Stanton Mons ... 62 C3
Stanton Nthumb ... 191 G8
Stanton Staffs ... 115 J2
Stanton Suffk ... 105 K8
Stanton by Bridge Derbys ... 116 B6
Stanton by Dale Derbys ... 116 D4
Stanton Drew BaNES ... 45 H6
Stanton Fitzwarren Swindn ... 47 J1
Stanton Harcourt Oxon ... 66 B6
Stanton Hill Notts ... 133 J7
Stanton in Peak Derbys ... 132 E6
Stanton Lacy Shrops ... 96 B7
Stanton Lees Derbys ... 132 E7
Stanton Long Shrops ... 96 D5
Stanton on the Wolds Notts ... 117 G5
Stanton Prior BaNES ... 45 K6
Stanton St Bernard Wilts ... 47 G7
Stanton St John Oxon ... 66 E5
Stanton St Quintin Wilts ... 46 C3

Stanton Street Suffk ... 89 J2
Stanton under Bardon Leics ... 100 A1
Stanton upon Hine Heath
Shrops ... 113 J6
Stanton Wick BaNES ... 45 J6
Stantway Gloucs ... 63 L4
Stanwardine in the Field
Shrops ... 112 F6
Stanwardine in the Wood
Shrops ... 113 G6
Stanway Essex ... 72 D2
Stanway Gloucs ... 64 F1
Stanway Green Essex ... 72 D2
Stanway Green Suffk ... 90 F1
Stanwell Surrey ... 50 D4
Stanwell Moor Surrey ... 50 D4
Stanwick Nhants ... 85 J1
Stanwix Cumb ... 177 L7
Staoinebrig W Isls ... 283 b10
Stape N York ... 162 D4
Stapehill Dorset ... 17 L3
Stapeley Ches E ... 113 L2
Stapenhill Staffs ... 115 L7
Staple Kent ... 41 L4
Staple Cross Devon ... 29 J6
Staple Cross E Susx ... 24 E3
Staplefield W Susx ... 37 L5
Staple Fitzpaine Somset ... 30 C7
Stapleford Cambs ... 87 K5
Stapleford Herts ... 69 J4
Stapleford Leics ... 117 L7
Stapleford Lincs ... 135 H8
Stapleford Notts ... 116 E4
Stapleford Wilts ... 33 J3
Stapleford Abbotts Essex ... 70 D8
Stapleford Tawney Essex ... 70 D7
Staplegrove Somset ... 30 B5
Staplehay Somset ... 30 B6
Staple Hill Worcs ... 98 B8
Staplehurst Kent ... 39 K5
Staplers IoW ... 19 H6
Staplestreet Kent ... 40 D3
Stapleton Cumb ... 178 C4
Stapleton Herefs ... 79 L2
Stapleton Leics ... 99 L4
Stapleton N York ... 169 H8
Stapleton Shrops ... 95 L3
Stapleton Somset ... 31 G6
Stapley Somset ... 30 B8
Staploe Bed ... 86 C3
Staplow Herefs ... 80 F7
Star Fife ... 222 E6
Star Pembks ... 75 M5
Star Somset ... 44 E7
Starbeck N York ... 150 D4
Starbotton N York ... 159 G7
Starcross Devon ... 14 A6
Stareton Warwks ... 83 H1
Starkholmes Derbys ... 132 F7
Starlings Green Essex ... 70 C1
Starr's Green E Susx ... 24 D4
Starston Norfk ... 106 E6
Start Devon ... 8 B6
Startforth Dur ... 168 D7
Startley Wilts ... 46 D3
Statenborough Kent ... 41 J4
Statham Warrtn ... 130 D2
Stathe Somset ... 30 E5
Stathern Leics ... 117 K5
Station Town Dur ... 169 L3
Staughton Green Cambs ... 86 C2
Staughton Highway Cambs ... 86 C2
Staunton Gloucs ... 63 H4
Staunton Gloucs ... 63 L3
Staunton in the Vale Notts ... 117 L3
Staunton on Arrow Herefs ... 79 L3
Staunton on Wye Herefs ... 79 L6
Staveley Cumb ... 156 E5
Staveley Cumb ... 157 G3
Staveley Derbys ... 133 H5
Staveley N York ... 150 E3
Staverton Devon ... 8 B2
Staverton Gloucs ... 64 C2
Staverton Nhants ... 83 M3
Staverton Wilts ... 46 B6
Staverton Bridge Gloucs ... 64 C2
Stawell Somset ... 30 E3
Stawley Somset ... 29 J6
Staxigoe Highld ... 280 E5
Staxton N York ... 163 J4
Staylittle Cerdgn ... 92 E5
Staylittle Powys ... 93 J5
Staynall Lancs ... 147 G6
Staythorpe Notts ... 117 K1
Stead C Brad ... 149 L6
Stean N York ... 159 K8
Stearsby N York ... 151 K2
Steart Somset ... 30 C2
Stebbing Essex ... 71 G2
Stebbing Green Essex ... 71 G2

Stechford Birm ... 98 E6
Stede Quarter Kent ... 39 L5
Stedham W Susx ... 36 C6
Steel Nthumb ... 179 L7
Steel Cross E Susx ... 38 E7
Steelend Fife ... 210 D1
Steele Road Border ... 188 F7
Steel Green Cumb ... 155 L6
Steel Heath Shrops ... 113 J4
Steen's Bridge Herefs ... 80 C4
Steep Hants ... 35 M6
Steephill IoW ... 19 J8
Steep Lane Calder ... 140 F3
Steeple Dorset ... 17 H6
Steeple Essex ... 72 D6
Steeple Ashton Wilts ... 46 C7
Steeple Aston Oxon ... 66 C2
Steeple Barton Oxon ... 66 C2
Steeple Bumpstead Essex ... 88 D7
Steeple Claydon Bucks ... 67 H2
Steeple Gidding Cambs ... 102 C7
Steeple Langford Wilts ... 33 H3
Steeple Morden Cambs ... 86 F6
Steeton C Brad ... 149 J7
Stein Highld ... 258 D5
Stella Gatesd ... 180 E6
Stelling Minnis Kent ... 40 F6
Stembridge Somset ... 30 F6
Stenalees Cnwll ... 5 G3
Stenhouse D & G ... 185 K4
Stenhousemuir Falk ... 210 A2
Stenigot Lincs ... 136 D3
Stenscholl Highld ... 259 H3
Stenson Fields Derbys ... 116 B5
Stenton E Loth ... 212 D4
Steornabhagh W Isls ... 282 g3
Stepaside Pembks ... 55 K5
Stepford D & G ... 185 L6
Stepney Gt Lon ... 51 K3
Stepping Hill Stockp ... 131 H2
Steppingley C Beds ... 85 K8
Stepps N Lans ... 209 H5
Sternfield Suffk ... 91 J3
Stert Wilts ... 46 F7
Stetchworth Cambs ... 88 C3
Stevenage Herts ... 69 G2
Steven's Crouch E Susx ... 24 C4
Stevenston N Ayrs ... 196 B3
Steventon Hants ... 35 H1
Steventon Oxon ... 48 C1
Steventon End Essex ... 88 B6
Stevington Bed ... 85 K4
Stewartby Bed ... 85 K6
Stewartfield S Lans ... 209 G7
Stewarton E Ayrs ... 196 E2
Stewkley Bucks ... 67 K2
Stewley Somset ... 30 D7
Stewton Lincs ... 137 G2
Steyne Cross IoW ... 19 L6
Steyning W Susx ... 21 L4
Steynton Pembks ... 54 E5
Stibb Cnwll ... 26 C3
Stibbard Norfk ... 121 L6
Stibb Cross Devon ... 27 G7
Stibb Green Wilts ... 47 J6
Stibbington Cambs ... 102 B4
Stichill Border ... 201 L5
Sticker Cnwll ... 5 G5
Stickford Lincs ... 136 F7
Sticklepath Devon ... 12 F4
Sticklepath Somset ... 29 J4
Stickling Green Essex ... 87 K8
Stickney Lincs ... 136 F8
Stiffkey Norfk ... 121 L3
Stifford's Bridge Herefs ... 81 G5
Stiff Street Kent ... 53 J6
Stile Bridge Kent ... 39 J4
Stileway Somset ... 31 G3
Stilligarry W Isls ... 283 b10
Stillingfleet N York ... 151 J7
Stillington N York ... 151 J2
Stillington S on T ... 169 K6
Stilton Cambs ... 102 D5
Stinchcombe Gloucs ... 63 L7
Stinsford Dorset ... 16 D4
Stiperstones Shrops ... 95 J3
Stirchley Birm ... 98 D7
Stirchley Wrekin ... 96 F2
Stirling Abers ... 257 L3
Stirling Stirlg ... 220 D8
Stirtloe Cambs ... 86 D2
Stirton N York ... 149 H5
Stisted Essex ... 71 J2
Stitchcombe Wilts ... 47 K5
Stithians Cnwll ... 3 J4
Stivichall Covtry ... 99 J8
Stixwould Lincs ... 136 C6
Stoak Ches W ... 129 K5
Stobo Border ... 199 L5
Stoborough Dorset ... 17 H5

Stoborough Green Dorset........... 17 H5
Stobs Castle Border 188 E4
Stobswood Nthumb.................. 191 J7
Stock Essex 71 G7
Stock N Som 44 F6
Stockbridge Hants...................... 34 D4
Stockbriggs S Lans................... 198 C6
Stockbury Kent 53 H6
Stockcross W Berk 48 B5
Stockdalewath Cumb............... 165 L2
Stocker's Hill Kent..................... 40 C5
Stockerston Leics..................... 101 H4
Stock Green Worcs 82 A3
Stocking Herefs 63 J1
Stockingford Warwks 99 J5
Stocking Pelham Herts 70 C1
Stockland Devon 14 F2
Stockland Bristol Somset 30 C2
Stockland Green Kent................. 38 E5
Stockleigh English Devon........... 13 K2
Stockleigh Pomeroy Devon 13 K2
Stockley Wilts 46 E5
Stockley Hill Herefs 79 L7
Stocklinch Somset...................... 30 F7
Stockmoor Herefs 79 M4
Stockport Stockp..................... 131 H2
Stockport Crematorium
    Stockp.................................... 131 H2
Stocksbridge Sheff.................. 141 L8
Stocksfield Nthumb.................. 180 C6
Stockton Herefs 80 C3
Stockton Norfk......................... 107 H4
Stockton Shrops 95 G3
Stockton Shrops 97 G3
Stockton Warwks 83 K3
Stockton Wilts 33 G3
Stockton Wrekin 114 B8
Stockton Brook Staffs.............. 114 E1
Stockton Heath Warrtn............. 130 B3
Stockton-on-Tees S on T 170 B6
Stockton on Teme Worcs 81 G2
Stockton on the Forest C York ... 151 L4
Stockwell Gloucs 64 D4
Stockwell End Wolves 97 K3
Stockwell Heath Staffs............. 115 G7
Stockwood Bristl........................ 45 J5
Stockwood Dorset 16 B1
Stock Wood Worcs 82 B3
Stodday Lancs 147 J4
Stodmarsh Kent......................... 41 H3
Stody Norfk.............................. 122 B4
Stoer Highld 270 D2
Stoford Somset 31 J8
Stoford Wilts 33 J4
Stogumber Somset..................... 29 K3
Stogursey Somset...................... 30 B2
Stoke Covtry 99 K7
Stoke Devon 26 D6
Stoke Hants 20 B6
Stoke Hants 48 B8
Stoke Medway............................ 53 H4
Stoke Abbott Dorset 15 K3
Stoke Albany Nhants................ 101 H5
Stoke Ash Suffk......................... 90 D1
Stoke Bardolph Notts 117 H3
Stoke Bliss Worcs 80 F3
Stoke Bruerne Nhants................ 84 E5
Stoke by Clare Suffk 88 E6
Stoke-by-Nayland Suffk 89 K7
Stoke Canon Devon 13 L3
Stoke Charity Hants 35 G3
Stoke Climsland Cnwll 11 L7
Stoke Cross Herefs..................... 80 E5
Stoke D'Abernon Surrey 50 E7
Stoke Doyle Nhants 102 A6
Stoke Dry Rutlnd...................... 101 J4
Stoke Edith Herefs..................... 80 E7
Stoke End Warwks 98 F4
Stoke Farthing Wilts 33 H5
Stoke Ferry Norfk..................... 104 D3
Stoke Fleming Devon................... 8 C5
Stokeford Dorset 17 G5
Stoke Gabriel Devon 8 C3
Stoke Gifford S Glos 45 J3
Stoke Golding Leics 99 L4
Stoke Goldington M Keyn 85 G5
Stoke Green Bucks 50 B3
Stokeham Notts 134 F4
Stoke Hammond Bucks 67 L1
Stoke Heath Shrops 113 L5
Stoke Heath Worcs 81 L2
Stoke Holy Cross Norfk........... 106 E3
Stokeinteignhead Devon 13 L8
Stoke Lacy Herefs...................... 80 E5
Stoke Lyne Oxon 66 E2
Stoke Mandeville Bucks 67 K5
Stokenchurch Bucks 67 J7
Stoke Newington Gt Lon 51 J2
Stokenham Devon 8 B6
Stoke-on-Trent C Stke.............. 114 D2

Stoke Orchard Gloucs............... 64 D2
Stoke Poges Bucks 50 B2
Stoke Pound Worcs................... 81 M2
Stoke Prior Herefs 80 C4
Stoke Prior Worcs...................... 81 L2
Stoke Rivers Devon 27 L4
Stoke Rochford Lincs 118 B6
Stoke Row Oxon 49 G2
Stoke St Gregory Somset 30 C5
Stoke St Mary Somset 30 C6
Stoke St Michael Somset 31 L2
Stoke St Milborough Shrops 96 D7
Stokesay Shrops 95 K7
Stokesby Norfk......................... 107 J1
Stokesley N York 161 H1
Stoke sub Hamdon Somset........ 31 J7
Stoke Talmage Oxon 67 G7
Stoke Trister Somset 32 B5
Stoke upon Tern Shrops 113 L6
Stoke-upon-Trent C Stke......... 114 D3
Stoke Wake Dorset 16 E1
Stoke Wharf Worcs..................... 81 L2
Stolford Somset 30 C2
Stondon Massey Essex 70 E7
Stone Bucks 67 J4
Stone Gloucs 63 K8
Stone Kent 52 C4
Stone Rothm............................ 133 L2
Stone Somset 31 J4
Stone Staffs 114 E5
Stone Worcs 97 J8
Stonea Cambs.......................... 103 J5
Stone Allerton Somset 30 F1
Ston Easton Somset 45 J8
Stonebridge N Som 44 D7
Stonebridge Norfk................... 105 J3
Stonebridge Warwks 99 G6
Stone Bridge Corner C Pete..... 102 F3
Stonebroom Derbys 133 H3
Stone Chair Calder 141 H2
Stone Cross E Susx 23 K6
Stone Cross E Susx 38 D7
Stone Cross E Susx 39 G7
Stone Cross Kent....................... 38 E5
Stone Cross Kent....................... 40 D7
Stone Cross Kent....................... 41 K4
Stonecross Green Suffk 89 G4
Stonecrouch Kent...................... 39 H6
Stone-edge-Batch N Som 44 F4
Stoneferry C KuH...................... 144 E2
Stonefield Castle Hotel Ag & B.. 206 D5
Stonegate E Susx 39 G7
Stonegate N York 162 D1
Stonegrave N York 161 L7
Stonehall Worcs 81 K5
Stonehaugh Nthumb................ 179 J4
Stonehaven Abers 245 J6
Stone Hill Donc 143 H6
Stonehouse C Plym 6 F4
Stone House Cumb.................. 158 D5
Stonehouse Gloucs 64 A6
Stonehouse Nthumb................ 179 G7
Stonehouse S Lans................... 198 C4
Stone in Oxney Kent 25 H2
Stoneleigh Warwks 83 H1
Stoneley Green Ches E 113 K1
Stonely Cambs........................... 86 C2
Stoner Hill Hants 35 M5
Stonesby Leics 117 L6
Stonesfield Oxon 66 B4
Stones Green Essex 73 H2
Stone Street Kent....................... 38 F2
Stone Street Suffk 89 K6
Stone Street Suffk 89 K7
Stone Street Suffk 107 H7
Stonestreet Green Kent............. 40 E7
Stonethwaite Cumb................. 165 J7
Stonewells Moray 266 F3
Stonewood Kent........................ 52 D4
Stoneybridge W Isls 283 b10
Stoneybridge Worcs 97 L8
Stoneyburn W Loth 210 C6
Stoney Cross Hants.................... 18 D1
Stoneygate C Leic 100 D3
Stoneyhills Essex 72 D7
Stoneykirk D & G 172 C3
Stoney Middleton Derbys 132 E4
Stoney Stanton Leics............... 100 B4
Stoney Stoke Somset................. 32 B4
Stoney Stratton Somset............. 31 L3
Stoney Stretton Shrops 95 J2
Stoneywood C Aber 245 K1
Stoneywood Falk..................... 209 L2
Stonham Aspal Suffk................. 90 D3
Stonnall Staffs 98 D3
Stonor Oxon 49 H1
Stonton Wyville Leics 101 G4
Stony Cross Herefs..................... 80 D1
Stony Cross Herefs..................... 81 G5
Stonyford Hants......................... 34 D7

Stony Houghton Derbys 133 K6
Stony Stratford M Keyn 84 F7
Stonywell Staffs 98 D1
Stoodleigh Devon 28 B4
Stoodleigh Devon 29 G3
Stopham W Susx 21 H3
Stopsley Luton 68 E2
Stoptide Cnwll 10 C7
Storeton Wirral 129 G3
Storeyard Green Herefs 81 G6
Storridge Herefs 81 H5
Storrington W Susx 21 J4
Storth Cumb............................ 157 G6
Storwood E R Yk 151 M7
Stotfield Moray 266 E2
Stotfold C Beds 86 E7
Stottesdon Shrops 96 F6
Stoughton Leics 100 E3
Stoughton Surrey....................... 50 C8
Stoughton W Susx 20 C4
Stoulton Worcs 81 L5
Stourbridge Dudley 97 K6
Stourbridge Crematorium
    Dudley 97 K6
Stourpaine Dorset 17 G1
Stourport-on-Severn Worcs 81 J1
Stour Provost Dorset 32 C6
Stour Row Dorset 32 D6
Stourton Leeds 141 M2
Stourton Staffs 97 K6
Stourton Warwks 83 G7
Stourton Wilts 32 C4
Stourton Caundle Dorset 32 B7
Stout Somset 31 G4
Stove Shet 281 e8
Stoven Suffk 107 J7
Stow Border 200 F4
Stow Lincs 135 H3
Stow Bardolph Norfk.............. 104 C2
Stow Bedon Norfk.................. 105 J4
Stowbridge Norfk.................... 104 B2
Stow-cum-Quy Cambs 87 L3
Stowe Gloucs 63 H5
Stowe Shrops 95 H8
Stowe by Chartley Staffs.......... 114 F6
Stowehill Nhants 84 C3
Stowell Somset 31 L6
Stowey BaNES 45 H7
Stowford Devon 12 B3
Stowford Devon 12 B5
Stowford Devon 14 D5
Stowford Devon 28 B3
Stowlangtoft Suffk..................... 89 J2
Stow Longa Cambs 86 C1
Stow Maries Essex 71 K7
Stowmarket Suffk 90 B3
Stow-on-the-Wold Gloucs 65 J2
Stowting Kent 40 F7
Stowting Common Kent.............. 40 F6
Stowupland Suffk....................... 90 C3
Straanruie Highld 253 J8
Strachan Abers 244 F5
Strachur Ag & B 217 H6
Stradbroke Suffk 106 E8
Stradbrook Wilts 46 D8
Stradishall Suffk 88 E5
Stradsett Norfk........................ 104 D2
Stragglethorpe Lincs 118 B1
Stragglethorpe Notts 117 H4
Straight Soley Wilts 47 L4
Straiton Mdloth 211 J5
Straiton S Ayrs 183 K2
Straloch Abers 256 F7
Straloch P & K.......................... 232 F3
Stramshall Staffs 115 H4
Strang IoM 154 e6
Strangeways Salfd................... 140 B7
Strangford Herefs 63 H2
Stranraer D & G 172 C3
Strata Florida Cerdgn 77 K2
Stratfield Mortimer W Berk 49 G6
Stratfield Saye Hants 49 G6
Stratfield Turgis Hants 49 G7
Stratford C Beds 86 D5
Stratford Gt Lon 51 K2
Stratford St Andrew Suffk 91 H3
Stratford St Mary Suffk 90 B8
Stratford sub Castle Wilts 33 K4
Stratford Tony Wilts 33 J5
Stratford-upon-Avon Warwks 82 F4
Strath Highld 260 C4
Strathan Highld 270 A4
Strathan Highld 277 K3
Strathaven S Lans 197 K2
Strathblane Stirlg..................... 208 F3
Strathcanaird Highld 270 F7
Strathcarron Highld 248 F3
Strathcoil Ag & B 227 K6
Strathdon Abers 243 K1

Strathkinness Fife 223 H4
Strathloanhead W Loth 210 B4
Strathmashie House Highld 241 G5
Strathmiglo Fife....................... 222 C5
Strathpeffer Highld 262 E8
Strathtay P & K......................... 232 D4
Strathwhillan N Ayrs 195 G4
Strathy Highld 278 E3
Strathy Inn Highld 278 E3
Strathyre Stirlg 219 J4
Stratton Cnwll 11 J1
Stratton Dorset 16 C4
Stratton Gloucs 64 E6
Stratton Audley Oxon 66 F2
Stratton-on-the-Fosse
    Somset.................................... 31 L1
Stratton St Margaret Swindn 47 H2
Stratton St Michael Norfk 106 C4
Stratton Strawless Norfk 122 E7
Stream Somset 29 K3
Streat E Susx 22 E4
Streatham Gt Lon 51 J4
Streatley C Beds 68 D2
Streatley W Berk 48 F3
Street Devon 14 C4
Street Lancs 147 K5
Street N York 162 C2
Street Somset 31 H3
Street Ashton Warwks 99 M7
Street Dinas Shrops 112 E4
Street End E Susx 23 K3
Street End Kent.......................... 40 F4
Street End W Susx 20 C4
Street Gate Gatesd 180 F7
Streethay Staffs 98 F1
Street Houses N York 151 H6
Streetlam N York 160 D3
Street Lane Derbys 116 C2
Streetly Wsall 98 D4
Streetly Crematorium Wsall...... 98 D4
Streetly End Cambs 88 C5
Street on the Fosse Somset....... 31 K3
Strefford Shrops 95 K6
Strelitz P & K 233 J7
Strelley Notts 116 E3
Strensall C York 151 K4
Strensham Worcs 81 L7
Stretcholt Somset...................... 30 D2
Strete Devon 8 C5
Stretford Herefs 80 B4
Stretford Herefs 80 C4
Stretford Traffd 130 F4
Strethall Essex 87 K7
Stretham Cambs 103 K8
Strettington W Susx 20 E5
Stretton Ches W 113 C4
Stretton Derbys 133 H7
Stretton Rutlnd........................ 118 B8
Stretton Staffs 97 K1
Stretton Staffs 115 C4
Stretton Warrtn 130 C3
Stretton en le Field Leics 99 J1
Stretton Grandison Herefs 80 C4
Stretton-on-Dunsmore
    Warwks.................................... 83 J1
Stretton on Fosse Warwks 82 F7
Stretton Sugwas Herefs 80 B4
Stretton under Fosse
    Warwks.................................... 99 M7
Stretton Westwood Shrops 96 D4
Strichen Abers 269 H5
Strines Stockp.......................... 131 J2
Stringston Somset...................... 30 B2
Strixton Nhants 85 H3
Stroat Gloucs 63 H7
Stroma Highld 280 E1
Stromeferry Highld 248 D5
Stromness Ork 275 b4
Stronachlachar Stirlg 218 F5
Stronafian Ag & B 207 G3
Stronchrubie Highld 271 H4
Strone Ag & B 207 K3
Strone Highld 239 J7
Strone Highld 250 F6
Stronenaba Highld 239 L6
Stronmilchan Ag & B 217 J2
Stronsay Ork 275 d4
Strontian Highld 228 C3
Strood Kent 39 L7
Strood Medway.......................... 52 F5
Strood Green Surrey 37 J1
Strood Green W Susx 36 F6
Stroud Gloucs 64 B6
Stroud Hants 35 L6
Stroude Surrey 50 C5
Stroud Green Essex 53 J1
Stroud Green Gloucs 64 A5
Stroxton Lincs 118 B5
Struan Highld 246 D1
Struan P & K 232 B2

Strubby - Talley 355

Strubby Lincs 137 H3
Strumpshaw Norfk 107 G2
Strutherhill S Lans 198 C3
Struthers Fife 222 F5
Struy Highld 250 C4
Stryd-y-Facsen IoA 124 F3
Stryt-issa Wrexhm 112 D2
Stuartfield Abers 257 H3
Stubbers Green Wsall 98 D3
Stubbington Hants 19 J3
Stubbins Lancs 140 B4
Stubbs Green Norfk 106 E4
Stubhampton Dorset 32 F8
Stubley Derbys 133 G4
Stubshaw Cross Wigan 139 H7
Stubton Lincs 118 A2
Stuckton Hants 33 L8
Studfold N York 148 E2
Stud Green W & M 49 L3
Studham C Beds 68 C4
Studholme Cumb 177 H7
Studland Dorset 17 K6
Studley Warwks 82 C2
Studley Wilts 46 D4
Studley Common Warwks 82 C2
Studley Roger N York 150 C2
Studley Royal N York 150 C2
Stuntney Cambs 103 L7
Stunts Green E Susx 23 K4
Sturbridge Staffs 114 C5
Sturgate Lincs 135 H2
Sturmer Essex 88 D6
Sturminster Common Dorset 32 C8
Sturminster Marshall Dorset 17 J3
Sturminster Newton Dorset 32 C8
Sturry Kent 41 G3
Sturton N Linc 144 B7
Sturton by Stow Lincs 135 H4
Sturton le Steeple Notts 134 F3
Stuston Suffk 106 C7
Stutton N York 151 G7
Stutton Suffk 90 D8
Styal Ches E 131 G3
Stydd Lancs 148 A8
Stynie Moray 267 G4
Styrrup Notts 134 C2
Succoth Ag & B 218 D6
Suckley Worcs 81 G5
Suckley Green Worcs 81 G4
Sudborough Nhants 101 L7
Sudbourne Suffk 91 J4
Sudbrook Lincs 118 C3
Sudbrook Mons 45 G2
Sudbrooke Lincs 135 L4
Sudbury Derbys 115 K5
Sudbury Gt Lon 50 F2
Sudbury Suffk 89 H7
Sudden Rochdl 140 C5
Sudgrove Gloucs 64 D5
Suffield N York 163 H4
Suffield Norfk 122 E5
Sugdon Wrekin 113 K8
Sugnall Staffs 114 B5
Sugwas Pool Herefs 80 B6
Suisnish Highld 247 J5
Sulby IoM 154 e3
Sulgrave Nhants 84 A6
Sulham W Berk 48 F4
Sulhamstead W Berk 48 F5
Sulhamstead Abbots W Berk 48 F5
Sulhamstead Bannister W Berk 48 F5
Sullington W Susx 21 J4
Sullom Shet 281 d4
Sullom Voe Shet 281 d4
Sully V Glam 43 J8
Summerbridge N York 150 B3
Summercourt Cnwll 4 E4
Summerfield Norfk 121 G4
Summerfield Worcs 97 J8
Summer Heath Bucks 49 H1
Summerhill Pembks 55 K5
Summerhill Staffs 98 D2
Summer Hill Wrexhm 112 D1
Summerhouse Darltn 169 G6
Summerlands Cumb 157 H5
Summerley Derbys 133 G4
Summersdale W Susx 20 D5
Summerseat Bury 140 B5
Summertown Oxon 66 D5
Summit Oldham 140 D6
Summit Rochdl 140 E4
Sunbiggin Cumb 157 L1
Sunbury-on-Thames Surrey 50 E5
Sundaywell D & G 185 K6
Sunderland Ag & B 204 C3
Sunderland Cumb 165 G4
Sunderland Lancs 147 H4
Sunderland Sundld 181 K7
Sunderland Bridge Dur 169 H3
Sunderland Crematorium Sundld 181 J7
Sundhope Border 200 D8
Sundon Park Luton 68 D2
Sundridge Kent 38 D2
Sunk Island E R Yk 145 H4
Sunningdale W & M 50 B5
Sunninghill W & M 50 B5
Sunningwell Oxon 66 D7
Sunniside Dur 168 F3
Sunniside Gatesd 180 F7
Sunny Brow Dur 169 G4
Sunnyhill C Derb 116 B5
Sunnyhurst Bl w D 139 K3
Sunnylaw Stirlg 220 D7
Sunnymead Oxon 66 D5
Sunton Wilts 47 K8
Surbiton Gt Lon 50 F5
Surfleet Lincs 119 H6
Surfleet Seas End Lincs 119 J6
Surlingham Norfk 107 G2
Surrex Essex 72 C3
Surrey & Sussex Crematorium W Susx 37 L3
Sustead Norfk 122 D4
Susworth Lincs 143 L7
Sutcombe Devon 26 F8
Sutcombemill Devon 26 F8
Suton Norfk 106 B4
Sutterby Lincs 137 G5
Sutterton Lincs 119 J4
Sutton C Beds 86 E5
Sutton C Pete 102 B4
Sutton Cambs 103 J7
Sutton Devon 7 K6
Sutton Devon 13 G2
Sutton Donc 142 E5
Sutton E Susx 23 H7
Sutton Gt Lon 51 H6
Sutton Kent 41 K5
Sutton N York 142 D3
Sutton Norfk 123 H6
Sutton Notts 117 K4
Sutton Oxon 66 B6
Sutton Pembks 54 E4
Sutton Shrops 96 C1
Sutton Shrops 97 G6
Sutton Shrops 112 E6
Sutton Shrops 113 L5
Sutton St Hel 129 M1
Sutton Staffs 114 B7
Sutton Suffk 91 G6
Sutton W Susx 21 G4
Sutton Abinger Surrey 37 H2
Sutton at Hone Kent 52 C5
Sutton Bassett Nhants 101 G5
Sutton Benger Wilts 46 D3
Sutton Bingham Somset 31 J8
Sutton Bonington Notts 116 E6
Sutton Bridge Lincs 120 B7
Sutton Cheney Leics 99 L3
Sutton Coldfield Birm 98 E4
Sutton Coldfield Crematorium Birm 98 F4
Sutton Courtenay Oxon 66 D8
Sutton Crosses Lincs 119 M7
Sutton cum Lound Notts 134 D3
Sutton Fields Notts 116 E6
Sutton Green Surrey 50 C8
Sutton Green Wrexhm 112 F2
Sutton Howgrave N York 160 D6
Sutton in Ashfield Notts 133 K7
Sutton-in-Craven N York 149 H7
Sutton in the Elms Leics 100 B4
Sutton Lane Ends Ches E 131 H5
Sutton Maddock Shrops 97 G3
Sutton Mallet Somset 30 E3
Sutton Mandeville Wilts 33 G5
Sutton Manor St Hel 129 L2
Sutton Marsh Herefs 80 D6
Sutton Montis Somset 31 K6
Sutton-on-Hull C KuH 144 E1
Sutton on Sea Lincs 137 K3
Sutton-on-the-Forest N York 151 J3
Sutton on the Hill Derbys 115 L5
Sutton on Trent Notts 134 F6
Sutton Poyntz Dorset 16 D6
Sutton St Edmund Lincs 103 H1
Sutton St James Lincs 119 L7
Sutton St Nicholas Herefs 80 C6
Sutton Scotney Hants 34 F3
Sutton Street Kent 39 K2
Sutton-under-Brailes Warwks 83 G7
Sutton-under-Whitestonecliffe N York 161 G6
Sutton upon Derwent E R Yk 151 L6
Sutton Valence Kent 39 K3
Sutton Veny Wilts 32 E3
Sutton Waldron Dorset 32 E7
Sutton Weaver Ches W 130 A4
Sutton Wick BaNES 45 H7
Sutton Wick Oxon 66 C8
Swaby Lincs 137 G4
Swadlincote Derbys 116 A7
Swaffham Norfk 105 G2
Swaffham Bulbeck Cambs 87 L3
Swaffham Prior Cambs 88 B2
Swafield Norfk 122 F5
Swainby N York 161 G2
Swainshill Herefs 80 B7
Swainsthorpe Norfk 106 E3
Swainswick BaNES 45 M5
Swalcliffe Oxon 83 J7
Swalecliffe Kent 40 F2
Swallow Lincs 144 F7
Swallow Beck Lincs 135 J6
Swallowcliffe Wilts 33 G5
Swallowfield Wokham 49 H6
Swallow Nest Rothm 133 J3
Swallows Cross Essex 70 F7
Swampton Hants 34 E1
Swanage Dorset 17 K6
Swanbourne Bucks 67 K2
Swanbridge V Glam 43 J8
Swancote Shrops 97 G4
Swan Green Ches W 130 E5
Swanland E R Yk 144 C2
Swanley Kent 52 B5
Swanley Village Kent 52 B5
Swanmore Hants 35 J7
Swannington Leics 116 C8
Swannington Norfk 122 C7
Swanpool Garden Suburb Lincs 135 J6
Swanscombe Kent 52 D4
Swansea Swans 57 J6
Swansea Crematorium Swans 57 J5
Swan Street Essex 72 C2
Swanton Abbot Norfk 122 F6
Swanton Morley Norfk 121 M8
Swanton Novers Norfk 121 M5
Swanton Street Kent 53 J7
Swan Village Sandw 98 C5
Swanwick Derbys 116 C1
Swanwick Hants 19 H2
Swarby Lincs 118 D3
Swardeston Norfk 106 D3
Swarkestone Derbys 116 B6
Swarland Nthumb 191 H5
Swarraton Hants 35 H3
Swartha C Brad 149 J6
Swarthmoor Cumb 156 C7
Swaton Lincs 118 F4
Swavesey Cambs 87 G2
Sway Hants 18 D4
Swayfield Lincs 118 C7
Swaythling C Sotn 34 F7
Sweet Green Worcs 80 F3
Sweetham Devon 13 K3
Sweethaws E Susx 38 D7
Sweetlands Corner Kent 39 K4
Sweets Cnwll 11 G3
Sweetshouse Cnwll 5 J3
Swefling Suffk 91 H3
Swepstone Leics 99 K1
Swerford Oxon 66 A1
Swettenham Ches E 130 F6
Swffryd Blae G 61 K7
Swift's Green Kent 39 L4
Swilland Suffk 90 E4
Swillbrook Lancs 138 F1
Swillington Leeds 142 B2
Swimbridge Devon 27 L5
Swimbridge Newland Devon 27 L5
Swinbrook Oxon 65 L4
Swincliffe Kirk 141 K2
Swincliffe N York 150 C4
Swincombe Devon 28 B3
Swinden N York 148 E5
Swinderby Lincs 135 H7
Swindon Gloucs 64 D2
Swindon Nthumb 190 D6
Swindon Staffs 97 J5
Swindon Swindn 47 H2
Swine E R Yk 153 J8
Swinefleet E R Yk 143 J3
Swineford S Glos 45 K5
Swineshead Bed 85 L2
Swineshead Lincs 119 H3
Swineshead Bridge Lincs 119 H3
Swiney Highld 275 H1
Swinford Leics 100 C7
Swinford Oxon 66 C5
Swingfield Minnis Kent 41 G6
Swingfield Street Kent 41 H6
Swingleton Green Suffk 89 K6
Swinhoe Nthumb 203 K7
Swinhope Lincs 145 G8
Swinithwaite N York 159 J5
Swinmore Common Herefs 80 F7
Swinscoe Staffs 115 J2
Swinside Cumb 165 H6
Swinstead Lincs 118 D7
Swinthorpe Lincs 135 L4
Swinton Border 202 C4
Swinton N York 160 B6
Swinton N York 162 D8
Swinton Rothm 142 C7
Swinton Salfd 140 A7
Swithland Leics 100 C1
Swordale Highld 263 G6
Swordland Highld 238 B5
Swordly Highld 278 C4
Sworton Heath Ches E 130 D3
Swyddffynnon Cerdgn 77 J2
Swyncombe Oxon 49 G1
Swynnerton Staffs 114 D4
Swyre Dorset 15 M5
Sycharth Powys 112 B6
Sychnant Powys 93 L7
Sychtyn Powys 94 B2
Sydallt Wrexhm 129 H8
Syde Gloucs 64 D5
Sydenham Gt Lon 51 K4
Sydenham Oxon 67 H6
Sydenham Damerel Devon 12 A7
Sydenhurst Surrey 36 E4
Syderstone Norfk 121 H5
Sydling St Nicholas Dorset 16 C3
Sydmonton Hants 48 C7
Sydnal Lane Shrops 97 H2
Syerston Notts 117 K2
Syke Rochdl 140 D4
Sykehouse Donc 143 G4
Syleham Suffk 106 E7
Sylen Carmth 56 F3
Symbister Shet 281 e5
Symington S Ayrs 196 D5
Symington S Lans 199 G6
Symondsbury Dorset 15 K4
Symonds Yat Herefs 63 H4
Sympson Green C Brad 150 A8
Synderford Dorset 15 J2
Synod Inn Cerdgn 76 D4
Syre Highld 278 B7
Syreford Gloucs 64 F3
Syresham Nhants 84 C7
Syston Leics 100 D1
Syston Lincs 118 B3
Sytchampton Worcs 81 J2
Sywell Nhants 84 F2

T

Tabley Hill Ches E 130 E4
Tackley Oxon 66 C3
Tacolneston Norfk 106 C4
Tadcaster N York 151 G7
Taddington Derbys 132 C5
Taddington Gloucs 65 G1
Taddiport Devon 27 H7
Tadley Hants 48 F6
Tadlow Cambs 86 F5
Tadmarton Oxon 83 J7
Tadwick BaNES 45 L5
Tadworth Surrey 51 G7
Tafarnaubach Blae G 61 H5
Tafarn-y-bwlch Pembks 75 J5
Tafarn-y-Gelyn Denbgs 128 E7
Taff's Well Rhondd 43 H5
Tafolwern Powys 93 J3
Taibach Neath 57 L7
Tain Highld 263 L3
Tain Highld 280 B3
Tai'n Lôn Gwynd 109 H2
Tairbeart W Isls 282 e5
Tai'r Bull Powys 60 F2
Takeley Essex 70 E3
Takeley Street Essex 70 E3
Talachddu Powys 78 F8
Talacre Flints 128 D3
Talaton Devon 14 C3
Talbenny Pembks 54 D4
Talbot Green Rhondd 43 G5
Talbot Village Bmouth 17 L4
Taleford Devon 14 C3
Talerddig Powys 93 K3
Talgarreg Cerdgn 76 D5
Talgarth Powys 79 G8
Talisker Highld 246 D3
Talke Staffs 114 C1
Talke Pits Staffs 114 C1
Talkin Cumb 178 D7
Talladale Highld 260 E6
Talla Linnfoots Border 187 H2
Tallaminnock S Ayrs 183 K3
Tallarn Green Wrexhm 113 G3
Tallentire Cumb 164 F4
Talley Carmth 59 H2

Tallington Lincs 102 B2
Tallwrn Wrexhm 112 D2
Talmine Highld 277 K4
Talog Carmth 58 B4
Talsarn Cerdgn 77 G4
Talsarnau Gwynd 109 L4
Talskiddy Cnwll 4 E2
Talwrn IoA 125 J4
Talwrn Wrexhm 112 F2
Tal-y-bont Cerdgn 92 E5
Tal-y-Bont Conwy 126 F6
Tal-y-bont Gwynd 109 L7
Tal-y-bont Gwynd 126 C5
Talybont-on-Usk Powys 61 H3
Tal-y-Cafn Conwy 126 F5
Tal-y-coed Mons 62 E4
Tal-y-garn Rhondd 42 F5
Tal-y-llyn Gwynd 92 F2
Talysarn Gwynd 109 J1
Tal-y-Waun Torfn 61 L6
Talywern Powys 93 H3
Tamer Lane End Wigan 139 J7
Tamerton Foliot C Plym 6 F3
Tamworth Staffs 99 G3
Tamworth Green Lincs 119 L3
Tancred N York 151 G4
Tancredston Pembks 74 E7
Tandridge Surrey 38 B3
Tanfield Dur 180 F7
Tanfield Lea Dur 180 F8
Tangiers Pembks 54 F3
Tangley Hants 47 L8
Tangmere W Susx 20 E5
Tangusdale W Isls 283 b13
Tan Hill N York 158 F1
Tankerness Ork 275 d4
Tankersley Barns 142 A7
Tankerton Kent 40 F2
Tannach Highld 280 D6
Tannachie Abers 245 H6
Tannadice Angus 234 D4
Tanner's Green Worcs 98 D8
Tannington Suffk 90 F2
Tannochside N Lans 209 J6
Tansley Derbys 132 F7
Tansor Nhants 102 B5
Tantobie Dur 180 E7
Tanton N York 170 C8
Tanwood Worcs 97 K8
Tanworth in Arden Warwks 82 D1
Tan-y-Bwlch Gwynd 110 C3
Tan-y-fron Conwy 127 J6
Tan-y-fron Wrexhm 112 D1
Tan-y-grisiau Gwynd 110 C3
Tan-y-groes Cerdgn 76 B5
Taobh Tuath W Isls 282 d6
Taplow Bucks 49 M3
Tarbert Ag & B 205 L6
Tarbert Ag & B 206 D5
Tarbert W Isls 282 e5
Tarbet Ag & B 218 D6
Tarbet Highld 238 C5
Tarbet Highld 276 B6
Tarbock Green Knows 129 K2
Tarbolton S Ayrs 196 E5
Tarbrax S Lans 199 H2
Tardebigge Worcs 82 B2
Tarfside Angus 244 B7
Tarland Abers 244 B3
Tarleton Lancs 138 F4
Tarlscough Lancs 138 E5
Tarlton Gloucs 64 D7
Tarnock Somset 44 D8
Tarns Cumb 164 F1
Tarnside Cumb 156 F4
Tarporley Ches W 130 A7
Tarr Somset 28 F4
Tarrant Crawford Dorset 17 H2
Tarrant Gunville Dorset 32 F8
Tarrant Hinton Dorset 32 F8
Tarrant Keyneston Dorset 17 H2
Tarrant Launceston Dorset 17 J1
Tarrant Monkton Dorset 17 J1
Tarrant Rawston Dorset 17 H1
Tarrant Rushton Dorset 17 H2
Tarring Neville E Susx 23 G6
Tarrington Herefs 80 E7
Tarskavaig Highld 247 J6
Tarves Abers 256 F5
Tarvin Ches W 129 L6
Tarvin Sands Ches W 129 L6
Tasburgh Norfk 106 D4
Tasley Shrops 96 F4
Taston Oxon 65 M3
Tatenhill Staffs 115 K7
Tathall End M Keyn 84 F6
Tatham Lancs 147 M2
Tathwell Lincs 136 F3
Tatsfield Surrey 51 L7
Tattenhall Ches W 129 L7

Tatterford Norfk 121 J6
Tattersett Norfk 121 J5
Tattershall Lincs 136 D8
Tattershall Bridge Lincs 136 C8
Tattershall Thorpe Lincs 136 D7
Tattingstone Suffk 90 D7
Tattingstone White Horse
    Suffk 90 D7
Tatworth Somset 15 H2
Tauchers Moray 267 H6
Taunton Somset 30 C6
Taunton Deane Crematorium
    Somset 30 B6
Taverham Norfk 122 D8
Taverners Green Essex 70 E3
Tavernspite Pembks 55 L4
Tavistock Devon 12 C7
Taw Green Devon 12 F3
Tawstock Devon 27 K5
Taxal Derbys 131 K4
Taychreggan Hotel Ag & B 217 G3
Tayinloan Ag & B 205 M7
Taynton Gloucs 63 L3
Taynton Oxon 65 K4
Taynuilt Ag & B 216 F1
Tayport Fife 223 H2
Tayvallich Ag & B 215 L7
Tealby Lincs 136 C2
Tealing Angus 234 B7
Team Valley Gatesd 181 G7
Teangue Highld 247 K6
Teanord Highld 263 G7
Tebay Cumb 157 K2
Tebworth C Beds 68 C2
Tedburn St Mary Devon 13 J4
Teddington Gloucs 81 M8
Teddington Gt Lon 50 F5
Tedstone Delamere Herefs 80 F3
Tedstone Wafer Herefs 80 F3
Teeton Nhants 84 D1
Teffont Evias Wilts 33 G4
Teffont Magna Wilts 33 G4
Tegryn Pembks 75 L5
Teigh Rutlnd 117 M8
Teigncombe Devon 12 F5
Teigngrace Devon 13 K7
Teignmouth Devon 13 L8
Teindside Border 188 D4
Telford Wrekin 96 F2
Telford Crematorium Wrekin 97 G1
Tellisford Somset 46 A7
Telscombe E Susx 22 F6
Telscombe Cliffs E Susx 22 F7
Tempar P & K 231 J4
Templand D & G 176 E2
Temple Cnwll 11 G2
Temple Mdloth 211 K7
Temple Balsall Solhll 99 G8
Temple Bar Cerdgn 76 F4
Temple Cloud BaNES 45 J7
Templecombe Somset 32 B6
Temple End Suffk 88 D5
Temple Ewell Kent 41 J6
Temple Grafton Warwks 82 D4
Temple Guiting Gloucs 65 G2
Temple Herdewyke Warwks 83 J5
Temple Hirst N York 142 F3
Temple Normanton Derbys 133 H6
Temple of Fiddes Abers 245 H7
Temple Sowerby Cumb 166 E5
Templeton Devon 28 F8
Templeton Pembks 55 J4
Templetown Dur 168 E1
Tempsford C Beds 86 D4
Tenbury Wells Worcs 80 E2
Tenby Pembks 55 K6
Tendring Essex 73 H2
Tendring Green Essex 73 H2
Tendring Heath Essex 73 H2
Ten Mile Bank Norfk 104 B4
Tenpenny Heath Essex 73 G3
Tenterden Kent 39 M6
Terling Essex 71 J4
Tern Wrekin 113 K8
Ternhill Shrops 113 L5
Terregles D & G 176 B3
Terrington N York 151 L2
Terrington St Clement Norfk 120 C7
Terrington St John Norfk 104 A1
Terry's Green Warwks 98 E8
Teston Kent 39 H3
Testwood Hants 34 D7
Tetbury Gloucs 64 C8
Tetbury Upton Gloucs 64 C8
Tetchill Shrops 112 F5
Tetcott Devon 11 L3
Tetford Lincs 136 F5

Tetney Lincs 145 J7
Tetney Lock Lincs 145 J7
Tetsworth Oxon 67 G6
Tettenhall Wolves 97 K3
Tettenhall Wood Wolves 97 K3
Teversal Notts 133 J7
Teversham Cambs 87 K3
Teviothead Border 188 C5
Tewin Herts 69 H4
Tewin Wood Herts 69 H4
Tewkesbury Gloucs 81 K8
Teynham Kent 40 B3
Thackley C Brad 149 M8
Thackthwaite Cumb 164 F6
Thackthwaite Cumb 166 A5
Thakeham W Susx 21 J3
Thame Oxon 67 H6
Thames Ditton Surrey 50 F5
Thamesmead Gt Lon 52 A3
Thanet Crematorium Kent 41 K2
Thanington Kent 40 F4
Thankerton S Lans 199 G5
Tharston Norfk 106 D4
Thatcham W Berk 48 D5
Thatto Heath St Hel 129 L1
Thaxted Essex 70 F1
Theakston N York 160 D5
Thealby N Linc 143 M4
Theale Somset 31 G2
Theale W Berk 48 F5
Thearne E R Yk 153 G8
The Bank Ches E 131 G8
The Bank Shrops 96 E3
The Beeches Gloucs 64 F6
Theberton Suffk 91 K2
The Blythe Staffs 115 G6
The Bog Shrops 95 J4
The Bourne Worcs 82 A4
The Braes Highld 247 H2
The Bratch Staffs 97 K4
The Broad Herefs 80 C3
The Brunt E Loth 212 F4
The Bungalow IoM 154 e5
The Burf Worcs 81 J2
The Butts Gloucs 64 C4
The Camp Gloucs 64 C5
The Chequer Wrexhm 113 H3
The City Bed 86 C3
The City Bucks 67 J7
The Common Oxon 65 L2
The Common Wilts 34 B3
The Common Wilts 46 F2
The Corner Kent 39 H5
The Counties Crematorium
    Nhants 84 E4
The Cronk IoM 154 d3
Theddingworth Leics 100 E6
Theddlethorpe All Saints Lincs 137 J2
Theddlethorpe St Helen Lincs 137 J2
The Den N Ayrs 196 C1
The Forest of Dean
    Crematorium Gloucs 63 J4
The Forge Herefs 79 L3
The Forstal Kent 40 D7
The Fouralls Shrops 113 L5
The Garden of England
    Crematorium Kent 53 J5
The Green Cumb 156 A5
The Green Essex 71 J3
The Green N York 162 D2
The Green Wilts 32 E4
The Grove Worcs 81 K7
The Haven W Susx 37 G5
The Haw Gloucs 64 B2
The Headland Hartpl 170 C4
The Hill Cumb 156 A6
The Holt Wokham 49 K3
The Hundred Herefs 80 C2
Thelbridge Cross Devon 28 D8
The Leacon Kent 40 C8
The Lee Bucks 67 L6
The Lhen IoM 154 e2
The Linn Crematorium E Rens 209 M4
Thelnetham Suffk 105 L7
The Lochs Moray 266 F4
Thelveton Norfk 106 D7
Thelwall Warrtn 130 C2
The Manchester
    Crematorium Manch 131 G1
The Marsh Powys 95 H4
Themelthorpe Norfk 122 B6
The Middles Dur 180 F8
The Moor Kent 39 J7
The Mumbles Swans 57 G6
The Murray S Lans 209 H8
The Mythe Gloucs 81 K8
The Narth Mons 63 G6
The Neuk Abers 245 G4
Thenford Nhants 83 M7
Theobald's Green Wilts 46 F5

The Park Crematorium Hants 36 C1
The Quarry Gloucs 63 L7
The Quarter Kent 39 M4
The Reddings Gloucs 64 C3
Therfield Herts 87 G7
The Rhôs Powys 61 J1
The Rose Hill Crematorium
    Donc 142 F7
The Ross P & K 220 D7
The Sands Surrey 36 C2
The Shoe Wilts 46 A4
The Smithies Shrops 96 F5
The Spike Cambs 87 K5
The Spring Warwks 83 G1
The Square Torfn 62 B7
The Stair Kent 38 F4
The Stocks Kent 25 G2
The Straits Hants 36 A3
The Strand Wilts 46 D7
Thetford Norfk 105 H6
Thethwaite Cumb 165 L2
The Towans Cnwll 2 E3
The Vale Crematorium Luton 68 E2
The Vauld Herefs 80 C5
The Wyke Shrops 97 G2
Theydon Bois Essex 70 C7
Thicket Priory N York 151 L7
Thickwood Wilts 46 B4
Thimbleby Lincs 136 D5
Thimbleby N York 161 G3
Thingwall Wirral 129 G3
Thirkleby N York 161 G6
Thirlby N York 161 G6
Thirlestane Border 201 H4
Thirn N York 160 B5
Thirsk N York 161 G6
Thirtleby E R Yk 144 F1
Thistleton Lancs 147 H8
Thistleton Rutlnd 118 B7
Thistley Green Suffk 104 D8
Thixendale N York 152 C4
Thockrington Nthumb 179 M3
Tholomas Drove Cambs 103 H2
Tholthorpe N York 151 G2
Thomas Chapel Pembks 55 J5
Thomas Close Cumb 166 B3
Thomastown Abers 255 L4
Thomas Town Warwks 82 C3
Thompson Norfk 105 J4
Thong Kent 52 E5
Thoralby N York 159 H5
Thoresby Notts 134 C5
Thoresthorpe Lincs 137 J4
Thoresway Lincs 144 F8
Thorganby Lincs 145 G8
Thorganby N York 151 L7
Thorgill N York 162 C3
Thorington Suffk 107 J8
Thorington Street Suffk 89 K8
Thorlby N York 149 H5
Thorley Herts 70 C3
Thorley IoW 18 F6
Thorley Houses Herts 70 C3
Thorley Street IoW 18 F6
Thormanby N York 161 H7
Thornaby-on-Tees S on T 170 B7
Thornage Norfk 122 B4
Thornborough Bucks 84 B8
Thornborough N York 160 D6
Thornbury C Brad 141 J1
Thornbury Devon 12 A1
Thornbury Herefs 80 C3
Thornbury S Glos 45 J1
Thornby Cumb 177 J8
Thornby Nhants 100 E8
Thorncliff Staffs 131 K7
Thorncliffe Crematorium
    Cumb 146 D2
Thorncombe Dorset 15 J2
Thorncombe Street Surrey 36 F3
Thorncott Green C Beds 86 C5
Thorncross IoW 19 G7
Thorndon Suffk 90 D1
Thorndon Cross Devon 12 D4
Thorne Donc 143 H5
Thorne Coffin Somset 31 H7
Thornecroft Devon 7 M2
Thornehillhead Devon 27 G3
Thorner Leeds 150 E7
Thornes Staffs 98 D3
Thornes Wakefd 141 M4
Thorne St Margaret Somset 29 K6
Thorney Bucks 50 D3
Thorney C Pete 102 F3
Thorney Notts 135 G6
Thorney Somset 30 F6
Thorney Hill Hants 18 B4
Thorney Island W Susx 20 C6
Thorney Toll Cambs 103 G3
Thornfalcon Somset 30 D6

Thornford Dorset...... 31 K8
Thorngrafton Nthumb...... 179 H6
Thorngrove Somset...... 30 E4
Thorngumbald E R Yk...... 145 G3
Thornham Norfk...... 121 G3
Thornham Magna Suffk...... 90 C1
Thornham Parva Suffk...... 90 D1
Thornhaugh C Pete...... 102 B3
Thornhill C Sotn...... 19 G1
Thornhill Caerph...... 43 J5
Thornhill Cumb...... 155 H1
Thornhill D & G...... 186 C7
Thornhill Derbys...... 132 D3
Thornhill Kirk...... 141 L4
Thornhill Stirlg...... 219 L7
Thornhill Crematorium Cardif...... 43 J5
Thornhill Lees Kirk...... 141 K4
Thornhills Calder...... 141 J3
Thornholme E R Yk...... 153 H3
Thornicombe Dorset...... 17 G2
Thornington Nthumb...... 202 D6
Thornley Dur...... 168 E3
Thornley Dur...... 169 K3
Thornley Gate Nthumb...... 179 J7
Thornliebank E Rens...... 208 F7
Thornythwaite Cumb...... 165 L6
Thorns Suffk...... 88 E4
Thorns Green Ches E...... 130 F3
Thornsett Derbys...... 131 K2
Thornthwaite Cumb...... 165 H5
Thornthwaite N York...... 149 L4
Thornton Angus...... 234 B6
Thornton Bucks...... 84 E8
Thornton C Brad...... 141 H1
Thornton E R Yk...... 152 A6
Thornton Fife...... 222 E7
Thornton Lancs...... 146 F7
Thornton Leics...... 100 A2
Thornton Lincs...... 136 D6
Thornton Middsb...... 170 B7
Thornton Nthumb...... 202 E4
Thornton Pembks...... 54 E5
Thornton Sefton...... 138 D7
Thornton Curtis N Linc...... 144 D4
Thornton Garden of Rest
    Crematorium Sefton...... 138 D7
Thorntonhall S Lans...... 209 G8
Thornton Heath Gt Lon...... 51 J5
Thornton Hough Wirral...... 129 G3
Thornton-in-Craven N York...... 148 F6
Thornton in Lonsdale N York...... 158 B8
Thornton-le-Beans N York...... 160 F4
Thornton-le-Clay N York...... 151 L3
Thornton le Dale N York...... 162 F4
Thornton le Moor Lincs...... 144 D8
Thornton-le-Moor N York...... 160 F5
Thornton-le-Moors Ches W...... 129 K5
Thornton-le-Street N York...... 160 F5
Thorntonloch E Loth...... 213 G4
Thornton Rust N York...... 159 G5
Thornton Steward N York...... 160 A5
Thornton Watlass N York...... 160 C3
Thornwood Common Essex...... 70 C6
Thornydykes Border...... 201 J3
Thornythwaite Cumb...... 165 L6
Thoroton Notts...... 117 K3
Thorp Arch Leeds...... 150 F6
Thorpe Derbys...... 115 J2
Thorpe E R Yk...... 152 F6
Thorpe Lincs...... 137 J3
Thorpe N York...... 149 H3
Thorpe Norfk...... 107 J4
Thorpe Notts...... 117 K2
Thorpe Surrey...... 50 C5
Thorpe Abbotts Norfk...... 106 D7
Thorpe Acre Leics...... 116 C2
Thorpe Arnold Leics...... 117 K7
Thorpe Audlin Wakefd...... 142 D4
Thorpe Bassett N York...... 162 F8
Thorpe Bay Sthend...... 53 K2
Thorpe by Water Rutlnd...... 101 K4
Thorpe Common Rothm...... 133 G1
Thorpe Constantine Staffs...... 99 H2
Thorpe End Norfk...... 106 F1
Thorpe Green Essex...... 73 H3
Thorpe Green Lancs...... 139 H3
Thorpe Green Suffk...... 89 J4
Thorpe Hesley Rothm...... 142 B8
Thorpe in Balne Donc...... 142 F5
Thorpe Langton Leics...... 101 G5
Thorpe Larches Dur...... 169 K5
Thorpe Lea Surrey...... 50 C5
Thorpe le Fallows Lincs...... 135 H4
Thorpe-le-Soken Essex...... 73 J3
Thorpe le Street E R Yk...... 152 C7
Thorpe Malsor Nhants...... 101 H7
Thorpe Mandeville Nhants...... 83 M6
Thorpe Market Norfk...... 122 E4
Thorpe Marriot Norfk...... 122 D8
Thorpe Morieux Suffk...... 89 J4
Thorpeness Suffk...... 91 L3

Thorpe on the Hill Leeds...... 141 M2
Thorpe on the Hill Lincs...... 135 H6
Thorpe St Andrew Norfk...... 106 F2
Thorpe St Peter Lincs...... 137 J7
Thorpe Salvin Rothm...... 133 K3
Thorpe Satchville Leics...... 100 F1
Thorpe Thewles S on T...... 169 L6
Thorpe Tilney Lincs...... 136 B8
Thorpe Underwood N York...... 151 G4
Thorpe Underwood Nhants...... 101 H7
Thorpe Waterville Nhants...... 102 A7
Thorpe Willoughby N York...... 142 F2
Thorpland Norfk...... 104 C2
Thorrington Essex...... 73 G3
Thorverton Devon...... 13 L2
Thrales End C Beds...... 68 E4
Thrandeston Suffk...... 106 C8
Thrapston Nhants...... 101 M7
Threapland Cumb...... 165 G3
Threapland N York...... 149 H4
Threapwood Ches W...... 113 G3
Threapwood Staffs...... 115 G3
Threapwood Head Staffs...... 115 G3
Threave S Ayrs...... 183 J2
Three Ashes Herefs...... 63 G3
Three Bridges W Susx...... 37 L3
Three Burrows Cnwll...... 4 B5
Three Chimneys Kent...... 39 K5
Three Cocks Powys...... 79 G7
Three Counties Crematorium
    Essex...... 71 J2
Three Crosses Swans...... 57 G6
Three Cups Corner E Susx...... 23 L3
Three Gates Worcs...... 80 F3
Threehammer Common Norfk...... 123 G7
Three Hammers Cnwll...... 11 J5
Three Holes Norfk...... 103 K3
Threekingham Lincs...... 118 E4
Three Leg Cross E Susx...... 39 H7
Three Legged Cross Dorset...... 17 L2
Three Mile Cross Wokham...... 49 H5
Threemilestone Cnwll...... 4 C6
Three Miletown W Loth...... 210 E4
Three Oaks E Susx...... 24 F4
Threlkeld Cumb...... 165 K5
Threshers Bush Essex...... 70 D5
Threshfield N York...... 149 H3
Thrigby Norfk...... 107 J1
Thringarth Dur...... 167 L6
Thringstone Leics...... 116 D8
Thrintoft N York...... 160 D4
Thriplow Cambs...... 87 J6
Throapham Rothm...... 133 K2
Throckenhalt Lincs...... 103 G2
Throcking Herts...... 69 J1
Throckley N u Ty...... 180 E5
Throckmorton Worcs...... 82 A5
Throop Bmouth...... 17 M3
Throop Dorset...... 16 F4
Throphill Nthumb...... 180 D2
Thropton Nthumb...... 190 E5
Throsk Stirlg...... 209 M1
Througham Gloucs...... 64 D5
Throughgate D & G...... 185 L6
Throwleigh Devon...... 12 F4
Throwley Kent...... 40 C4
Throwley Forstal Kent...... 40 C4
Thrumpton Notts...... 116 E5
Thrumpton Notts...... 134 D4
Thrumster Highld...... 280 D7
Thrunscoe NE Lin...... 145 J6
Thrunton Nthumb...... 190 F4
Thrup Oxon...... 65 L7
Thrupp Gloucs...... 64 B6
Thrupp Oxon...... 66 C4
Thrushelton Devon...... 12 B5
Thrussington Leics...... 117 H8
Thruxton Hants...... 34 C2
Thruxton Herefs...... 80 B8
Thrybergh Rothm...... 142 D8
Thulston Derbys...... 116 C5
Thundersley Essex...... 53 G1
Thurcaston Leics...... 100 C1
Thurcroft Rothm...... 133 K2
Thurdon Cnwll...... 26 E8
Thurgarton Norfk...... 122 D4
Thurgarton Notts...... 117 J2
Thurgoland Barns...... 141 L7
Thurlaston Leics...... 100 B4
Thurlaston Warwks...... 83 L1
Thurlbear Somset...... 30 C6
Thurlby Lincs...... 118 E8
Thurlby Lincs...... 135 H7
Thurlby Lincs...... 137 J3
Thurleigh Bed...... 85 L3
Thurlestone Devon...... 7 K6
Thurloxton Somset...... 30 C5
Thurlstone Barns...... 141 K7
Thurlton Norfk...... 107 J4
Thurlwood Ches E...... 130 F8

Thurmaston Leics...... 100 D2
Thurnby Leics...... 100 E3
Thurne Norfk...... 123 H8
Thurnham Kent...... 53 H7
Thurning Nhants...... 102 B6
Thurning Norfk...... 122 B5
Thurnscoe Barns...... 142 C6
Thursby Cumb...... 165 K1
Thursden Lancs...... 140 D1
Thursford Norfk...... 121 L5
Thursley Surrey...... 36 D3
Thurso Highld...... 279 K3
Thurstaston Wirral...... 128 F3
Thurston Suffk...... 89 J2
Thurston Clough Oldham...... 140 E6
Thurstonfield Cumb...... 177 K7
Thurstonland Kirk...... 141 J5
Thurston Planch Suffk...... 89 J2
Thurton Norfk...... 107 G3
Thurvaston Derbys...... 115 L4
Thuxton Norfk...... 105 L2
Thwaite N York...... 158 F3
Thwaite Suffk...... 90 D2
Thwaite Head Cumb...... 156 E4
Thwaites C Brad...... 149 K7
Thwaite St Mary Norfk...... 107 G4
Thwaites Brow C Brad...... 149 K7
Thwing E R Yk...... 153 G2
Tibbermore P & K...... 221 J3
Tibbers D & G...... 186 C6
Tibberton Gloucs...... 63 M3
Tibberton Worcs...... 81 L4
Tibberton Wrekin...... 113 L7
Tibbie Shiels Inn Border...... 187 K2
Tibenham Norfk...... 106 C5
Tibshelf Derbys...... 133 J7
Tibthorpe E R Yk...... 152 E5
Ticehurst E Susx...... 39 H7
Tichborne Hants...... 35 H5
Tickford End M Keyn...... 85 H6
Tickhill Donc...... 134 B1
Ticklerton Shrops...... 96 B5
Ticknall Derbys...... 116 B6
Tickton E R Yk...... 153 G7
Tidbury Green Solhll...... 98 E8
Tidcombe Wilts...... 47 L1
Tiddington Oxon...... 67 G6
Tiddington Warwks...... 82 F4
Tiddleywink Wilts...... 46 C4
Tidebrook E Susx...... 38 F7
Tideford Cnwll...... 6 C3
Tideford Cross Cnwll...... 6 C3
Tidenham Gloucs...... 63 H7
Tideswell Derbys...... 132 C4
Tidmarsh W Berk...... 48 F4
Tidmington Warwks...... 83 G7
Tidpit Hants...... 33 J7
Tidworth Wilts...... 34 B1
Tiers Cross Pembks...... 54 E5
Tiffield Nhants...... 84 D5
Tigerton Angus...... 234 E3
Tigh a Ghearraidh W Isls...... 282 b7
Tigharry W Isls...... 282 b7
Tighnabruaich Ag & B...... 206 F4
Tigley Devon...... 7 L3
Tilbrook Cambs...... 86 B2
Tilbury Thurr...... 52 D4
Tilbury Green Essex...... 88 E7
Tilbury Juxta Clare Essex...... 88 F7
Tile Cross Birm...... 98 F6
Tile Hill Covtry...... 99 H7
Tilehouse Green Solhll...... 98 F8
Tilehurst Readg...... 49 G4
Tilford Surrey...... 36 C2
Tilgate W Susx...... 37 L4
Tilgate Forest Row W Susx...... 37 L4
Tilham Street Somset...... 31 J4
Tillers Green Gloucs...... 80 F8
Tillicoultry Clacks...... 221 G7
Tillietudlem S Lans...... 198 D4
Tillingham Essex...... 72 E6
Tillington Herefs...... 80 B6
Tillington W Susx...... 36 E6
Tillington Common Herefs...... 80 B6
Tillybirloch Abers...... 244 F2
Tillyfourie Abers...... 244 E1
Tillygreig Abers...... 256 F7
Tillyrie P & K...... 221 K6
Tilmanstone Kent...... 41 J5
Tilney All Saints Norfk...... 120 C7
Tilney High End Norfk...... 120 C8
Tilney St Lawrence Norfk...... 120 C8
Tilshead Wilts...... 33 H1
Tilstock Shrops...... 113 J4
Tilston Ches W...... 113 G1
Tilstone Bank Ches W...... 130 A7
Tilstone Fearnall Ches W...... 130 A7
Tilsworth C Beds...... 68 B2

Tilton on the Hill Leics...... 101 G2
Tiltups End Gloucs...... 64 B7
Tilty Essex...... 70 E2
Timberland Lincs...... 136 B7
Timbersbrook Ches E...... 131 H7
Timberscombe Somset...... 29 G2
Timble N York...... 149 M5
Timewell Devon...... 29 H5
Timpanheck D & G...... 177 K4
Timperley Traffd...... 130 F2
Timsbury BaNES...... 45 K7
Timsbury Hants...... 34 D6
Timsgarry W Isls...... 282 d3
Timsgearraidh W Isls...... 282 d3
Timworth Suffk...... 89 H2
Timworth Green Suffk...... 89 H2
Tincleton Dorset...... 16 E4
Tindale Cumb...... 178 E7
Tindale Crescent Dur...... 169 G5
Tingewick Bucks...... 84 C8
Tingley Leeds...... 141 L3
Tingrith C Beds...... 68 C1
Tingwell Ork...... 275 c3
Tinhay Devon...... 12 A5
Tinker's Hill Hants...... 34 E2
Tinkersley Derbys...... 132 E6
Tinsley Sheff...... 133 H2
Tinsley Green W Susx...... 37 L3
Tintagel Cnwll...... 10 F5
Tintern Parva Mons...... 63 G7
Tintinhull Somset...... 31 H7
Tintwistle Derbys...... 140 F8
Tinwald D & G...... 176 D3
Tinwell Rutlnd...... 101 M2
Tippacott Devon...... 28 D2
Tipp's End Norfk...... 103 K4
Tiptoe Hants...... 18 C4
Tipton Sandw...... 98 B5
Tipton Green Sandw...... 98 B5
Tipton St John Devon...... 14 C4
Tiptree Essex...... 72 C4
Tiptree Heath Essex...... 72 C4
Tirabad Powys...... 78 B7
Tiree Ag & B...... 224 C6
Tiretigan Ag & B...... 206 A6
Tirley Gloucs...... 64 B2
Tirphil Caerph...... 61 H6
Tirril Cumb...... 166 C5
Tir-y-fron Flints...... 129 G7
Tisbury Wilts...... 32 F5
Tisman's Common W Susx...... 37 G4
Tissington Derbys...... 115 K1
Titchberry Devon...... 26 D5
Titchfield Hants...... 19 J3
Titchfield Common Hants...... 19 J2
Titchmarsh Nhants...... 102 A7
Titchwell Norfk...... 121 G3
Tithby Notts...... 117 J4
Titley Herefs...... 79 L3
Titmore Green Herts...... 69 G2
Titsey Surrey...... 51 L7
Titson Cnwll...... 11 J2
Tittensor Staffs...... 114 D4
Tittleshall Norfk...... 121 K7
Titton Worcs...... 81 J1
Tiverton Ches W...... 130 A7
Tiverton Devon...... 29 G8
Tivetshall St Margaret Norfk...... 106 D6
Tivetshall St Mary Norfk...... 106 D6
Tivington Somset...... 29 G2
Tivy Dale Barns...... 141 L6
Tixall Staffs...... 114 F7
Tixover Rutlnd...... 101 L3
Toab Shet...... 281 d9
Toadhole Derbys...... 133 H8
Toadmoor Derbys...... 116 B1
Tobermory Ag & B...... 226 F1
Toberonochy Ag & B...... 215 L3
Tobha Mor W Isls...... 283 b10
Tocher Abers...... 256 C5
Tochieneal Moray...... 267 K3
Tockenham Wilts...... 46 F3
Tockenham Wick Wilts...... 46 F3
Tocketts R & Cl...... 170 E7
Tockholes Bl w D...... 139 K3
Tockington S Glos...... 45 J2
Tockwith N York...... 151 G5
Todber Dorset...... 32 D7
Todburn Nthumb...... 191 G7
Toddington C Beds...... 68 C2
Toddington Gloucs...... 82 B8
Todds Green Herts...... 69 G2
Todenham Gloucs...... 82 F8
Todhills Angus...... 234 C7
Todhills Cumb...... 177 L6
Todhills Dur...... 169 G4
Todmorden Calder...... 140 E4
Todwick Rothm...... 133 K3
Toft Cambs...... 87 G4
Toft Ches E...... 130 E4

Toft Lincs 118 E8
Toft Shet 281 e4
Toft Warwks 83 L1
Toft Hill Dur 168 F5
Toft Hill Lincs 136 D7
Toft Monks Norfk 107 J4
Toft next Newton Lincs 135 L2
Toftrees Norfk 121 K6
Toftwood Norfk 105 K1
Togston Nthumb 191 J6
Tokavaig Highld 247 J6
Tokers Green Oxon 49 H3
Tolastadh W Isls 282 h2
Toldish Cnwll 4 F3
Tolland Somset 29 K4
Tollard Farnham Dorset 32 F7
Tollard Royal Wilts 32 F7
Toll Bar Donc 142 E6
Tollbar End Covtry 99 K8
Toller Fratrum Dorset 16 B3
Toller Porcorum Dorset 16 A3
Tollerton N York 151 H3
Tollerton Notts 117 G4
Toller Whelme Dorset 15 L2
Tollesbury Essex 72 D5
Tolleshunt D'Arcy Essex 72 D5
Tolleshunt Knights Essex 72 D4
Tolleshunt Major Essex 72 C5
Tolpuddle Dorset 16 F4
Tolsta W Isls 282 h2
Tolworth Gt Lon 51 G5
Tomatin Highld 252 E6
Tomchrasky Highld 239 M1
Tomdoun Highld 239 K3
Tomich Highld 250 B6
Tomich Highld 250 F2
Tomich Highld 263 J5
Tomich Highld 272 F7
Tomintoul Moray 254 D7
Tomlow Warwks 83 K3
Tomnacross Highld 250 F3
Tomnavoulin Moray 254 D6
Tompkin Staffs 114 E1
Ton Mons 62 C6
Ton Mons 62 D7
Tonbridge Kent 38 F4
Tondu Brdgnd 42 D5
Tonedale Somset 29 L6
Ton fanau Gwynd 92 C3
Tong C Brad 141 K2
Tong Kent 40 C4
Tong Shrops 97 H2
Tonge Leics 116 C7
Tong Green Kent 40 C4
Tongham Surrey 36 C1
Tongland D & G 175 H4
Tong Norton Shrops 97 H2
Tongue Highld 277 K5
Tongue End Lincs 118 F7
Tongwynlais Cardif 43 H5
Tonmawr Neath 42 B2
Tonna Neath 57 L5
Ton-teg Rhondd 43 H4
Tonwell Herts 69 J4
Tonypandy Rhondd 42 F3
Tonyrefail Rhondd 42 F4
Toot Baldon Oxon 66 E7
Toot Hill Essex 70 D6
Toothill Hants 34 E7
Toothill Swindn 47 G2
Tooting Gt Lon 51 H5
Tooting Bec Gt Lon 51 H4
Topcliffe N York 160 F7
Topcroft Norfk 106 F5
Topcroft Street Norfk 106 F5
Top End Bed 85 L3
Topham Donc 143 G4
Top of Hebers Rochdl 140 C6
Toppesfield Essex 88 E7
Toppings Bolton 139 L5
Toprow Norfk 106 D4
Topsham Devon 13 M5
Top-y-rhos Flints 128 F7
Torbeg N Ayrs 194 D5
Torboll Highld 273 H8
Torbreck Highld 251 H3
Torbryan Devon 8 B2
Torcastle Highld 239 J7
Torcross Devon 8 B6
Tore Highld 251 G1
Torfrey Cnwll 5 J4
Torinturk Ag & B 206 C6
Torksey Lincs 135 G4
Tormarton S Glos 45 M3
Tormore N Ayrs 194 D4
Tornagrain Highld 252 E2
Tornaveen Abers 244 D2
Torness Highld 251 G6
Toronto Dur 169 G4
Torpenhow Cumb 165 G3

Torphichen W Loth 210 C4
Torphins Abers 244 E3
Torpoint Cnwll 6 E4
Torquay Torbay 8 D2
Torquay Crematorium Torbay 8 D2
Torr Devon 7 H4
Torran Highld 259 K6
Torrance E Duns 209 G4
Torranyard N Ayrs 196 D2
Torre Somset 29 J3
Torridon Highld 260 E8
Torridon House Highld 260 D8
Torrin Highld 247 J4
Torrisdale Ag & B 194 B4
Torrisdale Highld 278 B4
Torrish Highld 274 C4
Torrisholme Lancs 147 J3
Torrobull Highld 272 E7
Torry C Aber 245 L3
Torryburn Fife 210 D2
Torteval Guern 9 h4
Torthorwald D & G 176 D3
Tortington W Susx 21 G6
Torton Worcs 81 J1
Tortworth S Glos 63 L8
Torvaig Highld 259 H7
Torver Cumb 156 C4
Torwood Falk 209 M2
Torwoodlee Border 201 G5
Torworth Notts 134 D2
Tosberry Devon 26 D6
Toscaig Highld 247 L1
Toseland Cambs 86 E3
Tosside Lancs 148 D4
Tostock Suffk 89 J3
Totaig Highld 258 B6
Tote Highld 259 G6
Tote Highld 259 J4
Tote Hill W Susx 36 C6
Totford Hants 35 H3
Tothill Lincs 137 H3
Totland IoW 18 E6
Totley Sheff 132 F4
Totley Brook Sheff 132 F4
Totnes Devon 8 B3
Toton Notts 116 E4
Totronald Ag & B 224 F4
Totscore Highld 258 F3
Tottenham Gt Lon 51 J1
Tottenhill Norfk 104 C1
Totteridge Gt Lon 69 H8
Totternhoe C Beds 68 C3
Tottington Bury 140 A5
Tottleworth Lancs 139 L2
Totton Hants 34 D8
Touchen End W & M 49 L4
Toulston N York 151 G7
Toulton Somset 30 B4
Toulvaddie Highld 264 D4
Tovil Kent 39 J3
Towan Cnwll 5 G5
Towan Cnwll 10 B7
Toward Ag & B 207 J5
Toward Quay Ag & B 207 J5
Towcester Nhants 84 D5
Towednack Cnwll 2 D3
Towersey Oxon 67 H6
Towie Abers 244 A1
Tow Law Dur 168 E3
Town End Cambs 103 J4
Town End Cumb 156 E1
Town End Cumb 156 F6
Town End Cumb 166 E5
Townend W Duns 208 C4
Towngate Cumb 166 C1
Towngate Lincs 102 C1
Town Green Lancs 138 E6
Town Green Norfk 107 G5
Townhead Barns 141 J7
Town Head Cumb 156 F2
Townhead Cumb 164 E3
Townhead Cumb 166 E4
Townhead D & G 176 D1
Town Head N York 148 E4
Townhead of Greenlaw D & G 175 J2
Townhill Fife 210 F1
Town Kelloe Dur 169 K3
Townlake Devon 12 A7
Town Lane Wigan 139 K7
Town Littleworth E Susx 22 F4
Town of Lowton Wigan 139 J8
Town Row E Susx 38 E7
Towns End Hants 48 E7
Townsend Somset 30 E7
Townshend Cnwll 2 F4
Town Street Suffk 104 F6
Townwell S Glos 45 L1
Town Yetholm Border 202 C7
Towthorpe C York 151 K4

Towthorpe E R Yk 152 D3
Towton N York 151 G7
Towyn Conwy 127 K4
Toxteth Lpool 129 H2
Toynton All Saints Lincs 137 G7
Toynton Fen Side Lincs 137 G7
Toynton St Peter Lincs 137 G7
Toy's Hill Kent 38 D3
Trabboch E Ayrs 196 E6
Trabbochburn E Ayrs 196 F6
Traboe Cnwll 3 J6
Tracebridge Somset 29 K6
Tradespark Highld 264 D8
Trallong Powys 60 E1
Tranent E Loth 211 L4
Tranmere Wirral 129 H2
Trantelbeg Highld 278 F5
Trantlemore Highld 278 F5
Tranwell Nthumb 180 F2
Trapp Carmth 59 J5
Traprain E Loth 212 D4
Trap's Green Warwks 82 D1
Trapshill W Berk 48 A6
Traquair Border 200 D6
Trash Green W Berk 49 G5
Trawden Lancs 148 F8
Trawscoed Cerdgn 77 J1
Trawsfynydd Gwynd 110 D4
Trealaw Rhondd 42 F3
Treales Lancs 138 F1
Trearddur Bay IoA 124 D4
Treaslane Highld 258 F6
Treator Cnwll 10 C7
Tre Aubrey V Glam 43 G7
Trebanog Rhondd 42 F4
Trebanos Neath 57 K4
Trebartha Cnwll 11 K7
Trebarwith Cnwll 10 E5
Trebeath Cnwll 11 J5
Trebetherick Cnwll 10 C7
Treborough Somset 29 H4
Trebudannon Cnwll 4 E3
Trebullett Cnwll 11 L7
Treburgett Cnwll 10 E6
Treburley Cnwll 11 L7
Treburrick Cnwll 10 B8
Trebyan Cnwll 5 J2
Trecastle Powys 60 C1
Trecogo Cnwll 11 K6
Trecott Devon 12 F3
Trecwn Pembks 74 F5
Trecynon Rhondd 60 F6
Tredaule Cnwll 11 J6
Tredavoe Cnwll 2 C5
Tredegar Blae G 61 J5
Tredethy Cnwll 10 F8
Tredington Gloucs 64 C1
Tredington Warwks 83 G6
Tredinnick Cnwll 5 H3
Tredinnick Cnwll 5 K6
Tredinnick Cnwll 5 M3
Tredinnick Cnwll 6 B3
Tredinnick Cnwll 10 C8
Tredomen Powys 61 H1
Tredrissi Pembks 75 J4
Tredrizzick Cnwll 10 D7
Tredunnock Mons 62 D8
Tredustan Powys 61 H1
Treen Cnwll 2 B6
Treen Cnwll 2 C3
Treesmill Cnwll 5 J4
Treeton Rothm 133 J2
Trefasser Pembks 74 E4
Trefdraeth IoA 125 G5
Trefecca Powys 61 J1
Trefeglwys Powys 93 L5
Trefenter Cerdgn 77 H2
Treffgarne Pembks 54 F2
Treffgarne Owen Pembks 74 E7
Trefforest Rhondd 43 G4
Treffynnon Pembks 74 D6
Trefil Blae G 61 H4
Trefilan Cerdgn 77 G4
Trefin Pembks 74 D5
Treflach Wood Shrops 112 C6
Trefnannau Powys 112 C8
Trefnant Denbgs 128 C5
Trefonen Shrops 112 C6
Trefor Gwynd 108 F2
Trefor IoA 124 F4
Trefrew Cnwll 10 F5
Trefriw Conwy 126 F7
Tregadillett Cnwll 11 K6
Tre-gagle Mons 63 G5
Tregaian IoA 125 H4
Tregare Mons 62 E5
Tregarne Cnwll 3 K6
Tregaron Cerdgn 77 J3
Tregarth Gwynd 126 B6
Tregaswith Cnwll 4 E2

Tregatta Cnwll 10 F5
Tregawne Cnwll 5 G2
Tregeare Cnwll 11 J5
Tregeiriog Wrexhm 112 B5
Tregele IoA 124 F1
Tregellist Cnwll 10 E7
Tregenna Cnwll 4 E6
Tregeseal Cnwll 2 B5
Tregew Cnwll 3 K4
Tre-Gibbon Rhondd 60 F6
Tregidden Cnwll 3 K6
Tregiskey Cnwll 5 G5
Treglemais Pembks 74 D6
Tregole Cnwll 11 H3
Tregolls Cnwll 3 J4
Tregonce Cnwll 10 C7
Tregonetha Cnwll 4 F2
Tregony Cnwll 4 F6
Tregoodwell Cnwll 11 G6
Tregorrick Cnwll 5 G4
Tregoss Cnwll 4 F3
Tregoyd Powys 79 H7
Tregrehan Mills Cnwll 5 H4
Tre-groes Cerdgn 76 D3
Tregullon Cnwll 5 H2
Tregunna Cnwll 10 D7
Tregunnon Cnwll 11 J6
Tregurrian Cnwll 4 D2
Tregynon Powys 94 D2
Tre-gynwr Carmth 58 D5
Trehafod Rhondd 43 G3
Trehan Cnwll 6 D3
Treharris Myr Td 43 H2
Treharrock Cnwll 10 E6
Trehemborne Cnwll 10 B7
Treherbert Carmth 77 G6
Treherbert Rhondd 42 E2
Trehunist Cnwll 6 C2
Trekenner Cnwll 11 L7
Treknow Cnwll 10 E5
Trelan Cnwll 3 J7
Trelash Cnwll 11 H4
Trelassick Cnwll 4 E4
Trelawne Cnwll 5 L4
Trelawnyd Flints 128 C4
Treleague Cnwll 3 K6
Treleaver Cnwll 3 K7
Trelech Carmth 58 A3
Trelech a'r Betws Carmth 58 C3
Treleddyd-fawr Pembks 74 B6
Trelew Cnwll 3 K4
Trelewis Myr Td 43 H2
Treligga Cnwll 10 E5
Trelights Cnwll 10 D6
Trelill Cnwll 10 E7
Trelinnoe Cnwll 11 K6
Trelion Cnwll 4 F4
Trelissick Cnwll 3 L3
Trellech Mons 63 G6
Trelleck Grange Mons 62 F6
Trelogan Flints 128 D4
Trelow Cnwll 4 F1
Trelowarren Cnwll 3 J6
Trelowia Cnwll 6 B3
Treluggan Cnwll 3 M3
Trelystan Powys 95 G3
Tremadog Gwynd 109 K3
Tremail Cnwll 11 H5
Tremain Cerdgn 75 M3
Tremaine Cnwll 11 J5
Tremar Cnwll 6 B1
Trematon Cnwll 6 D3
Trembraze Cnwll 6 B2
Tremeirchion Denbgs 128 C5
Tremethick Cross Cnwll 2 C5
Tremore Cnwll 5 G2
Tre-Mostyn Flints 128 D4
Trenance Cnwll 3 K6
Trenance Cnwll 4 D1
Trenance Cnwll 10 C8
Trenarren Cnwll 5 H5
Trench Wrekin 96 F1
Trench Green Oxon 49 G3
Trendeal Cnwll 4 E4
Trendrine Cnwll 2 D4
Treneague Cnwll 10 D7
Trenear Cnwll 3 H5
Treneglos Cnwll 11 H5
Trenerth Cnwll 2 F4
Trenewan Cnwll 5 K4
Trenewth Cnwll 10 F7
Trengune Cnwll 11 H4
Treninnick Cnwll 4 D3
Trenowah Cnwll 4 C3
Trenoweth Cnwll 3 K4
Trent Dorset 31 K7
Trentham C Stke 114 D3
Trentishoe Devon 28 A1
Trentlock Derbys 116 E5
Trent Port Lincs 135 G3

Trent Vale C Stke	114	D3
Trenwheal Cnwll	3	G4
Treoes V Glam	42	E6
Treorchy Rhondd	42	E2
Trequite Cnwll	10	E7
Tre'r-ddol Cerdgn	92	E5
Trerhyngyll V Glam	42	F6
Trerulefoot Cnwll	6	C3
Tresaith Cerdgn	76	A5
Tresawle Cnwll	4	E5
Tresco IoS	10	b2
Trescott Staffs	97	J4
Trescowe Cnwll	2	F5
Tresean Cnwll	4	C3
Tresham Gloucs	46	A1
Treshnish Isles Ag & B	225	H7
Tresillian Cnwll	4	E5
Tresinney Cnwll	10	F6
Treskinnick Cross Cnwll	11	H3
Tresmeer Cnwll	11	J5
Tresparrett Cnwll	11	G4
Tressait P & K	232	B3
Tresta Shet	281	d6
Tresta Shet	281	f3
Treswell Notts	134	F4
Treswithian Cnwll	3	G3
Treswithian Downs Crematorium Cnwll	3	G3
Tre Taliesin Cerdgn	92	E5
Trethevey Cnwll	10	F5
Trethewey Cnwll	2	B6
Trethomas Caerph	43	J4
Trethosa Cnwll	4	F4
Trethurgy Cnwll	5	H4
Tretio Pembks	74	C6
Tretire Herefs	63	G2
Tretower Powys	61	J3
Treuddyn Flints	128	F8
Trevadlock Cnwll	11	K6
Trevalga Cnwll	10	F4
Trevalyn Wrexhm	129	J8
Trevanger Cnwll	10	D7
Trevanson Cnwll	10	D8
Trevarrack Cnwll	2	E3
Trevarren Cnwll	4	E3
Trevarrian Cnwll	4	D2
Trevarrick Cnwll	5	G6
Trevarth Cnwll	3	J3
Trevaughan Carmth	55	L4
Tre-Vaughan Carmth	58	D4
Treveal Cnwll	2	D3
Treveal Cnwll	4	C3
Treveighan Cnwll	10	F6
Trevellas Downs Cnwll	4	B4
Trevelmond Cnwll	5	L2
Tremember Cnwll	4	D3
Treveor Cnwll	5	G6
Treverbyn Cnwll	4	E5
Treverbyn Cnwll	5	G3
Treverva Cnwll	3	J5
Trevescan Cnwll	2	B6
Trevethin Torfn	62	B6
Trevia Cnwll	10	F6
Trevigro Cnwll	6	C1
Trevilla Cnwll	3	L3
Trevilson Cnwll	4	D4
Treviscoe Cnwll	4	F4
Treviskey Cnwll	4	F6
Trevithick Cnwll	4	E2
Trevithick Cnwll	4	F6
Trevoll Cnwll	4	D3
Trevone Cnwll	10	B7
Trevor Wrexhm	112	C3
Trevorgans Cnwll	2	B6
Trevorrick Cnwll	10	C7
Trevose Cnwll	10	B7
Trew Cnwll	3	G5
Trewalder Cnwll	10	F6
Trewalkin Powys	61	J1
Trewarmett Cnwll	10	F5
Trewassa Cnwll	11	G5
Trewavas Cnwll	2	F5
Treween Cnwll	11	J6
Trewellard Cnwll	2	B4
Trewen Cnwll	11	J6
Trewennack Cnwll	3	H5
Trewent Pembks	55	G7
Trewern Powys	95	G1
Trewetha Cnwll	10	E6
Trewethern Cnwll	10	E7
Trewidland Cnwll	6	B3
Trewillis Cnwll	3	K7
Trewint Cnwll	6	B2
Trewint Cnwll	11	J6
Trewithian Cnwll	3	M4
Trewoodloe Cnwll	11	L8
Trewoon Cnwll	3	H7
Trewoon Cnwll	5	G4
Treworga Cnwll	4	E6
Treworgan Cnwll	4	D5

Treworlas Cnwll	4	E7
Treworld Cnwll	11	G4
Treworthal Cnwll	3	M3
Tre-wyn Mons	62	C3
Treyarnon Cnwll	10	B7
Treyford W Susx	20	D3
Trickett's Cross Dorset	17	L2
Triermain Cumb	178	E5
Triffleton Pembks	75	G7
Trillacott Cnwll	11	K4
Trimdon Dur	169	K4
Trimdon Colliery Dur	169	K4
Trimdon Grange Dur	169	K3
Trimingham Norfk	122	F4
Trimley Lower Street Suffk	91	G7
Trimley St Martin Suffk	91	G7
Trimley St Mary Suffk	91	G7
Trimpley Worcs	97	H7
Trimsaran Carmth	56	E4
Trims Green Herts	70	C4
Trimstone Devon	27	J2
Trinafour P & K	231	K3
Trinant Caerph	61	K7
Tring Herts	68	A5
Tringford Herts	67	M4
Tring Wharf Herts	68	A4
Trinity Angus	234	F3
Trinity Jersey	9	d2
Trinity Gask P & K	221	G3
Triscombe Somset	29	L4
Trislaig Highld	239	H8
Trispen Cnwll	4	D5
Tritlington Nthumb	191	J7
Troan Cnwll	4	E3
Trochry P & K	232	E7
Troedrhiwfuwch Caerph	61	H6
Troedyraur Cerdgn	76	B6
Troedyrhiw Myr Td	61	G6
Trofarth Conwy	127	G5
Trois Bois Jersey	9	c2
Troon Cnwll	3	G3
Troon S Ayrs	196	C5
Trossachs Pier Stirlg	219	H5
Troston Suffk	89	H1
Troswell Cnwll	11	J4
Trotshill Worcs	81	K4
Trottiscliffe Kent	52	D7
Trotton W Susx	36	B6
Troughend Nthumb	190	B7
Trough Gate Lancs	140	D3
Troutbeck Cumb	156	F2
Troutbeck Cumb	165	L5
Troutbeck Bridge Cumb	156	F3
Troway Derbys	133	H4
Trowbridge Wilts	46	B7
Trowell Notts	116	E3
Trowle Common Wilts	46	B7
Trowley Bottom Herts	68	D4
Trowse Newton Norfk	106	E2
Troy Leeds	150	C8
Trudoxhill Somset	32	C2
Trull Somset	30	B6
Trumfleet Donc	142	F5
Trumpan Highld	258	C4
Trumpet Herefs	80	F7
Trumpington Cambs	87	J4
Trumpsgreen Surrey	50	C5
Trunch Norfk	122	F4
Trunnah Lancs	147	G7
Truro Cnwll	4	D6
Truscott Cnwll	11	K5
Trusham Devon	13	K6
Trusley Derbys	115	L4
Trusthorpe Lincs	137	K3
Trysull Staffs	97	J4
Tubney Oxon	66	B7
Tuckenhay Devon	8	B4
Tuckhill Shrops	97	H5
Tuckingmill Cnwll	3	G3
Tuckingmill Wilts	32	F5
Tuckton Bmouth	18	A5
Tucoyse Cnwll	4	F5
Tuddenham Suffk	88	E1
Tuddenham Suffk	90	E5
Tudeley Kent	38	F4
Tudhoe Dur	169	H3
Tudorville Herefs	63	H3
Tudweiliog Gwynd	108	D4
Tuesley Surrey	36	E3
Tuffley Gloucs	64	B4
Tufton Hants	34	F2
Tufton Pembks	75	H6
Tugby Leics	101	G3
Tugford Shrops	96	D6
Tughall Nthumb	203	K7
Tullibody Clacks	220	E8
Tullich Highld	251	H6
Tullich Highld	264	D4
Tulliemet P & K	232	F5
Tulloch Abers	256	E5

Tullochgorm Ag & B	216	F8
Tulloch Station Highld	240	B7
Tullymurdoch P & K	233	J5
Tullynessle Abers	255	L7
Tulse Hill Gt Lon	51	J4
Tumble Carmth	58	F6
Tumbler's Green Essex	71	K2
Tumby Lincs	136	D7
Tumby Woodside Lincs	136	E6
Tummel Bridge P & K	231	L4
Tunbridge Wells Kent	38	F5
Tundergarth D & G	177	G3
Tungate Norfk	122	F5
Tunley BaNES	45	K7
Tunstall C Stke	114	D1
Tunstall E R Yk	145	J2
Tunstall Kent	40	A3
Tunstall Lancs	157	K8
Tunstall N York	160	B3
Tunstall Norfk	107	J2
Tunstall Staffs	114	B6
Tunstall Suffk	91	H4
Tunstall Sundld	181	J8
Tunstead Derbys	132	B5
Tunstead Norfk	122	F7
Tunstead Milton Derbys	131	K4
Tunworth Hants	35	K1
Tupsley Herefs	80	C7
Turgis Green Hants	49	G7
Turkdean Gloucs	65	G4
Tur Langton Leics	100	F4
Turleigh Wilts	46	A6
Turleygreen Shrops	97	H6
Turn Lancs	140	B4
Turnastone Herefs	79	L7
Turnberry S Ayrs	182	F2
Turnchapel C Plym	6	F4
Turnditch Derbys	116	A2
Turner Green Lancs	139	J2
Turner's Green E Susx	23	L3
Turner's Green Warwks	82	E2
Turner's Hill W Susx	38	A6
Turners Puddle Dorset	16	F4
Turnford Herts	69	K6
Turnhouse C Edin	211	G4
Turnworth Dorset	16	F1
Turriff Abers	268	C6
Turton Bottoms Bl w D	139	L4
Turves Cambs	103	G4
Turvey Bed	85	J5
Turville Bucks	49	J1
Turville Heath Bucks	49	H1
Turweston Bucks	84	B7
Tushielaw Inn Border	187	L3
Tutbury Staffs	115	L6
Tutnall Worcs	82	A1
Tutshill Gloucs	63	G8
Tuttington Norfk	122	E6
Tutwell Cnwll	11	M7
Tuxford Notts	134	E5
Twatt Ork	275	b3
Twatt Shet	281	d6
Twechar E Duns	209	J4
Tweedbank Border	201	H6
Tweedmouth Nthumb	202	F3
Tweedsmuir Border	187	G1
Twelveheads Cnwll	4	B6
Twelve Oaks E Susx	24	C3
Twemlow Green Ches E	130	F6
Twenty Lincs	118	F7
Twerton BaNES	45	L6
Twickenham Gt Lon	50	F4
Twigworth Gloucs	64	B3
Twineham W Susx	22	C3
Twineham Green W Susx	22	C3
Twinhoe BaNES	45	L7
Twinstead Essex	89	H7
Twitchen Devon	28	D5
Twitchen Shrops	95	J7
Twitham Kent	41	H4
Two Bridges Devon	12	E7
Two Dales Derbys	132	E7
Two Gates Staffs	99	G3
Two Mile Oak Cross Devon	8	C1
Two Pots Devon	27	J2
Two Waters Herts	68	D6
Twycross Leics	99	J3
Twyford Bucks	67	G2
Twyford Hants	35	G6
Twyford Leics	100	F2
Twyford Lincs	118	B6
Twyford Norfk	121	M6
Twyford Wokham	49	J4
Twyford Common Herefs	80	C8
Twyn-carno Caerph	61	H5
Twynholm D & G	175	G4
Twyning Green Gloucs	81	L7
Twynllanan Carmth	59	L4
Twyn-yr-Odyn V Glam	43	H7
Twyn-y-Sheriff Mons	62	E6

Twywell Nhants	101	L7
Tyberton Herefs	79	M7
Tyburn Birm	98	E5
Tycroes Carmth	57	H3
Ty Croes IoA	124	F5
Tycrwyn Powys	111	L7
Tydd Gote Lincs	120	A7
Tydd St Giles Cambs	119	M8
Tydd St Mary Lincs	119	M7
Tye Hants	20	B6
Tye Green Essex	70	D2
Tye Green Essex	71	J3
Tye Green Essex	88	B8
Tyersal C Brad	141	J1
Tyldesley Wigan	139	K7
Tyler Hill Kent	40	F3
Tylers Green Bucks	67	L8
Tyler's Green Essex	70	D6
Tylers Green Surrey	51	K8
Tylorstown Rhondd	42	F3
Tylwch Powys	93	L7
Ty-nant Conwy	111	J3
Ty-nant Gwynd	111	H6
Tyndrum Stirlg	218	E1
Ty'n-dwr Denbgs	112	C3
Tynemouth N Tyne	181	J5
Tynemouth Crematorium N Tyne	181	J5
Tynewydd Rhondd	60	E7
Tyninghame E Loth	212	D3
Tynron D & G	185	K4
Ty'n-y-bryn Rhondd	42	F4
Ty'n-y-coedcae Caerph	43	K4
Tynygongl IoA	125	J3
Tynygraig Cerdgn	77	J1
Ty'n-y-Groes Conwy	126	F5
Tyn-y-nant Rhondd	43	G4
Tyringham M Keyn	85	G6
Tyseley Birm	98	E6
Tythegston Brdgnd	42	C6
Tytherington Ches E	131	H4
Tytherington S Glos	45	K1
Tytherington Somset	32	C2
Tytherington Wilts	32	F3
Tytherleigh Devon	15	H2
Tytherton Lucas Wilts	46	D4
Tyttenhanger Herts	68	F6
Tywardreath Cnwll	5	J4
Tywardreath Highway Cnwll	5	J4
Tywyn Conwy	126	F4
Tywyn Gwynd	92	C3

U

Ubbeston Green Suffk	91	H1
Ubley BaNES	45	G7
Uckerby N York	160	C2
Uckfield E Susx	23	H3
Uckinghall Worcs	81	K7
Uckington Gloucs	64	C2
Uckington Shrops	96	D2
Uddingston S Lans	209	J6
Uddington S Lans	198	E6
Udimore E Susx	24	F3
Udny Green Abers	256	F6
Udny Station Abers	257	G6
Uffcott Wilts	47	H3
Uffculme Devon	29	K8
Uffington Lincs	102	B2
Uffington Oxon	47	L1
Uffington Shrops	96	C1
Ufford C Pete	102	B3
Ufford Suffk	91	G5
Ufton Warwks	83	J3
Ufton Nervet W Berk	48	F5
Ugadale Ag & B	194	B5
Ugborough Devon	7	K4
Uggeshall Suffk	107	J7
Ugglebarnby N York	162	F1
Ughill Sheff	132	E2
Ugley Essex	70	D2
Ugley Green Essex	70	D2
Ugthorpe N York	171	J8
Uibhist A Deas W Isls	283	c10
Uibhist A Tuath W Isls	283	b8
Uig Ag & B	224	F4
Uig Highld	258	B6
Uig Highld	258	F4
Uig W Isls	282	E3
Uigshader Highld	259	G7
Uisken Ag & B	226	D8
Ulbster Highld	280	D7
Ulcat Row Cumb	165	L6
Ulceby Lincs	137	H5
Ulceby N Linc	144	E5
Ulceby Skitter N Linc	144	E5
Ulcombe Kent	39	L4
Uldale Cumb	165	H3
Uley Gloucs	63	M7

Ulgham Nthumb 191 J7
Ullapool Highld 261 J1
Ullenhall Warwks 82 D2
Ullenwood Gloucs 64 D4
Ulleskelf N York 151 H7
Ullesthorpe Leics 100 B6
Ulley Rothm 133 J2
Ullingswick Herefs 80 E5
Ullinish Lodge Hotel Highld 246 D1
Ullock Cumb 164 E6
Ulpha Cumb 156 B4
Ulpha Cumb 157 G6
Ulrome E R Yk 153 J4
Ulsta Shet 281 e4
Ulting Wick Essex 71 K5
Ulva Ag & B 226 D4
Ulverley Green Solhll 98 E7
Ulverston Cumb 156 C7
Ulwell Dorset 17 K6
Ulzieside D & G 185 J1
Umberleigh Devon 27 L6
Unapool Highld 271 H2
Underbarrow Cumb 157 G4
Under Burnmouth Border 178 B2
Undercliffe C Brad 141 J1
Underdale Shrops 96 B1
Underling Green Kent 39 J4
Under River Kent 38 E3
Underwood Notts 116 D2
Undley Suffk 104 D7
Undy Mons 44 E2
Union Mills IoM 154 e6
Union Street E Susx 39 H7
Unst Shet 281 f2
Unstone Derbys 133 G4
Unstone Green Derbys 133 G4
Unthank Cumb 165 L1
Unthank Cumb 166 B3
Unthank Cumb 166 E3
Unthank Derbys 132 F4
Unthank Nthumb 202 F3
Upavon Wilts 47 H7
Up Cerne Dorset 16 C2
Upchurch Kent 53 H5
Upcott Devon 28 D5
Upcott Herefs 79 K5
Upend Cambs 88 D3
Up Exe Devon 13 L2
Upgate Norfk 122 C7
Upgate Street Norfk 106 B5
Upgate Street Norfk 106 F5
Uphall Dorset 16 A2
Uphall W Loth 210 E5
Upham Devon 13 K1
Upham Hants 35 H6
Uphampton Herefs 79 M3
Uphampton Worcs 81 J2
Uphill N Som 44 C7
Up Holland Lancs 139 G6
Uplawmoor E Rens 208 D8
Upleadon Gloucs 63 L2
Upleatham R & Cl 170 E6
Uplees Kent 40 C2
Uploders Dorset 15 L4
Uplowman Devon 29 J7
Uplyme Devon 15 H4
Up Marden W Susx 20 C4
Upminster Gt Lon 52 C2
Up Mudford Somset 31 J7
Up Nately Hants 49 G8
Upottery Devon 14 E1
Upper Affcot Shrops 95 K6
Upper Ardchronie Highld 263 G2
Upper Arley Worcs 97 H7
Upper Arncott Oxon 66 F4
Upper Astrop Nhants 83 L7
Upper Basildon W Berk 48 F4
Upper Batley Kirk 141 K3
Upper Beeding W Susx 22 B5
Upper Benefield Nhants 101 L5
Upper Bentley Worcs 82 B2
Upper Bighouse Highld 278 F5
Upper Birchwood Derbys 133 J8
Upper Boat Rhondd 43 H4
Upper Boddington Nhants 83 L5
Upper Borth Cerdgn 92 D5
Upper Brailes Warwks 83 G7
Upper Breakish Highld 247 L4
Upper Breinton Herefs 80 B7
Upper Broadheath Worcs 81 J4
Upper Broughton Notts 117 J6
Upper Bucklebury W Berk 48 D5
Upper Burgate Hants 33 K7
Upper Bush Medway 52 E6
Upperby Cumb 177 L8
Upper Caldecote C Beds 86 D6
Upper Canada N Som 44 D7
Upper Canterton Hants 18 D1
Upper Catesby Nhants 83 M3
Upper Catshill Worcs 98 B8

Upper Chapel Powys 78 D7
Upper Cheddon Somset 30 C5
Upper Chicksgrove Wilts 33 G5
Upper Chute Wilts 47 L8
Upper Clapton Gt Lon 51 K2
Upper Clatford Hants 34 D2
Upper Coberley Gloucs 64 E4
Upper Cokeham W Susx 21 K6
Upper Cotton Staffs 115 G2
Upper Cound Shrops 96 C2
Upper Cudworth Barns 142 B6
Upper Cumberworth Kirk 141 K6
Upper Cudworth Moray 267 J2
Upper Deal Kent 41 K5
Upper Dean Bed 85 L2
Upper Denby Kirk 141 K6
Upper Denton Cumb 178 A6
Upper Dicker E Susx 23 J5
Upper Dinchope Shrops 95 L6
Upper Dounreay Highld 279 H3
Upper Dovercourt Essex 73 K1
Upper Drumbane Stirlg 219 L6
Upper Dunsforth N York 150 F3
Upper Eashing Surrey 36 E2
Upper Eathie Highld 263 K7
Upper Egleton Herefs 80 E6
Upper Elkstone Staffs 131 L7
Upper Ellastone Staffs 115 J3
Upper End Derbys 132 B4
Upper Enham Hants 34 E1
Upper Farmcote Shrops 97 H5
Upper Farringdon Hants 35 L4
Upper Framilode Gloucs 63 L5
Upper Froyle Hants 35 M2
Upperglen Highld 258 E6
Upper Godney Somset 31 H2
Upper Gravenhurst C Beds 86 C8
Upper Green Mons 62 D3
Upper Green Suffk 88 E2
Upper Green W Berk 48 A6
Upper Grove Common Herefs 63 H2
Upper Hackney Derbys 132 F7
Upper Hale Surrey 36 B1
Upper Halliford Surrey 50 E5
Upper Halling Medway 52 E6
Upper Hambleton Rutlnd 101 K2
Upper Harbledown Kent 40 F4
Upper Hardres Court Kent 40 F5
Upper Hardwick Herefs 79 M4
Upper Hartfield E Susx 38 C6
Upper Hartshay Derbys 116 C2
Upper Hatherley Gloucs 64 D3
Upper Hatton Staffs 114 C4
Upper Haugh Rothm 142 C8
Upper Hayton Shrops 96 C7
Upper Heaton Kirk 141 J4
Upper Helmsley N York 151 L4
Upper Hergest Herefs 79 J4
Upper Heyford Nhants 84 C3
Upper Heyford Oxon 66 D2
Upper Hill Herefs 80 B4
Upper Hockenden Kent 52 B5
Upper Hopton Kirk 141 K4
Upper Howsell Worcs 81 H5
Upper Hulme Staffs 131 K7
Upper Ifold Surrey 36 F4
Upper Inglesham Swindn 65 J7
Upper Kilcott Gloucs 46 A1
Upper Killay Swans 57 G6
Upper Kinchrackine Ag & B 217 J2
Upper Lambourn W Berk 47 L3
Upper Landywood Staffs 98 C2
Upper Langford N Som 44 F7
Upper Langwith Derbys 133 K5
Upper Largo Fife 223 G6
Upper Leigh Staffs 115 G4
Upper Littleton N Som 45 H6
Upper Lochton Abers 244 F4
Upper Longdon Staffs 115 H8
Upper & Lower Stondon C Beds 86 D8
Upper Ludstone Shrops 97 H4
Upper Lybster Highld 275 H1
Upper Lydbrook Gloucs 63 J4
Upper Lyde Herefs 80 C6
Upper Lye Herefs 79 M2
Upper Maes-coed Herefs 79 K8
Upper Midhope Sheff 141 K7
Uppermill Oldham 140 F6
Upper Milton Worcs 81 J1
Upper Minety Wilts 46 E1
Upper Moor Worcs 82 A5
Upper Moor Side Leeds 141 K2
Upper Mulben Moray 267 G6
Upper Netchwood Shrops 96 E5
Upper Nobut Staffs 115 G4
Upper Norwood W Susx 20 F3
Upper Padley Derbys 132 E4
Upper Pennington Hants 18 D4
Upper Pollicott Bucks 67 H4
Upper Poppleton C York 151 J5

Upper Quinton Warwks 82 E6
Upper Ratley Hants 34 D6
Upper Rissington Gloucs 65 J3
Upper Rochford Worcs 80 E2
Upper Ruscoe D & G 174 E3
Upper Sapey Herefs 80 F3
Upper Seagry Wilts 46 D3
Upper Shelton C Beds 85 K6
Upper Sheringham Norfk 122 C3
Upper Skelmorlie N Ayrs 207 K5
Upper Slaughter Gloucs 65 H3
Upper Soudley Gloucs 63 K5
Upper Spond Herefs 79 K4
Upper Standen Kent 41 H7
Upper Staploe Bed 86 C3
Upper Stoke Norfk 106 E3
Upper Stowe Nhants 84 C4
Upper Street Hants 33 K7
Upper Street Norfk 106 D7
Upper Street Norfk 123 G7
Upper Street Norfk 123 G8
Upper Street Suffk 88 F5
Upper Street Suffk 90 C5
Upper Street Suffk 90 D8
Upper Strensham Worcs 81 K7
Upper Sundon C Beds 68 D2
Upper Swell Gloucs 65 H2
Upper Tankersley Barns 142 A7
Upper Tasburgh Norfk 106 E4
Upper Tean Staffs 115 G4
Upperthong Kirk 141 H6
Upperthorpe Derbys 133 J4
Upperthorpe N Linc 143 J7
Upper Threapwood Ches W 113 G3
Upperton W Susx 36 E6
Upper Town Derbys 115 L1
Uppertown Derbys 132 F6
Upper Town Dur 168 D3
Upper Town Herefs 80 D5
Uppertown Highld 280 D1
Upper Town N Som 45 G6
Upper Town Suffk 89 J2
Upper Tumble Carmth 59 G6
Upper Tysoe Warwks 83 H6
Upper Ufford Suffk 91 G4
Upperup Gloucs 64 F7
Upper Upham Wilts 47 J3
Upper Upnor Medway 53 G5
Upper Victoria Angus 234 E8
Upper Vobster Somset 32 B1
Upper Wardington Oxon 83 L6
Upper Weald M Keyn 84 F7
Upper Weedon Nhants 84 B3
Upper Welland Worcs 81 H7
Upper Wellingham E Susx 23 G4
Upper Weston BaNES 45 L5
Upper Weybread Suffk 106 E7
Upper Wick Worcs 81 J5
Upper Wield Hants 35 K3
Upper Winchendon Bucks 67 H4
Upperwood Derbys 132 F8
Upper Woodford Wilts 33 K3
Upper Wootton Hants 48 E7
Upper Wraxall Wilts 46 A4
Upper Wyche Worcs 81 H6
Uppincott Devon 13 L2
Uppingham Rutlnd 101 J3
Uppington Dorset 17 K2
Uppington Shrops 96 D2
Upsall N York 161 G5
Upsettlington Border 202 D4
Upshire Essex 69 L7
Up Somborne Hants 34 E4
Upstreet Kent 41 H3
Up Sydling Dorset 16 B2
Upthorpe Suffk 89 K1
Upton Bucks 67 J5
Upton C Pete 102 C3
Upton Cambs 102 D7
Upton Ches W 129 J6
Upton Cnwll 11 H2
Upton Cnwll 11 K8
Upton Cumb 165 K3
Upton Devon 7 K6
Upton Devon 14 C2
Upton Dorset 16 E6
Upton Dorset 17 J4
Upton E R Yk 153 J5
Upton Halton 129 L2
Upton Hants 34 E1
Upton Hants 47 M7
Upton Leics 99 K3
Upton Lincs 135 H2
Upton Nhants 84 D3
Upton Norfk 107 H1
Upton Notts 117 J1
Upton Notts 134 E4
Upton Oxon 48 D2
Upton Oxon 65 K4
Upton Pembks 55 G6

Upton R & Cl 171 G6
Upton Slough 50 B3
Upton Somset 29 H5
Upton Somset 31 G5
Upton Wakefd 142 D5
Upton Warwks 82 D4
Upton Wilts 32 E1
Upton Wirral 129 G1
Upton Bishop Herefs 63 K2
Upton Cheyney S Glos 45 K5
Upton Cressett Shrops 96 E5
Upton Crews Herefs 63 K2
Upton Cross Cnwll 11 K8
Upton End C Beds 86 C8
Upton Grey Hants 35 L1
Upton Heath Ches W 129 J5
Upton Hellions Devon 13 K2
Upton Lovell Wilts 32 F3
Upton Magna Shrops 96 C1
Upton Noble Somset 32 B3
Upton Pyne Devon 13 L3
Upton St Leonards Gloucs 64 B4
Upton Scudamore Wilts 32 E1
Upton Snodsbury Worcs 81 L4
Upton Towans Cnwll 2 F3
Upton-upon-Severn Worcs 81 K7
Upton Warren Worcs 81 L2
Upwaltham W Susx 20 F4
Upware Cambs 87 L1
Upwell Norfk 103 K3
Upwey Dorset 16 C5
Upwick Green Herts 70 C2
Upwood Cambs 102 E6
Urchfont Wilts 46 F7
Urdimarsh Herefs 80 C5
Ure Bank N York 150 D1
Urlay Nook S on T 169 L7
Urmston Traffd 130 E4
Urquhart Moray 266 F4
Urra N York 161 J2
Urray Highld 250 E1
Usan Angus 235 H4
Ushaw Moor Dur 169 G2
Usk Mons 62 D7
Usselby Lincs 136 A1
Usworth Sundld 181 H7
Utkinton Ches W 130 A6
Utley C Brad 149 J7
Uton Devon 13 J4
Utterby Lincs 136 F1
Uttoxeter Staffs 115 H5
Uwchmynydd Gwynd 108 B6
Uxbridge Gt Lon 50 D2
Uyeasound Shet 281 f2
Uzmaston Pembks 54 F4

V

Vale Guern 9 k2
Vale of Glamorgan
   Crematorium V Glam 43 H7
Valley IoA 124 E4
Valley End Surrey 50 B6
Valley Truckle Cnwll 10 F6
Valtos Highld 259 J4
Valtos W Isls 282 e3
Vange Essex 52 F2
Varteg Torfn 61 L6
Vatsetter Shet 281 e3
Vatten Highld 258 D7
Vaynor Myr Td 61 G5
Vazon Bay Guern 9 i2
Veensgarth Shet 281 e6
Velindre Powys 79 H7
Vellow Somset 29 G5
Velly Devon 26 E6
Venngreen Devon 26 F8
Vennington Shrops 95 H2
Venn Ottery Devon 14 C4
Venny Tedburn Devon 13 J3
Venterdon Cnwll 11 L7
Ventnor IoW 19 J8
Venton Devon 7 H3
Vernham Dean Hants 47 M7
Vernham Street Hants 47 M7
Vernolds Common Shrops 95 L7
Verwood Dorset 17 L3
Veryan Cnwll 4 E7
Veryan Green Cnwll 4 F6
Vicarage Devon 14 E7
Vickerstown Cumb 146 C2
Victoria Barns 141 J6
Victoria Blae G 61 J6
Victoria Cnwll 5 G3
Vidlin Shet 281 e5
Viewfield Moray 266 F3
Viewpark N Lans 209 J6
Vigo Kent 52 D6
Village de Putron Guern 9 k3

Ville la Bas Jersey 9 a1
Villiaze Guern 9 I3
Vinehall Street E Susx 24 D3
Vines Cross E Susx 23 K4
Vinters Park Crematorium
  Kent 39 K2
Virginia Water Surrey 50 C5
Virginstow Devon 11 M4
Vobster Somset 32 B1
Voe Shet 281 d5
Vowchurch Herefs 79 L7
Vulcan Village St Hel 130 B1

W

Waberthwaite Cumb 155 K4
Wackerfield Dur 168 F6
Wacton Norfk 106 D5
Wadborough Worcs 81 K5
Waddesdon Bucks 67 H4
Waddeton Devon 8 C3
Waddicar Sefton 138 E7
Waddingham Lincs 144 B8
Waddington Lancs 148 C7
Waddington Lincs 135 K6
Waddon Devon 13 K6
Waddon Dorset 16 B5
Wadebridge Cnwll 10 D8
Wadeford Somset 30 D8
Wadenhoe Nhants 101 M6
Wadesmill Herts 69 K4
Wadhurst E Susx 39 G7
Wadshelf Derbys 132 F5
Wadswick Wilts 46 B5
Wadworth Donc 142 F8
Waen Denbgs 127 K7
Waen Denbgs 128 D6
Waen Powys 112 C7
Waen Fach Powys 112 B8
Waen-pentir Gwynd 125 K6
Waen-wen Gwynd 125 K6
Wagbeach Shrops 95 J3
Wainfelin Torfn 62 B6
Wainfleet All Saints Lincs 137 J7
Wainfleet Bank Lincs 137 J7
Wainfleet St Mary Lincs 137 J8
Wainford Norfk 107 L5
Wainhouse Corner Cnwll 11 H3
Wainscott Medway 52 F5
Wain's Hill N Som 44 E5
Wainstalls Calder 141 G2
Waitby Cumb 158 C1
Waithe Lincs 145 H7
Wakefield Wakefd 142 A4
Wakefield Crematorium Wakefd .. 141 H4
Wake Green Birm 98 E6
Wakerley Nhants 101 L3
Wakes Colne Essex 72 C2
Walberswick Suffk 107 K8
Walberton W Susx 21 G5
Walbottle N u Ty 180 E5
Walbutt D & G 175 J1
Walby Cumb 178 B6
Walcombe Somset 31 J2
Walcot Lincs 118 E4
Walcot N Linc 143 M3
Walcot Shrops 95 J6
Walcot Shrops 96 D1
Walcot Swindn 47 H2
Walcot Warwks 82 D4
Walcote Leics 100 C6
Walcot Green Norfk 106 C7
Walcott Lincs 136 B8
Walcott Norfk 123 G5
Walden N York 159 H6
Walden Head N York 159 H6
Walden Stubbs N York 142 E4
Walderslade Medway 53 G6
Walderton W Susx 20 C5
Walditch Dorset 15 L4
Waldley Derbys 115 J4
Waldridge Dur 169 H1
Waldringfield Suffk 91 G6
Waldron E Susx 23 J3
Wales Rothm 133 J3
Wales Somset 31 K6
Walesby Lincs 136 B1
Walesby Notts 134 D5
Walford Herefs 63 H3
Walford Herefs 79 M1
Walford Shrops 113 G7
Walford Staffs 114 C5
Walford Heath Shrops 113 G7
Walgherton Ches E 113 M2
Walgrave Nhants 84 F1
Walhampton Hants 18 E4
Walkden Salfd 139 L7
Walker N u Ty 181 H6
Walkerburn Border 200 D5

Walker Fold Lancs 148 B7
Walkeringham Notts 134 F1
Walkerith Lincs 134 F1
Walkern Herts 69 H2
Walker's Green Herefs 80 C5
Walker's Heath Birm 98 D7
Walkerton Fife 222 C7
Walkford Dorset 18 C5
Walkhampton Devon 7 G1
Walkington E R Yk 152 F8
Walkley Sheff 133 G2
Walk Mill Lancs 140 C2
Walkwood Worcs 82 B2
Wall Nthumb 179 L5
Wall Staffs 98 E2
Wallacetown S Ayrs 183 H2
Wallacetown S Ayrs 196 C6
Wallands Park E Susx 22 F5
Wallasey Wirral 129 G1
Wall End Cumb 156 B6
Wall End Herefs 80 B4
Wallend Medway 53 J4
Waller's Green Herefs 80 F7
Wallhead Cumb 178 B6
Wall Heath Dudley 97 K5
Wall Houses Nthumb 180 C5
Wallingford Oxon 48 F1
Wallington Gt Lon 51 H6
Wallington Hants 19 K4
Wallington Herts 86 F8
Wallington Heath Wsall 98 C3
Wallis Pembks 75 G7
Wallisdown Poole 17 L4
Walliswood Surrey 37 H3
Walls Shet 281 c6
Wallsend N Tyne 181 H5
Wallthwaite Cumb 165 K5
Wall under Haywood Shrops 96 C5
Wallyford E Loth 211 L4
Walmer Kent 41 L5
Walmer Bridge Lancs 138 F3
Walmersley Bury 140 B5
Walmestone Kent 41 H3
Walmley Birm 98 F5
Walmley Ash Birm 98 F5
Walmsgate Lincs 137 G4
Walpole Somset 30 D3
Walpole Suffk 107 H8
Walpole Cross Keys Norfk 120 B7
Walpole Highway Norfk 120 B8
Walpole St Andrew Norfk 120 B8
Walpole St Peter Norfk 120 B8
Walrow Somset 30 E2
Walsall Wsall 98 C4
Walsall Wood Wsall 98 D3
Walsden Calder 140 D3
Walsgrave on Sowe Covtry 99 K7
Walsham le Willows Suffk 89 K1
Walshaw Bury 140 A5
Walshford N York 150 F5
Walsoken Norfk 103 K1
Walston S Lans 199 H4
Walsworth Herts 69 G1
Walter's Ash Bucks 67 K7
Walters Green Kent 38 D5
Walterston V Glam 43 G7
Walterstone Herefs 62 D2
Waltham Kent 40 E5
Waltham NE Lin 145 H7
Waltham Abbey Essex 69 K7
Waltham Chase Hants 35 H1
Waltham Cross Herts 69 K7
Waltham on the Wolds Leics ... 117 L6
Waltham St Lawrence W & M ... 49 K4
Waltham's Cross Essex 71 G1
Walthamstow Gt Lon 51 K1
Walton C Pete 102 D3
Walton Cumb 178 C6
Walton Derbys 133 G6
Walton Leeds 150 F6
Walton Leics 100 D6
Walton M Keyn 85 H7
Walton Powys 79 J3
Walton Shrops 95 L7
Walton Somset 31 G4
Walton Staffs 114 D5
Walton Staffs 114 D6
Walton Suffk 91 G8
Walton W Susx 20 D6
Walton Wakefd 142 A4
Walton Warwks 83 G4
Walton Wrekin 113 K7
Walton Cardiff Gloucs 64 C1
Walton East Pembks 55 H2
Walton Elm Dorset 32 C7
Walton Grounds Nhants 83 L8
Walton-in-Gordano N Som 44 E4
Walton Lea Crematorium
  Warrtn 130 B3
Walton-le-Dale Lancs 139 H2

Walton-on-Thames Surrey 50 E5
Walton-on-the-Hill Staffs ... 114 F7
Walton on the Hill Surrey ... 51 G7
Walton on the Naze Essex 73 K3
Walton on the Wolds Leics ... 117 G7
Walton-on-Trent Derbys 115 L7
Walton Park N Som 44 E4
Walton West Pembks 54 D4
Waltonwrays Crematorium
  N York 149 H5
Walwen Flints 128 D4
Walwen Flints 128 E4
Walwen Flints 128 E5
Walwick Nthumb 179 L5
Walworth Darltn 169 G7
Walworth Gt Lon 51 J3
Walworth Gate Darltn 169 G6
Walwyn's Castle Pembks 54 E4
Wambrook Somset 15 G1
Wampool Cumb 177 H7
Wanborough Surrey 36 D1
Wanborough Swindn 47 J2
Wandon End Herts 68 E3
Wandsworth Gt Lon 51 H4
Wangford Suffk 107 J7
Wanlip Leics 100 D1
Wanlockhead D & G 186 C4
Wannock E Susx 23 K6
Wansford C Pete 102 B3
Wansford E R Yk 153 G4
Wanshurst Green Kent 39 J4
Wanstead Gt Lon 51 L1
Wanstrow Somset 32 B3
Wanswell Gloucs 63 K6
Wantage Oxon 48 B1
Wants Green Worcs 81 H4
Wapley S Glos 45 L3
Wappenbury Warwks 83 J2
Wappenham Nhants 84 C6
Warbleton E Susx 23 K4
Warborough Oxon 66 F8
Warboys Cambs 102 F7
Warbreck Bpool 146 F8
Warbstow Cnwll 11 H4
Warburton Traffd 130 D2
Warcop Cumb 167 H7
Warden Kent 53 M5
Warden Nthumb 179 L5
Warden Street C Beds 86 C6
Ward End Birm 98 E5
Ward Green Suffk 90 B2
Ward Green Cross Lancs 148 A8
Wardhedges C Beds 85 L8
Wardington Oxon 83 L6
Wardle Ches E 130 B8
Wardle Rochdl 140 D4
Wardley Gatesd 181 H6
Wardley Rutlnd 101 H3
Wardley Salfd 140 A7
Wardlow Derbys 132 D5
Wardsend Ches E 131 J3
Wardy Hill Cambs 103 K7
Ware Herts 69 K4
Wareham Dorset 17 H5
Warehorne Kent 25 J1
Warenford Nthumb 203 J7
Waren Mill Nthumb 203 H5
Warenton Nthumb 203 H7
Wareside Herts 69 K4
Waresley Cambs 86 E4
Waresley Worcs 81 J1
Ware Street Kent 39 K2
Warfield Br For 49 L4
Warfleet Devon 8 C5
Wargate Lincs 119 H5
Wargrave Wokham 49 J3
Warham Herefs 80 B7
Warham All Saints Norfk 121 L3
Warham St Mary Norfk 121 L3
Wark Nthumb 179 K3
Wark Nthumb 202 C5
Warkleigh Devon 27 M6
Warkton Nhants 101 K7
Warkworth Nhants 83 L7
Warkworth Nthumb 191 K5
Warlaby N York 160 E4
Warland Calder 140 E4
Warleggan Cnwll 5 K1
Warleigh BaNES 46 A6
Warley Town Calder 141 G3
Warlingham Surrey 51 K7
Warmbrook Derbys 115 M1
Warmfield Wakefd 142 B4
Warmingham Ches E 130 D7
Warmington Nhants 102 B5
Warmington Warwks 83 K5
Warminster Wilts 32 E2
Warmley S Glos 45 K4
Warmsworth Donc 142 E7
Warmwell Dorset 16 E5

Warndon Worcs 81 K4
Warnford Hants 35 J6
Warnham W Susx 37 J4
Warnham Court W Susx 37 J4
Warningcamp W Susx 21 H5
Warninglid W Susx 37 K5
Warren Ches E 131 H5
Warren Pembks 54 F7
Warrenby R & Cl 170 D5
Warrenhill S Lans 198 F5
Warren Row W & M 49 K3
Warren's Green Herts 69 H2
Warren Street Kent 40 E5
Warrington M Keyn 85 H4
Warrington Warrtn 130 B2
Warriston C Edin 211 H4
Warriston Crematorium
  C Edin 211 H4
Warsash Hants 19 H2
Warslow Staffs 132 B7
Warsop Vale Notts 133 L6
Warter E R Yk 152 D5
Warthermaske N York 160 B6
Warthill N York 151 L5
Wartling E Susx 24 B5
Wartnaby Leics 117 J7
Warton Lancs 138 E2
Warton Lancs 147 K2
Warton Nthumb 190 E5
Warton Warwks 99 H3
Warwick Warwks 83 G2
Warwick Bridge Cumb 178 B7
Warwick-on-Eden Cumb 178 B7
Warwicksland Cumb 178 B3
Wasbister Ork 275 c3
Wasdale Head Cumb 156 B1
Wash Derbys 131 L3
Washall Green Herts 70 C1
Washaway Cnwll 5 H1
Washbourne Devon 8 B4
Washbrook Somset 30 F1
Washbrook Suffk 90 D6
Washfield Devon 29 G7
Washfold N York 159 J2
Washford Somset 29 J3
Washford Pyne Devon 28 E8
Washingborough Lincs 135 L5
Washington Sundld 181 H7
Washington W Susx 21 J4
Washwood Heath Birm 98 E5
Wasing W Berk 48 E6
Waskerley Dur 168 D2
Wasperton Warwks 83 G3
Wasps Nest Lincs 135 M6
Wass N York 161 J6
Watchet Somset 29 K2
Watchfield Oxon 47 K1
Watchfield Somset 30 E2
Watchgate Cumb 157 H3
Watchill Cumb 165 G2
Watcombe Torbay 8 D2
Watendlath Cumb 165 J7
Water Devon 13 H6
Water Lancs 140 C3
Waterbeach Cambs 87 K2
Waterbeach W Susx 20 E5
Waterbeck D & G 177 H3
Waterden Norfk 121 J4
Water Eaton Oxon 66 D5
Water Eaton Staffs 97 K1
Water End Bed 86 C5
Water End Bed 86 C5
Water End C Beds 85 L7
Waterend Cumb 164 F6
Water End E R Yk 152 B8
Water End Essex 88 B7
Water End Herts 68 D5
Water End Herts 69 G6
Waterfall Staffs 115 H1
Waterfoot E Rens 208 F7
Waterford Herts 69 J4
Water Fryston Wakefd 142 D2
Watergate Cnwll 11 G6
Waterhead Cumb 156 E2
Waterheads Border 200 B3
Waterhouses Dur 168 F3
Waterhouses Staffs 115 H2
Wateringbury Kent 39 H3
Waterlane Gloucs 64 D6
Waterloo Cnwll 10 F8
Waterloo Derbys 133 H7
Waterloo Herefs 79 L5
Waterloo Highld 247 K4
Waterloo N Lans 209 L6
Waterloo Norfk 122 E7
Waterloo P & K 233 G7
Waterloo Pembks 55 G6
Waterloo Poole 17 K4
Waterloo Sefton 138 C8
Waterloo Cross Devon 29 J8

Waterloo Port Gwynd.............. 125 J6
Waterlooville Hants.................. 19 M2
Watermillock Cumb................ 166 B6
Water Newton Cambs............... 102 C4
Water Orton Warwks................. 98 F5
Waterperry Oxon...................... 66 F6
Waterrow Somset..................... 29 J6
Watersfield W Susx.................. 21 G4
Waterside Bl w D.................... 139 L3
Waterside Bucks...................... 68 B7
Waterside Cumb..................... 165 H2
Waterside Donc...................... 143 H5
Waterside E Ayrs.................... 184 C1
Waterside E Ayrs.................... 196 F2
Waterside E Duns.................... 209 H4
Water's Nook Bolton............... 139 K6
Waterstein Highld................... 258 A7
Waterstock Oxon...................... 66 F6
Waterston Pembks.................... 54 F5
Water Stratford Bucks............... 84 C8
Water Street Neath................... 42 B5
Waters Upton Wrekin.............. 113 K7
Water Yeat Cumb.................... 156 D5
Watford Herts.......................... 68 E7
Watford Nhants....................... 84 B2
Wath N York.......................... 149 L2
Wath N York.......................... 160 D7
Wath upon Dearne Rothm....... 142 C7
Watlington Norfk.................... 104 C1
Watlington Oxon...................... 67 G8
Watnall Notts........................ 116 E2
Watten Highld....................... 280 D5
Wattisfield Suffk................... 105 K8
Wattisham Suffk...................... 89 K5
Watton Dorset......................... 15 K4
Watton E R Yk....................... 152 F6
Watton Norfk......................... 105 J3
Watton-at-Stone Herts.............. 69 J3
Watton Green Norfk............... 105 J3
Wattons Green Essex................. 70 D8
Wattston N Lans.................... 209 K5
Wattstown Rhondd.................... 42 F3
Wattsville Caerph..................... 43 K3
Wauldby E R Yk.................... 144 B2
Waulkmill Abers.................... 244 E5
Waunarlwydd Swans................. 57 H6
Waunfawr Cerdgn..................... 92 D7
Waunfawr Gwynd.................... 125 J7
Waungron Swans....................... 57 G4
Waunlwyd Blae G...................... 61 J5
Wavendon M Keyn..................... 85 H7
Waverbridge Cumb.................. 165 H1
Waverton Ches W................... 129 K7
Waverton Cumb...................... 165 H1
Wawne E R Yk....................... 153 H8
Waxham Norfk........................ 123 J6
Waxholme E R Yk.................. 145 J2
Way Kent............................... 41 K2
Waye Devon............................ 13 H8
Wayford Somset........................ 15 J1
Waytown Dorset........................ 15 L3
Way Village Devon.................... 28 F8
Way Wick N Som....................... 44 D6
Weacombe Somset...................... 29 K3
Weald Oxon............................. 65 L6
Wealdstone Gt Lon..................... 50 F1
Weardley Leeds....................... 150 D7
Weare Somset........................... 44 E8
Weare Giffard Devon.................. 27 H6
Wearne Somset.......................... 30 F5
Wear Valley Crematorium Dur... 169 H4
Weasdale Cumb....................... 158 B2
Weasenham All Saints Norfk.... 121 J7
Weasenham St Peter Norfk...... 121 J7
Weaste Salfd......................... 140 B8
Weatheroak Hill Worcs.............. 98 D8
Weaverham Ches W.................. 130 B5
Weaverslake Staffs.................. 115 J7
Weaverthorpe N York.............. 152 E2
Webbington Somset.................... 44 D7
Webb's Heath S Glos.................. 45 K4
Webheath Worcs........................ 82 B2
Webton Herefs.......................... 80 A7
Wedderlairs Abers.................. 256 F5
Wedding Hall Fold N York....... 149 G6
Weddington Kent....................... 41 J3
Weddington Warwks................... 99 K5
Wedhampton Wilts..................... 46 F7
Wedmore Somset........................ 31 G1
Wednesbury Sandw..................... 98 C4
Wednesfield Wolves................... 97 L3
Weecar Notts......................... 135 G6
Weedon Bucks.......................... 67 K3
Weedon Nhants......................... 84 C3
Weedon Lois Nhants................... 84 B6
Weeford Staffs......................... 98 F3
Week Devon.............................. 8 A2
Week Devon............................. 27 K5
Week Devon............................. 28 C7

Weeke Devon............................ 13 H2
Weeke Hants............................ 34 F5
Weekley Nhants....................... 101 J7
Week St Mary Cnwll.................. 11 J3
Weel E R Yk.......................... 153 G7
Weeley Essex........................... 73 H3
Weeley Crematorium Essex.......... 73 H3
Weeley Heath Essex.................... 73 H3
Weem P & K.......................... 232 B5
Weeping Cross Staffs............... 114 E7
Weethley Warwks....................... 82 C4
Weeting Norfk........................ 104 F5
Weeton E R Yk....................... 145 K4
Weeton Lancs......................... 138 D1
Weeton N York....................... 150 C6
Weetwood Leeds....................... 150 C8
Weir Lancs........................... 140 C3
Weirbrook Shrops.................... 112 E6
Weir Quay Devon........................ 6 E2
Weisdale Shet........................ 281 d5
Welborne Norfk....................... 106 B2
Welbourn Lincs....................... 118 C1
Welburn N York...................... 151 M2
Welbury N York...................... 160 F2
Welby Lincs.......................... 118 C4
Welches Dam Cambs.................. 103 K6
Welcombe Devon......................... 26 D7
Weldon Bridge Nthumb............. 191 G6
Welford Nhants....................... 100 F1
Welford W Berk........................ 48 B4
Welford-on-Avon Warwks............. 82 D5
Welham Leics......................... 101 G5
Welham Notts......................... 134 E3
Welham Green Herts.................... 69 G6
Well Hants............................ 36 A2
Well Lincs........................... 137 H5
Well N York.......................... 160 C6
Welland Worcs......................... 81 H7
Wellbank Angus...................... 234 D7
Well End Bucks........................ 49 L1
Well End Herts........................ 69 G7
Wellesbourne Warwks.................. 83 G4
Wellesbourne Mountford
  Warwks............................... 83 G4
Well Head Herts....................... 68 F2
Well Hill Kent........................ 52 B6
Wellhouse W Berk...................... 48 D4
Welling Gt Lon........................ 51 M4
Wellingborough Nhants................ 85 H2
Wellingham Norfk.................... 121 J7
Wellingore Lincs.................... 135 K8
Wellington Cumb..................... 155 K2
Wellington Herefs.................... 80 C5
Wellington Somset..................... 29 L6
Wellington Wrekin..................... 96 E1
Wellington Heath Herefs............. 81 H6
Wellington Marsh Herefs............. 80 C6
Wellow BaNES.......................... 45 L7
Wellow IoW............................ 18 F6
Wellow Notts......................... 134 D6
Wellpond Green Herts.................. 69 L3
Wells Somset.......................... 31 J2
Wellsborough Leics.................... 99 K3
Wells Green Ches E................... 113 M1
Wells Head C Brad................... 141 G1
Wells-next-the-sea Norfk.......... 121 K3
Wellstye Green Essex.................. 70 F3
Well Town Devon....................... 13 L1
Welltree P & K...................... 221 G3
Wellwood Fife....................... 210 E1
Welney Norfk......................... 103 L4
Welshampton Shrops.................. 113 G4
Welsh Bicknor Herefs................. 63 H4
Welsh End Shrops.................... 113 H4
Welsh Frankton Shrops............... 112 E5
Welsh Hook Pembks..................... 74 F6
Welsh Newton Herefs.................. 63 G3
Welshpool Powys....................... 94 F2
Welsh St Donats V Glam.............. 42 F6
Welton Cumb......................... 165 K2
Welton E R Yk....................... 144 B2
Welton Lincs......................... 135 K4
Welton Nhants......................... 84 B2
Welton le Marsh Lincs.............. 137 J6
Welton le Wold Lincs.............. 136 E2
Welwick E R Yk...................... 145 L3
Welwyn Herts.......................... 69 G4
Welwyn Garden City Herts........... 69 G4
Wem Shrops.......................... 113 H5
Wembdon Somset........................ 30 D3
Wembley Gt Lon........................ 50 F2
Wembury Devon.......................... 7 G5
Wembworthy Devon...................... 12 F1
Wemyss Bay Inver.................... 207 K5
Wenallt Cerdgn........................ 77 J1
Wendens Ambo Essex................... 87 K8
Wendlebury Oxon....................... 66 E3
Wendling Norfk....................... 105 J1
Wendover Bucks........................ 67 L5
Wendron Cnwll.......................... 3 H5

Wendy Cambs........................... 87 G5
Wenfordbridge Cnwll................... 10 F7
Wenhaston Suffk...................... 107 J8
Wennington Cambs.................... 102 E7
Wennington Gt Lon..................... 52 B3
Wennington Lancs.................... 147 M2
Wensley Derbys....................... 132 E7
Wensley N York...................... 159 K5
Wentbridge Wakefd................... 142 D4
Wentnor Shrops........................ 95 J5
Wentworth Cambs..................... 103 K7
Wentworth Rothm.................... 142 B8
Wentworth Castle Barns............ 141 M7
Wenvoe V Glam......................... 43 H7
Weobley Herefs........................ 79 M5
Weobley Marsh Herefs................. 80 A5
Wepham W Susx......................... 21 H5
Wereham Norfk........................ 104 D3
Wergs Wolves.......................... 97 K3
Wern Gwynd.......................... 109 K4
Wern Powys............................ 61 H3
Wern Powys............................ 95 G1
Wern Shrops.......................... 112 D4
Werneth Low Tamesd................. 131 J1
Wernffrwd Swans....................... 56 F2
Wern-y-gaer Flints.................. 128 F6
Werrington C Pete................... 102 D3
Werrington Cnwll...................... 11 L5
Werrington Staffs.................. 114 E2
Wervin Ches W....................... 129 K5
Wesham Lancs........................ 138 E1
Wessex Vale Crematorium
  Hants................................ 35 G7
Wessington Derbys.................. 133 G8
West Aberthaw V Glam................. 42 F8
West Acre Norfk..................... 121 G8
West Allerdean Nthumb............. 202 F4
West Alvington Devon................... 7 L6
West Amesbury Wilts.................. 33 K3
West Anstey Devon..................... 28 E5
West Appleton N York................ 160 B4
West Ashby Lincs.................... 136 E5
West Ashling W Susx.................. 20 D5
West Ashton Wilts..................... 46 C7
West Auckland Dur................... 168 F5
West Ayton N York................... 163 H5
West Bagborough Somset.............. 30 A4
West Bank Blae G...................... 61 K6
West Bank Halton.................... 129 L3
West Barkwith Lincs................. 136 C4
West Barnby N York.................. 171 J8
West Barns E Loth................... 212 E3
West Barsham Norfk.................. 121 K5
West Bay Dorset....................... 15 K4
West Beckham Norfk.................. 122 C4
West Bedfont Surrey................... 50 D4
Westbere Kent......................... 41 G3
West Bergholt Essex................... 72 D2
West Berkshire Crematorium
  W Berk............................... 48 D5
West Bexington Dorset................ 15 M5
West Bilney Norfk................... 120 F8
West Blatchington Br & H............ 22 D6
West Boldon S Tyne.................. 181 J6
Westborough Lincs................... 117 M3
Westbourne Bmouth.................... 17 L4
Westbourne W Susx..................... 20 B5
West Bourton Dorset................... 32 C5
West Bowling C Brad................. 141 J2
West Brabourne Kent................... 40 E6
West Bradenham Norfk................ 105 J2
West Bradford Lancs................. 148 C7
West Bradley Somset................... 31 J3
West Bretton Wakefd................. 141 L5
West Bridgford Notts................ 117 G4
West Briscoe Dur.................... 168 B6
West Bromwich Sandw.................. 98 C5
West Bromwich Crematorium
  Sandw................................ 98 C5
Westbrook Kent........................ 41 K1
Westbrook W Berk...................... 48 B4
Westbrook Wilts....................... 46 D5
West Buckland Devon................... 28 B4
West Buckland Somset................. 30 B6
West Burton N York.................. 159 H5
West Burton W Susx.................... 21 G4
Westbury Bucks........................ 84 B8
Westbury Shrops....................... 95 J2
Westbury Wilts........................ 46 C8
Westbury Leigh Wilts................. 32 G7
Westbury on Severn Gloucs............ 63 L4
Westbury-on-Trym Bristl.............. 45 H3
Westbury-sub-Mendip Somset........ 31 H1
West Butsfield Dur.................. 168 E2
West Butterwick N Linc.............. 143 L6
Westby Lancs........................ 138 D2
West Byfleet Surrey................... 50 D6
West Cairngaan D & G................ 172 E8
West Caister Norfk.................. 107 K1
West Calder W Loth.................. 210 D6

West Camel Somset..................... 31 J6
West Chaldon Dorset................... 16 E6
West Challow Oxon..................... 48 A1
West Charleton Devon................... 7 L6
West Chelborough Dorset.............. 15 M2
West Chevington Nthumb.............. 191 J6
West Chiltington W Susx.............. 21 H4
West Chinnock Somset................. 31 G8
West Chisenbury Wilts................ 47 H8
West Clandon Surrey................... 50 D8
West Cliffe Kent...................... 41 K6
Westcliff-on-Sea Sthend.............. 53 J2
West Coker Somset..................... 31 H8
West Combe Devon....................... 7 L2
Westcombe Somset...................... 31 L4
West Compton Somset................... 31 K2
West Compton Abbas Dorset.......... 16 A4
Westcote Gloucs....................... 65 J2
Westcote Barton Oxon................. 66 B2
Westcott Bucks........................ 67 H4
Westcott Devon........................ 14 B2
Westcott Surrey....................... 37 H1
West Cottingwith N York............ 151 L4
Westcourt Wilts....................... 47 J6
West Cowick E R Yk.................. 143 G3
West Cross Swans...................... 57 H7
West Curry Cnwll...................... 11 L4
West Curthwaite Cumb................ 165 K1
Westdean E Susx....................... 23 J7
West Dean W Susx...................... 20 E4
West Dean Wilts....................... 34 B2
West Deeping Lincs.................. 102 C2
West Derby Lpool.................... 129 J1
West Dereham Norfk.................. 104 D3
West Ditchburn Nthumb.............. 191 G7
West Down Devon....................... 27 J3
Westdown Camp Wilts.................. 33 H2
Westdowns Cnwll....................... 10 F6
West Drayton Gt Lon.................. 50 D3
West Drayton Notts.................. 134 D5
West Dunnet Highld.................. 280 D2
Wested Kent........................... 52 B2
West Ella E R Yk.................... 144 C2
West End Bed.......................... 85 J4
West End Br For....................... 49 L5
West End Caerph....................... 43 K3
West End Cambs........................ 87 G2
West End Cumb....................... 177 K7
West End E R Yk..................... 144 A2
West End E R Yk..................... 144 F2
West End E R Yk..................... 145 H2
Westend Gloucs........................ 64 A5
West End Hants........................ 34 F1
West End Hants........................ 35 K4
West End Herts........................ 69 H5
West End Herts........................ 69 J6
West End Lancs...................... 139 L4
West End Leeds...................... 150 B8
West End Lincs...................... 145 K8
West End N Som........................ 44 F5
West End N York..................... 151 H7
West End Norfk...................... 105 H2
West End Norfk...................... 107 K1
West End Oxon......................... 48 B2
West End S Glos....................... 45 L1
West End Somset....................... 31 L4
West End Surrey....................... 50 B6
West End Surrey....................... 50 E8
West End W & M........................ 49 K4
West End W Susx....................... 22 B4
West End Wilts........................ 33 F6
West End Wilts........................ 33 L8
West End Wilts........................ 46 E3
West End Green Hants.................. 49 G6
Westend Town Nthumb................ 179 H6
Westenhanger Kent..................... 40 F7
Westerdale Highld.................. 279 K6
Westerdale N York.................. 161 L2
Westerfield Suffk..................... 90 E5
Westergate W Susx..................... 20 F5
Westerham Kent........................ 51 L8
Westerhope N u Ty.................. 180 F5
Westerland Devon....................... 8 C2
Westerleigh S Glos.................... 45 K3
Westerleigh Crematorium
  S Glos................................ 45 L3
Western Isles W Isls................ 282 e6
Wester Ochiltree W Loth............ 210 D4
Wester Pitkierie Fife.............. 223 K6
Westerton W Susx...................... 20 E5
Westerton of Rossie Angus......... 235 G4
Westerwick Shet..................... 281 c6
West Ewell Surrey..................... 51 G6
West Farleigh Kent.................... 39 H3
West Farndon Nhants................... 83 M5
West Felton Shrops.................. 112 E6
Westfield BaNES....................... 45 K8
Westfield Cumb...................... 164 C5
Westfield E Susx...................... 24 E4
Westfield Highld.................... 279 J3

Westfield N Lans...... 209 J4
Westfield Norfk...... 105 K2
Westfield W Loth...... 210 B4
Westfields Dorset...... 16 D2
Westfields Herefs...... 80 C7
Westfields of Rattray P & K...... 233 J6
Westfield Sole Kent...... 53 G6
West Flotmanby N York...... 163 K6
Westford Somset...... 29 L6
Westgate Dur...... 167 L3
Westgate N Linc...... 143 K6
Westgate Norfk...... 121 L3
Westgate Hill C Brad...... 141 K2
Westgate on Sea Kent...... 41 K1
Westgate Street Norfk...... 122 D7
West Ginge Oxon...... 48 C2
West Grafton Wilts...... 47 K7
West Green Hants...... 49 H7
West Grimstead Wilts...... 33 L5
West Grinstead W Susx...... 37 J6
West Haddlesey N York...... 142 E2
West Haddon Nhants...... 84 C1
West Hagbourne Oxon...... 48 D2
West Hagley Worcs...... 97 K7
Westhall Suffk...... 107 J7
West Hallam Derbys...... 116 D3
West Hallam Common Derbys..... 116 C3
West Halton N Linc...... 144 A4
Westham Dorset...... 16 C6
Westham E Susx...... 23 L6
West Ham Gt Lon...... 51 K2
Westham Somset...... 30 F2
Westhampnett W Susx...... 20 E5
West Handley Derbys...... 133 H4
West Hanney Oxon...... 66 B8
West Hanningfield Essex...... 71 H7
West Harnham Wilts...... 33 K5
West Harptree BaNES...... 45 H7
West Harting W Susx...... 20 C3
West Hatch Somset...... 30 D6
West Hatch Wilts...... 32 F5
West Haven Angus...... 234 E8
Westhay Somset...... 31 G2
Westhead Lancs...... 138 F6
West Head Norfk...... 104 B2
West Heath Birm...... 98 C7
West Heath Hants...... 48 E7
West Helmsdale Highld...... 274 D5
West Hendred Oxon...... 48 C1
West Hertfordshire
   Crematorium Herts...... 68 E6
West Heslerton N York...... 163 G7
West Hewish N Som...... 44 D6
Westhide Herefs...... 80 D6
Westhill Abers...... 245 J2
West Hill Devon...... 14 C4
West Hoathly W Susx...... 38 A6
West Holme Dorset...... 17 G5
Westholme Somset...... 31 J3
Westhope Herefs...... 80 B5
Westhope Shrops...... 95 L6
West Horndon Essex...... 52 D1
Westhorp Nhants...... 83 L5
Westhorpe Lincs...... 119 H5
Westhorpe Suffk...... 90 B2
West Horrington Somset...... 31 J2
West Horsley Surrey...... 50 D8
West Horton Nthumb...... 203 G7
West Hougham Kent...... 41 H7
Westhoughton Bolton...... 139 K6
Westhouse N York...... 157 L7
Westhouses Derbys...... 133 H8
West Howe Bmouth...... 17 L3
West Howetown Somset...... 29 G4
Westhumble Surrey...... 50 F8
West Huntingtower P & K...... 221 K2
West Huntspill Somset...... 30 D2
West Hyde C Beds...... 68 E4
West Hyde Herts...... 50 C1
West Hythe Kent...... 40 F8
West Ilkerton Devon...... 28 C2
West Ilsley W Berk...... 48 C3
West Itchenor W Susx...... 20 C6
West Keal Lincs...... 137 G7
West Kennett Wilts...... 47 G5
West Kilbride N Ayrs...... 195 K1
West Kingsdown Kent...... 52 C6
West Kington Wilts...... 46 A3
West Kirby Wirral...... 128 F2
West Knapton N York...... 162 F7
West Knighton Dorset...... 16 D5
West Knoyle Wilts...... 32 E4
Westlake Devon...... 7 J4
West Lambrook Somset...... 233 D7
Westland Green Herts...... 70 B3
West Langdon Kent...... 41 K6
West Lavington W Susx...... 20 E3
West Lavington Wilts...... 46 E8
West Layton N York...... 168 F8

West Leake Notts...... 116 E6
West Learmouth Nthumb...... 202 C5
West Lees N York...... 161 G2
West Leigh Devon...... 13 G2
Westleigh Devon...... 27 H5
Westleigh Devon...... 29 J7
West Leigh Somset...... 29 L5
Westleton Suffk...... 91 K2
West Lexham Norfk...... 121 J8
Westley Shrops...... 95 J2
Westley Suffk...... 89 G2
Westley Waterless Cambs...... 88 C4
West Lilling N York...... 151 K3
Westlington Bucks...... 67 J5
West Linton Border...... 199 K3
Westlinton Cumb...... 177 L6
West Littleton S Glos...... 45 M4
West Lockinge Oxon...... 48 B2
West London Crematorium
   Gt Lon...... 51 G3
West Lulworth Dorset...... 16 F6
West Lutton N York...... 152 E2
West Lydford Somset...... 31 J4
West Lyn Devon...... 28 C1
West Lyng Somset...... 30 D5
West Lynn Norfk...... 120 D7
West Malling Kent...... 52 E7
West Malvern Worcs...... 81 H6
West Marden W Susx...... 20 C4
West Markham Notts...... 134 E5
Westmarsh Kent...... 41 J3
West Marsh NE Lin...... 145 H5
West Marton N York...... 148 F5
West Melbury Dorset...... 32 E6
West Melton Rothm...... 142 C7
West Meon Hants...... 35 K6
West Meon Hut Hants...... 35 K5
West Meon Woodlands Hants ... 35 K5
West Mersea Essex...... 72 E4
Westmeston E Susx...... 22 E4
West Mickley Nthumb...... 180 C6
Westmill Herts...... 69 J4
Westmill Herts...... 69 K2
West Milton Dorset...... 15 L3
Westminster Gt Lon...... 51 J3
West Minster Kent...... 53 K4
West Molesey Surrey...... 50 E5
West Monkton Somset...... 30 C5
West Moors Dorset...... 17 L2
West Morden Dorset...... 17 H3
West Morriston Border...... 201 J5
West Morton C Brad...... 149 K7
West Mudford Somset...... 31 J6
Westmuir Angus...... 234 A5
West Ness N York...... 162 B6
West Newbiggin Darltn...... 169 K7
Westnewton Cumb...... 164 F2
West Newton E R Yk...... 153 K8
West Newton Norfk...... 120 F6
West Newton Somset...... 30 D5
West Norwood Gt Lon...... 51 J4
West Norwood Crematorium
   Gt Lon...... 51 J4
Westoe S Tyne...... 181 J5
West Ogwell Devon...... 13 J8
Weston BaNES...... 45 L5
Weston Ches E...... 114 A1
Weston Devon...... 14 D3
Weston Devon...... 14 E5
Weston Dorset...... 16 D8
Weston Halton...... 129 L3
Weston Hants...... 35 M6
Weston Herefs...... 79 L4
Weston Herts...... 69 H1
Weston Lincs...... 119 J6
Weston N York...... 149 M6
Weston Nhants...... 84 B6
Weston Notts...... 134 F6
Weston Shrops...... 95 H8
Weston Shrops...... 96 D5
Weston Shrops...... 112 D6
Weston Staffs...... 114 F6
Weston W Berk...... 48 B4
Weston Beggard Herefs...... 80 D7
Westonbirt Gloucs...... 46 B1
Weston by Welland Nhants...... 101 G5
Weston Colley Hants...... 35 G3
Weston Colville Cambs...... 88 C4
Weston Corbett Hants...... 35 L2
Weston Coyney C Stke...... 114 E3
Weston Favell Nhants...... 84 F3
Weston Green Cambs...... 88 C5
Weston Heath Shrops...... 97 H1
Weston Hills Lincs...... 119 J7
Weston in Arden Warwks...... 99 K6
Westoning C Beds...... 85 K8
Weston-in-Gordano N Som...... 44 F4
Westoning Woodend C Beds...... 68 C1
Weston Jones Staffs...... 114 B6
Weston Longville Norfk...... 122 C8

Weston Lullingfields Shrops 112 F6
Weston Mill Crematorium
   C Plym...... 6 F3
Weston-on-Avon Warwks...... 82 E5
Weston-on-the-Green Oxon...... 66 D3
Weston Patrick Hants...... 35 L2
Weston Rhyn Shrops...... 112 D4
Weston-sub-Edge Gloucs...... 82 D7
Weston-super-Mare N Som...... 44 C6
Weston-super-Mare
   Crematorium N Som...... 44 D6
Weston Turville Bucks...... 67 K5
Weston-under-Lizard Staffs...... 97 H1
Weston under Penyard Herefs... 63 J3
Weston-under-Redcastle
   Shrops...... 113 J5
Weston under Wetherley
   Warwks...... 83 J1
Weston Underwood Derbys...... 115 M3
Weston Underwood M Keyn...... 85 G5
Weston-upon-Trent Derbys...... 116 C6
Westonzoyland Somset...... 30 E4
West Orchard Dorset...... 32 D7
West Overton Wilts...... 47 H5
Westow N York...... 152 A3
West Panson Devon...... 11 L4
West Park Abers...... 245 H4
West Parley Dorset...... 17 L3
West Peckham Kent...... 39 G3
West Peeke Devon...... 11 L4
West Pelton Dur...... 180 F8
West Pennard Somset...... 31 J3
West Pentire Cnwll...... 4 C3
West Perry Cambs...... 86 C2
West Porlock Somset...... 28 F2
Westport Somset...... 30 F6
West Pulham Dorset...... 16 D1
West Putford Devon...... 26 F7
West Quantoxhead Somset...... 29 K3
Westquarter Falk...... 210 B3
Westra V Glam...... 43 J7
West Raddon Devon...... 13 L2
West Rainton Dur...... 169 J1
West Rasen Lincs...... 135 L2
West Ravendale NE Lin...... 145 G7
Westray Ork...... 275 c2
West Raynham Norfk...... 121 J6
West Retford Notts...... 134 D3
Westridge Green W Berk...... 48 E3
Westrigg W Loth...... 210 B5
West Road Crematorium N u Ty...180 F6
Westrop Swindn...... 65 J8
West Rounton N York...... 160 F2
West Row Suffk...... 104 D8
West Rudham Norfk...... 121 H6
West Runton Norfk...... 122 D3
Westruther Border...... 201 K3
Westry Cambs...... 103 H4
West Saltoun E Loth...... 212 A5
West Sandford Devon...... 13 J2
West Sandwick Shet...... 281 e3
West Scrafton N York...... 159 K6
West Sleekburn Nthumb...... 181 G2
West Somerton Norfk...... 123 K7
West Stafford Dorset...... 16 D5
West Stockwith Notts...... 134 F1
West Stoke W Susx...... 20 D5
West Stonesdale N York...... 158 F2
West Stoughton Somset...... 30 F1
West Stour Dorset...... 32 C6
West Stourmouth Kent...... 41 H3
West Stow Suffk...... 89 G1
West Stowell Wilts...... 47 H6
West Stratton Hants...... 35 H3
West Street Kent...... 40 A4
West Street Kent...... 41 K4
West Street Medway...... 52 F4
West Street Suffk...... 89 K1
West Suffolk Crematorium
   Suffk...... 89 G2
West Tanfield N York...... 160 C7
West Taphouse Cnwll...... 5 K2
West Tarbert Ag & B...... 206 D5
West Tarring W Susx...... 21 J6
West Thirston Nthumb...... 191 H6
West Thorney W Susx...... 20 C6
Westthorpe Derbys...... 133 J4
West Thorpe Notts...... 117 G6
West Thurrock Thurr...... 52 C3
West Tilbury Thurr...... 52 E3
West Tisted Hants...... 35 K5
West Torrington Lincs...... 136 B3
West Town BaNES...... 45 G6
West Town Hants...... 20 B7
West Town Herefs...... 80 B3
West Town N Som...... 44 F5
West Town Somset...... 31 J4
West Town Somset...... 32 B3
West Tytherley Hants...... 34 C5
West Walton Norfk...... 103 K1

West Walton Highway Norfk...... 103 K1
Westward Cumb...... 165 J2
Westward Ho! Devon...... 27 G5
Westwell Kent...... 40 C6
Westwell Oxon...... 65 J5
Westwell Leacon Kent...... 40 C5
West Wellow Hants...... 34 C7
West Wembury Devon...... 7 G5
West Wemyss Fife...... 222 E8
Westwick Cambs...... 87 J2
Westwick Dur...... 168 D7
West Wick N Som...... 44 D6
Westwick Norfk...... 122 F6
West Wickham Cambs...... 88 C5
West Wickham Gt Lon...... 51 K5
West Williamston Pembks...... 55 H5
West Wiltshire Crematorium
   Wilts...... 46 C7
West Winch Norfk...... 120 E8
West Winterslow Wilts...... 34 B4
West Wittering W Susx...... 20 C7
West Witton N York...... 159 J5
Westwood Devon...... 14 B3
Westwood Kent...... 41 K2
Westwood Kent...... 52 D5
Westwood Notts...... 116 D1
Westwood Nthumb...... 179 H6
Westwood Wilts...... 46 A7
West Woodburn Nthumb...... 179 K2
West Woodhay W Berk...... 48 B6
Westwood Heath Covtry...... 99 H8
West Woodlands Somset...... 32 C2
Westwoodside N Linc...... 143 J7
West Worldham Hants...... 35 M3
West Worthing W Susx...... 21 K6
West Wratting Cambs...... 88 C5
West Wycombe Bucks...... 67 K8
West Wylam Nthumb...... 180 D6
West Yatton Wilts...... 46 B4
West Yoke Kent...... 52 D5
West Youlstone Cnwll...... 26 D7
Wetham Green Kent...... 53 H5
Wetheral Cumb...... 178 B7
Wetherby Leeds...... 150 F6
Wetherden Suffk...... 89 K3
Wetheringsett Suffk...... 90 D2
Wethersfield Essex...... 71 H1
Wetherup Street Suffk...... 90 D2
Wetley Rocks Staffs...... 114 F2
Wettenhall Ches E...... 130 C7
Wetton Staffs...... 132 B8
Wetwang E R Yk...... 152 E4
Wetwood Staffs...... 114 B5
Wexcombe Wilts...... 47 K7
Wexham Slough...... 50 C5
Wexham Street Bucks...... 50 C2
Weybourne Norfk...... 122 C3
Weybourne Surrey...... 36 C1
Weybread Suffk...... 106 E7
Weybread Street Suffk...... 106 E7
Weybridge Surrey...... 50 D6
Weycroft Devon...... 15 G3
Weydale Highld...... 279 L1
Weyhill Hants...... 34 D2
Weymouth Dorset...... 16 C6
Weymouth Crematorium
   Dorset...... 16 C6
Whaddon Bucks...... 84 F8
Whaddon Cambs...... 87 G6
Whaddon Gloucs...... 64 B4
Whaddon Wilts...... 33 L5
Whaddon Wilts...... 46 C6
Whale Cumb...... 166 C6
Whaley Derbys...... 133 K5
Whaley Bridge Derbys...... 131 K3
Whaley Thorns Derbys...... 133 K5
Whaligoe Highld...... 280 D8
Whalley Lancs...... 148 C8
Whalley Banks Lancs...... 139 L1
Whalsay Shet...... 281 f5
Whalton Nthumb...... 180 D3
Whaplode Lincs...... 119 K6
Whaplode Drove Lincs...... 103 G1
Wharf Warwks...... 83 K5
Wharfe N York...... 148 D2
Wharles Lancs...... 147 J3
Wharley End C Beds...... 85 J6
Wharncliffe Side Sheff...... 132 F5
Wharram-le-Street N York...... 152 C3
Wharton Ches W...... 130 C6
Wharton Herefs...... 80 C3
Whashton N York...... 159 L2
Whasset Cumb...... 157 H6
Whatcote Warwks...... 83 G6
Whateley Warwks...... 99 G3
Whatfield Suffk...... 89 L6
Whatley Somset...... 15 H1
Whatley Somset...... 32 B2
Whatley's End S Glos...... 45 K3
Whatlington E Susx...... 24 D4

Whatsole Street Kent........... 40 F6
Whatstandwell Derbys........... 116 B1
Whatton Notts........... 117 K4
Whauphill D & G........... 173 K5
Whaw N York........... 159 H2
Wheal Rose Cnwll........... 4 B6
Wheatfield Oxon........... 67 G7
Wheathampstead Herts........... 68 F4
Wheathill Shrops........... 96 E7
Wheathill Somset........... 31 J5
Wheatley Calder........... 141 G3
Wheatley Hants........... 36 A3
Wheatley Oxon........... 66 E6
Wheatley Hill Dur........... 169 K3
Wheatley Hills Donc........... 142 F6
Wheatley Lane Lancs........... 148 C8
Wheaton Aston Staffs........... 97 J1
Wheatsheaf Wrexhm........... 112 D1
Wheddon Cross Somset........... 29 G3
Wheelbarrow Town Kent........... 40 F6
Wheeler End Bucks........... 67 K8
Wheeler's Green Wokham........... 49 J4
Wheeler's Street Kent........... 39 L4
Wheelerstreet Surrey........... 36 E3
Wheelock Ches E........... 130 E7
Wheelock Heath Ches E........... 130 E8
Wheelton Lancs........... 139 J3
Wheldale Wakefd........... 142 C3
Wheldrake C York........... 151 L6
Whelford Gloucs........... 65 H7
Whelpley Hill Bucks........... 68 C6
Whelpo Cumb........... 165 J3
Whelston Flints........... 128 F4
Whempstead Herts........... 69 J3
Whenby N York........... 151 K2
Whepstead Suffk........... 89 G4
Wherstead Suffk........... 90 E7
Wherwell Hants........... 34 E3
Wheston Derbys........... 132 C4
Whetsted Kent........... 39 G4
Whetstone Gt Lon........... 69 H8
Whetstone Leics........... 100 C4
Wheyrigg Cumb........... 165 G1
Whicham Cumb........... 155 L6
Whichford Warwks........... 83 H8
Whickham Gatesd........... 180 F6
Whiddon Devon........... 12 B3
Whiddon Down Devon........... 13 G4
Whight's Corner Suffk........... 90 D6
Whigstreet Angus........... 234 D6
Whilton Nhants........... 84 C2
Whimble Devon........... 11 L2
Whimple Devon........... 14 B3
Whimpwell Green Norfk........... 123 H5
Whinburgh Norfk........... 105 K2
Whin Lane End Lancs........... 147 H7
Whinnie Liggate D & G........... 175 H4
Whinnow Cumb........... 177 J8
Whinnyfold Abers........... 257 K5
Whinny Hill S on T........... 169 K7
Whippingham IoW........... 19 H5
Whipsnade C Beds........... 68 C3
Whipton Devon........... 13 M4
Whirlow Sheff........... 132 F3
Whisby Lincs........... 135 H6
Whissendine Rutlnd........... 117 L8
Whissonsett Norfk........... 121 K7
Whistlefield Ag & B........... 218 C8
Whistlefield Inn Ag & B........... 217 J8
Whistley Green Wokham........... 49 J4
Whiston Knows........... 129 L2
Whiston Nhants........... 85 G3
Whiston Rothm........... 133 J2
Whiston Staffs........... 114 D8
Whiston Staffs........... 115 G2
Whiston Cross Shrops........... 97 H3
Whiston Eaves Staffs........... 115 G2
Whitacre Fields Warwks........... 99 H5
Whitbeck Cumb........... 155 K5
Whitbourne Herefs........... 81 G4
Whitburn S Tyne........... 181 K6
Whitburn W Loth........... 210 C6
Whitby Ches W........... 129 J4
Whitby N York........... 171 K8
Whitbyheath Ches W........... 129 J5
Whitchester Border........... 212 F7
Whitchurch BaNES........... 45 J5
Whitchurch Bucks........... 67 J3
Whitchurch Cardif........... 43 J5
Whitchurch Devon........... 12 C8
Whitchurch Hants........... 34 F1
Whitchurch Herefs........... 63 H4
Whitchurch Oxon........... 48 F7
Whitchurch Pembks........... 74 C7
Whitchurch Shrops........... 113 J3
Whitchurch Canonicorum
Dorset........... 15 J3
Whitchurch Hill Oxon........... 48 F3
Whitcombe Dorset........... 16 D5

Whitcot Shrops........... 95 J5
Whitcott Keysett Shrops........... 95 G6
Whiteacre Kent........... 40 E5
Whiteacre Heath Warwks........... 99 G5
Whiteash Green Essex........... 71 J1
White Ball Somset........... 29 K7
Whitebridge Highld........... 250 E8
Whitebrook Mons........... 63 G6
Whitecairns Abers........... 257 G8
Whitechapel Gt Lon........... 51 J3
White Chapel Lancs........... 147 L7
Whitechurch Pembks........... 75 K5
Whitecliffe Gloucs........... 63 H5
White Colne Essex........... 72 C1
White Coppice Lancs........... 139 J4
Whitecraig E Loth........... 211 K5
Whitecroft Gloucs........... 63 J6
Whitecrook D & G........... 172 F3
Whitecross Cnwll........... 2 E4
White Cross Cnwll........... 3 H6
Whitecross Cnwll........... 10 D8
Whitecross Falk........... 210 C4
White End Worcs........... 81 H8
Whiteface Highld........... 263 J2
Whitefarland N Ayrs........... 194 D3
Whitefaulds S Ayrs........... 183 H1
Whitefield Bury........... 140 B6
Whitefield Devon........... 28 C4
Whitefield Somset........... 29 K5
Whitefield Lane End Knows........... 129 K2
Whiteford Abers........... 256 C6
Whitegate Ches W........... 130 C6
Whitehall Hants........... 49 H8
Whitehall Ork........... 275 e3
Whitehall W Susx........... 37 H6
Whitehaven Cumb........... 164 C7
Whitehill Kent........... 40 C3
Whitehill Leics........... 99 L1
Whitehill and Bordon Hants........... 36 A4
Whitehills Abers........... 268 B3
Whitehouse Abers........... 256 A8
Whitehouse Ag & B........... 206 C6
Whitehouse Common Birm........... 98 E4
Whitekirk E Loth........... 212 D1
White Kirkley Dur........... 168 C3
White Lackington Dorset........... 16 D3
Whitelackington Somset........... 30 F7
White Ladies Aston Worcs........... 81 L4
Whiteleaf Bucks........... 67 K6
White-le-Head Dur........... 180 E7
Whiteley Hants........... 19 J2
Whiteley Bank IoW........... 19 J7
Whiteley Green Ches E........... 131 H4
Whiteley Village Surrey........... 50 E6
Whitemans Green W Susx........... 22 D2
White Mill Carmth........... 58 E4
Whitemire Moray........... 253 J1
Whitemoor C Nott........... 116 F3
Whitemoor Cnwll........... 5 G3
Whitemoor Derbys........... 116 B2
Whitemoor Staffs........... 131 H7
Whiteness Shet........... 281 d6
White Notley Essex........... 71 J3
Whiteoak Green Oxon........... 65 M4
White Ox Mead BaNES........... 45 L7
Whiteparish Wilts........... 34 B6
White Pit Lincs........... 137 G4
Whiterashes Abers........... 256 F7
White Roding Essex........... 70 E4
Whiterow Highld........... 280 E6
Whiterow Moray........... 265 G8
Whiteshill Gloucs........... 64 B5
Whitesmith E Susx........... 23 J4
White Stake Lancs........... 139 G3
Whitestaunton Somset........... 30 D8
Whitestone Devon........... 13 K4
White Stone Herefs........... 80 D6
Whitestone Cross Devon........... 13 L4
Whitestreet Green Suffk........... 89 K7
Whitewall Corner N York........... 152 B2
White Waltham W & M........... 49 K3
Whiteway BaNES........... 45 L6
Whiteway Gloucs........... 64 C5
Whitewell Lancs........... 148 B6
Whiteworks Devon........... 12 E8
Whitfield C Dund........... 234 C8
Whitfield Kent........... 41 J6
Whitfield Nhants........... 84 B7
Whitfield Nthumb........... 179 H7
Whitfield S Glos........... 63 K8
Whitfield Hall Nthumb........... 179 H7
Whitford Devon........... 14 F3
Whitford Flints........... 128 D4
Whitgift E R Yk........... 143 K3
Whitgreave Staffs........... 114 D6
Whithorn D & G........... 174 C6
Whiting Bay N Ayrs........... 195 G6
Whitkirk Leeds........... 142 B1
Whitland Carmth........... 55 L3
Whitlaw Border........... 188 E4

Whitletts S Ayrs........... 196 D6
Whitley N York........... 142 E4
Whitley Readg........... 49 H5
Whitley Sheff........... 133 G1
Whitley Wilts........... 46 C5
Whitley Bay N Tyne........... 181 J4
Whitley Bay Crematorium
N Tyne........... 181 J4
Whitley Chapel Nthumb........... 179 L7
Whitley Heath Staffs........... 114 C6
Whitley Lower Kirk........... 141 K4
Whitley Row Kent........... 38 D3
Whitlock's End Solhll........... 98 E8
Whitminster Gloucs........... 63 M5
Whitmore Dorset........... 17 L1
Whitmore Staffs........... 114 C3
Whitnage Devon........... 29 J7
Whitnash Warwks........... 83 H3
Whitney-on-Wye Herefs........... 79 J5
Whitrigg Cumb........... 165 G3
Whitrigg Cumb........... 177 H1
Whitrigglees Cumb........... 177 H7
Whitsbury Hants........... 33 K7
Whitsome Border........... 202 D3
Whitson Newpt........... 44 D2
Whitstable Kent........... 40 E2
Whitstone Cnwll........... 11 K3
Whittingham Nthumb........... 190 F4
Whittingslow Shrops........... 95 K5
Whittington Derbys........... 133 H4
Whittington Gloucs........... 64 E3
Whittington Lancs........... 157 K7
Whittington Norfk........... 104 E3
Whittington Shrops........... 112 E5
Whittington Staffs........... 97 J6
Whittington Staffs........... 98 F2
Whittington Warwks........... 99 J4
Whittington Worcs........... 81 K4
Whittington Moor Derbys........... 133 G5
Whittlebury Nhants........... 84 D6
Whittle-le-Woods Lancs........... 139 H3
Whittlesey Cambs........... 102 F4
Whittlesford Cambs........... 87 K5
Whittlestone Head Bl w D........... 139 L4
Whitton N Linc........... 143 M3
Whitton Nthumb........... 190 F6
Whitton Powys........... 79 J2
Whitton S on T........... 169 K6
Whitton Shrops........... 80 D1
Whitton Suffk........... 90 D5
Whittonditch Wilts........... 47 L4
Whittonstall Nthumb........... 180 C7
Whitway Hants........... 48 C7
Whitwell Derbys........... 133 K4
Whitwell Herts........... 68 F3
Whitwell IoW........... 19 J8
Whitwell N York........... 160 D3
Whitwell Rutlnd........... 101 K2
Whitwell-on-the-Hill N York........... 151 M3
Whitwell Street Norfk........... 122 B7
Whitwick Leics........... 116 D8
Whitwood Wakefd........... 142 B3
Whitworth Lancs........... 140 D4
Whixall Shrops........... 113 H4
Whixley N York........... 150 F4
Whorlton Dur........... 168 E7
Whorlton N York........... 161 G2
Whyle Herefs........... 80 D3
Whyteleafe Surrey........... 51 J7
Wibdon Gloucs........... 63 H7
Wibsey C Brad........... 141 J2
Wibtoft Warwks........... 100 B6
Wichenford Worcs........... 81 H3
Wichling Kent........... 40 B4
Wick Bmouth........... 18 B5
Wick Devon........... 14 E2
Wick Highld........... 280 E6
Wick S Glos........... 45 K4
Wick Somset........... 30 B2
Wick Somset........... 30 F5
Wick V Glam........... 42 D7
Wick W Susx........... 21 H6
Wick Wilts........... 33 L6
Wick Worcs........... 81 M6
Wicken Cambs........... 88 B1
Wicken Nhants........... 84 E7
Wicken Bonhunt Essex........... 87 K8
Wickenby Lincs........... 136 A3
Wick End Bed........... 85 K5
Wicken Green Village Norfk........... 121 J5
Wickersley Rothm........... 133 J2
Wicker Street Green Suffk........... 89 K6
Wickford Essex........... 71 H8
Wickham Hants........... 19 K2
Wickham W Berk........... 48 B5
Wickham Bishops Essex........... 71 K5
Wickhambreaux Kent........... 41 H3
Wickhambrook Suffk........... 88 E4
Wickhamford Worcs........... 82 C7
Wickham Green Suffk........... 90 C2

Wickham Green W Berk........... 48 B4
Wickham Heath W Berk........... 48 B5
Wickham Market Suffk........... 91 G4
Wickhampton Norfk........... 107 J2
Wickham St Paul Essex........... 89 G7
Wickham Skeith Suffk........... 90 C2
Wickham Street Suffk........... 88 F4
Wickham Street Suffk........... 90 C1
Wicklewood Norfk........... 106 B3
Wickmere Norfk........... 122 D5
Wick St Lawrence N Som........... 44 D4
Wickstreet E Susx........... 23 J5
Wickwar S Glos........... 45 L1
Widdington Essex........... 70 D1
Widdop Calder........... 140 D1
Widdrington Nthumb........... 191 K7
Widdrington Station Nthumb........... 191 J7
Widecombe in the Moor
Devon........... 13 G7
Widegates Cnwll........... 6 B3
Widemouth Bay Cnwll........... 11 H2
Wide Open N Tyne........... 181 G4
Widford Essex........... 71 G4
Widford Herts........... 70 B4
Widham Wilts........... 47 J3
Widley Hants........... 19 M2
Widmer End Bucks........... 67 L8
Widmerpool Notts........... 117 G6
Widmore Gt Lon........... 51 L5
Widnes Halton........... 129 L3
Widnes Crematorium Halton........... 129 L3
Widworthy Devon........... 14 F3
Wigan Wigan........... 139 H6
Wigan Crematorium Wigan........... 139 H6
Wigborough Somset........... 31 G7
Wiggaton Devon........... 14 C4
Wiggenhall St Germans Norfk........... 120 D8
Wiggenhall St Mary Magdalen
Norfk........... 104 B1
Wiggenhall St Mary the
Virgin Norfk........... 104 B1
Wiggens Green Essex........... 88 D6
Wiggenstall Staffs........... 132 B7
Wiggington Shrops........... 112 E4
Wigginton C York........... 151 J4
Wigginton Herts........... 68 B5
Wigginton Oxon........... 83 J8
Wigginton Staffs........... 99 G2
Wigginton Bottom Herts........... 68 B5
Wigglesworth N York........... 148 E4
Wiggonby Cumb........... 177 J8
Wiggonholt W Susx........... 21 H3
Wighill N York........... 151 G6
Wighton Norfk........... 121 L3
Wightwick Wolves........... 97 K4
Wigley Derbys........... 132 F5
Wigley Hants........... 34 C7
Wigmore Herefs........... 80 A2
Wigmore Medway........... 53 G6
Wigsley Notts........... 135 G5
Wigsthorpe Nhants........... 102 C4
Wigston Leics........... 100 D4
Wigston Fields Leics........... 100 D3
Wigston Parva Leics........... 100 A5
Wigthorpe Notts........... 134 B3
Wigtoft Lincs........... 119 J4
Wigton Cumb........... 165 H1
Wigtown D & G........... 174 C4
Wigtwizzle Sheff........... 141 L8
Wike Leeds........... 150 D7
Wilbarston Nhants........... 101 H5
Wilberfoss E R Yk........... 151 M5
Wilburton Cambs........... 103 K8
Wilby Nhants........... 85 G2
Wilby Norfk........... 105 L5
Wilby Suffk........... 90 F1
Wilcot Wilts........... 47 H6
Wilcott Shrops........... 112 F7
Wilcrick Newpt........... 44 E2
Wilday Green Derbys........... 132 F5
Wildboarclough Ches E........... 131 K6
Wilden Bed........... 86 B4
Wilden Worcs........... 81 J1
Wilde Street Suffk........... 104 C1
Wildhern Hants........... 34 D1
Wildhill Herts........... 69 H5
Wildmanbridge S Lans........... 209 L8
Wildmoor Worcs........... 98 B8
Wildsworth Lincs........... 143 K8
Wilford C Nott........... 116 F4
Wilford Hill Crematorium Notts........... 116 F4
Wilkesley Ches E........... 113 K3
Wilkhaven Highld........... 264 E3
Wilkieston W Loth........... 210 F5
Wilkin's Green Herts........... 69 G5
Wilksby Lincs........... 136 C1
Willand Devon........... 29 J8
Willards Hill E Susx........... 24 C2
Willaston Ches E........... 113 L1
Willaston Ches W........... 129 H4

Willen M Keyn............................. 85 G7
Willenhall Covtry........................ 99 K8
Willenhall Wsall......................... 98 B4
Willerby E R Yk......................... 144 C2
Willerby N York......................... 163 H6
Willersey Gloucs......................... 82 D7
Willersley Herefs........................ 79 K6
Willesborough Kent....................... 40 D7
Willesborough Lees Kent.................. 40 D7
Willesden Gt Lon......................... 51 L2
Willesleigh Devon........................ 27 L4
Willesley Wilts.......................... 46 B1
Willett Somset........................... 29 K4
Willey Shrops............................ 96 F3
Willey Warwks........................... 100 B6
Willey Green Surrey...................... 50 B8
Williamscot Oxon......................... 83 L6
Williamstown Rhondd...................... 42 F4
Willian Herts............................ 69 G1
Willicote Warwks......................... 82 E5
Willingale Essex......................... 70 E5
Willingdon E Susx........................ 23 K6
Willingham Cambs......................... 87 H1
Willingham by Stow Lincs................ 135 H3
Willingham Green Cambs................... 88 C4
Willington Bed........................... 86 C5
Willington Derbys....................... 116 A6
Willington Dur.......................... 169 G4
Willington Kent.......................... 39 K4
Willington Warwks........................ 83 G7
Willington Corner Ches W............... 129 M6
Willington Quay N Tyne................. 181 H5
Willitoft E R Yk........................ 143 J1
Williton Somset.......................... 29 K3
Willoughby Lincs........................ 137 J5
Willoughby Warwks........................ 83 M2
Willoughby Hills Lincs.................. 119 K2
Willoughby-on-the-Wolds
  Notts................................. 117 H6
Willoughby Waterleys Leics............. 100 C5
Willoughton Lincs....................... 135 J1
Willow Green Ches W..................... 130 B4
Willows Green Essex...................... 71 H3
Willsbridge S Glos....................... 45 K5
Willsworthy Devon........................ 12 D6
Willtown Somset.......................... 30 F6
Wilmcote Warwks.......................... 82 E4
Wilmington BaNES......................... 45 K6
Wilmington Devon......................... 14 F3
Wilmington E Susx........................ 23 J6
Wilmington Kent.......................... 52 B4
Wilmslow Ches E......................... 131 G3
Wilnecote Staffs......................... 99 G3
Wilpshire Lancs......................... 139 K1
Wilsden C Brad.......................... 149 K8
Wilsford Lincs.......................... 118 D3
Wilsford Wilts........................... 33 K3
Wilsford Wilts........................... 47 G7
Wilsham Devon............................ 28 D1
Wilshaw Kirk............................ 141 H6
Wilsill N York.......................... 150 A3
Wilsley Green Kent....................... 39 K6
Wilsley Pound Kent....................... 39 K6
Wilson Herefs............................ 63 H2
Wilson Leics............................ 116 C6
Wilsontown S Lans....................... 198 F2
Wilstead Bed............................. 85 L6
Wilsthorpe Lincs........................ 102 B1
Wilstone Herts........................... 67 L4
Wilstone Green Herts..................... 67 M4
Wilton Cumb............................. 164 D8
Wilton Herefs............................ 63 H2
Wilton N York........................... 162 F6
Wilton R & Cl........................... 170 D6
Wilton Wilts............................. 33 J4
Wilton Wilts............................. 47 K6
Wilton Dean Border...................... 188 E3
Wimbish Essex............................ 88 B7
Wimbish Green Essex...................... 88 C8
Wimbledon Gt Lon......................... 51 G5
Wimblington Cambs....................... 103 J5
Wimboldsley Ches W...................... 130 D7
Wimborne Minster Dorset.................. 17 K3
Wimborne St Giles Dorset................. 33 H8
Wimbotsham Norfk........................ 104 C2
Wimpole Cambs............................ 87 G5
Wimpstone Warwks......................... 82 F5
Wincanton Somset......................... 32 B5
Winceby Lincs........................... 136 F6
Wincham Ches W.......................... 130 C4
Winchburgh W Loth....................... 210 E4
Winchcombe Gloucs........................ 64 F2
Winchelsea E Susx........................ 25 G4
Winchelsea Beach E Susx.................. 25 G4
Winchester Hants......................... 35 G5
Winchet Hill Kent........................ 39 J5
Winchfield Hants......................... 49 J8
Winchmore Hill Bucks..................... 68 B8
Winchmore Hill Gt Lon.................... 69 J8
Wincle Ches E........................... 131 J6

Wincobank Sheff......................... 133 G1
Winder Cumb............................. 164 D7
Windermere Cumb......................... 156 F3
Winderton Warwks......................... 83 H7
Windhill Highld......................... 250 F2
Windlehurst Stockp...................... 131 J3
Windlesham Surrey........................ 50 A6
Windmill Cnwll........................... 10 B7
Windmill Derbys......................... 132 C4
Windmill Hill E Susx..................... 23 L1
Windmill Hill Somset..................... 30 D7
Windrush Gloucs.......................... 65 J4
Windsole Abers.......................... 267 L4
Windsor W & M............................ 50 B4
Windsoredge Gloucs....................... 64 B7
Windsor Green Suffk...................... 89 H4
Windy Arbour Warwks...................... 83 L5
Windygates Fife......................... 222 F7
Windyharbour Ches E..................... 131 G5
Windy Hill Wrexhm....................... 129 G8
Wineham W Susx........................... 22 C3
Winestead E R Yk........................ 145 J3
Winewall Lancs.......................... 148 F7
Winfarthing Norfk....................... 106 C6
Winford IoW.............................. 19 J6
Winford N Som............................ 45 K5
Winforton Herefs......................... 79 K6
Winfrith Newburgh Dorset................. 16 F5
Wing Bucks............................... 67 L3
Wing Rutlnd............................. 101 K3
Wingate Dur............................. 169 L3
Wingates Bolton......................... 139 K6
Wingates Nthumb......................... 191 G7
Wingerworth Derbys...................... 133 G6
Wingfield C Beds......................... 68 C2
Wingfield Suffk......................... 106 E7
Wingfield Wilts.......................... 46 B7
Wingfield Green Suffk................... 106 E7
Wingham Kent............................. 41 H4
Wingmore Kent............................ 41 G6
Wingrave Bucks........................... 67 L3
Winkburn Notts.......................... 134 E7
Winkfield Br For......................... 49 L4
Winkfield Row Br For..................... 49 L5
Winkhill Staffs......................... 115 H1
Winkhurst Green Kent..................... 38 D3
Winkleigh Devon.......................... 12 F1
Winksley N York......................... 150 C2
Winkton Dorset........................... 18 B4
Winlaton Gatesd......................... 180 E6
Winlaton Mill Gatesd.................... 180 E6
Winless Highld.......................... 280 D5
Winllan Powys........................... 112 C7
Winmarleigh Lancs....................... 147 J6
Winnall Hants............................ 35 G5
Winnersh Wokham.......................... 49 J5
Winnington Ches W....................... 130 C5
Winscales Cumb.......................... 164 D5
Winscombe N Som.......................... 44 E7
Winsford Ches W......................... 130 C6
Winsford Somset.......................... 28 F4
Winsham Devon............................ 27 J3
Winsham Somset........................... 15 J2
Winshill Staffs......................... 115 M7
Winshwen Swans........................... 57 J5
Winskill Cumb........................... 166 D4
Winslade Hants........................... 35 K1
Winsley Wilts............................ 46 A6
Winslow Bucks............................ 67 J2
Winson Gloucs............................ 65 G5
Winsor Hants............................. 34 D8
Winster Cumb............................ 156 F4
Winster Derbys.......................... 132 E7
Winston Dur............................. 168 F7
Winston Suffk............................ 90 E3
Winstone Gloucs.......................... 64 D5
Winswell Devon........................... 27 J8
Winterborne Came Dorset.................. 16 D5
Winterborne Clenston Dorset.............. 17 G2
Winterborne Herringston
  Dorset................................. 16 D5
Winterborne Houghton
  Dorset................................. 16 F2
Winterborne Kingston Dorset.............. 17 G3
Winterborne Monkton Dorset............... 16 C5
Winterborne Stickland Dorset............. 16 F2
Winterborne Tomson Dorset................ 17 G3
Winterborne Whitechurch
  Dorset................................. 17 G3
Winterborne Zelston Dorset............... 17 H3
Winterbourne S Glos...................... 45 J3
Winterbourne W Berk...................... 48 C4
Winterbourne Abbas Dorset................ 16 B4
Winterbourne Bassett Wilts............... 47 G4
Winterbourne Dauntsey Wilts.............. 33 L4
Winterbourne Earls Wilts................. 33 L4
Winterbourne Gunner Wilts................ 33 L4
Winterbourne Monkton Wilts............... 47 G4
Winterbourne Steepleton
  Dorset................................. 16 B4

Winterbourne Stoke Wilts................. 33 J3
Winterbrook Oxon......................... 48 F1
Winterburn N York...................... 149 G4
Winteringham N Linc.................... 144 A3
Winterley Ches E........................ 130 B4
Wintersett Wakefd....................... 142 B4
Winterslow Wilts......................... 34 B4
Winterton N Linc....................... 144 A4
Winterton-on-Sea Norfk................. 123 K7
Winthorpe Lincs......................... 137 K6
Winthorpe Notts......................... 135 G8
Winton Bmouth............................ 17 L4
Winton Cumb............................. 167 H8
Winton E Susx............................ 23 H6
Winton N York........................... 160 F3
Wintringham N York..................... 162 F8
Winwick Cambs........................... 102 B3
Winwick Nhants.......................... 100 D8
Winwick Warrtn.......................... 130 B1
Wirksworth Derbys....................... 115 M1
Wirswall Ches E......................... 113 L3
Wisbech Cambs........................... 103 J2
Wisbech St Mary Cambs................... 103 J2
Wisborough Green W Susx.................. 37 G5
Wiseman's Bridge Pembks.................. 55 K5
Wiseton Notts.......................... 134 E2
Wishanger Gloucs......................... 64 D5
Wishaw N Lans.......................... 209 L7
Wishaw Warwks............................ 98 E4
Wisley Surrey............................ 50 D7
Wispington Lincs........................ 136 D5
Wissenden Kent........................... 40 B7
Wissett Suffk........................... 107 H7
Wissington Norfk........................ 104 D4
Wissington Suffk......................... 89 J8
Wistanstow Shrops........................ 95 K6
Wistanswick Shrops...................... 113 L5
Wistaston Ches E........................ 113 L1
Wistaston Green Ches E.................. 130 D8
Wisterfield Ches E...................... 131 G5
Wiston Pembks............................ 55 H3
Wiston S Lans........................... 198 F6
Wiston W Susx............................ 21 K4
Wistow Cambs............................ 102 F7
Wistow Leics............................ 100 E4
Wistow N York........................... 142 F1
Wiswell Lancs........................... 148 C8
Witcham Cambs........................... 103 J7
Witchampton Dorset....................... 17 J2
Witchford Cambs......................... 103 K7
Witcombe Somset.......................... 31 G6
Witham Essex............................. 71 K4
Witham Friary Somset..................... 32 B3
Witham on the Hill Lincs................ 118 D8
Witham St Hughs Lincs................... 135 H7
Withcall Lincs.......................... 136 E3
Withdean Br & H.......................... 22 D5
Witherenden Hill E Susx.................. 23 L2
Witheridge Devon......................... 28 D8
Witherley Leics.......................... 99 J4
Withern Lincs........................... 137 H3
Withernsea E R Yk....................... 145 J2
Withernwick E R Yk...................... 153 J6
Withersdale Street Suffk................ 106 F7
Withersfield Suffk....................... 88 D5
Witherslack Cumb........................ 156 F5
Withiel Cnwll............................. 5 G2
Withiel Florey Somset.................... 29 H4
Withielgoose Cnwll........................ 5 G2
Withington Gloucs........................ 64 F4
Withington Herefs........................ 80 D6
Withington Manch........................ 131 G1
Withington Shrops........................ 96 D1
Withington Staffs....................... 115 G4
Withington Green Ches E................. 130 F6
Withington Marsh Herefs.................. 80 D6
Withleigh Devon.......................... 28 F8
Withnell Lancs.......................... 139 J3
Withybed Green Worcs..................... 82 B1
Withybrook Warwks........................ 99 L6
Withycombe Somset........................ 29 J3
Withyham E Susx.......................... 38 D6
Withy Mills BaNES........................ 45 K7
Withypool Somset......................... 28 E4
Withywood Bristl......................... 45 H5
Witley Surrey............................ 36 E3
Witnesham Suffk.......................... 90 E5
Witney Oxon.............................. 65 M5
Wittering C Pete....................... 102 B3
Wittersham Kent.......................... 25 G2
Witton Birm.............................. 98 D5
Witton Norfk............................ 107 G2
Witton Norfk............................ 123 G5
Witton Gilbert Dur..................... 169 G2
Witton Green Norfk...................... 107 J3
Witton le Wear Dur..................... 168 F4
Witton Park Dur........................ 168 F4
Wiveliscombe Somset...................... 29 K5
Wivelrod Hants........................... 35 K3
Wivelsfield E Susx....................... 22 E3

Wivelsfield Green E Susx................. 22 E3
Wivelsfield Station W Susx............... 22 E3
Wivenhoe Essex........................... 72 F3
Wivenhoe Cross Essex..................... 72 F2
Wiveton Norfk.......................... 122 A3
Wix Essex................................ 73 H2
Wixford Warwks........................... 82 C4
Wix Green Essex.......................... 73 H2
Wixhill Shrops.......................... 113 J6
Wixoe Suffk.............................. 88 E6
Woburn C Beds............................ 85 J8
Woburn Sands M Keyn...................... 85 H8
Wokefield Park W Berk.................... 49 G6
Woking Surrey............................ 50 C7
Woking Crematorium Surrey................ 50 B7
Wokingham Wokham......................... 49 K5
Wolborough Devon......................... 13 K8
Woldingham Surrey........................ 51 K7
Wold Newton E R Yk..................... 163 J8
Wold Newton NE Lin..................... 145 G8
Wolfclyde S Lans....................... 199 H6
Wolferlow Herefs......................... 80 F3
Wolferton Norfk........................ 120 E6
Wolfhampcote Warwks...................... 83 M2
Wolfhill P & K......................... 233 H8
Wolf Hills Nthumb...................... 179 G7
Wolf's Castle Pembks..................... 74 F6
Wolfsdale Pembks......................... 54 F3
Wollaston Dudley......................... 97 K6
Wollaston Nhants......................... 85 H3
Wollaston Shrops......................... 95 H1
Wollaton C Nott........................ 116 E4
Wolleigh Devon........................... 13 J6
Wollerton Shrops....................... 113 K5
Wollescote Dudley........................ 97 L6
Wolseley Bridge Staffs................. 115 G7
Wolsingham Dur......................... 168 D3
Wolstanton Staffs...................... 114 D2
Wolstenholme Rochdl.................... 140 C5
Wolston Warwks........................... 99 L8
Wolsty Cumb............................ 176 E8
Wolvercote Oxon.......................... 66 D5
Wolverhampton Wolves..................... 97 K4
Wolverley Shrops....................... 113 G5
Wolverley Worcs.......................... 97 J7
Wolverton Hants.......................... 48 E7
Wolverton Kent........................... 41 H6
Wolverton M Keyn......................... 84 F7
Wolverton Warwks......................... 82 F3
Wolverton Wilts.......................... 32 C4
Wolverton Common Hants................... 48 E7
Wolvesnewton Mons........................ 62 F7
Wolvey Warwks............................ 99 L6
Wolvey Heath Warwks...................... 99 L5
Wolviston S on T........................ 170 B5
Wombleton N York....................... 161 L6
Wombourne Staffs......................... 97 K5
Wombwell Barns......................... 142 B7
Womenswold Kent.......................... 41 H5
Womersley N York....................... 142 E4
Wonastow Mons............................ 62 F5
Wonersh Surrey........................... 36 F2
Wonford Devon............................ 13 L4
Wonson Devon............................. 12 F5
Wonston Dorset........................... 16 E1
Wonston Hants............................ 35 G3
Wooburn Bucks............................ 49 M2
Wooburn Green Bucks...................... 49 M1
Wooburn Moor Bucks....................... 49 M1
Woodacott Devon.......................... 11 M1
Woodale N York......................... 159 J6
Woodall Rothm.......................... 133 J3
Woodbank Ches W........................ 129 H5
Woodbastwick Norfk..................... 123 G8
Woodbeck Notts......................... 134 F4
Wood Bevington Warwks.................... 82 C4
Woodborough Notts...................... 117 G2
Woodborough Wilts........................ 47 G7
Woodbridge Devon......................... 14 E4
Woodbridge Dorset........................ 32 E7
Woodbridge Suffk......................... 91 G5
Wood Burcote Nhants...................... 84 D4
Woodbury Devon........................... 14 B5
Woodbury Salterton Devon................. 14 B5
Woodchester Gloucs....................... 64 B6
Woodchurch Kent.......................... 40 B8
Woodchurch Wirral...................... 129 G2
Woodcombe Somset......................... 29 G2
Woodcote Gt Lon.......................... 51 J6
Woodcote Oxon............................ 48 F3
Woodcote Wrekin........................ 114 B8
Woodcote Green Worcs..................... 81 L1
Woodcott Hants........................... 48 B7
Woodcroft Gloucs......................... 63 G7
Woodcutts Dorset......................... 33 G7
Wood Dalling Norfk..................... 122 B6
Woodditton Cambs......................... 88 D3
Woodeaton Oxon........................... 66 D5
Wood Eaton Staffs...................... 114 C7
Wooden Pembks............................ 55 J6

Wood End Bed............85 K6
Wood End Bed............86 B2
Wood End Cambs............103 H8
Wood End Gt Lon............50 E3
Wood End Herts............69 J2
Woodend Highld............228 B3
Woodend Nhants............84 B5
Woodend Staffs............115 K6
Woodend W Loth............210 B5
Woodend W Susx............20 D5
Wood End Warwks............82 D1
Wood End Warwks............99 H4
Wood End Warwks............99 J6
Wood End Wolves............97 L3
Wood Enderby Lincs............136 E6
Woodend Green Essex............70 E2
Woodfalls Wilts............33 L6
Woodford Cnwll............26 C8
Woodford Devon............8 B5
Woodford Gloucs............63 K7
Woodford Gt Lon............69 L8
Woodford Nhants............101 L8
Woodford Stockp............131 H3
Woodford Bridge Gt Lon............51 L1
Woodford Halse Nhants............84 A5
Woodford Wells Gt Lon............69 L8
Woodgate Birm............98 C6
Woodgate Devon............29 K7
Woodgate Norfk............121 K6
Woodgate Norfk............121 M8
Woodgate W Susx............20 F6
Woodgate Worcs............81 M2
Wood Green Gt Lon............51 J1
Woodgreen Hants............33 L7
Woodgreen Oxon............66 A5
Woodhall N York............159 H4
Woodhall Hill Leeds............141 K1
Woodhall Spa Lincs............136 C7
Woodham Bucks............67 H3
Woodham Dur............169 H5
Woodham Surrey............50 D6
Woodham Ferrers Essex............71 J7
Woodham Mortimer Essex............71 K6
Woodham Walter Essex............71 K5
Wood Hayes Wolves............97 L3
Woodhead Abers............256 E4
Woodhill Shrops............97 G6
Woodhill Somset............30 E5
Woodhorn Nthumb............181 H1
Woodhorn Demesne Nthumb............181 H1
Woodhouse Leeds............141 L1
Woodhouse Leics............116 F8
Woodhouse Sheff............133 H3
Woodhouse Wakefd............142 B3
Woodhouse Eaves Leics............116 F8
Woodhouse Green Staffs............131 H7
Woodhouselee Mdloth............211 H6
Woodhouselees D & G............177 L4
Woodhouse Mill Sheff............133 H3
Woodhouses Cumb............177 K8
Woodhouses Oldham............140 D7
Woodhouses Staffs............98 D2
Woodhouses Staffs............115 J7
Woodhuish Devon............8 D4
Woodhurst Cambs............103 G8
Woodingdean Br & H............22 E6
Woodkirk Leeds............141 L3
Woodland Abers............256 F7
Woodland Devon............7 J4
Woodland Devon............8 B1
Woodland Dur............168 D5
Woodland Kent............40 F7
Woodland S Ayrs............182 F4
Woodland Head Devon............13 H3
Woodlands Abers............245 H4
Woodlands Donc............142 E6
Woodlands Dorset............17 L1
Woodlands Hants............18 E1
Woodlands Kent............52 C6
Woodlands N York............150 D5
Woodlands Somset............29 L3
Woodlands (Coleshill)
Crematorium Warwks............98 F5
Woodlands Park W & M............49 L3
Woodlands St Mary W Berk............47 M4
Woodlands (Scarborough)
Crematorium N York............163 J5
Woodlands (Scunthorpe)
Crematorium N Linc............143 M5
Woodland Street Somset............31 J3
Woodland View Sheff............132 F2
Wood Lane Shrops............112 F5
Wood Lane Staffs............114 C2
Woodleigh Devon............7 L5
Woodlesford Leeds............142 B2
Woodley Stockp............131 J1
Woodley Wokham............49 J4
Woodmancote Gloucs............63 M7
Woodmancote Gloucs............64 E2
Woodmancote Gloucs............64 E5

Woodmancote W Susx............20 C5
Woodmancote W Susx............22 C4
Woodmancote Worcs............81 L6
Woodmancott Hants............35 H2
Woodmansey E R Yk............153 G8
Woodmansgreen W Susx............36 C5
Woodmansterne Surrey............51 H7
Woodmanton Devon............14 B5
Woodmarsh Wilts............46 B7
Woodmill Staffs............115 K7
Woodminton Wilts............33 H6
Woodnesborough Kent............41 J4
Woodnewton Nhants............102 A4
Woodnook Notts............116 D1
Wood Norton Norfk............121 M6
Woodplumpton Lancs............139 G1
Woodrising Norfk............105 K3
Wood Row Leeds............142 B2
Woodrow Worcs............97 K8
Wood's Corner E Susx............24 B3
Woods Eaves Herefs............79 K5
Woodseaves Shrops............113 M5
Woodseaves Staffs............114 B6
Woodsend Wilts............47 J4
Woodsetts Rothm............133 L3
Woodsford Dorset............16 E4
Wood's Green E Susx............39 G6
Woodside Br For............50 B5
Woodside Cumb............164 D4
Woodside Essex............70 C6
Woodside Fife............223 G5
Woodside Gt Lon............51 J5
Woodside Hants............18 E5
Woodside Herts............69 H5
Woodside P & K............233 J7
Woodside Green Kent............40 B4
Woodstock Oxon............66 C4
Woodstock Pembks............75 H7
Woodston C Pete............102 D4
Wood Street Norfk............123 H7
Wood Street Village Surrey............36 E1
Woodthorpe Derbys............133 J5
Woodthorpe Leics............116 F8
Woodthorpe Lincs............137 H4
Woodton Norfk............106 F4
Woodtown Devon............27 G6
Woodvale Sefton............138 C5
Woodvale Crematorium
Br & H............22 E6
Woodville Derbys............116 A7
Woodwall Green Staffs............114 B5
Wood Walton Cambs............102 E7
Woodyates Dorset............33 H7
Woofferton Shrops............80 C2
Wookey Somset............31 H2
Wookey Hole Somset............31 H2
Wool Dorset............17 G5
Woolacombe Devon............27 H2
Woolage Green Kent............41 H5
Woolage Village Kent............41 H5
Woolaston Gloucs............63 H7
Woolaston Common Gloucs............63 H6
Woolavington Somset............30 E3
Woolbeding W Susx............36 C6
Woolbrook Devon............14 D5
Woolcotts Somset............29 H4
Wooldale Kirk............141 J6
Wooler Nthumb............202 F7
Woolfardisworthy Devon............13 J1
Woolfardisworthy Devon............26 F6
Woolfold Bury............140 B5
Woolfords S Lans............199 G2
Woolhampton W Berk............48 E5
Woolhope Herefs............80 E8
Woolland Dorset............16 E1
Woollard BaNES............45 J6
Woollensbrook Herts............69 K5
Woolley BaNES............45 L5
Woolley Cambs............102 C8
Woolley Cnwll............26 D7
Woolley Derbys............133 G7
Woolley Wakefd............141 M5
Woolley Bridge Derbys............131 K1
Woolley Green W & M............49 K3
Woolmere Green Worcs............81 M3
Woolmer Green Herts............69 H3
Woolmerston Somset............30 D4
Woolminstone Somset............15 J1
Woolpack Kent............39 L6
Woolpit Suffk............89 K3
Woolpit Green Suffk............89 K3
Woolscott Warwks............83 L2
Woolsgrove Devon............13 J2
Woolsington N u Ty............180 F5
Woolstaston Shrops............95 L4
Woolsthorpe Lincs............117 L5
Woolsthorpe-by-
Colsterworth Lincs............118 B6
Woolston C Sotn............19 G2

Woolston Devon............7 L5
Woolston Devon............7 L6
Woolston Shrops............95 K6
Woolston Shrops............112 D6
Woolston Somset............29 K3
Woolston Somset............31 L5
Woolston Warrtn............130 C2
Woolstone Gloucs............64 D1
Woolstone M Keyn............85 G7
Woolstone Oxon............47 L2
Woolston Green Devon............8 A2
Woolton Lpool............129 K2
Woolton Hill Hants............48 B6
Woolverstone Suffk............90 E7
Woolverton Somset............46 A8
Woolwich Gt Lon............51 L3
Woonton Herefs............79 L5
Woonton Herefs............80 D3
Wooperton Nthumb............190 F2
Woore Shrops............114 A3
Wootten Green Suffk............90 F1
Wootton Bed............85 K6
Wootton Hants............18 C4
Wootton Herefs............79 L5
Wootton IoW............19 J5
Wootton Kent............41 H6
Wootton N Linc............144 D4
Wootton Nhants............84 E4
Wootton Oxon............66 B3
Wootton Oxon............66 C6
Wootton Shrops............112 E6
Wootton Staffs............114 C6
Wootton Staffs............115 H3
Wootton Bassett Wilts............46 F3
Wootton Bridge IoW............19 J5
Wootton Broadmead Bed............85 K6
Wootton Common IoW............19 J5
Wootton Courtenay
Somset............29 G2
Wootton Fitzpaine Dorset............15 J3
Wootton Rivers Wilts............47 J6
Wootton St Lawrence Hants............48 E8
Wootton Wawen Warwks............82 E3
Worcester Worcs............81 K4
Worcester Park Gt Lon............51 G6
Wordsley Dudley............97 K6
Worfield Shrops............97 G4
Worgret Dorset............17 H5
Workhouse End Bed............86 B5
Workington Cumb............164 D5
Worksop Notts............134 B4
Worlaby Lincs............136 F4
Worlaby N Linc............144 C5
Worlds End Bucks............67 L5
Worlds End Hants............19 L1
World's End W Berk............48 C3
Worlds End W Susx............22 E3
Worle N Som............44 D6
Worleston Ches E............130 C8
Worlingham Suffk............107 J5
Worlington Devon............28 D8
Worlington Suffk............104 D8
Worlingworth Suffk............90 F2
Wormald Green N York............150 D3
Wormbridge Herefs............62 E1
Wormegay Norfk............104 D1
Wormelow Tump Herefs............62 F1
Wormhill Derbys............132 C5
Wormhill Herefs............80 A7
Wormingford Essex............72 D1
Worminghall Bucks............66 F5
Wormington Gloucs............82 B7
Worminster Somset............31 J2
Wormit Fife............223 G2
Wormleighton Warwks............83 K4
Wormley Herts............69 K6
Wormley Surrey............36 E3
Wormleybury Herts............69 K6
Wormley Hill Donc............143 G4
Wormshill Kent............39 M2
Wormsley Herefs............80 A5
Worplesdon Surrey............50 B8
Worrall Sheff............132 F1
Worrall Hill Gloucs............63 J4
Worsbrough Barns............142 A7
Worsbrough Bridge Barns............142 A7
Worsbrough Dale Barns............142 B7
Worsley Salfd............139 M7
Worstead Norfk............122 F6
Worsthorne Lancs............140 C1
Worston Devon............7 H4
Worston Lancs............148 D7
Worth Kent............41 K4
Worth Somset............31 H2
Worth W Susx............37 L4
Wortham Suffk............106 B7
Worthen Shrops............95 H2
Worthenbury Wrexhm............112 F2
Worthing Norfk............121 M7
Worthing W Susx............21 K6

Worthing Crematorium W Susx............21 J5
Worthington Leics............116 C7
Worth Matravers Dorset............17 J7
Worthybrook Mons............62 G3
Worting Hants............48 F8
Wortley Barns............141 M7
Wortley Leeds............141 L1
Worton N York............159 G5
Worton Wilts............46 E7
Wortwell Norfk............106 F6
Wotherton Shrops............95 G3
Wothorpe C Pete............101 M2
Wotter Devon............7 H3
Wotton Surrey............37 H2
Wotton-under-Edge Gloucs............63 M8
Wotton Underwood Bucks............67 G4
Woughton on the Green
M Keyn............85 G7
Wouldham Kent............52 F6
Woundale Shrops............97 H5
Wrabness Essex............73 J1
Wrafton Devon............27 J4
Wragby Lincs............136 B4
Wragby Wakefd............142 C4
Wramplingham Norfk............106 C2
Wrangaton Devon............7 K3
Wrangbrook Wakefd............142 D5
Wrangle Lincs............119 M2
Wrangle Common Lincs............119 M1
Wrangle Lowgate Lincs............119 M1
Wrangway Somset............29 L5
Wrantage Somset............30 D6
Wrawby N Linc............144 C6
Wraxall N Som............44 F4
Wraxall Somset............31 K4
Wray Lancs............147 M2
Wray Castle Cumb............156 C3
Wraysbury W & M............50 C4
Wrayton Lancs............147 M2
Wrea Green Lancs............138 E2
Wreaks End Cumb............156 B5
Wreay Cumb............166 B1
Wreay Cumb............166 B6
Wrecclesham Surrey............36 B2
Wrekenton Gatesd............181 G7
Wrelton N York............162 D5
Wrenbury Ches E............113 K2
Wrench Green N York............163 H5
Wreningham Norfk............106 D4
Wrentham Suffk............107 K6
Wrenthorpe Wakefd............141 M3
Wrentnall Shrops............95 K3
Wressle E R Yk............143 H1
Wressle N Linc............144 B6
Wrestlingworth C Beds............86 E5
Wretton Norfk............104 D3
Wrexham Wrexhm............112 E2
Wribbenhall Worcs............97 H8
Wrickton Shrops............96 E6
Wrightington Bar Lancs............139 G5
Wright's Green Essex............70 D4
Wrinehill Staffs............114 B2
Wrington N Som............44 F6
Writhlington BaNES............45 K8
Writtle Essex............71 G6
Wrockwardine Wrekin............96 E1
Wroot N Linc............143 H7
Wrose C Brad............149 L8
Wrotham Kent............52 D7
Wrotham Heath Kent............52 D7
Wrottesley Staffs............97 J3
Wroughton Swindn............47 H3
Wroxall IoW............19 J7
Wroxall Warwks............82 F1
Wroxeter Shrops............96 D2
Wroxham Norfk............122 F8
Wroxton Oxon............83 K7
Wyaston Derbys............115 K3
Wyatt's Green Essex............70 F7
Wyberton East Lincs............119 K3
Wyberton West Lincs............119 J3
Wyboston Bed............86 D4
Wybunbury Ches E............113 M2
Wychbold Worcs............81 L2
Wych Cross E Susx............38 C5
Wychnor Staffs............115 K8
Wyck Hants............35 M3
Wyck Rissington Gloucs............65 J3
Wycliffe Dur............168 E7
Wycoller Lancs............149 G8
Wycomb Leics............117 K6
Wycombe Marsh Bucks............67 L8
Wyddial Herts............69 K1
Wye Kent............40 D6
Wyesham Mons............63 G5
Wyfordby Leics............117 L7
Wyke C Brad............141 J2
Wyke Devon............13 K3
Wyke Devon............15 G3
Wyke Dorset............32 D5

Wyke Shrops 96 E3
Wyke Surrey 50 A8
Wyke Champflower Somset 31 L4
Wykeham N York 163 H6
Wyken Covtry 99 K7
Wyken Shrops 97 H4
Wyke Regis Dorset 16 C7
Wykey Shrops 112 F6
Wykin Leics 99 L4
Wylam Nthumb 180 D6
Wylde Green Birm 98 E4
Wylye Wilts 33 H3
Wymeswold Leics 117 G6
Wymington Bed 85 J2
Wymondham Leics 117 M7
Wymondham Norfk 106 C3
Wyndham Brdgnd 42 E3
Wynford Eagle Dorset 16 B3
Wynyard Park S on T 169 L5
Wynyard Village S on T 169 L5
Wyre Forest Crematorium
    Worcs 97 J8
Wyre Piddle Worcs 81 M5
Wysall Notts 117 G6
Wyson Herefs 80 C2
Wythall Worcs 98 D8
Wytham Oxon 66 C5
Wythburn Cumb 165 K7
Wythenshawe Manch 131 G2
Wythop Mill Cumb 165 G5
Wyton Cambs 86 F1
Wyton E R Yk 144 F1
Wyverstone Suffk 90 B2
Wyverstone Street Suffk 89 L2
Wyville Lincs 118 A5

Y

Yaddlethorpe N Linc 143 M6
Yafford IoW 19 G7
Yafforth N York 160 E4
Yalberton Torbay 8 C3
Yalding Kent 39 H3
Yanwath Cumb 166 C5
Yanworth Gloucs 65 G4
Yapham E R Yk 152 B5
Yapton W Susx 21 G6
Yarborough N Som 44 D7
Yarbridge IoW 19 K6
Yarburgh Lincs 136 F1
Yarcombe Devon 14 F1
Yard Devon 28 D6
Yardley Birm 98 E6
Yardley Crematorium Birm 98 E6
Yardley Gobion Nhants 84 E6
Yardley Hastings Nhants 85 G4
Yardley Wood Birm 98 E7
Yardro Powys 79 J3
Yarford Somset 30 B5
Yarkhill Herefs 80 E6
Yarley Somset 31 H2
Yarlington Somset 31 L5
Yarm S on T 169 L8
Yarmouth IoW 18 E5
Yarnacott Devon 27 L5
Yarnbrook Wilts 46 C7
Yarner Devon 13 H7
Yarnfield Staffs 114 D5
Yarnscombe Devon 27 K6
Yarnton Oxon 66 C5
Yarpole Herefs 80 B2
Yarrow Border 200 D7
Yarrow Somset 30 E2
Yarrow Feus Border 200 D7
Yarrowford Border 200 E7
Yarsop Herefs 80 A6
Yarwell Nhants 102 B4
Yate S Glos 45 L3
Yateley Hants 49 K6
Yatesbury Wilts 46 F4
Yattendon W Berk 48 E4
Yatton Herefs 80 A2
Yatton N Som 44 E6
Yatton Keynell Wilts 46 C4
Yaverland IoW 19 K6
Yawl Devon 15 H4
Yawthorpe Lincs 135 H1
Yaxham Norfk 105 K1
Yaxley Cambs 102 D5
Yaxley Suffk 106 C8
Yazor Herefs 79 M6
Yeading Gt Lon 50 E3
Yeadon Leeds 150 B7
Yealand Conyers Lancs 157 H7
Yealand Redmayne Lancs 157 H7
Yealand Storrs Lancs 157 H7
Yealmbridge Devon 7 H4
Yealmpton Devon 7 H4
Yearby R & Cl 170 E6

Yearngill Cumb 164 F2
Yearsley N York 161 J7
Yeaton Shrops 113 G7
Yeaveley Derbys 115 K3
Yeavering Nthumb 202 E7
Yedingham N York 162 F6
Yelford Oxon 66 A6
Yell Shet 281 e3
Yelland Devon 27 J4
Yelling Cambs 86 F3
Yelvertoft Nhants 100 D8
Yelverton Devon 7 G1
Yelverton Norfk 106 F3
Yenston Somset 32 B6
Yeoford Devon 13 H3
Yeolmbridge Cnwll 11 L5
Yeo Mill Devon 28 E5
Yeo Vale Devon 27 G6
Yeovil Somset 31 J7
Yeovil Crematorium Somset 31 H7
Yeovil Marsh Somset 31 J7
Yeovilton Somset 31 J6
Yerbeston Pembks 55 H5
Yesnaby Ork 275 b4
Yetlington Nthumb 190 E4
Yetminster Dorset 31 K8
Yetson Devon 8 B4
Yettington Devon 14 B5
Yetts o'Muckhart Clacks 221 H6
Yews Green C Brad 141 H2
Yew Tree Sandw 98 C4
Y Felinheli Gwynd 125 J6
Y Ferwig Cerdgn 75 L2
Y Ffor Gwynd 109 G4
Y Gyffylliog Denbgs 128 C8
Yielden Bed 85 K2
Yieldingtree Worcs 97 K7
Yieldshields S Lans 198 E3
Yiewsley Gt Lon 50 D3
Y Maerdy Conwy 111 K3
Y Nant Wrexhm 112 D2
Ynysboeth Rhondd 43 G3
Ynysddu Caerph 43 J3
Ynysforgan Swans 57 J5
Ynyshir Rhondd 42 F3
Ynyslas Cerdgn 92 D5
Ynysmaerdy Rhondd 42 F3
Ynysmeudwy Neath 57 K4
Ynystawe Swans 57 J5
Ynyswen Powys 60 C4
Ynyswen Rhondd 42 E2
Ynysybwl Rhondd 43 G3
Ynysymaengwyn Gwynd 92 D3
Yockenthwaite N York 158 F6
Yockleton Shrops 95 K2
Yokefleet E R Yk 143 K3
Yoker C Glas 208 E5
York C York 151 J5
York Lancs 139 L1
York City Crematorium C York ... 151 J6
Yorkletts Kent 40 E3
Yorkley Gloucs 63 J5
York Town Surrey 49 L7
Yorton Heath Shrops 113 H7
Youlgreave Derbys 132 D6
Youlthorpe E R Yk 152 B5
Youlton N York 151 G3
Youngsbury Herts 69 K3
Young's End Essex 71 H3
Yoxall Staffs 115 J7
Yoxford Suffk 91 J2
Y Rhiw Gwynd 108 D6
Ysbyty Cynfyn Cerdgn 93 G7
Ysbyty Ifan Conwy 110 F2
Ysbyty Ystwyth Cerdgn 77 K1
Ysceifiog Flints 128 D5
Ysgubor-y-Coed Cerdgn 92 E4
Ystalyfera Neath 57 L3
Ystrad Rhondd 42 F3
Ystrad Aeron Cerdgn 76 F4
Ystradfellte Powys 60 D4
Ystrad Ffin Carmth 77 L6
Ystradgynlais Powys 60 B5
Ystrad Meurig Cerdgn 77 K2
Ystrad Mynach Caerph 43 J3
Ystradowen V Glam 42 F6
Ystumtuen Cerdgn 92 F7
Ythanbank Abers 257 G5
Ythanwells Abers 256 B4
Ythsie Abers 256 F5

Z

Zeal Monachorum Devon 13 G2
Zeals Wilts 32 C4
Zelah Cnwll 4 C4
Zennor Cnwll 2 C3
Zoar Cnwll 3 J7
Zouch Notts 116 E6

EXCLUSIVE
Half-price offer with this atlas
AA ALL–WEATHER
CAR KIT

Only £45.00* (£90.00 RRP)
Includes FREE P&P**

How To Purchase:

Visit **theAA.com/shop/AllWeather** add the kit to your shopping basket, then enter the promotional code: **ALLWEATHER** to receive your discount.

*Terms and conditions
Offer only available at theAA.com/shop/AllWeather in conjunction with AA 2015 UK Road Atlases and when the promotion code ALLWEATHER has been entered in the shopping basket. Offer only available while stocks last or until 31st December 2015, cannot be used in conjunction with any offer or promotion code. Pictures for illustration purposes only and may be subject to change. The AA reserve the right to replace kit components with other suitable products of the same value at its discretion. Please see website for details on returns and cancellations. **Free standard P&P to the UK mainland and Ireland addresses only. (Usually delivered within 7 working days).

RRP: £9.99

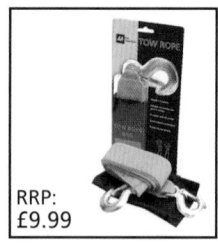
RRP: £9.99

RRP: £4.99

The All–Weather Car Kit includes:
Warning Triangle, High Visibility Vest, Tow Rope, Booster Cables, Snow & Ice Grips, Emergency Foil Blanket, Pack of 4 Ponchos, 3–Piece Torch Set, Picnic Blanket, Sunblinds, Canvas Carry Bag.

RRP: £16.99

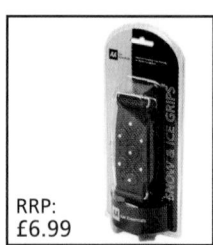
RRP: £6.99

RRP: £12.99

RRP: £7.99

RRP: £1.99

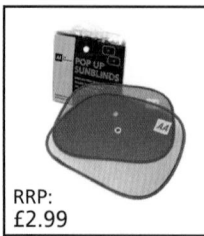
RRP: £2.99

Note: 3–Piece Headtorch Set not shown, RRP: £19.99

 Car Essentials

Map pages north

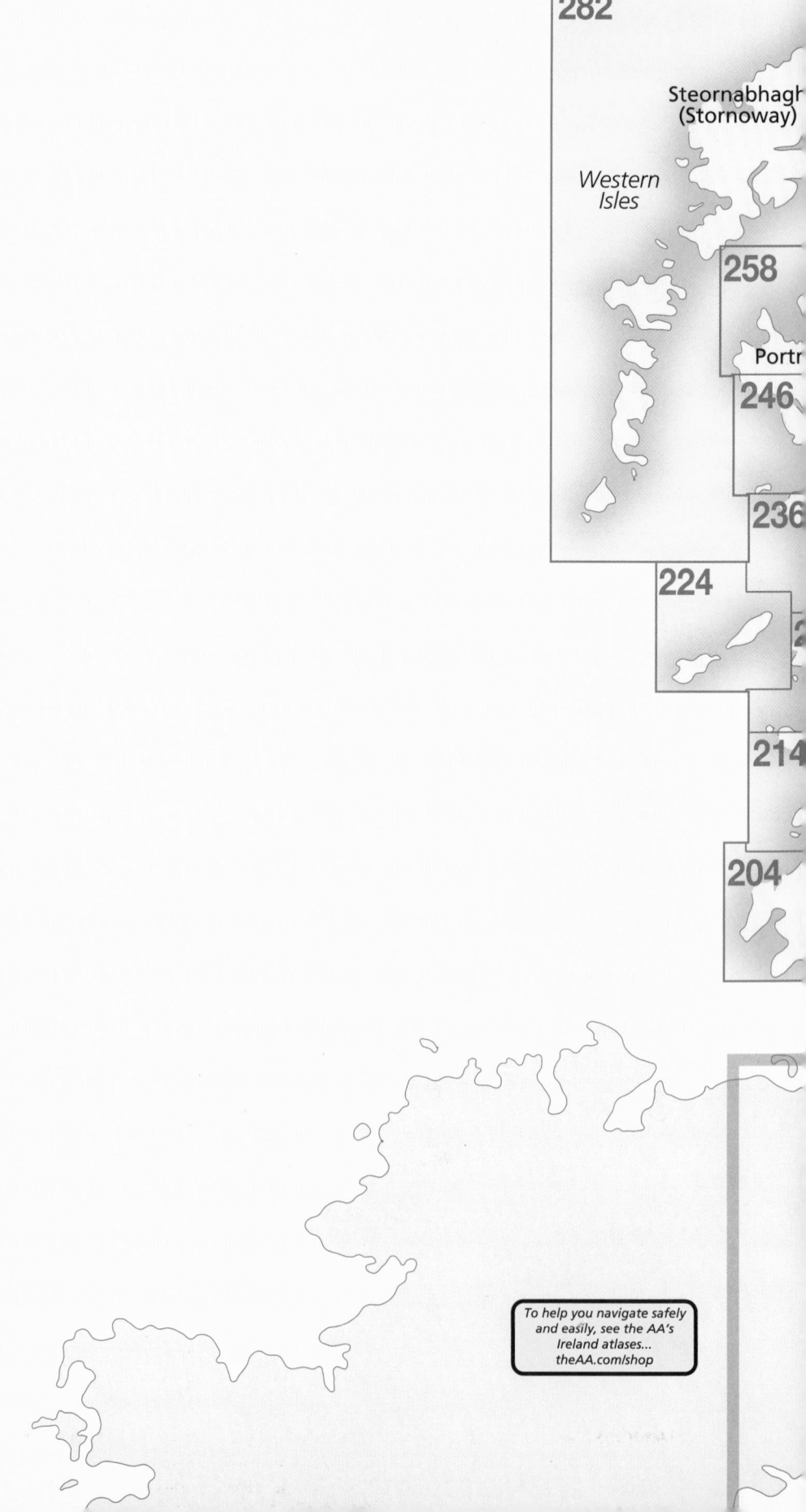

282

Steornabhagh
(Stornoway)

Western
Isles

258

Portr

246

236

224

214

204

To help you navigate safely
and easily, see the AA's
Ireland atlases...
theAA.com/shop